GED®TEST

PREMIER 2015

PUBLISHING

New York

ACKNOWLEDGEMENTS

Special thanks to the team that made this book possible:
Arthur Ahn, Mikhail Alexeeff, Gina Allison, Kim Bowers, Erik Bowman, Julie Choi, Margaret Crane, Alisha Crowley, Lola Disparte, Boris Dvorkin, Paula Fleming, Tom Flesher, Joanna Graham, Allison Harm, Gar Hong, Kevin Jacobson, Wyatt Kent, Jennifer Land, Heather Maigur, Terrence McGovern, Eli Meyer, Kathy Osmus, Anthony Parr, Rachel Pearsall, Neha Rao, Rachel Reina, Teresa Rupp, Scott Safir, Glen Stohr, Alexandra Strelka, Lee Weiss, and many others who have shaped this book over the years.

GED® is a registered trademark of the American Council on Education (ACE) and may not be used without permission. The GED® and GED Testing Service® brands are administered by GED Testing Service LLC under license. ACE and GED Testing Service LLC have not approved, authorized, endorsed, been involved in the development of, or licensed the substantive content of this material.

This publication is designed to provide accurate information in regard to the subject matter covered as of its publication date, with the understanding that knowledge and best practice constantly evolve. The publisher is not engaged in rendering medical, legal, accounting, or other professional service. If medical or legal advice or other expert assistance is required, the services of a competent professional should be sought. This publication is not intended for use in clinical practice or the delivery of medical care. To the fullest extent of the law, neither the Publisher nor the Editors assume any liability for any injury and/or damage to persons or property arising out of or related to any use of the material contained in this book.

CONTENTS

KAPLAN'S GED® TEST BOOK AND ONLINE CENTER

Congratulations on your decision to pursue high school equivalency, and thank you for choosing Kaplan for your GED® test preparation.

You've made the right choice in acquiring this book—you're now armed with a comprehensive GED® test preparation program that is the result of years of researching the GED® tests and teaching thousands of students the skills they need to succeed. You have what you need to pass the GED® tests and score higher; the next step is to make the commitment to your study plan.

The next section will tell you everything you need to know to take advantage of your book and your Online Center.

YOUR BOOK

This book contains a complete study program, including the following:

- Detailed instruction covering the essential concepts for Reasoning through Language Arts, Mathematical Reasoning, Social Studies, and Science
- Time-tested and effective methods and strategies for every question type
- Pretests featuring questions from all sections of the GED® tests, designed to help you diagnose your strengths and weaknesses
- Hundreds of practice questions, followed by answer explanations
- A timed, full-length Practice Test for each subject

YOUR ONLINE CENTER

Your Kaplan Online Center gives you access to additional instruction and practice materials to reinforce key concepts and sharpen your GED® test skills. The following list summarizes the resources available to you:

- An additional full-length Practice Test for each subject, so that you can practice the computer-based question formats used on the actual test
- Analysis of your performance on each section of your practice tests, including detailed answer explanations for the computer-based practice test
- Plenty of video lessons featuring Kaplan's top instructors

GETTING STARTED

Studying for the GED® test can be daunting, and with so many resources available to you, it may not be clear where to begin. Don't worry; we'll break it down one step at a time, just as we will with the GED® test questions that you will soon be on your way to mastering.

GETTING STARTED

1. Take the diagnostic Pretests.
2. Create a study plan.
3. Register your Online Center.
4. Learn and practice using both this book and your Online Center.
5. Work through the Practice Tests to gauge your progress.

STEP 1: TAKE THE DIAGNOSTIC PRETESTS

It's essential to take the diagnostic Pretests before you begin to study. Doing so will give you the initial feedback and diagnostic information that you will need to achieve your maximum score. Place enough importance on completing the Pretests—turn off your cell phone, give the tests your full attention, and learn from your performance.

Once you have finished your Pretests, check your answers starting on page 624. Mark the questions that you got correct and **carefully read the answer explanations** of those that you got wrong.

For each test, make a list of the questions that you got correct and use that list to fill out the Kaplan GED® Test Study Planners that begin on page xvi. Use the results to target your weak areas.

Another option is for you to go online and enter your answers so that the Kaplan Online Center can generate your results. Note which sections and which question types you need to target.

Review the detailed answer explanations in the book to better understand your performance. Look for patterns in the questions you answered correctly and incorrectly. Were you stronger in some areas than others? This analysis will help you target your study time to specific concepts.

STEP 2: CREATE A STUDY PLAN

Use what you've learned from your initial Pretest to identify areas for closer study and practice. Take time to familiarize yourself with the key components of your book and Online Center. Think about how many hours you can consistently devote to GED® test study.

Schedule time for study, practice, and review. It works best for many people to block out short, frequent periods of study time throughout the week. Check in with yourself frequently to make sure you're not falling behind your plan or forgetting about any of your resources.

STEP 3: REGISTER YOUR ONLINE CENTER

Register your Online Center using these simple steps:

1. Go to **kaptest.com/booksonline**.
2. Follow the on-screen instructions for GED®. Please have your book available.

Access to the Online Center is limited to the original owner of this book and is nontransferable. Kaplan is not responsible for providing access to the Online Center to customers who purchase or borrow used copies of this book. Access to the Online Center expires one year after you register.

STEP 4: LEARN AND PRACTICE

Your book and Online Center come with many opportunities to develop and practice the skills you'll need on Test Day. Depending on how much time you have to study, you can do this work methodically, covering every unit and lesson, or you can focus your study on those content areas that are most challenging to you. You will inevitably need more work in some areas than in others, but the more thoroughly you prepare, the better your score will be.

Initially, your practice should focus on mastering the needed skills and not on timing. Add timing to your practice as you become familiar with skills and methods.

STEP 5: WORK THROUGH THE PRACTICE TESTS

As you move through your GED® studies, take advantage of both the full-length Practice Test available in this book and also the one in your Online Center.

Review your Practice Test results thoroughly to make sure you are addressing the areas that are most important to your score. Allot time to review the detailed explanations so that you can learn from your mistakes and review the relevant chapters in the book for additional study.

If you find that you would like access to more of Kaplan's instructional content or practice material, look into our On Demand course option and other study resources available at **kaptest.com/GED**.

Thanks for choosing Kaplan. We wish you the best of luck on your journey to completing your high school equivalency and taking a vital step toward college and career readiness.

GED® TEST OVERVIEW

The GED® test is a widely used examination that demonstrates high school equivalency as well as college and career readiness. It includes the reading, writing, thinking, and problem-solving skills needed for postsecondary educational programs and for the world of work. This means that your high school equivalency diploma is not an end in itself—it is the springboard to more education, to better-paying jobs, and to more rewarding career paths.

TAKE FOUR SUBTESTS IN FOUR CONTENT AREAS

Reasoning through Language Arts—2.5 hours (one 10-minute break)

- Roughly 50–55 questions
- Includes 1 extended written response to reading passages—up to 45 minutes

Mathematical Reasoning—1 hour, 55 minutes

- Roughly 40–45 questions
- First section—5 questions, no calculator allowed
- Second section—calculator allowed (Texas Instruments TI-30XS MultiView™ calculator)

Social Studies—1.5 hours

- Roughly 30–35 questions
- Includes 1 extended written response to passages and/or graphics—up to 25 minutes

Science—1.5 hours

- Roughly 30–35 questions
- Includes 2 short-answer written responses to passages and/or graphics—up to 10 minutes each

You can read detailed information about each test in the four *About the Test* sections that introduce each content area in this book.

RESPOND TO SEVEN COMPUTER-BASED QUESTION FORMATS

To test a range of skills, the GED® test uses a variety of computer-based question formats. You will see examples of each type of question in *GED® Computer-Based Testing* and in the four *About the Test* sections. When you take the test, you will use these question formats:

- **Multiple-choice**—click to choose from four choices (A through D).
- **Fill-in-the-blank**—type a word, a phrase, or numbers in a box.
- **Drag-and-drop**—move words, numbers, or objects across the computer screen.
- **Drop-down**—select from menus embedded in text on the computer screen.
- **Hot spot**—click on graphics on the computer.
- **Short-answer**—write a paragraph or two of explanation in response to passages or graphics or a combination of the two.
- **Extended response**—compose a well-developed and supported response to passages or graphics or a combination of the two.

READ AND WRITE THROUGHOUT THE TEST

You will read and interpret passages and word problems on all four tests. In addition, three out of four subtests (*Reasoning through Language Arts, Social Studies,* and *Science*) require that you read a passage or two and compose a response about what you have read.

The type of writing that you will use is called *evidence-based writing*, which means that you need to cite specific evidence from the readings in your response. This is a key characteristic of the type of writing that is required in workplaces and in educational programs. This book contains special lessons and practice activities to help you write effectively on all three of the subtests.

PERFORM MATH SKILLS THROUGHOUT THE TEST

In addition to the questions on the *Mathematical Reasoning Test*, math items also appear on the *Science Test* and the *Social Studies Test*. Both of those sections of this book have specific instruction and practice activities to help you apply math skills to social studies and science materials.

On all three of these tests, you may use either a hand-held or an on-screen version of the Texas Instruments TI-30XS MultiView™ calculator to use with math items. If you wish to use a hand-held version of the calculator, you may need to take one with you on test day. **You are strongly encouraged to purchase a hand-held version of this calculator to use with this study guide**. You can buy this calculator at stores that carry office and school supplies and through online vendors. Specific lessons in the *Mathematical Reasoning* section of this book will help you learn to use this calculator.

USE THE GED TESTING SERVICE® MYGED™ INTERNET PORTAL

MyGED™ is a personalized online program that will be your entry point to all test activities, including scheduling testing and retesting (if necessary), viewing score reports, ordering transcripts and your diploma, and investigating your next steps in making the transition to college or to a career.

TAKE THE TEST: UNDERSTAND YOUR SCORE

Each GED® Test is scored on a scale from 100 to 200. There are three possible scores that you can receive on the GED® Test:

- **Not Passing**—lower than 150 on any of the four tests. You can reschedule up to two times a year to retake any or all of the tests.
- **GED® Passing Score**—at or higher than the minimum score (150 per test) needed to demonstrate high school equivalency–level skills and knowledge. Points on one test do not carry over to the others; that is, if you score 200 on one and 100 on another, that is not equivalent to scoring 150 on both. You need to score 150 on each of the four tests.
- **GED® Score with Honors**—at or higher than the minimum needed (170 per test) to demonstrate career and college readiness

Your score is determined by the number of points you earn on each test, but questions vary in point value. Therefore, there is no fixed number of questions you need to get correct on each test in order to pass or pass with honors.

GED® COMPUTER-BASED TESTING

The GED® Test is delivered on a computer. That means that you will need to familiarize yourself with basic computer skills and computer-based question formats in order to succeed on the test.

NOTE: *The GED® Test on computer is only offered at official Pearson Vue Testing Centers. Any Internet-based test that claims to be the GED® Test is not the actual test. At the MyGED™ portal, you can access study resources, take a practice test, or schedule your test. You cannot take the real GED® test online.*

Before you take the actual test, you can practice computer-based testing functions with the Practice Test available in Kaplan's Online Center and with the GED® Testing Service's GED Ready™ Test.

COMPUTER-BASED TESTING FUNCTIONS AND TOOLS

The GED® Test uses many computer **functions**, some of which you may already know. It also offers specific **tools** that you will utilize in different test areas.

Use the **mouse** to

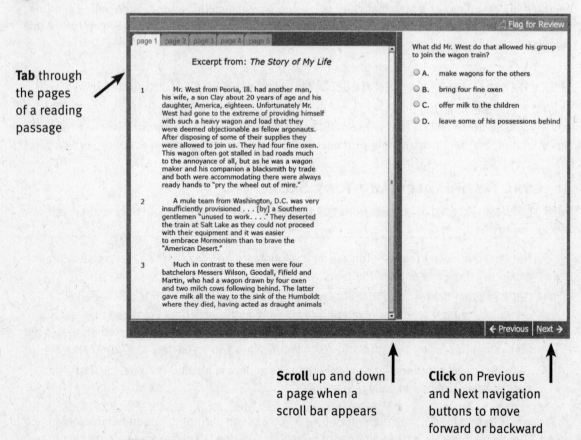

Tab through the pages of a reading passage

Scroll up and down a page when a scroll bar appears

Click on Previous and Next navigation buttons to move forward or backward

Use the **mouse** to (continued)

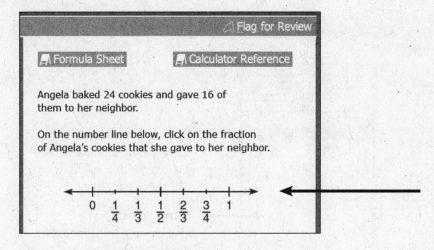

Click on an answer choice, a "Select" menu, or a point on a graphic

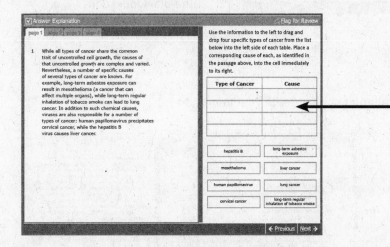

Drag and drop text, numbers, or images into a shape on the computer screen

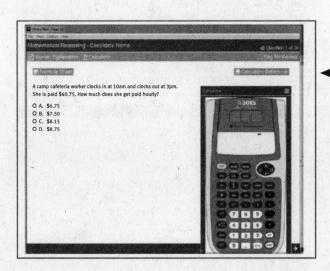

Click to open, move, and close information windows and math resources—such as the calculator, formula sheet, or symbol toolbar

Use **word processing skills** to

Click with the mouse to **cut, copy, paste, undo,** and **redo** on Extended-Response and Short-Answer items

Enter text with basic keyboarding skills in text boxes (shown here) and fill-in-the-blank questions

Use **the online highlighter** operated with your mouse, to

Highlight specific information that you will use as evidence in writing your Extended Responses and Short Answers.

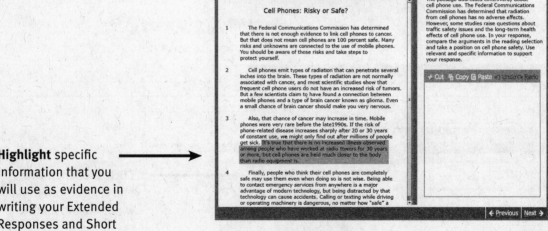

Use the offline, **erasable wipe-off board**, which will be provided at the testing center, to

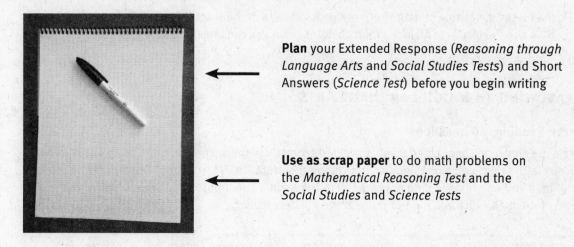

Plan your Extended Response (*Reasoning through Language Arts* and *Social Studies Tests*) and Short Answers (*Science Test*) before you begin writing

Use as scrap paper to do math problems on the *Mathematical Reasoning Test* and the *Social Studies* and *Science Tests*

Use three **onscreen test-tracking tools** at the top of the computer screen to

Test - Your Name   ⏱ Time Remaining 01:04:32
                                                           ☰ Question 32 of 50
                                                              🏳 Flag for Review

- **See how much time you have left:** *Time Remaining* shows how much time is left to complete each test.
- **Monitor your progress** through each test by viewing the *Question Line*. You can check how far you have progressed and how many more questions you need to answer. Budget your time carefully to allow for these writing tasks:
  - 45 minutes for the Extended Response at the end of the first section of the *Reasoning through Language Arts Test*
  - 25 minutes for the Extended Response at the end of the *Social Studies Test*
  - 10 minutes for <u>each</u> of the Short Answer questions that are interspersed with other questions in the *Science Test*
- **Click** on the *Flag for Review* if you are unsure of an answer. (You should never skip a question.) If you click on it, the flag will display in yellow and will be marked on the Review Screen.

At the end of each test, if you have time left, you can use the **Review Screen** to go back and review questions that you marked.

KAPLAN GED® TEST STUDY PLANNERS

Take the Pretests, starting on page 1. Check your answers in the Pretest Answer Key starting on page 624. Use the results to fill in the charts below so that you can target the areas that need the most work.

REASONING THROUGH LANGUAGE ARTS

Part I: Reading, 20 questions

Circle the *Question Numbers* that you answered correctly in the second column. Write the *Number Correct* in the third column. Compare your "number correct" to the "mastery" number in the fourth column. If you do not have time to review all of the *Reading* sections, target your study to the *Content Areas* in which you did not score at the mastery level.

Content Area	Question Numbers	Number Correct	Mastery/Total
Interpreting Nonfiction and Informational Text Pages 62–85	1, 2, 3, 4, 5, 6, 7, 12, 13	6/9	7 out of 9
Analyzing Nonfiction and Informational Text Pages 86–101	8, 9, 10, 11, 14, 15	4/6	4 out of 6
Interpreting Fiction Pages 102–117	16, 17, 18, 19, 20	3/3	3 out of 5

Part II: Writing and Language Skills, 18 questions

Circle the *Question Numbers* that you answered correctly in the second column. Write the *Number Correct* in the third column. Compare your "number correct" to the "mastery" number in the fourth column. If you do not have time to review all of the *Writing and Language* sections, target your study to the *Content Areas* in which you did not score at the mastery level.

Content Area	Question Numbers	Number Correct	Mastery/Total
Writing Effective Sentences and Connecting Ideas Pages 118–135 and 136–147	2, 6, 9, 10, 12, 17	3/6	4 out of 6
Polishing Your Writing Pages 174–183	4, 16	2/2	1 out of 2
Using Grammar Correctly Pages 184–199	1, 3, 8, 14, 15, 18	6/6	4 out of 6
Using Writing Mechanics Pages 200–213	5, 7, 11, 13	3/4	3 out of 4

Part III: Extended Response

Circle the *Question Numbers* that you answered correctly in the second column. Write the *Number Correct* in the third column. Compare your "number correct" to the "mastery" number in the fourth column and target your study to the *Content Areas* in which you did not score at the mastery level.

Content Area	Question Numbers	Number Correct	Mastery/Total
Unpack the Writing Prompt Pages 148–149	1, 2, 3, 4		**3 out of 4**
Identify a Writer's Arguments and Assumptions, Develop a Thesis Statement, and **Collect Supporting Evidence** Pages 150–155	5, 6, 7		**2 out of 3**
Plan Your Response Pages 156–159	8	My score is _____ based on the Planning Checklist, page 626.	**2 out of 3**
Draft Your Response Pages 160–165	9	My score is _____ based on the Drafting Checklist, page 627.	**4 out of 5**
Revise and Edit Your Response Pages 166–169	10	My score is _____ based on the Revising and Editing Checklist, page 627.	**4 out of 6**

MATHEMATICAL REASONING

Part I: Quantitative Reasoning, 18 Questions

Circle the *Question Numbers* that you answered correctly in the second column. Write the *Number Correct* in the third column. Compare your "number correct" to the "mastery" number in the fourth column. If you do not have time to review all of the *Quantitative Reasoning* sections, target your study to the *Content Areas* in which you did not score at the mastery level.

Content Area	Question Numbers	Number Correct	Mastery/Total
Number Sense and Problem Solving Pages 220–239	6, 8, 9, 13	3/4	3 out of 4 ✓
Decimals and Fractions Pages 240–261	3, 7, 14, 15	3/4	3 out of 4 ✓
Ratio, Proportion, and Percent Pages 262–281	2, 5, 11, 17	3/4	3 out of 4 ✓
Data, Statistics, and Probability Pages 282–313	1, 4, 10, 12, 16, 18	3/6	4 out of 6

Part II: Algebraic Reasoning and Geometric Measurement, 22 Questions

Circle the *Question Numbers* that you answered correctly in the second column. Write the *Number Correct* in the third column. Compare your "number correct" to the "mastery" number in the fourth column. If you do not have time to review all of the *Algebraic Reasoning and Geometric Measurement* sections, target your study to the *Content Areas* in which you did not score at the mastery level.

Content Area	Question Numbers	Number Correct	Mastery/Total
Algebra Basics, Expressions, and Polynomials Pages 314–347	1, 2, 3, 8, 10, 13		5 out of 6
Equations, Inequalities, and Functions Pages 348–377	6, 9, 11, 12, 15, 17, 19, 22		6 out of 8
Geometry Pages 378–402	4, 5, 7, 14, 16, 18, 20, 21		6 out of 8

SOCIAL STUDIES

Part I: Social Studies Practices, 10 Questions

Circle the *Question Numbers* that you answered correctly in the second column. Write the *Number Correct* in the third column. Compare your "number correct" to the "mastery" number in the fourth column. If you do not have time to review all of the *Social Studies Practices* sections, target your study to the *Content Areas* in which you did not score at the mastery level.

Content Area	Question Numbers	Number Correct	Mastery/Total
Determine Central Idea and Draw Conclusions, Interpret Words and Ideas, and Analyze Relationships Between Materials Pages 410–413 and 418–421	1, 2	1/2	**2 out of 2**
Analyze Author's Purpose and Point of View and Evaluate Author's Reasoning and Evidence Pages 414–417	3, 4, 5, 6	4/4	**3 out of 4** ✓
Interpret Data and Statistics Pages 422–423	7, 8, 9, 10	3/4	**3 out of 4** ✓

Part II: Social Studies Content, 25 Questions

Circle the *Question Numbers* that you answered correctly in the second column. Write the *Number Correct* in the third column. Compare your "number correct" to the "mastery" number in the fourth column. If you do not have time to review all of the *Social Studies Content* sections, target your study to the *Content Areas* that need the most work.

Content Area	Question Numbers	Number Correct	Mastery/Total
U.S. History Pages 430–443	1, 2, 10, 16, 17, 18, 19	4/7	**5 out of 7**
Civics and Government Pages 444–457	4, 5, 6, 7, 8, 9, 20, 21, 22, 23	9/10	**7 out of 10** ✓
Economics Pages 458–469	3, 11, 12, 24	3/4	**3 out of 4** ✓
Geography and the World Pages 470–485	13, 14, 15, 25	2/4	**3 out of 4**

Part III: Extended Response

Circle the *Question Numbers* that you answered correctly in the second column. Write the *Number Correct* in the third column. Compare your "number correct" to the "mastery" number in the fourth column. Target your study to the *Content Areas* in which you did not score at the mastery level.

The Social Studies Extended Response is discussed on pages 424–425. However, the chapter entitled *Writing About Text* in the *Reasoning Through Language Arts* unit is also relevant to the Social Studies Extended Response. The lessons mentioned in the left-hand column below are from the *Writing About Text* chapter.

Content Area	Question Numbers	Number Correct	Mastery/Total
Unpack the Writing Prompt Pages 148–149	1		**1 out of 1**
Identify a Writer's Arguments and Assumptions, Develop a Thesis Statement, Collect Supporting Evidence, and Plan Your Response Pages 150–159	2, 3		**1 out of 2**
Draft Your Response Pages 160–165	4	My score is_____ based on the Drafting Checklist, page 633.	**4 out of 5**
Revise and Edit Your Response Pages 166–169	5	My score is _____ based on the Revising and Editing Checklist, page 633.	**4 out of 6**

SCIENCE

Part I: Science Practices, 10 Questions

Circle the *Question Numbers* that you answered correctly in the second column. Write the *Number Correct* in the third column. Compare your "number correct" to the "mastery" number in the fourth column. If you do not have time to review all of the *Science Practices* sections, target your study to the *Content Areas* in which you did not score at the mastery level.

Content Area	Question Numbers	Number Correct	Mastery/Total
Comprehend Science Presentations Pages 492–493	1, 2	1/2	**1 out of 2** ✓
Use the Scientific Method Pages 494–495	3, 4	2/2	**2 out of 2** ✓
Reason with, Express, and Apply Scientific Information Pages 496–499	5, 6, 7, 8	2/4	**3 out of 4**
Use Statistics and Probability Pages 500–501	9, 10	1/2	**2 out of 2**

Part II: Science Content, 25 Questions

Circle the *Question Numbers* that you answered correctly in the second column. Write the *Number Correct* in the third column. Compare your "number correct" to the "mastery" number in the fourth column. If you do not have time to review all of the *Science Content* sections, target your study to the *Content Areas* in which you did not score at the mastery level.

Content Area	Question Numbers	Number Correct	Mastery/Total
Life Science Pages 508–527	1, 4, 5, 6, 9, 10, 16, 22, 24, 25	8/10	**7 out of 10** ✓
Earth and Space Science Pages 528–541	2, 8, 12, 13, 14, 15	4/6	**4 out of 6** ✓
Physical Science Pages 542–557	3, 7, 11, 17, 18, 19, 20, 21, 23	7/9	**7 out of 9** ✓

Part III: Short Answer

Compare your "number correct" to the "mastery" number in the fourth column. Study the *Short-Answer Content Areas* that need the most work. Target your study to the *Content Areas* in which you did not score at the mastery level.

Content Area	Score	Mastery/Total
Construct Short Answer Responses Pages 502–503	My score is _____ based on the Drafting Checklist, page 637.	**2 out of 3**
Construct Short Answer Responses Pages 502–503 (See also the *Reasoning through Language Arts* unit.)	My score is _____ based on the Revising and Editing Checklist, page 637.	**2 out of 4**

Pretests

The purpose of these Pretests is to help you decide what you need to study to pass the actual GED® Test. You will use the Pretests along with their answers and the study planners on pages xvi through xxii to determine what course of study works best for you.

These Pretests are specially designed to make your study as efficient as possible. If you want to see what the actual GED® Tests look like, look at the *Practice Tests* beginning on page 559.

1. **Take** the following pretests that correspond to the four GED® Test areas.

   - **Reasoning through Language Arts, pages 2–17**
     - Part I: Reading—20 Questions
     - Part II: Writing and Language Skills—18 Questions
     - Part III: Extended Response
   - **Mathematical Reasoning, pages 18–27**
     - Part I: Quantitative Reasoning—18 Questions
     - Part II: Algebraic Reasoning and Geometry—22 Questions
   - **Social Studies, pages 28–41**
     - Part I: Social Studies Practices—10 Questions
     - Part II: Social Studies Content—25 Questions
     - Part III: Extended Response
   - **Science, pages 42–54**
     - Part I: Science Practices—10 Questions
     - Part II: Science Content—25 Questions
     - Part III: Short Answer

   Most of the questions are in multiple-choice format; some require writing a short answer or a longer, extended response.

   - For the **multiple-choice questions**, you may fill in the circles next to the correct answers in this book, or you can write your answers on a separate piece of paper.
   - You can write **short answers** on the *Science Test* and the **extended responses** on the *Reasoning through Language Arts Test* and the *Social Studies Test* on a computer or, if one is not available, on a sheet of paper.

   NOTE: Writing your responses on a computer is preferable because you will be composing your responses on a computer when you take the GED® Test. However, if you do not have a computer available when you take these pretests, write your responses on paper so that you can evaluate your writing samples.

2. **Check** your answers with the *Pretest Answers and Explanations* that begin on page 624.

3. **Fill in** the *Kaplan GED® Test Study Planners*, starting on page xvi. These charts will allow you to target your problem areas so that you can study in the most efficient manner.

4. **Use the study planners** on pages xvi through xxii to map out your work. Work your way through the book, chapter by chapter. Always review your work using the explanations in the back of the book. Once you have completed your study, take the *Practice Tests* on pages 559–621.

PART I: READING

Directions: You may fill in the circles next to the correct answers or write your answers on a separate piece of paper.

Questions 1 through 5 refer to the following passage about introverts.

Excerpted from "Don't Call Introverted Children 'Shy'"

1   Imagine a 2-year-old who greets you with a huge smile, offering a toy. Now here's another child who regards you gravely and hides behind his parent's leg. How do you feel about these two children? If you're like most people, you think of the first child as social and the second as reserved or . . . "shy." . . . But this misses what's really going on with standoffish kids. Many were born with a careful, sensitive temperament that predisposes them to look before they leap. And this can pay off handsomely as they grow, in the form of strong academics, enhanced creativity, and even a unique brand of leadership and empathy.

2   One way to see this temperament more clearly is to consider how these children react to stimuli. When these children are at 4 months, if you pop a balloon over their heads, they holler and pump their arms more than other babies do. At age 2, they proceed carefully when they see a . . . toy robot for the first time. When they're school age, they play matching games with more deliberation than their peers. . . . Notice that none of these things—popping balloons, toy robots, matching games—has anything to do with people. In other words, these kids are not antisocial. They're simply sensitive to their environments. . . . [Children with this type of temperament are highly likely to grow up to be introverted, but s]hyness and introversion are not the same thing. Shy people fear negative judgment, while introverts simply prefer less stimulation. . . .

3   Children with an alert, sensitive temperament also pay close attention to social cues and moral principles. By age 6, they cheat and break rules less than other kids do—even when they believe they won't be caught. At 7, they're more likely than their peers to be described by parents and caregivers as empathetic or conscientious. As adults, introverted leaders have even been found to deliver better outcomes than extroverts when managing employees, according to a recent study by management professor Adam Grant of the Wharton School of the University of Pennsylvania, because they encourage others' ideas instead of trying to put their own stamp on things. And they're less likely to take dangerous risks. . . .

4   But we wouldn't want to live in a world composed entirely of cautious introverts. . . . The two types [introverts and extroverts] need each other. Many successful ventures are the result of effective partnerships between introverts and extroverts. The famously charismatic Steve Jobs teamed up with powerhouse introverts at crucial points in his career at Apple, cofounding the company with the shy Steve Wozniak and bequeathing it to its current CEO, the quiet Tim Cook. . . .

5   The ideal scenario is when those two toddlers—the one who hands you the toy with the smile and the other who checks you out so carefully—grow up to run the world together.

Reprinted with permission. Susan Cain, *Time*, January 26, 2012.

1. Which one of the following best expresses the main idea of the passage?

   ● A. Companies should include both introverted and extroverted workers on teams.
   ○ B. There are advantages to being sensitive and introverted.
   ○ C. Children who are sensitive are more deliberate when playing a game.
   ○ D. Introverts simply prefer less stimulation than others do.

2. According to the passage, children with sensitive temperaments are more likely to be which of the following?

   ● A. empathetic
   ○ B. risk-taking
   ○ C. antisocial
   ○ D. noisy

3. According to the passage, the partnership between Steve Jobs and Steve Wozniak is an example of which of the following?

   ○ A. the negative consequences of a mixture of different personality types in the workplace
   ○ B. a successful collaboration between two introverts
   ● C. a successful collaboration between an introvert and an extrovert
   ○ D. a combination of people who should "run the world"

4. Which one of the following is the best summary of the second paragraph?

   ○ A. Some children respond more dramatically than others to unfamiliar or startling events.
   ● B. Observing how children respond to stimuli is the best way to study different kinds of social behavior.
   ○ C. Children who are perceived as "shy" are actually more sensitive than other children to stimuli in their environments.
   ○ D. If sensitivity in a child is not corrected by around age 2, that child will grow up to be an oversensitive adult.

5. Based on the passage, which one of the following activities would an introvert most likely prefer?

   ● A. enjoying a quiet dinner with a handful of friends
   ○ B. going alone to a club to enjoy loud dance music
   ○ C. accompanying one friend to a crowded street festival
   ○ D. participating solo in a sport called "extreme ice-slope surfing"

Questions 6 through 10 refer to the following information about forklifts and the related diagram.

Excerpt from "Forklift Safety Guide"

1   Driving a forklift differs from driving a car. In a car or truck, the front wheels steer the vehicle. A forklift has the steering wheels in the rear. The rear end of the forklift swings in a circle around the front wheels, which support most of the load. The operator must check that there is room for the rear end to swing when making turns. This clearance can be maintained in your workplace by permanently marking aisles with painted lines or arranging storage racks in a way that creates obvious aisles for travel. However, these marked aisles will only be effective if you keep them clear of stored materials.

2   A forklift is not as responsive as a car when the steering wheel is turned. Rear-wheel steering makes it difficult to stop a forklift quickly or swerve and still maintain control. It is important, then, not to drive a forklift fast or around corners quickly.

3   Driving with the load downhill can result in loss of the load and control of the forklift. If you drive a forklift on an incline, you must keep the load on the uphill side. Otherwise, you may have no weight on the wheels that steer, and you can lose control! The load could also fall off or cause the forklift to tip.

4   Often a large forklift load obstructs the driver's view in one direction. It may be necessary to travel long distances with the load to the rear (in reverse for most forklifts). Use extra caution when traveling in reverse.

Adapted with permission from the State of Washington, Department of Labor and Industries.

6. According to the passage, which one of the following is an effect of rear-wheel steering on a forklift?

   ○ A. The front wheels carry most of the load.
   ● B. The driver may have some difficulty in controlling the forklift.
   ○ C. There is a danger that the forklift will tip over.
   ○ D. The forklift driver may have little visibility.

7. Which one of the following identifies a pair of things or ideas between which the author draws a contrast?

   ● A. driving a forklift and driving a car
   ○ B. the turning radius of a forklift and the turning radius of a car
   ○ C. a warehouse with clearly marked aisles and a highway with clearly marked lanes
   ○ D. driving a forklift in reverse and walking backward

8. Together, the passage and the graphic support which one of the following conclusions?

   ○ A. A forklift should never carry a load taller than the forklift itself.
   ○ B. A forklift should travel backward only when traveling downhill.
   ○ C. A forklift cannot drive uphill unless it is carrying a load.
   ● D. A forklift that is traveling downhill with a heavy load should travel backward.

9. Which of the following best describes the author's purpose?

   ○ A. to inform drivers of cars about the differences between driving a car and driving a forklift
   ○ B. to warn the general public about the dangers of forklifts
   ● C. to explain safe practices to forklift drivers
   ○ D. to describe the difference between skilled and unskilled forklift drivers

10. Which of the following best describes the organization of the passage?

   ○ A. The author lists potential dangers inherent in forklift driving and explains how to avoid them.
   ○ B. The author states that forklift driving is dangerous and gives examples of forklift accidents to support that idea.
   ○ C. The author lists the features of forklifts and describes their benefits.
   ● D. The author explains the pros and cons of forklift driving to present a balanced picture of the value of forklifts.

Questions 11 through 15 refer to the following selections about genetically modified organism (GMO) foods.

World Food Prize Goes to Three Biotech Scientists

1. The World Food Prize Foundation took the bold step of awarding this year's prize to three pioneers of plant biotechnology whose work brought the world genetically modified crops.

2. Van Montagu and Chilton independently developed the technology in the 1980s to stably transfer foreign genes into plants, a discovery that set up a race to develop tools to genetically engineer plants. It allowed other scientists to incorporate genetic traits that allow plants to better withstand drought and extreme heat and to fight off pests and disease. Fraley was the first to successfully transfer immunity to specific bacteria into a plant. Fraley genetically engineered the first herbicide-resistant soybean in 1996.

3. Genetically enhanced crops are grown on more than 420 million acres in nearly 30 countries by over 17 million farmers worldwide, the foundation said. More than 90 percent of the users are small, resource-poor farmers in developing countries.

4. Many U.S. farmers credited genetic modifications in corn with saving last year's crop from all but total devastation, as half of the nation endured the worst drought in 60 years. Modern corn plants are more stable and can withstand a wider variety of climate conditions because of genetically improved leaves, roots, and reproductive capability.

5. Fraley said biotechnology will enable the farming industry to meet the needs of a growing global population. "We know we need from a demand perspective to double food production around the world in the next 30 years," he said.

Adapted from David Pitt, "World Food Prize goes to 3 biotech scientists," Associated Press, June 19, 2013

Dangers of GMO Foods

1. The rise in autoimmune diseases, infertility, gastrointestinal problems, and chronic diseases may be associated with the introduction of GMO (genetically modified organism) foods. In a position paper by the American Academy of Environmental Medicine, the authors ask all physicians to consider the role of GMO foods in the nation's health crisis and advise their patients to avoid all GMO foods whenever possible. The Academy also recommends a moratorium on GMO seeds and calls for immediate independent safety testing and the labeling of all food items containing genetically modified products.

2. As the reliance on GMO seeds expands worldwide, concerns about food supply and safety continue to escalate. Genetically engineered seeds are identical in structure, and if a problem affects one particular crop, a major crop failure can result. For example, following the recent failure of three GMO corn crops in three South African provinces, the Africa Centre for Biosecurity has called for an investigation and immediate ban of all GMO food. Corn is a primary source of food for southern African nations.

3. Most GMO seeds are genetically engineered to be herbicide tolerant and resistant to insect infestation and disease. Environmentalists worry that the characteristics of GMO crops may encourage farmers to increase their use of herbicides and pesticides, which will raise human consumption of dangerous toxins. GMO crops also manufacture their own pesticides, which puts further poisons into humans and soil and may cause unforeseen changes in the environment.

Adapted from Susan Brassard, "Dangers of GMO Foods," Livestrong.com, September 2, 2010

11. The author of Passage 1 most likely notes that the majority of GMO crops are cultivated by "small, resource-poor farmers in developing countries" in order to

- ○ A. highlight how GMO foods can be harmful to struggling farmers.
- ● B. suggest that GMO foods can be beneficial to struggling farmers.
- ○ C. illustrate how GMO foods can be more expensive for consumers.
- ○ D. explain why GMO crops often fail.

12. Passage 2 is primarily concerned with

- ○ A. the uses and misuses of GMO foods
- ● B. the origin and development of GMO foods
- ○ C. the unexpected benefits of GMO foods
- ○ D. the safety and reliability of GMO foods

13. What can be inferred from the first paragraph of Passage 2?

- ○ A. American physicians, as a group, are completely unaware of the potential dangers of GMOs.
- ● B. The labels of some foods containing GMO ingredients do not indicate that the products contain genetically modified components.
- ○ C. GMO foods have been proven to cause certain chronic conditions.
- ○ D. Independent safety testing has been completed for most GMO foods.

14. The two passages primarily disagree about whether or not

- ● A. GMO foods can help support a growing world population
- ○ B. GMO foods are better able to withstand drought and insect infestation than natural foods
- ○ C. GMO foods are largely a positive development for global food production
- ○ D. scientists who study GMO foods are worthy of recognition

15. Passage 2 cites the example of a major crop failure in South Africa to illustrate the dangers of planting with GMO seeds. Which paragraph in Passage 1 offers a counterexample that weakens this position?

- ○ A. paragraph 1
- ○ B. paragraph 2
- ● C. paragraph 4
- ○ D. paragraph 5

Questions 16 through 20 refer to the following.

Excerpted from *Black Beauty*

1   The first place that I can well remember was a large, pleasant meadow with a pond of clear water in it. Some shady trees leaned over it, and rushes and water lilies grew at the deep end. Over the hedge on one side we looked into a plowed field, and on the other we looked over a gate at our master's house, which stood by the roadside. . .

2   One day, when there was a good deal of kicking, my mother whinnied to me to come to her, and then she said:

3   "I wish you to pay attention to what I am going to say to you. The colts who live here are very good colts, but they are cart-horse colts, and of course they have not learned manners. You have been well-bred and well-born; your father has a great name in these parts, and your grandfather won the cup two years at the Newmarket races; your grandmother had the sweetest temper of any horse I ever knew, and I think you have never seen me kick or bite. I hope you will grow up gentle and good, and never learn bad ways; do your work with a good will, lift your feet up well when you trot, and never bite or kick even in play."

4   I have never forgotten my mother's advice; I knew she was a wise old horse, and our master thought a great deal of her. Her name was Duchess, but he often called her Pet.

5   Our master was a good, kind man. He gave us good food, good lodging, and kind words; he spoke as kindly to us as he did to his little children. We were all fond of him, and my mother loved him very much. When she saw him at the gate she would neigh with joy, and trot up to him. . . . All the horses would come to him, but I think we were his favorites. My mother always took him to the town on a market day in a light gig.

6   There was a plowboy, Dick, who sometimes came into our field to pluck blackberries from the hedge. When he had eaten all he wanted, he would have what he called fun with the colts, throwing stones and sticks at them to make them gallop. We did not much mind him, for we could gallop off, but sometimes a stone would hit and hurt us.

7   One day he was at this game, and did not know that the master was in the next field, but he was there, watching what was going on; over the hedge he jumped in a snap, and catching Dick by the arm, he gave him such a box on the ear as made him roar with the pain and surprise. As soon as we saw the master, we trotted up nearer to see what went on.

From *Black Beauty*, by Anna Sewell. Used by permission of Random House, Inc.

16. Who is the narrator in this passage?

    ○ A. a servant
    ○ B. a hired plowboy
    ● C. a young horse
    ○ D. a child

17. What is the setting of the story?

    ○ A. a town
    ○ B. a racetrack
    ○ C. a forest
    ● D. a farm

18. The narrator's account of his youth can best be described as

    ● A. melancholy
    ○ B. contented
    ○ C. regretful
    ○ D. humorous

19. The narrator would most likely describe the master in the story as

    ● A. affectionate and protective
    ○ B. arrogant and abusive
    ○ C. playful and light-hearted
    ○ D. bold and aggressive

20. The mother's speech in paragraph 3 most likely serves to

    ○ A. correct the narrator for playing too roughly
    ● B. assure the narrator he will grow up to win races like his grandfather
    ○ C. reprimand the narrator for insulting the master
    ○ D. accuse the narrator of stealing blackberries

Answers and explanations for *Reasoning through Language Arts, Part I* start on page 624.

PART II: WRITING AND LANGUAGE SKILLS

Directions: You may fill in the circles next to the correct answers or write your answers on a separate piece of paper. Some of the questions in this section mimic the GED test's drop-down menu question format. Wherever the word "Select" appears, choose the option that best completes the passage.

Questions 1 through 6 refer to the following paragraphs.

To: Parents and Guardians
From: Sonia Vasquez, School Nurse

(1) A student in [Select... ▾] diagnosed with strep throat. (2) Strep throat is a highly contagious disease and a common illness in children. (3) Unlike most sore throats, which are caused by viruses, strep throat is caused by bacteria and is treatable with antibiotics. (4) The time between exposure to the disease and the appearance of symptoms is usually one to three days. (5) To safeguard your child's health, please take the following precautions. (6) Watch your child for strep [Select... ▾] sore throat, fever, swollen glands, and headache. (8) If your child [Select... ▾]. (9) If a throat culture is positive, treatment can be started. (10) It is extremely important to take all the prescribed medicine until it is gone.

(11) Children should get immediate treatment for several reasons. (12) For one, treatment reduces spread of the disease. (13) [Select... ▾] prevent rheumatic fever. (14) Treatment also prevents other rare but possibly dangerous complications.

(15) [Select... ▾] medicine for 24 hours, he or she may return to school. (16) Please call us with any questions or concerns you have.

1. A student in [Select... ▾] diagnosed with strep throat.

   ○ A. you're child's class has been
   ○ B. your child's class have been
   ○ C. your children's class has been,
   ● D. your child's class has been

2. Watch your child for strep [Select... ▾] sore throat, fever, swollen glands, and headache.

   ○ A. symptoms. Such as
   ○ B. symptoms, the best known are
   ● C. symptoms, such as
   ○ D. symptoms examples are

3. If your child [Select...▾].

    ○ A. develops any of these symptoms, take them to the doctor
    ◉ B. develops any of these symptoms, take him or her to the doctor
    ○ C. will develop any of these symptoms, take him or her to the doctor
    ○ D. developed any of these symptoms, take them to the doctor

4. Which revision would improve the effectiveness of the passage?

    Begin a new paragraph with

    ○ A. sentence 3
    ○ B. sentence 4
    ◉ C. sentence 5
    ○ D. sentence 6

5. [Select...▾] prevent rheumatic fever.

    ◉ A. In addition, antibiotics may
    ○ B. In addition antibiotics may
    ○ C. Additionally antibiotics, may
    ○ D. When taking antibiotics, may

6. [Select...▾] medicine for 24 hours, he or she may return to school.

    ◉ A. After the fever is gone and your child has taken
    ○ B. Your child must have no fever and having taken
    ○ C. Your child, once having no fever and having taken
    ○ D. The fever must be gone and once your child is taking

Compulsive Gambling

(A)

Most of us can [Select...▾] with little damage to our finances. In contrast, compulsive gamblers cannot stop even when their behavior [Select...▾] to ruin their lives.

(B)

Gambling frequently occupies the thoughts of compulsive gamblers. For instance, they may be reliving past gambling experiences or coming up with schemes to get more money for gambling. Although they may have tried several times to stop gambling, their efforts met with failure. When trying to stop gambling, they feel irritable and restless. They need to gamble with more and more money in order to enjoy [Select...▾] money increases their desire to gamble. They may even [Select...▾] to get the funds to continue their habit. Many of them have lost jobs, important relationships, or career opportunities because of their involvement with gambling.

(C)

Compulsive gambling is like any other addiction. As gamblers lose control over gambling, they lose control over their lives as well. They may become anxious and [Select...▾] may fail to live up to their obligations, causing others to stop trusting them.

7. Most of us can [Select...▾] with little damage to our finances.

- ○ A. bet on a football game, or buy a lottery ticket
- ○ B. make bets on football games, or lottery tickets
- ◉ C. bet on a football game or buy a lottery ticket
- ○ D. place bets on football games, or on lottery tickets

8. In contrast, compulsive gamblers cannot stop even when their behavior [Select...▾] to ruin their lives.

- ○ A. had threatened
- ○ B. will threaten
- ◉ C. threatens
- ○ D. having threatened

9. Which sentence would be most effective if inserted at the beginning of paragraph B?

- A. Compulsive gamblers have a lot of problems.
- B. Some people engage in compulsive gambling.
- C. Gamblers escape from negative emotions.
- D. Compulsive gamblers display a number of consistent traits.

10. They need to gamble with more and more money in order to enjoy [Select...▾] money increases their desire to gamble.

- A. it. Losing
- B. it but losing
- C. it, losing
- D. it and losing

11. They may even [Select...▾] to get the funds to continue their habit.

- A. commit fraud, forgery, or theft
- B. commit fraud forgery or theft,
- C. commit fraud or forgery or theft
- D. commit fraud forgery or theft,

12. They may become anxious and [Select...▾] may fail to live up to their obligations, causing others to stop trusting them.

- A. depressed, or they
- B. depressed, they
- C. depressed. And they
- D. depressed and they

Questions 13 through 18 refer to the following paragraphs.

Choosing a Pet

(A)

(1) [Select...▾] just because they see an adorable puppy or kitten. (2) Unhappily, these poor creatures are likely to end up at animal shelters [Select...▾]. (3) To avoid this outcome, choose your pet wisely. (4) Remember that your pet will become a member of your family and a daily responsibility.

(B)

(5) [Select...▾] when selecting a pet. (6) First of all, do you have the time to care for a pet? (7) While some pets require little care, puppies and kittens need to [Select...▾]. (8) If the animal needs exercise, is your home large enough? (9) Would you enjoy taking your pet outdoors for exercise? (10) Do you think people should get a lot of exercise? (11) Can you afford the costs of food, vaccinations, and health checkups? (12) Does your building allow pets? (13) Finally, if you must leave home for a few days, can you find someone to care for your pet?

(C)

(14) Once you choose a pet that is appropriate for your lifestyle, bring the animal to a veterinarian for examination. (15) You should be able to return the pet [Select...▾].

13. [Select...▾] just because they see an adorable puppy or kitten.

○ A. Being impulsive, people often make buys at Pet Stores

○ B. People often make impulse buys at pet stores

● C. Often, people buy on impulse at Pet Stores

○ D. It often happens that people buy on impulse at pet stores

14. Unhappily, these poor creatures are likely to end up at animal shelters [Select...▾].

○ A. when the owner find out he can't care for the animals

○ B. the owners having discovered they can't take care of the animals

○ C. their owners finding out that he can't care for the animals

● D. when the owners find they can't care for the animals

15. [Select...] when selecting a pet.

   ● A. There are several factors to consider
   ○ B. There is several factors to consider
   ○ C. There being several factors to consider
   ○ D. There are several factors considering

16. While some pets require little care, puppies and kittens need to [Select...].

   ○ A. be housebroken and to train them
   ○ B. housebreaking and training
   ● C. be housebroken and trained
   ○ D. be housebroken and training

17. Which revision should be made to the placement of sentence 10?

   ○ A. move sentence 10 to the beginning of paragraph B
   ○ B. move sentence 10 to follow sentence 6
   ○ C. move sentence 10 to the beginning of paragraph C
   ● D. remove sentence 10

18. You should be able to return the pet [Select...].

   ○ A. if the animal was unhealthy
   ○ B. if the animal were going to be unhealthy
   ○ C. if the animal will be unhealthy
   ● D. if the animal is unhealthy

Answers and explanations for *Reasoning through Language Arts, Part II* start on page 625.

Part III: Extended Response

Directions: Read both the selection and the writing prompt and answer the questions that follow.

<u>Questions 1–10</u> are based on the process of writing a response to a reading selection.
NOTE: Do not start writing your response until you are asked to do so at question 9.

Identity Theft

Identity theft happens when someone steals your personal information and uses it without your permission. It's a serious crime that can wreak havoc on your finances, credit history, and reputation — and can take time, money, and patience to resolve. If identity thieves have your personal information, they can drain your bank account, run up charges on your credit cards, open new utility accounts, or get medical treatment on your health insurance.

How do identity thieves get your personal financial information? They might go through trash cans and dumpsters, stealing bills and documents that have sensitive information. Or an identity thief might misuse the name of a legitimate business, and call or send emails that trick you into revealing personal information. Finally, an identity thief might steal your wallet, purse, backpack, or mail, and remove your credit cards, driver's license, passport, health insurance card, and other items that contain personal information.

There are three important ways in which you can protect yourself from identity thieves. First, keep your financial papers secure. Lock your financial documents and records in a safe place at home, and lock your wallet or purse in a safe place at work. When you go out, take only the identification, credit and debit cards you need, and leave your Social Security card at home. Shred receipts, credit offers, credit applications, insurance forms, physician statements, checks, bank statements, expired charge cards, and similar documents when you don't need them any longer. Take outgoing mail to post office collection boxes or the post office, and promptly remove mail that arrives in your mailbox. If you won't be home for several days, request a vacation hold on your mail. When you order new checks, don't have them mailed to your home, unless you have a secure mailbox with a lock.

Second, make sure you know who is getting your personal or financial information. Don't give out personal information on the phone, through the mail, or over the Internet unless you've initiated the contact or know who you're dealing with. If a company that claims to have an account with you sends email asking for personal information, don't click on links in the email. Instead, type the company name into your web browser, go to their site, and contact them through customer service. Ask whether the company really sent a request.

Finally, take steps to protect your online information as well. A "lock" icon on the status bar of your Internet browser means your information will be safe when it's transmitted. Look for the lock before you send personal or financial information online. Use strong passwords with your laptop, credit, bank, and other accounts. Install anti-virus software, anti-spyware software, and a firewall, and set your preference to update these protections often. Don't open files, click on links, or download programs sent by strangers.

Adapted from the Federal Trade Commission's website: www.consumer.ftc.gov.

Writing Prompt

The passage above outlines specific ways in which identity thieves go about stealing financial information from others. Read the passage closely.

Write a response to this passage that analyzes the mistakes that can make people vulnerable to identity theft. Use relevant and specific information from the reading selection to support your response.

Unpack the Writing Prompt

1. What is the topic of the writing prompt?

    Identity theft

2. What does the prompt ask you to do?

    read carefully for information.

3. What does the prompt tell you that you need to include in the response?

    relevant and specific information

4. Are you being asked to give your opinion or to explain something?

    explain

Develop Your Argument, Thesis Statement, and Evidence

5. What is the writer's main point about the topic?

    to be careful with your information

6. What will be your main point in response to the writing prompt?

    How you can improve your safety —

7. What are three pieces of evidence from the text that you will use to support your point?

    How people get the info

    How to dispose of your info

    why its important to be careful

Plan, Draft, Revise, and Edit Your Response

8. On a piece of paper, make a plan for your response.

9. On a computer or on a piece of paper, write a response to the prompt that includes an introduction, a body, and a conclusion.

10. On the computer or on the paper, make revisions to improve your response and edit to correct errors in grammar, usage, spelling, capitalization, and punctuation.

The *Extended Response Evaluation Guide for Reasoning through Language Arts,*
Part III starts on page 626.

MATHEMATICAL REASONING PRETEST

PART I: QUANTITATIVE REASONING—18 QUESTIONS

Directions: You may fill in the circles next to the correct answers or write your answers on a separate piece of paper. You MAY use a calculator.

Questions 1 and 2 refer to the following information and graph.

Video Warehouse has divided the surrounding community into four advertising zones. The graph shows the total number of customers from each zone for a three-week period.

Video Warehouse

1. During the three weeks, how many customers came from Zones 3 and 4?

   ○ A. between 900 and 1,000
   ○ B. between 1,000 and 1,100
   ◐ C. between 1,100 and 1,200
   ● D. between 1,200 and 1,300

2. Approximately what is the ratio of customers from Zone 1 to customers from Zone 3?

   ○ A. 3:5
   ○ B. 3:2
   ○ C. 2:1
   ● D. 1:2

3. A potter uses $\frac{3}{5}$ of a pound of clay to make a bowl. How many bowls could the potter make from 10 pounds of clay?

   ○ A. 6
   ○ B. 8
   ◐ C. 16
   ○ D. 17

4. Janelle has recently been hired for the job of library assistant. The following graph shows what percent of her time will be spent on each of five tasks each day.

Library Assistant Job Duties

Counter Duties 44%

Helping Patrons 19%

Processing New Books 9%

Repairing Bindings 6%

Reshelving Books 22%

The number of hours that Janelle will spend working at the counter is about how many times the number of hours that she will spend processing new books and repairing bindings?

   ○ A. 2
   ○ B. 3
   ◐ C. 4
   ○ D. 6

5. Fifteen percent of the workers at Nationwide Industries earn minimum wage. If 24 workers earn minimum wage, how many total workers are there at Nationwide Industries?

   ○ A.   4
   ○ B. 36
   ● C. 160
   ○ D. 360

6. An accountant is going to pay the following four bills:

Bill	Amount
W	$27.10
X	$261.00
Y	$2.80
Z	$27.20

   The accountant will pay the bills in order from smallest to largest. In what order will he pay them?

   ○ A. W, X, Z, Y
   ○ B. X, W, Z, Y
   ○ C. Y, X, W, Z
   ● D. Y, W, Z, X

7. A jar holds 16 ounces of honey. A cook is going to make two recipes. One of the recipes calls for 2.5 ounces of honey, and the other calls for 4.25 ounces of honey. After the cook has made those two recipes, how many ounces of honey will be left in the jar?

   ○ A.   6.75
   ● B.   9.25
   ○ C. 10.00
   ○ D. 11.75

8. All numbers that are evenly divisible by both 6 and 14 are also divisible by which of the following numbers?

   ○ A.   8
   ○ B. 12
   ○ C. 21
   ● D. 28

9. Alice, Kathy, and Sheila work as medical assistants at Valley Clinic. Alice has worked 8 years longer than Kathy. Kathy has worked half as long as Sheila. If Sheila has worked at the company for 10 years, how many years has Alice worked there?

   ○ A.   5
   ○ B.   8
   ○ C. 10
   ● D. 13

Question 10 is based on the spinner below.

10. The spinner shown in the drawing is divided into eight equal sections. If you spin the spinner one time, what is the probability of NOT getting blue?

   ○ A. $\frac{1}{8}$
   ○ B. $\frac{1}{4}$
   ○ C. $\frac{3}{4}$
   ● D. $\frac{7}{8}$

11. A computer monitor is regularly priced at $320. During a two-day sale, the price was decreased to $240. Which of the following is the percentage decrease of the monitor's price during the sale?

   ● A. 25%
   ○ B. 33%
   ○ C. 75%
   ○ D. 80%

12. For a 10-day period, a bank kept track of the number of new accounts opened each day. The results are shown in the table below. What is the median number of accounts opened per day during this 10-day period?

Day	Accounts	Day	Accounts
May 7	6	May 14	4
May 8	2	May 15	8
May 9	7	May 16	6
May 10	5	May 17	4
May 11	4	May 18	7

   ○ A. 5
   ● B. 5.3
   ○ C. 5.5
   ○ D. 6

13. Jim is a salesperson, and his employers expect him to sell at least $12,000 in merchandise per month. In April, Jim sold $2,500 in the first week of the month and twice that much in the second week. How much must he sell in the rest of April combined in order to sell the minimum expected of him?

   ● A. $4,500
   ○ B. $5,500
   ○ C. $9,500
   ○ D. $12,000

14. Angela likes to use two walking sticks when she goes hiking, but the two walking sticks she has been given recently are different lengths. One is $3\frac{4}{5}$ feet long, and the other is $3\frac{1}{2}$ feet long.

$3\frac{4}{5}$ feet $3\frac{1}{2}$ feet

Angela wants to cut the longer stick to match the shorter one. How much should she cut from the longer stick so that the two walking sticks will be the same length?

   ○ A. $\frac{3}{4}$ feet
   ○ B. $\frac{3}{5}$ feet
   ○ C. $\frac{3}{10}$ feet
   ● D. $\frac{1}{4}$ feet

Question 15 is based on the following number line.

0   $\frac{1}{2}$ 1 $1\frac{1}{2}$ 2 $2\frac{1}{2}$ 3 $3\frac{1}{2}$ 4 $4\frac{1}{2}$ 5

15. Which of the following is the decimal point value of the dot on the line above?

   ○ A. 3.25
   ○ B. 3.50
   ● C. 3.75
   ○ D. 4.00

Question 16 is based on the following information and graph.

Marjorie has a class of 35 students, and she tracked their performance on a recent math exam. The graph below represents how their scores were distributed along the range of possible scores, from F to A.

Based on the graph, which of the following is a true statement?

A. None of Marjorie's students received an F on the exam.

B. Most of Marjorie's students received either an A or a B on the exam.

C. If Marjorie gave the same exam again to another group of students, most of those students would receive a C.

D. More students received either an A or a B than received either a D or an F.

17. Jason deposits $5,000 in a bank account that will pay him 4% simple interest annually. If Jason deposits no more than the initial $5,000, how much money will be in the account at the end of five years? (The formula for simple interest is $I = prt$ or $interest = principal \times rate \times time$. Use a decimal to express the interest when using that formula.)

A. $200
B. $1,000
C. $5,000
D. $6,000

18. A local library shows movies on Thursday evenings. The library administrator has chosen the next six movies he will show, but he has not decided in which order to show them. How many possible orderings of the six movies are there?

A. 21
B. 36
C. 720
D. 1,012

Answers and explanations for *Mathematical Reasoning, Part I* start on page 628.

Below is a formula sheet that appears on the actual GED® Test. You can refer to this page on Part II of this Pretest.

Area of a:

square	$A = s^2$
rectangle	$A = lw$
parallelogram	$A = bh$
triangle	$A = \frac{1}{2}bh$
trapezoid	$A = \frac{1}{2}h(b_1 + b_2)$
circle	$A = \pi r^2$

Perimeter of a:

square	$P = 4s$
rectangle	$P = 2l + 2w$
triangle	$P = s_1 + s_2 + s_3$
Circumference of a circle	$C = 2\pi r$ OR $C = \pi d$; $\pi \approx 3.14$

Surface area and volume of a:

rectangular/right prism	$SA = ph + 2B$	$V = Bh$
cylinder	$SA = 2\pi rh + 2\pi r^2$	$V = \pi r^2 h$
pyramid	$SA = \frac{1}{2}ps + B$	$V = \frac{1}{3}Bh$
cone	$SA = \pi rs + \pi r^2$	$V = \frac{1}{3}\pi r^2 h$
sphere	$SA = 4\pi r^2$	$V = \frac{4}{3}\pi r^3$

(p = perimeter of base with area B; $\pi \approx 3.14$)

Data

mean	mean is equal to the total of the values of a data set, divided by the number of elements in the data set
median	median is the middle value in an odd number of ordered values of a data set, or the mean of the two middle values in an even number of ordered values in a data set

Algebra

slope of a line	$m = \dfrac{y_2 - y_1}{x_2 - x_1}$
slope-intercept form of the equation of a line	$y = mx + b$
point-slope form of the equation of a line	$y - y_1 = m(x - x_1)$
standard form of a quadratic equation	$y = ax^2 + bx + c$
quadratic formula	$x = \dfrac{-b \pm \sqrt{b^2 - 4ac}}{2a}$
Pythagorean theorem	$a^2 + b^2 = c^2$
simple interest	$I = Prt$ (I = interest, P = principal, r = rate, t = time)
distance formula	$d = rt$
total cost	total cost = (number of units) $\times$ (price per unit)

Provided by GED® Testing Service.

PART II: ALGEBRAIC REASONING AND GEOMETRY—22 QUESTIONS

Directions: You may fill in the circles next to the correct answers or write your answers on a separate piece of paper. Refer to the formula sheet on page 22 as needed. You MAY use your calculator.

1. Which point on the number line below represents the value $-\frac{16}{6}$?

- ○ A. Point A
- ● B. Point B
- ○ C. Point C
- ○ D. Point D

2. Evaluate the expression $2x - (4y - 3) + 5xz$, when $x = -3$, $y = 2$, and $z = -1$.

B - 3 = 5

- ○ A. 45
- ○ B. 16
- ● C. 4
- ○ D. −10

3. On April 1 of this year, the high temperature in Northville was 46 degrees Fahrenheit. Then a sudden snowstorm arose, and the temperature dropped sharply to a low of −8 degrees Fahrenheit. What was the magnitude of the change in temperature on that day?

- ● A. 54
- ○ B. 46
- ○ C. 36
- ○ D. −36

Question 4 refers to the following drawing.

4. A tower casts a shadow 11 feet long. The distance from the top of the tower to the end of the shadow is 61 feet. How many feet tall is the tower?

- ○ A. 50
- ○ B. 60
- ○ C. 61
- ● D. 72

Question 5 is based on the following information.

Designer Furnishings sells premade cabinets and cupboards, as shown below.

Model	Dimensions (in inches)
411R	32 by 22 by 10
412R	28 by 36 by 15
413S	24 by 72 by 18
414S	25 by 24 by 6

5. Each face of cabinet 413S is in the shape of a rectangle. What is the volume of Model 413S in cubic feet?

- A.   18
- ● B.   31
- C.   36
- D. 108

6. Together, Levy and Matthew earn $4,680 per month. Levy earns $520 more per month than Matthew earns. How much does Levy earn per month?

- A. $2,080
- B. $2,340 —
- ● C. $2,600
- D. $4,160

7. The design for a new cone-shaped closed container is shown below. What is the surface area of this container, in square inches? You can select the correct formula from the formula sheet on page 22.

slant height 6 in.

diameter 4 in.

- A.   4π
- B. 12π
- C. 16π
- D. 28π

8. Simplify this polynomial:
$3x^3 + x + 2x^3 - 4x^2 + 14y - 2(y + x)$.

- A. $3x^3 - 3x^2 + 14(-2y + 2x)$
- B. $5x^3 - 3x^2 + 14y - 2y - 2x$
- C. $3x^3 - x + 4x^2 + 12y$
- D. $5x^3 - 4x^2 - x + 12y$

9. A rectangle is drawn on a coordinate grid. Three of its four vertices are located at points (−1, −2), (−1, 4) and (2, −2) What is the location of the fourth vertex? Mark your answer on the coordinate grid below.

10. Which of the following expressions is equal to the expression $4x - 2(3x - 9)$?

○ A. $18 - 2x$
○ B. $-10x - 18$
○ C. $-2x - 18$
○ D. $10x - 18$

11. In the equation $3x^2 - 10x = 8$, which of the following values for x will make the equation true?

○ A. -4
○ B. -3
○ C. 3
○ D. 4

12. Solve for x: $12(x - 2) < 24$

○ A. $x < 0$
○ B. $x > 0$
○ C. $x < 12$
○ D. $x < 4$

13. Scientists estimate that Earth is 4,540,000,000 years old. What is that number expressed in scientific notation?

○ A. 4.54×10^7
○ B. 4.54×10^9
○ C. 454×10^{10}
○ D. $2(127 \times 10^7)$

$SA = \pi rs + \pi r^2$

$V = \frac{1}{3}\pi r^2 h$

14. Joe just purchased an oddly shaped piece of property, depicted in the figure below.

What is the area, in square yards, of Joe's new property?

- ○ A. 120
- ○ B. 134
- ○ C. 140
- ○ D. 204

15. The XYZ Company sells hats and will monogram them if customers choose. The price for each monogram varies depending on how many hats a customer would like to have monogrammed. The monogram prices for several order sizes are shown below:

Number of hats to be monogrammed (n)	Price per monogram (p)
1	$5
2	$4.50
3	$4.00
4	$3.50
5	$3.00
6	$2.50

Which of the following best expresses the relationship of price per monogram (for all nonnegative values of p) to number of hats monogrammed shown in the table above?

- ○ A. $p = \$5.00 - (n - 1)\$0.50$
- ○ B. $p = \$5.00 - n(\$0.50)$
- ○ C. $p = (n - 1)\$5.00$
- ○ D. $p = \$0.50(10n)$

16. A parallelogram has two obtuse angles and two acute angles. If the measure of one of the obtuse angles is 110°, what is the measure, in degrees, of one of the acute angles?

- ○ A. 10°
- ○ B. 70°
- ○ C. 110°
- ○ D. 240°

Question 17 refers to the following graph.

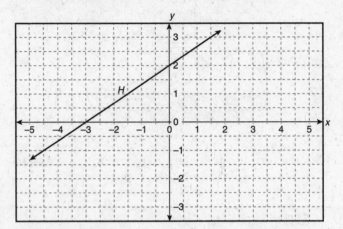

Line *H* is the graph of which of the following equations?

- ○ A. $y = \frac{1}{3}x + 2$
- ○ B. $y + 2 = \frac{2}{3}x$
- ○ C. $y = \frac{2}{3}x + 2$
- ○ D. $y = 3(x - 2) + 2$

18. A fountain's pool is enclosed by a circular plastic tank. The distance from the center of the pool to the wall of the tank is 10 feet. How long is the wall of the tank in feet?

- ○ A. 20π
- ○ B. $\frac{20}{\pi}$
- ○ C. 25π
- ○ D. 100π

19. Line *W* passes through the following points on the coordinate grid: (0, – 9) and (4, –1). What is the slope of line *W*?

   ○ A. -2

   ○ B. $-\frac{1}{2}$

   ○ C. $\frac{1}{2}$

   ○ D. 2

20. Beansey's Baked Beans, Inc., has developed a new can for its baked beans, shown below:

8 cm

12 cm

What is the volume of the new can, in cubic centimeters?

   ○ A. 48π
   ○ B. 96π
   ○ C. 192π
   ○ D. 768π

21. Tina is considering renting a commercial space for her business. The space is shown below.

70 ft

30 ft

40 ft

50 ft

What is the area of the commercial space, in square feet?

   ○ A.   290
   ○ B. 2,100
   ○ C. 2,800
   ○ D. 4,100

22. In the system of equations $3x - 3y = -9$ and $2x + y = 9$, solve for both *x* and *y*. You may use the coordinate grid below to help your work.

What is the solution set for *x* and *y*?

   ○ A. $(2, -5)$
   ○ B. $(0, 3)$
   ○ C. $(0, 9)$
   ○ D. $(2, 5)$

Answers and explanations for *Mathematical Reasoning, Part II* start on page 628.

PART I: PRACTICES—10 QUESTIONS

Directions: You may fill in the circles next to the correct answers or write your answers on a separate piece of paper. You MAY use your calculator if desired.

Question 1 refers to the following passage.

With the passage of the Fifteenth Amendment in 1870, all African Americans were given the right to vote throughout the United States. However, many Southern states quickly enacted legislative barriers to disenfranchise these new voters. Provisions such as poll taxes, literacy tests, and the grandfather clause prevented many African Americans from exercising their rights. For nearly one hundred years, these restrictions persisted in many Southern states. The civil rights movement, which gained national momentum in the 1950s, sought to address this unequal treatment in voting rights laws. Finally, in 1965, the Voting Rights Act provided for federal oversight of states that had previously raised unfair barriers to African American voting and outlawed discriminatory measures such as poll taxes and literacy tests. Voter participation among African Americans dramatically increased in the following years.

1. Which of the following describes the author's main idea?

   ○ A. The Voting Rights Act of 1965 ended discrimination in all areas of American society.
   ○ B. The main effect of the Voting Rights Act of 1965 was to empower individual states to end discriminatory measures against African American voting.
   ○ C. The Voting Rights Act of 1965 gave the federal government oversight of state elections to end barriers against African American voting.
   ● D. The Fifteenth Amendment did not end racism in Southern states.

Question 2 refers to the following passage.

To address the nation's financial insolvency after the Revolutionary War, George Washington turned to his secretary of the treasury, Alexander Hamilton. Hamilton proposed creating a national bank, which would help to pay back the nation's debt and stabilize the nation's currency. Immediately, Hamilton faced stiff opposition from those who believed in a **strict construction** of the Constitution; they believed that Congress and the president could only exercise powers specifically written in the Constitution. Because the Constitution did not give the power to create a national bank, Hamilton's actions would be unconstitutional. In response, Hamilton offered a justification for the constitutionality of his bank based on a **loose construction** of the Constitution, meaning that Congress could use the Necessary and Proper Clause of the Constitution to stretch its power beyond what was specified in the words of the document. In Washington's first great test of presidential leadership, he sided with Hamilton and the idea of a national bank.

2. What is meant by the term "construction" in the passage?

   ○ A. building
   ○ B. creation
   ● C. interpretation
   ○ D. structure

Questions 3 and 4 refer to the following passage.

In an attempt to make consumers more aware of the nutritional value of the foods they purchase, the Food and Drug Administration (FDA) is attempting to impose strict new regulations on all food retailers. These regulations would require that the caloric information of each food product be clearly posted on the premises, typically through signs that would be expensive to create and maintain. While these regulations would place a financial burden on all food retailers—an expense that would necessarily be passed on to consumers—the regulations would be particularly devastating to smaller restaurants, grocery stores, and convenience stores that offer fresh food items. To relieve this burden on smaller businesses, Congress has proposed the Common Sense Nutritional Disclosure Act, which would exempt smaller food establishments that primarily sell prepackaged foods from having to post on-site information. Also, under this legislation, restaurants that take most of their orders remotely can post caloric information online.

3. What is the author's point of view regarding the FDA's new food regulations?

    ● A. The FDA's new regulations would place a financial hardship on small food retailers.
    ○ B. The FDA's new regulations would help consumers choose foods of a higher nutritional value.
    ○ C. The FDA's new regulations would have a more severe financial impact on chain restaurants than on smaller food retailers.
    ○ D. The FDA's new regulations would give food retailers more diverse options for displaying caloric information.

4. Which one of the following words points to the author's viewpoint regarding the FDA's strict new regulations?

    ○ A. "aware"
    ○ B. "strict"
    ● C. "devastating"
    ○ D. "remotely"

Questions 5 and 6 refer to the following paragraph.

It is known that a significant quantity of oil exists within the Arctic National Wildlife Refuge (ANWR) of Alaska. Shockingly, there are many who would have us ignore this incredible resource housed right within our national borders. One commonly cited reason against drilling for oil in the ANWR is that the drilling process would endanger the existence of the porcupine caribou, whose calving grounds encompass much of the region. But science has shown us that as many as 99 percent of all the species that once existed on Earth are now extinct, and the vast majority of these extinctions were not caused by humans. Clearly, then, extinctions are a sad but natural aspect of life on Earth, and we have no reason not to drill in the ANWR.

5. Which of the following statements is a correct evaluation of the argument?

    ○ A. The argument is valid, because it relies on scientific evidence that has been shown to be true.
    ○ B. The argument is valid, because extracting oil would bolster the national economy.
    ○ C. The argument is invalid, because it confuses correlation with causation.
    ● D. The argument is invalid, because it attempts to refute one reason against doing something while ignoring other possible reasons.

6. Which of the following considerations, if true, best illustrates why the author's evidence is inadequate?

    ● A. Some people depend on the porcupine caribou for food.
    ○ B. People who call themselves "scientists" may make claims that are long held to be true yet are eventually shown to be false.
    ○ C. There is not enough oil in the ANWR to have a measurable impact on global oil prices.
    ○ D. Extracting oil from the ANWR would reduce the foreign trade deficit.

Questions 7 and 8 are based on the following information and map.

After World War II, Germany was split into two nations: democratic West Germany and communist East Germany. West Germany was under the control of the victorious Allies, who formed an alliance called the North Atlantic Treaty Organization (NATO). In 1955, NATO decided to allow West Germany to join NATO and to rearm. In response, the U.S.S.R. (that is, the Soviet Union) and a number of communist Eastern European countries formed what they called a "Treaty of Friendship, Co-operation, and Mutual Assistance," commonly referred to as the Warsaw Pact. In the Warsaw Pact, the communist countries agreed to band together if one of them was attacked, and the smaller communist countries agreed to put their military forces under the command of the Soviet Union.

Source: Central Intelligence Agency

7. Some historians believe that, in forming the Warsaw Pact, the Soviet Union wanted to create a buffer between itself and NATO countries. How does the map support that view?

   ○ A. The map indicates that many of the World War II Allies joined the Warsaw Pact, but not until the 1960s.
   ○ B. The map shows that most of the Warsaw Pact countries lay between the Soviet Union and Western countries, including France, West Germany, and Great Britain.
   ● C. The map shows that the Warsaw Pact involved the building of a wall between the Soviet Union and Western Europe.
   ○ D. The map indicates that the Soviet Union was made up of smaller republics on its western border.

8. The map could be used to dispute which one of the following claims?

   ● A. In forming the Warsaw Pact, the Soviet Union greatly increased its access to oceanic coastline.
   ○ B. In forming the Warsaw Pact, the Soviet Union wished to increase its trade with Africa.
   ○ C. The Warsaw Pact benefitted Bulgaria and Romania no less than the Soviet Union.
   ○ D. The Warsaw Pact initially included Albania.

Question 9 refers to the following table and map.

Average Yearly Rainfall in New England	
State	Avg. Rainfall/Year
Connecticut	47 inches
Maine	41 inches
Massachusetts	45 inches
New Hampshire	42 inches
Rhode Island	44 inches
Vermont	39 inches

Source: netstate.com

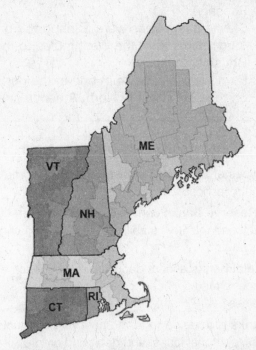

9. What is the average (arithmetic mean) yearly rainfall, in inches, of the three northernmost states in New England?

- ● A. $40\frac{2}{3}$
- ○ B. 41
- ○ C. 42
- ○ D. $43\frac{1}{3}$

Question 10 refers to the following graph.

The graph below shows the percent of people who voted in presidential elections from 1996 to 2012.

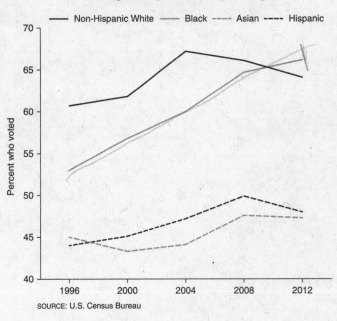

Voting Rates by Race and Hispanic Origin

——— Non-Hispanic White ——— Black ----- Asian ---- Hispanic

SOURCE: U.S. Census Bureau

10. Over the period illustrated by the line graph, the rate at which eligible black voters participated in presidential elections

- ○ A. fluctuated up and down, but ended higher than it began
- ● B. steadily increased, surpassing that of white voters in the 2012 elections
- ○ C. increased sharply in the middle of the time period shown on the graph before dropping back closer to its original level
- ○ D. was consistently lower than the rates of most other races and ethnic groups

Answers and explanations for *Social Studies, Part I* start on page 631.

Directions: You may fill in the circles next to the correct answers or write your answers on a separate piece of paper.

Questions 1 and 2 refer to the following map.

Colonial Triangular Trade

1. Based on this map, what were the three sides of the triangle in the triangular trade?

   ○ A. Europe to the West Indies; the West Indies to Africa; Africa to the British colonies

   ○ B. the West Indies to the British colonies; the British colonies to Africa; Africa to the West Indies

   ● C. the West Indies to England; England to the British colonies; the British colonies to Africa

   ○ D. South America to Africa; Africa to the West Indies; the West Indies to the British colonies

2. Which statement is a conclusion based on the map rather than a supporting detail from the map?

   ○ A. Cargo ships never had to sail empty on any leg of a profitable triangular journey.

   ○ B. The journey of Africans from Africa to the Americas was called the Middle Passage.

   ○ C. Slaves sometimes were transported on cargo ships from the West Indies to the British colonies.

   ● D. Rum was shipped from one of the ports on the east coast of North America.

Question 3 refers to the following information.

Several types of U.S. banking institutions and some of their main services are described below.

Federal Reserve Banks control the nation's monetary policy and maintain stability of the banking and financial systems.

Commercial banks accept deposits, make loans, and provide related services to corporations and other businesses.

Retail banks provide savings and checking accounts, mortgages, personal loans, and debit and credit cards to consumers.

Community development banks serve residents and spur economic development in low- to moderate-income areas.

Credit unions provide their members with checking and savings accounts, mortgages, and other services at a lower interest rate than other financial institutions.

3. At which type of financial institution would the ABC Printing Company be most likely to take out a loan to finance the purchase of a new printing press?

   ○ A. Federal Reserve Bank

   ○ B. commercial bank

   ● C. retail bank

   ○ D. community development bank

Questions 4 and 5 refer to the following passage.

Somerville has had a long history of corruption. From the 1960s to the 1980s, its mayor, councilors, and tax assessors were involved in a complex network of bribery and favors. The "strong-mayor" system of government is responsible for this corruption; in the history of Massachusetts, all but a single instance of municipal corruption occurred under a strong-mayor government. Because that tainted system is still in place to this day in Somerville, the current mayor must be viewed with strong suspicion.

4. Which of the following words or phrases is based on the author's opinion, not fact?

   ○ A. long history
   ○ B. tainted system
   ● C. bribery
   ○ D. mayors, councilors, and tax assessors

5. Is the author's conclusion properly supported by evidence?

   ○ A. Yes, because the corruption in Somerville spreads beyond the office of the mayor.
   ○ B. Yes, because 20 years of corruption can accurately be called a "long history."
   ○ C. No, because there is no mention of criminal investigation or charges.
   ● D. No, because no indication is given that the current mayor will behave as past mayors did.

6. Most Americans believe it is their duty as citizens to take part in our system of government.

   Which of the following actions represents participation in government?

   ○ A. pursuing higher education
   ○ B. displaying the American flag
   ○ C. volunteering at a hospital
   ● D. serving on a jury

7. In many Latin American countries, control passes back and forth between military and civilian rule. Generally, when a civilian government rules, it tries to improve conditions for the nation's citizens, but these attempts lead to turmoil and civil unrest. In response, the military takes power and imposes strict controls on the populace. Such shifts have taken place in Argentina, Peru, and Chile in recent decades.

   Which of the following is highly valued by those who favor military rule?

   ○ A. social welfare
   ○ B. freedom
   ○ C. democracy
   ● D. law and order

Questions 8 and 9 refer to the following chart.

Presidential Powers in Several Nations

Constitutional Power	U.S.A.	South Africa	France	Mexico
Controls armed forces	✔	✔	✔	✔
Approves legislation	✔	✔	✔	✔
Appoints executive branch officials	✔	✔	✔	✔
Appoints judges	✔	✔	✔	✔
Appoints prime minister			✔	
Dissolves legislature			✔	

8. Which of the following is a difference between the powers of the U.S. and French presidents?

   ○ A. The U.S. president controls the armed forces, and the French president does not.
   ○ B. The U.S. president approves legislation, and the French president does not.
   ◉ C. The French president has the power to dissolve the legislature, while the U.S. president does not.
   ○ D. The French president has the power to appoint judges, while the U.S. president does not.

9. Which of the following statements is a conclusion based on the chart rather than a detail?

   ○ A. The president of South Africa cannot dissolve the legislature.
   ◉ B. Of all the presidents shown, the French president has the greatest variety of powers.
   ○ C. The president of Mexico has the power to appoint judges.
   ○ D. The U.S. president has the power to approve legislation.

Question 10 refers to the following paragraph.

After the Civil War, southern states passed Jim Crow laws, which kept whites and blacks apart in public places like restaurants, buses, and restrooms. In an 1896 case, *Plessy v. Ferguson*, the U.S. Supreme Court upheld a Louisiana law requiring separate railroad cars for white and black passengers. The Court ruled that it was constitutional to have "separate but equal" facilities for whites and blacks and other minorities. The Court reasoned that "legislation is powerless to eradicate racial instincts or to abolish distinctions." One justice dissented, saying that the decision was "inconsistent with the personal liberty of citizens, white and black."

10. Which of the following statements is an opinion rather than a fact?

   ○ A. In the late 1800s, many southern states passed Jim Crow laws to keep whites and blacks separate in public places.
   ○ B. In Louisiana, a law required separate railroad cars for white and black passengers.
   ○ C. *Plessy v. Ferguson* was an 1896 Supreme Court case that challenged the Louisiana law related to segregated railroad cars.
   ◉ D. The U.S. Supreme Court ruling in *Plessy v. Ferguson* was wrong because it infringed on freedoms guaranteed in the Constitution.

Questions 11 and 12 refer to the following paragraph and chart.

When the U.S. government cannot cover its expenses, it borrows money by selling bonds. It pays back the principal and interest on the bonds over a period of many years. The national debt is the total amount the U.S. government owes at any particular point in time. In 2010, this was about $13.2 trillion.

One way of measuring the national debt is by computing the per capita national debt. The per capita national debt is the total national debt divided by the population of the United States. The graph below shows the per capita national debt every five years from 1990 to 2010.

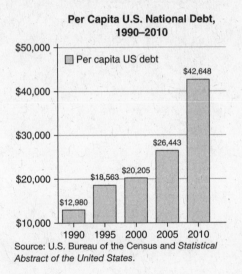

Per Capita U.S. National Debt, 1990–2010

□ Per capita US debt

1990: $12,980
1995: $18,563
2000: $20,205
2005: $26,443
2010: $42,648

Source: U.S. Bureau of the Census and *Statistical Abstract of the United States.*

11. Which of the following conclusions is supported by the data in the paragraph and the graph?

   ○ A. The nation's debt increased at a faster rate than did the U.S. population during the period shown on the graph.
   ○ B. Every person in the United States owed an average of $20,000 to the government in the year 2000.
   ○ C. In 1990, the U.S. government owed every American about $13,000.
   ○ D. The U.S. government sold about $5.7 trillion worth of bonds in 2000.

12. Which action would enable the U.S. government to reduce its debt?

   ○ A. postpone payment of that debt
   ○ B. pay interest to foreign investors
   ○ C. pay interest to U.S. investors
   ○ D. raise taxes and cut spending

Question 13 refers to the following paragraph.

The ninth-century BCE collapse of the Mayan empire is often attributed to a massive drought. But new geological and archaeological evidence from the Yucatan peninsula in Mexico shows that the Maya engaged in massive deforestation, clearing land for crops and burning the wood to bake bricks for their cities and temples. Modern weather models show that the destruction of native vegetation could have contributed to as much as 60 percent of the dry weather that is believed to have ended this civilization.

13. According to the theory presented in the paragraph, what was the effect of Mayan deforestation of the Yucatan peninsula?

   ○ A. The Mayans needed more land to grow crops.
   ○ B. Scientists discovered new evidence in the geological record.
   ● C. A drought was significantly worsened due to lack of native vegetation.
   ○ D. Baking bricks required an enormous amount of wood.

Question 14 refers to the following map.

Great Britain during the Industrial Revolution, 1830

14. Which of the following is a conclusion based on the map rather than a supporting detail from the map?

   ○ A. The Industrial Revolution took place in Great Britain around the year 1830.

   ○ B. More than 300,000 people lived in Sheffield around 1830.

   ◉ C. Many cities had large populations because nearby coal and iron ore deposits meant jobs.

   ○ D. There was a large area with coal deposits in southern Wales around 1830.

15. When a nation follows a policy of appeasement, it makes concessions to an aggressor in order to preserve the peace.

Which of the following is an example of appeasement?

   ○ A. Italy's support of Spanish Nationalists in the Spanish Civil War in the late 1930s

   ○ B. Great Britain's acceptance of Germany's takeover of Austria and Czechoslovakia in the late 1930s

   ○ C. Germany's 1939 invasion of Poland, which started World War II

   ◉ D. Japan's alliance with Germany and Italy in 1940, which created the Rome-Berlin-Tokyo Axis

Questions 16 through 18 refer to the following poster.

Source: Library of Congress. Artist Dan Sayre Groesbeck.

16. The person who designed this poster used irony to make a point. Behind this irony was an assumption with which the designer expected viewers to agree.

Which of the following statements summarizes this assumption?

○ A. People will give to the war effort because they are doing well economically.

○ B. Financing the war requires selling bonds and raising taxes.

○ C. During wartime, people have little money to spend on their sons.

◉ D. People value the lives of their children more than they value money.

17. During which war was this poster part of a government advertising campaign?

○ A. the Civil War

◉ B. World War I

○ C. World War II

○ D. the Vietnam War

18. If the government were running a similar advertising campaign today, which medium would probably reach the most people?

○ A. posters

○ B. leaflets and brochures

○ C. print ads in financial newspapers

◉ D. television ads on primetime

Question 19 refers to the following table.

The Five Most Populous American Colonies, 1750

Colony	Population (estimate)
Massachusetts	188,000
Pennsylvania	119,700
Connecticut	111,300
Maryland	141,000
Virginia	231,000

Source: U.S. Bureau of the Census

19. Which of the following statements is supported by the data in the chart?

◉ A. The population of all of the American colonies was less than 700,000.

○ B. Virginia had more than twice as many people as Maryland.

○ C. Most of the population of Massachusetts was of English origin.

○ D. The population of the colony of New York was smaller than that of Connecticut.

Questions 20 through 22 refer to the following paragraph and flowchart.

The U.S. Civil Service system is designed to ensure that people are appointed to government positions because of their skills and abilities rather than because of their political affiliation. Over 90 percent of federal jobs are covered by civil service rules. The typical steps in applying for a civil service job are shown below.

20. Which of the following is the best title for the flowchart?

   ○ A. A History of the Civil Service
   ○ B. The Qualifications of Civil Service Workers
   ● C. Applying for Civil Service Jobs
   ○ D. Interviewing for a Civil Service Job

21. What does a civil servant's GS rating probably affect most?

   ● A. salary
   ○ B. length of service
   ○ C. job security
   ○ D. education level

22. On which of the following values does the structure of the Civil Service system primarily rest?

   ○ A. patriotism
   ● B. equal opportunity
   ○ C. freedom of speech
   ○ D. respect for seniority

Questions 23 and 24 refer to the following graphs.

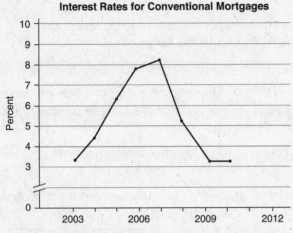

Interest Rates for Conventional Mortgages

Source: U.S. Bureau of the Census

U.S. Mortgage Debt Outstanding

Source: U.S. Bureau of the Census

23. In 2005, what were the approximate interest rate and approximate total mortgage debt outstanding for a conventional mortgage?

    ○ A. 8 percent and $13,000 billion
    ○ B. 4 percent and $11,000 billion
    ◑ C. 6 percent and $12,000 billion
    ○ D. 6 percent and $9,000 billion

24. Based on the graphs, how do mortgage interest rates and total mortgage debt outstanding compare?

    ○ A. Interest rates rise in direct proportion to decreases in total mortgage debt outstanding.
    ○ B. The higher the interest rate, the lower the total mortgage debt outstanding.
    ○ C. The lower the interest rate, the higher the total mortgage debt outstanding.
    ◉ D. As interest rates rise and then fall, the total mortgage debt will move similarly but not at the same rate.

25. A culture hearth refers to the center of a culture—the source of its ideas, values, customs, fashions, and practices. An example of an ancient culture hearth was the area along the Nile River in Egypt. The agricultural, economic, social, artistic, and religious ideas and practices that grew up there spread through trade to other areas of the ancient world.

Which of the following is an example of a modern culture hearth with worldwide influence?

    ○ A. Pyongyang, capital of North Korea, which has a 95 percent literacy rate
    ○ B. Ottawa, capital of Canada, with a population of about one million
    ◑ C. New Zealand, which exports wool and textiles
    ○ D. Hollywood, California, which produces movies and television shows, enjoyed around the world

Answers and explanations for *Social Studies, Part II* start on page 631.

SOCIAL STUDIES PRETEST

PART III: EXTENDED RESPONSE

Directions: Read both of the selections and the writing prompt and answer the questions that follow.

Questions 1 through 5 are based on the process of writing a response to a reading selection.
NOTE: Do not start writing your response until you are asked to do so at question 4.

First Amendment to the U.S. Constitution

Congress shall make no law respecting an establishment of religion, or prohibiting the free exercise thereof; or abridging the freedom of speech, or of the press; or the right of the people peaceably to assemble, and to petition the Government for a redress of grievances.

Public School Students Have Free Speech Rights: *Tinker v. Des Moines Independent Community School District* (1969)

This landmark U.S. Supreme Court decision recognizes that students have the same constitutional rights as every other American citizen. Students do not shed these rights as they pass through "the schoolhouse gate." The case arose when three students were suspended from school for wearing armbands to protest the Vietnam War. The Court found that the school officials had acted unconstitutionally in suppressing the students' free speech rights. The Court, however, recognized that school officials need some flexibility and control of students in order to fulfill the educational role of the school. Thus, school officials may prohibit student conduct which "materially disrupts or involves substantial disorder in the classroom."

Bill of Rights Curriculum Guide, American Civil Liberties Union of Minnesota

---

Writing Prompt

The first selection is the First Amendment to the U.S. Constitution, which is part of the Bill of Rights. The second selection is a summary of an important Supreme Court case relating this amendment to students' right to freedom of speech.

Write a response to these selections that analyzes how the case applies the concept of "free speech" in the First Amendment to students. Also explain the implications of the Court's statement that school officials need flexibility and therefore can prohibit some student conduct.

Use relevant and specific information from the reading selection and your general knowledge to support your response.

Unpack the Writing Prompt and Plan Your Response

1. What two things does the prompt ask you to write about?

   A. Explain the Implications of the courts statement

   B. Analizes - use relevant and specific info

2. What is the main point you will make about 1.A above?

   Why a proson yong and old should have freespeak

3. What are three main points you will make about 1.B above?

   Why this case was/is important

   Why the constatution needs to be challenged

   how important it is to stand for something

Draft, Revise, and Edit Your Response

4. On a computer or on a piece of paper, write a response to the prompt.

5. On the computer or on the paper, make revisions to improve your response and edit to correct errors in grammar, usage, spelling, capitalization, and punctuation.

The *Extended Response Evaluation Guide for Social Studies, Part III* starts on page 633.

PART I: SCIENCE PRACTICES—10 QUESTIONS

Directions: You may fill in the circles next to the correct answers or write your answers on a separate piece of paper.

<u>Questions 1 and 2</u> refer to the following passage.

For many years, scientists believed that all living things depended on sunlight for their energy. For example, human beings derive energy from food. Our food comes either from plants that require sunlight or from animals, which eat plants that require sunlight.

However, in the 1970s scientists discovered hot springs, called *hydrothermal vents*, in the ocean floor. These vents are miles below the surface of the ocean, far beyond the reach of sunlight. Yet these vents are surrounded by fascinating life forms, including giant red tube worms, eyeless shrimp, hairy-looking crabs, and communities of bacteria that grow like carpets on the ocean floor.

Those bacteria feed on minerals, like sulfur, that flow upward through the vents. The bacteria use a process called *chemosynthesis* to turn the minerals into nutrition. The bacteria, in turn, are eaten by many of the animals that live near the vents. Thus, those animals take in a source of energy that does not derive from sunlight.

1. Which of the following would be a good title for this passage?

   ○ A. "The Advantages and Disadvantages of Life Near Hydrothermal Vents"
   ◉ B. "Hydrothermal Vents: A Potential Fuel Source for Our Energy-Hungry Economy"
   ○ C. "Hydrothermal Vents Suggest That Not All Life Is Solar-Powered"
   ○ D. "Major 20th-Century Advances in Oceanography"

2. Which of the following is a detail that supports the main idea of the passage?

   ○ A. Many scientists believe that all living creatures depend on sunlight for their energy.
   ○ B. Hydrothermal vents were not discovered until the 1970s.
   ○ C. The hairy-looking crabs are covered in structures that enable them to catch tiny particles of food.
   ◉ D. No sunlight penetrates to the world of hydrothermal ocean vents.

<u>Questions 3 and 4</u> refer to the following passage.

In a *radioactive* element like uranium, atoms give off some of their particles. In the 19th century, chemist Marie Curie discovered that the radioactivity of a compound depends on the amount of a radioactive element it contains.

Then Curie noticed something strange. Pitchblende, a compound that contains radioactive uranium, gives off more radiation than pure uranium. Curie wondered why that would be the case. She guessed that pitchblende might contain another element that was even more radioactive than uranium.

To find out, Curie and her husband isolated the elements that make up pitchblende. After isolating each element, they measured its radioactivity. As a result of this process, the Curies discovered that pitchblende contains a highly radioactive element, which no one had identified before. They named their discovery *polonium*.

3. Which of the following restates Marie Curie's hypothesis about pitchblende?

   ○ A. Pitchblende contains uranium.
   ○ B. Uranium interacts with the nonradioactive elements in pitchblende to increase its radioactivity.
   ○ C. Polonium was discovered by the Curies as a result of their experiment.
   ◉ D. Pitchblende contains an element that is more radioactive than uranium.

4. Which of the following is a reasonable conclusion based on Curie's experiment?

   ◉ A. Pitchblende is more radioactive than pure uranium because it contains polonium.
   ○ B. Polonium is only one of many reasons why pitchblende is more radioactive than pure uranium.
   ○ C. Marie Curie would become famous.
   ○ D. The Curies were not the first physicists to isolate polonium.

Questions 5 and 6 refer to the following passage.

The **ozone layer** is a part of the upper atmosphere with high concentrations of ozone, a form of oxygen. The ozone layer absorbs between 97 percent and 99 percent of the sun's medium-frequency **ultraviolet light**, which can cause skin damage and even skin cancers. For this reason, depletion of the ozone layer is a potentially global health risk. The ozone layer has been decreasing in thickness for decades due to atmospheric pollution. In particular, **chlorofluorocarbons** (CFCs), used in aerosol sprays and refrigerators, were so harmful to the ozone layer that a global ban was implemented in 1994, and production had almost entirely ceased by 2004. However, this ban was not effective; the hole in the ozone layer that appeared over Antarctica reached its largest recorded size in 2006.

5. Which evidence from the passage supports the conclusion that CFCs remain in the atmosphere for some time after their use?

   ○ A. The ozone layer started thinning decades ago.
   ● B. The hole in the ozone layer reached its largest size after CFCs were banned from production and use.
   ○ C. CFCs are used both in aerosols and as refrigerants.
   ○ D. CFCs absorb medium-frequency ultraviolet light.

6. Which of the following additional pieces of evidence would best counter the author's opinion that the ban on CFCs was not effective?

   ○ A. The ozone hole is not literally a hole but rather an area in which the ozone layer is depleted by more than 50 percent.
   ○ B. While the ozone layer continues to thin, it is thinning at a rate much lower than it has in the past.
   ● C. Skin cancer rates near the equator, far from Antarctica, have not changed significantly since 1994.
   ○ D. The CFC ban contains a few extremely narrow exceptions for uses where no suitable replacement exists, such as in fire-suppression systems on airplanes.

Questions 7 and 8 refer to the following text.

Adenosine triphosphate (ATP) is one of the most important chemicals for the function of the cells of all known living organisms. It stores and transports energy within and between cells. When a cell needs to use this energy, a chemical reaction releases it. Adenosine triphosphate and water can combine to remove either a **phosphate** (P_i) or **pyrophosphate** (PP_i) from the ATP, leaving **adenosine diphosphate** (ADP) or **adenosine monophosphate** (AMP) respectively.

Equation	Energy released (in kilocalories per mole)
$ATP + H_2O \rightarrow ADP + P_i$	7.3
$ATP + H_2O \rightarrow AMP + PP_i$	10.9

7. Which answer choice describes the process in the equation $ATP + H_2O \rightarrow AMP + PP_i$?

   ○ A. Adenosine triphosphate is transported from one part of a cell to another.
   ○ B. Adenosine triphosphate is broken down into adenosine monophosphate and a pyrophosphate, releasing energy.
   ● C. Adenosine monophosphate is broken down into water and a pyrophosphate, releasing energy.
   ○ D. Adenosine monophosphate stores energy, which is transported to another cell.

8. Which of the following chemicals plays a role most similar to that of ATP?

   ○ A. Lactase, which breaks down the lactose sugar found in milk for easier digestion
   ○ B. DNA, which is found in the nucleus of every cell and contains instructions for the cell to manufacture proteins
   ○ C. Hemoglobin, which allows red blood cells to carry oxygen
   ● D. Glycogen, which stores sugars that can be broken off in differing amounts when the body needs energy

	P	**P**
w	Pw	Pw
w	Pw	Pw

	P	**w**
P	PP	Pw
w	Pw	ww

9. An equal number of seeds are produced from each of two pairs of flowers. One pair is a purebred pink plant with dominant pink genes (P) and a purebred white plant with recessive white genes (w). The other pair is made up of two hybrid plants, which are pink. The Punnett squares above show all possible combinations of alleles for the two pairs. If a seed is selected at random from the offspring of those two pairs, what is the probability that the selected seed will grow to be white?

A. $\frac{1}{8}$

B. $\frac{1}{4}$

C. $\frac{3}{4}$

D. $\frac{7}{8}$

Question 10 refers to the following graph.

Bounce Experiment Results

10. A ball was dropped onto a surface from different heights, and the height of the first bounce of each drop was recorded. The graph above illustrates the initial heights and bounce heights of the six trials in the experiment. What was the average (arithmetic mean) difference between the drop height and the first bounce height, in feet?

- A. $2\frac{1}{2}$
- B. $3\frac{1}{2}$
- C. 8
- D. 21

Answers and explanations for *Science*, *Part I* start on page 634.

PART II: SCIENCE CONTENT—25 QUESTIONS

Directions: You may fill in the circles next to the correct answers or write your answers on a separate piece of paper.

Question 1 refers to the following paragraph and diagram.

A neuron is the basic functional unit of the nervous system. Neurons transmit information throughout the body.

A Neuron

1. Which of the following is implied by the paragraph and the diagram?

   ○ A. Neurons are part of the endocrine system.
   ◉ B. Oxygen is carried throughout the body by neurons.
   ◉ C. Neurons transmit instructions regarding movement to muscles.
   ○ D. Nerve impulses travel from the axon to the cell body.

2. A comet is a small body made of ice and dust that orbits the sun in an elliptical, or oval, path. As the comet approaches the sun, its core heats up, releasing gas and dust. The gas and dust stream away from the comet in a tail that may be millions of miles long. Some scientists believe that comets formed when the solar system was born.

   Based on the paragraph, which of the following statements is an opinion rather than a fact?

   ○ A. Comets are small bodies of ice and dust.
   ○ B. The orbit of a comet has an elliptical shape.
   ○ C. Comets release gas and dust as they approach the sun.
   ◉ D. Comets formed when the solar system was born.

3. In a photochemical reaction, light starts the reaction. Light can start a chemical reaction by exciting atoms and molecules, making them unstable and more likely to react with other atoms and molecules.

   Which of the following is an example of a photochemical reaction?

   ○ A. polymerization, in which long-chain organic compounds are formed from repeating units called monomers
   ○ B. fractional distillation, in which various petroleum products are separated out of crude oil
   ○ C. neutralization, in which an acid and a base react to form a salt and water
   ◉ D. photosynthesis, in which green plants use the energy from sunlight to make carbohydrates from water and carbon dioxide

Questions 4 through 6 refer to the following chart.

Some Glands of the Endocrine System

Endocrine Gland	Hormone	Function
Pituitary gland	Growth hormone	Promotes bone and muscle growth
Ovary	Estrogen	Stimulates development of female secondary sexual characteristics
Testis	Testosterone	Stimulates development of male secondary sexual characteristics
Adrenal gland	Adrenaline	Increases heart activity, breathing rate, and blood flow to muscles for "fight or flight"
Thyroid	Thyroxine	Regulates metabolism and growth
Pancreas	Insulin	Regulates blood sugar levels

4. What is the function of the hormone thyroxine?

   A. It controls female secondary sexual characteristics.
   B. It controls male secondary sexual characteristics.
   C. It speeds up the pulse and breathing rate for "fight or flight."
   ● D. It helps control metabolism and growth.

5. People who have one form of the disease diabetes mellitus do not produce enough insulin. Based on the chart, what is the general effect of this disease?

   A. stunted growth
   B. excess growth
   C. overproduction of estrogen
   ● D. uncontrolled blood sugar levels

6. Paul, a child who was not growing as rapidly as he should, was given growth hormone to stimulate his growth. Paul anticipated that the hormone would enable him to reach an adult height of over six feet, even though his parents are both below average height. In fact, Paul's adult height was 5 feet 7 inches.

   What was wrong with Paul's thinking?

   A. Growth hormone is only one of several factors that determine a person's adult height.
   ● B. Growth hormone, when administered as a drug, does not affect a person's height.
   C. In order to grow to over six feet tall, Paul would have had to take insulin, too.
   D. In order to grow to over six feet tall, Paul would have had to take testosterone, too.

7. An emulsion is a mixture of two liquids whose particles are evenly scattered in one another without dissolving. Emulsions are unstable. After a time, the liquids separate.

   Which of the following is an emulsion?

   A. tea with sugar
   B. salt water
   ● C. oil and vinegar salad dressing
   D. food coloring and water

8. Earth science includes the study of Earth's atmosphere—the layer of gases that sur-rounds Earth—and Earth's hydrosphere—the oceans, rivers, lakes, and groundwater.

    Which of the following scientists would be most likely to apply knowledge from a study of both the atmosphere and hydrosphere to his or her work?

    ○ A. a geologist who studies volcanoes and mountain formation
    ○ B. an astronomer who studies the planets of the solar system
    ◉ C. a meteorologist who studies weather patterns and predicts weather
    ○ D. an ecologist who studies the distribu-tion of populations of organisms

Question 9 refers to the following chart.

Organisms in a Food Chain

Role	Description
Producer	A green plant, which produces its own food using energy from sunlight
Herbivore	An animal that gets nutrients by eating plants
Carnivore	An animal that gets nutrients by eating other animals
Omnivore	An animal that gets nutrients by eating both plants and animals
Decomposer	An organism that gets nutrients from feeding on dead organisms and returns nutrients to the soil in the process

9. Earthworms break down large pieces of dead organic material in the soil. What role do earthworms play in the food chain?

    ○ A. They are producers.
    ○ B. They are herbivores.
    ○ C. They are carnivores.
    ◉ D. They are decomposers.

Question 10 refers to the following graph.

Saturated Fat in Some Common Foods

Food	Grams per Serving
1 oz cheddar	6.0
1 oz low-fat cheddar	1.2
1 c whole milk	5.1
1 c 1% milk	1.6
1/2 c ice cream	4.5
1/2 c frozen yogurt	2.5
3 oz regular ground beef	7.2
3 oz extra lean ground beef	5.3
croissant	6.6
plain bagel	0.1

10. Suppose a child's diet usually includes two servings of cheese, four servings of milk, one serving of ice cream or frozen yogurt, one serving of ground beef, and a croissant or bagel every day.

    If the child's parent wanted to decrease the amount of saturated fat in the child's diet, which of the following actions would be most effective?

    ○ A. switch from regular to low-fat cheddar
    ○ B. switch from whole milk to 1 percent milk
    ○ C. switch from frozen yogurt to ice cream
    ◉ D. switch from regular to extra lean ground beef

11. Torque is the ability of a force to produce rotation. The torque of any force is equal to the amount of the force multiplied by the distance from the pivot point to the point where the force is applied. For example, when you go through a revolving door, you are applying force as you push. The torque of your force is equal to the force you apply times the distance between your hand and the axis of the revolving door.

Which of the following actions would decrease torque as you go through a revolving door?

- A. moving your hand closer to the center of the revolving door
- B. moving your hand closer to the outer edge of the revolving door
- C. pushing with two hands rather than one hand
- D. leaning toward the door as you push to increase your force

Question 12 refers to the following graph.

**U.S. Consumption of Energy by Source, 1997
(in common units of metric tons oil equivalent [TOE])**

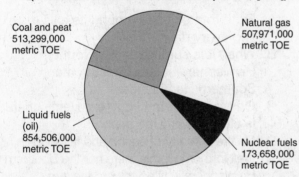

Coal and peat
513,299,000
metric TOE

Natural gas
507,971,000
metric TOE

Liquid fuels (oil)
854,506,000
metric TOE

Nuclear fuels
173,658,000
metric TOE

Source: World Resource Institute

12. Of the four energy sources shown, which two are the most similar in the proportion of energy they supply in the United States?

- A. coal/peat and natural gas
- B. natural gas and nuclear fuels
- C. nuclear fuels and liquid fuels
- D. liquid fuels and natural gas

Question 13 refers to the following paragraph and map.

In 1620, the eastern half of the United States was covered by virgin forest—forest that had never been cut down. Many parts of this region today are covered by second-growth forest—the ecosystem that eventually grows back after farmland is abandoned.

Virgin Forest of the United States 1620–1990

Virgin Forest
1620
1850
1990
Other ecosystem

Source: *National Geographic*

13. Which of the following conclusions is supported by the paragraph and the map?

- A. The western half of the United States had far less forest cover in 1620 than did the eastern half.
- B. As European Americans moved from the East Coast westward between 1620 and 1850, they cut down forests to build farms.
- C. A number of relatively large areas of virgin forest remain in the eastern half of the United States today.
- D. Today's second-growth forests in the eastern United States have fewer species of plants and animals than the virgin forest did.

Questions 14 and 15 refer to the following information and diagram.

The seasons occur because the axis of Earth is tilted. At different times of year, different parts of Earth get more hours of higher-intensity sunlight. As the diagram shows, summer begins in the Southern Hemisphere on December 21, when that hemisphere is tilted toward the sun.

Why Earth Has Seasons

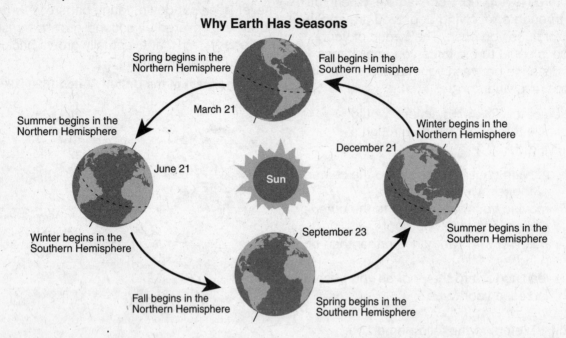

14. Which portion of Earth is tilted toward the sun on June 21?

  ○ A. the Southern Hemisphere
  ● B. the Northern Hemisphere
  ○ C. the axis
  ○ D. the equator

15. Which of the following statements is supported by the information in the diagram?

  ○ A. Earth rotates once around its axis each and every day.
  ● B. When it is summer in the Northern Hemisphere, it is summer in the Southern Hemisphere.
  ○ C. On March 21, the Northern Hemisphere is tilted toward the sun.
  ○ D. On the first day of spring and fall, neither the Northern Hemisphere nor the Southern Hemisphere is tilted toward the sun.

16. Ecologists use a tool called a quadrat when doing field studies of plant distribution. A quadrat is an open, four-sided structure about a meter square. It is placed on the ground, whether in a meadow, on a hillside, or at the beach. The ecologist then counts the plants of different species inside the quadrat. By using a quadrat, an ecologist can get a more accurate understanding of species distribution than by doing a random count.

Which of the following statements is a conclusion based on the given facts?

  ○ A. A quadrat is a tool used by ecologists.
  ○ B. A quadrat is a frame about a meter square.
  ○ C. To use a quadrat, the ecologist places it on the ground.
  ● D. A quadrat makes plant distribution estimates more reliable.

17. According to Charles's Law, when the pressure of a gas remains constant, the volume of a quantity of gas varies directly with the temperature. In other words, as the temperature of a gas rises, the volume of the gas increases.

Which of the following graphs illustrates Charles's Law?

○ A.

○ B.

○ C.

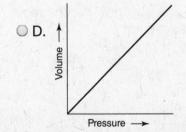

○ D.

18. At the beginning of the twentieth century, only three subatomic particles were known: protons, neutrons, and electrons. In the last half of the century, dozens of new particles were discovered using new technology. Machines called particle accelerators push particles to tremendous speeds. When two particles collide at high speed, they annihilate each other and new particles are formed.

Which of the following is not stated in the passage?

○ A. Protons, neutrons, and electrons are subatomic particles.
● B. Atoms are composed of subatomic particles.
○ C. In particle accelerators, particles are pushed to very high speeds.
○ D. Particles that collide at high speed annihilate each other, forming new particles.

19. Density is the amount of matter, or mass, in a given volume of a substance. To find the density of an object, you divide its mass by its volume. A student wanted to find the density of a 3-cm cube of lead. First, she used a scale to find the mass of the cube. Next, she calculated the volume by multiplying 3 cm × 3 cm × 3 cm. Finally, she divided the volume by the mass to find the density of the lead cube.

Why was the density the student calculated inaccurate?

○ A. A scale cannot be used for finding mass.
● B. Multiplying three sides of the cube will not give the cube's volume.
○ C. The student should have found the volume first.
○ D. The student should have divided the mass by the volume.

Questions 20 and 21 refer to the following information and diagram.

When the U.S. Mint had to design a new dollar coin to replace the old Susan B. Anthony dollar, it faced a problem. It wanted to design an appealing, distinctive golden-color coin that vending machines would recognize as an Anthony dollar, which looks like a quarter. Vending machines identify coins by their weight, size, and electromagnetic signature. They test a coin by passing an electric current through it and measuring the resulting magnetic field. Thus the new Sacagawea dollar coin had to be similar to the Anthony dollar in size, weight, and electromagnetic signature.

Size and weight were easy to imitate, but the electromagnetic signature was not. The Anthony dollar had a copper core covered by a silver-colored copper-nickel alloy. All the golden alloy sample coins had three times as much electrical conductivity as the Anthony dollar. Vending machines did not recognize them. Finally, metallurgists came up with the idea of adding manganese, which has low conductivity, to zinc and copper. The result was a coin consisting of 77 percent copper, 12 percent zinc, 7 percent manganese, and 4 percent nickel. The pure copper core was covered with a golden alloy of manganese, zinc, copper, and nickel. This golden coin has electromagnetic properties similar to those of the Anthony dollar, so it is recognized by U.S. vending machines.

20. It can be inferred from the passage above that an alloy is

○ A. a magnetic material
○ B. a material that stops electricity
◉ C. a mixture of metals
○ D. the core of a coin

21. The U.S. Mint could have solved its technical problems with the Sacagawea dollar by making it out of the same metals as the Anthony dollar. Why did the people at the Mint decide against this?

◉ A. The metals in the Anthony alloy were too rare and expensive to use in the new coin.
○ B. Like nickels, dimes, and quarters, the Anthony dollar was silver-colored and therefore not distinctive.
○ C. The electromagnetic signature of the Anthony coin was not recognized by vending machines.
○ D. The size and weight of the Anthony coin made it impractical for use in vending machines.

Question 22 refers to the following chart.

Types of Plants

Type	Characteristics
Annual	Completes life cycle in one growing season
Biennial	Completes life cycle in two growing seasons; flowers during second year
Perennial	Lives for years and flowers each year
Tender	Sensitive to cold (can be annual, biennial, or perennial)
Hardy	Can withstand frosts (can be annual, biennial, or perennial)

22. Marion has little interest in or time for gardening, yet she would like to have flowers in her front yard. Which of the following types of plants would probably give her the most flowers for the least effort?

○ A. annuals
○ B. biennials
○ C. tender plants
◉ D. hardy perennials

Question 23 refers to the following information and diagram.

How a Reflecting Telescope Works

23. If the flat mirror were removed from this telescope, what would happen as a result?

 ○ A. Light rays would not enter the telescope.
 ○ B. Light rays would not reflect off the curved mirror.
 ◉ C. A viewer could not see anything through the telescope.
 ○ D. A viewer could see only objects that were in focus.

24. The discovery of a new drug was once largely the result of trial and error, laboratory experiments, and clinical trials. Although these methods are still used, computer science is being applied to the drug discovery process to refine it and speed it up. For example, computers can analyze genetic material to locate genes that may hold promise in the development of new drugs. Computers can analyze data generated by lab experiments. Computer simulations can even help predict how a particular drug will work under specific circumstances.

What is the main reason that computers are now being used in the drug discovery process?

 ○ A. They enable scientists to abandon trial-and-error methods.
 ◉ B. They help scientists analyze large amounts of data in a systematic way.
 ○ C. They have made laboratory experiments unnecessary.
 ○ D. They have made clinical trials unnecessary.

25. People planning to visit tropical countries may need to be vaccinated against disease. For example, two to four weeks before a trip, travelers should be vaccinated against typhoid fever. The vaccine is 50 to 80 percent effective. Additional precautions against typhoid fever include avoiding food and water that may be dirty.

If a traveler is vaccinated against typhoid fever two to four weeks before a brief trip to the tropics, which of the following best explains why he or she should take extra precautions against contracting the disease?

 ○ A. The typhoid fever vaccination is effective for only a few months.
 ◉ B. The typhoid fever vaccination is only 50 to 80 percent effective.
 ○ C. The typhoid fever vaccination can cause soreness, fever, and headache.
 ○ D. Typhoid fever spreads only through air and water.

Answers and explanations for *Science, Part II* start on page 634.

PART III: SHORT ANSWER

Directions: Read the selection and the writing prompt and answer the questions that follow.

Threats to Coral Reefs

Coral reefs cover a tiny percentage of the world's ocean floor, but they serve as a habitat for millions of marine species, including starfish, sea anemones, octopuses, and many thousands of fish species such as the clownfish. Some species, such as *Atergatis subdentatus*—the red reef crab—cannot survive in any other habitat besides coral reefs.

The hard substance that forms the reef is actually the exoskeleton, or shell, of several species of marine invertebrates. These invertebrates, called corals, make their exoskeletons from calcium carbonate ions dissolved in seawater. Despite the tremendous diversity of animals that live on coral reefs, corals themselves are delicate organisms. Even a minor environmental stressor, such as a slight change in pH or in water temperature, can cause corals to sicken and die. When corals die, the fish that depend on them for food also die. Scavenger species such as the red reef crab may experience a brief population boom, but once they have eaten all the dead fish, the scavengers die as well. In fact, dying corals wreak havoc with the entire reef ecosystem.

Writing Prompt

Carbon dioxide emitted into the atmosphere through the burning of fossil fuels by humans dissolves in seawater. This dissolved carbon dioxide lowers the pH of the water. Moreover, increasing levels of carbon dioxide in the atmosphere are causing ocean temperatures to increase.

Explain how the burning of fossil fuels by humans could affect the red reef crab (*Atergatis subdentatus*). Support your answer with multiple pieces of evidence from the passage.

The *Short Answer Scoring Guide* appears on page 637.

Congratulations! You have completed the Pretests.

Reminder: Your next step is to check your answers using the
Pretests Answers and Explanations that begin on page 624
and fill in the study planners on pages xvi through xxii.

Reasoning through Language Arts

The GED® *Reasoning through Language Arts Test* (RLA) evaluates your reading and writing skills: You will have 2½ hours for about 46 questions that require you to

- answer questions based on single passages <u>and</u> on passages that are paired together (reading and thinking skills);
- review written text and select words and phrases so that the final product is written correctly (language skills); and
- compose an extended response to a writing prompt based on reading one or two passages or a passage accompanied by a graphic (writing skills).

The first section of the test includes reading and language questions and concludes with about 45 minutes for the Extended Response. You will have a 10-minute break before the second section, which includes reading and language questions only.

You will need a minimum score of 150 to pass the RLA Test, which is one of the four tests you will need to pass in order to earn a high school equivalency diploma.

Reading Content Areas

You will answer questions based on a wide range of types of reading materials. Seventy-five percent of the questions are based on **informational texts**, which include workplace- and community-based documents, **general nonfiction**, and **nonfiction related to general interest social studies and science** topics. Twenty-five percent of the questions are based on **fiction** selections.

Language Content Areas

The language skills model real-life editing to ensure correct **sentence structure**, **agreement** (subject-verb and pronoun-antecedent), **capitalization, punctuation, homonyms,** and **possessives**. The questions also assess appropriate **word choice** and **elimination of informal usage** to fit the purpose of the writing task.

Extended Response

The Extended Response requires reading text materials and responding to a writing prompt (assignment) by **developing an argument and supporting your ideas with evidence** from the text.

Computer-Based RLA Test Question Formats

You will work with several different question formats on the RLA Test. Many of the questions will be in the familiar multiple-choice format, but you will need to be acquainted with the other formats as well.

Multiple-choice questions have four options (A through D). You will **click** on the best answer.

In this passage, William tells Jordan about his life experiences and plans for the future. What do his stories indicate about his past?

- ○ A. He has already seen too much.
- ○ B. He has never been certain of his place in the world.
- ○ C. He wishes he had made different decisions in the past.
- ○ D. He is proud of his accomplishments and hopes to help others.

Fill-in-the-blank questions will require you to **type** a word, phrase, or number in a box that appears on the screen.

Which phrase from paragraph 2 describes how an employee should fill out the shipping authorization form? Type your answer in the box below.

[   ]

Drop-down questions give you the opportunity to **click** the word "Select" and choose the option that correctly completes the sentence. (This format is only used to assess language skills.)

Technical Corporation strives to provide excellent service. We have a history of providing outstanding technical and customer support and always aim to give 100%. When customers express concerns or complaints, we respond immediately to show that we value Select... ˅ feedback.

The words that appear in a drop-down menu when you **click** on "Select" are

his
her
its
their

You would choose **their** because the sentence should read: *When customers express concerns or complaints, we respond immediately to show that we value <u>their</u> feedback.*

Some of the questions in this book are designed to mimic this drop-down menu format. When you see the word "Select" in a question in this book, choose the option that best completes the sentence.

GED® TEST TIP

Test each one of the drop-down options in the context of the sentence before you make your final choice. Do not select an option that "seems" right until you have tested all of the choices and have a clear idea about why it is correct.

Drag-and-Drop items require you to **click** on a word or short phrase and to **drag** and **drop** it to a specified location on the computer screen.

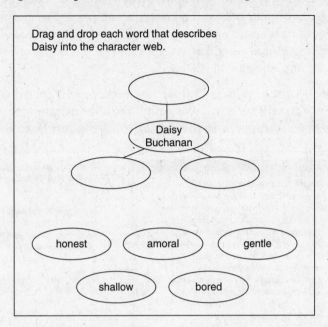

Drag and drop each word that describes Daisy into the character web.

Daisy Buchanan

honest   amoral   gentle

shallow   bored

An *Extended-Response* item requires you to **type** in a **text box** in response to a **prompt** (writing assignment) based on one or more short passages, a graphic, or a combination.

You will have 45 minutes to read the materials and to plan, write, and revise your response.

This article presents arguments from both sides of the debate about global warming.

In your response, analyze both arguments presented in the article to determine which one is best supported. Use specific, relevant evidence from the article in order to support your response.

✂ Cut   🗐 Copy   📋 Paste   ↩ Undo   ↪ Redo

Extended Response Question on the RLA Test

An important task on the RLA Test involves writing an extended response to a passage, two passages, or a passage accompanied by a graphic. This activity integrates reading and analytical skills with writing skills. The lessons in *Writing About Text*, on pages 148–173, give you a step-by-step approach to completing this task.

Look at how a sample passage and writing prompt will appear on the computer screen. You will need to **tab** through the reading passage or passages and **compose** your response in the word processing **text box**.

GED® TEST TIP

Preview the writing prompt before you read the passage(s). This will help you focus your reading to select key details and evidence that you will use to support your position.

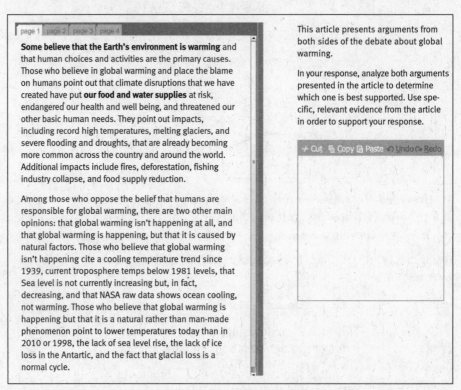

You can take up to 45 minutes at the end of the first section of the RLA Test to complete the assignment. This task has its own clock to help you manage your time. See page 156 for a suggested time management plan to do the following:

- *Preview* the writing prompt.
- *Read* the selection or selections, carefully using the **highlighter tool** to draw attention to information for later use.
- *Compose* a thesis statement.
- *Gather evidence* from the text to support your thesis statement.
- *Plan* your response (use the offline **wipe-off board**).
- *Draft* your response (in the **text box** that scrolls down).
- *Review your response* to improve your writing and correct any errors with the editing tools—**cut, copy, paste, undo,** and **redo**.

The Qualities of a Successful Extended Response

Your response can earn up to 6 points. It is reviewed for three different "traits" or qualities, and each trait is assigned a score from 0–2. So, *3 traits times a maximum of 2 points each equals a maximum of 6 points.*

Unlike other writing that you may have done in the past, this task is **"evidence-based writing,"** meaning that you need to base your position on the **information and arguments** in the reading materials.

<u>Trait 1:</u> **Creation of Arguments and Use of Evidence** To earn a score of 2 on Trait 1 you need to do the following:

- Create an **argument** by making a logical claim that clearly **states your position.**
- Use 3 or more **specific references** from the text(s) to support the claim.
- Identify **valid arguments and/or fallacious claims** in the text(s).
- Point out **supported and/or unsupported claims** in the text(s).

<u>Trait 2:</u> **Development of Ideas and Organizational Structure** To earn a score of 2 on Trait 2 you need to accomplish these tasks:

- Create an **effective organizational structure.**
- Sequence ideas **logically** so that one idea leads to the next.
- Elaborate main ideas and tie them to **specific evidence** from the text.
- Make effective transitions to **cohesively link** ideas.
- Use accurate and advanced **word choice.**
- Employ an appropriate level of **formality** (no slang, etc.).

<u>Trait 3:</u> **Clarity and Command of Standard English Conventions** To earn a score of 2 on Trait 3, you need to have few errors that would interfere with a reader's understanding of what you wrote. You should also do the following:

- Use varied and correct forms of **sentence structure.**
- Maintain **subject-verb** and **pronoun-antecedent** agreement.
- Adhere to the rules of **capitalization, punctuation,** and **spelling.**
- Distinguish between commonly confused words, such as **possessives** and **homonyms.**
- Avoid **wordiness** and **awkward constructions.**

Main Ideas and Details

The Main Idea

A writer has a message, or **main idea**, to get across. Sometimes the main idea is stated directly; often you have to figure it out yourself. You can find the main idea by asking, "What is the *most important* point the writer is making?" Most of the information in a passage will point to and explain the main idea.

As you read this passage, ask yourself what *main* point the writer is making. The answer will be the main idea.

> When I am reading a poem, I rarely feel alone in the room. The poet and I are together. It's as if the poet wrote a secret diary years ago. I am unlocking it as I sit alone and read.
>
> At times I don't understand what a poem means. I just like the way it sounds or the strange images that it provokes. The world is so peculiar in a poem. At the same time, it is so enticing. Sometimes I understand exactly, as if the poet is whispering to me, as if we shared the same experience.
>
> I must be fully concentrated on reading, or I cannot enter the world of a poem. There are too many daily tasks to attend to—tasks that are very far removed from the magic and imagination involved in a poem.
>
> On a cold, snowy day, I cuddle up inside my apartment and read and read. Then, I'm free to ride through the imagination of all those who came before me.

▶ Which of the following statements expresses the main idea?
  (1) The writer has a love of poetry.
  (2) The writer cuddles up on cold days to read.

You are correct if you chose **(1)**. While the passage mentions that the writer reads on cold days, the main point of all the information is how much the writer enjoys reading poetry.

Each paragraph has a main idea. To find the main idea of a passage with more than one paragraph, put together the ideas from all the paragraphs.

Supporting Details

A writer explains the main idea of a passage with supporting details. **Supporting details** include facts, examples, descriptions, and specific pieces of information. When you read, you need to identify details that support the main idea.

▶ Which detail helps you understand the writer's main point?
  (1) At times, the writer does not understand a poem.
  (2) The writer feels poetry is filled with magic and imagination.

You are correct if you chose **(2)**. That detail helps you see that the main idea is the writer's love of poetry. The fact that the writer doesn't always understand a poem is true, but it alone does not support the main idea.

Key Ideas

- The most important point of a passage is called the main idea.
- Sometimes a main idea is stated, but often you must figure it out.
- Supporting details point to and explain the main idea.

GED® TEST TIP

Be sure you don't confuse a supporting detail of a passage with the main idea. If you are asked for the main idea, choose the most important, general point.

PRACTICE 1

Questions 1 through 5 refer to the following passage from a diary.

EXCERPTED FROM *ARIADNE'S THREAD*

1   I feel I have never had a home. All my life moving from place to place. The only thing that remained the same, that was stable, was Oklahoma. Even the landscape never changed. The towns there never grew up into cities. The people were the same each year, wearing the same clothing, saying the same things.

2   The search for a homeland is part of the Chickasaw migration legend. It was ordained by the deities and began in the past when the people lived in the land of the "setting sun." During the days they would walk over the land, searching for their home. The priests carried a pole. They carried it in their hands by day and planted it each night. During the night it moved about and by morning it would be pointing the direction they were to travel. For a while it commanded the people to journey east, toward the morning sun. They crossed the Mississippi River eventually, and on the other side, the pole finally ceased to move during the night. The land was settled, crops were planted. It became known as the Old Fields. But one morning the pole leaned westward. The people gathered together and began the long journey back. They abandoned their village but did not feel sorrow because the pole had commanded it.

3   And I am still moving, looking for a home. I don't know if I will ever escape my tradition, my past. It goes with me everywhere, like a shadow.

By Linda Hogan from *Ariadne's Thread*, edited by Lyn Lifshin, New York: Harper & Row, 1982.

1. How does the author describe herself?

She feels as if she is

A. searching for a place to call home
B. doomed to stay in Oklahoma
C. tired of the sameness in her life
D. being shadowed by failure

2. Who do the Chickasaw believe are responsible for making them move?

A. the priests
B. white people
C. themselves
D. the gods

3. Why did the Chickasaw not feel sad when they left their homes in the east?

A. They knew they were headed to a better place to live.
B. They had been forced to move east to begin with.
C. They were returning to their ancient homeland.
D. It was simply part of their beliefs to follow the pole.

4. Which of the following best summarizes the main idea?

The writer

A. has always lived in Oklahoma and plans to stay there
B. feels trapped by tradition and wants to move far away
C. understands that her tendency to search is part of her Chickasaw heritage
D. believes that people in Oklahoma are all the same

5. How does the statement "I don't know if I will ever escape my tradition" (paragraph 3) support the main idea?

It shows that the writer

A. is trying to escape by moving around
B. lives in a more modern time
C. believes in the power of Indian legends
D. accepts that she is Chickasaw

Answers and explanations start on page 638.

Restatement and Summary

Key Ideas

- To restate an idea, put it in your own words.
- To summarize, choose the most important details that explain the main idea of a piece.

Restating Ideas

Restating an idea means putting it into your own words. For example, a friend may tell you that a movie wasn't worth the eight dollars she spent on it. You might then tell a co-worker that your friend said the movie was no good.

As you read the passage below, restate in your mind what you are reading.

> In Canton, Ohio, we take our desserts seriously. There are two local candy stores that receive over 90 percent of the city's candy business: Heggy's and Baldwin's. Those who prefer Heggy's won't befriend anyone who buys their sweets at Baldwin's.
>
> My family has always patronized Heggy's. At the Heggy's factory, Gerty wraps by hand each large chocolate candy in clear cellophane wrap. She's in the back of the store with her hairnet, seated at a table filled with hundreds of chocolates. My favorite chocolates at Heggy's are the dark chocolate creams, peanut clusters, and caramels.
>
> Heggy's aficionados point out that their candy of choice is a larger size and therefore superior. The rivalry runs deep . . . at Easter, Hanukkah, Christmas, Thanksgiving, and all occasions. Baldwin's loyal followers claim its sweets are sweeter. It's a feud over the best chocolate in town.

▶ How do the people of Canton feel about chocolate candy?
  (1) They consider it a serious health issue.
  (2) They feel it's important enough to take a stand on.

You are correct if you chose **(2)**. The phrase "take our desserts seriously" means that the candy is important to people.

On the *Reasoning through Language Arts* Test, the correct answer will not always use the exact words from the passage. You will have to recognize that the idea has been restated.

Summarizing

If you want to tell a friend about a movie you liked, you might **summarize** what happens in the movie. You certainly will not give all the details—that would take too long. A summary includes only the most important facts and ideas.

▶ Which of the following statements best summarizes the difference in opinion over the candy?
  (1) Some people prefer Heggy's candy because it's bigger, while others prefer Baldwin's because it's sweeter.
  (2) People argue whether to buy Heggy's or Baldwin's candy for different holidays.

You are correct if you chose **(1)**. The last paragraph sums up the difference in people's opinions. Statement (2) merely states a detail in the last paragraph.

GED® TEST TIP

As you read a GED® passage, check your understanding by pausing occasionally to see if you can restate and summarize what you are reading.

PRACTICE 2

Questions 1 through 3 refer to the following business letter.

EXCERPTED FROM *THE ENCYCLOPEDIA OF BUSINESS LETTERS*

Dear Richard,

1   Attached is a copy of my June 8th letter to Customer Service. After having my car serviced on June 30th, the list of problems has grown. These matters need your immediate attention.

2   Although I did finally receive my copy of the warranty after waiting two months, it is not bumper-to-bumper as Mr. Schecht promised. It also requires service at your facility unless the warranty administrator waives that requirement. I purchased the car from you at a premium price with the expectation that I would have a bumper-to-bumper warranty that I could use at any dealer. I never would have bought this car from you if I knew about these limitations. I expect two things: A written waiver from the warranty administrator that allows me to have warranty service performed at any dealer, and a wrap-around warranty, provided at your cost, that turns this limited warranty into the promised "bumper-to-bumper" warranty.

3   I expect an itemized list of registration costs, and the exact amount of credit I received from the Department of Motor Vehicles for the canceled plates voucher I gave to Mr. Schecht. If there is a refund due, I expect it within 15 days.

4   I expect a proper bill of sale that itemizes and describes the payments for the alarm system and the extended warranty, and includes all the items on the original bill of sale.

5   Your mechanic was unable to locate a cause for the burning smell. The smell persists. I expect your written assurance that if and when the cause for this smell becomes known, you will repair the problem at your cost.

6   The mechanic did *not* repair the left front marker light, although he promised he would. Enclosed is a copy of your invoice for this repair, which wasn't made, as well as an invoice from another dealer who actually made the repair. I expect reimbursement for $22.90.

cc: Joe Smith, Department of Consumer Affairs

Reprinted, with permission of the publisher, from *The Encyclopedia of Business Letters, Fax Memos, and Email* © 1999 Robert Bly. Published by Career Press, Pompton Plains, NJ. 800-227-3371. All rights reserved.

1. The problems that the writer mentions in the first paragraph and outlines in his letter include which of the following?

    A. receiving repairs the writer did not ask for
    B. rude treatment
    C. lack of proper paperwork
    D. the premium price paid for the car

2. What does the customer want done about the burning smell?

    A. the mechanic to find the cause of the smell
    B. the car to be repaired free of charge if the cause of the problem is discovered
    C. a refund of the money that was paid to have the problem fixed
    D. reimbursement for having the problem fixed by another dealer

3. Which of the following statements best summarizes this letter?

    A. A letter to customer service was never responded to and is being attached.
    B. Mechanics have been unable to fix one problem and did not fix a second.
    C. The service and warranty on the customer's car have been unacceptable.
    D. Some dealers and garages are better than others.

Answers and explanations start on page 638.

INTERPRETING NONFICTION AND INFORMATIONAL TEXT

Application of Ideas

When you **apply ideas**, you use information you already know in a new but similar situation. For example, suppose you know that a friend loves country music. When you need to buy a gift for that friend, you walk past the jazz and rock sections in the music store and head straight for the country. You're applying what you've learned about your friend to help you choose a gift.

To apply ideas when reading, look for elements in the new situation that are similar to elements in the passage you have read. Read this selection and then see if you can apply some of the ideas in it.

> When the delivery truck pulled up to my house the day before my mother's birthday, I knew her gift had finally arrived. I was excited. Not only had I ordered a beautiful art book for her, but I'd also ordered a mystery novel for myself and a book each for my nephew and niece. I couldn't resist buying them while I was choosing my mother's gift from an online bookstore. The carton looked bigger than I expected, but perhaps it had a lot of filler to keep the books from becoming damaged.
>
> I lugged the huge box into the kitchen so I could open it and begin wrapping my mother's gift. I tugged at the industrial staples and then tore open the carton. To my surprise, it was filled with many copies of the same book. To make matters worse, it was a book I had not ordered. *Who Moved My Cheese?* What kind of book was that? And who would order *one* copy of that book, let alone 11? I certainly didn't want these books. I knew my family wouldn't want them either. They wanted *The Art of Diego Rivera, Harry Potter,* and Dr. Seuss. So much for buying online. I'm sticking to in-store buying.

▶ Which of the following situations is most like the situation that happened to the writer?
  (1) buying groceries only to discover you brought someone else's bag home
  (2) buying 11 boxes of the same pasta at the store

Option **(1)** is correct. It shares the elements of intending to buy something and getting the wrong thing by mistake. The second option is wrong because the writer did not intentionally buy 11 copies of the book. Now try this question.

▶ If the writer attended an auction, she would be most likely to
  (1) decide which item to bid on and how much she would bid
  (2) get involved in the excitement and bid on many things

You are correct if you chose **(2)**. The writer states that she couldn't resist buying additional items when she was shopping online. Therefore, she seems the type to get caught up in buying things. If she had carefully chosen which book to buy her mother and had ordered only that one, then option (1) would be correct.

Key Ideas

- Applying ideas means using information in a new but similar situation.
- To apply ideas, ask yourself, "How is this new situation just like the situation in the passage?"

GED® TEST TIP

Remember that you can tab backward or forward in a passage on the computer screen to find information you need to answer a question.

PRACTICE 3

Questions 1 through 4 refer to the following excerpt.

EXCERPTED FROM *MAKING THE MOST OF YOUR MONEY*

1   Once you stop using credit cards, three things will happen.

2   You will buy less—and whatever you do buy will probably be a less expensive model or make. Studies have found that people spend more when they pay with plastic, because it doesn't feel like real money. When it is real money, you're more sensible.

3   Your total debt will shrink rapidly. You are paying *off* back bills, you are not adding new ones, and you have extra money because you're buying less. That surplus cash will reduce your debt faster than you could imagine.

4   You will grow incredibly smug. You're the first on your block to get out of debt. Others will follow, but you'll be the first.

5   I'm not against credit cards. They're easy to use. They're handy. If your card has a low annual fee and a 25-day, interest-free grace period for paying your bills, you're getting monthly loans for practically nothing. What I'm against is buying more on your credit cards than you can pay for at the end of the month.

6   Once you've fought your way out of debt you can start using credit cards again—but only for the convenience of not carrying cash. Your days of debt are done. A big expense may sometimes drive you over the limit. A stereo. A llama. A hot-air balloon. Whenever you limp home, back in debt, recite your mantra: "From now on, I'm not going to put down a charge card for anything." Stick with it until you're free again.

From *Making the Most of Your Money* by Jane Bryant Quinn, New York: Simon & Schuster, 1991.

1. According to the writer, becoming debt free is a behavior most similar to

   A. overcoming a bad habit
   B. learning a new trick
   C. forgetting a friend's birthday
   D. setting a good example

2. If you have five credit cards with high interest rates and no grace periods, how can you become debt free?

   A. pay your debt off slowly so that you have extra cash for necessities
   B. never use the credit cards
   C. use them only when it is not convenient to carry cash
   D. cut up four of the credit cards right away

3. Which of the following situations is most like the process of becoming debt free?

   A. driving a car
   B. wearing a patch to give up smoking
   C. losing weight by avoiding all-you-can-eat buffets
   D. running a marathon race

4. Earlier in the book, the author made the statement "It's so simple that I'm almost embarrassed to mention it. Don't borrow any more."

   Based on this information and the information in this passage, with which of the following statements would the author most likely agree?

   A. "Money is the root of all evil."
   B. "You can never have enough money."
   C. "Live within your means."
   D. "You deserve only the best."

Answers and explanations start on page 638.

Cause and Effect

When one event or idea influences another, there is a cause-and-effect relationship. For example, if you forget to fill your car with gas, the car will stall. The lack of gas is the **cause,** or the reason. The stalled car is the **effect**.

As you read this passage, look for cause-and-effect relationships.

> He is deceptively sweet upon waking up, and lets out a large yawn, showing his thin pink puppy tongue, and simultaneously letting out a high-pitched squeaking sound. Not two minutes later, he's eaten my favorite magazine and stuffed his entire head in the kitchen wastebasket to find a leftover turkey bone. The pup searches under the bed, on top of the dresser, and beside the nightstand for anything to chew. He's on a rampage in the morning—it's just his puppy nature.
>
> To calm him down, we head to the park for one hour of exercise with the other neighborhood dogs. Afterwards, he plays with his stuffed animal squeaky toy, sleeps for an hour, then finds his favorite bone. He lies down like an angel, chewing with contentment.

▶ What causes the puppy's owners to take him to the park?
  (1) They like to see the other neighborhood dogs.
  (2) The puppy is acting too wild and energetic.

You are correct if you chose **(2)**. The first paragraph describes wild behavior, and the second paragraph says, "To calm him down, we head to the park . . ."

▶ Why is the puppy so wild and energetic?
  (1) It is just the way a puppy is.
  (2) He has a behavioral problem.

You are correct if you chose **(1)**. The writer doesn't indicate that the puppy's behavior is a problem. In fact, she clearly states that it's just the puppy's nature.

▶ What effect does the activity in the park have on the puppy?
  (1) It calms him and tires him out.
  (2) It teaches him to obey his owner.

You are correct if you chose **(1)**. When they get back from the park, the puppy plays quietly, sleeps for an hour, and then lies down to chew.

▶ Why does a walk in the park have a calming effect on the puppy?
  (1) because the puppy enjoys seeing the other dogs
  (2) because the puppy gets plenty of exercise

You are correct if you chose **(2)**. The exercise brings on the effect—calm behavior. This cause is not directly stated. You have to apply what you know about exercise and its effects in order to understand the relationship.

Key Ideas

- To determine the cause of an event, answer the question "Why did this happen?"
- To determine an effect, ask yourself, "What was the result?"

ON THE GED® TEST

In a GED® passage, a writer might discuss one cause and all its effects, one effect and all its causes, or a chain of events in which each effect becomes the cause of another event.

PRACTICE 4

Questions 1 through 5 refer to the following excerpt from an essay.

EXCERPTED FROM "THE DEPRESSION"

1   Some events are so important that their influence cuts across class lines, affects all races and ethnic groups, and leaves no region untouched. The depression of the 1930s was such an event. No one who lived through those years in the United States could ever completely forget the bread lines, the millions of unemployed, or the forlorn and discouraged men and women who saw their mortgages foreclosed, their dreams shattered, their children hungry and afraid.

2   The depression was precipitated by the stock market crash in October 1929, but the actual cause of the collapse was an unhealthy economy. While the ability of the manufacturing industry to produce consumer goods had increased rapidly, mass purchasing power had remained relatively static. Most laborers, farmers, and white-collar workers, therefore, could not afford to buy the automobiles and refrigerators turned out by factories in the 1920s, because their incomes were too low. At the same time, the federal government increased the problem through economic policies that tended to encourage the very rich to over-save.

3   Herbert Hoover, a sensitive and humane engineer, had the misfortune of being President when the depression began. Even though he broke with the past and used the power of the federal government to stem the tide of depression, especially through loans to businesses and banks, his efforts proved to be too little and too late.

From "The Depression" from *Generations: Your Family in Modern American History*, 2nd ed., edited by James Watts and Allen F. Davis, New York: Alfred A. Knopf, 1974, 1978.

1. According to the authors, why was the depression of the 1930s so important?

   A. It could have been prevented.
   B. It was a time of economic hardship.
   C. It affected nearly everyone.
   D. It was unforgettable.

2. According to the passage, which of the following was an effect of the depression?

   A. Many people lost the mortgages on their homes.
   B. The stock market collapsed in October 1929.
   C. Herbert Hoover was elected president.
   D. The rich began to save too much of their money.

3. According to the passage, which of the following was one cause of the depression?

   A. a static stock market
   B. low worker incomes
   C. not enough productivity
   D. laborers refusing to buy products

4. In the early part of the depression, what effect did government policies have on the economy?

   A. Banks and businesses began to need loans.
   B. They had little effect.
   C. Some of the poorer people were helped.
   D. The very rich were helped.

5. One person who lived during the depression stated, "I can remember one time, the only thing in the house to eat was mustard. . . . And we can't stand mustard till today."

   This account supports which of the following ideas from the passage?

   A. Workers should have been paid more.
   B. The depression touched everyone.
   C. Herbert Hoover could have done more to help the economy.
   D. The depression left people emotionally scarred.

Answers and explanations start on page 638.

Compare and Contrast

You are probably familiar with comparing and contrasting whenever you go shopping. If you are looking at two cars or even two bottles of aspirin, you want to know if the price of the two is the same or different.

Writers **compare** to point out what is similar and **contrast** to point out what is different about ideas or things.

As you read this passage, look for things being compared and contrasted.

> In December, it seems everyone is hurrying to bake holiday treats, decorate, and buy gifts. Some holiday shoppers trek through store after store, while others prefer catalog or online shopping. Just two of the holidays that keep everyone so busy this time of year are Christmas and Hanukkah.
>
> These holidays are, of course, times of celebration. People plan parties and family get-togethers. Both involve gift giving. Both also coincide with the winter solstice in the Northern Hemisphere, a time when many ancient cultures rejoiced.
>
> Christmas is a celebration of the birth of Jesus, though celebrating Christmas on December 25 did not become common until the fourth century.
>
> Hanukkah, the Jewish Festival of Lights, celebrates the belief that a flask of oil sufficient for only one day miraculously burned for eight days in a temple in the second century B.C.E. That's why on Hanukkah an additional candle is lit each evening until, on the eighth night of the holiday, eight candles are burning.

▶ What is the writer comparing and contrasting?
  (1) methods of shopping
  (2) Christmas and Hanukkah

You are correct if you chose **(2)**. The similarities and differences between the two holidays are the focus of the discussion. Two methods of shopping are merely mentioned.

▶ What is one basis on which the writer compares the two?
  (1) time of year celebrated
  (2) kinds of meals served

You are correct if you chose **(1)**. The similarities discussed in this passage include the time of the winter solstice in the Northern Hemisphere, close to when each holiday is celebrated.

▶ What is one basis on which the writer contrasts the two?
  (1) gift giving
  (2) their histories

The correct answer is **(2)**. The two holidays have very different histories. Both holidays involve gift giving, so that is not a point of contrast.

Key Ideas

- To compare ideas or things, find out how they are alike.
- To contrast ideas or things, find out how they differ.
- A writer might compare two things, contrast two things, or compare and contrast in one passage.

ON THE GED® TEST

In a GED® passage, a writer may (1) compare in one paragraph and contrast in the next or (2) go back and forth, discussing similarities and differences on different points.

PRACTICE 5

<u>Questions 1 through 5</u> refer to the following excerpt from a diary.

EXCERPTED FROM *DIARIES OF THE WESTWARD JOURNEY*

1   Mr. West from Peoria, Ill. had another man, his wife, a son Clay about 20 years of age and his daughter, America, eighteen. Unfortunately Mr. West had gone to the extreme of providing himself with such a heavy wagon and load that they were deemed objectionable as fellow argonauts. After disposing of some of their supplies they were allowed to join us. They had four fine oxen. This wagon often got stalled in bad roads much to the annoyance of all, but as he was a wagon maker and his companion a blacksmith by trade and both were accommodating there were always ready hands to "pry the wheel out of mire."

2   A mule team from Washington, D.C. was very insufficiently provisioned . . . [by] Southern gentlemen "unused to work. . . ." They deserted the train at Salt Lake as they could not proceed with their equipment and it was easier to embrace Mormonism than to brave the "American Desert."

3   Much in contrast to these men were four batchelors Messers Wilson, Goodall, Fifield and Martin, who had a wagon drawn by four oxen and two milch cows following behind. The latter gave milk all the way to the sink of the Humboldt where they died, having acted as draught animals for several weeks after the oxen had perished. Many a cup of milk was given to the children of the train and the mothers tried in every way possible to express their gratitude.

By Catherine Haun from *Women's Diaries of the Westward Journey*, edited by Lillian Schlissel, New York: Schocken Books, 1982.

1. What did Mr. West do that allowed his group to join the wagon train?

  A. make wagons for the others
  B. bring four fine oxen
  C. offer milk to the children
  D. leave some of his possessions behind

2. What purpose did the cows serve?

  A. They led the oxen through rough terrain.
  B. They carried children when wagons were full.
  C. They provided milk and pulled wagons.
  D. They provided food and replaced the mules.

3. Which of the following is contrasted in this excerpt?

  A. the provisions of each group of travelers
  B. the stability of each of the wagons
  C. the number of people in each group
  D. the ability of each group to feed the children

4. Suppose the writer were comparing a woman with five children who could sew and cook to one man with an old ox. Which of the following would be her most likely response?

The writer would

  A. be happy to have people who could cook and sew
  B. prefer to add fewer people to the group of travelers
  C. feel sorry for the man and welcome him
  D. offer the man one of her own animals

5. Based on the information in this excerpt, how is this trip similar for all the travelers?

  A. They must cooperate and work together.
  B. They will be rewarded for their efforts.
  C. They have similar backgrounds and relate to each other.
  D. They have all been forced to go on the journey.

Answers and explanations start on page 638.

LESSON 6

Conclusions and Generalizations

Conclusions

A detective draws a **conclusion** when he looks at different pieces of evidence and figures out who committed a crime. A doctor draws a conclusion when she looks at different symptoms and figures out what illness a patient has. You, as a reader, can draw a conclusion when you take pieces of information and put them together to figure out something that the writer has not directly stated.

See what conclusions you can draw from this notice sent by an employer.

> Thank you for sending your resume in response to our newspaper advertisement. We consider our company—and especially our employees—to be the best. And we want to keep it that way. For that reason, we carefully review each resume that is sent to us. We want to ensure that our company and the new employee we hire are a perfect match.
>
> This process, of course, takes some time. We want to assure you that your resume is part of this process and will be reviewed. If we feel we have an opening that matches your qualifications, we will contact you. If you have not heard from us within ten business days of the postmark of this notice, be assured that we will keep your resume on file for one year and review it when future openings arise.

▶ If a job applicant has not heard from this company three weeks after reading this notice, what can she conclude?
  (1) The review process is taking longer than expected.
  (2) She did not get the job that she applied for.

Option **(2)** is correct. The notice says that the review process takes some time. It also says that the company will contact the applicant if it feels she matches the opening. Finally, if she doesn't hear from it within ten business days, her resume will go on file. You can conclude that the review process takes about ten business days, and if she hasn't been contacted in that time, she didn't get the job.

▶ What kind of notice can you conclude this is?
  (1) a personal note sent to this individual applicant
  (2) a form notice sent to all applicants

Again, you're correct if you chose **(2)**. The way the notice is worded, with no personal details, lets you conclude this. You can also use your knowledge of the real world and business form letters to conclude that this, too, is a form.

▶ What conclusion can you draw about the company's attitude?
  (1) It cares about its employees and their job satisfaction.
  (2) It cares only about profits and employee productivity.

You are correct if you chose **(1)**. The fact that the company states not only that it considers its employees to be the best but also that it takes the time to communicate sincerely with potential employees lets you conclude that.

Key Ideas

- A conclusion is an idea figured out from different pieces of information.
- You can use your knowledge of the real world to help you draw conclusions when you read.

GED® TEST TIP

Be sure to read an entire passage before answering the questions about it. That way, you'll take all the information into account and won't "jump to conclusions."

PRACTICE 6.1

Questions 1 through 5 refer to the following excerpt from an autobiography.

EXCERPTED FROM *THE STORY OF MY LIFE*

1   Once there were eleven tadpoles in a glass globe set in a window full of plants. I remember the eagerness with which I made discoveries about them. It was great fun to plunge my hand into the bowl and feel the tadpoles frisk about, and to let them slip and slide between my fingers. One day a more ambitious fellow leaped beyond the edge of the bowl and fell on the floor, where I found him to all appearance more dead than alive. The only sign of life was a slight wriggling of his tail. But no sooner had he returned to his element than he darted to the bottom, swimming round and round in joyous activity. He had made his leap, he had seen the great world, and was content to stay in his pretty glass house under the big fuchsia tree until he attained the dignity of froghood. Then he went to live in the leafy pool at the end of the garden, where he made the summer nights musical with his quaint love-song.

2   Thus I learned from life itself. At the beginning I was only a little mass of possibilities. It was my teacher who unfolded and developed them. When she came, everything about me breathed of love and joy and was full of meaning. She has never since let pass an opportunity to point out the beauty that is in everything, nor has she ceased trying in thought and action and example to make my life sweet and useful.

3   It was my teacher's genius, her quick sympathy, her loving tact which made the first years of my education so beautiful.

From *The Story of My Life* by Helen Keller.

1. What can you conclude about the writer's view of learning?

A. It is rewarding and one of life's joys.
B. It is better with a strict teacher.
C. It happens very slowly, if at all.
D. It happens most often when you are alone.

2. What conclusion can you draw about the writer's character?

The writer is

A. self-centered and demanding
B. confused and searching
C. fearful and shy
D. insightful and grateful

3. If Helen's teacher was trying to teach her addition, what method would the teacher most likely use?

A. make Helen stand and recite addition facts for one hour every day
B. assign an abundance of addition homework
C. show Helen how addition is used in everyday life
D. ask a well-known mathematician to teach the subject

4. How are the thoughts in this personal account organized?

A. as a comparison with a frog followed by a contrast
B. as a problem followed by its solution
C. in chronological order, or time sequence
D. as an anecdote followed by a generalization based on the anecdote

5. Later in her story, Helen compares a child's mind to a shallow brook "which ripples and dances merrily over the stony course of its education. . . ." Based on this information and the excerpt above, what is similar about the tadpole and a child?

A. They learn from others.
B. They are eager to grow into adulthood.
C. Youth can make them do dangerous things.
D. Their development is not entirely smooth.

Answers and explanations start on page 639.

Generalizations

A **generalization** is a broad statement about a group of people, objects, or things or about a type of event. Usually, it takes something that is true in one specific case and extends it to every possible case. For example, "My hometown celebrated Independence Day with fireworks last summer," is a fact about a specific Fourth of July in a specific town; a generalization could be "Every Independence Day, my hometown celebrates with fireworks."

► Identify one statement with *F* for a fact and the other with *G* for generalization.
    (1) Every clerk in the store focuses on customer service more than any other aspect of the job.
    (2) Tina, the manager of the women's shoe department, helps customers select just the right pair of shoes.

If you identified option **(2)** as being a fact and option **(1)** as being a generalization, you were correct. One hint that **(1)** is the generalization is the word "every." Words like *all*, *never*, and *always* show up in sentences that make broad, sweeping statements. The sentence about Tina, on the other hand, gives specific information about a specific person and so is not a generalization.

Generalizations can be valid and true when properly made. A writer can support a generalization with an example (like Tina, above) and information that shows why the example represents the whole group. Often, a generalization is too broad to apply to every member of a group, and a good writer will acknowledge that there are exceptions.

"Dogs are typically more attached to their owners than cats are, due in part to their evolution as pack animals. My dog will jump up to meet me as soon as I get home from work, while my cat will continue napping serenely until hunger motivates him to do otherwise."

► What example is given to support the generalization that "Dogs are typically more attached to their owners than cats"?
    (1) Dogs evolved as pack animals.
    (2) The author's dog jumps up to meet her, while her cat ignores her.

The example of the author's dog's attachment to her, **(2)**, illustrates and supports the generalization that most dogs show greater attachment to their owners. The specific example helps to show that the statement is based on experience.

Writers sometimes make the mistake of drawing **faulty generalizations** based on too little information. Imagine a person who bites into an apple, finds a worm, and concludes that all apples have worms in them. Since a generalization is a broad statement, a **valid generalization** requires broad knowledge to justify it. A generalization about American cities is more likely to be faulty if the writer bases on it only one city but more likely to be valid if the writer supports it with knowledge of 20 cities. With a larger sample, the writer is also better able to know whether to qualify a generalization as something that is true in most, but not all, cases.

► Identify one statement with *FG* for a faulty generalization and the other with *VG* for a valid generalization.
    (1) Every breed of dog has four legs, so almost all dogs have four legs.
    (2) Some dogs bark at kids, so all dogs must dislike or fear children.

You are correct if you chose **(1)** as the valid generalization: the writer shows awareness of many different types of dogs. Choice **(2)** is a faulty generalization; dogs may bark at children for reasons other than fear or dislike.

Key Ideas

- A generalization is a broad statement about a group or class.
- When assessing a generalization, evaluate the writer's evidence.
- An important factor in thoughtful reading is distinguishing between faulty and valid generalizations.

GED® TEST TIP

If you see a generalization, look for supporting evidence that may be introduced by phrases such as "for example," "such as," or "for instance."

PRACTICE 6.2

Questions 1 through 3 are based on the following newspaper editorial.

OPINION: DOUBTS ABOUT
GLOBAL WARMING

1   Shady Hollow was hit yesterday with record cold temperatures. And yet, despite this deep freeze, we'll continue to be subjected to the doctrine of global warming.

2   There is plenty to be said for fuel economy—anyone who lived through the energy crisis of the 1970s learned that lesson the hard way—but it's time we dispense with the terror campaign of doomsday climatology and recognize it for the pseudoscience that it is. Whenever Shady Hollow gets a big hit of winter weather, common sense tells us that the idea of "warming" seems fishy, yet climatologists insist on playing the same tune. More and more, this tune is taken up by policymakers and government bodies, who steer our administrations accordingly. It must be the case that ivory towers have good weather stripping and excellent heating systems; as for the man on the street, he's finding his street a chilly one these days.

3   The simple fact is that it is logically impossible to reconcile a record cold temperature with the idea that it's getting warmer. A record cold temperature, and this may be worth spelling out, means exactly this: it has never been colder on this date in recorded history. If "warming" means what it sounds like it means—that temperatures are rising, not falling—then there is a real problem here, because that is quite simply not what is happening.

4   It may take years to get out from under the orthodoxy of the accepted opinion on climate change, but the facts themselves will not go away. Sooner or later, we'll be forced to acknowledge that we're still bundling up, and when that happens, we can stop building policy discussions around fictions.

1. What is a generalization that is made in paragraph 3?

   A. Shady Hollow has the coldest temperatures in the region.
   B. Global warming can only be valid if it predicts high temperatures.
   C. On the whole, temperatures are not rising.
   D. If children are taught a simpler theory, then a more complex theory should be set aside.

2. What evidence does the author give to support his generalization about global warming?

   A. Shady Hollow was hit with a record cold temperature yesterday.
   B. Ivory towers have good weather stripping.
   C. It may take years to change opinions on climate change.
   D. There is plenty to be said for fuel economy.

3. Which of the following pieces of information would put the author in a better position to make a generalization about climate change?

   A. an account of the energy crisis of the 1970s
   B. minutes of policy discussions from the 1970s through today
   C. interviews with the "man on the street" from the 1990s through today
   D. nationwide data tables of temperatures from the 1980s through today

Answers and explanations start on page 639.

LESSON 7

Word Choice

Key Ideas

- Writers choose words carefully to make an impact on the reader.
- They deliberately choose words with positive, negative, or neutral connotations.
- Writers also use figurative language such as similes, metaphors, and personification to enhance descriptions.

GED® TEST TIP

Read closely to see how a writer's word choice affects how you picture something or feel about it. You may have to answer questions that require an awareness of the impact of both words' connotations and figurative language.

Writers make careful decisions to select words that will impact their audience. One choice that writers make is to select words that have a **connotation** associated with a particular image or feeling. Think of the different connotations of *dog*, *mutt*, and *man's best friend*. The word *dog* has a neutral connotation; it just describes the animal. To some, the word *mutt* would have a negative connotation, and the phrase *man's best friend* would have a positive connotation.

▶ Assign a *P* (positive) or an *N* (negative) to the following words to indicate the connotation that might be associated with them:
  (1) shack
  (2) villa

You are correct if you assigned an *N* to **(1)** and a *P* to **(2)**. The word *shack* probably brings to mind a small, poorly built or run-down building. On the other hand, the word *villa* might be associated with a house in the countryside or a vacation destination.

Writers use **figurative language** to make their descriptions clearer and more vivid. They use **similes**, which use the words *like* or *as* to compare two things; for example, "His voice was like velvet." This indicates that his voice was smooth. Another type of figurative language is a **metaphor**, which implies a comparison between two things. One familiar metaphor is "Life is a journey"; this compares two dissimilar things in order to describe life. A third figure of speech is **personification**, by which a writer assigns human characteristics to something that is not human. For example, a writer may describe a storm as "slashing at the windows and knocking on the door."

> If you look very carefully, you can find the island of Ascension on a map about midway between Angola, in Africa, and Brazil, in South America. This South Atlantic island has a population of about 1,000 people and is home to an important GPS ground antenna and a British air force base. Its volcanic terrain greets visitors with a forbidding aspect; place names like "Comfortless Cove" indicate how rocky and uninviting Ascension Island may appear. Even so, with its dry subtropical weather, excellent sport fishing, and unique wildlife, this barren outpost attracts about 1,000 tourists each year.

▶ What does the personification in the third sentence suggest about Ascension Island?
  (1) Tourists are forbidden to visit the island.
  (2) The island doesn't look like a good place to visit.

You are correct if you chose **(2)**. The writer refers to the island as if it were a person with an unfriendly appearance. Since the last sentence states that tourists do visit the island, you know that they are not forbidden to do so.

PRACTICE 7

Questions 1 through 5 refer to the following product description.

A COOL NEW BLANKET

1   Many people rely on electric blankets to keep warm on winter nights without turning on expensive central heating. In summer, though, there's no alternative to noisy fans and energy-hogging air conditioners if you want to stay cool . . . until now. The Starlight company recently introduced its newest product: an electric blanket that keeps you cool even on sweltering summer nights.

2   The CoolForter blanket works like an electric blanket, but it feels like a dream. The blanket contains a full tenth of a mile of flexible hose, fully insulated between layers of soft cotton. A small, quiet compressor refrigerates the safely enclosed cooling chemical and circulates it continuously through the coils. The CoolForter coddles you in refreshing comfort, and you never have to worry about waking up shivering. That's because your sleeping temperature is precisely controlled by the built-in thermostat, which can be adjusted to your exact temperature preference.

3   Your CoolForter blanket also matches your decorating preferences: the replaceable cover comes in a wide variety of bland colors to suit any décor. If you decide to redecorate, choose from a selection of fun and gaudy prints to liven up your room.

4   Best of all, the CoolForter saves you money every time you use it. Consuming an average of just 80 watts, the twin-size blanket is like a regular household lightbulb, costing just pennies per day to run. It's an investment in comfort that will pay for itself many times over the lifetime of its generous ten-year warranty and beyond.

1. In paragraph 2, what is compared to a dream?

A. an electric blanket
B. the flexible hose used in the CoolForter blanket
C. the cotton insulating layers
D. the CoolForter blanket

2. What could be a reason that the writer used the word "coddles" in paragraph 2?

A. to show that the blanket keeps its user warm
B. to show that the blanket is a pleasant indulgence
C. to show that the blanket keeps its user cool
D. to show that the user can wrap herself up in the blanket

3. What word could the writer have used instead of "chemical" in paragraph 2 that would have a less negative connotation?

A. fluid
B. antifreeze
C. contaminant
D. water

4. Which word in paragraph 3 means "neutral" and has a negative connotation?

A. decorating
B. replaceable
C. bland
D. gaudy

5. Why is "like a regular household lightbulb" from paragraph 4 an effective use of a comparison using figurative language?

A. It reminds the consumer that, while a lightbulb generates heat, the CoolForter blanket keeps its user cool.
B. It makes the CoolForter blanket seem ordinary.
C. It emphasizes the difference in cost between running a regular lightbulb and operating a compact fluorescent lightbulb.
D. It allows the consumer to compare the CoolForter's energy usage to that of a familiar item.

Answers and explanations start on page 639.

Writer's Tone and Point of View

Key Ideas

- The writer's attitude toward a subject is conveyed by the tone of the writing.
- To determine tone, look at word choice and manner of expression. How would the writer sound reading the piece?
- The writer's point of view is the position she is writing from.

Tone

A writer usually has a certain attitude toward the subject he or she is writing about. This attitude is the **tone** of the piece. The tone is not directly stated. You have to sense it by the writer's choice of words and manner of expression.

As you read this drama review, ask yourself, "What tone of voice would the author have if she were reading this aloud to me?"

> Watching actor Brian Dennehy as Willy Loman in the stage production of *Death of a Salesman* was transforming. I know intellectually that live theater is better than movies. Movie actors reshoot scenes until they are perfect. An actor on stage has one chance to get it right. It is immediate. The actors are breathing human beings in the same room with you. Theater provides the opportunity for strong emotions to surface, right there, in the moment. Seeing a play often envelops me in energy.
>
> But I've never gone so far as to cry at a theater performance until now. I cried because Dennehy's Loman reminded me of my father, of the brevity of our lives, of how easy it is to waste our lives. This was not an intellectual response. I suddenly heard what this man on stage was saying—his life wasn't worth living, though he had tried hard, had a devoted wife and two sons. It didn't matter that this play was written in the 1940s. Mr. Dennehy stood on stage and roared at us about our lives now. It was hard-hitting, emotional drama.

▶ Which of the following best describes the tone of this piece?
  (1) positive and somewhat awed
  (2) cool and objective

The correct response is **(1)**. The writer states positive opinions. She also chooses short, clipped expressions—"It is immediate" and "right there, in the moment"—that by themselves create a sense of drama and awe. If the tone were cool and objective, you would not sense the writer's emotional attitude toward the play.

ON THE GED® TEST

Some kinds of tone you might see in GED® passages are formal or informal, positive or negative, objective, sarcastic, arrogant, concerned, affectionate, or nostalgic.

Point of View

The **point of view** of a piece is "where the author is coming from"—that is, the writer's background and experiences that may affect her opinions. For example, when you read a column in a newspaper, you can usually tell whether the writer has a liberal or a conservative point of view.

▶ What point of view does the writer of the review above have?
  (1) that of a person who prefers sitting at home watching TV
  (2) that of an enthusiastic theatergoer

You are correct if you chose **(2)**. You can conclude that the writer goes to the theater ("Seeing a play often envelops me") and enjoys it ("theater is better than movies"). Knowing this helps you evaluate the merits of the review.

PRACTICE 8

Questions 1 through 5 refer to the following review.

EXCERPTED FROM "TALKING BACK TO THE TUBE"

1   CBS delivered a television low mark called *Big Brother*. Focusing on ten fame-seeking, people-pleasing, hair-teasing losers willing to submit to surveillance by a nation of snoops for three months, it was so bad that it wasn't even good. Forget about camp reversals that transform trash into the perversely fascinating, forget about the Cheese Factor, which allows a pop-cultural product to be moldy and musty and stinky and still taste good. *Big Brother* was so bad that even Jean-Paul Sartre would have yawned, and the dude wrote hundreds of pages about useless passion in *Being and Nothingness*.

2   But something good did come of *Big Brother*, something wicked and warped and witty, something created by people with way too much time on their hands and way too much venom in their bite. While the reality series was channeling banality through the cable cords and over the airwaves six nights a week, a small crew of writers were deconstructing and eviscerating the tedium on the Internet. They were taking hours and hours of prime-time dross and turning it into decadent, amoral, sharp, electronic gold.

3   Internet sass.

4   You gotta love it, if only because it keeps razor-tongued fanatics and uncensored savants off the streets and out of trouble.

5   Not only was there a site devoted entirely to the ridiculing of CBS, *Big Brother*, its ten cast members, their families, host Julie Chen, and the gaseous *Big Brother* house pug, but a number of other general interest sites, notably Salon.com, spent the summer providing wry daily updates on the non-goings-on of the non-people in the non-house. They, too, took the non-pulse of a DOA television series and gave it a semblance of life on the Internet.

Excerpt from "Talking Back to the Tube," by Matthew Gilbert. Reprinted courtesy of the *Boston Globe*.

1. Who are referred to as "razor-tongued fanatics and uncensored savants" (paragraph 4)?

   A. the television writers
   B. the television cast of *Big Brother*
   C. the Internet writers
   D. the Internet audience

2. Which of the following best summarizes the reviewer's point about *Big Brother*?

   A. The Internet reviews were much more interesting than the TV show.
   B. The TV show was so bad that it was funny.
   C. Internet writers are better than TV writers.
   D. The main problem was with the ten people on the TV show.

3. What opinion is supported by the statement "even Jean-Paul Sartre would have yawned, and the dude wrote hundreds of pages about useless passion" (paragraph 1)?

   A. The show was boring.
   B. The show should have been longer.
   C. The show needed more passion.
   D. The show was incomprehensible.

4. Which of the following best describes the tone of this review?

   A. apologetic
   B. nostalgic for earlier shows
   C. informal and hip
   D. objective

5. From whose point of view is this piece likely written?

   A. a television script writer
   B. a person who hates watching TV
   C. someone knowledgeable about the media
   D. a disgruntled fan

Answers and explanations start on page 639.

Text Structure

Writers make choices about how to organize informational and nonfiction materials based on their purpose. You have already seen two text structures: cause and effect, which shows how one thing made another happen, and compare and contrast, which illustrates similarities and differences.

There are other **text structures** often used for informational text:

- **Example**—introduces an unfamiliar topic and then follows with common examples to aid understanding.
- **Pros and Cons**—explains a situation by first presenting its benefits and then portraying its deficiencies in order to present both sides.
- **Chronological Order** or **Process**—presents details in the order in which they occur; also referred to as a **sequence** of events.
- **Elaboration**—makes a statement and indicates that additional information or an explanation will follow.

These text structures use different types of **transitions** to guide the reader from one idea to the next. Many of these are familiar to you.

Text Structure	Purpose	Sample Transitions
Example	Organizes illustrations that support a concept	for example, for instance, such as, to illustrate
Pros and Cons	Shows benefits and drawbacks	on the one hand, on the other hand
Chronological Order or Process	Describes events and procedures	before, after, next, following, meanwhile, until
Elaboration	Expands with additional details	additionally, furthermore, moreover

Practice using an understanding of text structure by reading the paragraph and answering the question below.

Today, there are millions of workers who are not employees in the traditional sense; they are called "contract workers." These are self-employed individuals who have contracts with different businesses. For example, a graphic artist may have several different clients and design a newsletter for one and a website for another. Contract workers pay for their own equipment, supplies, and benefits—such as health insurance.

▶ What is an example that explains the concept of "contract workers"?
(1) They are not employees in the traditional sense.
(2) They may have contracts with several businesses.

Choice **(2)** illustrates the concept of contract workers by explaining that they have several different clients rather than one employer. Choice **(1)** is not an example that helps to explain contract work; it just explains what contract workers are not.

Key Ideas

- Writers may use different text structures depending on what they are writing about.
- One of the main tools writers use to create different text structures is transition words, which create relationships between ideas.

GED® TEST TIP

You will need to be aware of different types of text structure to answer questions, but you will not need to identify any structures by their names.

PRACTICE 9

Questions 1 and 2 refer to this scientific experiment.

COWPOX, SMALLPOX, AND IMMUNITY

In 1796, British physician Edward Jenner conducted an experiment intended to help develop a viable treatment for the deadly smallpox disease. Some time before, he had noticed that dairymaids in his village commonly became infected with cowpox. Cowpox is an illness that is very similar to smallpox, but it is not deadly. The dairymaids who caught cowpox later turned out to be immune to smallpox. This led Jenner to experiment with whether he could make a test subject immune to smallpox by first infecting that person with cowpox. His test subject was a young boy named James. First, Jenner made small cuts on James's skin and inserted liquid from the cowpox sores of a local dairymaid. After being exposed to the disease, James caught cowpox and later recovered. After the boy's recovery from cowpox, Jenner exposed James to smallpox and found that the boy was immune. Today, scientists and medical professionals know that the cowpox and smallpox viruses are so similar that the body's immune system cannot tell them apart.

1. What step in the process came before James's recovery from cowpox?

   A. his immunity to smallpox
   B. exposure to the cowpox disease
   C. scientists' discovery that cowpox and smallpox are similar
   D. Jenner exposing James to smallpox

2. Which of the following phrases from the passage helps to understand the order of the steps in the process?

   A. "cannot tell them apart"
   B. "Jenner made small cuts"
   C. "After being exposed to the disease"
   D. "make a test subject immune"

Question 3 refers to this discussion of gardening.

THE UPS AND DOWNS OF GARDENING

Planting and maintaining a backyard garden can have many benefits, but it also brings challenges. On the one hand, successful gardeners often express deep feelings of accomplishment and satisfaction in their gardens. Gardening can involve good exercise and fresh air, and spending time outdoors can be a healthy escape from everyday responsibilities and concerns. A flower garden provides a beautiful view that often attracts delightful visitors, including butterflies and hummingbirds. A vegetable garden provides nutritious food and can add up to significant savings on your grocery bill. An herb garden can supply alternatives to unhealthy ingredients such as salt and oil.

On the other hand, planting and maintaining a garden can be very expensive and time-consuming, and a garden may fail despite your best efforts. Proper soil and fertilizers must be bought, and plants or seeds must be chosen. It is also important to consider the watering and feeding of the garden to ensure proper growth. A number of factors beyond your immediate control may affect the success of your garden. If the season's weather is extreme in any way—too dry, too rainy, too hot, or too cold—it can damage tender plants and undo your hard work, wasting your investment of time and money. Similarly, invasive pests and diseases can be devastating to your home garden and can be difficult and expensive to control.

3. Which of the following is one of the writer's arguments against planting and maintaining a backyard garden?

   A. Time outdoors often alleviates stress.
   B. A number of factors can damage a garden.
   C. Having too many daily chores is stressful.
   D. Rain is bad for a garden.

Answers and explanations start on page 639.

INTERPRETING NONFICTION AND INFORMATIONAL TEXT PRACTICE QUESTIONS

Questions 1 through 4 refer to the following excerpt from an autobiography.

EXCERPTED FROM *THE LIAR'S CLUB*

1   That fall my school career didn't go much better. I got suspended from my second-grade class twice, first for biting a kid named Phyllis who wasn't, to my mind, getting her scissors out fast enough to comply with the teacher, then again for breaking my plastic ruler over the head of a boy named Sammy Joe Tyler, whom I adored. A pale blue knot rose through the blond stubble of his crew cut. Both times I got sent to the principal, a handsome ex-football coach named Frank Doleman who let Lecia and me call him Uncle Frank. (Lecia and I had impressed Uncle Frank by both learning to read pretty much without instruction before we were three. Mother took us each down to his office in turn, and we each dutifully read the front page of the day's paper out loud to him, so he could be sure it wasn't just some story we'd memorized.)

2   He let me stay in his office playing chess all afternoon with whoever wandered in. He loved pitting me against particularly lunkheaded fifth- and sixth-grade boys who'd been sent down for paddlings they never got. He'd try to use my whipping them at chess to make them nervous about how dumb they were. "Now this little bitty old second-grader here took you clean in six plays. Don't you reckon you need to be listening to Miss Vilimez instead of cutting up?" When Mrs. Hess led me solemnly down the hall to Frank Doleman's office, I would pretend to cry, but thought instead about Brer Rabbit as he was being thrown into the briar patch where he'd been born and raised, and screaming *Please don't throw me in that briar patch!*

From *The Liar's Club* by Mary Karr, New York: Penguin Books, 1995.

1. If the writer had attended an elementary school dance, which of the following might she have done?

   A. made fun of everyone as they danced
   B. sat and played chess with the boys
   C. been too shy to dance with anyone
   D. hit a boy in the arm to get his attention

2. What is meant by the statement "I . . . thought instead about Brer Rabbit as he was being thrown into the briar patch where he'd been born and raised and screaming *Please don't throw me in that briar patch!*" (paragraph 2)?

   A. She was so upset that she wanted to scream.
   B. She was just pretending she didn't want to go to the principal's office.
   C. She hoped the teacher would let her back in class if she pleaded with her.
   D. She was afraid of what would happen in the principal's office.

3. What type of principal was Frank Doleman?

   A. strict
   B. ineffective
   C. unusual
   D. mean

4. Later in the autobiography, the narrator describes herself as "small-boned and skinny, but more than able to make up for that."

   Based on this description and the excerpt, which of the following best describes the narrator?

   A. confident
   B. serious
   C. friendly
   D. hopeful

Questions 5 through 9 refer to this article about soda.

TURNING BACK A SUGARY TIDE

1   The popular soft drinks known as soda, pop, or both trace their origins all the way back to 1767, when English chemist Joseph Priestley invented a method for carbonating water. Over the last two and a half centuries, soda has risen to prominence primarily as a sweet beverage for social occasions. By the mid-1990s, soda had become the beverage of choice for adolescents. This increase in consumption has not been without negative consequences. Since the early 1980s, obesity rates for young Americans have risen steadily, as has the incidence of juvenile diabetes, heart disease, and myriad other ailments related to poor diet.

2   To counteract the harmful effects of overindulging in soda, federal, state, and local governments have taken steps in recent years. First Lady Michelle Obama promotes healthier diet choices and campaigns against childhood obesity. Several states now require that restaurants post calorie information next to all menu items, including beverages. In a controversial move, New York City mayor Michael Bloomberg proposed banning the sale of sodas over 16 ounces in city eateries. Additionally, many school districts around the country have banned the sale of soda in school vending machines.

3   These efforts appear to be paying off: latest statistics indicate that the percentage of teens who consume soda daily has fallen from 75 percent in the 1990s to 62 percent in 2009. However, most teens who abandon soda as a daily beverage replace it with other high-sugar choices, such as juice or energy and sport drinks. While many of these products have slightly less sugar than soda, the net impact of regular consumption is likely to be just as damaging in the long term. Regulating the sale of soda is a step in the right direction, but more can be done to educate young people about the dangers of a diet overflowing with sugary beverages.

5. Which of the following best describes the tone of this article?

   A. playful but informative
   B. pessimistic and sarcastic
   C. concerned but hopeful
   D. neutral and inquisitive

6. Which of the following best describes the author's point of view on reducing consumption of sugared beverages?

   A. The sale of soda should be outlawed due to the beverage's negative impact on health.
   B. Consuming diet soda is healthier than consuming regular soda.
   C. A young person's decision to consume soda is a personal choice that must be respected.
   D. Young people will choose healthier beverages if they are better educated about the dangers of consumption of sugared beverages.

7. According to paragraph 3, what will likely be the "net impact" of regularly consuming juice, energy, and sport drinks instead of soda?

   A. Teenagers who consume these beverages instead of soda will avoid the health hazards associated with soda.
   B. Soda manufacturers will likely go out of business since fewer consumers will be purchasing their products.
   C. Young people who drink these beverages regularly will eventually suffer from the same ailments as those who drink soda regularly.
   D. Many of the teenagers who drink juice, energy, and sport drinks will choose healthier food options to supplement their diets.

8. According to the passage, the author most likely regards the steps to curb soda consumption described in paragraph 2 as

   A. disruptive but essential
   B. effective to some extent
   C. invasive and extreme
   D. well-intentioned but unenforceable

9. In the beginning of paragraph 3, the words "These efforts" refer to which of the following?

   A. creating soda from carbonated water
   B. recommending energy and sport drinks instead of soda
   C. reducing excessive consumption of soda
   D. increasing educational programs about the effects of soda

Questions 10 through 12 refer to the following business document.

EXCERPTED FROM *INDEPENDENT CONSULTANT'S BROCHURE AND LETTER HANDBOOK* BY HERMAN HOLTZ

1   The National Association of Temporary Services (NATS), which represents the nation's temporary help employers, testified today before the House Ways and Means Committee on the employer mandate and related provisions of the President's Health Security Act (H.R. 3600).

2   Edward A. Lenz, NATS senior vice president, legal and government affairs, said that the temporary help industry supports the principle of universal coverage, but has serious concerns that the cost of mandates could weaken the ability of the temporary help industry to act as a "jobs bridge" to regular, full-time employment.

3   According to Lenz, the temporary help industry has recently "assumed a new and vital role—by helping to ease the burden on individuals during the current restructuring of the American work force. Temporary work offers displaced workers a critical safety net of income, benefits, and skills training and often provides a bridge back to regular, full-time employment."

4   In addition, the Association is concerned that the mandates, as currently structured, would "also impose enormous administrative burdens" due to annual temporary employee turnover in the range of 400 to 600 percent. If employer mandates are adopted, Lenz urged Congress to create a mechanism that relates premium payments to hours worked, such as a simple payroll tax.

10. Which of the following states one of the main concerns of NATS?

A. NATS won't be able to offer skills training to temporary employees if the government mandates coverage.
B. There will be an increase in turnover of temporary employees if the government mandates coverage.
C. The cost of mandated coverage will lessen the ability of NATS to hire and supply temporary workers.
D. Restructuring the work force is a burden to all Americans.

11. According to the press release, why have businesses supplying temporary help become even more necessary?

A. Many workers are losing their jobs and need temporary jobs until they find permanent work again.
B. There is not enough work for everyone to have a full-time permanent job.
C. The job turnover rate has gone as high as 400 to 600 percent.
D. More and more workers do not want permanent full-time work.

12. What is the overall purpose of this piece?

A. to stimulate debate over universal health insurance coverage
B. to impress both the Congress and the president
C. to describe various alternatives to mandated coverage
D. to raise awareness of an issue

Questions 13 through 16 refer to the following excerpt from a historical feminist speech.

EXCERPTED FROM *A TREASURY OF THE WORLD'S GREAT SPEECHES*

1   We have met here today to discuss our rights and wrongs, civil and political, and not, as some have supposed, to go into the detail of social life alone. We do not propose to petition the legislature to make our husbands just, generous, and courteous, to seat every man at the head of a cradle, and to clothe every woman in male attire. None of these points, however important they may be considered by leading men, will be touched in this convention. As to their costume, the gentlemen need feel no fear of our imitating that, for we think it in violation of every principle of taste, beauty, and dignity; notwithstanding all the contempt cast upon our loose, flowing garments, we still admire the graceful folds, and consider our costume far more artistic than theirs. Many of the nobler sex seem to agree with us in this opinion, for the bishops, priests, judges, barristers, and lord mayors of the first nation on the globe, and the Pope of Rome, with his cardinals, too, all wear the loose flowing robes, thus tacitly acknowledging that the male attire is neither dignified nor imposing. No, we shall not molest you in your philosophical experiments with stocks, pants, high-heeled boots, and Russian belts. Yours be the glory to discover, by personal experience, how long the kneepan can resist the terrible strapping down which you impose, in how short time the well-developed muscles of the throat can be reduced to mere threads by the constant pressure of the stock, how high the heel of a boot must be to make a short man tall, and how tight the Russian belt may be drawn and yet have wind enough left to sustain life.

2   But we are assembled to protest against a form of government existing without the consent of the governed—to declare our right to be free. . . .

From a speech at a woman's-rights convention by Elizabeth Cady Stanton, as reprinted in *A Treasury of the World's Great Speeches*, edited by Houston Peterson, New York: Simon & Schuster, 1954, 1965.

13. Which of the following best restates the lines "Yours be the glory to discover . . . how long the kneepad can resist the terrible strapping down which you impose" (paragraph 1)?

A. Men do not understand how uncomfortable women's clothes are.
B. Women will not resort to wearing pants or other restrictive men's clothing.
C. Men will only understand women when women dress like them.
D. Men and women will be equal only when they both wear belts and collars.

14. What is a "stock" (paragraph 1)?

A. a man's jacket
B. a wooden frame holding a prisoner
C. a loose shirt
D. a cloth worn around the neck

15. If the speaker attended a fancy tea party, which of the following would she be most likely to do?

A. be on her best behavior
B. speak up about current events
C. treat the hostess like royalty
D. comment on everyone's clothing

16. Later in the speech, Stanton states that "over the horns of bigotry and prejudice will be our way." Based on this and the excerpt, you can conclude that Stanton is giving this speech for what reason?

A. Women are fighting for the right to vote.
B. Women are tired of being made to wear dresses.
C. Husbands need to be made just and generous.
D. Many people mistakenly judge others by their appearance.

Answers and explanations start on page 715.

Purpose of Text

When you read *GED® Reasoning through Language Arts* passages, it is important that you comprehend not only what the author is writing about but also the **purpose**—the reason *why* he or she is writing this passage. Authors of nonfiction passages have one or more of the following purposes:

- **Narrate**—Narrative passages typically recount events chronologically, that is, in the order in which they happened. Examples include a person's life story and hour-by-hour developments in a news story.

- **Inform**—The author seeks to present facts and data to explain a subject, situation, or idea. Examples include news articles, financial summaries, and scientific findings.

- **Persuade**—The author seeks to change readers' minds, and the passage includes the author's opinions, recommendations, or conclusions. Examples are political speeches, newspaper editorials, and entertainment reviews.

- **Entertain**—Authors writing to entertain are trying to amuse or interest their readers. Examples include a humorous memoir or articles about celebrities.

Read the paragraph and answer questions about the writer's purpose.

> According to market research, video game sales—including digital downloads and apps—in the United States topped $15 billion in 2010. The most popular game genres were Action (21.7 percent of sales), Sports (16.3 percent), and Shooter (15.9 percent). Family Entertainment games accounted for only 9.1 percent of sales.

▶ What is the writer's purpose for this paragraph?
  (1) to present facts about video game sales
  (2) to convince readers that Family Entertainment games' sales should be increased

▶ Imagine there is an additional sentence at the end of the paragraph. "Because popular games in the Action and Shooter genres may contain extremely graphic violence, parents must be educated about how to monitor their children's purchases and game play." What would be the purpose of the revised paragraph about video games?
  (1) to entertain readers with an amusing fact about video games
  (2) to persuade parents to become more involved in their children's use of video games

In the first question, choice **(1)** is correct because the writer gives facts and not persuasive information. In the second question, once the information about violence has been added, choice **(2)** is correct because the statement offers a recommendation to persuade, not entertain, parents.

Key Ideas

- Writers have different reasons, or purposes, for writing.
- The main purposes for writing are to narrate a story, to inform, to persuade, and to entertain.

GED® TEST TIP

As you are reading passages on the test, ask yourself, "Why did the author write this story, article, or speech?" That will help you to understand the purpose.

After an explosion damaged critical systems on the spacecraft of the Apollo 13 mission, the three astronauts aboard were forced to make the journey back to Earth inside the Lunar Module (LM), the small vessel originally designed to land on the Moon's surface. Using the LM as a "lifeboat" provided the astronauts with enough oxygen and water for the return trip, but it also introduced a new problem: there was no way to recycle used air. To solve the problem, engineers back on Earth cataloged all of the spare parts and detachable pieces inside the Apollo modules. From these, they prototyped various devices the astronauts might use to make filters to use inside the LM. The Earth-based engineers talked the astronauts through the process of constructing and installing the make-shift filters. The engineers' quick thinking and creativity provided the astronauts with a way to maintain breathable air throughout their journey back to Earth.

1. The purpose of the paragraph above is to

   A. explain how the Lunar Module worked
   B. tell how creative engineers saved astronauts
   C. inform about the space program's value
   D. convince that engineers are essential workers

Our state should cut all sales taxes on the purchase of new automobiles to encourage buying new cars. Older cars do not run as cleanly as new vehicles and, thus, contribute to air pollution. Additionally, older cars are less safe to operate. One study estimates that last year, as many as 500 deaths or serious injuries from accidents in our state could have been prevented by the sorts of safety features that are standard on newer-model cars.

2. The writer most likely includes the fact about preventable deaths or serious injuries in automobile accidents because it

   A. is the conclusion the writer is trying to prove
   B. supports the writer's main recommendation
   C. may shock readers into becoming safer drivers
   D. will encourage legislators to cut sales taxes

Questions 3 and 4 are based on this passage.

SILK: NOW AND THEN

Modern consumers do not appreciate the historical importance of the fabric silk. Silk fabric is valued for its smooth texture and shimmering appearance. It is also highly absorbent, making silk clothing comfortable in both high and low temperatures. Today, silk fabrics remain somewhat more expensive than cotton cloth and synthetic textiles, but many would be surprised to learn that silk was arguably the most important product in Asia and Europe for nearly 1,000 years.

Originally, sericulture—the technology of making silk cloth from silkworm cocoons—was known only in China. Around 2,000 years ago, nomads from Central Asia would travel to China to trade horses and other goods for silk cloth. As these nomads ventured West, silk became known to people in the Middle East and Europe. Over time, traders established routes over 4,000 miles long from China to Europe that became known as the Silk Road. Throughout the ancient and medieval world, silk was the preferred fabric for the robes of royalty and the very wealthy.

3. This purpose of this passage is to

   A. criticize ancient peoples for overvaluing silk
   B. explain how silk fabrics are made
   C. entertain readers who enjoy historical travel
   D. inform about the historical importance of silk

4. How does the information in the second paragraph support the purpose of the passage?

   A. It illustrates why silk remains an expensive product today.
   B. It refutes the notion that silk is a valuable product in the modern world.
   C. It provides examples of silk's historical importance in trade and culture.
   D. It compares the value of silk to that of other products from Asia.

Answers and explanations start on page 640.

LESSON 2

Effectiveness of Argument

- An argument is a statement that takes a position.
- An argument consists of a conclusion about the issue and supporting evidence.
- Critically reading an argument involves understanding the stated or implied assumptions behind the claim.

You may think of an argument as being a quarrel between people. However, in reading and writing, an **argument** consists of the following:

- A statement, which is a **conclusion** about something
- The **evidence**, which is support that is given for the argument
- The **premises** (and unstated premises, called assumptions) behind the argument

Writers should provide supporting evidence for their argument; otherwise, they are just making an unsupported claim. Sometimes writers clearly state the premises behind their argument, but in other cases, you may need to read carefully to **infer** their assumptions.

Read the argument below and answer the questions that follow.

> In the past few years, the majority of state governments have passed laws making it illegal to send text messages while driving. These laws are clearly a good decision for which legislators should be praised. Drivers are 23 times more likely to have accidents while texting than they are while driving undistracted. It is common sense that the government has a responsibility to protect its citizens from the recklessness of a careless few.

1. What is the writer's argument about anti-texting laws?
   (1) Such laws are a good idea because drivers are prone to accidents while texting.
   (2) The majority of state governments have passed laws making it illegal to text while driving.

2. What evidence is given in support of the author's argument?
   (1) Drivers are 23 times more prone to accidents while texting.
   (2) Members of state legislatures should be praised.

3. Which of the following is likely one of the author's unstated premises?
   (1) Drivers must police themselves to avoid dangerous situations.
   (2) A state government has a responsibility to ensure citizens' safety.

GED® TEST TIP

On some passages, writers may use terms such as "for these reasons," "it follows that," or "therefore" to indicate their conclusion. In other cases, you may have to carefully analyze the passage to find the argument.

The answer to Question 1 is **(1)**. The author's opinion is that anti-texting laws are "good" and "should be praised." The rest of the argument supports that opinion. The answer to Question 2 is **(1)**. A statistic such as "23 times more likely" is typical of the factual evidence you can expect to see on the GED® Test. The answer to Question 3 is **(2)**. We know that the assumption that governments should protect citizens is a premise of the author because he praises legislators for passing these laws to make roads and highways safer.

PRACTICE 2

Questions 1 through 4 **refer to this passage about the minimum wage.**

MAKING MINIMUM WAGE WORK FOR WORKERS

1   The minimum wage is the lowest salary that a company can legally pay its employees. The federal minimum wage is the lowest allowed in the nation, but many states have set minimum wages higher than the national number.

2   Several states have taken the sensible step of automatically raising their minimum wage to adjust for inflation and consumer price increases. This policy ensures that low-paid workers are paid a stable, livable income over the long term. Raising the federal minimum wage, however, requires direct action by lawmakers. As a result, over the past 40 years, the federal minimum wage has not kept pace with the rate of inflation. Nowadays, full-time minimum-wage workers earn so little money that many have fallen below the poverty line. In the case of the minimum wage, the federal government should follow the lead of the states. Congress needs to establish automatic wage increases triggered by increases in inflation and changes to the consumer price index. That is the only way to ensure sustainable earnings for hardworking citizens.

1. Which of the following is the main point of the passage?

  A. States' minimum wages differ from the federal minimum wage.
  B. The federal government should automatically raise the minimum wage to match price increases.
  C. The federal minimum wage ensures a comfortable living for people earning it.
  D. State minimum wages are the result of political games played with people's livelihoods.

2. What is the writer's argument about states that automatically raise their minimum wages?

  A. Those states' wages have not kept pace with the rate of inflation.
  B. People earning more than minimum wage in those states are wealthy.
  C. Those states have many workers in poverty.
  D. Those states have systems superior to the federal system of manual increases.

3. What evidence is given to support the author's argument?

  A. Some states have minimum wages lower than the federal minimum wage.
  B. The federal government should adjust its minimum wage automatically.
  C. Over the past 40 years, the federal minimum wage has not kept pace with inflation.
  D. As a result of inflation, $1 in 1972 was worth more than $5 is worth today.

4. Which of the following is most likely to be one of the author's assumptions?

  A. Employees under the age of 18 might be paid less than the minimum wage.
  B. Ensuring sustainable incomes for hardworking citizens is a responsibility of lawmakers.
  C. Employees earning the federal minimum wage cannot support themselves and their families.
  D. The past 40 years have experienced significantly higher inflation than was expected.

Answers and explanations start on page 640.

ANALYZING NONFICTION AND INFORMATIONAL TEXT

Validity of Arguments

Just because a writer makes an argument does not mean you have to accept it as **valid**, or convincing. You need to analyze the supporting evidence. Below are some types of **support for arguments** and ways that you can question their legitimacy.

Key Ideas

- An argument may or may not be valid.
- For the argument to be valid, it needs to be supported by relevant and provable evidence.
- Critical thinking requires questioning both the method of argument and the source of supporting evidence.

Type of Support	Description	Questions to Ask
Facts	Objective facts that can be tested or measured	Is the information complete, or is it partial or selectively chosen?
Data or Statistics	Numerical data that have been gathered or sampled	Do the numbers accurately represent the subject? How were they gathered?
Examples or Anecdotes	Stories to demonstrate the "truth"	Are the stories true? Are they relevant?
Authority	Testimonials from a recognized authority	Does the person really know the issue, or is he or she a spokesperson or celebrity?
Causality	Assertions that one thing caused another	Is this really a cause, or is it just a related factor?

In addition to analyzing the evidence, you need to be aware that sometimes writers use **emotional appeals** based on fear, pity, or getting you to "jump on the bandwagon."

> Gasoline prices spiked suddenly in the Weston metropolitan area last week when the local oil refinery went offline due to a facility-wide computer malfunction. Shortly thereafter, the average number of miles driven daily by Weston residents fell by a whopping 55 percent. Clearly, the higher gas prices were responsible for the decline in miles driven.

▶ What is the argument in the paragraph?
  (1) Higher gas prices were responsible for the decline in miles driven.
  (2) The spike in gas prices was due to a computer malfunction at the local refinery.

▶ Which of the following undermines the writer's argument?
  (1) Oil refineries have stopped production in the past.
  (2) Last week, a blizzard struck the Weston area, causing a state of emergency that required all nonemergency vehicles to stay off the roads.

GED® TEST TIP

When you are reading a writer's argument, don't evaluate it based on what you already believe. Think critically about whether or not the writer adequately and validly supports the argument.

For the first question, choice **(1)** is correct. The writer concludes that high gas prices caused the decline in driving and uses the background about the refinery shutdown as support. For the second question, choice **(2)** is correct. The writer's argument is faulty because she assumes that the high price of gasoline was the only cause of the reduction in driving. Choice **(2)** supplies another reasonable explanation for the reduced driving, thereby weakening the argument.

PRACTICE 3

Questions 1 through 4 refer to this passage about voting technology.

DIGITAL VOTING: A BETTER WAY TO COUNT

1   The large-scale adoption in 1996 of direct-recording electronic (DRE) voting marked the beginning of an era of superior voting technology. For as long as elections have been held, voting systems have been flawed in various ways. In mid-18th century America, voters called out their selections publicly. This assured an accurate count but meant voting could not be private. Paper ballots, on the other hand, were anonymous but could be easily forged or miscounted.

2   The next innovation was the mechanical-lever voting machine, introduced in the late 19th century. The use of this voting system peaked in the 1960s. Over the next several decades, the mechanical-lever machines were replaced by two early electronic voting systems: bubble sheets recorded by optical scanner and punch cards processed electronically. All of these systems were prone to glitches, such as the notorious "hanging chads" and unreadable ballots in Florida after the 2000 U.S. presidential election.

3   Now, many jurisdictions use all-electronic DRE systems. Every step of the voting process is electronic: the ballot appears on a screen, the voter indicates his or her selection via buttons or touch-screen technology, and results are stored on a memory card. In DRE voting, there is always a record of a voter's choices, and there is no chance of voters filling in the wrong bubble or of poorly punched cards that cause votes to go uncounted. For all of these reasons, DRE is clearly the most secure and accurate voting system available.

1. The main point of the passage is that

   A. unlike optical-scanning and punch-card voting systems, DRE voting is completely electronic
   B. punch-card voting systems caused a problem in the 2000 presidential election
   C. DRE systems offer more security and accuracy than other voting systems
   D. elections in America have changed greatly over the years

2. Which of the following is evidence to support the writer's argument?

   A. When technology changes, voting systems change along with it.
   B. DRE voting avoids problems associated with other voting systems.
   C. Several voting systems have become obsolete because they violated voters' privacy.
   D. No modern-day election would ever be conducted using a public voice vote.

3. What evidence is given to support the writer's argument?

   A. Each voter's choices are recorded in the DRE voting system.
   B. Mechanical-lever voting machines were replaced by other mechanical voting devices.
   C. Punch-card voting involves electronic processing.
   D. In the mid-18th century, public votes were popular.

4. Which of the following is an example of faulty reasoning that weakens the argument?

   A. The writer claims that punch-card systems contributed to problems in the 2000 presidential election without providing any support for the claim.
   B. The writer suggests that DRE voting was responsible for the demise of older voting systems, overlooking the possibility that there might have been another cause.
   C. The writer fails to consider that even if DRE voting addresses all the flaws of previous systems, it may introduce other flaws of its own.
   D. The author fails to provide evidence that voters in 18th-century America were wary of elections.

Answers and explanations start on page 641.

Text Related by Theme or Topic

On the GED® Test, you may need to read related **paired passages** and answer questions based on your understanding of both of them. The two texts will be related by **topic** (what the passages address) or **theme** (the writer's message about a topic). You will need to understand each passage on its own and be able to **synthesize** (blend) information to draw a conclusion.

Below are two paragraphs about the same topic. One is a news story, and the other is an opinion piece. Read both selections and answer the questions based on your understanding and analysis of both texts.

Key Ideas

- The GED® Test will present two selections on a related topic or theme.
- Some questions will require comprehension and analysis of each piece on its own.
- Other questions will require a synthesis of information from the two sources.

News Story

Candy, greasy meals, and high-calorie sodas may be banned in U.S. elementary and high schools. According to news reports, new standards proposed by the Department of Agriculture would replace such items as fried potato chips with baked chips and sugary sodas with lower-calorie sport drinks. These regulations are a result of a child nutrition law, passed by the U.S. Congress to combat childhood obesity.

Response Letter

The paper announced that the government will be mandating "healthier food" in school cafeterias. Doesn't the government have anything better to do than to "babysit" our schools? Shouldn't the schools be focused on improving education, not monitoring behavior? Where is the research to show that school meals account for childhood obesity? This is just one more government intrusion into our personal lives.

► What is the topic of both of these selections?
  (1) greasy food in school cafeterias
  (2) new guidelines for healthy school meals

► What information is given in the news story?
  (1) The government is "babysitting" our schools.
  (2) Certain unhealthy foods may be banned from public schools.

► Which relevant argument is made in the response letter?
  (1) The new regulations are a good way to help combat childhood obesity.
  (2) The new regulations are a poor idea because monitoring student behavior is not a school's responsibility.

GED® TEST TIP

When you answer questions related to two selections, skim the questions before you read the selections. That way, you can be thinking about how the test requires you to relate the pieces as you read them.

The correct choice in the first question is **(2)** because the news story reports on the regulations while the response letter criticizes them. In the second question, choice **(2)** is correct because it summarizes the factual information in the news story. The correct choice in the third question is **(2)** because the writer of the response letter clearly states her opposition to the new regulations.

PRACTICE 4

<u>Questions 1 through 4</u> refer to the paired passages below.

Passage 1

The online piracy of digital files is a major problem for the music industry. From 2004 to 2009, 30 billion songs were downloaded illegally, representing a loss of billions of dollars of revenue. Recent legislation, along with the shutdown of certain major file-sharing websites, has begun to stem the tide of piracy. The organization representing the music and recording industry, however, reports that the annual harm to the economy from piracy may be as high as $12.5 billion dollars a year. More must be done.

Passage 2

Online piracy is harmful to the music industry, but not only for the reasons the industry claims. The financial harm caused by piracy is often exaggerated. The recording industry's estimates are based on the prices of songs and the number of songs downloaded; in reality, a person who illegally downloaded 10,000 songs would download only a fraction of that number if forced to pay for each file. As a result, the actual loss of revenue caused by piracy is certainly much lower than the industry estimates. However, a fear of piracy has made investors cautious about signing new, experimental artists. That in itself is a cause for concern and a reason more needs to be done to halt illegal downloading.

---

1. The topic of both passages is

   A. ways in which industries can exaggerate financial harm
   B. examples of recent legislation to protect an industry
   C. online piracy of music files
   D. the signing of new, experimental musicians

2. The main argument of Passage 1 is that

   A. new, experimental artists are necessary for the music industry to succeed
   B. additional action to combat online piracy is warranted because piracy causes financial losses to the music industry
   C. the shutdown of major file-sharing websites was a positive development because they contributed to $12.5 billion per year in damages
   D. from 2004 to 2009, 30 billion songs were downloaded illegally

3. Which claim in Passage 2 supports the conclusion drawn in Passage 1?

   A. Fear of piracy makes it difficult for new, experimental acts to get signed.
   B. Recent legislation has begun to reduce the amount of online music piracy.
   C. A person who downloads music illegally would likely download fewer songs if he or she had to pay for them.
   D. Financial harm from illegal music downloads is often exaggerated.

4. With which of the following statements would the writers of both passages agree?

   A. Online piracy of digital files has a harmful effect on the music industry.
   B. Online piracy of digital files causes serious damage to the economy.
   C. The main reason to combat online piracy is to ensure that new, experimental artists can find investors.
   D. Music is important for a healthy society to function properly.

Answers and explanations start on page 641.

Texts with Opposing Arguments

You have learned about writers' arguments and have seen how the GED® Test requires you to work with two related texts. In some cases, you may read two selections that have **opposing arguments** about the same topic. Read the selections below and think about the authors' claims, the **assumptions** or the thinking behind their positions, and the supporting evidence for each.

Argument	Opposing Argument
Coal, the source of half the energy in the United States, has been the dirtiest of all fossil fuels because it creates harmful emissions when burned. Help is on the way with the development of new "clean coal" technologies that reduce coal's environmental impact. These new technologies purify exhaust gases as coal burns (wet scrubbers) and prevent the formation of harmful emissions in the first place (low-NOx burners). There is even gasification, which avoids burning coal altogether.	"Clean coal" amounts to just an advertising slogan. Don't be fooled by claims about new technologies making coal a clean-burning fuel. The hazards to our environment start well before that. Coal mining wastes huge amounts of water—70 to 260 million gallons daily. Today's mining companies now use mountaintop removal, instead of traditional mining, to extract coal. Forty-nine states have issued fish intake advisories due to high mercury concentration in water, much of it due to run-off from coal mining.

▶ What is the topic of both of these selections?
  (1) preventing air pollution from coal
  (2) the usefulness of "clean coal" technologies

You were right to pick choice **(2)**. The Argument suggests that "clean coal" will reduce coal's environmental impact, while the Opposing Argument contends that coal will continue to harm the environment.

▶ What type of evidence is provided in the Argument?
  (1) statistics demonstrating the effectiveness of "clean coal" technologies
  (2) facts about new "clean coal" technologies

Here, choice **(2)** is correct. The Argument lists and briefly describes the new technologies.

▶ How does the Opposing Argument confront the underlying assumption of the Argument?
  (1) It points out environmental damage caused by coal before it is burned, when "clean coal" technologies are not used.
  (2) It cites studies showing that "clean coal" technologies are less effective than their advocates claim they are.

Choice **(1)** is correct. Impacts from mining, water waste, and mercury run-off are among the other harms cited in the Opposing Argument.

PRACTICE 5

Questions 1 through 4 refer to the Argument and Opposing Argument below.

ARGUMENT: Rating Systems for Movies Are Beneficial

In 1968, the Motion Picture Association of America (MPAA) replaced the complicated, morals-based Hays Code with the current, user-friendly MPAA rating system. This system is designed specifically to help parents decide whether a movie is appropriate for their child. Every parent in America knows what G, PG, PG-13, and R mean and can use these ratings to quickly judge suitability. Moreover, ratings now include descriptions that give even more information that parents can use to assess content and make wise movie-viewing decisions for their children. MPAA ratings take the guesswork out of at least one aspect of parenting!

OPPOSING ARGUMENT: Movie Rating Systems Are a Joke

A movie's MPAA rating—G, PG, PG-13, or R—is a familiar tag that parents, in particular, use to make fundamental decisions about family entertainment. Sadly, the rating system is more a marketing tool for the industry than a useful guide for parents. Consider that, in the early 1980s, unknowing parents exposed their children to alarming gore and violence under the PG rating, prompting the creation of the PG-13 rating. The result is that now, a movie that includes violence, drug use, gore, and sexual content can be marketed as a family-friendly PG-13 experience. Parents are better off finding an unbiased source of realistic reviews than trusting the MPAA rating system.

---

1. The topic of both passages is

   A. violence in movies
   B. good and bad parenting decisions
   C. the MPAA movie rating system
   D. motion picture marketing strategies

2. Which of the following is the main point of the Argument?

   A. The MPAA rating system replaced the Hays Code.
   B. The MPAA rating system is a useful tool for parents.
   C. Parents should consult a variety of sources before deciding which movies to allow their children to watch.
   D. The G, PG, PG-13, and R ratings are familiar and easy to understand.

3. The writer of the Opposing Argument would agree with which of the following statements?

   A. Parents overreacted to movie content in the 1980s.
   B. The PG-13 rating introduced a helpful distinction to the system.
   C. Violence and drug use are examples of family-friendly movie content.
   D. The MPAA rating system should not be trusted.

4. Which of the following conclusions could be drawn about the writer of the Argument?

   A. She largely approves of the MPAA rating system as a guideline for parents.
   B. She allows her children to watch movies rated PG but not those rated PG-13.
   C. She is wary of how the MPAA rating system judges violent content in movies.
   D. She believes that the Hays Code was detrimental to the movie industry.

Answers and explanations start on page 641.

Texts with Related Graphic Information

ANALYZING NONFICTION AND INFORMATIONAL TEXT

Key Ideas

- The GED® Test will present some selections with accompanying graphics.
- Read the passage carefully and analyze the graphic.
- Evaluate whether each question is based on the text, the graphic, or a combination of the two.

GED® TEST TIP

When you see that a graphic accompanies a selection, ask yourself, "Is this graphic providing supporting material, or is it providing additional information?" If you understand that, you will be better able to answer the test questions.

When you read nonfiction and informational text in a textbook, magazine, or website, it is often accompanied by a **graphic**—an illustration, photograph, or diagram—that helps you to understand the information. On the GED® Test, you will need to combine information from text and graphics to draw conclusions and to make observations about how the graphic supports the information in the text. Practice with the text and graphic below.

"Mayfield" No More? The Changing American Household

Although *Leave It to Beaver* was a fictional television show, many advertisements, politicians, and movies still echo its portrayal of the typical American household of the 1950s: a married couple with children. A closer look at government statistics shows that it might be time to retool that image; today, fewer than half of American households are husband-wife households. In fact, more than a quarter of American households are now occupied by one person living alone—a significant group for marketers to target, as those who live alone are entirely responsible for all household purchases.

Percent Distribution of Households by Type

- One person alone — 26.7%
- Husband-wife family households — 48.4%
- Two or more nonrelated people — 6.8%
- Male homeowner/renter with other family — 5.0%
- Female homeowner/renter with other family — 13.1%

Source: U.S. Census Bureau

▶ What is the topic of the story and the graphic?
  (1) the composition of American households
  (2) advertising on *Leave It to Beaver*

If you answered **(1)**, you were correct. The story outlines the current makeup of American households, and the graphic supplies factual detail.

▶ How does the pie chart support the information in the story?
  (1) It provides statistics comparing American households in the 1950s with American households today.
  (2) It confirms the story's point about current household composition and provides additional details not discussed in the story.

Choice **(2)** is correct. The pie chart supplies statistics about husband-wife households (48.4%) and single-resident households (26.7%) that match the article's assertions and show the proportion of Americans living with other family and with roommates to whom they are not related.

PRACTICE 6

Questions 1 through 3 **refer to the following passage and the two figures.**

Gerrymandering: An Electoral Advantage

1   The term *gerrymander* is used to describe the process by which electoral districts are given curious shapes in order to favor the interests of the party in power of a state legislature. Through this process, the governing political party tailors the electoral map to group unfavorable neighborhoods into a few districts likely to vote for the opposition while configuring the majority of districts to favor the party in power.

2   Figures 2(a) and 2(b) show how a governing political party can benefit from gerrymandering. In both figures, there are 40 gray squares and 60 white squares, and the area is divided into four equal-sized districts. In Figure 2(a), the white-square party will win only two seats out of four, but in Figure 2(b), the white-square party will take three of the four districts, as most of the gray votes are consolidated into one oddly shaped and geographically divided district. In fact, Illinois's 4th Congressional District is similar in shape to the gray district in Figure 2(b).

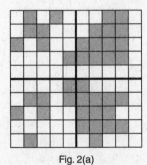

Fig. 2(a)

Geographically Uniform Districts.

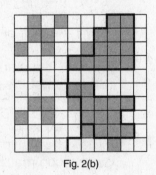

Fig. 2(b)

Gerrymandered Districts.

1. Which of the following is the main point of the passage and figures?

A. Illinois's 4th Congressional District has now been in existence for over 200 years.
B. Curiosity is the most important ingredient in the democratic process.
C. Gerrymandered congressional districts are a major threat to the democratic system.
D. Governing parties can use their power to shape electoral districts to their advantage.

2. Which of the following conclusions can be drawn from the passage and the figures?

A. Gerrymandering is more common in Illinois than in other American states.
B. Through gerrymandering, a governing party can be elected to a greater number of seats than its voter support might otherwise allow.
C. Through gerrymandering, impartial committees draw boundaries to keep elections fair.
D. Gerrymandering convinces citizens who would ordinarily be unfavorable to a party to change their votes.

3. In what way do the figures support the passage?

A. They illustrate the advantages a party can obtain through gerrymandering.
B. They predict victory for the gray party in the upcoming election.
C. They are more relevant to Chicago than to rural Illinois.
D. They show that voter turnout will continue to decline if governing parties continue to gerrymander districts.

Answers and explanations start on page 641.

ANALYZING NONFICTION AND INFORMATIONAL TEXT PRACTICE QUESTIONS

Questions 1 through 4 refer to the following passage about communication technology and the accompanying cartoon.

SOCIAL NETWORKING AT WHAT COST?

1   Sit in any restaurant or coffee shop long enough, and you're bound to witness a familiar scene: a couple, a family, or a group of friends gathered to enjoy a meal, but instead of conversing, each person at the table sits staring at his or her cell phone. In this age of social media, the question arises: does technology enhance or limit our ability to make strong emotional connections with other people?

2   Social networks have broadened with the expansion of communication technology. We connect easily with new acquaintances, old friends, potential clients, and complete strangers. For loved ones who are separated by distance, technology provides an important lifeline. Soldiers, deployed for long tours of duty, meet their newborn children over video chat. Grandparents, limited by ill health, watch their grandchildren grow through pictures and videos posted to social media sites.

3   With all the benefits of social media, however, come considerable costs. Each new connection we make (and old acquaintance we maintain) demands time, energy, and emotional investment. This often comes at the expense of time we could give to the most important people in our lives. Moreover, much of what we share through social media is superficial or entertaining. Only when technology is used to enhance our deepest, most valuable connections can it be considered real progress for humankind.

"A bunch of friends are coming over to stare at their phones."

1. What is the purpose of the passage and the graphic?

    A. to discuss different forms of social media
    B. to suggest a new form of communication technology
    C. to examine ways in which modern families use technology to communicate
    D. to discuss whether communication technology helps or hurts relationships

2. What is the topic of the passage and the graphic?

    A. maintaining long-distance relationships
    B. how technology affects interpersonal connections
    C. the limits of social media
    D. the expense of new technologies

3. Which of the following details in the graphic supports the author's point of view in the passage?

    A. The caption reveals that the woman is expecting friends to visit.
    B. The woman in the cartoon is speaking on the phone with a computer nearby.
    C. The woman in the cartoon is alone.
    D. The caption reveals that the woman's friends will use their phones during their visit.

4. Together, the graphic and the passage support which of the following conclusions?

    A. New communication technologies may offer exciting ways for people to establish new friendships.
    B. New communication technologies may adversely impact important human relationships.
    C. New communication technologies may offer positive solutions for friends who are separated by distance.
    D. New communication technologies may help people to complete several tasks at once.

Questions 5 through 8 refer to this passage about the giant squid.

THE GIANT SQUID: MORE THAN COLOSSAL?

1   The giant squid is the world's longest cephalopod. Based on measurements of over 100 full specimens (including adult and adolescent individuals) recovered from the stomachs of sperm whales and other predators, scientists have determined that the giant squid can reach a length of 13 meters.

2   Some have argued that the honor of longest cephalopod should instead go to the colossal squid, a distant relative of the giant squid, but this belief is incorrect. It is true that the colossal squid may outweigh its giant cousin. However, of the few specimens of the colossal squid (all of them juveniles) described in the scientific literature, the longest measured ten meters. Therefore, the giant squid wins the length contest.

3   No other cephalopod is even close in length to either of these animals. For example, the giant Pacific octopus, the world's longest octopus species, has a maximum arm span of only about six meters. The giant squid's status as the world's longest cephalopod remains uncontested.

5. The main point of the passage is that

   A. the colossal squid weighs more than the giant squid
   B. the giant squid is the world's longest cephalopod
   C. the giant Pacific octopus is the world's longest octopus species
   D. the giant squid can reach a length of 13 meters

6. Which of the following best summarizes the writer's argument in paragraph 2?

   A. The colossal squid is the world's longest cephalopod.
   B. The colossal squid is a distant relative of the giant squid.
   C. The giant Pacific octopus is not as long as the giant squid.
   D. The giant squid is longer than the colossal squid.

7. What evidence is given to support the writer's argument in paragraph 2?

   A. The colossal squid can weigh more than the giant squid.
   B. The giant squid is the world's longest cephalopod.
   C. The length of the longest known colossal squid specimen is ten meters.
   D. The giant Pacific octopus has a maximum arm span of only about six meters.

8. Which of the following is an example of faulty reasoning that weakens the writer's argument?

   A. The longest known colossal squid is ten meters long, so there is no colossal squid longer than the longest giant squid.
   B. The giant Pacific octopus is the world's longest species of octopus, but it is not as long as the giant squid.
   C. Many specimens of the giant squid have been measured.
   D. Because sperm whales prey on giant squid, they must also prey on colossal squid.

Passage 1

The use of mercury amalgam for dental fillings has already been banned in several European nations, and it should also be banned in the United States. The mercury contained in amalgam fillings slowly leaches into the mouth and is swallowed. It is then absorbed by the small intestine and accumulates in various body tissues, including the brain, kidney, and liver. This accumulated mercury causes a variety of health problems. In 2001, a study reported that patients with a higher number of amalgam fillings also had higher occurrences of cancer, respiratory disease, and diseases of the nervous system.

In addition to its health impact, the mercury released from dental amalgam has a number of damaging environmental consequences. Mercury waste produced by dental offices is sometimes directly disposed of into sewage water or landfills. Mercury can leach from landfills into groundwater and get into rivers and lakes. It has been estimated, for example, that dental amalgam is the source of 4 percent of the mercury found in the water of Lake Superior.

Due to the alarming health and environmental consequences of mercury amalgam, dental fillings should be made from resin composites instead. These composites are already becoming popular due to their cosmetic appeal, so banning mercury amalgam will create no consumer backlash. There are demonstrable advantages (and no disadvantages) to banning mercury dental amalgam in the United States.

Passage 2

In recent years, uneducated consumers have expressed a growing fear of the mercury commonly found in dental fillings. The environmental impact of mercury is serious, and the release of mercury into the environment must be better controlled. However, the health risks associated with mercury amalgam fillings are minimal.

It is well known that people who have mercury amalgam fillings absorb small amounts of mercury. However, most of this mercury is excreted in the urine. To date, no convincing scientific study has demonstrated that mercury absorbed from dental fillings causes any serious health problems. Because mercury amalgam fillings tend to last longer than resin composite fillings, amalgam is preferable for use whenever there is no cosmetic need for a tooth-colored filling.

However, the disposal of mercury amalgam in dental offices absolutely must be regulated. The Environmental Protection Agency estimates that 40 to 50 percent of the mercury in the wastewater processed at public treatment plants comes from dental amalgam. This is inexcusable, especially because devices that remove mercury from wastewater are inexpensive and easy for dental offices to use. While mercury amalgam should remain available because it is more durable than composites, every dental office must have a device to remove mercury from wastewater.

9. The topic of both passages is

   A. groundwater contamination
   B. mercury dental amalgam
   C. resin composite fillings
   D. dental health risks

10. What is the main argument of Passage 1?

   A. Mercury amalgam fillings are not unhealthy, but their disposal should be regulated for environmental reasons.
   B. Resin composite should replace mercury amalgam for dental fillings because it tends to last longer.
   C. Mercury amalgam fillings should be banned because they are unhealthy and bad for the environment.
   D. Mercury dental amalgam leaches mercury into a patient's mouth and can damage the liver.

11. Which statement best describes the supporting evidence in paragraph 3 of Passage 2?

   A. It appears convincing at first glance, but no source is cited.
   B. It is a seemingly convincing statistic, but the source is untrustworthy.
   C. It is an unconvincing statistic from an untrustworthy source.
   D. It is a convincing statistic from a reliable source.

12. In paragraph 3, the author of Passage 1 states that "These composites are already becoming popular due to their cosmetic appeal, so banning mercury amalgam will create no consumer backlash." Which of the following is an assumption the author of Passage 1 makes about consumers?

   A. Consumers have no other reason, such as cost or durability, to prefer mercury amalgam to composite fillings.
   B. Consumers will be happy with whatever material they are offered for dental fillings.
   C. Consumers are not generally vocal about their preferences.
   D. Consumers never discuss the choice of filling material with their dentists.

13. The writer of Passage 2 would be most likely to agree with which of the following statements?

   A. Mercury amalgam fillings should be banned because they are unhealthy.
   B. Resin composite fillings look better than mercury amalgam fillings when each is used on visible tooth surfaces.
   C. Mercury contamination of public wastewater is an unimportant issue.
   D. Resin composite fillings are preferable to mercury amalgam in all cases.

14. Which of the passages has weaker supporting evidence and why?

   A. Passage 1, because it cites no sources for the study or the statistic it cites
   B. Passage 1, because it argues that mercury should be banned in dental fillings
   C. Passage 2, because it cites the Environmental Protection Agency as the source of a statistic it cites
   D. Passage 2, because it argues that mercury used by dental offices should be better regulated

15. Which of the statements in Passage 1 is an example of faulty reasoning?

   A. Resin composites are already gaining in popularity.
   B. The use of mercury dental amalgam has already been banned in several European nations.
   C. The mercury released from dental amalgam has damaging environmental consequences.
   D. Mercury that accumulates in body tissues causes a variety of health problems.

Answers and explanations start on page 642.

INTERPRETING FICTION

Plot Elements

Key Ideas

- The plot is the series of events in a story. Understanding the order of the events helps you see how they are related.
- The conflict is a problem between characters, between a character and nature, or within a character.

GED® TEST TIP

To understand the events and conflict in a story, pay attention to the dialogue. Remember that every time the speaker changes, a new paragraph begins.

Plot refers to the events in a story. Generally, the events are told in order—what happened first, next, and so on. Understanding the order of events, the sequence, can help you see which events caused or affected others.

A story usually contains at least one **conflict**, or problem. The conflict may be between characters, within a character, or between a character and nature. Conflict creates tension. When it is resolved, the tension ends.

The following excerpt is about a brother and sister whose mother has a tumor. As you read it, look for the order of events and the conflict.

> Robert didn't phone until evening. His voice was fatigued and thin. "I've moved her to the university hospital," he said. "They can't deal with it at home."
>
> Kate waited, saying nothing. She concentrated on the toes of her shoes. They needed shining. *You never take care of anything,* her mother would say.
>
> "She has a tumor in her head." He said it firmly, as though Kate might challenge him.
>
> "I'll take a plane tomorrow morning," Kate answered, "I'll be there by noon."
>
> Robert exhaled. "Look," he said, "don't even come back here unless you can keep your mouth shut and do it my way."
>
> "Get to the point."
>
> "The point is they believe she has a malignancy and we're not going to tell her. I almost didn't tell you." His voice faltered. "They're going to operate but if they find what they're expecting, they don't think they can stop it."
>
> For a moment there was no sound except an oceanic vibration of distance on the wire. Even that sound grew still. Robert breathed. Kate could almost see him, in a booth at the hospital, staring straight ahead at the plastic instructions screwed to the narrow rectangular body of the telephone. It seemed to her that she was hurtling toward him.

From "Souvenir" by Jayne Anne Phillips, from *Black Tickets*, NY: Delacorte Press, 1979. Reprinted with permission of Jayne Anne Phillips.

▶ When did Robert decide not to tell his mother about the tumor?
   (1) before talking to Kate
   (2) after discussing the issue with Kate

(1) is correct. Robert has already decided what to do when he calls Kate.

▶ Which of the following identifies a conflict in this excerpt?
   (1) Kate tells Robert she will fly there tomorrow.
   (2) Robert tells Kate that she must do as he says.

(2) is correct. Robert challenges Kate. That creates tension.

PRACTICE 1

Questions 1 through 4 refer to the following excerpt from a short story.

EXCERPTED FROM "THE PIECE OF STRING"

1   The countryman looked at the Mayor in astonishment, already terrified by this suspicion resting on him without his knowing why.

2   "Me? Me? I picked up the pocketbook?"

3   "Yes, you, yourself."

4   "On my word of honor, I never heard of it."

5   "But you were seen."

6   "I was seen, me? Who says he saw me?"

7   "Monsieur Malandain, the harness-maker."

8   The old man remembered, understood, and flushed with anger.

9   "Ah, he saw me, the clodhopper, he saw me pick up this string, here, Mayor." And rummaging in his pocket he drew out the little piece of string.

10   But the Mayor, incredulous, shook his head.

11   "You will not make me believe, Maître Hauchecorne, that Monsieur Malandain, who is a man we can believe, mistook this cord for a pocketbook."

12   The peasant, furious, lifted his hand, spat at one side to attest his honor, repeating:

13   "It is nevertheless God's own truth, the sacred truth. I repeat it on my soul and my salvation."

14   The Mayor resumed:

15   "After picking up the object, you stood like a stilt, looking a long while in the mud to see if any piece of money had fallen out."

16   The old fellow choked with indignation and fear. . . .

17   He was confronted with Monsieur Malandain, who repeated and maintained his affirmation. They abused each other for an hour. At his own request, Maître Hauchecorne was searched. Nothing was found on him.

18   Finally the Mayor, very much perplexed, discharged him with the warning that he would consult the Public Prosecutor and ask for further orders.

From *Collected Novels and Stories* by Guy de Maupassant, translated by Ernest Boyd, copyright 1922 and renewed 1950 by Alfred A. Knopf, a Division of Random House, Inc. Used by permission of Alfred A. Knopf, a division of Random House, Inc.

1. What was the peasant doing when he "lifted his hand, spat at one side to attest his honor" (paragraph 12)?

   A. thinking of striking the Mayor
   B. swearing that he was telling the truth
   C. pleading to the Mayor for mercy
   D. performing a peasant ritual

2. How did the peasant react when confronted with Malandain, the harness-maker?

   He

   A. became choked with fear and indignation
   B. tried to explain what had actually happened
   C. became respectful and subdued
   D. confronted him and then asked to be searched

3. Which of the following statements best describes the conflict in this excerpt?

   A. A town mayor is abusing his authority.
   B. A peasant leads a harsh life and is often at odds with others.
   C. A peasant is accused of taking a pocketbook.
   D. Someone has lost a pocketbook with a great deal of money in it.

4. Place the numbers next to the actions to indicate the order in which the actions occurred in the excerpt.

The peasant and the harness-maker argue.	
The peasant explains that he picked up a piece of string, not a pocketbook.	
The mayor issues a warning to the peasant.	
The mayor states that the harness-maker witnessed the peasant stealing the pocketbook.	

1.	
2.	
3.	
4.	

Answers and explanations start on page 642.

INTERPRETING FICTION

Inferences

To understand a story, you can't just rely on what is directly stated. You also need to "read between the lines," or make **inferences**. An inference is based on information you are given *plus* what you have learned about the real world—the way things happen and the way people act.

As you read this excerpt from a story, look for suggested meanings behind people's actions and words.

> "Last night?" The old blue eyes looked blank, then brightened. "Ah no, I must have taken one of my Seconals. Otherwise I'd have heard it surely. 'Auntie,' my niece always says—'what if there should be a fire, and you there sleeping away?' Do what she says, I do sometimes, only to hear every pin drop till morning." She shook her head, entering the elevator. "Going up?"
>
> "N-no," said Mrs. Hazlitt. "I—have to wait here for a minute." She sat down on the bench, the token bench that she had never seen anybody sitting on, and watched the car door close on the little figure still shaking its head, borne upward like a fairy godmother, willing but unable to oblige. The car's hum stopped, then its light glowed on again. Someone else was coming down. . . .
>
> The car door opened. "Wssht!" said Miss Finan, scuttling out again. "I've just remembered. Not last night, but two weeks ago. And once before that. A scream, you said?"
>
> Mrs. Hazlitt stood up. Almost unable to speak, for the tears that suddenly wrenched her throat, she described it.

From "The Scream on Fifty-Seventh Street" by Hortense Calisher, from *Tales for the Mirror,* reprinted in *Women and Fiction,* edited by Susan Cahill, New York: New American Library, 1975.

▶ What happened before the beginning of this excerpt?
   (1) Mrs. Hazlitt heard a scream the night before and asked Miss Finan if she heard it too.
   (2) Mrs. Hazlitt asked Miss Finan about her health and whether she is sleeping well.

The correct answer is **(1).** You can infer it from details such as "Last night?" and "Not last night, but two weeks ago. And once before that. A scream, you said?"

▶ What is the most likely reason that "tears suddenly wrenched" Mrs. Hazlitt's throat?
   (1) She was upset at Miss Finan's inability to remember.
   (2) She was relieved that Miss Finan had heard a scream too.

You are correct if you chose **(2).** Mrs. Hazlitt is so relieved that someone else heard the scream that she has to fight back tears.

Key Ideas

- To understand a story, you must make inferences.
- Making inferences means that you look closely at the details in the story, think about your knowledge of the real world, and then ask yourself, "What does this information point to?"

GED® TEST TIP

Do not leave a question unanswered. If you read a tough question, do your best to think about it, look back at the passage for information you may need, and then choose the best answer.

PRACTICE 2

Questions 1 through 4 refer to the following excerpt from a short story.

EXCERPTED FROM "THE STORY OF AN HOUR"

1   She knew that she would weep again when she saw the kind, tender hands folded in death; the face that had never looked save with love upon her, fixed and gray and dead. But she saw beyond that bitter moment a long procession of years to come that would belong to her absolutely. And she opened and spread her arms out to them in welcome.

2   There would be no one to live for during those coming years; she would live for herself. There would be no powerful will bending her in that blind persistence with which men and women believe they have a right to impose a private will upon a fellow creature. A kind intention or a cruel intention made the act seem no less a crime as she looked upon it in that brief moment of illumination.

3   And yet she had loved him—sometimes. Often she had not. What did it matter! What could love, the unsolved mystery, count for in face of this possession of self-assertion, which she suddenly recognized as the strongest impulse of her being!

4   "Free! Body and soul free!" she kept whispering . . .

5   Some one was opening the front door with a latchkey. It was [her husband] Brently Mallard who entered, a little travel-stained, composedly carrying his grip-sack and umbrella. He had been far from the scene of accident, and did not even know there had been one. He stood amazed at [his wife] Josephine's piercing cry; at Richards' quick motion to screen him from the view of his wife.

6   But Richards was too late.

7   When the doctors came they said she had died of heart disease—of joy that kills.

From "The Story of an Hour" by Kate Chopin.

1. How did Brently Mallard generally feel toward his wife?

   He

   A. had always loved her
   B. kept her at arm's length
   C. liked to play practical jokes on her
   D. had cruel intentions toward her

2. Which detail best expresses Josephine's vision of her future?

   A. that bitter moment
   B. she'd weep again
   C. spread her arms out in welcome
   D. blind persistence

3. What was the doctors' meaning when they said that Josephine died of "joy that kills" (paragraph 7)?

   They thought that

   A. she was overcome and thrilled to see her husband
   B. she was excited about her upcoming life of freedom
   C. her heart was worn out from giving so much love
   D. her heart was weakened from the strain of living

4. Why did Josephine die?

   A. She was overcome with relief.
   B. She was shocked that she would not be free.
   C. She was confused by feelings of love and hate.
   D. She thought there would be no one to live for.

Answers and explanations start on page 643.

INTERPRETING FICTION

Character

Key Ideas

- Characters are the people in the story.
- You can understand a character by noting what the narrator tells you directly as well as by inferring from the character's appearance, actions, words, and thoughts.

Characters are the people who inhabit a story. The personalities and motivations of characters are often stated directly by the **narrator**—the person telling the story. Sometimes you can also infer characters' personalities or motivations by what they do, what they think, and what they say.

As you read this excerpt, look for details that describe each character.

> Axel Olsen was going to paint Helga Crane. Not only was he going to paint her, but he was to accompany her and her aunt on their shopping expedition. Aunt Katrina was frankly elated. Uncle Poul was also visibly pleased. Evidently they were not above kow-towing to a lion. Helga's own feelings were mixed; she was amused, grateful, and vexed. It had all been decided and arranged without her, and, also, she was a little afraid of Olsen. His stupendous arrogance awed her.
>
> The day was an exciting, not easily to be forgotten one. Definitely, too, it conveyed to Helga her exact status in her new environment. A decoration. A curio. A peacock. Their progress through the shops was an event; an event for Copenhagen as well as for Helga Crane. Her dark, alien appearance was to most people an astonishment. Some stared surreptitiously, some openly, and some stopped dead in front of her in order more fully to profit by their stares. "*Den Sorte*" dropped freely, audibly, from many lips.
>
> The time came when she grew used to the stares of the population. And the time came when the population of Copenhagen grew used to her outlandish presence and ceased to stare. But at the end of that first day it was with thankfulness that she returned to the sheltering walls of the house on Maria Kirkplads.

From "Quicksand" by Nella Larsen, in *The Norton Anthology of African American Literature,* edited by Henry Louis Gates, Jr., and Nellie Y. McKay, New York: W.W. Norton, 1997.

ON THE GED® TEST

A common kind of question asks you to choose how a character would act in a different situation, based on what you know about the character's personality.

▶ Which of the following describes Helga?
  (1) attractive, down-to-earth, embarking on a new life
  (2) self-centered, smug, enjoys being watched

Choice **(1)** is correct. An artist is painting her, suggesting she is attractive. Yet she prefers not to be the center of attention (see the end of the last paragraph).

▶ Which of the following would Olsen most likely do at a party?
  (1) snub the hostess if the wine was below his expectations
  (2) offer to drive anyone home who needed a ride

Choice **(1)** is correct. Apply what you know about people with "stupendous arrogance" (see the end of the first paragraph) to answer this question.

PRACTICE 3

Questions 1 through 3 refer to the following excerpt from a story.

EXCERPTED FROM "HIZAKURIGE"

1   "I shall never forget it," the witch went on. "When you were ill you gave your sickness to me. Our only child, who had to carry on our name, grew weak and thin because there was no rice to fill his empty stomach. Every day the bill collectors were knocking at the door and the rent remained unpaid. Yet I did not complain—not even when I slipped in the dogs' dirt in the lane."

2   "Don't talk of it," said Yaji. "You'll break my heart."

3   "And then, when through my labors I had saved enough money to buy a kimono, I had to pawn it for your sake and never saw it again. Never again did it come back to me from the pawnbroker's."

4   "At the same time you must remember what a pleasant place you are in now," said Yaji, "while I have to worry along down here."

5   "What? What is there pleasant about it? It is true that by the help of your friends you erected a stone over my grave, but you never go near it, and you never contribute to the temple to get the priests to say prayers for my soul. I am nothing to you. The stone over my grave has been taken away and put into the wall, where all the dogs come and make water against it. Not a drop of water is ever placed on my grave. Truly in death we suffer all sorts of troubles."

6   "True, true," said Yaji.

7   "But while you thus treat me with neglect," the witch went on, "lying in my grave I think of nobody but you and long for the time when you will join me in the underworld. Shall I come to meet you?"

8   "No, no, don't do that," said Yaji. "It's really too far for you."

9   "Well then, I have one request to make."

10   "Yes, yes. What is it?"

11   "Give this witch plenty of money."

12   "Of course, of course."

13   "How sad the parting!" cried the witch. "I have yet much to tell you, countless questions to ask you, but the messenger of Hell recalls me!"

14   Then, recovering from her trance, the witch twanged her bow.

From "Hizakurige" by Jippensha Ikku in *The Longwood Introduction to Fiction*, Boston: Allyn and Bacon, 1992.

1. Why does Yaji say, "No, no, don't do that . . . It's really too far for you" (paragraph 8)?

   A. He is trying to be more considerate than he had been in the past.
   B. He is frightened about seeing the ghost of his wife.
   C. He has no real interest in seeing his wife again.
   D. His wife can't really travel to him anyway.

2. Which of the following is the best description of the witch?

   A. caring
   B. straightforward
   C. untrustworthy
   D. thoughtful

3. Earlier in the story the witch, speaking as Yaji's wife, says, "Ah, what agony I went through when I was married to you—time and again suffering the pangs of hunger and shivering with cold in the winter."

   Based on this information and the excerpt, what kind of husband did Yaji seem to be?

   A. angry
   B. kind-hearted
   C. responsible
   D. neglectful

Answers and explanations start on page 643.

INTERPRETING FICTION

Theme

Key Ideas

- The subject of a story is what the story is about.
- The theme of a story is different from the subject. The theme goes beyond the subject and often expresses a point of view about life.

Every story has a subject. The subject might be about fighting a war or growing up in poverty. But there is more to a story than its subject. As a reader, look for what the author is trying to say about the subject. That is the **theme**—the message the author wants the reader to understand. In fiction, the theme is often a statement about life. For example, the theme might be that fighting in a war changes a person's life forever.

The theme may be directly stated. If it is not, you can infer the theme from the characters' thoughts and actions and from the things that happen in the story.

As you read the following excerpt, ask yourself what message about the people and their lives the author is trying to tell you.

> While the boys were getting the Doctor's horse, he went to the window to examine the house plants. "What do you do to your geraniums to keep them blooming all winter, Mary? I never pass this house that from the road I don't see your windows full of flowers."
>
> She snapped off a dark red one, and a ruffled new green leaf, and put them in his buttonhole. "There, that looks better. You look too solemn for a young man, Ed. Why don't you git married? I'm worried about you. . . ."
>
> Sometimes the Doctor heard the gossipers in the drugstore wondering why Rosicky didn't get on faster. He was industrious, and so were his boys, but they were rather free and easy, weren't pushers, and they didn't always show good judgment. They were comfortable, they were out of debt, but they didn't get much ahead. Maybe, Doctor Burleigh reflected, people as generous and warmhearted and affectionate as the Rosickys never got ahead much; maybe you couldn't enjoy your life and put it into the bank, too.

From "Neighbor Rosicky" by Willa Cather, from *Obscure Destinies.*

▶ Which of the following statements is the theme of the story?
  (1) A good life is measured in terms of love, not money.
  (2) People should not gossip about others.

You are correct if you chose **(1)**. Doctor Burleigh's thoughts at the end of the excerpt help you understand that this is the author's main message.

▶ Which of the following details supports the theme?
  (1) Mary Rosicky lovingly "worries" about the doctor.
  (2) The Rosickys keep out of debt.

Again, you are correct if you chose **(1)**. The flowers Mary grows, the fact that she snaps off one to give the doctor, and her expressed concern for him all show her warmth and happiness. They help support the theme that the doctor reflects on.

GED® TEST TIP

Read the whole passage carefully but not too slowly before you begin to answer the questions. If you read a question that really stumps you, skip it and go on. You can come back to it.

PRACTICE 4

<u>Questions 1 through 5</u> refer to the following excerpt from a short story.

EXCERPTED FROM "GONE FISHIN'"

1   Early morning is the best time. You're fully rested but not awake enough to remember how hard it all is. Morning is like being a child again, and morning before the sun is out is like those magic times that you hid under the bed and in between the clothes hanging in your mother's closet. Times when any kind of miracle could come about just as normal as a spider making her web.

2   I remember waking up in the dark once when I was very small. I jumped right out of bed and went up next to the screen door on the back porch to see what kind of fantastic thing was going on outside. At first I couldn't see anything but there was a clopping sound, nickering, and a deep voice that made me feel calm and wondering. Slowly, coming out from the darkness, I saw a gray shimmering next to a tall black pillar. The shimmer turned into a big horse and the pillar became my father holding out an apple and cooing in his bass voice, "Ho! Yeah, boy," even though the horse was tame and eating from his hand.

3   I drifted into sleep thinking that we were poor and didn't own a horse. When I woke up it was light and there was no horse to be seen. I asked my father about it but he told me that I was dreaming—where were poor people like us going to find big gray stallions?

4   But there were horse chips behind the barn and hoofprints too.

5   I decided that it was a magic horse and man that I'd seen. From that day on I believed that magic hides in the early morning. If you get up early enough you might find something so beautiful that it would be all right if you just died right then because nothing else in life could ever be better.

From "Gone Fishin'" by Walter Mosley, Baltimore: Black Classic Press, 1997.

1. In the story, the boy _____ after hearing his father's explanation.

   A. feels confused
   B. finds a new explanation
   C. no longer trusts his father
   D. tries to convince his father

2. Which of the following is the best description of the boy?

   A. hard-hearted
   B. imaginative
   C. skeptical
   D. chatty

3. What is the most likely reason the boy decides he saw a magic horse and man?

   A. He wants to reconcile what he saw with what his father told him.
   B. He enjoys magic and likes to make up stories.
   C. He wants to prove his father was mistaken.
   D. This kind of miracle can happen.

4. Which of the following would the father probably enjoy most?

   A. daydreaming about the future
   B. having enough money to pay some bills
   C. keeping his son's hopes up about getting a new bicycle for his birthday
   D. sharing ghost stories around a campfire

5. Which of the following statements fits the theme of this story?

   A. False hopes will not get you anywhere.
   B. Dreams really can come true.
   C. Adults cannot see what children see.
   D. Morning and youth are full of possibility.

Answers and explanations start on page 643.

Style and Point of View

Style

- The style of a piece of writing is determined by the choices a writer makes in words, sentence structure, images, and other devices.
- A story is written from a narrator's point of view. The narrator may be an "outsider" or a character who can reveal only what he or she sees and thinks.

A writer has many choices when deciding how to write a story. A writer may use long, complex sentences; short, clipped sentences; or anything in between. A writer may use flowery or formal language, slang, or spoken dialect. One writer may use vivid images or symbols, while another writes a plain, spare story. The individual characteristics that a writer chooses—sentence structure, choice of words, use of images, and other devices—are all part of the writer's **style.**

As you read this excerpt, look for the characteristics that this particular author chose. Ask yourself what effect they have on your understanding of the writing.

> The only part of the night I recall without feeling anger or sadness is loading the horses. Andy and I hardly had the fencing up before Brett came along with the first ten or twelve. . . . A couple of roans and an Appaloosa stood out in that first bunch in the starlight, and a bay with a roached mane. Then Ed brought up a second bunch, about fifteen mostly dark but a palomino and two paints in there, I remember. Andy and I shooed them up the ramp, which clattered and thundered under their hooves. It was a cool night, still. I could feel the horses on my skin, their body heat swirling around us. I could . . . hear their nostrils fluttering. I felt hard muscle ripple under my hand when I clapped a hip to steer them around. I felt their tails slap my back, and caught a glint in their bared eyes.

From "Stolen Horses" by Barry Lopez, from *Writers Harvest 3,* edited by Tobias Wolff, copyright © 2000 by Share Our Strength. Used by permission of Dell Publishing, a division of Random House, Inc.

► What is the effect of the author's description of the horses?
  (1) It creates a depth of feeling for the horses' vitality.
  (2) It provides insight into what the characters are doing.

You are correct if you chose **(1).** The vivid, descriptive details allow you to imagine the horses and sense their vitality and strength.

Point of View

ON THE GED® TEST

You will not have to identify and use terms such as third person *and* first person, *but you should be able to understand and appreciate the effect of the writers' choices.*

Another choice a writer makes is which **point of view** to write from. Will the narrator be outside the story, watching and revealing the characters' actions and perhaps even their thoughts and feelings? If so, the writer will use *third person* point of view. Or will the narrator be a character in the story, able to report only what he or she thinks? In that case, the writer will use *first person* point of view.

► Which of the following indicates that the narrator is a character and so we can know only his thoughts?
  (1) "The only part of the night I recall . . ."
  (2) "Then Ed brought up a second bunch . . ."

(1) is correct. The narrator tells his own thoughts. A clue is the word *I.*

PRACTICE 5

Questions 1 through 4 refer to the following excerpt from a short story called "Coach."

EXCERPTED FROM *AN AMATEUR'S GUIDE TO THE NIGHT*

1   "This apartment your mom found is like an office or something. A studio for her to go to and get away every now and then. . . ."

2   "She wants to get away from us," Daphne said.

3   "Definitely not. She gave me a list, is how this whole thing started. She's got stuff she wants to do, and you with your school problems and me with the team—we're too much for her, see? She could spend her entire day on us, if you think about it, and never have one second for herself. If you think about it fairly, Daphne, you'll agree." . . .

4   She made a sigh and marched over to a trash can to deposit her slumping cone. Then she washed up at the children's drinking fountain and rejoined Coach, who had finished his Brown Cow but had kept the plastic spoon in the mouth.

5   "What was on this list of Mom's?" Daphne asked.

6   "Adult stuff," Coach said.

7   "Just give me an example."

8   Coach removed the plastic spoon and cracked it in half.

9   "Your mother's list is for five years. In that time, she wants to be speaking French regularly. She wants to follow up on her printmaking."

10   "This is adult stuff?" Daphne said.

11   Coach raised a hand to Bobby Stark. Stark had three malt cups in a cardboard carrier and he was moving toward the parking lot.

12   "Hey, those all for you?" Coach called out.

13   "I got a month to get fat, Coach. You'll have five months to beat it off me," the boy called back.

14   The people at some of the tables around Coach's lit up with grins. Bobby Stark's parents were grinning.

15   "Every hit of that junk takes a second off your time in the forty—just remember that!" Coach shouted.

16   Stark wagged his head ruefully, his cheeks blushing. He pretended to hide the malts behind his arm.

From *An Amateur's Guide to the Night* by Mary Robison, copyright © 2001, reprinted with the permission of The Wylie Agency, Inc.

1. What is Bobby Stark's attitude?

   A. He worries about his weight problem.
   B. He takes things in stride.
   C. He is looking forward to the sports season.
   D. He feels unfairly criticized by the coach.

2. Because of the narrator's point of view, what does the reader know?

   A. only Bobby Stark's actions
   B. thoughts and feelings of the characters
   C. the actions and speech of the characters
   D. only Daphne's thoughts and feelings

3. Through their dialogue, what kind of relationship can you conclude the characters have with each other?

   A. informal
   B. tense
   C. suspicious
   D. deteriorating

4. Later in the story, Coach has this discussion with his wife, Sherry: "'It's like my apartment,' Sherry said. 'A place apart.' Coach cut her off. 'Don't go on about how much you love your apartment.'"

   Based on this information and the excerpt, which of the following best describes Coach in his discussion with Daphne?

   A. brutally frank
   B. angry and hostile
   C. loving and warm
   D. not entirely honest about his feelings

Answers and explanations start on page 643.

INTERPRETING FICTION

Figurative Language

Key Ideas

- Fiction writers and poets use figurative language—words that do not have their literal meaning—to compare different things.
- Some comparisons are introduced by *like* or *as*; others are not. Some comparisons give human characteristics to nonhuman things.

Figurative language refers to words that are being used to mean something other than their actual, literal meaning. Writers and poets use figurative language to help paint a mental picture in the reader's mind. Instead of saying, "His voice was soothing and pleasing," for example, a writer might say, "His voice was like velvet."

Figurative language often compares two different things. Sometimes the comparison is signaled by the words *like* or *as*, but not always. A writer might also say, "His voice was velvet." Another favorite technique of writers and poets is to give a human characteristic to something nonhuman, such as, "The wind sighed."

As you read this poem, look for figurative language and what it might mean.

The School Children

The children go forward with their little satchels.
And all morning the mothers have labored
to gather the late apples, red and gold,
like words of another language.

And on the other shore
are those who wait behind great desks
to receive these offerings.

How orderly they are—the nails
on which the children hang
their overcoats of blue or yellow wool.

And the teachers shall instruct them in silence
and the mothers shall scour the orchards for a way out,
drawing to themselves the gray limbs of the fruit trees
bearing so little ammunition.

From "The House on Marshland" from *The First Four Books* by Louise Gluck.
Copyright 1968, 1971, 1972, 1973, 1974, 1975, 1976, 1977, 1978, 1980, 1985, 1995.

▶ What is suggested by comparing apples to "words of another language" in the fourth line?
(1) a sense of strangeness, not a part of one's world
(2) useless things that have no meaning

You are correct if you chose **(1)**. A language different from your own can seem strange and removed. The mothers feel removed from the world of teachers and schoolchildren.

▶ What does the word *shore* in the fifth line refer to?
(1) the farthest edge of a lake
(2) the world of the classroom

You are correct if you chose **(2)**. The mothers in the poem think of school as far away from them.

GED® TEST TIP

You are not penalized for wrong answers on the GED® Test, so do not leave any answers blank. If you return to a skipped multiple-choice question and still cannot determine the answer, narrow the choices to the two most reasonable and then select the one that makes the most sense.

PRACTICE 6

<u>Questions 1 through 5</u> refer to the following poem.

EXCERPTED FROM "DÉJEUNER SUR L'HERBE" ("LUNCH ON THE GRASS")

1 It's pleasant to board the ferry in the sunscape
As the late light slants into afternoon;
The faint wind ruffles the river, rimmed with foam.
We move through the aisles of bamboo
Towards the cool water-lilies.

2 The young dandies drop ice into the drinks,
While the girls slice the succulent lotus root.
Above us, a patch of cloud spreads, darkening
Like a water-stain on silk.

3 *Write this down quickly, before the rain!*

4 Don't sit there! The cushions were soaked by the shower.
Already the girls have drenched their crimson skirts.
Beauties, their powder streaked with mascara, lament their ruined faces.

5 The wind batters our boat, the mooring-line
Has rubbed a wound in the willow bark.
The edges of the curtains are embroidered by the river foam.

6 Like a knife in a melon, Autumn slices Summer.

7 *It will be cold, going back.*

Tu Fu, "Déjeuner sur l'herbe," translated by Carolyn Kizer, from *Carrying Over: Poems from the Chinese, Urdu, Macedonian, Yiddish, and French African.* Copyright © 1988 by Carolyn Kizer. Reprinted with the permission of The Permissions Company, Inc., on behalf of Copper Canyon Press, www.coppercanyonpress.org.

1. What is compared to "a water-stain on silk" (Stanza 2)?

 A. foam on the edge of the river
 B. rain clouds approaching
 C. lotus root juice on a tablecloth
 D. ice cubes dropping into cold drinks

2. What is meant by the statement "lament their ruined faces" (Stanza 4)?

 A. They could no longer smile.
 B. They were growing old.
 C. The rain caused their makeup to run.
 D. The wind was chapping their faces.

3. Why is "The edges of the curtains are embroidered by the river foam" (Stanza 5) an effective use of figurative language?

 It helps the reader see that

 A. the people forgot to close the windows and curtains
 B. the wind is so strong that it is blowing spray from the river into the boat
 C. the curtains are beautifully edged with lace
 D. the river is rising quickly

4. According to the speaker, how was the change from summer to autumn (Stanza 6)?

 A. quick and easy
 B. halting and uncertain
 C. slow and predictable
 D. pleasant and smooth

5. Which of the following words best describe the tone of this poem?

 A. gentle and calm
 B. humorous and playful
 C. wry and observant
 D. dry and formal

Answers and explanations start on page 643.

INTERPRETING FICTION PRACTICE QUESTIONS

<u>Questions 1 through 3</u> refer to the following excerpt from a story.

EXCERPTED FROM *SHILOH & OTHER STORIES*

1   Leroy Moffitt's wife, Norma Jean, is working on her pectorals. She lifts three-pound dumbbells to warm up, then progresses to a twenty-pound barbell. Standing with her legs apart, she reminds Leroy of Wonder Woman.

2   "I'd give anything if I could just get these muscles to where they're real hard," says Norma Jean. "Feel this arm. It's not as hard as the other one."

3   "That's cause you're right-handed," says Leroy, dodging as she swings the barbell in an arc.

4   "Do you think so?"

5   "Sure."

6   Leroy is a truckdriver. He injured his leg in a highway accident four months ago, and his physical therapy, which involves weights and a pulley, prompted Norma Jean to try building herself up. Now she is attending a body-building class. Leroy has been collecting temporary disability since his tractor-trailer jackknifed in Missouri, badly twisting his left leg in its socket. He has a steel pin in his hip. He will probably not be able to drive his rig again. It sits in the backyard, like a gigantic bird that has flown home to roost. Leroy has been home in Kentucky for three months, and his leg is almost healed, but the accident frightened him and he does not want to drive any more long hauls. He is not sure what to do next. In the meantime, he makes things from craft kits. He started by building a miniature log cabin from notched Popsicle sticks. He varnished it and placed it on the TV set, where it remains. It reminds him of a rustic Nativity scene. Then he tried string art (sailing ships on black velvet), a macramé owl kit, a snap-together B-17 Flying Fortress, and a lamp made out of a model truck, with a light fixture screwed in the top of the cab. At first the kits were diversions, something to kill time, but now he is thinking about building a full-scale log house from a kit. It would be considerably cheaper than building a regular house, and besides, Leroy has grown to appreciate how things are put together. He has begun to realize that in all the years he was on the road he never took time to examine anything. He was always flying past scenery.

Excerpt from *Shiloh & Other Stories* by Bobbie Ann Mason. Reprinted by permission of International Creative Management, Inc. Copyright © 1982 by Bobbie Ann Mason.

1. Which of the following best describes Leroy's wife, Norma Jean?

   A. shy
   B. loving
   C. self-concerned
   D. grumpy

2. By comparing Leroy's truck to a bird that has flown home to roost, the author suggests that Leroy

   A. comes and goes as he pleases
   B. always preferred to be at home "nesting"
   C. won't be driving his truck for a while
   D. is a bit "flighty" and unpredictable

3. Why might Leroy be continually making things from craft kits?

   Because he

   A. is impatient with his leg healing
   B. has always enjoyed working with his hands
   C. grew tired of bodybuilding
   D. doesn't want to face what to do next

Questions 4 through 7 refer to this excerpt from a story.

EXCERPTED FROM *WINTER'S TALES*

1   A small sailor-boy, named Simon, stood on the wet, swinging deck, held on to a shroud, and looked up towards the drifting clouds, and to the upper top-gallant yard of the main-mast.

2   A bird, that had sought refuge upon the mast, had got her feet entangled in some loose tackle-yarn of the halliard, and, high up there, struggled to get free. The boy on the deck could see her wings flapping and her head turning from side to side.

3   Through his own experience of life he had come to the conviction that in this world everyone must look after himself, and expect no help from others. But the mute, deadly fight kept him fascinated for more than an hour. He wondered what kind of bird it would be. These last days a number of birds had come to settle in the barque's rigging: swallows, quails, and a pair of peregrine falcons; he believed that this bird was a peregrine falcon. He remembered how, many years ago, in his own country and near his home, he had once seen a peregrine falcon quite close, sitting on a stone and flying straight up from it. Perhaps this was the same bird. He thought: "That bird is like me. Then she was there, and now she is here."

4   At that a fellow-feeling rose in him, a sense of common tragedy; he stood looking at the bird with his heart in his mouth. There were none of the sailors about to make fun of him; he began to think out how he might go up by the shrouds to help the falcon out. He brushed his hair back and pulled up his sleeves, gave the deck round him a great glance, and climbed up. He had to stop a couple of times in the swaying rigging.

5   It was indeed, he found when he got to the top of the mast, a peregrine falcon. As his head was on a level with hers, she gave up her struggle, and looked at him with a pair of angry, desperate yellow eyes.

6   He had to take hold of her with one hand while he got his knife out, and cut off the tackle-yarn. He was scared as he looked down, but at the same time he felt that he had been ordered up by nobody, but that this was his own venture, and this gave him a proud, steadying sensation, as if the sea and the sky, the ship, the bird and himself were all one.

From *Winter's Tales* by Isak Dinesen, Random House, Inc ©1942.

4. What can you infer about the boy's decision to climb the rig?

   A. It took some courage.
   B. It was a familiar task.
   C. It felt like a chore.
   D. He was ordered to do it.

5. Which of the following best describes both the boy and the bird at the beginning of the excerpt?

   A. confident
   B. alone
   C. scared
   D. wary

6. Which ideas are most clearly contrasted in this excerpt?

   A. love and hate
   B. youth and experience
   C. fear and fearlessness
   D. loneliness and sense of belonging

7. The word _____ best describes the mood created by the author in this excerpt.

   A. mournful
   B. nostalgic
   C. peaceful
   D. triumphant

EXCERPTED FROM "THE LEGEND OF SLEEPY HOLLOW"

1   "Who are you?" He received no reply. He repeated his demand in a still more agitated voice. Still there was no answer. Once more he cudgelled the sides of the inflexible Gunpowder, and, shutting his eyes, broke forth with involuntary fervor into a psalm-tune. Just then the shadowy object of alarm put itself in motion, and, with a scramble and a bound, stood at once in the middle of the road. Though the night was dark and dismal, yet the form of the unknown might now in some degree be ascertained. He appeared to be a horseman of large dimensions, and mounted on a black horse of powerful frame. He made no offer of molestation or sociability, but kept aloof on one side of the road, jogging along on the blind side of old Gunpowder, who had now got over his fright and waywardness.

2   Ichabod, who had no relish for this strange midnight companion, and bethought himself of the adventure of Brom Bones with the Galloping Hessian, now quickened his steed, in hopes of leaving him behind. The stranger, however, quickened his horse to an equal pace. Ichabod pulled up, and fell into a walk, thinking to lag behind—the other did the same. His heart began to sink within him; he endeavored to resume his psalm-tune, but his parched tongue clove to the roof of his mouth, and he could not utter a stave. There was something in the moody and dogged silence of this pertinacious companion, that was mysterious and appalling. It was soon fearfully accounted for. On mounting a rising ground, which brought the figure of his fellow-traveller in relief against the sky, gigantic in height, and muffled in a cloak, Ichabod was horror-struck, on perceiving that he was headless!—but his horror was still more increased, on observing that the head, which should have rested on his shoulders, was carried before him on the pommel of the saddle: his terror rose to desperation; he rained a shower of kicks and blows upon Gunpowder, hoping, by a sudden movement, to give his companion the slip—but the spectre started full jump with him.

3   Away then they dashed, through thick and thin; stones flying, and sparks flashing at every bound. Ichabod's flimsy garments fluttered in the air, as he stretched his long lank body away over his horse's head, in the eagerness of his flight.

From "The Legend of Sleepy Hollow" by Washington Irving.

8. What is meant by "he endeavored to resume his psalm-tune" (paragraph 2)?

Ichabod Crane tried to

A. remind himself to stay calm
B. ride more steadily
C. start singing again
D. think of a realistic solution

9. What is the effect of the author's use of words such as "dashed," "stones flying," and "sparks flashing" (paragraph 3)?

The words create a feeling of

A. panic
B. clumsiness
C. playfulness
D. magic

10. Which of the following best describes the mood of this excerpt?

A. angry
B. sorrowful
C. suspenseful
D. sentimental

11. Later in the story, the narrator implies that the horseman had a pumpkin on the pommel of his saddle. Given this additional information, Ichabod can best be described as _____ given his actions in the excerpt.

A. brave in the face of great danger
B. too scared to think rationally
C. moving too quickly
D. quick thinking in his escape

Questions 12 through 16 refer to this excerpt from a story.

EXCERPTED FROM "THE WEDDING OF HENRY MARKOWITZ"

Those sprawling universities Henry left behind long ago. America, with its mass-produced undergraduates processed through seedy lecture halls where, under flickering lights, they slump with their knees up and take in lectures as they might see movies. Where the familiar passes into the wide pupils of their eyes and the rest dribbles down the aisles to collect with the dirt and candy wrappers at the professor's feet. Has he not been a professor at Queens College and then NYU? And the graduate students. Hasn't he seen them at Princeton clustering at the office doors? Young Calibans eager for praise. They can tear open the Italian Renaissance before lunch, strangle a Donne sonnet and crush its wings, battering away with blunt instruments. As for the older scholars—like students at a cooking school, they cook up Shakespeare, serve him up like roast goose, stuffed with their political-sexual agendas, carve and quarter him with long knives. For Henry, reading had always been a gentle thing, a thing as delicate as blowing eggs. Two pinpricks and the meaning came, whole, unbroken, into the bowl. Now reading is a boiling and a breaking, something to concoct. It's a deviling of art, history, social theory, politics—all mixed and piped back in and served up on a platter. These are the scholars in the journals now. They are at war with the beautiful. . . .

Excerpt from "The Wedding of Henry Markowitz" from *The Family Markowitz* by Allegra Goodman. Copyright © 1996 by Allegra Goodman. Reprinted by permission of Farrar, Straus and Giroux, LLC.

12. Which of the following is Henry most interested in?

    A. teaching
    B. reading
    C. students
    D. history

13. Based on the passage, it is most likely that Henry would use the term/phrase _____ to describe younger college students.

    A. bright
    B. open to new ideas
    C. a dime a dozen
    D. insightful about literature

14. When the author compares Shakespeare to a roast goose in the middle of the paragraph, what is she suggesting about the older students?

    The older students

    A. dissect literature too much and ruin the meaning
    B. enjoy literature as they would a fine meal
    C. throw Shakespeare back in Henry's face
    D. have trouble finding meaning in literature

15. What is the tone of this excerpt?

    A. upbeat
    B. scholarly
    C. disapproving
    D. sentimental

16. Later, Henry refers to his brother as a "shaper himself of the tawdry yellow thing they sell now as the humanities."

    Based on this information and the excerpt, what is Henry's attitude toward college education?

    A. indifferent
    B. appreciative
    C. admiring
    D. disapproving

Answers and explanations start on page 644.

WRITING EFFECTIVE SENTENCES

Simple Sentences

A complete simple sentence has at least one subject and one verb. The **subject** is the person, place, or thing that the sentence is talking about. The subject performs an action or is described. The **verb** is the word that tells what action the subject is doing or links the subject to a modifier.

Action verb: Elaine took notes on the meeting.
        subject verb

Linking verb: They were long.
          subject verb modifier

If a sentence is missing either the subject or the verb, it is incomplete. An incomplete sentence is called a **fragment**.

EXAMPLES
No subject: Typed up her notes.
Complete sentence: Elaine typed up her notes.

No verb: The computer in the main office.
Complete sentence: The computer in the main office crashed several times.

A complete sentence must also express a complete thought. The reader should not be left asking questions.

Incomplete thought: When she lost her work. (What happened when she lost her work?)
Complete thought: Elaine was very frustrated when she lost her work.

Incomplete thought: The person in charge of computer support. (What about that person?)
Complete thought: Elaine called the person in charge of computer support.

Incomplete thought: By replacing the hard drive.
Complete thought: Elaine can fix the computer by replacing the hard drive.

Finally, a complete sentence should have correct end punctuation. A statement should end with a period, and so should a command. A question should end with a question mark. An exclamation should end with an exclamation point.

Statement: Elaine has lost several files this way.
Command: Turn off the computer.
Question: Will the computer ever be fixed?
Exclamation: What a mess we're in!

If you find a fragment in your writing, rewrite to make it a complete sentence.

- If the sentence does not have a subject, add a subject.
- If the sentence does not have a verb, add a verb.
- If the thought is incomplete, add words or combine the incomplete thought with a complete sentence.

Key Ideas

- Make sure each sentence has a subject and verb and expresses a complete thought.
- If a sentence doesn't express a complete thought, you may need to add a subject, verb, or other words.
- Use correct end punctuation.

GED® TEST TIP

Read each sentence in a GED® passage to yourself and pause at its end. That may help you "hear" whether the sentence is actually an incomplete thought or a sentence fragment.

PRACTICE 1

A. Directions: Write *C* if the sentence is complete or *F* if the sentence is a fragment. Rewrite any fragments to make them complete.

EXAMPLE

Talks all the time on the telephone. *F Dave talks all the time on the telephone.* _____

1. Drives his girlfriend crazy. _____

2. As soon as he comes home from work. _____

3. He calls everyone he knows. _____

4. Dave's sister and his best friend. _____

B. <u>Questions 5 through 7</u> refer to the following advertisement.

What Is Three-Way Calling?

Three-way calling is a unique service that enables you to conduct a conference [Select...▾] the privacy of your own home. You can talk to your sister in Florida and your mother in Nebraska at the same time. It's even possible to seek a third person's advice when you're in the middle of a regular call. For instance, [Select...▾] .

Why wait? This useful and convenient [Select...▾] be yours for only pennies a month.

5. Three-way calling is a unique service that enables you to conduct a conference [Select...▾] the privacy of your own home.

   A. call. And from
   B. call. It from
   C. call from
   D. calling from

6. For instance, [Select...▾] .

   A. if you're closing a deal, can bring in your lawyer into the conversation
   B. if you're closing a deal, can be bringing your lawyer into the conversation
   C. if you're closing a deal, you can bring your lawyer into the conversation
   D. if you're closing a deal, you might could bring your lawyer into the conversation

7. This useful and convenient [Select...▾] be yours for only pennies a month.

   A. service is
   B. service it can
   C. service can
   D. service. That can

Answers and explanations start on page 644.

WRITING EFFECTIVE SENTENCES

Compound and Complex Sentences

Compound Sentences

The simple sentences described in Lesson 1 are also called **independent clauses.** An independent clause has a subject and a verb and expresses a complete thought. You can join two or more independent clauses in one **compound sentence.** To make a compound sentence, you should:

- Choose a logical **coordinating conjunction** to join the independent clauses. The coordinating conjunctions are *and, but, or, nor, for, so,* and *yet.*
- Insert a comma before the coordinating conjunction.

EXAMPLES

Two independent clauses: Sam saw a design flaw. He wrote a memo.
Joined correctly: Sam saw a design flaw, so he wrote a memo.

No coordinating conjunction: Sam asked his boss, she told him to send it.
Correct: Sam asked his boss, and she told him to send it.

No comma: Sam's boss was busy so she asked Sam to write the memo.
Correct: Sam's boss was busy, so she asked Sam to write the memo.

Be sure the coordinating conjunction expresses the correct relationship between the ideas in the two independent clauses.

Relationship between Ideas	Coordinating Conjunction
join two equally important ideas	and
contrast two ideas	but, yet
show a cause	for
show an effect	so
give a choice	or
give no choice	nor

Incorrect conjunction: Sam showed initiative, **yet** his boss praised him.
Correct conjunction: Sam showed initiative, **and** his boss praised him.

Be sure that you are actually joining two independent clauses and not just two subjects or two verbs.

Incorrect: The designers, and the builders got the memo.
Correct (no comma): The designers and the builders got the memo.

Incorrect: The designers needed the information, and appreciated the memo.
Correct (two independent clauses): The designers needed the information. They appreciated the memo.
Correct (no comma): The designers needed the information and appreciated the memo.

PRACTICE 2.1

A. Directions: Using the list on page 120, choose a coordinating conjunction for each sentence. Rewrite the sentence using the conjunction preceded by a comma.

EXAMPLE

I didn't want to seem timid, _____*so*_____ I didn't tell anyone about my experience.

1. It was late _____ I was walking home from work.

2. My coworker, Judy, had offered to drive me _____ I had refused.

3. It was a warm night _____ I decided to get some fresh air.

4. It was really my choice. I could have taken a cab _____ I could have walked.

5. I heard a loud noise _____ I ran the last block to my house. Later, I learned that it was only a car backfiring.

B. Questions 6 through 8 refer to the following paragraph.

Air Couriers

If you want to travel abroad but don't have a lot of money, one option is to be an air courier. `Select... ▾` gets a cheap ticket in return. Companies use couriers because it often costs less to check freight as baggage than to ship it as cargo. Air couriers fly on the major `Select... ▾` sometimes they can't check any baggage of their own. Couriers usually book their trips `Select... ▾`.

6. `Select... ▾` gets a cheap ticket in return.

   A. An air courier carries shipping documents on an international flight, and
   B. An air courier carries shipping documents on an international flight and
   C. An air courier, carries shipping documents on an international flight, and
   D. An air courier carries shipping documents, on an international flight, and

7. Air couriers fly on the major `Select... ▾` sometimes they can't check any baggage of their own.

   A. airlines, but
   B. airlines but
   C. airlines nor
   D. airlines, or

8. Couriers usually book their trips `Select... ▾`.

   A. in advance but they get their tickets on the day of the flight
   B. in advance, but they get their tickets on the day of the flight
   C. in advance getting their tickets on the day of the flight
   D. in advance, but they get their tickets, on the day of the flight

Answers and explanations start on page 644.

Complex Sentences

A **complex sentence** is made up of an independent clause and a **subordinate clause.** A subordinate clause has a subject and verb, but it does not express a complete thought.

Key Ideas

- Join a subordinate and an independent clause to form a complex sentence.
- Use a subordinating conjunction that shows the correct relationship between ideas.
- Put a comma after the subordinate clause when it comes at the beginning of a sentence.

EXAMPLES
Subordinate clause: Because their pay was too low.
Complex sentence: Teachers went on strike because their pay was too low.

                               independent clause   subordinate clause

Every subordinate clause begins with a **subordinating conjunction** that shows the relationship between the subordinate clause and the independent clause. Below is a list of common subordinating conjunctions.

Relationship between Clauses	Subordinating Conjunction
cause/reason	because
effect/result	in order that, so that
time	after, as, before, once, since, until, when, whenever, while
place	where, wherever
choice	if, whether
contradiction	although, even though, though

Choose the subordinating conjunction that conveys the meaning you are trying to express.

Incorrect meaning: The strike continued for more than a month once it finally ended.
Correct meaning: The strike continued for more than a month before it finally ended.

ON THE GED® TEST

You may need to select the correct subordinating conjunction to link two clauses. Choose the word or phrase that correctly conveys the relationship between the ideas.

When a subordinate clause comes at the beginning of a sentence, put a comma after it. If the subordinate clause comes at the end of a sentence, you generally don't need a comma before it.

At beginning of sentence: While teachers were on the picket line, kids stayed home.
At end of sentence: Kids stayed home while teachers were on the picket line.

However, when a subordinate clause at the end of a sentence begins with *although, though,* or *even though,* put a comma before the clause.

At beginning of sentence: Even though the public supported the teachers, the school board did not concede to the teachers' demands.
At end of sentence: The school board did not concede to teachers' demands, even though the public supported the teachers.

A subordinate clause cannot stand independently. By itself, a subordinate clause is a sentence fragment. Make sure that every subordinate clause is joined to an independent clause.

Incorrect: After the strike finished. The school year began.
Corrected by joining independent and subordinate clauses: After the strike finished, the school year began.

PRACTICE 2.2

A. Directions: Join the clauses to form complex sentences. Use the subordinating conjunctions in parentheses.

EXAMPLE

(if) You buy a smoke detector. You can protect your family.
If you buy a smoke detector, you can protect your family.

1. Most fatal fires occur. (when) A family is asleep.

_____

2. (because) A smoke alarm wakes you up. It can allow you to escape.

_____

3. Try to replace the smoke detector's battery. (before) It goes dead.

_____

4. (although) Smoke detectors cost money. The expense is worth it.

_____

B. Questions 5 through 7 refer to the following paragraph.

Phone Etiquette

When you [Select... ▾] it's wise to keep a few key rules in mind. First of all, be prepared. Have paper and pencil ready so that you won't have to fumble for them. [Select... ▾] the person whether this is a good time to talk. Get to the point quickly. Before you hang [Select... ▾] the person for his or her time. Finally, put the phone down gently. Slamming down the receiver makes a poor impression.

5. When you [Select... ▾] it's wise to keep a few key rules in mind.

   A. are making a business call
   B. are making a business call,
   C. will make a business call
   D. business call make

6. [Select... ▾] the person whether this is a good time to talk.

   A. After you identify yourself, ask
   B. Whenever you identify yourself, ask
   C. After you identify yourself ask
   D. After identifying yourself and asking

7. Before you hang [Select... ▾] the person for his or her time.

   A. up and then Thank
   B. up and thank
   C. up thank
   D. up, thank

Answers and explanations start on page 644.

WRITING EFFECTIVE SENTENCES

Run-Ons and Comma Splices

Key Ideas

- A run-on sentence is two or more sentences that are connected without correct punctuation.
- In a comma splice, two sentences are joined with only a comma.
- To correct a run-on or comma splice, make a compound or complex sentence or separate the sentences.

Run-Ons

There are two errors people commonly make when they join independent clauses to form a sentence. The first type of error is called a **run-on.** In a run-on, two independent clauses are combined without proper punctuation.

Run-On: Banks offer many helpful services you should check them out.

You can correct a run-on in one of several ways:
- Break the run-on into two separate sentences.
  Correct: Banks offer many services. You should check them out.
- Make a compound sentence (add a coordinating conjunction and a comma).
  Correct: Banks offer many services, so you should check them out.
- Make a complex sentence (add a subordinating conjunction and, if necessary, a comma).
  Correct: Because banks offer many services, you should check them out.

A run-on can also consist of independent clauses strung together with *and.* Correct this kind of run-on by dividing it into one or more compound sentences or by combining ideas into one sentence.

Run-On: Banking is getting more and more convenient and you can check on your account using bank-by-phone services and it's even possible to do your banking on the Internet.
Correct: Banking is getting more and more convenient. You can check on your account using bank-by-phone services, and it's even possible to do your banking on the Internet.

Run-On: Friday I got paid and I went to the bank and I cashed my check.
Correct: Friday I got paid, went to the bank, and cashed my check.

Comma Splices

The second type of error people sometimes make when joining independent clauses is called a **comma splice.** A comma splice occurs when two sentences are joined with just a comma. To correct a comma splice, add a coordinating conjunction after the comma:

Comma splice: You can check on your account using bank-by-phone services, it's even possible to do your banking on the Internet.
Correct: You can check on your account using bank-by-phone services, and it's even possible to do your banking on the Internet.

You can also correct a comma splice using the methods described above for correcting a run-on. You can also join two related ideas with a semicolon.

Comma splice: There are fewer bank tellers today, banks do offer other services.
Corrected by creating a complex sentence: Although there are fewer bank tellers today, banks do offer other services.

GED® TEST TIP

When you read a run-on sentence or a comma splice, look for the place where you would pause if you read the sentence aloud. That is the place where you would make the correction.

PRACTICE 3

A. Directions: Correct the following run-ons and comma splices using the methods explained on page 124. Try to use each method at least once.

1. Jeff just got his driver's license, he's very excited.

_____

2. He bought a car that has a lot of miles on it it wasn't very expensive.

_____

3. He doesn't have a lot of free time, he'd like to take a car trip.

_____

4. He needs to find out about car insurance and he needs to get a good map and he needs to join an auto club.

_____

B. Questions 5 through 7 refer to the following paragraph.

Photography Tips

It's not hard to take great [Select...▼] keep these tips in mind. For one thing, you need to get close to your subject, or you won't get a good shot. [Select...▼] for the right moment to shoot. Make sure the lighting is sufficient. Even outdoors, you can use a flash to fill in shadows.

Think about what you want to emphasize in your picture. You don't have to use [Select...▼] allow you to select the focus point you prefer. For example, many photographs of people focus on the eyes.

5. It's not hard to take great [Select...▼] keep these tips in mind.

  A. pictures if you just
  B. pictures just
  C. pictures, you just
  D. pictures that just

6. [Select...▼] for the right moment to shoot.

  A. Be patient, wait
  B. Be patient and wait
  C. Be patient wait
  D. Be patient and you wait

7. You don't have to use [Select...▼] allow you to select the focus point you prefer.

  A. the autofocus option, most cameras
  B. the autofocus option most cameras
  C. the autofocus option, because most cameras
  D. the autofocus option most cameras therefore

Answers and explanations start on page 645.

WRITING EFFECTIVE SENTENCES

Subordinate Ideas

Key Ideas

- Use smooth, flowing sentences rather than short, choppy sentences.
- Form compound or complex sentences from short sentences.
- Combine two predicates to make a compound predicate or combine two subjects to make a compound subject.

Writing is more effective when it flows smoothly. Therefore, try to eliminate short, choppy sentences whenever possible. You can do this by using **subordination** in a variety of ways.

You already know how to form a complex sentence with a subordinating clause. You also know how to create compound sentences. Either of these methods can be used to combine short sentences.

EXAMPLES
Short and choppy: Carla ran for the bus. She missed it.
Complex sentence: <u>Although</u> Carla ran for the bus, she missed it.
Compound sentence: Carla ran for the bus<u>, but</u> she missed it.

If two sentences have the same subject, you can combine them to form one sentence with a compound predicate. The **predicate** includes the verb plus anything else that is not part of the subject:

Short and choppy: Carla sat on the bench. She looked at her watch.
With compound predicate: Carla <u>sat on the bench and looked at her watch</u>.

Likewise, when two sentences have the same predicate, you can combine them to form one sentence with a compound subject. The resulting sentence will be less repetitive and wordy:

Short, choppy, and repetitive: Carla missed the bus. Dave missed the bus, too.
With compound subject: <u>Carla and Dave</u> missed the bus.

GED® TEST TIP

Read the passages on the test to yourself as if you could hear them in your mind. That "silent hearing" will help you notice sentences that are choppy or repetitive.

Finally, several short sentences that are related can be combined into one longer and more detailed sentence:

Short and choppy: Carla missed the bus. It was the 7:45 bus. She was on her way to work.
More detailed sentence: Carla missed <u>the 7:45 bus on her way to work</u>.

Sometimes, you can use two methods at the same time. For instance, in the sentence below, you can make a complex sentence with combined details:

Short and choppy: Carla found a pay phone near the bus stop. She called her boss. Then she called one of her coworkers.
Complex sentence with combined details: After Carla found a pay phone near the bus stop, she called <u>her boss and one of her coworkers</u>.

Repetitive: Her boss thanked her for calling. Her coworker thanked her for calling, and they both offered to pass along any messages.
With compound subject and compound predicate: <u>Both her boss and her coworker</u> thanked her for calling <u>and offered</u> to pass along any messages.

PRACTICE 4

A. Directions: Write each set of short, choppy sentences as one longer, smooth sentence.

EXAMPLE

If you are in a tornado, keep the windows closed. You should go to a safe place.
If you are in a tornado, keep the windows closed and go to a safe place.

1. Tornadoes can cause a lot of damage. Earthquakes are also capable of causing a lot of damage.

   _____

2. Earthquakes are somewhat common in California. Many Californians do not seem to mind.

   _____

3. On May 20, 2013, there was a tornado. It happened in Oklahoma. Twenty-four people were killed. Almost 400 people were injured.

   _____

4. Tornadoes can occur anywhere in the United States. They can happen any time of year.

   _____

B. Questions 5 through 7 refer to the following warranty.

Limited Warranty

If there is any defect, Pantronics will repair this unit free of charge. Audio components will be [Select... ▼] to one year after the date of purchase. The unit [Select... ▼]. A proof of purchase, such as a receipt, must be presented in order to receive service. This warranty does not cover damage [Select... ▼] faulty installation.

5. Audio components will be [Select... ▼] to one year after date of purchase.

   A. repaired. Repairs will then take up
   B. repaired and repairs will take place up
   C. repaired, the repairs will take place up
   D. repaired up

6. The unit [Select... ▼].

   A. may be brought or mailed to the service center
   B. may be brought to the service center. Or it can be mailed
   C. may be brought to the service center. It can be mailed, too
   D. may be brought, or mailing it, to the service center

7. This warranty does not cover damage [Select... ▼] faulty installation.

   A. due to accidents. It does not cover damage due to mishandling or
   B. due to accidents, nor it does not cover damage due to mishandling or
   C. due to accidents or cover damage due to mishandling or
   D. due to accidents, mishandling, or

Answers and explanations start on page 645.

WRITING EFFECTIVE SENTENCES

Modify Ideas

Key Ideas

- Modifiers make writing clearer and more interesting.
- Correct a dangling modifier by turning it into a subordinate clause or by making the word that is modified the subject of the sentence.
- Place a modifier as near as possible to the word or phrase it describes.

Modifiers are words and phrases used to add descriptive details. A modifier might be a word like *sweaty*, a verb phrase like *dragging the heavy box*, a prepositional phrase like *from the storage room*, or a clause like *that we packed this morning*. Modifiers make writing clearer, more specific, and more interesting.

EXAMPLES

Without modifiers: Our friends Jack and Tina helped us while we were moving.
With modifiers: Our <u>good</u> friends Jack and Tina helped us while we were moving, <u>watching our baby in their home.</u>

Without modifiers: We realized the weather would not cooperate.
With modifiers: <u>Sweating profusely at 9 a.m.,</u> we realized the weather would be <u>uncooperatively hot.</u>

Use modifiers carefully, or your meaning will be unclear. A **dangling modifier** is a word or phrase at the beginning of the sentence that has no clear subject to describe. To correct a dangling modifier, turn it into a subordinate clause, or make the word that the modifier describes into the subject of the sentence.

Dangling modifier: Driving the truck, one of the boxes fell out. (Who was driving the truck—one of the boxes?)
Correct: <u>As we were driving the truck,</u> one of the boxes fell out.
Correct: Driving the truck, <u>we heard</u> one of the boxes fall out.

Dangling modifier: Parking in a tow zone, a police officer gave us a ticket. (It sounds as if the police officer were parking in the tow zone.)
Correct: <u>Because we parked in a tow zone,</u> a police officer gave us a ticket.

Dangling modifier: Never having planned a move before, the real estate agent gave us some tips. (It sounds as if the real estate agent is the one who had never planned a move.)
Correct: Never having planned a move before, <u>we asked</u> the real estate agent for some tips.

A **misplaced modifier** is poorly placed in the sentence. It is not clear which word it modifies, or it modifies the wrong word in the sentence. To correct a misplaced modifier, put the modifier next to the word it describes.

Misplaced modifier: The moving van was just large enough <u>that we rented.</u>
Correct: <u>The moving van that we rented</u> was just large enough.

Misplaced modifier: We hoisted and lugged all our furniture up two flights of stairs <u>panting heavily.</u> (What was panting heavily—*we* or *the stairs*?)
Correct: <u>Panting heavily, we</u> hoisted and lugged all our furniture up two flights of stairs.

GED® TEST TIP

When a modifying phrase is at the beginning of a sentence, use a comma to separate it from the rest of the sentence.

PRACTICE 5

A. Directions: Revise each sentence, correcting the misplaced or dangling modifier.

1. Trent's sister encouraged him to become a nurse, who is a health professional.

    _____

2. Waking up the patients to take their blood pressure, they get rather annoyed.

    _____

3. He writes their temperature and blood pressure on their charts carefully.

    _____

4. Talking with the patients, it is hard to make visitors leave at 9 p.m.

    _____

B. Questions 5 through 7 refer to the following passage about adoption.

Adoption

Adoption is a legal procedure that gives [Select... ▾]. This practice dates back to ancient Greece. People without heirs used it to perpetuate their estates.

Adoptions may be handled through an agency or by independent placement. [Select... ▾] whether prospective parents will be fit. In an independent placement, there is no study. Lawyers [Select... ▾].

5. Adoption is a legal procedure that gives [Select... ▾].

   A. a person the rights of a son or daughter, who is not the adopter's birth child
   B. a person who is not the birth child of the adopter the rights of a son or daughter
   C. a person a son's or daughter's rights, who is not a birth child
   D. a person the rights of a birth child, who is not a son or daughter of the adopter

6. [Select... ▾] whether prospective parents will be fit is required.

   A. Going through an agency, a "home study" is required to determine
   B. Undergoing a "home study," an agency determines
   C. An agency requires a "home study" to determine
   D. Requiring a "home study," parents undergo such a study to determine

7. Lawyers [Select... ▾].

   A. handle these adoptions when parents ask them to frequently
   B. handle these adoptions when frequently asked to do so by parents
   C. handle these adoptions when parents ask them to, frequently
   D. frequently handle these adoptions when parents ask them to

Answers and explanations start on page 645.

Parallel Structure

When you write a sentence that lists two or more words, phrases, or clauses, the elements in the list must be in the same grammatical form. In other words, the sentence must have **parallel structure**. Writing that has parallel structure is clearer and easier to follow.

Key Ideas

- Listed items should be parallel in form and structure.
- Each phrase should have the same elements as other phrases in the series.
- Don't put words and clauses together in the same series.

Examples

Not parallel: Jim wants to eat less, exercise more, and be getting more sleep.
Parallel: Jim wants to <u>eat</u> less, <u>exercise</u> more, and <u>get</u> more sleep.

Not parallel: Walking and to swim are good aerobic exercises.
Parallel: <u>Walking</u> and <u>swimming</u> are good aerobic exercises.

Not parallel: Try to lose weight slowly, sensibly, and be careful.
Parallel: Try to lose weight <u>slowly</u>, <u>sensibly</u>, and <u>carefully</u>.

To be sure that your sentences have parallel structure, follow the guidelines below.

Make sure that verbs in a list are in the same form and tense:

Not parallel: Jim went to the store, bought an exercise mat, and is doing exercises.
Parallel: Jim <u>went</u> to the store, <u>bought</u> an exercise mat, and <u>did</u> exercises.

Be sure that phrases in a list are parallel in form and wording. For example, if one phrase in a list begins with a preposition, the others should, too. If one phrase begins with the word *the*, the others should, too.

Not parallel: Avoid exercising on busy streets, near traffic jams, and polluted areas.
Parallel: Avoid exercising <u>on busy streets</u>, <u>near traffic jams</u>, and <u>in polluted areas</u>.

Not parallel: He left the gym shoes, sweatpants, and the shirt in the gym.
Parallel: He left <u>the</u> gym shoes, <u>the</u> sweatpants, and <u>the</u> shirt in the gym.

Each list must have single words, short phrases, or clauses. Don't put single words and clauses together in the same series:

Not parallel: The most effective fitness programs are low impact, informal, and you can do them at home.
Parallel: The most effective fitness programs are <u>low impact</u>, <u>informal</u>, and <u>home based</u>.

Finally, notice that a comma separates each item within a list of three or more: *low impact, informal, and home based.*

GED® TEST TIP

When you revise a sentence to use parallel stracture, use the comma to separate each element as shown in these examples.

PRACTICE 6

A. Directions: Rewrite each sentence to make the structure parallel.

EXAMPLE
Jenna works quickly, carefully, and is thorough.
Jenna works quickly, carefully, and thoroughly.

1. Jenna has worked in a factory, a store, and has a waitressed.

   _____

2. She would like putting her kids in a better school and to get a better job.

   _____

3. She thinks the kids' father is irresponsible, lazy, and doesn't care about them.

   _____

4. He doesn't have the time, the energy, or money to give them what they deserve.

   _____

B. Questions 5 through 7 refer to the following memo.

TO: All Employees

A new alarm system has been installed. It is designed to make our workplace [Select... ▼]. However, we need everyone's cooperation.

If you are the last one to leave, turn off all lights, [Select... ▼] coffee makers. Then go to the alarm system located by the door. Punch in [Select... ▼]. Lock the door behind you.

5. It is designed to make our workplace [Select... ▼].

   A. safer, more comfortable, and pleasant
   B. safer and make it more comfortable and pleasant
   C. safer, more comfortable, and more pleasant
   D. safer, more comfortable, and make it more pleasant

6. If you are the last one to leave, turn off all lights, [Select... ▼] coffee makers.

   A. and computers, and the
   B. computers, and check the
   C. computers, and checking the
   D. computers, and

7. Punch in [Select... ▼].

   A. the secret code, press ON, and leaving immediately
   B. the secret code, pressing ON, and immediately leaving
   C. the secret code, press ON, and leave immediately
   D. the secret code, press ON, and then you will leave immediately

Answers and explanations start on page 645.

WRITING EFFECTIVE SENTENCES PRACTICE QUESTIONS

<u>Questions 1 through 5</u> refer to the following paragraphs.

Conserving Household Energy

According to the Department of Energy, many families spend an average of 14 percent of their yearly income on heating and cooling costs. Although you can't do much about high fuel prices, you can try some energy-saving measures.

To reduce wintertime energy costs, keep the shades drawn at night. [Select... ▾] the cracks. You can use sealing material available at any hardware store. If you have an air conditioner, cover it with thick plastic. Keep your thermostat at 68°F [Select... ▾].

In the summer, use fans and natural breezes rather than air-conditioning whenever possible. If you have windows that get direct [Select... ▾] the shades down during the day. Don't leave your air conditioner running when you're not at [Select... ▾] the filter every summer. With a clogged filter, the air conditioner's energy use can go up as much as 5 percent. Put your air conditioner on a low setting. Your home [Select... ▾].

1. [Select... ▾] the cracks.

   A. Sealing your windows, so that cold air can't get through
   B. Seal your windows so that cold air can't get through
   C. Seal your windows, so that cold air couldn't get out
   D. Your windows being sealed, cold air won't get through

2. Keep your thermostat at 68°F [Select... ▾].

   A. day, and it should be kept at 62° at night
   B. day and 62° at night
   C. day. Keep it at 62° at night
   D. day. At night, it should be kept at 62°

3. If you have windows that get direct [Select... ▾] the shades down during the day.

   A. sun and
   B. sun and to keep
   C. sun keep
   D. sun, keep

4. Don't leave your air conditioner running when you're not at [Select... ▾] the filter every summer.

   A. home and change
   B. home change
   C. home, so change
   D. home. Do change

5. Your home [Select... ▾].

   A. will not cool down any faster when your air conditioner is on full blast
   B. any faster will not cool down having your air conditioner on full blast
   C. will not cool down having your air conditioner on full blast any faster
   D. will not cool down when any faster your air conditioner is on full blast

Questions 6 through 10 refer to the following letter of complaint.

Cole Electronics
2514 Broadway
New York, NY 10057

Dear Manager:

    On August 2, I purchased a television at your store. [Select...▾] that the picture was fuzzy. [Select...▾] be fixed easily. I assumed that there would be no problem because I had just purchased the set.

    The customer service personnel said they had no time to handle my complaint. They were extremely rude and unprofessional. Finally, a salesman told me that I would have to send the TV to a service center in Detroit. At that point, I demanded a refund. [Select...▾] it could not be returned.

    I am [Select...▾]. I would now like to receive a full [Select...▾] the TV repaired locally. Please contact me to let me know what action will be taken. My phone number is (212) 555-2719.

Sincerely,
Jeffrey Barnes

6. [Select...▾] that the picture was fuzzy.

    A. When I got the television home I discovered
    B. When I got the television home, I discovered
    C. When I got the television home. I discovered
    D. When I got the television home I discovered,

7. [Select...▾] be fixed easily.

    A. I returned to the store to see if the problem could
    B. Returned to the store, I wanted to see if the problem could
    C. Returning to the store, the problem could
    D. Returning to the store to see if the problem could

8. [Select...▾] it could not be returned.

    A. He claimed that because the TV had been used,
    B. Claiming that because the TV had been used,
    C. The TV was claimed to be used, and therefore
    D. Claimed that the TV had been used and said

9. I am [Select...▾].

    A. angry and frustrated about the treatment I received
    B. angry about the treatment I received. I am also very frustrated
    C. angry about the treatment I received, I am also frustrated
    D. angry about the treatment I received I am also frustrated

10. I would now like to receive a full [Select...▾] the TV repaired locally.

    A. refund, getting
    B. refund, or getting
    C. refund or get
    D. refund to getting

Questions 11 though 15 refer to the following paragraphs.

Workplace Friendships

Should you make friends at work or keep your distance? Most experts agree that it's not wise to get too chummy with your boss. Relationships with coworkers, however, are a more complex matter. Although workplace friendships between peers can be beneficial, they can also cause problems.

Workplace friendships have many positive aspects. It's hard to [Select...▼]. Having friends at work [Select...▼]. Friends can serve as a sounding board for problems and help you succeed.

However, like any other friendship, workplace friendships can turn sour. [Select...▼] in plain view of your boss and coworkers. Discrimination and harassment suits have even been brought in some cases.

Experts recommend keeping your social life with work friends out of the workplace. For instance, don't exchange presents at [Select...▼] about your evening out. Avoid praising a friend publicly if it could make someone else resentful. Keeping your work life separate from your social life [Select...▼].

11. It's hard to [Select...▼].

   A. work productively if you feel alone
   B. work if you feel alone and in a productive way
   C. work in a productive way and feeling alone
   D. work, it isn't easy if you feel alone, productively

12. Having friends at work [Select...▼].

   A. can make your day more pleasant. And can give you energy
   B. can make your day more pleasant, and give you energy
   C. can make your day more pleasant and give you energy
   D. can make your day, giving you energy, more pleasant

13. [Select...▼] in plain view of your boss and coworkers.

   A. Things get messy, when the friendship unravels
   B. Things get messy when the friendship unravels
   C. Things are getting messy, when the friendship unravels
   D. Things getting messy when the friendship unravels

14. For instance, don't exchange presents at [Select...▼] about your evening out.

   A. work or talk
   B. work, or talk
   C. work, or talking
   D. working or talking

15. Keeping your work life separate from your social life [Select...▼].

   A. is worth the effort although it be hard
   B. may be hard, but it's worth the effort
   C. is worth the effort it may be hard
   D. may be hard but, it's worth the effort

Computer Virus Hoaxes

If you use email, you've probably received at least one message warning you of a terrible virus that will ruin your computer. Most of these messages are [Select... ▾] to scare you. Though some messages about viruses are accurate, most are just inaccurate rumors.

Virus hoax messages are similar to one another. Frequently, they describe viruses that will destroy your hard drive or computer. These hoaxes also claim that a respected authority, such as a government agency, has issued a warning about the virus. You can [Select... ▾]. Finally, hoaxes urge you to send the message to everyone you [Select... ▾] just creates panic.

If you receive a virus warning, don't pass it on. However, you don't have to worry about opening the email message itself. Your computer can't get a virus that way. Don't open any suspicious attachments, though, as you might infect your computer with a real virus. By following these guidelines, you can [Select... ▾].

16. Most of these messages are [Select... ▾] to scare you.

   A. hoaxes and they are designed
   B. hoaxes and they designed
   C. hoaxes, designing
   D. hoaxes designed

17. You can [Select... ▾].

   A. check a claim like this. Contacting the agency is a good way to check
   B. check a claim like this by contacting the agency
   C. check a claim like this, is contacting the agency
   D. check a claim like this, contact the agency

18. Finally, hoaxes urge you to send the message to everyone you [Select... ▾] just creates panic.

   A. know and this
   B. know, this
   C. know. This
   D. know that this

19. By following these guidelines, you can [Select... ▾].

   A. keep your computer equipment safe, and avoid spreading hysteria
   B. avoid spreading hysteria, keep your computer equipment safe
   C. avoiding spreading hysteria by keeping your computer equipment safe
   D. keep your computer equipment safe and avoid spreading hysteria

Answers and explanations start on page 645.

CONNECTING IDEAS

Organize Ideas into Paragraphs

Key Ideas

- Each paragraph should have one main idea. Each sentence in the paragraph should relate to the main idea.
- Break long paragraphs into two if possible.
- Join short paragraphs if they both relate to the same main idea.

Effective Paragraphs

A **paragraph** is a group of sentences that relate to one main idea. If the sentences do not help develop the same main idea, the paragraph seems disorganized, and the writer's meaning is unclear.

Incorrect: Group of sentences that do not relate to the same main idea:
Houseplants make a home more beautiful, but many people find them difficult to take care of. I water my houseplants once a week. There are many different kinds of houseplants. If you are buying a houseplant as a gift, consider how much light the person's home gets.

In the example above, each sentence is about houseplants, but there is no main idea. In the paragraph below, however, each sentence supports one idea: *helping houseplants adjust to a new home.*

Correct: Paragraph with sentences that relate to one main idea:
Houseplants need help to adjust to a new environment. Your home is probably less bright and humid than a greenhouse or plant store. Therefore, when you get a new houseplant, keep it near a south-facing window at first. Move it away from the light over a period of four weeks. Use a humidifier to make the air in your home more humid. These actions will help avoid the loss of foliage that often occurs when plants change locales.

One paragraph should stop and a new one begin when the main idea shifts. In the example below, the first four sentences describe what road rage is, while the last four sentences tell how to react to road rage. The writer should have started a new paragraph with sentence 5.

Incorrect: One paragraph that should be divided into two paragraphs:
(1) Road rage is an episode of violent behavior that takes place when one driver's actions anger another driver. (2) Young males are the most likely to lose their cool on the road. (3) Most road rage incidents take place during rush hour, when people often get frustrated. (4) Warm weather is another factor in road rage. (5) If you're a victim of an aggressive driver, try to stay calm. (6) Don't react or make eye contact. (7) Try not to brake or swerve in retaliation. (8) These actions will only infuriate the other driver, and you might lose control of your car.

Sometimes the ideas in two paragraphs really belong in one:

Incorrect: Two paragraphs that should be combined:
To make chicken broth, boil a pot of water. Take some chicken, onions, parsnips, carrots, and herbs, and wrap them up in cheesecloth.

Make sure it is real cotton cheesecloth, or you won't be able to eat the broth! Simmer the cheesecloth-wrapped vegetables and chicken in the water for several hours; then remove them. Add salt and pepper to taste.

GED® TEST TIP

If a paragraph is especially long, check to see if the main idea shifts at some point. If so, that is where the paragraph should be divided in two.

PRACTICE 1.1

A. Directions: Read each group of sentences. If there is a main idea, underline it. If there is no main idea, write "No MI."

_____ 1. The pharmacist at the local drugstore is very helpful. She can always get the medicines we need. She arranges deliveries of our prescriptions when we're sick. When we don't have money, she lets us pay the next time. Many people have written to thank her.

_____ 2. Keep your toolbox well equipped, and you'll always be able to make home repairs. Common home repairs include replacing lighting fixtures and fixing furniture. The community center offers a class on this subject. You can pay someone to do home repairs.

_____ 3. Some people don't vote because they think their vote doesn't count. However, elections have been won by just a few hundred votes. If people don't vote, they are giving up their voice. Every vote counts, so let your voice be heard and vote!

_____ 4. When you are traveling, it's a good idea to mark your luggage clearly. Put a luggage tag on every piece you intend to bring, including hand luggage like backpacks. To recognize your luggage quickly, put a brightly colored ribbon on it.

_____ 5. Listening to music can benefit you in many ways. When you are feeling stressed, music can help soothe and relax you. When you need energy, rock 'n' roll or hip-hop can give you a boost. If you have a baby or small child, soft music can help lull the child to sleep.

B. Questions 6 and 7 refer to the following paragraphs.

The Common Cold

(A)

(1) How frequently you get colds depends on your age. (2) The average young adult gets two to four colds a year. (3) Adults over 60 have fewer than one cold a year, while children have six to ten colds annually. (4) Colds are caused by viruses. (5) Contrary to popular belief, being cold will not cause you to get a cold. (6) Vitamin C is thought to prevent colds, but there is no proof.

(B)

(7) Because there is no cure for the common cold, prevention is key. (8) Washing your hands is the best way to avoid getting a cold. (9) Encourage others who have colds to sneeze into a tissue and throw it away immediately.

(C)

(10) Refrain from touching your eyes and nose, and stay far from people who have colds.

6. Which revision would improve the effectiveness of the article?

   Begin a new paragraph with

   A. sentence 2
   B. sentence 3
   C. sentence 4
   D. sentence 5

7. Which revision would improve the effectiveness of the article?

   A. remove sentence (1)
   B. remove paragraph B
   C. remove paragraph C
   D. join paragraphs B and C

Answers and explanations start on page 646.

- A topic sentence states the main idea of a paragraph.
- Each sentence in a paragraph should provide details to support the main idea.
- An essay should have a main idea statement that states the main point of the entire essay.

Topic Sentences in Paragraphs

Every paragraph should have a **topic sentence** that states the main idea. The other sentences in the paragraph are **supporting details**. These details tell more about the topic sentence. The topic sentence usually appears at the beginning of the paragraph, though it may appear elsewhere.

A topic sentence must do two things:

- Identify the topic, or subject, of the paragraph
- State the central point that the writer wants to make about the topic

In the paragraph below, the topic sentence is underlined. Notice how the topic sentence tells the subject of the paragraph (*graffiti in our neighborhood*) and states the central point about the topic (*graffiti is a serious problem in the neighborhood and should be addressed*).

EXAMPLE

We need to do more to stop the problem of graffiti in our neighborhood. Recently, several bus stops and the exterior walls of many buildings have been defaced with unsightly graffiti. The neighborhood is fast becoming a much less desirable place to live. As a result, prospective renters feel frightened and look elsewhere.

A topic sentence should not be too specific or too general. If it is, readers won't know what the overall point is. A topic sentence like "The market is covered with gang symbols" would be too specific for the paragraph above. "There is graffiti in our neighborhood" would be too general.

Main Idea Statements in Essays

Just as every paragraph should have a topic sentence, so every essay should have a **main idea statement**. Whereas a topic sentence states the main idea, or "point," of a single paragraph, a main idea statement expresses the central point of all the paragraphs in an essay. In the essay below, the main idea statement is underlined. Notice that while the main idea statement appears in the first paragraph, it is not the first sentence.

EXAMPLE

While graffiti is indeed a serious problem facing our neighborhood, other issues also need to be addressed. Two of the most pressing neighborhood issues are the crime rate and the lack of decent housing.

In recent months, crime has increased. For example, a number of muggings have occurred. As a result, residents are nervous about going out at night. The number of apartment break-ins has increased as well. We need a stronger police presence to combat the crime problem.

In addition, much of the housing in this neighborhood is in poor condition. Every day, residents are put in danger by peeling paint, broken locks, and rundown fences. We must put pressure on landlords to resolve their tenants' complaints, perhaps by showing them that, in the long run, it is in their financial interest to do so.

If we do not act immediately, our neighborhood will decline even more. Therefore, I recommend that we form a community task force to tackle these issues. We should ask our city councilwoman to be an advocate for us. With full participation of community members, we will be on our way to a safer, more livable neighborhood.

PRACTICE 1.2

A. Directions: Write topic sentences for each of the following paragraphs.

1. _____

Weather satellites send us information about weather around the world. Thanks to satellite TV, we have an ever-widening range of programs to choose from. Satellites even play a role in long-distance telephone communication.

2. _____

First of all, stock prices are falling. Second, home sales have slowed to a crawl. Finally, many consumers have cut back on big purchases such as cars, home improvements, and vacations.

3. _____

According to the new dress code, employees of the library may now wear "semi-casual" clothing. Khakis, blue jeans with no holes, and other slacks are acceptable for men and women. Skirts must be knee-length or longer. Sandals are acceptable in the summer. Employees are requested not to wear gym shoes.

B. Questions 4 and 5 refer to the following paragraphs.

Repetitive Strain Injury

(A)

Repetitive strain injury is a problem. The injury can affect factory workers, computer users, and meatpackers, among others. Anyone who uses his or her hands all day may be affected, even if the work does not seem to require a lot of physical effort. When fine hand movements are repeated for many hours a day, they eventually strain the forearms, wrists, and fingers.

(B)

Maintaining a stiff and constrained posture, as is required for working at a computer, places a lot of stress on the body. Likewise, holding muscles still for long periods causes fatigue and discomfort. In addition, many jobs require workers to work at top speed all day long. Consistently working quickly deprives the body of natural rest breaks, forcing workers to push themselves to the limit.

4. Which is the most effective revision of sentence 1?

A. Some workers get repetitive strain injury.
B. Just what, you may ask, is repetitive strain injury?
C. Workers suffer many injuries on the job, and repetitive strain injury is just one of them.
D. Repetitive strain injury is a painful condition resulting from repeated use of the hands.

5. Which sentence would be most effective if inserted at the beginning of paragraph B?

A. Repetitive movements cause muscle strain.
B. A number of factors contribute to repetitive strain injury.
C. Watch your posture as you work.
D. Repetitive strain injury is very common.

Answers and explanations start on page 646.

CONNECTING IDEAS

Use Logical Order and Relevant Ideas

Key Ideas

- The sentences in a paragraph should follow a logical order.
- Keep reasons and examples close to the point you are making with them.
- Eliminate any irrelevant details.

When you are writing a paragraph, it is important to put your sentences in a logical order. For instance, you may choose to sequence supporting details from most important to least important, from least important to most important, or in time order. All the sentences in the paragraph should follow the same order. If not, your readers may get confused. Look at the sample paragraphs below:

Incorrect: Sentences not in time order:

> To clear a clogged drain using a plunger, fill the sink with enough water to cover the plunger cup. Put petroleum jelly on the rim of the cup to form a tight seal. Before you begin, check to make sure that the plunger's suction cup is big enough to cover the drain. Block the sink overflow with rags. Plunge 15 or 20 times.

Correct: Sentences in time order:

> To clear a clogged drain using a plunger, <u>first check to make sure that the plunger's suction cup is big enough to cover the drain</u>. Fill the sink with enough water to cover the plunger cup. Put petroleum jelly on the rim of the cup to form a tight seal. Block the sink overflow with rags. Plunge 15 or 20 times.

The reasons and examples you use to support your points should come immediately after you make each point. If they come later, they will be less effective.

Incorrect: Reason far from point:

> Don't make a habit of using chemicals to clear your drain. Always wear rubber gloves to protect your hands when using chemical drain cleaners. These powerful cleaners can damage the pipes.

Correct: Reason close to point:

> Don't make a habit of using chemicals to clear your drain. <u>These powerful cleaners can damage the pipes</u>. Always wear rubber gloves to protect your hands when using chemical drain cleaners.

ON THE GED® TEST

Make sure that every supporting sentence is relevant to the topic sentence. Ask yourself, "Does this support the main idea of the paragraph?" If not, delete it or move it to where it belongs.

Sometimes a sentence in a paragraph relates to the topic in a general way but does not support the topic sentence. This mistake is a type of **irrelevant detail**, as shown in the paragraph below:

> In many cultures, blonde is considered a desirable hair color. Perhaps blonde hair is valued because few people are naturally blonde. The practice of bleaching one's hair blonde is very old, dating back to ancient Roman times, and it continues to be popular today. <u>My sister dyed her hair last year</u>. A number of hair-bleaching products are sold in drugstores and supermarkets.

The sentence "My sister dyed her hair last year," is an irrelevant detail. While it relates to the topic of bleaching one's hair, it does not support the idea that blonde is a popular hair color in many cultures. This sentence should be deleted.

PRACTICE 2

A. Directions: Cross out the irrelevant detail in each paragraph.

1. Why do people blame themselves when things go terribly wrong? Some psychologists believe that by blaming themselves, people find a reason for the upsetting event. Getting very ill is one bad thing that could happen. Finding a reason is more comforting than believing that the event took place for no reason at all.

2. It's almost time for the back-to-school rush. This year, come to Carter's to make sure that your child is outfitted with all the things that he or she needs. We have school supplies at rock-bottom prices. Adult students can also use school supplies. Check out our backpacks and lunch boxes in colors your kids will love. At Carter's, we have everything your kids will ever need!

3. Tenants: On Friday, April 23, the boiler in this building will be fixed. This job will be extremely expensive! There will be no water from 8 A.M. to 5 P.M. Please plan in advance, and draw out water the night before to be used the next day. We apologize for the inconvenience.

B. Questions 4 through 6 refer to the following cover letter.

(A)

Dear Mr. Soros:

(1) Thank you very much for taking the time to speak with me about the carpentry position. (2) It was a pleasure to meet you and to learn about your organization. (3) I enjoyed meeting you and learning about your organization.

(B)

(4) As you will see from the enclosed resume, I recently completed a program in carpentry at Dade Community College. (5) I have also worked in the carpentry field. (6) In addition, I held a secretarial job.

(C)

(7) With my education and experience, I believe that I could make a valuable contribution to your company. (8) Thank you for considering me for this position. (9) I look forward to hearing from you soon. (10) I would be honored to take the job if it were offered to me.

Sincerely,

Sandra Barnes

4. Which revision would improve the effectiveness of paragraph A?

A. remove sentence 1
B. move sentence 1 to follow sentence 2
C. move sentence 2 to the beginning of paragraph B
D. remove sentence 3

5. Sentence 6: In addition, I held a secretarial job.

Which revision should be made to the placement of sentence 6?

A. move sentence 6 to follow sentence 4
B. move sentence 6 to follow sentence 8
C. move sentence 6 to follow sentence 10
D. remove sentence 6

6. Sentence 10: I would be honored to take the job if it were offered to me.

Which revision should be made to the placement of sentence 10?

A. move sentence 10 to follow sentence 2
B. move sentence 10 to follow sentence 4
C. move sentence 10 to follow sentence 5
D. move sentence 10 to follow sentence 8

Answers and explanations start on page 646.

CONNECTING IDEAS

Relate Sentences and Paragraphs

Good writing flows smoothly and logically from one sentence to the next and from one paragraph to the next. To make your writing flow, use **transitions** to show how ideas are related. Here are some common transitions and their uses.

Transitional Word or Phrase	Use it to . . .
for example, for instance	give an example
also, furthermore, in addition, in the same way, likewise, moreover, similarly	compare ideas or add to an idea
however, nevertheless, on the other hand, in contrast	contrast ideas
first, second, then, next, after that, later, at last, finally, in conclusion	show steps in a process or time order
because	show a cause
as a result, consequently	show a result
therefore, thus	draw a conclusion

Key Ideas

- Use transitions to help your writing flow from sentence to sentence and from paragraph to paragraph.
- Choose the transition that expresses the correct relationship between ideas.

You can link two sentences using transitions in the following ways:

EXAMPLES

Begin the second sentence with a transition followed by a comma: Raquel has many hobbies. For example, she paints furniture and sews clothes.

Put the transition within the second sentence and set it off with commas: Raquel has many hobbies. She paints furniture, for example, and sews clothes.

Combine the two sentences into one. Put a semicolon before the transition and a comma after it: Raquel has many hobbies; for example, she paints furniture and sews clothes.

Transitions can also be used to link one paragraph to another, highlighting the relationship between the two paragraphs.

EXAMPLE

Top performance in sports depends on "mental economy." Mental economy involves focusing the mind on the task at hand. When athletes think too much about what they're doing or worry about the outcome, they interfere with the communication between the brain and the muscles.

In addition, athletes must strive for "physical economy." Although athletes put forth a tremendous amount of effort, they must take care to pace themselves in order to conserve energy for the end of the event.

GED® TEST TIP

When you use a transition at the beginning of a sentence, be sure you put a comma after the transition.

To decide which transition to use, see how the paragraph is organized and what you are trying to accomplish. For example, are you comparing two things? If so, you will want to use transitions that compare ideas. Similarly, when choosing transitions to introduce paragraphs, consider the organization of the entire essay.

PRACTICE 3

A. Directions: Rewrite each pair of sentences using a transition from the chart on page 142. Change the punctuation if necessary. Write your answers on a separate sheet of paper.

Example: We have worked very hard this year. Sales are at an all-time high.
We have worked very hard this year. As a result, sales are at an all-time high.

1. Our marketing efforts need to be enhanced. We will soon begin another marketing initiative.

2. Sales representatives say their jobs are extremely demanding. The salary is attractive.

3. The marketing director has instructed sales representatives to try some new ideas. Sales representatives can give away free samples.

4. A new ad campaign will be launched in just a few weeks. We expect sales to increase.

B. Questions 5 through 7 refer to the following paragraphs.

Library Cafés

Until very recently, eating was not something that most people associated with libraries. A patron would likely be chased out for munching on a sandwich in a corner. `Select... ▾` and a croissant in some public libraries.

Following the lead of successful bookstores, libraries across the country are installing cafés. Some library cafés have menus that offer just as much variety as a regular `Select... ▾`, one of them offers 20 varieties of coffee, hot cider, and muffins. These refreshments make going to the library more pleasant and may therefore increase library patronage.

`Select... ▾` may benefit a library financially. The income from the café adds to library revenues. Also, as more people enjoy coming to the library, they may be more likely to approve tax increases for it.

5. `Select... ▾` and a croissant in some public libraries.

   A. Times however are changing, and these days patrons can even buy coffee
   B. Times are changing, however, and these days patrons can even buy coffee
   C. Times are changing, and these days, however patrons can even buy coffee
   D. Times are changing, and these days patrons can even buy coffee, however

6. Some library cafés have menus that offer just as much variety as those of a regular `Select... ▾` one of them offers 20 varieties of coffee, hot cider, and muffins.

   A. restaurant, in addition,
   B. restaurant. For example,
   C. restaurant. Nevertheless,
   D. restaurant. Thus,

7. `Select... ▾` may benefit a library financially.

   A. In addition, having a café
   B. On the other hand, having a café
   C. A café, by benefiting a library,
   D. Financially a café

Answers and explanations start on page 646.

CONNECTING IDEAS PRACTICE QUESTIONS

The Effects of Lack of Sleep

(A)

(1) Research shows that about 70 million North Americans have experienced the problem of sleep disruption. (2) Losing sleep is more than just an annoyance. (3) In some cases, it can have catastrophic results. (4) In the United States, sleepy drivers are responsible for at least 100,000 car crashes each year. (5) Most people need at least eight hours of shut-eye a night but get only six or seven. (6) Their fast-paced lives leave them little time for sleep. (7) Another factor is poor bedtime habits. (8) Family stresses may also cause sleep loss.

(B)

(9) A study of high school students showed that students with low grades went to bed 40 minutes later and got 25 minutes less sleep than students with high [Select...▾] another study shows that when one gets fewer than six to eight hours of sleep, it is harder to learn new skills.

(C)

(11) If you have trouble sleeping, avoid caffeine and alcohol. (12) Get regular exercise during the day, when it won't make you too energized to sleep. (13) Exercise can also help you lose weight.

(D)

(14) Set times for going to bed and getting up each day, and stick to them. (15) Don't watch TV or use a computer late at night, since these stimulate visual response and interfere with sleep. (16) If you find you still can't sleep, get up and do something.

1. Which revision would improve the effectiveness of the article?

   Begin a new paragraph with

   A. sentence 3
   B. sentence 4
   C. sentence 5
   D. sentence 6

2. Which sentence would be most effective if inserted at the beginning of paragraph B?

   A. Some high school students get better grades than others.
   B. High-achieving students get more sleep.
   C. Lack of sleep interferes with mathematical ability.
   D. People need more sleep than they used to.

3. A study of high school students showed that students with low grades went to bed 40 minutes later and got 25 minutes less sleep than students with high [Select...▾] another study shows that when one gets fewer than six to eight hours of sleep, it is harder to learn new skills.

   A. grades. Similarly,
   B. grades, likewise,
   C. grades. As a result,
   D. grades. Therefore,

4. Exercise can also help you lose weight.

   Which revision should be made to the placement of sentence 13?

   A. move sentence 13 to follow sentence 11
   B. move sentence 13 to follow sentence 14
   C. move sentence 13 to follow sentence 15
   D. remove sentence 13

5. Which revision would improve the effectiveness of the article?

   A. join paragraphs B and C
   B. move sentence 11 to the end of paragraph B
   C. remove sentence 14
   D. join paragraphs C and D

Questions 6 through 10 refer to the following paragraphs.

Getting Out Those Troublesome Stains

(A)

(1) Have you ever ruined a nice piece of clothing by staining it? (2) If so, the following information on stain removal may interest you. (3) By learning a few simple rules and keeping some household cleaners on hand, you can preserve your clothing. (4) First of all, the faster you act, the better. (5) With time, the stain will set. (6) Be sure to blot the stain rather than scrubbing it. (7) Scrubbing can actually drive the stain into the fabric.

(B)

(8) Use hot water on a grease stain such as salad dressing and cold water on a water-based stain such as wine, pasta sauce, or blood. (9) If you don't know what the stain is or where it came from, use room-temperature water. (10) Otherwise you might set the stain.

(C)

(11) Sometimes other liquids are more effective than water. (12) Lemon [Select...▾] ink, rust, and iodine. (13) White vinegar takes out alcohol, coffee, deodorants, and glue. (14) Liquid shampoo can be used on oil, tar, and grease. (15) Not surprisingly, it works the same way on an oil stain as it does on oil in your hair. (16) Rubbing alcohol removes stains from grass and soft drinks.

(D)

(17) If you find that a stain is not going away or is getting worse, stop and take your clothes to a dry cleaner. (18) Professionals know best. (19) Home remedies may not work on every stain.

6. Which revision would improve the effectiveness of the article?

   Begin a new paragraph with

   A. sentence 3
   B. sentence 4
   C. sentence 5
   D. sentence 6

7. Which sentence would be most effective if inserted at the beginning of paragraph B?

   A. Hot and cold water have many uses.
   B. Choose the right water temperature for cleaning each stain.
   C. Hot water takes out tough stains.
   D. The second step is to determine the proper use of hot water.

8. Lemon [Select...▾] ink, rust, and iodine.

   A. juice, for example removes
   B. juice, for example. Removes
   C. juice for example removes
   D. juice, for example, removes

9. Which revision would improve the effectiveness of paragraph C?

   A. move sentence 11 to follow sentence 12
   B. move sentence 12 to follow sentence 14
   C. remove sentence 14
   D. remove sentence 15

10. Home remedies may not work on every stain.

   Which revision should be made to the placement of sentence 19?

   A. move sentence 19 to the beginning of paragraph C
   B. move sentence 19 to follow sentence 13
   C. move sentence 19 to the beginning of paragraph D
   D. move sentence 19 to follow sentence 17

Questions 11 through 14 refer to the following memo.

To: All Employees
From: Denise Ellis, Benefits Manager

(A)

(1) Starting on January 1, Allcity will no longer be our insurance carrier. (2) Instead, you will have a choice of two other insurance carriers: HealthPlan and Rainbow Insurance Company.

(B)

(3) HealthPlan is an HMO. (4) You will not have to pay any money to doctors in advance with this plan, but you must go to doctors listed with the insurance company. (5) HMOs are becoming increasingly popular. (6) With Rainbow Insurance, you may choose any doctor you wish. (7) [Select... ▼] you receive the service. (8) Afterwards, you submit the receipts to Rainbow Insurance. (9) Representatives of both companies will be here on December 2 to discuss the details of their plans. (10) Please sign up for an informa-tional session on that day. (11) The sign-up sheet is on the door of the conference room, where the meetings will take place.

(C)

(12) At the meeting, you will receive a card on which you must indicate your choice of company. (13) Please mark your choice in the appropriate box and submit it to me by December 5.

(D)

(14) If you do not submit your card in time, you may not be insured for the month of January. (15) If you are not able to attend any of the informational sessions, please let me know right away. (16) Feel free to contact me at ext. 2453 with any questions you may have about this process.

11. Which revision would improve the effectiveness of paragraph B?

   A. remove sentence 3
   B. move sentence 5 to the beginning of paragraph B
   C. remove sentence 5
   D. remove sentence 10

12. [Select... ▼] you receive the service.

   A. However, you must pay the health providers when
   B. However you must pay, the health providers when
   C. However you must pay the health providers when,
   D. However you must pay the health providers, when

13. Which revision would improve the effectiveness of the memo?

   Begin a new paragraph with

   A. sentence 7
   B. sentence 8
   C. sentence 9
   D. sentence 10

14. If you do not submit your card on time, you may not be insured for the month of January.

   Which revision should be made to the placement of sentence 14?

   A. move sentence 14 to the end of paragraph C
   B. move sentence 14 to follow sentence 15
   C. move sentence 14 to follow sentence 16
   D. remove sentence 14

Questions 15 through 19 refer to the following paragraphs.

Repairing a Flat Bicycle Tire

(A)

(1) The first step in fixing a flat bicycle tire is to remove the wheel. (2) Next, release the brake. (3) Before you begin, let out any air in the tire. (4) If you are removing the back wheel, put the derailleur in high gear. (5) Then take off the axle nuts by unscrewing counterclockwise. (6) If your bike has safety washers, remove these also. (7) Then remove the wheel.

(B)

(8) Remove the tire, and mark the valve stem position on it. (9) If possible, remove the tire without using tools, because the inner tube punctures easily. (10) Use tire levers or the backs of forks and spoons if necessary. (11) When you find the leak, scrape the spot with sandpaper. (12) Remove the inner tube and inflate it, listening and feeling for air leaks. (13) Then apply cement to the tube, and let it dry completely before putting the patch on.

(C)

(14) First, inflate the tube and make sure the leak has been fixed. (15) Next, slip the inner tube back into the tire, and put the tire back on the rim. (16) Then inflate the tube to the correct pressure. (17) The pressure is right when there is enough air to steady the tire but not so much air that the tire cannot be squeezed between the brake pads.

(D)

(18) Put the bike back on its wheels, and then tighten the wheel nuts. (19) [Select... ▾] ready to ride!

15. Which revision would improve the effectiveness of paragraph A?

   A. move sentence 2 to follow sentence 3
   B. begin a new paragraph with sentence 5
   C. move sentence 5 to follow sentence 7
   D. remove sentence 6

16. Which revision would improve the effectiveness of paragraph B?

   A. move sentence 11 to follow sentence 8
   B. move sentence 11 to follow sentence 9
   C. move sentence 11 to follow sentence 12
   D. move sentence 11 to follow sentence 13

17. Which sentence would be most effective if inserted at the beginning of paragraph C?

   A. All you have to do now is take care of the tire pressure.
   B. Fixing a flat tire is a long process that requires a lot of patience.
   C. The next step is to put the tire and tube back onto the rim.
   D. Patching the leak properly is also very important.

18. Which sentence would be most effective if inserted at the beginning of paragraph D?

   A. The final step is to reinstall the wheel.
   B. Fixing a flat tire requires careful planning.
   C. Whether you are an experienced cyclist or just a beginner, you can fix a flat tire.
   D. Try not to use sharp tools to fix a flat tire.

19. [Select... ▾] ready to ride!

   A. Then readjust the tire pressure, and you're
   B. Moreover, readjust the tire pressure, and you're
   C. Moreover, readjusting the tire pressure, you're
   D. Also, having readjusted the tire pressure, you will be

Answers and explanations start on page 647.

Unpack the Writing Prompt

Key Ideas

- The Extended Response will require reading one or two passages and writing a response to a prompt.
- To draft an acceptable response to the text, the first step is to "unpack" the prompt—to focus on the specific question you need to address.
- Your response must be evidence based, which means that it needs to be grounded in facts, details, and examples from the text.

The writing activity on the GED® *Reasoning through Language Arts Test* is called an **Extended Response**. This task involves reading one passage or two paired passages and producing a piece of writing in a word-processing box on the computer screen. Page 60 shows how the reading and writing formats will look on the computer.

To master this assignment, you need to understand the purpose of **evidence-based writing**. This type of writing requires that you develop an argument by using evidence from the text(s) to support your claim.

On pages 634–633, you looked at writers' **arguments** as a reading activity alone. On the Extended Response activity, you will look at them in order to develop your *own* argument and supporting text in response to the writing **prompt**, or assignment.

Below are two arguments that you read on page 94. On the facing page is a writing prompt based on them. While these readings are much shorter than the ones on the *Reasoning through Language Arts Test,* they give a good starting point for understanding how to **unpack the writing prompt**.

What does it mean to "unpack" a prompt? When you unpack a suitcase, you take things out and think about what you are going to do with them—wash them, fold them, hang them up, or put them in a drawer. Similarly, with a writing prompt, you will take it apart in your mind and plan how you are going to accomplish the task.

Reread the selections and the writing prompt on the facing page. Then practice unpacking the writing prompt by answering the questions numbered 1–6 and reading the explanation below.

GED® TEST TIP

It is advisable to read the prompt <u>before</u> you read the passages. That will help you to focus on the argument and the supporting evidence in the passage or passages.

Passage A

Coal, the source of half the energy in the United States, has been the dirtiest of all fossil fuels because it creates harmful emissions when burned. Help is on the way with the development of new "clean coal" technologies that reduce coal's environmental impact. These new technologies that purify exhaust gases as coal burns (wet scrubbers) and prevent the formation of harmful emissions in the first place (low-NO*x* burners). There is even gasification, which avoids burning coal altogether.

Passage B

"Clean coal" amounts to just an advertising slogan. Don't be fooled by claims about new technologies making coal a clean-burning fuel. The hazards to our environment start well before that. Coal mining wastes huge amounts of water—70 to 260 million gallons daily. Today's mining companies now use mountaintop removal, instead of traditional mining, to extract coal. Forty-nine states have issued fish intake advisories due to high mercury concentration in water, much of it due to coal-fired power plants.

Coal Writing Prompt

While the writer of Passage A proposes the benefits of clean coal, the writer of Passage B identifies drawbacks to this position.

In your response, analyze both selections to determine which position is better supported.

Use relevant and specific information from both selections to support your response.

Type your response in the box. This task will take 45 minutes to complete.

Unpacking the Writing Prompt

1. What is the writing assignment about?

2. What does the prompt ask you to do? Turn it into a question.

3. What are you being asked to include in your response?

4. Are you being asked for your opinion on the topic?

5. Are you being asked to take a position about the writers' arguments?

6. Where are you writing? How long do you have?

---

1. The writing assignment is about **the two selections that take different positions on clean coal**.

2. The prompt asks me: **Which of the positions about clean coal is better supported?**

3. The prompt states that I have to use **both relevant and specific information from the passage**.

4. No. I am **not being asked for my opinion about clean coal**.

5. Yes. I am being asked to take a position about **which writer I think made a stronger case**.

6. I am to **type in the box on the computer screen**. I will have **45 minutes** for the entire writing task.

PRACTICE 1

Questions 1 through 4 refer to the following writing prompt. (For this practice, there are no passages.)

Writing Prompt

Passage A cites Federal Communications Commission determinations and scientific studies that have concluded that radiation from cell phones has no adverse effects. However, Passage B cites studies that raise questions about traffic safety issues and the long-term health effects of cell phone use.

In your response, compare and analyze both selections to determine whether you agree with the writer of Passage A or Passage B. Use relevant and specific information from both selections to support your response.

Unpacking the Writing Prompt

1. What is the topic of the writing prompt?

_____

2. What does the prompt ask you to do? (Put this in the form of a question.)

_____

3. What are you asked to include in your response?

_____

4. Are you being asked for your opinion on the topic or to take a position on the writers' arguments?

_____

Answers and explanations start on page 647.

WRITING ABOUT TEXT

Identify a Writer's Arguments and Assumptions

Key Ideas

- Your response to the writing assignment will be based on identifying a writer's argument.
- A writer's argument is a conclusion, which is supported by facts, details, and other evidence.
- While a writer may not directly state them, he or she has assumptions about the topic.

On the Reasoning through Language Arts Test, you will be writing a response based on one or two passages. On page 88 you read that a written **argument** consists of the following:

- A statement, which is a **conclusion** about something
- The **evidence**, which is support that is given for the argument
- The **premises**, or the **assumptions**, behind the argument

Read a short passage. Identify the writer's conclusion about the topic and the assumptions behind it.

Secondhand smoke is the smoke that comes either from the lighted end of a cigarette, pipe, or cigar or from the exhalation of a smoker. Most people consider secondhand smoke to be less dangerous than the nicotine that a cigarette user intakes. However, the particles that come from the smoke of the lighted end of a cigarette, called sidestream smoke, contain higher concentrations of carcinogens, which are chemicals that cause cancer. These particles can be breathed in easily by people around smokers, especially in enclosed areas. Therefore, all restaurants should ban smoking inside.

1. What is the writer's topic?
   (1) Secondhand smoke and its effects
   (2) The most common carcinogens

2. What is the writer's conclusion about the topic?
   (1) Sidestream smoke contains high concentrations of carcinogens.
   (2) Smoking should be banned inside restaurants.

3. Which of the following is the writer's unstated assumption?
   (1) Carcinogens only come from sidestream smoke.
   (2) Restaurants should take steps to protect the health of their patrons.

GED® TEST TIP

When you are reading the passages for the extended-response questions, ask yourself: What is the writer's conclusion?

In question 1, choice **(1)** is correct. The writer focuses on secondhand smoke throughout. In question 2, choice **(2)** is correct. The writer uses the information about secondhand smoke as support for the claim that smoking should be banned inside restaurants. In question 3, choice **(2)** is correct. The writer mentions that cancer-causing carcinogens can be breathed in easily in enclosed areas as the premise for how smoking indoors can be dangerous to others.

PRACTICE 2

Directions: For each passage, answer the questions about topic, conclusions, and assumptions.

Passage 1

Some U.S. representatives advocate a bill requiring all young people to perform two years of military service by the age of 25. Proponents of the bill argue that this will not only prepare the U.S. military for any potential threat from other nations but will also build a greater spirit of patriotism among U.S. citizens. Citizens will be able to appreciate the service of the military and acquire a deeper respect toward honoring their country. However, making service a requirement for all citizens will have the opposite effect; people will feel burdened and resentful toward their government. Instead of focusing on increasing participation in the military, the government should more heavily promote volunteer programs to encourage citizens to help the poor or marginalized within their communities.

1. What is the writer's topic?

    _____

    _____

2. The writer's conclusion about the topic is

    _____

    _____

3. What is the writer's unstated assumption about the topic?

    _____

    _____

Passage 2

To best protect children from being subjected to portrayals of violence, we must reduce the amount of violence that is present in video games. Numerous studies done by various groups show a positive correlation between video game usage and violence.

Many people consider violence in video games a recent trend, but one of the earliest and most controversial video games was Death Race, released in 1976. In this game, the players controlled cars that ran over gremlins. The game was later pulled from stores due to public outcry. With the successful protest against Death Race as a model, we should be as proactive now to reduce or eliminate violence in video games.

4. What is the writer's topic?

    _____

5. What is the writer's conclusion about the topic?

    _____

    _____

6. What is the writer's unstated assumption about the topic?

    _____

    _____

Answers and explanations start on page 647.

Develop a Thesis Statement

You have been reading and analyzing writers' arguments. Now it is your turn to develop a response to what writers have to say.

Once you have unpacked the prompt and read the reading passages, you will construct a **thesis statement** for your writing. This is your central argument. It differs from an **opinion** because it makes a claim that you will defend with evidence from the text.

A thesis statement does the following:
  • makes your argument clear
  • provides the reader with a road map of what you will be discussing

▶ Compare these two statements about the clean coal selections from page 148. Label the thesis statement with *TS* and the opinion with *O*.

_____ I think that Passage A is better than Passage B because it does a good job of explaining the new technologies and reminds us that coal is responsible for half of our electricity.

_____ I think that Passage B makes a better argument because it backs up its conclusion with information about overuse of water, mountaintop removal, and potential mercury poisoning.

The first statement should have *O* for opinion next to it because it is an assertion without any support. It is **subjective**—in that it tells what the reader likes, not what ideas the passage presents. It also repeats the **irrelevant** point—that half of our electricity depends on coal. While that may be factually true, it is **off-topic** when discussing whether or not coal can be a clean source of energy.

The second statement should have *TS* next to it because it meets the criteria for a thesis statement: it makes a claim and demonstrates that the writing that follows will discuss **specific** and **relevant** support for the claim.

Keep in mind that your conclusion may need to recognize a limitation or a problem. That problem may be contained in the passage writer's **unstated assumption**. For Passage B on page 148, the writer has already decided that the notion of clean coal is deceptive. You may strengthen your thesis statement by acknowledging and dealing with a problem.

> Even though the writer of Passage B is biased against the idea of clean coal, I believe that he makes the stronger argument. He backs up his conclusions with specific information about the environmental impact of today's coal-mining processes.

Key Ideas

• A thesis statement makes a claim and indicates that the passage will support the claim with specific and relevant information.

• A thesis statement differs from an opinion, which is a feeling or belief about the topic of the passage.

• A thesis statement is strengthened if it confronts any problems in a passage.

GED® TEST TIP

Although writers have different approaches, it is best to introduce your extended response with your thesis statement. This will let a reader know your position right away. Also, come back to your thesis statement as you write. This will keep you on track.

PRACTICE 3

Directions: Read each paragraph. Write a thesis statement for a possible response to each.

ADVERTISING FOR PRESCRIPTION DRUGS ON TV

Sit down to enjoy any television show today, and you'll find that almost every other commercial seems to be pushing a prescription drug. Although this form of direct-to-consumer (DTC) advertising of prescription medication has become commonplace in American programming, it remains a relatively new development in the medical world. In fact, the practice is currently legal in only two countries, the United States and New Zealand. Patient advocates and those who wish to maintain high standards of healthcare argue that DTC advertising should be eliminated altogether. Advertising prescription medications on television creates a popular demand for the drugs, and it may lead individuals to pressure their health-care providers for treatments that are inappropriate or even dangerous. At the same time, because prescription commercials must name all potential side effects of a certain medication, the ads may frighten other individuals away from using drugs that are both safe and effective for the general public. While such DTC advertisements serve to increase the profits of drug companies, they do little to ensure that the public is better educated about its health-care choices.

1. What is the writer's argument about prescription drug advertising on TV?_____

_____

2. Write a thesis statement in response to the argument. State your position and indicate how you will support it.

_____

_____

_____

MANY AMERICANS DON'T SPEAK A SECOND LANGUAGE

In an era in which people from different continents can connect in seconds by phone, email, or videochat, there is a growing demand for individuals who can speak multiple languages. Additionally, rapid immigration, particularly (in recent years) from Spanish- and Chinese-speaking countries, has ensured that America's population becomes more multilingual every day. Despite this, the majority of Americans are still fluent in American English only and know just a few key phrases of another language for polite but limited exchanges. With almost 18 percent of the country's population citing languages other than English as their primary tongues, many Americans recognize that their inability to speak a foreign language fluently places them at a disadvantage. Particularly in the fields of technology, business, education, and medicine, those who can competently communicate in the native languages of their peers, clients, students, or patients, respectively, will be better equipped to find common ground, work collaboratively, make advances, and build deeper relationships. To remain competitive both at home and internationally, Americans must make foreign language fluency the keystone of a well-rounded education.

3. What is the writer's argument about Americans not knowing a second language?

_____

_____

_____

4. Write a thesis statement in response to the argument. State your position and indicate how you will support it.

_____

_____

Answers and sample thesis statements start on page 647.

WRITING ABOUT TEXT

Collect Supporting Evidence

Key Ideas

- Formulate your thesis statement and collect supporting evidence while you read by using the tools provided.
- Gather supporting evidence that is specific and ties back to your thesis statement.
- Avoid facts that are interesting but not relevant to your central argument.

Once you have formulated your thesis statement, you need to use **evidence** from the passage or passages to support your claim. You should preview the **prompt** before you read the passage or passages. That benefit of this strategy is that you can:

- formulate your thesis statement while you are reading
- gather specific and relevant evidence to support your thesis

How can you gather information while you are reading? The computer-based GED® Test provides you with two essential tools for gathering evidence:

- an online **highlighter** that you can use to mark specific facts and examples to use in your response
- an offline **write-on board and erasable marker** that you can use to write your thesis statement and to take notes as you read

---

Thesis statement: Family time is a thing of the past because too many distractions interfere with conversation and other interactions.

Practice gathering evidence with the passage below. Circle specific pieces of evidence that support the thesis statement above.

> I know it sounds corny, but I miss the way my family was together when I was growing up. Even though Mom and Dad worked, we usually had breakfast together. Now, I work the night shift and sleep in the morning, while my husband is too harried with getting the kids to eat and making their lunches to get a preview of their day.
>
> After school, our kids have part-time jobs, and everyone gets home at different times. Even though I have dinner ready before I leave at 8:00 p.m., someone is doing homework, someone is on the Internet, and someone is texting friends that he or she saw an hour before. I can't remember the last time we all ate together and had a conversation. Even when I try to organize a movie night, it seems that one of us has social or work obligations. We all love each other, but it is hard to have what we can call family time. Thank goodness for holidays and vacations when we can slow down and enjoy each other.

Evidence statements that support the thesis statement:

- Breakfast time is hectic and one parent is asleep.
- After school, people are working or engaged in distractions.
- Family members don't eat dinner together.
- Not everyone is available for common activities, like movie night.

GED® TEST TIP

When you cite the writer's evidence, use phrases such as "The passage stated . . ."; "In the text . . ."; and "One example from the text is . . ."

PRACTICE 4

Directions: Read the prompt, the reading selection, and the writer's conclusion. List three pieces of supporting evidence from the passage that you could use in a response to the prompt. Add one piece of supporting evidence from your own experience or observations. <u>You will not be writing a response to this prompt</u>.

Drinking Age Prompt

The writer of this passage has a position on keeping the minimum legal drinking age at 21. Take a position in response to the writer's argument, using relevant and specific information from the selection to support your response.

The Case for Keeping the Minimum Drinking Age at 21

We owe it to young adults, teens, and children to keep the minimum drinking age right where it is: at 21. The dangers of alcohol are often overlooked due to the fact that it is not a prohibited substance, but make no mistake: it is eminently dangerous, particularly to our youth.

In larger doses—consistent with binge drinking—alcohol wreaks havoc on the sensitive chemistry of the brain. The feast-and-famine pattern of drinking that is typical of teenage drinkers can lead to permanent damage to the prefrontal cortex, the part of the brain responsible for planning and decisions. Since this portion of the brain continues to develop later in life, younger brains are particularly vulnerable to the effects of alcohol. Even in moderate doses, it causes long-term damage to the heart, the liver, and the stomach.

Proponents of a lower drinking age maintain that the allure of the taboo of alcohol encourages abuse among youth. The United Kingdom, however, has a long history of social drinking, and the legal drinking age is 18 in bars and 16 in restaurants; despite this, alcohol-related deaths had doubled in the U.K. in the decade before 2008. Indeed, a 2008 BBC documentary ranked alcohol as the fifth most dangerous drug in the U.K., ahead of speed, LSD, ecstasy, and cannabis.

As a nation, we recognized the dangers that alcohol represented to our citizens and communities when we united to pass a constitutional amendment against it a century ago. That experiment was abandoned only due to challenges of enforcement, but Al Capone could never have built a crime empire on the dimes of 18- to 20-year-olds alone. We owe it to our youth—and the future of our nation—to protect their brains and their lives.

Writer's Conclusion

The conclusion is that despite some reasons for lowering the legal drinking age, it should remain at 21.

1. Three pieces of evidence used in the passage to support this conclusion are . . .
   a. The passage states that _____
   _____
   _____

   b. Another fact from the passage is
   _____
   _____

   c. In support of this position, the text further says that _____
   _____
   _____

2. I (agree/disagree) with the position of this piece.

3. One piece of personal evidence I would use to support my position is _____
   _____
   _____
   _____

Answers begin on page 648.

Plan Your Response

You will have 45 minutes to complete the Extended-Response activity. An online clock at the top of your screen will let you know how much time you have left. Check it as you work through your response. You want to use that time wisely, and the best thing you can do is to take 10 minutes for **prewriting**, or planning, what you are going to write.

Successful test takers do this type of planning. It ensures that you understand the prompt, write a thesis statement, gather the relevant evidence, and have your ideas in place before you begin to write.

Extended-Response Strategy

This **Extended-Response Strategy** will maximize your ability to use the 45 minutes efficiently and effectively. As you work through the rest of this unit, practice managing each stage of the strategy.

Plan: 10 minutes

- Preview the writing prompt.
- Read the passage(s), highlighting or making notes of key details on the write-on board.
- Use the write-on board to write your thesis statement and plan your response with either an outline or an idea map

Draft: 25 minutes

- Write a thesis statement as the introduction to your response.
- Use your plan, citing specific evidence from the text to support your ideas.
- Provide other relevant information based on your own knowledge and perspective.
- Write a closing that summarizes your position or restates the thesis statement in another way.

Revise: 10 minutes

- Reread your thesis statement and review your response to make sure your response stayed focused on the prompt.
- Use the **Revision Questions** on page 166 to improve the response.
- Use the **Editing Questions** on page 168 to correct errors.

Key Ideas

- Take ten minutes to unpack the prompt, read the passage(s), and plan your response.
- As you read the passages, develop your thesis statement and collect supporting evidence with the online highlighter or by taking notes.
- Plan your response by either outlining or mapping the key ideas that you will use in the response.

GED® TEST TIP

Follow through on all of the planning steps before you write. You will have plenty of time to execute your plan, and your score will be higher if you have thought your response through and mapped it out.

Prewriting Strategies

Two of the most useful prewriting strategies for any kind of writing, including evidence-based writing, are outlining and mapping. Look at both methods of grouping ideas based on the same thesis statement.

> **Thesis statement:** *People need both close friends and acquaintances because they meet our social needs in different ways.*

An **outline** depicts each main topic by using a system of numbers and letters stressing a logical progression of ideas. Here is an outline based on the thesis statement above.

I. Benefits of close friends

    a. Will always be there for you

    b. Can always be yourself with them

    c. Can have intimate conversations that are satisfying but confidential

    d. Stand the test of time

II. Benefits of acquaintances

    a. Add variety to your life

    b. Expand your world

III. Acquaintances fulfill some special needs

    a. Social needs—if you can't see closest friends every day

    b. Networking needs—when you need to search for a job, find a new day care provider, etc.

    c. Can make a party or other social event more interesting

An **idea map** uses a drawing to visually group ideas. To make a map, write your main idea in the center. Then draw lines from there to your main topics. From there, you attach the supporting ideas.

PRACTICE 5

Directions: Follow these steps to plan a response. You should allow <u>10 minutes</u> for this task.

- Read the writing prompt to understand your task.
- Read the passage. Think about your thesis statement. Underline and take notes on key points that you will want to summarize or respond to.
- Write a thesis statement based on responding to the prompt and the passage.
- Make an outline and an idea map based on the selection.

Family Pets Writing Prompt

The writer of this passage explains the reasons a family should not own a pet. Read the selection and take a stand for or against the author's viewpoint, using relevant and specific information from the selection to support your response.

When you are trying to decide whether or not to buy a household pet, you need to weigh the pros and cons of doing so. Your children will make heartfelt pleas for an animal and will make wild claims about what they will do to help. However, the negative reasons outweigh the positive ones in terms of time, money, and inconvenience.

One major disadvantage is that you simply will have more household chores. You will need to take the pet on walks or clean out a box, cage, or fish bowl. Trust me. I've done them all. You will have to buy food regularly, sometimes even specialty food for particular pets or aging or sick animals. Finally, ongoing cleanup is needed for animals that shed fur, feathers, or skin.

There are other inconveniences as well for you and your family. You need specialized knowledge to care properly for the pet's health and safety. You will make more trips to the vet than you do to the doctor's office. This gets expensive. It can be time-consuming and expensive to go away for a weekend or a vacation, unless you have a cousin or a friend who owes you a favor.

Owning a pet may also create unexpected problems for family and friends. Some people are allergic to animals and might suffer an adverse reaction when they come to your home. Also, if a new baby arrives in the house, the animal may express its jealousy in unwelcome ways.

I do have to recognize the positive side of having a pet. Animals can be great companions and return your love unconditionally. They can provide security (or at least a sense of security). Also, that walking I belittled at the outset can actually be good exercise. Finally, I have to admit that with all of the work involved, caring for an animal is still less work than taking care of a child.

On balance, I think the wisest course of action for a family is to forgo the joys of pet ownership. The children will get over their discontent and find something else that fires their interest. The time and money saved can be put to different uses, which hopefully will give you satisfaction and companionship as well.

1. **Thesis Statement** According to the prompt, you are to take a position in agreement or disagreement with the writer of "Family Pets." Decide what you think and write your thesis statement below.

I. I think that the writer's position on owning a family pet is _____

because _____

_____

Then, on Test Day, either write an outline or make an idea map. Practice both approaches on this page.

2. **Outline** Write an outline, using this as a model. **Keep your outline; you will use it in Lesson 6.**

Also address related reasoning issues, either by stating and contradicting the **counterargument** (main argument against your position) and/or by addressing the writer's **faulty reasoning** (if any).

   I. Thesis statement
  II. Main supporting reason related to the text
 III. Another supporting reason related to the text
 IV. Another supporting reason related to the text
  V. Related arguments
     A. Counterargument
        i. Argument against my position
       ii. My rejection of the counterargument, with example
     B. Writer's faulty reasoning (if any)
        i. Why the writer's reasoning is faulty
       ii. Supporting example

3. **Idea Map** Make a map of your response to the passage. Use facts and evidence from the passage as well as your own ideas. Draw it on a sheet of paper. **Keep your map; you will use it in Lesson 6.**

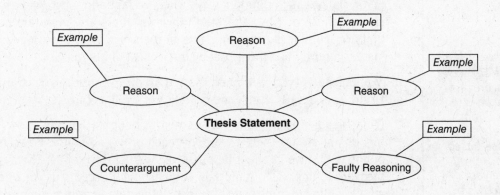

4. **Reflect** Which way worked better for you—outline or map? Practice both until you find the method that will work best for you on the test.

Sample responses start on page 648.

WRITING ABOUT TEXT

Draft Your Response

You have practiced the first part of the **Extended-Response Strategy: Planning**. Once you have planned your writing, the next stage is to **draft** your response. You should take about 25 minutes to do the following:

- Use your thesis statement to **introduce** your argument and how you intend to support it.
- Use your plan to write the **body** of your response, **citing specific evidence from the text** to support your ideas.
- Provide **additional relevant information** based on your own knowledge and perspective.
- Consistently **check back** with your thesis statement to make sure that you are staying on track.
- Write a **closing** that summarizes your position or restates the thesis statement in another way.

Review the planning on page 157 for writing on the topic of close friends and acquaintances. See how that planning was used to draft the writing below. (Note that an underlined **topic sentence** introduces each paragraph.)

An **introduction** lays out your argument and how you will support it:

<u>People need both close friends and acquaintances because they meet our social needs in different ways.</u> The special bond a person has with close friends can't be replicated. However, there are important needs that acquaintances can fulfill, and, in their own way, these needs are just as important as those met by the closest of friends.

Body paragraphs (you will need more than one) elaborate on your support with evidence, details, facts, and related personal examples.

<u>Close friendships certainly have numerous benefits.</u> For one thing, loyal friends are always there to support each other, no matter what. A big bonus is that we can just be ourselves with close friends. There is no pressure to impress or entertain someone who accepts us for who we are. Some friendships last years, becoming deeper and more meaningful with time. For example, even though I am now 35, my best friend from high school and I are still in touch, sharing stories about our two-year-old boys.

A **closing paragraph** restates your main point to reinforce it.

<u>So while it is important to have close friends, it is really rewarding to have a wide circle of acquaintances as well.</u> Even though the quality of the relationship may not be as deep, these people broaden our lives, experiences, and networks to enrich our experiences and help us to grow.

Key Ideas

- Take 25 minutes to draft your response.
- Use your thesis statement to begin your introductory paragraph and to keep you focused as you write.
- Write several body paragraphs based on the facts, details, and evidence in your outline or idea map.
- Wrap up the response with a concluding paragraph that reinforces your thesis.

GED® TEST TIP

One key to a good score on the Extended Response is to cite specific evidence from the reading passage(s). This is called an "evidence-based" writing activity because you are expected to base your response on evidence from the texts.

PRACTICE 6.1

Part A: Introduction

Directions: Practice writing an introduction based on the prompt and passage from page 158 and your planning from page 159. Write your introduction on a computer if possible. Save the file as *Family Pets Introduction*. If it is not possible to write it on a computer, compose your introduction neatly on paper so that you can revise it later.

Family Pets Writing Prompt

The writer of this passage explains the reasons a family should not own a pet. Read the selection and take a stand for or against the author's position, using relevant and specific information from the selection to support your response.

- Begin with <u>a topic sentence</u> that summarizes your thesis statement from page 159.
- Support your topic sentence with either
  - a preview of the main points you will be covering based on your outline or idea map; or
  - an example, description, or personal story—tied to the thesis statement—that will interest the reader.

Part B: Concluding Statement

Directions: Practice writing a concluding statement based on the prompt above and your planning from page 159. Write your conclusion on a computer if possible. Save the file as *Family Pets Conclusion*. If writing it on a computer is not possible, compose the concluding statement neatly on paper.

- Restate your thesis statement from page 159 in different words. (Don't just repeat what your reader has already read.)
- Make a statement that answers the question "So what?" Give your reader a reason to care about your argument.
- Don't introduce new arguments but leave the reader with something to think about that wraps up the paper.

Sample responses start on page 649.

PRACTICE 6.2

Directions: Plan and draft an extended response to the prompt below and the passage on the facing page. Write your response on a computer if possible. If you cannot, write neatly on paper so that you can revise it later.

Step 1—Plan: <u>Take 10 minutes</u> to read the prompt and the passage. Under the prompt, make an outline *or* draw an idea map to organize the following:

- your thesis statement
- your main points and <u>supporting evidence</u> from the passage
- counterarguments and your response *or* faulty reasoning in the passage

Step 2—Draft: <u>Take 25 minutes</u> to draft your response, which will include the following:

- an introductory statement with your thesis statement as the topic sentence
- body paragraphs, with your reasons accompanied by supporting evidence from the text
  - use phrases such as "As the writer says . . . ," "The information in the passage states . . . ," "This is supported in the passage by . . ."
- a concluding statement wrapping up the piece

It would be best to write the response on a computer. If that is not possible, write it out on a piece of paper. **Save your response, since you will be revising and editing it in Lesson 7.**

Cell Phone Writing Prompt

The passage addresses controversy about cell phone use. The Federal Communications Commission has determined that radiation from cell phones has no adverse effects. However, some studies raise questions about traffic safety issues and the long-term health effects of cell phone use.

In your response, compare the arguments in the reading selection and take a position on cell phone safety. Use relevant and specific information to support your response.

K Writing About Text

Cell Phones: Risky or Safe?

1 The Federal Communications Commission has determined that there is not enough evidence to link cell phones to cancer. But that does not mean cell phones are 100 percent safe. Many risks and unknowns are connected to the use of mobile phones. You should be aware of those risks and take steps to protect yourself.

2 Cell phones emit types of radiation that can penetrate several inches into the brain. These types of radiation are not normally associated with cancer, and most scientific studies show that frequent cell phone users do not have an increased risk of tumors. But a few scientists claim to have found a connection between mobile phones and a type of brain cancer known as glioma. Even a small chance of brain cancer should make you very nervous.

3 Also, that chance of cancer may increase in time. Mobile phones were very rare before the late 1990s. If the risk of phone-related disease increases sharply after 20 or 30 years of constant use, we might only find out after millions of people get sick. It's true that there is no increased illness observed among people who have worked at radio towers for 30 years or more, but cell phones are held much closer to the body than radio equipment is.

4 Finally, people who think their cell phones are completely safe may use them even when doing so is not wise. Being able to contact emergency services from anywhere is a major advantage of modern technology, but being distracted by that technology can cause accidents. Calling or texting while driving or operating machinery is dangerous, no matter how "safe" a piece of equipment your phone may be.

5 Be cautious with your cell phone. You may find that you need it to function in today's modern society, but your health and well-being are too important to risk through careless use of this technology. Do not assume that today's science proves that your phone is completely free of danger.

The *Extended Response Evaluation Guide* appears on page 722.

PRACTICE 6.3

Directions: Plan and draft an extended response to the prompt and the paired passages on the facing page. Write your response on a computer, if possible. If you cannot, write neatly on a sheet of paper so that you can revise it later.

Step 1—Plan: Take 10 minutes to read the prompt below and the passages. Take notes as you read, or underline evidence that you will want to use. Make an outline *or* an idea map to organize:

- your thesis statement
- your main points and supporting evidence from the passages
- counterarguments and your response *or* faulty reasoning in either of the passages

Step 2—Draft: Take 25 minutes to draft your response with:

- an introductory statement with your thesis statement as the topic sentence
- body paragraphs, with your reasons accompanied by supporting evidence from the text
- a concluding statement wrapping up the piece

It would be best to write the response on a computer. If that is not possible, write it out on paper. **Save your response, since you will be revising and editing it on pages 177 and 179.**

Gettysburg Address Writing Prompt

Abraham Lincoln's Gettysburg Address is renowned as one of the most significant speeches of all time. Delivered in the midst of a brutal civil war, this address places that war in the context of U.S. history—past, present, and future. However, it was not universally acclaimed at the time, as shown by the excerpt from the *Chicago Times* newspaper.

Read both of the passages closely. Take a stand on which passage does a better job of explaining the significance of the Battle of Gettysburg's casualties. There were a total of more than 45,000 casualties on both sides, Union and Confederacy.

Use relevant and specific information from both passages to support your response.

Abraham Lincoln's Gettysburg Address

Fourscore and seven years ago our fathers brought forth on this continent a new nation, conceived in liberty and dedicated to the proposition that all men are created equal. Now we are engaged in a great civil war, testing whether that nation or any nation so conceived and so dedicated can long endure. But in a larger sense, we cannot dedicate, we cannot consecrate, we cannot hallow this ground. The brave men, living and dead who struggled here have consecrated it far above our poor power to add or detract. The world will little note nor long remember what we say here, but it can never forget what they did here. It is for us the living rather to be dedicated here to the unfinished work which they who fought here have thus far so nobly advanced. It is rather for us to be here dedicated to the great task remaining before us—that from these honored dead we take increased devotion to that cause for which they gave the last full measure of devotion—that we here highly resolve that these dead shall not have died in vain, that this nation under God shall have a new birth of freedom, and that government of the people, by the people, for the people shall not perish from the earth.

—Abraham Lincoln, November 19, 1863

Critical Review of the Gettysburg Address

. . . The President's exhibition . . . was an insult at least to the memories of a part of the dead, whom he was there professedly to honor—in its misstatement of the cause for which they died, it was a perversion of history so flagrant that the most extended charity cannot regard it as otherwise than willful. As a refutation. . . . we copy certain clauses in the Federal constitution:

"Representatives and direct taxes shall be apportioned among the several States which may be included in this Union, according to their respective numbers, which shall be determined by adding to the whole number of free persons, including those bound to service for a term of years, and excluding Indians not taxed, three-fifths of all other persons.

"The migration or importation of such persons as any of the States now existing shall think proper to admit shall not be prohibited by the Congress prior to the year 1808, but a tax or duty may be imposed on such importation, not exceeding ten dollars for each person. . . . No amendment to the constitution, made prior to 1808, shall affect the preceding clause.

"No person held to service or labor in one State under the laws thereof, escaping into another, shall, in consequence of any law or regulation therein, be discharged from such service or labor, but shall be delivered up on claim of the party to whom such service or labor may be due."

Do these provisions in the constitution dedicate the nation to "the proposition that all men are created equal"? Mr. Lincoln occupies his present position by virtue of this constitution, and is sworn to the maintenance and enforcement of these provisions. It was to uphold this constitution, and the Union created by it, that our officers and soldiers gave their lives at Gettysburg. How dared he, then, standing on their graves, misstate the cause for which they died, and libel the statesmen who founded the government?

Excerpted from the *Chicago Times*,
November 23, 1863

Evaluation criteria begins on page 722.

Revise and Edit Your Response

WRITING ABOUT TEXT

Key Ideas

- Take ten minutes to revise and edit your response.
- Reread the response to improve the clarity of your arguments; sufficiency of evidence from the text; and organization of sentences, paragraphs, and the entire piece.
- Use the delete, copy, and paste features on the computer to make these revisions.

GED® TEST TIP

When you practice revising before you take the test, read your drafts out loud. This will help you to "hear" weaknesses in your organization, sentence structure, and word choice.

Revising Your Work

Once you have completed your draft, you need to **revise**. You should take about five of the ten remaining minutes to read over your response and make improvements by using the copy, delete, and paste functions on the computer. Ask yourself:

- Does the introductory paragraph contain the **thesis statement** and lay out the main point of my response?
- Does each paragraph have **one main idea**, begin with a **topic sentence**, and support the thesis statement?
- Is there **specific and relevant supporting evidence from the text** for each main idea?
- Have I assessed the **validity** of the arguments in the passages?
- Is there a **clear flow of ideas** from one paragraph to the next, using transitional words, phrases, and ideas?
- Are there any **irrelevant ideas or sentences** that can be removed?
- Are there any **short, choppy sentences** that could be combined?
- Can I improve my **word choice** to be more specific or interesting?
- Is there a concluding paragraph that **restates and reinforces** the thesis?

Read the writing sample below and review the revisions that were made by hand to improve the draft. Think about why each change was made.

A job is much more pleasant when you like and admire your supervisor. A good supervisor must have excellent communication skills and must make it a priority to help workers get ahead. *Communication is a key part of management.* Supervisors need to give clear directions to spare the workers many hours of frustration. In addition, supervisors should be confident *and decisive.* ~~They should also be decisive.~~ Finally, supervisors should be as honest as possible. Once they make a decision, they should stick to it, so *that* everyone knows what the policy is.

Good bosses want to see their workers progress. Therefore, supervisors should give lots of encouragement and reward workers who display initiative and problem-solving abilities. *Also,* Supervisors should offer opportunities for workers to improve their skills *and education*.

PRACTICE 7.1

A. Directions: Read the response below, and revise the problems in sentence structure and organization. Try to complete your revisions in five minutes, but use more time if needed.

Most of us are aware of the consequences of speeding, which range from receiving a speeding ticket to getting into an accident. A quick survey of any highway will show that many drivers exceed the speed limit. Why do people speed? One common reason is that people do not think they will suffer any consequences. If they have never been stopped by the police or crashed their car, they don't see any reason to worry.

People simply need to get somewhere in a hurry. They realize that they are speeding but they have such a need to arrive on time that they don't care. They've got ants in their pants. A final reason is lack of respect for other drivers, one driver who is speeding makes road conditions less safe for everyone. Drivers who act as though they are in the Indy 500 they have no regard for the safety of others.

We know that people speed because of impatience and they don't fear the consequences. Another reason is no respect. Let's figure out what will make them stop.

B. Directions: Revise the response that you wrote on the topic below on page 162. Time yourself. Try to complete the revision in ten minutes. Save your work. You will use the response again.

> ### Cell Phone Writing Prompt
>
> The passage addresses controversy about cell phone use. The Federal Communications Commission has determined that radiation from cell phones has no adverse effects. However, some studies raise questions about traffic safety issues and the long-term health effects of cell phone use.
>
> In your response, compare the arguments in the reading selection and take a position on cell phone safety. Use relevant and specific information to support your response.

C. Directions: After you check your answers to the exercise above, complete the strategy box below. If you need more practice with specific skills and concepts, review "Connecting Ideas" on pages 136–147 and "Polishing Your Writing" on pages 174–183.

MY TEST-TAKING STRATEGY

I need to pay special attention to these areas of revising. (Check all that apply.)

❏ Writing introductory paragraphs	❏ Putting in paragraph breaks
❏ Writing concluding paragraphs	❏ Remembering to use transitions
❏ Writing topic sentences	❏ Deleting irrelevant details
❏ Adding support to body paragraphs	❏ Combining short, choppy sentences
❏ Putting sentences in logical places	❏ Making sure each sentence makes sense

---

Answers and explanations start on page 649.

Key Ideas

- Edit your work to make sure there are no errors in sentence structure, grammar, usage, or mechanics.
- An editing checklist can help you find errors as you practice for the Reasoning through Language Arts test.

Editing Your Work

Once you're satisfied with the organization and clarity of your essay, check for other errors in sentence structure, as well as errors in grammar, usage, and mechanics. To edit your response, take another five minutes to reread your response, and ask yourself these questions:

- Are all the sentences complete?
- Are there any run-ons or comma splices that should be corrected?
- Are all lists parallel in structure?
- Are nouns and pronouns used correctly?
- Are verb forms and tenses used correctly?
- Does the subject of each sentence match the verb?
- Is the punctuation correct?
- Is capitalization used correctly?
- Are all words correctly spelled?
- Are there any inappropriate word choices?

▶ Read the paragraph below, and notice how the errors were corrected.

A job is much more pleasant when you like and admire your supervisor. A good supervisor must have excellent communication skills, and must make it a priority to help workers get ahead. In addition, a supervisor should be a fair and moral person.

Clear communication is a key part of management. Supervisors need to give clear directions, to spare the workers many hours of frustration. In addition, supervisors should be confident and decisive. Once they make a decision, they should stick to it so everyone knows what the policy is. Finally, supervisors should be as honest as possible.

Good bosses want to see their workers progress. Therefore, supervisors should give lots of encouragement and reward workers who display initiative and problem-solving abilities. Also, supervisors should offer opportunities for workers to improve their skills, and education.

Top-notch supervisors have a high level of moral character. They reward honesty and fire workers who have lied or cheated. Some bosses keep employees who lie if their skills are valuable to the company, but I feel that this is an example of poor management.

Knowing the qualities of a good supervisor is important for both bosses and workers. The next time you apply for a job, think about whether your prospective boss is a moral person and a clear communicator who wants you to succeed.

PRACTICE 7.2

A. Directions: Read the body of the writing sample. Correct errors in sentence structure, grammar, usage, mechanics, and word choice. Try to finish editing in five minutes, but use more time if needed.

One common reason for speeding is that people don't think they will suffer any consequences. If they have never been stopped by the Police or crashed there car they don't see any reason too worry.

Another reason is that people simply are needing to get somewhere in a hurry. They realize that they are speeding, but they have such a need to arrive on time that they dont care. There impatience get the better of them.

A final reason is lack of respect for other drivers, one driver who is speeding make road conditions less safe for everyone. Drivers who act as though they are in the indy 500 got no regard for the safety of others.

B. Directions: Edit the response that you wrote on the topic below, which you saw on page 162. Time yourself and try to complete the edit in five minutes.

Cell Phone Writing Prompt

The passage addresses controversy about cell phone use. The Federal Communications Commission has determined that radiation from cell phones has no adverse effects. However, some studies raise questions about traffic safety issues and the long-term health effects of cell phone use.

In your response, compare the arguments in the reading selection and take a position on cell phone safety. Use relevant and specific information to support your response.

C. Directions: After you check your answers to the exercise above, complete the strategy box below. If you need more practice with specific skills and concepts, review the sections in the book that correspond to these skills.

MY TEST-TAKING STRATEGY

I need to pay special attention to these areas of editing. (Check all that apply.)

❏ Making sure my sentences are complete
❏ Correcting run-ons and comma splices
❏ Using parallel structure
❏ Using nouns and pronouns correctly
❏ Using verb forms and tenses correctly

❏ Matching subjects and verbs
❏ Making sure punctuation is correct
❏ Using capitalization correctly
❏ Making sure words are spelled correctly
❏ Choosing appropriate words

Answers and explanations start on page 649.

WRITING ABOUT TEXT PRACTICE

Part A

Directions: Plan and draft an extended response to the prompt below and the passage on the facing page. Write your response on a computer if possible. If you cannot, write neatly on paper so that you can revise it later.

Step 1—Plan: <u>Take 10 minutes</u> to read the prompt and the passage. Under the prompt, make an outline *or* draw an idea map to organize:

- your thesis statement
- your main points and <u>supporting evidence</u> from the passage
- counterarguments and your response *or* faulty reasoning in the passage

Step 2—Draft: <u>Take 25 minutes</u> to draft your response, which will include the following:

- an introduction, with your thesis statement as the topic sentence
- body paragraphs, with your reasons accompanied by supporting evidence from the text
  - use phrases such as "As the writer says . . . ," "The information in the passage states . . . ," "This is supported in the passage by . . ."
- a concluding statement wrapping up the piece

Step 3—Revise and Edit: <u>Take 10 minutes</u> to reread your response to:

- revise to improve organization, cohesion, and clarity of sentences, paragraphs, and the entire piece
- edit to correct errors in sentence structure, grammar, punctuation, capitalization, and spelling

---

Social Networking on the Internet—Positive or Negative?

The passage addresses the serious impact that the explosion of social networking has had on our lives. In recent years, social relations have developed online that allow us to connect with friends or create communities around common interests. Supporters feel that these networks create greater interaction and increased information. Critics say that this trend actually limits social interactions and creates short- and long-term risks for the users.

In your response, compare the arguments in the reading selection and take a position favoring either the benefits or the drawbacks of social networking. Use relevant and specific information to support your response.

"Social Networking on the Internet—Positive or Negative?"

In a hundred years, humanity will look back and try to pinpoint the moment in its history when it overcame the clumsy limits of flesh-and-blood existence. When it does, Internet social networking will stand out as an important change, not just in the ways in which we communicate with each other but also, and perhaps more importantly, in the ways in which we perceive ourselves.

At this primitive moment, our contacts on social networks are still people we have met in person, for the most part. And there was a time when this was natural: you have to choose your friends from the selection available to you. But the menu has changed. The great promise of Internet socialization is that congregation is no longer at the mercy of geography. If I join an online community of checkers enthusiasts whose members are scattered across four continents, our interactions will be little different than if we all lived in the United States. Our shared interest, rather than where our bodies happen to live, is what brings us together.

As our online friendships increasingly supplant our in-person friendships, our online personalities begin to replace our old selves, too. What happens when two-thirds of my acquaintances know me by an invented username rather than by my real name, or by an animated icon of a dancing stickman rather than by my face? The answer: I learn that I can essentially define myself for this group of people. I can be exactly who I want to be.

With time, we will all come to shift to interest-based interactions almost exclusively. If you've always felt alone because you've never been able to find anyone who shares your greatest passion—and that passion happens to be watching macramé competitions—then the Internet opens up a new world of like-minded individuals to you. You'll share experiences, pictures, and tips and live as you never could have 30 years ago, when you would have been forced to endure your isolation.

At the same time, we must ask ourselves: Is this something we want to encourage? One of the great protective mechanisms of the flesh-and-blood version of human communities is shame. As unfair as it may sound to ridicule our poor macramé enthusiast, social disapproval is an important tool for discouraging destructive behavior and extremism. When online communities offer a meeting place for outcasts, the shunning of these tendencies loses its force. It is no coincidence that online communities are the single most fertile recruiting ground for terrorism. And isn't accepting differences in others—rather than surrounding ourselves with homogeneous communities of like-minded friends—an important part of the human experience?

For children of the 20th century, there is something else very alarming in the idea of channeling so many of our interactions through the Internet. In the heyday of the Soviet Union, a video camera in every home was presented as the greatest tool a totalitarian state could wish for. If all my interactions pass through the Internet, won't the government be watching me? Regardless of whether it will or won't, it certainly seems now to have that option.

We also must wonder what will become of our most cherished traits as we transition to an existence of ones and zeroes. As biological beings, we have emotional needs tied to touch and warmth. None of my online friends can give my dancing stickman a hug!

Ultimately, the new possibilities that the online world opens up to us are irresistible and herald a new era of finely tuned communities with unprecedented potential. The challenge will lie in making the most of this new world without losing the vital elements of our nonelectronic human experience.

Evaluation criteria begins on page 722.

Part B

Directions: Develop an extended response to the prompt below and the paired passages on the facing page. Write your response on a computer if possible. If you cannot, write neatly on paper so that you can revise it later.

Step 1—Plan: <u>Take 10 minutes</u> to read the prompt and the passages. Under the prompt, make an outline *or* draw an idea map to organize:

- your thesis statement
- your main points and <u>supporting evidence</u> from the passage
- counterarguments and your response *or* faulty reasoning in the passage

Step 2—Draft: <u>Take 25 minutes</u> to draft your response, which will include the following:

- an introductory statement, with your thesis statement as the topic sentence
- body paragraphs, with your reasons accompanied by supporting evidence from the text
  - use phrases such as "As the writer says . . . ," "The information in the passage states . . . ," "This is supported in the passage by . . ."
- a concluding statement wrapping up the piece

Step 3—Revise and Edit: <u>Take 10 minutes</u> to reread your response and do the following:

- revise to improve organization, cohesion, and clarity of sentences, paragraphs, and the entire piece
- edit to correct errors in sentence structure, grammar, punctuation, capitalization, and spelling

---

Health and Safety on the Job

The first passage presents regulations of the U.S. Occupational Safety and Health Administration (OSHA). The second passage is a newspaper article about workers who successfully sued their employer, claiming that they were fired because they had reported injuries on the job.

Read both the OSHA regulations and the news report carefully. Take a position on whether or not you think that the court decision was correct based on the OSHA guidelines.

Use relevant and specific information from both passages to support your response.

OSHA Standards and Worker Protection

OSHA standards are rules that describe the methods that employers must use to protect their employees from hazards. There are OSHA standards for Construction work, Agriculture, Maritime operations, and General Industry, which are the standards that apply to most worksites. These standards limit the amount of hazardous chemicals workers can be exposed to, require the use of certain safe practices and equipment, and require employers to monitor hazards and keep records of workplace injuries and illnesses. Examples of OSHA standards include requirements to: provide fall protection, prevent trenching cave ins, prevent some infectious diseases, assure that workers safely enter confined spaces, prevent exposure to harmful substances like asbestos, put guards on machines, provide respirators or other safety equipment, and provide training for certain dangerous jobs.

You Cannot Be Punished or Discriminated Against for Using Your OSHA Rights

The OSHA Act protects workers who complain to their employer, OSHA or other government agencies about unsafe or unhealthful working conditions in the workplace or environmental problems. You cannot be transferred, denied a raise, have your hours reduced, be fired, or punished in any other way because you used any right given to you under the OSHA Act. Help is available from OSHA for whistleblowers.

If you have been punished or discriminated against for using your rights, you must file a complaint with OSHA within 30 days of the alleged reprisal for most complaints.

Source: U.S. Occupational Safety and Health Administration

OSHA fines Norfolk Southern $802K for firing workers

The U.S. Occupational Safety and Health Administration announced Monday that it was fining a Norfolk Southern Corp. subsidiary more than $800,000 for firing three workers who had reported injuries on the job.

OSHA, a division of the U.S. Department of Labor, ordered Norfolk Southern Railway Co. to pay the former workers a total of $802,169 in damages. The agency also said the railroad company must clear the workers' disciplinary records and post workplace notices and offer training on whistleblower rights.

"OSHA's investigations have found that the company continues to retaliate against employees for reporting work-related injuries and has effectively created a chilling effect in the railroad industry," the Labor Department said in a news release.

Norfolk Southern spokesman Robin Chapman said the company would appeal the decisions on all three workers before an administrative law judge at the Labor Department.

Two of the three incidents occurred in 2010, according to the agency's release. An engineer in Louisville, Ky., and a conductor in Harrisburg, Pa., were fired after reporting injuries from falls in or near company bathrooms.

Norfolk Southern accused the employees of falsifying their injuries, the agency said. The company also accused the conductor of failing to promptly report the injury. "The day before the injury, the employee had been lauded for excellent performance, highlighted by no lost work time due to injuries in his 35-year career," according to the Labor Department release.

OSHA found that the company hearings for both workers were "flawed." In the case of the engineer, the hearing "was orchestrated to intentionally support the decision to terminate the employee," the release said.

In the third incident, an employee in Greenville, S.C., was fired after he reported being hit by a company truck. Norfolk Southern accused him of "improper performance of duties." The agency found he was treated "disparately in comparison to four other employees involved in the incident," none of whom had reported injuries.

"Firing workers for reporting an injury is not only illegal, it also endangers all workers," David Michaels, an assistant U.S. secretary of labor, said in a statement. "To prevent more injuries, railroad workers must be able to report an injury without fear of retaliation."

Reprinted with permission from *The Virginian-Pilot*.

The *Extended Response Evaluation Guide* appears on page 722.

Strengthen Sentences

Key Ideas

- Read your work as a whole to make sure that it is clear and logical.
- Imagine that you are reading your work for the first time.
- Correct any sentences that have errors in structure or punctuation.

GED® TEST TIP

To prepare for the Extended Response, practice prewriting, drafting, and revising often. Frequent practice will help you feel more comfortable and confident as a writer.

Revising Unclear and Incorrect Sentences

When you write your response, your first step is to get your ideas down. To do this, you follow a prewriting and drafting plan like the ones on pages 148–165. When you are finished drafting, go back and reread what you have written. As you read each sentence, ask yourself:

- Do the ideas in the sentence make sense? If not, how can I make the sentence clearer? Add some words? Drop or move a confusing word or phrase? Insert or delete punctuation? Change the words?
- Is the sentence structure correct? If not, how can I correct it?

Read the paragraph below, and think about how you would revise the errors in clarity and sentence structure. Then compare it with the revised paragraph.

Paragraph with unclear and incorrect sentences:

Working outdoors has many advantages over working indoors. When you are outside you are in contact with nature. You can enjoy the sunshine on your face, hear the birds, and to smell the flowers. You don't have to consult the weather forecast on TV. In contrast, sitting in a climate-controlled cubicle, it is not known whether the sky is sunny or cloudy. Also, most outdoor jobs require you to use your body, that can be a huge advantage. Finally, if you work indoors, you might be sitting down at a desk, and typing all day long. After work, instead of relaxing. You'll probably have to go to the gym to work out.

Paragraph with revised sentence structure:

Working outdoors has many advantages over working indoors. When you are <u>outside, you</u> are in contact with nature. You can enjoy the sunshine on your face, hear the birds, and <u>smell</u> the flowers. You don't have to consult the weather forecast on TV. In contrast, <u>when you sit in a climate-controlled cubicle, you don't know</u> whether the sky is sunny or cloudy. Also, most outdoor jobs require you to use your <u>body, and that</u> can be a huge advantage. Finally, if you work indoors, you might be sitting down at a <u>desk and typing</u> all day long. After work, instead of <u>relaxing, you'll</u> probably have to go to the gym to work out.

Use these **revision marks** when you revise your sentences on paper:

- To delete a word or punctuation mark, cross it out.
- To add a word or punctuation mark, insert a caret (^) in the line where you want it to go, and then write it in above the line.
- To change a word, cross it out and write the new word above it.
- To move a word or phrase, circle it and draw an arrow to its new position.
- To capitalize a letter, draw three lines under it.

PRACTICE 1

A. Directions: Read and revise the sentences. Correct these problems by using revision marks.

☑ fragments, run-ons, and comma splices
☑ incorrect coordination and subordination
☑ misplaced or dangling modifiers
☑ problems in parallel structure

EXAMPLE: It's fun to do a family tree you can learn a lot.

1. First, write down what you know about your family then interview relatives.
2. Videotaping or to record the interviews is a good idea.
3. Ask relatives to provide exact names, dates, and give other details.
4. Making copies of documents such as birth certificates and marriage licenses.
5. Interviewing older family members, they'll often tell you stories you never heard.
6. Record all the information you get and put it in a three-ring binder carefully.
7. Some people use their computers to do genealogy searches, they get very good results.
8. However, one must have the time, the patience, and know-how to use the Internet.
9. If you decide to learn more about your roots don't be surprised to find yourself at a huge family reunion.
10. The whole process of putting together a family tree and contacting long-lost family members.

B. Directions: Read the paragraphs below. Use revision marks to correct problems with sentences.

It was a beautiful day, the blue ocean sparkled in the sunlight. A perfect day for going to the beach. Looking across the sand, two little girls were building a sandcastle and made a moat next to it. Renelle spread out her towel she anchored it with her shoes and beach bag and began to read a magazine. Suddenly she heard a voice. "Are you going to get in the water, or are you just going to lie there?" Renelle looked up, and saw her friend Terry. She laughed softly and she got up and she greeted Terry. Putting on her sandals, the two of them walked across the burning sand to the water's edge.

Renelle loved going to the beach. Going to the beach relaxed her. Going to the beach helped her forget about her problems. It didn't cost money like most other forms of entertainment. Most of Renelle's friends also spent a lot of time at the beach so that was another incentive.

Answers and explanations start on page 649.

Improve Organization

Key Ideas

- Revise your response so that the organization is clear to the reader.
- Make sure that paragraph breaks fall in the right places.
- Check for faulty transitions and irrelevant details.

GED® TEST TIP

When you write a draft on paper, leave wide margins and space between lines so that you can more easily use the revision marks. On a computer, you can use the cut, copy, and paste functions to revise.

Revising Problems in Organization

When you reread your response, you may also need to make changes in organization to make the response clearer to the reader. As you read, ask yourself:

- Is my main idea clear?
- Are there a clear introduction, body of support, and conclusion?
- Is the paragraphing correct? Does each paragraph relate to only one main idea? Should any paragraphs be split into two? Should any be combined?
- Does each paragraph have a topic sentence that tells the main idea? Are any of the other sentences in a place that doesn't make sense? Are there any irrelevant details that should be removed?
- Does the writing flow smoothly from sentence to sentence and from paragraph to paragraph? If not, where can I add transitions?

Read the sample paragraph below. Think about how you would correct the errors in organization. Then compare it with the revised paragraph.

Paragraph with problems in organization:

(1) Many people believe that changes in technology have improved our communication with others. (2) I believe that the opposite is true. (3) So-called technological improvements have led to a marked decline in the quality of interpersonal communication. (4) In the old days, when you called someone, the person was likely to pick up the phone to find out who was calling. (5) Nowadays, screening devices make that unnecessary. (6) By listening to your voice on the answering machine or by seeing your phone number pop up on his caller identification box, the other person can decide that he doesn't care to speak to you. (7) This encourages long games of "phone tag." (8) Television is another example—you can barely get a word out of someone who is glued to the tube.

Paragraphs with revised organization:

(1) Many people believe that changes in technology have improved our communication with others. (2) <u>However</u>, I believe that the opposite is true. (3) So-called technological improvements have led to a marked decline in the quality of interpersonal communication.

(*) <u>Phone use is one area in which communication has suffered.</u> (4) In the old days, when you called someone, the person was likely to pick up the phone to find out who was calling. (5) Nowadays, screening devices make that unnecessary. (6) By listening to your voice on the answering machine or by seeing your phone number pop up on his caller identification box, the other person can decide that he doesn't care to speak to you. (7) This encourages long games of "phone tag."

In the revised paragraphs, the transition *however* was added to sentence 2. The piece was divided into two paragraphs—an introductory paragraph and a body paragraph about phone use. A topic sentence (marked with *) was added. Sentence 8 of the original, which was not related to telephones, was deleted.

Use these symbols to revise essay organization:

- To change whole sentences, use the same marks you used to change words.
- To start a new paragraph, use the paragraph symbol (¶).

PRACTICE 2

A. Directions: Using the revision marks, revise the paragraphs below. One revision has been made for you.

We've all heard countless advertising campaigns warning us not to litter. Yet some people still think nothing of throwing a soda can out of their car window onto the highway or dropping a candy wrapper on the sidewalk. Most of us realize that we are upsetting a delicate ecological balance when we don't dispose of our trash properly. Why do people continue to litter? One reason people litter is that they just don't care about others. It doesn't bother them to leave their trash in front of someone else's apartment building, forcing another person to deal with the problem.

This inconsiderate attitude is also reflected in the refusal to recycle plastic, glass, and newspapers. People figure that they won't be around in the future when the landfills are used up, so who cares? Another possible reason for littering is low self-esteem. If people don't feel good about themselves, they won't be motivated to keep their environment looking attractive. Low self-esteem can cause many other problems, including depression and lack of self-confidence. People who have high self-esteem believe that it's important to keep their home, the planet Earth, clean and beautiful.

B. Directions: Revise the response that you wrote to the Gettysburg Address writing prompt on page 164.

Be sure to check for:

- ☑ clear main idea
- ☑ introduction, body, and conclusion
- ☑ correct paragraphing
- ☑ topic sentences
- ☑ logical placement of sentences
- ☑ irrelevant details that should be removed
- ☑ clear transitions

Save your work. You will use it in the next step of the writing process, editing.

Answers and explanations start on page 650.

Word Choice

Key Ideas

- Use precise words instead of vague ones.
- Express your ideas in as few words as possible.
- When writing a response, use formal language instead of slang.

GED® TEST TIP

When you read your draft, focus on the specific words and ask yourself, "Can I make this clearer or more concise?" If so, revise accordingly to improve your score on the response.

After you have written and revised your response, you will need to edit it. In the editing stage of the writing process, you check for correct grammar, usage, and word choice. You may already have made some organizational changes. The kinds of changes you make when you are editing will be smaller—more like fine-tuning.

Word choice is an important aspect of writing. There are several aspects of word choice to look at when you are editing: using precise words, avoiding wordiness, and avoiding slang.

People often use vague terms when they are speaking. They say things like, "It was a great party!" or "The weather is nice today." General words like *great* and *nice* are okay in conversation because the listener can ask questions such as, "What was so great about the party?" In writing, however, you should try to write specific words that create a clear picture for the reader.

With vague words: Tim took a <u>long</u> hike in the <u>beautiful</u> mountains.
With precise words: Tim took a <u>12-mile</u> hike in the <u>rocky, snowy</u> mountains.

With vague words: He <u>walked</u> through a forest where the ground was <u>covered</u> with pine needles.
With precise words: He <u>meandered</u> through a forest where the ground was <u>carpeted</u> with pine needles.

It's also helpful to your reader if you write concisely and avoid wordiness. Being brief helps the reader focus on your message. If you notice that you have said the same thing twice, cut out the extra words.

Too wordy: Tim's dream and the thing he hopes for most of all is to make a home for himself and live in a cabin in the woods.
More concise: Tim's most cherished dream is to live in a cabin in the woods.

Too wordy: The only thing getting in the way of his having this dream come true is that his wife isn't so sure that it's such a fantastic idea.
More concise: The only obstacle to realizing his dream is his wife's resistance.

Finally, avoid using slang when writing your essay. Though people sometimes use informal language when speaking, essay writing calls for more formal language. Take care to express yourself appropriately.

With slang: Tim is going to <u>hit the road</u> at seven tonight.
With more formal language: Tim is going to <u>leave town</u> at seven tonight.

With slang: He needs a better map because <u>he's totally clueless about</u> directions.
With more formal language: He needs a better map because <u>he has difficulty understanding</u> directions.

PRACTICE 3

A. Directions: Replace each of the underlined words or phrases with more appropriate language. Write your answers on a separate sheet of paper.

1. Families International is a <u>nonprofit organization that does not make any money</u>.

2. We give aid to <u>many</u> children in the Third World every year.

3. These children must endure <u>lousy</u> living conditions.

4. Your donation, even if it is only five <u>bucks</u>, will help a child get food and clothing.

5. Please send your donation <u>as soon and as quickly as possible</u> to the following address.

B. Directions: Edit the paragraphs below for correct grammar and usage, paying special attention to nouns and pronouns, subject-verb agreement, and regular and irregular verbs.

If you ever order merchandise from a catalog, you should be aware of your rights. All companies, regardless of what state they are located in, is required to ship your order within 30 days unless they have advertise a different shipping time. If a company is unable to meet the shipping deadline, they must send you an "Option Notice." You can choose to wait longer or get a refund.

Some consumers complaining about receiving merchandise that they did not order. They were told that companies that engaged in this practice broken the law. If they send you a product you haven't order, it is yours to keep.

If you receive a package that been damaged, don't open it. Write "REFUSED" on the package, and return it to the seller. There's no need to add new postage as long as the package come by regular mail.

C. Directions: Revise the response you wrote to the Gettysburg Address writing prompt on page 164.

Be sure to check for:

☑ Correct use of nouns and pronouns
☑ Correct use of regular and irregular verbs
☑ Subject-verb agreement
☑ Word choice

Answers and explanations start on page 650.

POLISHING YOUR WRITING PRACTICE QUESTIONS

Questions 1 through 5 refer to the following paragraphs.

Gardening for success

(A)

(1) Flowers, herbs, and shrubs can beautify both small and large spaces in your home or yard. (2) In addition, growing your own vegetables can be enjoyable and healthful. (3) If you want to be a successful [Select...▾] you follow some simple guidelines.

(B)

(4) First, determine whether you'll be gardening indoors or outdoors. (5) This might depend on what type of home you live in, or it might depend on the climate. (6) If you live in an apartment building and don't have access to a community garden, an indoor garden might be right for you. (7) An indoor garden is also an [Select...▾] for the plants that you'd like to grow.

(C)

(8) Indoors, you'll need to place your plants near a window where they'll get some sunlight each day. (9) Choose your growing space carefully, whether indoors or outdoors. (10) Outdoors, find a spot that doesn't have a lot of rocks or clay. (11) Likewise, you should choose your plants carefully.

(D)

(12) Investigate various [Select...▾] find out how much sunlight and water they need and what temperature they prefer. (13) You might be surprised to find, for instance, that you shouldn't try to grow basil in a shady side yard or impatiens in full sun. (14) A little extra effort up front will help you avoid common gardening pitfalls and enjoy your garden more.

1. If you want to be a successful [Select...▾] you follow some simple guidelines.

   A. gardener, importantly
   B. gardener, but it's important that
   C. gardener, it's important that
   D. gardener. And it's important that

2. An indoor garden is also an [Select...▾] for the plants that you'd like to grow.

   A. option if you live in a climate that is too extreme
   B. option if one lives in a climate that is not good
   C. option, if you live in a climate that is not good
   D. option if you live in a climate that is not good

3. Which revision would improve the effectiveness of paragraph C?

   A. move sentence 11 to the beginning of paragraph C
   B. move sentence 8 to follow sentence 9
   C. move sentence 8 to follow sentence 10
   D. move sentence 8 to follow sentence 11

4. Which revision would improve the effectiveness of the article?

   A. move sentence 12 to the end of paragraph C
   B. move sentence 3 to the beginning of paragraph B
   C. move sentence 7 to the beginning of paragraph C
   D. move sentence 11 to the beginning of paragraph D

5. Investigate various [Select...▾] find out how much sunlight and water they need and what temperature they prefer.

   A. plants, but
   B. plants or
   C. plants to
   D. plants, and then

Questions 6 through 10 refer to the following paragraphs.

Rowing Across the Atlantic

When I was a child, my grandmother often told me stories about her father. He was born in [Select...▼] the United States when he was 2 years old. His trip to this country was a mystery to me.

"Dad always said he came over in a rowboat," Granny explained. I tried to imagine a 2-year-old boy rowing across the [Select...▼] seemed impossible that he could have done that. [Select...▼] Atlantic Ocean *in a rowboat*?

I had many questions for Granny. "Were his parents with him?" I asked. "No, I think he came by himself," she explained, laughing. Was she [Select...▼]? The stories always ended with Granny wiping tears from her eyes. She had several grandchildren. "Oh, how I wish you had known him," she cried.

6. He was born in [Select...▼] the United States when he was 2 years old.

   A. Wales and had come to
   B. Wales which coming to
   C. Wales which had come to
   D. Wales, which had come to

7. I tried to imagine a 2-year-old boy rowing across the [Select...▼] seemed impossible that he could have done that.

   A. ocean however it
   B. ocean, thus it
   C. ocean. Thus it
   D. ocean; it

8. [Select...▼] Atlantic Ocean *in a rowboat*?

   A. Could he had crossed to
   B. He could have crossed the really big
   C. Could he have crossed the vast
   D. Could he crossed the really big

9. Was she [Select...▼]?

   A. totally pulling my leg
   B. kidding me
   C. totally joking
   D. for real

10. Which sentence should be removed from the last paragraph?

   A. Sentence 10
   B. Sentence 11
   C. Sentence 12
   D. Sentence 13

Southern Gothic Writer

(A)

Flannery O'Connor was a gifted Southern writer. She wrote many short stories and two novels. She is known for writing in a Southern gothic style and exploring topics of religion, ethics, Select... ⌄ explored the dark side of human nature.

(B)

One of O'Connor's most popular stories, "A Good Man is Hard to Find" was written in 1953 and focuses on a man called The Misfit. Select... ⌄ her most shocking story. It raises important questions of good and evil, morality and immorality, and Southern historical issues.

(C)

When Flannery was just 26, she was diagnosed with lupus. The disease that had killed her father. To manage her health, she returned to her family's farm, Andalusia, in Milledgeville, Georgia. There, she lived with her mother Regina and wrote many of her most important works. She delighted in raising birds of all varieties, including peafowl.

(D)

During her time at Andalusia, Select... ⌄ . Although she was only expected to live for five years after her lupus diagnosis, she managed to survive for fourteen.

11. She is known for writing in a Southern gothic style and exploring topics of religion, ethics, Select... ⌄ explored the dark side of human nature.

    A. and morality she also frequently
    B. and morality she also, frequently
    C. and morality frequently
    D. and morality. She also frequently

12. Select... ⌄ her most shocking story.
    A. Many figure this is
    B. Many consider this
    C. Many think it ought to be a
    D. Many reckon this ought to be her

13. When Flannery was just 26, she was diagnosed with lupus. The disease that had killed her father.

    Which is the best way to revise these two sentences?

    A. Switch the order of the two sentences.
    B. Insert the second sentence after the comma in the first sentence.
    C. Combine the two sentences by replacing the period with a comma.
    D. Remove the second sentence.

14. During her time at Andalusia, Select... ⌄ .

    A. Flannery maintained many fulfilling correspondences that gave her the insight into human behavior that is evident in her writing
    B. Flannery also maintained many correspondences with friends, family, and other writers, which is why she had a special insight into human behavior that is displayed in her writing
    C. Flannery also maintained many fulfilling correspondences with friends, family, and other writers which is why she is believed to have had a special insight into human behavior that is in her writing
    D. Flannery maintained many correspondences with friends, family, and other writers which is why she is believed to have had a special insight into human behavior

Questions 15 through 19 refer to the following paragraphs.

Notification of Utility Repairs

Universal Utilities will soon begin repairs of the underground lines in your neighborhood. This [Select...▾] to receive the exceptional service you have come to expect from us.

We will begin by installing a new pipeline under your street. [Select...▾] the smaller line that runs from the street to your home. Lastly we will install a new meter at your home.

This work will require our company's trucks to be in your neighborhood. We apologize for any inconvenience this may cause during peak travel [Select...▾] may experience a temporary disruption in your utility service. [Select...▾]

If you have any questions [Select...▾]. We can be reached by telephone, or you may visit our website. Thank you for allowing us to serve your utility needs.

15. This [Select...▾] to receive the exceptional service you have come to expect from us.

    A. will ensure you continue
    B. will ensure you always continue
    C. is ensuring you always continue
    D. will ensure they always continue

16. [Select...▾] the smaller line that runs from the street to your home.

    A. Than next we will replace
    B. Then we will replace
    C. Then next we will replace
    D. Then next we will have replaced

17. We apologize for any inconvenience this may cause during peak travel [Select...▾] may experience a temporary disruption in your utility service.

    A. times, you
    B. times but you
    C. times. You
    D. times, and so you

18. [Select...▾]

    A. However we will adjust your bill accordingly if your service is interrupts.
    B. However we will adjust your bill accordingly if your service is interrupted.
    C. However we will adjust your bill accordingly thus your service is interrupted.
    D. However, we will adjust your bill accordingly if your service is interrupted.

19. If you have any questions [Select...▾].

    A. about the scheduled repairs. Please contact our office
    B. about the scheduled repairs, please contact our office
    C. about the scheduled repairs please contact our office
    D. , about the scheduled repairs. Please contact our office

Answers and explanations begin on page 650.

USING GRAMMAR CORRECTLY

Noun and Pronoun Agreement

Key Ideas

- A noun names a person, place, thing, or idea.
- A pronoun takes the place of a noun.
- Use subject, object, and possessive pronouns in the proper places.

Using Nouns and Pronouns

A **noun** names a person (such as *woman* or *Anne*), a place (such as *drugstore* or *Florida*), a thing (such as *car* or *Titanic*), or an idea (*truth* or *Buddhism*). A **proper noun** refers to a specific person, place, thing, or idea; a **common noun** is more general. For example, *Anne* is a proper noun; *woman* is a common noun.

A **pronoun** is a word that replaces a noun. The **antecedent** is the noun that is being replaced, as shown below:

EXAMPLE

Steven lost his <u>address book</u>. <u>It</u> held many important phone numbers.
            antecedent   pronoun

There are three types of pronouns: subject, object, and possessive.

EXAMPLES

A **subject pronoun** replaces the subject of a sentence.

<u>Steven</u> called home. <u>He</u> was very worried.
 subject   subject pronoun

An **object pronoun** replaces the object of a verb or of a preposition.
His wife called Steven. She asked <u>him</u> what the problem was.
                              object pronoun (object of a verb)

She and Steven looked for <u>it</u>.
                      object pronoun (object of a preposition)

A **possessive pronoun** replaces a possessive noun.
Steven needed <u>Kelly's</u> number. He called 411 to get <u>her</u> number.
       possessive noun   possessive pronoun

Use this chart for help in remembering the three types of pronouns:

Subject Pronoun: replaces subject	Object Pronoun: replaces object	Possessive Pronoun: shows ownership
I	me	my, mine
you	you	your, yours
he	him	his
she	her	her, hers
it	it	its
we	us	ours
they	them	their, theirs

Avoid these mistakes with pronouns in compound subjects and objects:

Incorrect pronoun in compound subject: Linda and <u>me</u> went to the movies.
Correct: Linda and <u>I</u> went to the movies.

Incorrect pronoun in compound object: We saw Kareem and <u>he</u> at the theater.
Correct: We saw Kareem and <u>him</u> at the theater.

GED® TEST TIP

To choose the option with the correct pronoun in a compound like "They went to the party with James and I," take out "James and" and ask yourself whether the sentence still sounds correct.

PRACTICE 1.1

A. Directions: Write the correct pronoun to replace each underlined noun.

1. Laurie and Paul just moved to California. _____

2. A neighbor told Laurie and Paul that saving water was important there. _____

3. He said they should turn the water off when brushing their teeth. _____

4. Laurie's sister suggested getting a special shower head that saves water. _____

5. Laurie and Laurie's sister will go shopping for it on Sunday. _____

B. Questions 6 through 8 refer to the following letter.

To Whom It May Concern:

    I am writing to recommend Bonetta Williams for the position of managerial assistant in your firm. I believe that she is highly qualfied for the position, and I urge you to strongly consider her candidacy.

    [Select... ▾] have worked together for three years. As my secretary, she has proven to be responsible and efficient. [Select... ▾] her work done on time and looks for ways to help others. In addition, I find her extremely intelligent and likable. I will be sorry to see her go.

    My supervisor, Walter Constantine, has also worked with Bonetta and would be happy to speak with you if necessary. Please contact [Select... ▾] if you need any further information.

Sincerely,

Carol Rhodes

6. [Select... ▾] have worked together for three years.

  A. Bonetta and me
  B. We (Bonetta and me)
  C. Bonetta and me,
  D. Bonetta and I

7. [Select... ▾] her work done on time and looks for ways to help others.

  A. She always getting
  B. Her always getting
  C. Her always gets
  D. She always gets

8. Please contact [Select... ▾] if you need any further information.

  A. Walter and I
  B. Walter or me
  C. him or I
  D. he or me

Answers and explanations start on page 651.

Key Ideas

- A pronoun should match its antecedent in person and number.
- Make sure it is clear which antecedent a pronoun refers to.
- If necessary, use a noun in place of a pronoun, or construct the sentence differently so that the antecedent is clear.

Pronoun-Antecedent Agreement

Pronouns should agree with their antecedents, or the nouns they refer to. For example, a pronoun and its antecedent must agree in number. If the antecedent is singular, the pronoun should be singular. If the antecedent is plural, the pronoun should be plural.

EXAMPLES

Andy's <u>company</u> is very progressive. <u>It</u> pays for his college classes.
    singular antecedent   singular pronoun

Many <u>employees</u> want to learn more skills, so <u>they</u> take classes.
    plural antecedent   plural pronoun

Incorrect: Any <u>employee</u> who is interested should submit <u>their</u> application.
Correct: Any <u>employee</u> who is interested should submit <u>his or her</u> application.
Correct: <u>Employees</u> who are interested should submit <u>their</u> applications.

Note that for collective nouns (such as *company, jury, family, team, committee, union*), you generally use the singular pronoun *it*.

Incorrect: The <u>committee</u> announced that <u>they</u> will hold weekly meetings.
Correct: The <u>committee</u> announced that <u>it</u> will hold weekly meetings.

A pronoun and its antecedent must agree in person. To agree, they both must be first person (referring to the speaker), second person (the person spoken to), or third person (the person or thing spoken about).

First person	Second person	Third person
I, me, my mine	you, your, yours	he, him, his
we, us, our, ours		she, her, hers
		it, its
		they, them, their, theirs

GED® TEST TIP

Take into account the whole passage when you are determining which pronoun is correct. A common error to watch for is when a paragraph begins with the third-person form one *and then shifts to the second-person form* you.

The indefinite pronoun *one* is like a third-person personal pronoun. A common error in writing (and one that is tested on the Reasoning through Language Arts Test) is an incorrect shift between the third-person *one* and the second-person *you*.

Incorrect shift: If <u>one</u> attends college classes, <u>you</u> can be reimbursed.
Correct: If <u>one</u> attends college classes, <u>one</u> can be reimbursed.
Correct: If <u>one</u> attends college classes, <u>he or she</u> can be reimbursed.
Correct: If <u>you</u> attend college classes, <u>you</u> can be reimbursed.

It must be clear which antecedent a pronoun refers to. If necessary, use a noun in place of the pronoun, or reconstruct the sentence.

Unclear: Carlos spoke to his boss, and he told him about the program.
Clear (noun replaces pronoun): Carlos spoke to his boss, and <u>his boss</u> told him about the program.
Clear (different construction): Carlos spoke to his boss, <u>who told him</u> about the program.

Unclear: Michelle helped Shania fill out the financial aid application that she had picked up.
Correct (different construction): After picking up a financial aid application for Shania, Michelle helped her fill it out.

PRACTICE 1.2

A. Directions: Correct any errors in pronoun use. If there are no errors, write *C*. You may also have to change some verbs.

                                                          they have
EXAMPLE: People who live in small towns know ~~one has~~ access to fewer amenities than big-city dwellers.

___ 1. Sally is moving to a small town. Her mother is concerned about the health-care options they offer.

___ 2. Sally tried to reassure her mother, but it was hard for her to believe her.

___ 3. Sally asked a friend who lives in the town for information about it's health-care facilities.

___ 4. The town has a freestanding clinic where a person can go when they are sick.

___ 5. There is also a nearby hospital, and they have a very good reputation.

___ 6. If one is concerned about health care, you should sign up for a good insurance plan.

B. Questions 7 through 9 refer to the following paragraphs.

The Best Discipline

What should parents do when their children act up? Parents often like the idea of punishment, but punishment may not be the most effective solution. If the punishment results from the parent's anger, it won't work. Instead, children [Select...▼] parents angry.

One parenting expert feels that [Select...▼] should be clear about their expectations from the outset so that children will not unknowingly violate rules. They should respond to children's misbehavior in a calm and neutral fashion. It's also important to choose a consequence related to the action. If a child hits or bites in a play group, for example, it would be most appropriate not to allow [Select...▼] for a short time. He or she will begin to see the connection.

7. Instead, children [Select...▼] parents angry.

   A. will learn only that they shouldn't make one's
   B. will have learned only that they shouldn't make one's
   C. will learn only that you shouldn't make one's
   D. will learn only that they shouldn't make their

8. One parenting expert feels that [Select...▼] should be clear about their expectations from the outset so that children will not unknowingly violate rules.

   A. he
   B. we
   C. one
   D. parents

9. If a child hits or bites in a play group, for example, it would be most appropriate not to allow [Select...▼] for a short time.

   A. the child to play with them
   B. them to play with them
   C. the child to play with the group
   D. the child to plays with them

Answers and explanations start on page 651.

Verb Forms and Tenses

Key Ideas

- Each verb has four forms: present, present participle, past, and past participle.
- Verb forms are used to create different tenses, which show time relationships.
- Use clues in the sentence and paragraph to help decide which tense to use.

Regular Verbs

An important part of writing correctly is using the right verb forms. A **verb** is a word that indicates action or being. Each verb has a base form and four other forms. A **regular verb** follows a consistent pattern to create each verb form.

Base form: look

Tense	Verb form	How to write it
Present	look/looks	with *I, you, we, they*: use the base form
		with *he, she, it*: add *-s* to the base form
Present participle	looking	add *-ing*
Past	looked	add *-ed* (*-d* if verb ends with *e*)
Past participle	looked	add *-ed* (*-d* if verb ends with *e*)

The forms are used to create different **verb tenses,** or times. The table below shows how verb tense and form are related. Notice that when you use certain tenses, you must also use a **helping verb**—often a form of *be* or *have*.

Tense	Verb form	Use
Present	look/looks	a habitual action, general truth, or state of being: *I look at the newspaper every day.*
Past	looked	an action that has been completed: *I looked at it this morning.*
Future	will look	an action that has not yet happened: *I will look at it tonight, too.*
Present progressive	am/is/are looking	an action in progress: *I am looking at it right now.*
Present perfect	have/has looked	an action that began in the past and continues until now: *I have looked at it every day this week.*
Past perfect	had looked	an action that was completed before a specific time in the past: *I had looked at it before it got wet.*
Future perfect	will have looked	an action that will be completed by a specific time in the future: *I will have looked at it by the time I get home.*

GED® TEST TIP

Some passages on the GED® Test have a verb-tense question based on the tense of the entire passage. Make sure you select verb forms that are consistent with the tense of the passage.

Sentences often contain clues that tell you which tense to use. For instance, time words and phrases like *yesterday* or *last week* show that the past should be used, *tonight* and *next month* indicate the future, and *by tonight, since 2000,* and *for seven years* indicate the perfect tenses.

Other verbs in the sentence can be clues: *I look at the newspaper whenever I get the chance.* Finally, verbs in other sentences also can be clues. The verbs in a paragraph or passage are generally in the same tense.

PRACTICE 2.1

A. Directions: Rewrite each verb in its correct tense. Use clues in each sentence for help in choosing the tense.

EXAMPLE: Between 1892 and 1924, about 12 million immigrants _entered_ (enter) the U.S. through Ellis Island in New York.

1. By the 1950s, Ellis Island _____ (cease) to be an important immigration checkpoint.

2. The government _____ (close) Ellis Island to immigration in 1954.

3. Now Ellis Island _____ (function) as a national monument.

4. Since the island was reopened as a museum in 1990, many tourists _____ (visit) it.

5. Soon, a genealogical center _____ (open).

6. The island _____ (look) different than it did originally because 24 acres of landfill have been added.

7. Now we _____ (think) about taking a trip to Ellis Island next month.

B. Questions 8 through 10 refer to the following advertisement.

Don't Miss Your Chance!

The Express Lane credit card [Select...▼] a fantastic deal right now, for a limited time only. [Select...▼], you will receive a 20 percent discount on your first five purchases!

The Express Lane card carries no monthly charge. You'll pay a low $35 fee just once a year. Become an Express Lane member now. Your savings opportunities [Select...▼]!

8. The Express Lane credit card [Select...▼] a fantastic deal right now, for a limited time only.

  A. offered
  B. is offering
  C. offers
  D. will offer

9. [Select...▼], you will receive a 20 percent discount on your first five purchases!

  A. If you are signing up for Express Lane before April 9
  B. If you have signed up for Express Lane before April 9
  C. If you will sign up for Express Lane before April 9
  D. If you sign up for Express Lane before April 9

10. Your savings opportunities [Select...▼]!

  A. will have been amazing you
  B. would be amazing you
  C. will be amazing you
  D. will amaze you

Answers and explanations start on page 651.

Key Ideas

- Irregular verb forms do not follow a single pattern.
- Some irregular verbs follow an *i, a, u* pattern.

GED® TEST TIP

When you choose an answer that changes a verb, read the sentence again, with your choice in it. Doing so may help you "hear" whether the verb form is correct.

Irregular Verbs

Most verbs are regular verbs; their past and participle forms follow the same pattern. Some verbs, however, are **irregular verbs**. Although some irregular verbs follow a pattern, most do not.

A common error with irregular verbs is using the past participle in place of the past—for instance, *I been there* instead of *I was there*. Discover which irregular verb forms, if any, give you problems. Then learn the correct forms. Here are some tips for learning the forms of irregular verbs:

- If you find two verbs that rhyme in the present form (for example, *grow* and *throw*), check to see if they have the same forms in the past and past participles (*grew, grown; threw, thrown*). If so, learn them together.
- Learn which verbs follow the *i, a, u* pattern: *sing, sang, sung; drink, drank, drunk; sink, sank, sunk*. However, be aware that there are exceptions (*bring, brought, brought*).

Here is a list of common irregular verbs.

Present Form	Past Form	Past Participle Form
am, are, is	was, were	been
become	became	become
begin	began	begun
blow	blew	blown
break	broke	broken
bring	brought	brought
buy	bought	bought
choose	chose	chosen
come	came	come
do	did	done
drink	drank	drunk
eat	ate	eaten
fall	fell	fallen
fly	flew	flown
freeze	froze	frozen
get	got	gotten
give	gave	given
go	went	gone
grow	grew	grown
have, has	had	had
know	knew	known
leave	left	left
lose	lost	lost
ride	rode	ridden
run	ran	run
see	saw	seen
shake	shook	shaken
show	showed	shown
speak	spoke	spoken
steal	stole	stolen
take	took	taken
throw	threw	thrown
wear	wore	worn
write	wrote	written

PRACTICE 2.2

A. Directions: Write the correct form of the verb shown in parentheses.

EXAMPLE: Since November, the school's heating system ___*has broken*___ (break) down several times.

1. Yesterday the technician _____ (come) to resolve the problem once and for all.

2. School employees _____ (show) him the boiler.

3. The technician said, "If you _____ (speak) to me about this sooner, it would have been easier to fix."

4. He _____ (take) parts out of the heating system and replaced them with new ones.

5. He said, "I've never _____ (see) such a poorly installed system."

B. Questions 6 through 8 refer to the following paragraphs.

TV Rating Systems

In 1996, television industry representatives announced that the industry had formed TV Parental Guidelines. This rating system, designed to give parents advance warning about the content of TV shows, [Select...▾] TV in 1997. The ratings system [Select...▾] down into six different categories, ranging from "All Children" to "Mature Audiences Only."

Six months later, after pressure from advocacy groups, the television industry agreed to include additional labels to advise viewers if a show they were about to view contained violence, sexual activity, coarse language, or sexually suggestive language. These labels [Select...▾] more specific and therefore more helpful information about an upcoming show.

6. This rating system, designed to give parents advance warning about the content of TV shows, [Select...▾] TV in 1997.

   A. begun to appear on
   B. began to appearing on
   C. had begun to appear on
   D. began to appear on

7. The ratings system [Select...▾] down into six different categories, ranging from "All Children" to "Mature Audiences Only."

   A. broke itself
   B. broke
   C. was broken
   D. had broken

8. These labels [Select...▾] more specific and therefore more helpful information about an upcoming show.

   A. now given viewers
   B. now give viewers
   C. now will give viewers
   D. now have given viewers

Answers and explanations start on page 651.

USING GRAMMAR CORRECTLY

Subject-Verb Agreement

Key Ideas

- A verb must match its subject in number.
- Collective nouns are singular when they refer to a group as a single unit.
- Indefinite pronouns may be singular, plural, or both.

Agreement with a Simple Subject

In the present tense, subjects and verbs must agree in number. To understand the basics of subject-verb agreement, study the chart below. Notice that present tense verbs take an -s ending when they are used with the pronoun subjects *he, she,* and *it* or their noun equivalents.

Verb Forms for Singular Subjects	Verb Forms for Plural Subjects
I jump	*we* jump
you jump	*you* jump
he, she, it jumps	*they* jump

To master subject-verb agreement for the GED® Test, be aware of these special nouns and pronouns:

Collective nouns are usually singular, even though they may seem plural. A collective noun names a group, such as *army, crew, crowd, staff, family, herd,* or *flock.* If the group is considered to be a single unit, it is singular.

EXAMPLES
The <u>army is</u> a good place to learn discipline.
The <u>church choir sings</u> each Sunday.

Some nouns that end in -s may look plural, but in fact they are not.

EXAMPLE
<u>Politics is</u> an interesting topic.

Indefinite pronouns do not refer to a specific person. Some indefinite pronouns are singular, some are plural, and some may be either.

Singular	anyone, everyone, someone, no one, one, anybody, everybody, somebody, nobody, anything, everything, something, nothing, another, other, either, neither, each, much
Plural	many, several, few, both
Singular or plural	all, none, some, any, part, most

EXAMPLES
Singular: These days, it seems as if almost <u>everyone is</u> joining a health club.
Singular: <u>Most</u> of the equipment <u>is</u> easy to use.
Plural: <u>Most</u> of the exercise classes <u>are</u> fun
Plural: A <u>few are</u> advanced classes for those already in great shape.

PRACTICE 3.1

A. Directions: Underline the correct verb form to complete each sentence.

EXAMPLE: Every Monday, the National Orchestra (perform, <u>performs</u>) live on the radio.

1. The public (is, are) invited to listen free of charge.

2. Free tickets (becomes, become) available one hour before the performance.

3. The performance (is, are) usually held in Barnes Hall.

4. Many well-known musicians (has, have) played there.

5. Everyone (seem, seems) to enjoy these concerts very much.

6. The concert series (is, are) very popular.

B. **Questions 7 through 9 refer to the following article.**

The Speed of Sound

Most of us [Select...▾] airplane noise that is so loud it sounds like an explosion. [Select...▾] fly faster than the speed of sound. Listeners on the ground hear the noise, but it is not audible to passengers.

The speed of sound is 1,088 feet per second at 32°F at sea level. It is different at other temperatures and in other substances. For example, sound travels faster in water than in air. Sound takes about one second to move a mile under water, but five seconds to move a mile through air. It travels through ice cold vapor at 4,708 feet per second and through ice cold water at 4,938 feet per second. Surprisingly, [Select...▾] very well. For instance, sound travels through glass at speeds up to 19,690 feet per second.

7. Most of us [Select...▾] airplane noise that is so loud it sounds like an explosion.

A. were hearing
B. have heard
C. having heard
D. hears

8. [Select...▾] fly faster than the speed of sound.

A. That noise occurs when a plane start to
B. That noise occurred when a plane start to
C. That noise occurs when a plane starts to
D. That noise occur when a plane start to

9. Surprisingly, [Select...▾] very well.

A. some other materials conducts sound
B. some other materials conduct sound
C. some other materials conducted sound
D. any other material conducts sound

Answers and explanations start on page 651.

- If a compound subject is joined by *and*, use a plural verb.
- If a compound subject is joined by *or*, *either . . . or*, or *neither . . . nor*, the verb should agree with the subject closer to it.
- When checking subject-verb agreement, ignore interrupting phrases and watch for inverted structure.

Agreement with a Compound Subject

A compound subject is made up of two or more subjects joined by *and* or *or*. To make a verb agree with a compound subject, follow these guidelines:

When two or more subjects are joined by *and*, the compound subject is plural. Use the correct verb form for the plural.

EXAMPLE: Tricia and her sister are caring for their mother.

If two subjects are joined by *or*, the verb agrees with the subject closer to it:

EXAMPLE: A health aide or a nurse visits each day.

When subjects are joined by *either . . . or* or *neither . . . nor*, the verb agrees with the subject closer to it.

EXAMPLE: Neither the sisters nor their brother has medical training.

Interrupting Words

Sometimes a word or group of words comes between the subject and the verb. In that case, locate the subject by asking yourself, What is this sentence really about? Mentally cross out the interruptor. Then make the verb agree with the subject.

EXAMPLE: The medicine prescribed by the doctors is on a high shelf.
              subject   interruptor   verb

Interrupting phrases often begin with prepositions, such as *of, in, on, from, with, to,* and *for.*

EXAMPLE: A pile of medical supplies rests in the front hallway.

Interrupting phrases may be set off by commas. Watch especially for phrases beginning with words like *along with, as well as, besides,* and *in addition to.*

EXAMPLES
Dr. Silva, who is one of the surgeons, consults with the family.
The sisters, along with the medical team, keep the patient comfortable.

Inverted Structure

Checking subject-verb agreement can be tricky when the sentence structure is **inverted**—that is, when the subject comes after the verb. Most questions and sentences that begin with *here* or *there* are inverted.

EXAMPLES
Does the pharmacy have enough medicine to fill the prescription?
Here are the hospital supplies that Tricia ordered.

Incorrect: What is Tricia and her family going to do?
Correct: What are Tricia and her family going to do?

Incorrect: Do Tricia want to send her mother to a hospital?
Correct: Does Tricia want to send her mother to a hospital?

Incorrect: There's the bandages. (Remember that *There's* is short for *There is.*)
Correct: There are the bandages.

PRACTICE 3.2

A. Directions: If a sentence contains an interrupting phrase, cross out the interruptor. Then underline the correct verb to complete the sentence.

EXAMPLE: Brushing and flossing ~~with regularity~~ (is, <u>are</u>) key to good dental health.

1. Many toothpastes on the market (carry, carries) a seal of approval from the American Dental Association.

2. Products carrying the seal (are, is) tested to guarantee that they are safe and effective.

3. Fluoride, an important ingredient in many toothpastes, (strengthens, strengthen) teeth and (attacks, attack) bacteria that cause tooth decay.

4. There (is, are) toothpastes that claim to have special benefits, like tartar control or whitening.

5. Some pharmacies and supermarkets (offers, offer) store-brand toothpaste at a low price.

6. Any toothpaste with fluoride and good flavor (is, are) fine to use, even if it's not a brand-name toothpaste.

B. Questions 7 through 9 refer to the following paragraphs.

Unemployment Insurance

Unemployment insurance provides workers who have lost their jobs with partial replacement of their salaries. Each state [Select...▾] its own laws. [Select...▾] the amount received. When the unemployment rate rises above a certain level, states are required to extend the benefits. The state and federal governments share the cost of the additional benefits.

In most states, employer contributions pay for this program. Unemployed workers who wish to [Select...▾] public employment office to learn about job openings.

7. Each state [Select...▾] its own laws.

  A. administers its own program and have
  B. administer its own program and have
  C. administers its own program and has
  D. administers it's own program and have

8. [Select...▾] the amount received.

  A. Wage level and the length of employment determine
  B. Wage level and the length of employment determines
  C. Wage level and the length of employment would be determined by
  D. Wage level and the length of employment will then determine

9. Unemployed workers who wish to [Select...▾] public employment office to learn about job openings.

  A. draw benefits reports regularly to their
  B. draw benefits, reports regularly to their
  C. draw benefits report regularly to their
  D. draw benefits reports regularly to there

Answers and explanations start on page 651.

USING GRAMMAR CORRECTLY PRACTICE QUESTIONS

Unorthodox Tennis Stars

Venus and Serena Williams are not your typical tennis stars. For one thing, they are African Americans in a game that few African Americans have become famous for playing; those who preceded them were Althea Gibson, Arthur Ashe, and Zina Garrison. For another, Venus and Serena are sisters.

Tennis players often receive hours of instruction from [Select...▾] that way for Venus and Serena. Instead, their father, the former owner of a security-services business, taught them how to play on public courts, after teaching himself through books and films. The family lived in a rough neighborhood, and gang members watched over the girls while [Select...▾] practiced.

The practice paid off. Venus had won 63 tournaments by the time she turned 12, and she became a professional at 14. In just a few years, she [Select...▾] millions of dollars in endorsements and prizes. Serena, turning professional a year after Venus, had a slower start. However, some experts think she may now be better than her sister.

The two sisters, [Select...▾]. Though they sometimes face each other on the court, [Select...▾].

1. Tennis players often receive hours of instruction from [Select...▾] that way for Venus and Serena.

   A. highly paid coaches, but it doesn't happen
   B. highly paid coaches but it doesn't happen
   C. highly paid coaches, but it didn't happen
   D. highly paid coach, but it doesn't happen

2. The family lived in a rough neighborhood, and gang members watched over the girls while [Select...▾] practiced.

   A. they
   B. the girls
   C. each
   D. them

3. In just a few years, she [Select...▾] millions of dollars in endorsements and prizes.

   A. is earning
   B. earned
   C. earn
   D. will earn

4. The two sisters, [Select...▾].

   A. who live in Palm Beach Gardens, Florida, is best friends
   B. who lives in Palm Beach Gardens, Florida, is best friends
   C. who live in Palm Beach Gardens, Florida is best friends
   D. who live in Palm Beach Gardens, Florida, are best friends

5. Though they sometimes face each other on the court, [Select...▾].

   A. there been no trace of sibling rivalry
   B. there had not been a trace of sibling rivalry
   C. there will be no trace of sibling rivalry
   D. there is no trace of sibling rivalry

Questions 6 through 10 refer to the following paragraphs.

Getting the Best Service for Your Car

Have you had trouble finding a good mechanic? By following these tips, you can improve your chances of getting quality service.

Even before your car breaks down, look for a shop you like and trust. Ask [Select...▼] good service at a reasonable price. Don't [Select...▼] to home, for another shop may have a better deal. Be wary of ads that offer rock-bottom prices. Specials like [Select...▼].

Be as specific as possible when you describe your car's problem to the mechanic. If the technician must spend time trying to determine [Select...▼] cost more. You also need to request information about both estimates and guarantees before the repair work starts. Ask for a price range rather than an exact estimate. Find out how long the guarantee lasts and whether [Select...▼] any time or mileage limits.

If you don't understand a repair explanation, ask for clarification right away. In addition, keep records of all repairs and billing in case of a dispute.

6. Ask [Select...▼] good service at a reasonable price.

 A. people where they will receive
 B. people where they have received
 C. people where they receiving
 D. them where they will receive

7. Don't [Select...▼] to home, for another shop may have a better deal.

 A. have picked a shop just because it's close
 B. be picking a shop just because it's close
 C. have picked a shop just because its close
 D. pick a shop just because it's close

8. Specials like [Select...▼].

 A. these often comes with restrictions attached
 B. this often comes with restrictions attached
 C. these often came with restrictions attached
 D. these often come with restrictions attached

9. If the technician must spend time trying to determine [Select...▼] cost more.

 A. what's wrong, it will
 B. what are wrong, it will
 C. what's wrong it will
 D. what's wrong, the repair job will

10. Find out how long the guarantee lasts and whether [Select...▼] any time or mileage limits.

 A. there is
 B. there be
 C. there are
 D. there were

Taxpayer Notification

We have received your tax return and have noted some inconsistencies in it. We are therefore proposing a number of changes to your return. These `Select...▾` on your refund are outlined below.

First, the amount you claimed for self-employed income differs from our records. If you wish to contest this change, please `Select...▾`. Second, you have made an error in your calculations. Please review `Select...▾`.

Because of these changes to your return, the amount of taxes you owe `Select...▾`. Your refund has therefore been reduced accordingly.

Contact us if you have any questions about these specific problems or about the documents you must send to contest the changes. Be sure to send the last page of this letter when replying by mail. If we determine that your return was correct as filed, we `Select...▾` your account.

11. These `Select...▾` on your refund are outlined below.

A. changes and its effect
B. changes and their effect
C. changes, and its effect
D. changes and it's effect

12. If you wish to contest this change, please `Select...▾`.

A. send photocopies of one's records
B. to send photocopies of one's records
C. send photocopies of your records
D. send photocopies of their records

13. Please review `Select...▾`.

A. our calculations, which is appended to this letter
B. are calculations, which is appended (to this letter)
C. our calculations which is appended to this letter
D. our calculations, which are appended to this letter

14. Because of these changes to your return, the amount of taxes you owe `Select...▾`.

A. has increased
B. have increased
C. is increasing
D. are increasing

15. If we determine that your return was correct as filed, we `Select...▾` your account.

A. are crediting
B. will credit
C. will have credited
D. had credited

Questions 16 through 20 refer to the following paragraphs.

Disability Etiquette

Many of us [Select...▼] know how to act when meeting someone who has a disability. The main thing to remember [Select...▼] just like everyone else. They want to be treated with respect and dignity. Beyond that, try the following tips.

When you meet a person with a disability, speak and act with [Select...▼] as you would with anyone else. Use your usual tone of voice. A person who has trouble hearing you will let you know. Don't talk down to the person or stare. Refrain from using a term like *handicap,* which focuses on the disability rather than on the person. Instead, use a term such as *physically disabled* or say, "He uses a wheelchair."

Any assistive equipment, [Select...▼]. Unless you have the person's express permission, you should not touch it. Also, don't pet a blind person's guide dog because distracting [Select...▼] could put the owner in danger.

Finally, if you have a child with you, don't prevent him or her from talking to the person or asking questions. Children are often more accepting than adults.

16. Many of us [Select...▼] know how to act when meeting someone who has a disability.

    A. does not
    B. don't
    C. didn't
    D. never does

17. The main thing to remember [Select...▼] just like everyone else.

    A. is that people with disabilities has feelings
    B. are that people with disabilities has feelings
    C. is that people with disabilities have feelings
    D. is that those with disabilities has feelings

18. When you meet a person with a disability, speak and act with [Select...▼] as you would with anyone else.

    A. he or her
    B. him or her
    C. him or she
    D. them

19. Any assistive equipment, [Select...▼].

    A. such as a wheelchair, cane or communication board, is the person's property
    B. such as a wheelchair, cane, or communication board, is the person's property
    C. such as wheelchair, cane, or communication board, are the person's property
    D. such as a wheelchair, such as a cane, or a communication board, are the person's property

20. Also, don't pet a blind person's guide dog because distracting [Select...▼] could put the owner in danger.

    A. a blind person's guide dog
    B. it
    C. her
    D. them

Answers and explanations start on page 651.

Comma Use

As a general rule, **commas** indicate where readers would pause in a sentence if they were reading it aloud. Below are specific guidelines for using commas.

Key Ideas

- In a compound sentence, use a comma before the coordinating conjunction.
- Be careful not to use a comma between two words or phrases joined by *and*.
- Insert a comma after an introductory word, phrase, or clause.

GED® TEST TIP

Read a sentence out loud to see if you hear a pause. Before you insert a comma, be sure that you can base your decision on a comma rule.

Commas in Compound Sentences

In a compound sentence, place a comma immediately before the coordinating conjunction.

EXAMPLES

Some people are insecure about hosting a party, but others are relaxed and confident.

Many hosts have years of practice, and they have some organizational tips.

Watch out, though, for sentences that appear to be compound but are not. Some sentences have one main clause but have a compound subject or a compound predicate. If a sentence does not have two independent clauses, a comma is not needed before the coordinating conjunction.

Incorrect: Planning, and list making are two key organizational techniques.
Correct: Planning and list making are two key organizational techniques.

Incorrect: Making a list reduces disorganization, and helps you feel in control.
Correct: Making a list reduces disorganization and helps you feel in control.

Commas after Introductory Elements

In general, a comma should follow an introductory word, phrase, or clause to separate the introductory element from the main part of the sentence.

EXAMPLES
Introductory words:
Yes, listing your ideas can be very helpful.
However, making a list is only the first step.

Introductory phrases:
Giving it some thought, carefully draw up a guest list.
For a casual feel, have an open house.
On the day of the party, do as much as you can first thing in the morning.
By party time, you should be able to relax.

Introductory clauses:
Before you make a list, decide what kind of party you will have.
If you are a good cook, you might choose to have a dinner party.

Remember that only a subordinate clause at the beginning of a sentence requires a comma after it. A subordinate clause at the end of the sentence generally does not.

No comma: Decide what kind of party you will have before you make a list.

PRACTICE 1.1

A. Directions: Insert commas where needed in the sentences below. If no commas are required, write *NC*.

_____ 1. Train travel is more pleasant than riding a bus but it can be more expensive.

_____ 2. When you're on a train you can stand up and stretch if you need to.

_____ 3. Most trains have club cars where passengers can get snacks and sometimes even sit at tables.

_____ 4. Unlike buses trains sometimes have seats that face each other.

_____ 5. Traveling through a scenic area you may find that your train has a double-decker car that offers a better view.

_____ 6. Lowered airfares and many people's unwillingness to spend long hours in a train have contributed to the declining popularity of rail travel.

B. <u>Questions 7 through 9 refer to the following paragraphs.</u>

Low-Fat Cooking

To have a more healthful diet, try cooking with less fat. It's not as hard as you think! [Select... ▾] such as steaming, poaching, or baking. When you do include oil in the preparation of your dish, use less of it. Vinegar can be used without oil in salad [Select... ▾] the flavor can be enhanced with fresh herbs.

Another tactic is to cut down on dairy fat. Avoid regular milk, cream, and sour cream. Add low-fat dairy products or another liquid to your dish instead. Many dairy foods come in a [Select... ▾] to the palate, some are.

7. [Select... ▾] such as steaming, poaching, or baking.

A. For starters, use cooking methods that require little or no oil or butter,
B. For starters use cooking methods that require little or no oil or butter
C. For starters use cooking methods that require little or no oil or butter,
D. For starters use cooking methods that require little, or no oil or butter,

8. Vinegar can be used without oil in salad [Select... ▾] the flavor can be enhanced with fresh herbs.

A. dressing, and
B. dressing and,
C. dressing, or
D. dressing, for example

9. Many dairy foods come in a [Select... ▾] to the palate, some are.

A. low-fat version and though, not all of them may be pleasing
B. low-fat version, and though, not all of them may be pleasing,
C. low-fat version, and though, not all of them may be pleasing
D. low-fat version, and though not all of them may be pleasing

Answers and explanations start on page 652.

Key Ideas

- Separate the items in a series with commas.
- Put commas around an appositive only if it gives nonessential details about a noun.
- Don't put a comma between a subject and a verb.
- Don't use a comma between two items joined by *and* or *or*.

Commas in a Series

When three or more items are listed in a series, place commas *between* the items:

EXAMPLES

Keith, Darnelle, Marisol, and Doug are ready to take the GED® Test.
They have taken a class, studied together, and prepared well.

The comma before the final *and* or *or* is optional (for example, *March 7, March 14, or March 21*). Placing a comma there is not tested on the *Reasoning through Language Arts Test*, but using one there will help you place commas correctly in the series. To use commas between the items in a series, count the number of items listed and subtract one. That is the number of commas you should use.

Commas with Appositives

An **appositive** is a word or group of words that gives more information about a noun by renaming it.

EXAMPLES

Marisol, an experienced writer, feels confident about the essay.
Doug's only sister, Gina, was the first in the family to receive a high school equivalency degree.

To decide whether to set off an appositive with commas, mentally cross out the appositive. Then ask, *"Can I still identify the person, place, or thing described in the sentence?"* If you can, use commas around the appositive.

EXAMPLES

Mann College, a local community college, offers GED® test courses.
Keith, who attended GED® test classes for a year, has done well there.

Here you can identify the noun without the appositive. Each appositive adds more information, but it is not essential to your understanding. Usually when an appositive is renaming a proper noun, it is not essential.

On the other hand, if you cannot identify the person, place, or thing without the appositive, do not set off the appositive with commas.

EXAMPLES

Keith and his friend Antoine plan to work in construction.
Students who study faithfully usually do well on the test.

In these examples, you cannot identify the nouns without the appositives. You would ask, *"Which friend?"* and *"Which students?"* The appositives are essential to your understanding and should not be set off by commas.

Comma Errors to Avoid

It is easy to overuse commas. Avoid this error by following these guidelines:

Do not use a comma between the subject and the verb.

Incorrect: Park College, is the school Doug hopes to attend.

Do not use a comma between two subjects, two verbs, or two other items joined by *and* or *or*.

Incorrect: Science, and math are hard subjects for Keith.
Incorrect: Darnell writes practice essays, and reads.
Incorrect: They will review his application, and transcript.

PRACTICE 1.2

A. Directions: Insert commas where needed in the sentences below. If no commas are required, write *NC*.

_____ 1. Kwanzaa is a week-long African American holiday that celebrates culture community and family.

_____ 2. Kwanzaa a wintertime holiday is based on an ancient African harvest celebration.

_____ 3. It was developed in modern times by scholar Maulana Karenga.

_____ 4. Kwanzaa celebrations include rituals such as singing dancing drumming and poetry reading.

_____ 5. The family lights one candle every day for each of seven principles: unity self-determination responsibility cooperative economics purpose creativity and faith.

_____ 6. A day during which people consider their moral worthiness marks the end of Kwanzaa.

B. Questions 7 through 9 refer to the following paragraphs.

Childproofing Your Home

If you have small children, you no doubt appreciate the need to make your home as safe as possible. It is a fact that [Select...▾]. Taking a few simple measures might reduce the number of times you take your kids to the emergency room.

Start by putting childproof locks on all cupboards in which [Select...▾]. To keep babies and toddlers from entering dangerous areas, put baby gates in doorways and install sleeves on doorknobs. Install safety locks on doors and windows. Make sure that older [Select...▾] can open them in an emergency. To prevent burns in the bathtub, keep the water temperature below 120°F. Cover unused outlets with outlet plugs.

7. It is a fact that [Select...▾].

A. home accidents are responsible for more children's injuries than all childhood diseases combined

B. home accidents, is responsible for more children's injuries than all childhood diseases combined

C. home accidents, are responsible for more children's injuries, than all childhood diseases combined

D. home accidents, being responsible for more children's injuries than all childhood diseases combined

8. Start by putting childproof locks on all cupboards in which [Select...▾].

A. medicines poisons, or fragile objects are stored

B. medicines, poisons, or fragile objects are stored

C. medicines poisons, or fragile objects, are stored

D. medicines poisons, or fragile objects is stored

9. Make sure that older [Select...▾] can open them in an emergency.

A. children those ten and up
B. children, those ten, and up,
C. children, those ten and up,
D. children those ten and up,

Answers and explanations start on page 652.

Capitalization

To recognize capitalization errors on the Reasoning through Language Arts test and to use capital letters correctly in your response, follow these guidelines.

Capitalize proper nouns. A **proper noun** is the name of a specific person, place, thing, or idea. If a proper noun has two or more words, capitalize each word.

EXAMPLES

Claude Normand is a major contributor to Portland Community Hospital. The hospital is located on Camden Road in Portland, Maine.
The hospital and charities such as the American Cancer Society rely on contributions from citizens.
All major religions, from Islam to Christianity, support giving to charity.

Note that the key words in addresses are proper nouns and are capitalized. The key words include the names of streets, cities, states, and countries.

Do not capitalize common nouns, which do not refer to a specific person, place, or thing.

EXAMPLE

Incorrect: Many Doctors volunteer at Clinics in the City.
Correct: Many doctors volunteer at clinics in the city.

Capitalize the names of proper adjectives. A **proper adjective** is formed from a proper noun.

EXAMPLE

Mr. Normand has a French Canadian heritage.

Capitalize a title before a person's name. Do not capitalize a title when it appears without a person's name unless it is used in direct address.

EXAMPLES

Title before name: Mr. Normand met recently with Dr. Halverson and Mayor Maresky.
Title without name: The doctor and mayor were very receptive to his ideas.
Direct address: He said, "Thank you, Mayor, for listening to my proposal."

Capitalize names of holidays, days of the week, and months. Do not capitalize the names of seasons.

EXAMPLES

Memorial Day is always the last Monday in May and is a paid holiday.
The project will be completed by the end of spring.

Capitalize names of specific school courses and all languages.

EXAMPLE

I am taking Introduction to Computers 101, English, and math.

Key Ideas

- Capitalize proper nouns and adjectives.
- Capitalize days of the week, months, and names of holidays but not seasons.
- Capitalize titles if they come before a person's name or are used to address the person.

GED® TEST TIP

Use the "proper noun" test to determine if a word should be capitalized. To capitalize, make sure the word or phrase is the name of a person, place or thing: "my uncle" is fine, and so is "Uncle Leo."

PRACTICE 2

A. Directions: Correct the capitalization errors in the sentences below.

EXAMPLE:

I am writing to thank the $\overset{s}{\cancel{S}}$taff of the Waterside Physical Therapy $\overset{C}{\cancel{c}}$enter.

1. Last Spring, I broke my arm in a car accident.

2. My internist, doctor claudia McNally, referred me to Waterside.

3. The center's Director, Ilana Harris, assigned me a physical therapist named Ellie Royce.

4. Ellie studied physical therapy in her native London and used british methods of treatment that relieved my pain quite effectively.

5. She also did therapy with me in the pool at Rainbow health club.

6. I finished my treatments just before labor day, and I feel 100 percent better, thanks to Ellie.

B. Questions 7 through 9 refer to the following paragraphs.

An Unusual Breed

The Akita is a Japanese dog breed that dates to ancient times. The breed has a special spiritual meaning for many. For example, when a child is born, well-wishers give the family small statues of Akitas to express hopes for future happiness and health. In the past, Select...▾ allowed to own his breed.

Akitas are massive, powerful dogs, used for hunting game and guarding. Starting in the 17th century, Select...▾ . In 1937, Akitas were brought to Select...▾ .

7. In the past, Select...▾ allowed to own this breed.

   A. only Emperors and nobles were
   B. only emperors and nobles were
   C. only Emperors and Nobles were
   D. only Emperors and nobles are

8. Starting in the 17th century, Select...▾ .

   A. they were trained to hunt game and water-fowl in the Mountains of Japan
   B. they were trained to hunt game and water-fowl, in the Mountains of Japan
   C. they were trained to hunt game and water-fowl in the mountains of Japan
   D. they were trained to hunt game, and water-fowl in the Mountains of Japan

9. In 1937, Akitas were brought to Select...▾ .

   A. america by author Helen Keller
   B. America by author Helen Keller
   C. america by Author Helen Keller
   D. america by author helen keller

Answers and explanations start on page 652.

USING WRITING MECHANICS

Possessives and Contractions

Key Ideas

- Use apostrophes with possessive nouns but not with possessive pronouns.
- Use an apostrophe to replace the missing letters in a contraction.
- To decide whether to use a possessive or contraction, test to see whether the full form of the contraction makes sense in the sentence.

Some of the most common spelling errors involve possessives and contractions. Follow these guidelines when spelling these words:

A **possessive** shows ownership. Use apostrophes with possessive nouns. Do not use apostrophes with possessive pronouns.

EXAMPLES
Possessive nouns: friend's car   Marta's map   the dogs' leashes
Possessive pronouns: his, hers, ours, yours, theirs, its
Correct: The car's tires are new. The map is hers.

If a noun is singular or if it is plural but does not end in s, add an apostrophe + s to form the possessive.

Singular possessive: cat's   boss's   women's

If a noun is plural and ends in s, add an apostrophe after the final s.

Plural possessive: workers'   ladies'

A singular possessive often sounds like a plural noun. Use an apostrophe only with the possessive.

Correct: My company's benefits (possessive) make it one of the best companies (plural) to work for.

A **contraction** shortens two words by combining the second word with the first and leaving out one or more letters. An apostrophe takes the place of the missing letters. Some contractions combine pronouns with verbs.

EXAMPLES
here is → here's   there is → there's   I am → I'm

Other contractions combine verbs with the word not.

EXAMPLES
have not → haven't   do not → don't   will not → won't

Be careful to use the apostrophe in place of the missing letter or letters. Notice that the correct position is not necessarily the point at which the two words come together.

Incorrect: You do'nt have to come with us tonight. (*do'nt* should be *don't*)

Some possessives and contractions sound the same (*your* and *you're*, *its* and *it's*, *their* and *they're*). To determine whether to use a possessive or a contraction, substitute the two words that make up the contraction. If the substitution makes sense, the contraction is correct. If not, use a possessive.

GED® TEST TIP

Contractions are acceptable in informal speech and writing. However, try to avoid them in more formal writing situations, such as the GED® Extended Response.

PRACTICE 3

A. Directions: Underline the correct word or words to complete each sentence.

EXAMPLE: I'm (your, you're) downstairs neighbor, and (I've, Iv'e) been having trouble sleeping lately because of noise late at night.

1. (Theirs, There's) a noise that sounds like the thumping beat of rock music.

2. I (ca'nt, can't) be sure (who's, whose) responsible, but (its, it's) coming from your apartment.

3. My roommates and I have discussed this, and (were, we're) running out of patience.

4. You should talk to your children if the stereo is (theirs, there's).

5. Please be considerate of your neighbors just as we are considerate of (our's, ours).

B. Questions 6 through 8 refer to the paragraphs that follow.

Sales Trainees Wanted

Do you have a warm smile? Do people feel comfortable with you? Do you have a friendly phone manner? Do you have good organizational skills? Are you good at solving problems? If you've answered yes to these [Select...▾] skills at Macro Software.

Macro Software is one of the industry leaders in software distribution. [Select...▾] to offer a mail order service that was the first of its kind. We pride ourselves on our high-quality products, quick delivery times, and excellent customer service.

We are currently hiring sales trainees for our Miami office. Interested [Select...▾] to Jim Burns, Macro Software, 904 Ocean Drive, Miami, Florida.

6. If you've answered yes to these [Select...▾] skills at Macro Software.

   A. questions, we need you're
   B. questions we need you're
   C. questions, we needs you're
   D. questions, we need your

7. [Select...▾] to offer a mail order service that was the first of its kind.

   A. In addition to hour chain of stores, we're proud
   B. In addition to our chain of stores, we're proud
   C. In addition to our chain of stores, were proud
   D. In addition, to our chain of stores, were proud

8. Interested [Select...▾] to Jim Burns, Macro Software, 904 Ocean Drive, Miami, Florida.

   A. party's should send they're resumes
   B. parties should send their resumes
   C. parties should send they're resume's
   D. parties should send they're resumes

Answers and explanations start on page 653.

Homonyms

Homonyms are words that sound alike but are spelled differently and have different meanings. The following chart lists homonyms and other commonly confused words that people often misspell.

Key Ideas

Homonyms are words that sound the same but have different spellings and different meanings.

Word	Meaning	Word in Sentence
accept	to receive willingly	I accept responsibility for my actions.
except	excluding	Everyone went except Molly.
affect	to have an impact	Did the medicine affect you?
effect	a result	The effects will wear off soon.
board	a piece of wood	Nail that board to the other one.
bored	not interested	Rami was bored in wood shop class.
brake	to stop; something that stops	Put your foot on the brake!
break	to shatter in pieces	Be careful, or you'll break your arm.
close	to shut	Please close that bag.
clothes	something to wear	I'm going to return those clothes.
desert	to leave behind; arid land	Don't desert a friend in need.
dessert	sweet food served after dinner	They offer dessert to their guests.
fare	money paid by a passenger	The subway fare was just raised.
fair	just, right	A lot of people think it's not fair.
forth	forward	Let's go forth!
fourth	in the 4th position	It is our fourth trip in three days.
grate	to shred	We need to grate some potatoes.
great	fantastic; of large size	It's going to be a great casserole.
hole	opening	There's a hole in the sweater.
whole	entire	Soon the whole thing will fall apart.
know	to understand	I don't know what's wrong with him.
no	opposite of *yes*	He has no sense.
led	past of the verb *lead;* brought	He led the worker to the supply room.
lead	a material in pencils	They gave her some lead pencils.
lessen	to decrease	Will you lessen the sugar in the recipe?
lesson	something you learn; moral	That will teach him a lesson.
male	a boy or man	There are both females and males in the Army.
mail	to send a message through the post office; a message sent	Send the letter through the mail.
passed	went by	Have you passed the post office?
past	opposite of *future*	Yes, in the past.
peace	opposite of *war*	When will there be world peace?
piece	a part	That's only a piece of the problem.
principal	head of a school	The principal has called a meeting.
principle	a guiding rule; a moral	He has no principles.
than	compared with	I used to have more money than you.
then	after that; at that time	Then I spent most of mine.
there	at that place	The car is over there.
their	belonging to them	It is their car.
they're	they are	They're going to sell it.
to	indicates a direction	Go to the grocery store.
too	also, in addition	Sharmaine will go, too.
two	the number 2	Buy me two loaves of bread.

GED® TEST TIP

Possessives, contractions, and homonyms are the kinds of spelling items that appear on the GED® Test. Study the ones that give you problems.

PRACTICE 4

A. Directions: Underline the correct word or words to complete each sentence.

EXAMPLE: The chairman of the (board, bored) has called this meeting.

1. This is our (fourth, forth) meeting on the topic of funding.

2. We don't (no, know) any other sources of funding.

3. The director of the organization brought up this (whole, hole) issue.

4. Next (weak, week), we plan to submit a proposal.

5. We worry that a request for funding may (affect, effect) our nonprofit status.

6. In the (past, passed), we could rely on government funding.

B. Questions 6 through 8 refer to the paragraphs that follow.

Equal Pay for Equal Work?

In 1963, women earned only 59 percent of the wages men earned. In 1997, the figure was still just 74 percent. Women [Select... ▾]?

One explanation is that the statistics include older women. [Select... ▾] prevail. In contrast, women under the age of 25 earn about 92 percent of what men earn. However, upon closer examination, this theory falls flat. Women in entry-level jobs have always earned salaries similar to those of their male peers. The problem is that women don't receive the same raises and promotions that men get. [Select... ▾]

7. Women [Select... ▾]?

   A. have logged grate achievements in the workforce, so why don't they receive fair pay
   B. has logged great achievements in the workforce, so why don't they receive fair pay
   C. have logged great achievements in the workforce, so why don't they receive fair pay
   D. have logged great achievements in the workforce, so why don't they receive fare pay

8. [Select... ▾] prevail.

   A. In principle, the age gap could account for the wage gap because older women still work in jobs in which attitudes and conditions of the past
   B. In principal, the age gap could account for the wage gap because older women still working in jobs in which attitudes and conditions of the past
   C. In principal, the age gap could account for the wage gap because older women still work in jobs in which attitudes and conditions of the passed
   D. In principal, the age gap could account four the wage gap because older women still work in jobs in which attitudes and conditions of the past

9. [Select... ▾]

   A. The effect is that, as women get older, the gap between men's and women's salaries becomes greater.
   B. The affect is that, as women get older, the gap between men's and women's salaries become greater.
   C. The affect is that, as women get older, the gap between men's and women's salaries becomes grater.
   D. The affect is that as women get older, the gap between men's and women's salaries becomes greater.

Answers and explanations start on page 653.

Using Writing Mechanics Practice Questions

Questions 1 through 5 refer to the following paragraphs.

Single Parents and Relationships

Children of single parents don't exactly cheer their parents on at the start of a new relationship. [Select...▾] and generally try to ruin their parents' chances. If you are a parent in this situation, you need to [Select...▾] your children that you love them. However, also let [Select...▾] doing the right thing.

Your children may become quickly attached to a new date, even within the course of an evening. Alternatively, they may fear that you plan to marry each potential partner you bring home. For these reasons, it makes sense not to introduce all your dates to your children. Try to see your dates at times when [Select...▾].

Once you become committed to a particular person, it's important to include your partner in family events gradually. Don't be surprised if your children have a negative reaction to your new partner. This time may be difficult for your kids. They're not used to seeing you with a new partner, and they may be realizing that a reconciliation with your ex-spouse is impossible. If communication breaks [Select...▾] family counseling. Children may be more willing to share their worries and complaints in that setting.

1. [Select...▾] and generally try to ruin their parents' chances.

   A. Instead children may have tantrums erase phone messages,
   B. Instead, children may have tantrums, erase phone messages,
   C. Instead, children may have tantrums, erase phone messages,
   D. Instead children, may has tantrums, erase phone messages,

2. If you are a parent in this situation, you need to [Select...▾] your children that you love them.

   A. understand, and showing
   B. understand. And show
   C. understand and show
   D. understand, and you show

3. However, also let [Select...▾] doing the right thing.

   A. you're kids know that you feel your
   B. you're kids know that you feel you're
   C. your kids know that you feel your
   D. your kids know that you feel you're

4. Try to see your dates at times when [Select...▾].

   A. you're children are'nt at home
   B. your children are'nt at home
   C. your children aren't at home
   D. your children isn't at home

5. If communication breaks [Select...▾] family counseling.

   A. down will consider
   B. down, consider
   C. down. Consider
   D. down, and consider

Questions 6 through 10 refer to the following paragraphs.

The History of Daylight Saving Time

We set our clocks forward every spring and back every fall, but few of us stop to think about why we do this. One of the main reasons for daylight saving [Select...▾]. In the evening, we use lights, TVs, and electrical appliances. Daylight saving time makes the period between sunset and bedtime one hour shorter, and therefore less electricity is used.

With daylight saving time, each time zone changes [Select...▾]. Time zones were introduced by the railroads to make schedules standard across the country. In 1918, [Select...▾] the rail time zones official. That same year, a second law put the country on daylight saving time for the rest of World War I. The law was unpopular, however, and it was repealed seven months later. Daylight saving time was also in force during most of World War II.

From 1945 to 1966, each state and town could decide whether to observe daylight saving time. The resulting inconsistencies created a great deal of confusion. [Select...▾] to put out new schedules every time a state started or ended daylight saving time. Then came the Uniform Time Act of 1966, which established starting and [Select...▾]. This law was amended in 1986, when the starting date was moved almost a month earlier to save energy.

6. One of the main reasons for daylight saving [Select...▾].

    A. time, is to save energy
    B. time is to save energy
    C. time, are to save energy
    D. times, is to save energy

7. With daylight saving time, each time zone changes [Select...▾].

    A. it's standard time by an hour
    B. its standard time by an hour
    C. it's standard time by an our
    D. it's standard time, by an hour

8. In 1918, [Select...▾] the rail time zones official.

    A. congress passed a law making
    B. Congress passed a law making
    C. congress past a law making
    D. congress passed a law made

9. [Select...▾] to put out new schedules every time a state started or ended daylight saving time.

    A. For example, radio and TV stations had
    B. For example radio and TV stations have
    C. For example radio and TV stations had
    D. For example radio and TV stations, had

10. Then came the Uniform Time Act of 1966, which established starting and [Select...▾].

    A. ending dates for daylight savings time, in the spring and fall
    B. ending date's for daylight savings time, in the spring and fall
    C. ending dates for daylight savings time in the spring and fall
    D. ending dates for daylight savings time, in the Spring and Fall

Questions 11 through 15 refer to the following paragraphs.

Rules and Regulations

Thank you [Select...▾]. Before using our facility, please read these rules and regulations carefully.

[Select...▾] When you enter the pool or exercise room, a security guard will request to see your card and will deny you entrance without it.

Guests are welcome to use the pool and exercise room, but only when accompanied by members. The guest fee is $10 per day. When bringing guests, please have them sign in at the desk in the lobby. They will be given a guest card for the day.

Pool safety is very important. [Select...▾] and other flotation devices are available for your use. Do not hesitate to ask lifeguards for help. Children under the age of 12 must swim in the [Select...▾] by an adult. Swimming classes are available to help both children and adults improve their skills.

You must [Select...▾] for any class you wish to take. Members receive a significant discount. Registration may be limited to a certain number of participants.

11. Thank you [Select...▾].

    A. for joining Spring Valley Community center
    B. for joining Spring Valley community center
    C. for joining Spring Valley Community Center
    D. for joining, Spring Valley Community center

12. [Select...▾]

    A. Please have your membership card with you at all times when your in the building.
    B. Please have you're membership card with you at all times when you're in the building.
    C. Please have your membership card with you at all times' when your in the building.
    D. Please have your membership card with you at all times when you're in the building.

13. [Select...▾] and other flotation devices are available for your use.

    A. If you are a weak swimmer, life jackets
    B. If you are a week swimmer life jackets
    C. If you are a week swimmer, life jackets
    D. If you are a week swimmer, live jackets

14. Children under the age of 12 must swim in the [Select...▾] by an adult.

    A. children's pool, unless they're supervised
    B. childrens' pool, unless they're supervised
    C. children's pool, unless their supervised
    D. children's pool unless they're supervised

15. You must [Select...▾] for any class you wish to take.

    A. register, pay
    B. register and pay
    C. register. And pay
    D. register. Pay

Questions 16 through 20 refer to the following paragraphs.

Racial Profiling

African American and Hispanic motorists are much more likely to be stopped by police [Select...▾] no apparent reason. What's their offense? It may be that these individuals have been targeted because of their race.

Blacks and Hispanics, who some police officers believe are more likely to commit crimes, have been systematically targeted by police. Police statistics [Select...▾] occurs in every geographic location. Motorists, pedestrians, and airline passengers have been searched. The police do not make class [Select...▾] of every station in life have been victims of this practice.

The statistical evidence shows a clear pattern. On one Maryland highway, 73 percent of those stopped by police were African American, even though blacks represented only 17 percent of all drivers. Hispanics make up only 8 percent of the population in [Select...▾] of drivers stopped there are Hispanic. [Select...▾] dispute the studies that document racial profiling. They maintain that the problem has been confined to a small number of officers and can be remedied easily.

16. African American and Hispanic motorists are much more likely to be stopped by police [Select...▾] no apparent reason.

   A. then their white counterparts, often for
   B. then, their white counterparts, often for
   C. than their white counterparts, often for
   D. then their white counterparts, often four

17. Police statistics [Select...▾] occurs in every geographic location.

   A. from 23 States show that this policy, called racial profiling
   B. from 23 states, show that this policy, called racial profiling
   C. from 23 states show that this policy, called racial profiling,
   D. from 23 states show that this policy, called racial profiling

18. The police do not make class [Select...▾] of every station in life have been victims of this practice.

   A. distinctions. For nonwhites
   B. distinctions, for nonwhites
   C. distinctions moreover nonwhites
   D. distinctions nonwhites

19. Hispanics make up only 8 percent of the population in [Select...▾] of drivers stopped there are Hispanic.

   A. illinois, yet 30 percent
   B. Illinois, yet 30 percent
   C. illinois yet 30 percent
   D. illinois, and 30 percent

20. [Select...▾] dispute the studies that document racial profiling.

   A. However police superintendents chiefs of police, and other law enforcement officials
   B. However, police superintendents, chiefs of police, and other law enforcement officials
   C. However, police superintendents chiefs of police, and other law enforcement officials,
   D. However, police superintendents chiefs of police and other law enforcement officials

Answers and explanations start on page 653.

Mathematical Reasoning

The GED® *Mathematical Reasoning Test* evaluates your ability to solve mathematical problems and apply mathematics to a variety of contexts. You will have 90 minutes to answer approximately 46 questions based on the following:

- **Quantitative Reasoning (45%)**, which includes problems with positive and negative whole numbers, decimals, and fractions; ratios, proportions, and percents; data and statistics; and geometric measurement
- **Algebraic Reasoning (55%)**, which includes expressions, polynomials, equations, inequalities, linear equations, quadratic equations, and patterns and functions. A variety of formats will assess evaluating, solving, and graphing skills in algebra.

You will need a minimum score of 150 to pass the *Mathematical Reasoning Test*, which is one of the four tests you will need to pass in order to earn a high school equivalency diploma.

Tools

Calculator For most of the test, you will be able to use either a hand-held or an online version of the **Texas Instruments TI-30XS MultiView™ scientific calculator**. You can access the online calculator by clicking on this icon. You can also take your own hand-held TI-30XS MultiView™ calculator to use on test day.

For the first five questions on the test, you will not be able to use the calculator. You can take up to 12 of the 90 minutes with these questions. Check all of your work carefully before you leave this section of the test. You will not be able to return to these problems once the online calculator is enabled.

If you forget how to use a specific calculator function, you will be able to access a *Calculator Reference Sheet* from the computer screen by clicking on this icon.

Formula Sheet A copy of this formula sheet appears on page 403 of this book. You will be able to access these formulas by clicking on this icon. Other formulas that appear in this book should be memorized.

Symbol Selector On some fill-in-the-blank problems, you will need to use a symbol from the symbol selector toolbar. You can enable it when the icon to the right shows up on the light blue toolbar at the top of your screen.

At the testing center, you will be given a dry erase marker and a **wipe-off board** that you can use as scratch paper.

Computer-Based Mathematics Test Formats

Many of the questions will be *multiple-choice* with four options (A through D). You will **click** on the best answer.

> A painter needs to cover the walls of four rooms in two coats of paint. Each room measures 4 ft by 8 ft, and the ceiling is 10 feet high in each. Each gallon of paint covers 32 square feet. How many gallons of paint does he need?
>
> ○ A.   2
> ○ B.   64
> ○ C. 128
> ○ D. 256

GED® TEST TIP

Follow all directions carefully. For example, in this fill-in-the-blank problem, you are asked to type the answer, simplify the expression, and use the symbol selector to complete the result.

Fill-in-the-blank questions will require you to **type** a numerical answer to a problem or to enter an equation by **clicking** to open the symbol selector and then **inserting** the symbol in the box. You may also be asked to **type** a word or phrase in the box to answer a question about your thought process.

> Type your answer in the box. You may use numbers, symbols, and/or text in your answer.
>
> Simplify the expression completely. Leave your answer in radical form.
>
> $$\sqrt{60} \div \sqrt{5}$$
>
> (**NOTE:** Click the symbol selector when you need to insert the radical sign.)
>
> ☐

Drop-down questions give you the opportunity to **click** the word "Select" and choose the option that correctly completes the statement.

> Sarah runs an open babysitting service on Saturday nights so that parents in the neighborhood can enjoy a night out. The chart below shows the number of children in attendance each hour.
>
> | Hour | # of children |
> |---|---|
> | 5 pm | 2 |
> | 6 pm | 4 |
> | 7 pm | 5 |
> | 8 pm | 6 |
> | 9 pm | 5 |
> | 10 pm | 2 |
> | 11 pm | 2 |
>
> The number of children in attendance ranged from Select... ▾ to Select... ▾.

Drag-and-drop items require you to **click** on an image, number, or symbol and to **drag** and **drop** it to a specified location on the computer screen to create an expression, equation, or inequality.

A clown creates an equation that relates his data of each child's head size to the length of the balloon he needs to make them a proper balloon-animal hat. For each child, he needs a balloon five times as long as the child's head size, plus $\frac{4}{5}$ of an inch extra. Complete a linear equation for child A, where x is the size of the child's head in inches and y is the length of the balloon in inches.

Click on the variables and numbers you want to select and drag them into the boxes.

Equation for Child A

Hot-spot questions are based on a graphic such as a number line, coordinate grid, or geometric figure. You will need to **click** on a specific place or places on the figure.

GED® TEST TIP

You may need to click on one point or on more than one point to correctly answer a hot-spot question. Check the finished graphic against the question before moving on. Make sure that you have completed the task by creating all required points.

Jessica has 20 hours a week to spend making scarves. Each week, she spends 2 hours purchasing the materials. Each scarf takes 3 hours to complete. The inequality $2 + 3s \leq 20$ represents the number of scarves, s, Jessica can make in one week.

Using the number line below, click each number to plot each possible value for s.

(**NOTE:** If you need to remove a point, hold the cursor over the point and left-click the mouse.)

Using the Texas Instruments TI-30XS MultiView™ Calculator

Throughout this unit, you will practice using the **TI-30XS MultiView™** calculator. Remember: You <u>do not have to</u> use the calculator to solve problems; only use it if it is relevant to the problem or if you believe it will be helpful.

Below is a picture of the hand-held version and some issues to keep in mind.

Photo used with permission from TI. http://education.ti.com.

- The <u>hand-held version</u> has an On/Off button at the lower-left hand side.

- To use the <u>online version</u> of the calculator, **click** the calculator icon (see page 215) to open the calculator in a new window. Use your mouse to **drag** the calculator to the side of the computer screen so that it does not cover the problem. When you are finished with a calculation, **click** on the "X" at the top of the window to close the calculator.

TI-30XS MultiView™ Calculator

- When you are finished with a calculation, use the *enter* button. (There is no "equal sign" button on this calculator.)

- Use the *white numeric keypad* to enter numbers, the decimal point, and the negative sign (−) for a negative number such as −13 .

- The *operation keys*, on the right, allow you to add, subtract, multiply, and divide. (Use the minus sign here for subtraction; use the negative sign (−) on the keypad to indicate a negative number.)

- Use the bright green *2nd button* at the left of the calculator to activate the *2nd functions* (in bright green) above the keys. Some of the main ones are square root, exponent, percent, and mixed number functions.

- The *four arrows* at the top right of the calculator allow you to move the *onscreen cursor* up, down, left, or right as needed. The *delete* key to the left of the arrows allows you to correct mistakes as you work.

- Every time you begin a calculation, press the *clear* button above the *operation keys* to clear the calculator's memory.

Accessing the Symbol Selector Toolbar

Some questions will instruct you to use a particular symbol from the "symbol selector." This is not available for all problems, but this icon shows up when you need the toolbar: Æ Symbol

When you **click** on this icon, a new window will open up with these symbols:

Æ Symbol

∏	f	≥	≤	≠	²	³			×	÷	±	∞	√
+	–	(	)	>	<	=

Click on a symbol to insert it in the correct place in an expression, equation, or inequality. When you are finished with the toolbar, **click** on the "X" at the top of the window to close the window.

Using the Wipe-Off Board

Even with all of the computer-based tools, you may still feel the need for some scratch paper to do the following:

- Write down the relevant numbers that you need to answer a specific question.
- Solve the problem by hand and use the calculator to check your work.
- Make a drawing or a diagram to help you picture a situation that is described in a word problem. This is an important strategy when working with measurement and geometry problems that do not contain a graphic.

At the testing center, you will be provided with a wipe-off board and dry erase marker, similar to the material shown at the right. Make use of the board throughout the *Mathematical Reasoning Test* and ask for a new one if you feel that you need it.

NUMBER SENSE AND PROBLEM SOLVING

Compare and Order Numbers

Place Value

Numbers are part of your everyday life. Whether you're paying with cash, reading bus schedules, or changing television channels, you're using whole numbers.

The value of a number depends on the **place value** of its digits. On the place-value chart below, note that the value of a digit increases as you move to the left.

In the whole number shown on the chart, 1 has the greatest value. The number would be read as "one thousand four hundred seventy-nine."

Comparing and Ordering Values

To **order** numbers, you need to compare the value of their digits. Align the place values of the numbers you are comparing. Start at the left and compare the value of the first digit of each number.

Example 1: Place the numbers 342, 98, and 317 in order from least to greatest.

1. Compare the first digit in each number. Since 98 is a two-digit number, and the other numbers are three-digit numbers, 98 has the smallest value.

   hundreds tens ones

   342
   98
   317

2. Next, compare the first digit of the remaining numbers. Since both numbers have the same digit (3) in the hundreds place, compare the digits in the tens place. Since 1 is less than 4, 317 is less than 342.

   From least to greatest:
   98, 317, 342

Rounding Numbers

Place value is also essential to **rounding** numbers.

Example 2: Round 2451 to the nearest hundred.

2451

1. Locate the place value that you want to round to. Then look at the place value to the right. If the digit to the right is 5 or greater, round up. If the digit to the right is less than 5, don't change the number in the hundreds place.

   The value to the right of the hundreds place is a 5. Round up.

2. Round up the digit in the hundreds place. Then change the digits to the right of the hundreds place to zeros.

   2451 rounds up to **2500**

Key Ideas

- When ordering numbers, compare the same place values between numbers.
- Round numbers to estimate answers or eliminate answer choices in multiple-choice questions.

GED® TEST TIP

It's important to know the inequality symbols below.
< means "is less than"
≤ means "is less than or equal to"
> means "is greater than"
≥ means "is greater than or equal to"

PRACTICE 1

A. Write the digit from the number below that corresponds to the listed place value. The first one is done for you.

1,436,879

__4__ 1. hundred thousands   ____ 5. thousands

____ 2. hundreds   ____ 6. tens

____ 3. ones   ____ 7. ten thousands

____ 4. millions

B. Round these numbers as directed.

8. Round 544 to the nearest hundred.   11. Round 11,632 to the nearest thousand.

9. Round 76 to the nearest ten.   12. Round 1525 to the nearest thousand.

10. Round 1058 to the nearest hundred.   13. Round 84 to the nearest hundred.

C. In each of the following pairs, which number is greater?

14. 100 or 89   16. 1099 or 1145

15. 339 or 341   17. 125,391 or 119,450

D. Write these numbers in order from <u>least to greatest</u>.

18. 23 18 45 39   21. 1429 1420 1432 1425

19. 111 89 109 91   22. 12,071 11,098 12,131

20. 1087 932 909 1139   23. 15,356 15,309 15,298

E. Choose the <u>one best answer</u> to each question.

24. When stacking items, the heaviest items should be placed at the bottom. Starting at the bottom, in what order should items weighing 45 pounds, 40 pounds, 50 pounds, and 48 pounds be stacked?

    A. 40, 45, 48, 50
    B. 45, 50, 40, 48
    C. 50, 48, 45, 40
    D. 50, 40, 45, 48

25. Which of the following correctly shows 1,543,976 rounded to the nearest hundred thousand?

    A. 2,000,000
    B. 1,600,000
    C. 1,500,000
    D. 1,540,000

Answers and explanations begin on page 654.

Whole Number Operations

Addition and Subtraction

You use **addition** when you need to combine amounts. The answer in an addition problem is called the **sum**, or **total**. When you are adding, it's helpful to stack the numbers in a column. Be sure to line up the place-value columns and then work from right to left, starting with the ones column.

Sometimes the digits in a place-value column add up to 10 or more. When this happens, you will need to **regroup** to the next place value.

Example 1: Add 40 + 129 + 24.

1. Align the numbers you want to add on the ones column. Working from right to left, add the ones column first. Since the ones column totals 13, write the 3 in the ones column and regroup, or **carry**, the 1 ten to the tens column.

$$\begin{array}{r} 1 \\ 40 \\ 129 \\ + 24 \\ \hline 3 \end{array}$$

2. Add the tens column, including the regrouped 1.

$$\begin{array}{r} 1 \\ 40 \\ 129 \\ + 24 \\ \hline 93 \end{array}$$

3. Then add the hundreds column. Since there is only one value, write the 1 hundred in the answer.

$$\begin{array}{r} 1 \\ 40 \\ 129 \\ + 24 \\ \hline 193 \end{array}$$

You **subtract** when you want to find the **difference** between amounts. Write the greater number on top, and align the amounts on the ones column. You may also need to regroup as you subtract.

Example 2: If Sue is 57 and Kathy is 38, how many years older is Sue?

1. Find the difference in their ages. Start with the ones column. Since 7 is less than the number being subtracted (8), regroup, or **borrow**, 1 ten from the tens column. Add the regrouped amount to the ones column. Now subtract $17 - 8$ in the ones column.

$$\begin{array}{r} 4\,17 \\ \cancel{5}\cancel{7} \\ - 38 \\ \hline 9 \end{array}$$

2. Regrouping 1 ten from the tens column left 4 tens. Subtract $4 - 3$ and write the result in the tens column of your answer. Check: $19 + 38 = 57$.

$$\begin{array}{r} 4\,17 \\ \cancel{5}\cancel{7} \\ - 38 \\ \hline 19 \end{array}$$

Sue is **19 years older** than Kathy.

Key Ideas

- Add when combining amounts and subtract when finding the difference.
- Align place-value columns when adding or subtracting.
- Always look to the next place-value column to regroup.

GED® TEST TIP

Another way to check answers is to round the numbers in a problem and find an approximate answer.

Example 3: Find the difference between 205 and 67.

1. Subtract. Start with the ones column. Since 5 is less than the number being subtracted (7), regroup. Since there are 0 tens in the tens column, regroup 1 hundred from the hundreds column. From 10 tens, regroup 1 ten to the ones column. Now subtract $15-7$ in the ones column.

$$\begin{array}{r} \overset{9}{\underset{1\ \cancel{10}\ 15}{\cancel{2}\ \cancel{0}\ \cancel{5}}} \\ -\ 6\ 7 \\ \hline 8 \end{array}$$

2. Regrouping 1 ten from the tens column left 9 tens. Subtract $9-6$, and write the result in the tens column of your answer.

$$\begin{array}{r} \overset{9}{\underset{1\ \cancel{10}\ 15}{\cancel{2}\ \cancel{0}\ \cancel{5}}} \\ -\ 6\ 7 \\ \hline 3\ 8 \end{array}$$

3. Regrouping 1 hundred from the hundreds column left 1 hundred. Subtract the hundreds column: $1-0$. Check: $138+67=205$.

$$\begin{array}{r} \overset{9}{\underset{1\ \cancel{10}\ 15}{\cancel{2}\ \cancel{0}\ \cancel{5}}} \\ -\ 6\ 7 \\ \hline 1\ 3\ 8 \end{array}$$

PRACTICE 2.1

A. Solve.

1. $\begin{array}{r} 54 \\ +23 \\ \hline \end{array}$

3. $\begin{array}{r} 73 \\ -21 \\ \hline \end{array}$

5. $\begin{array}{r} 105 \\ +85 \\ \hline \end{array}$

7. $\begin{array}{r} 100 \\ -57 \\ \hline \end{array}$

2. $\begin{array}{r} 46 \\ +54 \\ \hline \end{array}$

4. $\begin{array}{r} 55 \\ -19 \\ \hline \end{array}$

6. $\begin{array}{r} 2386 \\ +1692 \\ \hline \end{array}$

8. $\begin{array}{r} 2500 \\ -383 \\ \hline \end{array}$

B. Rewrite the problems in columns before solving.

9. $20+12+33=$

10. $245-131=$

11. $30+75+75=$

12. $378-85=$

13. $144+238+101=$

14. $545-89=$

15. $2095+324=$

16. $1250-350=$

17. $10,326+982=$

18. $15,890-705=$

19. $108,755+22,442=$

20. $44,789-13,890=$

C. Choose the one best answer to each question.

21. What is the total weight of the boxes below?

   A. 78
   B. 88
   C. 150
   D. 160

22. Celia's share for lunch is $7. If she pays with a $20 bill, how much change should she get?

   A. $3
   B. $7
   C. $13
   D. $27

Answers and explanations begin on page 654.

Multiplication and Division

You **multiply** to combine the same amount multiple times. For example, instead of adding $24 + 24 + 24$, you could multiply 24 by 3. If a problem asks you to find the **product** of two or more numbers, you should multiply.

Example 4: Find the product of 24 and 63.

1. Align place values as you rewrite the problem in a column. Multiply the ones place of the top number by the ones place of the bottom number: $4 \times 3 = 12$. Write the 2 in the ones place in the first partial product. Regroup the 1 ten.

$$\begin{array}{r} 1 \\ 24 \\ \times\,63 \\ \hline 2 \end{array}$$

2. Multiply the tens place in the top number by 3: $2 \times 3 = 6$. Then add the regrouped amount: $6 + 1 = 7$. Write the 7 in the tens place in the partial product.

$$\begin{array}{r} 1 \\ 24 \\ \times\,63 \\ \hline 72 \end{array}$$

3. Now multiply by the tens place of 63. Write a **placeholder** 0 in the ones place in the second partial product, since you're really multiplying by 60. Then multiply the top number by 6: $4 \times 6 = 24$. Write 4 in the partial product and regroup the 2. Multiply $2 \times 6 = 12$. Add the regrouped 2: $12 + 2 = 14$.

$$\begin{array}{r} 2 \\ 24 \\ \times\,63 \\ \hline 72 \\ +1440 \\ \hline \mathbf{1512} \end{array}$$

4. Add the partial products to find the total product: $72 + 1440 = \mathbf{1512}$.

To **divide** means to find how many equal parts an amount can be divided into. The amount being divided is called the **dividend.** The number you are dividing by is the **divisor,** and the answer to a division problem is the **quotient.**

Example 5: At a garage sale, 3 children sold their old toys for a total of \$54. If they share the money equally, how much money should each child receive?

1. Divide the total amount (\$54) by the number of ways the money is to be split (3). Work from left to right. How many times does 3 go into 5? Write the answer 1 directly above the 5 in the dividend. Since $3 \times 1 = 3$, subtract $5 - 3 = 2$.

$$\begin{array}{r} 1 \\ 3\overline{)\$54} \\ -3 \\ \hline 2 \end{array}$$

2. Continue dividing. Bring down the 4 from the ones place in the dividend. How many times does 3 go into 24? Write the answer 8 directly above the 4 in the dividend. Since $3 \times 8 = 24$, subtract $24 - 24 = 0$.

Each child should receive \$18.

$$\begin{array}{r} 18 \\ 3\overline{)\$54} \\ -3 \\ \hline 24 \\ -24 \\ \hline 0 \end{array}$$

Example 6: Divide $1006 \div 4$.

1. Divide the total amount (1006) by 4. Work from left to right. Since 4 doesn't divide into 1, use the next place value in the dividend. How many times does 4 go into 10? Write the answer 2 directly above the first 0 in the dividend. Since $4 \times 2 = 8$, subtract $10 - 8 = 2$.

$$\begin{array}{r} 2 \\ 4\overline{)1006} \\ -8 \\ \hline 2 \end{array}$$

2. Continue dividing. Bring down the 0 from the tens place in the dividend. How many times does 4 go into 20? Write the answer 5 directly above the second 0 in the dividend. Since $4 \times 5 = 20$, subtract $20 - 20 = 0$. Bring down the 6 from the ones place in the dividend. How many times does 4 go into 6? Write the answer 1 above the 6 in the dividend. Since $4 \times 1 = 4$, subtract $6 - 4 = 2$. Write the **remainder** of 2 as part of the quotient.

$$
\begin{array}{r}
251\ r2 \\
4\overline{)1006} \\
-8 \\
\hline
20 \\
-20 \\
\hline
06 \\
-4 \\
\hline
2
\end{array}
$$

By reviewing and memorizing multiplication tables, you can save yourself precious time on the GED® *Mathematical Reasoning Test*.

PRACTICE 2.2

A. Solve.

1. $\begin{array}{r} 121 \\ \times 4 \\ \hline \end{array}$

4. $5\overline{)65}$

7. $\begin{array}{r} 45 \\ \times 30 \\ \hline \end{array}$

10. $10\overline{)280}$

2. $\begin{array}{r} 250 \\ \times 4 \\ \hline \end{array}$

5. $7\overline{)735}$

8. $\begin{array}{r} 105 \\ \times 25 \\ \hline \end{array}$

11. $15\overline{)225}$

3. $\begin{array}{r} 342 \\ \times 8 \\ \hline \end{array}$

6. $9\overline{)189}$

9. $\begin{array}{r} 211 \\ \times 16 \\ \hline \end{array}$

12. $19\overline{)114}$

B. Solve. If multiplying more than two numbers, find the product of two numbers before multiplying by the next number, and so on.

13. $50 \times 5 =$

16. $1004 \div 5 =$

19. $10,760 \div 20 =$

14. $179 \div 4 =$

17. $25 \times 3 \times 2 =$

20. $12 \times 8 \times 4 =$

15. $5 \times 6 \times 10 =$

18. $7452 \times 9 =$

21. $144,140 \div 12 =$

C. Choose the one best answer to each question.

22. A fruit juice container holds 16 servings. If the serving size is 6 ounces, how many ounces does the container hold in all?

    A. 10
    B. 22
    C. 76
    D. 96

23. A cashier has fifteen $5 bills. How much does he have in $5 bills?

    A. $15
    B. $25
    C. $75
    D. $150

D. For question 24, write your answer on the line provided.

24. How many 2-foot lengths can be cut from the string shown below?

    _____
                12 ft

    _____

    Answers and explanations begin on page 654.

3

NUMBER SENSE AND PROBLEM SOLVING

GED® Test Calculator Skills

Key Ideas

- For many questions, you may use either a hand-held or online version of the TI-30XS MultiView™ scientific calculator.
- Use the calculator when you think it will save you time or improve your accuracy.
- Learn the placement of the keys and how to perform specific functions before you take the test.

You will have access to an online or hand-held calculator for many questions on the *Mathematical Reasoning Test* and for some questions on the *Social Studies* and *Science Tests*. If you wish to use a hand-held calculator, you will likely need to bring your own. It must be the Texas Instruments TI-30XS MultiView™, shown here. The online version will be available when the calculator icon appears at the top of the computer screen. You will click on the icon to open the calculator and use the mouse to move it so that it does not cover the problem. See page 218 for more calculator basics.

Look at the reproduction of the calculator below and follow the examples that demonstrate how to use the calculator's **operation keys**.

Calculations you enter appear here.

Delete key

Digit keys

On

Solution to a problem displays here.

Arrows (allow you to navigate in the display)

Clear key

Operations keys

Enter key

GED® TEST TIP

You can buy a handheld TI-30XS MultiView™ calculator for practice as you work through this study guide. It may be available online, at office supply stores, or other places where calculators are sold.

Example 1: Add $63 + 97 + 58 + 32 + 81$.

1. Always clear a calculator before starting a new computation. On the TI-30XS MultiView™, use the *clear* key.

   (clear)

2. Enter each number followed by the plus sign. As you type, the numbers and plus signs will appear on the calculator's screen. If you make a mistake, press *delete* to go back and reenter a number.

   $63 + 97 + 58 + 32 + 81$

3. Press *enter* to find the total.

   (enter)

The total, **331**, will appear on the right-hand side of the display:

331

Example 2: Find the difference between 15,789 and 9,332.

1. Always clear a calculator before starting a new computation.   (clear)
2. Enter the greater number first, followed by the minus operator.   15789 (−)
   NOTE: Use the minus key that is on the right side of the calculator
   with the other operation symbols. Don't use the (−) key at the bottom of the calculator; that key is used to enter a negative number.
3. Enter the number being subtracted.   9332
4. Press the *enter* key to find the answer.   (enter)

The answer **6457** will appear on the right-hand side of the display.   **6457**

Example 3: Find the product of 309 and 68.

1. Always clear a calculator before starting a new computation.   (clear)
2. Enter the first number, followed by the multiplication operator.   309 (×)
   (The multiplication sign will appear in the display as an asterisk
   rather than an ×, but the *multiplication key* looks like an ×.)
3. Enter the next number.   68
4. Press the *enter* key to find the product.   (enter)

The answer **21012** will appear on the right-hand side of the display.   **21012**

Example 4: Divide 12,456 by 12.

1. Always clear a calculator before starting a new computation.   (clear)
2. Enter the number to be divided first, followed by the division   12456 (÷)
   operator.
3. Enter the number you are dividing by.   12
4. Press the *enter* key to find the quotient.   (enter)

The answer **1038** will appear on the right-hand side of the display.   **1038**

PRACTICE 3.1

A. Practice solving the following problems on your calculator.

1. $19 + 26 + 85 + 23 =$
2. $2579 - 1392 =$
3. $4 \times 28 \times 7 =$
4. $2568 \div 107 =$
5. $12,356 + 14,728 =$
6. $107,899 - 93,457 =$
7. $209 \times 56 =$
8. $972 \div 18 =$
9. $20,540 \div 13 =$

B. Choose the one correct answer to each question.

10. Dan bought a used car with 16,741 miles on it. If the car now has 42,920 miles on it, how many miles has Dan put on the car?

   A. 16,741
   B. 26,179
   C. 42,920
   D. 59,661

11. A shipment of 20 computers arrived at a warehouse. If each computer is valued at $995, what is the total value of the shipment?

   A. $995
   B. $1015
   C. $1990
   D. $19,900

Answers and explanations begin on page 654.

Using the *2nd* Key for a Second Function

To access some of the functions on the TI-30XS MultiView™, you need to press the *2nd* key in the upper left corner of the keypad. This bright green key will activate the second function also shown in green above the corresponding key. To access the second function of a key, press the *2nd* key first—do not press it at the same time as the function key. Highlighted below are two commonly used second functions—square root and percent. Use the process shown here for all *2nd* function keys.

2nd key.

Square root (√☐) is the 2nd function of the x^2 key.

Percent (%) is the 2nd function of the left parenthesis key.

Example 5: Find the square root of 169.

	Keys to Press	On the Display
1. Always clear a calculator before starting a new computation.	clear	
2. Recognize that square root is a *2nd* function over the x^2 key. Press the *2nd* key. (Note that the term *2nd* now appears in the upper left corner of the display.)	2nd	2nd
3. Next, press the x^2 key to activate the square root function in green over the key. You will see a blinking cursor under the square root.	√⎵ x^2	√☐
4. Now that you have the square root function, enter the number. The number will appear under the square root symbol in the display.	169	√169▶
5. Press the *enter* key to find the square root. The answer, **13**, will appear on the right-hand side of the display.	enter	√169 13

For more information about square roots, see page 318.

Remember: For all *2nd functions*, (1) press the *2nd* key first to activate the *2nd* function, (2) press the key, and (3) enter the numbers.

Example 6: Find the part if you are given the percent and the whole. Find 10 percent of 500.

1. Always clear a calculator before starting a new computation.	(clear)
2. Enter the number you want to find the percent of.	500
3. Press the multiplication sign.	⊗
4. Enter the percent number.	10
5. Press the *2nd* key and then press the open, or left, parenthesis key to activate the percent function.	(2nd) %⟮(
6. Press the *enter* key to find the answer.	(enter)

The answer, **50**, will appear on the right-hand side of the display. Ten percent of 500 is 50.   **50**

Example 7: Find the percent if you are given the whole and the part. What percent of 240 is 60?

1. Always clear a calculator before starting a new computation.	(clear)
2. Enter the part.	60
3. Press the division sign.	÷
4. Enter the whole.	240
5. Press the *2nd* key and then press the close, or right, parenthesis symbol. This tells the calculator to translate the answer into a percent.	
6. Press the *enter* key to find the answer.	(enter)

The answer, **25%**, will appear on the right-hand side of the display. Sixty is 25% of 240.   **25%**

For more information about percents, see pages 266–277.

PRACTICE 3.2

A. Practice solving the following problems on your calculator.

1. $\sqrt{625}$

2. $\sqrt{324}$

3. $\sqrt{1225}$

4. Find 20% of 680.

5. Find 10% of 1250.

6. 15 is what percent of 300?

7. Find 5% of 40.

8. Find 30% of 450.

9. 20 is what percent of 400?

B. Choose the <u>one best</u> answer to each question.

10. Tanya paid 20% of $1680 as a down payment. How much was the down payment?

  A. $20
  B. $168
  C. $336
  D. $840

11. Aaron received a credit of $48 on a purchase of $960. What percent of $960 is $48?

  A. 5%
  B. 20%
  C. 48%
  D. 912%

Answers and explanations begin on page 654.

Word Problems

To pass the *Mathematical Reasoning Test*, you will need to solve word problems. These questions are easier to manage if you use a **five-step problem-solving process**. Practice this process with word problems in this book.

Step 1. What is the **question** asking me to find?

> *Read the problem carefully. State the question in your own words.*

Step 2. What **information** from the problem do I need?

> *Select only the information you need to answer the question.*

Step 3. Which **operation** do I need to perform—addition, subtraction, multiplication, or division?

> *Choose from one of the four operations above based on your understanding of the question.*

Step 4. What is my **solution**?

> *Carry out the operation with the numbers you chose in step 2.*

Step 5. Does my answer **make sense**?

> *Look back to make sure that you answered the question. Check that your answer makes sense.*

Key Ideas

- Successful math problem solvers use a five-step process.
- Read carefully to understand the question and select only the information needed to answer it.
- When you have found an answer, check that it makes sense.

ON THE GED® TEST

Many Mathematical Reasoning Test questions include information that is not needed to answer the specific question. In multiple-choice questions, wrong answer choices may be based on mistakenly using this "extra" information, so read carefully.

To help you decide which operation to use, keep the following ideas in mind.

You...	in order to...
add	combine amounts of different sizes
subtract	find the difference between amounts
multiply	combine the same amount multiple times
divide	separate one amount into equal-sized groups

Example 1: To cover a sofa, Sophia needs 12 yards of fabric that costs $14 per yard. How many yards does Sophia need for 3 sofas?

    A. 4
    B. 36
    C. 42
    D. 168

The correct answer is **B. 36 yards** of fabric. The question asked you to find the total number of yards of fabric Sophia needs for 3 sofas. Note that the cost of a yard of fabric is not needed to answer the question.

Since you were asked to find the amount of fabric for 3 sofas, you should multiply 12 yards × 3 sofas = 36 yards. Here are two common errors to avoid:

- If you had mistakenly divided, you would have gotten the incorrect answer of 4 yards of fabric for 3 sofas.

- If you had used the $14 price per yard and multiplied by either 3 sofas or 12 yards, you would have been tempted by wrong answers 42 or 168. However, the cost per yard is not needed.

PRACTICE 4.1

1. Peter wants to repaint his 700-square-foot apartment. He calculates that he has 3500 square feet of wall space to paint. (He will not paint the floor or the ceiling.) If each gallon of paint will cover 350 square feet of wall space, how many gallons will Peter need?

   A. 2
   B. 5
   C. 10
   D. 15

2. For a family get-together, Darryl wants to be sure that each child gets 2 party favors. The party favors cost $3 each, and there are 11 children coming. How many party favors will Darryl need?

   A. 9
   B. 11
   C. 18
   D. 22

3. Sarah and Kate live 18 miles apart, and they both work at the same office. If Sarah lives 25 miles from the office and Kate lives 30 miles from the office, how many miles farther from the office does Kate live than Sarah?

   A. 5
   B. 7
   C. 12
   D. 15

For question 4, <u>write your answer</u> on the line provided.

4. The Navarro family uses an average of 225 gallons of water per day, 5 gallons of which goes through the family's water filter. The Navarros' water filter can process 450 gallons before it needs to be replaced. After how many days of average water use will the family need to replace their filter?

_____

<u>Questions 5 and 6</u> are based on the following information.

Joyce owns a beauty salon, and she has posted the following information in her salon.

Service	Minutes to complete	Price
Manicure	30	$15
Pedicure	30	$25
Manicure & Pedicure	45	$35
Facial	45	$45
Makeover	60	$60

5. How many minutes will it take Joyce to give 3 pedicures?

   A. 30
   B. 55
   C. 75
   D. 90

6. How much more does a customer pay for the makeover than for the manicure & pedicure combination?

   A. $15
   B. $20
   C. $25
   D. $35

_____

For questions 7 and 8, <u>write your answers</u> on the lines provided.

7. Brandon is planning his part of the local community garden. He has calculated that he can plant 6 seedlings per row, and the garden allots 7 rows to each gardener. What is the maximum number of seedlings Brandon could plant?

_____

8. Sumayyah knits gloves and hats each winter and sells them through a local shop. If Sumayyah received $189 from the sale of her hats and gloves this past winter, and she spent $27 on yarn, how much money did she earn from her knitting?

   $ _____

Answers and explanations begin on page 654.

Multi-Step Word Problems

The word problems on the previous two pages involved only one operation to solve. However, on the GED® *Mathematical Reasoning Test* and other tests, you may need to do several math processes to solve a problem. These are called **multi-step problems**.

When you are working on multi-step problems, there are two important ideas to keep in mind. *What is the question asking me to find?* and *Did I answer the question?*

Review this example of a multi-step problem and the problem-solving process below.

Example 1: To win a prize, Sarah's daughter has to sell 75 boxes of cookies in 3 days. If she sold 16 boxes on day 1 and 34 boxes on day 2, how many boxes would she need to sell on day 3 to win the prize?

       (1) 18
       (2) 25
       (3) 50

Step 1. What is the question asking me to find?

The question asks me to find how many boxes Sarah's daughter needs to sell on the third day to make her goal of 75 boxes.

Step 2. What information from the problem do I need?

I know the total number of boxes she needs to sell (75 boxes).

I know how many boxes she sold on day 1 (16 boxes) and day 2 (34 boxes).

Step 3. Do I need to do only one operation, or do I need to do more than one?

I can add to find how many boxes Sarah's daughter has sold so far: 16 + 34 = 50.

However, that doesn't tell me <u>how many boxes she needs to sell on day 3</u>. I need one more step.

Step 4. What is my solution?

*75 boxes total − 50 boxes sold = 25 boxes for day 3. The correct answer is (2) **25**.*

Step 5. Does my answer make sense? Did I answer the question?

By taking the additional step, I answered the question of how many boxes need to be sold on day 3.

This sample multi-step problem involved only two operations: adding and subtracting. On the actual test, you may need to do three or more operations to answer a question, so read and think carefully about each problem.

As you think about the example, note the most common mistake people make with multi-step problems. Often they stop short of answering the question. Notice that choice (3) 50 is a **partial solution**, but it is not the answer to the question. Using the five-step problem-solving process will help you avoid that mistake.

PRACTICE 4.2

<u>Questions 1–3 are based on the information below.</u>

Farhana's produce company distributes to several restaurants. The table below shows how many cases of different produce each restaurant ordered from Farhana's company in July.

Produce Orders in July					
	Asparagus	Boston lettuce	Carrots	Romaine lettuce	Tomatoes
Restaurant A	2	3	1	4	3
Restaurant B	4	4	2	2	1
Restaurant C	0	0	3	4	3
Restaurant D	1	2	2	3	4
Restaurant E	3	0	3	2	1

1. If Boston lettuce costs $17 per case and romaine lettuce costs $23 per case, how much did Restaurant D spend on lettuce ordered from Farhana in July?

   A. $85
   B. $93
   C. $103
   D. $143

2. Delivery costs $2 per case for the first 5 cases and $1 per case for each additional case of produce. What was Restaurant B's delivery charge in July?

   A. $13
   B. $18
   C. $20
   D. $26

3. If asparagus costs $22 per case and tomatoes cost $15 per case, which of the following restaurants spent the most on asparagus and tomatoes combined?

   A. Restaurant A
   B. Restaurant B
   C. Restaurant C
   D. Restaurant D

4. At a certain store, loose-leaf paper comes only in packages of 400 sheets. If a student buys enough paper at this store to fill 3 binders with 150 sheets of paper each, how many sheets will be left over?

   A. 17
   B. 50
   C. 350
   D. 450

5. Three friends are baking cupcakes for a bake sale. Each batch of 24 cupcakes requires 2 cups of flour. The friends have a single 5-pound bag of flour that contains 19 cups of flour. How many whole batches of cupcakes can they bake?

   A. 9
   B. 38
   C. 216
   D. 228

6. A certain health insurance plan costs $3000 per year for a family of six. If each member of the family has $750 in medical expenses in a year, and the plan pays 100% of those expenses, how much will the family save by purchasing the plan?

   A. $1500
   B. $2000
   C. $2500
   D. $3000

Answers and explanations begin on page 654.

NUMBER SENSE AND PROBLEM SOLVING

Distance and Cost

Key Ideas

- The following all indicate multiplication:

  $n \times r \quad nr \quad n(r) \quad n \cdot r$

- The following indicate division:

  $c \div n \quad \dfrac{c}{n}$

- A formula can be rewritten to solve for each of its variables.

  $c = nr \quad \dfrac{c}{n} = r \quad \dfrac{c}{r} = n$

  $d = rt \quad \dfrac{d}{r} = t \quad \dfrac{d}{t} = r$

Distance

On the *Mathematical Reasoning Test*, you'll see questions that will require you to apply formulas. When a relationship is constant, use a formula to set up the information about how the different parts relate to each other. One of the most commonly tested formulas deals with distance, rate, and time. Distance is a product of the rate at which something travels and the amount of travel time:

$$\text{distance} = \text{rate} \times \text{time}, \quad \text{or} \quad d = rt$$

Notice that letters, or variables, can be used to represent the different parts of a formula. A formula allows you to substitute known values for certain variables and solve for the unknown variable.

Example 1: How many miles can you travel if you drive at an average speed of 55 miles per hour for 3 hours?

1. You know the rate (55 miles per hour) and the time (3 hours). Substitute the values in the distance formula.

   $\text{distance} = 55 \times 3$

2. Multiply to find the distance.

   $55 \times 3 = \textbf{165 miles}$

Cost

Another helpful formula is the cost formula. It expresses the relationship between cost, the number of units, and rate (price per unit). **NOTE:** The word *per* means for every one unit. The cost formula can be written as follows:

$$\text{total cost} = (\text{number of units}) \times (\text{price per unit}), \quad \text{or} \quad c = nr$$

Example 2: At a bakery, a package of frosted cookies is priced at $3 per package. If a teacher treats her class by buying 4 packages, how much would the cookies cost before tax?

1. You know the number of units (4 packages) and the price per unit ($3 per package). Substitute the values in the cost formula.

   $c = nr$
   $\text{total cost} = 4 \times \$3$

2. Multiply to find the total cost.

   $4 \times \$3 = \textbf{\$12}$

If you know any two of the three variables in a formula, you can solve for the third variable.

Example 3: Max bought a set of 4 floor mats for $44. How much was the price per floor mat?

1. You know the total cost ($44) and the number of units (4 floor mats). Rewrite the formula to solve for the price per unit (r).

   $c = nr$
   $r = \dfrac{c}{n}$

2. Substitute the known values in the cost formula. Divide to find the price per unit.

   $\dfrac{\$44}{4} = \textbf{\$11}$

ON THE GED® TEST

Substitute all of the values for variables back into a formula to check your answer.

PRACTICE 5

A. Each problem below includes two of the three variables from either the distance formula or the cost formula. Write the missing variable you need to solve for. Then decide which of the following formula variations you would use in each situation. The first one is done for you.

$$d = rt \qquad \frac{d}{r} = t \qquad \frac{d}{t} = r \qquad c = nr \qquad \frac{c}{n} = r \qquad \frac{c}{r} = n$$

1. Given: distance and time

   Solve for: rate

   Formula: $\frac{d}{t} = r$

2. Given: rate and time

   Solve for: _____

   Formula: _____

3. Given: distance and rate

   Solve for: _____

   Formula: _____

4. Given: cost and number of units

   Solve for: _____

   Formula: _____

5. Given: number of units and price per unit

   Solve for: _____

   Formula: _____

6. Given: cost and price per unit

   Solve for: _____

   Formula: _____

B. Use the formulas provided in part A above to help you set up the problems. Solve for the unknown variable.

7. Find the total cost of 4 flats of plants at $12 each.

8. Find the total cost of 12 boxes of cookies if each box costs $3.

9. If 4 tires cost $320, how much does a single tire cost?

10. How many tickets would you get for $25 if raffle tickets cost $5 apiece?

11. If you paid $20 for 10 bus transfer tickets, how much did you pay per ticket?

12. Find the distance traveled by a car averaging 60 miles per hour for 3 hours.

13. Find the distance traveled by a train averaging 50 miles per hour for 4 hours.

14. How long does it take for a bus to travel 25 miles at an average rate of 25 miles per hour?

15. If a train travels 270 miles in 3 hours, what is the train's average speed?

16. How long does it take to complete a delivery route of 75 miles at a rate of 25 miles per hour?

C. Choose the <u>one best answer</u> to each question.

17. A company sold a total of $640 in gift boxes. If the gift boxes cost $20 apiece, how many gift boxes did the company sell?

    A.   32
    B.   320
    C.   660
    D. 1280

18. A truck driver traveled 275 miles in 5 hours. What was his average speed in miles per hour?

    A. 1375
    B.   280
    C.   270
    D.   55

Answers and explanations begin on page 654.

NUMBER SENSE AND PROBLEM SOLVING PRACTICE QUESTIONS

Directions: You MAY use your calculator.

1. A beverage container holds 12 servings. If the serving size is 8 ounces, how many ounces does the container hold in all?

   A. 20
   B. 32
   C. 48
   D. 96

2. Sales at 3 concession stands are $839, $527, and $726. What is the total amount in sales?

   A. $1581
   B. $2092
   C. $2178
   D. $2517

3. If you want to cut 24 two-foot braces, how many boards of the length shown below would you need?

   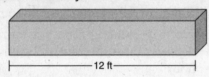

   A. 4
   B. 6
   C. 12
   D. 24

4. Using your calculator, find the value of $\sqrt{441}$.

   A. 11
   B. 21
   C. 221
   D. 441

5. Angelo bought a used car with 39,451 miles on it. If the car now has 70,040 miles on it, how many miles has Angelo driven the car?

   A. 30,589
   B. 39,459
   C. 70,040
   D. 109,491

6. Use your calculator to solve this problem. If Emory paid 20% of $3280 as a down payment, how much was the down payment?

   A. $164
   B. $328
   C. $656
   D. $6560

7. Inventory shows that a warehouse has 45 printers in stock. If each printer is valued at $125, what is the total value of the printer inventory?

   A. $5625
   B. $170
   C. $80
   D. $45

8. Lydia can drive 180 miles in 3 hours. On Tuesday, she drove for 7 hours at that rate. How many miles did she drive on Tuesday?

   A. 60
   B. 420
   C. 600
   D. 1260

9. Janelle wants to drive from Danville to Brownsville. If she averages 60 miles per hour, how many hours will it take her to drive the distance?

480 miles

Danville   Brownsville

A.   6
B.   8
C.   60
D. 540

10. A company sold a total of $1440 in gift bears for Valentine's Day. If the gift bears cost $15 apiece, how many gift bears did it sell?

A.   15
B.   96
C.   144
D. 1440

11. In addition to interest charges, Richard's credit card company charges a $25 late fee for payments made after the payment due date. If he was charged a late fee for 8 different monthly bills, how much could he have saved by paying the bills on time?

A. $200
B. $80
C. $33
D. $25

12. A waiter has seven $5 bills and eighteen $1 bills from tips. In all, how much does he have in tips?

A. $18
B. $25
C. $35
D. $53

13. April has taken her car in for the recommended oil and filter change every 3,500 miles. If April bought her car brand-new, and the odometer now shows just over 17,500 miles, how many oil changes has her car received?

A.   5
B.   14
C.   123
D. 1236

14. A clinic treated 536 children over a 4-month period. At this rate, how many children did the clinic treat in 1 month?

A.   134
B.   536
C.   540
D. 2144

15. Attendance at a local play was 438 Friday night, 820 Saturday night, and 636 Sunday afternoon. How many more people attended the play on Sunday than on Friday?

Write your answer on the line below.

_____

16. Raquel has 4 payments left on her car. If each payment is $268, how much does she still owe on her car?

Write your answer on the line below.

_____

17. In what order should items weighing 51 pounds, 40 pounds, 48 pounds, and 44 pounds be stacked if you want them in order from <u>heaviest to lightest</u>?

    A. 51, 44, 40, 48
    B. 40, 44, 48, 51
    C. 51, 48, 44, 40
    D. 51, 40, 44, 48

18. Which of the following correctly shows 2,354,769 rounded to the nearest ten thousand?

    A. 2,400,000
    B. 2,355,000
    C. 2,350,000
    D. 2,000,000

19. What is the total weight in pounds of the packages below?

    A. 83
    B. 65
    C. 60
    D. 42

20. Jason paid a $14 dinner bill with a $20 bill. How much change should he receive?

    A. $6
    B. $7
    C. $14
    D. $34

21. Maria spent 8 minutes installing a new showerhead, 33 minutes rodding out a drain, and 18 minutes fixing a leaking faucet. <u>About</u> how many minutes did it take Maria to complete all three tasks?

    A. 90
    B. 60
    C. 30
    D. 20

22. Carla drove 248 miles in 4 hours. What was her average rate of speed, in miles per hour?

    Write your answer on the line below.

    _____

23. A bulk bag of nuts contains 144 ounces of nuts. If the nuts are packaged in smaller 8-ounce bags, how many bags will there be?

    A.   8
    B.   12
    C.   18
    D. 136

24. If you drove 299 miles on 9 gallons of gasoline, <u>about</u> how many miles per gallon did the car get?

    A.   10
    B.   30
    C. 270
    D. 300

25. A shipment of 33 crates like the one shown below is delivered. <u>Approximately</u> how many pounds did workers unload?

41 pounds

   A.   40
   B.   120
   C. 1200
   D. 2000

26. Four friends bought a birthday cake for $21 and balloons for $15. If they divided the cost equally, how much did each friend pay toward the birthday party?

   A. $4
   B. $5
   C. $9
   D. $36

27. David paid $20 toward a dinner bill of $128. If the remainder of the bill is divided equally among the remaining 9 people in the group, how much should each person other than David pay?

   A. $12
   B. $18
   D. $20
   E. $108

28. A driver traveled 4 hours at an average rate of 65 miles per hour. How many miles did the person drive?

   A.   61
   B.   69
   C. 240
   D. 260

29. Using the following information, how much would a large pizza with 3 toppings cost?

Large 1-Topping Pizza for $14
$2 for Each Additional Topping

   A. $20
   B. $18
   C. $16
   D. $14

30. Bagels are 2 for $1. What is the maximum number of bagels you could buy for $7?

   A.   7
   B. 10
   C. 14
   D. 15

31. How many months would it take to save $1800 at $75 per month?

Write your answer on the line below.

_____

32. How many 45-page documents would a binder hold if its maximum capacity is 630 sheets of paper?

Write your answer on the line below.

_____

Answers and explanations begin on page 655.

DECIMALS AND FRACTIONS

Decimal Basics

- The decimal point separates the whole number from the decimal part.
- To round decimals, use the same rules as with rounding whole numbers.
- Adding zeros to the right of the last digit after the decimal does not change the number's value.

The Decimal System

Decimals are numbers that use place value to show amounts less than 1. You already use decimals when working with money. For example, in the amount $10.25, you know that the digits to the right of the **decimal point** represent cents, or hundredths of a dollar.

The first four decimal place values are labeled on the chart below.

The number 2.375 is shown on the chart. Read *and* in place of the decimal point. After reading the decimal part, say the place value of the last decimal digit. This number would be read "two *and* three hundred seventy-five *thousandths*."

Rounding

Round decimals the same way you round whole numbers.

Example 1: A calculator display reads 3.62835. Round to the hundredths place.

1. Look at the digit to the right of the hundredths place.

   $3.62\boxed{8}35$

2. If the digit to the right is 5 or greater, round up. If the digit is less than 5, don't change the number. Then drop all digits to the right of the place you are rounding to.

   Since 8 is greater than 5, round up. 3.62835 rounds to **3.63.**

Comparing and Ordering

Comparing decimals is similar to comparing whole numbers.

Example 2: Matt ran the 400-meter race in 45.8 seconds. Alonzo ran the same race in 45.66 seconds. Which runner had the faster time?

1. Line up the decimal points. Add a zero at the **end** of 45.8 so that both times have the same number of digits after the decimal.

   45.80
   45.66

2. Compare the decimal parts of the numbers as though they were whole numbers. **Alonzo's time was faster.**

   80 is greater than 66, so 45.8 is greater than 45.66.

When you compare more than two numbers, it is helpful to compare one place-value column at a time, working from left to right.

Example 3: Arrange the numbers 0.85, 1.8, 0.8, and 0.819 in order from greatest to least.

1. Write the numbers in a column, lining up the decimal points. Add zeros so that the numbers have the same number of decimal places.

    0.850
    1.800
    0.800
    0.819

2. Compare the digits, working from left to right. Only 1.8 has a whole number part, so it is greatest. The remaining numbers each have 8 in the tenths column. Looking at the hundredths column, 0.85 is next, followed by 0.819. The least number is 0.8.

In order: **1.8**
          0.85
          0.819
          0.8

PRACTICE 1

A. Round these numbers as directed.

1. Round 3.75 to the tenths place.
2. Round 5.908 to the ones place.
3. A calculator display reads 0.4285714. Round to the nearest hundredth.
4. Round 0.66667 to the nearest thousandth.
5. Round 8.125 to the nearest tenth.
6. A calculator display reads 2.7142857. Round to the nearest thousandth.

B. In each of the following pairs, which number is greater?

7. 0.45 or 0.449
8. 0.008 or 0.08
9. 4.68 or 4.086
10. 0.75 or 1.85
11. 1.0275 or 1.029
12. 0.14 or 0.104

C. Write these numbers in order from <u>least to greatest</u>.

13. 5.6 5.08 5.8 5.802
14. 0.1136 0.12 0.2 0.115
15. 14.005 4.52 4.8 4.667
16. 0.8023 0.8 0.803 0.823

D. Choose the <u>one best answer</u> to each question.

17. In a circuit board assembly, the weights of three parts are 0.572 grams, 0.0785 grams, and 0.6 grams. Which of the following lists the weights in order from <u>greatest to least</u>?

    A. 0.0785 g, 0.572 g, 0.6 g
    B. 0.6 g, 0.0785 g, 0.572 g
    C. 0.6 g, 0.572 g, 0.0785 g
    D. 0.572 g, 0.6 g, 0.0785 g

18. Which of the following correctly shows 1.3815 rounded to the nearest hundredth?

    A. 1.4
    B. 1.382
    C. 1.381
    D. 1.38

Answers and explanations begin on page 655.

Decimal Operations

Key Ideas

- Always add and subtract like place-value columns.
- Always line up the decimal points when you write a problem in columns.
- When adding or subtracting, place the decimal point in the answer directly below the decimal point in the problem.

Addition and Subtraction

Adding decimals is much like adding whole numbers. The trick is to make sure you have lined up the place-value columns correctly. You can do this by writing the numbers in a column and carefully lining up the decimal points.

Example 1: Add $0.37 + 13.5 + 2.638$.

1. Write the numbers in a column, lining up the decimal points.

2. You may add placeholder zeros so that the decimals have the same number of decimal places.

3. Add. Start on the right and add each column. Regroup, or carry, as you would with whole numbers.

4. Place the decimal point in the answer directly below the decimal points in the problem.

$$\begin{array}{r} 0.370 \\ 13.500 \\ +\,2.638 \\ \hline \end{array}$$

$$\begin{array}{r} 1\ 1 \\ 0.370 \\ 13.500 \\ +\,2.638 \\ \hline 16.508 \end{array}$$

To find the difference between decimals, write the numbers in a column with the greater number on top. Make sure the decimal points are in a line.

Example 2: Find the difference between 14.512 and 8.7.

1. Write the numbers in a column, lining up the decimal points. Add placeholder zeros so that the numbers have the same number of decimal places.

$$\begin{array}{r} 14.512 \\ -\,8.700 \\ \hline \end{array}$$

2. Subtract. Regroup, or borrow, as needed. Place the decimal point in the answer directly in line with the decimal points in the problem.

$$\begin{array}{r} {\scriptstyle 13\ 15} \\ 1\cancel{4}.\cancel{5}12 \\ -\,8.700 \\ \hline 5.812 \end{array}$$

The greater number may have fewer or no decimal places. In the next example, a decimal is subtracted from a whole number.

Example 3: What does 9 minus 3.604 equal?

1. Line up the place-value columns. Put a decimal point after the whole number 9 and add placeholder zeros.

$$\begin{array}{r} 9.000 \\ -\,3.604 \\ \hline \end{array}$$

2. Subtract, regrouping as needed. Place the decimal point in the answer.

$$\begin{array}{r} {\scriptstyle 8\ 9\ 9\ 10} \\ \cancel{9}.\cancel{0}\,\cancel{0}\,\cancel{0} \\ -\,3.6\,0\,4 \\ \hline 5.3\,9\,6 \end{array}$$

A. Solve. You MAY NOT use a calculator.

1. 4.025
    + 3.971

2. 6.5
    + 4.008

3. 2.8
    + 9.46

4. 8.04
    − 2.19

5. 8.5
    − 1.074

6. 10
    − 7.89

7. 17.294
    + 0.8

8. 4.07
    + 1.047

9. 17.52
    + 3.8

10. 3.8
    − 2.905

11. 14.64
    − 10.8

12. 100.5
    − 98.15

13. $0.236 + 2.4 + 2.87 =$

14. $38.06 - 16.9 =$

15. $0.006 + 0.09 + 0.549 =$

16. $8.5 - 6.074 =$

17. $1.02 - 0.87 =$

18. $0.45 + 1.8 + 0.07 + 2.56 =$

19. $12.5 - 0.7 =$

20. $25 - 10.984 =$

21. $0.01 + 2.052 + 0.96 + 1.5 =$

22. $12.9 - 10.54 =$

23. $0.68 + 12.3 + 4.9 =$

24. $32.9 - 15.675 =$

B. Choose the one best answer to each question.

25. James ran 3 miles. His times for the individual miles were 7.2 minutes, 6.8 minutes, and 8.25 minutes. How long did it take him, in minutes, to run the 3-mile distance?

    A. 22.25
    B. 22.7
    C. 23.35
    D. 96.5

26. Claudia earns overtime pay when she works more than 40 hours in one week. How many hours of overtime pay did she work for the week of March 4?

    Work Record for March 4–10

March 4	8.5
March 5	Off
March 6	9.25
March 7	8.75
March 8	10
March 9	Off
March 10	7.75

    A. 44.25
    B. 40.0
    C. 4.25
    D. 2.25

27. A plumber cut two lengths of pipe measuring 2.8 and 1.4 meters from a 6-meter length.

    Assuming there was no waste when the cuts were made, what is the length in meters of the remaining piece?

    A. 1.8
    B. 3.2
    C. 4.2
    D. 7.4

28. Mona purchased the following art supplies: a storage box for $16.98, a set of art markers for $31.78, and a pad of paper for $6.50. What was the cost of the three items?

    A. $48.76
    B. $53.26
    C. $55.26
    D. $61.76

Answers and explanations begin on page 655.

Multiplication and Division

The rules you used to multiply whole numbers can be used to multiply decimals. You don't have to line up the decimal points. You will wait until you are finished multiplying before you place the decimal point in the answer. The number of decimal places in the answer equals the total number of decimal places in the numbers you are multiplying.

Example 4: Find the product of 2.6 and 0.45.

1. Set up the problem as though you were multiplying the whole numbers 26 and 45.

$$\begin{array}{r} 2.6 \\ \times .45 \\ \hline \end{array}$$

2. Ignore the decimal points while you multiply.

3. Now count the decimal places in the numbers you multiplied. The number 2.6 has one decimal place, and 0.45 has two decimal places, for a total of three.

$$\begin{array}{r} 2.6 \\ \times .45 \\ \hline 130 \\ 1\,040 \\ \hline 1.170 \\ \end{array}$$

4. Starting from the right, count three places to the left and insert the decimal point. Thus, the answer is **1.17**.

When you divide decimals, you must figure out where the decimal point will go in the answer before you divide.

Example 5: Divide 14.4 by 6.

1. Set up the problem. Since the divisor (the number you are dividing by) is a whole number, place the decimal point in the answer directly above the decimal point in the dividend (the number you are dividing).

$$\begin{array}{r} 2.4 \\ 6\overline{)14.4} \\ -12 \\ \hline 24 \\ -24 \\ \hline 0 \end{array}$$

2. Divide. Use the rules you learned for dividing whole numbers. The answer is **2.4**.

If the divisor is a decimal, you must move the decimal points in both the divisor and the dividend before you divide.

Example 6: Divide 4.9 by 0.35.

$$.35\overline{)4.90}$$

1. Set up the problem. There are two decimal places in the divisor. Move the decimal point in *both* the divisor and the dividend two places to the right. Note that you need to add a zero in the dividend in order to move the decimal two places.

2. Place the decimal point in the quotient directly above the decimal point in the dividend.

$$\begin{array}{r} 14. \\ 35\overline{)490.} \\ -35 \\ \hline 140 \\ -140 \\ \hline 0 \end{array}$$

3. Divide. The correct answer is **14**.

Note: You may not need to finish dividing in order to choose the correct answer. You may be able to eliminate all but one of the answer choices after only one or two division steps.

PRACTICE 2.2

A. Solve. You <u>MAY NOT</u> use a calculator.

1. $\begin{array}{r} 5.3 \\ \times\,0.5 \\ \hline \end{array}$

4. $6\overline{)3.12}$

7. $\begin{array}{r} 6.25 \\ \times\,1.4 \\ \hline \end{array}$

10. $1.25\overline{)30}$

2. $\begin{array}{r} 64 \\ \times\,0.2 \\ \hline \end{array}$

5. $8\overline{)28.8}$

8. $\begin{array}{r} 13.5 \\ \times\,0.25 \\ \hline \end{array}$

11. $2.8\overline{)39.76}$

3. $\begin{array}{r} 12.4 \\ \times\,0.04 \\ \hline \end{array}$

6. $5\overline{)20.45}$

9. $\begin{array}{r} 9.62 \\ \times\,1.005 \\ \hline \end{array}$

12. $0.003\overline{)47.4}$

13. $15.5 \times 2.2 =$

16. $1.32 \div 0.5 =$

19. $3.36 \times 1.1 =$

14. $0.944 \div 0.4 =$

17. $2.75 \times 0.6 =$

20. $15.03 \div 15 =$

15. $2.05 \times 0.32 =$

18. $12.825 \div 3 =$

21. $0.12 \times 0.06 =$

B. Choose the <u>one best answer</u> to each question.

22. One container of floor cleaner holds 3.79 liters. If Zachary bought 4 containers, how many liters of cleaner did he buy?

   A. 0.9475
   B. 7.79
   C. 12.83
   D. 15.16

23. Ribbon costs $0.45 per foot. A sewing project calls for 20.5 feet of ribbon. To the nearest cent, what will be the cost of the ribbon for the project?

   A. $0.92
   B. $9.23
   C. $9.90
   D. $45.56

24. Armando drove 278.7 miles over a 3-day period. On average, how many miles did he drive each day?

   A. 9.3
   B. 90.3
   C. 92.9
   D. 836.1

Questions 25 and 26 are based on the following information.

Cereal	Net Weight	Servings per Box
Toasted Oats	22.8 oz	19
Crisp Rice	16.9 oz	13
Honey Mix	12.5 oz	10

25. A box of Toasted Oats cereal is priced at $4.94. What is the cost per serving? (*Hint:* Divide the price by the number of servings.)

   A. $0.49
   B. $0.29
   C. $0.26
   D. $0.22

26. Lee bought 4 boxes of Honey Mix cereal. How many ounces of cereal did she buy?

   A. 31.25
   B. 50.0
   C. 67.6
   D. 91.2

Answers and explanations begin on page 655.

DECIMALS AND FRACTIONS

Fraction Basics

A **fraction** uses two numbers to represent part of a whole. The bottom number, called the **denominator,** tells how many equal parts are in the whole group or item. The top number, called the **numerator,** tells how many parts you are working with.

Key Ideas

- The bottom number of a fraction tells how many parts the group or object has.
- The top number tells how many parts you are working with.
- When the top number is greater than the bottom number, the fraction is greater than 1.

There are 4 equal parts in this rectangle. Since 3 are shaded, we say that $\frac{3}{4}$ of the rectangle is shaded.

In a proper fraction, the numerator is less than the denominator. A **proper fraction** represents a quantity less than 1. An **improper fraction** is equal to or greater than 1.

There are 6 equal parts in the figure, and 6 are shaded; therefore, $\frac{6}{6}$ of the figure is shaded. $\frac{6}{6} = 1$

In this grouping, each figure is divided into 2 equal parts. A total of 3 parts are shaded, so $\frac{3}{2}$ are shaded.

A **mixed number** is another way to show an amount greater than 1. It consists of a whole number and a proper fraction. Another name for the shaded portion in the last figure is $1\frac{1}{2}$. The improper fraction $\frac{3}{2}$ equals $1\frac{1}{2}$.

You can also change an improper fraction to a whole or mixed number.

Example 1: Change $\frac{16}{5}$ to a mixed number.

1. Divide the numerator (16) by the denominator (5). Since 16 is not evenly divisible by 5, there is a remainder of 1.

$$16 \div 5 = 3 \text{ r } 1.$$

2. The answer becomes the whole number, and the remainder becomes the numerator of the proper fraction. The denominator is the same as the original fraction.

$$\frac{16}{5} = 3\frac{1}{5}$$

GED® TEST TIP

If you have trouble visualizing the fractions in a problem, draw a quick sketch of the information presented in the problem similar to the ones on this page.

You can also change a mixed number to an improper fraction.

Example 2: Change $7\frac{2}{3}$ to an improper fraction.

1. Multiply the whole number (7) by the denominator of the fraction (3), and add the numerator (2).

$$7 \times 3 = 21$$
$$21 + 2 = 23$$

2. Write the sum over the denominator of the original fraction.

$$7\frac{2}{3} = \frac{23}{3}$$

To perform operations with fractions, you need to be able to write equal fractions in higher or lower terms. The **terms** are the numerator and the denominator. A fraction is **reduced to lowest terms** when the two terms do not have any common factor except 1.

To **raise** a fraction, multiply both terms by the same number: $\frac{3}{4} = \frac{3 \times 3}{4 \times 3} = \frac{9}{12}$.

To **reduce** a fraction, divide both terms by the same number: $\frac{10}{15} = \frac{10 \div 5}{15 \div 5} = \frac{2}{3}$.

PRACTICE 3

A. Write a proper fraction for the shaded portion of each figure.

1. 　　　　2. 　　　　3.

B. Write an improper fraction and a mixed number for the shaded portion of each figure.

4.　　　　5.　　　　6.

C. Write improper fractions as mixed numbers and mixed numbers as improper fractions.

7. $\frac{17}{3} =$　　　9. $\frac{24}{6} =$　　　11. $\frac{19}{4} =$　　　13. $\frac{43}{9} =$　　　15. $\frac{33}{4} =$

8. $3\frac{3}{5} =$　　　10. $5\frac{2}{9} =$　　　12. $2\frac{5}{12} =$　　　14. $1\frac{3}{4} =$　　　16. $5\frac{7}{10} =$

D. Write an equal fraction with the given denominator.

17. $\frac{3}{4} = \frac{}{16}$　　　18. $\frac{1}{3} = \frac{}{21}$　　　19. $\frac{4}{5} = \frac{}{60}$　　　20. $\frac{3}{8} = \frac{}{40}$　　　21. $\frac{6}{25} = \frac{}{100}$

(*Hint for question 17: $4 \times ? = 16$*)

E. Reduce each fraction to lowest terms.

22. $\frac{21}{28} =$　　　23. $\frac{4}{24} =$　　　24. $\frac{12}{20} =$　　　25. $\frac{26}{30} =$　　　26. $\frac{60}{90} =$

F. Choose the one best answer to each question.

27. Eighteen out of every 24 people surveyed say they went to at least one movie in December. What fraction of the people surveyed went to a movie in December?

   A. $\frac{3}{4}$

   B. $\frac{2}{3}$

   C. $\frac{1}{3}$

   D. $\frac{1}{4}$

28. Which of the following fractions equals $\frac{2}{5}$?

   A. $\frac{15}{100}$

   B. $\frac{30}{100}$

   C. $\frac{40}{100}$

   D. $\frac{80}{100}$

Answers and explanations begin on page 656.

DECIMALS AND FRACTIONS

Fraction Operations

Addition and Subtraction

You can add or subtract **like fractions**. Like fractions have a **common denominator**. In other words, their denominators are the same.

Example 1: Add $\frac{3}{10} + \frac{5}{10}$.

1. Since the denominators are the same, add the numerators. $\qquad \frac{3}{10} + \frac{5}{10} = \frac{8}{10}$

2. Reduce the answer to lowest terms. $\qquad \frac{8}{10} = \frac{8 \div 2}{10 \div 2} = \frac{4}{5}$

Example 2: Subtract $\frac{2}{9}$ from $\frac{7}{9}$.

Subtract the numerators. The answer is already in lowest terms. $\qquad \frac{7}{9} - \frac{2}{9} = \frac{5}{9}$

If the denominators are not the same, raise one or both fractions to higher terms so that they become like fractions.

Example 3: Add $\frac{5}{6} + \frac{1}{4}$.

1. One way to find a common denominator is to think of the multiples of both denominators. The lowest is 12.

   Multiples
   of 6: 6, [12], 18
   of 4: 4, 8, [12], 16

2. Raise each fraction to higher terms with a denominator of 12. $\qquad \frac{5 \times 2}{6 \times 2} = \frac{10}{12}, \frac{1 \times 3}{4 \times 3} = \frac{3}{12}$

3. Add the like fractions. Rewrite the sum as a mixed number. $\qquad \frac{10}{12} + \frac{3}{12} = \frac{13}{12} = 1\frac{1}{12}$

Use the same process to add or subtract mixed numbers. Example 4 shows how to regroup when subtracting mixed numbers.

Example 4: Subtract $4\frac{1}{16} - 1\frac{3}{8}$.

1. Raise the second fraction so that it also has a denominator of 16. $\qquad \frac{3 \times 2}{8 \times 2} = \frac{6}{16}$

2. Set up the problem. To subtract the fractions, you need to regroup 1 from the whole number column and add it to the top fraction. $\qquad 4\frac{1}{16} = 3\frac{16}{16} + \frac{1}{16} = 3\frac{17}{16}$

3. Subtract the fractions and then the whole numbers. $\qquad 3\frac{17}{16} - 1\frac{6}{16} = 2\frac{11}{16}$

Key Ideas

- You can add or subtract fractions, but they must have the same denominator.
- If denominators are not the same, find a common denominator and raise one or both fractions.
- Always reduce answers to lowest terms and change improper fractions to mixed numbers.

GED® TEST TIP

If your solution to a fraction problem is not one of the given answer choices, make sure that you reduced your answer to lowest terms. On the Mathematical Reasoning Test, *answer choices are always written in lowest terms.*

PRACTICE 4.1

A. Solve. Reduce answers to lowest terms. Simplify improper fractions as mixed numbers.

1. $\begin{array}{r} \frac{3}{8} \\ +\frac{1}{8} \\ \hline \end{array}$

3. $\begin{array}{r} \frac{8}{9} \\ -\frac{5}{9} \\ \hline \end{array}$

5. $\begin{array}{r} \frac{1}{4} \\ +\frac{2}{3} \\ \hline \end{array}$

7. $\begin{array}{r} \frac{9}{10} \\ -\frac{3}{5} \\ \hline \end{array}$

9. $\begin{array}{r} 2\frac{1}{5} \\ +1\frac{2}{3} \\ \hline \end{array}$

2. $\begin{array}{r} \frac{1}{6} \\ +\frac{5}{6} \\ \hline \end{array}$

4. $\begin{array}{r} \frac{7}{12} \\ -\frac{5}{12} \\ \hline \end{array}$

6. $\begin{array}{r} \frac{1}{2} \\ +\frac{5}{8} \\ \hline \end{array}$

8. $\begin{array}{r} \frac{7}{9} \\ -\frac{1}{2} \\ \hline \end{array}$

10. $\begin{array}{r} 4\frac{1}{2} \\ -2\frac{3}{4} \\ \hline \end{array}$

11. $5\frac{5}{6} + 2\frac{2}{3} =$

12. $6\frac{7}{8} + 4\frac{3}{4} =$

13. $12\frac{1}{10} + 9\frac{3}{5} =$

14. $2\frac{2}{9} + \frac{2}{3} + 4\frac{5}{6} =$

15. $3\frac{1}{3} + 5\frac{2}{3} + 3\frac{5}{6} =$

16. $\frac{3}{8} + \frac{7}{12} + 1\frac{2}{3} =$

17. $16\frac{2}{3} + 25\frac{3}{4} =$

18. $10\frac{1}{2} + 8\frac{4}{5} + 3\frac{1}{4} =$

19. $8\frac{1}{2} - 3\frac{4}{9} =$

20. $15 - 3\frac{7}{8} =$

21. $14\frac{1}{4} - 10\frac{3}{7} =$

22. $9\frac{11}{12} - 8\frac{5}{8} =$

23. $6 - 3\frac{4}{7} =$

24. $13\frac{1}{3} - 4\frac{4}{9} =$

25. $5\frac{5}{7} - 4\frac{4}{5} =$

B. Choose the one best answer to each question.

26. To make the top of a dining room table, Craig glues a piece of oak that is $\frac{5}{16}$ inch thick to a piece of pine that is $\frac{7}{8}$ inch thick. What is the total thickness, in inches, of the tabletop?

    A. $\frac{9}{16}$

    B. $1\frac{3}{16}$

    C. $1\frac{1}{4}$

    D. $1\frac{9}{16}$

27. Carol will use the two bolts shown below to assemble a book cart. How much longer, in inches, is bolt A than bolt B?

    A $2\frac{7}{8}$ in

    B $1\frac{1}{4}$ in

    A. $\frac{5}{8}$

    B. $1\frac{3}{8}$

    C. $1\frac{5}{8}$

    D. $1\frac{3}{4}$

28. At a fabric store, Melissa sold $8\frac{7}{8}$ yards of cloth to a customer. If the material was cut from a bolt of fabric containing $23\frac{1}{4}$ yards, how many yards are left on the bolt?

    A. $14\frac{3}{8}$

    B. $15\frac{3}{8}$

    C. $15\frac{3}{4}$

    D. $31\frac{7}{8}$

29. A batch of salad dressing requires $1\frac{2}{3}$ cups of olive oil, $\frac{1}{2}$ cup of vinegar, and $\frac{3}{4}$ cup of water. How many cups of salad dressing will this recipe produce?

    A. $1\frac{2}{3}$

    B. $2\frac{5}{6}$

    C. $2\frac{11}{12}$

    D. $3\frac{7}{12}$

    Answers and explanations begin on page 656.

Multiplication and Division

It isn't necessary to find a common denominator to multiply and divide fractions. To multiply fractions, simply multiply the numerators and then the denominators. Reduce the answer, if necessary.

Example 5: What is the product of $\frac{7}{8}$ and $\frac{1}{2}$?

Multiply the numerators together and then the denominators. The answer is in lowest terms.

$$\frac{7}{8} \times \frac{1}{2} = \frac{7 \times 1}{8 \times 2} = \frac{7}{16}$$

Before multiplying a mixed number, change it to an improper fraction.

Example 6: What is $\frac{1}{3}$ of $3\frac{3}{4}$?

1. Change $3\frac{3}{4}$ to an improper fraction.

$$3\frac{3}{4} = \frac{15}{4}$$

2. Multiply the numerators and the denominators.

$$\frac{15}{4} \times \frac{1}{3} = \frac{15 \times 1}{4 \times 3} = \frac{15}{12}$$

3. Change to a mixed number and reduce to lowest terms.

$$\frac{15}{12} = 1\frac{3}{12} = \mathbf{1\frac{1}{4}}$$

You can use a shortcut called **canceling** to reduce the fractions as you work the problem. To cancel, divide both a numerator and a denominator by the same number. The numerator and the denominator can be in different fractions.

Example 7: Multiply $1\frac{1}{2}$ by $1\frac{1}{5}$.

1. Change to improper fractions.

$$1\frac{1}{2} = \frac{3}{2} \text{ and } 1\frac{1}{5} = \frac{6}{5}$$

2. Set up the multiplication problem. Both 6 (a numerator) and 2 (a denominator) are evenly divisible by 2. Divide them by 2. Then multiply using the new numerator and denominator. Finally, change the improper fraction to a mixed number.

$$\frac{3}{2} \times \frac{6}{5} = \frac{3}{\cancel{2}} \times \frac{\overset{3}{\cancel{6}}}{5} = \frac{9}{5} = \mathbf{1\frac{4}{5}}$$

The slash marks show that the numbers have been divided.

You will need two additional steps to divide fractions. Before dividing, **invert** the divisor (the fraction you are dividing by). To invert the fraction, switch the numerator and the denominator. Finally, change the division symbol to a multiplication symbol and multiply.

Example 8: Jim has an 8-pound bag of nuts. He wants to fill smaller $\frac{1}{2}$-pound bags using the nuts. How many small bags can he make?

1. Divide 8 by $\frac{1}{2}$. Set up the division problem. Always write whole or mixed numbers as improper fractions.

$$8 \div \frac{1}{2} = \frac{8}{1} \div \frac{1}{2} =$$

2. Invert the fraction you are dividing by. Then change the operation sign to multiplication. Multiply, following the rules for multiplying fractions. Jim can make **16 small bags**.

$$\frac{8}{1} \times \frac{2}{1} = \frac{16}{1} = \mathbf{16}$$

NOTE: When you multiply by a fraction less than 1, the answer is smaller than the number you started with because you are finding a "part of." When you divide by a fraction less than 1, the answer is greater than the number.

PRACTICE 4.2

A. Solve. Reduce answers to lowest terms. Simplify improper fractions as mixed numbers.

1. $\frac{2}{3} \times \frac{1}{4} =$

2. $1\frac{5}{6} \times \frac{1}{2} =$

3. $\frac{2}{3} \times 21 =$

4. $50 \times \frac{3}{8} =$

5. $3\frac{1}{2} \times \frac{1}{4} =$

6. $\frac{3}{4} \times \frac{7}{8} =$

7. $2\frac{1}{3} \times 3\frac{2}{5} =$

8. $15 \times 2\frac{3}{4} =$

9. $\frac{5}{8} \times 3\frac{1}{4} =$

10. $\frac{7}{8} \div \frac{1}{16} =$

11. $\frac{4}{5} \div \frac{2}{5} =$

12. $12 \div \frac{1}{4} =$

13. $6 \div 2\frac{1}{2} =$

14. $3\frac{3}{4} \div 1\frac{2}{3} =$

15. $9 \div \frac{1}{3} =$

16. $26\frac{2}{3} \div 3\frac{1}{3} =$

17. $40\frac{3}{8} \div 4\frac{1}{4} =$

18. $3\frac{7}{8} \div 5\frac{1}{6} =$

B. Choose the one best answer to each question.

19. A city is considering raising taxes to build a football stadium. A survey of registered voters yielded the following results:

Position	Fraction of Those Surveyed
Against Tax Hike	$\frac{7}{16}$
For Tax Hike	$\frac{3}{16}$
Undecided	$\frac{3}{8}$

If 400 people were surveyed, how many support the tax hike?

A. 48
B. 75
C. 150
D. 175

20. A tailor has 20 yards of shirt fabric. How many shirts can she <u>complete</u> if each shirt requires $2\frac{3}{4}$ yards of fabric?

A. 6
B. 7
C. 8
D. 10

21. An insurance agent estimates that it takes $\frac{2}{3}$ hour to process a customer's claim. If the agent spends 22 hours per week processing claims, about how many claims does he process in a week?

A. $14\frac{2}{3}$
B. 33
C. 44
D. 66

22. A fluorescent lighting panel is $12\frac{5}{8}$ inches wide. If three of the panels are installed as shown below, what will be the width in inches of the combined panels?

A. $13\frac{7}{8}$
B. $36\frac{5}{8}$
C. $37\frac{7}{8}$
D. $42\frac{7}{8}$

Answers and explanations begin on page 656.

DECIMALS AND FRACTIONS

Fraction and Decimal Equivalencies

Fractions and decimals are two ways to show part of a whole. You can change fractions to decimals by dividing.

Example 1: Change $\frac{3}{8}$ to a decimal.

The fraction $\frac{3}{8}$ means $3 \div 8$. Use a calculator to divide.

$$3 \div 8 = \mathbf{0.375}$$

You can also change a decimal to a fraction.

Example 2: Change 0.35 to a fraction.

Write the decimal number over the place value name of the last decimal digit on the right. The last digit, 5, is in the hundredths column. Reduce to lowest terms.

$$\frac{35}{100} = \frac{35 \div 5}{100 \div 5} = \frac{7}{20}$$

You will find it useful to memorize the most common fraction and decimal equivalents. These equivalents will also help you solve percent problems.

Decimal	Fraction	Decimal	Fraction	Decimal	Fraction
0.1	$\frac{1}{10}$	0.375	$\frac{3}{8}$	0.7	$\frac{7}{10}$
0.125	$\frac{1}{8}$	0.4	$\frac{2}{5}$	0.75	$\frac{3}{4}$
0.2	$\frac{1}{5}$	0.5	$\frac{1}{2}$	0.8	$\frac{4}{5}$
0.25	$\frac{1}{4}$	0.6	$\frac{3}{5}$	0.875	$\frac{7}{8}$
0.3	$\frac{3}{10}$	0.625	$\frac{5}{8}$	0.9	$\frac{9}{10}$
$0.33\overline{3}$	$\frac{1}{3}$	$0.66\overline{6}$	$\frac{2}{3}$		

The decimal equivalents for $\frac{1}{3}$ and $\frac{2}{3}$ are marked with a bar. The bar shows that the decimal repeats indefinitely.

You can use fraction and decimal equivalents to save time when solving math problems.

Example 3: Each dose of cough medicine contains 0.25 ounce of medication. How many ounces of medication are in 48 doses?

To solve the problem, you need to multiply 48 by 0.25, a time-consuming calculation. However, since $0.25 = \frac{1}{4}$ you can find $\frac{1}{4}$ of 48 to solve the problem. The answer is **12 ounces**.

$$48 \times \frac{1}{4} = \frac{48}{4} = \mathbf{12}$$

Key Ideas

- To change a fraction to a decimal, divide the numerator by the denominator.
- To change a decimal to a fraction, write the number without the decimal point over the place value of the last decimal digit. Reduce.
- Avoid time-consuming calculations by using fraction-decimal equivalents.

GED® TEST TIP

Look at the answer choices before you begin working a multiple-choice problem. Knowing whether you need an answer in fraction or decimal form may affect how you approach the problem.

Knowing fraction-decimal equivalents can also help you interpret remainders when using a calculator.

Example 4: Ray inspects machine assemblies. He must inspect 12 assemblies during his 40-hour workweek. On average, how many hours can he spend on each inspection?

Using a calculator, divide 40 by 12: 40 $\div$ 12 enter. The right side of the display reads 3.333333333.

Since you know that $0.33\overline{3} = \frac{1}{3}$, the answer is $3\frac{1}{3}$ **hours.**

PRACTICE 5

Solve. When possible, use fraction and decimal equivalents to make the work easier. You MAY use a calculator on questions 5 and 6.

1. During a 25%-off sale, store clerks find the amount of the discounts by multiplying the regular price by 0.25. What is the discount on an item with a regular price of $80?

    A. $32.00
    B. $20.00
    C. $16.40
    D. $2.00

2. At Linton Products, $\frac{3}{10}$ of the workers are in the company's ride-share program. If there are 480 workers, which of the following expressions could be used to find the number in the ride-share program?

    A. 480×0.7
    B. $480 \div 0.7$
    C. 480×0.3
    D. $480 \div 0.3$

3. Sharon is using a calculator to find out how many hours she has spent on a certain job. She divides, and her display reads:

    $\boxed{4.666666666}$

    Assuming her calculations are correct, how many hours did she spend on the job?

    A. $4\frac{1}{6}$

    B. $4\frac{2}{3}$

    C. $4\frac{6}{7}$

    D. 46

4. A gourmet candy company charges the following prices per pound.

Jelly Beans	$9.60
Peanut Brittle	$12.00
Almond Toffee	$28.50

    How much would a customer pay for 1.5 pounds of peanut brittle?

    A. $6.00
    B. $14.40
    C. $18.00
    D. $42.75

5. At 1 p.m., the amount of rain in a rain gauge is 1.125 inches. At 3 p.m., the gauge holds 1.875 inches. What fraction of an inch of rain fell between 1 p.m. and 3 p.m.?

    A. $\frac{7}{8}$

    B. $\frac{3}{4}$

    C. $\frac{7}{10}$

    D. $\frac{1}{8}$

6. A steel rod, 3 meters in length, is cut into 8 equal pieces. What is the length in meters of each piece?

    A. 0.125
    B. 0.333
    C. 0.375
    D. 2.333

Answers and explanations begin on page 656.

Decimals and Fractions on the Number Line

Key Ideas

- A number line is a picture that helps you compare the sizes of numbers. Numbers on the left are smaller than numbers on the right.
- Number lines can also be used to represent and compare decimals.
- Fractions and mixed fractions can also be represented on a number line.

On the GED® *Mathematical Reasoning Test* you may need to recognize or locate fractions, mixed fractions, or decimals on a **number line**. A number line represents numbers in order from least to greatest. As you move to the left along a number line, numbers decrease in value. As you move to the right, numbers increase in value.

The arrows on the ends indicate that numbers continue forever in both directions. If you imagine zooming in on a portion of that number line, it might look like this:

Thus, a number line can include decimals and whole numbers. For example, the point represents 0.75, which is greater than 0.5 and less than 1.

A number line can also represent fractions and mixed fractions in order from least to greatest:

Use this question to practice working with number lines:

Example 1: John works five shifts per week. His boss asks him to spend exactly half of his time this week working on a specific project. How many work shifts will John devote to that project? Circle the answer on the number line below.

If you circled $2\frac{1}{2}$, you are correct. Multiply 5 by $\frac{1}{2}$ to determine that John will spend $2\frac{1}{2}$ shifts on the project.

PRACTICE 6

A. Choose the <u>one best answer</u> to each question.

1. What is the value of the point on the number line below?

   A. 0
   B. $\frac{1}{2}$
   C. $\frac{2}{3}$
   D. $1\frac{1}{3}$

2. What is the value of the point on the number line below?

   A. 2
   B. 2.5
   C. 2.7
   D. 2.8

3. In the number line below, what is the value of *A* minus *B*?

   A. 1
   B. $1\frac{1}{2}$
   C. 2
   D. $3\frac{1}{2}$

4. Angela baked 24 cookies and gave 16 of them to her neighbor. On the number line below, circle the fraction of Angela's cookies that she gave to her neighbor.

B. Write the decimal values of the points on the number lines.

For each of the number lines below, fill in the value of the point using decimals.

5.

6.

C. Write the fraction values of the points on the number lines.

For each of the number lines below, fill in the value of the point using mixed fractions.

7.

8.

Answers and explanations begin on page 656.

DECIMALS AND FRACTIONS

Decimal and Fraction Calculator Skills

Several important calculator keys are used to work with decimals and fractions.

Key Ideas

- Fraction and decimal operations are entered in the same order as whole-number operations.
- On the TI-30XS MultiView™ calculator, use the decimal point key (.) for decimals and the fraction key, $\frac{n}{d}$, for fractions.
- To work with mixed fractions, use the 2nd function, $U\frac{n}{d}$, which is in green over the fraction key.

Cursor keys move the cursor on the screen up, down, left, and right.

The **fraction key** is used to enter fractions; the **mixed number 2nd function** is in green above it.

The **toggle key** changes between equivalent fraction and decimal forms of a number.

The **decimal point** key enters a decimal point.

Calculator **decimal operations** are performed in the same way that you use operations with whole numbers. You need to use the **decimal point key** ⊙ under the 2 in the white **numeric keypad**. Practice with these examples:

To solve this problem...	Press these keys...	The right-hand side of the display reads...
$3.89 + 2.5$	3.89 (+) 2.5 (enter)	6.39
$5.2 - 0.78$	5.2 (−) .78 (enter)	4.42
0.9×15	.9 (×) 15 (enter)	13.5
$1.7 \div 2$	1.7 (÷) 2 (enter)	0.85

You will use several calculator functions to work with **fractions** and **mixed fraction operations**. First practice entering fractions and converting to decimals.

Example 1: Reduce $\frac{56}{448}$ to lowest terms and then convert to a decimal.

GED® TEST TIP

A fraction answer may appear in the form of an improper fraction. In order to change to an equivalent mixed number, use the green 2nd function over this key:

On the Display

1. Clear the calculator.
2. Press the $\frac{n}{d}$ button to enter a fraction. Enter 56 at the blinking cursor, in the numerator.

3. Use the down cursor key ▼ to enter 448 in the denominator.

4. Press (enter) to reduce the fraction to lowest terms, which appears on the right of your screen: $\frac{1}{8}$

5. To express the fraction as a decimal, press the *toggle* button: ◀▶. The decimal **0.125** appears on the right display.

Now practice operations with **mixed fractions** using the *2nd function* key.

Example 2: A plastic pipe is to be cut into pieces measuring $1\frac{7}{8}$ feet. The original pipe was $20\frac{5}{8}$ feet long. How many pieces can be cut from the pipe?

	Keys to Press	**On the Display**
1. Clear the calculator	clear	

2. Recognize that a mixed fraction is a green *2nd* function: $\left(\cup\frac{n}{d}\right)$ over the $\frac{n}{d}$ key. Press the (2nd) key and the $\frac{n}{d}$ key. Note both a whole number and a blinking fraction cursor on the display.

Keys to Press: (2nd) $\frac{n}{d}$

On the Display:

3. Enter the number being divided first—the whole pipe: $20\frac{5}{8}$. Enter 20, then follow the direction of the onscreen arrow and press the right arrow button to move to the fraction cursors. Enter 5 and then use the down arrow to enter the 8. Exit the fraction by pressing the right arrow again.

Keys to Press: 20 ▶ 5 ▼ 8 ▶

On the Display: $20\frac{5}{8}$

4. Press the division key. Then follow the same process with the second number: $1\frac{7}{8}$, starting with the 2nd function: $\left(\cup\frac{n}{d}\right)$

Keys to Press: ÷ (2nd) $\frac{n}{d}$ 1 ▶ 7 ▼ 8 ▶

On the Display: $20\frac{5}{8} \div 1\frac{7}{8}$

5. Press the (enter) button for the solution. The answer 11 for **11 pieces** appears on the right side of the screen.

Keys to Press: enter

On the Display: $20\frac{5}{8} \div 1\frac{7}{8}$ 11

PRACTICE 7

A. Solve the following problems using your calculator.

1. $3.5 + 1.87 + 2.009$ 2. $3\frac{2}{3} - 1\frac{5}{12}$ 3. $\$25.35 \times 15$ 4. $10\frac{1}{2} \div \frac{1}{4}$

5. Linda earns $95 per day. If she works $\frac{8}{9}$ of a day, how much will she earn?

6. Aaron bought a refrigerator for $956.88. The price includes tax and interest charges. If he makes 12 equal monthly payments, how much will he pay each month?

7. An insurance agent estimates the annual cost of insurance on a home by multiplying the sale price of the home by 0.0125. What will be the yearly cost of insurance on a home priced at $118,000?

8. In a recipe, the total liquid added to a mixture is $1\frac{1}{2}$ cups of water and $2\frac{3}{4}$ cups of chicken broth. How many cups of liquid are used in the recipe?

9. A quilt costs $84.99 and weighs 5.56 pounds. The shipping charge is $1.20 per pound. To the nearest cent, what would be the shipping charge on the quilt?
   A. $5.56
   B. $6.67
   C. $8.26
   D. $10.20

10. A state park contains 64 acres. A wildlife preserve makes up $\frac{3}{8}$ of the park. How many acres are in the preserve?
    A. 8
    B. 21
    C. 24
    D. 27

Answers and explanations begin on page 656.

DECIMALS AND FRACTIONS PRACTICE QUESTIONS

Directions: You MAY use your calculator.

1. A wooden flooring strip is $20\frac{1}{2}$ inches long. If you cut off $4\frac{3}{4}$ inches from one end, what will be the new length of the strip in inches?

   A. $16\frac{3}{4}$

   B. $16\frac{1}{4}$

   C. $15\frac{3}{4}$

   D. $15\frac{1}{4}$

2. A box of cereal costs $4.69. The package label says that the box contains 19 servings. What is the cost of 1 serving to the nearest cent?

   A. $0.02
   B. $0.25
   C. $0.47
   D. $2.46

3. How much would a computer system cost if it is priced as shown below?

Pay $200 down and make 12 monthly payments of only $98.85.

   A. $3586.20
   B. $2400.00
   C. $1386.20
   D. $1186.20

4. Unleaded gasoline sells for $2.869 per gallon. How much would $10\frac{1}{2}$ gallons cost? Round your answer to the nearest cent.

   A. $13.40
   B. $28.69
   C. $30.12
   D. $301.20

5. Three packages weigh $1\frac{1}{2}$ pounds, $4\frac{3}{4}$ pounds, and $2\frac{3}{10}$ pounds. What is the average weight, in pounds, of the packages? (*Hint:* Add the weights, then divide by the number of packages.)

   A. 2.14
   B. 2.85
   C. 4.75
   D. 8.55

6. Gina is paid $8 an hour. If she earned $258 in 1 week, how many hours did she work?

   A. $34\frac{1}{2}$

   B. $32\frac{1}{3}$

   C. $32\frac{1}{4}$

   D. $32\frac{1}{5}$

7. A developer plans to build homes on $20\frac{1}{2}$ acres. She estimates that $6\frac{1}{4}$ acres will be used for roads. The remaining land will be divided into $\frac{1}{4}$-acre lots. How many lots can the subdivision include?

   A.   7
   B.   57
   C.   81
   D.   107

8. A school buys 1000 white-board markers. Below is the price per marker for two brands. How much did the school save by buying Brand A instead of Brand B?

   Brand A: $0.27 each
   Brand B: $0.36 each

   A. $0.09
   B. $0.90
   C. $9.00
   D. $90.00

Questions 9 and 10 refer to the following information.

Madison Small Animal Clinic Scheduling Guidelines	
New-Patient Appointment	$\frac{3}{4}$ hr
Immunizations	$\frac{1}{4}$ hr
Routine Physical	$\frac{1}{3}$ hr
Dental Scaling	$\frac{3}{4}$ hr
Sick Animal Visit	$\frac{1}{2}$ hr
Serious-Injury Visit (includes X-rays)	$1\frac{1}{4}$ hr

9. Ray is a veterinarian at the small-animal clinic. He has four appointments scheduled for Monday morning: two new-patient appointments, a serious-injury visit, and a dental scaling. In hours, how much time should these appointments take?

A. $2\frac{3}{4}$
B. $3\frac{1}{2}$
C. $3\frac{3}{4}$
D. 4

10. Jennifer works $3\frac{1}{2}$ hours each morning at the clinic. How many routine physicals could she complete in one morning?

A. 4
B. 9
C. 10
D. 11

11. A minor-league baseball stadium has 6000 seats. On Beach Towel Night, the stadium sold 5500 of its available seats. What fraction of the seats were sold?

A. $\frac{5}{6}$
B. $\frac{8}{9}$
C. $\frac{9}{10}$
D. $\frac{11}{12}$

12. The City Center parking garage charges $3.50 for the first hour and $1.25 for each additional $\frac{1}{2}$ hour. How much would it cost to park at the garage for $2\frac{1}{2}$ hours?

A. $4.75
B. $6.25
C. $7.25
D. $9.75

13. Susan scheduled 84 appointments for patients at a hospital outreach clinic. Only 56 patients kept their appointments. What fraction of the scheduled appointments were kept?

Write your answer on the line below.

_____

14. This portion of a gas bill compares a household's natural gas usage for December of this year and last year.

Gas Bill Comparison Average Daily Usage			
This Year		Last Year	
Dec	3.13 therms	Dec	3.97 therms

How many more therms of natural gas did the household use in December of last year than December of this year? Express your answer as a decimal.

Write your answer on the line below.

_____

15. Jim and Carl have until 1 p.m. to load 250 boxes. By 12:30 p.m., 175 of the boxes are loaded. What fraction of the boxes has <u>not</u> been loaded?

A. $\frac{1}{5}$

B. $\frac{3}{10}$

C. $\frac{3}{5}$

D. $\frac{7}{10}$

16. On the number line below, what is the value of *A* minus *B*?

A. $\frac{1}{4}$

B. $\frac{5}{8}$

C. $\frac{7}{8}$

D. $1\frac{1}{8}$

17. Scott is driving about 380 miles from Los Angeles to San Francisco. He plans to cover $\frac{3}{4}$ of the distance before noon. How many miles does he plan to drive before noon?

A. 285

B. 254

C. 126

D. 95

18. A cookie recipe calls for $1\frac{2}{3}$ cups of sugar. If you wanted to make half the quantity shown in the recipe, how many cups of sugar would you use?

A. $\frac{2}{5}$

B. $\frac{2}{3}$

C. $\frac{5}{6}$

D. $1\frac{1}{6}$

Question 19 is based on the following information.

Carbide Steel Drill Bits		
Description	**Size (inches)**	**Price**
Cutter	$\frac{9}{16}$	$6.19
Core Box	$\frac{5}{32}$	$16.40
Classic	$\frac{3}{8}$	$17.85
Bevel	$\frac{1}{2}$	$10.50

19. Which of the following shows the drill bits arranged in order from least to greatest in size?

A. cutter, bevel, classic, core box

B. core box, bevel, classic, cutter

C. bevel, classic, cutter, core box

D. core box, classic, bevel, cutter

20. Joe is going to order a pizza. He will eat at least $\frac{1}{2}$ of it. If he's very hungry, he might eat as much as $\frac{7}{8}$ of it. Place two points on the number line below to represent the minimum fraction of the pizza Joe might have left over and the maximum fraction of the pizza Joe might have left over.

21. A project should take no more than 60 hours. If John can spare 7.5 hours per day to work on the project, what is the maximum number of days it will take him to finish?

A. 6

B. 7

C. 8

D. 9

22. How many miles would a map distance of $\frac{5}{8}$ inch represent if 1in. = 240 mi?

A. 40

B. 130

C. 150

D. 200

23. A survey shows that $\frac{2}{3}$ of all homeowners have a pet. Of those, $\frac{3}{4}$ have either a dog or cat. Of the homeowners surveyed, what fraction has either a dog or a cat?

    A. $\frac{1}{2}$

    B. $\frac{3}{4}$

    C. $\frac{5}{7}$

    D. $\frac{6}{7}$

24. At Wyman Shipping, 140 employees work during the day shift. At night, the crew is $\frac{2}{5}$ the size of the day shift. How many workers are scheduled to work the night shift?

    A. 28
    B. 56
    C. 70
    D. 94

Question 25 refers to the following map.

The map below shows the distance, in miles, between four stores.

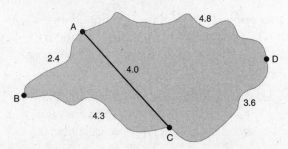

25. Maya drives a van that delivers supplies to each of the stores. On Friday, she traveled the following route.

    Store A to Store B
    Store B to Store C
    Store C to Store D
    Store D to Store C
    Store C to Store A

    How many miles did she drive in all?

    A. 13.9
    B. 15.1
    C. 17.9
    D. 19.1

26. From a wooden dowel $12\frac{1}{2}$ feet long, Jamie cut two pieces, each $3\frac{3}{4}$ feet long. How long, in feet, is the remaining piece?

    A. $8\frac{3}{4}$

    B. $7\frac{1}{2}$

    C. $6\frac{1}{2}$

    D. 5

27. Luis bought 20 shares of stock, priced at $26.38 per share. He also paid an $8 transaction fee. How much did he pay?

    A. $687.60
    B. $535.60
    C. $527.60
    D. $519.60

28. A mat board is 60 inches wide. How many strips measuring 0.75 inches wide can be cut from the board? (Assume no waste from the cuts.)

    Write your answer on the line below.

    _____

29. Of his take-home pay each month, Jerry spends $\frac{1}{6}$ on a car payment and $\frac{1}{4}$ on food. What fraction of his take-home pay is left after paying for these two items?

    Write your answer on the line below.

    _____

Answers and explanations begin on page 657.

Ratio and Proportion

Ratio

A **ratio** compares two numbers. You can write a ratio using the word *to*, using a colon (:), or using fraction form.

Example 1: A softball pitcher strikes out four batters for every one batter that she walks. What is the ratio of strikeouts to walks?

Always write the numbers in the ratio in the same order in which they appear in the question.

$$\text{4 to 1} \qquad \text{4:1} \qquad \frac{4}{1}$$

Ratios are similar to fractions. They have two terms, and they can be simplified by reducing to lowest terms.

Example 2: Frank manages a small drugstore. During a two-hour period, he counts 25 cash sales and 15 credit card sales. What is the ratio of credit card to cash sales?

1. Write the ratio as a fraction with the terms in the correct order: credit card to cash sales.

$$\frac{\text{credit card sales}}{\text{cash sales}} = \frac{15}{25}$$

2. Reduce to lowest terms. The ratio of credit card to cash sales is **3 to 5.**

$$\frac{15 \div 5}{25 \div 5} = \frac{3}{5}$$

There are some fraction rules that ratios do not follow. Do not change a ratio that is an improper fraction to a mixed number. Also, if a ratio in fraction form has a denominator of 1, <u>do not</u> write it as a whole number. Leave it in fraction form.

Another important difference is in the use of labels. The terms in a fraction have the same unit labels: $\frac{5}{6}$ of a pie means 5 slices out of 6 slices. Ratios <u>may</u> have different labels: *The sale advertised 6 cans for $1, a 6:1 ratio.*

To write a ratio, you may need to perform one or more basic operations to find one of the terms.

Example 3: A football team won 12 games and lost 8. There were no tied games. What is the ratio of games won to games played?

1. The problem does not tell you the number of games played. Add the games won to the games lost to find the games played.

$$12 \text{ won} + 8 \text{ lost} = 20 \text{ played}$$

2. Write the ratio in the correct order and simplify. **The team won 3 games for every 5 games it played, a 3:5 ratio.**

$$\frac{\text{games won}}{\text{games played}} = \frac{12}{20} = \frac{12 \div 4}{20 \div 4} = \frac{3}{5}$$

Key Ideas

- A ratio has two terms and can be written in words, with a colon, or as a fraction.
- Ratios are simplified by reducing to lowest terms.
- The terms in a ratio can have different labels.

GED® TEST TIP

The terms in a ratio must be written in the order given by the words of the question. Don't be fooled by an answer choice on a multiple-choice question that reverses the order of the numbers.

PRACTICE 1.1

A. Write each ratio as a fraction in lowest terms.

1. Stan made 24 sales in 6 hours. What is the ratio of sales to hours?

2. Carol's monthly take-home pay is $1500. She spends $250 a month on food. What is the ratio of food costs to take-home dollars?

3. A toy rocket travels 180 ft in 15 sec. What is the ratio of feet to seconds?

4. At Phil's work, there are 12 part-time workers and 18 full-time workers. What is the ratio of part-time workers to total workers?

5. Juanita drove 336 miles on 14 gallons of gasoline. What is the ratio of miles to gallons?

6. Lynn estimates that a roofing job will cost $1500. Bo estimates that the same job will cost $2400. What is the ratio of Lynn's estimate to Bo's estimate?

7. A basketball player attempted 32 free throws and made 20. What is the ratio of free throws made to free throws missed?

8. There are 10 men and 14 women in Kathleen's math class. What is the ratio of women to the total number of students in the class?

9. To paint his apartment, Alex bought 6 gallons of paint to cover 1440 square feet. What is the ratio of square feet to gallons of paint?

B. Choose the one best answer to each question.

Questions 10 through 12 refer to the following information.

Three candidates are running for mayor. Below are the results of a survey of 600 registered voters.

Candidate	Number of Supporters
Stothard	220
Mesa	180
Newmark	50
Undecided	150

10. What is the ratio of Mesa's supporters to Stothard's supporters?

    A. 9:11
    B. 11:9
    C. 11:20
    D. 20:11

11. What is the ratio of voters who prefer Mesa to the total number surveyed?

    A. 3 to 7
    B. 3 to 10
    C. 3 to 13
    D. 11 to 30

12. What is the ratio of undecided voters to voters who have made a decision?

    A. $\frac{1}{4}$
    B. $\frac{1}{3}$
    C. $\frac{3}{1}$
    D. $\frac{4}{1}$

13. Soan made a $400 down payment on a washer and dryer that cost a total of $1200. What is the ratio of the amount Soan has paid to the amount he still owes?

    A. 1 to 4
    B. 1 to 3
    C. 1 to 2
    D. 2 to 3

14. A team played 77 games and won 56 of them. There were no tied games. What is the ratio of wins to losses?

    A. 3:8
    B. 8:11
    C. 11:8
    D. 8:3

Answers and explanations begin on page 657.

Proportion

A **proportion** is an equation that shows that two ratios are equal. The **cross products** in a true proportion are equal. In other words, when you multiply diagonally across the equals sign, the products are equal.

Example 4: The directions on a can of powdered drink mix say to add 3 cups of water to every 2 scoops of drink mix. Matt adds 12 cups of water to 8 scoops of drink mix. Did he make the drink correctly?

1. Write a proportion, making sure the terms of the ratios are in the same order.

$$\frac{\text{Cups}}{\text{scoops}} \quad \frac{3}{2} \diagup\!\!\!\!\diagdown \frac{12}{8}$$

2. Cross multiply and compare the products. Since the products are the same, the ratios are equal. **Matt made the drink correctly.**

$$3 \times 8 = 24$$
$$2 \times 12 = 24$$

In most proportion problems, you are asked to solve for a missing term.

Example 5: A map scale says that 2 inches = 150 miles. What actual distance would a map distance of 5 inches represent?

1. Write a proportion with both ratios in the same form: inches to miles. The variable x represents the unknown distance.

$$\frac{\text{inches}}{\text{miles}} \quad \frac{2}{150} = \frac{5}{x}$$

2. Locate the term in the first ratio that is diagonal from the known term in the second ratio. Cross multiply.

$$\frac{2}{150} \diagup \frac{5}{x}$$
$$150 \times 5 = 750$$

3. Divide the result by the remaining known term to find the value of x.

$$750 \div 2 = \textbf{375 miles}$$

Some proportion problems ask you to find a **rate.** A rate compares a quantity to 1. When a rate is written in fraction form, its denominator is always 1. In word form, rates are often expressed using the word *per.*

Example 6: Connie drove 276 miles on 12 gallons of gasoline. How many miles per gallon did she get on the trip?

1. Gas mileage is one kind of rate. You need to find how many miles Connie drove on one gallon of gasoline.

$$\frac{\text{miles}}{\text{gallons}} \quad \frac{276}{12} = \frac{x}{1}$$

2. Solve.

$$276 \times 1 = 276$$
$$276 \div 12 = \textbf{23 miles per gallon}$$

Using your calculator, you can solve proportion problems in one series of calculations.

Example 7: Find the value of x in the proportion $\dfrac{6}{16} = \dfrac{21}{x}$.

You need to multiply 16 and 21, then divide by 6. On the TI-30XS MultiView™ calculator:

1. Press 16 ⊠ 21 ÷ 6.

2. Then press enter. The right side of the display will read 56.

The missing term is **56.**

NOTE: When working a problem, ask yourself if it can be solved using proportion. This may be possible when two quantities are compared or when three values are given and you are asked to find a fourth.

PRACTICE 1.2

A. Solve for the missing term in each proportion problem. You MAY use your calculator for questions 9 through 16. NOTE: Answers will not always be whole numbers.

1. $\frac{2}{3} = \frac{x}{18}$

2. $\frac{3}{5} = \frac{27}{x}$

3. $\frac{6}{5} = \frac{3}{x}$

4. $\frac{15}{2} = \frac{x}{8}$

5. $\frac{4}{\$212} = \frac{7}{x}$

6. $\frac{25}{6} = \frac{400}{x}$

7. $\frac{7}{30} = \frac{x}{9}$

8. $\frac{0.5}{12} = \frac{3}{x}$

9. $\frac{20}{2.5} = \frac{100}{x}$

10. $\frac{\$5.96}{2} = \frac{x}{3}$

11. $\frac{12}{5} = \frac{3}{x}$

12. $\frac{4}{60} = \frac{2.5}{x}$

13. $\frac{3}{19} = \frac{x}{114}$

14. $\frac{9}{\$80.10} = \frac{x}{\$284.80}$

15. $\frac{\$26.00}{4} = \frac{x}{7}$

16. $\frac{24}{96} = \frac{7}{x}$

B. Choose the one <u>best answer</u> to each question. You MAY use your calculator for questions 20 through 22.

17. A store is advertising the following sale:

Tomato Soup
4 cans for $0.98

    To the nearest cent, how much would five cans of tomato soup cost?

    A. $0.25
    B. $1.23
    C. $2.45
    D. $4.90

18. The Bay City Cardinals have won 5 out of 8 games. At the same rate, how many games will they have to play to win 60 games?

    A. 180
    B. 120
    C. 96
    D. 12

19. Carla drove her truck 414 miles on 18 gallons of gasoline. How many miles did she drive per gallon?

    A. 18
    B. 23
    C. 74
    D. 95

20. The scale on a map reads, "2 cm = 150 km." How many kilometers would be represented by a distance of 4.6 centimeters?

    A. 300
    B. 345
    C. 690
    D. 1380

21. Two ingredients in a recipe are $2\frac{1}{2}$ cups of flour and $1\frac{1}{2}$ cups of sugar. If June keeps the proportion the same, how many cups of flour should she add to 4 cups of sugar?

    A. $6\frac{2}{3}$
    B. 6
    C. 5
    D. $3\frac{3}{4}$

22. Claudia drove 155 miles in 2.5 hours. Which of the following expressions could be used to find how many miles she can drive in 7 hours?

    A. $155 \times 7 \div 2.5$
    B. $2.5 \times 7 \div 155$
    C. $155 \times 2.5 \div 4\,7$
    D. $7 \times 2.5 \times 155$

Answers and explanations begin on page 658.

RATIO, PROPORTION, AND PERCENT

Percents

Percent means "per hundred" or "out of one hundred." For example, if you have $100 and you spend $25, you spent $25 out of $100, or 25% of your money.

Since percent is a way of showing part of a whole, it has much in common with fractions and decimals. To convert a percent to a fraction, write the percent over 100 and reduce. To convert percents to decimals, drop the percent symbol and move the decimal point two places to the left.

Key Ideas

- The percent symbol (%) means "out of 100."
- The three elements of a percent problem are the base, the part, and the rate.
- Percent problems can be solved by writing a proportion that has a denominator of 100.

Percent to Fraction
$$25\% = \frac{25}{100} = \frac{1}{4}$$

Percent to Decimal
$$25\% = .25 = 0.25$$

In any percent problem, there are three elements: the base, the part, and the rate. The **base** is the whole quantity, or amount, that the problem is about. The **part** (also called a **percentage**) is a portion of the base. The **rate** is a number followed by the percent symbol (%).

Example 1: At a restaurant, Janice's bill is $20. She gives the waiter a tip of $3, which is 15% of her bill. Identify the base, part, and rate in this situation.

The entire bill of $20 is the base. The $3 tip is part of the base, and the rate is 15%.

One way to think of a percent problem is as a proportion. In Example 1, there are two ratios. The $3 tip is part of the $20 total bill, and 15% is the same as $\frac{15}{100}$. Since the two ratios are equal, they can be written as a proportion.

$$\frac{\text{part}}{\text{base}} \quad \frac{3}{20} = \frac{15}{100}$$

Cross multiply to prove the ratios are equal.

$$20 \times 15 = 300$$
$$3 \times 100 = 300$$

You can solve percent problems by setting up a proportion and solving for the missing elements. Just remember to express the percent as a number over 100.

Example 2: At a plant that manufactures lighting fixtures, it is expected that about 2% of the fixtures assembled each day will have some type of defect. If 900 fixtures are completed in one day, how many are expected to be defective?

1. Write a proportion. Remember that 2% means 2 out of 100. Use the variable x to stand for the number of defective fixtures.

$$\frac{\text{part}}{\text{base}} = \frac{\text{rate}}{100}$$
$$\frac{x}{900} = \frac{2}{100}$$

2. Solve for x. Cross multiply and divide by the remaining number. **The company can expect about 18 defective fixtures.**

$$900 \times 2 = 1800$$
$$1800 \div 100 = 18$$

A. For each situation, identify and label the base, part, and rate.

1. Victor owes his uncle $1000. Recently, he gave his uncle $200. The payment was 20% of the money he owes.

2. On a test with 80 problems, Sophie got 72 problems right. In other words, she answered 90% of the problems correctly.

3. The Kang family made a down payment of $2,740 on a new car. The down payment was 20% of the purchase price of $13,700.

4. Zoe's take-home pay each month is $2000. She spends $500 on rent each month, which is 25% of her take-home pay.

5. This year, Rafael has 60 regular customers, which is 150% of the 40 regular customers he had last year.

6. Kayla bought a dress for $38. She paid $3.23 in sales tax. The sales tax rate in her state is 8.5%.

7. Misako's employer withholds 15% of her salary each paycheck for taxes. Misako earns $900 each week, and her tax withholding is $135.

8. Harrison got a 10% raise. Before the raise, his hourly wage was $10.70. Now he earns an additional $1.07 per hour.

9. Kim Industries has 800 employees. Of those, 200 workers, or 25%, work part-time.

10. In an election, 5,000 of the 12,500 registered voters actually voted. Only 40% of the registered voters actually voted.

B. Choose the one best answer to each question. Use the proportion $\dfrac{\text{part}}{\text{base}} = \dfrac{\text{rate}}{100}$ to solve each problem.

Questions 11 and 12 refer to the following information.

A local newspaper printed the following high school basketball standings:

Team	Wins	Losses
Fairfax	9	3
Hamilton	8	4
Bravo	6	6
Mountain View	4	8
Lincoln	3	9

11. Which of the following expressions could be used to find what percent of its total games Fairfax has won?

A. $\dfrac{9 \times 100}{12}$

B. $\dfrac{3 \times 100}{12}$

C. $\dfrac{12 \times 100}{9}$

D. $\dfrac{6 \times 100}{12}$

12. What percent of its games did Bravo win?

A. 100%
B. 75%
C. 60%
D. 50%

13. A jacket with a price tag of $128 is on a rack with the following sign:

> All Items:
> 25% off marked price
> Discount taken at register

By how much will the price be reduced when the jacket is taken to the register?

A. $4
B. $25
C. $32
D. $96

Answers and explanations begin on page 658.

RATIO, PROPORTION, AND PERCENT

Using the Percent Formula

Key Ideas

- You can use a formula to solve percent problems: *Base × Rate = Part.*

- To change a percent to a decimal, drop the % sign and move the decimal point two places to the left.

- To change a decimal to a percent, move the decimal point two places to the right and add the % sign.

Solving for Part

You have seen how to use proportion to solve percent problems. You can also solve percent problems using the formula ***Base × Rate = Part***.

Study the diagram at the right to learn how to use the formula. To use the diagram, cover the element you need to solve for: B = Base, R = Rate (percent), and P = Part. Then perform the operation that connects the remaining elements.

Example 1: A company offers its employees two health plans. In a recent newsletter, the personnel department stated that 70% of the employees chose Plan A. If the company has 320 workers, how many chose Plan A?

1. The rate is 70%, and the base is 320, the total number of workers. You need to solve for the part. Using the diagram, cover P for part. You can see that you need to multiply to solve the problem.

2. Change the percent to a decimal and multiply.
   Out of 320 workers, 224 chose Plan A.

   $70\% = 0.7$

   $320 \times 0.7 = \mathbf{224}$

Solving for Rate

Rewrite the percent formula to solve for rate. Use the formula ***Part ÷ Base = Rate***. You can use the diagram to help you remember the formula.

Example 2: A computer system is regularly priced at $1600. On Friday, the manager reduced the price by $640. By what percent did the manager discount the computer system?

1. The base is $1600, the regular price. The part is $640, the amount the price was reduced. You are asked to find the rate of the discount. Cover R for rate (percent). You need to divide the part by the base to solve the problem.

2. Divide 640 by 1600.

3. Convert the decimal answer to a percent by moving the decimal point two places to the right and adding the percent sign. The price reduction was a **40% discount.**

$$1600\overline{)640.0}$$
$$\underline{640.0}$$
$$0.4 = 40 = \mathbf{40\%}$$

GED® TEST TIP

When you take the Mathematical Reasoning Test, make a quick sketch of the percent diagram on the wipe-off board to help you analyze percent problems.

Always ask yourself whether your answer seems reasonable. For example, you know that 40% is a little less than $\frac{1}{2}$, and $\frac{1}{2}$ of $1600 is $800. Since $640 is a little less than $800, it is a reasonable answer.

PRACTICE 3.1

A. Solve. You MAY use a calculator for questions 9 through 16.

1. What is 20% of $25?
2. Find 90% of 200.
3. What is 35% of 400?
4. What percent is 19 out of 20?
5. 42 is what percent of 168?
6. What percent is $18 out of $600?
7. Find $33\frac{1}{3}$% of 51. (*Hint:* $33\frac{1}{3}\% = \frac{1}{3}$)
8. What is 125% of $48?

9. 240 is what percent of 120?
10. What percent is 3 out of 60?
11. $52 is what percent of $650?
12. Find $8\frac{1}{2}$% of $46.
13. $0.65 is what percent of $10.00?
14. Find 28% of $1300.
15. What percent is 2.5 out of 4?
16. Find $66\frac{2}{3}$% of 108. (*Hint:* $66\frac{2}{3}\% = \frac{2}{3}$)

B. Choose the one best answer to each question. You MAY use your calculator.

17. Pat called 120 customers to offer a software upgrade. Of those he called, 72 purchased the upgrade. What percent agreed to the purchase?

    A. 40%
    B. 48%
    C. 60%
    D. $66\frac{2}{3}$%

18. Douglas received a 6% raise. If his old monthly salary was $2,250, what is his monthly salary now? (*Hint:* Find the amount of the raise. Then add the raise to the previous monthly salary.)

    A. $2,256
    B. $2,385
    C. $3,600
    D. $13,500

19. At a restaurant, Levy's total bill is $46. If he wants to tip 15%, how much should he leave as a tip?

    A. $690.00
    B. $31.00
    C. $15.00
    D. $6.90

20. The following advertisement for sporting goods appeared in the newspaper. What percent of the original price is the sale price?

    > Little League Package
    > Magnum bat, tote bag, and youth cleats
    > Only $45.50
    > Originally $65

    A. 20%
    B. 31%
    C. 44%
    D. 70%

21. Lydia pays $3 sales tax on a $50 purchase. Which of the following expressions could be used to find the sales tax rate in her state?

    A. $\dfrac{\$3 \times 100}{\$50}$

    B. $\dfrac{\$3 \times \$50}{100}$

    C. $\$3 \times \$50 \times 100$
    D. $\$3 \div \$50$

Answers and explanations begin on page 658.

Solving for Base

Some problems on the *Mathematical Reasoning Test* may require you to solve for the base in a percent situation. Remember, the base represents the whole item or group. Read each situation carefully to figure out which element is missing. Then choose the correct method for solving the problem.

Example 3: In a math class, 75% of the students got at least a B grade on the final exam. If 18 students got at least a B, how many students are in the class?

1. Analyze the situation. The 18 students are part of the larger class. You know that the 18 students are 75% of the whole group, so 75% is the rate and the base is unknown.

   Use the diagram. Cover *B* for base. You need to divide the part by the rate to solve the problem.

2. Convert the rate to a decimal (75% = 0.75) and divide. There are **24 students** in the class.

$$\begin{array}{r} 24 \\ 0.75\overline{)18.00} \\ \underline{150} \\ 300 \\ \underline{300} \end{array}$$

Most of the time, we work with percents that are less than 100%. When a percent is less than 100%, the part is less than the base. However, it is possible to have a situation in which the part is greater than the base. When this occurs, the percent will be greater than 100%.

Example 4: The workforce at Eastland Inc. is growing rapidly. The number of employees this year is 225% of the number last year. If there are 135 employees this year, how many employees did the company have last year?

1. The base is the number of employees the company had last year. This year's number is a percent of last year's number. Therefore, the rate is 225%, the part is 135, and the base is unknown.

2. Convert 225% to a decimal. Drop the % sign and move the decimal point two places to the left.

   $225\% = 2.25 = 2.25$

3. Divide the part (135) by the rate (2.25). Last year, there were only **60 employees.**

   $$\begin{array}{r} 60 \\ 2.25\overline{)135.00} \\ 135.0 \end{array}$$

There is often more than one way to approach the solution to a problem. Both the percent formula presented in this lesson and the proportion method from Lesson 1 can be used to solve Example 4.

Formula method: $\dfrac{135}{2.25}$ Proportion method: $\dfrac{135 \times 100}{225}$

If you evaluate both methods using a calculator, both expressions equal 60, the correct solution.

NOTE: Don't begin calculations before you completely analyze a situation. Every percent problem has three elements. Make sure you know which one is missing before you multiply or divide.

PRACTICE 3.2

A. Find the missing element in each set. You MAY NOT use a calculator.

1. $35 is 20% of what amount?
2. 5% of what number is 14?
3. 3.2 is 50% of what number?
4. $170 is 85% of what amount?
5. 24 is 80% of what number?
6. $105 is 125% of what amount?
7. 190 is 95% of what number?
8. What number is 15% of 60?
9. 90% of $15 is what number?

10. $42 is what percent of $168?
11. $150 is 200% of what amount?
12. 15% of $62 is what amount?
13. 9 is 1% of what number?
14. What percent is 126 of 140?
15. 65% of $1200 is what amount?
16. 5% of an amount is $156. What is the amount?
17. $2\frac{1}{2}$% of a number is 100. What is the number?
18. What percent is $15.60 of $156.00?

B. Choose the one best answer to each question. You MAY use your calculator.

19. Kevin's total payroll deductions are 30% of his earnings. If his deductions add up to $369 for a two-week period, how much were his earnings for the period?

    A. $110.70
    B. $123.00
    C. $1,230.00
    D. $11,070.00

20. A city council established the following budget to improve public transportation.

	Project Budget
Salaries	50%
Office lease	35%
Equipment	6%
Supplies	2%
Miscellaneous	7%

    If $72,000 is allotted for equipment, what is the total budget for the project?

    A. $432,000
    B. $940,000
    C. $1,200,000
    D. $120,000,000

21. Jack earns a 5% commission on each sale. If he is paid a $160 commission, which of the following expressions could be used to find the amount of the sale?

    A. $\dfrac{5 \times 100}{160}$

    B. $\dfrac{160 \times 100}{5}$

    C. $\dfrac{5 \times 160}{100}$

    D. $5 \times 100 \times 1.60$

22. American Loan Company mailed 3600 customers an application for a new credit card. Only 20% of the customers returned the application. How many customers returned the application?

    A.   72
    B.   180
    C.   720
    D. 180,000

Answers and explanations begin on page 658.

RATIO, PROPORTION, AND PERCENT

Percent Calculator Skills

By changing a percent to either a fraction or decimal, you can use a calculator to solve percent problems.

Example 1: What is 25% of 120? Try both decimals and fractions.

Change 25% to the decimal (.25), multiply times 120, and press (enter). **30** is on the right of the display.

On the Display

.25*120	30

Change 25% to the fraction $\frac{25}{100}$ using the $\boxed{\frac{n}{d}}$ key, multiply times 120, and press (enter). **30** is on the right of the display.

$\frac{25}{100}$*120	30

Using either decimals or fractions, you can find that **30** is 25% of 120.

When you use the *percent 2nd* function, you don't have to convert the percent to a fraction or decimal. Practice this function below to multiply to find the **part** when you are given the rate (percent).

Example 2: What is 65% of $360?

	Keys to Press	On the Display
1. Type the base, 360, and press the multiplication sign.	360 $\boxed{\times}$	360*
2. Type the rate (65). Press the 2nd function key and engage the percent 2nd function—over the $\boxed{(}$ key. Then press (enter).	65 $\boxed{2nd}$ $\boxed{\%}$ $\boxed{enter}$	360*65% 234

The amount **$234** is 65% of $360.

You can use the percent function to divide to find the **base** when given the rate.

Example 3: Ned paid $150 for a stereo. The amount Ned paid was 20% of the original cost. What was the original cost of the stereo?

	Keys to Press	On the Display
1. Enter the base, 150, and press the division sign.	150 $\boxed{\div}$	150÷
2. Enter 20 and press the 2nd function key and the $\boxed{(}$ key. Then press *enter*.	20 $\boxed{2nd}$ $\boxed{\%}$ $\boxed{enter}$	150÷20% 750

The original cost of the stereo appears on the right of the display: **$750**.

Key Ideas

- One way to solve percent problems on the calculator is to change the percent to a decimal or a fraction.
- On the TI-30XS MultiView™ calculator, you can use the percent 2nd function to find the part and the base.
- To create a percent, use the 2nd function, %, which is in green over the left parenthesis $\boxed{(}$ key.

GED® TEST TIP

Practice using the Delete *key when you make a mistake in a problem. That will erase your latest entry. The* Clear *key will erase the entire entry.*

PRACTICE 4

A. Solve. You MAY use your calculator.

1. Find 46% of $130.

2. 14% of what amount is $13.44?

3. What is 12% of $126?

4. What number is $62\frac{1}{2}$% of 64?

5. 12 is what percent of 400?

6. A number is 32% of 6500. What is the number?

7. 36 is what percent of 144?

8. 90% of what number is 63?

9. Find 7% of 360.

10. What number is $33\frac{1}{3}$% of 237?

11. 25 is what percent of 1000?

12. What is $12\frac{1}{2}$% of 384?

13. 390 is what percent of 500?

14. Find 2% of $800.

15. 32% of what number is 80?

16. What number is $87\frac{1}{2}$% of 16?

17. $112 is what percent of $1600?

18. A number is $66\frac{2}{3}$% of 414. What is the number?

B. Choose the one best answer to each question. You MAY use your calculator.

Questions 19 and 20 refer to the following chart.

Shipping and Handling Information	
For items costing:	**% of order + handling:**
$20 or less	3% + $1.50
$20.01 to $50	4% + $2.50
$50.01 to $100	5% + $4.00
$100.01 or more	8%

19. Chanel placed an $84 order. How much shipping and handling will she be charged on her order?

   A. $4.20
   B. $4.40
   C. $8.20
   D. $8.36

20. Jason placed an order totaling $110. Zola placed a $90 order. How much more did Jason pay in shipping and handling than Zola?

   A. $0.30
   B. $4.30
   C. $4.50
   D. $20.00

21. In an election, 3190 out of 3625 registered voters voted against a tax increase. What percent of the registered voters voted against the increase?

   A. 43%
   B. 83%
   C. 88%
   D. 98%

22. A baseball player has the following statistics. To the nearest percent, what percent of the player's at bats were strikeouts?

At Bats	Hits	Home Runs	Walks	Strikeouts
410	108	2	70	63

   A. 90%
   B. 58%
   C. 26%
   D. 15%

Answers and explanations begin on page 658.

Simple Interest

Interest is a fee paid for the use of someone else's money. If you put money in a savings account, you receive interest from the bank. If you borrow money, you pay interest. In each case, the amount that you invest or borrow is called the **principal.**

Simple interest is a percent of the principal multiplied by the length of the loan. The formula for finding simple interest is given on the formulas sheet of the *Mathematical Reasoning Test* (see page 403). It reads:

simple interest Interest = principal × rate × time

You may find it easier to remember the formula using **variables** (letters that stand for numbers): $I = prt$, where I = interest, p = principal, r = rate, and t = time. Writing variables next to each other means that they are to be multiplied.

Example 1: Asher borrows $2500 from his uncle for three years at 6% simple interest. How much interest will he pay on the loan?

1. Write the rate as a decimal.

$6\% = 0.06$

2. Substitute the known values in the formula. Multiply.

$I = prt$
$= \$2500 \times 0.06 \times 3$
$= \mathbf{\$450}$

Asher will pay **$450** in interest.

Some problems ask you to find the **amount paid back.** This adds an additional step to an interest problem. In Example 1, Asher will owe $450 in interest at the end of three years. However, he will pay back the interest ($450) plus the principal ($2500): $2500 + $450 = $2950. When he has finished paying the loan, Asher will have paid his uncle $2950.

In a simple interest problem, the rate is an annual, or yearly, rate. Therefore, the time must also be expressed in years.

Example 2: Eva invests $3000 for 9 months. She will be paid 8% simple interest on her investment. How much interest will she earn?

1. Write the rate as a decimal.

$8\% = 0.08$

2. Express the time as a fraction of a year by writing the length of time in months over 12, the number of months in a year.

$9 \text{ months} = \frac{9}{12} = \frac{3}{4} \text{ year}$

3. Multiply.

$I = prt$
$= \$3000 \times 0.08 \times \frac{3}{4}$
$= \mathbf{\$180}$

Eva will earn **$180** in interest.

Key Ideas

- Simple interest is found by multiplying principal, rate, and time: $I = prt$.
- The time must be written in terms of years. Write months as a fraction of a year.
- To find the amount paid back, add the principal and the interest.

GED® TEST TIP

An onscreen formula sheet (see page 403) is provided when you take the Mathematical Reasoning Test. *The formula for simple interest is printed close to the bottom of that sheet. Every time you see a formula in this book, check to see if it is on the formula sheet. If the formula is not there, you will need to memorize it.*

PRACTICE 5

A. Solve these problems using the formula for simple interest. You MAY use your calculator.

1. Leah borrows $1500 for 2 years at a 12% interest rate. Find the interest on the loan.

2. How much interest would you pay on a loan of $800 for 6 months at 14% interest?

3. Dominica invested $2000 for 3 years at an interest rate of 7%. How much interest did she earn on her money?

4. How much interest would you earn on an investment of $600 for 8 years at 10% interest?

5. Todd invests $6500 for $3\frac{1}{2}$ years at 5% interest. How much interest will he be paid at the end of the time period?

6. Ricardo borrows $1850 for 8 months at 12% interest. What is the amount he will pay back at the end of the loan period?

7. Yanira puts $5000 in an investment account for 4 years. If she is paid $8\frac{1}{2}\%$ simple interest, how much interest will she earn?

B. Choose the one best answer to each question. You MAY use your calculator.

8. Jean borrowed $1300 to buy tools for her job as an auto mechanic. The loan is for 1 year 6 months at 9% simple interest. Which of the following expressions could be used to find the amount she will pay back at the end of the loan period?

   A. $1300 × 1.5 × 0.09
   B. $1300 × 1.5 × 9
   C. $1300 + ($1300 × 9 × 1.5)
   D. $1300 + ($1300 × 0.09 × 1.5)

9. Noah borrows $8000 for 5 years to make improvements to his home office. If the simple interest rate is 6%, how much will he pay in interest?

   A. $2400
   B. $1040
   C. $420
   D. $400

10. Caleb borrowed $1500 from his aunt. He plans to pay his aunt back in 9 months. If he pays 4% interest on the loan, what is the total amount he will pay back in 9 months?

    A. $1455
    B. $1545
    C. $1560
    D. $2040

Questions 11 and 12 refer to the following information.

Option	Length of Loan	Simple Interest Rate
A	$2\frac{1}{2}$ years	12%
B	3 years	10%
C	4 years	9%

11. Charlotte needs to borrow $2400. She is considering the three loan options shown above. How much more interest would Charlotte pay if she takes loan option C instead of option A?

    A. $108
    B. $144
    C. $720
    D. $864

12. Charlotte chooses Option B, but she decides to borrow $2800. What is the total amount she will pay back when the loan is due?

    A. $2830
    B. $3240
    C. $3556
    D. $3640

Answers and explanations begin on page 659.

RATIO, PROPORTION, AND PERCENT

Percent of Change

Percent is often used to show change.

Example 1: Michelle recently started her own business. Last month, she earned $1000. This month, she earned $2000. How could she describe the increase in her earnings?

All of the following statements accurately describe the change.

- Michelle's earnings doubled from last month to this month.

- This month, her earnings increased by 100%.

- This month's earnings are 200% of last month's earnings.

Percent of change compares a new number, which shows an **increase** or a **decrease**, to the original number—the number before the change.

Example 2: Before her raise, Lisa earned $10.50 per hour. Now she earns $11.34 per hour. What percent raise did her boss give her?

1. Subtract to find the amount of change. $11.34 - $10.50 = $0.84

2. Divide the amount of change by $10.50, $\frac{\$0.84}{\$10.50} = 0.08 = \mathbf{8\%}$
Lisa's wage before the change. Convert the
decimal to a percent. Lisa's hourly wage
increased by 8%.

Think carefully about a situation to decide which number is the original amount.

Example 3: A jacket is on sale for $90. Three days ago, the jacket was on sale for $120. By what percent was the price of the jacket reduced?

1. Subtract to find the amount of change. $120 - $90 = $30

2. The price of the jacket was $120 before it was $\frac{\$30}{\$120} = 0.25 = \mathbf{25\%}$
$90, so $120 is the original price. Divide the
amount of change by $120. The new price is
25% less than the price three days ago.

Percent of increase may be greater than 100%.

Example 4: Calvin started his business with 10 employees. Now he has 60 employees. By what percent has his workforce increased?

1. Subtract to find the amount of change. $60 - 10 = 50$

2. Divide by the original number. Convert the $\frac{50}{10} = 5.0 = \mathbf{500\%}$
number to a percent. Calvin's workforce has
increased by 500%.

Key Ideas

- The amount of change is the difference between the new number and the original number.
- Find the percent of change by dividing the amount of change by the original number.
- Percent of increase may be greater than 100%.

GED® TEST TIP

You can work backward to check your answers. For example, if a price has decreased by 25%, the new price should be 75% of the original price, since 25% + 75% = 100%.

PRACTICE 6

A. Solve as directed. If necessary, round your answer to the nearest percent. You MAY use your calculator for questions 7 through 10.

1. Find the percent of increase from 2000 to 3000.

2. Find the percent of decrease from $2.00 to $1.25.

3. What is the percent of increase from 30 to 90?

4. Find the percent of decrease from 20 to 11.

5. Find the percent of increase from $25 to $30.

6. What is the percent of decrease from 500 to 340?

7. Find the percent of increase from $1.89 to $2.29.

8. What is the percent of decrease from 21 to 3?

9. Find the percent of increase from 65 to 338.

10. What is the percent of decrease from $1550 to $1025?

B. Choose the one best answer to each question. You MAY use your calculator.

11. Justin recently moved from a part-time to a full-time job. Because of the change, his weekly pay increased from $280 to $448. To the nearest percent, by what percent did his income increase?

    A. 38%
    B. 60%
    C. 168%
    D. 267%

12. David bought a computer game on sale for $36. The game was originally $48. What was the percent of decrease in the game's price?

    A. 12%
    B. 25%
    C. $33\frac{1}{3}$%
    D. 75%

13. The Utleys' rent increased from $600 to $636 per month. By what percent did the rent increase?

    A. 4%
    B. 5%
    C. 6%
    D. 7%

Questions 14 and 15 refer to the following information.

Marc sells computer equipment. He buys printers at wholesale and sells them at retail price. Customers who join his discount club pay the member's price.

Printer Pricing Chart

Model Number	Wholesale Price	Retail Price	Member's Price
L310	$63.00	$141.75	$92.15
L1430	$86.00	$150.50	$105.35

14. What is the percent of increase from wholesale to retail price of the L310 model?

    A. 56%
    B. 78%
    C. 125%
    D. 225%

15. For the L1430 model, what is the percent of decrease from retail price to member's price?

    A. 26%
    B. 30%
    C. 43%
    D. 53%

Answers and explanations begin on page 659.

RATIO, PROPORTION, AND PERCENT PRACTICE QUESTIONS

Directions: You MAY use your calculator.

1. From a total yearly budget of $360,000, the Kimball Foundation spends $30,000 on leasing office space. What is the ratio of dollars spent on office space to dollars spent on other costs?

   A. 12:1
   B. 11:1
   C. 1:11
   D. 1:12

2. A worker can assemble 5 motors in 2 hours. Which of the expressions below could be used to find how long it would take the worker to assemble 50 motors?

   A. $2 \times \dfrac{50}{5}$

   B. $\dfrac{5 \times 50}{2}$

   C. $\dfrac{5}{2 \times 50}$

   D. $2 \times 5 \times 50$

3. Frank owns a discount music store. The table below shows how much Frank pays for certain merchandise items.

Item	Wholesale Price
CDs	$7.20
Posters	$5.60

   To find his selling price, Frank increases each price by 35%. What is the selling price of a poster?

   A. $9.72
   B. $7.56
   C. $5.95
   D. $1.96

4. Neva's car is now worth $12,000. This is 60% of what she paid for it. How much did she pay for the car?

   A. $7,200
   B. $18,000
   C. $19,200
   D. $20,000

5. At a shop, the ratio of union to non-union workers is 7 to 3. If there are 18 nonunion workers at the shop, how many union workers are there?

   A. 21
   B. 25
   C. 42
   D. 126

6. Camilla earned $954 in commission on $15,900 in sales. What is her rate of commission?

   A. 6%
   B. 9%
   C. $16\frac{2}{3}$%
   D. 60%

7. John spent the following amounts of time building a workbench:

drawing the plans:	2 hours
cutting the wood:	$1\frac{1}{2}$ hours
assembling the workbench:	2 hours
sanding and sealing:	$3\frac{1}{2}$ hours

   What is the ratio of time spent cutting wood to total time spent on the project?

   A. 1:9
   B. 1:6
   C. 1:5
   D. 3:7

Ford County Farmland Usage Total Acreage: 40,000	
Usage	Number of Acres
Dairy	22,000
Nursery/greenhouse	3,600
Vegetables/fruits	5,200
Grains	9,200

8. What percent of Ford County farmland is used for the growing of grains, vegetables, or fruits?

   A. 23%
   B. 36%
   C. 57%
   D. 64%

9. One dairy farmer in Ford County is considering selling her farm to developers, who will convert it from a dairy farm to a resort. If this happens, the amount of farmland devoted to dairy in Ford County will decrease by 20%. How many acres of farmland will Ford County then have if the dairy farmer decides to sell?

   A. 35,600
   B. 32,000
   C. 17,600
   D. 4,400

10. A serving of peanut butter contains 3 grams of saturated fat and 13 grams of unsaturated fat. This amount of fat is 25% of the recommended amount of fat in a 2000-calorie diet. What is the ratio of grams of saturated fat to total fat in a serving of peanut butter?

   A. $\frac{3}{16}$
   B. $\frac{3}{13}$
   C. $\frac{13}{16}$
   D. $\frac{16}{3}$

11. A drawing of a company logo is 4 inches wide and 5 inches long. If the drawing is enlarged so that it is 12.5 inches long, and the original proportions remain unchanged, how many inches wide will the enlarged drawing be?

   A. 7.5
   B. 10
   C. 15.625
   D. 20

12. A local hospital currently has 184 male patients. If the ratio of male to female patients is 4:3, how many female patients are there in the hospital?

   Write your answer on the line below.

   _____

13. A newspaper advertisement contains the following information.

Busy Body Fitness Center Inventory Reduction Blowout! All sale prices are 20% off original price!	
Equipment	Sale Price
Treadmill	$1512
Upright bike	$720
Home gym	$3148

   In dollars, what was the original price of the upright bike?

   Write your answer on the line below.

   _____

14. The Tigers' ratio of wins to losses is 5 to 4. If the team continues winning at the same rate, how many games will the Tigers win in a 72-game season?

   A. 20
   B. 40
   C. 37
   D. 52

15. A television station called 400 adults and asked the following question: "Do you approve of the governor's new education program?" The table below shows the results of the survey:

Response	Percent
Undecided	16%
Yes	32%
No	52%

Of the people called, how many did NOT answer "no"?

   A. 64
   B. 128
   C. 192
   D. 208

16. The price of a carton of computer paper decreased from $25 to $20. What was the percent decrease in the price?

   A. 80%
   B. 50%
   C. 20%
   D. 5%

17. Six months ago, Sandra had 55 regular customers. Now, she has 220% as many regular customers as she had six months ago. How many regular customers does Sandra have now?

   A. 121
   B. 90
   C. 66
   D. 25

18. If 1 gram of fat equals 9 calories, what percent of the calories in a Munchies roast beef sandwich come from fat?

Munchies Sandwich Facts		
Sandwich	Fat (grams)	Calories
Roast Beef	6	300
Club Classic	5	335

   A. 2%
   B. 3%
   C. 6%
   D. 18%

19. For every $8 in their budget, the Parks spend $3 on food. If their weekly budget is $704, how much do they spend on food each week?

   A. $88
   B. $192
   C. $235
   D. $264

20. Suddeth Travel estimates that 80% of its employees have more than 12 days of unused sick leave. If 140 employees have more than 12 days of unused sick leave, how many employees work at the agency?

   A. 112
   B. 164
   C. 175
   D. 700

21. The Gladstone Theater has 900 seats. At a recent show, the ratio of tickets sold to tickets unsold was 11 to 1. How many tickets were sold?

    A.   75
    B. 810
    C. 818
    D. 825

22. Matthew put $2200 in a savings account for one year and six months. If he earns simple interest at an annual rate of 8%, how much will he have in the account at the end of the time period?

    A. $2212
    B. $2376
    C. $2464
    D. $2640

23. A television set that is regularly priced at $410 is on sale for 20% off. What is the sale price of the television set?

    A. $82
    B. $328
    C. $390
    D. $492

24. On a county map shown below, the map scale reads, "0.5 in. = 60 mi."

What is the actual distance in miles between Lakeview and Riverside?

    A.   23
    B. 165
    C. 300
    D. 330

Question 25 refers to the following information.

Leo's Bookstore kept track of the number of customers who visited the store over a 3-day period. Employees also recorded the number of customers who made a purchase for each day during the same period.

Day	Number of Customers	Number of Customers Who Made a Purchase
Friday	112	83
Saturday	138	45
Sunday	140	91

25. Which of the following could be used to find what percent of Sunday's customers did NOT make a purchase?

    A. $\dfrac{91}{140}$

    B. $\dfrac{91}{140} \times 100$

    C. $\dfrac{(140 - 91)}{140} \times 100$

    D. $\dfrac{(140 - 91)}{91} \times 100$

26. A school admits 9 out of every 14 who apply. At that rate, how many students will be admitted if 420 apply?

Write your answer on the line below.

27. In a 40-hour workweek, Marcie spends 15 hours answering telephones. What is the ratio of hours spent answering telephones to hours doing other types of work? (Record your answer as a fraction.)

Write your answer on the line below.

Answers and explanations begin on page 659.

DATA, STATISTICS, AND PROBABILITY

Tables and Pictographs

Data are facts and information. By analyzing data, we can make predictions, draw conclusions, and solve problems. To be useful, data must be organized in some way. A **table** organizes data in columns and rows. The labels on the table will help you understand what the data mean.

Example 1: The table below shows population figures for selected counties in 2000 and 2010 and the land area in square miles for each county.

County	2000 Pop.	2010 Pop.	Land Area in sq mi
Adams	11,128	15,295	4,255
Bell	25,199	22,707	2,523
Cook	6,532	6,518	2,398
Davis	82,204	90,834	1,139
Evans	139,510	130,748	921

Which county showed the greatest percent of increase in population from 2000 to 2010?

1. **Read the labels.** The first column shows the county names. The second and third columns show population figures. The fourth column shows land area data. You don't need land area to answer this question.

2. **Analyze the data.** Only Adams and Davis counties show increases from 2000 to 2010.

3. **Use the data.** Find the percent of increase for Adams and Davis counties.

Adams: $\frac{15,295-11,128}{11,128} \approx 0.374 \approx 37\%$; Davis: $\frac{90,834-82,204}{82,204} \approx 0.105 \approx 10\%$

Adams County shows the greatest percent of increase in population from 2000 to 2010.

A **pictograph** is another way to display data. Pictographs use symbols to compare data. A key shows what value each symbol represents.

Example 2: A city has three public library branches. A librarian kept track of the numbers of books checked out from each branch in a week. He used the data to create the pictograph below.

From March 4 to March 10, how many books were checked out from the South and West branches combined?

1. There are $4\frac{1}{2}$ symbols for the South Branch and 9 symbols for the West branch. Add: $4\frac{1}{2} + 9 = 13\frac{1}{2}$ symbols.

2. Find the value of the symbols. The key states that each symbol equals 150 books. Multiply by 150: $13\frac{1}{2} \times 150 = $ **2025 books.**

PRACTICE 1

A. Use the table on page 282 to answer questions 1 and 2. Use the pictograph on page 282 to answer questions 3 and 4. You MAY use a calculator.

1. On average, how many people were there per square mile in Bell County in 2010?

2. To the nearest percent, what was the percent of decrease in Evans County's population from 2000 to 2010?

3. How many more books were checked out from North Branch than from South Branch during the week of March 4?

4. How many books were checked out from all three branches combined?

B. Choose the one best answer to each question.

Questions 5 and 6 refer to the following table.

Percent of 3-year-old children with school-readiness skills for the years 2004 and 2010		
	2004	**2010**
Recognizes all letters	11%	17%
Counts to 20 or higher	37%	47%
Writes own name	22%	34%
Reads or pretends to read	66%	67%

5. If 100 children were surveyed in each year, which category showed the least percent of increase from 2004 to 2010?

   A. Recognizes all letters
   B. Counts to 20 or higher
   C. Writes own name
   D. Reads or pretends to read

6. A community had 350 three-year-old children in 2010. If the chart is representative of the community, how many were able to write their own name?

   A. 34
   B. 97
   C. 119
   D. 134

Questions 7 and 8 refer to the following graph.

Mayfair Parking Garage
Daily Average of Parked Cars by Timed Period

Time of Day	Average Number of Cars
8:00 a.m. – noon	🚗🚗🚗🚗🚗🚗
12:01 – 4:30 p.m.	🚗🚗🚗🚗🚗🚗🚗🚗
4:31 – 8:00 p.m.	🚗🚗🚗🚗

Key 🚗 = 50 cars

7. How many cars are parked in the garage from 12:01 to 4:30 p.m.?

   A. 275
   B. 350
   C. 375
   D. 650

8. How many more cars are parked from 8 a.m. to noon than are parked after 4:30 p.m.?

   A. 75
   B. 100
   C. 175
   D. 200

Answers and explanations begin on page 660.

DATA, STATISTICS, AND PROBABILITY

Bar and Line Graphs

Working with Bar Graphs

A **bar graph** uses bars to represent values. Bar graphs have two axis lines. One line shows a number scale, and the other shows labels for the bars. By comparing the length of a bar to the scale, you can estimate what value the bar represents.

Example 1: A national corporation made a bar graph (shown below) to show the number of discrimination complaints made by employees during a six-year period. About how many more complaints were made in 2010 than in 2009?

1. **Read the labels.** Each bar represents the number of complaints made within a year. The years are shown beneath the bars.

2. **Analyze the data.** Compare the bars for 2009 and 2010 to the scale. There were 20 complaints in 2009 and about 32 complaints in 2010.

3. **Use the data.** Subtract: $32 - 20 = 12$. There were **about 12 more** complaints in 2010 than in 2009.

A **double-bar graph** compares more than one type of data.

Example 2: A studio released four films in one year. The graph below compares the cost of making each movie to its box-office receipts, or ticket sales. Film B's cost is what percent of its box-office receipts?

1. **Read the labels.** Read the key to find the meaning of the bars. Notice that the scale represents millions of dollars.

2. **Analyze the data.** Film B's cost is about $30 million. It brought in about $65 million in receipts.

3. **Use the data.** Find what percent $30 is of $65.

$$\frac{\$30}{\$65} \approx 0.462 \approx 46\%$$

Key Ideas

- A bar graph uses bars to represent numbers.
- To find the value of a bar, compare its length to the scale shown on one of the axis lines. Estimate the value.
- A double-bar graph compares groups of data. Read the key to find the meaning of the bars.

GED® TEST TIP

You may not be able to find the exact value of a bar. If the bar falls about halfway between two numbers on the scale, use a whole number that lies in the middle.

PRACTICE 2.1

A. For questions 1 through 3, use the bar graph entitled "Employee Discrimination Complaints" on page 284. For questions 4 through 6, use the bar graph entitled "Profit Analysis for Four Films" on page 284.

1. To the nearest 10, how many employee discrimination complaints were there in 2006 and 2007?

2. To the nearest 5, how many more complaints were there in 2011 than in 2006?

3. By what percent did the number of complaints decrease from 2008 to 2009?

4. About how much more did it cost to make Film A than Film D?

5. Which film made the greatest amount of profit? (*Hint:* profit = receipts − cost)

6. Film C's cost was what percent of its box-office receipts?

B. Choose the one best answer to each question.

Questions 7 and 8 refer to the following graph.

Items Sold for the Week of September 20

Games
Toys
Books
Movies
T-shirts

0   20   40   60   80   100   120
Number sold

Questions 9 and 10 refer to the following graph.

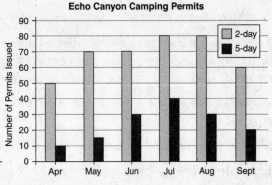

Echo Canyon Camping Permits

7. Approximately how many more T-shirts were sold than books and toys combined?

   A. 40
   B. 70
   C. 80
   D. 90

8. One-half of the games sold during the week of September 20 were on sale for $16. The rest sold for the full price of $24. Approximately how much money did the store take in for games sold during the week of September 20?

   A. $400
   B. $600
   C. $800
   D. $1000

9. In May, what was the ratio of the number of 2-day permits to the number of 5-day permits?

   A. 2:5
   B. 3:17
   C. 14:3
   D. 14:17

10. In which month was there a <u>total</u> of 80 permits issued?

   A. June
   B. July
   C. August
   D. September

Answers and explanations begin on page 660.

Working with Line Graphs

A **line graph** is useful for showing changes over time. By analyzing the rise and fall of the line, you can tell whether something is increasing, decreasing, or staying the same. Like a bar graph, a line graph has two axis lines. One is marked with a scale; the other is marked in regular time intervals.

Example 3: The graph below shows the number of patients who visited an emergency room for the treatment of scooter-related injuries.

In which month did the greatest increase in scooter-related injuries occur?

The points on the graph are positioned above the months, which are arranged in calendar order. By examining the line that connects the points, you can tell whether there was an increase or decrease from one month to the next.

A steeper line shows a greater increase; therefore, the **greatest increase was from July to August**.

If a line graph has more than one line, a key will tell you what the lines represent.

Example 4: The graph below shows the changes in ticket prices for two amusement parks.

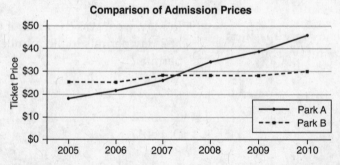

What was the last year in which the admission price to Park B was greater than the admission price to Park A?

The admission prices for Park A are represented by a solid line. Park B's prices are shown with a dotted line. The graph begins in 2005. In 2005, Park B's ticket price is greater than Park A's. Follow the two lines to the right. Between 2007 and 2008, the lines cross, and Park A's prices climb higher than Park B's. **The year 2007** was the last time that Park B charged more than Park A for a ticket.

NOTE: The steepest line shows the greatest increase or decrease, but it may not show the greatest <u>percent</u> of change. When the original value is small, a small change may result in a high percent of change.

PRACTICE 2.2

A. For questions 1 through 3, use the graph from Westside Hospital on page 286. For questions 4 through 6, use the graph "Comparison of Admission Prices" on page 286.

1. In which month did the number of scooter-related injuries decrease?

2. To the nearest 10, how many emergency room visits were due to scooter injuries in August, September, and October combined?

3. Which of the following shows the greater percent of increase: the change in injuries from June to July or the change from August to September?

4. About how much more did it cost to buy a ticket to Park A than a ticket to Park B in 2009?

5. What was the percent of increase in the ticket prices at Park B from 2005 to 2010?

6. To the nearest 10, how much more did it cost to buy a ticket to Park A in 2010 than in 2005?

B. Choose the <u>one best answer</u> to each question.

<u>Questions 7 and 8 refer to the graph below.</u>

Inflation Facts

If a purchase cost $100 in the year 2000, what would its cost have been in the past?

<u>Questions 9 and 10 refer to the graph below.</u>

Lamp Depot has two stores. The graph shows the sales data from the two stores for an 8-week period.

7. Over what period of time did the price of goods actually decrease?

   A. 1930 to 1940
   B. 1940 to 1950
   C. 1960 to 1970
   D. 1970 to 1980

8. Goods purchased in 1970 were about what fraction of their cost in the year 2000?

   A. $\frac{4}{5}$
   B. $\frac{1}{2}$
   C. $\frac{1}{3}$
   D. $\frac{1}{5}$

9. About how many more sales were there at Store 2 than at Store 1 in week 6?

   A. 110
   B. 50
   C. 40
   D. 25

10. During which week did Store 1 experience the greatest increase in sales from the week before?

   A. Week 2
   B. Week 3
   C. Week 4
   D. Week 5

Answers and explanations begin on page 660.

DATA, STATISTICS, AND PROBABILITY

Circle Graphs

Key Ideas

- In a circle graph, the circle represents a whole amount, and the sections represent parts of the whole.
- Sections are usually labeled with percents, but they can show amounts.
- The size of each section of a circle graph is equal to the fraction or percent it represents.

A **circle graph** is used to show how a whole amount is broken into parts. The sections of a circle graph are often labeled with percents. The size of each section corresponds to the fraction it represents. For example, a section labeled 25% is $\frac{1}{4}$ of the circle.

Example 1: A graph below shows how a children's sports camp spends its weekly budget.

Sports Camp Weekly Budget $2250

How much does the sports camp spend on lunches each week?

1. **Analyze the graph.** According to the heading, the entire circle represents the camp's weekly budget of $2250. Find the section labeled "lunches." According to the section label, lunches make up 35% of the weekly budget.

2. **Use the data.** To find the amount spent on lunches, find 35% of $2250: $2250 \times 0.35 =$ **$787.50.**

A circle graph may also be labeled using fractions or decimals. One common kind of circle graph labels each section in cents to show how a dollar is used.

Example 2: According to the graph, what percent of the average energy bill is spent on drying clothes, lighting, and heating water?

Where Do Your Energy Dollars Go?

1. **Analyze the graph.** The entire circle represents $1. The amounts in the sections mentioned in the problem are $0.03, $0.05, and $0.17.

2. **Use the data.** Add the amounts: $0.03 + $0.05 + $0.17 = $0.25. Since $0.25 is 25% of a dollar, **25%** of an average bill is spent on these items.

GED® TEST TIP

Since a circle graph represents a whole, or 100%, amounts can easily be converted to percents. For example, $0.05 on a circle graph can also represent 5%.

PRACTICE 3

A. For questions 1 through 3, use the Sports Camp Weekly Budget circle graph on page 288. For questions 4 through 6, use the Where Do Your Energy Dollars Go circle graph on page 288.

1. What percent of the total sports camp budget is spent on equipment and umpires?

2. What <u>fraction</u> of the sports camp budget is spent on permits?

3. What amount does the camp spend each week on busing?

4. A family's energy bill is $180. Assuming the family's energy use is typical, how much did the family spend on water heating?

5. Which section is greater than 50% of an energy dollar?

6. Which energy cost is about $\frac{1}{10}$ of the energy dollar?

B. Choose the <u>one best answer</u> to each question.

Questions 7 and 8 refer to the following graph.

Time Spent on Tasks by Records Clerks, Woods County Recorders Office

7. During a 40-hour workweek, how many hours does a records clerk spend preparing documents?

   A. 10
   B. 15
   C. 25
   D. 30

8. What percent of a records clerk's time is spent on tasks other than data entry?

   A. 25%
   B. 31%
   C. 44%
   D. 56%

Questions 9 and 10 refer to the following graph.

The employees of National Bank are given the following graph to explain how their retirement fund is invested.

How Your Retirement Dollar Is Invested

9. What percent of each retirement dollar is invested in real estate and the stock market?

   A. 4%
   B. 10%
   C. 40%
   D. 90%

10. Steve contributes $120 of each paycheck to his National Bank retirement fund. How much of each contribution is invested in public bonds?

   A. $36
   B. $40
   C. $48
   D. $84

Answers and explanations begin on page 661.

DATA, STATISTICS, AND PROBABILITY

Measures of Central Tendency

Using a Frequency Table

A **frequency table** shows how often an item appears in a data set. The data is in the form of tally marks next to a list of items.

Example 1: The sales manager at Montana Motors asked her sales staff to keep a record of the color of the cars that were chosen for test-drives in one month. Then she combined the data to make the frequency table shown below.

Montana Motors—Car Color Preferences	
white	⊞⊞ ⊞⊞ ⊞⊞ ⊞⊞ ⊞⊞ ⊞⊞
black	⊞⊞ ⊞⊞ ⊞⊞ ⊞⊞ ⊞⊞ ‖
red	⊞⊞ ⊞⊞ ⊞⊞
green	⊞⊞ ⊞⊞ ‖
silver	⊞⊞ ‖‖‖‖
other	⊞⊞ ⊞⊞ ⊞⊞ ‖

What was the ratio of black cars driven to silver cars driven?

1. Count the tally marks. There are 27 marks for black and 9 for silver.

2. Write the ratio and reduce to lowest terms. $\frac{27}{9} = \frac{3}{1}$

The ratio of black to silver is **3 to 1**. You can also say that the black cars are 3 times as popular as the silver cars.

Numerical data is often grouped in intervals. The table below shows data grouped in intervals of 18 to 24, 25 to 40, and so on. This way of presenting data is called a **grouped frequency table**.

Example 2: The table below shows the ages of the customers at Louise's Diner for a four-day period. What percent of the customers were from 25 to 40 years old?

Louise's Diner Customers by Age Group, February 19–22	
under 18	⊞⊞ ‖
18–24	⊞⊞ ⊞⊞ ⊞⊞ ‖‖‖
25–40	⊞⊞ ⊞⊞ ⊞⊞ ⊞⊞ ⊞⊞ ‖‖‖
41–55	⊞⊞ ⊞⊞
over 55	⊞⊞ ‖‖‖

1. Find the data you need. There are 28 marks for the 25–40 age group. Add the tally marks for all age groups to find the total number of customers for the three-day period: $6 + 18 + 28 + 10 + 8 = 70$.

2. Find the percent. The base is 70, the total number of customers. The part is 28, the number of customers in the desired age group. Solve for the rate: $\frac{28}{70} = \frac{4}{10} = 0.4 = \mathbf{40\%}$.

Key Ideas

- A frequency table is used to show how often data occurs.
- Tally marks are made next to a list to record the data.
- Numerical data is often grouped in intervals.

GED® TEST TIP

If several problems refer to a frequency table, you may want to count the tally marks for each line and record the numbers on the wipe-off board provided at the testing center. Then use the numbers to solve all related problems.

PRACTICE 4.1

A. For questions 1 through 3, use the frequency table from Montana Motors on page 290. For questions 4 through 6, use the frequency table from Louise's Diner on page 290.

1. What was the total number of test drives of black and white cars combined?

2. How many more drivers chose red than silver cars?

3. What was the ratio of red cars to white cars chosen for test-drives?

4. What is the ratio of customers under 18 to those over 55?

5. What was the total number of customers from 18 to 40 years of age?

6. What percent of the total customers were from 41 to 55 years of age? (Round your answer to the nearest whole percent.)

B. Choose the **one best answer** to each question.

Questions 7 and 8 refer to the following information.

The frequency table shows the reasons customers gave for returning clothing merchandise to a store.

Reason	Number
Wrong size	⊪⊪ ⊪⊪ ⊪⊪ I
Unwanted gift	⊪⊪ ⊪⊪ ⊪⊪ ⊪⊪
Found flaw after purchase	III
Changed mind	⊪⊪

7. What is the ratio of customers saying the clothes were the wrong size to all the returns represented?

A. $\frac{4}{15}$

B. $\frac{4}{11}$

C. $\frac{4}{7}$

D. $\frac{4}{5}$

8. Approximately what percent of the customers who returned clothing said that the clothes were an unwanted gift?

A. 20%

B. 25%

C. 45%

D. 50%

Questions 9 and 10 refer to the following information.

A personnel office gives typing tests to people applying for a job. The test shows how many words per minute (wpm) a job applicant can enter correctly. After testing 90 applicants, the manager made the following table.

Typing Speed	Number
Under 30 wpm	⊪⊪ ⊪⊪ ⊪⊪ ⊪⊪ ⊪⊪ ⊪⊪ ⊪⊪
30–45 wpm	⊪⊪ ⊪⊪ ⊪⊪ ⊪⊪ ⊪⊪
46–60 wpm	⊪⊪ ⊪⊪ ⊪⊪ III
Over 60 wpm	⊪⊪ ⊪⊪ II

9. What percent of the applicants had a speed of under 30 wpm?

A. 14%

B. 25%

C. 28%

D. 39%

10. What is the ratio of applicants who could type at a speed above 45 wpm to those who could type at a speed of 45 wpm or less?

A. 1:3

B. 1:2

C. 2:3

D. 6:5

Answers and explanations begin on page 661.

Mean, Median, and Mode

Suppose you were asked how much money you usually spend on groceries in a week. Some weeks, you may spend a great deal; other weeks, much less. You would probably choose an amount in the middle to represent what you typically spend. This middle value is called an **average**, or **measure of central tendency**.

The most common type of average is the **mean**, or the arithmetic average.

Example 3: In five football games, a team scored 14, 21, 3, 20, and 10 points. What is the mean, or average, score per game?

1. Add the values. $14 + 21 + 3 + 20 + 10 = 68$

2. Divide by the number of items in $68 \div 5 = \textbf{13.6 points per game}$
   the data set.

Although it is impossible for a football team to score 13.6 points in a game, the number represents the center of the scores from the five games.

A calculator is useful for finding the mean. Do the calculations in two steps. Enter the addition operations. Then, if you are using the TI-30XS MultiView™, press *enter* to find the sum. Then key in the division operation. Try Example 1 above with a calculator.

Another measure of average is the median. The **median** is the middle value in a set of data.

Example 4: During a 7-hour period, a bookstore recorded the following numbers of sales. Find the median number of sales.

Hour 1	Hour 2	Hour 3	Hour 4	Hour 5	Hour 6	Hour 7
43	28	24	36	32	37	48

1. Arrange the values by size.   24, 28, 32, 36, 37, 43, 48

2. Find the middle number.   24, 28, 32, 36, 37, 43, 48

If there is an even number of values, the median is the mean of the two middle values.

Example 5: Robert has the following test scores in his math class: 90, 72, 88, 94, 91, and 80. What is the median score?

1. Arrange the values by size and find the   72, 80, 88, 90, 91, 94
   middle.

2. Find the mean of the two middle values. The   Add: $88 + 90 = 178$
   median score is **89**.   Divide by 2: $178 \div 2 = \textbf{89}$

The **mode** is the value that occurs most often in a set of data. A set of data could have more than one mode if several items occur the same number of times. If each item of data occurs only once, there is no mode.

Example 6: Six weather stations recorded the following temperatures at 3:00 p.m.: 45°, 44°, 45°, 47°, 46°, and 45°. What is the mode of the data?

The temperature 45° occurs most often (3 times). The mode is **45°**.

PRACTICE 4.2

A. For each data set, find the mean, median, and mode. Round calculations to the nearest hundredth or cent. You MAY use a calculator.

1. Golf scores for 7 rounds:
   76, 82, 75, 87, 80, 82, and 79

2. Sales totals for 6 weeks:
   $5,624; $10,380; $8,102; $6,494; $12,008; and $8,315

3. Cost of lunch for 8 days:
   $4.50, $5.25, $4.50, $3.75, $4.50, $5.25, $6.10, and $4.25

4. Miles driven per day for 5 days:
   330, 286, 342, 300, and 287

5. Grocery bills for 4 weeks:
   $97.48, $106.13, $110.98, and $92.74

6. Scores on 7 quizzes:
   90, 72, 86, 100, 88, 78, and 88

7. High temperatures for 10 days:
   96°, 103°, 98°, 101°, 98°, 100°, 100°, 97°, 98°, and 100°

8. Inches of rainfall over 3-day period:
   2.5, 1.8, and 1.4

9. Attendance figures at a play:
   305, 294, 328, 296, 305, 315, and 292

10. Hours worked per week for 5 weeks:
    36, 40, 38, 40, and 40

B. Choose the one best answer to each question. You MAY use your calculator.

Questions 11 and 12 refer to the following information.

Homes Sold in Fairfield Heights in June		
Home	**Asking Price**	**Selling Price**
#1	$124,600	$116,500
#2	$132,400	$124,800
#3	$118,900	$116,500
#4	$98,500	$103,600
#5	$105,800	$109,000
#6	$122,400	$118,400

11. What was the mean asking price of the homes sold in Fairfield Heights in June?

    A. $117,100
    B. $116,500
    C. $115,450
    D. $114,800

12. What was the median selling price of the homes sold in Fairfield Heights in June?

    A. $112,750
    B. $114,800
    C. $116,500
    D. $117,450

13. The numbers of patients enrolled at four health clinics are 790, 1150, 662, and 805. Which expression could be used to find the mean number of patients per clinic?

    A. $\dfrac{790 + 1150 + 662 + 805}{4}$
    B. $790 + 1150 + 662 + 805$
    C. $\dfrac{662 + 1150}{2}$
    D. $(790 + 1150 + 662 + 805) \div 2$

14. What is the median value of $268, $1258, $654, $1258, $900, $1558, and $852?

    A. $1258
    B. $964
    C. $900
    D. $852

15. What is the mode of the following points scored: 14, 17, 14, 12, 13, 15, 22, and 11?

    A. 13.5
    B. 14
    C. 14.75
    D. 16.5

Answers and explanations begin on page 661.

Line Plots

The same kind of information that can be expressed in a frequency table (see page 290) can also be expressed in a **line plot**. A line plot shows the frequency of data along a number line. Study the following example.

Key Ideas

- A line plot is a graph that shows the frequency of data along a number line.
- Based on frequency tables, line plots consist of a horizontal scale and points or *x*'s placed over corresponding numbers.
- Line plots help us to interpret the distribution of data.

Example 1: The student health services department at a university surveyed several students and asked them how many times per week they visited the school's gym. The following frequency table shows the results for several students.

Weekly Gym Visits	Number of Students
0	I
1	II
2	II
3	III
4	0
5	I
6	0
7	I

Next, the health services department decided to create a line plot in order to see the distribution of gym visits. Each *x* represents a student.

```
              x
        x  x  x
     x  x  x  x        x           x
     +--+--+--+--+--+--+--+--+-->
     0  1  2  3  4  5  6  7
```

You can see from this line plot that there is an uneven **distribution**, or arrangement, of students across the numbers of possible gym visits. Three visits per week has the **highest frequency**, meaning that more students go to the gym three times per week than any other number of visits. You can also see that the data **range** extends from zero visits per week to seven visits per week—no student visits the gym more often than that. The data point showing the one student who visits the gym seven times per week is an **outlier**— that is, a data point that is distant from where most of the data is clustered.

The *Mathematical Reasoning Test* may ask you to identify highest frequency, range, and outliers, or it may give you some data and ask you to place *x*'s or dots on a number line to create a line plot.

Use the following example to study these concepts further.

Example 2: Students in Ms. Jones's class took a math test. Their scores on the test are displayed on the line plot below. Each dot represents a student. Which grade displayed the highest frequency?

More students received a C than received any other grade. Therefore, grade C has the highest frequency of any grade on the line plot.

The range of grades on the math test was from D (the lowest grade received by any student) to A (the highest grade received by any student).

PRACTICE 5

For questions 1 and 2, <u>choose the line plot</u> that matches each frequency table. Use choices A–D below for both questions.

1. Zoologists have counted the number of stripes on certain zebras in a zoo. The set of data from these observations is represented by the following frequency table:

Number of stripes per side	Number of zebras with that many stripes
24	I
25	0
26	II
27	0
28	II
29	0
30	II
31	0
32	I

Which line plot below represents this data?

A.

B.

2. At a certain elementary school, classes may have different numbers of students. The following frequency table represents how many students are in the classes this year:

Number of students	Number of classes with that many students
24	0
25	0
26	0
27	I
28	I
29	III
30	0
31	I
32	II

Which line plot below represents this data?

C.

D.

Questions 3 and 4 are based on the following information.

Juana runs a community garden. She is interested in how many different types of vegetables garden members are planting. She collects the following data:

Garden Member	Types of Vegetables Planted
Alberta	4
Paul	3
Eileen	6
Donato	2
Vijay	3
Janelle	2
Zara	1
Wahib	8
Bill	4
Yeo	3

3. The line plot below is based on the information in the table. Each point represents one of the members of the community garden. Place as many additional points as necessary to complete the line plot.

4. Which value (number of types of vegetables) has the highest frequency in the data?

   A. 2
   B. 3
   C. 4
   D. 8

Answers and explanations begin on page 661.

Histograms

Like line plots, **histograms** display **frequencies**, but they do so in a very different way. Consider the following example:

Example 1: Graham is a veterinarian. Last year he decided to track client appointments for spring shots. The following table and histogram represent his results:

Week of	Number of Appointments
March 1–7	2
March 8–14	4
March 15–21	8
March 22–28	11
March 29–April 4	14
April 5–11	17
April 12–18	13
April 19–25	7
April 26–May 2	5

Number of Graham's Appointments by Week

The **histogram** above on the right has two axes: a **vertical axis** (or *y*-axis) representing numbers of appointments and a **horizontal axis** (also called an *x*-axis) that has increments representing the weeks. The **area** of each bar represents the number of appointments for that week. Thus, you can see not only how many appointments were in any given week but also how the **frequency** of appointments changed over the weeks in the chart.

Finally, histograms can also be used to show percentages. If we alter the histogram about Graham's appointments so that each bar represents the *percent* of total appointments each week, it would look like the one on the right.

Because the percentages add up to 100%, the areas of all the bars add up to 100.

Percent of Graham's Appointments by Week

Example 2: What percent of appointments for spring shots occurred during the first two weeks of March?

You can figure this out by adding the percentages for those weeks (you can approximate based on the histogram): for March 1–7, about 2%; for March 8–14, about 5%. Approximately **7%** of appointments for spring shots occurred during those two weeks.

PRACTICE 6

A. Choose the <u>histogram</u> that matches each frequency table. Use choices A–D below for <u>both</u> questions 1 and 2.

1. Josefina runs a retail business. She posted a coupon to a social media site from 9:00 a.m. to 5:00 p.m. The table shows how many people downloaded or printed the coupon.

Hour Beginning With:	Number of People Who Down-Loaded or Printed Coupon:
9:00 a.m.	30
10:00 a.m.	56
11:00 a.m.	80
12:00 p.m.	71
1:00 p.m.	56
2:00 p.m.	31
3:00 p.m.	22
4:00 p.m.	14

2. Mike administered a skills assessment to his employees. Possible scores on the skills assessment ranged from 200 to 1800. The following table shows how his employees performed on the assessment:

Score Range	Number of Employees
200–399	15
400–599	22
600–799	35
800–999	62
1000–1199	80
1200–1399	69
1400–1599	47
1600–1800	20

A. B. C. D.

B. Choose the <u>one best answer</u> to each question.

<u>Question 3</u> refers to the following histogram and information.

Influenza, or "flu," season in the United States tends to last from fall through spring.

Percent of Total Flu Cases Reported to CDC per Week, 2012–2013 Flu Season in the U.S.

Source: Centers for Disease Control and Prevention

3. Approximately what percentage of flu cases was reported to the CDC during the 2012–2013 season during the time period of December 9 to January 5?

A. 7%
B. 15%
C. 36%
D. 50%

Answers and explanations begin on page 661.

DATA, STATISTICS, AND PROBABILITY

Probability

Key Ideas

- Probability is a ratio. It can be expressed as a ratio, fraction, decimal, or percent.
- Theoretical probability is the ratio of favorable outcomes to possible outcomes.
- Experimental probability is the ratio of favorable outcomes to the number of trials in an experiment.

Simple Probability

Probability tells whether something is likely or unlikely to happen. The probability of any event can be expressed by a number from 0 to 1. If an event has 0 probability, the event is impossible. An event with a probability of 1 is certain to happen. Most events are somewhere in between.

To find the probability of a simple random event, we must identify favorable and possible outcomes. A **favorable outcome** is the event that we are interested in. The **possible outcomes** are all the possible events that could occur. **Theoretical probability** (sometimes called **simple probability**) is the ratio of favorable outcomes to possible outcomes.

Example 1: The spinner is divided into 8 equal sections. What is the probability of spinning a 4 on the spinner?

1. There are two sections labeled 4 on the spinner, and there are 8 sections in all.

2. Use the probability ratio: $\frac{\text{favorable outcomes}}{\text{possible outcomes}} = \frac{2}{8} = \frac{1}{4}$.

The probability of spinning a 4 on the spinner is **1 out of 4, $\frac{1}{4}$, 0.25, or 25%.**

In Example 1, probability was based on what we knew could happen. Another type of probability, called **experimental probability**, is based on what actually happens during the trials of an experiment. The number of trials are the number of times you try the experiment.

Example 2: Ricardo and Scott used the same spinner to play a game. They kept track of the numbers that they got on each spin for 20 spins. The numbers are shown below.

2, 4, 4, 6, 4, 3, 4, 6, 4, 3, 1, 6, 2, 2, 5, 2, 4, 2, 1, 2

Based on their results, what is the experimental probability of spinning a 4?

1. Ricardo and Scott spun a 4 six times out of twenty.

2. Use this ratio: $\frac{\text{favorable outcomes}}{\text{number of trials in experiment}} = \frac{6}{20} = \frac{3}{10}$**, 0.3, or 30%.**

Notice that experimental probability is close to, but not necessarily equal to, theoretical probability. Theoretical probability can tell you what will probably happen, but it can't predict what will actually happen.

GED® TEST TIP

In a multiple-choice probability problem, skim the answer choices to see if they are in fraction, percent, or ratio form. Knowing the answer form will help you decide how to do your calculation.

PRACTICE 7.1

A. Express probability as a fraction, decimal, and percent for questions 1 through 5. Do not use a calculator.

1. A game has 50 wooden tiles. Players draw tiles to spell words. If 20 of the tiles are marked with vowels, what is the probability of drawing a vowel from the tiles?

2. A spinner has five equal sections colored either red, white, or blue. After 40 spins, a player has the following results:

Color	Frequency
red	⊞
white	⊞ II
blue	⊞ ⊞ ⊞ ⊞ ⊞ III

What is the experimental probability of not spinning blue on the spinner?

3. There are four red, four blue, and two green marbles in a bag. If one marble is chosen at random from the bag, what is the probability that the marble will be green?

4. A movie theater sells 180 adult tickets and 60 children's tickets to a movie. As part of a special promotion, one ticket will be chosen at random, and the winner will receive a prize. What is the probability that the winner will be a child?

5. A spinner has six equal sections numbered from 1 to 6. What is the probability of spinning either a 5 or 6?

B. Choose the one best answer to each question. You MAY use your calculator.

Questions 6 and 7 refer to the following information.

A deck of 12 cards is marked with the following symbols.

6. If a card is chosen at random, what is the probability of selecting a diamond (♦)?

    A.   6%
    B. 12%
    C. 50%
    D. 60%

7. If a card is chosen at random, what is the probability of selecting something other than a club (♣)?

    A. $\frac{3}{4}$
    B. $\frac{2}{3}$
    C. $\frac{1}{3}$
    D. $\frac{9}{100}$

Questions 8 and 9 refer to the following information.

Erin flipped a coin 40 times and made this table to show how many outcomes were "heads" and how many were "tails."

| heads | ⊞ ⊞ ⊞ ⊞ IIII |
| tails | ⊞ ⊞ ⊞ I |

8. Based on Erin's data, what is the experimental probability of getting tails on a coin flip?

    A. 3 out of 5
    B. 3 out of 4
    C. 2 out of 3
    D. 2 out of 5

9. Based on Erin's data, what is the experimental probability of getting heads on a coin flip?

    A. 3 out of 5
    B. 3 out of 4
    C. 2 out of 3
    D. 1 out of 2

Answers and explanations begin on page 661.

Dependent and Independent Probability

You know how to find the probability of a single event. You can use this knowledge to find the probability of two or more events.

Example 3: Brad tosses two quarters into the air. What is the probability that both will land so that the heads' sides are showing?

One way to solve the problem is to list or diagram all the possible outcomes.

If quarter #1 is heads,
quarter #2 could be <u>heads</u>.　　H <u>H</u>
or
quarter #2 could be <u>tails</u>.　　H <u>T</u>

If quarter #1 is tails,
quarter #2 could be <u>heads</u>.　　T <u>H</u>
or
quarter #2 could be <u>tails</u>.　　T <u>T</u>

There are four possible outcomes, and only one is favorable (HH). Therefore, the probability of having both land with the heads side up is $\frac{1}{4}$, or **25%**.

You can also use multiplication to find the probability.

1. Find the probability of the individual events. The probability that one coin will be heads is $\frac{1}{2}$, and the probability that the other will be heads is $\frac{1}{2}$.

2. Multiply to find the probability of both events: $\frac{1}{2} \times \frac{1}{2} = \frac{1}{4}$.

The two coin tosses in Example 3 are **independent events**. When events are independent, one does not affect the probability of another. In Example 4 below, the events are **dependent**. Once the first event takes place, the probability of the second event is changed.

Example 4: A box contains four blue marbles and two red marbles. If you select two marbles, what is the probability that both will be blue?

(*Hint:* Even though the marbles in the box are taken out at the same time, think of one as the first marble and the other as the second marble.)

1. There are six marbles in the box, and four are blue. The probability that the first marble will be blue is $\frac{4}{6}$, which reduces to $\frac{2}{3}$.

2. Assume the first marble selected is blue. Now there are only five marbles in the box, and three are blue. The probability that the second marble will be blue is $\frac{3}{5}$.

3. Multiply to find the probability of the two events: $\frac{2}{3} \times \frac{3}{5} = \frac{6}{15}$, or $\frac{2}{5}$.

The probability that both marbles will be blue is **2 out of 5**.

NOTE: The events in Example 4 would not be dependent if the first marble were replaced before the second marble was selected. Always think carefully about the situation to decide whether two events are dependent or independent.

PRACTICE 7.2

A. Solve as directed. Express answers as fractions.

1. Kim rolls two standard six-sided dice. What is the chance that both will be 4s?

2. Ten cards are numbered from 1 to 10. Toni draws out a card, replaces it, and then draws another card. What is the probability that both cards will be numbers greater than 5?

3. A spinner has four equal sections. Two sections are red, one is green, and one is blue. If the spinner is spun three times, what is the probability that all three spins will be red?

4. Twenty marbles are placed in a bag. Ten are red, and ten are black. One marble is drawn from the bag and set aside. Another marble is drawn from the bag. What is the chance that both marbles will be red?

5. Allison tosses a coin four times. What is the chance that the coin will be heads all four times?

6. If you roll two standard dice, what is the probability that both will be an odd number?

B. Choose the one best answer to each question. You MAY use your calculator.

Questions 7 and 8 refer to the following information.

In a game a player rolls a die, numbered from 1 to 6, and spins a spinner. The spinner is shown below.

7. What is the probability of rolling a 5 and then spinning an even number?

    A. $\frac{1}{9}$

    B. $\frac{1}{6}$

    C. $\frac{2}{3}$

    D. $\frac{5}{6}$

8. What is the chance that a player will get the same number on both the die and the spinner?

    A. $\frac{5}{6}$

    B. $\frac{2}{3}$

    C. $\frac{1}{3}$

    D. $\frac{1}{6}$

Daniel uses the ten cards below in a magic trick.

9. Daniel shuffles the cards and asks an audience member to choose and hold two cards. If the cards are chosen randomly, what is the chance that both will be marked with a square?

    A. 8 out of 14

    B. 3 out of 5

    C. 1 out of 3

    D. 1 out of 5

10. There are 15 colored chips in a bag. Eight are green, and seven are white. Five white chips are removed. What is the probability that the next chip selected will be green?

    A. 100%

    B. 80%

    C. 75%

    D. 25%

Answers and explanations begin on page 662.

Combinations

Combinations with One Type of Item

Sometimes the GED® *Mathematical Reasoning Test* will ask you how many ways you can combine a set of items. Sometimes you may have only one type of item to combine, and sometimes you may have more than one type to combine. This difference will determine your problem-solving strategy.

Consider an example with *only one type of item:*

Example 1: Pablo is going shopping at a fruit stand that sells apples, bananas, grapes, and pears. Pablo will buy two different kinds of fruit. How many combinations of two kinds of fruit could Pablo buy?

The question is asking you to list possible groups of two out of the overall set of four. Notice that order doesn't matter—that is, *apples and bananas* is no different from *bananas and apples*. To solve this problem, you can make a list. Start with apples and list all of the **combinations** that include apples: AB, AG, AP. Then make a list of groups that start with bananas and include the remaining fruits: BG, BP. Don't include BA because that's the same as AB. Then make a list of groups that start with grapes and include only the remaining fruits: GP. There are no remaining groups that start with P. You may find it easier to make this list in columns, as follows:

AB

AG   BG

AP   BP   GP

There are **6** possible combinations.

You can also draw a quick table like the following. Include a column for each of the fruits, and let each row represent a possible combination. Place two *x*'s in each row to represent a combination of two fruits.

Apples	Bananas	Grapes	Pears
x	x		
x		x	
x			x
	x	x	
	x		x
		x	x

Notice that you could not draw any more rows with two *x*'s without duplicating some of the existing rows. Count the rows: there are **6** possible combinations of two fruits.

PRACTICE 8.1

A. Use counting, an organized list, or a table to solve the following problems.

1. As a supervisor, Rob is choosing four of his employees to work on a special project. The employees are Angela, Barbara, Colin, David, and Elizabeth. Of those five employees, how many teams of four are possible?

2. Jessica wants to take three books on vacation with her. She has five books to choose from. How many possible combinations of three books could she take on vacation?

3. Grant is cooking a homemade pizza, and he has the following toppings available: anchovies, ham, mushrooms, and sausage. He will choose three of those toppings. How many ways could Grant combine those toppings?

4. Five friends want to play a video game designed for two players. How many different combinations of two friends are possible, if the order of the friends does not matter?

B. Choose the one best answer to each question about combinations.

5. Celia is going to plant a small flower bed with four flowers. She can choose from begonias, fuchsias, hellebore, daisies, and salvia. How many combinations of four flowers are possible?

   A. 5
   B. 20
   C. 24
   D. 120

6. Regan owns a small business, and she wants to send three people from her business to an upcoming trade show. Regan plans to attend, and she will also choose two of her four employees to attend. How many combinations of employees could Regan choose to send to the trade show?

   A. 4
   B. 6
   C. 10
   D. 24

7. A book club, which has two women and three men, can send three of its members to a book signing. How many possible combinations of members could attend the book signing?

   A. 1
   B. 5
   C. 10
   D. 120

8. Given six people, how many combinations of three are possible if order does not matter?

   A. 20
   B. 120
   C. 180
   D. 720

9. The Sarkesian brothers own a hardware store. There are five items the owners might display in the window. Joe Sarkesian thinks that the window should have two items, but his brother Rick thinks the window should have three items. Counting both Joe's ideas and Rick's ideas for the window, how many possible combinations of items might go into the window display?

   A. 10
   B. 20
   C. 30
   D. 120

Answers and explanations begin on page 662.

Combinations with More Than One Type of Item

Sometimes you may be asked to count possible combinations with more than one type of item. Consider the following example:

Example 2: Sarah is deciding what to wear. She has three shirts, two pairs of pants, and two pairs of shoes. How many possible outfits does she have, if an outfit is one shirt, one pair of pants, and one pair of shoes?

This question differs from the question about Pablo on page 302. In that question, Pablo was choosing from one overall group of fruits. Here, Sarah is choosing one out of each of three groups—shirts, pants, and shoes. If you are given more than one type of item and must choose one of each type, you can use a tree diagram to figure out all the possible combinations. Study the following example:

Each "branch" of the tree represents a possible combination. The number of branches on the right-hand side represents the possible number of combinations; in this case, there are **12** possible outfits.

However, you can solve the same type of problem (where you have more than one type of item and are choosing one of each type) using the **fundamental counting principle,** which works like this:

Start with shirts: for each shirt, Sarah has two pants options. That's $3 \times 2 = 6$. Additionally, for each of those six options, she has two options for shoes. That's $3 \times 2 \times 2 = $ **12**.

Use the fundamental counting principle to solve the following problem:

Example 3: Gordon is at a restaurant that serves a three-course meal: an appetizer, an entrée, and a dessert. There are three appetizers, six entrees, and four desserts to choose from. Gordon will order one of each. How many different meals could he order?

Multiply three appetizers by six entrees by four desserts: $3 \times 6 \times 4 = 72$. There are **72** possible ways Gordon could order his meal.

PRACTICE 8.2

A. Use a tree diagram or the fundamental counting principle to solve the following problems.

1. Frank is making a sandwich. His sandwich will have one type of bread, one type of meat, and one condiment. He has four types of bread: white, wheat, rye, and a Kaiser roll. Meats he can choose from are chicken, turkey, and roast beef. For condiments, Frank can choose mayonnaise, mustard, vinaigrette, or horseradish. How many ways can Frank make his sandwich?

2. Van Ahn attended a trivia contest and won three rounds. For the first round she won, she could choose one of three restaurant gift certificates. The prize for another round was one of two T-shirts. Winning the third round allowed her to choose one of four souvenir hats. How many possible combinations of prizes were available to Van Ahn?

3. Henry is wrapping a gift for his daughter. He will use one type of wrapping paper, one type of ribbon, and one bow. He has three different types of wrapping paper, three different types of ribbon, and three different bows. How many ways can Henry wrap the gift?

4. Julio is looking forward to a three-day weekend. On Friday, he will either go to the beach or attend a street festival. On Saturday, he plans to visit a museum, but he is trying to decide among three different museums. On Sunday, he will try one of four new restaurants. How many ways could Julio combine these weekend activities?

B. Choose the <u>one best answer</u> to each question about combinations. Determine whether you are being asked to find possible combinations from one type of item or from multiple types of items. You MAY use your calculator.

5. The Nu Mu Beta fraternity is deciding what secret passphrase it should require its members to say before being admitted to meetings. The first and third words of the passphrase will be the names of Greek letters. There are 24 letters in the Greek alphabet. The second word will be a number from one to nine. How many possible passphrases are there?

   A.   24
   B.   57
   C.   576
   D. 5,184

6. A video game designer is creating a new superhero, who will have three of five potential superpowers. How many combinations of superpowers could the new superhero have?

   A. 10
   B. 15
   C. 100
   D. 125

7. A chef will make a soup with five ingredients: one of four meats, one of four vegetables, one of four kinds of noodles, one of four kinds of broth, and one of four spices. How many possible combinations of ingredients could the chef put into the soup?

   A.   20
   B.   256
   C. 1,024
   D. 3,125

8. A doctor is deciding how to treat a given disease. The doctor will prescribe one medication, one dietary change, and one type of vitamin supplement. There are five medications, five dietary changes, and five types of vitamins the doctor might prescribe. How many combinations are possible?

   A. 125
   B. 625
   C. 1,250
   D. 3,125

Answers and explanations begin on page 662.

DATA, STATISTICS, AND PROBABILITY

Permutations

On the *Mathematical Reasoning Test*, you may be asked how many possible permutations, or sequences, are possible given a group of items. Consider the following example:

Example 1: Eliza is planning her day off. She wants to visit the art museum, try the new coffee shop, call her mom, and take a walk, but not necessarily in that order. How many possible sequences of those four activities are there?

This question asks you for all possible permutations, or ways to sequence the items. Thus, *coffee-art-mom-walk* and *art-coffee-mom-walk* are two different possible outcomes. Consider how this problem differs from the combinations problems on pages 302–305. In those cases, order did not matter; in a permutations problem, order does matter.

To find how many ways you can sequence all the items in a list, multiply the possibilities like this. Start with how many things could go first: here, there are four possibilities for Eliza's first activity. Once she has done that first activity, three possibilities remain. After she has done a first and second activity, two possibilities remain, and then only one. So you simply multiply: $4 \times 3 \times 2 \times 1$. There are **24** possible permutations.

Some permutations questions may ask you to determine the possible orderings for only some of the items in a list. Consider this example:

Example 2: Ten runners are competing in a race. There are prizes for first, second, and third place. How many possible sequences of the top three prize winners are there?

Notice that you are not simply figuring out how many groups of three can be made out of the ten. Rather, you are figuring out how many sequences of three can be made out of the ten. That can sometimes be represented on the GED® Test with the notation P(10, 3).

Now, multiplying $10 \times 9 \times 8 \times 7 \times 6 \times 5 \times 4 \times 3 \times 2 \times 1$ would give you all the possible permutations of all ten runners, so that approach will not work here. Instead, start with how many people could win first place: here, ten. Once someone has won first, there are nine possibilities for second place. Once someone has won first and someone else has won second, there are eight possibilities for third place. And then you stop multiplying: $10 \times 9 \times 8 = 720$. There are **720** possible ways that the runners could be arranged in the top three prize-winning slots. (Note that simply multiplying 10 by 3 will not work.)

Key Ideas

- Permutations are used to find the number of possible outcomes when the order does matter.
- Use the total number of people or items and the number of possible outcomes to find the number of permutations that are possible.

ON THE GED® TEST

When you are reading a question that suggests that you may want to find a combination or a permutation, ask yourself, "Am I finding a number of groups (combinations), or am I finding the number of possible sequences (permutations)?"

PRACTICE 9

A. Read the problems and decide whether you are being asked to find combinations or permutations. Then solve.

1. Noemi is trying to remember the password for her email. She knows that it has the following characters in it: M, Q, \$, L, 7. But she can't remember the order they go in. How many possible sequences of those five characters are there?

2. Bilal is going to the museum. She wants to see the contemporary art exhibit, the Impressionists, the Greek vases, and a special Picasso exhibit but not necessarily in that order. How many sequences of those exhibits are possible?

3. Five students in a class have volunteered for a special project. Only three can actually help with the project. How many possible groupings of three out of the five are possible?

4. Tyrell is the curator at a gallery and is deciding how to arrange six paintings that will be displayed in a line along one wall. All six paintings will be included. How many possible sequences could Tyrell choose?

B. Choose the <u>one best answer</u> to each question about combinations or permutations. You MAY use your calculator.

5. Soraya has been given six tasks to do at work, but she has time to complete only four of them. She must decide in what order to do the tasks. How many possible orderings of four tasks are available to Soraya?

   A. 24
   B. 36
   C. 360
   D. 720

6. In a certain public garden, the gardener wanted to show the different visual effects that arranging flowers in different sequences can have. So he chose three kinds of flowers and planted flower beds showing each of the possible sequences of the three kinds. How many such flower beds did the gardener plant?

   A. 3
   B. 6
   C. 9
   D. 12

7. Ten people hope to become extras in a movie. The movie's casting director will choose four people to fill the following specific roles in the movie: Bystander #1, Bystander #2, Bystander #3, and Bystander #4. How many ways could those four roles be filled?

   A. 24
   B. 40
   C. 540
   D. 5,040

Questions 8 and 9 refer to the following information:

Clark and his daughter are at the amusement park, and Clark is offering his daughter a choice. They don't have time to ride all six rides at the amusement park, but they can ride three of them.

8. How many combinations of three rides could Clark's daughter choose?

   A. 18
   B. 20
   C. 120
   D. 720

9. Clark's daughter can also choose the order in which she wants to enjoy the rides. How many possible orderings of three out of the six rides are possible?

   A. 18
   B. 20
   C. 120
   D. 720

Answers and explanations begin on page 663.

DATA, STATISTICS, AND PROBABILITY PRACTICE QUESTIONS

Directions: You MAY use your calculator.

Questions 1 and 2 refer to the following graph.

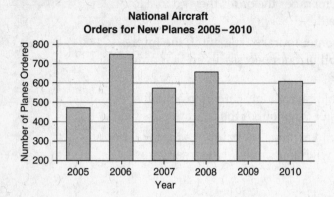

**National Aircraft
Orders for New Planes 2005–2010**

1. The mean number of aircraft orders for the six years shown on the graph is 573 planes. In which year was the number of orders closest to the mean?

   A. 2006
   B. 2007
   C. 2008
   D. 2009

2. By about what percent did orders at National Aircraft decrease from 2008 to 2009?

   A. 30%
   B. 40%
   C. 68%
   D. 75%

---

3. At a convention, Jim and his three friends each bought three raffle tickets. At the time of the drawing, 400 tickets had been sold. What is the probability that either Jim or one of his friends will win?

   A. $\frac{3}{100}$
   B. $\frac{1}{25}$
   C. $\frac{3}{50}$
   D. $\frac{9}{100}$

Questions 4 through 6 are based on the following table.

Southland Weather March 9			
Area	**High Temp.**	**Low Temp.**	**Precipitation (in inches)**
Downtown	65° F	53° F	0.45
Airport	62° F	50° F	0.63
Woodland Hills	68° F	50° F	1.34
East Village	56° F	48° F	3.53
Ventura	62° F	49° F	2.57
Highland Park	64° F	55° F	0.84

4. Based on the data in the table, what was the median low temperature for March 9?

   A. 62.8°
   B. 51.5°
   C. 50.8°
   D. 50°

5. What was the mean amount of precipitation (in inches) on March 9 for the areas listed in the table?

   A. 0.65
   B. 1.09
   C. 1.56
   D. 1.99

6. For which area on the table was there the greatest range, or difference, between the high and low temperatures?

   A. Ventura
   B. East Village
   C. Woodland Hills
   D. Downtown

Questions 7 and 8 refer to the graph.

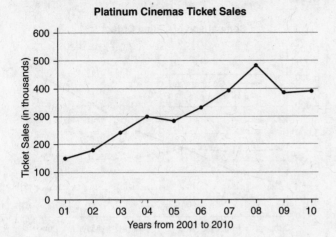

Platinum Cinemas Ticket Sales

7. Platinum Cinemas opened its first theaters in 2001. The company's ticket sales increased steadily until what year, when there was a drop in sales?

   A. 2004
   B. 2005
   C. 2008
   D. 2009

8. Which year had the sharpest increase in ticket sales over the previous year?

   A. 2002
   B. 2006
   C. 2008
   D. 2009

9. At Nelson Stationers, the first 25 customers who visited the store on Monday morning received their choice of a gift. The table below shows how many customers chose each gift.

pen and pencil set	ⴑⴑⴑⴑⴑ
calculator	ⴑⴑⴑⴑⴑ ⴑⴑⴑⴑⴑ ‖
mouse pad	ⴑⴑⴑⴑⴑ ‖‖‖

What percent of the customers chose a mouse pad?

   A. 17%
   B. 25%
   C. 32%
   D. $33\frac{1}{3}$%

10. A standard deck of playing cards has 52 cards, with 13 cards each of hearts, diamonds, clubs, and spades. If a card is drawn randomly from the deck, what is the probability that it will be either hearts or diamonds?

    A. 1 in 2
    B. 1 in 4
    C. 1 in 8
    D. 1 in 16

11. Nita worked the following overtime hours over a six-week period.

    Week 1: 5 hours

    Week 2: $3\frac{1}{2}$ hours

    Week 3: 4 hours

    Week 4: 0 hours

    Week 5: $1\frac{1}{2}$ hours

    Week 6: 7 hours

    What is the mean number of overtime hours Nita worked each week?

    Write your answer on the line below.

12. A spinner has five equal sections, and they are numbered from 1 to 5. What is the probability of spinning a number greater than 3? (Express the answer as a fraction.)

    Write your answer on the line below.

Questions 13 through 15 refer to the following graph.

In a recent election, five candidates ran for the city council seat from District 11. The results of the race are shown in the graph below.

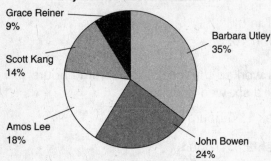

City Council Election Results

Grace Reiner 9%
Scott Kang 14%
Amos Lee 18%
John Bowen 24%
Barbara Utley 35%

13. The three city council candidates who received the fewest votes received what percent of the total vote?

    A. 23%
    B. 41%
    C. 56%
    D. 77%

14. Which two candidates combined received about $\frac{3}{5}$ of the votes cast?

    A. Reiner and Utley
    B. Kang and Utley
    C. Bowen and Utley
    D. Lee and Bowen

15. If 5100 votes were cast in the election, which of the following expressions could be used to find out how many votes Grace Reiner received?

    A. 5100×0.9

    B. $\frac{5100}{0.9}$

    C. $\frac{5100}{0.09}$

    D. 5100×0.09

Questions 16 through 18 refer to the following graph.

Comparison of Online Orders

16. In which month did Company A and Company B receive about the same number of online orders?

    A. February
    B. March
    C. April
    D. May

17. Based on the trends shown by the data, what would be the best prediction for the number of online orders in July for Company A?

    A. 7200
    B. 5900
    C. 5200
    D. 4900

18. About 18% of the online orders in April at Company A are returned for credit or exchange. How many orders at Company A were returned for credit or exchange in the month of April?

    A. 180
    B. 360
    C. 540
    D. 600

Questions 19 and 20 are based on the following information.

A basketball player's statistics for an eight-game series are shown in the table below.

Game	Shots Attempted	Shots Made
1	25	10
2	23	12
3	26	10
4	24	13
5	29	15
6	18	7
7	24	12
8	27	10

19. What was the median number of shots attempted by this player in the series?

    A. 24
    B. 24.5
    C. 25
    D. 26.5

20. What is the mode of the shots made by this player during the series?

    A. 12
    B. 11
    C. 10 and 12
    D. 10

21. A bag contains 24 marbles. Eight are red, six are blue, and ten are white. A marble is drawn from the bag and replaced. A second marble is chosen at random from the bag. What is the probability that the first marble is red and the second is white?

    A. $\frac{2}{5}$
    B. $\frac{5}{36}$
    C. $\frac{5}{48}$
    D. $\frac{1}{48}$

22. A company has 36 employees. For three months, the owner has kept track of the number of sick days used by her employees per month.

Month	Sick Days
Sept.	34
Oct.	31
Nov.	42

Which expression could be used to find the average number of sick days taken each month?

    A. $\frac{34 + 31 + 42}{36}$
    B. $\frac{34 + 31 + 42}{3}$
    C. $\frac{34 + 31 + 42 + 36}{4}$
    D. $(34 + 31 + 42) \times 3$

For questions 23 through 27, write your answers on the lines provided.

23. Andy rolls two standard six-sided dice. What is the probability of rolling two 1s? Express your answer as a fraction.

    _____

24. Kate drove 158 miles on Monday, 276 miles on Tuesday, 54 miles on Wednesday, 305 miles on Thursday, and 210 miles on Friday. In miles, what was the median distance she drove for the five days?

    _____

25. Angelique, a teacher, is making a reading list for her students. She wants to include one historical novel, one work of science fiction, one book of poetry, and one graphic novel. She has five of each type of book to choose from. How many possible combinations of books could she include in her reading list?

    _____

26. There are four children in Mr. Martin's class. Three of them will be selected to be hall monitors. How many combinations of hall monitors are possible?

    _____

27. A charity's board has ten members. One of the members will be elected president, then another will be elected treasurer, and then a third will be elected secretary. If no member can hold more than one position, how many ways can the members fill those positions?

_____

Questions 28 and 29 are based on the following information.

The frequency table below displays the reasons why patients visited a walk-in clinic during a certain week.

Reason	Number of Patients
Colds and Flu	∥∥∥ ∥∥∥ ∥∥∥ ∥
Cuts and Scrapes	∥∥∥ ∥∥∥ ∥∥∥
Sprained Muscles	∥∥∥ ∥∥∥ ∥∥
Tetanus Shots	∥∥∥ ∥∥
Severe Headaches	∥∥∥ ∥∥∥ ∥∥

28. Write your answer on the line below. What percent of the patients represented in the table visited the walk-in clinic because of sprained muscles?

_____

29. In the week represented in the table, what was the ratio of the number of patients with colds or flu to the number of patients with severe headaches?

A. 4:15
B. 4:3
C. 3:4
D. 1:5

Questions 30 and 31 are based on the following information and graph.

A hundred people are participating in a medical study. As a first step, the researchers collected information about participants' weight. The graph below represents how many people fell into each weight category.

Weight of Participants

30. Which weight category displays the highest frequency?

A. 120–139 lbs
B. 180–199 lbs
C. 200–219 lbs
D. 260–279 lbs

31. Consider only the 100 individuals represented in the graph. Which one of the following groups contains the most people?

A. Participants weighing 200 lbs or more
B. Participants weighing less than 200 lbs
C. Participants weighing 180–199 lbs
D. Participants weighing less than 180 lbs

The owner of a taxi company measures the gas
mileage of each of the cars in her fleet. The frequency table below shows her results.

Average miles per gallon	Number of cars
15	I I
20	HHI I I
25	HHI
30	HHI I
35	I

32. Which of the values (average miles per gallon)
displays the highest frequency?

A. 15 miles per gallon
B. 20 miles per gallon
C. 30 miles per gallon
D. 35 miles per gallon

33. What is the ratio of taxis that get 35 miles per
gallon on average to the number of taxis that
get 15 miles per gallon on average?

A. $\frac{1}{2}$

B. $\frac{3}{2}$

C. $\frac{4}{5}$

D. $\frac{1}{10}$

34. The line plot below is based on the information in the table. Place additional points on
the line to accurately represent the data.

35. Ahmed works at the ticket window of a theater, and one night he decides to track when
the patrons arrive for a 7:30 p.m. show. The
table below represents his data.

Time period	Percent of patrons who arrive
5:30 to 5:59 p.m.	2%
6:00 to 6:29 p.m.	14%
6:30 to 6:59 p.m.	25%
7:00 to 7:29 p.m.	48%
7:30 to 8:00 p.m.	11%

Which one of the histograms below accurately
represents Ahmed's data?

Answers and explanations begin on page 663.

ALGEBRA BASICS, EXPRESSIONS, AND POLYNOMIALS

The Number Line and Signed Numbers

Key Ideas

- If numbers have like signs, add and keep the same sign.
- If numbers have unlike signs, find the difference and use the sign from the larger number.
- To subtract signed numbers, change the operation to addition and change the sign of the number you are subtracting.

Understanding Signed Numbers

Signed numbers include zero, all positive numbers, and all negative numbers. Zero is neither positive nor negative. On a number line, the positive numbers are shown to the right of zero, and the negative numbers are shown to the left.

A positive number may be written with a plus (+) symbol. If a number has no symbol at all, we assume that it is positive. A negative number *must* be preceded by a minus (−) symbol.

A signed number provides two important facts. The sign tells the direction from zero, and the number tells you the distance from zero. For example, −5 lies five spaces to the left of zero, and +4 lies four spaces to the right of zero.

Adding and Subtracting Signed Numbers

You can use a number line to model the addition of signed numbers.

Examples: $1 + (-4) = -3$ Begin at +1; move 4 in a negative direction (left).

$-5 + 4 = -1$ Begin at −5; move 4 in a positive direction (right).

$-2 + (-3) = -5$ Begin at −2; move 3 in a negative direction (left).

To add without a number line, follow these steps:

- If numbers have like signs, add the numbers and keep the same sign.
- If the numbers have unlike signs, find the difference between the two numbers and use the sign of the larger number.

Example 1: Add $15 + (-25)$.

1. Since the numbers have unlike signs, subtract: $25 - 15 = 10$.

2. Use the sign from the larger number: $15 + (-25) = \mathbf{-10}$.

Subtraction is the opposite of addition. To rewrite a subtraction problem as an addition problem, change the operation symbol to addition and change the sign on the number you are subtracting. Then apply the rules for adding signed numbers.

Example 2: Subtract $3 - 8$.

1. Change the operation symbol and the sign of the number you are subtracting:

$3 - 8$ becomes $3 + (-8)$.

2. Add: $3 + (-8) = -5$.

You can use the same rules to combine several signed numbers.

Example 3: $(-5) + 6 - 4 - (-2) = ?$

1. Rewrite each subtraction as addition: $(-5) + 6 + (-4) + 2$.

2. Add the positive terms: $6 + 2 = 8$. Add the negative terms: $-5 + (-4) = -9$.

3. Combine the results: $8 + -9 = -1$.

PRACTICE 1.1

A. Solve.

1. $8 + (-3)$
2. $50 - 5$
3. $11 - (-2)$
4. $-1 + 2$
5. $-4 - (-5)$
6. $8 - (-2)$
7. $6 - 9$
8. $2 + 11$

9. $(-7) - (-3)$
10. $(-4) + 6$
11. $-15 + (-7)$
12. $36 - 4$
13. $-60 - (-10)$
14. $-5 - 6$
15. $12 + 13$
16. $-55 + 20$

17. $7 + (-3) + (-5) - 10$
18. $66 + (-22) - 33$
19. $-14 - (-6) + 18$
20. $80 - (-15) - 20$
21. $6 - (-3) + (-5) + 8$
22. $-23 + (-11) - (-15) + 21$
23. $3 + 9 - 5 + 12 - 9 - 11$
24. $-7 - 20 - (-14)$

B. Choose the <u>one best answer</u> to each question.

<u>Question 25</u> refers to the following number line.

$-5\ -4\ -3\ -2\ -1\ \ 0\ \ 1\ \ 2\ \ 3\ \ 4\ \ 5$

25. The number line above shows which of the following expressions?
    A. $2 + (-3)$
    B. $2 + (-5)$
    C. $-3 + 2$
    D. $-3 - (+2)$

26. At noon, the temperature in the high desert was 92°F. A scientist observed the following temperature changes over the course of the next two hours: $+12$°F, -5°F, $+6$°F, -3°F, and $+13$°F. What was the temperature, in degrees Fahrenheit at the end of the two-hour period?
    A. 95°F
    B. 103°F
    C. 115°F
    D. 131°F

Answers and explanations begin on page 664.

Multiplying and Dividing Signed Numbers

In algebra, multiplication is not shown using the times sign (×) because the symbol could be easily mistaken for the variable x. Instead, multiplication is shown using a dot or by placing two numbers next to each other. To avoid confusion, one or both of the numbers may be enclosed in parentheses. For example, the expressions $-5 \cdot 6$ and $-5(6)$ and $(-5)(6)$ all mean "-5 times 6."

In algebra, division can be written with the $\div$ symbol, but it is usually shown with a line that means "divided by." The expression $\frac{20}{-5}$ means "20 divided by -5," as does $20/-5$. When multiplying or dividing signed numbers, use the following rules:

- If the signs are the same, the answer is positive.
- If the signs are different, the answer is negative.

Example 1: Multiply $4(-25)$.

1. Multiply the numbers only: $4 \times 25 = 100$.

2. Determine the sign. Since the signs on the numbers are different, the answer is negative: $4(-25) = -\mathbf{100}$.

Example 2: Divide $\frac{-160}{-8}$.

1. Divide the numbers only: $160 \div 8 = 20$.
2. Determine the sign. Since the signs on the numbers are the same, the answer is positive:

$$\frac{-160}{-8} = \mathbf{20}.$$

A problem may contain more than two factors. Remember that each pair of negative factors will equal a positive product. Therefore, if there is an even number of negative terms, the product will be positive. If there is an odd number of negative terms, the product will be negative.

Example 3: $(-5)(6)(-1)(-2)(2) = ?$

1. Multiply: $5 \times 6 \times 1 \times 2 \times 2 = 120$.

2. There are three negative terms. Since 3 is an odd number, the product is negative: $-\mathbf{120}.$

When a problem contains more than one operation, follow this **order of operations**. Do multiplication and division operations first, working from left to right. Do addition and subtraction operations last, also working from left to right. If a problem contains division presented with a division bar, do any operations above and below the bar first and then divide.

Example 4: $(-4)(6) - \dfrac{3 + (-9)}{-2}$

1. Multiply: $-24 - \dfrac{3 + (-9)}{-2}$.

2. Do the operation above the fraction bar: $-24 - \dfrac{-6}{-2}$.

3. Divide: $-24 - (+3)$.

4. Subtract: $-24 - (+3) = -24 + (-3) = -\mathbf{27}.$

NOTE: *Notice how parentheses clarify meaning:* $4 - 5$ *means "four minus five," but* $4(-5)$ *means "four times negative five."*

PRACTICE 1.2

A. Solve. You MAY NOT use a calculator.

1. $(5)(4)$
2. $(7)(-3)$
3. $(-8)(6)$
4. $(-2)(-9)$
5. $(-10)(1)$

6. $9 \div 3$
7. $12 \div (-4)$
8. $-25 \div 5$
9. $(-18) \div (-9)$
10. $\frac{40}{-8}$

11. $(14)(-2)$
12. $(-75) \div 25$
13. $13 \div (-13)$
14. $(-5)(15)$
15. $\frac{18}{3}$

B. Solve. You MAY use a calculator.

16. $\frac{25(4)}{-5}$
17. $(-3)(-5)(2)(-10)$
18. $20 \div (-5) \div (-2)$
19. $\frac{6(5)}{(-3)(2)}$

20. $(-11)(2)(-5)(6)$
21. $(12)(-2) \div (-2)$
22. $(-4)(-6)(-5)$
23. $50 \div (2)(-5)$

24. $(-1)(2)(-3)(2)(-1)$
25. $\frac{(3)(-4)(2)(5)}{-6}$
26. $\frac{4(-4)}{-8(-2)}$
27. $(-5)(-2)(0)(-1)$

C. Choose the <u>one best answer</u> to each question.

28. Janice is creating a computer spreadsheet. A portion of her work is shown below.

	A	B	C
1	−3	4	7
2	2	−5	−8
3	−1	3	−2

Using the information from the spreadsheet, what is the value of the expression A1*C1*A3/(B3*A3)? (*Hint*: In a spreadsheet, the symbol * means multiplication.)

A. −21
B. −7
C. $\frac{-1}{7}$
D. 21

29. The product of 2 and 8 is divided by −8 . Which of the following expressions could be used to find the value of the statement?

A. $\frac{\frac{2}{8}}{-8}$

B. $2(8)(-8)$

C. $\frac{2(8)}{(-8)}$

D. $\frac{2(-8)}{8}$

30. Which of the following is a true statement about the value of the expression $(52)(-103)(-45)(-8)(3)$?

A. The result is a fraction.
B. The result is greater than 1.
C. The result is a negative number.
D. The result is a positive number.

Answers and explanations begin on page 664.

Powers and Roots

Key Ideas

- In the expression 2^3, the base is 2 and the exponent is 3.
- To raise a number to a certain power, write the base the number of times shown by the exponent and then multiply.
- To find a square root, think, "What number times itself equals this number?"

Powers are a special way to show repeated multiplication. For example, suppose you needed to multiply $5 \times 5 \times 5 \times 5$. This series of operations can be expressed as "five to the fourth power." In other words, the number 5 appears in the multiplication problem four times.

We can write the operations algebraically using **exponents**. In the expression $5 \times 5 \times 5 \times 5$ above, the number 5 is the base. The exponent, a small number written above and to the right of the **base**, tells how many times the base is repeated: $5 \times 5 \times 5 \times 5 = 5^4$.

To evaluate an expression, perform the multiplication indicated by the exponent.

Example 1: Find the value of 2^5.

Write the base the number of times indicated by the exponent and then multiply:

$$2^5 = 2 \times 2 \times 2 \times 2 \times 2 = \mathbf{32}.$$

You may encounter some special uses of exponents on the *Mathematical Reasoning Test*. An exponent can be any positive number, or it can be 0, 1, or a negative number. Memorize the situations described below.

1. A number raised to the first power equals itself: $8^1 = 8$.

2. A number other than zero raised to the power of zero equals 1: $6^0 = 1$.

3. A number raised to a negative exponent is equal to a fraction with a numerator of 1: $4^{-2} = \dfrac{1}{4^2} = \dfrac{1}{4 \times 4} = \dfrac{1}{16}$.

You can use a calculator to raise numbers to any power. Use the $\boxed{x^2}$ or $\boxed{\wedge}$ key.

Example 2: Find the square of 24.

Press: $24 \boxed{x^2}$ $\boxed{\text{enter}}$. The right side of the display reads 576.

The square of 24 is **576**.

Example 3: Find the value of 9^4.

Enter the base, press $\boxed{\wedge}$, and enter the exponent. Then press $\boxed{\text{enter}}$.

Press $9 \boxed{\wedge} 4$ $\boxed{\text{enter}}$. The right side of the display reads 6561.

Nine raised to the fourth power is **6561**.

NOTE: To raise a negative number to a power using the TI-30XS MultiView™ calculator, you must enter that number in parentheses: $\boxed{(} \boxed{(-)} 4 \boxed{)} \boxed{x^2}$ $\boxed{\text{enter}}$.

To square a number, multiply the number by itself. For example, $6^2 = 6 \times 6 = 36$. In the expression $6 \times 6 = 36$, the number 36 is the square, and the number 6 is the **square root** of 36.

GED® TEST TIP

Make a list of common square roots by squaring the numbers from 1 to 15. Memorize them. You will need to know common square roots to solve geometry problems about area and right triangles.

The symbol for square root is $\sqrt{\ }$. To find a square root, think, "What number multiplied by itself is equal to the number in the bracket?"

Example 4: Find the value of $\sqrt{144}$.

You know that $12 \times 12 = 144$, so the square root of 144 is **12**.

Although $(-12) \times (-12)$ also equals 144, you will only be expected to find positive roots on the GED® Test.

You may have to approximate the value of a square root.

Example 5: What is the square root of 90?

You know that $9 \times 9 = 81$ and $10 \times 10 = 100$. Therefore, the square root of 90 is **between 9 and 10**.

You can also use your calculator to find a square root. On the TI-30SX MultiView™, you must first press the (2nd) key to access the square root function. The $\sqrt{\ }$ function is directly above the (x²) key. (Other calculators may not require the use of the (2nd) key.)

Example 6: Use your calculator to find $\sqrt{90}$ to the nearest tenth.

On the TI-30SX MultiView™, press (2nd)(x²)90 (enter). The right side of the display reads $3\sqrt{10}$.

Press the toggle key, (◀▶), to change the format of the answer into a decimal.

The right side of the display now reads 9.486832981.

Rounding to the tenths place, $\sqrt{90} \approx$ **9.5**.

PRACTICE 2

A. Solve each expression. You MAY NOT use a calculator.

1. 3^2
2. 4^1
3. $\sqrt{9}$

4. 25^0
5. $(-3)^2$
6. $\sqrt{49}$

7. 5^3
8. 4^{-2}
9. 2^4

10. $\sqrt{64}$
11. 10^{-3}
12. $\sqrt{121}$

B. Solve each expression below. You MAY use your calculator. Round your answer to the nearest tenth.

13. 3^8
14. $(-6)^4$
15. $\sqrt{150}$

16. 20^3
17. 1^{15}
18. $(-4)^{-2}$

19. $\sqrt{242}$
20. $(3.3)^2$
21. $\sqrt{57}$

22. $\sqrt{536}$
23. 112^0
24. $(-2)^8$

C. Choose the <u>one best answer</u> to each question.

25. The cube shown below measures 6 inches on each side. You can find the volume of the cube by multiplying $\text{length} \times \text{width} \times \text{height}$. Which of the following expressions represents the volume of the cube?

    A. 6^1
    B. 6^2
    C. 6^3
    D. 6^6

6 in.
6 in.
6 in.

26. Which of the following expressions has the least value?

    A. 3^{-3}
    B. 4^0
    C. 4^1
    D. 2^{-4}

Answers and explanations begin on page 664.

Scientific Notation

Key Ideas

- In scientific notation, a number equal to or greater than 1 and less than 10 is multiplied by a power of ten.
- Very small numbers are expressed by multiplying by a negative power of ten.
- In scientific notation, the number with the greatest power of ten has the greatest value.

Scientific notation uses the powers of ten to express very small and very large numbers. In scientific notation, a decimal number (greater than or equal to 1 and less than 10) is multiplied by a power of ten.

Look for patterns as you review these powers of ten.

$10^1 = 10$	$10^2 = 100$	$10^3 = 1,000$	$10^4 = 10,000$ and so on.
$10^{-1} = 0.1$	$10^{-2} = 0.01$	$10^{-3} = 0.001$	$10^{-4} = 0.0001$ and so on.

Did you find the patterns? In the row with positive exponents, the exponent is the same as the number of zeros in the number written in standard form. In the row with negative exponents, the exponent is the same as the number of decimal places in the number.

You can use these patterns to change scientific notation to standard form.

Example 1: Write 6.2×10^5 in standard form.

6.20000

Move the decimal point five places to the *right* (the same number as the exponent). Add zeros as needed.

620,000

Example 2: Write 3.82×10^{-3} in standard form.

Move the decimal point three places to the *left* (the same number as the exponent). Add zeros as needed.

0.00382

Work backward to write large and small numbers in scientific notation.

Example 3: To reach Mars, the Viking 2 spacecraft traveled 440,000,000 miles. What is the distance traveled in scientific notation?

1. Move the decimal point to the left until there is only a single digit in the ones place.

4.40000000

2. Multiply by 10 raised to a power equal to the number of places you moved the decimal point.

4.4×10^8

GED® TEST TIP

Always try to save time. Suppose the multiple-choice answers are written in scientific notation. Instead of changing each choice to standard notation, change your answer to scientific notation.

Example 4: Scientists find that a kind of bacteria moves at a rate of 0.00016 kilometers per hour. Write the measurement in scientific notation.

1. Move the decimal place to the right until there is a single digit in the ones place.

0001.6

2. Multiply by 10 raised to a negative exponent equal to the number of places you moved the decimal point.

1.6×10^{-4}

You may be asked to compare numbers in scientific notation.

Example 5: Which is greater: 4.5×10^3 or 9.8×10^4?

You don't need to change the numbers to standard notation. Simply consider the powers of ten. Multiplying by 10^4, or 10,000, must have a greater result than multiplying by 10^3, which equals 1,000. In scientific notation, the number with the greater power of 10 has the greater value. Therefore, **9.8×10^4 is greater than 4.5×10^3.**

PRACTICE 3

A. Write each number in scientific notation.

1. 2300
2. 0.00042
3. 12,400,000

4. 14,320,000,000
5. 36,000,000
6. 0.0095

7. 0.00000058
8. 150,000,000,000
9. 0.000000009

B. Convert from scientific notation to standard notation.

10. 5.173×10^{-4}
11. 3.7×10^6

12. 4.8×10^8
13. 1.7×10^{-5}

14. 7.2×10^{-3}
15. 9.16×10^5

16. 8.591×10^7
17. 9.56×10^{-6}

C. Answer the following questions.

18. Many domestic satellites maintain an orbit approximately 23,500 miles above Earth. What is that distance, in miles, in scientific notation?

19. Modern technology measures very fast transactions in nanoseconds. One nanosecond equals 1.0×10^{-9} of a second. How many seconds is a nanosecond, in standard notation?

20. The average distance of Neptune from Earth is 2.67×10^9 miles. Write the distance, in miles, in standard notation.

21. Light in the vacuum of space travels at a speed of nearly 300 million meters per second. Write the speed, in meters, in scientific notation.

D. Choose the one best answer to each question.

Questions 22 and 23 refer to the following table.

Unit	U.S. Equivalent	Metric Equivalent
1 ton	2,000 lb	0.907 metric ton
1 acre	43,560 sq ft	4,047 square m

22. What is the number of square feet in an acre, written in scientific notation?

A. 0.4356×10^6
B. 4.356×10^4
C. 4.356×10^3
D. 43.56×10^3

23. A shipment of goods weighs 5 tons. Which of the following expressions could be used to express the weight in metric tons?

A. $5 \times 0.907 \times 10^{-1}$
B. $5 \times 9.07 \times 10^1$
C. $5 \times 9.07 \times 10^{-2}$
D. $5 \times 9.07 \times 10^{-1}$

Answers and explanations begin on page 664.

ALGEBRA BASICS, EXPRESSIONS, AND POLYNOMIALS

Order of Operations

When a mathematical expression contains more than one operation, its value may depend upon the order in which the operations are performed. To avoid confusion, mathematicians have agreed to perform operations in a certain order.

Key Ideas

- To evaluate an expression correctly, you must follow the order of operations.
- If an expression uses more than one set of grouping symbols, start with the inside set and work to the outside.
- The division bar may be used as a grouping symbol.

The Order of Operations
1. Parentheses or any other grouping symbols that enclose operations
2. Exponents and roots
3. Multiplication and division, working from left to right
4. Addition and subtraction, working from left to right

Study the following example to see how to apply the order of operations. Notice that parentheses are used in two places in the expression; however, only the first set of parentheses encloses an operation.

Example 1: Evaluate the expression $\dfrac{(5+3)^2}{4} + 3(-1)$.

1. Perform the addition operation in parentheses. $\qquad \dfrac{(8)^2}{4} + 3(-1)$

2. Raise 8 to the second power. $\qquad \dfrac{64}{4} + 3(-1)$

3. Divide, then multiply. $\qquad 16 + (-3)$

4. Add. $\qquad 13$

The value of the expression $\dfrac{(5+3)^2}{4} + 3(-1)$ is **13**.

In more complicated expressions, one set of grouping symbols may be nested within another set. To avoid confusion, you can also use brackets [ ] or braces { } to group operations. To evaluate an expression with more than one set of grouping symbols, work from the inside to the outside.

Example 2: Evaluate the expression $4[5(-4) + 3) + 2]$.

1. Perform the operation in the inner set of grouping symbols: $(-4 + 3)$. $\qquad \begin{array}{l} 4[5(-4+3) + 2] \\ 4[5(-1) + 2] \end{array}$

2. Do the operations inside the brackets. Since multiplication comes before addition in the order of operations, multiply 5 and -1 and then add 2. $\qquad \begin{array}{l} 4[-5 + 2] \\ 4[-3] \end{array}$

3. Multiply 4 and -3. $\qquad \mathbf{-12}$

The division bar is also a grouping symbol. Before you divide, perform any operations shown above and below the bar.

Example 3: Evaluate the expression $\dfrac{15+25}{2(5)} + 6$.

1. Perform the operations above and below the fraction bar.

$$\dfrac{15+25}{2(5)} + 6$$

$$\dfrac{40}{10} + 6$$

2. Divide, then add.

$$4 + 6 = \mathbf{10}$$

PRACTICE 4

A. Solve. You MAY NOT use a calculator.

1. $4(3) - 2 + (6 + 4 \cdot 2)$
2. $16 \div (10 - 6)^2$
3. $5^2 - (5-7)(2)$
4. $3(-3) + (7+4)$
5. $\dfrac{3^3}{5-2} - \dfrac{(4-2)^2}{2}$

6. $\dfrac{25}{(4+1)} \cdot 3 + (6-1)$
7. $2^3 + (8-5)^2 - 3$
8. $(4-12)(-6) + (10-3)$
9. $30 \div 3(5-4)$
10. $15 + (4)(3) - 2^2$

11. $(4+2)^2 + (7-2)^3$
12. $7^2 \div (11-4) + (9+14)$
13. $2\left[(17-11)^2 \cdot \dfrac{(15-5)}{2}\right]$
14. $(5^2 + 6 - 3) \div (16 - 3^2)$
15. $150 - 4\left[\dfrac{3+9}{4-1} \cdot (14-11)^2\right]$

B. Choose the _one best answer_ to each question.

Question 16 refers to the following information.

Susan is in charge of planning Midvale Hospital's parent education classes. She uses the table below to determine the cost of each class to the hospital.

Midvale Hospital Parenting Workshops	
Type of Workshop	Cost per Participant
Childbirth Classes	$35 per couple
Infant Care	$30 per person
Teaching Your Child to Read	$60 per person

16. A local foundation has offered to pay 75% of the cost of infant care classes. The hospital will cover any remaining costs. There are 28 parents enrolled in the upcoming class. Which of the following expressions could be used to find the amount the hospital will pay?
    A. $(75)(28)(30)$
    B. $(28)(30) - (0.75)(30)$
    C. $(1 - 0.75)(28)(30)$
    D. $(1 - 0.75)(30) + 28$

17. In the expression

$$5 + 2\left[7\left(\dfrac{10^2}{10}\right) + (6-2)(3)\right],$$

what is the last operation you should perform to find the value of the expression?
    A. Subtract 2 from 6.
    B. Add 5.
    C. Multiply by 2.
    D. Find the square of 10.

18. Find the value of the expression
    $22 + 6[(14 - 5) \div 3(17 - 14)]$.
    A. 2.73
    B. 28
    C. 76
    D. 97

Answers and explanations begin on page 665.

Absolute Value

The **absolute value** of a number is its distance from zero on the number line. For example, the absolute value of 5 is 5, since 5 is five spaces away from zero on the number line. But the absolute value of −5 is also 5, since −5 is also five spaces away from zero on the number line. Because **distance** is always **positive**, the absolute value of any positive or negative number is always positive.

Absolute value is written as two straight lines around a number, like this: |−5|.

$$|{-5}| = 5 \qquad\qquad\qquad |5| = 5$$

Example 1: Which of the following is equal to |−13|?

    (1) 13

    (2) −13

The correct answer is **(1)**. Absolute value is always positive.

Treat the absolute value sign as you would treat parentheses in the order of operations. If numbers inside the absolute value sign are being added, subtracted, multiplied, or divided, then do that operation before you do anything else.

Example 2: Which of the following is equal to $-20\,|17-34|$?

    (1) 340

    (2) −340

The correct answer is **(2)**. First perform the subtraction within the absolute value sign. Because you first found the absolute value, change −17 to 17. Then multiply by −20, like this:

$$-20\,|17-34| = -20\,|{-17}| = -20\,(17) = \mathbf{-340}.$$

We often think in terms of absolute value in real life, though we might not bother to call it that. For example, imagine that you have $314 in a checking account but you write a check for $400. You've overdrawn your account by $86. The bank will record your balance as −$86.00. But you'll think, "I'm $86 short." You'll just think of the absolute value, or **magnitude**, of the overdraft, without the negative sign.

Key Ideas

- The magnitude of a number, without a sign, is called the absolute value.
- Absolute value is used to determine distance of a positive or negative number from zero.
- In the order of operations, absolute value is treated the same as a set of parentheses.

GED® TEST TIP

A signed number, positive or negative, is used to show its direction *in relation to zero. However, when you see a number inside two straight lines, you are working with its* distance *from zero—which is always positive.*

A. Find the absolute values.

1. $|18|$
2. $|-107|$
3. $|423|$

4. $|95|$
5. $|-7026|$
6. $|-18|$

7. $|-5,708,432|$
8. $|-85.6|$
9. $|42|$

10. $|10.5|$
11. $|-163.24|$
12. $|-3.14|$

B. Use absolute value to find the solutions.

13. $5 + |-6|$
14. $-3|52|$
15. $3|-52|$
16. $12 \div |-4|$

17. $-|110 - 201|$
18. $-14 + |-28 \div 2|$
19. $706.2 - |-86.4 + 0.2|$
20. $49 \div (-|-7|)$

21. $-5|-4|$
22. $|-6| - |-7|$
23. $|17| \div |-8|$
24. $|-5.5| \times (-2)$

C. Choose the one best answer to each question.

25. The temperature in Northville at 9:00 p.m. was $-5°$F. By 5:00 a.m. the following morning, the temperature was $-15°$F. By how many degrees did the temperature change?

    A. -15 degrees
    B. -5 degrees
    C. 5 degrees
    D. 10 degrees

26. Bob has errands to run. He walks 5 blocks east from his apartment to the barber shop, then walks 6 blocks west to the grocery store, then walks another 2 blocks west to the post office, and finally walks back home. Assuming that Bob's apartment, the barber shop, the grocery store, and the post office are all located on the same street, how many blocks did Bob walk in completing his errands?

    A. 6
    B. 11
    C. 13
    D. 16

27. Milania has a score of -65 points, and Chris has a score of 55 points. By how many points is Milania losing to Chris?

    A. 55
    B. 65
    C. 120
    D. 150

28. Absolute error is the absolute value of the difference between an actual value and its measurement. A deli scale gives a measurement of 25 ounces for a cut of meat that actually weighs only 23.5 ounces. What is the absolute error, in ounces, of the deli scale in this instance?

    A. 1.5
    B. 23.5
    C. 25
    D. 48.5

Answers and explanations begin on page 665.

Algebraic Expressions

Key Ideas

- Algebraic expressions show mathematical relationships using numbers, symbols, and variables.
- Variables are letters that take the place of unknown numbers.

Writing Algebraic Expressions

An **algebraic expression** uses numbers, operations, and variables to show number relationships. **Variables** are letters (such as x and y) that represent unknown numbers. Each time a letter is used within the same expression, it represents the same number.

To solve algebra problems, you will need to be able to translate number relationships described in words into algebraic expressions. Study the following examples.

Algebraic Expressions in Words	In Symbols
the product of 5 and a number	$5x$
a number decreased by 12	$x - 12$
the sum of 3 and the square of a number	$3 + x^2$
6 less than the quotient of a number and 2	$\frac{x}{2} - 6$
one-half a number increased by 15	$\frac{1}{2}x + 15$
4 times the difference of -3 and a number	$4(-3 - x)$
a number less another number	$x - y$
10 less the square root of a number plus 3	$10 - \sqrt{x + 3}$

To do well on algebra questions on the GED® *Mathematical Reasoning Test*, you must be able to translate a common life situation into mathematical symbols. You will use this skill to write equations and functions, to apply formulas, and to solve word problems.

GED® TEST TIP

To check whether the expression you have chosen is correct, substitute easy numbers into the expression and complete the operations. Then see if the result is reasonable for the situation.

Example 1: Kyle processes sales for an online bookstore. The shipping and handling on an order is equal to 4% of the total cost of the order plus $0.95 per book. If c represents total cost and n represents the number of books in an order, which of the following expressions could be used to find the shipping and handling for an order?

(1) $\frac{4}{100}nc + 0.95$

(2) $(0.04 + 0.95)n + c$

(3) $0.04c + 0.95n$

This kind of problem is called a **setup problem.** You need to recognize the correct way to find the shipping and handling based on the total cost and number of items. The relationship is described in the second sentence.

shipping and handling = 4% of total cost (c) plus $0.95 per book ($n$)

$$= \quad 0.04c \quad + \quad 0.95n$$

The correct answer is option **(3), $0.04c + 0.95n$.**

PRACTICE 6.1

A. Write an algebraic expression for each description. Use the variables x and y.

1. a number decreased by 7

2. the product of 3 and the square of a number increased by that number

3. the product of 8 and a number less 10

4. the difference of -3 multiplied by a number and the product of 2 and another number

5. 5 less than the quotient of 10 and a number

6. the sum of -8 and the product of 7 and a number

7. the sum of 16 times a number and the number less another number times 3

8. a number squared plus the number raised to the fourth power

9. the sum of the square of a number and 4 divided by 7

10. 6 subtracted from the sum of 15 and the square root of a number

11. a number less the sum of another number and 13

12. the square of the sum of a number and 6

13. 17 less the sum of 2 times a number plus another number

14. a number increased by the quotient of 24 and the number

15. the difference of the product of 2 and a number and 15

16. 4 times the difference of two different numbers

17. 5 multiplied by the difference of a number squared and 3

18. the product of a number and the difference of 11 and the square root of 100

B. Choose the <u>one best answer</u> to each question.

19. A minor-league baseball team is giving a local charity the sum of $1500 and $0.50 for each ticket over 2000 sold for one game. Let x represent the number of tickets sold. If the team sells more than 2000 tickets, which of the following expressions could be used to find the amount of the donation?

    A. $\$1500 + \$0.50x$
    B. $\$1500 + \$0.50(2000 - x)$
    C. $\$1500 + \$0.50(x - 2000)$
    D. $\$1500(2000 - x)(\$0.50)$

20. The sum of 3 times a number and 4 times another number is divided by the sum of 2 and a third number. Which of the following expressions represents this series of operations?

    A. $(3x + 4y) \div (2 + z)$
    B. $3x + 4y \div (2 + z)$
    C. $3x + 4y \div 2 + z$
    D. $(3x + 4y) \div 2z$

Question 21 refers to the following information.

Appliance City employees earn an hourly wage plus commission. Wage options are shown below.

Option	Hourly Wage	Commission on Sales
A	$7.50	1%
B	$6.00	3%

21. Chandra is paid under Option B. If h represents the number of hours worked and s represents Chandra's total sales, which of the following expressions could be used to find her weekly pay?

    A. $6 + h + 0.03s$
    B. $6h + 0.03s$
    C. $6s + 0.03h$
    D. $0.03(h)(s)$

Answers and explanations begin on page 665.

Simplifying and Evaluating Expressions

Simplifying an expression means to perform all the operations you can within an expression. When working with variables, you must remember an important rule: you can add or subtract like terms only.

A **term** is a number, a variable, or the product or quotient of numbers and variables. A term cannot include a sum or a difference.

Examples: $5x$ $3y^2$ 13 x^3 $\frac{x}{2}$

Like terms have the same variable raised to the same power. For example, $3x^2$ and $5x^2$ are like terms. $8y$ and $4y$ are also like terms. However, $6x$ and $2x^2$ are not like terms because the variables are not raised to the same power.

To simplify an expression, combine like terms.

Example 2: Simplify $2x - 5 + 4x^2 - 8 + 6x$.

Combine like terms. It is customary to write the term with the greatest exponent first and to continue in descending order.

$$2x - 5 + 4x^2 - 8 + 6x$$
$$= (2x + 6x) + (-5 + -8) + 4x^2$$
$$= 8x + (-13) + 4x^2$$
$$= 4x^2 + 8x - 13$$

The **distributive property** allows you to remove grouping symbols to simplify expressions. We can state the distributive property using symbols.

$$a(b + c) = ab + ac \quad \text{and} \quad a(b - c) = ab - ac$$

In other words, each term inside the parentheses is multiplied by the term outside the parentheses, and the results are added or subtracted depending on the operation inside the parentheses. Example 3 applies the distributive property.

Example 3: Simplify $4x - 3(x + 9) + 15$.

1. Change subtracting to adding a negative number.
2. Use the distributive property. Multiply –3 by each term in the parentheses.

3. Combine like terms.
   (**NOTE:** $1x$ means x.)

$$4x - 3(x + 9) + 15$$
$$= 4x + -3(x + 9) + 15$$
$$= 4x + (-3x) + (-3)(9) + 15$$
$$= 4x + (-3x) + (-27) + 15$$
$$= (4x + -3x) + (-27 + 15)$$
$$= x - 12$$

Evaluating an expression means finding its value. To evaluate an expression, substitute a given number for each variable. Follow the order of operations.

Example 3: Find the value of the expression $\frac{3x + 2y}{4}$ when $x = 6$ and $y = 5$.

1. Replace the variables with the values given in the problem.

$$\frac{3x + 2y}{4} = \frac{3(6) + 2(5)}{4}$$

2. Perform the operations above the fraction bar. Then divide.

$$\frac{3(6) + 2(5)}{4} = \frac{18 + 10}{4} = \frac{28}{4} = 7$$

NOTE: To remove parentheses from an operation that follows a minus sign, imagine that the parentheses are preceded by 1. Then use the distributive property.

$$-(2x + 3)$$
$$= -1(2x + 3)$$
$$= -1(2x) + (-1)(3)$$
$$= -2x + (-3) \text{ or } -2x - 3$$

PRACTICE 6.2

A. Simplify.

1. $5 + x^2 - 3 + 3x$

2. $2y + 5 + 17y + 8$

3. $3x - 6(x - 9)$

4. $6x^3 + 4 + 2x^2(15) + x^2$

5. $4(y + 8) + 3(y - 6)$

6. $5 - (x - 3) + 4x$

7. $16x + 6(x - 2)$

8. $5y^2 + 4 - 3y^2 + 5 + y$

9. $-3(x + 3) - 2(x + 4)$

10. $5x - (x + 4) - 3$

B. Evaluate each expression as directed.

11. Find the value of $6(x + 2) + 7$ when $x = 2$.

12. Find the value of $3x^2 + 3(x + 4)$ when $x = 3$.

13. Find the value of $\frac{(x + y)^2}{2} - 10$ when $x = 2$ and $y = 4$.

14. Find the value of $y^2 + 16 - (y - 5)^2$ when $y = 3$.

15. Find the value of $8x + 9y - (2x + y)$ when $x = 4$ and $y = 6$.

16. Find the value of $x^2 + 3y - 4 + 2(x - z)$ when $x = 7$, $y = 5$, and $z = -3$.

17. Find the value of $(14 - x)^2 + 20\sqrt{x}$ when $x = 9$.

18. Find the value of $\frac{3(2x - y)}{3} + 6(y - 5)$ when $x = -2$ and $y = 3$.

19. Find the value of $x^2 - (x^3 + 3)$ when $x = -2$.

20. Find the value of $30x + 2 + 2y^2 - 3(x - 2)^2$ when $x = 1$ and $y = 4$.

C. Choose the one best answer to each question.

21. Which of the following expressions is equal to $3x^2 + 3(x - 3) + x + 10$?

    A. $x^2 + 9x + 1$

    B. $3x^2 + 4x + 19$

    C. $3x^2 - 2x + 19$

    D. $3x^2 + 4x + 1$

22. Given the expression $4x^2 - 3(y + 6)$, which of the following values for x and y will result in a value of -11?

    A. $x = 2, y = 3$

    B. $x = -2, y = 4$

    C. $x = -1, y = 2$

    D. $x = 1, y = 0$

Question 23 refers to the following information.

Temperature Conversion Formulas	
To convert Fahrenheit (F) to Celsius (C)	$C = \frac{5}{9}(F - 32)$
To convert Celsius (C) to Fahrenheit (F)	$F = \frac{9}{5}C + 32$

23. If the temperature is 68° Fahrenheit, what is the temperature in Celsius?

    A. 20°

    B. 36°

    C. 154.4°

    D. 180°

Answers and explanations begin on page 665.

ALGEBRA BASICS, EXPRESSIONS, AND POLYNOMIALS

Expressions and Calculator Skills

When you take the GED® *Mathematical Reasoning Test*, you may use either a hand-held or an online version of a scientific calculator (TI-30XS MultiView™) to use on the second part of the test items. This calculator, like most scientific calculators, uses algebraic logic, which means that it follows the order of operations that you saw on page 322.

You need to practice using a scientific calculator with algebraic logic. You can find out whether your calculator uses algebraic logic by running this simple test.

Press: 4⊗3 x^2 enter. (Your calculator may have an equal sign instead of an *enter* button.)

If the display reads **36**, your calculator uses algebraic logic.

If the display reads **144**, your calculator does not use algebraic logic. You should find another calculator to practice for the *Mathematical Reasoning Test*.

You can use a calculator to evaluate an expression that contains several operations.

Example 1: Find the value of the expression $2x^2 + 3x - 5$ when $x = -4$.

When you come to the variable x, enter –4 by pressing (–)4. The (–) key is called the **change sign key**.

Press: 2 ((–) 4) x^2 + 3 × (–) 4 – 5 enter.
The right side of the display reads 15.

The value of the expression is **15**.

Expressions sometimes contain grouping symbols to show a different order of operations. You can enter grouping symbols on a scientific calculator. On the TI-30XS MultiView™, the grouping symbols (and) are found above the 8 and 9, respectively. When you enter the left, or open, parenthesis, (, the calculator waits until you enter the right, or closing, parenthesis,), before it calculates what is inside the symbols.

Example 2: Find the value of the expression $2(x + 4) + \frac{5x}{3}$ when $x = 6$.

Press: 2 × (6 + 4) + 5 × 6 ÷ 3 enter.
The right side of the display reads 30.
The value of the expression is **30**.

You can also use your calculator for only part of an expression.

Example 3: Find the value of the expression $\frac{3x + 6}{2} + \sqrt{225}$ when $x = 4$.

Substitute 4 for x in the first part of the expression and calculate the results by hand or using your calculator: $\frac{3(4) + 6}{2} = \frac{12 + 6}{2} = \frac{18}{2} = 9.$
Now use your calculator to find the square root of 225.

Press: 2nd x^2 225 enter. The right side of the display reads 15.

Add the results of the two steps: $9 + 15 = \textbf{24}.$

Key Ideas

- On the *Mathematical Reasoning Test*, you will use a scientific calculator that follows the order of operations.
- Use the *change sign* key to enter a negative number.
- Use the *grouping symbol* keys to change the order of operations.

GED® TEST TIP

To check your work when using a calculator, enter each calculation twice. If the results are the same, you probably pressed the keys that you intended.

PRACTICE 7

A. Use a calculator as needed to find the value of the expressions as directed.

1. What is the value of $5x^2 - 3x + 5$ when $x = 2$?

2. Find the value of $\sqrt{7x} + 2x$ to the nearest tenth when $x = 5$.

3. If $x = -3$, what is the value of $7x^2 + 2x - 6$?

4. What is the value of $\frac{1}{2}x + 15$ when $x = 3$?

5. Find the value of $3(2x + 3 + y) - 14$ when $x = -2$ and $y = 9$.

6. If $y = -3$, what is the value of $4y^3 + 2(y^2 - 4)$?

7. What is the value of $2(x^2 + 6) + 3(x - 1)$ when $x = 5$?

8. If $x = 4$ and $y = -4$, what is the value of the expression $6x^2 + 3y^2 + 2$?

9. Find the value of $-2(x^3 + 3) + 16x + 2$ when $x = 2$.

10. If $x = 7$, what is the value of the expression $7 + 3(x - 2) - 2x^2$?

11. Find the value of $-(x + y) + 3(2z - y)$ if $x = -5$, $y = -7$, and $z = 4$.

12. What is the value of the expression $x^2 - 7(3 - y) + 4$ when $x = 5$ and $y = 4$?

13. If $x = -2$ and $y = 8$, what is the value of $x^2 + y - 6(y + 3)$?

14. What is the value of $\sqrt{760 - 4x^2}$ to the nearest tenth when $x = 6$?

15. If $x = 20$, what is the value of the expression $4(x + 7) - 3(x - 2)$?

16. Find the value of $\dfrac{x(25 + 2x - y)}{-z}$ when $x = -3$, $y = 4$, and $z = -1$.

17. What is the value of $5y^2 + 4x^2 - 6(x - y)$ when $x = 5$ and $y = -2$?

18. Find the value of $3x^2 \cdot \dfrac{2(x - 3y)}{6}$ when $x = 6$ and $y = 1$.

19. What is the value of the expression $(x^2 + 5)(x^2 - x + 2) - 3$ when $x = -4$?

20. Find the value of $(x + y)(x - y)(2x + y)$ when $x = 9$ and $y = 4$.

B. Choose the _one best answer_ to each question.

Width = 5.6 m

Length = 12.5 m

21. Jake has to buy enough fencing to enclose the rectangular garden shown above.

    The formula for finding the perimeter of (or distance around) a rectangle is $P = 2l + 2w$, where $P =$ perimeter, $l =$ length, and $w =$ width. Using the values from the drawing, what is the perimeter in meters of the garden?

    A. 18.1
    B. 36.2
    C. 70
    D. 140

22. If $x = -5$ and $y = 2$, which of the following expressions has the greatest value?

    A. $x + y$
    B. $-x + y$
    C. xy
    D. $-2xy$

23. What is the value of the expression $2 \div x^{-4}$ when $x = 2$?

    A. 32
    B. 16
    C. 8
    D. -16

Answers and explanations begin on page 665.

Understand Polynomials

Key Ideas

- A polynomial is an expression with more than one term—any combination of coefficients, variables, exponents, and constants.
- Specific types of polynomials include monomials, binomials, and trinomials.

The GED® *Mathematical Reasoning Test* will expect you to understand polynomials. A **polynomial** is made up of terms, and since the prefix *poly-* means "many," a polynomial is a term in which many parts are being combined. Each term in a polynomial may be made up of a combination of coefficients, variables, exponents, and constants.

Coefficients include numbers such as 4, −25, or $\frac{1}{2}$ and will come before the variables. Coefficients can be negative, like −25. If there is no coefficient next to a variable, assume the coefficient is 1. In the expression $x + y + z$, the coefficient in front of each variable is equal to 1.

Variables are letters such as x and y in polynomial terms. In the polynomial $45a^2b$, the variables are a and b.

Exponents, or powers, are a way of showing repeated multiplication. This is also known as raising a number or variable to a power. Polynomials must be raised to whole number exponents. There are no negative or fractional powers in polynomials. In the polynomial $6x^3y^4$, the exponents are 3 and 4. The **degree** of a polynomial with only one variable is the largest exponent of that variable. For example, in the expression $4x^3 + 3x^2 - 5$, the degree is 3 (the largest exponent of x.)

A **constant** is a number on its own that will always remain the same. It is not next to a variable. A constant can be either positive or negative, depending on whether it is being added or subtracted. In the expression $4x^3 + 3x^2 + 5$, the constant is 5. No matter what value you substitute for x, 5 will always be just 5.

Polynomials are built out of all of the components above, and there are different types of polynomials, including monomials, binomials, and trinomials. These are important to know.

- A **monomial** is a polynomial with only one term. An example of a monomial is $4xy^2$. This term is made up of a coefficient (4), two variables (x and y), and an exponent (the power of 2).

- A **binomial** is a polynomial with two terms. An example of a binomial is $3x + 2$. The first term is made up of a coefficient (3) and a variable (x), and the second term consists of a constant (2).

- A **trinomial** is a polynomial with three terms. An example of a trinomial is $4x + 3y^2 - 4$. The first term is made up of a coefficient (4) and a variable (x). The second term is made up of a coefficient (3), a variable (y), and an exponent (the power of 2). The third term is made up of a constant, and this time it is a negative number (−4).

A few types of numbers are not categorized as polynomials and cannot be present in polynomial terms. These include the following:

- Division by a variable, such as $\frac{3}{x+3}$ or $\frac{1}{x}$
- Negative exponents, such as $4xy^{-2}$ (exponents can only be 0, 1, 2, etc.)
- Fractional exponents, such as $3a^{\frac{1}{2}}$
- Variables inside radicals, such as $\sqrt{x}$

In a polynomial term, however, you can divide by a constant or have numbers inside a radical. For example, $\frac{4x}{12}$ is allowed, as is $\sqrt{10}$.

PRACTICE 8

A. Identify whether each of the following is a monomial, binomial, or trinomial.

1. $25a$
2. $2xy^2z$
3. $x - 4$
4. $x^3 + y - 1$
5. $7y - 1$
6. $2x^4 + 3x + 4$
7. $\dfrac{x}{3}$
8. y^2
9. $g^2h^2i^2j^2$
10. $x^2 + x^2$
11. $x^2 + 14x + 3$
12. $x^2y + x^2 + y$
13. $g + h$
14. $\sqrt{49}$
15. $3x^2 - 5$

B. For each polynomial, identify the terms. Remember that a coefficient can be positive or negative.

16. $3x^4 - 2x^2 + 3$
17. $12a^2bc$
18. $3g - 4h$
19. $x^2 + y$
20. $-4a - 3b^2 + c$
21. 25
22. $x^2 + 3x - 7$
23. $\dfrac{3x}{8}$
24. $\sqrt{25}$
25. $\dfrac{x^2}{9}$
26. $49x^2y^2z^2$
27. $18y^2 - 4y^2 + 8$
28. $3h - 4$
29. $x^2 - x + y^2 - 2$
30. $ab + ab^2 + b^2 - 4$

C. Choose the <u>one best answer</u> to each question.

31. What is the sum of the exponents in the expression $4x^3 + 3x^2 + 5$?

    A. 3
    B. 5
    C. 12
    D. 17

32. What is the sum of the coefficients in the expression $a - 3b - c + 2d$?

    A. -3
    B. -1
    C. 2
    D. 3

Answers and explanations begin on page 666.

Simplify Polynomials

Combine Like Terms

When working with polynomials, you must work to combine like terms. **Like terms** have variables that are the same or are terms that have the same variable raised to the same power, or exponent. For example, $8x^3$ and $4x^3$ are like terms, and $5y$ and $3y$ are also like terms.

Unlike terms have variables that are different or have the same variable raised to different powers. For example, $3a$ and $5b$ are unlike terms. The terms $9x$ and $7x^2$ are also unlike terms because the variables are raised to different powers.

You can only combine like terms when simplifying polynomials. Unlike terms cannot be combined. For example, in the polynomial $7x^2 + 4x^3$, you cannot combine the terms because x is raised to different powers in each term. However, in the polynomial $7x^2 + 4x^2$, you can combine terms that all have the same variable and the same exponent: $7x^2 + 4x^2 = 11x^2$.

Example 1: Combine like terms in the polynomial $4y^3 + 2x^3 - 7y^3$.
1. First, identify and group the like terms. $4y^3 - 7y^3 + 2x^3$

The two y^3 terms are alike; the x^3 term cannot be combined with them.

2. Combine the like terms. $-3y^3 + 2x^3$

Simplify Polynomials

Some polynomials may contain both like and unlike terms. The following example shows how like and unlike terms are handled when you have to simplify a polynomial. Start by combining like terms from the exponent with the largest number, or degree, and proceed to the exponent with the smallest number.

Example 2: Simplify the polynomial $7x^4 - 13x^2 + x^4 + 2x^2 + 5x + 3 + x$.

1. Combine like terms with the largest degree, which is 4. Add: $7x^4 + x^4 = 8x^4$.
2. You now have $8x^4 - 13x^2 + 2x^2 + 5x + 3 + x$. Combine like terms from the exponent with the next largest degree, which is 2. Add: $-13x^2 + 2x^2 = -11x^2$.
3. You now have $8x^4 - 11x^2 + 5x + 3 + x$. Finally, combine like terms with the next largest degree, which is 1. Add: $5x + x = 6x$.
4. You now have $\mathbf{8x^4 - 11x^2 + 6x + 3}$.

This is as much as you can simplify this polynomial by combining like terms. The simplified polynomial has no more like terms and must remain as is.

Key Ideas

- Like terms can be combined; unlike terms cannot.
- Like terms are either numbers—positive or negative— or variables with the same degree of exponents.
- Polynomials with unlike terms cannot be simplified.

GED® TEST TIP

When working with polynomials, treat the minus sign before a coefficient or constant as an indicator of a negative number. This will help you to combine like terms using the rules of signed numbers that you learned on pages 314–315.

PRACTICE 9

A. For each pair of terms, indicate if they are like terms or unlike terms.

1. $4x^3, x^3$ _____ terms

2. $3x, x$ _____ terms

3. b, b^2 _____ terms

4. $-2x, 7y$ _____ terms

5. $-2x, 7x$ _____ terms

6. $4a, 4$ _____ terms

7. g^2, g^2hi _____ terms

8. $2x^2y, 8x^2y$ _____ terms

9. $-5m, -5m^2$ _____ terms

10. x^2y, xy^2 _____ terms

11. $ab, 8ab$ _____ terms

12. $3y, 3y^2$ _____ terms

13. $14g, \frac{1}{3}g$ _____ terms

14. $12x^2, x^2$ _____ terms

15. a, ab^2 _____ terms

16. $15x^2, -x^2$ _____ terms

17. $10y, 11yz$ _____ terms

18. $x^2, \frac{x^2}{2}$ _____ terms

19. $g, -g^2$ _____ terms

20. $\frac{x}{8}, x^2$ _____ terms

B. Simplify each expression by combining like terms.

21. $3x^2y + 4x^2y$

22. $3b + b$

23. $a - 7a + 3$

24. $14ab + ab^2 + 2ab + 3$

25. $x^2 - 3x^2 + 7$

26. $ab + 2ab + ab$

27. $7g + 7gh + 7g + 7gh$

28. $g^2 + h^2 - 4g^2h^2 + g^2 + h^2 - 4$

29. $9y + y - y^2 - y$

30. $x^2 - 8x^2 + y - 3$

31. $11y + 11y - 7$

32. $9x^2y - 3x^2y + 4y^2 - 21 + y^2 - 2$

33. $8x^2 - 4x + 7 + 4x^3 - x^2 + 7x - 2$

34. $-3x^2 + 6x - 2x^2 - 10x + 5$

35. $9x^2 - 3x^3 + x - 2x^2$

C. Choose the <u>one best answer</u> to each question.

36. What is the simplified form of the expression $3a^2b + 4ab + 3a^2b + 5ab$?

    A. $6a^3b^2 + 8a^3b^2$

    B. $6a^2b + 9ab$

    C. $6a^2b + 8ab$

    D. $15a^6 + b^4$

37. When simplified, how many terms are in the polynomial $j^2 + k^3 - 2j^3 + 5k^3 - 2j^2$?

    A. 2

    B. 3

    C. 4

    D. 5

Answers and explanations begin on page 666.

LESSON

10

Add and Subtract Polynomials

Add Polynomials with One Variable

On the *Mathematical Reasoning Test*, you may be required to add polynomials that have one variable. You can add polynomials when they have like terms, including variables and exponents. When you see polynomials within parentheses linked by an addition sign, add them by combining the like terms across the polynomials.

Example 1: Add $(3x^2 + x + 4) + (2x^2 + 2x - 16)$.

1. To add these polynomials, simply combine like terms. Add: $3x^2 + 2x^2 = 5x^2$.
2. Add: $x + 2x = 3x$.
3. Add: $4 + (-16) = -12$.
4. Combine the results into one polynomial: $\mathbf{5x^2 + 3x - 12}$.

Sometimes, an expression needs to be simplified before you add and combine like terms.

Example 2: Add $(5x^2 + 8x - 4) + (2x^2 - 6x + 14x)$.

1. Simplify within the second parentheses. Add: $-6x + 14x = 8x$.
2. Combine like terms across the polynomials. Add: $5x^2 + 2x^2 = 7x^2$.
3. Use the simplified expression from step 1. Add: $8x + 8x = 16x$.
4. Combine the results into one polynomial: $\mathbf{7x^2 + 16x - 4}$.

Subtract Polynomials with One Variable

The only difference between adding and subtracting polynomials is the minus sign between the parentheses. You must distribute the negative sign across the second polynomial. To distribute the negative sign across the second polynomial, simply reverse the signs of each term. Then drop the parentheses and combine like terms across both polynomials.

Example 3: Subtract $(3x^2 + x + 4) - (7x^2 + 2x - 16)$.

1. Distribute the negative sign to everything in the second set of parentheses by reversing the sign of each term: $-7x^2 - 2x + 16$.
2. Drop the parentheses from the entire expression and combine like terms:
   $3x^2 + x + 4 - 7x^2 - 2x + 16$

   $-4x^2 + x + 4 - 2x + 16$
   $-4x^2 - x + 4 + 16$
   $-4x^2 - x + 20$

Note that subtracting a negative constant or coefficient is the same as adding a positive. In the next example, watch what happens to the negative coefficient inside the second set of parentheses when the sign is distributed.

Key Ideas

- Monomials, binomials, or trinomials can be added or subtracted.
- In some cases, a polynomial needs to be simplified before it can be added or subtracted.
- When subtracting polynomials, distribute the second polynomial, changing the signs for coefficients, and then combine all the like terms.

GED® TEST TIP

When you subtract, you are simply reversing the signs within the second polynomial. Be careful to make all negative signs positive. Study Examples 3 and 4 carefully to avoid common errors.

Example 4: Subtract $(x^2 + 2x + 3) - (4x^2 - x + 6)$.

1. Distribute the negative sign to everything in the second set of brackets by reversing the sign of each term:
$-4x^2 + x - 6$

2. Drop the brackets and combine like terms:

$x^2 + 2x + 3 - 4x^2 + x - 6$

$x^2 - 4x^2 + 2x + x + 3 - 6$

$-3x^2 + 3x - 3$

PRACTICE 10.1

A. Add the following polynomials.

1. $(3x + 4) + (2x + 2)$
2. $(17y - y + 3) + (4y + 3y + 3)$
3. $(5x^2 - 3x - 4) + (3x^2 - 2x + 6)$
4. $(-a^2 + 2a) + (16a^2 + 6a)$
5. $(9x^2 - 3x - 2) + (2x^2 + 5x + 5)$

6. $(6a + 6) + (-5a - 5)$
7. $(-8g^2 + 7g + 6) + (8g^2 - 7g - 5)$
8. $(2x^2 + 5x) + (2x^2 + 4x + 7x - 9)$
9. $(13y + 4y + 4) + (7y - 7)$
10. $(-a^2 - a^2 - a - 4) + (-a^2 - a^2 - a - 5)$

B. Subtract the following polynomials.

11. $(3y - 4) - (2y - 2)$
12. $(x + 16) - (4x + 3)$
13. $(2a + 1) - (-a - 1)$
14. $(5x^2 + 2x + 4) - (2x^2 + x + 2)$
15. $(7y + 5y + 5) - (2y - 2)$
16. $(9x^2 + 4x + 5x + 4) - (7x^2 + 6x - 9)$

17. $(-g + g - 1) - (-g - g - 2)$
18. $(17a^2 - 4a - 4) - (16a^2 + 6a - 6)$
19. $(7b^2 + b - 8) - (7b^2 + b + 8)$
20. $(21x^2 + 3x^2 - 2x - 4 - 1) -$
$(3x^2 + x^2 + x + 2x - 5 - 1)$

C. Choose the <u>one best answer</u> to each question.

21. What is the sum of the polynomials

$(2xy + 3xy^2 - 4x^2y) + (5x^2y - 3xy^2 + 2xy)$?

A. $x^2y + 4xy$

B. $4xy + 3x + y$

C. $7x - 2y$

D. $7x^2y - 2xy$

22. Which of the following equals

$(5x^2 - 2x + 1) - (3x^2 - 3x - 2)$?

A. $x - 5x - 1$

B. $2x^2 - x + 3$

C. $2x^2 + x + 3$

D. $2x^2 - 5x + 3$

Answers and explanations begin on page 666.

Simplifying Polynomials with More Than One Variable

Some polynomials contain terms with different variables—for example, the binomial $2x + 3y$ contains an x term and a y term. You add, subtract, and simplify polynomials with more than one variable just as you do polynomials with just a single variable. However, you have to be careful to add and subtract only like terms. Remember that in all polynomials, like terms have the *same variable* and the *same exponent*. For example, in the polynomial $x^2 + 2x + y^2 + 3x + 2y$, the only like terms are the two x^1 terms. You can combine the $2x$ and the $3x$, but you cannot combine x^2 with any other term, nor can you combine the y^2 or the $2y$ with any other term. The most simplified version of this polynomial is $x^2 + 5x + y^2 + 2y$.

A term that consists of two or more variables multiplied together cannot be combined with terms that contain only one of those variables. For example, you cannot combine $2xy + 7x$. However, you can combine $2xy + 7xy$ to get $9xy$.

Example 1: Simplify $6xy^4 - 20x^2 - 3 + xy^4 + 12x^2 - 30$.

Start by grouping the like terms together. Then add and subtract as appropriate.

$$6xy^4 - 20x^2 - 3 + xy^4 + 12x^2 - 30$$
$$= 6xy^4 + xy^4 - 20x^2 + 12x^2 - 3 - 30$$
$$= 7xy^4 - 8x^2 - 33$$

Adding Polynomials with More Than One Variable

Adding polynomials that contain more than one variable requires the same process as adding polynomials that have only one variable. Just remove the brackets and combine like terms across both polynomials. Remember that only like terms can be combined.

Example 2: Add $(3x^2 + 6x + 3xy) + (5x^2 - 6xy + 14y)$.

$$(3x^2 + 6x + 3xy) + (5x^2 - 6xy + 14y)$$
$$= 3x^2 + 5x^2 + 6x + 3xy - 6xy + 14y$$
$$= 8x^2 + 6x - 3xy + 14y$$

Subtracting Polynomials with More Than One Variable

Subtracting polynomials that contain more than one variable is exactly the same as subtracting polynomials that contain only a single variable. Remember to distribute the minus sign across the second polynomial when you remove the parentheses. Also remember that only like terms can be combined.

Example 3: Subtract $(3xy^2 + x + 2xy + 4) - (7xy^2 + 2xy - 16)$.

$$3xy^2 + x + 2xy + 4) - (7xy^2 + 2xy - 16)$$
$$= 3xy^2 + x + 2xy + 4 - 7xy^2 - 2xy + 16$$
$$= -4xy^2 + x + 20$$

Notice that there is no xy term in the final simplified expression because $2xy - 2xy = 0$.

PRACTICE 10.2

A. Simplify the following polynomials.

1. $a^2 + 2a + b^2 + 3a + 3b^2$

2. $x + 3xy + y + 16 - 5x - 4xy$

3. $yz^2 - z^2 + 5 + 3yz - 3z^2 + 4yz$

4. $ab - b + c + 17 + 6ab - 34$

5. $a^4 + c^2 + 3ac - 5a^4 - 2c^2 + 5$

6. $19xyz + x - y + 3xyz + 6 + y$

7. $ef + ef^2 - 10 + 6ef + f$

8. $p + pq - q - p + 3pq - 3 - q + 7$

B. Add the following polynomials.

9. $(ab + b - c + 6) + (3ab - b + c - 6)$

10. $(x^2 + xy - y - 3) + (-x^2 - xy + y + 3)$

11. $(p^6 + p^5 + pq - p^2) + (2p^6 - p^5 + 3pq - q^2)$

12. $(x + xy + 7) + (y - xy + 8)$

13. $(9a + bc + c^2) + (-9a - b + bc - c^2)$

14. $(4xyz + 4x - 4y) + (6xyz - 4x - 4y + 16)$

15. $(5a + 5b + 4c - 6) + (a - b - 4c + d + 6)$

16. $(pq - q + 15) + (6pq - 15)$

C. Subtract the following polynomials.

17. $(ab + a + b + 6) - (8ab + a - b - 6)$

18. $(xy + x + y) - (xy + x + y)$

19. $(p^2 + q^2 + 14) - (3p^2 - 4q^2 + 7)$

20. $(x^4 + yz + z^4) - (yz + z^5)$

21. $(bc^2 + bc + c - 7) - (2bc - c - 7)$

22. $(xy + xz - xyz) - (4xy + xyz)$

23. $(c^3d^7 + c^2 - d + 35) - (2c^2 - 3d + 35)$

24. $(ef^2g - fg + 16) - (ef^2 + fg + 8)$

D. Choose the <u>one best answer</u> to each question.

25. Which of the following equals
$(x + y + z) - (-2x + 2y + z)$?

    A. $-x + 3y + 2z$

    B. $-2x - y + 2z$

    C. $3x - 2y + 2z$

    D. $3x - y$

26. Which of the following equals
$(2g^2 + 3h - 5k) + (g^2 + 2h + 3k)$?

    A. $g^2 + h - 8k$

    B. $3g^2 + 5h - 2k$

    C. $2g^2 + 6h^2 - 15k^2$

    D. $2g^4 + 5h - 2k$

Answers and explanations begin on page 666.

Multiply Polynomials

Multiply a Monomial by a Monomial

To multiply two monomials, multiply each component separately. Start by multiplying the coefficients (or numbers). If there is no coefficient given, assume that the coefficient is 1 (for example, $xy = 1xy$). Then, multiply each variable separately by adding the exponents of like variables. Remember that a variable with no exponent is a variable raised to the first power (for example, $x = x^1$). So $x(x^3) = x^1(x^3) = x^4$.

Example 1: Multiply $(2ab)(4b)$.

$$2 \times 4 \times a \times b^1 \times b^1 = \mathbf{8ab^2}$$

Multiply a Monomial by a Binomial

To multiply a monomial by a binomial, multiply the monomial by the first term in the binomial, then multiply the monomial by the second term in the binomial. Finally, add the resulting terms.

Example 2: Multiply $-2z^2(z + 3yz)$.

1. Distribute the negative sign:

   $-2z^2(z + 3yz) = 2z^2(-z - 3yz)$.

2. Multiply the monomial by each term in the binomial:

   $2z^2(-z - 3yz) = [2 \times (-1) \times z^2 \times z^1] + [2 \times (-3) \times z^2 \times y^1z^1]$.

3. Add: $-2z^3 + (-6yz^3) = \mathbf{-2z^3 - 6yz^3}$.

Multiply Two Binomials

To multiply two binomials, multiply the first terms, then the outer terms, then the inner terms, and, finally, the last terms. Add the results and combine like terms. You can remember this process by the acronym FOIL, which stands for *First, Outer, Inner, Last*.

Example 3: Multiply $(2g^2 + 9)(3g^2 - 4)$.

1. Multiply using FOIL:

   $(2g^2 + 9)(3g^2 - 4) = (2g^2)(3g^2) + (2g^2)(-4) + (9)(3g^2) + (9)(-4)$.

2. Add: $6g^4 - 8g^2 + 27g^2 - 36$.

3. Combine like terms:

   $6g^4 - 8g^2 + 27g^2 - 36 = \mathbf{6g^4 + 19g^2 - 36}$.

PRACTICE 11

A. Multiply the monomials.

1. $(6x)(5x)$

2. $(2xy)(3y)$

3. $(7abc)(4bc)$

4. $(12y)(z)$

5. $(a)(9bc)$

6. $(5xyz)(2xy^2z^4)$

7. $(4ab)(bc^2)$

8. $(17f^2gh^3)(2fh^4)$

B. Multiply the binomials by the monomials.

9. $3z^2(6xy + 4z)$

10. $6x(7x - 6z)$

11. $-5ab(3b + 11c)$

12. $-3f^3(6h - 8fgh^2)$

13. $10z(7x^7 - 5z)$

14. $-z(-z - 6xy)$

15. $8b(9ab + 8a)$

16. $-9(-2x^4 + 3xy^2)$

C. Multiply the binomials by using FOIL. Remember to complete by combining like terms wherever possible.

17. $(x + 5)(x - 6)$

18. $(x + y)(x + y)$

19. $(z + 9)(z - 9)$

20. $(yz^2 + x)(yz^2 - 3x)$

21. $(3x + 3)(3x + 5)$

22. $(x + y)(x - y)$

23. $(y^2 - 6)(y^4 + 10)$

24. $(ab + 3)(ab - 4)$

D. Choose the <u>one best answer</u> to each question.

25. Which of the following expressions is equal to $(4a^3b^2)(3a^2c)$?

   A. $12a^5b^2c$
   B. $7a^5b^2c$
   C. $12a^6bc$
   D. $7a^6b^2c$

26. Martha has $2pc^2$ board games, and John has $6p^2c$ board games. Which of the following expressions represents the product of the number of board games that Martha and John have?

   A. $8p^3c^3$
   B. $8p^2c^2$
   C. $12p^2c^2$
   D. $12p^3c^3$

27. Which of the following expressions is equal to $(4ab + 2)(3ab - 7)$?

   A. $7a^2b^2 + 22ab + 5$
   B. $12a^2b^2 - 22ab - 14$
   C. $12a^2b^2 + 22ab + 14$
   D. $7a^2b^2 - 22ab - 5$

Answers and explanations begin on page 667.

ALGEBRA BASICS, EXPRESSIONS, AND POLYNOMIALS

Divide Polynomials

Divide Polynomials by a Number

The *Mathematical Reasoning Test* will sometimes ask you to simplify a polynomial that is written as a fraction. To simplify, divide the numerator and denominator by a common term. A common term can be the following:

- a number

- a variable with a number as a coefficient

- a more complicated expression

You may need to factor the common term out of the numerator or denominator before you can do the division.

Example 1: Simplify $\dfrac{3x+6}{3}$.

$$\frac{3x+6}{3} = \frac{3(x+2)}{3} = \frac{\cancel{3}(x+2)}{\cancel{3}} = x + 2$$

Divide Polynomials by an Expression

Dividing a polynomial by an expression is really no different from dividing by a number. You need a common term in the numerator and denominator, and you may have to factor out that common term (including any variables) before you can do the division.

Example 2: Simplify $\dfrac{25x^3 - 45x^2}{5x}$.

$$\frac{25x^3 - 45x^2}{5x} = \frac{5x(5x^2 - 9x)}{5x} = \frac{\cancel{5x}(5x^2 - 9x)}{\cancel{5x}} = 5x^2 - 9x$$

When the numerator has two added or subtracted expressions that both include the common term, it may be easier to split the polynomial into two separate fractions and simplify them separately. Doing it this way will help you keep straight exactly which terms you can cancel.

Example 3: Simplify $\dfrac{x(x+7) - 3(x+7)}{x+7}$.

$$\frac{x(x+7) - 3(x+7)}{x+7} = \frac{x(x+7)}{x+7} - \frac{3(x+7)}{x+7}$$

$$= \frac{x\cancel{(x+7)}}{\cancel{x+7}} - \frac{3\cancel{(x+7)}}{\cancel{x+7}} = x - 3$$

Key Ideas

- You can divide a polynomial by numbers, expressions, or other polynomials.
- The key to dividing a polynomial is to isolate a common factor that divides into the numerator and denominator.
- Common factors can be numbers, variables, or a combination of the two such as addition, subtraction, or multiplication expressions.

GED® TEST TIP

Remember that you will be provided with a wipe-off board during the Mathematical Reasoning Test. *You will be able to use that board to carefully work through the steps needed to solve these types of problems.*

PRACTICE 12

A. To simplify, divide each polynomial by a number. (You may need to factor the numerator and/or denominator to find the common term.)

1. $\dfrac{2y + 30}{2}$

2. $\dfrac{7x + 21}{7}$

3. $\dfrac{4x + 20}{4}$

4. $\dfrac{3a + 3b}{3}$

5. $\dfrac{11x^2 + 22x}{11}$

6. $\dfrac{26x^2 + 39x + 13}{13}$

7. $\dfrac{5x + 10y}{5}$

8. $\dfrac{21a + 14b}{7}$

9. $\dfrac{48x + 32y}{32}$

10. $\dfrac{9a - 15b}{12}$

11. $\dfrac{6b + 24c}{18}$

12. $\dfrac{25a + 5b + 15c}{10}$

B. Divide each polynomial. Decide whether it is easier for you to divide the original numerator by the common term (as in Example 2) or whether to split the numerator first (as in Example 3).

13. $\dfrac{18x^2 + 6x}{3x}$

14. $\dfrac{10x^2 + 6x}{2x}$

15. $\dfrac{40y^2 + 10y}{5y}$

16. $\dfrac{42xy + 49x}{7x}$

17. $\dfrac{38xy + 38x}{19x}$

18. $\dfrac{3x + 18}{x + 6}$

19. $\dfrac{x(x + 4) - 6(x + 4)}{x + 4}$

20. $\dfrac{y(y + 3) + 7(y + 3)}{y + 3}$

21. $\dfrac{z(z + 2) - 5(z + 2)}{z + 2}$

22. $\dfrac{22x^2 + 66x}{11x}$

23. $\dfrac{x(y - 2) - 6(y - 2)}{y - 2}$

24. $\dfrac{a(b + 3) + 3(b + 3)}{b + 3}$

C. Choose the <u>one best answer</u> to each question.

25. Which of the following is equal to $\dfrac{21a + 14b}{7}$?

   A. $5a + 5b$
   B. $3a + 14b$
   C. $3a + 2b$
   D. $21a + 2b$

26. James has $27x$ apples, Rachel has $51y$ oranges, and Glen has $60z$ peaches. Which of the following expressions represents the average number of pieces of fruit that James, Rachel, and Glen have in their baskets?

   A. $9x + 51y + 60z$
   B. $46x + 46y + 46z$
   C. $9x + 17y + 60z$
   D. $9x + 17y + 20z$

27. Which of the following expressions is equal to $\dfrac{2z^2 - 12z + 2(z + 4) - 8}{2z}$?

   A. $z - 5$
   B. $z(z + 2) - 5$
   C. $z(z + 2) - 5(z + 2)$
   D. $z - 3$

Answers and explanations begin on page 667.

ALGEBRA BASICS, EXPRESSIONS, AND POLYNOMIALS PRACTICE QUESTIONS

1. Which of the following expressions is equal to $6 - 4(x + 3)$?

   A. $4x + 3$
   B. $4x - 9$
   C. $-4x + 9$
   D. $-4x - 6$

2. If Kris makes d dollars and Heidi makes 75 dollars less than 3 times Kris's wage, what does Heidi make in terms of d?

   A. $d + 75$
   B. $d - 225$
   C. $3d - 75$
   D. $3d - 225$

3. What is the product of 700 and 180,000 written in scientific notation?

   A. 12.6×10^9
   B. 1.26×10^8
   C. 1.26×10^9
   D. 1.26×10^{10}

4. If there are $4x$ identical schools in a region and each school has $3y$ classrooms each with $7x$ desks, how many desks are there in the region?

   A. $11x + 3y$
   B. $28x + 3y$
   C. $84xy^2$
   D. $84x^2y$

5. Which of the following is equivalent to $x^2 - 25$?

   A. $x(x - 25)$
   B. $(x - 5)^2$
   C. $(x + 5)(x - 5)$
   D. $(x - 25)^2$

6. If Tom has $9x$ baseball cards, Adam has 13 more than Tom, and Dave has $2y$ baseball cards, together they would have how many cards?

   A. $9x + 2y + 13$
   B. $18xy + 13$
   C. $18xy + 2y$
   D. $18x + 2y + 13$

Questions 7 and 8 refer to the figure below.

The figure below is a multiplication box. Each place represents the horizontal number multiplied by the vertical number; for example, the 9 in the lower right corner equals 3 multiplied by 3.

	5	y	3
1	5		3
c	20	a	
3	b	d	9

7. Which of the following is equal to ab?

   A. $5y$
   B. $60y$
   C. $100y$
   D. $500y$

8. Which of the following is equal to $a - d$?

   A. b
   B. c
   C. x
   D. y

9. Multiply $7c^2(a^2 + 5b + 7c^2)$.

   A. $7a^2c^2 + 35bc^2 + 49c^4$
   B. $7(ac)^2 + 35(bc)^2 + 49c^4$
   C. $7a^2 + 35b + 49c^4$
   D. $a^2 + 5b + 14c^2$

10. A Little League pie sale fundraiser generated $900 in revenue. If there were $6x$ pies sold, how much did each pie cost?

    A. $10
    B. $15
    C. $\dfrac{x}{150}$
    D. $\dfrac{150}{x}$

11. Simplify the expression
    $$\frac{(a-4)^2\,(6b)}{2(3b)\,(a+4)\,(a-4)}.$$

    A. $\dfrac{a-4}{a+4}$

    B. $\dfrac{a+4}{a-4}$

    C. $\dfrac{a-2}{2}$

    D. 1

12. Emilie buys x ounces of chicken for each of her guests at a dinner party. There are $8y$ people coming, and chicken is z a pound. How much will the total amount of chicken cost in dollars? (*Hint*: There are 16 ounces in one pound.)

    A. $8xyz$
    B. $16xyz$
    C. $\dfrac{xyz}{2}$
    D. $\dfrac{xyz}{8}$

13. What is the value of the expression $6(x - y) - 8x$ when $x = -2$ and $y = 5$?

    A. -58
    B. -26
    C. 2
    D. 34

14. Which of the following would be equal to $x^2 + 6z$ multiplied by $2y - 4z$ if $x = 2$, $y = 4$, and $z = 3$?

    A. -88
    B. -72
    C. 0
    D. 104

15. What is the value of the following expression?
    $$\frac{4^3 - [3(12 + 2^2)]}{6 + 5(4) - 15}$$

Write your answer on the line below.

_____

16. If every member of a team is paid $5p$ dollars for his or her participation, and Team Alpha has $6k$ members, Team Beta has $4p$ members, and Team Delta has $9h$ members, which of the following represents the total amount paid to the members of all three teams?

    A. $1080hkp$
    B. $1080hkp^2$
    C. $120p^2k + 45ph$
    D. $30kp + 20p^2 + 45hp$

17. Which of the following is equal to $7x - [(5y)2x - 9y + 8x]$?

   A. $x - 9y + 10xy$
   B. $-3x - 4y$
   C. $-x + 9y - 10xy$
   D. $15x - 9y + 10xy$

18. If Stephanie has $5c$ CDs for every DVD Alyshia has, and Jeff has $4d$ DVDs, which is 15 more than Alyshia has, how many CDs does Stephanie have?

   A. $20cd - 75c$
   B. $20cd + 15$
   C. $80cd - 15$
   D. $80cd - 75d$

19. Divide $\dfrac{56x^4 + 49x^3y^3 - 84x^3 - 7x^2}{7x^2}$.

   A. $8x^2 + 7xy^3 - 12x - 1$
   B. $8x^4 + 7x^3y^3 - 12x^3 - x^2$
   C. $8x^4 + 7y^3 - 5x^3 - 1$
   D. $49x^2 + 42xy^3 - 77x$

20. A charity with a yearly budget of $80d$ gets all of its money from either its yearly ball or from private donations. If the charity raised $64d$ from the silent auction at the ball and $4a$ from ticket sales at the ball, what will need to be raised in private donations to meet the budget?

   A. $16d$
   B. $16d - 4a$
   C. $16d + 4a$
   D. $144d - 4a$

21. Divide $\dfrac{x^4 + 4x^2y^4 - 8x - y^2}{2y^2}$.

   A. $\dfrac{x^4}{2y^2} + 2x^2y^2 - \dfrac{4x}{y^2} - \dfrac{1}{2}$

   B. $\dfrac{x^2}{2y} + \dfrac{2x^2y^2 - 4x}{y^2 - \dfrac{1}{2}}$

   C. $\dfrac{2x^4y^2 + 8x^2y^2 - 16x}{y^2 + 2y^4}$

   D. $\dfrac{x^4 - 4x}{2y^2 + 2x^2y^2 - \dfrac{1}{2}}$

22. If $12k$ privates, $8f$ lieutenants, and $6r$ captains are divided into $2r$ equal squads, which of the following would express the number of members of one squad?

   A. $6k + 4f + 3r$
   B. $\dfrac{6k + 4f}{r} + 3$
   C. $12k + 8f + 4r$
   D. $12k + 8f + 3r$

23. If $q = 2$ and $r = 4$, which of the following would equal $\dfrac{r^2 x^2 + q^3 x}{(q^2 x)}$?

   A. $4x + 2$
   B. $4x^2 + 2$
   C. $16x^2 + 8x - 2$
   D. $16x^2 + 21$

24. Simplify:
$$\dfrac{44x^6 + 55x^3y^4 + 88x^2 - 11y^2}{11x^2} - 6x^4 - 8$$

   A. $4x^4 + 5xy^2 + 8x - 1$

   B. $2x^4 + 5xy^3 - y^2 - 8$

   C. $-2x^4 + 5xy^4 - \dfrac{y^2}{x^2}$

   D. $10x^4 + 5y^4 - \dfrac{y^2}{x^2} - 8$

25. Simplify:

$(6x^2 + 5xy^2)(y) - (4xy - 9x)(4xy)$.

A. $5xy^3 - 16x^2y^2 + 42x^2y$
B. $5xy^3 - 16x^2y^2 - 30x^2y$
C. $6x^2y - 11x^2y^2 - 36xy^2$
D. $6x^2y + 5x^2y^2 - 36xy^2 + 16xy$

26. There are $4x$ workers, including managers, in an office. If the salaries of the 3 managers are not included, the average salary of each employee is $5x - 6$. What do the nonmanagerial employees earn in total?

A. $20x^2 - 24x$
B. $20x^2 - 24x - 3$
C. $20x^2 - 9x + 18$
D. $20x^2 - 39x + 18$

27. What is the value of $\dfrac{45xy + 63y^2}{9y}$ if $x = 6$ and $y = 3$?

A. 12
B. 51
C. 108
D. 153

28. Simplify

$\dfrac{3x(x^2 + 3) - 2x(x^2 + 3) - (x^2 + 3)}{x^2 + 3}$

A. $x^3 - 1$
B. $x^3 - 3x - 1$
C. $3x - 1$
D. $x - 1$

29. If the $3h$ people in one country and the $4k$ people in the neighboring country each consume $h - 17$ pounds of rice per year on average, how much rice would be consumed by both countries in one year?

A. $4h + 4k - 17$
B. $4h^2 + 4k - 68k$
C. $12hk + h - 17$
D. $3h^2 + 4hk - 51h - 68k$

30. Simplify:

$\dfrac{4x^2(x + y) - 2(x + y)^2(x - y) - xy(x + y)}{x + y}$

A. $2x^2 + 2y^2 - xy$
B. $4x^2 + xy - 2x - 2y$
C. $4x^2 - xy - 2x - 2y$
D. $3x^2 - 2xy^2 - xy$

Questions 31 and 32 refer to the figure below.

The figure below is a multiplication box. Each place represents the horizontal number multiplied by the vertical number; for example, the 20 in the lower right corner equals 5 multiplied by 4.

	a^2	ab	5
a			ab
c	$8b$		
4		40	20

31. Which of the following is equal to a?

A. 2
B. 4
C. 5
D. 10

32. Which of the following is equal to a^2c?

A. 13
B. 40
C. 42
D. 60

Answers and explanations begin on page 667.

EQUATIONS, INEQUALITIES, AND FUNCTIONS

Equations

- An equation states that two expressions are equal.
- To solve an equation, isolate the variable by applying inverse operations to both sides of the equation.
- Check your work by substituting your solution for the variable in the original equation and simplifying.

Writing and Solving One-Step Equations

An **equation** is a mathematical statement that two expressions are equal.

Examples: $3 + 5 = 4 \times 2$ $10 - 1 = 3^2$ $5(3 + 4) = 35$

An equation can contain one or more variables. Solving an equation means finding a value for the variable that will make the equation true.

Examples: $4 + x = 11$ $3x = 24$ $x - 5 = -2$
$$x = 7 \qquad x = 8 \qquad x = 3$$

The basic strategy in solving an equation is to isolate the variable on one side of the equation. You can do this by performing **inverse**, or opposite, operations. However, you must always follow one basic rule: whatever you do to one side of the equation, you must also do to the other side.

Example 1: Solve $x - 23 = 45$.

On the left side of the equation, the number 23 is subtracted from x. The inverse of subtraction is addition. Add 23 to both sides of the equation.

$$x - 23 = 45$$
$$x - 23 + \mathbf{23} = 45 + \mathbf{23}$$
$$x = \mathbf{68}$$

To check your work, replace the variable with your solution and simplify.
When $x = \mathbf{68}$, the equation is true.

Check: $x - 23 = 45$
$$68 - 23 = 45$$
$$45 = 45$$

The following examples use the inverse operations of multiplication and division.

If you are unsure about a multiple-choice algebra problem, substitute each of the answer choices for the variable in the equation. You may be able to do this quickly using your calculator.

Example 2: Solve $\dfrac{x}{2} = 17$.

The variable x is divided by 2. Since multiplication is the inverse of division, you must multiply each side of the equation by 2.

$$\frac{x}{2} = 17$$
$$2\left(\frac{x}{2}\right) = 2(17)$$
$$x = \mathbf{34}$$

When $x = \mathbf{34}$, the equation is true.

Check: $\dfrac{34}{2} = 17$
$$17 = 17$$

Example 3: Solve $5x = 75$.

Since the variable x is multiplied by 5, divide both sides of the equation by 5.

$$5x = 75$$
$$\frac{5x}{5} = \frac{75}{5}$$
$$x = \mathbf{15}$$

When $x = \mathbf{15}$, the equation is true.

Check: $5(15) = 75$
$$75 = 75$$

PRACTICE 1.1

A. Solve for the variable in each equation.

1. $7x = 63$

2. $23 + m = 51$

3. $-13 = y - 12$

4. $\frac{x}{4} = -16$

5. $5a = 625$

6. $y - 17 = -30$

7. $x + 6 = 33$

8. $4c = 28$

9. $\frac{12}{x} = -3$

10. $26 = b + 33$

11. $93 = 3x$

12. $s + 16 = 8$

13. $36 = \frac{x}{3}$

14. $t + 14 = 53$

15. $\frac{x}{6} = 8$

16. $16y = -48$

17. $r - 35 = 75$

18. $24 = \frac{120}{x}$

19. $5y = -45$

20. $d + 45 = 20$

21. $16 = 4x$

22. $-4x = 24$

23. $19 = h - 7$

24. $\frac{x}{11} = 6$

25. $m + 24 = 14$

26. $5y = 45$

27. $14 - w = 42$

28. $18 = \frac{y}{4}$

B. Choose the one best answer to each question.

Questions 29 and 30 refer to the following table.

April Time Sheet Summary
Hours Worked per Week

Week	1	2	3	4
Kayla Sax	36	40	40	
Erin Grady		24	28	38

29. Kayla and Erin worked a total of 77 hours during Week 1. Let $x = $ Erin's hours for Week 1. Which of the following equations could be used to solve for Erin's hours during Week 1?

    A. $x - 36 = 77$
    B. $x + 77 = 36$
    C. $x + 36 = 77$
    D. $x - 77 = 36$

30. Erin worked twice as many hours as Kayla did during Week 4. Let $y = $ Kayla's hours for Week 4. Which of the following equations could be used to solve for Kayla's hours during Week 4?

    A. $\frac{y}{2} = 38$
    B. $38y = 2$
    C. $2y = 38$
    D. $\frac{1}{2y} = 38$

31. The quotient of a number divided by 4 is 32. What is the number?

    A. 8
    B. 28
    C. 128
    D. 512

32. The solution $x = -5$ makes which of the following equations true?

    A. $14 - x = 9$
    B. $\frac{x}{5} = 1$
    C. $x + 3 = 8$
    D. $12x = -60$

33. Mike had $572.18 in his checking account. After writing a check, he had $434.68. Which of the following equations could be used to find the amount of the check (c)?

    A. $\$572.18 + c = \$434.68$
    B. $\$572.18 - c = \$434.68$
    C. $\$572.18c = \$434.68$
    D. $\dfrac{\$572.18}{c} = \$434.68$

Answers and explanations begin on page 668.

Solving Multi-Step Equations

Most equations require more than one operation in order to find a solution. Follow these basic steps:

- Simplify by combining like terms.

- Perform addition and subtraction steps.

- Perform multiplication and division steps.

Example 1: Solve $6x + 5 - 2x = 25$.

1. Combine like terms ($6x - 2x = 4x$).

2. Subtract 5 from both sides.

3. Divide both sides by 4.

4. Check by substituting the solution for x in the original equation.

$$6x + 5 - 2x = 25$$
$$4x + 5 = 25$$
$$4x + 5 - 5 = 25 - 5$$
$$4x = 20$$
$$\frac{4x}{4} = \frac{20}{4}$$
$$x = 5$$
$$6(5) + 5 - 2(5) = 25$$
$$30 + 5 - 10 = 25$$
$$25 = 25$$

In this example, the distributive property is used to simplify an expression. Notice that not every step is written out. As you gain experience, you can perform an operation on both sides of an equation mentally.

Example 2: Solve $-4(x - 6) = 2x$.

1. Use the distributive property to remove the grouping symbols.
2. Add $4x$ to each side.
3. Divide each side by 6.

$$-4(x - 6) = 2x$$
$$-4x + 24 = 2x$$
$$24 = 6x$$
$$4 = x$$

4. Check.

$$-4(4 - 6) = 2(4)$$
$$-4(-2) = 8$$
$$8 = 8$$

Some of the time you will be expected to write an equation from information given in the problem. The problem will describe two expressions that are equal. Write each expression in symbols and connect the expressions with the equal sign (=). In many problems, the word *is* indicates the = symbol.

Example 3: The product of a number and 6 is 44 more than twice the number. What is the number?

1. Write an equation. The word *is* represents the equal sign.
2. Subtract $2x$ from both sides.
3. Divide both sides by 4.

$$6x = 44 + 2x$$
$$4x = 44$$
$$x = \mathbf{11}$$

4. Check.

$$6(11) = 44 + 2(11)$$
$$66 = 44 + 22$$
$$66 = 66$$

The number described in the problem is **11**.

NOTE: Subtraction and division operations must be written in the order indicated by the words. "The difference between x and y" must be written $x - y$, <u>not</u> $y - x$. "The quotient of x and y" must be written $\frac{x}{y}$, <u>not</u> $\frac{y}{x}$.

PRACTICE 1.2

A. Solve for the variable in each equation.

1. $3x - 20 = 130$

2. $2y - 8 = -3y - 18$

3. $6m = 14m - 16$

4. $2x + 5 + 6x = -27$

5. $5y + 3(y + 2) = 54$

6. $17 - 4z + 2z = 13$

7. $6m - 4 = m + 11$

8. $35 = x + 7 + 6x$

9. $5p - 2 = 6p - 9$

10. $50 = 3(s + 16) - 2(s - 2)$

11. $\dfrac{5(2x - 10)}{2} + 14 = 19$

12. $3(3 + r) = 2r + 4$

13. $5y = 2y + 22 + y$

14. $38 = 5(2b - 3) + 3b + 1$

15. $-5 - x = 2x - (4x + 6)$

16. $\dfrac{3h}{2} = 30$

17. $4(3 + 2x) + 8 = 92$

18. $-5(3 - z) = z + 1$

19. $10 - 3b + 3 = -1 + (b + 2)$

20. $5n + 8 - n = 6(n - 1)$

B. Choose the <u>one best answer</u> to each question.

21. Three times a number increased by 9 is 15 less than six times the number. Let $x =$ the unknown number. Which of the following equations could be used to find the value of x?

   A. $3(9x) = 6(15x)$
   B. $3x(9) = 6x - 15x$
   C. $3x + 9 = 15 - 6x$
   D. $3x + 9 = 6x - 15$

22. Dave has 500 baseball cards, which is as many as Eric and Travis have combined. Eric has three times as many cards as Travis has.

Dave	Eric	Travis
500	$3x$	x

From the information, you can write the equation $3x + x = 500$. How many cards does Eric have? (*Hint:* Solve for x. Then find how many cards Eric has.)

   A. 150
   B. 250
   C. 350
   D. 375

23. The difference of four times a number and 7 is 15 plus the quotient of the number and 3. Which of the following equations could be used to find the value of x?

   A. $4x - 7 = \frac{x}{3} + 15$
   B. $7 - 4x = \frac{x}{3} + 15$
   C. $7 - 4x = \frac{3}{x} + 15$
   D. $4x - 7 = \frac{3}{x} + 1$

24. Kim earned x dollars at his part-time job on Friday. His wife earned $12 more than twice Kim's pay $(2x + 12)$. Together, they earned $174. How much did Kim earn on Friday?
(*Hint:* Use the equation $x + (2x + 12) = \$174$

   A. $54
   B. $87
   C. $108
   D. $120

Answers and explanations begin on page 668.

EQUATIONS, INEQUALITIES, AND FUNCTIONS

Equation Word Problems

Algebra problems describe how several numbers are related. One number is the unknown, which you will represent with a variable. Using the relationships described in the problem, you can write an equation and solve for the variable.

Example 1: There are twice as many women as men in a class on auto repair. If there are 24 students in the class, how many are women?

1. Express the numbers in the problem in terms of the same variable. Let x represent the number of men. Since there are twice as many women, let $2x$ represent the number of women.

2. Write and solve an equation. The total number of men and women is 24, so $x + 2x = 24$. Solve:
$$x + 2x = 24$$
$$3x = 24$$
$$x = 8$$

Since $x = 8$, $2x = 2(8) = 16$. There are 8 men and **16 women** in the class.

Consecutive numbers are numbers that follow in counting order. For example, 1, 2, and 3 are consecutive numbers. The numbers 2, 4, and 6 are consecutive even numbers, and 1, 3, and 5 are consecutive odd numbers.

Example 2: The sum of three consecutive numbers is 105. What is the greatest of the three numbers?

1. Let x represent the first number and $x + 1$ and $x + 2$ represent the other numbers.

2. Write an equation and solve:
$$x + (x + 1) + (x + 2) = 105$$
$$3x + 3 = 105$$
$$3x = 102$$
$$x = 34$$

3. Find the answer. The variable x represents the first number in the sequence, so the three numbers are 34, 35, and 36. The problem asks for the greatest number, which is **36**.

You may need to use the difference between numbers to write equations.

Example 3: The ticket prices for a play are $12 for adults and $8 for children. One evening, the box office sold 200 tickets. If the total box office receipts were $2240, how many adult tickets were sold?

1. Let x represent the number of adult tickets. Since 200 tickets were sold, the number of children's tickets sold can be written as $200 - x$.

Key Ideas

- To solve a word problem, decide what quantity will be represented by x. Then write expressions for the other quantities in terms of x.
- Write and solve an equation. Answer the question asked in the problem.

GED® TEST TIP

When you find x, you may not be finished solving a problem. Always reread the question. As shown in Examples 1 and 2, you may need to use the value of x to calculate the solution in a multi-step problem.

2. Multiply each term by the cost for that type of ticket. Set the total equal to $2240, and solve for x.

$$12x + 8(200 - x) = 2240$$
$$12x + 1600 - 8x = 2240$$
$$4x + 1600 = 2240$$
$$4x = 640$$
$$x = 160$$

3. There were **160 adult tickets** sold.

PRACTICE 2

A. Solve.

1. Two houses are for sale on the same street. The second house has 1000 square feet less than twice the square feet of the first house. Together the houses have 4400 square feet. What is the square footage of the first house?

2. Julia has 24 coins in her pocket. The coins are either dimes or quarters. The total value of the coins is $4.50. How many coins are dimes? (*Hint:* The value of the dimes is $0.10x$, and the value of the quarters is $0.25(24 - x)$.)

3. The Bulldogs won twice as many games as they lost. If they played a total of 36 games, how many did they win? (There were no tied games.)

4. The sum of four consecutive even numbers is 212. What is the third number? (*Hint:* Let $x =$ the first number, $x + 2 =$ the the second number, $x + 4 =$ the the third, and so on.)

5. A children's store is selling pants for $6 each and shirts for $4. Brenda bought 13 items and paid $62. How many shirts did she buy?

6. The sum of three consecutive numbers is 180. What is the least number in the series?

7. In a month Andrew spends twice as much on rent as he does on food for his family. Last month, he spent $1650 on rent and food. How much did he spend on rent?

8. George spends four times as much time helping customers as he does stocking shelves. Last week, he spent 35 hours on the two tasks. How many hours were spent helping customers?

B. Choose the <u>one best answer</u> to each question.

9. Sylvia scored 10 points better than Wiley on their science exam. Greg scored 6 points less than Wiley. Altogether, the students earned 226 points. How many points did Sylvia earn?

   A. 74
   B. 78
   C. 84
   D. 94

10. Two adults and four children paid $48 to get into the fair. A child's ticket is $6 less than an adult's ticket. What is the cost of an adult's ticket?

    A. $15
    B. $12
    C. $9
    D. $6

11. Jenny is four times as old as her niece Tina. In 12 years, Jenny will be only twice as old as Tina. The chart shows expressions for Tina and Jenny's ages now and in 12 years.

	Jenny's Age	Tina's Age
Now	$4x$	x
In 12 Years	$4x + 12$	$x + 12$

How old is Tina now?

    A. 4
    B. 6
    C. 8
    D. 12

Answers and explanations begin on page 669.

EQUATIONS, INEQUALITIES, AND FUNCTIONS

Inequalities

An **inequality** is a mathematical statement that connects two unequal expressions. The inequality symbols and their meanings are as follows:

$>$ greater than $\geq$ greater than or equal to

$<$ less than $\leq$ less than or equal to

An inequality is solved much as is an equation. Use inverse operations to isolate the variable.

Example 1: Solve for x in the inequality $3x + 2 < 8$.

1. Subtract 2 from both sides.
$$3x + 2 < 8$$
$$3x < 6$$
2. Divide both sides by 3.
$$x < 2$$

The solution $x < 2$ states that any number less than 2 makes the inequality true. Check by substituting 1 (a number less than 2) for x: $3(1) + 2 < 8$, which simplifies to $5 < 8$, a true statement.

There is one important difference between solving equalities and inequalities. Whenever you multiply or divide both sides of an inequality by a <u>negative</u> number, you must <u>reverse</u> the inequality symbol.

Example 2: Solve for n in the inequality $-2n - 5 \geq 3$.

1. Add 5 to both sides to remove -5 from the left side of the equation.
$$-2n - 5 + 5 \geq 3 + 5$$
$$-2n \geq 8$$
2. Divide both sides by -2 and *reverse the inequality symbol.*
$$\frac{-2n}{-2} \geq \frac{8}{-2}$$
$$n < -4$$

Check your work by substituting a number that is less than or equal to -4 into the <u>original</u> inequality. Here -5 is used for n. Since $5 \geq 3$ is a true statement, the answer is correct.
$$-2n - 5 \geq 3$$
$$-2(-5) - 5 \geq 3$$
$$5 \geq 3$$

When an inequality contains a variable, there are usually several numbers that make the inequality true. For that reason, we often graph the solution. In the examples below, a closed dot means that the number is included in the solution set. An open dot means the number is not included.

Examples: $x < 2$

$x > -3$

$x \leq 1$

$x \geq -2$

A **compound inequality** combines two inequalities. To solve a compound inequality, separate the inequalities and solve both. Then combine the solutions.

Example 3: Solve $3x + 4 < 5x < 16 + x$.

1. Write two inequalities and solve each separately.

$$3x + 4 < 5x \qquad\qquad 5x < 16 + x$$
$$4 < 2x \qquad\qquad\qquad 4x < 16$$

2. Write the result as a compound inequality. $2 < x < 4$

$$2 < x \qquad\qquad\qquad x < 4$$

In other words, any quantity that is greater than 2 *and* less than 4 will make the compound inequality true.

PRACTICE 3

A. Solve.

1. $3x - 7 > 5$

2. $13 < 2x - 1$

3. $4 + 2x \leq -2$

4. $\dfrac{4 + x}{5} \leq 8$

5. $2(x + 3) < 4$

6. $3 + 9x \geq 4(x + 7)$

7. $-4(x + 2) < 24$

8. $-2x + 9 < 1$

9. $\dfrac{x - 2}{3} > 2x + 11$

10. $6x < 5x + 2$

11. $x + 6 \leq 8x - 15$

12. $5x + 14 > 2 + 7x$

13. $13x - 7 > 25 - 3x$

14. $x - 6 < 2(x + 2)$

15. $-5 + 3x \geq 4(3x - 8)$

16. $36 > 4(x - 12)$

17. $6 \leq 3(x + 3)$

18. $\dfrac{4x}{3} > 8x - 20$

19. $x - 2 < \dfrac{2x + 6}{4}$

20. $x \geq 4x - 9$

21. $30 \geq 5(x + 4) \geq 10$

22. $-7x > -2(x + 15) < 10$

23. $3 < 5x - 27 < 53$

24. $22 \leq 6x - 2 \leq 4x + 16$

B. Choose the <u>one best answer</u> to each question.

25. The perimeter of a square can be found using the formula $P = 4s$, where s is one side of the square.

The perimeter of a square is less than or equal to 64 inches. Which of the following represents the possible measures of the side of the square in inches?

A. $s \leq 16$

B. $s \geq 16$

C. $s \geq 8$

D. $s \leq 64$

26. Three added to the product of -4 and a number (x) is less than 5 added to the product of -3 and the number. Which of the following is a graph of the solution set of x?

A.
$$\xleftarrow{\quad} \; |{-5}\;|{-4}\;|{-3}\;|{-2}\;|{-1}\;|{0}\;|{1}\;\circ{2}\;|{3}\;|{4}\;|{5} \;\xrightarrow{\quad}$$

B.
$$\xleftarrow{\quad} \; |{-5}\;|{-4}\;|{-3}\;|{-2}\;|{-1}\;|{0}\;|{1}\;\circ{2}\;|{3}\;|{4}\;|{5} \;\xrightarrow{\quad}$$

C.
$$\xleftarrow{\quad} \; |{-5}\;|{-4}\;\circ{-3}\;|{-2}\;|{-1}\;|{0}\;|{1}\;|{2}\;|{3}\;|{4}\;|{5} \;\xrightarrow{\quad}$$

D.
$$\xleftarrow{\quad} \; |{-5}\;|{-4}\;\circ{-3}\;|{-2}\;|{-1}\;|{0}\;|{1}\;|{2}\;|{3}\;|{4}\;|{5} \;\xrightarrow{\quad}$$

Answers and explanations begin on page 669.

EQUATIONS, INEQUALITIES, AND FUNCTIONS

Quadratic Equations

Key Ideas

- A quadratic equation can have two solutions.
- Set the quadratic equation equal to 0 and factor.
- Find the values for x that will make each factor equal 0.

A **quadratic equation** contains a squared variable, for example, $x^2 - 3x = 4$. One way to solve quadratic equations is by factoring. This is the simplest method and the one you should use on the GED® *Mathematical Reasoning Test*. When you factor an expression, you find the terms that divide evenly into the expression.

Example 1: Factor the expression $15x^2 + 9x$.

1. Look for a term that divides evenly into both $15x^2$ and $9x$. Both terms can be divided by $3x$.
    $15x^2 \div 3x = 5x$
    $9x \div 3x = 3$
2. Factor out $3x$. Write the terms as factors.
    $15x^2 + 9x = \mathbf{3x(5x + 3)}$

Study Example 2 to learn how to multiply factors with more than one term.

Example 2: Multiply $\overset{\text{(factor)}}{(2x + 3)}\ \overset{\text{(factor)}}{(x - 4)}$.
$\underset{\text{four terms}}{}$

1. Multiply each term in the first factor by each term in the second factor.
    $2x \cdot x = 2x^2$
    $2x \cdot -4 = -8x$
    $3 \cdot x = 3x$
    $3 \cdot -4 = -12$

2. Combine the results.
    $2x^2 + (-8x) + 3x + (-12) =$
    $\mathbf{2x^2 - 5x - 12}$

This method of multiplying factors is called the FOIL method. The letters in FOIL stand for First, Outer, Inner, and Last. Use the word FOIL to make sure you have performed all the necessary operations.

You factor a quadratic equation to solve it. A quadratic equation may have two solutions. Find values that make the factors equal to 0. Since a number multiplied by 0 is 0, each of the values is a solution.

GED® TEST TIP

Trial and error can help you factor quadratic equations. The more you practice, the better you will get at solving them.

Example 3: Solve $x^2 - 3x = 4$.

1. Set the equation equal to 0 by subtracting 4 from both sides.
    $x^2 - 3x = 4$
    $x^2 - 3x - 4 = 0$

2. Factor by trial and error. Think: What factors of the last term, -4, when added, will equal -3, the number part of the middle term?
$-4 \cdot 1 = -4$ and $-4 + 1 = -3$
    $(x\ \ \ )(x\ \ \ ) = 0$
    $(x + 1)(x - 4) = 0$

3. If either one of the factors equals 0, then the product of the factors will be 0. Set each factor equal to 0 and solve for x.
    $x + 1 = 0$
    $x = -1$
    $x - 4 = 0$
    $x = 4$

The solutions to the quadratic equation are -1 and 4.

PRACTICE 4

A. Multiply.

1. $(x+4)(x+2)$

2. $(x-3)(x+5)$

3. $(x-1)(x+4)$

4. $(x-6)(x-3)$

5. $(x+8)(x-2)$

6. $(2x+1)(x-2)$

7. $(x-9)(x-5)$

8. $(x+1)(3x-2)$

9. $(x-2)(x+7)$

10. $(3x+8)(x+2)$

11. $(x-6)(x+5)$

12. $(x-10)(x-3)$

13. $(2x+1)(2x+2)$

14. $(x+9)(x-4)$

15. $(x-5)(x-5)$

B. Factor each expression.

16. $x^2 + 4x + 3$

17. $x^2 + 4x - 5$

18. $x^2 + 8x + 12$

19. $x^2 - x - 6$

20. $x^2 + 5x - 14$

21. $x^2 - x - 12$

22. $x^2 + 2x - 35$

23. $x^2 - 12x + 36$

24. $x^2 - 6x - 7$

25. $x^2 + 4x - 32$

26. $2x^2 + 5x - 3$

27. $2x^2 - 8x - 10$

28. $x^2 + 5x - 50$

29. $4x^2 + 4x - 3$

30. $x^2 + x - 56$

C. Choose the <u>one best answer</u> to each question.

31. What are two solutions for the equation $x^2 - x = 20$?

    A. −4 and 5
    B. 4 and −5
    C. −10 and 2
    D. −2 and 10

32. For which of the following equations is $x = -4$ a solution?

    A. $2x^2 - 8 = 0$
    B. $x^2 - 8x + 64 = 0$
    C. $x^2 - 2x - 15 = 0$
    D. $2x^2 + 2x - 24 = 0$

33. What is the only positive solution for the equation $2x^2 - 7x - 30 = 0$?

    A. 5
    B. 6
    C. 7
    D. 8

34. The area of a rectangle is found by multiplying the length by the width. In the rectangle below, the area of the rectangle is equal to the expression $2x^2 - 27x + 70$.

    ?

    2x − 7

    An expression equal to the length is shown on the diagram. Which of the following expressions is equal to the width of the rectangle?

    A. $x + 10$
    B. $x - 10$
    C. $2x + 10$
    D. $2x - 10$

Answers and explanations begin on page 669.

Algebra Problem Solving

Key Ideas

- Guess-and-check is a strategy for answering complicated multiple-choice problems.
- Choose an answer from the options and try the value in the problem. If it works, you have found the correct answer.

One strategy that can help you save time on the more complicated algebra problems is **guess-and-check**. Guess-and-check means selecting one of the answer choices and trying that value in the problem. If you guess correctly, you can move on to the next question. If not, guess again. Guess-and-check is a good strategy for problems involving quadratic equations and expressions.

Example 1: Which of the following is a solution for the equation $2x^2 - 12 = 2x$?

    A.   4
    B.   3
    C.   0
    D. −1

To solve the problem, you would have to rewrite the equation so that the quadratic expression equals zero, factor the expression, and solve.

Instead, substitute each answer choice into the equation.

Option (A):
$$2x^2 - 12 = 2x$$
$$2(4)^2 - 12 = 2(4)$$
$$20 \neq 8$$

Option (B):
$$2x^2 - 12 = 2x$$
$$2(3)^2 - 12 = 2(3)$$
$$6 = 6$$

Option (B) 3 makes the equation true.

Guess-and-check can also save time when writing an equation seems difficult.

Example 2: Terry is ten years older than his brother Tomas. Twenty years ago, Terry was twice as old as Tomas. How old is Terry now?

    A. 25
    B. 30
    C. 40
    D. 45

Instead of writing an equation, try each age in the answer choices for Terry.

  A. If Terry is 25 now, Tomas is 15. Twenty years ago, Tomas would not have been born.
  B. If Terry is 30 now, Tomas is 20. Twenty years ago, Tomas would have been 0 years old, and Terry would have been 10.
  C. If Terry is 40 now, Tomas is 30. Twenty years ago, Tomas would have been 10, and Terry would have been 20, which is twice as old as 10.

Therefore, **option (C) 40** is correct.

> ### GED® TEST TIP
>
> *Use your judgment. Do not use guess-and-check if you can quickly see how to solve the problem. Trying each answer choice may take longer than simply solving the problem.*

PRACTICE 5

A. Use guess-and-check to solve the following problems.

1. A number divided by 2 is equal to 12 less than the original number. What is the number?
   A. 12
   B. 20
   C. 24
   D. 28

2. For a fund-raiser, Sandra raised three times as much money as Barbara, and Barbara raised $50 more than Matt. Together they raised $950. How much money did Barbara raise?
   A. $150
   B. $175
   C. $200
   D. $325

3. The three packages below weigh a total of 15 pounds.

   The first package weighs twice as much as the second package. The third package weighs three times as much as the second package. How many pounds does the first package weigh?
   A. 2
   B. 4
   C. 5
   D. $6\frac{1}{2}$

4. Hannah scored a total of 170 points on two math tests. The score of the first test was 6 points lower than the score of the second test. How many points did Hannah score on the first test?
   A. 76
   B. 82
   C. 88
   D. 90

5. Nelson is twice as old as Maria. Six years ago, Nelson was five times as old as Maria. How old was Nelson six years ago?
   A. 5
   B. 10
   C. 15
   D. 20

6. Which of the following is a solution for the quadratic equation $2x^2 + x - 15 = 0$?
   A. −3
   B. −1
   C. 2
   D. 3

7. An amusement park sells adults' and children's passes. An adult's pass is $25, and a child's pass is $15. A group spent $440 on 20 passes. How many children's passes did the group purchase?
   A. 5
   B. 6
   C. 9
   D. 14

8. The rectangular garden below is twice as long as it is wide. If the total distance around the garden is 120 feet, what is the width of the garden in feet?

   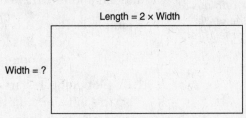

   A. 15
   B. 20
   C. 30
   D. 40

Answers and explanations begin on page 670.

EQUATIONS, INEQUALITIES, AND FUNCTIONS

The Coordinate Plane

Key Ideas

- A coordinate grid is formed by two intersecting axes, or number lines.
- The *x*-axis is horizontal, and the *y*-axis is vertical.
- The location of a point is shown by two numbers called an ordered pair: (*x*, *y*).

A **coordinate grid** is a way to locate points that lie in a **plane,** or flat surface. The grid is formed by two intersecting lines, an *x*-axis and a *y*-axis. The *x*-axis is actually a horizontal number line, and the *y*-axis is a vertical number line. The point at which the two axes intersect is called the **origin.**

Each point on the grid can be named using two numbers called an **ordered pair.** The first number is the distance from the origin along the *x*-axis. The second number is the distance from the origin along the *y*-axis. The numbers are written in parentheses and are separated by a comma: (*x, y*).

Example 1: Write the ordered pairs for points *M* and *P*.

1. Point *M* lies 2 spaces to the right of the origin along the *x*-axis and 3 spaces above the origin along the *y*-axis. The coordinates are **(2, 3).**

2. Point *P* lies 1 space to the left along the *x*-axis and 3 spaces down along the *y*-axis. The coordinates are **(−1, −3).**

To plot points on the grid, use the number lines located at the axes. Remember that right and up are the directions for positive numbers and left and down are the directions for negative numbers.

Example 2: Point *A* is located at (−2, 1), and point *B* is located at (3, −2). Plot these points on a coordinate grid.

1. To plot point *A*, start at the origin. Count 2 spaces left along the *x*-axis. Count 1 space up along the *y*-axis.

2. To plot point *B*, start at the origin. Count 3 spaces right along the *x*-axis. Count 2 spaces down along the *y*-axis.

A. Write the ordered pair for each point.

1. Point *A*
2. Point *B*
3. Point *C*
4. Point *D*
5. Point *E*
6. Point *F*
7. Point *G*
8. Point *H*

B. Plot the points on the coordinate grid.

9. Plot the following points:

   J at $(-3, -2)$

   K at $(4, 0)$

   L at $(1, -3)$

   M at $(-4, 2)$

10. Plot the following points:

    N at $(0, -1)$

    O at $(-4, -4)$

    P at $(3, 1)$

    Q at $(-3, 0)$

C. Choose the one best answer to each question.

11. On the coordinate grid below, a line passes through points *A* and *B*.

Which of the following ordered pairs also lies on the line?

A. $(1, 0)$
B. $(1, -1)$
C. $(0, -1)$
D. $(-1, 0)$

12. Two of the corners of a triangle are located at $(3, -3)$ and $(2, 3)$. What is the location of the third corner as shown in the diagram below?

A. $(-3, -2)$
B. $(-3, 2)$
C. $(-2, -3)$
D. $(3, -2)$

Answers and explanations begin on page 670.

EQUATIONS, INEQUALITIES, AND FUNCTIONS

Graphing a Line

Using the coordinate system, we can graph equations. When an equation has only two variables, x and y, and neither is raised to a power, the graph of the equation will be a line. When the graph of an equation is a straight line, the equation is a **linear equation.**

Key Ideas

- A linear equation has two variables, x and y.
- When the solutions to a linear equation are graphed on a coordinate grid, the graph forms a line.
- To find a point on the line, substitute a value for x and solve for y.
- You must solve for at least two points in order to draw the line.

To graph an equation, you need to solve for two points on the line.

Example 1: Graph the equation $y = 3x - 4$.

1. Choose any value for x and solve for y. Let $x = 1$.

$$y = 3(1) - 4$$
$$y = 3 - 4$$
$$y = -1$$

If $x = 1$, then $y = -1$. The ordered pair for the first point is $(1, -1)$.

2. Choose another value for x and solve for y. Let $x = 2$.

$$y = 3(2) - 4$$
$$y = 6 - 4$$
$$y = 2$$

If $x = 2$, then $y = 2$. The ordered pair for the second point is $(2, 2)$.

3. Plot the points on a coordinate grid and draw a line through them.

The line is the graph of all the possible solutions for the equation $y = 3x - 4$. Arrows at both ends of the line indicate that the line continues in both directions. From this, you can see that there is an infinite number of solutions to a linear equation.

GED® TEST TIP

If a linear equation is not written with y *on one side of the equation, use inverse operations to isolate* y*. Example:* $2x + y = 15$*. Subtract 2x from each side.* $y = -2x + 15$*.*

Some linear equation problems don't require you to draw a graph.

Example 2: Point A lies at $(5, -6)$ on a coordinate grid. The graph of which of the following equations passes through point A?

      (1) $y = -5x + 18$
      (2) $y = -4x + 14$
      (3) $y = -2x - 13$

Use the ordered pair given in the problem. Substitute the x-coordinate, 5, for x in each equation and solve for y. If $y = -6$, the value of the y-coordinate from the ordered pair, you have found the correct equation.

Option (2) is correct.

$$y = -4x + 14$$
$$y = -4(5) + 14$$
$$y = -20 + 14 = -6$$

PRACTICE 7

A. Fill in the y column in each table and graph the equation.

1. $y = \frac{1}{2}x + 3$

If $x =$	then $y =$
−2	
0	
2	

2. $y + 3x = -1$

If $x =$	then $y =$
−1	
0	
1	

3. $-2 + y = -x$

If $x =$	then $y =$
1	
2	
3	

4. $y = 3 - 2x$

If $x =$	then $y =$
0	
1	
2	

B. Choose the <u>one best answer</u> to each question.

<u>Questions 5 and 6</u> refer to the following coordinate grid.

5. The graph of the equation $y = \frac{1}{4}x$ will pass through which of the following pairs of points?

   A. point S and $(-1, 2)$
   B. point S and $(0, -2)$
   C. point T and $(0, 0)$
   D. point T and $(0, -2)$

6. Line P is the graph of which of the following equations?

   A. $y = 4x + 1$
   B. $y = -4x - 1$
   C. $y = 4x + 2$
   D. $y = -4x - 2$

7. Point C is located at $(-3, 5)$. A graph of which of the following equations would pass through point C?

   A. $3x + 2y = 5$
   B. $2x + 3y = 9$
   C. $4x - 2y = 8$
   D. $3x - 3y = 6$

Answers and explanations begin on page 670.

EQUATIONS, INEQUALITIES, AND FUNCTIONS

Slope of a Line

Key Ideas

- Slope is the ratio of rise to run.
- Moving from left to right, a line that goes upward has a positive slope, and a line that moves downward has a negative slope.
- You can find slope by counting spaces and writing a ratio or by using the slope formula.

Slope is the measurement of the steepness of a line. Imagine a road going up a hill. If the road must climb upward over a short forward distance, the road will be very steep. Slope measures the relationship between **rise** (how high the road must climb) and **run** (the distance the road goes forward).

On a coordinate grid, a line that moves upward from left to right has a **positive slope.** A line that moves downward from left to right has a **negative slope.** You can find the slope of a line on a coordinate grid by writing the ratio of rise to run.

Example 1: What is the slope of line P shown on the coordinate grid?

1. Find two points on line P. Count to find the rise and run. The line moves up 1 space for every 2 spaces it goes to the right.

2. Write the ratio: $\dfrac{\text{rise}}{\text{run}} = \dfrac{1}{2}$. The slope is $\dfrac{1}{2}$.

Example 2: What is the slope of line S shown on the coordinate grid?

1. Find any two points on line S. The line moves down 6 spaces (a negative direction) and 2 spaces to the right.

2. Write the ratio: $\dfrac{\text{rise}}{\text{run}} = \dfrac{-6}{2} = -3$.

The slope of line S is **−3.**

You can also find slope using the slope formula on the GED® Formula Sheet. The formula will appear as follows:

slope of a line $(m) = \dfrac{y_2 - y_1}{x_2 - x_1}$, where (x_1, y_1) and (x_2, y_2) are two points on a line.

Example 3: A line passes through points at coordinates (1, 4) and (−5, 2). What is the slope of the line?

1. Choose one point to be (x_1, y_1). The other will be (x_2, y_2). It doesn't matter which you choose. For this example, $(x_1, y_1) = (1, 4)$ and $(x_2, y_2) = (-5, 2)$.

2. Substitute the values into the slope formula and solve:

$$\frac{y_2 - y_1}{x_2 - x_1} \qquad \frac{2-4}{-5-1} = \frac{-2}{-6} = \frac{1}{3} \qquad \text{The slope is } \frac{1}{3}.$$

Since the slope is positive, you know that the line rises from left to right. You also know that it goes up 1 space for every 3 spaces it moves to the right.

In working with slope, there are a few special circumstances that you should memorize. A horizontal line, just like a flat stretch of roadway, has a **slope of 0**. The slope of a vertical line is **undefined**; in other words, our definition of slope will not work for a line that has no run at all.

PRACTICE 8

A. Find the slope of each line.

1.

2.

3.

B. Use the slope formula to find the slope of a line that passes through the following pairs of points.

4. (3, 5) and (−1, 2)

5. (0, 2) and (4, 0)

6. (4, 2) and (2, 2)

7. (6, 1) and (0, 3)

8. (1, 4) and $(-2, -2)$

9. (4, −2) and (2, 4)

C. Choose the one best answer for each question.

Question 10 refers to the following graph.

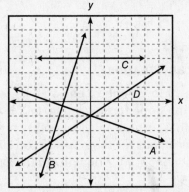

10. Which of the following lines shown on the graph has a slope of $-\frac{1}{3}$?

A. line *A*
B. line *B*
C. line *C*
D. line *D*

11. Line *N* passes through the following points: (0, 4), (1, 2), (2, 0), and (3, −2). What is the slope of line *N*?

A. −4
B. −2
C. 2
D. 4

12. Line *L* passes through point (1, 0) and has a slope of 3. Which of the following points also lies on line *L*?

A. (0, 3)
B. (1, 3)
C. (2, 3)
D. (2, 5)

Answers and explanations begin on page 671.

EQUATIONS, INEQUALITIES, AND FUNCTIONS

Slope and Equations

Use the Slope-Intercept Form to Find an Equation

Lesson 8 showed how to find the slope of a line and graph it. The examples in this lesson show how you can use the slope and a point on the line to find the equation of a line in two different forms. (You might also need to find the equation of a line from two points. In this case, you would calculate the slope first, then use the slope and one of the points to find the equation.)

The first of these forms is the **slope-intercept form:** $y = mx + b$. In this form of the equation, the variable m stands for the **slope** of the line. The variable b stands for the **y-intercept,** which is the y-value at the point where the line crosses the y-axis. The variables x and y are the **x-** and **y-coordinates** of any point on the line and are usually written as an ordered pair.

Follow these steps to find the equation of a line in the slope-intercept form.

1. Substitute the values that you are given for the slope (m) and the x- and y-coordinates (x, y) into the slope-intercept equation. Be careful not to mix up x and y.

2. Use inverse operations to isolate b.

3. Rewrite the equation in slope-intercept form, leaving x and y as variables and substituting values for m and b.

Example 1: Use the slope-intercept form to find the equation of a line that has the slope $m = 4$ and passes through the point $(-1, -6)$.

1. $-6 = (4) \times (-1) + b$

   $-6 = -4 + b$

2. $-2 = b$

3. $y = 4x - 2$

Use the Point-Slope Form to Find an Equation

The second important form that is used to describe a line on the *Mathematical Reasoning Test* is the **point-slope form:** $y - y_1 = m(x - x_1)$. In this form, (x_1, y_1) is an ordered pair that corresponds to a point on the line. As in the slope-intercept form, m stands for the slope. If you simplify an equation in point-slope form by solving for y, you will get the slope-intercept form of the equation.

Follow these steps to find the equation of a line in the point-slope form.

1. Call the point that you are given (x_1, y_1).

2. Put the x_1 and y_1 values into the point-slope equation.

3. Put the slope value in the point-slope equation for m.

Example 2: Use the point-slope form to find the equation of the line that passes through the point (4, 3) and has a slope of 2.

1. $(x_1, y_1) = (4, 3)$

2. $y - 3 = m(x - 4)$

3. $y - 3 = 2(x - 4)$

Notice that you can simplify the equation to find the slope-intercept form:

$$y - 3 = 2(x - 4)$$
$$y - 3 = 2x - 8$$
$$y = 2x - 5$$

PRACTICE 9

A. Use the slope-intercept form, $y = mx + b$, to find the equation of the line that passes through the given point and has the given slope.

1. $(1, -2); m = -4$ 2. $(-1, -4); m = 2$ 3. $(-4, 2); m = -\frac{1}{3}$

B. Use the point-slope form, $y - y_1 = m(x - x_1)$, to find the equation of the line that passes through the given point and has the given slope.

4. $(2, 1); m = 3$ 5. $(2, 0); m = -\frac{1}{3}$ 6. $(1, -2); m = 1$

C. Find the equation of the line that passes through the given points. Write your answer in slope-intercept form.

7. $(-5, 3), (1, 1)$ 8. $(-3, 0), (-2, 4)$ 9. $(-3, -4), (7, 1)$

D. Choose the <u>one best answer</u> for each question.

10. Which of the following is an equation for the line that passes through $(-1, 0)$ and $(2, -3)$?

     A. $y = 3x + 3$
     B. $y = -3x + 9$
     C. $y = -x - 1$
     D. $y = x - 5$

11. Which of the following is an equation for the line that passes through $(-3, 4)$ and $(1, 4)$?

     A. $y = 0$
     B. $y = 4$
     C. $y = x + 3$
     D. $y = x + 7$

12. Which of the following equations describes the same line as $y - 2 = \frac{1}{2}(x - 6)$?

     A. $y = 3x + 2$
     B. $y = \frac{1}{2}x - 4$
     C. $y = -x + 12$
     D. $y = \frac{1}{2}x - 1$

Question 13 refers to the following graph.

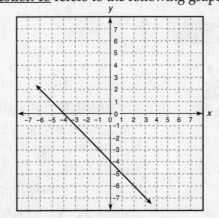

13. Which of the following equations correctly describes the line on the graph?

     A. $y = x - 4$
     B. $y = -x - 4$
     C. $y = x + 4$
     D. $y = -x + 4$

Answers and explanations start on page 671.

EQUATIONS, INEQUALITIES, AND FUNCTIONS

Systems of Linear Equations

Graph to Solve the System of Equations

The equations in Lessons 7 and 9 are **linear equations**: they have two variables, *x* and *y*, and represent straight lines in the coordinate plane. Two or more linear equations make up a **system of linear equations**. Solving a system of two equations means finding the values of both variables. The **solution** will give the *x*- and *y*-coordinates of the point at which the two lines intersect. You can express this solution as an ordered pair: (x, y).

One way to solve a system of equations is by graphing each equation using a **T-chart**—like those that you filled in for the Lesson 7 practice. Graphing a system of linear equations provides a picture of the intersection. Follow these steps to solve a system of equations by graphing.

1. Set up an *x* and *y* T-chart for each equation. Find two ordered pairs for each equation: use $x = 0$ and find *y* and then use $y = 0$ and find *x*.
2. Graph both lines, using the ordered pairs that you generated in step 1.
3. Find the point of intersection and express it in the form (x, y).

Example 1: Graph the equations $6x + 3y = 12$ and $5x + y = 7$ to find the solution.

1.

$6x + 3y = 12$

X	Y
0	4
2	0

$5x + y = 7$

X	Y
0	7
$\frac{7}{5}$	0

2.

3. The point of intersection—that is, the solution—is **(1, 2)**.

Substitute to Solve the System of Equations

You can also use **substitution** to solve a system of linear equations. Follow these steps to solve a system of linear equations by substitution.

Example 2: Solve the equations $6x + 3y = 12$ and $5x + y = 7$ by substitution.

1. Solve the first equation so that *y* is expressed in terms of *x*.

$$6x + 3y = 12$$
$$3y = 12 - 6x$$
$$y = 4 - 2x$$

2. Substitute that value of *y* into the second equation and solve for *x*.

$$5x + (4 - 2x) = 7$$
$$3x + 4 = 7$$
$$3x = 3$$
$$x = 1$$

3. Substitute that value of *x* into the first equation and solve for *y*.

$$6(1) + 3y = 12$$
$$6 + 3y = 12$$
$$3y = 6$$
$$y = 2$$

The solution is **(1, 2)**.

PRACTICE 10

A. Find two pairs of coordinates for each equation by making a T-chart. Use the coordinates to graph the lines and find the solution.

1. $y = 3x - 15$
   $x + y = 13$

2. $4x + 2y = 10$
   $y = -5x - 4$

B. Find the solution for the two equations by substitution. Express as an ordered pair in the form (x, y).

3. $7x - y = 22$
   $4x + 2y = 10$

4. $x + y = 9$
   $2x - 3y = 8$

5. $y = 3x + 15$
   $5x - 2y = -26$

6. $10x - y = -1$
   $y = 12x$

C. Choose the <u>one best answer</u> for each question.

7. Where does the line with the equation $x - 2y = 4$ intersect with the line with the equation $6y + 5x = 4$?

   A. $(2, -1)$
   B. $(3, -2)$
   C. $(-2, 1)$
   D. $(-1, 2)$

8. Where does the line with the equation $y = x$ intersect with the line with the equation $y = -x$?

   A. $(1, -1)$
   B. $(-1, 1)$
   C. $(0, 0)$
   D. $(1, 0)$

9. Where does the line with the equation $y = -2$ intersect with the line with the equation $3y = 2x + 3$?

   A. $(-\frac{2}{9}, -2)$
   B. $(-\frac{1}{3}, -2)$
   C. $(-\frac{9}{2}, -2)$
   D. $(\frac{9}{2}, 2)$

10. Which of the following is the equation of a line that intersects $y = 4x + 2$?

    A. $2y = 8x + 2$
    B. $y = 4x - 2$
    C. $y = -4x + 2$
    D. $\frac{1}{2}y = 2x - 7$

Answers and explanations start on page 672.

Patterns and Functions

Key Ideas

- A pattern is a sequence of numbers determined by a mathematical rule.
- A function is a rule that shows how one set of numbers is related to another set of numbers.
- To use a function, substitute values for variables and solve.

A **pattern** is a series of numbers or objects whose sequence is determined by a particular rule. You can figure out what rule has been used by studying the terms you are given. Think: What operation or sequence of operations will always result in the next term in the series? Once you know the rule, you can continue the pattern.

Example 1: Find the seventh term in the sequence: 1, 2, 4, 8, 16, . . .

1. Determine the rule. Each number in the sequence is two times the number before it.

2. Apply the rule. You have been given five terms and must find the seventh. Continue the pattern. The sixth term is $16 \times 2 = 32$, and the seventh term is $32 \times 2 = \mathbf{64}$.

A **function** is a rule that shows how the terms in one sequence of numbers are related to the terms in another sequence. Each distinct number entered into the function produces a unique output. For example, a sidewalk vendor charges $1.50 for a slice of pizza. The chart below shows how much it would cost to buy one to six slices.

Number of Pizza Slices	1	2	3	4	5	6
Cost	$1.50	$3.00	$4.50	$6.00	$7.50	$9.00

Each number in the first row corresponds to a price in the second row. We could say that the amount a customer will pay is a function of (or depends upon) the number of slices the customer orders. This function could be written:

Cost = number of slices $\times$ $1.50, or $C = n(\$1.50)$.

If you know the function and a number in the first set of numbers, you can solve for its corresponding number in the second set.

Example 2: Using the function $y = 3x + 5$, what is the value of y when $x = -3$?

1. Substitute the given value of x. $y = 3(-3) + 5$
2. Solve for y. $y = -9 + 5$
                                            $y = \mathbf{-4}$

Example 3: Using the function $n = 100 - 4(3 + m)$, what is the value of n when $m = 6$?

1. Substitute the given value of m. $n = 100 - 4(3 + 6)$
2. Solve for n. $n = 100 - 4(9)$
                                            $n = 100 - 36$
                                            $n = \mathbf{64}$

GED® TEST TIP

To figure out what rule has been used to form a pattern, begin by finding the difference between each term and the term that follows it in the sequence.

PRACTICE 11

A. Solve.

1. Which number should come next in the following pattern?

    $-12, -9, -6, -3,$ _____

2. What is the next number in the sequence?

    $21, 26, 31, 36,$ _____

3. In the function $y = 4x + 10$, if $x = -2$, what is the value of y?

4. In the function $y = 2x(4 + x) - 2$, if $x = 3$, what is the value of y?

5. Each term in the second row is determined by the function $y = 2x - 1$.

x	1	2	3	4	5	. . .	12
y	1	3	5	7	9	. . .	

    What number belongs in the shaded box?

6. In the function $y = \dfrac{x+3}{6} - 8$, if $x = 21$, what is the value of y?

7. What is the next term in the pattern below?

    $1000, 500, 250, 125, 62.5,$ _____

8. What is the next number in the sequence?

    $3, -5, 7, -9, 11,$ _____

9. Each term in the second row is determined by the function $y = 3x + 5$.

x	-2	-1	0	1	2	. . .	9
y	-1	2	5	8	11	. . .	

    What number belongs in the shaded box?

10. In the function $y = (x - 7) + 12$, if $x = -10$, what is the value of y?

B. Choose the <u>one best answer</u> to each question.

Question 11 refers to the following drawing.

11. How many blocks would be needed to build the 25th construction in the sequence?

    A. 47
    B. 49
    C. 51
    D. 55

12. What is the sixth term in the sequence below?

    $-14, -8, -2, 4, \ldots$

    A. 10
    B. 14
    C. 16
    D. 22

13. The price per scarf is a function of the number of scarves purchased. The table shows the price per scarf for purchases of up to four scarves.

number (n) of scarves	1	2	3	4
cost (c) per scarf	$5.00	$4.75	$4.50	$4.25

    Which of the following functions was used to determine the prices shown in the table?

    A. $c = n(\$5.00 - \$0.25)$
    B. $c = \$5.00 - \$0.25(n - 1)$
    C. $c = \$5.00 - \$0.25n$
    D. $c = \$5.00n - \$0.25n$

14. Which of the following sequences of values of y could be created using the function
    $y = 4x - 3$?

    A. $1, 4, 7, 10, 13, \ldots$
    B. $1, 5, 9, 13, 17, \ldots$
    C. $1, 4, 8, 13, 19, \ldots$
    D. $1, -1, -3, -5, -7, \ldots$

Answers and explanations begin on page 672.

EQUATIONS, INEQUALITIES, AND FUNCTIONS

Function Applications

Functions are used in many business applications. For instance, they can be used to calculate profit, cost, employee wages, and taxes. On the *Mathematical Reasoning Test*, you will read about common work and life situations. The problems may contain or describe a function that you can use to solve the problem.

Key Ideas

- Functions are used to make many common work calculations.
- Functions can be used to make comparisons.
- To use a function, you must know the meaning of the variables. This information should be given in the text of the problem.

Example 1: Celino Advertising is finishing a series of print ads for a client. Finishing the project will cost $2000 per day for the first seven days and $3500 per day after seven days. The finishing costs can be found using the function $C = \$2000d + \$1500(d - 7)$, where C = the cost of finishing the project and d = the number of days. If the project takes 12 days to complete, what will the project cost?

Use the function to solve the problem.

$$C = \$2000d + \$1500(d - 7)$$
$$= \$2000(12) + \$1500(12 - 7)$$
$$= \$24000 + \$1500(5)$$
$$= \$24000 + \$7500$$
$$= \mathbf{\$31,500}$$

You may be asked to use functions to make comparisons.

Example 2: Nita decides to join a health club. She gets brochures from two health clubs and compares the plans. Healthstars Fitness charges a one-time membership fee of $250 and $8 per month. Freedom Health Center charges $25 per month. At both health clubs, the price (P) Nita will pay is a function of the number of months (m) she attends the club. The functions are as follows:

Healthstars Fitness $\qquad P = \$250 + \$8m$

Freedom Health Center $\qquad P = \$25m$

Nita plans to move in 18 months. If she attends a health club until she moves, which one offers the better price?

1. Find the price at Healthstars Fitness:

$$P = \$250 + \$8m$$
$$= \$250 + \$8(18)$$
$$= \$250 + \$144$$
$$= \$394$$

2. Find the price at Freedom Health Center:

$$P = \$25m$$
$$= \$25(18)$$
$$= \$450$$

3. Compare the results. Even though Nita will have to pay a large amount up front, **Healthstars Fitness** offers the better price.

GED® TEST TIP

There is often more than one way to work a problem, even when a function is given. Solve using the function. If you see another way to solve the problem, use it to check your answer.

PRACTICE 12

A. Solve. You MAY use a calculator.

1. The Chimney Sweep charges $25 for a chimney inspection. If the customer purchases additional services, $15 of the inspection fee is deducted. Let $s = $ the cost of any additional services. The total cost (C) of an inspection and services can be determined by the function $C = \$25 + (s - \$15)$ where s is not 0.

   a. Jan has her chimney inspected and purchases a smoke guard for $89. How much will she be charged?

   b. After an inspection, Ahmed decides to have a new damper installed for $255. How much will he pay?

2. Ricardo does a great deal of driving for his work. He generally estimates his driving time in hours (t) using the function $t = \frac{m}{60}$, where $m = $ the number of miles.

   a. How many hours will it take Ricardo to drive 330 miles?

   b. How many hours will it take Ricardo to drive 255 miles?

3. A customer's phone charges are a function of the number of minutes of long-distance calls made. The graph shows a comparison of two plans available.

Long-Distance Plan Cost Comparison

   a. Michelle looks at her previous phone bills and finds that she makes about 350 minutes of long-distance calls per month. Which plan is better for her?

   b. Craig usually makes about 150 minutes of long-distance calls per month. Which plan is better for him?

B. Choose the one best answer to each question. You MAY use a calculator.

Questions 4 and 5 refer to the following information.

Alicia is considering three job opportunities. At all three jobs, weekly pay (P) is a function of the number of hours (h) worked during the week. The functions are shown below:

Job 1	$P = \$9.75h$
Job 2	$P = \$70 + \$8.40h$
Job 3	$P = \$380 \times \frac{h}{38}$

4. If Alicia works 30 hours in a week, how much more will she earn at Job 2 than at Job 1?

   A. $5.33
   B. $29.50
   C. $40.50
   D. $59.00

5. If Alicia works 40 hours per week, which of the following is a true statement?

   A. Alicia will earn the least at Job 3.
   B. Job 1 will pay more than Job 3.
   C. Job 3 will pay more than Job 2.
   D. Alicia will earn the most at Job 2.

6. A company is awarded a $95,000 job that will cost $5,400 per day in expenses. Profits (P) can be calculated using $P = \$95,000 - \$5,400d$, where $d = $ days. What is the company's profit if the job takes 14 days to complete?

   A. $10,800
   B. $19,400
   C. $66,100
   D. $75,600

Answers and explanations begin on page 673.

EQUATIONS, INEQUALITIES, AND FUNCTIONS
PRACTICE QUESTIONS

Directions: You MAY use your calculator.

1. Which of the following expressions is equal to $6 - 4(x + 3)$?

   A. $4x + 3$
   B. $4x - 9$
   C. $-4x - 3$
   D. $-4x - 6$

2. Three increased by the product of 4 and a number is equal to the same number decreased by 6. What is the number?

   A. -3
   B. -1
   C. 1
   D. 3

3. What is the equation of a line with a slope of -4 that passes through the point $(1, 2)$?

   A. $y = -4x + 2$
   B. $y = -4x + 6$
   C. $y = 4x + 1$
   D. $y = 4x + 6$

4. The ordered pair $(-2, -1)$ is a solution to which of the following equations?

   A. $-4x - y = 7$
   B. $4x + y = -7$
   C. $4x - y = -7$
   D. $-4x + y = -7$

5. For a two-week period, Jan earned $150 less than twice Tom's earnings. Together Jan and Tom earned $1380. How much did Tom earn?

   A. $720
   B. $660
   C. $510
   D. $360

Questions 6 and 7 refer to the following graph.

6. If the graph of the equation $y = -x - 5$ were drawn on the grid, which of the points would be on the line?

   A. A
   B. B
   C. C
   D. D

7. If a line were drawn through points B and C, what would be the slope of the line?

   A. -3
   B. $-\frac{1}{3}$
   C. $\frac{1}{3}$
   D. 3

8. Samuel is paid $350 per month plus a 10% commission on his total sales for the month. If he needs to earn at least $2100 per month, which of the following expressions represents the total sales (s) Samuel needs to achieve?

   A. $s \geq \$17,500$
   B. $s \leq \$17,500$
   C. $s \leq \$21,000$
   D. $s \geq \$21,000$

9. For its Checking Plus account, a bank charges $3.95 per month plus $0.10 for each check written after the first ten checks written that month. The function to find the total monthly fee (F) is $F = \$3.95 + \$0.10(n - 10)$, where n = number of checks written.

Greg writes 24 checks in March. How much will he pay in fees for the month?

A. $6.35
B. $5.35
C. $2.40
D. $1.40

10. The sum of four consecutive odd numbers is 104. What is the largest number?

A. 23
B. 25
C. 27
D. 29

11. Which value for x makes the inequality $x > 400$ true?

A. 7^3
B. 4^4
C. 3^6
D. 6^3

12. Four less than the product of a number (x) and 5 is equal to 8 more than 2 added to 3 times the number. Which of these equations could be used to find the value of x?

A. $4 - 5x = 8 + 2 + 3x$
B. $5x - 4 = 8 + 2 + 3x$
C. $5x = 4 - 8 + 2 + 3x$
D. $5x - 4 = 8 + 2 + 3$

13. What is the slope of a line that passes through the points (2, 4) and (4, 6)?

A. −2
B. 1
C. 2
D. 4

14. What is the next number in the sequence?

1, 7, 14, 22, ...

A. 30
B. 31
C. 32
D. 33

15. What is the y-intercept of the line with a slope of 2 that passes through the point (1, 2)?

A. −2
B. $-\frac{1}{2}$
C. 0
D. $\frac{1}{2}$

16. The graphs of the equations $y = x + 3$ and $y = -2x - 3$ are drawn on a coordinate grid.

In the coordinate plane below, darken the circle corresponding to the point at which the two lines intersect.

17. Which of the following shows the product of −7 and x decreased by the sum of 8 and y?

   A. $-7x - (8 + y)$
   B. $-7x - 8 + y$
   C. $(8 + y) - 7x$
   D. $(7 + x) - (8 + y)$

18. What are the possible solutions for the quadratic equation $x^2 - 5x = 24$?

   A. −8 and 3
   B. −6 and 4
   C. 8 and −3
   D. 4 and −6

19. Cynthia is 6 times as old as Rebecca. In 6 years, Cynthia will be only 3 times as old as Rebecca. How old is Rebecca now?

   A. 3
   B. 4
   C. 8
   D. 12

20. The graph of which equation will pass through points (0, −3) and (5, 7)?

   A. $x = \frac{1}{2}x - 3$
   B. $y = 2x - 3$
   C. $y = 2x + 7$
   D. $y = -2x + 3$

21. Which of the following graphs represents the solution set of the inequality $-2(x - 6) > 8$?

   A. ![number line −5 −4 −3 −2 −1 0 1 2 3 4 5, open circle at −1]
   B. ![number line −5 −4 −3 −2 −1 0 1 2 3 4 5, closed circle at 2]
   C. ![number line −5 −4 −3 −2 −1 0 1 2 3 4 5, open circle at −2]
   D. ![number line −5 −4 −3 −2 −1 0 1 2 3 4 5, open circle at 2]

Questions 22 and 23 refer to the following graph.

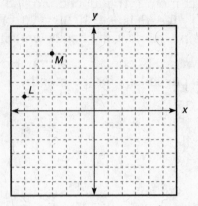

22. Which of the following ordered pairs shows the location of point L?

   A. (−5, −1)
   B. (−5, 1)
   C. (−1, 5)
   D. (1, −5)

23. What is the slope of the line that passes through points L and M?

   A. $\frac{-3}{2}$
   B. $\frac{-2}{3}$
   C. $\frac{2}{3}$
   D. $\frac{3}{2}$

24. Bob, Celia, Sam, and Daniel contributed money to buy their boss a retirement gift. Sam and Daniel each gave the same amount of money. Celia gave $12 more than Daniel. Bob gave half as much as Celia gave. If the four workers gave a total of $81, how much did Sam give?

   A. $9
   B. $15
   C. $18
   D. $21

25. What is the solution set of the inequality
$-7x - 4 \geq x - 28$

    A. $x \leq 3$
    B. $x \geq 3$
    C. $x \leq -3$
    D. $x \geq -4$

26. A line goes through the points (0, 2) and (1, 3). What is the equation of the line?

    A. $y = -\frac{1}{2}x + 3$
    B. $y = \frac{1}{2}x + 2$
    C. $y = x + 2$
    D. $y = x + 3$

27. In a recent election, Perez got 5512 more votes than $\frac{1}{3}$ of the leading candidate's votes. Together the two candidates received 18,072 votes. How many people voted for Perez?

    A. 6,024
    B. 8,652
    C. 9,420
    D. 12,560

28. What is the value of x in the equation
$-4(x + 2) - 10 = 5x$?

    A. $x = -18$
    B. $x = -2$
    C. $x = 2$
    D. $x = 18$

29. Marcia counts the $5 bills and $10 bills in her cash register drawer. She counts a total of 35 bills with a total value of $240. If $x =$ the number of $5 bills in the drawer, which of the following equations could be used to find the number of $5 bills in the drawer?

    A. $\$5x + \$10x = 35$
    B. $\$5x + \$10x + 35 = \$240$
    C. $\$5(35 - x) + \$10x = \$240$
    D. $\$5x + \$10(35 - x) = \$240$

30. The sum of five consecutive numbers is 370. What is the fourth number in the sequence?

    A. 73
    B. 74
    C. 75
    D. 76

31. A baseball pitcher's earned run average (E) is a function of the number of earned runs (r) given up and innings pitched (i). The function is written $E = \dfrac{9r}{i}$. What is the earned run average of a pitcher who gives up 8 runs in 18 innings?

Write your answer on the line below.

_____

32. Point B is located halfway between $(-1, 5)$ and $(-1, -3)$. Name the location of point B.

In the coordinate plane below, darken the circle corresponding to the location of point B.

Answers and explanations begin on page 674.

GEOMETRY

Plane Figures

Four-Sided Plane Figures

A **plane figure** is a set of line segments, all lying on a single plane. To prepare for the GED® *Mathematical Reasoning Test*, learn the properties of each shape. You will need to identify the characteristics of different types of four-sided plane figures and draw conclusions about their angles and sides.

You are already familiar with rectangles and squares. A **rectangle** is a four-sided figure with four right angles. The opposite sides (sides across from each other) are the same length, and they are parallel.

Sides with the same markings are equal.

A **square** is actually a kind of rectangle. It, too, has four right angles with parallel opposite sides. However, a square has one additional property: its four sides are all the same length.

A **parallelogram** is a four-sided figure whose opposite sides are parallel and the same length. In addition, its opposite angles (the angles diagonally across from each other) are also equal in measure. A special parallelogram, called a **rhombus** (not shown), has four sides of equal length.

A **trapezoid** is a four-sided figure with exactly one pair of parallel sides. The definition of a trapezoid does not dictate the measure of the angles or the lengths of the sides.

All four-sided plane figures have one important property in common. The sum of the measures of the interior angles is 360°. You can use this fact to find a missing angle measure.

Example: In figure *ABCD*, the opposite sides are parallel. What is the measure of ∠*A*?

1. Identify the figure. The notation on the drawing tells you that the opposite sides are equal in measure. Since they are also parallel, the figure is a parallelogram.

2. Find the measure of ∠*C*. The opposite angles of a parallelogram are equal in measure; therefore, $m\angle C = m\angle B$. Both ∠*B* and ∠*C* measure 110°.

3. Find the measure of $\angle A$. You know the measures of $\angle A$ and $\angle D$ are equal and that the sum of all four angles equals 360°. Let $x = m\angle A$. Therefore, $2x =$ the sum of $m\angle A$ and $m\angle D$. Write an equation and solve.

$$2x + 110° + 110° = 360°$$
$$2x + 220° = 360°$$
$$2x = 140°$$
$$x = 70°$$

The measure of $\angle A$ is **70°**.

PRACTICE 1

A. List the names of four-sided plane figures introduced on page 378 that can exhibit the following properties. Write *None* if no four-sided plane figure has the given property.

1. four right angles
2. opposite sides are equal in length
3. exactly one pair of parallel sides
4. all angles are equal in measure
5. only three right angles
6. opposite angles are equal in measure
7. all four sides are equal in length
8. sum of interior angles is 360°
9. sides are all of different lengths
10. four equal angles and four equal sides

B. Choose the <u>one best answer</u> to each question.

<u>Questions 11 and 12</u> refer to the following figure.

11. Angle F is 20° more than three times the measure of $\angle H$. What is the measure of $\angle F$?

    A. 40°
    B. 120°
    C. 140°
    D. 180°

12. In order for figure *EFGH* to be a trapezoid, which of the following must be a true statement?

    A. *EF* is the same length as *FH*.
    B. $EF \parallel GH$.
    C. $m\angle F = m\angle H$.
    D. $m\angle G = m\angle F$.

<u>Question 13</u> refers to the following figure.

13. If the opposite sides in figure *RSUT* are parallel, what is the measure of $\angle R$?

    A. 5°
    B. 20°
    C. 90°
    D. 270°

14. A four-sided plane figure has sides measuring 10, 15, 10, and 15. The opposite angles are equal, but there are no right angles. What is the figure?

    A. rhombus
    B. rectangle
    C. parallelogram
    D. trapezoid

Answers and explanations begin on page 674.

GEOMETRY

Triangles

The Properties of Triangles

A **triangle** is a closed three-sided plane figure. From the definition, we can infer other properties. Since a triangle has three sides, it must also have three interior angles and three vertices.

A triangle is named by writing its vertices in any order. The triangle shown at right could be named $\triangle DEF$. Its sides are DE, EF, and DF.

Triangles can be classified by the lengths of their sides and by the measures of their angles. In the figures below, sides with the same number of marks are equal.

Classified by Side Lengths

equilateral triangle
All sides are equal in length. Note that the angles also are equal.

isosceles triangle
Exactly two sides are equal in length. Note that the two angles opposite these sides are equal.

scalene triangle
No sides are equal in length, and no angles are equal.

Classified by Angle Measures

right triangle
One angle measures 90°.

acute triangle
All angles measure less than 90°.

obtuse triangle
One angle is greater than 90°.

Each triangle can be classified in two ways.

Example 1: What kind of triangle is $\triangle PQR$?

1. Classify by its sides: Two sides have the same length, so $\triangle PQR$ is an isosceles triangle.

2. Classify by its angles: $\angle P$ is a right angle, so $\triangle PQR$ is a right triangle.

$\triangle PQR$ is a **right isosceles triangle**.

The sum of the measures of the interior angles of any triangle is 180°. We can use this fact to solve for a missing angle.

Example 2: In △ABC, ∠A measures 55° and ∠B measures 100°. What is the measure of ∠C?

Write an equation and solve.

$$55° + 100° + ∠C = 180°$$
$$155° + ∠C = 180°$$
$$∠C = 25°$$

The measure of ∠C is **25°**.

PRACTICE 2

A. Classify each triangle in two ways.

1.

2.

3.

B. Find the measure of the unknown angle in each triangle.

4.

5.

6.

C. Choose the <u>one best answer</u> to each question.

<u>Questions 7 and 8</u> refer to the following figure.

7. If ∠DAB measures 115° and ∠DCB measures 95°, what is the length of side AC in centimeters? (*Hint*: Use the facts in the problem to find *m*∠BAC and *m*∠BCA.)

A. 6
B. 8
C. 14
D. 22

8. What kind of triangle is △ACD?
   A. isosceles
   B. acute
   C. right
   D. obtuse

---

9. One angle in a scalene triangle measures 38°, and another angle measures 56°. What is the measure of the third angle?

   A. 38°
   B. 56°
   C. 86°
   D. 124°

Answers and explanations begin on page 674.

GEOMETRY

Pythagorean Relationship

As you know, a right triangle has one right angle. The side directly across from the right angle, called the **hypotenuse**, is the longest side of the right triangle. The remaining sides, the rays of the right angle, are the **legs** of the triangle.

Key Ideas

- The hypotenuse is the longest side of a right triangle. It is found opposite the right angle.
- The sum of the squares of the legs of a right triangle equals the square of the hypotenuse.

Thousands of years ago, people found a special relationship, called the **Pythagorean relationship**, among the sides of a right triangle. You can use this relationship to find the measure of any side of a right triangle if the other two side measures are known.

Pythagorean relationship $a^2 + b^2 = c^2$; a and b are legs, and c is the hypotenuse of a right triangle

In other words, the square of the hypotenuse is equal to the sum of the squares of the two legs of the right triangle.

Example 1: What is the length of the hypotenuse of the right triangle shown in the diagram?

1. The lengths of the legs are 3 ft and 4 ft. Let one leg equal a and the other equal b.

2. Solve for c. Substitute the values.

$$a^2 + b^2 = c^2$$
$$3^2 + 4^2 = c^2$$
$$9 + 16 = c^2$$

3. When one side of an equation equals a squared variable, isolate the variable by finding the square root of both sides.

$$25 = c^2$$
$$\sqrt{25} = c$$
$$5 = c$$

The length of the hypotenuse is **5 feet**.

The Pythagorean relationship can also be used to solve for the length of a leg.

GED® TEST TIP

Watch for right triangles with sides in a 3-4-5 or 5-12-13 ratio. These triangles often appear on math tests because the measures of the sides are all whole numbers.

Example 2: If John places a 13-foot ladder 3 feet from the base of a wall, how far up the wall will the ladder reach to the nearest tenth of a foot?

The wall, ground, and ladder form a right triangle. The hypotenuse is 13 ft in length. One leg is 3 ft. You need to find the length of the other leg.

$$a^2 + b^2 = c^2$$
$$3^2 + b^2 = 13^2$$
$$9 + b^2 = 169$$
$$b^2 = 160$$
$$b = \sqrt{160}$$
$$b \approx 12.6$$

The ladder will extend **12.6 feet** up the wall.

NOTE: Most of the time, you will need to use your calculator for the final step when using the Pythagorean relationship. To find the square root of 160 on the TI-30XS MultiView™ calculator, press: 2nd x² 160 enter (use ◄► to convert the result from a radical to a decimal format).

Some right triangles display special proportions, which are worth memorizing.

- A right triangle whose angles are 45°, 45°, and 90° displays the following relationship:
  leg : leg : hypotenuse = $x : x : x\sqrt{2}$.

- A right triangle whose angles are 30°, 60°, and 90° displays the following relationship:
  leg : leg : hypotenuse = $x : x\sqrt{3} : 2x$.

PRACTICE 3

A. **The lengths of two sides of a right triangle are given. Find the length of the remaining side to the nearest tenth unit. You MAY use a calculator.**

1. leg *a*: 8 in.
   leg *b*: 8 in.
   hypotenuse *c*: ? in.

2. leg *a*: 9 yd
   leg *b*: 12 yd
   hypotenuse *c*: ? yd

3. leg *a*: 1.5 cm
   leg *b*: 2 cm
   hypotenuse *c*: ? cm

4. leg *a*: ? m
   leg *b*: 3 m
   hypotenuse *c*: 6 m

5. leg *a*: 6 mm
   leg *b*: ? mm
   hypotenuse *c*: 10 mm

6. leg *a*: ? ft
   leg *b*: 5 ft
   hypotenuse *c*: 18 ft

7. leg *a*: 7 cm
   leg *b*: 10 cm
   hypotenuse *c*: ? cm

8. leg *a*: 15 in.
   leg *b*: ? in.
   hypotenuse *c*: 30 in.

9. leg *a*: 4 km
   leg *b*: 5 km
   hypotenuse *c*: ? km

B. **Choose the one best answer to each question.**

10. On a coordinate plane, points *A*, *B*, and *C* can be connected to form a right triangle.

What is the distance from *A* to *C*, to the nearest tenth unit? (*Hint:* Count units to find the lengths of the sides and use the Pythagorean relationship to find the distance between the points.)

A. 5.2
B. 6.7
C. 8.4
D. 10.1

11. The two shorter sides of a right triangle measure 18 ft and 24 ft. What is the measure in feet of the third side?

A. 25
B. 28
C. 30
D. 42

12. Jan has built a rectangular frame out of wood to use for the bottom of a platform. He wants to add a diagonal brace as shown in the drawing below.

5 ft

11 ft

What will the length of the brace be, to the nearest tenth of a foot?

A. 16.0
B. 13.7
C. 12.8
D. 12.1

13. The hypotenuse of a right triangle measures 39 inches. If one leg measures 15 inches, what is the measure of the other leg, in inches?

A. 36
B. 24
C. 18
D. 12

Answers and explanations begin on page 675.

GEOMETRY

Perimeter and Area

Perimeter is the distance around a figure. To find perimeter, simply add the lengths of the sides. For common figures, you can apply a formula to find the perimeter. You need to memorize these formulas.

square	Perimeter $= 4 \times$ side	$P = 4s$
rectangle	Perimeter $= 2 \times$ length $+ 2 \times$ width	$P = 2l + 2w$
triangle	Perimeter $=$ side$_1 +$ side$_2 +$ side$_3$	$P = a + b + c$

Example 1: A rectangle is 16 inches long and 9 inches wide. What is the perimeter of the rectangle?

Use the formula: Perimeter $= 2 \times$ length $+ 2 \times$ width

$$= 2 \times 16 + 2 \times 9$$
$$= 32 + 18$$
$$= \mathbf{50 \ in.}$$

Area is the measure of the space inside a flat figure. Area is measured in square units. For example, if the sides of a figure are measured in inches, its area will be measured in square inches. The formulas for finding area are shown below.

square	Area $=$ side^2	$A = s^2$
rectangle	Area $=$ length $\times$ width	$A = lw$
parallelogram	Area $=$ base $\times$ height	$A = bh$
triangle	Area $= \frac{1}{2} \times$ base $\times$ height	$A = \frac{1}{2}bh$
trapezoid	Area $= \frac{1}{2} \times$ height (base$_1 +$ base$_2$)	$A = \frac{1}{2}h(b_1 + b_2)$

Three of the formulas mention two new measures: base and height. The **base** is one side of the figure. The **height** is the length from the vertex to the base, forming a right angle to the base.

Example 2: Find the area of figure *ABCD*.

1. Identify the figure. *ABCD* is a parallelogram.

2. Find the facts you need. To use the formula for finding the area of a parallelogram, you need to know the height and the length of the base. Ignore the length of side *BD*.

3. Use the formula Area $=$ base $\times$ height.

   Area $= 12 \times 7$

   $= \mathbf{84 \ sq \ cm \ or \ 84 \ cm^2}$

PRACTICE 4

A. Find the area and perimeter of each figure.

1.

2.

3.

4.

5.

6.

B. Choose the <u>one best answer</u> to each question.

<u>Question 7</u> refers to the following figure.

7. What is the area in square inches of the shaded portion of the rectangle?

   A. 38
   B. 40
   C. 56
   D. 88

8. The four sides of a retangle measure 9 feet, 6 feet, 9 feet, and 6 feet. What is the area of the retangle in square feet?

   A. 30
   B. 36
   C. 54
   D. 81

9. Martin is building a rectangular patio centered on one side of his yard. The rest of his yard, shown in the diagram, is planted in grass.

   If the measurements in the diagram are in feet, what is the square footage of the grass portion of Martin's yard?

   A. 108
   B. 162
   C. 324
   D. 432

10. A square measures 6 centimeters on one side. What is the perimeter of the square in centimeters?

   A. 12
   B. 24
   C. 36
   D. 216

Answers and explanations begin on page 675.

GEOMETRY

Circles

Circumference and Area

A **circle** is a closed set of points that are all the same distance from a single point, the center of the circle. The **circumference** of a circle is its perimeter, or the distance around the circle. The **area** of a circle is the space inside the circle.

To find perimeter and area of a circle, you need to know two other measures of a circle. The **diameter** is a line segment with endpoints on the circle that passes through the center of the circle. The **radius** is a line segment that connects the center of the circle to any point on the circle. As you can see from the diagram, the radius is one-half the diameter.

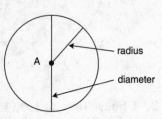

The formulas for circumference and area use a special quantity called **pi** (π). Pi is the ratio of the circumference to the diameter. It is equal to approximately 3.14. As far as we know, the digits for pi continue infinitely, so calculations with pi are always approximations. For the *Mathematical Reasoning Test*, you will use 3.14 as the value of pi. Below is the formula for finding the circumference of a circle.

Circumference $= \pi \times$ diameter, or $C = \pi d$

Example 1: A china plate has a gold rim. If the plate's diameter is 10.5 inches, what is the distance around the rim to the nearest tenth of an inch?

Use the formula: $C = \pi d$

$= 3.14(10.5)$

$= 32.97$, which rounds to **33.0 inches**

Use this formula to find the area of a circle: Area $= \pi \times$ radius^2, or $A = \pi r^2$.

Example 2: The circular surface of a satellite component must be covered with heat-resistant tiles. If the radius of the component is 4 meters, what is the area in square meters?

Use the formula: $A = \pi r^2$

$= 3.14(4^2)$

$= 3.14(16)$

$= $ **50.24 square meters**

In some situations, you may need to solve for either the diameter or radius. Remember, the diameter is twice the radius ($d = 2r$), and the radius is one-half the diameter: $r = \frac{1}{2}d$.

Key Ideas

- Pi, expressed as 3.14, is the ratio of the circumference of a circle to its diameter.
- To find circumference, multiply pi by the diameter (distance across) the circle.
- The radius is the distance from the center to the edge of the circle. To find area, multiply pi by the square of the radius.

GED® TEST TIP

You will need to memorize the formulas for circumference and area of a circle. They do not appear on the GED® Formulas Sheet.

Example 3: What is the circumference of circle B to the nearest tenth of a centimeter?

1. The radius of the circle is 5 cm. Therefore, the diameter is 2×5, or 10 cm.

2. Use the formula: $C = \pi d$
$$= 3.14(10)$$
$$= \mathbf{31.4 \, cm}$$

PRACTICE 5

A. **Find the circumference and area of each circle. Round answers to the nearest tenth.**

1.

10 in.

2.

2 cm

3.

4 m

B. **Choose the <u>one best answer</u> to each question.**

<u>Questions 4 and 5 refer to the following drawing.</u>

$d = 12$ ft

4. If workers lay a tile border around the edge of the fountain shown in the diagram, how many feet long will the border be to the nearest foot?

    A. 19
    B. 36
    C. 38
    D. 57

5. Which of the following expressions could be used to find the area of the bottom surface of the fountain?

    A. 3.14×6
    B. 3.14×6^2
    C. 3.14×12
    D. 3.14×12^2

6. The radius of a circle is 6.5 cm. What is the diameter of the circle in centimeters?

    A. 3.25
    B. 13.0
    C. 33.16625
    D. 132.665

7. On the target below, the 5- and 10-point bands are each 2 inches wide, and the inner circle has a diameter of 2 inches.

25

10

5

To the nearest inch, what is the outer circumference of the 10-point band?

    A. 6
    B. 13
    C. 19
    D. 113

Answers and explanations begin on page 675.

GEOMETRY

Volume

Rectangular Solids, Cubes, Cylinders, and Spheres

Volume, also called **capacity**, is the measure of space inside a three-dimensional object. You measure volume in cubic units. In other words, if the sides of an object are measured in inches, the volume is the number of cubes (one inch per side) you would need to fill the object.

Many common three-dimensional objects have at least two identical and parallel faces. Think of a cereal box or a soup can. Both objects have identical faces at the top and bottom of the container. Either of these faces can be called the base of the object. To find the volume of any container with identical bases, multiply the area of one base by the height of the object: Volume = area of base × height .

Another way to find the volume of an object is to use the formula that applies specifically to that object.

rectangular prism	Volume = base × height	$V = Bh$
cube	Volume = edge^3	$V = e^3$
cylinder	Volume = pi × radius^2 × height	$V = \pi r^2 h$
sphere	Volume = $\frac{4}{3}$ × pi × radius^3	$V = \frac{4}{3}\pi r^3$

In the examples below, formulas are used to find the answers, but the problems can also be solved by simply multiplying the area of the base by the height.

A **rectangular prism** has two identical rectangular bases. The remaining sides of the figure are also rectangles.

Example 1: A cardboard box has the dimensions shown in the diagram. What is the volume of the box in cubic feet?

Use the formula: $V = Bh$, where B is *length × width*
$$= (4 \times 5)(3) = \textbf{60 cubic feet}$$

A **cube** is a rectangular prism with six identical faces. In a cube, each edge (where the sides meet) is the same length.

Example 2: A wood block measures 2 inches per edge. What is the volume of the block?

Use the formula: $V = e^3$
$$= 2^3 = \textbf{8 cubic feet}$$

A **cylinder** has two circular bases. The bases are connected by a curved surface. Cans, barrels, and tanks are often in the shape of cylinders.

Example 3: A storage tank has a radius of 1.5 meters and a height of 3 meters. What is the volume of the tank to the nearest cubic meter?

Use the formula: $\quad V = \pi r^2 h$
$\quad\quad\quad\quad\quad\quad = 3.14(1.5^2)(3) = 21.195 \text{ m}^3,$
$\quad\quad\quad\quad$ which rounds to **21 cubic meters**

PRACTICE 6.1

A. Find the volume of each object to the nearest whole unit.

1.

4
5
8

3.

6
5

5.

1.5
1.5
1.5

2.

3
3
3

4.

7
6
10

6.

3
5

B. Choose the <u>one best answer</u> to each question.

Question 7 refers to the following drawing.

4 ft
4 ft

7. A rectangular box with a volume of 80 cubic feet has the length and width shown in the drawing. What is the height of the box?

A. 5
B. 10
C. 16
D. 20

_____

8. A wooden crate measures 5 feet along each edge. What is the crate's volume in cubic feet?

A. 15
B. 25
C. 125
D. 150

Question 9 refers to the following drawing.

9. Linda adds a water stabilizer to her children's swimming pool once a week. The instructions tell her to add one scoop of the product for every 20 cubic feet of water. About how many scoops should she add per week?

12 ft
3 ft

A. 3
B. 6
C. 17
D. 36

Answers and explanations begin on page 675.

Volume of Pyramids and Cones

A **pyramid** is a three-dimensional object with four triangle faces that connect to the same vertex. The base of a pyramid can be any closed figure, but the pyramids that you will see on the GED® *Mathematical Reasoning Test* will all have square bases.

The rectangular prism and the pyramid shown here both have identical square bases and the same height. Compare the two figures. As you can see, the pyramid holds much less than the rectangular prism. In fact, it holds only one-third of the rectangular prism's volume.

The formula for finding the volume of a pyramid is as written below. Notice that B equals the area of the square base. The height of a pyramid is the perpendicular distance from the base to the vertex at the top.

square pyramid   Volume $= \frac{1}{3} \times$ base $\times$ height

Example 1: Find the volume of the pyramid shown below.

The length of a base edge is 5 cm. The height of the pyramid is 6 cm. Ignore the diagonal edges.

Apply the formula: $V = \frac{1}{3}Bh$

$$= \frac{1}{3}(5^2)(6)$$

$$= \frac{1}{3}(25)(6)$$

$$= \textbf{50 cm}^3$$

A **cone** is similar to a cylinder. Both have a circular base and a curved side. The curved side of a cone slants inward so that it meets at a point, or vertex. The volume of a cone is $\frac{1}{3}$ of the volume of a cylinder with the same size base and height.

On the GED® Formula Sheet, the formula for volume of a cone is based on the following relationship. Notice that the formula contains the formula for finding the area of a circle (πr^2).

cone   Volume $= \frac{1}{3} \times \pi \times$ radius$^2 \times$ height

Example 2: Find the volume of the cone shown below.

The radius of the base is 2 inches, and the height is 9 inches.

Apply the formula: $V = \frac{1}{3}\pi r^2 h$

$$= \frac{1}{3}(3.14)(2^2)(9)$$

$$= \frac{1}{3}(3.14)(4)(9)$$

$$= \textbf{37.68 in}^3$$

NOTE: In volume formulas for cones and square pyramids, the factor $\frac{1}{3}$ is shown first. Don't begin with this factor. Multiply the other factors first and then divide by 3, unless one of the numbers is easily divided by 3.

PRACTICE 6.2

A. Find the volume of each object to the nearest unit.

1.

3 in.
3 in. 3 in.

3.

5 cm
12 cm

5.

2 in. 8 in.
2 in.

2.

6 in.
9 in.

4.

10 m
13.1 m
12 m 12 m

6.

18 cm
15 cm

B. Choose the <u>one best answer</u> to each question.

7. Advertisers have designed this pyramid-shaped package to hold action figures.

h = 15 cm

10 cm 10 cm

After testing the design, the manufacturer decides to increase both the length and width of the base by 4 cm. How many more cubic centimeters will the new package hold than the package shown above?

A. 480
B. 500
C. 980
D. 2940

8. The height of a cone is half the diameter of its base. If the cone's height is 4 inches, what is the cone's volume to the nearest cubic inch?

A. 21
B. 48
C. 67
D. 268

9. Which of the following is a true statement about the figures shown below?

4 cm
2 cm
3 cm
Figure A

h = 6 cm
3 cm 3 cm
Figure B

A. The volume of A equals the volume of B.
B. The volume of B is greater than the volume of A.
C. Both A and B have a volume greater than 20 cubic centimeters.
D. The volume of B is less than the volume of A.

10. A cone's base is a circle with a radius of 8 inches. The cone's height is 15 inches. What is the cone's approximate volume in cubic inches?

A. 125
B. 250
C. 500
D. 1000

Answers and explanations begin on page 675.

GEOMETRY

Surface Area

The **surface area** is the total area of the outside **faces** of three-dimensional figures. This is different from the **volume**, which is the capacity of what a figure can hold. Surface area is expressed in square units.

Surface Area of a Square Prism

The surface area of a **square prism (cube)** is the sum of the areas of the six squares that form the prism. The area of one square is s^2. Since these sides are the same, find the area of one side and multiply by 6.

Example 1: Find the surface area of a cube with sides of 3 inches each.

$$SA = 6s^2$$
$$SA = 6(3 \text{ in})^2 = 6\,(9 \text{ in}^2) = 54 \text{ in}^2$$

Surface Area of a Rectangular Prism

The surface area of a **rectangular prism** is the sum of the areas of the six rectangles that form the prism.

Example 2: Find the surface area of this box.

$$SA = ph + 2B$$
$$SA = \text{perimeter} \times \text{height} + 2(\text{area of base})$$
$$SA = (5 \text{ m} + 6 \text{ m} + 5 \text{ m} + 6 \text{ m}) \times 7 \text{ m} + 2(6 \text{ m} \times 5 \text{ m})$$
$$SA = (22 \text{ m})7 \text{ m} + 2(30 \text{ m}^2) = 154 \text{ m}^2 + 60 \text{ m}^2 = \mathbf{214 \text{ m}^2}$$

Surface Area of a Pyramid

The surface area of a **pyramid** is $\frac{1}{2}$ the perimeter of the base (p) times the **slant height** (s) plus the area of the base (B). The slant height is the length of a line segment from the **apex** (top) to the **base**.

Example 3: What is the surface area of a pyramid with a slant height of 5 feet, a base with a perimeter of 14 feet, and a base with an area of 12 feet?

slant height

$$SA = \tfrac{1}{2}\,ps + B$$
$$SA = \tfrac{1}{2}\,\text{perimeter} \times \text{slant height} + \text{base area}$$
$$SA = \tfrac{1}{2}(14 \text{ ft})\,(5 \text{ ft}) + 12 \text{ ft}^2$$
$$SA = \tfrac{1}{2}(70 \text{ ft}^2) + 12 \text{ ft}^2 = 35 \text{ ft}^2 + 12 \text{ ft}^2 = \mathbf{47 \text{ ft}^2}$$

PRACTICE 7.1

A. Find the surface area of each object in square units. Use the formulas on page 392.

1.
3
4
6

3.
2
2
2

5.
12 in.
4 in.
5 in.

2.
5 in.
3 in.   3 in.

4.
8 m
12 m   12 m

6.
8 in.
8 in.
8 in.

B. Choose the <u>one best answer</u> to each question. Use the formulas on page 392.

7. All the edges of a metal box are of equal length. If the surface area is 150 square inches, what is the length, in inches, of each edge of the box?

A. 5
B. 6
C. 25
D. 50

8. Which of the following is a true statement about the figures shown below? (Measurements indicated are all in the same units.)

5
5
5

3
3
10

Figure *A*   **Figure *B***

A. The surface area of Figure *A* is equal to the surface area of Figure *B*.
B. The surface area of Figure *A* is half of the surface area of Figure *B*.
C. The surface area of Figure *A* is greater than the surface area of Figure *B*.
D. The sum of the surface areas of both Figure *A* and Figure *B* is greater than 300.

9. If the dimensions of the box below are doubled, by how many square centimeters does the surface area increase?

A. 8
B. 54
C. 162
D. 216

3 cm
3 cm
3 cm

Answers and explanations begin on page 676.

Finding the surface areas of cylinders, cones, and spheres involves using some dimensions of circles.

Surface Area of a Cylinder

To find the surface area of a cylinder, multiply the circumference ($2\pi r$) by the **height** (h) and add the product to the area of the two ends of the cylinder, each of which is the area of a circle (πr^2).

Example 1: Find the surface area of a cylinder with a radius (r) of 4 inches and a height (h) of 3 inches.

$$SA = 2\pi rh + 2\pi r^2$$
$$SA = (2 \times 3.14 \times 4 \times 3) + (2 \times 3.14 \times 4^2)$$
$$SA = (6.28 \times 12) + (6.28 \times 16) = 75.36 \text{ in}^2 + 100.48 \text{ in}^2$$
$$= \textbf{175.84 in}^2$$

You may find the on-screen calculator helpful to complete these calculations effectively.

Surface Area of a Cone

The surface area of a **cone** is found by combining the **lateral side surface** (πrs) with the area of its **base** (πr^2).

Example 2: Find the surface area of a cone with a radius of 2 feet and a slant height of 5 feet.

$$SA = \pi rs + \pi r^2$$
$$SA = \text{lateral side surface with slant height} + \text{area of base}$$
$$SA = \pi(2)(5) + \pi(2^2)$$
$$SA = 10\pi \text{ ft}^2 + 4\pi \text{ ft}^2 = 14\pi \text{ ft}^2 = 14 \text{ ft}^2 \times 3.14 \cong \textbf{43.96 ft}^2$$

Surface Area of a Sphere

The surface area of a **sphere** is four times the area of a circle with the same radius as the sphere.

Example 3: What is the surface area of this sphere with a radius of 10 feet?

$$SA = 4\pi r^2$$
$$SA \approx 4 \times 3.14 \times 10^2 \approx \textbf{1256 ft}^2$$

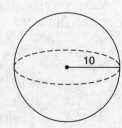

PRACTICE 7.2

A. Find the surface area of each object in square units. Express your answer in terms of pi (for example, 36π). Use the formulas on page 394.

1.

3.

5.

6.

2.

4.

B. Choose the <u>one best answer</u> to each question. Use the formulas on page 394.

7. If the length of the diameter of a sphere is 8, how many square units is its surface area?

    A. 16π
    B. 64π
    C. 256π
    D. 512π

8. A cone, pictured below, has a slant height of 8 inches and a diameter of 8 inches. If the cone's slant height is doubled, and the diameter is halved, which of the following statements must be true?

    A. The new cone will have the same surface area as the original cone.
    B. The new cone will have a surface area exactly half of the surface area of the original cone.
    C. The new cone will have a surface area exactly double that of the surface area of the new cone.
    D. The new cone will have a surface area less than the surface area of the original cone.

9. In the cylinder below, the diameter of the circular base is equal to the height of the cylinder. What is the surface area of the cylinder, to the nearest square inch?

    A. 57
    B. 113
    C. 170
    D. 339

Answers and explanations begin on page 676.

GEOMETRY

Combined Figures

Breaking Combined Figures into Parts

A combined figure puts together geometric figures to form a new shape. To find the perimeter of a combined figure, simply add the lengths of the sides. You may need to solve for one or more missing lengths.

Example 1: A family room has the dimensions shown in the diagram. All measures are in feet. What is the perimeter of the room?

1. Find the missing measures. Measurement x equals the combined lengths of the two opposite walls: $x = 8 + 4 = 12$ ft. You also know that $18 - 10 = y$, so $y = 8$ ft.

2. Add all distances to find the perimeter: $12 + 18 + 8 + 8 + 4 + 10 = \textbf{60 ft}$.

To find the area or volume of a combined figure, break the figure into parts. Then apply the correct formula to each part.

Example 2: What is the area of the figure in square centimeters?

1. Divide the figure into two shapes and find any missing measurements. Here the figure is divided into a trapezoid and a rectangle.

2. Calculate the area of each shape.
   Rectangle: $A = lw$
   $$= 2(5) = 10 \text{ cm}^2$$

   Trapezoid: $A = \frac{1}{2}h(b_1 + b_2)$
   $$= \frac{1}{2}(3)(5 + 7) = 18 \text{ cm}^2$$

3. Combine: $10 + 18 = \textbf{28 cm}^2$.

Example 3: Find the volume of the container shown below.

Break the figure into a cylinder and a cone and find the volume of each.

1. Cylinder: $V = \pi r^2 h$
   $$= (3.14)(1^2)(2) = 6.28 \text{ m}^3$$

2. Cone: $V = \frac{1}{3}\pi r^2 h$
   $$= \frac{1}{3}(3.14)(1^2)(1.5) = 1.57 \text{ m}^3$$

3. Combine: $6.28 + 1.57 = \textbf{7.85 m}^3$ or **7.85 cu m.**

PRACTICE 8

A. Find the perimeter and area of each figure.

1.

2.

(*Hint:* Think of the figure as a rectangle and a half circle.)

3.

B. Find the volume of each figure to the nearest cubic unit.

4.

5. $h = 8$

6.

C. Choose the one best answer to each question.

7. A slab of concrete will have four concrete blocks in each corner as shown in the drawing below.

If each corner block has the same dimensions, what is the volume of the structure in cubic feet?

A. 72
B. 168
C. 288
D. 360

8. A candy package is in the shape of a cylinder with a cone on each end.

If the radius of the cylinder is 2 inches and the cones are identical, what is the capacity of the container to the nearest cubic inch?

A. 33
B. 100
C. 134
D. 201

Answers and explanations begin on page 676.

Geometry

Geometry Calculator Skills

- When a problem involves many calculations, use the order of operations to decide which operation to do first.
- Check your work by estimating an answer or by quickly repeating the keystrokes to see if the result is the same.

When solving problems with formulas, you can generally save time by performing some or all of the operations on a calculator. Remember the order of operations when solving formulas and always check your work, either by reentering the key sequence or by estimating an answer and comparing your answer to the estimate.

Example 1: A pyramid has a height of 81 feet. The base is in the shape of a square with each side measuring 40 feet. What is the volume in cubic feet of the pyramid?

Use the formula for the volume of a pyramid: $\frac{1}{3} Bh$. Begin by calculating the area of the base: 40×40, or 40^2. Multiply that by the height, 81. In the last step, dividing by 3 is the same as multiplying by $\frac{1}{3}$.

Evaluate the exponent.	40 $\boxed{x^2}$
Multiply by 81.	$\boxed{\times}$ 81
Divide by 3.	$\boxed{\div}$ 3 $\boxed{\text{enter}}$
The right side of the display shows the correct answer, **43,200**.	**43200**

To enter this formula using a fraction using one series of keystrokes on the TI-30XS MultiView™ calculator, enter the following: $\boxed{\frac{n}{d}}$ 1 $\boxed{\blacktriangledown}$ 3 $\boxed{\times}$ 40 $\boxed{x^2}$ $\boxed{\times}$ 81 $\boxed{\text{enter}}$.

The right side of the display shows **43200**.

The volume of the pyramid is **43,200 square feet**.

You may need your calculator to find the exact answer to problems that involve the Pythagorean relationship. These problems can also be done in one series of keystrokes.

Example 2: A right triangle has legs 10 inches and 24 inches in length. What is the length of the hypotenuse?

Use the formula $a^2 + b^2 = c^2$. You will need to add the squares of the legs and then find the square root of the total.

Press: 10 $\boxed{x^2}$ $\boxed{+}$ 24 $\boxed{x^2}$ $\boxed{\text{enter}}$. The display will read 676. Then press $\boxed{\text{2nd}}$ $\boxed{x^2}$ 676 $\boxed{\text{enter}}$. The right side of the display shows **26**.

The hypotenuse is **26 inches** in length.

If you need to include the quantity pi (π) in a calculation, the TI-30XS MultiView™ calculator includes a *pi* key, located three keys below the *2nd* key on the left-hand side of the keypad.

Example 3: What is the area of a circle with radius 2.4 cm? Round your answer to the nearest tenth.

Use the formula Area $= \pi r^2$. Press $\boxed{\pi}$ $\boxed{\times}$ 2.4 $\boxed{\sqrt{x^2}}$ and then press $\boxed{\text{enter}}$. The right side of the display reads 18.09557368.

Round that to find the answer: **18.1 cm²**.

Watch the calculator display while you are entering all of these keystrokes. If you make a mistake, use the delete *key to remove that mistake and then replace it with the correct number or function. Practice that with these examples.*

PRACTICE 9

A. Use your calculator to evaluate each formula.

1. Find the perimeter of a rectangle with a length of 16 inches and a width of 5 inches.
   Perimeter = 2 × length + 2 × width

2. Find the area of a triangle with a base of 26 centimeters and a height of 15 centimeters.
   Area = $\frac{1}{2}$ × base × height

3. What is the volume of a cube if the edge measures 3.5 feet? Round to the nearest cubic foot.
   Volume = edge^3

4. What is the measure of the hypotenuse of a right triangle when the legs measure 13 cm and 9 cm? Round your answer to the nearest tenth.
   Pythagorean relationship: $a^2 + b^2 = c^2$

5. Find the circumference of a circle with a diameter of 12 inches. Round to the nearest tenth.
   Circumference = π × diameter

6. Find the volume of a cone with a radius of 12 cm and a height of 20 cm. Round to the nearest cm^3.
   Volume = $\frac{1}{3}$ × π × radius^2 × height

B. Choose the one best answer to each question. You MAY use your calculator.

Question 7 refers to the following drawing.

20 in.

12 in.

8 in. 20 in. 4 in.

7. For a woodworking project, Paul cuts the shape shown above from plywood. What is the area in square inches of the piece? (*Hint:* Think of the shape as a triangle removed from a rectangle.)

   A. 400
   B. 480
   C. 520
   D. 640

8. To the nearest cubic meter, what is the volume of a cylinder with a radius of 1.5 meters and a height of 5 meters?

   A. 25
   B. 35
   C. 45
   D. 141

Questions 9 and 10 refer to the drawing.

32

28

26 12

22 8

All measurements are in centimeters.

9. How many cubic centimeters greater is the volume of Box A than the volume of Box B?

   A. 64
   B. 1,448
   C. 4,928
   D. 5,056

10. An advertiser plans to print advertisements on one side panel of each of the boxes (the shaded faces in the drawing). What is the total area, in square centimeters, that the advertiser will cover?

    A. 224
    B. 384
    C. 608
    D. 1448

Answers and explanations begin on page 676.

GEOMETRY PRACTICE QUESTIONS

1. What is the surface area, in square centimeters, of a cube with each edge length of 5 cm?

   A. 15
   B. 25
   C. 125
   D. 150

2. What is the surface area, in square centimeters, of a cylinder with a height of 10 cm and a radius of 6 cm?

   A. 136π
   B. 160π
   C. 192π
   D. 256π

3. What is the surface area, in square centimeters, of a cylinder that measures 8 cm tall with a diameter of 6 cm on its base?

   A. 48π
   B. 57π
   C. 66π
   D. 132π

4. A pyramid has a square base. If each edge of the pyramid is 4, what is the total surface area of the entire pyramid?

   A. $8\sqrt{3}$
   B. $8\sqrt{3} + 16$
   C. $16\sqrt{3} + 16$
   D. $64\sqrt{3}$

Question 5 refers to the following figure.

5. A toy factory paints all of its rubber balls with 2 coats of latex for durability. How many square centimeters of latex are needed to cover a rubber ball with a circumference of 16π cm?

   A. 64π
   B. 128π
   C. 256π
   D. 512π

6. The floor of a walk-in closet measures 7 feet by 4 feet. If the ceiling height is 8 feet, what is the volume in cubic feet of the closet?

   A. 28
   B. 56
   C. 112
   D. 224

Question 7 refers to the following figure.

7. An ice cream cone has a spherical scoop of ice cream placed inside. Exactly one-half of the ice cream is visible above the rim of the cone. What is the surface area of the entire ice cream treat, in units squared?

   A. 24π
   B. 30π
   C. 48π
   D. 60π

8. The radius of Sphere A is 2, and the radius of Sphere B is 1. What is the ratio of the volume of Sphere A to that of Sphere B? (*Hint*: Use the formula for the volume of a sphere on page 388.)

   A. 1:2
   B. 4:1
   C. 8:1
   D. 8:3

9. A parallelogram has a base of 6 centimeters and a height of 10 centimeters. This parallelogram has the same area as a triangle with a height of 5 centimeters. What is the measure, in centimeters, of the base of the triangle?

   Write your answer in the box.

Question 10 refers to the following figure.

18 in.

10. Three identical rectangular boxes are stacked one on top of another. The total height of all three boxes is the same as the width of one box. The length of the boxes is 18 in., and the width is half the length. What is the combined volume, in cubic inches, of all three boxes?

A. 1458
B. 1800
C. 2124
D. 3136

11. Using a compass, Max hikes 300 yards due north of his campsite. From that point, he hikes 400 yards due east. If he were to hike directly to his campsite from this point, how many yards would he have to hike?

A. 400
B. 500
C. 600
D. 700

12. The rectangular base of a container is 9 inches long and 7 inches wide. By how many cubic inches will the volume of the container increase if you increase the length of the base by 2 inches?

A. 84
B. 126
C. 168
D. 216

12 in.

9 in. 7 in.

13. In a right triangle, the hypotenuse measures 15 inches. If one leg of the triangle measures 6 inches, which of the following equations could be used to find the length of the other leg (x) in inches?

A. $x = \sqrt{15-6}$
B. $x = 15-6$
C. $x^2 = 15^2 + 6^2$
D. $x^2 = 15^2 - 6^2$

14. The length of a rectangle is three times its width. If the perimeter of the rectangle is 96 inches, what is its length in inches?

A. 12
B. 24
C. 36
D. 48

Question 15 refers to the following figure.

7 cm

16π cm

15. Sarah is making party hats for a birthday party. Each hat is in the shape of a cone and will have a circumference of 16π cm and a slant height of 7 cm. She will be making 20 hats. What is the total surface area, in square centimeters, of all 20 hats combined?

A.   32π
B.   56π
C.   112π
D. 1120π

Question 16 refers to the following figure.

16. Use your calculator to make the following calculation. In the figure above, a square contains a circle such that each of the sides of the square is touching a point on the circle. What is the area, in square inches, of the shaded portion?

A. 3.43
B. 12.57
C. 16.00
D. 28.57

Questions 17 and 18 refer to the following.

A classroom is 40 feet long and 25 feet wide. The ceiling height is 12 feet. The school district plans to repaint the room and put in air-conditioning. The ceiling tile will not be painted.

17. What is the approximate total square footage of the four walls of the room? Ignore space taken up by windows and doors.

A. 1200
B. 1560
C. 1920
D. 4000

18. To choose an air-conditioning system, the school district must know the volume of the room. What is the volume in cubic feet?

A. 1000
B. 3120
C. 12000
D. 15625

Question 19 refers to the following figures.

19. Laura is painting model pyramids for an art project. She needs one tube of paint for every 30 square inches of surface area. If Laura paints each pyramid and its base, approximately how many tubes of paint should she buy?

A. 4
B. 16
C. 48
D. 109

Answers and explanations begin on page 676.

2015 GED® Test Mathematics Formula Sheet

Area of a:

square	$A = s^2$
rectangle	$A = lw$
parallelogram	$A = bh$
triangle	$A = \frac{1}{2}bh$
trapezoid	$A = \frac{1}{2}h(b_1 + b_2)$
circle	$A = \pi r^2$

Perimeter of a:

square	$P = 4s$
rectangle	$P = 2l + 2w$
triangle	$P = s_1 + s_2 + s_3$
Circumference of a circle	$C = 2\pi r$ OR $C = \pi d$; $\pi \approx 3.14$

Surface area and volume of a:

rectangular/right prism	$SA = ph + 2B$	$V = Bh$
cylinder	$SA = 2\pi rh + 2\pi r^2$	$V = \pi r^2 h$
pyramid	$SA = \frac{1}{2}ps + B$	$V = \frac{1}{3}Bh$
cone	$SA = \pi rs + \pi r^2$	$V = \frac{1}{3}\pi r^2 h$
sphere	$SA = 4\pi r^2$	$V = \frac{4}{3}\pi r^3$

(p = perimeter of base with area B; $\pi \approx 3.14$)

Data

mean	mean is equal to the total of the values of a data set, divided by the number of elements in the data set
median	median is the middle value in an odd number of ordered values of a data set, or the mean of the two middle values in an even number of ordered values in a data set

Algebra

slope of a line	$m = \dfrac{y_2 - y_1}{x_2 - x_1}$
slope-intercept form of the equation of a line	$y = mx + b$
point-slope form of the equation of a line	$y - y_1 = m(x - x_1)$
standard form of a quadratic equation	$y = ax^2 + bx + c$
quadratic formula	$x = \dfrac{-b \pm \sqrt{b^2 - 4ac}}{2a}$
Pythagorean Theorem	$a^2 + b^2 = c^2$
simple interest	$I = Prt$ (I = interest, P = principal, r = rate, t = time)
distance formula	$d = rt$
total cost	total cost = (number of units) × (price per unit)

Provided by GED® Testing Service.

ABOUT THE TEST

Social Studies

The GED® *Social Studies Test* evaluates your ability to understand, interpret, and apply information. You will have 90 minutes to answer 35 questions that are based on reading passages and interpreting graphics such as charts, graphs, diagrams, editorial cartoons, photographs, and maps.

You will need a minimum score of 150 to pass the *Social Studies Test*, which is one of the four tests you will need to pass in order to earn a high school equivalency diploma.

Content Areas

Civics and Government (50%) topics include modern and historic governments, constitutional government, levels and branches of the U.S. government, the electoral system, and the role of the citizen.

U.S. History (20%) topics stretch from colonialism and the American Revolution through the Civil War and Reconstruction into the modern era of industrialization, immigration, two world wars, the Cold War, and the movements for equal rights.

Economics (15%) topics include basic economics concepts and systems, the government and the economy, and labor and consumer economics issues.

Geography and the World (15%) topics cover major stages in world history as well as the relationship among resources, the environment, and societies.

Social Studies Practices

In addition to testing your understanding of social studies passages and graphics, questions are based on your understanding of major skills, called **Social Studies Practices,** and these skills introduce this unit on pages 410–429. After you study these practices, you will reinforce them as you work through the unit. They include the following:

- Determine **Central Ideas, Inferences, Hypotheses,** and **Conclusions.**
- Analyze **Words, Events,** and **Ideas** in Social Studies Contexts.
- Analyze Author's **Purpose** and **Point of View.**
- Evaluate Author's **Reasoning** and **Evidence.**
- Analyze and Integrate **Relationships Within and Between Social Studies Materials.**
- Interpret Data and Statistics in **Graphs** and **Charts.**
- Find the Center in a Statistical Data Set, Including **Average, Median,** and **Mode.**

Computer-Based Social Studies Test Question Formats

You will work with six question formats on the Social Studies Test. Many of the questions will be in the familiar multiple-choice format, but you will need to be acquainted with the other formats as well.

Multiple-choice questions have four options (A through D). You will **click** on the best answer.

Which statement correctly describes a significant way that aristocracy differs from democracy as a political system?

○ A. In an aristocracy, power is always directly exercised by the people.

○ B. In an aristocracy, power is concentrated in the hands of a small group.

○ C. In an aristocracy, all adults are equal before the law.

○ D. In a democracy, all laws are seen as divinely ordained.

Fill-in-the-blank questions will require you to **type** a word, phrase, or number in a box that appears on the screen.

Type the appropriate state name in the box.

The number of representatives in Congress from the state of ⬚ is twice the number of representatives in Congress from the state of Pennsylvania.

Drop-down questions give you the opportunity to **click** on the correct response to complete a statement.

An industrial economy exists within a web of complex relationships. Goods must first be [Select...▾] before they can be sold, but no goods can be sold without [Select...▾] to buy them. The largest group of buyers are ordinary citizens, who cannot buy without [Select...▾], the most common source of which is [Select...▾], frequently earned through employment in the production of goods.

Hot-spot items consist of a graphic image or images. You will need to **click** on one or more "points" or graphics on the screen.

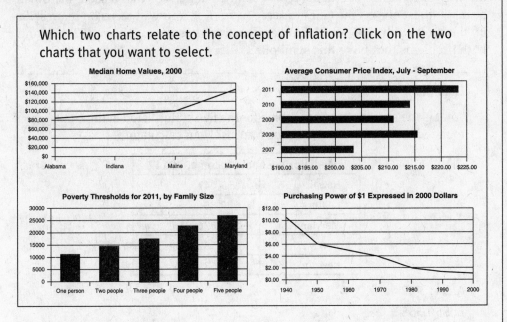

Which two charts relate to the concept of inflation? Click on the two charts that you want to select.

Drag-and-drop items require you to **click** on a small image, words, or numerical expression and to **drag** and **drop it** in a specified location on the computer screen.

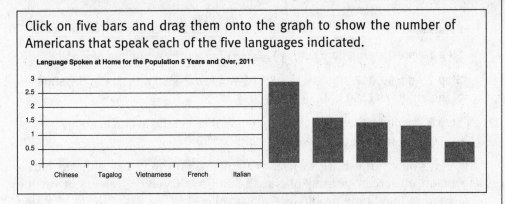

Click on five bars and drag them onto the graph to show the number of Americans that speak each of the five languages indicated.

An **Extended-Response** item requires you to **type** in a *text box* in response to a **prompt** based on one or more short passages, a graphic, or a combination.

You will have 25 minutes at the end of the *Social Studies Test* to read the materials and to plan, write, and revise your response.

In your response, develop an argument for the main cause behind the Great Depression, and the major step taken to recover. Incorporate relevant and specific examples from the paragraph and your own knowledge of the issue and the circumstances surrounding the time of the Great Depression.

Type your response in the box. This task may require 25 minutes to complete.

+ Cut 📋 Copy 📋 Paste ↺ Undo ↻ Redo

Math Problems on the *Social Studies Test*

Many social studies investigations use mathematics. For that reason, there will be math questions on the *GED® Social Studies Test*. You will focus on math skills in this unit with the Social Studies Practices lesson on pages 422–423 and with problems that have this symbol: 🖩 Calculator .

Example

What is the average median income for the five states listed in the chart, rounded to the nearest dollar? You MAY use your calculator.

Median Household Income, 2011	
Hawaii	$59,047
Kentucky	$39,856
Maryland	$68,876
New Mexico	$41,982
New York	$50,636

A. $41,952

B. $50,338

C. $52,079

D. $52,200

Solution

Step 1 Write the equation: Average = sum of amounts ÷ number of amounts.

Step 2 Add $59,047 + 39,856 + 68,876 + 41,982 + 50,636$ to get the sum of the amounts (260397).

Step 3 Divide by the number of amounts (5) to get the average: $60397 ÷ 5 = 52079.$; round to the nearest dollar: C. $52,079.

Although you do not have to use a calculator, you may use either a hand-held or an on-screen version of the TI-30XS MultiView™ calculator on the *Social Studies Test*. Some problems will say: *You MAY use your calculator.* When you see that language, the calculator icon appears at the top of the screen. If you cannot remember how to use the calculator, you can open the online *Calculator Reference Sheet.* Both links are shown below.

🖩 Calculator   📄 Calculator Reference

You can **click** the links to *open, move,* and *close* both the online *Texas Instruments TI-30XS MultiView™* calculator and the *Calculator Reference Sheet.* You will want to move them on the computer screen so that they don't block the problem. Also remember that you will have an *off-line wipe-off board* that you can use as scratch paper.

Extended-Response Questions on the Social Studies Test

Social scientists and students communicate about their work in writing. To reflect that, the *GED® Social Studies Test* has an Extended-Response item. You will focus on writing Extended Responses in this unit with the Social Studies Practices lesson on pages 424–425.

The Extended-Response items are based on one passage, two passages, a graphic, or a combination. You will compose your answer in a textbox similar to the one below.

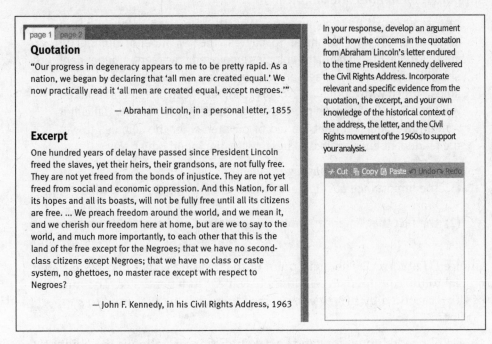

page 1 page 2

Quotation

"Our progress in degeneracy appears to me to be pretty rapid. As a nation, we began by declaring that 'all men are created equal.' We now practically read it 'all men are created equal, except negroes.'"

— Abraham Lincoln, in a personal letter, 1855

Excerpt

One hundred years of delay have passed since President Lincoln freed the slaves, yet their heirs, their grandsons, are not fully free. They are not yet freed from the bonds of injustice. They are not yet freed from social and economic oppression. And this Nation, for all its hopes and all its boasts, will not be fully free until all its citizens are free. ... We preach freedom around the world, and we mean it, and we cherish our freedom here at home, but are we to say to the world, and much more importantly, to each other that this is the land of the free except for the Negroes; that we have no second-class citizens except Negroes; that we have no class or caste system, no ghettoes, no master race except with respect to Negroes?

— John F. Kennedy, in his Civil Rights Address, 1963

In your response, develop an argument about how the concerns in the quotation from Abraham Lincoln's letter endured to the time President Kennedy delivered the Civil Rights Address. Incorporate relevant and specific evidence from the quotation, the excerpt, and your own knowledge of the historical context of the address, the letter, and the Civil Rights movement of the 1960s to support your analysis.

Cut   Copy   Paste   Undo Redo

Read the prompt carefully and use the **online highlighter** to target specific facts and information that you will use in your response. An effective response must answer the questions and use relevant and specific evidence from the source material as well as your knowledge about the issue.

Your response is expected to be an example of "**evidence-based writing**." Since the Extended Response is worth more than other kinds of questions, take time to understand the question, write a thesis statement to articulate your position, plan your response, and cite at least three relevant facts from the information to back up your position. Conclude with a strong summary of your position.

As with other writing tasks on the GED® Test, you have word processing tools that you can **click** on at the top of the toolbox that will allow you to do the following:

- **Cut** (remove extraneous ideas or correct mistakes)
- **Copy** and **Paste** (move words and ideas to improve your writing)
- **Undo** or **Redo** (use if you change your mind or want to change it back)

SOCIAL STUDIES PRACTICES

Determine Central Idea and Draw Conclusions

Key Ideas

• *Social Studies Test* presentations consist of text, graphics, or a combination of the two.
• Comprehending social studies material requires understanding the central idea or point and its supporting details.
• *Social Studies Test* questions also require you to make inferences in order to draw conclusions.

The **central idea** of a passage or graphic is its topic or main point. This is supported by **details** or **examples**.

> At the outset of the Revolutionary War, the American colonies had a small navy of only 31 ships. To contest the far superior number of vessels in the British fleet, the colonies employed privateers, independent ships authorized to harass and capture enemy merchant and cargo ships. Armed with more than 14,000 guns, American privateers captured well over 2,000 enemy ships. These figures demonstrate how difficult it would have been, without the aid of privateers, for the colonies to win their independence against a larger, better equipped British Navy.

▶ What is the topic of this passage?
  (1) the importance of colonial privateers to winning the Revolutionary War
  (2) the fact that American privateers captured well over 2,000 enemy ships

Choice **(1)** is correct. The main point of the passage is that privateers were crucial to the colonies' success in their war for independence. The number of ships captured by privateers, referred to in choice (2), is used to support that point.

One skill needed to understand social studies information is the ability to **draw conclusions** from what you read or see. This skill requires you to go beyond what is directly stated and make an inference about what is meant or implied.

▶ Which of the following conclusions can be drawn based on this graph?

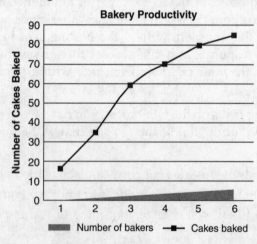

Bakery Productivity

(1) The productivity of a bakery is based on a number of factors.
(2) The productivity of the bakery rises when more bakers are added.

You were correct if you selected choice **(2)**. As you look at the graph, the line—the number of cakes baked—rises steeply when more bakers are added. This associates the productivity of the bakery with the number of bakers. Choice (1) may well be true, but it is not a conclusion based on this graph.

GED® TEST TIP

To answer GED® test questions based on a passage or graphic, ask yourself, "What is the main point? What evidence or details are used to support it? What conclusion can I draw?"

PRACTICE 1

<u>Questions 1 through 3</u> are based on the following passage.

Theater was one of the most popular forms of art in ancient Greece, and one form of drama—tragedy—was central to Greek culture. Tragedies told familiar stories from Greek myths and epics, but actors portrayed the main roles, and a chorus narrated the background of the story and commented upon the action. These serious dramas centered on a main character who displayed exceptional attributes but also had a tragic flaw that caused his downfall. This flaw was often hubris, which is excessive pride or overconfidence.

1. Which of the following is the topic of the paragraph?

    A. the superiority of Greek theater
    B. the standard forms of Greek drama
    C. the characteristics of Greek tragedy
    D. the most popular Greek tragedies

2. Which of these details supports the central idea?

    A. Theater was one of the most popular Greek art forms.
    B. Tragedies were more important than comedies in ancient Greece.
    C. Greeks thought flaws other than hubris were not tragic.
    D. The main character in Greek drama has a tragic flaw that causes his downfall.

3. Which of these conclusions is supported by the paragraph?

    A. Ancient Greeks did not expect to see an original story each time they attended the theater.
    B. Playwrights in ancient Greece also wrote myths and epics.
    C. Tragedies in ancient Greece were judged on the basis of how serious their stories were.
    D. Only highly cultured people attended tragedies in ancient Greece.

<u>Questions 4 and 5</u> are based on this graphic.

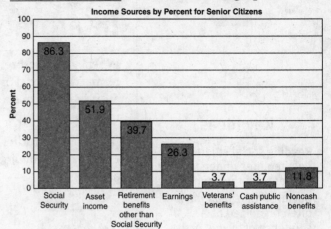

Income Sources by Percent for Senior Citizens

Source: Social Security Administration

4. The graph answers which of the following questions?

    A. What is the dollar value of the income for senior citizens?
    B. How much do senior citizens have in savings accounts?
    C. How many senior citizens are dependent upon veterans' benefits for their retirement income?
    D. Where do the incomes of senior citizens come from?

5. Which of the following conclusions can be drawn from this graph?

    A. More senior citizens need to continue to work in order to make ends meet now than in the past.
    B. Social Security benefits are the most widespread means of support for most senior citizens.
    C. Senior citizens who receive income from veterans' benefits also receive benefits from public assistance.
    D. Senior citizens who do not receive Social Security benefits get income from one or more other sources.

Answers and explanations start on page 678.

Interpret Words and Ideas

Key Ideas

- Reading social studies materials requires understanding key terms in their context.
- Social studies material is often organized as a sequence of events or as steps in a process.
- Analyzing social studies materials often involves relating causes to effects.

When you interpret social studies materials, you need to understand key **terms** in context. For instance, on page 446, the word *articles* is presented. You already know an everyday use of the word, such as "articles of clothing," but in the context on page 446, an *article* refers to a section of the U.S. Constitution.

Some social studies material is organized in **chronological** or time order. Look at the timeline below and answer a question about the sequence of events.

Inventions in the 1870s

Blasting gel	Telephone	Cylinder phonograph Carbon arc lightbulb	Cash register Carbon filament lightbulb
1875	1876	1877	1879

▶ Which of the following events preceded the invention of the carbon arc lightbulb?

   (1) invention of the telephone

   (2) invention of the carbon filament lightbulb

Timelines are read left to right from oldest to most recent, so choice **(1)** is correct. Choice (2) refers to the carbon filament lightbulb, invented in 1879, a year after the carbon arc lightbulb.

Another way that social studies material is organized is by **cause and effect**, which is another way of asking "What resulted from this action?" or "What made this event happen?" Read the following paragraph to practice this skill.

The prices of goods and services are determined by the relationship between supply and demand. When supply exceeds demand, sellers must lower prices to stimulate sales; on the other hand, when demand exceeds supply, consumers bid up prices as they compete to purchase items or services that they desire.

▶ Based on the theory of supply and demand, under which of the following scenarios would prices be most likely to rise?

   (1) The demand for a product exceeds that product's supply.

   (2) Producers and sellers advertise a product in order to stimulate demand for that product.

Choice **(1)** is correct. According to the law of supply and demand, prices rise when demand outpaces supply. Choice (2) describes a situation in which producers and sellers advertise to stimulate demand for their product, but without knowing whether the supply is limited, we cannot conclude that this would cause the price to increase.

GED® TEST TIP

*To learn key social studies terms, pay close attention to the meaning of the words in **bold type** in the history, government, economics, and geography sections of this unit.*

PRACTICE 2

Questions 1 through 3 are based on this passage.

From 1820 to 1870, more than 7.5 million immigrants arrived on U.S. shores. That was more people than the entire U.S. population in 1810. Almost all of these immigrants came from Northern Europe, and a majority were Catholic. Historians have often focused on what "pushed" these emigrants out of Europe. During the 1840s, for example, Germany experienced a series of crop failures that, combined with social upheaval triggered by rapid industrialization in urban areas, produced riots, civil unrest, and open rebellion. During the same years, Ireland saw the infamous "potato famine" strike poor and working-class Irish families, killing an estimated 700,000 people.

While those crises spurred Europeans to emigrate, a variety of factors created a simultaneous "pull" to immigrate to the United States. Letters home from friends and family members who had immigrated earlier often described the United States as a "land of plenty" and related stories of successful employment and plentiful land. Steamship companies offering passage across the Atlantic advertised with posters that showed majestic scenes of American abundance.

1. According to the passage, which of the following was a cause of Northern European immigration to the United States in the 1840s and 1850s?

   A. Americans' desire to double the population of the United States
   B. efforts by Northern European governments to reduce the number of people living in poverty
   C. political and social instability in some Northern European countries
   D. efforts to spread Catholicism to the United States

2. Based on the passage, which one of the following was most likely to have been featured on a steamship company poster?

   A. a folk-art painting depicting the life of the rural poor in the United States
   B. a portrait of an American politician from the 1840s
   C. a poster advertising an American product
   D. a painting of pioneers settling and farming productive prairie land

3. Which of the following results of Northern European immigration to the United States in the mid-1800s can be inferred from the passage?

   A. a spread of poverty in the United States
   B. a decline in political upheaval in Northern Europe
   C. a growth in the population of the United States
   D. a number of Americans converting to the Catholic faith

Questions 4 and 5 are based on this timeline.

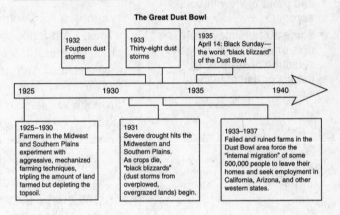

The Great Dust Bowl

4. Given the information in the timeline, which of the following would be a flawed inference?

   A. Mechanized farming contributed to dust storms.
   B. Internal migration led to overgrazing.
   C. Severe drought contributed to "black blizzards."
   D. Some farmers left the Dust Bowl before the worst dust storm hit the region.

5. Which of the following could have been a cause of the Great Dust Bowl?

   A. "black blizzards"
   B. internal migration
   C. depleted topsoil
   D. failed farms

Answers and explanations start on page 678.

SOCIAL STUDIES PRACTICES

Analyze Author's Purpose and Point of View

Any author of social studies material has a viewpoint and a purpose. Social studies material can have many purposes, such as to inform or educate (for example, a textbook or magazine article). Other materials, such as newspaper editorials and online blogs, are used to convince people of a point of view.

An author's **point of view** is his or her way of looking at the world. Some social scientists follow a method of examining the facts and coming to a conclusion. In other cases, an author may start with a point of view and assemble facts or evidence to support it.

When you read social studies materials, determine whether an author has a **bias**, a tendency to see one point of view. A bias is not a bad thing in and of itself (after all, we all have biases), but you should take the author's bias into account. An extreme form of bias is **propaganda**, in which an author tries to convince people to act and think as the author wants. Authors of propaganda selectively include certain facts and ignore others, or they use loaded words to trigger emotional responses. Use the following example to practice finding the author's point of view.

> Until the 1980s, most anthropologists mistakenly estimated the native population in North America at the time of Columbus's expedition in 1492 to be somewhere between 2 million and 7 million people. They based these estimates on the number of Native Americans alive at the time of their first contact with European explorers and settlers. However, the estimates ignored the impact of infectious diseases, such as smallpox, which traveled much faster than humans did and would have decimated the native population before Europeans made contact with native people.

▶ What is the author's point of view about the population of North America in 1492?

   (1) that it was not exactly 2 million people or 7 million people but was somewhere in between those two numbers

   (2) that it was probably much larger than 7 million people

Choice **(2)** is correct. The author points out a reason to think that anthropologists prior to the 1980s undercounted the native population. Answer (1) gives the estimate of most anthropologists prior to the 1980s.

▶ Which of the following words is a clue to the author's viewpoint?

   (1) ignored

   (2) estimated

The correct choice is **(1)**. The author believes that the anthropologists' estimates were flawed because they ignored relevant information about the impact of diseases on the native population. Choice (2) misses the author's point; he doesn't fault them for estimating, but rather for ignoring evidence when they made their estimates.

Key Ideas

- Social studies material may be written to inform or to persuade.
- Thoughtful readers need to take an author's purpose and point of view into account.
- Some authors may express a bias or point of view by the selection of supporting details or use of loaded words.

GED® TEST TIP

You may be provided with a newspaper editorial, an online blog commentary, or a speech. Ask yourself, "What is the author's viewpoint? How are facts and evidence organized to be convincing? How are words chosen to have an impact?"

PRACTICE 1

Questions 1 through 3 are based on the paragraph and poster below.

During World War I, the U.S. National War Garden Commission began a campaign to encourage private citizens to grow their own food as a means of supporting the war effort. This practice became very popular. With increased private food production, the government could reserve much of the cheaper, mass-produced food for the troops. The money saved in feeding soldiers freed up resources for other military needs. In addition, planting war gardens, also known as victory gardens, gave American citizens a sense of empowerment.

Source: Library of Congress Poster by James Montgomery Flagg

1. Which of the following best describes the poster's use of the word *victory*?

   A. ambiguous
   B. informative
   C. propagandistic
   D. impersonal

2. What is meant by the poster's caption "Every Garden a Munition Plant"?

   A. War gardens require a great deal of time to cultivate.
   B. Citizens who plant war gardens encourage a sense of community in their hometowns.
   C. Citizens who plant war gardens help supply the war effort with essential resources.
   D. War gardens provide an excellent opportunity to learn about gardening, canning, and food drying.

3. The author's primary purpose in writing the paragraph accompanying the poster is most likely to

   A. describe war gardens and explain their popularity in the United States
   B. encourage patriotism and continued support for a strong United States military
   C. distinguish the efforts of American citizens during World War I from those of citizens in other countries
   D. rebut the accusations of those who claimed that civilians did not do enough to support the U.S. war effort in World War I

Question 4 is based on the following dialogue.

Congresswoman Burns: The new organic food safety regulations are likely to increase the average cost of some food staples. The costs are justified, however, by the peace of mind that comes from knowing your food is safe and healthy.

Concerned Citizen: Rising prices are a cancer eating away at our families. High costs will drive people away from healthy foods and wind up harming our children's diets. Instead of buying wholesome, natural products, parents will feed their kids fast food.

4. Which of the following constitute "loaded" words the Concerned Citizen uses to support her point?

   A. high costs
   B. fast food
   C. a cancer
   D. our children's diets

Answers and explanations start on page 678.

SOCIAL STUDIES PRACTICES

Evaluate Author's Reasoning and Evidence

Key Ideas

- An author's point of view may be supported by facts, opinions, and reasoned judgment.
- While reading, analyze whether information is a fact, an opinion, or a conclusion based on reasoning or evidence.
- A careful reader evaluates whether an author supports his or her claims with evidence.

Social studies authors in print and online publications use a variety of strategies to support their viewpoints. They may use the following:

- **Facts**—information that can be proven to be true
- **Opinions**—beliefs about a concept or situation
- **Judgments**—conclusions that are supported by reasons and evidence

On the GED® *Social Studies Test*, you need to read carefully to distinguish among these three concepts.

▶ Indicate whether each of the following statements is a fact (F), an opinion (O), or a judgment (J).

(1) ___ Because it raises the amount employers will pay in payroll taxes, the new tax bill may contribute to higher unemployment.

(2) ___ Last year, manufacturing output in our state rose by 4.6 percent over the previous year.

(3) ___ We should limit the role played by the federal government in formulating energy policy for our region of the country.

Statement (1) is a **judgment;** the author's conclusion (that the bill may increase unemployment) is based on evidence (that the bill raises payroll taxes). Statement (2) is a **fact;** the truth or falsity of the statement can be checked against empirical data. Statement (3) is an **opinion;** the author makes a recommendation (limit the role of the federal government) but offers no evidence or reasoning to support it.

To be credible, a author needs to support his or her claims with evidence. Part of your job on the Social Studies Test is to answer questions about whether or not an author's claims are supported.

GED® TEST TIP

When you read an author's viewpoint, ask yourself, "What is the claim being made? Is evidence provided to support this claim? Is the evidence relevant to the claim and sufficient and credible enough to support it?"

Delaware was the first state to ratify the U.S. Constitution. Because of its history of favorable corporate tax policies, Delaware is today home to 63 percent of Fortune 500 corporations. There is no doubt then that Delaware's freedom-of-information act, requiring the state government to respond within 15 days of a request, should serve as a model for similar acts in other U.S. states.

▶ Does the author support the claim of the passage?

(1) Yes, because he believes and asserts that there is no doubt about the truth of the claim.

(2) No, because he asserts the truth of the claim without offering evidence relevant to the claim.

Choice **(2)** is correct. The author's claim is that Delaware's freedom-of-information act should serve as a model for similar acts in other states, but the other statements in the passage are irrelevant to that claim. Choice (1) is incorrect because stating a claim firmly ("no doubt") does not provide *support* for the claim.

1. Consultant: A reliable energy supply is vital to developing a stable economy in Cambodia, a country still recovering from decades of civil war and genocide in the late 1970s in which millions of Cambodians were killed. Damming the Mekong River could solve Cambodia's energy supply problems. However, since the Mekong flows through China, Myanmar, Laos, and Thailand before it reaches Cambodia, regional cooperation will be necessary.

    Which of the following is an opinion, and not a fact, presented by the consultant?

    A. Damming the Mekong could solve Cambodia's energy problems.
    B. The Mekong River flows through several countries before reaching Cambodia.
    C. Cambodia experienced civil war.
    D. Millions of Cambodians were killed in the late 1970s.

Question 2 is based on this cartoon referencing the labor movement of the early 20th century.

Source: Literary Digest 9/6/19. Originally from the George Matthew Adams Service (Morris).

2. Which of the following represents the viewpoint of the cartoonist?

    A. Strikes can achieve better working conditions.
    B. Strikes have a detrimental impact on workers.
    C. Farmworkers are more likely to engage in strikes than are factory workers.
    D. Strikes should hamper production.

3. Historian: Ancient Greece was the greatest of the early civilizations. While the Babylonians may have had arithmetic and ancient Egypt built the pyramids, ancient Greece gave us our first taste of democracy.

    Which of the following is a fact that the historian uses to support her opinion?

    A. Ancient Greece was the greatest early civilization.
    B. Babylonians made use of arithmetic.
    C. The pyramids were built in ancient Egypt.
    D. Ancient Greece pioneered democracy.

Question 4 is based on the following chart.

The Articles of Confederation were the predecessor to the United States Constitution.

	The Articles of Confederation	The Constitution
Federal Court System	No system of federal courts	Court system exists to deal with issues between citizens, states
Regulating Trade	No provision to regulate interstate trade	Congress has the right to regulate trade between states
Executive Power	No executive with power; president merely presided over Congress	Executive branch is headed by president who chooses Cabinet and has checks on power of judiciary and legislature
Raising an Army	Congress could not draft troops; depended on states to contribute forces	Congress can raise an army to deal with military situations
Sovereignty	Sovereignty resides in states	The Constitution is the supreme law of the land
Taxes	Congress could ask states to pay taxes	Congress has the right to levy taxes on individuals

4. Which of the following is a conclusion supported by the table above, rather than a detail stated in the table?

    A. The Constitution allows Congress to enforce collection of taxes, whereas the Articles of Confederation did not.
    B. The Constitution grants more power to the federal government than did the Articles of Confederation.
    C. There were no national armed forces before the Constitution was drafted.
    D. Trade was not nationally regulated by the Articles of Confederation.

Answers and explanations start on page 678.

SOCIAL STUDIES PRACTICES

Analyze Relationships Between Materials

Key Ideas

- Social studies materials may use graphics to illustrate key concepts.
- Circle, bar, and line graphs visually portray social studies information.
- Maps are drawings that show places and regions with keys, compasses, and scales.

Content Presented in Graphic Format

Social studies content is often presented in graphic form. Two of the most useful displays are graphs and maps.

Circle graphs are used to show how a whole is divided into parts; they show fractions or percents.

Line graphs and **bar graphs** organize material by using labels on the bottom axis and values on the side.

Sanchez Family Budget

Food
Car
Entertainment
Housing
Other

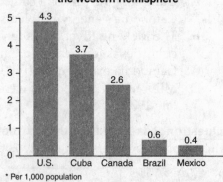

Divorce Rates for Five Countries in the Western Hemisphere*

* Per 1,000 population

Maps may use a **legend** (also called the **key**) to explain symbols, a **compass rose** to indicate directions, and **scales** to determine distances.

Europe's Climate

Hot and Humid

Mild and Humid

Cold and Humid

Dry

Alpine

► According to the map, what is England's climate?
  (1) mild and humid
  (2) cold and humid

The correct answer here is choice **(1)**. To interpret information on a map, note any labels printed directly on the map—in this case, England appears just to the left and slightly above the center. Then check the legend to see whether the color, shading, or symbols shown give additional information. On this map, England is shown in gray, indicating that its climate is "mild and humid."

PRACTICE 5.1

1. According to the circle graph on p. 418, the greatest portion of the Sanchez family's budget is spent on which two items?

   A. housing and food
   B. housing and entertainment
   C. food and car
   D. entertainment and other

2. Which of the following statements is supported by the bar graph on p. 418?

   A. Cuba has the highest divorce rate in the hemisphere.
   B. Mexico has the lowest divorce rate in the hemisphere.
   C. Mexico's divorce rate is decreasing.
   D. Brazil has a higher divorce rate than Mexico.

Questions 3 and 4 refer to the following graph.

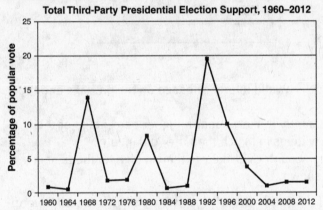

Total Third-Party Presidential Election Support, 1960–2012

3. Based on the graph, you may validly infer that support for third-party candidates ⟨Select...▾⟩ during the 1980s and 1990s.

   • steadily increased
   • steadily decreased
   • neither increased nor decreased
   • fluctuated

4. The graph can be used to disprove which one of the following claims?

   A. Third-party candidates have not enjoyed significant support in the 21st century.
   B. The third-party candidate who garnered the most support since 1960 was Ross Perot in 1992.
   C. Third party candidates have never captured more than 10 percent of the popular vote in any presidential election.
   D. In most elections, all third-party candidates combined get less than 5 percent of the popular vote.

Questions 5 and 6 are based on the following map.

5. What does this map show?

   A. political boundaries in the ancient Americas
   B. physical features of the Americas
   C. how agriculture spread in the Americas
   D. all ancient civilizations of the Americas

6. Which of the following statements is supported by the information on the map?

   A. Both the Andes civilization and Mesoamerica domesticated maize.
   B. Both the Andes civilization and Mesoamerica domesticated beans.
   C. Agriculture developed in the Andes civilization before it did in Mesoamerica.
   D. Agriculture spread more rapidly northward than southward.

Answers and explanations start on page 679.

Integrating Text and Graphic Content

In reading social studies materials and the materials you encounter in daily life, you often have to combine text information with a graphic. For example, an online article about a conflict in Africa may have a map. A newspaper graph with information about new immigrants in your community may accompany a story about their contributions to local health care and manufacturing industries.

Practice combining information with the passage and graphic below.

> Consumer confidence is an economic indicator that reflects how optimistic consumers are about their personal finances, given the state of the economy. When consumer confidence shows a monthly trend of decline month after month, consumers are pessimistic about their chances of finding and keeping good jobs. When their confidence is low, consumers spend less—especially on nonessential items—and tend to save more of their money. On the other hand, when confidence is high, consumers will make more discretionary, or optional, purchases.

Consumer Confidence by Month in Country X

▶ Which of the following is a valid inference based on the passage and the graph above?

(1) Consumers in Country X likely spent a higher percentage of their income on luxury items in March than they did in July.

(2) Unemployment in Country X is likely to remain high for the remainder of the year shown.

Choice **(1)** is correct. The graph shows that the trend in consumer confidence has generally been in decline from March through July. The text tells you that when consumer confidence is lower, consumers are less likely to spend, especially on nonessential goods. These two statements combined support choice (1). Choice (2) cannot be inferred from the information in the passage or that in the graph. Neither of those sources provides a basis to make a prediction about future unemployment.

Key Ideas

- Some situations combine text information with a graphic.
- To better understand the main point or supporting evidence, you need to combine information from both sources.

GED® TEST TIP

When you see text accompanied by a graphic, read the questions carefully. Some questions may ask about the text or the graphic individually. Others may ask you to combine information from both sources.

PRACTICE 5.2

Questions 1 through 3 relate to the following passage and map.

The sea otter (*Enhydra lutris*) is a marine mammal native to the coasts of the northern and eastern North Pacific Ocean. At one time, sea otters populated the entire coast of what is now the state of California and farther south along Mexico's Baja California coastline. Prior to 1741, the sea otter population worldwide is estimated to have been 150,000–300,000.

Between 1741 and 1911, however, sea otters were hunted extensively for their fur, and the world population fell to just 1,000–2,000 individuals. By 1911, the wild sea otter population in California was limited exclusively to a small area around Monterey Bay.

Fortunately, an international ban on hunting, conservation efforts, and programs to reintroduce the sea otter into previously populated areas have contributed to numbers rebounding, and the species now occupies about two-thirds of its former range. Despite these successes, sea otter populations in California have declined, and the sea otter remains classified as an endangered species.

Current Range of the Sea Otter in California

* Maps and ranges not to scale

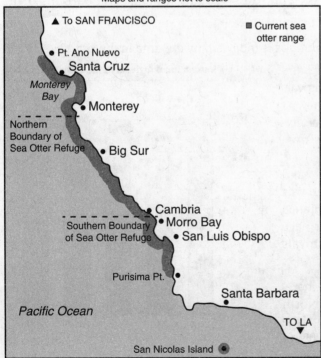

1. According to the passage, which one of the following statements about the sea otter is true?

   A. Sea otter conservation efforts have been more successful in areas outside of California than they have been within California.
   B. Sea otter populations were threatened by water pollution as well as by extensive hunting.
   C. The sea otter population is now about two-thirds of its pre-1741 number.
   D. Sea otters have been able to live in habitats from which they were once eliminated.

2. Which of the following conclusions can be drawn from the information in the passage and the map?

   A. Sea otters will soon have the same range they had prior to 1741.
   B. Sea otter habitat has been restored only within the boundaries of the Sea Otter Refuge.
   C. Sea otters are still hunted in the area north of Point Ano Nuevo.
   D. The current range of the sea otter in California is larger than it was in 1911.

3. The author of the passage would be most likely to agree with which of the following statements about the information in the map?

   A. The range of sea otters shown on the map indicates that sea otter conservation programs are no longer needed.
   B. The range of sea otters shown on the map is identical to the range of sea otters prior to 1741.
   C. Without conservation efforts and reintroduction programs, the range of sea otters in California would be smaller than what is shown on the map.
   D. Ten years from now, the range of sea otters in California will be larger than what is currently shown on the map.

Answers and explanations start on page 679.

SOCIAL STUDIES PRACTICES

Interpret Data and Statistics

Understanding social studies materials requires calculations to analyze data or statistics, so you will do some math on the *GED® Social Studies Test*. This work will include interpreting tables, finding measures of **central tendency**, making **comparisons**, and spotting **trends**. You may want to review pages 284–293 of *Unit 2: Mathematical Reasoning*. Practice your skills with the table below.

Key Ideas

- Tables and graphs are commonly used to present data in social studies materials.
- A measure of central tendency is used to summarize data with one number.
- Bar graphs are used to compare data, and line graphs are used to show trends.

Franklin County Family Finances			
Year	Median income (family of 4)	Average % to taxes	Average % to savings
2009	$40,800	27%	5.2%
2010	$41,500	28%	6.0%
2011	$42,300	29%	5.5%
2012	$44,100	29%	5.1%

▶ What is the average (arithmetic mean) percentage of income that a family of four in Franklin County saved each year between 2009 and 2012?

  (1) 5.45 percent
  (2) 5.35 percent

Choice **(1)** is correct. To find the *average* percentage saved per year, add up the figures from the column "Average % to Savings" and divide the total by 4, since 2009 to 2012 is four years. Thus, $5.2 + 6 + 5.5 + 5.1 = 21.8$, and dividing that number by 4 gives you 5.45.

Some questions may ask you to use graphs to make comparisons or to identify trends.

▶ What of the following trends is indicated by the data in the chart?

  (1) Between 2003 and 2007, foreign arrivals from overseas grew at a faster pace than foreign arrivals from North America.
  (2) Between 2003 and 2007, foreign arrivals from North America grew at a faster pace than foreign arrivals from overseas.

Choice **(2)** is correct here. Foreign arrivals from North America grew from a little over 23 million in 2003 to almost 33 million in 2007, an increase of around 41 percent. Meanwhile, overseas arrivals rose from roughly 18 million in 2003 to just under 24 million, a change of approximately 33 percent growth.

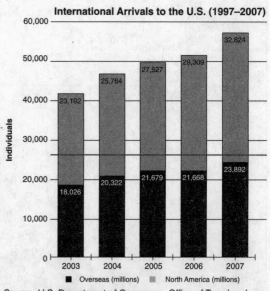

International Arrivals to the U.S. (1997–2007)

Source: U.S. Department of Commerce, Office of Travel and Tourism Industries

PRACTICE 6

Question 1 is based on the following table.

New Mexico: Population by Age, 2010	
Under 18	518,672
18–19	61,169
20–24	142,370
25–34	267,245
35–49	393,362
50–64	404,106
65 & over	272,255
Total	2,059,179

Adapted from U.S. Census Bureau

1. Which of the following could have been the median age in New Mexico in 2010?

   A. 30
   B. 32
   C. 34
   D. 36

Question 2 is based on the following line graph.

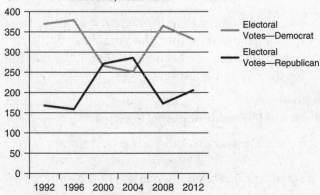

2. The information in the graph supports the conclusion that in the presidential elections from 1992 to 2012,

   A. Democrats and Republicans won the presidency an equal number of times
   B. the average margin of victory was higher in years when a Democrat won than in years when a Republican won
   C. the average margin of victory was higher in years when a Republican won than in years when a Democrat won
   D. more electoral votes were cast in the 2008 presidential election than were cast in the 1996 presidential election

Questions 3 and 4 are based on the following chart.

Source: U.S. Census (adapted)

3. According to the bar graph, in what year were there approximately as many Americans living in rural locations as there were in urban settings?

   A. 1860
   B. 1910
   C. 1920
   D. 1930

4. Approximately how much larger was the range of the urban population than the range of the rural population in the United States between 1860 and 1930?

   A. 10 million
   B. 23 million
   C. 34 million
   D. 43 million

Answers and explanations start on page 679.

SOCIAL STUDIES PRACTICES

Write an Extended Response

The *GED® Social Studies Test* will require you to compose a written response to a passage, graphic, or combination of the two. *About the Test* on pages 405–409 includes more information about the format and criteria for evaluation of your response of the extended response question. Additional practice with the extended-response format appears on pages 170–173 of the *Reasoning Through Language Arts* section of this study guide.

You will be asked to write a response to a question based on one or two passages or a passage and a graphic. A response that receives a high score does the following:

- Presents a <u>well-supported argument</u> that cites three or more pieces of <u>specific evidence</u> from the text or graphic
- Stays <u>focused</u> on the question prompt throughout the piece
- Consistently <u>links</u> either (a) the two texts or (b) the text and graphic (if there are two passages or a passage and graphic)
- Organizes ideas <u>logically</u> and demonstrates a <u>progression</u> of ideas
- Maintains a <u>formal</u> style (no slang) and <u>objective</u> (unbiased) tone
- Demonstrates <u>limited errors</u> in sentence structure, grammar, spelling, and punctuation

Since the extended response is worth more than individual multiple-choice questions, it is well worth your time to carefully plan, organize, and write it. You should budget about 25 minutes out of the total 90 minutes on the *GED® Social Studies Test* for this type of question.

Practice this process with the extended-response questions on the next page and throughout the social studies unit in this book.

1. Read the question carefully and mentally put it in your own words.
2. Develop a thesis statement based on an analysis of the author's point of view or argument.
3. Reread the information that is provided and use the online high-lighter to emphasize the facts, details, and evidence that you will use in your response.
4. Use the provided wipe-off board to organize your response.
5. Compose a clear multi-paragraph response with the following:
   a. Introduction that lays out your thesis statement
   b. Supporting paragraphs based on the evidence from the piece
   c. Conclusion that summarizes your main point
6. Use the online editing tools (cut, copy, paste, undo, and redo) to improve your writing.

Key Ideas

- Take about 25 minutes to plan and write your response.
- Develop a thesis statement based on a well-reasoned response to the material.
- Use specific details, facts, and evidence from the source materials—as well as your own knowledge—to compose a logical and organized analysis.

GED® TEST TIP

If you are presented with two passages or a passage and a graphic, be sure that your response draws from both source materials.

PRACTICE 7

Directions: Use 25 minutes to read, plan, and write an analysis of the two quotes below. Incorporate evidence from both materials and your own knowledge in your response. Compose your answer on a computer if one is available, or write your answer on a separate sheet of paper.

Quote A

A decade before assuming office as the second president of the United States, John Adams wrote the following in his *Defence of the Constitutions of Government of the United States of America*:

"If a majority are capable of preferring their own private interest, or that of their families, counties, and party, to that of the nation collectively, some provision must be made in the constitution, in favor of justice, to compel all to respect the common right, the public good, the universal law, in preference to all private and partial considerations. [. . .]

"And that the desires of the majority of the people are often for injustice and inhumanity against the minority, is demonstrated by every page of history of the whole world."

—**John Adams**, *A Defence of the Constitutions of Government of the United States of America*

Quote B

After touring the United States for nine months in 1831–1832, Frenchman Alexis de Tocqueville published his observations from and reflections on his visit in a two-volume work, *Democracy in America*, including this excerpt:

"A majority taken collectively is only an individual, whose opinions, and frequently whose interests, are opposed to those of another individual, who is styled a minority. If it be admitted that a man possessing absolute power may misuse that power by wronging his adversaries, why should not a majority be liable to the same reproach? Men do not change their characters by uniting with each other; nor does their patience in the presence of obstacles increase with their strength. For my own part, I cannot believe it; the power to do everything, which I should refuse to one of my equals, I will never grant to any number of them."

—**Alexis de Tocqueville**, *Democracy in America*

In your response, develop an argument about how both President Adams and Alexis de Tocqueville discuss the tension between the will of the majority and the enduring issue of protection of the minority in a democracy. Incorporate relevant and specific evidence from the quotes and your own knowledge of the United States government.

Refer to the *Social Studies Extended Response Evaluation Guide* on
page 723 to evaluate your response.

SOCIAL STUDIES PRACTICES PRACTICE QUESTIONS

Questions 1 and 2 are based on the following line graph and timeline.

Unemployment Rates During the New Deal : Percentage of Jobless Nonfarm Workers, 1926–1946

Source: U.S. Census Bureau, Bureau of Labor Statistics, Global insifht.

1. According to the Census Bureau's data on the graph, it can be concluded that the onset of World War II contributed to which change in the U.S. unemployment rate?

   A. The unemployment rate stabilized at the beginning of World War II and remained stable until the war's end.
   B. The unemployment rate declined consistently until shortly before the war's end.
   C. The unemployment rate decreased during World War II but remained above the normal rate throughout the war.
   D. The unemployment rate increased gradually throughout the war.

2. According to the graph, the most significant and uninterrupted change in the U.S. unemployment rate between 1926 and 1946 occurred immediately after

   A. the stock market crash
   B. FDR's first New Deal
   C. New Deal, Part 2, began
   D. the U.S. enters World War II

Questions 3 and 4 are based on the following passage.

The women's rights movement in the United States gained strength with the 1848 Seneca Falls Convention. The defining document of this gathering was the Declaration of Sentiments, which was patterned after the Declaration of Independence but focused on the fact that women lacked basic freedoms that men enjoyed. The revolutionary nature of the Seneca Falls Convention was apparent in the public's response to the event. One newspaper described Seneca Falls as "the most shocking and unnatural event ever recorded in the history of womanity."

3. Which of the following statements based on the passage is an opinion, not a fact?

   A. The Seneca Falls Convention helped the women's rights movement gain strength.
   B. The Declaration of Sentiments was modeled on the Declaration of Independence.
   C. The Declaration of Sentiments described how women's rights were limited.
   D. The Seneca Falls Convention was a shocking and unnatural event that undermined the nature of women.

4. Which of the following states the main idea of the passage above?

   A. Women lacked basic freedoms that men had, and they were angry.
   B. The Seneca Falls Convention was open to both men and women.
   C. The women's rights movement was stronger in Seneca Falls than in the rest of the United States.
   D. The Seneca Falls Convention was important in the fight for women's rights.

Questions 5 and 6 refer to the following map.

Reported Cases of Human Plague—United States, 1970–2010

1 dot placed in county of exposure for each plague case

Source: Centers for Disease Control

5. Which of the following conclusions is supported by this map?

   A. More than half of the reported cases of human plague in the United States between 1970 and 2010 were reported in four states.
   B. More than 99 percent of diphtheria-related deaths in the United States between 1970 and 2010 occurred in the western half of the United States.
   C. The majority of reported cases of plague in the American Southwest spread from one infected person.
   D. In the United States, human plague most frequently occurs within larger cities, where the risk of contagion is greatest.

6. The map above could be used to disprove which of the following claims?

   A. There were more cases of plague in the United States between 2000 and 2010 than there were between 1990 and 2000.
   B. Although many cases of plague have been reported in the United States since 1970, no deaths have been reported.
   C. Several cases of plague were reported on the East Coast of the United States between 1970 and 2010.
   D. Plague is less virulent in colder climates than it is in warmer climates.

Questions 7 and 8 are based on the following passage and chart.

The invention of the cotton gin by Eli Whitney in 1784 revolutionized the cotton industry in the American South. The separation of the cotton seeds and fibers, once a painstaking task that slaves performed by hand, could now be done quickly by machine. This made cotton goods more affordable, thereby increasing international demand for these goods and, consequently, the profits of cotton farmers. Ironically, however, the cotton gin did not reduce the South's reliance on slavery. In fact, with the boom of the cotton industry, more slaves were used to pick the cotton at a faster rate to keep up with the increasing demand for cotton.

Growth of Slavery and Cotton in America

■ Number of Slaves in the U.S.
■ National Cotton Production in Bales

7. Which of the following conclusions is supported by the passage?

   A. Eli Whitney invented the cotton gin with the hope that it would reduce slavery.
   B. The cotton gin had little impact on the cotton industry in the South.
   C. After the invention of the cotton gin, many plantation owners found that they needed fewer slaves.
   D. The effects of the cotton gin on the cotton industry actually led to an increased demand for slaves in the South.

8. According to the graph, approximately how much greater was the increase in the number of cotton bales produced between 1840 and 1860 than the increase in the number of slaves during the same interval?

   A. 750,000
   B. 1,500,000
   C. 2,000,000
   D. 4,000,000

Questions 9 and 10 are based on the following graph:

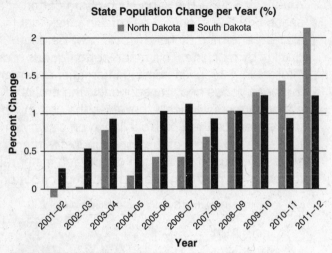

State Population Change per Year (%)

■ North Dakota ■ South Dakota

Source: United States Census Bureau

The above graph shows the percent increase, year by year, in the populations of each of North Dakota and South Dakota over eleven years.

9. Which of the following statements about the eleven-year period is supported by the graph above?

   A. North Dakota's population increased every year, while South Dakota's stayed the same.

   B. The population of South Dakota was originally greater than that of North Dakota, but in 2012, the population of North Dakota was greater than that of South Dakota.

   C. In most years, the percent population increase in South Dakota was greater than that in North Dakota.

   D. In most years, the percent population increase in North Dakota was greater than that in South Dakota.

10. Based on the graph above, the average percent increase in population per year for North Dakota was [Select...▾] the average percent increase in population per year for South Dakota for the period shown.

   • greater than
   • equal to
   • less than

Question 11 is based on the following graphic.

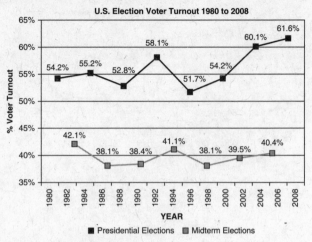

U.S. Election Voter Turnout 1980 to 2008

■ Presidential Elections ■ Midterm Elections

Source: weathertrends360.com

The chart above shows the percentage of registered voters who voted in presidential and midterm elections from 1980 to 2008.

11. The average voter turnout for midterm elections is approximately [Select...▾] of the average voter turnout for presidential elections.

   • 10 percent
   • 25 percent
   • 50 percent
   • 70 percent

Question 12 is based on the following chart.

Average Federal Tax Rates for All Households, by Household Income Quintile, 2005–2009					
Year	Lowest Quintile	Second Quintile	Middle Quintile	Fourth Quintile	Highest Quintile
2005	5.4	9.9	13.8	17.6	25.4
2006	5.7	9.9	13.9	17.7	25.4
2007	5.1	10.3	14.0	17.5	24.7
2008	1.5	7.3	11.6	15.6	23.6
2009	1.0	6.8	11.1	15.1	23.2

12. According to the chart, from 2005 to 2009, the median tax rate for households in the middle income quintile was

   A. 11.6 percent
   B. 12.8 percent
   C. 13.8 percent
   D. 14.0 percent

Answers and explanations start on page 680.

13. **Directions: Use 25 minutes to read, plan, and write an analysis of the two speech excerpts below. Incorporate evidence from both materials and your own knowledge in your response. Compose your answer on a computer if one is available, or write your answer on a separate sheet of paper.**

In this 1821 speech, Secretary of State John Quincy Adams spoke to the U.S. House of Representatives in celebration of the anniversary of Independence Day. In this speech, he touched on his ideal role for America in foreign affairs.

SPEECH EXCERPT

[America] goes not abroad, in search of monsters to destroy. She is the well-wisher to the freedom and independence of all. She is the champion and vindicator only of her own. She will commend the general cause by the countenance of her voice, and the benign sympathy of her example. She well knows that by once enlisting under other banners than her own, were they even the banners of foreign independence; she would involve herself beyond the power of extrication, in all the wars of interest and intrigue, of envy, and ambition, which assume the colors and usurp the standard of freedom. The fundamental maxims of her policy would insensibly change from liberty to force. She might become the dictatress of the world. She would be no longer the ruler of her own spirit.

—**John Quincy Adams, July 1821**

In the following speech, "The March of the Flag," Senator Albert Beveridge spoke of American imperialism as part of his 1898 campaign. His campaign followed President McKinley's success in the Spanish-American War and the American acquisition of Cuba, Puerto Rico, and Guam from the Spanish. At the time of this speech, the status of these newly acquired territories remained an open issue.

SPEECH EXCERPT

Therefore, in this campaign, the question is larger than a party question. It is an American question. It is a world question. Shall the American people continue their march toward the commercial supremacy of the world?

Shall free institutions broaden their blessed reign as the children of liberty wax in strength, until the empire of our principles is established over the hearts of all mankind?

. . .

Shall we be as the man who had one talent and hid it, or as he who had ten talents and used them until they grew to riches? And shall we reap the reward that waits on our discharge of our high duty; shall we occupy new markets for what our farmers raise, our factories make, our merchants sell—aye, and, please God, new markets for what our ships shall carry?

Hawaii is ours; [Puerto Rico] is to be ours; at the prayer of her people, Cuba finally will be ours.
. . .

. . .

The Opposition tells us that we ought not to govern a people without their consent. I answer: The rule of liberty that all just government derives its authority from the consent of the governed, applies only to those who are capable of self-government. We govern the Indians without their consent, we govern our territories without their consent, we govern our children without their consent. How do they know that our government would be without their consent?

—**Albert Beveridge, September 1898**

In your response, develop an argument comparing and contrasting John Quincy Adams's and Senator Beveridge's views of the role of America in foreign affairs. Discuss how these speeches may or may not apply to America and the world today. Incorporate relevant and specific evidence from the speeches and from your own knowledge.

Refer to the *Social Studies Extended Response Evaluation Guide* on page 723 to evaluate your response.

U.S. HISTORY

Exploration, Colonialism, and the American Revolution

The first Americans traveled from Asia across the Bering Strait into North America and, over many generations, down to South America. Called **Native Americans**, they established extensive tribal cultures and several advanced civilizations.

In the late 1400s, **explorers** from Europe searched for a sea route to Asia so they could trade for Asian gold and spices. They traveled around the tip of Africa. However, in 1492 Christopher Columbus convinced Spain to finance a trip west, across the Atlantic Ocean. When he reached land, he thought he had found India and called the inhabitants Indians. Later explorers realized that they had found a "New World," and many European nations set out to establish **colonies** there. The first explorers were searching for valuable resources and for the glory of conquest. This colonization led to tragedy for many Native Americans who died from diseases or were killed, enslaved, or forced off their lands.

In the 1500s and 1600s, European nations, including Spain, France, England, and the Netherlands, established settlements in North America. Settlements were established to gain power and wealth or to provide colonists a place for permanent residence. The first permanent English settlement was established in Jamestown, Virginia, in 1607. In 1620, the **Pilgrims** sailed to the Americas aboard the *Mayflower* and established a second English colony in Massachusetts. Beginning about 1675, colonists began importing a large number of slaves who had been forcibly taken from Africa. Many were put to work on the plantation system in the Southern colonies.

The colonies grew rapidly in the early 1700s. When England defeated France in the French and Indian War (1754–1763), England acquired many of France's American colonies. After the war, England sought to regain more control over the Thirteen Colonies. It also sought to recover economically from the debts caused by the costly war. New British taxes and policies troubled the colonists; however, it was not until 1775 that a war for independence seemed inevitable. After a series of skirmishes, the **Continental Congress** assigned George Washington to lead the Continental Army and ordered publication of the **Declaration of Independence** on July 4, 1776.

Despite the superiority of the well-trained British forces, the Americans had the advantage of defending their own land and eventually forged a fighting force with strong military leaders. The **American Revolution** lasted until the surrender of the British at Yorktown in 1781. In 1783, the final treaty to end the war resulted in the recognition of American independence. The new nation initially formed a weak national government through the **Articles of Confederation**. This first effort stressed a loose confederation of the states with strong local control. Over time, many colonial leaders recognized the need for a centralized government. The principles of this government were established in the **U.S. Constitution**, which was ratified in 1788. To counter fears of an overly powerful government, the first ten amendments to the Constitution, the **Bill of Rights**, promised many individual freedoms, such as freedom of speech and assembly.

Key Ideas

- European explorers sought wealth and conquest in the New World from the 1400s to the 1600s.
- The Thirteen Colonies declared independence from England in 1776.
- America won its independence in 1783 and ratified the U.S. Constitution in 1788.

GED® TEST TIP

*Reviewing key vocabulary can help you prepare for the GED® Test. As you review, look up any words that you do not understand. Pay special attention to the words in **bold** type.*

PRACTICE 1

Questions 1 and 2 refer to the following map.

European Colonial Settlements, 1650

St. Lawrence River

Quebec

Montreal

Boston

Plymouth

New Haven

New Amsterdam

Atlantic Ocean

Jamestown

Roanoke Island

N
W   E
S

St. Augustine

Legend	
Dutch	
English	
French	
Spanish	
Swedish	

1. Choose the correct phrase that would fill in the blank.
   Based on the map, [Select... ▾] had the southernmost colony in 1650.

   • the Dutch
   • the English
   • the Spanish
   • the Swedish

2. Which of the following conclusions is supported by the map?

   A. By 1650, Spain had conquered most of North America.
   B. The English established several colonies in the New World.
   C. The Dutch established their colonies in the western part of North America.
   D. French colonies extended along the East Coast between Boston and Jamestown.

3. Some of the early colonists did not come to the New World to gain power and wealth. These groups came seeking freedom from persecution.

   Which immigrant group is most similar to those early colonists?

   A. African slaves who were involuntarily brought to work on plantations
   B. Mexican workers who came to the United States to earn better wages than they could at home
   C. British businessmen who visited the United States to invest in media companies
   D. Haitian refugees who fled to the United States to escape a dictatorship

4. According to the information on page 430, which of the following was a cause of the American Revolution?

   A. France's defeat in the French and Indian War
   B. increased British taxes and restrictions on the colonies
   C. Britain's acquisition of France's colonies in North America
   D. the publication of the Declaration of Independence

5. The first amendment to the U.S. Constitution states: "Congress shall make no law abridging the right of the people peaceably to assemble, and to petition the government for a redress of grievances."

   Based on the passage on page 430, what is the most likely reason the framers of the Constitution included these guarantees?

   A. They were planning to organize assemblies.
   B. They were concerned about the government becoming tyrannical.
   C. They were hoping to petition the government.
   D. They were attempting to prevent a redress of grievances.

Answers and explanations start on page 681.

U.S. HISTORY

Westward Expansion, the Civil War, and Reconstruction

Key Ideas

- The economy of the South was based on slavery. The Northern economy was based on paid labor.
- Conflict over whether slavery should be allowed in the nation's new western territories led to the Civil War.
- The North won the war and ended slavery. During Reconstruction, the South was rebuilt.

Early on in the history of the United States, the North and the South diverged economically. The North developed a varied economy that included industry and commerce as well as agriculture. Slavery had been legal throughout the North during the colonial period. However, by the early 1800s, it was **abolished** in all Northern states. Women and **immigrants**, as well as men, provided labor for the growing economy in the North.

The Southern economy was based largely on agriculture. By the 1800s, there was one major crop in the South: cotton. Planting and harvesting cotton required a lot of labor. Southern farmers came to depend more and more on slaves to do the work, and the number of enslaved persons grew in the South.

As the United States expanded during the early 1800s, the North and the South worked to maintain a balance of power. New states were generally added in pairs, one slave and one free. But there was increasing tension over the vast western territory that had become part of the United States by the mid-1800s. In the 1850s, Congress voted that the territories themselves should decide whether or not to allow slavery. This soon led to war in Kansas. People from both the North and the South rushed to settle the territory. Voter fraud in the 1855 elections led to the setup of two warring governments. The violence in Kansas foreshadowed the violence that soon tore up the nation.

In the late 1850s, political parties fractured over the slavery issue. Four candidates ran for president in 1860. Abraham Lincoln, who promised to halt the spread of slavery (although not abolish it where it already existed) won. Opposed to Lincoln's policies, most slave states **seceded** from the United States. They set up their own government, called the **Confederacy**. By April 1861, the United States (called the **Union**) and the Confederacy were at war.

At first it seemed as if the Confederacy might win. They had well-trained military leaders and soldiers who were willing to fight hard to hold onto their way of life, so the Confederacy won many early battles. However, by the summer of 1863, the Confederacy began to wear down. Ammunition, uniforms, and shoes were in short supply for Confederate soldiers because the South lacked industry. There were food shortages for soldiers and civilians alike. The war was fought mostly in the South, and the destruction was terrible. After four long years, in 1865, Confederate general Robert E. Lee surrendered to Union general Ulysses S. Grant. The Civil War ended.

For the next 12 years, federal troops oversaw the rebuilding of the South. This period was called **Reconstruction**. Schools were established for former slaves, who were all freed when the war ended. However, the **sharecropping** system, which kept black farmers enslaved economically, soon came into being. Whites who came back to power as Reconstruction ended in the South in the 1870s prevented African Americans from exercising their right to vote. The Civil War ended slavery, but it did not end racism.

PRACTICE 2

1. Based on the passage on page 432, which of the following disagreements was a main cause of the Civil War?

   A. whether cotton should be the main crop in the South
   B. whether slavery should continue to exist
   C. whether the United States should expand westward
   D. whether slavery should be permitted in territories in the West

2. In 1820, Missouri proposed to enter the Union as a slave state. Based on the passage, what do you think was the response of Northerners in Congress?

   A. They supported having another slave state join the Union.
   B. They lobbied against having Missouri join the Union at all.
   C. To balance the admission of Missouri, they agreed to a compromise in which Maine was admitted as a free state.
   D. They started a war to prevent Missouri from attaining statehood.

3. In the mid-1950s, the country of Vietnam was divided. There was a communist government in the North and a noncommunist government in the South. The two fought for control of Vietnam. In 1975, the communists won. Vietnam was united under this form of government.

   Because both wars [Select... ▾], the Vietnam War and the U.S. Civil War can be said to share some similarities.

   • involved racial conflict
   • saw the addition of new territory upset the balance of power
   • concluded with the formation of new nations
   • concluded with the reunification of the nation

Questions 4 and 5 refer to the following photographs of people who served in South Carolina's state government in 1868.

Photography by Katherine Wetzel. Reprinted with the permission of The Museum of the Confederacy, Richmond, Virginia.

4. Which of the following is a fact confirmed by information in the photographs?

   A. Southern Democrats were treated very well during Reconstruction.
   B. It was unfair that former Confederate soldiers could vote during Reconstruction.
   C. In 1868, many African Americans served in the government of South Carolina.
   D. The most qualified leaders in South Carolina government in 1868 were African Americans.

5. Which of the following conclusions is supported by the photographs and the passage on page 432?

   A. Over the course of Reconstruction, African Americans in the South gained and then lost political power.
   B. Over the course of Reconstruction, African Americans in the South lost and then gained political power.
   C. Over the course of Reconstruction, whites in the South gained and then lost political power.
   D. In the early years of Reconstruction, African Americans served in government in each Southern state.

Answers and explanations start on page 681.

U.S. HISTORY

Industrialization, Immigration, and the Progressive Era

Key Ideas

- The U.S. underwent rapid industrialization starting in the mid-1800s.
- Immigrants came from many places to work in the expanding American industries.
- Rapid industrialization brought problems, which labor unions and reformers tried to solve, especially during the Progressive Era.

ON THE GED® TEST

The GED® Social Studies Test examines your ability to interpret graphs, charts, maps, and other visual sources of information.

In the mid-1800s, American industries, which had been growing steadily since the late 1700s, began a period of extremely fast growth. This rapid **industrialization** occurred for several interconnected reasons. With the addition of the vast western territories, the United States gained plentiful **natural resources**. Among these resources were materials, such as metals, needed to manufacture new products and machines, and fuels, such as coal, needed to run these machines. Another reason for rapid industrialization was the invention of many new machines and new industrial processes. With these new inventions and processes, manufactured goods could be produced more easily, more efficiently, and less expensively. A third reason for the rapid industrialization was the nation's booming population. The U.S. population more than doubled in the last 40 years of the 1800s. There were more people to buy more goods, spurring commerce and further industrial growth.

Rapid industrialization meant that many new factories were built in the mid- and late-1800s. Most were built in or near the nation's large cities, including New York, Boston, Chicago, Philadelphia, and Pittsburgh. These urban centers had large groups of people who could work in the factories and large groups of people who would buy the goods the factories produced.

U.S. factory jobs drew many **immigrants** to American cities. Although the United States has always been a "nation of immigrants," the late 1800s saw a sharp rise in the number of people moving here from foreign countries. The majority came from Europe, including Germany, Italy, Russia, and Eastern European countries. Many also came from Mexico and Central America. Asian immigration was declining because the government had passed laws barring Chinese from moving to the United States. However, thousands of Japanese came to this country, taking jobs in farm fields and mines.

America's factory workers, whether native- or foreign-born, worked very hard at grueling, dangerous work. Many received low pay for long hours on the job. Over time, workers began to unionize. By joining a **union**, workers pledged to work together for better and safer working conditions and higher wages. They called **strikes** when their employers cut their pay or refused to grant raises. Many of the laws we have today, including the eight-hour workday and the five-day workweek, came about through the bitter struggles for better working conditions that unions waged in the late 1800s and the early 1900s.

Unions weren't the only groups working to solve problems brought on by America's rapid industrialization. Some reformers worked to clean up slums, improve health care, and stop child labor. Others worked to preserve the nation's natural beauty by creating national parks. Still others worked to give more people a voice in government. For example, many women lobbied to gain the right to vote. In the early 1900s, groups were working toward so many sweeping social and political improvements that the time is called the **Progressive Era**.

PRACTICE 3

<u>Questions 1 through 4 are based on the information on page 434.</u>

1. Which of the following always occurs during a period of rapid industrialization?

   A. the annexation of new territory
   B. an increase in manufacturing
   C. an increase in population
   D. an increase in immigration

2. Which event directly contributed to the growth of American industries in the mid-1800s?

   A. the passage of the Chinese Exclusion Act, which banned Chinese immigration
   B. the passage of the Sherman Antitrust Act, which helped prevent businesses from forming monopolies
   C. the development of the Bessemer process, which made it easier to produce steel
   D. the development of settlement houses to aid impoverished immigrants and city dwellers

3. Based on the passage, which of the following would early union workers have valued the most?

   A. productivity in the workplace
   B. contact with people of all different backgrounds
   C. cooperation with others to improve worker safety
   D. the freedom to work whenever they pleased

4. What was a strong ideal held by people working toward reforms during the Progressive Era?

   A. efficiency
   B. wealth
   C. artistic beauty
   D. fairness

<u>Questions 5 and 6 refer to the following graphs.</u>

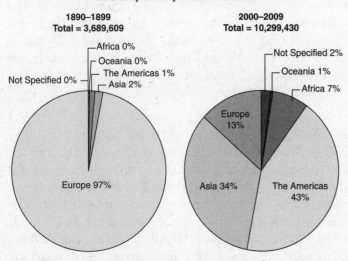

Persons Obtaining Legal Permanent Resident Status in the U.S. by Country of Last Residence

1890–1899
Total = 3,689,609

Africa 0%
Oceania 0%
The Americas 1%
Asia 2%
Not Specified 0%
Europe 97%

2000–2009
Total = 10,299,430

Not Specified 2%
Oceania 1%
Africa 7%
Europe 13%
Asia 34%
The Americas 43%

5. Which of the following best completes this statement? In the 1890s, the vest majority of persons gaining permanent legal residency came from Europe, whereas in the early 2000s, a majority of such persons came from [Select... ▾].

   • Europe and Asia
   • Asia and the Americas
   • Africa, Oceania, and Europe

6. **You MAY use your calculator to answer this question.**
   Based on the graphs, which of the following is true of the number of persons who came from Europe and gained legal permanent resident status?

   A. In the 1890s, that number was roughly seven times what it was in the period of 2000–2009.
   B. In the 1890s, that number was less than what it was in the period of 2000–2009.
   C. In the 1890s, that number was roughly three times what it was in the period of 2000–2009.
   D. In the 1890s, that number was the same as what it was in the period of 2000–2009.

   Answers and explanations start on page 681.

U.S. HISTORY

The United States as an Emerging World Power

The expansion of U.S. industries in the mid-1800s had an effect not only on the nation's economy but also on its politics. Business and government leaders wanted access to more natural resources, which industries needed to continue growing. They also wanted to be able to sell more goods overseas. Regions in Africa, Asia, and Latin America had rich natural resources. People in these regions might buy what Americans wanted to sell. To promote industrial growth and increase its power, the United States became imperialistic. **Imperialism** is the policy by which a stronger nation extends economic, military, and/or political control over a weaker nation or region.

European nations had been engaging in imperialism for many centuries. In the late 1800s, the United States joined in. In 1898, the United States fought the Spanish-American War. Ostensibly, the United States declared war on Spain because of Spain's mistreatment of Cuba, which was a Spanish colony. Yet, after winning the war, the United States took over Spain's colonies of Cuba, Puerto Rico, the Philippines, and Guam. It granted independence to none of them.

The next war the United States was involved in was World War I, which began in Europe in 1913. It pitted two groups of nations against each other. One group was called the **Allies;** the leading Allied nations included Great Britain, Russia, and France. The other group was called the **Central Powers,** which included Germany, Austria-Hungary, and the Ottoman Empire. The Allies and Central Powers fought for three years in what fast became a deadly stalemate. Then, in 1917, the United States, alarmed over Germany's sinking of American ships, joined the Allies. With American help, in November 1918 the Allies defeated the Central Powers, and World War I ended.

Because the destruction was so terrible, some people called World War I "the war to end all wars." However, this was not to be. Within 12 years, by 1929, the world had fallen into a serious economic downturn, which Americans called the **Great Depression**. Economic problems aided the rise of **fascism** in Europe and elsewhere. Fascist nations squelched democracy and advocated the takeover of other nations. Germany, led by fascist dictator Adolf Hitler, started attacking smaller nations in Europe in the mid-1930s. Italy fought to take over Ethiopia, in Africa. Japan attacked China. Hitler built an alliance with Italy and Japan, which came to be called the **Axis**. By 1939, war again broke out between the Axis and the Allies.

The United States did not enter World War II until 1941, when the Japanese bombed the U.S. naval base at Pearl Harbor in Hawaii. This time, Americans fought not only in Europe but also in Africa and Asia as well. With its horrific battles, the fire-bombing of cities, the **Holocaust**, and the dropping of two atomic bombs on Japan, World War II led to massive destruction. The United States, which played a major part in the Allied victory in World War II in 1945, also played a major part in helping to rebuild war-scourged nations after the war was over.

PRACTICE 4

Question 1 refers to the following chart.

Factors Related to the Growth of Imperialism

Economic	Desire for greater access to natural resources or new markets
Military	Desire for control of ports that could serve as refueling stations for long sea voyages or air flights
Political	Desire to spread the institutions of democracy or other political systems
Religious	Desire to spread Christianity or other faith
Cultural/Racial	Lack of respect for different cultures or races

1. Cuba lies about 90 miles off the coast of Florida. After the United States freed Cuba from Spanish rule in 1898, the U.S. Navy built an important base there.

   Circle the factor in the chart above that best explains the situation in Cuba after 1898.

2. What assumption do you need to make to fully understand the last sentence in paragraph 4 on page 436?

   A. In World War I, the Allies fought the Central Powers.
   B. In World War II, the Allies included England, France, and Russia.
   C. In World War II, the Allies included the Germans, Austrians, and Ottoman Turks.
   D. In World War II, the Axis included Germany, Italy, and Japan.

3. Franklin D. Roosevelt became president during the height of the Great Depression, in 1933. He soon instituted a set of federal programs called the New Deal to try to lower unemployment.

   Which conclusion about the effectiveness of New Deal programs does the text on page 436 and graph below support?

U.S. Unemployment Rate, 1929–1944

Source: *Historical Statistics of the United States*

   A. Within a year, the New Deal had raised unemployment to its pre-Depression level.
   B. Within a year, the New Deal had lowered unemployment to its pre-Depression level.
   C. Unemployment fell after the start of the New Deal and continued to fall sharply as the United States entered World War II.
   D. The New Deal lowered unemployment, but Allied victory in World War II lowered it further.

4. Which statement best summarizes the main idea of paragraph 5 on page 436?

   A. America entered World War II in 1941.
   B. Americans fought in Europe, Africa, and Asia.
   C. World War II involved more nations than any other war ever fought.
   D. America took a strong leadership role during and after World War II.

Answers and explanations start on page 682.

LESSON 5

U.S. History

The Cold War and the Civil Rights Era

Key Ideas

- The Cold War dominated U.S. foreign policy from the end of WWII until the fall of the Soviet Union.
- Social changes in the U.S. in the mid-1900s included the expansion of civil rights for minorities.
- Technological advances have introduced benefits but also caused problems.

ON THE GED® TEST

The GED® Social Studies Test will include some questions that focus on the role of the United States in the world.

After World War II ended, the capitalist and communist nations soon began engaging in a power struggle called the **Cold War**. Leading the capitalist nations was the United States; leading the communist nations was the Soviet Union. The Cold War never led to direct fighting between these two superpowers, although there was a constant threat of nuclear war. Clashes between communism and capitalism did lead to numerous smaller conflicts. These included the Korean War of the early 1950s and the Vietnam War, which lasted from 1954 to 1975. The United States sent soldiers to both. The Vietnam War was long and difficult and caused deep division among Americans. The United States sent massive military aid to the non-communist South Vietnamese, but they kept losing to the communist North Vietnamese. Although a few Americans wanted to continue fighting, in 1973 America pulled out of Vietnam. In 1975, the communists took over the country.

The Cold War ended in 1991 with the breakup of the Soviet Union and the end of communism there. In the late 1980s, Soviet leader Mikhail Gorbachev had tried to reform the communist government. But the loosening of Soviet control had led to the collapse of many communist governments of Eastern Europe. The Berlin Wall, which had separated East and West Germany, was torn down. With communism no longer so threatening, world politics became less tense but also more unpredictable.

During the second half of the 20th century, the United States continued to face many challenges. In the 1950s, African American leaders launched the **civil rights movement** to try to end segregation and discrimination in the United States. Among their victories included the integration of public schools and other public facilities, the passage of laws protecting the voting rights of minorities, and the striking down of laws that permitted overt discrimination based on race or cultural background. However, minority groups and people of all backgrounds concerned about fair application of the law have continued to be vigilant in insisting that civil rights laws be upheld.

Another area of challenge in recent decades has been **technology**. Technology has led to many advances in science, medicine, and our personal lives. Computers, for instance, make many jobs easier and more productive. They allow almost instantaneous communication with co-workers, family, and friends. Furthermore, they allow people from around the world to share information quickly and easily, giving us the sense that we live in a "global village." However, our reliance on the use of technology has led us to pollute the air with exhaust from a growing number of cars. It has led us to pollute the water with acid rain, resulting from burning coal to generate increased electricity. It has led us to pollute our land with mountains of trash and tons of hazardous wastes.

PRACTICE 5

1. The conflict during the second half of the twentieth century between the United States and the Soviet Union was called the Cold War because it involved (1) `Select...▼`. In 1991, the (2) `Select...▼` finally brought the Cold War to an end.

Select (1)	Select (2)
• communists and capitalists	• destruction of the Berlin Wall
• two countries at the far north of Earth	• dissolution of the Soviet Union
• the threat of nuclear war	• separation of East and West Germany
• no direct combat	• death of Mikhail Gorbachev

2. Which of the following best summarizes the message of the cartoon below?

© 1980 Mark Alan Stamaty. Reprinted with permission of the artist.

   A. Nuclear bombs are extremely destructive.
   B. Expanding U.S. nuclear capabilities is a good idea.
   C. The buildup of nuclear arms increases fear and instability, not peace.
   D. The threat of nuclear war is lessened if both superpowers have equally powerful weapons.

3. Which of the following statements about the Vietnam War is a false generalization?

   A. Some Americans served in both Korea and Vietnam.
   B. The United States sent massive military aid to South Vietnam.
   C. Americans were in complete agreement about pulling out of Vietnam.
   D. The Vietnam War lasted much longer than the Korean War.

4. Which of the following goals would a civil rights activist be most likely to pursue?

   A. getting Congress to enact laws to restrict the sale of firearms
   B. petition for a city ordinance requiring those selling real estate to select a buyer without regard to race
   C. getting local companies to stop polluting the environment
   D. working with local clergy to publicize a worship service open to people of all religions

5. Which of the following is a conclusion about technology rather than a supporting detail?

   A. Reliance on technology has increased pollution.
   B. Cars cause air pollution.
   C. Coal-generating power plants cause acid-rain pollution.
   D. The ease of manufacturing disposable items has led to land pollution at landfill sites.

Answers and explanations start on page 682.

U.S. HISTORY PRACTICE QUESTIONS

Questions 1 and 2 refer to the timeline below.

Important Events in Early Cherokee History

1. Which of the following is a conclusion based on multiple details in the timeline?

   A. The Cherokee had begun farming around 800, before Europeans came to America.
   B. Although the Cherokee adopted many aspects of white culture, they were driven off their ancestral lands.
   C. The Cherokee traditionally considered land ownership to be a tribal matter rather than a right of individuals acting on their own.
   D. The Bible was one of the first books the Cherokee translated into their written language.

2. When President Andrew Jackson mandated that the Cherokee move west in 1830, he claimed that the U.S. government would be better able to protect the Cherokee from whites who might try to get their new land in the West. The Cherokee considered this to be illogical.

   Which of the following summarizes the logical fallacy?

   A. If the government can't protect us from white settlers here, now, how could it protect us from whites moving west in the future?
   B. If you ask us to move to the West now, how do we know you won't ask us to move back to the South in the future?
   C. If the land we have in the South is good, why wouldn't the land in the West be better?
   D. If the state governments are protecting us now, why can't the U.S. government help later?

3. In the late 1700s, Abigail Adams—wife of John Adams, who was our nation's second president—wrote the following in a letter to her sister:

   I will never consent to have our sex considered in an inferior point of light. Let each planet shine in their [its] own orbit . . . if man is Lord, woman is *Lordess*—that is what I contend for.

   Based on this letter, which of the following principles was Abigail Adams advocating?

   A. the separation of church and state
   B. the abolition of slavery
   C. the promotion of scientific learning
   D. equal rights and opportunities for women

Questions 4 and 5 refer to the following map.

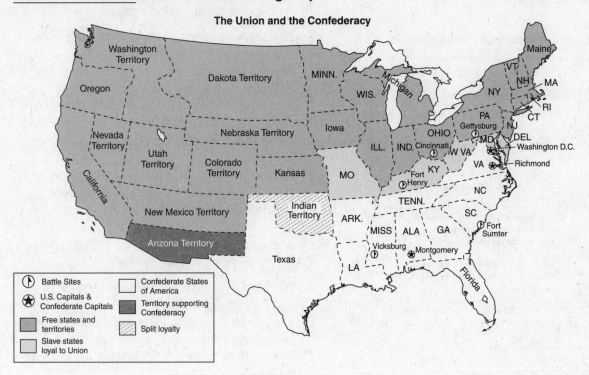

The Union and the Confederacy

4. List four states that permitted slavery but did not join the Confederacy.

_____

_____

_____

_____

5. The loyalty of Maryland was of crucial importance to the Union. Based on the map, which statement best explains why this was so?

A. The nation's capital was located nearby.
B. The Confederate capital was located there.
C. It was close to Fort Sumter, where the Civil War began.
D. Important rail lines ran through Baltimore, Maryland.

6. In the Emancipation Proclamation, issued in 1863, President Lincoln freed all people enslaved in the states that had seceded from the Union. This proclamation was explicitly not to be put into effect in slave states that had remained in the Union. The proclamation went on to say:

I hereby enjoin upon the people so declared to be free to abstain from all violence . . . and make known that such persons of suitable condition will be received into the armed services of the United States to garrison forts, positions, stations, and other places, and to man vessels of all sorts.

Based on the information given about the Emancipation Proclamation and the text of the order itself, which of the following was a major reason Lincoln issued the proclamation?

A. to encourage states to secede from the Union
B. to punish slaveholders throughout the South
C. to weaken the North by enlisting former slaves in the Confederate army
D. to weaken the South by enlisting former slaves in the Union army

Questions 7 through 9 refer to the following chart.

Civil Rights Amendment and Laws

14th Amendment (1868)	Granted citizenship and equal protection of the law to all persons born in the United States (not applied to American Indians)
15th Amendment (1870)	Granted voting rights to African Americans
Civil Rights Act of 1875	Gave African Americans the right to serve on juries Banned racial segregation in public places
Civil Rights Act of 1964	Outlawed segregation by race in public places and racial discrimination in employment
Voting Rights Act of 1965	Prohibited literacy tests for voting Allowed the federal government to register voters
Civil Rights Act of 1968	Outlawed discrimination in the sale or rental of homes

7. An Asian American registers to vote and is given a reading test. Place a dot in the cell from the chart above containing the civil rights amendment or law relevant to this situation.

8. Which statement best summarizes what this chart shows about voting rights?

   A. African Americans were granted the vote five years after the Civil War ended.
   B. African Americans were granted the vote 100 years after the Civil War ended.
   C. African Americans were granted the vote soon after the Civil War, but laws enforcing these rights had to be passed a century later.
   D. African Americans were granted the vote in 1870 but American Indians were never granted these same rights.

9. How are the Civil Rights Act of 1875 and the Civil Rights Act of 1964 similar?

   A. They both guaranteed African Americans citizenship rights.
   B. They both prohibited the legal separation of people by race in public places.
   C. They both ensured that African Americans could serve on juries.
   D. They both make job discrimination illegal.

10. Alexander Graham Bell invented the telephone in the spring of 1876. In the fall, he exhibited it at an exposition in Philadelphia. When leading scientists saw Bell's invention, they said, "Here is the greatest marvel ever achieved in electrical science."

    Which of the following statements related to the passage is an opinion, not a fact?

    A. Bell invented the telephone in 1876.
    B. Bell exhibited the telephone at an exposition in Philadelphia.
    C. Scientists admired Bell's invention.
    D. The telephone was the greatest electrical invention ever.

Questions 11 through 13 are based on the paragraph and the political cartoon below.

In 1974, President Richard Nixon resigned from office. He had been involved in a scandal known as Watergate. The Watergate scandal implicated Nixon in covering up crimes committed by members of his reelection committee. These crimes ranged from illegally harassing political opponents to burglary and bribery. With Congress investigating him, he was sure to be impeached. This cartoon was published before Nixon resigned to avoid impeachment.

Hey guys, do you really think we need that clause about impeachment in there?

Cartoon by Robert Lawlor. Reprinted with permission of the *Philadelphia Daily News*.

11. In this cartoon, whom is Nixon addressing?

    A. the writers of the Declaration of Independence
    B. the framers of the U.S. Constitution
    C. the past presidents of the United States
    D. the present session of Congress

12. Which value was Congress furthering by investigating Nixon and Watergate?

    A. the pursuit of justice
    B. the duty of obedience
    C. loyalty to a friend
    D. love of mercy

13. About Watergate, one historian has written, "In a society in which distrust of leaders and institutions of authority was already widespread, the fall of Richard Nixon seemed to confirm the most cynical assumptions about the character of American public life."

Based on the information on page 438, which of the following was most likely a reason for Americans' growing distrust of their government in the years just prior to Watergate?

    A. mismanagement of the New Deal
    B. the beginning of rock music
    C. the escalation and failure of the Vietnam War
    D. the scandals of previous presidents, including John Kennedy and Bill Clinton

Questions 14 and 15 refer to the graph below.

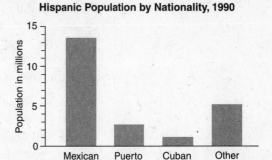

Hispanic Population by Nationality, 1990

Source: U.S. Census Bureau

14. In 1990, approximately how many people of Cuban nationality lived in the United States?

    A.   100
    B.   100,000
    C. 1,000,000
    D. 5,000,000

15. A Hispanic family moved into an apartment next door to yours in 1990. Based solely on the bar graph, which place was the family most likely to be from?

    A. Cuba
    B. Mexico
    C. Puerto Rico
    D. Spain

Answers and explanations start on page 682.

CIVICS AND GOVERNMENT

Historic Basis for U.S. System

- The idea of democracy originated with the Ancient Greeks who spoke of the 'rule of the people.'
- The historic basis of the U.S. government came from the British system that limited the king's powers and protected individual rights.
- The U.S. system evolved from the British idea of a parliamentary democracy to a representative democracy.

ON THE GED® TEST

While you will not need to memorize dates, it will be helpful to be familiar with key terms, such as the ones in **bold** *type.*

The system of government in the United States is known as **representative democracy**. In this form of government, the citizens vote to elect representatives who make and execute laws. To understand this form of democracy, it is helpful to first distinguish democracy from other types of government. Then, you can trace the historical development of democracy and see how representative democracy differs from other types of democracy employed over time and around the globe.

The origins of **democracy** are ancient. The term *democracy*, which means "rule of the people" in Greek, arose in approximately 500 BCE in the Greek city-state of Athens. This distinguishes democracy from **monarchy**, the "rule of one person" (such as a king or queen); **aristocracy**, the "rule of an elite class" (lords or barons, for example); **theocracy**, the "rule of the church"; and **anarchy**, the "rule of the mob" (arguably not a form of government at all). Democracy is also distinct from forms of **authoritarian rule**, such as dictatorship, military rule, and fascism.

In ancient Athenian democracy, laws were voted upon by a council of all citizens, a system known as **direct democracy**. In ancient Athens, however, a "citizen" was defined as a free male landowner over the age of 20. Women, foreigners, slaves, non-landowners, and minors were excluded from the vote.

For the eventual development of democracy in the U.S., one of the most important events was the signing of the **Magna Carta** (Latin for Great Charter) in England in 1215. England was a monarchy, but some protested the king's absolute power. The result was the signing of the Magna Carta, a document limiting the king's rule and subjecting his decisions to review. This same period also saw the development of the legal doctrine of **habeas corpus**, which made it illegal for the government to hold or imprison individuals without granting them trials.

Over time, the group allowed by the Magna Carta to review the king's decisions developed into a **parliament** of lawmakers appointed by title and/or elected by citizens. As the power of the parliament grew, England transformed into a **parliamentary democracy**. In this system, a government is formed by the party holding a majority of seats in the parliament. In most parliamentary democracies, the majority party appoints or authorizes the chief executive, such as the president.

Known as the Age of Enlightenment, the 17th and 18th centuries saw the spread of democracy to many other European countries. England, France, Holland, and other European powers also adopted **bills of rights** for individuals during this period. The philosophies dominant in this era emphasized reason and individual rights and encouraged government by the people. Enlightenment philosophers such as Adam Smith, John Locke, and Voltaire strongly influenced the founders of the United States.

PRACTICE 1

Questions 1 through 5 are based on the information on page 444.

Directions: Match each choice in the box corresponding to the form of government that best matches the description.

1.

Direct democracy	
Monarchy	
Representative democracy	
Aristocracy	

Choices:

In <u>Country A</u>, laws are made and administered by lords who inherit their lands and titles.
In <u>Country B</u>, laws are made by a sovereign king and are subject to no review.
In <u>Country C</u>, laws are made by Congress, an elected group of representatives.
In <u>Country D</u>, laws are made by the vote of all citizens.

Directions: For <u>Questions 2 through 5</u>, choose the <u>one best answer</u> to each question.

2. Which of following can be inferred about the Founding Fathers of the United States?

   A. They sought to establish the power of the king of England in the United States.
   B. They were concerned about protecting the rights of individuals.
   C. They argued that the United States should adopt a system of direct democracy.
   D. They thought representatives from the United States should sit in Parliament.

3. In the United States, laws are enacted by Congress, a group of representatives elected by the people. Which of the following was most likely the chief historical model for the U.S. Congress?

   A. Athenian council of citizens
   B. Magna Carta
   C. Parliament of England
   D. Declaration of the Rights of Man and the Citizen adopted in France in 1789

4. Some nations have been ruled by a form of government known as constitutional monarchy. While a king or queen is the single, sovereign ruler of the country, his or her power is limited by a constitution, a formal document outlining which of the monarch's decisions are subject to review or may be overruled by a court of law.

   Which of the following was most likely a constitutional monarchy?

   A. the ancient city-state of Athens
   B. any country ruled by fascism
   C. the United States at the time of its founding
   D. England during the Age of Enlightenment

5. If the United States were a parliamentary democracy, which of the following would be most likely to occur?

   A. The office of the president would decrease in power.
   B. The office of the president would increase in power.
   C. The president would be elected by a majority vote of all citizens.
   D. The president would be appointed by the majority party in parliament.

Answers and explanations start on page 683.

CIVICS AND GOVERNMENT

Constitutional Government

Key Ideas

- The U.S. Constitution is the basis for our government structure and legal system.
- The Bill of Rights—the first ten constitutional amendments—define the rights of citizens.
- Amendments to the Constitution require wide support, but many important amendments have gained enough support to be ratified.

The Constitution of the United States is the foundation of our national government and legal system. The United States is a **republic**, a form of government in which citizens elect the people who will govern them. A republic is very different from a government system in which citizens do not choose their political leaders, such as a **monarchy** or **dictatorship**.

The people who wrote the Constitution set particular goals for the new nation, which they stated in the **preamble**, or introduction. They wanted to unite the states under one government, establish a nation where people could live peacefully and safely under the rule of law, and make prosperity and freedom possible for all citizens.

Following the preamble are the original seven **articles** of the U.S. Constitution. These articles provide for the three branches of government (see page 448), establish the rights of states, and set forth procedures for ratifying and amending the Constitution. Article 6 states that all government officials must uphold the Constitution as "the supreme law of the land" and that no other laws can contradict any part of the Constitution.

According to Article 5, a constitutional **amendment** can be proposed by Congress if it is supported by two-thirds majorities in both the House and Senate. The proposed amendment then must be ratified by three-fourths of the states. This process ensures that amendments have very broad national support.

The original Constitution did not specifically describe citizens' rights. Even as the Constitution was being written, some political leaders insisted that a bill of rights was needed to help develop citizens' trust in the new government. However, they agreed to wait to make amendments to the Constitution until after it was **ratified**. As a result of this compromise, the first ten amendments to the U.S. Constitution, passed in 1791, became the **Bill of Rights**. These rights are well known to many Americans. The First Amendment, for example, guarantees freedom of religion, freedom of speech, and freedom of the press. The Sixth and Seventh Amendments guarantee citizens' rights to trial by jury.

As Americans' ideas about citizenship and government have evolved, the amendment process has allowed the Constitution to evolve as well. The Thirteenth Amendment (1865) outlawed slavery; the Fifteenth Amendment (1870) established that the rights of citizens "shall not be denied or abridged ... on account of race, color, or previous condition of servitude."

A number of constitutional amendments have extended voting rights to citizens. The Nineteenth Amendment (1920) gave women the right to vote. The Twenty-fourth Amendment (1964) banned poll taxes, which some states were using to prevent African Americans from voting. The Twenty-sixth Amendment (1971) lowered the voting age to 18.

PRACTICE 2

1. Based on the information on page 446, which of the following is the main characteristic of a republic?

   A. voting rights extended to few adult citizens
   B. elected representatives exercising government power on behalf of citizens
   C. people governing themselves by voting directly on all issues
   D. power concentrated among a small group

2. The Constitution is a relatively brief document containing only about seven thousand words. It establishes the structure and powers of the U.S. government but does not give many specifics.

   What assumption were the drafters of the Constitution working under as they kept the document general and brief?

   A. There was not enough time to draft a long, detailed document before the states had to ratify it.
   B. Most of the power of the federal government would be reserved to the president, who could govern as he saw fit.
   C. The details of government would be worked out in the future, as the need arose, within the framework of the Constitution.
   D. Written constitutions were an untested basis for democratic government, so it was better to keep such a document brief.

3. Franklin Delano Roosevelt was elected to the presidency four times between 1933 and 1945. In reaction to this, the Twenty-second Amendment, ratified in 1951, allowed presidents a maximum of two terms in office.

   People who favored presidential term limits would most likely have valued which of the following?

   A. responsibility but no authority
   B. authority but no responsibility
   C. the power of an office, not an individual
   D. the power of an individual, not an office

4. The third paragraph of the passage on page 446 includes a summary of Article 6 of the Constitution, also called the supremacy clause.

   _____ is an example of the supremacy clause in action.

   • Congress voting to appropriate $2 billion for a federal highways program
   • The Environmental Protection Agency issuing new regulations on a pollutant
   • The U.S. Supreme Court refusing to hear a case
   • The U.S. Supreme Court declaring an Illinois state law unconstitutional

Question 5 refers to the following chart.

Methods of Amending the Constitution

Proposal	Ratification Method	When Used
Two-thirds vote in both houses of Congress to propose an amendment	By three-quarters of the state legislatures	For every amendment except one
	By special conventions in three-fourths of the states	Twenty-first Amendment (repealing Prohibition)
Two-thirds of states request Congress to call a constitutional convention to consider an amendment	By three-quarters of the state legislatures	Never used
	By special conventions in three-fourths of the states	Never used

5. Which of the following would best explain why the third and fourth methods of amending the Constitution have never been used?

   A. State governments do not usually act together.
   B. Only Congress can propose amendments.
   C. State legislatures can vote on an amendment.
   D. Conventions meet more frequently than Congress and state legislatures do.

Answers and explanations start on page 683.

CIVICS AND GOVERNMENT

Levels and Branches of Government

Key Ideas

- Under our Constitution, the federal government must share power with the states.
- The federal government has three major branches—executive, legislative, and judicial.
- The three branches of the government balance each other's power.

The U.S. government works in layers with different responsibilities at the national, or **federal**, level; the state level; and local levels, including cities, villages, and counties. The federal government works across all 50 states, and its decisions and actions affect everyone. States have their own constitutions, similar to the U.S. Constitution. State governments also are quite powerful in shaping the lives of people in their states.

Federalism, which is a basic principle of the U.S. Constitution, means that power is shared between the national and state levels of government. Dividing power between federal and state government protects the rights of individual states, but also allows our national government to enforce certain rights of citizenship. The Constitution gives some powers only to the national government, some only to state government, and some to both. For example, only the federal government can declare war. States are given the power to establish schools. Both federal and state governments can levy taxes and set up court systems.

There are three branches of government at the federal level, each with different roles to play. The powers of each branch are described in the Constitution. The **executive branch** consists of the president and various advisors (including the president's cabinet) and government departments. The executive branch enforces the nation's laws and provides national leadership, setting goals and policies. The **legislative branch** consists of two houses of **Congress**: the **Senate** and the **House of Representatives**. Congress is responsible for making laws that all citizens, organizations, and businesses must follow. The **judicial branch**, made up of the federal court system including the Supreme Court, decides disputes related to laws, including the U.S. Constitution.

U.S. citizens vote for the president and all members of Congress. As a result, these politicians have a responsibility to represent and serve their **constituents**—the people who elected them. The president may be elected to only two terms of four years each. Representatives are elected for two years and Senators for six years; these members of Congress may be reelected for any number of terms.

ON THE GED® TEST

Editorial cartoons like the one on page 449 use pictures and humor to make a political point.

Federal judges, in contrast, are appointed by the president and **confirmed** by the Senate. They can serve in these positions for life. As citizens, we have a right to expect our federal judges to make **impartial** decisions based on the Constitution and the laws of the United States.

The people who wrote the U.S. Constitution were afraid to give any government body too much power. Therefore, the Constitution limits the power of each branch of the federal government. Each branch has separate powers. Each branch also has the power to act in ways that affect the other branches, in a system called **checks and balances**. For example, the president can **veto** laws made by Congress. Congress can override a presidential veto by repassing the law with a two-thirds majority. The Constitution is also now interpreted to mean that judges can review laws and declare them **unconstitutional**.

PRACTICE 3

<u>Questions 1 through 4</u> are based on the information on page 448.

1. What is the key characteristic of federalism?

   A. division of power between national and state governments
   B. concentration of power in one government
   C. concentration of power at the local level
   D. a judicial system with trial, appellate, and supreme courts

2. Which of the following is an example of a government entity that is part of the executive branch?

   A. the Democratic National Committee
   B. Congress's House Rules Committee
   C. the U.S. Court of Appeals
   D. the State Department

3. Why do lifetime appointments help ensure that federal judges rule impartially on legal issues?

   A. Federal judges need not worry about pleasing their constituents in order to be reelected.
   B. Only people who demonstrate loyalty to the ruling political party are appointed.
   C. Lifetime appointments mean that federal judges acquire a great deal of experience.
   D. A federal judge must be impartial or he or she will not be reelected.

4. Match each of the following definitions to the matching term.

Terms

Checks and balances	
Veto	
Senators	
Constituents	
Representatives	

Definitions

Limits that one branch of government can place on the other branches
The people whom political leaders represent
The president's power to strike down a law
Legislators who serve two-year terms
Legislators who serve six-year terms

<u>Question 5</u> refers to the following cartoon.

"Let's never forget that the constitution provides for three equally important branches of government: the legislative and the other two."

5. Which of the following people is most likely depicted in the cartoon?

   A. the president
   B. a member of Congress
   C. the head of a government department
   D. a federal judge

6. Although the states have the power to make their own laws in many areas, in practice they cooperate with one another to a great extent. For example, when a person travels, his or her driver's license, which was issued by one state, will be honored in other states.

   On which of the following principles is this type of cooperation based?

   A. mutual respect and convenience
   B. centralization of authority
   C. common law
   D. division of power

Answers and explanations start on page 683.

CIVICS AND GOVERNMENT

The Electoral System

Key Ideas

- U.S. politics are dominated by the Democratic and Republican parties.
- Political parties hold primaries to select candidates for the general election.
- Political campaigns are very expensive, and many people believe that we must reform our campaign finance laws.

At the national level in particular, two **political parties** dominate the political arena in the United States: the **Democrats** and the **Republicans**. These parties represent different ideas about the role of government in our nation. In each election season, the parties and candidates work to promote their views, or **platforms**—their positions on issues like tax reform, Social Security, education spending, environmental protection, and so on.

The political parties have developed large organizations for raising money and getting their candidates elected. Each party runs its own **primary** election, in which candidates within the party compete with each other for the party's **nomination**. After the primary elections, the winners from each party's primary face off in the general election. In presidential elections, the primary season ends with a party **convention**, where delegates from each state gather to select the party's candidate. Citizens vote in a general election, and the results are tallied by state. Following the general election, electors from each state cast their state's votes in the **Electoral College**. The electors generally must cast their votes for the candidate who won the general election in their state. The candidate who wins the greatest number of electoral votes becomes president.

Although Democrats and Republicans are by far the largest political parties, there are small parties as well. At times, a "third-party candidate" like Ralph Nader or Ross Perot attracts enough support to influence the outcome of the national election. Even when small parties offer interesting new ideas or solutions to problems, they have great difficulty attracting money and public attention because the Democratic and Republican parties are so well established.

Although many voters consider themselves to be either Republicans or Democrats, many others are **independent**. Candidates and their political parties rely heavily on **opinion polls** to find out what voters think; they try to tailor their campaign messages to appeal to large numbers of voters. Groups of voters who might "swing" an election one way or another are particularly important targets for political campaigns. Sometimes opposing candidates participate in public **debates**.

Political campaigns can be very expensive, and the higher the office, the more expensive the campaign. To reach the public, candidates pay for mailings, TV ads, and events, including personal appearances; they need campaign staff and offices; they must pay for travel expenses. As a result, fund-raising has become a very important part of running for office.

In recent decades, Americans have become more and more concerned about the high cost of running for office. Many Americans believe that a candidate should not have to be wealthy to begin with, or be overly obligated to contributors, in order to gain political office. We now have laws that restrict the size of campaign contributions. We also have restrictions on how **Political Action Committees** (PACs) operate. However, many people believe that more reforms are needed.

PRACTICE 4

<u>Questions 1 through 3</u> are based on the information on page 450.

1. Which of the following is necessary for a candidate to win the presidency?

   A. earning a majority of primary wins
   B. receiving a majority of the popular vote
   C. receiving a majority in the Electoral College
   D. having no third-party opponent

2. An exit poll is one that surveys people as they leave a voting location. Instead of waiting for votes to be counted, the media often announce the winners of elections based on exit polls.

   Which of the following is an important drawback of using exit polls?

   A. Exit polls may be inaccurate if the people polled are not representative of the political unit as a whole or if the election is very close.
   B. Exit polls allow the media to present election results during prime time on election night instead of waiting until later in the evening.
   C. Exit polls have undue influence on the way politicians running for office conduct their campaigns.
   D. Exit polls are likely to be unreliable when there is a wide margin between the candidates.

3. Which of the following is an example of a primary election?

   A. A Democrat and a Republican oppose one another in a race for the U.S. Senate.
   B. A Republican and an independent candidate oppose one another in a race for the state senate.
   C. Once presidential candidates are chosen, they select their running mates.
   D. Two city council members are on a ballot to determine which one will run for mayor as a Democrat.

<u>Questions 4 and 5</u> refer to the following graphs.

2010 Election
Senate Candidates' Funds $597,600,000

Other 13%
PACs* 13%
Self 13%
Individuals 61%

House Candidates' Funds $949,300,000

Self 6%
Other 4%
PACs* 33%
Individuals 57%

*PACs are Political Action Committees – groups that raise money for candidates.

Source: Federal Election Commission.

4. How do the campaign funding sources of Senate and House candidates compare?

   A. Individual donations provided a larger percentage of funds raised by House candidates than of those raised by Senate candidates.
   B. In total, individuals contributed a greater dollar amount to House candidates than they did to Senate candidates.
   C. Political parties provided a greater percentage of the funds raised by House candidates than they did of funds raised by Senate candidates.
   D. On average, Senate candidates received a greater percentage of their funds from PACs than did House candidates.

5. Which of the following statements is supported by the graphs?

   A. In 2010, self-funding was a larger source of funds for Senate candidates than it was for House candidates.
   B. In 2010, individual donations were the largest source of funds for Senate candidates but not for House candidates.
   C. In 2010, PACs were the largest source of funds for House candidates but not for Senate candidates.
   D. Fund-raising accounts for most of the work on a congressional campaign.

Answers and explanations start on page 684.

CIVICS AND GOVERNMENT

The Role of the Citizen

Citizenship is a special relationship between a person and a nation: the nation owes the person certain rights and guarantees; the person has certain obligations to the nation. Thus citizens of the United States have both rights and responsibilities.

People born in the United States, no matter what the circumstances, automatically become U.S. citizens. Regardless of where you were born, if one of your parents was a U.S. citizen, then you are also a U.S. citizen. People who **immigrate** to the United States from other countries can become U.S. citizens through a legal process called **naturalization**; underage children are naturalized along with their parents.

Our rights of citizenship are established in the first ten amendments to the U.S. Constitution—the Bill of Rights (see page 446)—and in other sections of the Constitution. One of the most fundamental rights of U.S. citizens is our right to participate in our nation's political life. We are eligible to vote and to hold public office, and we elect representatives to govern us. In a famous phrase in the Gettysburg Address, Abraham Lincoln said that we have a government "of the people, by the people, and for the people."

As Lincoln's famous remark implies, a government "by the people" requires that citizens take responsibility. First and foremost, we must uphold the laws of our country. As citizens, we also make contributions to the national welfare. Our taxes pay for services that the government provides to benefit everyone. By voting, we not only choose our government representatives, but we also help to make the political process meaningful for everyone. Through national service—such as military service, holding public office, or participating in intensive volunteer programs like Teach for America—citizens may devote years of their lives to the responsibilities of citizenship.

Our **jury** system is an important example of the give-and-take of citizenship. Each of us is guaranteed the right to a fair and speedy trial, heard by "a jury of peers," if we are accused of a crime. However, we are also obligated to serve on juries or as **witnesses** when we are called by the court system. The fairness of our legal system depends on citizens participating in that system. Therefore, our employers are obligated to release us from work at the request of the courts.

In addition to the rights and responsibilities established by law, many citizens contribute their time and money in other ways that serve society as a whole. People volunteer to serve organizations in their communities or within their professions—serving meals in shelters, fund-raising for schools, offering free medical services, etc. People also give money to causes they think are important, from political campaigns to food pantries to environmental organizations. Many citizens also work hard to conduct their daily lives in ways that contribute to the general welfare: by recycling, cleaning up trash, and looking out for their neighbors and family members.

PRACTICE 5

Question 1 is based on the information on page 452.

1. _____ outlines the rights of U.S. citizens.

   - The Declaration of Independence
   - The U.S. Constitution
   - A U.S. passport
   - A person's naturalization papers

Questions 2 and 3 refer to the following information.

Noncitizens can be classified into five groups:

Resident alien: A foreigner who has established permanent residence in the United States.

Nonresident alien: A foreigner who is staying in the United States for a brief, specified period.

Enemy alien: A foreigner who is a citizen of a nation at war with the United States.

Refugee: A foreigner fleeing his or her country to escape persecution or danger.

Illegal alien: A foreigner who comes to the United States without legal documentation.

2. Louvina married an American and moved to the United States from Trinidad in 2010. Three years later, she filed a legal petition requesting U.S. citizenship. In what category of alien does Louvina belong?

   A. resident alien
   B. nonresident alien
   C. enemy alien
   D. refugee

3. What would happen to the legal status of noncitizens living in the United States if their country declares war on the United States?

   A. They would become nonresident aliens.
   B. They would become resident aliens.
   C. They would become enemy aliens.
   D. They would become refugees.

4. The United States must balance the right of society to protect itself against the rights of an accused criminal. One aspect of this tension is the Fourth Amendment guarantee of "the right of people to be secure in their persons, houses, papers, and effects, against unreasonable searches and seizures."

   Which of the following values is supported by the Fourth Amendment?

   A. free speech
   B. privacy
   C. civic duty
   D. volunteerism

Question 5 refers to the following graph.

Reported U.S. Voter Turnout by Age, 2012 Presidential Election

Source: United States Census Bureau

5. Which of the following is a conclusion based on the graph rather than a detail of the graph?

   A. About 63 percent of people aged 45 to 64 reported voting in the 2012 presidential election.
   B. Those aged 65+ reported the highest voter turnout in the 2012 presidential election, at 70 percent.
   C. If the 2012 presidential election is representative of elections generally in the United States, voter turnout increases with age.
   D. Only about 38 percent of young people reported voting in the 2012 presidential election.

Answers and explanations start on page 684.

CIVICS AND GOVERNMENT PRACTICE QUESTIONS

Question 1 refers to the following chart.

Political Divisions in the 113th Congress, 2013

Party	House	Senate
Republicans	234	45
Democrats	201	53
Others	—	2 (In case of a tie, Vice President Joe Biden (D) would vote.)
Vacant	—	—

1. Which of the following is the best summary of the chart above?

   A. Congress is made up of the House and the Senate.
   B. In 2013, a different major party controlled the House than controlled the Senate.
   C. In 2013, the narrow margin of control in each body of Congress made it difficult to pass legislation.
   D. In 2013, the vice president was likely to cast the deciding vote on many bills before the Senate.

---

2. In 1215, English nobles limited royal power by forcing King John to accept the Magna Carta. This document gave certain rights to nobles, such as protection of private property, trial by jury, and religious freedoms.

   Therefore, the [Select...▾] shares essential characteristics with the Magna Carta.

   - Mayflower Compact, which established a government for Plymouth colony,
   - Bill of Rights of the U.S. Constitution, which guarantees citizens certain rights,
   - Albany Plan of Union, which called for a colonial confederation,
   - *Federalist Papers*, which encouraged ratification of the U.S. Constitution,

Questions 3 and 4 refer to the following passage.

In 1979, Congress passed legislation to allow political parties to raise unlimited amounts of general-purpose money not designated for particular candidates. In 1991, a lawsuit forced disclosure of such "soft money" contributions, and concern grew about the size of individual donations, the extent of total donations, and the ways in which the money was being spent. During the presidential elections of 1996 and 2000, campaign fund-raising, especially the raising and spending of soft money, was an issue, with the candidates promising reform. Finally, in 2001, after several years of hearings, the Senate passed the McCain-Feingold bill, which would eliminate the unregulated soft money contributions that make up a large proportion of the parties' budgets.

3. Which of the following is an example of a soft money contribution?

   A. a $250 ticket to a fund-raising dinner-dance to benefit a mayoral candidate
   B. a $3,000 donation to the campaign fund of an incumbent senator
   C. a $3,000 contribution to a party fund for TV ads on political issues
   D. a $1,000 gift to a senator's campaign fund in response to a direct mail solicitation

4. Which of the following is the most likely reason soft money was not a major issue in the 1980s?

   A. People were less aware of soft money because disclosure was not required at that time.
   B. Political campaigns were publicly financed, so soft money was not needed.
   C. Most candidates spent part of their campaign funds on television ads.
   D. McCain and Feingold had not submitted their campaign finance reform bill.

Questions 5 and 6 refer to the following paragraph and graphs.

In order to win a presidential election, a candidate must win a majority of the vote in the Electoral College. Each state has as many electors as it has senators and representatives in Congress. In most states, the winner of the popular vote gets all the electoral votes of the state. These graphs show the popular and Electoral College votes in the election of 2012.

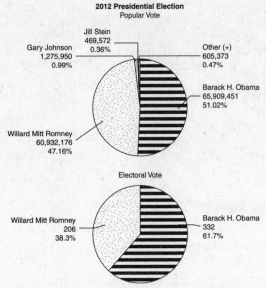

2012 Presidential Election
Popular Vote

Jill Stein
469,572
0.36%

Gary Johnson
1,275,950
0.99%

Other (+)
605,373
0.47%

Barack H. Obama
65,909,451
51.02%

Willard Mitt Romney
60,932,176
47.16%

Electoral Vote

Willard Mitt Romney
206
38.3%

Barack H. Obama
332
61.7%

5. Which one of the following statements is supported by the information in the paragraph and the graphs?

   A. A presidential candidate will receive the same percentage of electoral votes as he or she received of the popular vote.

   B. Romney won a greater percentage of the electoral vote than of the popular vote in 2012.

   C. Jill Stein won a greater percentage of the popular vote than of the electoral vote in 2012.

   D. The total of popular votes cast for all candidates other than Barack Obama was greater than the total of those cast for Barack Obama.

6. Which of the following would be the best title for the paragraph and the graphs?

   A. 2012 Presidential Election: How Obama Defeated Romney

   B. 2012 Presidential Election: Third-Party Influence

   C. 2012 Presidential Election: Winning the Electoral College

   D. 2012 Presidential Election: Popular and Electoral Votes

Question 7 refers to the following passage.

Where do I vote? Your voting district is determined by your place of residence. Watch your local newspaper for an announcement indicating polling locations and times, or contact your local board of election to determine your voting location.

You may also obtain your polling place location by accessing the website of the Office of the Secretary of State at www.anystate.us. You may also call the Office of the Secretary of State for assistance.

7. Which of the following is assumed but not stated outright in the voter guide above?

   A. The board of election is the county, city, or town office responsible for local voting.

   B. A voter's polling place is determined by his or her address.

   C. A voter can find his or her polling place on the Internet.

   D. A voter can call the Office of the Secretary of State to find out where to vote.

8. An interest group is an organization with specific goals that seeks to influence government policies.

Place a ★ into the box next to each entity that constitutes an interest group. There may be more than one.

The Democratic Party, which nominates candidates and tries to win elections	
The National Association of Manufacturers, which lobbies for businesses	
The Federal Communications Commission, which regulates broadcasters	
The Cabinet, an advisory body for the president	
Public Citizen, a nonprofit consumer rights advocacy group	

WAYNE STAYSKAL
Courtesy Tampa Tribune

© 1998 Wayne Stayskal, Tampa Tribune. Reprinted by permission of Wayne Stayskal.

9. What is the main idea of this cartoon?

A. Most voters are working people.
B. Most registered voters don't vote.
C. Voters should establish another political party.
D. A non-voters' party would lose every election.

10. Which of the following values is the cartoonist appealing for?

A. the work ethic
B. majority rule
C. civic duty
D. national pride

---

11. An oligarchy is a system of government in which a small group of people holds power.

Which of the following is an oligarchy?

A. China, where the top leaders of the communist party control the government
B. Iraq, when it had a dictator, Saddam Hussein
C. Great Britain, with a monarch, a prime minister, and an elected parliament
D. Greece, with a prime minister and an elected parliament

12. Three typical laws from the code of Hammurabi, written about 1700 B.C.E., are "If a son strike his father, his hands shall be hewn off. If a man put out the eye of another man, his eye shall be put out. If he break another man's bone, his bone shall be broken."

What principle underlies these laws?

A. retribution
B. rehabilitation
C. incarceration
D. mediation

Questions 13 and 14 refer to the following map and table.

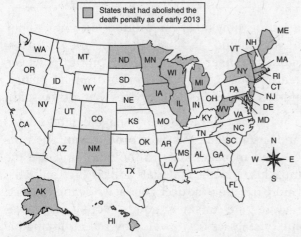

The Death Penalty in the United States, 2013

States that had abolished the death penalty as of early 2013

NOTE: By early 2013, Connecticut, Maryland, and New Mexico had abolished the death penalty prospectively. Anyone convicted of a capital offense that occurred prior to abolition of the death penalty in these states may be legally executed.

Homicide Rate per 100,000 Population, 2010

Highest	Lowest
Louisiana, 11.9	Vermont, 1.3
Mississippi, 9.6	New Hampshire, 1.4
Alabama, 8.2	Idaho, 1.5
Maryland, 7.6	Wyoming, 1.6
New Mexico, 7.4	Hawaii, 1.8

Source: National Center for Health Statistics and U.S. Bureau of the Census.

13. How many states have the death penalty?

   A. 12
   B. 18
   C. 32
   D. 40

14. People who favor capital punishment usually argue that it prevents serious crimes like homicide. Based on the map and chart, what is a logical flaw with this argument?

   A. A life sentence without parole costs taxpayers more than executing an inmate.
   B. Some executed inmates turn out to have been innocent based on newly discovered evidence.
   C. Two of the five states with the highest per capita homicide rates have abolished the death penalty.
   D. Two of the five states with the lowest per capita homicide rates have abolished the death penalty.

15. The U.S. Constitution gives the president the power to make treaties with foreign nations, and it gives the Senate the power to "advise and consent" on all treaties. Thus a two-thirds majority of the Senate must ratify any treaty presented by the president. In 1978, President Jimmy Carter persuaded the Senate to ratify treaties with Panama that transferred control of the Panama Canal from the United States to Panama. Many Americans were outraged and believed that U.S. interests had been given away.

Which of the following is an opinion rather than a statement of fact?

   A. Presidents have the power to enter into treaties with foreign nations.
   B. A two-thirds majority of the Senate is needed to ratify a treaty.
   C. The 1978 Panama treaties sold out U.S. interests to Panama.
   D. The 1978 Panama treaties gave control of the Panama Canal to Panama.

16. In the mayor-council form of city government, voters elect both a mayor and a city council. The mayor is the city's chief executive, operating the city on a day-to-day basis and also serving a ceremonial function. The city council is a legislative body, in charge of the city's finances and passing city laws. In the council-manager form of city government, voters elect a city council that makes city policies and laws. The council may elect a mayor who has a largely ceremonial function. It appoints a professionally trained city manager to oversee day-to-day operations.

What is the main similarity between the mayor's role in the mayor-council and in the council-manager forms of city government?

   A. The mayor sets policy.
   B. The mayor runs day-to-day operations.
   C. The mayor is elected by voters.
   D. The mayor has ceremonial duties.

Answers and explanations start on page 685.

ECONOMICS

Basic Economics Concepts

Key Ideas

- Businesses utilize capital, labor, and materials to create goods and services to sell.
- Markets are systems that bring sellers' goods and services to buyers.
- The prices of goods and services are determined in part by supply and demand.

ON THE GED® TEST

Use the direction of lines on line graphs to spot trends and make predictions.

In economics, *capital* is a term for things that can produce income. Money can be capital; so can equipment, land, and buildings. Businesses invest capital in order to create **goods** and **services** to sell for profit. However, capital by itself cannot create value. **Labor**, the work of human beings, transforms capital and materials into goods and services that can be sold.

For example, a business that makes computers must make capital investments to build a factory and install equipment for **production**. Then the business must hire workers and managers to run the plant and use the equipment. The business must also buy the materials and parts to build the computers. The materials and parts are **producer goods**, while the finished computers, ready to sell in stores, are **consumer goods**. Not all businesses make or build objects. Some businesses create value by selling intangible services to their customers—such as an employment agency that offers the service of matching people with jobs.

Markets are established routines and networks for selling and buying goods and services. There are producers' markets for producer goods; there are **retail** and **wholesale** markets for consumer goods; there are markets for **raw materials** such as minerals; there are financial markets for selling stocks and bonds. Some markets are more highly organized than others, and all markets are regulated by law to some extent. But markets, by definition, are not completely under the control of any government or agency.

Goods and services are **distributed** through markets so that they can be **consumed** where they are wanted. Through the market system, sellers and buyers negotiate prices and contracts; they **compete** for the best terms possible in that market. For example, a computer manufacturer might enter the consumer electronics market, competing with other manufacturers to sell its goods at a fair price to retailers. The retailers negotiate contracts specifying how many computers they are willing to buy and distribute to consumers through their stores or catalogs.

How are prices determined in the market system? In economics, price is related to **supply** and **demand**. Sellers need to earn money on the goods they have produced. Buyers want to spend as little as possible. When the supply of something is large, buyers shop around looking for the best price, and sellers lower their prices in order to move their **inventory**. On the other hand, if a product is **scarce**, buyers are less able to shop around, and sellers can raise their prices. When Florida has a hard freeze and fruit growers lose their citrus crops, the price of oranges goes up. That is because there are fewer oranges to buy and fewer sellers to buy them from, so those sellers can charge more.

Supply and demand most clearly influence price in a **free market economy**. The U.S. economy operates primarily, but not completely, as a free market. For example, governmental **price supports** ensure that farmers can sell certain agricultural products at prices that allow them to earn a profit.

PRACTICE 1

Questions 1 through 4 are based on the information on page 458.

1. What is the main role of labor in an economy?

    A. to provide capital to start new businesses
    B. to convert capital and raw materials into products and services
    C. to purchase all the goods and services that are produced
    D. to purchase raw materials in retail and wholesale markets

2. Which of the following is an example of a producer good rather than a consumer good?

    A. a pencil
    B. a can opener
    C. a cell phone
    D. a plastic material

3. When there are very few houses for sale in an area, the real estate market is said to be a seller's market.

    Why is this name appropriate?

    A. When the supply of houses is low and demand is high, sellers can raise their prices.
    B. When the supply of houses is low and demand is high, sellers will accept an offer lower than list price.
    C. Sellers are always at an advantage in the real estate market.
    D. Competition among sellers raises prices.

4. Why might the U.S. government offer price supports to farmers but not to toy manufacturers?

    A. Toy sales vary widely, depending on the appeal of a particular toy.
    B. Toys are not critical to a nation's economic and political well-being.
    C. Toys are sold to adults for use by children.
    D. Toys are distributed through conventional wholesale and retail channels.

Questions 5 and 6 refer to the following graph.

Keisha's Monthly Apple Purchases

5. When apples cost 30 cents each, how many apples does Keisha buy each month?

    A.   4
    B.   8
    C. 12
    D. 16

6. Which of the following conclusions is supported by the data on the graph?

    A. As the supply of apples rises, Keisha buys fewer apples.
    B. As the supply of apples rises, the demand for apples falls.
    C. As the price of apples rises, Keisha buys fewer apples.
    D. As the price of apples falls, Keisha buys the same number of apples.

7. Place a ★ into the box corresponding to each service business in the list below.

    | a tool manufacturer | a bicycle repair shop |
    | a paper mill | a microchip factory |
    | a car wash | a beauty salon |

Answers and explanations start on page 685.

ECONOMICS

The U.S. Economic System

Key Ideas

- The U.S. economy is built on principles of laissez-faire capitalism.
- The U.S. economy moves through cyclical phases of growth, slowdown, recession, and recovery.
- Saving and investing contribute to the economy by making money available for businesses to grow.

ON THE GED® TEST

A short reading passage may accompany a graphic, such as a map. Some questions may require you to use information from both the passage and the graphic.

In the United States, the economic activity of individual people and businesses primarily determines our economic health and growth. We make our own decisions about how to save and spend most of our income. We can accept employment as we choose, become **entrepreneurs** and build businesses of our own, and seek education and training to whatever level best serves our goals. These freedoms are based on **laissez-faire capitalism**, the ideas of 18th-century economist Adam Smith, who believed that if individuals are free to act in their own best interests economically, the sum total of their actions will be in the best interests of the society as a whole.

Throughout the history of the United States, **free enterprise** and **competition** have played important roles in the development of our economy. Businesses have incentives to grow larger—either by expanding their **capacity** or by integrating a broader set of functions into their **operations**—in order to make more **profit**. However, businesses are expected to compete with each other on the merits of their products and operations. Businesses are not allowed to form **monopolies**—single companies that control whole industries—and they also are not allowed to form **oligopolies**—tight-knit groups of companies that control whole industries.

Because the U.S. economy is not under government control, no one can predict or control exactly how the economy will behave. Our economy tends to move through a **business cycle** with identifiable phases, but the length and strength of a cycle and its phases vary greatly. The first phase of a cycle is the growth phase, in which businesses invest and expand optimistically. At some point, growth is slowed or stopped by one or more factors—limited resources, limited production capacity, tight employment, or market **saturation**—and the economy enters a slowdown phase. As businesses lay off workers, stop investing their capital, and cut back production, the economy enters a **recession** or **depression** phase. Unemployment rises, consumer spending slows down, and businesses act very conservatively, holding down wages and prices, avoiding risks, and managing cash flow tightly. Eventually, the economy moves into a recovery phase, perhaps initiated by a government action. Recovery may be slow or uneven across economic sectors, but eventually the economy moves into a new growth phase. **Inflation**, in which the combined price of goods and services grows faster than the purchasing power of the currency, is only partly related to these business cycle phases.

Banking and investment services, like most U.S. industries, are conducted on principles of free enterprise. A major role of **banks** and **savings and loan associations** is to create pools of savings in order to make money available as credit to businesses and consumers. **Stock exchanges** have a similar purpose; they allow investors to purchase shares of stock, which represent part ownership of a business. Both saving and investing make funds available for businesses to use to grow. When people invest in stock, they take risks because the value of the stock depends on the success of the business. However, the potential **return** is generally much higher than the **interest rate** on a savings account.

PRACTICE 2

Questions 1 through 4 are based on the information on page 460.

1. Why are monopolies not permitted in the United States?

    A. Monopolies are too efficient.
    B. Monopolies are part of laissez-faire capitalism.
    C. Monopolies result from free enterprise.
    D. Monopolies shut out competition.

2. According to the passage, Select... ▾ is one characteristic of a recession.

    *   increased job growth
    *   large investments of capital
    *   increased consumer spending
    *   rising unemployment

3. Private ownership of property (land or buildings) is a key characteristic of the free enterprise system. Owning property gives people a strong incentive to take care of it and use it productively.

    What is the basis for this incentive?

    A. Property owners have a stake in the future value of the property.
    B. Property owners work harder than tenants do.
    C. Property owners are given tax incentives by the federal government.
    D. Property owners must pay real estate taxes to local government.

4. Which of the following investments carries the most risk?

    A. opening a savings account at a local bank
    B. buying a certificate of deposit at a savings and loan institution
    C. buying stock in a new company, such as an Internet startup
    D. buying stock in an established company, such as Microsoft

Question 5 refers to the following paragraph and graph.

At different times during the business cycle, the gross domestic product—the total value of goods and services produced in a year—rises and falls.

The Business Cycle

5. Which of the following conclusions is supported by the paragraph and the graph?

    A. High points in the business cycle are generally followed by recoveries.
    B. Low points in the business cycle are generally followed by slowdowns.
    C. During recessions, the rate of unemployment drops.
    D. Despite ups and downs, the gross domestic product generally increases over time.

6. Based on the passage on page 460, what do saving and investing in stocks have in common?

    A. They provide capital for businesses to grow.
    B. They provide a sure rate of return.
    C. They pay a fixed rate of interest.
    D. They are without risk.

Answers and explanations start on page 686.

ECONOMICS

The Economy and the U.S. Government

Key Ideas

- The U.S. government plays a major part in the nation's economy.
- The federal government facilitates the free market system while protecting workers and consumers.
- The free market system cannot effectively provide for all our needs, so government fills some gaps.

ON THE GED® TEST

Charts, such as the one on page 463, are used to summarize information. You may be asked to find specific information from the chart or to apply information from the chart to a specific situation.

Although the United States has primarily a free market economy, the U.S. government does have important economic functions. Both the executive and the legislative branches of government are involved in setting the U.S. government **budget**. The government has considerable impact on our economy, since it determines our taxes, employs many people, and borrows and spends much money. The federal budget may have a **surplus** of **revenue**, in which case elected leaders may either spend the additional funds or cut taxes; or the budget may have a revenue **deficit**, requiring the government to borrow money to cover its expenses. Government spending sometimes has a very direct impact on the economy. For example, if the government wants to boost the national economy out of a recession, it may spend extra money on projects that create new jobs.

The federal government is also responsible for maintaining good conditions for our free market system. The government must have laws and courts in place to maintain property rights. It must enforce fair legal standards for operating a business. The federal government provides a stable **currency** and operates the U.S. Mint, which makes coins and prints paper money. Our central banking system, the **Federal Reserve System**, manages the total amount of money available for lending and borrowing in the private banking system and partially controls interest rates. The **Federal Deposit Insurance Corporation** (FDIC) insures the money in individual bank accounts in case of bank fraud or failure.

One of the fundamental purposes of the federal government is to promote the general welfare of the nation. Therefore, the government takes over many functions that the free market system does not provide. For example, the free market does not distribute wealth according to what people need to live on, so the government collects taxes to redistribute some money to people who don't earn enough. The government also provides **infrastructure**, such as interstate highways, that indirectly supports economic activity.

Another role for government in the economy is protecting workers from health dangers and exploitation. The **Occupational Safety and Health Administration** (OSHA) is a special federal agency charged to protect workers on the job, particularly in hazardous industries. Many federal and state laws also protect the interests of workers. For example, all states regulate the hours and types of work that children may perform. A number of agencies are involved in enforcing safe and fair working conditions; they visit businesses, investigate reports of problems, identify violations, and initiate prosecution in some cases.

Another group of agencies protects consumers from fraudulent business practices and unsafe products. The **Food and Drug Administration** (FDA) is responsible for making sure that food products are safe, drugs are effective, and cosmetics and drugs are labeled properly. The **Federal Trade Commission** (FTC) ensures that product claims in advertising and on package labels are true and complete.

PRACTICE 3

Questions 1 through 3 are based on the passage on page 462.

1. When the U.S. government [Select... ▾], it is an indication that the government has a budget surplus.

   - issues bonds through the U.S. Treasury
   - attempts to boost the economy by cutting the discount rate
   - registers expenditures that exceed its revenues
   - registers revenues that exceed its expenditures

2. Which of the following legislative actions would lead to a direct increase in consumer spending?

   A. raising Social Security contributions
   B. decreasing spending on federal work projects
   C. cutting the federal income tax
   D. ratifying an international trade agreement

3. Which of the following is an example of infrastructure that supports economic activity?

   A. consumer demand
   B. the annual federal budget
   C. local sales taxes
   D. the air traffic control system

4. The federal government has two main ways to manipulate the economy. The first is fiscal policy, in which the government increases or decreases taxes and spending to influence the economy. The second is monetary policy, in which the government increases or decreases the supply of money in order to stimulate or slow the economy.

   What is the main similarity between fiscal and monetary policy?

   A. Both involve raising taxes.
   B. Both involve lowering taxes.
   C. Both are budgetary tools of state governments.
   D. Both affect the amount of money circulating in the economy.

Questions 5 and 6 refer to the following paragraph and chart.

Monetary policy affects the amount of money in circulation. When there is rapid economic growth and a risk of inflation, the Federal Reserve System (the "Fed") slows it down by tightening the money supply. This makes it more difficult for people and businesses to borrow and spend money. When the economy is sluggish, the Fed increases the money supply to stimulate borrowing and spending.

The Fed's Monetary Policy Options

To Take Money out of Circulation		To Put Money into Circulation	
Sell government securities (bonds and Treasury bills) to investors	○	Buy back government securities from bond holders	○
Raise the discount rate member banks are charged to borrow from the Fed	○	Lower the discount rate member banks are charged to borrow from the Fed	○
Raise the reserve requirement, the amount banks must keep on hand to cover deposits	○	Lower the reserve requirement	○

5. Place a dot in the circle in each box that indicates a step the government might take in order to stimulate the economy.

6. Since the Fed's monetary policy options have such specific effects, why does the Fed sometimes fail to head off recession or stimulate recovery?

   A. The Fed's board meets only four times a year.
   B. The people on the Fed's board lack experience.
   C. Our complex economy takes time to respond.
   D. Our economy can be controlled only by international economic forces.

Answers and explanations start on page 686.

ECONOMICS

Labor and Consumer Issues

Key Ideas

- Workers earn wages and some benefits and protections in exchange for their labor.
- The U.S. economy is now in a time of rapid change, and workers must prepare themselves to adapt.
- Consumers must protect themselves by being aware of risks and by spending their money wisely.

As workers, we earn **wages** and other **benefits** in exchange for our labor. People who are paid hourly wages are paid only for the number of hours they work. Their earnings may fluctuate depending on how much their labor is needed. People who earn salaries typically receive the same constant pay all the time, although the hours they work may fluctuate. Some people are paid for "piecework"—that is, for each piece of work they complete. Many workers receive benefits in addition to their wages, such as health insurance, vacation pay, and special savings plans. A worker's total **compensation** for a job is the combined value of wages and benefits.

Workers and their employers must pay taxes and buy insurance to cover work-related problems, including injury, disability, and **unemployment**. Workers who lose their jobs because they are fired or laid off usually can receive unemployment benefits for a time or until they find new jobs. Sometimes workers lose their jobs because of major economic changes. For example, rapid changes in the steel industry drove out much of the steel manufacturing in the United States. Plants closed, and workers who thought they would spend their lives making good wages in steel mills suddenly found their skills worthless. In most cases, these workers had to learn new skills. This kind of rapid change is common in our modern times. Because so many markets are international, and because transportation, communication, and shipping are possible even over very long distances, businesses can change strategies very quickly and change their workforce as a result. Workers need to anticipate changes in their industries and continually seek new training in order to be prepared for change.

Most workers have direct individual agreements with their employers. However, **labor unions** are common in certain industries and professions. Through **collective bargaining**, unions negotiate contracts for wages and working conditions on behalf of all union members. If these negotiations fail, the union can call a **strike**, in which workers refuse to work. When labor-management negotiations break down, federal **mediators** may be asked to intervene. The National Labor Relations Board helps companies and unions resolve disputes.

We all participate in the U.S. economy as **consumers**. The free market system offers U.S. consumers an amazing array of choices for the goods and services we want. As retailers and marketers woo our business relentlessly, we should all remember the maxim, "Let the buyer beware." Although government agencies must protect consumers, consumers must also protect themselves. For example, federal laws require that potentially hazardous products have special labeling and instructions. But these will not protect us as consumers unless we read them. Parents are required by law to strap their small children into automobile safety seats. But if the seats are incorrectly installed, the children are still at risk. Retailers who offer credit payment plans are required to disclose the interest rate, payment amount, and number of payments, but it's up to consumers to work out the total expense and compare the total with the purchase price of the item.

PRACTICE 4

Questions 1 through 4 are based on the information on page 464.

1. What is a worker's total compensation?

   A. wages only
   B. benefits only
   C. wages and benefits
   D. the amount received in unemployment benefits

2. Reread the second paragraph on page 464. Which of the following statements is a conclusion rather than a supporting detail related to the paragraph?

   A. Workers must learn skills throughout their lives to be prepared for changes in their industries.
   B. Most steel manufacturing moved out of the United States.
   C. Many steelworkers had to retrain themselves and learn new skills.
   D. Workers sometimes lose their jobs because of major economic restructuring.

3. A [Select... ▾] is acting as a consumer.

   • person working in a shopping mall
   • professor teaching economics at a community college
   • woman buying a computer
   • teen starting a babysitting cooperative

4. Which of the following proverbs or slogans expresses the principle that underlies labor unions?

   A. All for one and one for all.
   B. Strike while the iron is hot.
   C. Work expands to fill the time available.
   D. Many hands make light work.

Questions 5 and 6 refer to the following graph.

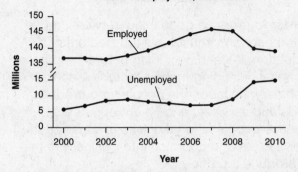

Civilian Unemployment, 2000–2010

5. When was civilian unemployment at its lowest during the decade shown on the graph?

   A. in 2000
   B. in 2002
   C. in 2006
   D. in 2008

6. Which of the following statements is supported by the data in the graph?

   A. People who have stopped looking for work are not counted among the unemployed.
   B. As the number of employed civilians rose steadily from 2003 to 2006, the number of unemployed slowly declined.
   C. The rate of civilian unemployment during the 2000s exceeded the rate of civilian employment.
   D. Unemployed civilians made up about 25 percent of the total civilian workforce from 2000 to 2010.

Answers and explanations start on page 686.

ECONOMICS PRACTICE QUESTIONS

<u>**Questions 1 through 3 refer to the following passage.**</u>

In order to produce goods and services, a free market economy must have four factors of production: (1) land, including natural resources; (2) capital, including money, factories, and machinery; (3) labor, the people who produce goods and services; and (4) entrepreneurs, business people who take risks to organize the other factors of production into businesses that will produce a profit.

1. Which of the following best defines the factors of production?

    A. the political organizations that support an economy
    B. the various types of resources needed for an economy to produce goods and services
    C. the way in which the work flow is organized in a factory or office
    D. all the transactions involved in producing goods and services

2. In a communist economy, a central government makes all of the economic decisions.

    Which factor of production is not part of a communist economy?

    A. land
    B. natural resources
    C. labor
    D. entrepreneurs

3. Which of the following is an example of capital?

    A. an office building
    B. a deposit of iron ore
    C. a skilled engineer
    D. the founder of a publishing business

4. Many fiscal conservatives believe that the U.S. budget should be balanced, with spending equal to income. They think it is wrong for the government to influence the economy by manipulating taxes or by borrowing. Instead, they feel that a balanced budget reassures business leaders that the economy is solid.

    Which of the following statements is a fact?

    A. In a balanced budget, revenues equal expenditures.
    B. The government should not use the budget to tinker with the economy.
    C. The government should not borrow money to balance the budget.
    D. A balanced government budget is the best indicator that the economy is healthy.

<u>**Question 5 refers to the following graph.**</u>

U.S. Personal Income Sources, February 2013
(Billions of Dollars)

5. Which of the following statements is supported by the data on the graph?

    A. More than half of all personal income was earned through work in February 2013.
    B. Government social benefits accounted for more than one-quarter of personal income in February 2013.
    C. Interest and dividends accounted for one-third of personal income in February 2013.
    D. Per capita income was roughly $8,565 in February 2013.

Reprinted with permission of the *Green Bay Press-Gazette*, Green Bay, Wisconsin.

6. Who does the man in the plaid shorts represent?

A. a retiree
B. an American taxpayer
C. a corporate executive
D. an investor

7. Why is the man in the plaid shorts calm about his ride on the roller coaster?

A. He enjoys riding on roller coasters.
B. He has made money buying bonds.
C. He is accustomed to stock market ups and downs.
D. All of his retirement savings are in stocks.

8. Employers withhold, or take out, federal income tax from their employees' paychecks. However, some people need to make estimated tax payments. According to the Internal Revenue Service, "Estimated tax is the method used to pay tax on income that is not subject to withholding (for example, earnings from self-employment, interest, dividends, rents, alimony, etc."

A [Select...▼] is most likely to need to make estimated tax payments.

• factory worker
• student working part-time at the university
• person who runs a home day-care center
• gas station attendant

9. In a free market economy, people make their own decisions about working, buying goods and property, and starting businesses. Which of the following is most likely to be highly valued in nations with free market economies?

A. cooperation
B. individualism
C. job security
D. economic equality

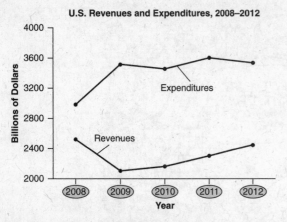

U.S. Revenues and Expenditures, 2008–2012

10. At the bottom of the chart, select the year between 2008 and 2012 in which the United States ran its largest budget deficit.

11. If a family wanted to make a graph of its economic situation similar to this graph of U.S. revenues and expenditures, what set of documents for the years 2008 to 2012 would be most useful?

    A. records showing all family members' sources of income
    B. income tax returns and expense records
    C. credit card bills and rent or mortgage statements
    D. records showing the value of the family's possessions

12. The Interstate Highway System, begun in 1956, consists of more than 45,000 miles of four- to eight-lane highways connecting most large U.S. cities. The federal government pays for almost 90 percent of the building and maintenance of interstate highways out of receipts from excise taxes on gasoline, tires, truck parts, and other related products.

    Which of the following best summarizes this information?

    A. In 1956, the federal government established the Interstate Highway System.
    B. The Interstate Highway System consists of thousands of miles of large highways.
    C. The federal government collects excise taxes on transportation-related items.
    D. The national network of interstate highways is paid for mostly by federal excise taxes.

13. In recent years, the United States has lowered protective tariffs (charges on goods imported from other countries), arguing that lower tariffs encourage free trade and benefit consumers by decreasing the cost of imported goods.

    From the perspective of a U.S. factory worker, what is the flaw in this argument?

    A. When cheaper imported goods force out U.S.-made goods, U.S. factory workers often lose their jobs.
    B. Free trade leads to cheaper imported goods because the cost of labor is less in many other nations.
    C. Factory workers cannot afford to buy imported consumer goods even if they are cheaper than U.S.-made goods.
    D. Lower protective tariffs actually raise the prices of all goods whether they are made in the United States or in foreign countries.

Question 14 refers to the following chart.

U.S. Consumer Protection

Agency		Function
Food and Drug Administration	◯	Protects public from poorly processed and improperly labeled foods and drugs
Federal Trade Commission	◯	Protects consumers from misleading and/or fraudulent advertising
Consumer Product Safety Commission	◯	Protects consumers from risk of injury or death from hazardous products
Securities and Exchange Commission	◯	Protects investors from being misled about stocks and bonds
National Highway Traffic Safety Administration	◯	Protects consumers by testing vehicle safety and monitoringn ationwide speed limits

14. In the table above, place a dot or dots in the circle(s) next to the agency or agencies that could be involved in a dispute over a commercial that implied something about a product that was not true.

15. Equilibrium occurs when the supply of a product or service equals the demand for it. A product tends to be priced at the equilibrium point. When the price is greater than the equilibrium point, demand decreases and there is an oversupply of the product on the market.

   [Select... ▾] is the result of the price falling below the equilibrium point.

   • A shortage of the product
   • A surplus of the product
   • The equilibrium point decreasing
   • The equilibrium point increasing

16. One approach to the study of economics is called macroeconomics. Macroeconomics deals with economies as a whole. For instance, a macroeconomist might study the causes of inflation or the factors that determine why some national economies grow quickly and others do not.

   Which of the following is most likely to be studied by a macroeconomist?

   A. how a firm prices its products or services
   B. what causes high rates of unemployment
   C. what determines consumer demand for a product
   D. how a factory makes production decisions

Question 17 refers to the following graph.

17. Which of the following conclusions is supported by the data on the graph?

   A. As the price per eraser decreases, manufacturers supply more erasers.
   B. As the price per eraser increases, manufacturers supply fewer erasers.
   C. As the price per eraser increases, manufacturers supply more erasers.
   D. As the supply of erasers increases, the demand for erasers decreases.

Answers and explanations start on page 687.

GEOGRAPHY AND THE WORLD

Early Civilizations

Key Ideas

- Ancient civilizations developed where people could settle in one place with a secure food supply.
- The ancient republics of Greece and Rome were incubators for important ideas in modern government.
- Ancient civilizations also left legacies in art, architecture, science, and astronomy.

One of the earliest known **civilizations** is ancient Egypt. By 5000 B.C.E., people who lived along the **Nile River** had begun to take advantage of the fertile soil left behind by floods. The river and irrigation systems allowed the Egyptians to grow enough food to support a large population. Around 3000 B.C.E., Egyptian civilization grew under the rule of Egypt's kings, or **pharaohs**. Believing their pharaohs to be part god, Egyptians built the famous **pyramids** to house these rulers in their next lives. Many who built the pyramids and did the hard work to build this civilization were slaves.

Around the same time, in the **Fertile Crescent**—an area northeast of Egypt—**Sumerian** city-states were also developing irrigation and flood control methods. They also created a system of writing. In about 1800 B.C.E., the Sumerians were conquered by the Babylonians. One of the Babylonian kings, Hammurabi, is remembered for codifying laws. The **Code of Hammurabi** was written on a huge stone in a public place so all Babylonians could know and follow the law.

The civilization of **ancient Greece** did not develop around a river, but around the sea. The Greeks built an **empire**: they established colonies on the Mediterranean Sea and the Black Sea; then they imported food from the colonies. However, Greece itself was not politically unified. As its city-states fought for control of each other's land, Sparta, a particularly warlike state, took over a number of other city-states. Athens, another city-state, is known as the first political **democracy**. All Athenian citizens could vote—but less than half of Athenians were citizens. Women could not vote, nor could the many slaves. The Greek Empire lasted only a few hundred years, but its original ideas, such as democracy, and its stunning arts, including architecture and literature, remain influential even now.

Eventually, the Greek Empire fell to **Roman** conquerors. Rome began as a city on the Italian Peninsula, governed by its wealthy citizens through an elected Senate. Roman citizens were governed by a system of laws that is still influential in the United States. For example, the Romans believed that a person accused of a crime was innocent until proven guilty. The power of Rome grew, and the Romans took over many lands surrounding the Mediterranean Sea, pushing north as far as England and east into Asia by about 100 C.E. Roman leaders built systems and infrastructure to make their empire strong: schools, roads and bridges, hospitals, a tax system, and an army. The ancient Roman Empire lasted until 476 C.E.

Ancient Egypt, Greece, and Rome were only a few of the early civilizations in which people made important scientific discoveries and developed enduring ideas. In Central America, the **Maya**, whose culture was strongest from 300 to 900 C.E., invented a pictographic writing system in which they recorded remarkable discoveries in mathematics and astronomy. The **Inca Empire** in South America had a sophisticated system of government. The Incas built amazing roads and bridges in their rugged mountain lands. In Mexico, the **Aztecs** invented a written language and a calendar system and expanded their farmlands by dredging mud from lakes.

PRACTICE 1

Questions 1 through 4 are based on the information on page 470.

1. Which of the following Central American civilizations is particularly noted for achievements in both mathematics and astronomy?

    A. the Sumerians
    B. the Maya
    C. the Aztecs
    D. the Incas

2. According to the information on page 470, two ancient civilizations were particularly influential on the form of government adopted by the United States of America. Select the two civilizations that had the greatest impact on America's systems of law and government and write them into the blanks below.

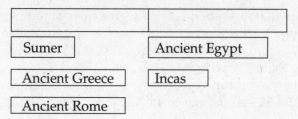

Sumer   Ancient Egypt

Ancient Greece   Incas

Ancient Rome

3. What did the ancient civilizations of Egypt and the Fertile Crescent have in common?

    A. Both developed flood control and irrigation technologies to boost food production.
    B. Both had a public code of law engraved on a huge stone.
    C. Both were centered on the shores of the Mediterranean Sea.
    D. Both developed systems of political democracy in which citizens could vote.

4. Once a society developed agriculture and domesticated animals, food surpluses and rising populations made possible which of the following developments?

    A. a nomadic lifestyle
    B. towns
    C. stone tools
    D. stone carvings

Questions 5 and 6 refer to the following map.

Ancient China

Mongolia
Gobi Desert
Manchuria
Yellow River
Anyang
Korea
Yellow Sea
Loyang   Chengchow
China
Yangtze River
South China Sea

▨ Shang dynasty from about 1600 B.C. to 1122 B.C.

5. In the Yellow River valley, floods deposit a fertile yellow soil called loess that is easily worked by farmers.

    Which of the following civilizations arose under geographic conditions similar to those in ancient China?

    A. the Aztecs
    B. ancient Greece
    C. ancient Rome
    D. ancient Egypt

6. Which of the following statements is supported by the information in the map?

    A. The Yellow River is the only major river in China.
    B. The Shang dynasty, or ruling family, controlled China for almost a thousand years.
    C. The Yellow River was probably the main trade route between Loyang and Chengchow.
    D. The Shang civilization traded more with Korea than with Manchuria.

Answers and explanations start on page 688.

GEOGRAPHY AND THE WORLD

Feudalism to Nation States

Key Ideas

- During the Middle Ages, the feudal system helped to stabilize Europe.
- A by-product of the Crusades was the opening up of trade routes and city growth.
- During the Renaissance, education grew in importance, and people left the Catholic Church to establish Protestantism.

GED® TEST TIP

To summarize a graph such as the one on page 473, ask yourself: What is the topic of the graph? What is the main point of the data? How could I say this in a sentence or two?

The **Middle Ages** in Europe lasted from about A.D. 500 to 1500. As the once strong government of Rome weakened, Europe became vulnerable to invasions from warring groups or tribes. A tribal ruler named **Charlemagne** conquered most of Europe by 800. Charlemagne was able to stabilize this large territory for a time. He established laws, spread Christianity, and encouraged education and commerce. When Charlemagne died in 814, the territories of Europe became unstable again, and the system of **feudalism** emerged.

Under feudalism, kings granted control of land to nobles. A noble's soldiers, or knights, protected the noble's estate, or manor. **Peasants** farmed at the manor. Nobles paid taxes to kings; peasants paid taxes to nobles. As the political boundaries among the kings' lands became established, the feudal system made life in Europe more peaceful over several hundred years.

To the east, the religion of **Islam** was founded during the early Middle Ages by the prophet Muhammad, who was born in A.D. 570. The followers of Islam, called **Muslims**, conquered large territories in the Middle East, northern Africa, Spain, Persia, and India. They established a series of empires. Many people in these conquered lands converted to Islam while contributing their own knowledge and arts to the Muslim culture. Although the Islamic Empire itself did not last, Islam and its culture have remained strong.

During the late Middle Ages, Christians and Muslim Turks fought over the holy city of Jerusalem in a series of wars called the **Crusades**. Christians gained control of Jerusalem from the Turks, but they ruled the city for less than 90 years. A more lasting effect of the Crusades was to open up trade between Europe and the Middle East and even China. As trade, money, and merchants grew in importance in Europe, feudalism declined. People left the manors and went to live and work in cities, where opportunities were greater. Cities gained political, economic, and cultural importance.

During the Middle Ages, European nations began to form as **monarchs** combined territories of small rulers and took advantage of the wealth of cities. England's monarchy was established by 1100. France won the Hundred Years' War against England and emerged as a strong nation under its monarch. Spain united through the marriage of two rulers, Ferdinand and Isabella, who had each controlled smaller states.

The **Renaissance**, which spread from Italy across Europe between 1300 and 1600, brought growth in education, science, and the arts. The Renaissance also led to changes in the Catholic Church. During the **Reformation** in the 1500s, reformers criticized the church for abusing its power. Those who believed that people should read the Bible themselves rather than follow the pope split from the Catholic Church and formed the **Protestant** religion. King Henry VIII of England broke from the Catholic Church and formed the Church of England so he would not have to obey the pope.

1. According to the passage on page 472, what was the role of the knights in feudal Europe?

   A. to collect taxes for the king
   B. to take care of livestock
   C. to protect their noble's land from attack
   D. to administer justice

Question 2 is based on the text on page 472 and the following map.

2. Given the information on page 472, select the modern European nation in which you are most likely to find evidence of Muslim arts and culture.

_____

3. During the late Middle Ages, the growth of trade spurred a migration of peasants from the manors to the towns. To which of the following events is this most similar?

   A. the migration of Puritans to the New World to escape religious persecution in the 1600s
   B. the migration of people from farms to industrial cities in the 1800s
   C. the migration of political refugees to the United States in the 1900s
   D. the migration of individuals with health problems from cold, damp regions to warm, dry regions

4. At the time of the Reformation, which of the following was one of the main differences between Roman Catholics and Protestants?

   A. Roman Catholics accepted the authority of the pope and Protestants did not.
   B. Roman Catholics lived on the manors and Protestants lived in the towns.
   C. Roman Catholics supported the monarchies in their nations and Protestants did not.
   D. Roman Catholics led the Church of England under Henry VIII and Protestants did not.

5. In England in the 1100s, any free man could bring a case before a royal court headed by a circuit judge, who formed juries of local people. The decisions of these courts were recorded and formed the basis for common law, which was applied to everyone in the kingdom. In contrast, justice in the manor courts, which were run by the nobles, could be fickle. There were few written laws, and the verdicts could be overturned by the lord.

   People usually preferred to be tried in royal courts rather than manor courts because the royal courts valued which of the following?

   A. accepted legal principles
   B. harsh punishment
   C. power for the local lord
   D. fines rather than imprisonment

Question 6 refers to the following graph.

Source: Carlo M. Cippola, ed. *The Fontana Economic History of Europe: The Middle Ages* and Carlo M. Cippola *Before the Industrial Revolution: European Society and Economy, 1000–1700.*

6. Which of the following best summarizes the information shown on the graph?

   A. The population of Western Europe showed the most growth between the years 750 and 1000.
   B. There were fewer than 50 million people living in Western Europe at any given time.
   C. The population of Western Europe showed almost constant growth with only brief periods of decline.
   D. The population of Western Europe fell to its lowest around the year 1450.

Answers and explanations begin on page 688.

The Age of Revolutions

Key Ideas

- In the American and French Revolutions, people fought against unjust governments.
- Revolution spread to Latin America, ending many colonial governments there.
- The Industrial Revolution caused sweeping changes in work, living conditions, and social mobility.

ON THE GED® TEST

As part of the GED® Social Studies Test, you may be provided with basic historic information and asked to make comparisons—such as the similarities and differences between two revolutions.

Political revolutions often happen when people are unhappy about the conditions resulting from their system of government. Political revolutions may also be fueled by new ideas about who is best suited to govern. In the Age of Revolutions, many people wanted more political power.

One important cause of the **American Revolution** was British taxation. Although British citizens in England were represented in government through **Parliament**, the American colonists did not have representatives in that body. The colonists believed that they should not have to pay the special taxes levied on them, since they had had no voice in determining the tax laws. Although the colonists began by arguing for representation in the British government, by 1776 they had declared themselves a sovereign nation, the United States of America.

Revolutionaries in France were inspired by democratic ideas expressed in the American colonies' **Declaration of Independence** and the **U.S. Constitution**. Unlike England, France had no Parliament; the French monarch had absolute power. The nobility and the Church had many privileges and paid no taxes, while ordinary citizens paid heavy taxes and had few rights or freedoms. In 1789, the French people organized a National Assembly—a law-making body to represent them. When King Louis XVI fought against the establishment of the National Assembly, the **French Revolution** began. Its turmoil lasted for ten years.

In Latin America, many colonized people, inspired in part by the American and French Revolutions, began to shake off European rule. In Haiti, an island in the Caribbean Sea, slaves led by Toussaint L'Ouverture overturned French rule and established an independent nation in 1804. Mexican revolutionaries finally won their independence from Spain in 1821. In South America, revolutions rocked the continent until 1824, by which time most countries had gained their independence.

Important revolutions are not always political. The **Industrial Revolution** started in the late 1700s in the textile industry, when new equipment was invented for spinning thread and weaving cloth. Instead of workers using their own tools at home, factories could house many workers using machines to produce much greater quantities. This factory model for large-scale production spread along with **steam engines** and electricity. Workers moved into factory towns and cities to work for wages. The Industrial Revolution brought a mixture of benefits and problems—useful inventions, increasing wealth, and new **social mobility** were offset by dangerous factory jobs, **child labor**, crowded cities, and **pollution**.

The Industrial Revolution also brought sweeping social changes. The economic mainstay of the European **aristocracy** had been farmland. After the Industrial Revolution, manufacturing and trade became more important economically than agriculture. Thus, the merchant classes became more powerful. New ideas about political equality affected how people thought about social equality as well.

PRACTICE 3

1. According to the passage on page 474, which of the following had a great influence on the French Revolution?

    A. the Industrial Revolution
    B. the Mexican Revolution
    C. the U.S. Declaration of Independence
    D. the British monarchy

Question 2 refers to the following paragraph and graph.

Before the French Revolution, the French were divided into three groups by law, each with different privileges. In the First Estate were the higher clergy, who were nobles, and the parish priests, who were commoners. The Second Estate consisted of nobles who were not members of the clergy. The Third Estate was made up of commoners, including the middle class and peasants.

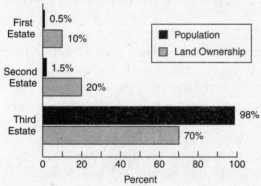

Population and Land Ownership in France, 1789

First Estate: 0.5%, 10%
Second Estate: 1.5%, 20%
Third Estate: 98%, 70%

Legend: Population, Land Ownership

2. Which of the following statements is supported by the paragraph and the graph?

    A. All members of the nobility belonged to the First Estate.
    B. The members of the First Estate owned more property than members of the Second Estate.
    C. The distribution of wealth in prerevolutionary France favored the Third Estate.
    D. Members of the Third Estate owned the least amount of land per person.

3. According to the information on page 474, the main difference between the English and French governments before 1789 is that England (1) [Select...▾], while France (2) [Select...▾].

Select (1)	Select (2)
was a monarchy	was not a direct democracy
had a parliament	did not have a parliament
was a democratic republic	was not a monarchy

4. On what was the economic power of the aristocracy based in 18th-century Europe?

    A. moral superiority
    B. attaining a high level of education
    C. possessing large landholdings
    D. belonging to the Church bureaucracy

5. Which of the following does the writer of the text on page 474 take for granted that you know, but does not state outright?

    A. The American colonists demanded representation in the British government before they declared independence.
    B. A sovereign nation is independent, having the power to govern itself.
    C. Many colonies were influenced by the American and French revolutions to seek independence.
    D. As manufacturing and trade became more important, the merchant classes gained power.

6. The Information Revolution of the late 20th century, spurred by the availability of personal computers and the Internet, is most similar to which of the following revolutions?

    A. the American Revolution
    B. the French Revolution
    C. the Mexican Revolution
    D. the Industrial Revolution

Answers and explanations start on page 688.

Exploration, Colonialism, and Wars

Key Ideas

- Two devastating world wars occurred during the first half of the 20th century.
- The United States and Soviet Union emerged as superpowers after World War II.
- The superpowers faced off during the Cold War, which ended with the breakup of the Soviet Union in 1991.

World War I resulted from **nationalism** and **imperialism**—the desire of nations to extend their empires. This desire for expansion led to military buildup. When war broke out in 1914 between Serbia and Austria-Hungary over the assassination of an Austrian leader visiting Serbia, a chain reaction started as other countries also declared war. Germany and Austria-Hungary were the mainstays of the **Central Powers**, who fought against the **Allies**— England, France, Russia, Serbia, and eventually the United States. When the Central Powers finally lost the war, millions of people had been killed. The war had devastated Europe, leaving many people jobless and homeless. In the 1918 **Treaty of Versailles**, Germany was blamed for the war and forced to pay **reparations** to the Allies.

Revolution in Russia began during World War I. The Russian **Czar** refused to pull out of the war, even though most Russians did not support involvement. In 1917, the Czar and his family were assassinated, and the **Russian Revolution** ended with Bolshevik leader Vladimir Lenin in power. The Bolsheviks founded the Soviet Union as a **communist** nation with one political party—the Communist Party.

The Great Depression, which began in the United States when the stock market crashed in 1929, affected many countries. One hard-hit nation was Germany, which was still suffering economically and politically from its defeat in World War I. By 1933, nearly half of German workers were unemployed, and people were starving. Adolf Hitler, leader of the Nazi Party, rose to power by appealing to German nationalism and promising to put people back to work. Hitler's terrible form of nationalism involved imprisoning and killing people who were not part of "the Aryan race." Jews were the main targets of Hitler's campaign, now called the **Holocaust**. Hitler wanted to take over all Europe, and because other powerful nations wanted to avoid war, they let him annex Austria, then Czechoslovakia. But when Hitler invaded Poland in 1939, England and France declared war on Germany, and **World War II** began. Many nations went to war, including the United States. Once again, Germany and the other **Axis Powers** (including Italy and Japan) were defeated by the Allies. The United States dropped the first **atomic bomb** on Hiroshima to end the war.

After World War II, the United States and the Soviet Union emerged as **superpowers**. Former allies, they each led opposing groups of countries, one group democratic, the other group communist. The two groups of nations so distrusted each other that the period following World War II was called the **Cold War**—a war fought through political and diplomatic contests instead of battles. To catch up with the United States, the Soviet Union started to build its own nuclear weapons, and the **arms race** began, soon followed by the "space race."

However, by 1990 the Soviet bloc was falling apart. The Soviet Union itself split into 15 countries in 1991. People who had lived under repressive governments for many years struggled to establish democracy—not only in the former Soviet bloc, but also in Africa, Latin America, and Asia.

PRACTICE 4

Questions 1 through 4 are based on the information on page 476.

1. As a result of the 1918 Treaty of Versailles, what did Germany have to do?

   A. pay the Allies money to repair war damages
   B. develop its military forces to protect Europe
   C. adopt a communist government
   D. promote nationalism among its people

2. What event was the immediate cause of England and France declaring war on Germany at the beginning of World War II?

   A. the annexation of Austria
   B. the annexation of Czechoslovakia
   C. the invasion of Poland
   D. the invasion of France

3. Before the atomic bomb was dropped on Hiroshima, the Allies warned Japan they would suffer "complete and utter destruction" unless they surrendered. Despite the fact that 80,000 people were killed and 40,000 wounded by the bombing of Hiroshima, Japan still refused to surrender. The United States then dropped a second atomic bomb on the city of Nagasaki, killing 40,000 more people. After the second bombing, the Japanese surrendered.

   Japan's refusal to surrender after the bombing of Hiroshima suggests that the Japanese placed a high value on which of the following?

   A. negotiation
   B. national pride
   C. the lives of military personnel
   D. a lasting peace

4. Which of the following is a similarity between World War I and World War II?

   A. Both were confined to Europe.
   B. Both occurred after the Russian Revolution.
   C. Both involved the use of atomic weapons.
   D. Both were won by the Allies.

Questions 5 and 6 refer to the following chart.

Casualties in World War II

Nation	Military Dead	Military Wounded	Civilian Dead
Great Britain	398,000	475,000	65,000
Soviet Union	7,500,000	14,102,000	15,000,000
United States	292,000	671,000	very few
Germany	2,850,000	7,250,000	5,000,000
Japan	1,576,000	500,000	300,000

Source: *The Second World War* by Henri Michel.

5. What was the main difference between the casualties sustained by the United States and those sustained by other nations in World War II?

   A. The United States had more military dead than wounded.
   B. The United States sustained only a few civilian casualties.
   C. The United States had the fewest wounded.
   D. The United States had more civilian than military casualties.

6. The main reason that the Soviet Union had so many casualties is that it was invaded by the German army, which got as far as the outskirts of Moscow and Leningrad. There the Germans halted in 1941. Severe winters, long supply lines back to Germany, and stiff resistance from the Soviets ultimately defeated the Germans.

   Which of the following events is most similar to the German invasion of the Soviet Union?

   A. the 1812 French invasion of Russia, which failed due to harsh weather and lack of supplies
   B. the occupation of Singapore by Japan in World War II, which gave Japan control of Malaya
   C. the 1941 Japanese attack on Pearl Harbor, which drew the United States into World War II
   D. the 1945 Allied invasion of Europe, which liberated Europe from German control

Answers and explanations start on page 689.

GEOGRAPHY AND THE WORLD

Humans and the Environment

Key Ideas

- When populations grow, decline, or shift, changes in geographic regions occur.
- Populations change as a result of many different political and economic factors.
- Population growth and urbanization have a negative impact on the environment.

GED® TEST TIP

Some questions give a definition and ask you to apply it. To answer an application question such as number 2 on page 479, check each of the answer options against the given definition.

Populations—particularly the movement and growth of population groups—play a major role in defining and altering geographic regions. A population may be **native** to a geographic area, as the Taino, for example, were native to the Caribbean when Columbus arrived there. Sometimes population groups **migrate** over long distances, as did many Irish people who came to the United States during the Potato Famine in the mid-1800s. However, when people feel strong ties to a place, they may stay there even when conditions are unfavorable; they may even develop new economic and cultural strategies that strengthen their population. The **distribution** of population within a region depends on many factors, not all of which humans can control. People tend to move where there are resources, jobs, and other favorable conditions. But these conditions are ever changing, depending on politics, climate, economic development, and so on.

Urban and **rural** development have a strong impact on the distribution of a population. Industrialized regions generally see their populations shift away from rural areas into cities and towns. **Suburban** development very often follows urban growth. As cities become crowded, the urban population spreads into the countryside, often taking up agricultural lands for housing and commercial development. Agriculture also changes in most industrialized regions. Farming is done on a larger scale by fewer people using more mechanized tools. Industrialized regions usually can support a larger population at a higher standard of living than noindustrialized regions. However, these regions also may lose some of their distinctive traditional cultures, arts, farming methods, and so on.

When political boundaries are in dispute, or ethnic groups declare war on each other, local population shifts may dramatically change the character of a region. For example, during World War II, Hitler depopulated Europe of millions of Jews through deportation and death camps. After World War II, the state of Israel was established in the Middle East, drawing many Jews to the region. Continuing conflicts within the Middle East have led to further population shifts of different Arab and Jewish groups there.

When human populations grow, they significantly affect the natural environment. **Manufacturing** and **urbanization** cause air and water **pollution**. Commercial agriculture tends to degrade both soil and water. Eventually food and water supplies become endangered. For example, these problems, along with a loss of farmland to urbanization, are very prominent in China today, where the government has been trying since the 1970s to reduce population growth.

Overall, government policies and international agreements have not been strong enough nor widely enforced when it comes to reducing the destructive impact of growing populations, large cities, and damaging agricultural methods in many parts of the world.

PRACTICE 5

Questions 1 through 4 are based on the information on page 478.

1. What is migration?

   A. a form of society in which people move on after they consume an area's resources
   B. temporary travel to another geographic region to scout for resources
   C. the move of an individual or population from one geographic area to settle in another
   D. the relative distribution of populations in urban and rural areas

2. Migration within a country's borders is called internal migration. Which of the following is an example of internal migration?

   A. the movement of the Irish to the United States during the Potato Famine in the 1800s
   B. the westward movement of the American population from the 1700s to the present
   C. the movement of Mexican workers into the southwest United States during the 1900s
   D. the movement of people from former British colonies to Great Britain

3. Urban areas Select... ▾ suburban areas.

   • are more densely populated than
   • have been more recently settled than
   • contain more remnants of farms than
   • have more agricultural workers than

4. Which of the following technologies was the most likely contributor to the rapid growth of suburbs in the United States?

   A. the telephone
   B. the telegraph
   C. the airplane
   D. the automobile

Questions 5 and 6 refer to the following graph.

Source: Population Reference Bureau

5. What does the figure 9,039,000,000 represent?

   A. the projected population of less developed nations in 2025
   B. the projected population of less developed nations in 2050
   C. the projected population of more developed nations in 2050
   D. the projected total world population in 2050

6. Which of the following conclusions is supported by the data on the graph?

   A. The total world population will double in the 50 years from 2000 to 2050.
   B. About half the world's population lives in the more developed nations.
   C. Most of the population growth in the 50 years from 2000 to 2050 will occur in the less developed nations.
   D. Most of the population growth in the 50 years from 2000 to 2050 will occur in the more developed nations.

Answers and explanations start on page 689.

Using Resources Wisely

Key Ideas

- Conservation means carefully using natural resources to help preserve them for the future.
- Conflicts over natural resources require the balancing of different interests.
- Government programs can promote conservation and encourage people to develop alternative energy sources.

ON THE GED® TEST

Some questions are based on important current topics such as the development and conservation of resources. Reading the newspaper will help you become familiar with many of these issues.

Conservation means using natural resources—such as soil, plant and animal life, water, air, and mineral reserves—carefully. Conservationists encourage the **sustainable use** of resources—using resources in ways that do not exhaust them for the future. Natural resources are either **renewable** or **nonrenewable.** Renewable resources can be sustained through replacement. For example, harvested plants can be replanted. Solar and wind energy are also renewable, since their supply never runs out. Nonrenewable resources are materials that humans use but cannot replace—such as petroleum and natural gas, as well as minerals such as coal, copper, and iron.

Natural resources need to be protected for many reasons. Some reasons for conservation are economic: natural resources are needed to produce goods and services of economic value. Petroleum provides fuel to run equipment in factories and to transport materials and goods. We also need wood and wood products for building structures, making furniture, and manufacturing paper. Other reasons for conserving resources relate to our need to sustain the diverse **ecosystems** of Earth to help keep the planet healthy. These diverse ecosystems help maintain the following resources: water; air; and plant, animal, and human life. Finally, natural resources inspire our sense of beauty and wonder; natural areas and materials play important roles in people's cultural and spiritual traditions.

When natural resources are **scarce** or become threatened, different people's interests can come into conflict. For example, water resources in a region might not be adequate to provide clean drinking water, irrigate local farms, sustain wildlife, and supply water for industrial development. If these interests are not balanced, some people will lose what they need. These problems become even more difficult when political boundaries are involved. Perhaps one nation's water supply comes from a river that flows through another nation; if the second nation builds a dam on the river, it could cut back the flow of water to the first nation. Such conflicts can be very difficult to negotiate. Industry, agriculture, natural ecosystems, clean air and water, and historical and cultural preservation—all these factors influence how people decide to allocate natural resources.

Many countries have laws that protect **endangered species** of plants and animals. Industrial and agricultural interests have to be balanced against **biodiversity**—the maintenance of many different species of organisms. New international agreements attempt to protect the **ozone layer** in the atmosphere, which is critical to maintaining Earth's climate patterns. In some nations—although not in the United States—high taxes on gasoline pay for clean air programs and encourage people to reduce their use of cars. **Fossil fuels** are relatively inexpensive and available, so industrialized regions are highly dependent on them. But they are nonrenewable and cause a great deal of pollution. Globally, we will have to develop more sustainable sources of energy on a large scale—such as **solar** and **wind energy**—to keep our planet healthy in the long run.

PRACTICE 6

Questions 1 through 5 are based on the information on page 480.

1. What are renewable resources?

    A. materials that will never run out or can be replaced if used
    B. materials that we do not use and so can use at a later date
    C. materials that we use but cannot replace
    D. an incentive to conserve materials

2. Which of the following is an example of the sustainable use of a resource?

    A. burning fossil fuels
    B. strip mining
    C. overgrazing livestock
    D. rotating crops

3. Since conflicts over scarce or polluted resources sometimes cross national boundaries, which of the following methods would be most likely to solve problems related to these resources?

    A. negotiating in an international forum
    B. taking unilateral action
    C. importing resources
    D. selling resources

4. In the United States, there is disagreement about how to reduce dependence on foreign oil. Some favor exploiting domestic sources of oil even if that means polluting the environment. Others prefer to concentrate on developing alternative, renewable sources of energy.

    Which of the following best characterizes the underlying difference in points of view between the pro-oil and pro-alternative energy factions?

    A. self-sufficiency versus interdependence
    B. competition versus cooperation
    C. short-term benefit versus long-term benefit
    D. patriotism versus internationalism

5. Which of the following actions could a family take to conserve nonrenewable resources?

    A. incinerate the trash
    B. carpool to work and school
    C. plant trees in the yard
    D. burn more firewood

Questions 6 and 7 refer to the following chart.

Current Natural Gas Resources and Reserves
(in trillion cubic feet)

Region	Current Production	Proved Reserves	Reserves to Production Ratio
N. America	25.5	312.7	12/1
S. America	2.1	189.1	90/1
Europe	9.2	216.3	24/1
Former U.S.S.R.	25.7	2,057.5	80/1
Africa	2.6	341.6	131/1
Middle East	3.9	1,594.3	409/1
Asia/Oceania	6.5	350.6	54/1

Source: Congressional Research Service.

6. Select the world region that currently produces the most natural gas.

7. Natural gas is a nonrenewable resource. As gas is produced for consumption, reserves are depleted. Assume that each of the regions listed above continues to produce natural gas at its current rate and does not discover any additional reserves. Rank the regions below in the order in which they will run out of natural gas, with (1) meaning the region will run out of natural gas first and (4) meaning the region will run out of natural gas last.

(1)	
(2)	
(3)	
(4)	

North America	Europe
Former U.S.S.R.	Africa

Answers and explanations start on page 689.

GEOGRAPHY AND THE WORLD PRACTICE QUESTIONS

1. The Germanic tribes that invaded the Roman Empire had relatively simple governments. There were few government officials and taxes. Rulers depended on the loyalty of their warriors rather than on a government bureaucracy. Germanic laws were based on custom and designed to prevent warfare between families.

Which of the following is the best title for this passage?

A. How Germanic Tribes Governed
B. Germanic Tribes and the Roman Empire
C. The Invasion of the Roman Empire
D. Loyalty Among the Germanic Tribes

2. The mechanization of the textile industry, the invention of the steam engine, and the development of the coal and iron industries contributed to Great Britain's lead in the Industrial Revolution. However, after 1850, other nations began to challenge Great Britain's lead. Belgium, France, and Germany all industrialized quickly. By 1900, natural resources and railroad building helped make the United States the leading industrial nation.

Which of the following is the best summary of this passage?

A. The development of natural resources made Great Britain the leader in the Industrial Revolution.
B. The Industrial Revolution started in Great Britain and spread throughout the world.
C. The Industrial Revolution started in Great Britain and spread to Europe, but by 1900 the United States was the leading industrialized nation.
D. Plentiful natural resources and a vast railroad system were the underpinnings of the Industrial Revolution in the United States.

Questions 3 and 4 refer to the following map.

Early Civilizations in Africa

3. Select the area on the map where the earliest civilizations in Africa developed.

4. Which of the following statements is supported by information on the map?

A. Over 800 years, several civilizations succeeded one another in western Africa.
B. The Kingdom of Mali dominated western Africa for more than 500 years.
C. Timbuktu was an important center of learning in Songhai.
D. Gold and salt were transported along caravan trade routes in western Africa.

Questions 5 through 8 refer to the following timeline.

5. Portugal dominated trade in the East Indies for most of the 1500s. Select the event on the timeline that most likely first triggered Portugal's superiority in the region.

6. Which of the following statements is supported by information on the timeline?

   A. Spanish and Portuguese domination of exploration gave way to that of the Dutch, French, and English.
   B. Henry Hudson discovered more places in North America than did Marquette and Joliet and Cartier.
   C. Both Cartier and Da Gama explored North America on behalf of France.
   D. French explorers cooperated with American Indians in establishing trade.

7. Instead of financing expeditions themselves, the rulers of Spain allowed conquistadors to establish outposts in the Americas. The conquistador financed his own expedition, but if he succeeded, he was allowed to keep four-fifths of any treasure he found. Cortés was a conquistador who became rich by conquering the Aztecs in Mexico.

   [Select...▼] was also a conquistador.

   • Da Gama
   • Pizarro
   • Cartier

8. Which of the following is the best title for this timeline?

   A. The Spanish Explorers and Empire
   B. The Age of Exploration
   C. History of the 16th and 17th centuries
   D. European Colonies in the Americas

Question 9 refers to the following graph.

U.S. National Defense Spending, 1976–1995

9. Which of the following statements is supported by the graph?

   A. Before the Cold War began, defense spending was at an all-time high.
   B. Defense spending remained steady throughout the Cold War.
   C. Defense spending declined steadily during the period 1976 to 1990.
   D. After the Cold War ended, defense spending began to fall.

10. When establishing colonies, European nations wanted their colonies to be economically self-sufficient. That meant that each colony paid for its government salaries and the cost of building and maintaining roads, railroads, and government buildings. To do this, European colonists or the colonial governments exported natural resources like gold or copper or grew cash crops like sugar or rubber.

   Which of the following statements is an opinion rather than a fact?

   A. European countries had similar goals in establishing their colonies.
   B. Colonies should be economically independent.
   C. European nations built railroads, roads, and government buildings in their colonies.
   D. Colonies provided natural resources that colonists could export.

Questions 11 and 12 refer to the following passage.

Desertification, the spread of deserts, is usually caused in part by human activity. Agricultural practices, such as clearing trees and brush, depleting the soil through plowing and planting, overgrazing, and irrigation, contribute to the sterilization and erosion of the land. A period of drought is often enough to tip the balance toward a desert ecosystem.

For example, in the 1930s, excessive plowing, overgrazing, and well-digging left the American Great Plains vulnerable to desertification. A lengthy drought led to conditions so severe the topsoil was blown away, creating what is known as the Dust Bowl. Formerly valuable farmland became almost worthless in a period of years. The area was spared permanent desertification only because normal rainfall eventually resumed.

11. Which of the following was the most likely result of the Dust Bowl?

   A. the Great Depression of the 1930s, an economic downturn
   B. the migration of thousands of farm families to other regions
   C. the permanent cessation of agriculture in the Great Plains
   D. restoration of the Great Plains ecosystem as it was before agriculture

12. Which of the following is an example of desertification?

   A. the shrinking of the Greenland ice sheet
   B. the shifting sandbars along the coast of Lake Michigan
   C. the extension of grazing onto land that is part of the National Forest system
   D. the spread of the Sahara into the grazing land on its southern border

13. According to experts in world agriculture, the poor nutrition and starvation of millions of people stems not from a global scarcity of resources, but from the uneven distribution of resources among nations. Experts claim the world has the resources to feed its population if the political will of the richer nations were brought to bear on this problem.

Which of the following is an opinion rather than a fact?

A. Millions of people worldwide are under-nourished.
B. The world has abundant natural resources.
C. Natural resources are distributed unevenly among nations.
D. The problem of feeding the world's population is a matter of political will rather than one of resources.

14. The 2000 Census showed that the United States has 281,421,906 people, an increase of 13.2 percent over the 1990 Census. Population growth and immigration accounted for this increase. The state population counts showed the largest relative gains in the South and West, with Nevada's population increase the highest at 66.3 percent. Because state population figures are used to allocate seats in the House of Representatives, every ten years a shift in political power occurs. In 2000, states in the Northeast and Midwest lost seats, and states in the West and South picked up seats.

Which of the following is implied by the paragraph?

A. Nevada had a 66.3 percent population increase.
B. Nevada gained seats in the House.
C. People moved away from the Northeast and Midwest.
D. The U.S. population in 2000 was about 281 million people.

Questions 15 and 16 refer to the following map.

15. Which of the following people is most likely to use the map above?

A. a geologist surveying land features in the Philadelphia area
B. a visitor to Philadelphia
C. an employee of the Federal Aviation Administration
D. a commercial airline pilot

16. Which of the following statements is supported by the data on the map?

A. More than 20 airlines have landing rights at Philadelphia International Airport.
B. Route 95 borders the south side of Philadelphia International Airport.
C. It is possible to get to Philadelphia International Airport by plane, car, or rail.
D. Labels for terminals and parking areas are coordinated to provide convenient parking.

Answers and explanations start on page 690.

Science

The GED® *Science Test* evaluates your ability to understand, interpret, and apply *science* information. You will have 90 minutes to answer 34 questions that are based on reading passages, graphics such as diagrams, tables, graphs, and maps, or a combination of the two.

You will need a minimum score of 150 to pass the *Science Test*, which is one of the four tests you will need to pass in order to earn a high school equivalency diploma.

Content Areas

Life Science (40%) topics include cell structures and processes, human body systems, health and nutrition, heredity and reproduction, genetics and DNA, evolution and natural selection, and the organization of ecosystems.

Earth and Space Science (20%) topics include the structure of Earth, plate tectonics, geological cycles and processes, renewable and nonrenewable natural resources, weather and climate, the solar system, and the universe.

Physical Science (40%) topics include atoms and molecules, properties and states of matter, chemical reactions, energy and work, motion and forces, waves, electricity, and magnetism.

Science Practices

In addition to testing your understanding of science passages and graphics, *Science Test* questions are based on your understanding of skills that are used in scientific study and investigation. These skills are called **Science Practices**, and they introduce this unit on pages 492–507. After you study these practices, you will reinforce them as you work through the unit. The science practices include the following:

- **Comprehend Scientific Presentations** to interpret passages and graphics.
- **Use the Scientific Method** to design investigations, reason from data, and work with findings.
- **Reason with Scientific Information** to evaluate conclusions with evidence.
- **Apply Concepts and Formulas** to express scientific information and apply scientific theories.
- **Use Probabilities and Statistics** in a science context.

Computer-Based Science Test Question Formats

You will work with six question formats on the *Science Test*. Many of the questions will be in the familiar multiple-choice format, but you will need to be acquainted with the other formats as well.

Multiple-choice questions have four options (A through D). You will **click** on the best answer.

> A scientist concludes that frog and toad populations worldwide are in decline due to stratospheric ozone depletion, which results in more ultraviolet radiation from the sun reaching the earth's surface.
>
> Which excerpt from the text most directly supports this conclusion?
>
> ○ A. "Embryos were examined at 12-hour intervals and the time from egg-laying to hatching was recorded for both groups."
>
> ○ B. "Ultraviolet radiation causes genetic mutations and abnormally slow growth rates in the embryos of most species of frogs and toads, thus negatively impacting survival rates."
>
> ○ C. "The control group was kept in a fully shaded enclosure, and UV levels were measured in both enclosures on a daily basis."
>
> ○ D. "For example, increased exposure to ultraviolet radiation may cause skin cancer in cattle."

Fill-in-the-blank questions will require you to **type** a word, phrase, or number in a box that appears on the screen.

> Type your answers in the boxes:
>
> A supplier of snapdragon seeds to the retail market is considering the genetics of snapdragon flower color. Red and white alleles display incomplete dominance; a plant with one red and one white allele will have pink flowers.
>
> The seed supplier crosses a homozygous red snapdragon and homozygous white snapdragon. What is the likelihood that each seed produced will result in a certain flower color?
>
> Red [   ] %
>
> White [   ] %
>
> Pink [   ] %
>
> Yellow [   ] %

Drop-down questions give you the opportunity to **click** on the correct response to complete a statement.

> The sugar glider is a pouched mammal, or [Select... ▾], that is native to [Select... ▾]. It is one of several gliding [Select... ▾] that behave similarly to flying squirrels. However, sugar gliders and flying squirrels are not close relatives; rather, their similar behavior is the result of [Select... ▾] evolution.

Hot-spot items consist of a graphic image. You will need to **click** on one or more "points" on the graphic as shown at the top of the next page.

The graph shows the relationship between an urban population of Peregrine Falcons and their primary prey species, feral rock pigeons, over time.

Select the area on the graph that represents the Peregrine Falcon population at time A.

To remove a point, place the arrow over the point and click the left mouse button.

Drag-and-drop items require you to **click** on a small image, words, or numerical expression and to **drag** and **drop** it in a specified location on the computer screen.

Identify the independent and dependent variable in the experiment.
Drag and drop the correct variable into each box.

Independent

Dependent

Variables:

Biomass of algae present in aquarium

Phosphorus concentration

Water temperature

Behavior of fish

Two *Short-Answer* items require you to **type in a text box with editing tools** to write a summary, create an experiment design, or explain how evidence supports a hypothesis or conclusion. Each Short-Answer question is expected to take about 10 minutes.

Desertification is a process in which relatively dry land such as grassland loses its plant and animal life and becomes a desert. Desertification can happen as a result of deforestation, overgrazing of livestock, and other human activities. It is currently happening in many regions around the world, including the Sahel region south of the Sahara desert.

Explain how desertification could disrupt the life cycle of *Adenium obesum*, a flowering plant native to the Sahel. Include multiple pieces of evidence from the text to support your answer.

Type your response in the box. This task may require approximately 10 minutes to complete.

Cut   Copy   Paste   Undo   Redo

GED® TEST TIP

The two Short-Answer responses are interspersed within the Science Test. *Try to spend about 10 minutes per short answer. That means you can take a maximum of 20 out of the 75 minutes on them.*

Math Problems on the Science Test

Many science investigations use mathematics. For that reason, there will be math questions on the GED® *Science Test*. You will focus on math skills in this unit with the Science Practices lesson on pages 500–501.

Day	Noontime temperature in degrees Fahrenheit
April 15	58.0
May 15	65.4
June 15	76.9
July 15	88.2
August 15	87.3

$$C = \frac{5}{9}(F - 32)$$

What was the approximately temperature in degrees Celsius at noon on July 15?

You MAY use the calculator.

- A. 10.5
- B. 31.2
- C. 42.8
- D. 58.6

Solution:

Step 1: Write the equation $C = \frac{5}{9}(F - 32)$.

Step 2: Substitute 88.2 for F in the equation because the Fahrenheit temperature on July 15 was 88.2.

Step 3: Use the calculator to find the answer. $C = \frac{5}{9}(88.2 - 32) = 31.2$

Although you do not have to use a calculator, you may use either a hand-held version or an on-screen version of the TI-30XS MultiView™ calculator on the *Science Test*. Some problems will say: *You MAY use your calculator*. When you see that language, the calculator icon appears at the top of the screen. If you cannot remember how to use the calculator, you can open the online *Calculator Reference Sheet*.

You can **click** the links to **open, move,** and **close** both the online **Texas Instruments TI-30XS MultiView**™ calculator and the Calculator Reference Sheet. You will want to move them on the computer screen so that they don't block the problem. Also remember that you will have an *off-line wipe-off board* that you can use as scratch paper.

Short-Answer Questions on the Science Test

Scientists and science students communicate about their work in writing. To reflect that, the GED® *Science Test* contains two Short-Answer items. You will focus on writing Short-Answers in this unit with the Science Practices lesson on pages 502–503.

The Short-Answer items are based on one passage, two passages, a graphic, or a combination. You will compose your answer in a text box similar to the one below.

What are some features of a fossilized skeleton a paleontologist might examine in order to determine the species the skeleton belonged to? What might these features tell the paleontologist about this particular skeleton?

Type your answer in the box.

Cut   Copy   Paste   Undo   Redo

Read the prompt carefully and use the **online highlighter** to target specific facts and information that you will use in your response. Because this is a Short-Answer response, it is expected to be about one or two paragraphs long, with complete sentences and well-developed ideas.

An effective response must answer the questions and use specific information from the source materials. It should not be based on your opinions or personal experiences. Since the Short-Answer responses are worth up to 3 points each, take time to understand the question, plan your response, and choose several facts from the information to back up your position.

As with other writing tasks on the GED® Test, you have word processing tools that you can click on at the top of the toolbox that will allow you to do the following:

- **Cut** (remove extraneous ideas or correct mistakes)
- **Copy** and **Paste** (move words and ideas to improve your writing)
- **Undo** or **Redo** (use if your change your mind or want to restore)

SCIENCE PRACTICES

Comprehend Scientific Presentations

The GED® *Science Test* consists of questions based on science passages and graphics. To comprehend science presentations, you need to understand main ideas and their supporting details.

The **main idea** of a science presentation or graphic is its topic or the writer's point. Use this science diagram to practice finding the main idea.

Dry Cell Battery

► What is the topic of this diagram?
   (1) the components of a dry cell battery
   (2) how a dry cell battery powers machinery

The correct answer is choice **(1)**. The diagram displays the different components (that is, the parts) of a dry cell battery. It does not show the process by which the battery actually operates or powers machinery, so choice **(2)** is incorrect.

Science writers support their main ideas with **details**, **facts**, and **evidence**.

Read the paragraph below and answer the question.

> Earthquakes can be classified as either surface earthquakes or deep-focus earthquakes. Scientists agree that surface earthquakes occur when rock in Earth's crust fractures to relieve stress. Deep-focus earthquakes originate from seismic activity more than 300 kilometers below Earth's surface. The causes of deep-focus earthquakes remain a subject of debate, but scientists believe they may be caused by the pressure of fluids trapped in Earth's tectonic plates.

► Which of the following details supports the main point of this paragraph?
   (1) The causes of deep-focus earthquakes remain a subject of debate among scientists.
   (2) Surface earthquakes are caused by stress in Earth's crust, while deep-focus earthquakes may be caused by pressure.

The correct answer is choice **(2)**. The main point of the paragraph is that earthquakes can be classified into two types based on their causes, and choice **(2)** provides supporting details that illustrate the differences between the two types. While **(1)** is mentioned in the paragraph, it is not a fact that supports the main point about the classification of earthquakes.

PRACTICE 1

<u>Questions 1 through 3 are based on the passage</u> below.

Despite the prevalence of type 2 diabetes, the causes of the disease remain somewhat uncertain. It is likely that some combination of genetics and lifestyle contributes to the development of type 2 diabetes. However, scientists have not fully determined the roles played by various lifestyle factors (such as diet and exercise).

For Americans, one contributing factor may be high sugar consumption. Sugar from food is broken down and absorbed into the bloodstream, and insulin is required for the body to be able to use that sugar. In a study of individuals 18–25 years old who consumed more than the recommended amount of sugar daily, it was shown that the majority had significantly elevated levels of glucose (that is, sugar) in their blood but normal levels of insulin. In other words, these subjects could not produce enough insulin to allow their bodies to use the amount of sugar they were consuming. Elevated blood glucose levels may put individuals consuming high amounts of sugar at higher risk of developing type 2 diabetes.

1. Which one of the following is the topic of the entire passage?

   A. sources of sugar in Americans' diet
   B. the role of insulin in metabolizing sugar from food
   C. the causes of type 2 diabetes
   D. how to prevent type 2 diabetes

2. Which of the following is the main idea of the first paragraph?

   A. It is likely that sugar consumption contributes to the development of type 2 diabetes.
   B. It is likely that genetics plays a role in the development of type 2 diabetes.
   C. Researchers have discovered the causes of type 2 diabetes.
   D. The causes of type 2 diabetes are not fully understood.

3. The main idea of the second paragraph is that high sugar consumption may put individuals at greater risk of developing type 2 diabetes. Which of the following details from the second paragraph supports that main idea?

   A. Sugar from food is absorbed into the bloodstream.
   B. A study of 18–25 year olds showed that a majority did not produce enough insulin to offset the high amounts of sugar they were consuming.
   C. A study of 18–25 year olds showed that high sugar consumption interacted with genetic factors in a majority of those individuals in order to suppress insulin production.
   D. It has not been proven that sugar is a contributing factor to the development of type 2 diabetes.

Question 4 is based on this graphic.

How Topography Contributes to Precipitation

Source: U.S. Geological Survey

4. Which statement correctly describes the process depicted in the graphic above?

   A. As moist, flowing air encounters rising elevations, it cools, which causes condensation, a stage that precedes precipitation and cloud development.
   B. Once above the tree line, flowing air is likely to slow down and stop moving, and then collect in the form of snow.
   C. Clouds dissipate before encountering mountain peaks.
   D. Moist air flows from the west, while drier air usually flows from the east.

Answers and explanations begin on page 691.

SCIENCE PRACTICES

Use the Scientific Method

SCIENCE PRACTICES

The **scientific method** is a set of techniques that scientists use to investigate observable facts and occurrences and to acquire new knowledge. Here are the steps in the scientific method:

1. **Observe a phenomenon** and **formulate a question** about it. The scientific method starts with a **question** about something that you observe. Formulate the question about something that you can measure.
2. **Collect data** about the phenomenon you are studying. Scientific study is founded on **data**, or observable facts, which are used to describe a phenomenon.
3. **Form a hypothesis**. A **hypothesis** is an educated guess about the answer to your question.
4. **Test the hypothesis through an experiment**. Your experiment should be a fair test of the hypothesis. You may need to adjust the experiment. You would do so by changing only one factor at a time while **controlling** other factors. You should also repeat the experiment to make sure the first results are valid.
5. **Draw a conclusion** about the hypothesis based on the experiment. When the experiment is complete, you may conclude that your hypothesis was supported by the data or that it was not, in which case you may formulate a new hypothesis.

Read about scientific observation and answer the question below.

> Scientists observed unusual plant and algae growth in a pond. They sampled the water and also discovered very high concentrations of bacteria. Significant increases in the growth of plants, algae, and bacteria in ponds are often caused by an excess of phosphates and nitrates in the water. The pond was fairly close to neighboring farmland, and two streams carried water from the farm to the pond.

▶ What could be a sound hypothesis about the growth in the pond?
  (1) Runoff from the neighboring farm may be carrying excessive phosphates and nitrates from fertilizers into the pond.
  (2) Proximity to farmland is the cause of plant and algae growth in ponds and other bodies of water.

If you chose **(1)**, you are correct. That hypothesis is an educated guess about the reason for the unusual plant and algae growth in the pond. It could be tested by an experiment that compares samples from the pond water to samples from streams coming from neighboring fields. Choice **(2)** is an assertion that is very general and cannot be measured in this specific situation.

The phenomenon you are studying is called the **dependent variable**. A factor that you believe might be affecting that phenomenon is called the **independent variable**. In the example above, the unusual plant and algae growth would be the dependent variable. The runoff from the neighboring farm would be the independent variable.

Key Ideas

- The scientific method is used to investigate events and to acquire knowledge.
- Scientists follow a series of procedures involving observing, collecting information, and forming a hypothesis.
- After the hypothesis has been tested in an experiment or study, scientists draw a conclusion.

ON THE GED® TEST

The GED® Science Test may present an experiment and ask you to answer multiple-choice questions or to write a Short Response to a question about it.

PRACTICE 2

<u>Questions 1 through 3 are based on this passage.</u>

A majority of teenagers develop acne, but scientists still struggle to explain its cause. It has long been thought that bacteria play a role, although until recently it was assumed that role was purely detrimental—contributing to acne. However, a team of researchers began to wonder whether different strains of bacteria might impact acne in different ways.

The research team studied 49 individuals with acne and 52 individuals without acne, and the researchers collected samples of bacteria from the nasal pores of all those individuals. The researchers found that some combinations of bacterial strains were highly likely to be found in clear-skinned individuals, while other combinations were highly likely to be found in individuals with acne.

After carefully analyzing their data, the scientists concluded that, while some bacterial combinations likely contribute to acne, other bacterial combinations may actually help to ward it off. The researchers suggested that, if further studies confirm these findings, we may want to treat acne by encouraging the growth of helpful bacteria.

1. Use the boxes below to identify the researchers' independent and dependent variables.

Independent variable	Dependent variable

acne symptoms	combinations of bacteria
teenagers	treatments for acne

2. What was the researchers' hypothesis?
   A. Combinations of bacteria are a major cause of acne.
   B. Different kinds of bacteria may impact acne differently.
   C. We may want to change the way we treat acne, treating it by encouraging the growth of beneficial bacteria.
   D. Some combinations of bacteria may actually help ward off acne.

3. What conclusion did the researchers reach based on their data?
   A. Combinations of bacteria are a major cause of acne.
   B. Acne sufferers have more types of bacterial strains in their facial pores than do non-sufferers.
   C. The way we currently treat acne is misguided.
   D. Some combinations of bacteria may actually help ward off acne.

<u>Question 4 is based on the following information.</u>

Suppose that you notice your right knee hurts every time you play softball. You suspect that one of the movements involved in playing softball is causing your knee to hurt, but you are not sure which movement is the culprit. You decide to do a scientific investigation to find out more.

4. Match each of the following steps of the scientific method with a phase of your investigation (listed below the table).

a) Form a hypothesis.	
b) Design a test for your hypothesis.	
c) Collect data to test your hypothesis.	
d) Form a conclusion based on the data from your test.	

i) You make a list of each of the movements involved in softball. In the off season (when you are not playing entire games), you plan to perform each movement several times without performing the others.

ii) Based on the data you collected in your experiment, you think it is likely that stopping suddenly after running a short distance is indeed the cause of your knee pain.

iii) Based on your experience, you make a guess about which of the movements involved in playing softball puts the greatest stress on the knees. You suspect that it may be stopping suddenly after running a short distance.

iv) After performing each movement in isolation, record how your knee feels. Let your knee recover between tests of each type of movement.

Answers and explanations start on page 691.

Reason with Scientific Information

Key Ideas

- Reasoning with scientific information requires citing specific evidence to support a conclusion.
- In some cases, an existing theory can be challenged by new data or evidence.
- One of the ways scientists use information is in making predictions.

Some GED® *Science* questions require recognizing or citing specific evidence to support a conclusion. Another type of question may ask you to judge whether a **conclusion** or a **scientific theory**—a substantiated explanation of the natural world—is challenged by particular data or evidence.

Use the graph below to practice scientific reasoning.

Rates of Infant Mortality, 1940–2009

Source: CDC/NCHS, National Vital Statistics System, Mortality.

▶ Which conclusion is supported by the data on the graph?
   (1) The rate of infant deaths in the United States experienced its sharpest decline between roughly 1940 and the late 1950s.
   (2) In each year between 1940 and 2009, there were fewer infant deaths than in the year before.

The correct answer is choice **(1)**. The graph shows that the rate of infant mortality decreased most sharply between the years of 1940 and the late 1950s. After the late 1950s, it continued to decrease, but more gradually. Choice **(2)** is not a true statement based on the graph: around 1960, there was an uptick in the rate of infant deaths.

Other questions will ask you to make a **prediction** based on evidence or data that the test provides to you. Based on the **trend** observed, scientists use data to predict, or forecast, what they think may happen in the future.

▶ Which of the following predictions is based on the graph above?
   (1) Since there has not been an increase in infant deaths since 1960, there will likely be such an increase sometime soon.
   (2) The rate of infant deaths is unlikely to experience sharp declines in the near future.

Choice **(2)** is correct: the line on the graph shows the trend in infant mortality has been one of very gradual decrease since the 1950s. A good prediction based on that pattern would be that the trend of gradual decline is likely to continue. The graph shows a downward trend, but gives no information to suggest a future increase, so choice **(1)** is incorrect.

> **GED® TEST TIP**
>
> *When you interpret a line graph, carefully follow the direction of each line to see its trend. You can use trends to make predictions based on data.*

PRACTICE 3

1. Inertia causes an object to resist changes in its state of motion. In other words, inertia causes an object at rest to resist any attempt to set it in motion. Similarly, inertia causes an object in motion to resist any attempt to stop its motion. Objects with greater mass have greater inertia.

These figures represent the mass of two objects:

Brick: 100 grams
Block of wood: 70 grams

Which of the following is supported by the information above?

A. It would require more effort to break the brick than to break the block of wood.
B. If both objects were currently sitting still, it would require more effort to push the block of wood across the floor than it would to push the brick across the floor.
C. If both objects were currently sitting still, it would require more effort to push the brick across the floor than it would to push the block of wood across the floor.
D. The brick would absorb water more readily than would the block of wood.

2. In the last several decades, the spider population has exploded on the island of Guam: parts of the island have as many as 40 times more spiders than nearby islands do. One scientist has concluded that the explosion in the Guam spider population is due to an increase in the population of an invasive species of brown tree snake. The snake was introduced into Guam in the 1940s but was not introduced into the neighboring islands. The brown tree snake preys on birds.

Which one of the following, if true, makes the scientist's conclusion more likely?

A. The birds that the brown tree snake eats are the primary predators of spiders on Guam.
B. The brown tree snake is typically introduced into islands via ships carrying tourists. Guam and the islands nearby have long been popular tourist spots.
C. Brown tree snakes eat spiders as well as birds.
D. In the rainy season, the island of Guam can have more than 40 times as many spiders as it did ten years ago.

Questions 3 and 4 are based on the following passage:

Melting ice sheets in Greenland and Antarctica have the potential to contribute significantly to rising sea levels in the next century. Some ice sheets melt more quickly than others, and scientists have wondered why. A team of researchers recently used data from both satellites and radar to study the composition of many of the ice sheets in Greenland and Antarctica. They found that some of the ice sheets formerly thought to sit on rock actually sit on water. This finding could be significant because it may be the case that ice sheets sitting on water tend to melt more quickly than those sitting on rock.

3. Which of the following is a prediction scientists might make based on the information above?

A. If large areas of ice sheets sit on rock, the rising of sea levels may proceed more quickly than had previously been predicted.
B. If large areas of ice sheets sit on water, the rising of sea levels may proceed more quickly than had previously been predicted.
C. Ice sheets in Greenland will likely melt more quickly than ice sheets in Antarctica.
D. All the ice sheets that are melting more quickly will be found to be sitting on water.

4. A scientist predicts that the ice sheets sitting on water will collectively discharge more water into the ocean than will those sitting on rock. Which of the following facts, if true, might weaken that prediction?

A. Most of the ice sheets sitting on water are covering inland lakes with no access to the ocean.
B. Water sitting under ice sheets flows directly into the ocean.
C. Ice in a glass of water will melt even if the room is very cold.
D. Radar used alone is an unreliable way to assess the composition of ice sheets.

Answers and explanations start on page 692.

SCIENCE PRACTICES

Express and Apply Scientific Information

Scientific information can be expressed in different forms. On the GED® *Science Test*, you may be asked to find relationships among science passages, graphics, formulas, or equations.

Scientific equations for **chemical reactions** often use these symbols:

Symbol	Meaning
+	Positive symbol separates two or more **reactants** or **products** from one another.
$\rightarrow$	Yield symbol separates reactants from products and shows the reaction direction.
$\leftrightarrows$	Reversible reaction symbol indicates that the reaction can proceed in both directions.

For example, here is the general chemical formula for what happens when carbon (C) is burned:

$$C + O_2 \rightarrow CO_2$$

▶ Which statement describes the process in the formula?
  (1) Carbon combines with oxygen to produce carbon dioxide.
  (2) Carbon creates oxygen, which takes on another oxygen atom in order to produce carbon dioxide.

The correct answer is statement **(1)**. In this case, carbon and oxygen (O_2) combine without losing any of their components. The result is carbon dioxide, a molecule made up of one carbon atom and two oxygen atoms. (The prefix *di-* means "two," so *carbon dioxide* means "a C and two Os.") The plus sign on the left-hand side of the formula indicates that carbon and oxygen are separate reactants, not that carbon creates oxygen. Thus, statement **(2)** is incorrect.

Other questions may ask you to understand a science concept and **relate** it to a specific situation.

The term *desertification* describes a chain of events in which so much soil erodes from land that the land can no longer support plant or animal life. The lack of plant life allows for further soil erosion, making the land even more barren. It is very difficult to reverse desertification.

▶ Which of the following could be an example of the early stages of desertification?
  (1) In a certain valley, overgrazing has nearly eliminated plant life. This lack of vegetation has led to rapid soil erosion.
  (2) In a certain valley, the climate is arid, and soil erosion has occurred when the infrequent rains arrive. Farmers have devised an irrigation system to grow crops and thus reverse the rate of soil erosion.

Choice **(1)** is correct. Soil erosion is the cause of desertification, so the valley may be in the early stages of desertification. In choice **(2)**, farmers have found a way to combat erosion, so this valley does not appear to be undergoing desertification.

PRACTICE 4

Questions 1 through 4 are based on the information below.

Imagine a substance (such as salt or sugar) dissolved in a liquid (such as water or alcohol). The liquid in which the substance is dissolved is called the *solvent*. *Osmosis* is the diffusion (movement) of a solvent across a semipermeable membrane (a barrier that allows some substances to pass through it). The solvent moves from the side of the membrane with less dissolved material to the side of the membrane with more dissolved material. The result of osmosis is an equilibrium: the state in which the rate at which the solvent flows across the membrane at the same rate in both directions.

Gillian conducted an experiment to see how quickly various liquids with a specific amount of sugar dissolved in them would undergo osmosis. She used vats of the same size with semipermeable membranes separating one side of the vat from the other, and she put equal quantities of various liquids in both sides:

Container Used for Studying Osmosis

Semipermeable membrane

1. Gillian used one of the vats to test the rate of diffusion of liquid acetone in the process of osmosis. What did she most likely put on the two sides of the semipermeable membrane in that vat?

	Side A	Side B
A.	Pure acetone	Sugar in a glass container, submerged in acetone
B.	A 50 percent solution of sugar in acetone	A 50 percent solution of sugar in acetone
C.	Pure acetone	A solution of sugar in acetone
D.	Pure acetone	Pure acetone

Gillian's experiment yielded the following results.

Solvent	Time Required to Reach Equilibrium
Water	20 minutes
Acetone	25 minutes
Acetic acid	18 minutes
Formic acid	15 minutes

2. Based on the table above, which solvent had the highest rate of diffusion?

A. water
B. acetone
C. acetic acid
D. formic acid

3. Based on the table above, calculate the average (mean) time required for the solvents to reach equilibrium. [   ]

4. Osmosis is the reason why it is unhealthy and potentially dangerous to drink seawater. If you drink seawater, which contains a high concentration of salts and other dissolved material, some of the dissolved material will be absorbed into your bloodstream, causing your blood to have a higher-than-normal concentration of dissolved material. As that blood circulates through your body, water will move from your body's tissues into your blood vessels, causing your tissues to lose water and dry out.

Fill in the blank with one of the choices: Based on the information above, your tissues would begin to lose water and dry out when your blood has a level of dissolved material [Select... ▾] that of your body's tissues.

- greater than
- less than
- equivalent to

Answers and explanations start on page 692.

SCIENCE PRACTICES

Use Statistics and Probability

Because scientists often need to perform calculations, you will do some math on the GED® *Science Test*. This math work will include the following:

- Central tendency—average (mean), median, mode, and range
- Independent and dependent probabilities
- Counting techniques for combinations and permutations

You may want to review these topics on pages 290–215 and 296–307 of the unit on *Mathematical Reasoning*. For some of these questions, you may have access to an on-screen calculator. See pages 215–219 and 226–229 of the unit on *Mathematical Reasoning* to learn more about the on-screen calculator.

Scientists use **measures of central tendency** (mean, median, mode, and range) to summarize many pieces of data with one number.

Use the graph below to answer a question about central tendency.

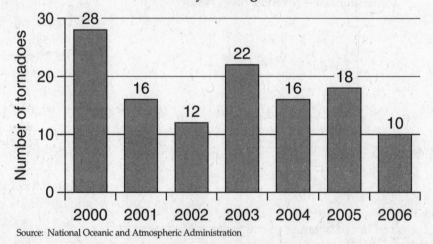

Annual Tornadoes, 2000–2006, Goodland (Kansas) 19-County Warning Area

Source: National Oceanic and Atmospheric Administration

▶ Calculate the mean (arithmetic average) number of tornadoes that struck the Goodland area per year in the years 2002 through 2005.

To find the mean of a set of quantities, sum the quantities and divide by the number of items in the set. The list from 2002 to 2005 is 12, 22, 16, and 18. The sum of those numbers is 68. Divide by the number of items in the list (4), and the result is **17**.

Scientists frequently use data to investigate the **probability** that an event will happen. You may wish to review pages 298–301, *Mathematical Reasoning*, to refresh your memory about working with probability.

Key Ideas

- A measure of central tendency is used to summarize data.
- Probabilities are used to make predictions.
- Combinations and permutations are used to calculate numbers of ordered and unordered arrangements, respectively.

ON THE GED® TEST

When you need to compute on the GED® *Science Test, a calculator symbol with the word "Calculator" will appear on the toolbar at the top of your screen. Click on it to open the online calculator.*

PRACTICE 5

Questions 1 through 4 are based on the following information.

Metabolism is a set of chemical processes that occur in the tissues of living organisms. One example of a metabolic process in animals is the breaking down of carbohydrates from food into substances the body can store. Another example is the transformation of those same substances into energy that the animal can use. The *rate of metabolism* describes the speed at which these processes take place. Metabolic rate varies among different species. The graph below compares several animal species by both average metabolic rate and average body weight.

Metabolic Rates of Seven Species

1. Of the species in this graph, which has the median body weight? [   ]

2. Of the species in this graph, which has the median metabolic rate? [   ]

3. Imagine that you could calculate the average (mean) of metabolic rates of all the animal species in this graph. Now imagine that the shrew were removed from the graph and that you recalculated the average of the remaining species. Without the shrew, the new average metabolic rate would be [Select... ▾].

   - higher than the previous average
   - lower than the previous average
   - about the same as the previous average

4. Adult elephants weigh more than adult horses. Based on the graph above, what would you predict would be true of elephants?

   A. Their metabolic rate would resemble that of cactus mice, which, like elephants, live in warm climates.
   B. Their metabolic rate would be equivalent to that of horses.
   C. Their metabolic rate would be slightly lower than that of horses.
   D. Their metabolic rate would be significantly higher than that of horses.

5. Growing the same crop on a field year after year can cause crop yields to decline as the soil becomes depleted and insect populations become firmly established. Crop rotation, or growing different crops in different years, is one way to avoid these problems. However, discovering the most effective rotation of a number of different crops is difficult, because there are so many possible orders in which to grow them and testing any given crop rotation takes several years.

   For example, imagine a proposed rotation of corn, peanuts, onions, beets, and carrots, with a different crop grown each year for five years. How many different orderings of these five crops are possible?

   A. 15
   B. 25
   C. 120
   D. 125

Answers and explanations begin on page 700.

SCIENCE PRACTICES

Construct Short–Answer Responses

The GED® *Science Test* will require you to write *two* written responses to a passage, graphic, or combination of the two. Pages 489 and 491 have more information about Short-Answer responses on the GED® *Science Test*.

You could be asked to complete one or both of the following types of writing tasks within a writing text box that will appear on your computer screen:

- **Cite specific evidence** to support inferences, conclusions, or analyses of scientific information.
- **Design a scientific experiment** to test a hypothesis. As you read in Lesson 2: Use the Scientific Method on page 494, this involves how data are collected, tested, and evaluated.

A response to a question based on text, graphics, or a combination of the two should contain the following:

- A complete and well-developed explanation
- Specific facts, details, or evidence from source material

A plan for a scientific experiment should include the following:

- A clearly stated hypothesis
- A well-formulated design of how the experiment would be conducted
- A logical method to collect the data
- Sound criteria for evaluating the results in relation to the hypothesis

Since each of the Short-Answer responses are worth more than individual multiple-choice questions, they are well worth your time to carefully plan, organize, and write. You should budget 10 minutes for *each* Short-Answer question out of the total 75 minutes on the *Science Test*.

Practice this five-step process with the Short-Answer response questions on the next page and throughout the science units in this book.

1. **Read the question** carefully and mentally put it in your own words.
2. **Develop a thesis statement** that (a) explains your position or (b) describes your experiment design.
3. Reread the information that is provided and use the online high-lighter to **emphasize the facts, details, and evidence** you will use in your response.
4. Use the provided wipe-off board to **plan your response**.
5. **Write a one- or two-paragraph response**, using the online tools (cut, copy, paste, undo, and redo) to improve your work.

Key Ideas

- You can take about ten minutes to plan and write each of the two Short-Answer responses on the GED® *Science Test*.
- You may be asked to respond to a question about a passage, graphics, or both.
- You might also be asked to write a design for an experiment.

GED® TEST TIP

Each Short-Answer response is worth up to 3 points. You can improve your score when you use two or three specific facts, details, or pieces of evidence from the passage in your response.

PRACTICE 6

Directions: For each of the two passages, take ten minutes to read the passage and plan and write a one- or two-paragraph response to the questions in the boxes. Use multiple pieces of evidence from the text to support your response. Compose your answer on a computer if one is available or write your answer on a sheet of paper.

Short-Answer Practice: Explanation

How did the moon form? Scientists have suggested a number of answers to that question over time. Some have suggested that the moon was originally part of Earth and somehow broke off early in the history of the solar system. Others have suggested that the moon was formed separately from Earth and then at some point was drawn into Earth's gravitational field, where it remains.

Another possible answer involves rings. Earth (and other planets with a moon or moons) may have originally had rings like those of the planet Saturn. A team of scientists has recently suggested that all moons in our solar system were formed from rings. According to their idea, a moon begins to coagulate, or come together, out of debris near the outer edges of planetary rings. At those outer edges, the newly formed moon has a better chance of holding together without being broken up again by the planet's gravity. (Small objects orbiting close to a planet tend to be pulled toward the planet by gravity; they often ultimately crash into the planet.) The initial products of this process of coagulation are small "moonlets," which spin outward from the planet, colliding and fusing with other moonlets as they do so. The process is somewhat similar to that of a snowball rolling downhill, gathering more material as it rolls. This hypothesis has at least one source of appeal, in that it explains why the larger moons of planets like Neptune and Uranus (which have more than one moon) are farther away from the planet than the smaller moons.

Formation of the Moon Writing Prompt

Earth does not currently have rings. If Earth originally had rings, what happened to them? Using information from the passage, suggest a hypothesis to answer that question. Cite specific information from the passage as support for why your suggestion is plausible.

Short-Answer Practice: Experiment

Human blood is composed of approximately 45 percent *formed elements* (which include red blood cells, white blood cells, and platelets) and approximately 55 percent *plasma*, a liquid that holds the formed elements in suspension. The ratio of formed elements to plasma can vary according to an individual's diet, health, and genetic makeup. The ratio can be measured by taking a sample of blood and spinning it for 20 minutes in a centrifuge (a device used to separate substances) to force the formed elements to separate from the plasma. The plasma can then be siphoned off, measured, and compared to the quantity of formed elements.

Researchers are interested in learning the ways in which diet can affect the ratio of formed elements to plasma. They suspect that consumption of caffeine may have short-term effects on plasma levels relative to levels of formed elements in the blood.

Caffeine and Blood Components Writing Prompt

Design a controlled experiment that the researchers can use to test their hypothesis. Include descriptions of data collection and explain how the researchers would know whether their hypothesis is well supported by the experimental data.

Writing evaluation criteria begins on page 693.

SCIENCE PRACTICES PRACTICE QUESTIONS

Questions 1 through 3 are based on the following passage.

The 1543 publication of Nicolaus Copernicus's heliocentric, or sun-centered, theory of the universe marked a crucial moment in the history of science. Copernicus's theory that the planets revolve around the sun was controversial: at first, many refused to accept that Earth could be hurtling through space. However, we now know that Copernicus's theory was accurate in many ways.

Despite its importance as a breakthrough, Copernicus's theory contained a number of ideas that today seem primitive. For example, Copernicus maintained that the planets were embedded in crystalline spheres. Additionally, while Copernicus developed the novel, and later widely accepted, idea that Earth rotates on its axis, he also believed that the planets orbit around the sun in perfect circles. We now know that the planets move in elliptical orbits.

1. Which of the following is the main idea of the second paragraph?

   A. Primitive astronomers accepted Copernicus's theory when it was first published.
   B. While Copernicus's theory was an important development, it included elements that are outdated today.
   C. Copernicus believed that Earth moved around the sun, rather than the other way around.
   D. Earth does not hurtle through space.

2. Which of the following would be an appropriate title for this passage?

   A. "Important Landmarks in 16th-Century Science"
   B. "Copernicus: The Life of an Astronomer"
   C. "The Significance and Limitations of the Copernican Theory"
   D. "The Earth-Centered Universe"

3. Which of the following can be inferred from the passage?

   A. Astronomers now believe that the planets are not embedded in crystalline spheres.
   B. Astronomers now know that Earth does not move around the sun in an ellipse.
   C. All aspects of the Copernican theory have now been disproven.
   D. Copernicus took inspiration from the primitive astronomers who came before him.

4. Matter is generally found in one of three phases: solid, liquid, and gas. A substance can be converted from a solid to a liquid and then from a liquid to a gas by adding heat. Once the temperature of a solid substance reaches its melting point, any heat added is used to change the solid to the liquid phase. So, while the phase is changing, the temperature of the substance remains constant. Once the phase change is complete, the temperature of the liquid continues to rise. Similarly, once the temperature of a liquid reaches the boiling point, any heat added is used to change the liquid to the gas phase, and the temperature remains constant while the phase is changing.

Temperature and Phase Changes of a Substance

At which points are phase changes occurring in the graph above?

   A. A and E
   B. A, C, and E
   C. B and D
   D. C, D, and E

5. While all types of cancer share the common trait of uncontrolled cell growth, the causes of that uncontrolled growth are complex and varied. Nevertheless, a number of specific causes of several types of cancer are known. For example, long-term asbestos exposure can result in mesothelioma (a cancer that can affect multiple organs), while long-term regular inhalation of tobacco smoke can lead to lung cancer. In addition to such chemical causes, viruses are also responsible for a number of types of cancer: human papillomavirus precipitates cervical cancer, while the hepatitis B virus causes liver cancer.

Use the information above to place four specific types of cancer from the list below into the left side of the table. Place a corresponding cause of each, as identified in the passage above, into the cell immediately to its right.

Type of Cancer	Cause

hepatitis B	mesothelioma
human papillomavirus	cervical cancer
long-term asbestos exposure	liver cancer
lung cancer	long-term inhalation of tobacco smoke

Questions 6 through 8 are based on the following paragraph and graphic.

Record high temperatures were recorded in numerous Australian cities in the summer of 2012. The chart below indicates current and former record temperatures for seven of those cities. For instance, Hobart's previous record was a little below 41°C, and its current record is a little above 41°C.

Record High Temperatures in Australian Cities

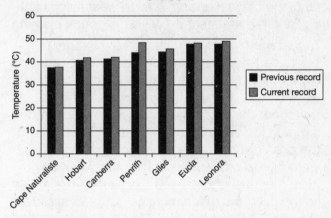

6. According to the chart, which city experienced the largest increase from its previous record to its current record?

A. Hobart
B. Penrith
C. Eucla
D. Leonora

7. Which of the following cities had a previous record equal to the median of all the cities' previous records?

A. Cape Naturaliste
B. Canberra
C. Penrith
D. Eucla

8. According to the chart, which of the following statements is true?

A. Temperatures will likely continue to increase.
B. Temperatures increased 5 degrees or less.
C. Temperatures increased more than 5 degrees.
D. Temperatures usually increase 2–5 degrees in the summer.

An office manager noticed that each time she touched the metal filing cabinet next to her desk, she experienced an electrostatic shock (commonly known as "static"). Her assistant, however, only rarely experienced such shocks when touching the cabinet. The office manager wondered why this might be.

The office manager developed a hypothesis: perhaps differences in clothing could explain why she was experiencing more shocks than her assistant. The office manager liked to wear nylon clothing, and her assistant usually wore cotton clothing.

To test her hypothesis, the office manager convinced her assistant to wear nylon clothing to work every day for a week, while she herself wore cotton clothing. The next week, they switched: the office manager wore nylon clothing, and the assistant wore cotton. To control for the possibility that the differences in shocks were due to differences in their footwear, they wore identical shoes each day. During the experiment, both the office manager and her assistant recorded the number of times they touched the metal filing cabinet each day, and they also recorded the number of times they experienced electrostatic shocks when doing so.

At the end of the first week, they found that the assistant had experienced 73 electrostatic shocks, while the office manager had experienced 10. During the second week, the office manager experienced 68 shocks, and her assistant 12. The office manager concluded that these results supported her hypothesis, and as a result she decided to switch to wearing mostly cotton clothing.

9. Scientific investigations begin with a question. Which of the following is the question that formed the basis for the office manager's experiment?

A. Is it better to wear cotton clothing or nylon clothing?

B. Why does touching the metal filing cabinet produce more electrostatic shocks than touching other office furniture?

C. Why, when I touch the metal filing cabinet, do I experience more electrostatic shocks than my assistant does when she touches it?

D. Could my shoes be causing me to experience more electrostatic shocks than my assistant experiences?

10. Which of the following best summarizes how the office manager conducted her experiment?

A. The office manager suspected that her nylon clothing was causing her to experience electrostatic shocks.

B. The office manager switched to cotton clothing after seeing that her hypothesis was supported by her data.

C. The office manager wore shoes of a different material than those of her assistant.

D. The office manager wore one type of clothing, while her assistant wore another type of clothing, and they recorded the number of shocks they experienced.

11. Why did the office manager and her assistant wear the same type of shoes while conducting the experiment?

A. They wanted to test the effect of their clothing on the number of shocks they experienced, and wearing different types of shoes might have confused their results.

B. They wanted to test whether the office manager's shoes were causing the high number of electrostatic shocks she was experiencing.

C. They believed that wearing cotton might cause the wearer to experience more electrostatic shocks.

D. They wanted to protect themselves from the effects of electrostatic shock.

12. Imagine that the results of the office manager's experiment had demonstrated that her clothing was not in fact responsible for the large number of electrostatic shocks she was experiencing. After reviewing those findings, the office manager then wondered if her footwear might be responsible, and she decided to conduct a new experiment to test this idea. Before she conducted that experiment, the idea that her shoes might be responsible would be which of the following?

A. a new conclusion based on findings

B. a general principle from the study of physics

C. a new hypothesis

D. an experiment design

Directions: You MAY use your calculator to figure out the answers to questions 13 and 14.

13. Common garden snails are hermaphroditic. That is, each individual snail produces both sperm and eggs. Mating between two garden snails involves the transfer of sperm from each partner to the other. A high school science teacher has created a large terrarium for his classroom that contains 6 adult garden snails. Assuming that all 6 snails are healthy, how many different mating pairs are possible?

   A. 2
   B. 12
   C. 15
   D. 36

14. The sun is a class G star, which is a type of main-sequence star. Approximately 90 percent of all stars in the Milky Way galaxy are main-sequence stars, and approximately 7 percent of all main-sequence stars are class G stars. What is the probability that any given star in the Milky Way galaxy is a class G star? Express your answer as a percentage: _____

Directions: Use ten minutes to read, plan, and write a one- or two-paragraph response to this short-answer activity. Compose your answer on a computer if one is available or write your answer on a separate sheet of paper.

15. The table below contains data observed in a group of 58-year-old Swedish men. The study examined the relationship between tobacco use and formations called plaques that build up on the walls of arteries, which are blood vessels that carry blood from the heart to the body's tissues. The carotid and femoral arteries are two large and very important arteries.

Average Characteristics of 58-Year-Old Swedish Men, by Smoking Status

	Never Smokers	Ex-Smokers	Current Smokers
Waist circumference (cm)	93.8	99.1	95.4
Cholesterol			
Total Cholesterol	5.98	6.11	5.90
HDL Cholesterol	1.31	1.28	1.21
LDL Cholesterol	4.08	4.09	3.95
Carotid plaques (%)			
None	62	55	53
Small	15	23	16
Large	23	22	31
Femoral plaques (%)			
None	80	54	45
Small	10	13	14
Large	10	33	41

Swedish Men and Smoking Writing Prompt

Discuss the conclusions that can be drawn from the information recorded in the table above, making specific reference to the data. In addition, identify any further information that would need to be obtained in order to better evaluate the relationship between plaque formation and smoking.

Answers and explanations start on page 693.

LIFE SCIENCE

Cell Structures and Functions

Key Ideas

- The basic unit of all living things is the cell, which carries out the life functions, including movement, growth, and reproduction.
- All cells have a cell membrane, cytoplasm, and genetic material.
- Unlike an animal cell, a plant cell contains a cell wall—a structure that gives the cell rigidity and shape.

All living things are made of **cells**, the basic unit of life. Some organisms, like bacteria and protozoa, are **unicellular**—they consist of a single cell. Others, like plants and animals, are **multicellular**, consisting of many different types of specialized cells. For example, humans have skin cells, blood cells, and nerve cells, to name just a few. All cells carry out the basic life functions: movement, growth, cell maintenance, reproduction, and the manufacture of specialized substances.

Although cells differ widely in size and appearance, they all have basic structures in common. All cells have a **cell membrane**, a structure that keeps the cell's contents separate from its external environment. The cell membrane is selectively permeable, which means that it allows certain substances, such as water, nutrients, and wastes, to pass between the cell's interior and the surrounding environment. Inside the cell membrane is the **cytoplasm**, a watery, jellylike substance that can include other cell structures. Finally, all cells have **genetic material**, which contains coded instructions for carrying out the cell's activities. In bacteria, the genetic material consists of a single molecule suspended in the cytoplasm. Bacteria are called **prokaryotes**. In all other cells, the genetic material is contained within a **nucleus**. Such cells are called **eukaryotic cells**. All plant and animal cells are eukaryotic. A typical plant cell is shown below. Note that a plant cell has a **cell wall**, which gives the cell shape and rigidity, and an animal cell does not.

GED® TEST TIP

The title and labels of a diagram usually tell you the main idea of the diagram. Here, the main idea is that plant cells have cell structures with specialized functions.

A Plant Cell

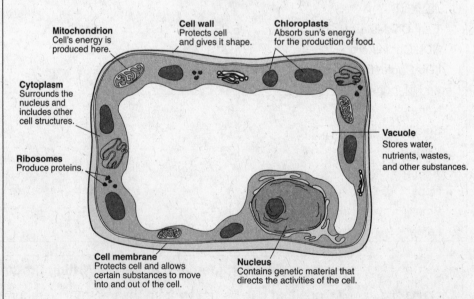

Mitochondrion
Cell's energy is produced here.

Cell wall
Protects cell and gives it shape.

Chloroplasts
Absorb sun's energy for the production of food.

Cytoplasm
Surrounds the nucleus and includes other cell structures.

Vacuole
Stores water, nutrients, wastes, and other substances.

Ribosomes
Produce proteins.

Cell membrane
Protects cell and allows certain substances to move into and out of the cell.

Nucleus
Contains genetic material that directs the activities of the cell.

PRACTICE 1

Questions 1 through 3 are based on the information on page 508.

1. According to the diagram on page 508, the function of the [Select... ▾] is to supply energy to the cell.

   - nucleus
   - ribosomes
   - mitochondrion

2. In addition to the cell wall, the water stored in a plant cell's vacuole helps give the plant firmness and shape. When a plant is not taking in enough water from the soil through its roots, it uses up its stored water and its vacuoles shrink. When the vacuoles shrink, the plant wilts.

   Which of the following is a conclusion based on the paragraph above rather than a given fact?

   A. Cell walls help give a plant cell firmness and shape.
   B. Vacuoles help give a plant cell firmness and shape.
   C. Plants take in water from the soil through their roots.
   D. Cell walls cannot maintain a plant's shape and rigidity when the plant lacks water.

3. A student is examining a cell using a microscope. She is able to identify the cell membrane, cytoplasm, a small vacuole, and the nucleus, but she does not see a cell wall or any chloroplasts. She concludes that the cell is a eukaryotic cell.

   Which of the following is evidence that her conclusion is correct?

   A. the presence of a nucleus
   B. the presence of cytoplasm
   C. the absence of chloroplasts
   D. the absence of a cell wall

4. Cells were first seen during the 1600s, when English scientist Robert Hooke observed cork cell walls through a microscope that could magnify a specimen a couple of hundred times its original size. In the 1800s, the compound light microscope, which magnifies up to a thousand times, was developed. Electron microscopes, which can magnify up to a million times, were invented during the 1900s.

   Which of the following best explains why our knowledge of cells has grown with improvements in microscope technology?

   A. Each time the microscope is improved, scientists can see cell structures more clearly.
   B. With the first microscopes, all cell structures were clearly visible.
   C. Compound light microscopes can magnify cells up to a thousand times.
   D. Robert Hooke's microscope only allowed him to see the largest cell structures.

5. Diffusion is a process by which particles move from an area of higher concentration to an area of lower concentration. For example, oxygen diffuses through the cell membrane of a unicellular pond organism from the water, where there is lots of oxygen, into the cell, where there is less oxygen. Eventually, the concentration of oxygen inside and outside the unicellular organism is the same.

   What would happen if the concentration of oxygen were greater in the unicellular organism than in its watery environment?

   A. Water would diffuse from the unicellular organism into the pond water.
   B. Oxygen would diffuse from the unicellular organism into the pond water.
   C. Oxygen would diffuse from the pond water into the unicellular organism.
   D. Diffusion of oxygen between the organism and the pond water would stop entirely.

Answers and explanations start on page 694.

LIFE SCIENCE

Cell Processes and Energy

Key Ideas

- In photosynthesis, plants use light energy to form glucose from carbon dioxide and water. Oxygen is a by-product.
- In cellular respiration, glucose is broken down in the presence of oxygen to release energy. Carbon dioxide is a by-product.
- These two processes help maintain oxygen and carbon dioxide levels in the atmosphere.

ON THE GED® TEST

About 40% of the questions on the Science Test *are about life science topics.*

All cells need energy to carry out the life functions, such as growth and reproduction. Green plants, some algae, and some bacteria use energy from sunlight to make food in a process called **photosynthesis**.

In photosynthesis, plants use sunlight to power chemical reactions that convert carbon dioxide gas and water into oxygen and the simple sugar **glucose**. In the first stage of photosynthesis, light energy is captured by chloroplasts inside plant cells. Chloroplasts contain **chlorophyll**, a pigment that gives plants their green color. Chlorophyll absorbs light energy for photosynthesis. In the second stage, water (H_2O) that the plant gets from the soil and carbon dioxide (CO_2) that the plant gets from the air undergo a complex series of chemical reactions inside the chloroplasts. The products of these reactions are oxygen (O_2) and glucose $(C_6H_{12}O_6)$. Plant cells use the energy that is stored in glucose to power cell processes. Photosynthesis can be summarized in the chemical equation shown below:

$$\text{light energy}$$
$$6CO_2 + 6H_2O \rightarrow C_6H_{12}O_6 + 6O_2$$

In words, this means that carbon dioxide plus water, in the presence of light energy, yields glucose plus oxygen.

As a result of photosynthesis, energy is stored in sugars and other **carbohydrates** in the plant. To meet their energy needs, other organisms eat plants or eat organisms that eat plants. When energy is needed in a cell, carbohydrates are broken down to release the energy in a process called **cellular respiration**. In this process, oxygen from the air reacts with glucose from food to yield carbon dioxide, water, and energy. Cellular respiration can be summarized in the following chemical equation:

$$C_6H_{12}O_6 + 6O_2 \rightarrow 6CO_2 + 6H_2O + \text{energy}$$

In words, this means that glucose plus oxygen yields carbon dioxide, water, and energy.

If you examine the two equations, you will notice that the products of photosynthesis are the raw materials of cellular respiration, and the products of cellular respiration are the raw materials of photosynthesis. These two processes are part of a cycle. Plants release oxygen, a waste product of photosynthesis, into the atmosphere. Animals breathe in the oxygen and use it in cellular respiration. They breathe out carbon dioxide, a waste product of cellular respiration. The carbon dioxide is then used by plants in photosynthesis, and the cycle repeats. Between them, photosynthesis and cellular respiration help keep the amounts of oxygen and carbon dioxide in the atmosphere fairly constant.

PRACTICE 2

Questions 1 through 3 are based on the information on page 510.

1. Which of the following are the products of cellular respiration?

    A. glucose and light energy
    B. carbon dioxide and oxygen
    C. glucose, oxygen, and energy
    D. carbon dioxide, water, and energy

2. A horticulturist wants to grow large, healthy plants by maximizing the rate of photosynthesis.

    Which of the following actions would be most likely to get the results she wants?

    A. increasing the amount of light the plants receive each day
    B. increasing the amount of oxygen the plants receive each day
    C. decreasing the amount of oxygen the plants receive each day
    D. decreasing the amount of carbon dioxide the plants receive each day

3. Carbon dioxide is one of the "greenhouse gases" that help keep Earth warm by trapping radiated heat in the atmosphere. Global warming is thought to be caused in part by increased amounts of carbon dioxide in the atmosphere.

    Which of the following would help reduce the level of carbon dioxide in the atmosphere and thus perhaps slow the global warming trend?

    A. increasing the population of domestic animals
    B. increasing the number of green plants
    C. increasing the harvest of trees
    D. increasing the amount of glucose in our food

Questions 4 and 5 refer to the following information and diagram.

In most plants, photosynthesis takes place primarily in the palisade cells of leaves.

Cross Section of a Leaf

Sunlight passes through epidermal cells to palisade cells.
Epidermal cell
Palisade cell
Chloroplasts
Xylem
Water diffuses from xylem
Spongy cell
Stoma
Carbon dioxide enters through stoma

4. <u>Fill in the blank</u> using one word from the diagram.

    A(n) _____ is an opening in the lower surface of the leaf through which gases such as carbon dioxide can pass.

5. Chloroplasts are structures found within some of the cells in a leaf. They help in the process of photosynthesis. In the diagram, they are represented by small gray spots on the cells.

    Which of the following statements is supported by the information in the diagram?

    A. Palisade cells provide a means of transporting water through a plant.
    B. Most of a leaf's chloroplasts are found in its palisade cells.
    C. The spongy cells are soft, like a sponge.
    D. The epidermis blocks light from reaching the palisade cells.

Answers and explanations start on page 695.

LIFE SCIENCE

Human Body Systems

There are four levels of organization in the human body: (1) **cells**, the smallest unit of life; (2) **tissues**, groups of similar cells that perform a specific function, such as muscle tissue; (3) **organs**, groups of tissues that perform a function, such as the stomach; and (4) **body systems**, groups of organs working together to perform a function, such as digestion. Human body systems include the circulatory, respiratory, digestive, nervous, immune, endocrine, reproductive, urinary, skeletal, and muscular systems.

The **circulatory system**, sometimes called the cardiovascular system, consists of the heart and the blood vessels. Its main function is to move the blood, which transports substances like oxygen and nutrients, throughout the body. The major **organ** of the circulatory system is the **heart**, a muscle that contracts to pump blood. Blood moves through the blood vessels from large **arteries**, to smaller arteries, to **capillaries**, to small **veins**, to large veins, and back to the heart. Through the thin walls of the capillaries, oxygen, nutrients, and other substances pass from the blood into the body's cells, and carbon dioxide and other wastes pass from the cells into the blood.

The **respiratory system** consists of the nose, throat, **trachea** (windpipe), and **lungs**. Its function is to take oxygen from the air into the body when we inhale and to get rid of waste in the form of carbon dioxide when we exhale. The trachea branches into two tubes called the **bronchi**, one of which goes into each lung. The bronchi branch into smaller tubes called **bronchioles**, each of which ends in an **alveolus**, a tiny spherical sac. Inside the capillaries of the alveoli, oxygen diffuses into the blood and carbon dioxide diffuses out of the blood.

The **digestive system** consists of the mouth, **esophagus**, **stomach**, **small intestine**, and **large intestine**. Its function is to break down food into nutrients, which are used for cell processes including the production of energy, and to get rid of digestive wastes. Digestion begins in the mouth, where the teeth grind food into smaller pieces, and **saliva** begins to break it down chemically. Food is pushed by muscular action down through the esophagus into the stomach, where it is churned and further broken down by **enzymes** and stomach acids. From the stomach it travels to the small intestine, where most of the nutrients are absorbed into the blood through tiny capillaries in the **villi**. What remains goes to the large intestine, which removes water, leaving solid waste to be excreted through the **rectum**.

The **nervous system** consists of the **brain**, **spinal cord**, and **nerves**. Its function is to receive, process, and transmit information, controlling body activities. The brain has three main parts: the **cerebrum**, which controls functions such as thinking, seeing, and speaking; the **cerebellum**, which coordinates movement and position; and the **brainstem**, which controls breathing and heart rate. Information is transmitted to and from the brain through the nerves, which are bundled in the spinal cord and branch out from there into all parts of the body.

Key Ideas

- The circulatory system moves blood around the body, delivering and taking away substances.
- The respiratory system brings oxygen into the body and gets rid of carbon dioxide.
- The digestive system breaks down food into nutrients that cells can use.
- The nervous system controls body activities.

ON THE GED® TEST

On the Science Test, *you will have to answer questions that require you to use information from both text and a graphic, as in questions 4 and 5 on page 513.*

PRACTICE 3

Questions 1 through 3 are based on the information on page 512.

1. Which human body system interacts with each cell of the body?

   A. the circulatory system
   B. the digestive system
   C. the muscular system
   D. the skeletal system

2. How are the alveoli in the lungs and the villi in the small intestine similar?

   A. Both are structures located in the respiratory system.
   B. Both are structures located in the digestive system.
   C. Both are structures in which substances pass through capillary walls into the blood.
   D. Both are structures involved in coordination and movement.

3. In the 17th century, English physician William Harvey concluded that blood in the veins flows toward the heart.

   Which of the following facts helps support Harvey's conclusion?

   A. The heart pumps about 1,800 gallons of blood per day.
   B. The heart has four chambers: two atria and two ventricles.
   C. Large veins branch into smaller blood vessels called capillaries.
   D. Veins have valves that allow blood to flow in one direction only.

Questions 4 and 5 refer to the following information and diagram.

The kidneys of the urinary system remove cellular wastes and excess water from the blood. This material, called urine, is stored in the bladder until it is excreted from the body.

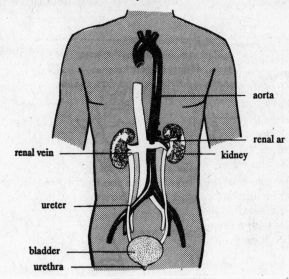

4. On the diagram, circle the name(s) of the structure(s) through which urine passes from the kidneys to the bladder.

5. A urologist is a doctor who specializes in disorders of the urinary system.

   Which of the following patients is most likely to be treated by a urologist?

   A. a patient with low levels of iron in her blood
   B. a patient with a painful kidney stone
   C. a patient with swollen veins in the anus, called hemorrhoids
   D. a patient with chronic indigestion

Answers and explanations start on page 695.

LIFE SCIENCE

Health Issues

Health can be affected by infections, nutrition, and substance abuse.

An **infection** is the invasion of the body by germs—microorganisms that cause disease. It is often characterized by fever and other symptoms. Germs can enter the body through breaks in the skin (for example, tetanus), with air (for example, influenza), in contaminated food and water (for example, food poisoning), by contact with contaminated blood or saliva (for example, rabies), or through sexual activity (for example, gonorrhea). Infections can be grouped according to the type of microorganisms that cause them. The most common germs are **bacteria** and **viruses**, although infections can also be caused by fungi, protozoans, and worms.

The body has natural defenses against infection, such as the skin, the mucous membranes in the nose, tears, and acid in the stomach. If germs get past these defenses, the **immune system** produces **antibodies** that destroy the germs. In developed nations, infectious diseases are less common than they used to be because of better nutrition and living conditions, safer water and sewage systems, **immunization** (which provides protection against specific infectious diseases), and **antibiotics**, drugs that fight bacteria.

Nutrients are substances that are needed for growth, normal functioning, and maintenance of cells. The body does not produce nutrients; instead we get them from the food we eat. The nutrients that humans need for good health include **proteins**, **carbohydrates** (sugars and starches), **fats**, **vitamins**, **minerals**, and water. In a well-balanced diet, people get enough nutrients to provide energy as well as the right nutrients needed for all the body's functions. Too much or too little of a nutrient can cause problems. For example, a diet with too much fat can lead to obesity and contribute to heart disease. Too little vitamin C can cause scurvy, a painful disease.

Drugs are substances that affect the structure or function of the body. They are usually used to treat disease or relieve its symptoms, although some drugs, like nicotine in tobacco, have no medicinal purpose. The nonmedical use of a drug to the point that it interferes with a person's normal functioning is called **drug abuse**, or substance abuse. Drug abuse can lead to **addiction**, a severe form of dependence that causes physical changes in the body so that when the drug wears off or is stopped, withdrawal symptoms such as nausea and pain occur. Heroin, speed, alcohol, nicotine, and barbiturates are frequently abused addictive drugs. A milder form of dependence than addiction is **psychological dependence**, or **habituation**. In this type of dependence, the urge to take the drug is strong, even though there are no withdrawal symptoms. Examples of drugs that can cause habituation in humans are marijuana and hallucinogens. People also abuse substances that are not drugs, like glue, gasoline, and aerosols. Most of these substances are **inhalants**—they are sniffed for their effect on the nervous system. Inhalants generally depress, or slow, the functioning of the nervous system, sometimes causing their users to lose control or become unconscious.

PRACTICE 4

Questions 1 and 2 are based on the information on page 514.

1. Which of the following is among the body's first barriers against germs?

   A. the immune system
   B. antibiotics
   C. antibodies
   D. the skin

2. Each evening, Sara has a glass of wine. If there is no wine in the house, she feels a strong urge to get some, although she feels no ill effects if she does not.

   What is Sara's relationship to alcohol?

   A. addiction
   B. physical dependence
   C. habituation
   D. withdrawal

Questions 3 and 4 are based on the following table.

Nutrients in the Diet

Nutrient	Description	Function	Source
Proteins	Complex molecules (amino acids) made of oxygen, carbon, nitrogen, hydrogen	Growth and maintenance of cells and metabolism	Meat, fish, eggs, dairy products, legumes, nuts, seeds
Carbohydrates	Molecules containing oxygen, carbon, and hydrogen	Body's main energy source, providing 4 calories of energy per gram; roughage for digestion	Bread, pasta, cereal, rice, fruits, potatoes
Fats	Fatty acids containing oxygen, carbon, and hydrogen	Concentrated source of energy, providing 9 calories of energy per gram; insulation; cell maintenance	Fish oils, vegetable oils, and animal fats
Vitamins	Substances used in very small quantities that are vital for body chemistry	Growth maintenance, repair of cells; protein synthesis; metabolism; and other functions	Various foods, daylight on skin (vitamin D), microorganisms in the bowel (vitamin K)
Minerals	Substances, such as iron and calcium, necessary for normal development	Many functions, including making red blood cells and building strong bones	Various foods
Water	A liquid made of oxygen and hydrogen atoms	Involved in almost all body processes	Beverages, soups, foods

3. Which of the following statements is supported by the information in the table?

   A. Fats are a more concentrated source of energy than carbohydrates.
   B. Vitamins are more important in the diet than minerals.
   C. A good source of vitamin C is citrus fruits.
   D. Minerals provide a low-fat source of energy.

4. Which of the following is a fact, rather than an opinion, based on the table?

   A. Eating meat is the best way to get sufficient protein in your diet.
   B. Carbohydrates come from fruits as well as from bread and rice.
   C. Iron is the only mineral you need.
   D. Everyone should drink eight glasses of water each day.

Answers and explanations start on page 695.

LIFE SCIENCE

Reproduction and Heredity

All **species** of organisms reproduce in some way. There are two types of reproduction. In **asexual reproduction**, an individual organism produces offspring identical to the parent. For example, in a type of asexual reproduction called budding, a tiny freshwater animal called a hydra grows buds that develop into offspring. In **sexual reproduction**, two sex cells combine to form unique offspring with characteristics from both parent cells. In humans and many other species, those specialized sex cells are called **sperm** and **ova**.

Physical characteristics of organisms are called **traits**. The passing of traits from parents to offspring in sexual reproduction is called **heredity**. The first person to study heredity in a systematic way was an Austrian monk, **Gregor Mendel** (1822–1884). He bred plants and observed that sometimes offspring plants had the same traits as the parents and sometimes they did not. Mendel experimented with **purebred** pea plants—plants that always produced offspring with the same form of a trait as the parent. For example, purebred short plants always produced short offspring. First he crossed purebred short plants with purebred tall plants. In the first generation of offspring, all the plants were tall—the shortness trait had vanished. When the first-generation offspring reproduced, about three-quarters of the next generation of plants were tall, and one-quarter were short. The shortness trait had reappeared.

Mendel repeated his pea plant experiments with other traits over a ten-year period. Eventually he concluded that individual factors from each parent plant control the **inheritance** of specific traits. An offspring plant inherited one factor from the female parent and one from the male parent. Mendel concluded that one factor in a pair can hide the other factor. For example, the tallness factor hid the shortness factor in the first generation of offspring.

The factors that control traits are called **genes**. Different forms of a gene are called **alleles**. The gene that controls pea plant height, for example, has one allele for tallness and one allele for shortness. Each pea plant inherits one allele for the height gene from each parent. Therefore, any particular pea plant may have (1) two alleles for tallness, (2) two alleles for shortness, or (3) one allele for shortness and one for tallness. In the third case, the **dominant allele**, the tallness allele, controls the appearance of the trait. The **recessive allele**, the shortness allele, is hidden. For a recessive trait to appear in an individual, the individual must inherit two recessive alleles.

In Mendel's original experiment, the parent plants were purebred tall and purebred short. Thus, one parent had two dominant alleles for tallness, and the other parent had two recessive alleles for shortness. All the offspring in the first generation were **hybrid**—each had one allele for tallness and one for shortness. Because the tallness allele is dominant, all of the first generation plants were tall. In the next generation, some plants inherited two dominant alleles, some inherited two recessive alleles, and some inherited one dominant and one recessive allele, producing a mix of plants.

Key Ideas

- In asexual reproduction, an offspring is identical to its parent; in sexual reproduction, an offspring is unique, inheriting traits from each parent.
- Gregor Mendel was the first to observe patterns of trait inheritance.
- Traits are controlled by genes, which come in forms called alleles. A dominant allele hides a recessive allele.

GED® TEST TIP

As you take the test, pace yourself. If you are unsure of an answer, do your best and mark Flag for Review at the top of your computer screen. At the end of the test, you may have time to review these "flagged" questions.

PRACTICE 5

Questions 1 through 3 refer to the following paragraph and diagram.

The Punnett square below shows all the possible combinations of alleles for height in offspring pea plants when two tall hybrid pea plants are crossed. A capital *T* represents the dominant tallness allele, and a lowercase *t*, the recessive shortness allele. One parent's alleles are shown along the top of the square; the other's are shown on the left side. The **genotypes** of the offspring are shown in the boxes.

	T	t
T	T T	T t
t	T t	t t

1. The parent pea plants are both [Select... ▼].

   - tall
   - short
   - of medium height

2. What chance is there that an offspring will be short?

   A. 0 out of 4
   B. 1 out of 4
   C. 2 out of 4
   D. 3 out of 4

3. If you wanted to grow only tall pea plants in your garden over several growing seasons, which of the following genotypes would give you the best results?

   A. tt
   B. Tt
   C. tT
   D. TT

4. Fill in the blank with a numeral.

   According to the passage on page 516, in order to show a recessive trait, an organism must inherit _____ recessive alleles for that trait.

5. Why are organisms that reproduce sexually more genetically diverse than organisms that reproduce asexually?

   A. Organisms that reproduce sexually tend to produce more offspring than those that reproduce asexually.
   B. Organisms that reproduce sexually produce offspring that inherit diverse traits from only one parent.
   C. Organisms that reproduce sexually produce offspring with entirely new traits unlike those of either parent.
   D. Organisms that reproduce sexually produce offspring that have inherited a mix of traits from their parents.

6. A student is trying to repeat Mendel's experiments using the trait of fur color in rabbits. Black fur is dominant, and white fur is recessive. She starts with what she assumes is a purebred white female rabbit and a purebred black male rabbit. She crosses them and is surprised when one of the offspring has white fur.

   What probably was wrong with the student's experiment?

   A. The white female was actually a hybrid.
   B. The black male was actually a hybrid.
   C. Most of the offspring were hybrids.
   D. Most of the offspring were purebred.

   Answers and explanations start on page 695.

LIFE SCIENCE

Modern Genetics

Years after Mendel died, scientists identified **chromosomes**, rod-shaped structures in the nucleus of each cell, as responsible for carrying genes from parent organisms to their offspring. Reproductive cells have half the number of chromosomes of an organism's other cells. When a sperm cell and an ovum unite, the resulting offspring has a full set of chromosomes. For example, human sex cells have 23 chromosomes and our other cells have 46.

One chromosome can contain thousands of genes on a single long molecule of **deoxyribonucleic acid (DNA)**. A DNA molecule is shaped like a spiral ladder. The sides of the ladder are made of deoxyribose—a sugar— and phosphate. Each rung of the ladder is made of a pair of nitrogen bases. There are four of these bases: adenine (A), guanine (G), thymine (T), and cytosine (C). The four bases pair up in a specific way: *A* always pairs with *T*, and *C* always pairs with *G*.

DNA

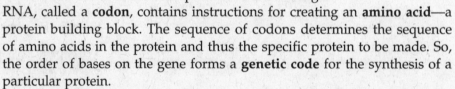

DNA controls the cell's production of proteins, which help determine all the characteristics and processes of the organism. During **protein synthesis**, the information from a gene in the cell's nucleus is used to produce a protein on ribosomes in the cytoplasm. Messenger **ribonucleic acid (RNA)**, transmits the code from the DNA. Each set of three base pairs on the messenger RNA, called a **codon**, contains instructions for creating an **amino acid**—a protein building block. The sequence of codons determines the sequence of amino acids in the protein and thus the specific protein to be made. So, the order of bases on the gene forms a **genetic code** for the synthesis of a particular protein.

There have been many recent advances in genetics, some controversial. Dolly the sheep and other animals have been cloned from single cells. Cloning bypasses sexual reproduction, raising the possibility that one day humans will be cloned—an idea that many find unethical. Through genetic engineering, the DNA of one organism can be introduced into the DNA of another organism, changing the second organism's traits. Genetic engineering has been used to produce medicines, such as insulin. It has been more controversial when used to improve foods. Finally, the entire **human genome**, or genetic code, has been decoded, making possible many advances in medicine. Scientists have identified genes involved in genetic disorders such as cystic fibrosis. They have also identified genes that predispose people to diseases such as breast cancer and Alzheimer's disease. Through genetic testing, people can find out whether they have any of these disease-related genes. In some cases, they can take steps to prevent the disease or to seek early treatment. In recent years, scientists have also succeeded in correcting certain genetic disorders through gene therapy.

PRACTICE 6

Questions 1 and 2 are based on the information on page 518.

1. Which of the following provides the code needed for a cell to make proteins?

   A. the number of chromosomes in the cell
   B. the amino acids in the cytoplasm
   C. the sequence of base pairs in a gene
   D. the pairing of adenine with thymine

2. A mutation is any change in the DNA of a gene. Which of the following is the most likely result of a mutation?

   A. the loss of one or more chromosomes
   B. an extra chromosome
   C. too much RNA in the cytoplasm
   D. a change in protein synthesis

3. Some animals have been genetically engineered to grow larger. Plants have been engineered to resist diseases or insects. Some fruits have been engineered to ripen more slowly. Genetic engineering of domesticated plants and animals is controversial. According to some people, these foods pose a risk because their effects on consumers and the environment are unknown. Others claim that genetically engineered foods are safe.

   Which of the following statements is an opinion about genetic engineering rather than a fact?

   A. Scientists have used genetic engineering to produce animals that grow larger.
   B. Disease-resistant plants have been produced by genetic engineering.
   C. Some genetically engineered fruit takes longer to ripen than its unaltered counterpart.
   D. Genetically engineered foods are safe for consumers and the environment.

4. When a cell reproduces through cell division, scientists call the reproducing cell the parent cell, and the two cells that result from the division are called daughter cells. The daughter cells are genetically identical to the parent cells. Before a parent cell starts to divide, the DNA in its nucleus replicates, or makes a complete copy of itself.

   Why is this process necessary?

   A. so that the parent cell will have an extra copy of DNA
   B. so that each daughter cell receives a complete set of DNA
   C. so that each daughter cell will not need to synthesize proteins
   D. so that each daughter cell will receive half its DNA from each parent cell

5. Which of the following statements is supported by the diagram and the passage on page 518?

   A. The DNA molecule unzips between the sugar and phosphate segments.
   B. The base guanine pairs only with the base cytosine.
   C. In a sequence of DNA bases, guanine always comes before adenine.
   D. About 10 percent of DNA contains genes; the remainder is "junk" DNA.

6. According to the passage on page 518, proteins, which perform a variety of functions, are built from chains of ⌊Select...▾⌋.

   • amino acids
   • RNA
   • codons
   • enzymes

   Answers and explanations start on page 696.

LIFE SCIENCE

Evolution and Natural Selection

In 1831, the British ship the *Beagle* set sail with naturalist Charles Darwin (1809–1882) aboard. Darwin's job was to observe living things he encountered. His observations during this five-year trip around the world led him to formulate an important scientific theory, the theory of **evolution**.

One of the *Beagle*'s stops was the Galápagos Islands, a group of islands in the Pacific Ocean off the South American coast. There Darwin saw great diversity of life forms. He noticed that many of the plants and animals resembled those he had seen on the South American mainland. However, there were also important differences between mainland and island organisms. For example, the iguanas on the mainland had small claws that allowed them to climb trees to eat leaves. On the Galápagos, iguanas had large claws that allowed them to grip wet, slippery rocks and eat seaweed. As Darwin traveled among the Galápagos Islands, he also observed that similar species of organisms sometimes differed from island to island. For example, small birds called ground finches had strong, wide beaks well-suited for breaking and eating seeds. However, different species of ground finches had different sized beaks, depending on which island they lived on. The sizes of the iguanas' claws and the birds' beaks are examples of **adaptations**, traits that help an organism survive in its environment. From these observations, Darwin concluded that organisms had originally come from the mainland and had changed, or evolved, over many generations to become better adapted to their new island environments.

Darwin explained that species evolve because of **natural selection**. By this process, individuals that are better adapted to their environments are more likely to survive and reproduce, passing their favorable adaptations to their offspring. Several factors are involved in natural selection:

1. Most species produce far more offspring than can survive.
2. These offspring compete with one another for scarce resources in their environment.
3. Members of a species have different traits, called **variations**. Some variations make individuals better adapted to survive in their environment.
4. Individuals with favorable variations are more likely to survive, reproduce, and pass the favorable traits to their offspring.
5. Over generations, helpful variations spread through a species, causing the species to change, or evolve.

Evolution through natural selection explains how species change over time. But how do new species evolve? Geographic isolation seems to play a big role in the evolution of new species. When a group of individuals remains separated from the rest of its species long enough, it may become a new species. This means that members of the new species will be unable to interbreed with members of the original species. For example, there are 13 species of finches on the various Galápagos Islands. They all probably evolved from a single ancestral species.

Key Ideas

- Charles Darwin's observations in the Galápagos Islands led him to formulate the theory of evolution.
- Adaptations are traits that help an organism survive in its environment.
- Natural selection is the process by which individuals with favorable variations survive, reproduce, and pass the variations to their offspring.

ON THE GED® TEST

The GED® Science Test will not test memorized definitions of terms such as "adaptation" and "natural selection." However, you could be asked a question about the meaning of a term in the context of a science passage.

PRACTICE 7

Questions 1 and 2 refer to the following paragraph and diagram.

The forelimbs of humans, penguins, birds that fly, and alligators are similar. The similar pattern of the bones is evidence that these animals evolved from a common ancestor. Similar structures that organisms have inherited from a common ancestor are called homologous structures.

Homologous Structures

Human arm
- Humerus
- Carpals
- Radius
- Ulna

Penguin's flipper
- Humerus
- Radius
- Carpals
- Ulna

Bird's wing
- Radius
- Humerus
- Ulna
- Carpals

Alligator's leg
- Humerus
- Radius
- Carpals
- Ulna

1. The forelimbs of frogs are homologous to those of human arms, penguins' flippers, birds' wings, and alligators' legs. Based on the diagram and paragraph, which of the following is likely to be true of frogs' forelimbs?

   A. Frogs use their forelimbs for swimming.
   B. Frogs' forelimbs contain carpal bones.
   C. Frogs' forelimbs resemble wings more than they resemble human arms.
   D. Frogs are more closely related to humans than they are to alligators.

2. Which of the following statements is supported by the paragraph and the diagram?

   A. The tip of a bird's wing is homologous to the upper arm of a human.
   B. Penguins are more closely related to humans than they are to birds.
   C. In penguins, flying birds, humans, and alligators, the forelimbs have similar structures despite performing different functions.
   D. Homologous structures have similar functions in modern organisms but had different functions in modern organisms' ancestors.

3. What are **adaptations**, according to the passage on page 520?

   A. traits that make an organism better able to survive in its environment
   B. traits that all members of a species possess
   C. traits that are learned and not inherited
   D. traits that appear only when two recessive alleles are inherited

4. The more similar the DNA of two species, the more closely related they are. Scientists have used modern DNA analysis to trace the evolutionary relationships among Darwin's 13 species of finches. DNA analysis revealed that the finch species all had very similar DNA. Thus, Darwin was correct when he proposed that they had evolved from a common ancestor.

   Which of the following best explains why DNA analysis provides better evidence to support the hypothesis that Darwin's finches evolved from a common ancestor than the scientific methods that Darwin used?

   A. DNA analysis takes less time than observation.
   B. DNA analysis is easier to do than observing birds in the wild.
   C. DNA analysis provides more objective data than observation does.
   D. Technological methods of obtaining evidence are inferior to observation.

Answers and explanations start on page 696.

LIFE SCIENCE

Organization of Ecosystems

Key Ideas

- An ecosystem is a community of organisms and their physical environment.
- Energy passes through an ecosystem from the sun, to producers (green plants), to consumers.
- Carbon, oxygen, nitrogen, and water cycle through the biosphere from the living to the nonliving components and back again.

An **ecosystem** is an area consisting of a community of organisms—plants, animals, fungi, bacteria—and the physical environment in which they live—soil, air, water, and climate. Earth as a whole is an enormous ecosystem called the **biosphere**. Smaller ecosystems include meadows, ponds, wetlands, and tidal zones. A healthy ecosystem contains a diversity of organisms. Some of the organisms, such as green plants, are called **producers** because they use energy from the sun to make their own food through photosynthesis. Other organisms, called **consumers**, depend on producers to meet their energy needs. These organisms eat plants, or eat organisms that eat plants, to get energy. The complex pattern in which energy passes through an ecosystem is called a **food web**. A simple food web for a wooded area is shown here.

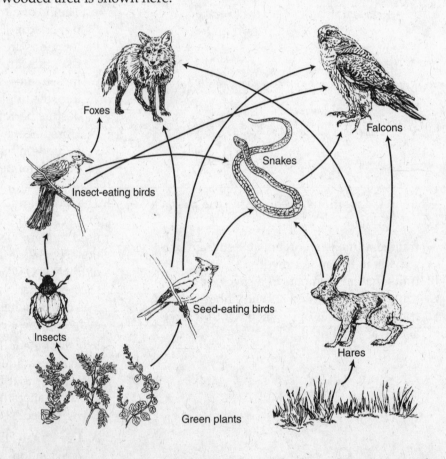

Foxes

Falcons

Snakes

Insect-eating birds

Seed-eating birds

Insects

Hares

Green plants

ON THE GED® TEST

On the GED® Science Test, you may see diagrams, like the one on this page, which contain arrows. Follow the directions of the arrows to understand the process.

Carbon, oxygen, nitrogen, and water also cycle through ecosystems from the living to the nonliving components and back again. As discussed in Lesson 2, carbon and oxygen cycle through the biosphere as a result of photosynthesis and cellular respiration. Nitrogen cycles between the land, organisms, and the air through chemical processes. Water cycles between the oceans and other surface water, the air, land, and organisms through evaporation, condensation, precipitation, and transpiration from plants.

PRACTICE 8

1. According to the passage, what is the ultimate source of energy for the food web on page 522?

   A. green plants
   B. mammals
   C. soil, air, and water
   D. the sun

2. Suppose most of the foxes in the woodland ecosystem on page 522 were hunted and killed. Which of the following is most likely to happen as a result?

   A. The amount of plant life in the woodland would increase.
   B. The populations of hares and seed-eating birds would increase.
   C. The populations of insects and insect-eating birds would decrease.
   D. The population of snakes would decrease.

3. Which of the following is most similar to a naturally occurring ecosystem?

   A. a diorama with dried vegetation and stuffed animals
   B. an aquarium with aquatic plants and herbivorous tropical fish
   C. a house with central air conditioning and heating
   D. a supermarket with a large section of fresh fruits and vegetables

4. In most cases, changes in one aspect of an ecosystem result in reactions in other parts of the ecosystem, restoring balance. In some cases, however, changes can be so great that the original ecosystem is replaced with another. When this occurs naturally, as when grasses are replaced by taller plants, shrubs, and eventually trees, it is called succession.

   Which of the following statements is supported by the information above?

   A. When changes are introduced into an ecosystem, its balance is permanently disrupted.
   B. Succession is usually caused by human destruction of an ecosystem.
   C. The intentional replacement of a wooded area by a field of cultivated wheat is an example of succession.
   D. The natural replacement of lichens by mosses and ferns, and then shrubs, is an example of succession.

5. Although more than three-quarters of the atmosphere is nitrogen, atmospheric nitrogen cannot be used directly by plants and animals. Instead, certain bacteria and blue-green algae take nitrogen from the air and, through a process called nitrogen fixation, turn it into compounds that plants can use. Nitrogen-fixing bacteria are found in the roots of some plants such as peas and beans. When these plants are present, the nitrate content of the soil is increased. Nitrates are absorbed by plants, which are eaten by consumers. Eventually the nitrogen returns to the soil in excrement and when organisms die.

   What is the role of nitrogen-fixing bacteria in the nitrogen cycle?

   A. to decompose dead plants and animals
   B. to add nitrogen to the atmosphere
   C. to turn atmospheric nitrogen into compounds plants and animals can use
   D. to take nitrogen from blue-green algae and turn it into compounds plants can use

   Answers and explanations start on page 696.

LIFE SCIENCE PRACTICE QUESTIONS

1. Cell membranes are selectively permeable, allowing some substances to pass through and blocking others. The movement through the cell membrane takes place by means of passive or active transport. In passive transport, materials like water move through the cell's membrane without using any of the cell's energy. Active transport is the movement of materials in the cell from areas of low concentration to areas of high concentration. In active transport, the cell uses energy to move substances in and out. For example, transport proteins use energy when they carry molecules into and out of the cell.

What is the main difference between passive transport and active transport?

A. Active transport involves the passage of water, and passive transport does not.
B. Active transport requires the cell to use energy, and passive transport does not.
C. Active transport is used by animal cells, and passive transport is used by plant cells.
D. Active transport takes substances out of the cell, and passive transport brings them in.

2. Ben set up an experiment to prove that ivy plants take in water through their roots. He took a jar, put an ivy plant in the open jar, and filled the jar with water to cover only the roots of the ivy. After a week, he checked the water level in the jar and found it had gone down. Ben concluded that the plant had absorbed water through its roots.

Why does Ben have insufficient proof for his conclusion?

A. Ben should have put more ivy plants in the open jar.
B. Ben should have put several plants of different species in the open jar.
C. The water level in the jar might have gone down because of evaporation.
D. There should have been soil in the jar rather than water.

Questions 3 and 4 refer to the following information and diagram.

A pedigree shows the pattern of inheritance of a trait in a family. In a pedigree, circles represent females; squares represent males. A completely shaded shape indicates that the person has the trait. A half-shaded shape indicates the person carries the recessive form of the gene for the trait but does not have the trait. An unshaded shape indicates the person neither has nor carries the trait. In the following pedigree, Megan is a carrier of the genetic disorder cystic fibrosis, although she is healthy.

3. In the diagram above, one of Cailin's grandfathers is a carrier of cystic fibrosis. Circle that individual on the diagram.

4. Which of the following best explains why Megan's and Will's families were surprised to learn Cailin had inherited cystic fibrosis?

A. Megan and Will are carriers of cystic fibrosis.
B. Some of Will's distant ancestors had cystic fibrosis.
C. Megan's father and Will's mother are carriers of cystic fibrosis.
D. No one in either Megan's or Will's immediate family has cystic fibrosis except Cailin.

Questions 5 through 7 refer to the following paragraph and diagram.

Mitosis is a type of cell division in which two daughter cells are formed that have the same genetic material as the parent cell. Before mitosis starts, each chromosome in the nucleus duplicates itself to produce two sections, called chromatids, which are linked. Those chromatids then split, so that each daughter cell has DNA identical to that of the parent cell and to that of the other daughter cell. The function of the spindle fiber in mitosis is to control the movement of chromatids during mitosis. During the metaphase, for example, the spindle fiber helps to align the chromatids in a line across the middle of the cell so that the chromatids can divide evenly. The spindle fibers then direct the movement of the chromatids after they split, ensuring that each daughter cell has a full set of identical chromatids.

The Process of Mitosis

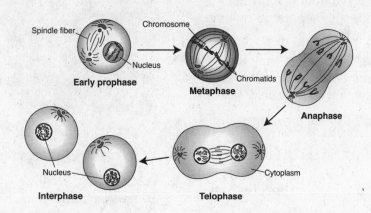

5. During which stage do the chromosomes line up across the middle of the cell?

  A. early prophase
  B. metaphase
  C. telophase
  D. interphase

6. Which of the following is true based on the paragraph and diagram?

  A. After mitosis, one of the resulting daughter cells is larger than the other one.
  B. After mitosis, the two daughter cells have their own nuclei.
  C. The first stage of mitosis is the division of the cell into two separate cells.
  D. The first stage of mitosis involves the formation of cytoplasm.

7. **Directions:** Use ten minutes to review the passage and diagram above, plan, and write a one- or two-paragraph response to the question below. Compose your answer on a computer if one is available, or write your answer on a separate sheet of paper. Include multiple pieces of evidence from the text to support your answer.

Spindle Fibers Writing Prompt

Explain why the function of the spindle fibers is important for the creation of identical daughter cells. Suggest an answer using multiple pieces of information from the paragraph and the diagram.

8. Charles Darwin thought that evolution took place gradually, with tiny changes eventually adding up to major change in a species. If this view is right, then there should be fossils, remains of long-dead organisms, that show the intermediate stages of evolution in a species. However, the fossil record often shows no intermediate forms for long periods of time. Instead, fossils of a species appear to suddenly become distinctly different. To account for this, some modern scientists have hypothesized that species evolve during short periods of rapid, major change, separated by long periods of relative stability.

Which of the following hypotheses may also explain why evolutionary change sometimes seems to occur rapidly and dramatically?

A. Organisms with soft tissues may form fossils.
B. Fossils usually form in layers of sedimentary rock.
C. The fossil record for any given species may be incomplete.
D. Fossils do not provide evidence for evolution.

9. Blood consists of blood cells and proteins suspended in a yellowish liquid called plasma. Red blood cells carry oxygen to the body. White blood cells protect the body against infection. Plasma transports nutrients and hormones to the body's cells and removes waste.

Which answer choice below describes some of the main functions of blood?

A. energy production and movement
B. movement and cell repair
C. cell repair and respiration
D. nutrient transport and immune defense

Questions 10 and 11 refer to the following diagram.

Tooth Cross Section

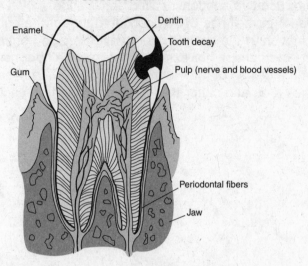

10. Which material covers the tooth's top surface?

A. enamel
B. nerve fibers
C. blood vessels
D. periodontal fibers

11. Tooth decay can eat away at the structure of a tooth. Tooth decay begins at the surface, but it must reach the pulp, which contains many nerve endings, before it will cause extreme pain. That suggests that the dentin contains [Select... ▾] .

- few or no nerve endings
- many nerve endings
- more minerals than the enamel

12. The carrying capacity of an ecosystem is the maximum number of organisms it can support. If the carrying capacity is exceeded, there will not be enough resources, and one or more species will decline until a balance of organisms and resources is reached.

Which of the following is an example of people overloading the carrying capacity of an ecosystem?

A. using a park for recreation
B. grazing too many cattle on grassland
C. adding a room to a suburban house
D. banning shellfishing in polluted waters

13. Classification is the grouping of organisms based on similarities in their traits and their evolutionary histories. In the past, scientists classified organisms based primarily on a visual analysis of their structures and on the fossil record. Today, DNA analysis of selected genes is overturning many traditional classifications. For example, it was thought that sperm whales and dolphins, both of which have teeth, were closely related. However, DNA analysis revealed that sperm whales are actually more closely related to baleen whales, which do not have teeth.

What is the reason that DNA analysis has led to changes in the classification of organisms?

A. DNA analysis provides more fundamental, accurate data than does a visual analysis of structures and fossils.
B. Traditional classification was based on the erroneous assumption that organisms could be grouped by similarities.
C. When organisms possess similar structures, it always means that they are closely related.
D. When data from DNA analysis conflict with data from structural analysis, usually the structural data are correct.

14. *Homeothermy* refers to the maintenance of a constant body temperature in warm-blooded animals, such as dogs and human beings. Warm-blooded animals have specific body processes to help them gain or lose heat. For example, sweating helps cool the body through the evaporation of water, and shivering helps generate heat in cold environments.

Which of the following is most likely an example of a homeothermic process in dogs?

A. panting
B. healing after a wound
C. reproduction
D. grooming

Questions 15 through 17 refer to the following graph.

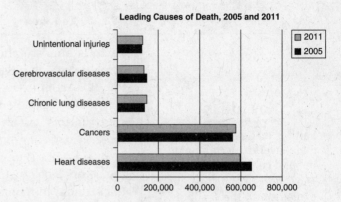

Leading Causes of Death, 2005 and 2011

Source: National Center for Health Statistics

15. Provide a numerical response.

How many of the five causes of death depicted in the graph produced more deaths in 2011 than in 2005? _____

16. Compare the number of deaths from heart disease in 2005 to the number of deaths from heart disease in 2011. That difference represents the [Select... ▾] of all the causes of death depicted in the graph.

- biggest increase
- biggest decrease
- smallest increase

17. Which of the following approximately expresses the percentage change in deaths from heart diseases from 2005 to 2011? You MAY use your calculator.

A. 8% increase
B. 8% decrease
C. 92% increase
D. 92% decrease

Answers and explanations start on page 696.

EARTH AND SPACE SCIENCE

Structure of Earth

Key Ideas

- Earth is made up of three main layers: the crust, mantle, and core.
- The theory of plate tectonics explains how the seafloor spreads, how major landforms are created, and how the continents move.
- At the margins between plates, plates move away from or toward each other, or they slide past each other.

Earth is almost spherical, flattened at the poles, and bulging at the equator. It is composed of three main layers: the crust, the mantle, and the core. Earth's outer layer, its solid **crust**, is made of granite, basalt, gabbro, and other types of rock. Under the oceans, the crust is 3 to 6.8 miles thick; under the continents, the crust is from 12 to 40 miles thick. Below the crust is the molten **mantle**; it consists of silica and metal-rich minerals. The **core** has two layers: the outer core, which is mostly liquid iron, and the inner core, which is mostly solid iron. Extreme heat and pressure characterize the core.

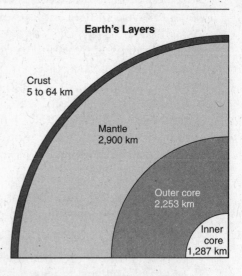

Earth's Layers

Crust 5 to 64 km

Mantle 2,900 km

Outer core 2,253 km

Inner core 1,287 km

The **theory of plate tectonics** explains phenomena of Earth's crust: seafloor spreading, the formation of major landforms, and the movement of continents. According to this theory, Earth's crust is made up of **tectonic plates** that fit together like a crude jigsaw puzzle. These plates move relative to one another at a rate of up to 15 centimeters (6 inches) a year. At the boundaries between plates, major landforms such as mountain ranges, volcanoes, ocean trenches, and mid-ocean ridges form, and earthquakes occur. There are three types of plate boundaries, or **margins**.

- At a **constructive margin**, two plates are moving apart and new crust is forming. Molten material from the mantle below wells up in the space between the plates, hardens, and forms new crust, usually at a mid-ocean ridge. For example, at the Mid-Atlantic Ridge, new crust is forming, causing the seafloor to spread and grow by about 5 centimeters (2 inches) a year.

- At a **destructive margin**, two plates are colliding and crust is being destroyed. When a continental plate collides with an oceanic plate, the denser oceanic crust may be forced under the other plate, forming a deep trench. When two plates consisting of continental crust collide, the crust crumples to form mountain ranges such as the Andes.

- At a **transform**, or **conservative**, **margin**, two plates are sliding by one another, and no crust is created or destroyed. For example, the San Andreas fault in California is the boundary between the North American plate and the Pacific plate, which is sliding northwest, causing many earthquakes.

As the plates move, they carry the continents with them. Scientists believe that a single large continent, **Pangaea**, existed about 250 million years ago. It gradually broke apart, and over millions of years the pieces (which are today's continents) drifted into the locations they are in today.

GED® TEST TIP

When you read a multiple-choice question, try to answer it before you read the choices. If one of the choices is similar to your answer, it is probably correct.

PRACTICE 1

1. What does the theory of plate tectonics explain?

   A. changes in Earth's crust
   B. changes in Earth's mantle
   C. changes in the composition of Earth's layers
   D. why there is extreme heat and pressure in Earth's core

2. Fill in the blanks with the options below.
   One similarity between Earth's inner and outer cores is that both (1) [Select... ▼], although the two are different because the inner core (2) [Select... ▼] while the outer core (3) [Select... ▼].

Select (1)	Select (2)	Select (3)
consist primarily of iron	is mostly gaseous	is mostly gaseous
consist primarily of granite	is mostly liquid	is mostly liquid
consist primarily of silica	is mostly solid	is mostly solid

3. The Japan Trench off the coast of Japan is part of the boundary between an oceanic plate called the Pacific plate and a continental plate called the Eurasian plate. At the trench, the Pacific plate is forced beneath the Eurasian plate, causing earthquakes in Japan.

   The Japan Trench is an example of which type of crustal feature?

   A. a tectonic plate
   B. a mid-ocean ridge
   C. a constructive margin
   D. a destructive margin

4. Which of the following provides evidence that the present-day continents were once one large continent that broke apart?

   A. Australia is a large, continent-sized island.
   B. Eurasia is the largest land mass on Earth today.
   C. Australia and Antarctica are located in the Southern Hemisphere.
   D. The west coast of Africa seems to fit into the east coast of the Americas.

5. Which of the following is implied by the fact that seafloor spreading at the Mid-Atlantic Ridge is causing the Atlantic Ocean to widen by about 5 centimeters a year?

   A. The Mid-Atlantic Ridge is thousands of miles long.
   B. The Mid-Atlantic Ridge is the largest underwater structure in the Atlantic Ocean.
   C. The continents of North America and Europe are moving apart.
   D. The continents of North America and Europe are growing larger at the Mid-Atlantic Ridge.

6. Which of the following is a theory rather than a fact?

   A. The San Andreas fault is the boundary between the North American and Pacific plates.
   B. A single large landmass called Pangaea existed about 250 million years ago.
   C. The Earth's crust is composed of rocks like granite, basalt, and gabbro.
   D. Earthquakes often occur along tectonic plate boundaries.

   Answers and explanations start on page 697.

LESSON 2

Earth's Resources

Key Ideas

- Natural resources include air, water, soil, minerals, and energy.
- Resources are either renewable (having an endless supply) or nonrenewable (having a limited supply).
- Conservation efforts limit the consumption, overuse, and pollution of the natural environment.

A **resource** is anything that is needed by humans to survive. Natural resources include air, water, soil, minerals, and energy. Air is involved in respiration, climate, and weather. Water is used for drinking, cooking, bathing, agriculture, and industrial processes. Less than 3 percent of the world's water is fresh water. **Soil** is the layer of loose disintegrated rock, organic matter, living organisms, air, and water in which rooted plants, including agricultural plants, grow. **Minerals** are the naturally forming inorganic substances with a crystalline structure of which rocks are made; they have many uses—from talcum powder to uranium fuel rods to diamond drill bits. **Energy resources** include fossil fuels, flowing water, wind, **solar energy**, and **geothermal energy**.

Resources can be classified as nonrenewable or renewable. **Nonrenewable resources** are those that take millions of years to form naturally; when they are used up, there is no replacement for them. For example, fossil fuels, including peat, coal, natural gas, and oil, are nonrenewable resources because they form over millions of years from decaying plant remains. Fossil fuels are our main source of energy for heating, transportation, and the generation of electricity. Soil and minerals are also nonrenewable resources.

Renewable resources are those whose supply will not run out, either because there is an unlimited supply, as is the case with **solar energy** (energy from the sun), or because the resource cycles through the environment, as is the case with water. In addition to solar energy, renewable energy resources include the water power of flowing rivers, tidal and wave power from the movement of ocean water, wind power from the movement of air, and geothermal power from the heat in the Earth's crust. All of these are used as alternative sources of energy to generate electricity.

People harm or destroy natural resources through consumption, overuse, and pollution. For example, some scientists estimate that we have already consumed between one-tenth and one-quarter of the world's supply of oil. Soil is subject to agricultural overuse and erosion. Air is polluted by fossil fuel emissions and its **ozone layer** is depleted by the release of compounds called chlorofluorocarbons (CFCs) into the atmosphere. Water is polluted by sewage, industrial waste, and agricultural and urban runoff.

Conservation is any action taken to preserve natural resources and protect the natural environment. Conservation involves a wide range of activities, including building more efficient combustion engines to reduce gasoline consumption; using catalytic converters to reduce the harmful emissions of burning fossil fuels; developing technologies to exploit renewable sources of energy; recycling glass, plastic, and metal wastes; using agricultural methods that protect the soil; building water treatment and sewage treatment plants; safely disposing of radioactive wastes; and cleaning up sites heavily polluted by industry.

ON THE GED® TEST

Some Earth and space science questions may deal with the impact of humans on natural resources and the environment.

PRACTICE 2

<u>Questions 1 through 3</u> refer to the following graph.

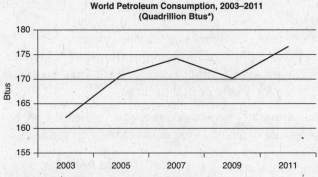

World Petroleum Consumption, 2003–2011
(Quadrillion Btus*)

Source: US Energy Information Administration
* Btus are British thermal units, a measure of energy

1. Approximately how many quadrillion Btus of petroleum were consumed in 2011?

A. 160
B. 170
C. 174
D. 177

2. Between its low point in 2003 and its high point in 2011, the approximate range of the data regarding world petroleum consumption was _____ quadrillion Btus.

- 10
- 14
- 176

3. Which of the following sentences best summarizes the information in the graph?

A. World petroleum consumption increased by about 14 quadrillion Btus between 2003 and 2011.
B. World petroleum consumption fell by about 4 quadrillion Btus between 2005 and 2009.
C. World petroleum consumption increased by roughly 50 percent between 2003 and 2007.
D. World petroleum consumption fell by roughly 50 percent between 2007 and 2009.

4. Which of the following proverbs best expresses the views of a conservationist?

A. All that glitters is not gold.
B. Every cloud has a silver lining.
C. Oil and water don't mix.
D. Waste not, want not.

5. The overall demand for water in the developed nations is rising. But it is not rising as quickly as people had predicted it would. In fact, the rate of water consumption per person per year in developed nations has actually dropped. This means that even though population has increased and industrial output has grown, the rate at which people withdraw water from reservoirs, rivers, and aquifers has slowed.

Which of the following is a likely reason for the drop in per person consumption of water in developed countries?

A. Vast new supplies of water have been found in the developed nations.
B. Developed nations have started using water more efficiently than they did in the past.
C. Developed nations are sharing water resources with each other.
D. Some developed nations export fresh water to other nations that lack it.

6. Soil erosion occurs when soil is worn away by the natural action of wind, water, and ice or by deforestation and poor farming practices. If soil erosion continues for a long time, it can lead to the formation of deserts. Some scientists estimate that the world lost about 20 percent of its farm topsoil between 1950 and 1990. Contour plowing, planting trees to serve as windbreaks, and other techniques can all reduce soil erosion.

Which of the following statements is supported by the information above?

A. All deserts originally formed as a result of soil erosion.
B. Most soil erosion is caused by poor farming practices.
C. Improved farming techniques can completely halt soil erosion.
D. Soil erosion is caused by both natural forces and the actions of people.

Answers and explanations start on page 698.

EARTH AND SPACE SCIENCE

Weather and Climate

Key Ideas

- Weather is the day-to-day change in atmospheric conditions at a particular place. Climate is the average long-term weather conditions in a region.
- Weather and climate are influenced by global air patterns and ocean currents.
- Daily weather is caused by the movement of air masses and is predicted by meteorologists.

ON THE GED® TEST

About 20% of the questions on the Science Test *will cover Earth and space science topics.*

Weather is the day-to-day change in conditions in the **atmosphere** at a particular place on Earth. **Climate**, on the other hand, is the average weather conditions of a large region over a long period of time.

All weather and climate ultimately arise from the uneven heating of the Earth. The sun's rays fall more directly at the equator than they do at the North and South Poles. This resulting uneven heating causes global wind circulation patterns: the warm air at the equator rises, creating an area of low pressure, and moves toward the poles. Cold air at the poles sinks, creating an area of high pressure, and moves toward the equator. The result is a pattern of **prevailing winds** in both the Northern and Southern hemispheres.

Global Wind Patterns

Another major influence on weather and climate, also caused by the uneven heating of Earth, is the worldwide pattern of **ocean currents**. Ocean currents are caused by the wind and by variations in the density of water (warm water is less dense than cold water). Ocean currents help transfer heat from the equatorial regions to the poles.

Daily weather patterns are caused by the movements of **air masses**, large bodies of air with similar temperature, humidity, and pressure. The boundary between two air masses is called a **front**. A **cold front** occurs where a cold air mass overtakes and displaces a warm air mass. A **warm front** occurs where a warm air mass rises over a cold air mass. An **occluded front** occurs when a cold front catches up with a warm front and the two weather systems merge. Clouds and **precipitation** are characteristic of fronts.

Meteorologists study the short-term weather patterns and data of particular areas. At meteorological stations around the world, temperature, humidity, cloud cover, wind, and other weather data are collected. Satellites and radar are also used to collect weather data. Weather predictions are based on comparing present weather conditions to computer models of previous weather conditions and storm systems in an area. When hurricanes, tornadoes, blizzards, or floods are forecast, meteorologists issue storm watches and warnings. For example, if a hurricane might reach an area in 24 to 36 hours, a hurricane watch is issued. If a hurricane is expected in an area in less than 24 hours, a hurricane warning is issued, and people are urged to take precautionary measures against the storm.

PRACTICE 3

Questions 1 through 4 are based on the information on page 532.

1. The diagram of global wind patterns on page 532 suggests that weather systems between 30°N and 60°N generally move in which direction?

A. northeast to southwest
B. northwest to southeast
C. southeast to northwest
D. southwest to northeast

2. Based on the diagram on page 532, how do the prevailing winds in the Northern Hemisphere compare to the prevailing winds in the Southern Hemisphere?

A. The winds in the Northern Hemisphere blow faster than those in the Southern Hemisphere.
B. The winds in the Northern Hemisphere are a mirror image of those in the Southern Hemisphere.
C. The winds in the Northern Hemisphere blow east and those in the Southern Hemisphere blow west.
D. The winds in the Northern Hemisphere blow west and those in the Southern Hemisphere blow east.

3. Hurricanes are violent storms with high winds and rain that form over the ocean. They cover an area 300 to 600 miles across and move relatively slowly—between 5 and 15 miles per hour. Meteorologists can now predict their paths with a great deal of accuracy.

Which of the following technologies best accounts for accurate hurricane tracking?

A. anemometers, which measure wind speed
B. thermometers, which measure air temperature
C. the Beaufort wind scale, a method of estimating wind speed
D. satellites, which transmit cloud photos and weather data

4. Which of the following help even out the unbalanced heating of Earth as a whole?

A. precipitation associated with fronts
B. local air masses
C. tornadoes, blizzards, and floods
D. global wind and ocean current patterns

Questions 5 and 6 refer to the following chart.

Layers of the Atmosphere

Layer	Altitude	Temperature
Troposphere	0 to 6 miles	Average 59°F
Stratosphere	6 to 31 miles	–76°F to 32°F
Mesosphere and ionosphere	31 to 50 miles	32°F to –212°F
Thermosphere	50 to 435 miles	Up to thousands of degrees

5. For which of the following statements does the chart provide evidence?

A. The higher you go in the atmosphere, the colder it gets.
B. The higher you go in the atmosphere, the less oxygen there is to breathe.
C. The highest layer of the atmosphere is the stratosphere.
D. The highest temperatures in the atmosphere are in the thermosphere.

6. In the chart, draw a stick-figure inhabitant in the atmospheric layer in which most human activity takes place.

Inhabitant

Answers and explanations start on page 698.

EARTH AND SPACE SCIENCE

Earth in the Solar System

The **solar system** consists of the sun, a star; the **planets**; their **satellites**, or moons; the **asteroids**, sometimes called the minor planets; and the comets. The sun contains more than 99 percent of the **mass** (amount of matter) in the solar system, and all the other celestial bodies revolve around it, held by the force of **gravity**.

The eight planets of the solar system include (in order from the sun) Mercury, Venus, Earth, Mars, Jupiter, Saturn, Uranus, and Neptune. Mercury, Venus, Earth, and Mars are called the **inner planets** because they are relatively close to the sun. They are all small, rocky planets. Jupiter, Saturn, Uranus, and Neptune are called the **outer planets** because of their great distance from the sun. The outer planets are gas giants. Some facts about the planets are presented in the following chart.

Key Ideas

- The solar system consists of the sun; the planets; their satellites, or moons; the asteroids; and the comets.
- There are eight planets: Mercury, Venus, Earth, Mars, Jupiter, Saturn, Uranus, and Neptune.
- The moon revolves around Earth every 27 days and appears to go through phases.

GED® TEST TIP

Some Science Test questions are based on detailed charts similar to the one on this page. Read the question carefully and select only the specific information needed to answer the question.

The Planets of Our Solar System

Planet	Distance from sun	Diameter	Number of moons	Rotation period (day)	Revolution period (year)
Mercury	36 million mi	3,030 mi	None	59 Earth days	88 Earth days
Venus	67 million mi	7,500 mi	None	243 Earth days	225 Earth days
Earth	93 million mi	7,923 mi	1	23 hr 56 min 4.1 sec	365 days 5 hr 48 min 46 sec
Mars	142 million mi	4,210 mi	2	24 hr 37 min	687 Earth days
Jupiter	484 million mi	88,700 mi	50	9 hr 51 min	11.86 Earth years
Saturn	0.9 billion mi	75,000 mi	53	10 hr 14 min	29.46 Earth years
Uranus	1.8 billion mi	31,600 mi	27	17 hr 12 min	84 Earth years
Neptune	2.8 billion mi	30,200 mi	13	16 hr 7 min	164.8 Earth years

Earth is unusual among the planets in that about 70 percent of its surface is covered by water. It is the only celestial body in the solar system on which life is known to exist. Earth's rocky satellite, the moon, is the fifth largest satellite in the solar system. It has no atmosphere, but it does have some surface ice, which was discovered in 1998. The moon revolves around Earth once every 27 days. During the lunar month, the moon appears to go through a series of **phases**—changes in the proportion of its surface that is in shadow. The cycle of phases takes approximately 29 days. U.S. astronauts landed on the moon in several missions from 1969 to 1972, making it the only celestial body visited by crewed spacecraft.

PRACTICE 4

Questions 1 through 4 are based on the information on page 534.

1. According to the chart on page 534, which of the planets takes the shortest time to revolve, or complete its orbit, around the sun?

   A. Mars
   B. Saturn
   C. Neptune
   D. Mercury

2. According to the chart, which of the following planets is most similar to Earth?

   A. Mercury
   B. Venus
   C. Jupiter
   D. Neptune

3. Before 1781, the only planets that were known were the ones visible to the naked eye: Mercury, Venus, Mars, Jupiter, and Saturn. In 1781, William Herschel, an astronomer who made his own superb and powerful telescopes, discovered a strange "star" that appeared as a greenish disk rather than a point of light. A few nights later, he observed that this "star" had moved relative to the background of the other stars. Herschel realized he had discovered another planet. It was named Uranus, after the Greek sky god. Later it was found that Uranus had actually been observed at least 20 times before, as far back as 1690, but each time it had been identified as a star.

   Which of the following is an unstated assumption that could help account for the fact that Uranus was misidentified as a star prior to 1781?

   A. Uranus takes 84 earth years to revolve around the sun.
   B. The length of a day on Uranus is about 17 hours.
   C. Uranus was not clearly visible with the telescopes generally in use at the time.
   D. Uranus was not visible when it was on the other side of the sun.

4. According to the chart on page 534, which of the following planets has the most moons?

   A. Jupiter
   B. Saturn
   C. Uranus
   D. Neptune

5. According to some estimates, it would cost about ten times more to send a crewed mission to Mars to collect geologic samples and look for life than it would cost to send a robotic mission. Some people think that a human mission would yield much more relevant data, justifying the additional cost. Others think there is no scientific reason to send crewed missions, which are costly and risky, when robotic missions will do.

   Which of the following values is most likely to provide the motivation to send a crewed mission to Mars despite the risk and the additional cost?

   A. a desire to provide equal opportunities for astronauts of all nationalities
   B. a desire for economic development
   C. a desire to demonstrate the superiority of computers over humans
   D. faith in human judgment and decision-making skills

6. The structure of the solar system, with the massive sun at the center and many objects revolving around it, is most similar to the structure of which of the following?

   A. a DNA molecule, with its twisted spiral shape
   B. an atom, with a dense nucleus and electrons orbiting the nucleus
   C. the electromagnetic spectrum, with waves of different lengths and frequencies
   D. the planet Earth, with its layers of crust, mantle, and core

Answers and explanations start on page 698.

EARTH AND SPACE SCIENCE

The Expanding Universe

Key Ideas

- Stars are globes of hydrogen and helium that produce their own heat and light through nuclear reactions.
- The sun is one star in the Milky Way galaxy, a large group of stars.
- The Big Bang theory helps explain the origin of the universe. According to this theory, the universe began as a compact spot of matter that exploded.

Our sun is a medium-sized yellow **star**, a globe of helium and hydrogen gas that produces its own heat and light through nuclear reactions. Stars like our sun generally have a 10-billion-year life cycle. They begin as **protostars**, which form from clouds of condensing gases and dust called **nebulae**. As a protostar reaches a certain density and temperature, nuclear reactions begin, releasing huge amounts of energy. At this point, the star is known as a **main-sequence star**, the longest stage in the stellar life cycle. After billions of years, the star begins to run out of hydrogen fuel. It may become a **red giant**. In time, the red giant becomes unstable and collapses, either exploding as a **supernova** and leaving behind a **neutron star** or losing mass slowly to become a **white dwarf**. A neutron star can be very dense, and gravity sometimes causes it to collapse in on itself, producing a **black hole**. Black holes are so called because their gravity is so great that light cannot escape from them.

The sun is just one star in a huge group of stars called the **Milky Way** galaxy. **Galaxies** consist of between one million and one trillion stars, along with clouds of gas and dust, which are held together by the force of gravity. Galaxies are classified according to their shape: spiral, barred-spiral, elliptical, and irregular. The Milky Way is a spiral galaxy. A spiral galaxy has a dense circular center with arms spiraling out from the core. Our solar system is located in one of the arms, called the Orion arm, of the Milky Way galaxy.

The Milky Way galaxy is part of a group of galaxies called the **Local Group**. There are 27 known galaxies in the Local Group, of which the Milky Way and the Andromeda galaxy are the largest.

The **universe** consists mostly of empty space with galaxies scattered throughout. Besides galaxies with stars at every stage of the life cycle, the universe has other bodies: **brown dwarfs** are objects that are less massive than a star but more massive than a planet; **pulsars** are thought to be rotating neutron stars that emit pulses of energy at regular intervals; and **quasars** are distant starlike objects that emit more energy than a hundred galaxies.

Cosmologists study the origin, properties, and evolution of the universe. One theory about the beginning of the universe is called the **Big Bang**. According to this theory, the universe began in a hot, superdense state smaller than an atom. The Big Bang caused all this compacted material to be flung outward, accounting for the still-expanding universe. There is evidence to support the Big Bang theory. First, galaxies appear to be moving away from one another in every direction, as if they had originated at a common point. Second, scientists have detected cosmic background radiation left over from the Big Bang. Cosmologists do not know what caused the Big Bang, but from the current rate of expansion of the universe, they estimate its age to be between 10 and 20 billion years.

PRACTICE 5

Questions 1 through 3 refer to the following paragraph and chart.

In astronomy, magnitude is an indication of the brightness of a celestial body. Magnitudes are measured along a scale from positive to zero to negative, with brightness increasing as magnitude decreases. Apparent magnitude is the brightness as seen from Earth, either by the naked eye or photographically. Absolute magnitude is a measure of the actual brightness of an object. It is defined as the apparent magnitude the object would have if it were located 32.6 light-years from Earth.

The Five Brightest Stars

Star	Distance from Earth (light-years)	Apparent magnitude	Absolute magnitude
Sirius	8.7	− 1.47	+ 1.41
Canopus	180	− 0.71	− 4.7
Alpha Centauri	4.3	− 0.1	+ 4.3
Arcturus	36	− 0.06	− 0.2
Vega	26	+ 0.03	+ 0.5

1. Choose information from the chart below to fill in the blanks. As seen from Earth, (1) [Select... ▼] is the brightest star. However, if all the stars listed in the chart were 32.6 light-years from Earth, then (2) [Select... ▼] would be brightest.

Select (1)	Select (2)
Sirius	Sirius
Canopus	Canopus
Alpha Centauri	Alpha Centauri
Arcturus	Arcturus
Vega	Vega

2. Which of the following would be true of a star with a position 32.6 light-years from Earth?

   A. The star's absolute magnitude would be less than that of Alpha Centauri.
   B. The star's apparent magnitude would be greater than its absolute magnitude.
   C. The star's apparent magnitude would be equal to its absolute magnitude.
   D. The star's apparent magnitude would be greater than that of Arcturus.

3. A magazine article makes the following statement about stars: A star's apparent magnitude and its absolute magnitude must always be close in value.

   Which of the following explains why the magazine's statement is incorrect?

   A. Stars form from huge masses of dust and gas.
   B. The absolute magnitude of a star indicates how bright the star looks to viewers on Earth.
   C. The apparent magnitude of a star is a measure of the amount of light the star puts out.
   D. Not all stars are located about 32.6 light-years from Earth.

4. The sun is about 4.7 billion years old. Based on the information on page 536, at which stage of its life cycle is the sun?

   A. It is a protostar.
   B. It is a main-sequence star.
   C. It is a neutron star.
   D. It is a white dwarf.

5. Pluto has a diameter of just 1,438 miles. It is made mostly of ice and frozen rock. It is very small and has an irregular orbit. It was originally classified as the ninth planet from the Sun, but it has been recategorized as a dwarf planet within the Kuiper belt.

   Which of the following is not a factual detail about Pluto?

   A. Pluto has a diameter of 1,438 miles.
   B. Pluto is made mostly of ice and frozen rock.
   C. Pluto has an irregular orbit.
   D. Pluto should be classified as a dwarf planet.

Answers and explanations start on page 699.

EARTH AND SPACE SCIENCE PRACTICE QUESTIONS

1. Tides are the twice-daily rise and fall of water along the shores of the oceans. Tides are caused mainly by the gravitational pull of the moon, and secondarily by the gravitational pull of the sun. The highest tides, called spring tides, occur when the sun, moon, and Earth are in line. Other high tides, called neap tides, occur when the sun and moon are at right angles with respect to Earth.

   Which of the following statements is supported by the information above?

   A. The moon and the sun exert the greatest pull on Earth's oceans when these bodies are all in a line.
   B. When the moon is at right angles to the sun with respect to Earth, tides do not occur along the ocean shore.
   C. Spring tides occur only in the spring, and neap tides occur only in the fall.
   D. Neap tides are generally higher than spring tides.

2. Geothermal energy is energy extracted from naturally occurring steam, hot water, or hot rocks in Earth's crust. It is used to heat buildings and generate electricity in areas where hot magma (melted rock) is close to the surface.

   In which of the following places is geothermal energy most likely to be used?

   A. Arizona, a state where abundant sunshine provides solar energy
   B. Cape Cod, a peninsula formed from glacial deposits of sand
   C. Iceland, an island nation in the Atlantic with active volcanoes
   D. Saudi Arabia, a Middle Eastern nation with ample oil and gas reserves

Questions 3 and 4 refer to the following paragraph and graph.

Scientists think there may be more matter and energy in the universe than has been directly observed because of some gravitational effects that cannot be explained otherwise. Dark matter and dark energy, so-called because they do not interact with light, may account for most of the stuff of the universe. In fact, ordinary matter, made of the chemical elements, may form only 4 percent of the universe.

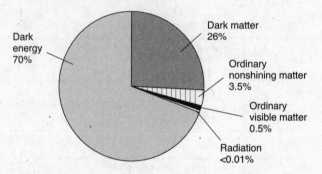

Source: Ostriker, Jeremiah and Paul Steinhardt, "The Quintessential Universe" *Scientific American,* January, 2001

3. According to the graph, about what percentage of the universe may consist of matter that does not interact with light?

   A. less than 0.01 percent
   B. 0.5 percent
   C. 4 percent
   D. 26 percent

4. Which of the following statements is a fact rather than a hypothesis about the makeup of the universe?

   A. Dark energy may account for 70 percent of the universe.
   B. Dark matter may account for 26 percent of the universe.
   C. Dark energy may cause gravitational effects.
   D. Ordinary matter is made of the chemical elements.

Questions 5 through 8 refer to the following map.

World Climate Zones

Polar
Temperate-snow
Desert-steppe
Tropical-subtropical
Highland

5. Which type of climate is characteristic of areas along the equator?

   A. polar
   B. temperate-snow
   C. desert-steppe
   D. tropical-subtropical

6. Which of the following statements is supported by information on the map?

   A. The continent with the least area of desert-steppe climate is Europe.
   B. Australia's climate is entirely tropical-subtropical.
   C. Africa and South America do not have areas with highland climate.
   D. Only North America has a large temperate-snow climate zone.

7. Temperate-snow climate zones hold only one-third of the world's people yet produce about two-thirds of the world's wealth. Historically, the fact that temperate-snow climate zones have more [Select...▼] than other climate zones do is the most likely explanation for this discrepancy between population and productivity.

   • farm output
   • seasons
   • tropical rain forests

8. The continents shown above have, on average, how many different climate zones? Write your answer on the line below. You MAY use your calculator.

_____

Questions 9 and 10 are based on the following diagrams.

Lunar Eclipse

Solar Eclipse

9. Fill in the blanks using the options below. Based on the diagram, a lunar eclipse occurs when (1) [Select...▾] passes between (2) [Select...▾] and the sun.

Select (1)	Select (2)
the moon	the sun
the sun	Earth
Earth	the moon
the moon's umbra	the moon's penumbra

10. Which of the following statements is supported by the information in the diagram?

   A. During a solar eclipse, the sun passes through Earth's umbra.

   B. During a lunar eclipse, the sun passes through the moon's umbra.

   C. A lunar eclipse can be seen only at night and a solar eclipse can be seen only during the day.

   D. A maximum of five solar eclipses and thirteen lunar eclipses are possible during each year.

Questions 11 and 12 are based on the following passage.

Acid rain is a form of precipitation caused by the release of sulfur dioxide and nitrogen oxide into the atmosphere. Acid rain is comprised of a mixture of wet and dry deposition. If the acidic chemicals in the air blow into places with wet weather, the acids fall to the ground in the form of rain or fog, affecting plant and animal life. In drier climates, the acidic chemicals mix into dust or smoke, which will then fall to the ground or on trees or buildings. These deposits are later washed off by rainstorms. The addition of water to these chemicals makes the resulting mixture more acidic.

The acidic chemicals themselves form as a byproduct of burning fossil fuels, such as coal, oil, diesel, and gasoline. Acid rain alters the chemical balance of lakes, affecting aquatic life. It also alters the chemical balance of soil, harming plant life. In addition, it damages buildings and statues.

11. Which of the following technologies can help reduce acid rain?

   A. a diesel locomotive, which burns diesel fuel to produce energy that is used to turn the wheels

   B. an electric power plant that burns coal to heat water and produce steam to drive turbines, which power the generator

   C. a refinery, which purifies metals, petroleum, and other substances into a more useful form

   D. a catalytic converter, a device in the exhaust system of a vehicle that reduces harmful emissions from the engine

12. **Directions:** Use ten minutes to read, plan, and write a one- or two-paragraph response to this short-answer activity. Compose your answer on a computer if one is available or write your answer on a separate sheet of paper.

Acid Rain Writing Prompt

A certain pond has been affected by acid rain. Explain how it might be the case that the pond was affected by both wet deposition and dry deposition.

The Rock Cycle

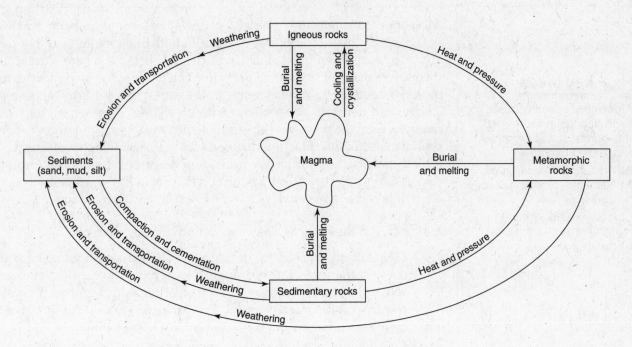

13. Which of the following statements is supported by the information in the diagram?

    A. The rock cycle is a continuous process of rock formation, destruction, and reformation.
    B. Sedimentary rocks form under conditions of heat and pressure.
    C. Metamorphic rocks form under conditions of compaction and cementation.
    D. Sediments form only from sedimentary rocks.

14. Fossils can form when plant or animal remains are buried under sand, mud, or silt. These materials can be compacted to form rock. A hiker knew she had found a(n) [Select... ▾] because it contained the fossilized imprint of a fish.

    • igneous rock
    • sedimentary rock
    • rock formed from magma

15. What is magma?

    A. melted rock
    B. crystallized rock
    C. cooled rock
    D. eroded rock

16. In open-pit mining, surface layers of soil and rock are stripped to obtain coal, ores, or minerals. It is cheaper than shaft mining because there is no underground work.

    Which of the following is the most likely reason that some countries restrict open-pit mining?

    A. There are no underground deposits.
    B. Open-pit mining is more dangerous than shaft mining.
    C. Open-pit mining destroys valuable land.
    D. Open-pit mining yields low-grade coal, ores, and minerals.

Answers and explanations start on page 699.

PHYSICAL SCIENCE

Atoms and Molecules

All matter is made of tiny particles called atoms. An **atom** is the smallest unit of matter that can combine chemically with other matter and that cannot be broken down into smaller particles by chemical means. Atoms are themselves made of **subatomic particles**. The major subatomic particles are protons, neutrons, and electrons. **Protons** are particles with a positive charge, and **neutrons** are particles with no charge. Together, protons and neutrons form the nucleus of all atoms except hydrogen, which has just one proton in its nucleus. **Electrons** are particles with negative charge. Electrons orbit the nucleus of an atom. When an atom has an equal number of protons and electrons, it is electrically neutral. When an atom gains or loses electrons, it becomes a negatively charged or positively charged **ion**.

Matter can be classified as elements, compounds, or mixtures.

- **Elements** are substances that cannot be broken down into other substances. They are made of a single type of atom. Gold, iron, hydrogen, sodium, oxygen, and carbon are some familiar elements. Each element has a **chemical symbol**. For example, gold is Au, iron is Fe, hydrogen is H, sodium is Na, oxygen is O, and carbon is C.
- **Compounds** are substances formed of two or more elements chemically combined in a definite proportion. Compounds have properties that differ from the properties of the elements that they contain. For example, at room temperature, water is a liquid compound made of the elements hydrogen and oxygen, which, uncombined, are both gases. Compounds are represented by **chemical formulas**. The chemical formula for water is H_2O, indicating that a water molecule is made of two atoms of hydrogen and one atom of oxygen.
- **Mixtures** are physical combinations of two or more substances that keep their own properties. For example, salt water is a mixture.

When elements combine to form **molecules** or ionic compounds, their constituents are held together by **bonds**. There are two main types of bonds: covalent and ionic. In a **covalent bond**, atoms share a pair of electrons, each atom contributing one electron. For example, the compound water is held together by covalent bonds. In an **ionic bond**, atoms gain or lose electrons to become ions, and the attraction between positively ($+$) and negatively ($-$) charged ions holds the compound together. For example, sodium chloride (NaCl), commonly called table salt, is an ionic compound.

Covalent Bond

H   O   H
Water (H_2O)

Ionic Bond

Na⁺   Cl⁻
Sodium chloride (NaCl)

PRACTICE 1

Questions 1 through 3 are based on the information on page 542.

1. Sodium is represented by the chemical symbol Na and chlorine is represented by the chemical symbol Cl. According to the text and the diagram on page 542, what happens when sodium chloride forms?

   A. The sodium atom loses an electron, becoming positively charged, and the chlorine atom gains an electron, becoming negatively charged.
   B. The sodium atom gains an electron, becoming negatively charged, and the chlorine atom loses an electron, becoming positively charged.
   C. The sodium atom gains an electron, becoming positively charged, and the chlorine atom loses an electron, becoming negatively charged.
   D. The sodium and chlorine atoms share a pair of electrons, becoming ions and forming a covalent bond.

2. Water is composed of two atoms of hydrogen and one atom of oxygen and has the formula H_2O. Glucose, a simple sugar, consists of 6 atoms of carbon, 12 atoms of hydrogen, and 6 atoms of oxygen.

   Which of the following is the chemical formula for glucose?

   A. CHO
   B. $_6C_{12}H_6O$
   C. $C^6H^{12}O^6$
   D. $C_6H_{12}O_6$

3. Choose statements from the chart below to fill in the blanks.

   Based on the information on page 542, atoms are (1) [Select... ▾] and ions are (2) [Select... ▾].

Select (1)	Select (2)
not necessarily either positively or negatively charged	not necessarily either positively or negatively charged
positively charged	positively charged
negatively charged	negatively charged
either positively or negatively charged	either positively or negatively charged

4. In 1911, British scientist Ernest Rutherford performed experiments that increased our knowledge of atomic structure. He bombarded an extremely thin sheet of gold foil with helium nuclei. (Helium nuclei, also called alpha particles, consist of two protons and two neutrons). He found that most of the helium nuclei passed right through the foil. Only a few were deflected back toward the source. On the basis of this experiment, Rutherford concluded that an atom has a dense nucleus with electrons orbiting it, but consists mostly of empty space.

   Which of the following is evidence that atoms consist mostly of empty space?

   A. Helium nuclei consist of two protons and two neutrons.
   B. Most of the alpha particles passed right through the gold foil.
   C. A few alpha particles were deflected off the gold foil and bounced back toward the source.
   D. Electrons orbit a dense nucleus consisting of protons and neutrons.

5. The number of protons in the nucleus of an atom is called the atomic number. Each element has a unique number of protons in its nucleus and therefore a unique atomic number.

   The atomic number of the element sodium is 11. How many electrons does a non-ionic sodium atom have?

   A. 10
   B. 11
   C. 12
   D. 22

Answers and explanations start on page 700.

PHYSICAL SCIENCE

Properties and States of Matter

Key Ideas

- Matter has mass and occupies space.
- The three states of matter include solid, liquid, and gas. A substance's state of matter can be changed by adding or removing heat.
- Solutions are a type of mixture. The solute is the dissolved substance. The solvent is what the solute is dissolved in. Solvents and solutes can be any of the states of matter.

Matter is anything that has mass and takes up space. The **mass** of an object is the amount of matter that it contains, and its **weight** is a measure of the gravitational force exerted on it. The mass of an object like a shovel never changes, but its weight can change. For example, a shovel weighs less on the moon than it does on Earth because the gravitational pull of the moon is less than that of Earth.

Under most conditions, there are three **states of matter**, as described below:

- **Solids** have a definite shape and volume because the molecules of which they are made occupy fixed positions and do not move freely. In some solids, such as minerals, the molecules form an orderly pattern called a **crystal**.
- **Liquids** have a definite volume but no definite shape because the molecules in a liquid are loosely bound and move freely. For this reason, a liquid conforms to the shape of its container.
- **Gases** have no definite shape or volume. The attraction between the molecules of a gas is very weak. In consequence, the molecules of a gas are far apart and are always in motion, colliding with one another and with the sides of the container.

The states of matter can be changed by adding or removing heat energy. When heat is applied to a solid, it melts. This happens because the motion of the solid's molecules increases until the bonds between them are loosened, allowing them to flow freely. The temperature at which a solid becomes a liquid is its **melting point**. When heat is applied to a liquid, it boils and evaporates, turning into a gas as the motion of its molecules increases. The temperature at which a liquid becomes a gas is called its **boiling point**. When heat is removed from a gas, the motion of its molecules decreases and it turns into a liquid. The temperature at which a gas becomes a liquid is its **condensation point**. When heat is removed from a liquid, the motion of its molecules slows until it solidifies. The temperature at which a liquid becomes a solid is its **freezing point**. The temperatures at which a substance changes state are unique properties of that substance. For example, water boils at 100°C (212°F) and freezes at 0°C (32°F). Water is also the only substance that is found naturally in all three states on Earth.

ON THE GED® TEST

Approximately 40% of the questions on the Science Test *are about physical science topics.*

As you learned in Lesson 1, mixtures are physical combinations of two or more substances that keep their original properties. A **solution** is a mixture (such as salt water) that is uniform throughout and that contains ions, atoms, or molecules of two or more substances. The substance in a solution that is dissolved is called the **solute**. The substance in which the solute is dissolved is the **solvent**. In salt water, for example, salt is the solute and water is the solvent. Water is called the universal solvent because so many substances dissolve in it. However, solutions are not always liquids. They can be solids, as when two or more metals are combined in an **alloy**, or they can be gases, as when oxygen and nitrogen are combined in the air.

PRACTICE 2

Question 1 is based on page 544.

1. Which of the following physical changes involve adding heat to a substance?

   A. melting and boiling
   B. boiling and condensing
   C. condensing and freezing
   D. evaporating and condensing

2. Density is the amount of mass in a particular volume of a substance. It can be expressed in grams per cubic centimeter. The chart shows the densities of some common substances.

Densities of Substances

Substance	Density (g/cm³)
Solids	
Lead	11.35
Iron	7.87
Aluminum	2.70
Liquids	
Chloroform	1.49
Water	1.00
Ethyl alcohol	0.79
Gases	
Oxygen	0.0013
Nitrogen	0.0012
Helium	0.0002

Which of the following statements is supported by the information provided?

   A. Water is the least dense liquid on Earth.
   B. Solids are usually denser than liquids and gases.
   C. Density increases as the volume of a substance increases.
   D. Density decreases as the force of gravity decreases.

3. It is well known that the boiling point of water is 100° Celsius. More viscous, or thicker, substances often have higher boiling points. Glycerin, for example, boils at 290° Celsius, while olive oil boils at 300° Celsius.

   By what percentage is the boiling point of glycerin greater than that of water? You MAY use your calculator. Write your answer on the line below.

4. Water is different from most other substances. It changes from gas to liquid to solid at temperatures that are common on Earth. When it freezes, its molecules form a crystal lattice, so that its solid form is less dense than its liquid form. It is the most common solvent.

   Which of the following is a conclusion about water rather than a supporting statement?

   A. Water is a unique substance on Earth.
   B. Water changes state at temperatures typical on Earth.
   C. Frozen water is less dense than liquid water.
   D. Water is Earth's most common solvent.

5. When a solute is dissolved in a liquid solvent, the freezing point of the solution is lower than the freezing point of the pure liquid.

   In which of the following situations is this property of liquid solutions applied?

   A. Sugar dissolves in water more quickly if the solution is heated.
   B. Antifreeze added to water in a car's radiator lowers the freezing point below 0°C.
   C. The oil and vinegar in salad dressing is mixed more thoroughly by shaking.
   D. Spherical ice "cubes" freeze more quickly than regular ice cubes do.

6. A suspension is a mixture in which the distributed particles are larger than those of the solvent and in which the particles, in time, will settle out.

   Which of the following is a suspension?

   A. pure gold
   B. pure oxygen
   C. salt water
   D. dusty air

Answers and explanations start on page 700.

PHYSICAL SCIENCE

Chemical Reactions

In a **chemical reaction,** the atoms or ions of one or more substances, called the **reactants,** are rearranged, resulting in one or more different substances, called the **products.** For example, iron, water, and oxygen react to form hydrated iron oxide, or rust. Matter is neither created nor destroyed during a chemical reaction, so the mass of the products always equals the mass of the reactants. This principle is known as the **law of conservation of mass**.

Chemical reactions can be represented by **chemical equations**. Chemical equations show the reactants on the left side and the products on the right side. They also show the proportions of the reacting substances—how many units of each reactant and each product are involved. Because of the law of conservation of mass, a chemical equation must balance. That is, the total number of atoms of an element on the left side must be equal to the total number of atoms of the element on the right side. Here is the chemical equation that represents the burning of hydrogen and oxygen to yield water.

$$2H_2 + O_2 \rightarrow 2H_2O$$

Restated in words: two molecules of hydrogen (H_2) combine with one molecule of oxygen (O_2) to form two molecules of water (H_2O). The equation balances because there are four hydrogen atoms on the left side and four on the right; there are two oxygen atoms on the left side and two on the right. To balance a chemical equation, you can change the coefficients—the number of units of any reactant or product. However, you *cannot* change the subscripts of any reactant or product.

Energy is involved in all chemical reactions. A reaction in which the reactants absorb energy from their surroundings is an **endothermic reaction**. For example, when you scramble an egg, you add heat energy and the egg solidifies. A reaction in which energy is given off with the products, usually in the form of heat or light, is an **exothermic reaction**. When you burn wood in a fireplace, for example, heat and light energy are given off. **Activation energy** is the amount of energy needed to get a reaction going. These energy relationships can be shown in graphs like those below.

Endothermic Reaction

Exothermic Reaction

PRACTICE 3

1. Which of the following chemical formulas represents the reaction in which copper (Cu) and oxygen gas (O_2) combine to form copper oxide (CuO)?

   A. $2CuO \rightarrow 2Cu + O_2$
   B. $Cu + O_2 \rightarrow 2CuO$
   C. $2Cu + O_2 \rightarrow 2CuO$
   D. $Cu + 2O_2 \rightarrow 2CuO$

2. Which of the following procedures would provide evidence for the law of conservation of mass?

   A. Weigh the reactants, conduct the reaction in an open container, and weigh the products.
   B. Weigh the reactants, conduct the reaction in a sealed container, and weigh the products.
   C. Measure the volume of the reactants, conduct the reaction in a sealed container, and measure the volume of the products.
   D. Write the chemical formula for the reaction and balance it.

3. Juanita would like to cook a scrambled egg on her gas stove. When she first turns on the stove's burner, the electronic ignition produces a spark that sets the gas burning. As the gas burns, it heats the frying pan. As the egg cooks, it absorbs the heat energy from the pan and solidifies.

   Match the correct form of energy needed with each step of Juanita's cooking process.

Juanita ignites the gas.	The gas burns.	The egg solidifies.

   Choices:

activation energy	endothermic energy

exothermic energy

4. In the graphs on page 546, what does the horizontal axis represent?

   A. the instant the reaction starts
   B. the instant the reaction stops
   C. the time during which the reaction occurs
   D. the energy level in the reaction

5. Organic compounds are those containing linked carbon atoms that form bonds with other atoms, usually hydrogen, oxygen, nitrogen, and/or sulfur. Organic compounds consist of chains, branching chains, rings, and other complex arrangements of carbon atoms with which other atoms bond. One type of organic compound is a polymer, a large long-chain or branching structure made up of many repeated simple units, called monomers. Natural polymers include cellulose. Synthetic polymers include polyethylene and other types of plastics.

   Which of the following is taken for granted and not stated by the writer of the paragraph above?

   A. Compounds are substances consisting of two or more elements chemically combined in a definite proportion.
   B. Organic compounds have linked carbon atoms forming bonds with other atoms, usually hydrogen, oxygen, nitrogen, and/or sulfur.
   C. Chains are among the arrangements carbon atoms in an organic compound can take.
   D. Plastics are synthetic polymers and cellulose is a natural polymer.

6. An acid is a compound that releases hydrogen ions (H^+), or protons, in the presence of water. Strong acids, like battery acid and stomach acid, are corrosive. Most dilute acids, like lemon juice, have a sour taste.

   A base is a compound that accepts hydrogen ions, or protons. Household cleaners like ammonia, lye, and bleach are bases. When an acid reacts with a base, the product is a salt and water. This reaction is called neutralization.

   Which of the following is the best title for this passage?

   A. "Corrosive Substances"
   B. "Acids and Bases"
   C. "Acids and Bases in the Lab"
   D. "Neutralization Reactions"

   Answers and explanations start on page 700.

PHYSICAL SCIENCE

The Nature of Energy

Energy is defined as the capacity to do work. **Work** is done whenever a force is applied to an object to set it in motion. Thus, anything that can force matter to move, change direction, or change speed has energy.

Energy comes in many forms. **Heat energy** can change a solid to a liquid and a liquid to a gas. It is also involved in most chemical reactions. **Light energy** can create an image by causing the chemicals on a piece of film to react. It provides the energy needed for the process of photosynthesis in green plants. **Electrical energy** can turn a motor, plate a set of flatware with a layer of silver, or store data on a hard drive. **Chemical energy** in food provides the energy humans need for life functions. It heats our buildings when we burn oil, gas, coal, or wood. Chemical energy in batteries provides electricity when the batteries are connected in a circuit. **Nuclear energy** from breaking apart the nuclei of atoms provides energy to produce electricity or power a submarine. **Mechanical energy** turns the axles of a car or the blades of a fan.

Energy can be converted from one form to another. Consider the production and use of electricity. In most electric plants, a fossil fuel (chemical energy) is burned, producing heat energy that turns water to steam. The energy in the steam turns the blades of a turbine, producing mechanical energy. The turbine powers the generator, which produces electrical energy. Electrical energy is used in homes to provide heat energy (in stoves and toasters), light energy (in light bulbs), sound energy (in the stereo), and mechanical energy (in a blender). Even though energy undergoes changes in form, the amount of energy in a closed system remains the same. This principle is known as the **law of conservation of energy**.

Two basic types of energy are **potential energy** and **kinetic energy**. An object has potential energy because of its position; it has kinetic energy when it moves. For example, when you raise a hammer, at the top of your upswing the hammer has potential energy. When you lower the hammer to hit a nail, the hammer has kinetic energy, the energy of motion. When the hammer hits the nail, it transfers energy to the nail. The energy transferred is equal to the work done by the hammer on the nail, and it can be measured in **joules**. The rate of doing work or consuming energy is called **power**, and it can be measured in horsepower (in the English system) or **watts** (joules per second in the metric system).

Physicist Albert Einstein discovered the relationship between energy and mass and expressed it in the equation $E = mc^2$, in which E represents energy, m represents mass, and c represents the speed of light. Since the speed of light is a very large number, the equation indicates there is a great deal of energy in even the tiniest bit of matter. So, for example, in nuclear bombs and nuclear power plants, mass is changed to energy when large atoms are split into two or more smaller atoms with less mass than the original large atom.

Key Ideas

- Anything that can force matter to move, change direction, or change speed has energy.
- Energy comes in many forms and can be converted from one form to another.
- The law of conservation of energy states that energy can neither be created nor destroyed, only changed in form.

ON THE GED® TEST

Since many Science Test questions are based on diagrams and graphs, it is important to carefully read the titles and all of the other information on all graphics. Make sure you understand a graphic before answering questions based on it.

PRACTICE 4

Questions 1 through 4 are based on the information on page 548.

1. Which of the following states the law of conservation of energy?

   A. Potential energy is the energy of position; kinetic energy is the energy of motion.
   B. Energy can be created and destroyed as well as changed in form.
   C. Energy cannot be created or destroyed, but can only change in form.
   D. Energy cannot be created, destroyed, or changed in form.

2. During a power outage, George relied upon his flashlight to move around his home. The flashlight is constructed with wires and a lightbulb enclosed in a plastic casing. It requires batteries to operate.

   Write in the three types of energy involved in turning on and using the flashlight.

   Options:

sound	light
nuclear	electrical
chemical	

3. An oak tree may grow very tall very slowly. It may take the tree a hundred years to absorb light energy and store it as chemical energy, yet only a single winter to be turned into heat energy in someone's wood stove. Which concept does this fact best relate to?

   A. work
   B. power
   C. force
   D. kinetic energy

4. What does Einstein's equation $E = mc^2$ express?

   A. the relationship between electricity and magnetism
   B. the relationship between energy and mass
   C. the speed of light in a vacuum
   D. the relationship between electrical energy and nuclear energy

Question 5 refers to the following diagram.

A Pendulum's Energy

3. Pendulum has only potential energy

1. Pendulum has only potential energy

2. Pendulum has only kinetic energy

5. Which of the following statements is supported by the information in the diagram?

   A. At the high point of its swing, a pendulum has kinetic energy.
   B. At the high point of its swing, a pendulum has potential energy.
   C. As a pendulum swings through one arc, it loses all its energy.
   D. A pendulum can swing forever because of kinetic energy.

6. Heat energy is present in all matter in the form of the kinetic energy of its atoms and molecules. Heat energy can pass from one place to another through conduction: the transfer of kinetic energy from molecules in greater motion (hot areas) to molecules of lesser motion (cold areas). Solid metals like silver and copper are good conductors of heat energy; gases like air are poor conductors.

   What is the reason that air is a poor conductor of heat?

   A. The molecules in air are far apart.
   B. The molecules in air are very large.
   C. The molecules in air do not move.
   D. The molecules in air are very small.

Answers and explanations start on page 683.

PHYSICAL SCIENCE

Motion and Forces

Everything in the universe is in motion. Even objects that seem to be at rest, like a building, are moving with Earth's rotation. **Speed** is the rate at which an object moves; **velocity** is its speed in a particular direction. **Acceleration** is the rate at which velocity changes. So a car's speed may be 40 miles per hour; its velocity may be 40 miles per hour toward the north; and it may accelerate by 10 feet per second until its velocity is 50 miles per hour to the north. A **force** is anything that tends to change the state of rest or motion of an object. A push or a pull on an object is a force, as are gravity and friction. So, for example, if you allow a car to coast on a level road, the force of friction will eventually bring it to a stop.

Sir Isaac Newton (1642–1727), an English physicist and mathematician, set down three laws by which the planets and all other objects move when acted upon by a force. These are called the **laws of motion**.

Newton's first law of motion, the **law of inertia**, states that an object at rest will stay at rest until a force acts upon it, and an object in motion will stay in motion at a constant speed in a straight line until a force acts upon it. Objects moving on Earth eventually slow down and stop because of the forces of friction and gravity. A bullet, for example, would continue its forward motion in a straight line, but friction from the air slows it down and the force of gravity pulls it toward the ground.

The second law of motion, sometimes called the **law of motion** or **acceleration**, states that the acceleration of an object depends on its mass and the force acting upon it. The greater the force, the greater the acceleration. The more massive the object, the more force it takes to accelerate it. Additionally, if a constant force acts upon an object, the object will move with constant acceleration in the direction of the force. This is why truck engines are more powerful than car engines: it takes more force to accelerate an object with more mass (a truck) than an object with less mass (a car).

Newton's third law of motion states that for every action, there is an equal and opposite reaction. This law was used to derive the law of conservation of momentum. **Momentum** is related to the amount of energy that a moving object has, and it depends on the mass of the object and its velocity. In fact, momentum is defined as an object's mass multiplied by its velocity. Newton's third law states that when an object is given a certain amount of momentum in a particular direction, some other object must receive an equal momentum in the opposite direction. Another way to state this is to say that all forces exist in pairs, and that all forces are interactions between objects. So, for example, when a bullet is fired out of a gun, the bullet's forward momentum causes the gun to recoil, or move backward.

Key Ideas

- Speed is the rate at which an object moves; velocity is speed in a given direction; acceleration is the rate at which velocity changes.
- A force is anything that changes the state of rest or motion of an object.
- Newton stated three laws of motion that explain the inertia, acceleration, and momentum of objects.

GED® TEST TIP

If you are asked to apply a general law or principle of science to a particular situation, ask yourself: "What is similar about this situation and the general principle?"

PRACTICE 5

Questions 1 through 3 are based on page 550.

1. What is a force?

    A. the rate at which an object moves in a particular direction

    B. any change in an object's acceleration or deceleration

    C. the inertia and momentum of an object at rest

    D. anything that changes the rest or motion of an object

2. What is inertia?

    A. the speed at which an object is moving

    B. changes in an object's speed or direction

    C. the force needed to move an object a certain distance

    D. the tendency of an object to remain at rest or in motion

3. The force that is needed to keep an object moving in a circular path is called centripetal force.

Which of the following is an example of motion that requires centripetal force?

    A. the tides occurring as a result of the moon's gravitational pull

    B. the International Space Station orbiting Earth

    C. a parachute slowing as it falls to the ground

    D. a gun recoiling as a bullet is fired

---

4. Select the phrase from the choices below that correctly completes the paragraph.

A car is traveling at a velocity of 30 miles per hour across a narrow bridge when it is approached on a collision course by another car traveling at 30 miles per hour. The momentum of each car is propelling it forward, and there is no way to completely avoid an impact. Because the momentum of the car `Select... ▾`, each driver should attempt to decrease his car's speed to lessen the severity of impact.

- decreases when its velocity decreases
- increases when its velocity increases
- decreases when its velocity increases

Question 5 refers to the following graph, the paragraph below, and the information on page 550.

Graphs are often used to convey information about motion. One type of motion graph shows distance and time. Distance is measured from a particular starting point. If the distance graph has a straight, horizontal line, the distance is unchanging and the object is not moving. If the distance graph has a straight line with an upward slope, the distance is changing at a constant rate; this means that the object is moving at a constant speed. If the distance graph is a curve, the object is accelerating or decelerating, depending on the shape of the curve.

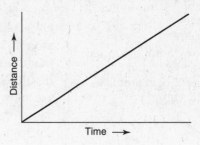

5. What does the graph above show?

    A. an object that is not moving

    B. an object that has a constant speed

    C. an object that is accelerating

    D. an object that is decelerating

---

6. A machine is a device that transmits a force, changing the direction or size of the force and doing work. The force applied to a machine is the effort force; the force it overcomes is the load. Types of simple machines include the inclined plane, wedge, lever, pulley, and wheel-and-axle.

Which of the following statements is supported by the information given?

    A. The force a machine overcomes is called the effort force.

    B. Work can be done only with machines.

    C. Some machines simply change the direction of a force.

    D. All machines change both the direction and size of a force.

Answers and explanations begin on page 701.

PHYSICAL SCIENCE

Electricity and Magnetism

As you recall from your study of atoms, electrons have a negative charge (−), and protons have a positive charge (+). This **electric charge** causes them to exert forces on one another. Particles with like charges repel one another, and particles with unlike charges attract one another. Sometimes electrons are temporarily pulled away from atoms, creating stationary areas of positive and negative charge. This can happen when two objects, like a balloon and a rug, are rubbed together, creating **static electricity**.

The movement of charged particles, usually electrons, is an **electric current**. Direct current flows in one direction only, and it is used in battery-operated devices. Alternating current flows back and forth rapidly, and it is used in household wiring. A material that allows electrons to move freely from atom to atom is called a **conductor**. Metals are good conductors. A material that does not allow electrons to move freely from atom to atom is called an **insulator**. Rubber and plastic are examples of insulators. **Semiconductors** are substances whose ability to conduct electricity is midway between that of a conductor and an insulator. Semiconductors like silicon are used in electronic devices.

An electric current produces a **magnetic field** that affects magnetic substances such as iron in the same way a permanent magnet does. Magnetic fields are produced by moving charged particles. In an **electromagnet**, the charged particles move along a coil of wire connected to a battery or other power source. In a **permanent magnet**, the spinning of electrons creates a magnetic field. Every magnet has two ends, called the north and south poles. The north pole of one magnet attracts the south pole of another magnet; like poles repel one another.

Just as an electric current produces a magnetic field, a moving magnetic field produces an electric current. This principle underlies electric motors, generators, and transformers. In an **electric motor**, for example, magnetic fields are produced by electric currents. The magnetic fields push against one another, turning the shaft of the motor. In a **generator**, a moving magnetic field produces electric current. In a **transformer**, an incoming electric current in coiled wire produces fluctuating magnetic fields, which in turn produce an outgoing electric current of a different **voltage**. The difference in voltage is caused by the differing sizes of the wire coils.

Key Ideas

- Particles with like electric charges repel one another, and particles with unlike electric charges attract one another.
- The flow of electrons through a substance is called an electric current.
- An electric current produces a magnetic field, and a moving magnetic field produces an electric current.

GED® TEST TIP

You can use your knowledge of everyday things like electricity and motors to help you answer questions on the Science Test.

Magnetic Fields

Bar magnet

Unlike poles

Like poles

PRACTICE 6

<u>Questions 1 through 3 are based on page 552.</u>

1. Suppose a drawing of two magnets with their north poles facing one another were added to the diagram on page 552. What would the new drawing show?

   A. two poles attracting one another
   B. two poles repelling one another
   C. magnetic lines of force connecting the poles
   D. magnetic lines of force flowing southward

2. What is the reason copper and aluminum are used for electrical wiring?

   A. Copper and aluminum are conductors.
   B. Copper and aluminum are insulators.
   C. Copper and aluminum are semiconductors.
   D. Copper and aluminum are magnetic.

3. Based on the information on page 552, which of the following devices is most likely to use direct current?

   A. a washing machine
   B. a desktop computer
   C. a toaster
   D. a flashlight

4. In an electric power plant, generators may produce electric current at about 10,000 volts. The current may be stepped up and transmitted along high voltage lines at 230,000 volts, and then stepped down to about 2,300 volts for transmission in a city. Finally, before it enters houses, the current is stepped down to 110 volts.

   Based on the information above and that on page 552, which of the following devices steps current up and down for efficient transmission?

   A. a conductor
   B. an electromagnet
   C. an electric motor
   D. a transformer

<u>Questions 5 and 6 refer to the following paragraph and diagram.</u>

An electric circuit is a complete pathway for the flow of electric current. It consists of a source of electricity, such as a battery, wires along which the current travels, devices called resistors powered by the current, and often a switch to start and stop the flow of current.

A Series Circuit

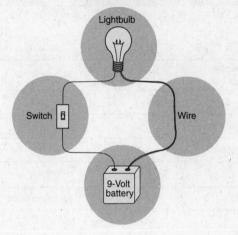

5. Circle the element of the diagram that acts as a resistor in the circuit.

6. A student was asked how the current in the circuit shown above could be stopped without using the switch. He answered that the only way to stop the current was to disconnect the battery.

   What was wrong with the student's response?

   A. Disconnecting the battery will not stop the current.
   B. Removing the fuse will also stop the current.
   C. Disconnecting the lightbulb will also stop the current.
   D. There is no way to stop the current without using the switch.

Answers and explanations start on page 701.

PHYSICAL SCIENCE PRACTICE QUESTIONS

Questions 1 and 2 refer to the following paragraph and chart.

When the nuclei of unstable elements disintegrate, emitting radioactive radiation, the unstable elements change into other elements, becoming more stable. The amount of time it takes for half of a sample of a radioactive element to decay into its stable product is called the radioactive element's half-life.

Radioactive Decay

Radioactive element	Decays into	Half-life
Radon-222	Polonium-218	3.82 days
Carbon-14	Nitrogen-14	5,730 years
Uranium-235	Lead-207	713 million years
Uranium-235	Lead-206	4.5 billion years
Rubidium-87	Strontium-87	50 billion years

1. What is the half-life of carbon-14?

   A. 3.82 days
   B. 5,730 years
   C. 713 million years
   D. 4.5 billion years

2. Uranium is used as fuel in nuclear power plants, resulting in radioactive waste, which is dangerous to living things.

   Which of the following arguments is likely to be used by opponents of nuclear power?

   A. Uranium is a plentiful source of fuel for generating electricity.
   B. Uranium is a renewable resource, and therefore its use is limitless.
   C. During the three days that radioactive waste is unstable, it may harm living things.
   D. Uranium produces radioactive waste that may harm living things for millions of years.

Questions 3 and 4 refer to the following paragraph and diagram.

An oscillation is a back-and-forth or up-and-down movement. When an oscillation travels through matter or space and transfers energy, it is called a wave.

Longitudinal Wave

Transverse Wave

3. What is the main similarity between longitudinal and transverse waves?

   A. Both involve up-and-down displacement of particles.
   B. Both involve back-and-forth displacement of particles.
   C. Both involve compressions in which particles are pushed together.
   D. Both involve the transfer of energy through matter or space.

4. After a transverse wave passes through a substance, no particle ever ends up far from its original position.

   Which of the following illustrates this principle?

   A. A cork in water bobs up and down as waves pass.
   B. Sound waves travel through air.
   C. When two waves overlap, they interfere with one another.
   D. A stone dropped into a pond causes ripples to radiate outward.

5. According to the kinetic theory of matter, all matter is made up of molecules in a state of constant motion. The motion of molecules can be inferred by observing particles in a fluid (a liquid or a gas) as they are hit by molecules of the fluid. The random, zigzag movement of the particles is called Brownian motion.

Which of the following is an example of Brownian motion?

A. dust motes dancing in a shaft of sunlight
B. the ground vibrating as a truck passes
C. water evaporating from a puddle
D. an inflatable raft floating on a lake

6. In a chemical reaction, the surface area of the reactants affects the rate at which the reaction occurs. The greater the surface area of the reactants, the faster the reaction rate will be.

When dilute sulfuric acid reacts with marble, carbon dioxide gas is produced. Among the options below, one will increase the rate of reaction, and one will decrease the rate of reaction. Match the appropriate action to the corresponding box for each effect—increasing and decreasing the rate of reaction.

Increase Rate of Reaction	Decrease Rate of Reaction

Options:

Use a larger container.	Use a smaller container.
Use powdered marble.	Use larger chunks of marble.

7. Boyle's law states that at a constant temperature, the volume of a fixed amount of gas varies inversely with the pressure exerted on the gas. Therefore, the volume of a gas [Select...▼] when the pressure on the gas increases.

- increases
- decreases
- remains the same

Questions 8 and 9 refer to the following paragraph and chart.

All of the elements are arranged in the periodic table according to atomic number—the number of protons in an atom of each element. The rows of the periodic table show elements according to the structure of their electron orbits. The columns, or groups, show elements with similar properties. A portion of the periodic table is shown below.

Part of the Periodic Table

13	14	15	16	17	18
					He 2
B 5	C 6	N 7	O 8	F 9	Ne 10
Al 13	Si 14	P 15	S 16	Cl 17	Ar 18
Ga 31	Ge 32	As 33	Se 34	Br 35	Kr 36
In 49	Sn 50	Sb 51	Te 52	I 53	Xe 54
Tl 81	Pb 82	Bi 83	Po 84	At 85	Rn 86

8. Group 18 is also called the noble gases. Their electron orbits are completely filled, and they rarely react with other elements. Which of the following is a noble gas?

A. nitrogen (N)
B. chlorine (Cl)
C. xenon (Xe)
D. fluorine (F)

9. Which of the following statements is supported by the information given?

A. Silicon (Si) is a very common element.
B. Chlorine (Cl) and iodine (I) have similar properties.
C. Arsenic (As) and antimony (Sb) have very different properties.
D. Arsenic (As) has 85 protons in its nucleus.

Questions 10 and 11 refer to the following paragraph and diagram.

Electromagnetic radiation consists of electric and magnetic fields that oscillate back and forth. There is a wide range of types of electromagnetic radiation, which together form the electromagnetic spectrum.

The Electromagnetic Spectrum

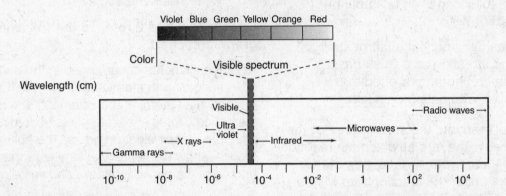

10. Which of the following types of electromagnetic radiation has a wavelength longer than those in the visible spectrum?

  A. microwaves
  B. ultraviolet light
  C. X-rays
  D. colored light

11. Which of the following generalizations is supported by the diagram?

  A. Unlike people, some insects can see ultraviolet light.
  B. Warm colors like yellow have a shorter wavelength than cool colors like blue.
  C. People can see only a small portion of the electromagnetic spectrum.
  D. In medicine, X rays are used to make images of bones.

12. Objects are attracted to one another by the force of gravity. Gravity is proportional to the mass—the amount of matter—objects have; gravity decreases as the distance between the objects increases. An object's weight is a measurement of the Earth's gravitational pull on the object.

What happens to the mass and weight of a rocket as it travels beyond Earth's orbit?

  A. Its mass remains the same, and its weight increases.
  B. Its mass remains the same, and its weight decreases.
  C. Its mass decreases, and its weight decreases.
  D. Its mass increases, and its weight remains the same.

13. Heat energy can be transferred from one object to another. In summer, when you hold an ice-cold can of soda against your face, your face feels cooler. However, what is really happening is that the can is being warmed by heat from your body. You are actually losing a little body heat.

Which of the following is an unstated assumption related to the paragraph?

  A. Heat can be transferred.
  B. Coldness cannot be transferred.
  C. A cool object can be warmed by your body.
  D. You can lose body heat.

Questions 14 and 15 refer to the following table and paragraph. You MAY use your calculator.

An aviation engineer tests five newly developed airplanes by measuring and recording the top speed of each plane. Unbeknownst to the engineer, the radar she used to measure the planes' speeds is faulty: it gives the speed of any object in motion as 3.7 km/hour faster than it really is. The following table shows the speeds that the engineer recorded using the faulty radar and the actual speed of each plane:

Airplane	Recorded speed (km/hour)	Actual speed (km/hour)
1	214.4	210.7
2	362.1	358.4
3	410.0	406.3
4	214.4	210.7
5	359.6	355.9

Using the speeds recorded from the faulty radar, the engineer then calculated the mean, median, mode, and range of the planes' speeds.

14. Which one of the engineer's calculations using the recorded speed is identical to what it would have been had the engineer made the same calculation using the actual speed of each plane?

    A. the mean
    B. the median
    C. the mode
    D. the range

15. After completing her measurements, the engineer selects at random two planes to demonstrate at an upcoming air show. What is the probability that the actual speeds of both planes selected are less than 360 km/hour?

    A. $\dfrac{1}{5}$

    B. $\dfrac{3}{10}$

    C. $\dfrac{3}{5}$

    D. $\dfrac{4}{5}$

Directions: Use ten minutes to read the following passage, plan, and write a one- or two-paragraph response to the question below. Compose your answer on a computer if one is available or write your answer on a separate sheet of paper. Include multiple pieces of evidence from the text to support your answer.

16. A pharmaceutical company sells a popular decongestant in capsule form. Market research shows that a new product combining the decongestant with the company's most popular pain reliever and sold in liquid form would be a big seller during cold and flu season. One problem is that the decongestant is extremely bitter when dissolved in water and the proposed product would require a flavor to be added to make it palatable to customers. The company tested several flavors and found that customers preferred a particular cherry flavor to all others. When the company's chemists created a sample of the decongestant, the pain reliever, and the cherry flavor, however, they discovered that the resulting compound coagulated into a liquid too thick to be easily swallowed. Chemist A hypothesized that the problematic ingredient was the pain reliever and suggested that the decongestant, the flavor, and an alternative pain reliever could be combined into a successful product. Chemist B disagreed; she suggested that the flavor was the ingredient causing the product to thicken and that a new flavor should be substituted into the product along with the popular decongestant and the popular pain reliever.

Decongestant Writing Prompt

Describe an experiment or series of experiments that the chemists could conduct to determine which of the chemists' hypotheses is correct or whether they are both wrong and further research is needed for the proposed product.

Answers and explanations start on page 702.

Practice Tests

1. To practice for the actual GED® Tests, you can take the following four tests. When you take the tests, <u>follow the same time limits</u> you will face on the actual tests.

   - **Reasoning through Language Arts, 53 Questions and Extended Response, 2½ Hours, Pages 560–581**
     - First Section—30 minutes: reading and language skills
     - Second Section—45 minutes: extended written response to two passages
     - Break—10 minutes
     - Third Section—65 minutes: reading and language skills
   - **Mathematical Reasoning, 46 Questions, 1 Hour, 55 Minutes, Pages 583–595**
     - First Section—no calculator allowed
     - Second Section—calculator allowed
   - **Social Studies, 34 Questions and one Extended Response, 1½ Hours, Pages 596–609**
   - **Science, 32 Questions and 2 Short Answers, 1½ Hours, Pages 610–621**

   Just as on the actual tests, you will work with a variety of formats:

   - For the **multiple-choice questions**, you may fill in the circles next to the correct answers in this book, or you can write your answers on a separate piece of paper.
   - For **other formats**, directions will indicate where you can write in boxes, write on lines, or place a dot on a specific place on a graphic.
   - You can write **Short Answers** on the *Science Test* and the **Extended Response** on the *Reasoning through Language Arts Test* and the *Social Studies Test* on a computer or, if one is not available, on a sheet of paper.

   NOTE: Writing your responses on a computer is preferable because you will be composing your responses on a computer when you take the GED® Test. However, if you do not have a computer available when you take these tests, write your responses on paper so that you can evaluate your writing samples.

2. **You MAY use your calculator** beginning on page **584** of the *Mathematics Test* and as needed during the *Science* and *Social Studies Tests*.

3. **Check** your answers using the *Practice Test Answers and Explanations* that begin on page 704 and **fill in** the *Practice Test Evaluation Charts*. These charts will allow you to see which study areas may still need work.

4. **Confirm** your readiness to take the actual GED® Test.

REASONING THROUGH LANGUAGE ARTS PRACTICE TEST

Directions: Use 30 minutes to answer the following 20 questions. You may fill in the circles next to the correct answers or write your answers in boxes or on lines as indicated. Some of the questions in this section mimic the GED test's drop-down menu question format. Wherever the word "Select" appears, choose the option that best completes the passage.

<u>Questions 1 through 6</u> refer to the following excerpt from an article.

Excerpted from "Sizing Up the Interviewer"

1   It is intrinsic to human nature to take the measure of the people we meet. We do it all the time, automatically. We develop an instinctive way of reading others that is sometimes the saving of us and at other times can prove to be our undoing. It is this instinct that makes us form instant, lifelong relationships with some people or causes us to give a wide berth to others because we get a "funny" feeling about them. With some careful consideration and planning, though, these "feelings" can be honed into a useful tool for gauging the personality and character of interviewers and, by extension, their expectations of potential employees. Let's examine some clues.

2   **Their e-mail.** You can tell a lot about your interviewer by his or her e-mail messages. Some interviewers are very warm, writing in a conversational style, addressing you by your first name. Others are witty, mixing little jokes and humorous remarks in with job-related questions. Still others get right down to business—no chit-chat or informality. Before you ever meet the interviewer, you begin to form certain "pictures" of the person, based on his or her approach and style. But it still remains for you to check him or her out face-to-face.

3   **Their office.** Let's begin with the physical setting of interviewers' offices. Some put a desk the size of a 747 between themselves and you. This is a clear message to you to keep your distance. A straight-backed, rigid chair for the applicant says, "O.K. Let's get down to business, and then you leave so I can get back to mine." Here, you would be advised to adopt a crisp, businesslike style, with brief, professional answers. And, for heaven's sake, **don't touch that desk!**

4   Then, there is the homey, comfortable environment—kids' pictures on the desk, executive "toys" around, soft chairs, and a sofa. There may not even be a desk between the applicant and the interviewer, but rather two chairs grouped around a coffee table. This environment invites more intimacy. It says, "Be yourself. Tell me about who you are so I can get to know you." Here, your manner, though still professional, should be relaxed and open, more personable. It would be a mistake with this employer to sit ramrod straight and give cool, truncated responses to the questions.

by Fred Jandt and Mary Nemnich, Indianapolis: JIST Works.

1. The purpose of this article is to

   ○ A. raise awareness about incompetent interviewers
   ○ B. describe types of interviewers and how to approach them
   ○ C. guarantee a perfect interview with an employer
   ○ D. explain how to email an interviewer

2. Which of the following is a generalization made in paragraph 1 but NOT supported with evidence?

   ○ A. Your "feelings" can be honed into a useful tool for gauging the personality and character of interviewers.
   ○ B. An interviewer's office can tell you a great deal about that interviewer.
   ○ C. Our ability to "read" others makes us form instant, lifelong relationships with some people.
   ○ D. There is more than one type of clue you can use to gauge the personality of your interviewer.

3. Which of the following are contrasted in this passage?

   ○ A. interviewers who welcome questions about themselves and those who do not
   ○ B. interviewers who frequently use email and interviewers who do not
   ○ C. interviewers who ask difficult questions and interviewers who ask very few questions
   ○ D. interviewers with homey, comfortable offices and interviewers whose offices seem less welcoming

4. Which of the following is an assumption the author of this passage makes?

   ○ A. Interviewers have some influence or control over their office arrangements.
   ○ B. Because email can be impersonal, it is a poor way to communicate with a potential employer.
   ○ C. Managers who enjoy chatting informally with employees never have large desks in the middle of their offices.
   ○ D. In preparing for a job interview, it is more important to "read" your interviewer than to research the company where you have applied to work.

5. Arrange the following boxes in order from first to last in the order they appear in the passage.

1st	
2nd	
3rd	
4th	

   ○ a. The author claims that an interviewer's email style tells you something about that interviewer.
   ○ b. The author claims that the arrangement of an interviewer's office tells you something about that interviewer.
   ○ c. The author makes a generalization about how your ability to "read" an interviewer can be useful.
   ○ d. The author cites specific evidence about why an interviewer's email style may be helpful to you.

6. Which of the following best summarizes the author's main point?

   ○ A. You should never respond to an interviewer who expects crisp answers with a rambling story about yourself.
   ○ B. You should focus on details when attempting to understand your interviewer, since details are important.
   ○ C. You should help your interviewer get to know you during the interview and beforehand.
   ○ D. You should try to understand your interviewer's personality and tailor your responses to him or her accordingly.

Excerpted from *The Living Is Easy*

1   He gave them each a copper, too, though he could hardly spare it, what with four of them to feed and Mama wanting yard goods and buttons and ribbons to keep herself feeling proud of the way she kept her children. Time was, he gave them kisses for toting his bucket. But the day Cleo brazenly said, I don't want a kiss, I want a copper, the rest of them shame-facedly said it after her. Most times Pa had a struggle to dig down so deep. Four coppers a day, six days a week, was half a day's pay gone up in smoke for candy.

2   Pa couldn't bring himself to tell Mama. She would have wrung out of him that Cleo had been the one started it. And Cleo was his eldest. A man who loved his wife couldn't help loving his first-born best, the child of his fiercest passion. When that first-born was a girl, she could trample on his heart, and he would swear on a stack of Bibles that it didn't hurt.

3   The sisters put their coppers in their pinafore pockets and skipped back through the woods. Midway Cleo stopped and pointed to a towering oak. "You all want to bet me a copper I can't swing by my feet from up in that tree?"

4   Lily clapped her hands to her eyes. "I doesn't want to bet you," she implored. "I ain't fixing to see you fall."

5   Serena said severely, "You bust your neck, you see if Mama don't bust it again."

6   Charity said tremulously, "Cleo, what would us do if our sister was dead?"

7   Cleo saw herself dressed up fine as Josie Beauchamp, stretched out in a coffin with her sisters sobbing beside it, and Pa with his Sunday handkerchief holding his tears, and Mama crying, I loved you best, Cleo. I never said it when you were alive. And I'm sorry, sorry, I waited to say it after you were gone.

8   "You hold my copper, Charity. And if I die, you can have it."

9   Lily opened two of her fingers and peeped through the crack. "Cleo, I'll give you mine if you don't make me see you hanging upside down." It was one thing to hear Cleo tell about herself. It was another thing to see her fixing to kill herself.

10   "Me, too," said Serena, with a little sob, more for the copper than for Cleo, whom she briefly hated for compelling unnecessary sacrifice.

Dorothy West, excerpt from *The Living is Easy*. Copyright 1948, © 1975 by Dorothy West. Reprinted with the permission of The Permissions Company, Inc., on behalf of The Feminist Press at the City University of New York, www.feministpress.org.

7. Which of the following would Cleo probably enjoy?

   ○ A. jumping from a roof before an audience
   ○ B. sewing clothes with her mother
   ○ C. reading a good book
   ○ D. treating her sisters to candy

8. Whose point of view is explained by this quote from paragraph 2? "A man who loved his wife couldn't help loving his first-born best, the child of his fiercest passion."

   ○ A. Cleo's
   ○ B. Mama's
   ○ C. the narrator's
   ○ D. Pa's

9. Arrange the following plot elements in order from the earliest to the latest.

1st	
2nd	
3rd	
4th	

○ a. Cleo envisions her own funeral.
○ b. Cleo's sisters offer her their coppers.
○ c. One day Cleo said that she did not want a kiss but wanted a copper instead.
○ d. Cleo asks her sisters to bet on whether she can swing from her feet in an oak tree.

10. Why did Serena offer Cleo her own copper?

   ○ A. Serena wanted Cleo to get in trouble for taking the others' money.
   ○ B. Serena had placed a bet that Cleo could not swing from the oak tree.
   ○ C. Serena felt that she had no choice but to give Cleo her copper to stop Cleo from doing something unsafe.
   ○ D. Serena wanted to show how much she loved her sister.

11. What is meant by the following quote from paragraph 1? "Most times Pa had a struggle to dig down so deep."

   ○ A. It was difficult for Pa to find it within himself to be generous.
   ○ B. Pa had so few coins that they were usually far down in his pockets.
   ○ C. Pa often searched for reasons not to give coppers to Cleo and her sisters.
   ○ D. Pa could not really afford to give Cleo and her sisters money.

12. Which of the following statements best describes the theme of the passage?

   ○ A. Cleo is wrong to take advantage of her sisters and her father.
   ○ B. Cleo's boldness and her family's love for her sometimes make them feel powerless to resist her.
   ○ C. Cleo's longing to be loved makes her vulnerable.
   ○ D. Cleo and her sisters are becoming greedy as they learn how to extract money from each other and from their parents.

Questions 13 through 16 refer to the following paragraphs.

Painting a Room

Would you like to redecorate a room in your home? Painting [Select... ▾] new look. First, remove the furniture, or move it to the center of the room and cover it with drop cloths. Prepare the room by [Select... ▾] a coat of primer if necessary.

Now you're ready to paint. Use a brush to paint a clean line along all edges where paint stops, such as where the wall meets the door frame, and in places where the ceiling meets a wall of a different color. This is called "cutting in."

The next step [Select... ▾] to paint the room in the following order: ceiling, walls, trim, doors, and windows. Put no more than 3/4 of an inch of paint in the paint pan. Run your roller through the paint, being careful not to overload the roller. Apply paint to the ceiling and walls in a "W" or "Z" zigzag pattern.

Spread the paint evenly by rolling either side to side or up and down, using gentle strokes so as not to leave roller marks. After finishing an area, look for spots you [Select... ▾] over them with your relatively dry roller.

13. Painting [Select... ▾] new look.
   - A. is a fast inexpensive way to give that room a hole
   - B. are a fast, and inexpensive way to give that room a whole
   - C. is a fast and inexpensive way to giving that room a whole
   - D. is a fast and inexpensive way to give that room a whole

14. Prepare the room by [Select... ▾] a coat of primer if line break necessary.
   - A. stripping paint and excess wallpaper, fill cracks, and add
   - B. strip paint and wallpaper, fill cracks, and add
   - C. stripping paint and wallpaper, fill cracks, and adding
   - D. stripping paint and wallpaper, filling cracks, and adding

15. The next step [Select...▾] to paint the room in the following order: ceiling, walls, trim, doors, and windows.

   ○ A. was
   ○ B. being
   ○ C. is
   ○ D. had been

16. After finishing an area, look for spots you [Select...▾] over them with your relatively dry roller.

   ○ A. missed, and go
   ○ B. missed, and going
   ○ C. missed go
   ○ D. missed, but go

Starting a Community Garden

(A)

(1) In many cities, neighborhood groups are forming community gardens in vacant lots, in parks, or on rooftops. (2) These gardens [Select...▾] to work with nature while making the neighborhood more beautiful. (3) [Select...▾] people are truly interested in the project. (4) If they are, organize a meeting of interested people, and choose someone to be the garden coordinator.
(5) Form committees for tasks like finding money for the garden.

(B)

(6) Once your group is organized, approach a sponsor—a group or individual who can support your garden. (7) Keep in mind that contributions of seeds, tools, and land are just as important as money. (8) Schools, churches, citizen groups, and private businesses are all potential sponsors.

(C)

(9) Find out how the land has been used in the past to avoid places that may be contaminated. (10) Pick a site that gets at least six hours of direct sunlight a day, and make sure that water is available. (11) Contact the owner of the site try to get a lease that allows you to use the land for at least three years.

(D)

(12) After choosing a site, the group of gardeners needs to decide how to organize the garden. (13) What size should each plot be, and how will plots be assigned? (14) Finally, establish a procedure to follow so that the garden stays tidy and peaceful.

17. These gardens [Select...▼] to work with nature while making the neighborhood more beautiful.

- ○ A. is an ideal way for both children, and adults
- ○ B. are an ideal way for both children and adults
- ○ C. are an ideal way for both children, and adults,
- ○ D. ideal, since both children and adults

18. If you [Select...▼] people are truly interested in the project.

- ○ A. will like to start a community garden, first determine whether
- ○ B. would like to start a community garden, first determine whether
- ○ C. would like to start a community garden first determine whether
- ○ D. would like to start a community garden, first determine weather

19. Which sentence would be most effective if inserted at the beginning of paragraph C?

- ○ A. Next, choose a site for the garden.
- ○ B. Land use is a very significant factor.
- ○ C. We all know that you are going to need land for your garden.
- ○ D. Learn about the history of your site.

20. Which of the following would improve the effectiveness of paragraph A?

- ○ A. Start a new paragraph before sentence 2.
- ○ B. Start a new paragraph before sentence 3.
- ○ C. Combine sentences 2 and 3 into a compound sentence.
- ○ D. Combine paragraphs A and B.

Directions: Based on both passages on pages 568 and 569, write a response to the prompt on page 569. This task may take up to 45 minutes to complete.

Passage A: Why Physical Education Should No Longer Be a Requirement for Graduation

This is the text of Councilwoman Juanita Sanchez's speech at last week's school board meeting.

The job market is increasingly competitive. Because of this, we must ensure that our students' education fully prepares them to succeed in the future. A limited budget and limited time during the school day force us to make difficult decisions concerning what we teach. We must be willing to make these decisions with the best interests of our students at heart. With these goals in mind, I support the proposal to eliminate physical education as a core requirement for high school graduation in our district.

Time spent completing physical education requirements is time away from more productive educational pursuits. While our state's standardized test scores have continued to rise in past years, we are still seeing results that are below average in both mathematics and reading. Added instructional time is necessary to see our test scores meet the standards set for us. This additional time spent on core subjects will also better prepare students for a pursuit of higher education after high school graduation.

No one is suggesting that physical education and fitness classes be completely eliminated from our curriculum. Physical education is a worthwhile pursuit and should be provided for those students who are interested. But it should be an elective, or optional, course in the same way that music, art, and theater classes are offered as electives. Thus, this outdated requirement will no longer get in the way of more academically important pursuits.

Passage B: Physical Education Is an Important Requirement for Students

Letter from concerned parent published in the City Journal *newspaper*

No one would disagree that preparing our students for a successful future is essential. Changes need to be made in order to help our children compete for college scholarships and career advancement. But as we make these changes, we have to be careful not to cause more harm than good. The current proposal places us in danger of damaging successful programs in our efforts to make improvements.

Having a healthy lifestyle is at least as important to a happy and successful future as mathematics and reading skills are. We currently are in the middle of an epidemic of health problems caused by lack of physical fitness among the children in our community. In our state, almost 20 percent of children between the ages of 12 and 18 are classified as obese. And obesity is linked to a number of life threatening health problems including diabetes and heart disease. Thus, this is a trend that we must make every effort to reverse.

Programs to offer healthier lunch choices for students have already been introduced. It would be ridiculous to now eliminate requirements that teach our children about other aspects of healthy living. What good is longer time spent in so-called "core classes" if students aren't healthy enough to fully participate?

I understand that the School Board members have students' best interests at heart. And I agree that it is important to find ways to improve the math and reading scores of our students. Unfortunately, the current plan to eliminate physical education will do much more harm than good. There is a reason P.E. has been a part of our school curriculum for so many years!

Write an Extended Response to Both Passages

While Councilwoman Sanchez makes her case for the benefits of eliminating physical education from the required curriculum, the editorial response identifies the drawbacks of this proposal.

In your response, analyze both the speech and the editorial. Explain which position you believe is best supported by its advocate. Use relevant and specific evidence from both sources to support your response.

Type your response on a computer, if one is available. If one is not available, write your response neatly on paper. This task may require approximately 45 minutes to complete.

Use the *Reasoning Through Language Arts Extended Response Evaluation Guide* on page 722 to evaluate your response.

You may take a 10-minute break before proceeding.

Questions 21 through 27 refer to the following book excerpt.

Excerpt from *Small Business for Dummies*

1   The domestic automakers had a huge market share coming into the 1970s but, unfortunately, were upsetting customers left and right. The Detroit auto manufacturers were able to keep their costs low and profits high in part by producing sub-par cars. Sure, their cars looked nice on the auto dealer's lot, but after a short time in use, many of the U.S.-manufactured cars developed far more problems than their foreign equivalents. And, to add insult to injury, U.S. auto customers didn't get particularly good customer service when they brought their cars in for needed tune-ups and repairs.

2   The chief bean counters and the management of the major U.S. automakers weren't considering the bigger picture when they analyzed their companies' financial statements during the 1970s. These companies were too focused on their short-term profitability and weren't considering the after-sales service that was required as a result of their initially shoddy products.

3   Not surprisingly, the U.S. automakers lost tremendous market share at the expense of the best foreign automakers during the 1970s and 1980s. In fact, one of the big four U.S. automakers—Chrysler—nearly went bankrupt and was saved only because of a government bailout.

4   In the long run, the Detroit automakers learned the hard way that getting your product right the first time is less costly and more profitable than retrenching to play catch-up. Customers aren't stupid, and if you continually sell them shoddy merchandise (especially when better merchandise is available from other sources), they won't come back the next time they're in the market for the products and services you have to offer. What's more, they'll tell others of their lousy experience with your company.

5   Although the major U.S. automakers ultimately got their act together in the 1990s and have stopped the erosion of market share, they still feel the financial pain from the millions of customers they alienated and lost to foreign competitors in the two preceding decades.

From *Small Business for Dummies* by Eric Tyson and Jim Schell, Foster City, Calif.: IDG Books, 2000.

21. The passage states that in the 1970s and 1980s, the management of the major U.S. automakers was too focused on which of the following?

○ A. Attractiveness of the cars they manufactured
○ B. After-sales service
○ C. Manufacturing shoddy merchandise
○ D. Short-term profitability

22. According to the passage, which of the following is a lesson learned by the Detroit automakers?

○ A. Getting your product right the first time is more profitable than fixing mistakes later.
○ B. Servicing your product is not profitable and therefore unimportant.
○ C. Bankruptcy is profitable for large companies due to government bailouts.
○ D. It is easy to win back customers a company has lost to a competitor.

23. What do the authors suggest was one of the goals of foreign automakers?

Foreign automakers

○ A. studied and then improved on the design of U.S. cars
○ B. deliberately underpriced their cars to get a share of the U.S. market
○ C. wanted to build quality cars with few repair problems
○ D. put short-term profitability above all else

24. The author uses the phrase "chief bean counters" most probably in order to

○ A. underscore the fact that customers will not return once they have had a poor experience with a certain company
○ B. argue that foreign automakers provided better customer service than U.S. automakers
○ C. emphasize U.S. automakers' preoccupation with keeping costs low and profits high in the short term, at the expense of their long-term outlook
○ D. indicate that domestic automakers enjoyed tremendous market share at the beginning of the 1970s

25. Which of the following are causes, and which are effects? Place the following four causes and effects into the table below:

Causes	Effects

a. U.S. automakers manufactured cars of low quality

b. A customer chooses not to do business with a company

c. A customer has a bad experience when doing business with a company

d. U.S. automakers lost business to foreign automakers in the 1970s and 1980s

26. Which of the following best describes the authors' tone toward U.S. automakers?

○ A. critical
○ B. proud
○ C. approving
○ D. arrogant

27. Later, the authors advise: "As a small-business owner, remember that if you don't get your product right the first time, you may not have a second chance."

Based on this information and the excerpt, who did get a second chance?

○ A. U.S. automakers
○ B. foreign automakers
○ C. small-business owners
○ D. the government

Excerpted from "The Twins"

1   After a while, there was a ring at the back door. The children scampered in from the garden, while Jennie answered the ring.

2   "Baker," said the man.

3   "Oh, yes," said Jennie: "wait, I'll get my purse."

4   I went on writing my letter, only half hearing the sound of Jennie's small-change as she, presumably, paid the baker's man.

5   In a moment, Marjie was by my side.

6   "Hallo," I said.

7   Marjie did not answer.

8   "Hallo, Marjie," I said. "Have you come to keep me company?"

9   "Listen," said little Marjie in a whisper, looking over her shoulder. "Listen."

10   "Yes," I said.

11   She looked over her shoulder again, as if afraid her mother might come in.

12   "Will you give me half-a-crown?" whispered Marjie, holding out her hand.

13   "Well," I said, "what do you want it for?"

14   "I want it," said Marjie, looking furtively behind her again.

15   "Would your mummy want you to have it?" I said.

16   "Give me half-a-crown," said Marjie.

17   "I'd rather not," I said. "But I'll tell you what, I'll buy you a—"

18   But Marjie had fled, out of the door, into the kitchen. "She'd rather not," I heard her say to someone.

19   Presently, Jennie came in, looking upset.

20   "Oh," she said, "I hope you didn't feel hurt. I only wanted to pay the baker, and I hadn't enough change. He hadn't any either; so just on the spur of the moment I sent Marjie for a loan of half-a-crown till tonight. But I shouldn't have done it. I never borrow anything as a rule."

21   "Well, of course!" I said. "Of course I'll lend you half-a-crown. I've got plenty of change. I didn't understand and I got the message all wrong; I thought she wanted it for herself and that you wouldn't like that."

22   Jennie looked doubtful. I funked explaining the whole of Marjie's act. It isn't easy to give evidence against a child of five.

23   "Oh, they never ask for money," said Jennie. "I would never allow them to ask for anything. They never do that."

24   "I'm sure they don't," I said, floundering a bit.

From "The Twins" by Muriel Spark, from the book *The Go-Away Bird and Other Stories*, J. B. Lippincott Company.

28. What does Marjie's looking over her shoulder suggest to the narrator?

The narrator thinks Marjie

- A. is imagining what she'll do with the money
- B. has forgotten something in the other room
- C. is shy and lacks confidence
- D. is hoping her mother won't hear her asking for money

29. Which of the following becomes evident during the discussion between Jennie and the narrator?

- A. Jennie knows the narrator wanted to lend her the money.
- B. Jennie can't believe that the narrator wouldn't lend her the money.
- C. Jennie is perplexed when the narrator blames Marjie.
- D. The narrator and Jennie eventually forget the misunderstanding.

30. If Jennie were criticized by her boss at work, what would she most likely do?

- A. resent it in silence
- B. discuss it defensively
- C. not take it seriously
- D. argue forcefully

31. The first person point of view allows the reader to know

- A. the narrator's thoughts
- B. the thoughts and actions of all characters
- C. only the actions of the narrator
- D. Marjie's opinions about the narrator

32. What kind of relationship do Jennie and the narrator have?

- A. They are cool and indifferent to each other.
- B. They frequently disagree on matters.
- C. They know each other but are not close.
- D. Jennie takes advantage of the narrator.

33. Which of the following best describes the situation presented in this excerpt?

- A. humorous
- B. sad
- C. uncomfortable
- D. sentimental

34. Match the following descriptions with the characters they best describe.

Marjie	
Jennie	
Narrator	

Obedient
Diplomatic
Proud

How Should We Measure the Rate of Poverty?

1   The rate of poverty appears to be increasing. Each year, the U.S. Census Bureau estimates the rate of poverty, or how many people in the U.S. are living in poverty. According to the Census Bureau, about 15.9 percent of the U.S. population was poor in 2011. That was a 15.3 percent increase over 2010. Moreover, the rate of poverty rose each year from 2007 to 2011.

2   It has been argued that the estimated rate of poverty is too low—that, in fact, more Americans are poor. To understand this, it is important first to understand how the Census Bureau determines who is poor. The Bureau surveys people about their income and then compares that income to the official "poverty threshold" (often called the "poverty line"). This poverty threshold varies depending on age, family size, and number of children. For example, in 2011 the poverty threshold for a single individual under 65 was $11,702. For a family of four, it was $23,021.

3   Some researchers have argued that these poverty thresholds do not account for taxes, living expenses, medical costs, or differences in cost of living. For example, in a major city, higher rents may leave individuals with less money for food. If the poverty thresholds were adjusted to account for these considerations, the estimated rate of poverty might be higher.

4   A panel of experts has proposed a different measure of poverty, which they call the Supplemental Poverty Measure, or SPM. The graph below shows what percentage of people are living in poverty as measured by the official poverty threshold and compares it to the percentage of people who would be considered poor by the SPM.

5   Why does it matter how many people are considered poor by the Census Bureau? One answer is that the Bureau's estimate of the rate of poverty is used by the federal government to allot resources to states and local communities. Local governments also use the estimate to figure out how many people are eligible for anti-poverty programs.

Poverty Rates Using Two Measures for Total Population and by Age Group, 2011

*Includes unrelated individuals under age 15.
Source: U.S. Census Bureau, Current Population Survey, 2012 Annual Social and Economic Supplement.

Adapted with permission from the U.S. Census Bureau

35. Which of the following best states the main idea of the passage and graph?

   ○ A. The Census Bureau uses a set of poverty thresholds to determine the rate of poverty.
   ○ B. If the Census Bureau adopted the SPM, the estimate of the rate of poverty among seniors would increase.
   ○ C. There may be more people in poverty than the Census Bureau official estimate suggests.
   ○ D. It is important that the government take action to combat poverty.

36. Which of the following is a supporting detail, rather than a main idea, in paragraph 1?

   ○ A. The rate of poverty rose each year from 2007 to 2011.
   ○ B. The rate of poverty appears to be increasing.
   ○ C. The Census Bureau may underestimate the number of people living in poverty.
   ○ D. Differences in cost of living should be accounted for in how the government measures poverty.

37. How does the bar graph support the information in the passage?

   ○ A. The bar graph supports the claim that some people who do not think they are poor may actually be poor.
   ○ B. The bar graph supports the claim that the government should do more to combat poverty.
   ○ C. The bar graph supports the claim that a different way to measure poverty would produce a different estimate of the rate of poverty.
   ○ D. The bar graph supports the claim that 15.9% of people in the U.S. were poor in 2011.

38. Which of the following describes a cause and effect relationship mentioned in the passage?

   ○ A. The poverty thresholds cause individuals to have lower income.
   ○ B. The Census Bureau's estimated rate of poverty can cause government officials to care about poverty.
   ○ C. Higher rents can cause people to have less money for food.
   ○ D. The SPM would cause more money to be spent on programs for senior citizens.

39. Place each of the factors below into the column that best describes it. You may or may not fill up each column.

Estimates that would be higher if the SPM were adopted	Estimates that would be lower if the SPM were adopted

The overall rate of poverty
The rate of poverty among people 65 and older
The rate of poverty among people under 18
The rate of poverty among people 18–64

40. A student reviewed this passage and graph and then said: "It's clear to me that if the Census Bureau adopted the SPM, then local governments would get significantly more federal money to spend on anti-poverty programs." Which of the following best describes the flaw in the student's reasoning?

   ○ A. The student has confused the causes of poverty with the effects of poverty.
   ○ B. The student has overlooked the fact that other factors might impact how much money local governments receive from the federal government.
   ○ C. The student has overlooked the possibility that not all local governments work to combat poverty.
   ○ D. The student has overlooked the fact that other countries have even higher rates of poverty.

41. This piece was most likely written by someone who _____.

   ○ A. worries that the government spends too much money on anti-poverty programs
   ○ B. thinks poverty is too emotional a topic to be discussed publicly
   ○ C. wants governmental actions to be based on an accurate estimate of the rate of poverty
   ○ D. thinks that there is little that government can do about poverty

Directions: <u>Questions 42 through 45</u> refer to the following two passages.

Glenwood Community Improvement Council Member:

As a member of the Glenwood Community Improvement Council, I fully support spending money to beautify our public parks. Over the last few years, several of our community parks have fallen into disrepair. Walking paths through the parks are not clearly marked, graffiti is visible on picnic shelters, and garden areas are overgrown with weeds. My neighbors tell me that they do not visit our parks because of the parks' condition. Some even said that they worry the parks are dangerous! We should spend money to ensure that our parks are good places to spend time with your family.

Improving and maintaining the parks would have a positive effect on crime and vandalism. If the parks are established as a source of pride for all of the community, vandals will be less likely to deface them. Well-maintained basketball and volleyball courts, picnic areas, and special events such as concerts in the parks would provide activities for the whole town and help neighbors spend time together.

Furthermore, beautiful public spaces are essential to community pride. Without community pride, Glenwood residents and others are unlikely to invest in creating and supporting small businesses. And small businesses are the heart of a thriving community. We must present Glenwood as a beautiful place to live in order to attract successful entrepreneurs from the surrounding area. If we do so, our investment in the parks will quickly pay for itself. Thus, we must improve our public parks.

Concerned Local Business Owner:

I think I speak for most of the business owners in Glenwood when I say that spending money to improve parks would be a complete waste of resources. The parks are not popular, and we do not know that they would become popular after being improved.

If we want a shining example of our town's successes to attract businesses, our growing business district is all we need! In the last four years, six new businesses have moved into vacant locations on Main Street. On top of that, several restaurants and shops downtown have survived the recent economic downturn and are now seeing more customers.

The city should do more to support these businesses. We should spend money to improve the infrastructure and appearance of the downtown business district. Improvements could be made to streetlights, signs, and building exteriors along our historic Main Street. We also currently are not able to plant public flower beds or clean and maintain the sidewalks. Investments in these areas would make downtown inviting to both customers and small business owners.

Beautifying our town is important if we want economic growth. But we should make sure that our beautification efforts are in the most important places. Clearly, beautifying downtown would help us build a healthy local economy. And once we have done so, then we can put money toward our parks.

42. The topic of both passages is

   ○ A. the best way to enjoy public spaces
   ○ B. what businesses should exist in Glenwood
   ○ C. whether beautification projects create economic growth
   ○ D. how best to spend public money

43. The writers of the passages disagree about which of the following claims about Glenwood Public Parks?

   ○ A. They are in a state of disrepair.
   ○ B. They are a current source of pride for the community.
   ○ C. Improving them is a good use of funds right now.
   ○ D. Park activities can lower the amount of crime.

44. How does the local business owner feel about projects that improve the appearance of the city?

   ○ A. They are good when done in the best locations.
   ○ B. They are always a waste of taxpayer money.
   ○ C. The city parks are good enough the way they are.
   ○ D. They have no impact on local business.

45. Which of the following would the two writers most likely agree on?

   ○ A. Improving Glenwood Public Parks will have an immediate impact on local business.
   ○ B. Investing in our community is important for the future of Glenwood.
   ○ C. The parks would be used regularly if they were in better repair.
   ○ D. Public activities are more important than encouraging new local business.

Questions 46 through 49 refer to the following paragraphs.

Sick Building Syndrome

Do you [Select... ▾]? Do you experience symptoms such as coughing, sneezing, nausea, headaches and difficulty breathing? Do these [Select... ▾]? If so, you may be working in a sick building.

"Sick building syndrome" is a term that refers to working in a building that makes you sick. The syndrome may be caused by improper building design. Over the past 20 years, architects have designed office buildings with an eye to saving energy. The buildings are tightly sealed so that little heat escapes, and the air inside the buildings is recirculated to avoid the cost of heating fresh air. Although this design reduces energy costs, the lack of ventilation causes a buildup of toxins in the air. On the other hand, [Select... ▾] the syndrome. Even if [Select... ▾] originally opened to let in fresh air, adding insulation, caulking, and weather stripping at a later date may have made the windows airtight.

Toxins in the air come from a variety of sources. Biological agents, including bacteria, viruses, fungi, and pollen, may be found in poorly maintained air circulation systems and dirty washrooms. The deadly gas carbon monoxide can seep into a building's air through an improperly ventilated garage or a leaky duct. Formaldehyde is frequently found in furniture, paneling, draperies, glues, and upholstery.

It is possible to "cure" a sick building. Steps to take include eliminating tobacco smoke, providing good ventilation, keeping the ventilation system in good repair, and removing all sources of pollution.

46. Do you [Select...▾]?

   A. often feel sick when at you're work-place?
   B. often feel sickly when at your work-place?
   C. often feel sick when at your workplace?
   D. often feeling sick when at your work-place?

47. Do these [Select...▾]?

   A. symptoms seem to disappear magically once you leave work?
   B. symptoms seem to disappear once you leave work magically?
   C. symptoms seems to disappear once you leave work magically?
   D. symptoms seem to disappear once magically you leave work?

48. On the other hand, [Select...▾] the syndrome.

   A. an older building isn't necessarily immune to
   B. an older isn't necessarily immune to
   C. an older isn't necessarily immune too
   D. an older building isn't necessarily immune, to

49. Even if [Select...▾] originally opened to let in fresh air, adding insulation, caulking, and weather stripping at a later date may have made the windows airtight.

   A. them
   B. it
   C. the building
   D. the windows

Questions 50 through 53 refer to the following flyer.

Save Compton Point!

(A)

(1) Compton Point, home to many animal species that are threatened with extinction, now faces a threat of its own. (2) Developers are attempting to change the zoning in order to build a hotel, a tourist center, and an observation tower. (3) If they succeed in getting the rights to build, construction will begin next August.

(B)

(4) Sam Wanamaker, director of the Society for the Protection of Nature, warns that construction of the development is likely to drive out more than 30 animal species that live on the point. (5) [Select... ▾].

(C)

(6) The Compton Point area is zoned as natural parkland. (7) There are several other areas in the county that are zoned as natural parkland. (8) However, because this project is potentially so lucrative for the city, the zoning board seems to be bending to the will of the developers.

(D)

(9) Developers argue that the new jobs [Select... ▾]. (11) Certainly, everyone in the community agrees that the economy around here could use a lift, but this is not the way to do it.

(E)

(12) Register your opposition to the development of Compton Point! (13) Come to a demonstration at 10 A.M. on [Select... ▾]. (14) Bring signs with slogans that tell how you feel. (15) A strong turnout at this demonstration will send a message to developers.

50. Select... ▾.

   ○ A. Tourism increases both air pollution and litter, which will further reduce the animals' chances for survival.

   ○ B. Air pollution from tourist traffic will further reduce the animals' chances for survival, not to mention litter left behind by floods of tourists.

   ○ C. Air pollution from tourist traffic and also litter from tourists flooding through the area will further reduce the animals' chances for survival.

   ○ D. Tourism will further reduce animals' chances for survival because of air pollution from tourist traffic and floods of litter from tourists.

51. Which revision would improve the effectiveness of paragraph C?

   ○ A. remove sentence 6

   ○ B. move sentence 6 to follow sentence 7

   ○ C. remove sentence 7

   ○ D. move sentence 7 to follow sentence 8

52. Developers argue that the new jobs Select... ▾.

   ○ A. resulting from their development would boost the region's sagging economy, and the influx of tourism would too.

   ○ B. and influx of tourism resulting from their development would boost the region's sagging economy.

   ○ C. resulting from their development would help along the economy of the region. The influx of tourism would too.

   ○ D. and also the influx of tourism, that would result from their development, would cause the region's economy to boost.

53. Come to a demonstration at 10 A.M. on Select... ▾.

   ○ A. Saturday, May 7, in front of the mayor's office 34 wilton road.

   ○ B. saturday, May 7, in front of the mayor's office, 34 Wilton road.

   ○ C. Saturday, may 7, in front of the mayor's office, 34 Wilton road.

   ○ D. Saturday, May 7, in front of the mayor's office, 34 Wilton Road.

End of *Reasoning through Language Arts* Test

Answers and explanations begin on page 704.

MATHEMATICAL REASONING PRACTICE TEST

You may use formulas from this sheet to answer questions on the test.

Area of a:

square	$A = s^2$
rectangle	$A = lw$
parallelogram	$A = bh$
triangle	$A = \frac{1}{2}bh$
trapezoid	$A = \frac{1}{2}h(b_1 + b_2)$
circle	$A = \pi r^2$

Perimeter of a:

square	$P = 4s$
rectangle	$P = 2l + 2w$
triangle	$P = s_1 + s_2 + s_3$
Circumference of a circle	$C = 2\pi r$ OR $C = \pi d$; $\pi \approx 3.14$

Surface area and volume of a:

rectangular/right prism	$SA = ph + 2B$	$V = Bh$
cylinder	$SA = 2\pi rh + 2\pi r^2$	$V = \pi r^2 h$
pyramid	$SA = \frac{1}{2}ps + B$	$V = \frac{1}{3}Bh$
cone	$SA = \pi rs + \pi r^2$	$V = \frac{1}{3}\pi r^2 h$
sphere	$SA = 4\pi r^2$	$V = \frac{4}{3}\pi r^3$

(p = perimeter of base with area B; $\pi \approx 3.14$)

Data

mean	mean is equal to the total of the values of a data set, divided by the number of elements in the data set
median	median is the middle value in an odd number of ordered values of a data set, or the mean of the two middle values in an even number of ordered values in a data set

Algebra

slope of a line	$m = \dfrac{y_2 - y_1}{x_2 - x_1}$
slope-intercept form of the equation of a line	$y = mx + b$
point-slope form of the equation of a line	$y - y_1 = m(x - x_1)$
standard form of a quadratic equation	$y = ax^2 + bx + c$
quadratic formula	$x = \dfrac{-b \pm \sqrt{b^2 - 4ac}}{2a}$
Pythagorean Theorem	$a^2 + b^2 = c^2$
simple interest	$I = Prt$ (I = interest, P = principal, r = rate, t = time)
distance formula	$d = rt$
total cost	total cost = (number of units) × (price per unit)

Directions: Use 20 or fewer minutes to answer the following 5 questions. You may fill in the circles next to the correct answers or write your answers in boxes. Refer to the formula sheet on page 583 as needed. YOU MAY NOT USE YOUR CALCULATOR ON THIS SECTION.

1. Mike borrowed $400 from his brother for six months. He agreed to pay simple interest at the annual rate of 5%. Including interest and principal, how much will Mike have paid his brother at the end of the six months?

   - ○ A. $10
   - ○ B. $120
   - ○ C. $410
   - ○ D. $500

2. What is the value of the expression $3(2x - y) + (3 + x)^2$ when $x = 4$ and $y = 5$?

   - ○ A. 49
   - ○ B. 58
   - ○ C. 61
   - ○ D. 82

3. Which of the following is equal to the expression below?

   $(3x + 2y)(5x - 6y)$

   - ○ A. $8x - 4y$
   - ○ B. $15x^2 - 12y^2$
   - ○ C. $15x^2 + 10xy - 12y^2$
   - ○ D. $15x^2 - 8xy - 12y^2$

4. John needs to replace the boards on a 22-foot section of his fence. He plans to place the boards as shown below.

   If the boards are $5\frac{1}{2}$ inches wide, how many boards should he buy to cover the distance?

   - ○ A. 4
   - ○ B. 12
   - ○ C. 48
   - ○ D. 121

5. What is the value of this expression?

   $$-3 \times 5^2 + 2(4 - 18) + 3^3$$

   Write your answer in the box below.

Directions: Use a maximum of 1 hour and 35 minutes to answer 42 questions. You may fill in the circles next to the correct answers or write your answers in boxes. Refer to the formula sheet on page 583 as needed. YOU MAY USE YOUR CALCULATOR ON THIS SECTION.

6. A storage shelf has room for only two containers on the bottom shelf. The heaviest boxes should be placed on the bottom. Which two boxes should be placed on the bottom shelf? Write the letters of the boxes in the spaces below.

7. Brad's average golf score after six rounds was 81. For the first five rounds his scores were 78, 86, 82, 81, and 82. What was his score on the sixth round?

Write your answer in the box below.

8. A kayaker spends 2 hours paddling up a stream from point A to point B, quickly turns her kayak around, and immediately heads back downstream. It takes her only 1 hour to float back down the stream from point B to point A. If points A and B are 6 miles apart, what was the kayaker's average rate of speed in miles per hour?

○ A. 12 mph
○ B. 6 mph
○ C. 4 mph
○ D. 2 mph

9. In quadrilateral ABCD, side AB is parallel to side CD. Sides AD and BC are not parallel. What is the area of the figure to the nearest square centimeter?

Write your answer in the box below.

10. Simplify the following expression:

$2x^2 - 2xy + 4xy$

- ○ A. $x(x + y)$
- ○ B. $x(x - y)$
- ○ C. $2x(x - y)$
- ○ D. $2x(x + y)$

11. A scientist measures the outside temperature at noon each day over a 3-day period.

Day	Temperature at noon (°F)
Saturday	−1
Sunday	2
Monday	−4

What was the average temperature on these three days? Place an X on the number line below to represent your answer.

12. What is the value of 4^7?

Write your answer in the box below.

13.

	A	B	C
1	−2	−4	1
2	8	4	3
3	5	2	−1

In the computer spreadsheet above, $-[A1 - (C2 - A3) + C2 * B1]$ is equal to which of the following? (*Hint: on a spreadsheet,* *means multiplication*)

- ○ A. −22
- ○ B. −12
- ○ C. 12
- ○ D. 22

14. Simplify the expression:
$(6x^4 + 7x + 5x^3) - (4x^4 - 2x^3 + 3x)$

   ○ A. $10x^4 + 7x^3 + 18x$
   ○ B. $2x^4 + 7x^3 + 4x$
   ○ C. $2x^4 + 7x^3 + 18x$
   ○ D. $10x^4 + 3x^3 + 12x$

15. The perimeter of the trapezoid below is 50. What is its area?

   ○ A. 12
   ○ B. 60
   ○ C. 120
   ○ D. 150

16. Risa wants to order business cards. A printing company determines the cost (C) to the customer using the following function, where $b =$ the number of boxes of cards and $n =$ the number of ink colors.

$$C = \$25.60b + \$14.00b(n - 1)$$

If Risa orders 4 boxes of cards printed in 3 colors, how much will the cards cost?

   ○ A. $214.40
   ○ B. $168.00
   ○ C. $144.40
   ○ D. $102.40

17. The graph of the equation $y = -\frac{3}{4}x + 1$ is a line that passes through points C and D on the coordinate plane. Which of the following points also lies on the graph of the equation?

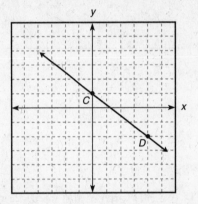

   ○ A. (3, 1)
   ○ B. (8, −5)
   ○ C. (5, 3)
   ○ D. (10, 6)

18. Which of the following equations correctly describes the line on the graph?

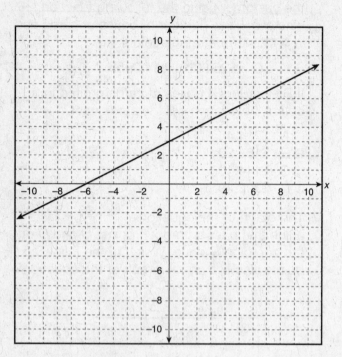

- ○ A. $y = -\frac{1}{2}x - 6$
- ○ B. $y = 2x + 3$
- ○ C. $y = \frac{1}{2}x - 6$
- ○ D. $y = \frac{1}{2}x + 3$

19. What is the 6th term in the sequence below?

1, 3, 7, 15, 31, __ , 127

- ○ A. 62
- ○ B. 63
- ○ C. 68
- ○ D. 77

20. Evening tickets to a play are $24.50 each. Tickets for the afternoon show are $19 each. Janice wants to buy 6 tickets. Arrange terms from the options below to construct the expression Janice would use to determine how much less she would spend if she chooses an afternoon show instead of an evening show. (You do not need to use all of the terms offered as options. Use any term only once.)

+		$19
(		÷
)		$24.50
6		$\frac{1}{2}$
−		

21. In a certain state, the legislature has 100 seats. In 2010, Party X held 54 seats. In the 2012 election, the party gained two seats. If, in the 2014 election, Party X loses 6 seats, but gains 2 seats in the 2016 election, what will the absolute change in the number of seats held by Party X from 2010 to 2016 be?

Write your answer in the box below.

22. What is the surface area of the cylinder below?

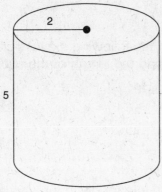

- A. 20π
- B. 28π
- C. 32π
- D. 50π

23. $\dfrac{2x^2 - 6x - 36}{2x - 12} =$
- A. $x - 6$
- B. $x - 3$
- C. $x + 3$
- D. $x^2 + 3x + 18$

24. Customers of Paul's Beauty Supply can make purchases online, from a catalog, or in the store.

About how much more did the company make from catalog sales than from online sales in March?

- A. $35,000
- B. $65,000
- C. $130,000
- D. $195,000

25. Which of the following is a graph of the inequality $-2 \le x < 4$?

A.
   -5 -4 -3 -2 -1 0 1 2 3 4 5

B.
   -5 -4 -3 -2 -1 0 1 2 3 4 5

C.
   -5 -4 -3 -2 -1 0 1 2 3 4 5

D.
   -5 -4 -3 -2 -1 0 1 2 3 4 5

26. At what point does the line with the equation $y = 2x + 3$ intersect with the line with the equation $y = -\frac{1}{2}x - 7$?

○ A. $(-4, -5)$
○ B. $(0, -7)$
○ C. $(0, 3)$
○ D. $(2, 7)$

27. A pole is supported by a cable as shown. The cable is attached to the ground 9 feet from the base of the pole, and it is attached to the pole 12 feet above the ground.

Which of the following expressions could be used to find the length of the cable?

○ A. $9^2 + 12^2$
○ B. $12^2 - 9^2$
○ C. $\sqrt{9^2 + 12^2}$
○ D. $\sqrt{12^2 - 9^2}$

28. Meg is an interior designer who is looking to place two chairs against an accent wall. She has four different chairs from which to choose, each a different color: yellow, red, green, and blue. How many different combinations of chairs can Meg use in her design?

Write your answer in the box below.

29. The Whitmans are trying to pay off their credit card debt, so they developed the following budget based on their monthly take-home pay.

Whitman Family Budget

Other 12%
Housing 27%
Credit Card Debt 24%
Transportation 4%
Clothing 5%
Food 28%

If the Whitmans' monthly take-home pay is $2500, about how much do they plan to pay each month on their credit card debt?

- A. $600
- B. $450
- C. $300
- D. $240

30. A market sells all varieties of pasta at a rate of 4 boxes for $5.00. Jennifer needs 3 boxes of ziti and 3 boxes of spaghetti. At this rate, how much will she spend for the pasta?

Write your answer in the box below.

31. Inge has been finding spiders in her apartment. In order to help her landlord understand the problem, she has kept track of how many spiders she found each week over an eight-week period. This is her record:

Week	Number of spiders found
1st	3
2nd	4
3rd	6
4th	5
5th	4
6th	4
7th	7
8th	2

The line plot below is based on the table Inge created, above. However, it is incomplete. Place additional dots on the line plot until it accurately reflects Inge's records over the eight week period.

Number of Spiders

32. If the area of circle O is 36π, what is its diameter?

   ○ A. 6
   ○ B. 6π
   ○ C. 12
   ○ D. 18

33. In 2011, Karen's base salary was $52,500, and she earned an end-of-year bonus of $6250. In 2012, her base salary was raised to $56,300 and her end-of-year bonus was $4100. What was the percent increase or decrease in her overall earnings from 2011 to 2012?

   Write your answer in the box below. Round your answer to the nearest tenth of a percent.

   | |

34. Imtaez works as a server in a restaurant. On a certain night, he collected $157 in tips and paid y dollars to the food runner who helped him. The amount Imtaez had remaining after paying the runner was equal to ($101 + y).

   Arrange terms from the options below to construct the equation you would use to determine how much Imtaez paid to the food runner. (You may not need to use all of the terms offered as options. Use any term only once.)

=		$+ y$
$101		$157
x		$\div$
$-y$		y^2

35. Place a dot on the coordinate plane below to represent the solution to the following system of equations:

$y = x + 4$

$2y + 4x = 44$

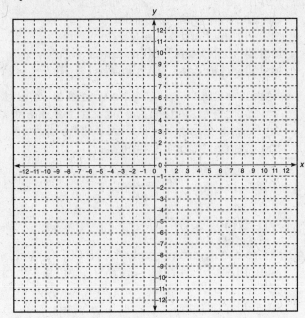

36. A bag contains 12 red, 3 blue, 6 green, and 4 yellow marbles. If a marble is drawn from the bag at random, what is the probability that the marble will be either blue or yellow?

   A. 7%
   B. 12%
   C. 25%
   D. 28%

37. The right cone shown below has a base with a radius of 6.4 cm.

6.4 cm

12 cm

To the nearest cubic centimeter, what is the volume of the cone? (Use 3.14 for π.)

   A.   40
   B.   81
   C. 129
   D. 514

38. Ten artists have entered an art show. There are three prizes to be awarded in the art show: first prize, second prize, and third prize. How many possible ways could those prizes be awarded among the ten artists?

Write your answer in the box below.

39. Archie has made a huge pot of chili. He cannot eat it all himself, so he is going to share some with his neighbors and family. Archie will give 1/4 of the chili to his parents. He will give 1/8 of it to his neighbor Cecilia. He will give another 1/8 of it to his neighbor Chang. How much of the chili will Archie have left over? Place a dot on the number line below to reflect the correct answer.

40. At the end of baseball season, 5% of the children enrolled in a local youth baseball program will be chosen to play in the state tournament. If 12 children will be chosen to play in the tournament, how many children are enrolled in the program?

   ○ A.   60
   ○ B. 120
   ○ C. 240
   ○ D. 600

41. Fabio has his own computer repair business. He uses the following guidelines to estimate how long a project will take.

   Install operating system: 1 hour
   Replace motherboard: $1\frac{1}{2}$ hours
   Reimage hard drive: 2 hours
   Upgrade memory: 20 minutes
   Install new hard drive: 45 minutes
   Install sound card: 30 minutes
   Install video card: 30 minutes

   Fabio needs to install a new hard drive and an operating system for a customer. If Fabio charges $65 per hour, what will he charge the customer for his time?

   ○ A. $94.25
   ○ B. $105.00
   ○ C. $113.75
   ○ D. $146.25

42. There are approximately 1,335,000,000 cubic kilometers of water in Earth's oceans. Which of the following expresses that number in scientific notation?

   ○ A. $1.335 \times 100 \times 100$
   ○ B. 1.335×10^3
   ○ C. 1.335×10^6
   ○ D. 1.335×10^9

43. What is the slope of the line shown below?

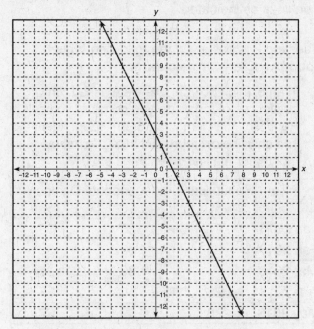

Write your answer in the box below.

44. One number is 12 more than 3 times another number. The sum of the two numbers is −20. What are the numbers?

○ A. 8 and 12
○ B. 8 and −12
○ C. −2 and −18
○ D. −8 and −12

45. Which of the following pairs of numbers is a solution to the equation $3x^2 - 54 = -21x$?

○ A. −6 and 3
○ B. −2 and 9
○ C. −3 and 6
○ D. −9 and 2

46. Match the solutions to the equations.

Equation	Value of the variable
$x - 2 = 9$	
$\frac{a}{10} = 5$	
$3y = -21$	
$14 + m = 6$	

50
−8
−7
11

End of *Mathematical Reasoning* Test

Answers and explanations begin on page 708.

SOCIAL STUDIES PRACTICE TEST

Directions: Use 65 minutes to answer the following 34 questions. You may fill in the circles next to the correct answers or write your answers in boxes or on lines as indicated.

Question 1 is based on the following paragraph and graph.

When the value of exported goods – those sold abroad—is greater than the value of imported goods—those bought from foreign nations—there is a favorable balance of trade. On the other hand, when imports are greater than exports, there is an unfavorable balance of trade.

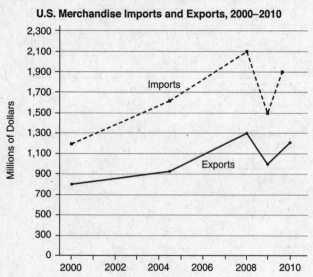

U.S. Merchandise Imports and Exports, 2000–2010

Source: *Statistical Abstract of the United States*

1. Which of the following statements is supported by the paragraph and the graph?

    ○ A. Exports equaled imports at the start of the 2000s.
    ○ B. Exports exceeded imports throughout the 2000s.
    ○ C. The United States had a favorable balance of trade in merchandise during the 2000s.
    ○ D. The United States had an unfavorable balance of trade in merchandise during the 2000s.

Question 2 is based on the following table.
You MAY use your calculator.

2. In an opinion poll, people were asked, "In politics, as of today, do you consider yourself a Republican, a Democrat, or an independent?" The chart below represents the results, by month, for the first six months of 2013.

	Republicans %	Independents %	Democrats %
Jan 2013	27	38	33
Feb 2013	28	38	32
Mar 2013	27	36	35
Apr 2013	26	40	33
May 2013	28	39	32
Jun 2013	26	41	31

Source: Gallup

During the first six months of 2013, what percent of the people surveyed, on average, considered themselves independents? (Assume that the same number of people were surveyed each month.) Round your answer to the nearest percentage and write your answer in the box below.

Questions 3 and 4 are based on the following information and graph.

What standard of living do people in other countries enjoy? There are different ways to answer that question. Many economists hold that one good way is to calculate *gross domestic product* (GDP) *per capita*. GDP per capita is found by adding up the value of all the goods produced and services performed in a given country in a year and then dividing that total (the GDP) by the number of people living in that country.

The map below shows GDP per capita for each country in the world in 2008. Some, but not all, of the countries are labeled with the name of the country.

Map of GDP Per Capita by Country

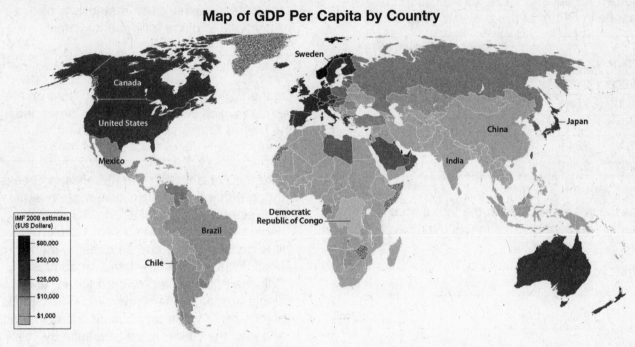

3. In the map above, place a dot on the continent that, in 2008, had the highest percentage of countries with a GDP per capita of less than $10,000 per year.

4. Place the countries below in order from highest GDP per capita to lowest GDP per capita.

Highest	
Second highest	
Third highest	
Lowest	

Democratic Republic of Congo
United States
Mexico
India

Question 5 refers to the following information and chart.

The Consumer Price Index (CPI) is a measure of the average prices paid by consumers for a typical assortment of goods and services, including housing, food, clothing, transportation, recreation, and medical care. A higher CPI indicates that prices have risen. The table below shows the CPI for several years, as well as the percent change in CPI over the previous year.

Year	CPI	Percent change in CPI over previous year
2008	215.3	3.8
2009	214.5	−0.4
2010	218.1	1.6
2011	224.9	3.2
2012	229.6	2.1

Source: Bureau of Labor Statistics

For the years included in the table, what was the median percent change in CPI over the previous year?

Write your answer in the box below.

```

```

6. The 15th Amendment to the Constitution, ratified in 1870, declared that U.S. citizens' right to vote "shall not be denied ... on account of race." However, some states found ways to continue to restrict voting rights for almost a century. For example, Mississippi's 1890 constitution restricted African Americans' voting rights by imposing a poll tax and a literacy test. In the Voting Rights Act of 1965, Congress outlawed such restrictions and put protections in place for minority voters.

1870 1880 1890 1900 1910 1920 1930 1940 1950 1960 1970

On the timeline above, place two dots on the years in which voting rights were expanded in the United States.

7. Like the ancient Chinese, the ancient Greeks thought that a sound political system and well-established social relationships were necessary for a stable society. Greek rule was decentralized, and as a result, many political structures coexisted. In contrast, Chinese rule was largely centralized, and a single political system prevailed. The Greeks placed more value on councils, participation, and law; the Chinese, on bureaucracy, hierarchy, and rules.

Based on the paragraph, what did the ancient Greeks and the ancient Chinese have in common in regard to politics and government?

- A. Both governed through a hierarchical bureaucracy.
- B. Both valued a stable political framework for society.
- C. Both had centralized councils.
- D. Both had decentralized political systems.

Question 8 refers to the following chart.

The Effect of World War II on Industry

Measure	1939	1940	1941
Index of manufacturing output (1939 = 100)	100	116	154
Corporate profits before taxes	$6.4 billion	$9.3 billion	$17 billion
Corporate profits after taxes	$5 billion	$6.5 billion	$9.4 billion

Source: Fute, Gilbert C., and Reese, Jim E. *An Economic History of the United States*

8. Which of the following best explains why the war had the effect on industry indicated by the chart?

   ○ A. Even before the United States entered the war, corporate profits had increased sharply.
   ○ B. Manufacturing output increased by over 50 percent in two years.
   ○ C. The war created a huge demand for military equipment and supplies.
   ○ D. With men gone to serve as soldiers, more women were employed in factories.

9. The U.S. president has a great deal of influence over foreign policy. In part, this is because international relations often require quick and decisive action, which is best undertaken by an individual. In times of foreign crisis, the public usually rallies to the support of the president, at least at first.

   Which of the following values probably underlies Americans' initial approval of a president's emergency foreign policy actions?

   ○ A. patriotism
   ○ B. imperialism
   ○ C. self-expression
   ○ D. self-sacrifice

10. To combat the anticompetitive nature of monopolies or "trusts" such as US Steel, Standard Oil, and the American Tobacco Company, the US Congress passed the Sherman Antitrust Act in 1890. That act made it illegal for an individual to monopolize or conspire to monopolize an industry or to act with others to restrain trade or commerce among the States or abroad. While the Sherman Antitrust Act was, and remains, very influential, it was not sufficient to solve all of the problems raised by monopolies. Because of its broad language and its focus on the intent to create monopolies, courts interpreted the Sherman Antitrust Act differently and inconsistently in the many cases to which it was applied. As a result, Congress passed the Clayton Antitrust Act in 1914, which targeted specific actions—such as favorable price discrimination and exclusive dealings contracts—that were used to create monopolies.

In the passage above, the writer's main point is that

   ○ A. courts struck down the Sherman Antitrust Act because its broad language made it unconstitutional
   ○ B. problems with consistently enforcing the Sherman Antitrust Act led to further legislation to prevent monopolies
   ○ C. monopolies like US Steel, Standard Oil, and the American Tobacco Company successfully avoided prosecution under the Sherman Antitrust Act
   ○ D. the Sherman Antitrust Act ended monopolies like US Steel, Standard Oil, and the American Tobacco Company, but did not prevent new monopolies from arising

11. Since the mid-twentieth century, environmental scientists have been warning the United States about the impact of unchecked carbon emissions into the atmosphere, a threat that many researchers conclude has already led to climate change. Of the many long-term dangers of climate change, which refers to the trend toward greater global temperature extremes, some of the most destructive involve lengthy droughts, diminishing fresh water supplies, and decreased world food production. Although some point to the potential benefits of the temperature changes in particular hemispheres, benefits such as longer growing seasons and more temperate climates for certain populations, the hazards far outweigh any potential advantages. Since the United States has the second highest rate of carbon emissions per person, it must lead the way by dramatically cutting industrial emissions and finding alternate sources of fuel that do not release carbon dioxide as a byproduct. Positive efforts are underway, particularly through the Environmental Protection Agency, which has fostered several international partnerships to limit the production of carbon dioxide, among other greenhouse gases.

Place the letter of each statement within the correct column. You may or may not fill up each column.

The author would agree with this statement:	The author would disagree with this statement:	The author does not address this information:

a. The United States has failed to take any action against carbon emissions.
b. The dangers of climate change are more significant than the possible benefits.
c. Wind energy is preferable to solar energy.
d. Climate change will not impact the world food supply.

Questions 12 through 13 refer to the following map.

Forced Resettlement of American Indians, 1830s

12. Which of the following is the most likely reason that American Indians were forcibly relocated in the 1830s?

    A. Whites wanted lands in the Kansas and Nebraska territory for settlement.
    B. Whites wanted to take over Indian lands in the eastern states.
    C. Indians of different tribes wanted to settle in a single Indian territory.
    D. Indians in the eastern states wanted to look for gold in the West.

13. Which American Indian tribe was moved the farthest from its tribal lands?

    A. the Sauk/Fox
    B. the Cherokee
    C. the Chocktaw
    D. the Seminole

Question 14 refers to the following cartoon.

"I THOUGHT HE WAS A MEMBER OF A SPECIAL INTEREST GROUP...
BUT I FOUND OUT HE'S ONLY A VOTER!"

© 1989 Wayne Stayskal, Tampa Tribune. Reprinted by permission of Wayne Stayskal.

14. With which of the following opinions would the cartoonist be most likely to agree?

- A. People shouldn't have to stand around waiting to see their elected representatives.
- B. Senators should pay attention to special interest groups as well as to voters.
- C. Special interest groups are treated better than voters by members of Congress.
- D. Senators are nicer to their constituents than are members of the House.

15. In the late 1800s, industrialization caused a large-scale migration from rural to urban areas in the United States. Parents who moved to cities with their children left behind the social support of their extended families. In addition, city families found that children, who were an asset on the farm because they could work at an early age, were more of an economic drawback in the city. As a consequence, the birthrate dropped during this period and average family size shrank.

Which of the following is the best summary of this passage?

- A. Industrialization led to increased urbanization in the late 1800s.
- B. City families lost the social support of their extended families back on the farm.
- C. Industrialization and urbanization caused many changes in family life in the late 1800s.
- D. In the late 1800s, average family size shrank due to the fall in the birthrate.

Questions 16 and 17 refer to the following chart.

Acts of Parliament Directed at the American Colonies

Act	Description
Revenue Act of 1764 (Sugar Act)	Imposed duties (tariffs) on foreign sugar and luxuries to raise money for Great Britain
Quartering Act of 1765	Required colonists to provide food and shelter for British soldiers
Stamp Act of 1765	Required colonists to purchase revenue stamps for all important documents, including legal documents, newspapers, and ads
Declaratory Act of 1766	Asserted the right of Parliament to make laws for the colonies
Townshend Acts of 1767	Imposed new duties on the import of tea, glass, and paper

16. How did the Declaratory Act differ from all the other acts of Parliament shown in the chart?

- A. It did not involve the quartering of British soldiers.
- B. It related only to the import of luxury goods.
- C. It did not impose direct economic costs on the colonists.
- D. It was enacted long after the other acts of Parliament.

17. The information in this chart would have been most useful for the writing of which of the following documents?

- A. The Declaration of Independence, which explained why the colonies broke away from Great Britain
- B. The Articles of Confederation, which established a central government consisting of a congress
- C. The U.S. Constitution, which established the structure of government for the newly independent nation
- D. Washington's Farewell Address, in which he warned the new nation of policies and practices he thought unwise

Questions 18 and 19 are based on the following map.

Percentage of Undernourished People Worldwide

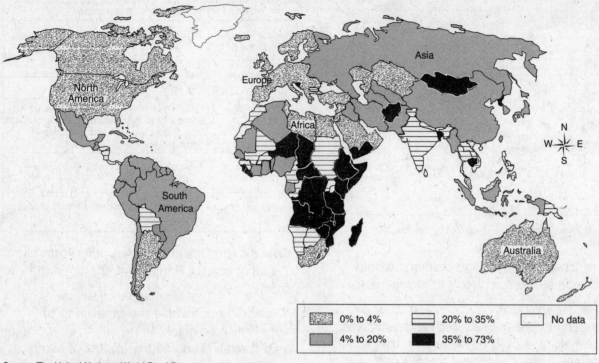

Source: The United Nations, World Food Program.

18. According to the map, what is the percent-age range of people in the United States who do not get enough food and nutrients?

   ○ A. 0% to 4%
   ○ B. 4% to 20%
   ○ C. 20% to 35%
   ○ D. 35% to 73%

19. Which of the following statements is supported by the information on the map?

   ○ A. All areas with more than 35% of the population undernourished are inland nations.
   ○ B. World hunger would disappear if food were distributed more fairly.
   ○ C. There are no areas of hunger in Europe or Australia.
   ○ D. Hunger is a major problem in many countries in Africa.

Questions 20 through 22 refer to the following chart.

Important Political Documents Preceding the Declaration of Independence and the U.S. Constitution

Year	Document	Description
1215	Magna Carta	Limited the power of the English king and granted rights to the nobles
1620	Mayflower Compact	Set rules by which the Pilgrims would govern themselves in Plymouth colony
1628	Petition of Right	Limited the English king's powers further
1636	Great Fundamentals	Established the first basic system of laws in the English colonies, in Massachusetts Bay Colony
1688	English Bill of Rights	Declared that the king rules with the consent of the people's representatives in Parliament; granted ordinary people certain rights

20. What do the Mayflower Compact and the Great Fundamentals have in common?

   ○ A. Both limited the power of the king.
   ○ B. Both granted rights to the nobles.
   ○ C. Both established methods of self-government in English colonies.
   ○ D. Both applied to the government in England.

21. One of the major grievances the American colonists had against the British was that the British taxed the colonists without granting them representation in the British Parliament. Part of the Declaration of Independence is a list of political and economic rights that American colonists complained that the British king had deprived them of.

   By which of the following documents were the writers of the Declaration probably most influenced as they drafted their list?

   ○ A. the Mayflower Compact
   ○ B. the Petition of Right
   ○ C. the Great Fundamentals
   ○ D. the English Bill of Rights

22. Which document first set limits on the British monarch's powers?

   ○ A. the Magna Carta
   ○ B. the Mayflower Compact
   ○ C. the Petition of Right
   ○ D. the English Bill of Rights

23. The civil rights movement of the 1950s and 1960s inspired historians to reinterpret slavery's impact on U.S. society in general and on African Americans in particular. One interpretation that emerged was that slaves and owners were always in conflict and that slavery was destructive. The extent of slavery's destructiveness was debated. Some historians argued that slavery destroyed the culture and self-respect of the slaves and their descendants. Others thought that slaves overcame hardship by developing a unique African American culture that included, among many different things, strong religious and musical traditions.

Based on the paragraph, which of the following statements is an opinion rather than a fact?

   ○ A. The civil rights movement took place during the middle of the twentieth century.
   ○ B. The civil rights movement caused historians to take another look at slavery.
   ○ C. Historians debated slavery's negative effects on slaves and their descendants.
   ○ D. Slavery destroyed the culture of the slaves, diminishing their self-respect.

Questions 24 and 25 refer to the following paragraph and graph.

The market price of a product tends to change in a way that brings supply and demand into balance, a condition called equilibrium. This is illustrated in the graph below, which shows supply and demand for apples.

Supply and Demand for Apples

S = Supply of apples
D = Demand for apples
E = Equilibrium

24. According to this graph, what is the market price of apples—also known as the price at equilibrium?

   ○ A. 45 cents
   ○ B. 30 cents
   ○ C. 20 cents
   ○ D. 15 cents

25. Which of the following would result if part of the apple crop were destroyed but demand remained the same?

   ○ A. Supply would increase.
   ○ B. The market price would remain the same.
   ○ C. The market price would go down.
   ○ D. The market price would go up.

Question 26 refers to the following paragraph and map.

The Battle of Fort Sumter was the first battle of the American Civil War. South Carolina had seceded from the Union and insisted that Union troops in South Carolina leave. A small band of Union soldiers was finally forced to evacuate Fort Sumter, on the South Carolina coast. After that, President Lincoln called for 75,000 volunteers to help put down the rebellion in the south. Following his call, four additional states seceded from the Union and joined the Confederacy. The progress of secession is shown here.

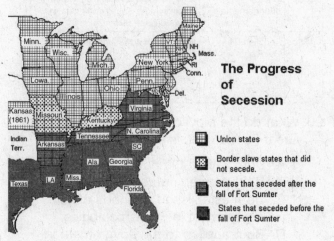

The Progress of Secession

▦ Union states

▨ Border slave states that did not secede.

▧ States that seceded after the fall of Fort Sumter

■ States that seceded before the fall of Fort Sumter

Reprinted from "The South Secedes," U.S. History Online Textbook, ushistory.org.

26. Match each of the following states to the appropriate column(s) in the table. A state may be matched to both columns, or to none at all. You may or may not fill up each column.

Belonged to the Confederacy before the battle of Fort Sumter	Belonged to the Confederacy after the battle of Fort Sumter

Iowa

North Carolina

Delaware

Alabama

Questions 27 through 29 refer to the following paragraph and diagram.

Most cases that arise under federal law are tried in the federal court system. The federal court system has several levels of courts and several routes by which cases may be appealed to a higher court.

Routing Cases Through the Federal Court System

27. A U.S. import-export firm files a lawsuit against a foreign trading company. In which court is the suit most likely to be filed?

  A. the United States Claims Court
  B. the United States Court of Appeals
  C. the Court of International Trade
  D. the United States Tax Court

28. The U.S. Constitution established only the Supreme Court, but it gave Congress the power to create inferior (lower) federal courts.

Which of the following is the most likely reason that Congress established other federal courts?

  A. The justices of the U.S. Supreme Court were not well versed enough in the law to handle all federal cases.
  B. The volume and variety of federal cases were too great for a single court to handle.
  C. A system of inferior federal courts gave the United States prestige in the eyes of the rest of the world.
  D. The Supreme Court's power to interpret the Constitution was established in *Marbury v. Madison.*

29. If cases are not resolved in any of the lower federal courts, to which court may they eventually, finally be appealed?

  A. the Supreme Court of the United States
  B. the United States Courts of Appeals
  C. the Court of Appeals for the Federal Circuit
  D. the Court of Military Appeals

Question 30 refers to the following poster.

The poster below was published during World War I.

Source: Library of Congress. Poster by James Montgomery Flagg

30. Which of the following opinions is the artist attempting to propagate?

○ A. Americans are not yet part of civilization.
○ B. The war effort needs the help of everyone, including men, women and children.
○ C. Every man, woman and child should rest in preparation for the war effort.
○ D. Americans are part of a lazy civilization.

Questions 31 and 32 refer to the following paragraph and maps.

Mapmakers have devised many solutions to the problem of projecting the curved surface of Earth onto a flat piece of paper. However, all map projections involve some distortion, and each type of projection has advantages and disadvantages. Two types of projections are shown here.

Mercator Projection

Interrupted Projection

31. Approximately where is there the least distortion on these projections?

○ A. at 60° north and south latitude
○ B. at 40° north and south latitude
○ C. at 20° north and south latitude
○ D. at 0° latitude

32. A sailor who wanted to plan an around-the-world sailing trip decided to use the interrupted projection. What was wrong with his decision?

○ A. The interrupted projection distorts distances across the continents at midlatitudes.
○ B. The interrupted projection distorts distances across the oceans.
○ C. The interrupted projection distorts the shapes of mid-latitude land masses.
○ D. The interrupted projection shows only a few of the world's oceans.

Question 33 refers to the following paragraph and map.

After the Roman Empire had reached its greatest extent in the 2nd century C.E. emperors consolidated its borders in various ways: where the frontiers were over land, they were seen as vulnerable, and so the emperors often built <u>heavy</u> fortifications, such as forts or walls to defend the borders; where there was a natural barrier like a river or a desert, <u>light</u> fortifications, such as watchtowers, were viewed as adequate; and where there were major barriers, such as the ocean, the emperors concluded that <u>no</u> defense was needed.

Northwestern Frontiers of the Roman Empire, 2nd Century C.E.

- – – Sea frontier
- ···· River frontier
- - - - Land frontier

33. Based on the information in the paragraph above, match the appropriate degree of fortification to each part of the frontier on the map. You may use some labels twice.

| **Heavy** |

| **Light** |

| **None** |

34. Constitutional guarantees of fairness and equality under the law, our basic civil liberties, are called due process of law. The Fifth and Fourteenth Amendments state that government shall not deprive anyone of "life, liberty, or property, without due process of law." The Fifth Amendment protects people from actions of the federal government. The Fourteenth protects people specifically from actions of governments of the individual states.

What is a main difference between the Fifth and Fourteenth Amendments?

- A. The Fifth Amendment applies to adults, and the Fourteenth Amendment, to children.
- B. The Fifth Amendment applies to due process, and the Fourteenth Amendment, to freedom of speech.
- C. The Fifth Amendment applies to the federal government, and the Fourteenth Amendment, to state governments.
- D. The Fifth Amendment applies to life, and the Fourteenth Amendment, to liberty.

Directions: Based on both articles, write a response to the prompt on page 609. This task may take up to 25 minutes to complete.

Passage A

In 1963, a group of civil rights activists began a campaign of sit-ins and other demonstrations in the highly segregated city of Birmingham, Alabama. As part of that campaign, the group broke laws forbidding demonstrations and requiring racial segregation. Dr. Martin Luther King, Jr., one of the leaders of the Birmingham Campaign, was arrested and wrote a famous letter from his jail cell. The passage below is excerpted from that letter.

Excerpted from "Letter from a Birmingham Jail"

You may well ask: "Why direct action? Why sit-ins, marches and so forth? Isn't negotiation a better path?" You are quite right in calling for negotiation. Indeed, this is the very purpose of direct action. . . . I have earnestly opposed violent tension, but there is a type of constructive, nonviolent tension which is necessary for growth. . . .

. . . Perhaps it is easy for those who have never felt the stinging darts of segregation to say, "Wait." But when you have seen vicious mobs lynch your mothers and fathers at will and drown your sisters and brothers at whim; when you have seen hate-filled policemen curse, kick and even kill your black brothers and sisters; when you see the vast majority of your twenty million Negro brothers smothering in an air-tight cage of poverty in the midst of an affluent society; . . . I hope, sirs, you can understand our legitimate and unavoidable impatience.

You express a great deal of anxiety over our willingness to break laws. This is certainly a legitimate concern. Since we so diligently urge people to obey the Supreme Court's decision of 1954 outlawing segregation in the public schools, at first glance it may seem rather paradoxical for us consciously to break laws. One may well ask: "How can you advocate breaking some laws and obeying others?" The answer lies in the fact that there are two types of laws: just and unjust. . . . One has not only a legal but a moral responsibility to obey just laws. Conversely, one has a moral responsibility to disobey unjust laws. I would agree with St. Augustine that "an unjust law is no law at all."

Now, what is the difference between the two? How does one determine whether a law is just or unjust? A just law is a man-made code that squares with the moral law or the law of God. An unjust law is a code that is out of harmony with the moral law. . . . Thus it is that I can urge men to obey the 1954 decision of the Supreme Court, for it is morally right; and I can urge them to disobey segregation ordinances, for they are morally wrong.

. . . Let me give another explanation. A law is unjust if it is inflicted on a minority that, as a result of being denied the right to vote, had no part in enacting or devising the law. Who can say that the legislature of Alabama which set up that state's segregation laws was democratically elected? Throughout Alabama all sorts of devious methods are used to prevent Negroes from becoming registered voters, and there are some counties in which, even though Negroes constitute a majority of the population, not a single Negro is registered. Can any law enacted under such circumstances be considered democratically structured?

—Martin Luther King, Jr., "Letter from a Birmingham Jail"

In 1872, Susan B. Anthony broke the law by voting in a federal election. At that time, women were not permitted by law to vote. She was arrested, convicted, and ordered to pay a fine, which she never paid. The passage below is an excerpt from a public speech Anthony gave around the time of her trial.

Excerpted from "Is It a Crime for a Citizen of the United States to Vote?"

I stand before you to-night, [accused of] the alleged crime of having voted at the last Presidential election, without having a lawful right to vote. It shall be my work this evening to prove to you that in thus voting, I not only committed no crime, but, instead, simply exercised my citizen's right, guaranteed to me and all United States citizens by the National Constitution, beyond the power of any State to deny. . . .

[The Declaration of Independence says:] "All men are created equal, and endowed by their Creator with certain unalienable rights. Among these are life, liberty and the pursuit of happiness. That to secure these, governments are instituted among men, deriving their just powers from the consent of the governed."

. . . And here, in this very first paragraph of the declaration, is the assertion of the natural right of all to the ballot; for, how can "the consent of the governed" be given, if the right to vote be denied. . . .

. . . One-half of the people of this nation to-day are utterly powerless to [erase] from the statute books an unjust law, or to write there a new and a just one. The women, dissatisfied as they are with this form of government, that enforces taxation without representation, that compels them to obey laws to which they have never given their consent, that imprisons and hangs them without a trial by a jury of their peers, that robs them, in marriage, of the custody of their own persons, wages and children, are this half of the people left wholly at the mercy of the other half. . . .

[The Fourteenth Amendment to the Constitution says:] "No states shall make or enforce any law which shall abridge the privileges or immunities of citizens; nor shall any state deprive any person of life, liberty or property, without due process of law, nor deny to any person within its jurisdiction the equal protection of the laws."

. . . [W]omen are citizens, and no state has a right to make any new law, or to enforce any old law, that shall abridge their privileges or immunities. Hence, every discrimination against women in the constitutions and laws of the several states, is to-day null and void [that is, invalid], precisely as is every one against negroes.

—Susan B. Anthony, "Is It a Crime for a Citizen of the United States to Vote?"

Write an Extended Response to Both Passages

Both Dr. Martin Luther King, Jr., and Susan B. Anthony were arrested for breaking the law. The passages describe their reactions to being arrested and their attitudes toward the law.

Write an essay in which you compare and contrast King's and Anthony's responses to their arrests. What ideas did they seem to have in common? In what ways did their explanations of their actions differ? Use specific and relevant details from both passages in your essay.

Type your response on a computer, if one is available. If one is not, write your response neatly on paper. This task may require 25 minutes to complete.

Use the *Social Studies Extended Response Evaluation Guide* on page 723 to evaluate your response.

End of *Social Studies* Test

Answers and explanations begin on page 712.

SCIENCE PRACTICE TEST

Directions: Use 35 minutes to answer the following 16 questions. You may fill in the circles next to the correct answers or write your answers in boxes or on lines as indicated.

<u>Question 1</u> refers to the following paragraph and diagram.

Newton's third law of motion states that when one object exerts a force upon another object, the second object exerts an equal force on the first, in the opposite direction. An airplane in motion changes the speed and direction of the air, exerting a force on it. The opposing force of the air keeps the airplane aloft.

How an Airplane Flies

1. What vertical force holds the airplane up?

   ○ A. lift
   ○ B. Newton's third law
   ○ C. weight
   ○ D. air resistance

2. Sleep may have evolved in humans for several reasons. First, people were unable to hunt, gather food, or travel in the dark. Second, sleep provides an opportunity to repair our body's cells, especially those in the brain. Third, our body temperature is lower during sleep, which conserves energy. Fourth, during deep sleep the pituitary gland releases a growth hormone, so sleep may play a role in growth.

   Which of the following is the best title for this paragraph?

   ○ A. "Sleep and Growth"
   ○ B. "Our Brains During Sleep"
   ○ C. "Why We Sleep"
   ○ D. "The Role of Deep Sleep"

3. You MAY use your calculator on this question.

   A scientist shines a laser through six beakers, each containing a different liquid substance, and measures the laser beam's angle of refraction. The scientist records her measurements for liquids A–E in the table below; her measurement for liquid F is lost.

Liquid	Angle of Refraction (degrees)
A	15
B	32
C	12
D	47
E	15
F	?

   However, the scientist recalls that the mean of all six angle measurements was 23 degrees. What must the laser beam's angle of refraction through liquid F have been?

   Write your answer in the box below.

Questions 4 through 6 are based on the following information and graphic.

The processes that circulate nitrogen between the atmosphere, land, and organisms are called the nitrogen cycle.

The Nitrogen Cycle

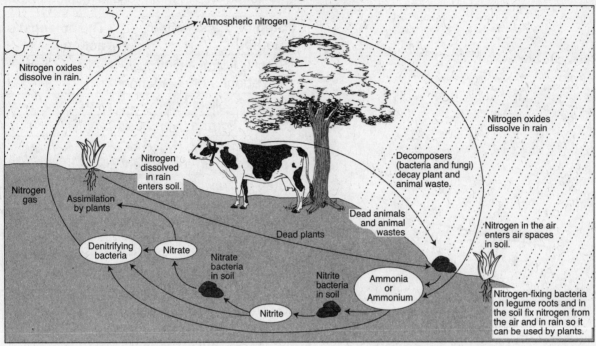

4. Nitrogen-fixing bacteria are found both in the soil and on the roots of legumes like peas and beans. From where do these bacteria get nitrogen?

   ○ A. ammonia and ammonium
   ○ B. the air and rainwater in the soil
   ○ C. animals and animal wastes
   ○ D. animal wastes and decaying plants

5. Which of the following statements is a conclusion about the nitrogen cycle rather than a detail in the diagram?

   ○ A. Nitrogen oxides dissolve in rainwater.
   ○ B. Nitrogen-fixing bacteria are found both in the soil and on the roots of legumes.
   ○ C. The recycling of nitrogen through the biosphere involves many complex processes.
   ○ D. Nitrite bacteria turn ammonia and ammonium into nitrites.

6. To increase the nitrogen content of the soil, many farmers spread synthetic fertilizers containing nitrogen compounds. What might an organic farmer, who does not use synthetic fertilizers, do to improve the fertility of the soil?

   ○ A. switch to crops requiring more potassium
   ○ B. compost with plant and animal wastes
   ○ C. plant more nonleguminous plants
   ○ D. switch to crops requiring more nitrogen

Question 7 refers to the following graph.

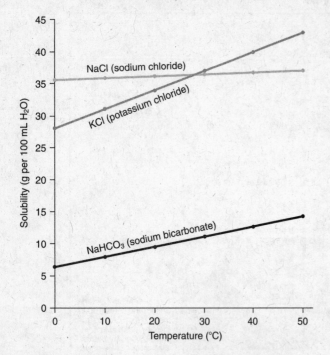

Solubility of Common Compounds in Grams of Solute per 100 mL of Water

7. Which of the following statements is supported by the information in the graph?

○ A. About 15 grams of sodium bicarbonate will dissolve in 100 mL of water at 10°C.

○ B. About 30 grams of potassium chloride will dissolve in 100 mL of water at 30°C.

○ C. Sodium chloride shows the greatest increase in solubility with increase in temperature.

○ D. For the three compounds shown, solubility increases as temperature increases.

8. Directions: Following the scientific method, a researcher conducted an experiment using houseplants. Match each action the scientist took to the step in the scientific method below.

Step of the scientific method	The scientist's action
Step 1. Formulate a question about a phenomenon	
Step 2. Collect data	
Step 3. Form a hypothesis	
Step 4. Test the hypothesis through an experiment	
Step 5. Draw a conclusion	

a. For 6 weeks, the scientist used water at 75 degrees to water plants in Group A and used water at 55 degrees to water plants in Group B. He recorded their growth during this period.

b. The scientist wondered whether water at different temperatures might affect houseplants differently.

c. The scientist researched the growth rate of plants at various greenhouses, some of which use cool water and some of which use warm water to water their plants.

d. At the end of 6 weeks, the plants in Group A were, on average, 2" taller than plants in Group B. The scientist interpreted this to mean that warm water is better for plants than cool water.

e. The scientist guessed that warm water might be better for plants than cool water.

9. Atoms are composed of protons (positive charge), neutrons (no charge), and electrons (negative charge). Because an atom has an equal number of protons and electrons, it has a total charge of zero.

What would happen if an atom lost an electron?

○ A. Its charge would become positive.
○ B. Its charge would become negative.
○ C. Its charge would remain neutral.
○ D. Its neutrons would gain a positive charge.

10. Weathering is the breaking down of rock by rain, frost, wind, and other elements. No transport is involved in weathering. The weathered rock remains in place. Weathering can be physical, involving abrasion—the wearing away of a surface—or changes in temperature; it can be chemical, involving chemical reactions; or it can be organic, involving the action of living things.

Which of the following is an example of physical weathering?

○ A. the cracking of granite from the expansion of freezing water
○ B. the breakdown of calcite by reaction with acids in fertilizer
○ C. the transport of sand by the wind
○ D. the breakdown of crumbling rock in the soil by burrowing worms

11. When removed from the body, large organs live only a few hours or days under cold conditions. Therefore, organ transplants must be performed quickly. Many organs go to waste because the organ cannot be transported to an appropriate patient in the short time available. Unfortunately, it is not yet possible to freeze large organs to preserve them for a longer period. That's because they contain many different types of cells, all of which react differently to freezing. Some cells are even destroyed by the ice crystals that form during freezing.

Which of the following studies is most likely to yield information that might help solve the specific problem of freezing whole organs for transplant?

○ A. how the time it takes to locate patients who need organs can be decreased
○ B. how the time it takes to transport organs to their destinations can be decreased
○ C. how special fluids keep insects alive during subfreezing weather
○ D. how radioactive isotopes can be used to diagnose the condition of donated organs

12. Most animals have bodies that exhibit either bilateral symmetry or radial symmetry. If you drew a straight line down the middle of an animal exhibiting bilateral symmetry, the two sides would be mirror images of one another. Such animals have a front end and a rear end. On the other hand, an animal exhibiting radial symmetry has a body consisting of similar parts arranged around a center.

Circle the image of the animal(s) below displaying a radially symmetrical body plan.

A. salt marsh greenhead fly

B. sea star

C. dogfish   D. horseshoe crab

13. Hydrogen peroxide molecules are composed of two hydrogen atoms and two oxygen atoms. Water is also composed of hydrogen and oxygen, but water has one fewer oxygen atom than hydrogen peroxide does. Which of the following statements best describes the chemical reaction shown in the equation below?

$$2H_2O_2 \rightarrow 2H_2O + O_2$$

○ A. Hydrogen peroxide is being made out of water and air.
○ B. Hydrogen peroxide is decomposing into pure water.
○ C. Hydrogen peroxide is decomposing into water and oxygen.
○ D. Water and oxygen are combining to make hydrogen peroxide.

Question 14 refers to the following chart.

Melting and Boiling Points

Element	Melting Point, F	Boiling Point, F
Mercury	−38	675
Bromine	19	138
Iron	2,795	5,184
Carbon	6,420	8,720
Gold	1,945	5,379

14. Which of the following statements is supported by the information in the chart?

   A. Mercury and bromine are liquids at room temperature.
   B. Iron has a higher melting point than carbon.
   C. Iron has a higher boiling point than gold.
   D. Mercury, bromine, iron, carbon, and gold are all metals.

15. In 1969, the U.S. Surgeon General announced that infectious bacterial diseases would soon become a thing of the past because antibiotic drugs had become so effective against them. However, since that time, strains of disease-causing bacteria that are resistant to antibiotics have evolved. Some types of pneumonia and gastrointestinal infections are now untreatable by antibiotics. About 17 million people worldwide still die annually from infectious diseases.

Which of the following best explains why the U.S. Surgeon General's prediction was wrong?

   A. Antibiotic drugs are not effective against most disease-causing bacteria.
   B. Infectious diseases are also caused by viruses and parasites.
   C. Infectious diseases have remained a problem outside the United States.
   D. Bacteria quickly evolved resistance to antibiotic drugs.

16. A student did an experiment to see how far a ball would roll on different surfaces. She made five different ramps, each with a different surface: a plain pine board, a painted board, a board covered with sandpaper, a board covered with artificial turf, and a board covered with shag carpet. She set up his experiment on a smooth, level floor. To make the ramps, she raised one end of each board with a book. She collected four copies of the science textbook her class was using and set up four of the ramps with these books. She couldn't find a fifth copy of the book, so she used a thinner science study guide to set up the fifth ramp. She rolled a tennis ball down each ramp and measured how far the ball traveled each time. Then she compiled his data and drew conclusions.

Why was the student's experiment flawed?

   A. The student should have used a ball with a smooth surface rather than a tennis ball.
   B. The student should have used books of the same height for all of the ramps.
   C. The student should not have used sandpaper as one of the surfaces.
   D. For a control, the student should have rolled the ball across a piece of wood that was level.

Directions: Read the article and respond to the writing prompt below. Type your response on a computer, if one is available. If you do not have access to a computer, write your response neatly on paper. This task may require approximately 10 minutes to complete.

1   A local candy company has had great success with its new neon candy bars. The neon candy bars are featured in a range of five bright colors. They were designed to entice children with their visual appeal and have been selling extremely well since their release.

2   Recently, the company has been flooded with complaints that children are experiencing extreme hyperactivity shortly after consuming the neon candy bars. The company's original candy bars have not generated similar complaints. The only differences between the original candy bars and the new neon candy bars are the neon color of the bar, increased sugar content, and a design change on the outside of the packaging.

3   The candy company's development team has been debating what could be causing the hyperactivity. Developer A suggests that the type of food coloring used in the neon candy bars is causing the hyperactivity and a new type of food coloring should be explored. This claim has a basis in a study conducted a few years earlier that showed a competitor's candy bar increasing hyperactivity when the same food coloring was used.

4   Developer B doesn't believe that the food coloring responsible. She suggests that the increased sugar content of the neon candy bars is to blame for the hyperactivity the children are experiencing. While there is little scientific evidence linking sugar to hyperactivity, many parents of hyperactive children claim that sugar makes their children's behavior problems worse.

5   Developer C believes it is the new ink used on the packaging. On some items, the ink can leak through the thin wrapper and affect the product. The new design incorporates neon colors, and the ink used to produce those colors is made of harsher chemicals than were previously used.

Write a Short Answer Response

As part of an experiment conducted by the candy company, a group of children is given a new candy bar formulated with less sugar than the neon candy bars. This group of children experiences extreme hyperactivity. What could be causing the hyperactivity? Using information from the passage, suggest a hypothesis in answer to this question. Cite specific information from the passage as support for why your suggestion is plausible.

Directions: Use 35 minutes to answer the following 16 questions. You may fill in the circles next to the correct answers or write your answers in boxes or on lines as indicated.

Question 17 refers to the following paragraph and diagram.

Herbivores are animals that eat only plants; carnivores are animals that eat animals. Typical herbivore and carnivore teeth patterns are shown below.

Typical Teeth Patterns in Carnivores and Herbivores

Carnivore (dog)

Incisors

Canines

Premolars

Molars

Herbivore (sheep)

Incisors

Premolars

Molars

17. What is the most notable difference between the dog's teeth and the sheep's teeth?

○ A. The dog has fewer teeth than the sheep does.

○ B. The dog has molars and the sheep does not.

○ C. The dog has incisors and the sheep does not.

○ D. The dog has canines and the sheep does not.

Question 18 refers to the following chart.

The Five Largest Asteroids

Name	Average distance from sun (Earth = 1)	Time to orbit sun
Ceres	2.77	4.6 years
Pallas	2.77	4.6 years
Vesta	2.36	3.6 years
Hygeia	3.13	5.5 years
Interamnia	3.06	5.4 years

18. Which of the following statements is supported by the information in the chart?

○ A. Pallas is further away from the sun than Hygeia is.

○ B. Of the five largest asteroids, Vesta has the longest orbital period.

○ C. The five largest asteroids are all farther from the sun than Earth is.

○ D. Of the five largest asteroids, only Interamnia takes more than five years to orbit the sun.

19. The American lobster, *Homerus americanus,* is typically bluish-green to brown in coloration. However, a rare genetic mutation, estimated to occur in 1 in 2 million lobsters, can result in a bright blue-colored shell. In 2011, 220 million pounds of lobsters, typically weighing 1–9 pounds each, were caught; two blue lobsters were reported in that time.

In 2011, the experimental probability of catching a blue lobster was [Select...▾] the estimated probability of a lobster having the blue mutation.

- greater than
- approximately the same as
- less than

Question 20 is based on the following diagram.

Structure of a Volcano

Lava plug

Pressure forces magma up the main vent and branch pipes

Cone of lava and ash layers

Hot magma collects in the magma chamber underground

20. Based on the diagram, what causes a volcano to erupt?

○ A. Pressure builds up inside the magma chamber and vent.

○ B. Magma flows down toward the underground chamber.

○ C. The lava plug at the top of the main vent wears away.

○ D. The lava plug at the top of the main vent collapses inward.

21. In a chemical reaction, the atoms of the reactants are rearranged to form products with different chemical and physical properties. A catalyst is a substance that speeds the rate at which a chemical reaction takes place. The catalyst itself is unchanged at the end of the reaction. In which of the following reactions is a catalyst at work?

○ A. when an acid is neutralized, as when hydrochloric acid is added to sodium hydroxide yielding sodium chloride and water

○ B. when food is digested, as when an enzyme in saliva called ptyalin breaks down starch into sugars without itself changing

○ C. when copper is oxidized by combining with nitric acid to yield copper nitrate, nitrogen dioxide, and water

○ D. when baking soda is heated, causing the sodium bicarbonate to break down, yielding carbon dioxide gas as a byproduct

22. For five years, researchers at the University of Wisconsin Medical School ran an experiment in which they evaluated the hearing of 3,753 people between the ages of 48 and 92. Of the group, 46 percent were nonsmokers, 30.3 percent were former smokers, and 14.7 percent still smoked. The scientists found that smokers were nearly 1.7 times as likely as nonsmokers to suffer hearing loss. The study suggests that age-related hearing loss might be preventable.

Which of the following statements is most likely to have been the researchers' hypothesis?

○ A. Smoking has been shown to harm health in many different ways.

○ B. People can reduce their chances of developing age-related hearing loss by not smoking.

○ C. The University of Wisconsin study group consisted of 3,753 people between the ages of 48 and 92.

○ D. Smokers were nearly 1.7 times as likely as nonsmokers to suffer hearing loss.

Question 23 refers to the following graphs.

Elements in Humans and Bacteria

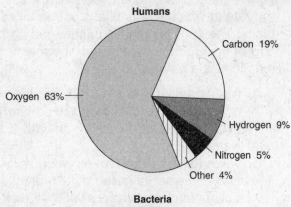

Question 24 refers to the following diagrams.

24. What do the wheel and axle and the screw have in common?

○ A. Both increase the effort needed to move a load.

○ B. Both involve effort applied with circular motion.

○ C. Both involve effort applied with horizontal motion.

○ D. Both involve effort applied with vertical motion.

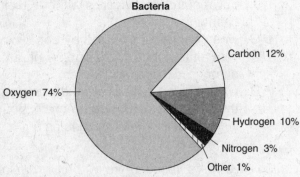

23. What is one of the main differences between the composition of humans and that of bacteria?

○ A. Humans contain elements other than oxygen, carbon, nitrogen, and hydrogen and bacteria do not.

○ B. Humans contain a higher percentage of oxygen than bacteria do.

○ C. Humans contain a higher percentage of hydrogen than bacteria do.

○ D. Humans contain a higher percentage of carbon than bacteria do.

25. During various periods in Earth's history, average global temperatures have dropped, resulting in ice ages. During an ice age, glaciers cover large regions of Earth. Scientists disagree about what causes ice ages. One hypothesis suggests that there have been long term changes in Earth's orbit, causing the planet to periodically move farther from the sun. Another view proposes that a periodic increase in volcanic activity increases the dust in the atmosphere, blocking the sun's rays. Still another hypothesis suggests that changes in Earth's own radiant energy cause ice ages. And finally, other scientists propose that changes in the direction of ocean currents cause ice ages.

Which of the following statements is a fact and NOT an opinion or hypothesis?

○ A. During an ice age, temperatures drop and ice covers vast areas of Earth.

○ B. Changes in Earth's orbit cause temperature fluctuations and ice ages.

○ C. Large amounts of volcanic dust blocking the sun's energy cause ice ages.

○ D. Changes in Earth's own radiant energy cause ice ages.

Question 26 refers to the following diagram.

Ether (C₂H₆O)

```
     H        H
     |        |
H  — C  — O — C  — H
     |        |
     H        H
```

Key

C = Carbon

H = Hydrogen

O = Oxygen

Ethanol (C₂H₅OH)

```
   H   H
   |   |
H — C — C — OH
   |   |
   H   H
```

26. What is the main difference between the hydrocarbons ether and ethanol?

A. Ether has carbon, hydrogen, and oxygen atoms, and ethanol has only carbon and hydrogen atoms.

B. Ether has three carbon atoms and ethanol has two carbon atoms.

C. Ether has one oxygen atom and ethanol has two oxygen atoms.

D. The arrangement of the carbon, hydrogen, and oxygen atoms in the two hydrocarbons is different.

27. In 1861, Charles Darwin, a naturalist who formulated the theory of evolution, remarked that the science of geology had made much progress in his lifetime. He wrote, "About thirty years ago there was much talk that geologists ought only to observe and not theorize; and I well remember someone saying that at this rate a man might as well go into a gravel-pit and count the pebbles and describe the colors. How odd it is that anyone should not see that all observation must be for or against some view if it is to be of any service!"

Which of the following statements best summarizes Darwin's view of the role of observation in science?

A. Observation is the best way to gather facts about any aspect of nature.

B. Observation is useful as long as it is supported by statistics.

C. Observation should be used only in the field of geology.

D. Observation is useful as long as the results are used to support or disprove a hypothesis.

28. Directions: Match each process to an example of that process.

The four types of processes that create minerals in Earth's crust are called *magmatic, hydrothermal, metamorphic*, and *surficial*. Magmatic processes involve the heating and cooling of magma deep inside the Earth's mantle to form crystals. Hydrothermal processes are caused by the movement of water within Earth's crust. Metamorphic processes involve combinations of heat, pressure, time, water, and various solutions to change existing mineral deposits and form new ones. Surficial processes are physical processes that affect rock at Earth's surface or in the loose material—soil and dust—that covers Earth's crust.

Type of process	Example of process
Magmatic	
Hydrothermal	
Metamorphic	
Surficial	

a. Wind eroding away the softer components in sandstone
b. A gradual increase in temperature in the mantle, followed by a sudden drop in temperature
c. Movement of seawater through fractured rock underground
d. Fault lines fracturing rock into particles underground and then those particles undergoing great heat and pressure

Question 29 refers to the following graph.

Rainfall in 5 Cities in California, 2008–2010

	2008–2009 Rain (in.)	2009–2010 Rain (in.)
Crescent City	49.35	62.77
Eureka	29.75	44.51
Ukiah	22.68	40.52
Redding	23.71	30.45
Sacramento	16.33	20.74

Source: Golden Gate Weather Services

29. Which city had the median increase in rainfall between the two time periods displayed in the table? Write your answer in the box below.

30. Brock's physics teacher has assigned everyone in his class the task of conducting an experiment. To write up their experiments, everyone must use the outline provided below.

Match each summary of the steps in Brock's experiment to the appropriate category in the experiment outline.

Experiment outline	Brock's steps
Step 1. Formulate a question about a phenomenon	
Step 2. Collect data	
Step 3. Form a hypothesis	
Step 4. Test the hypothesis through an experiment	
Step 5. Draw a conclusion	

a. Brock placed wooden cubes that were 1 cc, 10 cc, and 100 cc in water. He observed their buoyancy. Then he placed iron cubes of 1 cc, 10 cc, and 100 cc in water and observed their buoyancy.
b. Brock noted that ice floats in water, whether it is a small ice cube or a huge iceberg.
c. Brock said: "Since all wooden cubes float and all iron cubes sink, size does not affect the buoyancy of an object in water."
d. Brock asked, "Does size affect the buoyancy of an object in water?"
e. Brock thought: "For an object made of a given material, increasing the size of the object won't affect its buoyancy in water."

31. In 1993, after years of fluctuating water levels in their reservoir, the residents of Weyland County built a dam at one end of the reservoir to regulate and stabilize the water levels. Circle the X on the graph below that most likely represents 1993.

32. One property of a gas is that its molecules spread out to fill their container. Which of the following best illustrates this property of gases?

    ○ A. A teacher's perfume can be detected at the back of the classroom.
    ○ B. Rain puddles evaporate more quickly when the sun comes out.
    ○ C. Water is produced when hydrogen gas is burned in oxygen gas.
    ○ D. Liquid oxygen is denser than gaseous oxygen.

Directions Read the article and respond to the writing prompt below. Type your response on a computer, if one is available. If you do not have access to a computer, write your response neatly on paper. This task may require approximately 10 minutes to complete.

Plants grow faster when humans talk to them, but it is not clear why. Some scientists have hypothesized that it is the actual air involved that makes the difference. When we speak, we exhale carbon dioxide. Increased levels of carbon dioxide improve a plant's ability to grow, so this may explain why talking helps plants. Others have hypothesized that the benefit to plants comes from the content of what is being said. They hypothesize that it is the words themselves and their positive meaning that increase a plant's growing ability.

Write a Short Answer Response

Describe an experiment that could be used to test the two hypotheses described above.

End of the *Science Test*

Answers and explanations begin on page 715.

GED®
Answers and Explanations

GED® PRETEST ANSWERS AND EXPLANATIONS
REASONING THROUGH LANGUAGE ARTS

Part I: Reading, page 2

1. **B. There are advantages to being sensitive and introverted.** The main idea of a passage is the idea that is most important to the author. The author wrote this passage to convey the idea that being introverted can be beneficial. Choices (C) and (D) both contain ideas the author expresses, but neither of those are the main idea of the entire passage. Choice (A) might be a reasonable inference based on the fourth paragraph, but it is not the author's main point.

2. **A. empathetic** The third passage states that children with sensitive temperaments "are more likely than their peers to be described by parents and caregivers as empathetic or conscientious." Choice (B) is contradicted by the author's statements that sensitive children tend to grow up to be introverts, and that introverts are less likely than others "to take dangerous risks." The author says explicitly that sensitive children "are not antisocial," so choice (C) is incorrect. Choice (D) is not supported by the passage.

3. **C. a successful collaboration between an introvert and an extrovert** The author mentions the partnership between Jobs and Wozniak in order to support her point that "[m]any successful ventures are the result of effective partnerships between introverts and extroverts."

4. **C. Children who are perceived as "shy" are actually more sensitive than other children to stimuli in their environments.** The author's purpose in the second paragraph is to help her readers understand the temperaments of the so-called "shy" children introduced in the first paragraph.

5. **A. enjoying a quiet dinner with a handful of friends** The author explains that introverts are not antisocial, so an introvert will not necessarily prefer to be alone.

However, introverts are more sensitive to stimuli in their environment, so an introvert would not be likely to prefer (B) loud dance music or (C) a crowded street festival. Moreover, the author says that introverts are "less likely to take dangerous risks," and you can infer that (D) "ice slope surfing" is a dangerous sport.

6. **B. The driver may have some difficulty in controlling the forklift.** Paragraphs one and two discuss rear-wheel steering in forklifts. According to the second paragraph, rear-wheel steering is the reason why forklifts are not as responsive as cars and can be difficult to control.

7. **A. driving a forklift and driving a car** The first and second paragraphs discuss the differences between driving a car and driving a forklift.

8. **D. A forklift that is traveling downhill with a heavy load should travel backward.** The third paragraph explains that, when driving a forklift with a load on an incline, "you must keep the load on the uphill side." The graphic reinforces this by showing a forklift with the load on the uphill side. The arrow above the graphic points in two directions, and this suggests that the forklift should keep its load on the uphill side and travel backwards when going downhill.

9. **C. to explain safe practices to forklift drivers** The author is primarily concerned with helping drivers of forklifts understand and use safe practices. The author's primary focus is on safety, not on convincing people that forklifts are dangerous, as choice (B) suggests, or describing different kinds of forklift drivers, as choice (D) suggests. The differences between driving a car and driving a forklift, mentioned in choice (A), are discussed in the passage. However, the author's purpose in discussing those

differences is to help forklift drivers understand how to operate forklifts safely.

10. **A. The author lists potential dangers inherent in forklift driving and explains how to avoid them.** Each paragraph discusses a different potential danger of forklift driving: first paragraph: the forklift's wide swing when turning; second paragraph: the difficulty of controlling a forklift; third paragraph: the dangers of driving on an incline with the load facing downhill; fourth paragraph: large loads that obstruct the driver's view. Each paragraph also discusses how best to deal with those dangers.

11. **B. suggest that GMO foods can be beneficial to struggling farmers.** This detail supports the overall purpose of the passage—to highlight the benefits of GMO foods for world food production. The fact that "small, resource-poor farmers" would choose to produce GMO crops implies that these are more reliable and potentially more lucrative than natural crops.

12. **D. the safety and reliability of GMO foods** Passage 2 primarily discusses how GMO foods can pose a threat to human health and how GMO crops can be especially susceptible to massive failures.

13. **B. The labels of some foods containing GMO ingredients do not indicate that the products contain genetically-modified components.** The last sentence of the first paragraph states that the American Academy of Environmental Medicine called for "the labeling of all food items containing genetically-modified products." Therefore, at least some GMO foods do not yet have this labeling.

14. **C. GMO foods are largely a positive development for global food production** The authors of the two passages disagree primarily about whether

GMO foods are beneficial or dangerous.

15. **C. Paragraph 4** In Passage 1, paragraph 4 details how GMO corn crops survived a devastating drought that natural corn crops would not have been able to withstand. This addresses the issue of reliability raised by the example of the South African corn in Passage 2.

16. **C. a young horse** The context clues in the passage indicate that the speaker is actually a horse. In paragraph 2, we learn that the speaker's mother "whinnied," and in paragraph 4, she is specifically referred to as a horse. In paragraph 5, the speaker mentions that he and his mother are the master's favorites among all of the horses.

17. **D. a farm** The description of the setting in paragraph 1 indicates that the story takes place in a rural location. In paragraph 6, the speaker's reference to an event that occurred in his "field" also supports this setting.

18. **B. contented** The overall tone of the speaker's account is positive. The passage describes the pleasant setting of his childhood, the respect he had for his mother, and the kind treatment he received from his master. Even the one negative memory, the occasional teasing by the plowboy, serves to show how the speaker was cared for by his master.

19. **A. affectionate and protective** Paragraph 5 describes the master's gentle way of treating his horses. Paragraph 7 recounts how the master punished the young boy who was harming the horses.

20. **A. correct the speaker for playing too roughly** The mother's speech is introduced in paragraph 2 after the phrase "when there was a good deal of kicking." Toward he end of the speech in paragraph 3, the mother implores the speaker to

"grow up gentle and good" and "never to bite or kick even in play."

Part II: Writing and Language Skills, page 10

1. **D. your child's class has been** The third-person singular subject student requires the verb form has.

2. **C. symptoms, such as** Choice (C) correctly joins the list of symptoms to the main clause. Choice (A) creates a sentence fragment. Choices (B) and (D) create two independent clauses without joining them with conjunctions.

3. **B. develops any of these symptoms, take him or her to the doctor** The verb should be in the present tense because the action is occurring in the present. Moreover, the present tense is consistent with the majority of verbs in the passage. Also, because "child" is singular, the plural pronoun "them" is incorrect.

4. **C. sentence 5** Sentences 1–4 explain basic facts about strep throat. Sentences 5–10 explain what parents should do if their child has strep throat.

5. **A. In addition, antibiotics may** Generally, an introductory phrase is followed by a comma.

6. **A. After the fever is gone and your child has taken** Combining the detail about taking medicine and the detail about the fever into an introductory subordinate clause results in a smooth, effective sentence.

7. **C. bet on a football game or buy a lottery ticket** No comma is needed between two verbs in a compound predicate (*bet on a football game or buy a lottery ticket*).

8. **C. threatens** The action is always true, so the present tense is correct. Moreover, the present tense is consistent with the majority of verbs in the passage.

9. **D. Compulsive gamblers display a number of consistent traits.**

This is the only topic sentence that sums up the main point and is neither too specific nor too general.

10. **A. it. Losing** Choice (A), which forms two complete sentences, is the only choice given that avoids errors. Choice (B) joins two independent clauses but omits the necessary comma. Choice (C) creates a comma splice. Choice (D) is incorrect because a comma must precede *and* in a compound sentence.

11. **A. commit fraud, forgery, or theft** Commas are required between items in a series.

12. **A. depressed, or they** A comma should precede a coordinating conjunction that joins independent clauses.

13. **B. People often make impulse buys at pet stores** This term *pet stores* should not be capitalized, because it is not the name of a store; it is just a type of store. That eliminates choices (A) and (C). Choice (D) is needlessly wordy.

14. **D. when the owners find they can't care for them** The antecedent *owners* is plural, so *they* is the correct pronoun to use. Choice (B) is incorrect because of its awkward construction.

15. **A. There are several factors to consider** The verb agrees with the subject, "several factors," which is plural. Choice (D) is incorrect because it suggests that the factors are doing the considering.

16. **C. be housebroken and trained** Only choice (C) has both verbs in parallel structure and creates a correct sentence.

17. **D. remove sentence 10** The sentence about exercise and people is not relevant to pets, the topic of the article.

18. **D. if the animal is unhealthy** The statement is always true, so the present tense is correct. Moreover, the present tense is consistent with the majority of verbs in the passage.

Part III: Extended Response, page 16

Your responses to questions 1 through 5 may vary but should be similar to the following:

1. identity theft

2. explain how people can become vulnerable to identity theft

3. specific information from the reading selection

4. to explain something

5. There are several things you can do to protect yourself from identity theft.

Your responses to questions 6 and 7 may vary. Sample responses are below.

6. People might become vulnerable to identity theft if they are careless about papers, information access, or online activities.

7. (1) Identity thieves might go through a person's garbage looking for financial papers. (2) You shouldn't have checks sent to your mailbox unless your mailbox locks. (3) You should update your anti-spyware software to protect yourself from identity theft.

8. **Planning Checklist** Check off each task that you performed. Give yourself a score of 0–3 based on how many checks you made.

_____ I wrote a central idea (thesis statement) for my response.

_____ I made a plan for what I wrote.

_____ In my plan, I related each point to a piece of evidence or information in the text.

9. **Drafting Checklist** Check off each task that you performed. Give yourself a score of 0–5 based on how many checks you made.

_____ I wrote an introduction to my response based on my central idea (thesis statement).

_____ I developed several paragraphs responding to the prompt.

_____ In my response, I cited specific evidence from the text to support my central idea.

_____ In my response, I provided additional relevant information based on my own knowledge and perspectives.

_____ I wrote a conclusion that summarized my position or restated my central idea in a different way.

10. **Revising and Editing Checklist** Give yourself a score of 0–6 based on how many checks you made.

_____ My piece was well organized, or I improved its organization so that one idea relates to another.

_____ I made sure that my sentences were complete, clear, and correct.

_____ Each of my paragraphs has a central idea and supporting evidence from the text.

_____ My piece has a clear beginning, middle, and ending.

_____ I corrected subject-verb agreement, pronoun agreement, and verb tense errors.

_____ I have corrected punctuation, capitalization, and spelling.

MATHEMATICAL REASONING

Part I: Quantitative Reasoning, page 18

1. **D. between 1,200 and 1,300** The graph shows that roughly 900 customers came from Zone 3 during this period, and that somewhere between 300 and 400 customers came from Zone 4 during the same period. Thus, adding them together will result in a number between 1,200 and 1,300.

2. **D. 1:2** The bar for Zone 1 is a little less than halfway between 400 and 500, so round up to 450. The best estimate for the bar for Zone 3 is 900. Make sure you write the ratio in the order stated in the problem. Zone 1: Zone 3 = 450:900, which simplifies to 1:2.

3. **C. 16** Divide 10 by $\frac{3}{5}$. The answer is 16 with a remainder. Since the question asks for how many bowls the potter can complete, ignore the remainder.

4. **B. 3** The graph doesn't give the actual number of hours Janelle will work, but it does show how her time spent at one activity compares to another. If she works 100 hours, she will spend 44 hours working at the counter, 9 hours processing new books, and 6 hours repairing bindings. Compare 44 to 15. The number 44 is about 3 times as great as 15.

5. **C. 160** To solve, set up a ratio. 15 percent $= \frac{15}{100}$. Set that equal to the ratio of employees who make minimum wage to the total number of employees, and use a variable to represent the total number of employees. $\frac{15}{100} = \frac{24}{x}$. Cross multiply: $24 \times 100 = 2400$. Divide: $2400 \div 15 = 160$.

6. **D. Y, W, Z, X** Compare the numbers and list in order from smallest to largest: $2.80, $27.10, $27.20, $261.00.

7. **B. 9.25** Add together the amounts of honey the cook will use in the two recipes: $2.5 + 4.25 = 6.75$. Subtract that amount from the total amount of honey in the jar. $16 - 6.75 = 9.25$.

8. **C. 21** One way to solve the problem is to find a number that is evenly divisible by 6 and 14, and then try dividing that number by each of the answer choices. Go through the multiples of 14 until you find one that is divisible by 6: 14, 28, 42. The number 42 is divisible by both 14 and 6. Then review the answer choices. 42 cannot be evenly divided by 8, 12, 28, or 35. It can be evenly divided by 21.

9. **D. 13** Work backward through the facts. Sheila has worked 10 years. Kathy has worked half as long as Sheila, which equals 5 years. Alice has worked 8 years longer than Kathy. $5 + 8 = 13$ years.

10. **C. $\frac{3}{4}$** Two sections, which equal $\frac{2}{8}$ or $\frac{1}{4}$, are marked "blue." Thus, the chance of not getting blue is $1 - \frac{1}{4} = \frac{3}{4}$.

11. **A. 25%** To find percent of change, divide the amount of change by the original price. Then multiply by 100 to change the result from a decimal to a percent: $\frac{\$320 - \$240}{\$320} \times 100 = \frac{\$80}{\$320} \times 100 = 0.25 \times 100 = 25\%$.

12. **C. 5.5** The median is the middle number of a group of numbers. Arrange the numbers of accounts in order: 2, 4, 4, 4, 5, 6, 6, 7, 7, 8. The middle numbers are 5 and 6. When there are two numbers in the middle, find the mean of those two numbers: $\frac{5+6}{2} = 5.5$.

13. **A. $4,500** Add together the amounts that Jim has sold so far in April: $2,500 + $5,000 = $7,500. Then subtract that amount from the minimum his employers expect him to sell: $12,000 - $7,500 = $4,500.

14. **C. $\frac{3}{10}$ feet** Subtract the length of the shorter stick from the length of the longer one: $3\frac{4}{5} - 3\frac{1}{2}$. To solve, find a common denominator: $3\frac{8}{10} - 3\frac{5}{10} = \frac{3}{10}$.

15. **C. 3.75** The number line is divided into increments, each of which equals one-fourth, or .25. The dot is three increments to the right of the number 3, so its value is 3.75.

16. **D. More students received either an A or a B than received either a D or an F.** Based on the graph, 6 students received an A and 7 students a B. $7 + 6 = 13$. Also, 7 students received a D, and 3 received an F. $7 + 3 = 10$. Since 13 is greater than 10, the A-and-B group is larger than the D-and-F group. Choice (A) is not supported because some students did fail the exam. Choice (B) suggests that most—more than half—of Marjorie's students received an A or B. However, the A-and-B group (13 students) is smaller than the total number of students who got a C (12 students), a D (around 7 students), or an F (3 students, for a total of 22 students). Choice (C) is unsupported because the graph has no information about how any other group of students would perform.

17. **D. $6,000** Use the formula provided to find the interest Jason's deposit would earn over the five years. As directed, express the percent interest as a decimal, 0.04. $5000 × 5 (years) × 0.04 = $1000. Then, to find out how much is in the account at the end of the five years, add that interest to Jason's original deposit: $5,000 + $1,000 = $6,000.

18. **C. 720** To find out how many possible orderings, or sequences, of six items are possible, multiply. There are six possibilities for the first movie. Then after the first movie has been chosen, there are five possibilities for the second movie, then four for the third movie, and so on: $6 \times 5 \times 4 \times 3 \times 2 \times 1 = 720$.

Part II: Algebraic Reasoning and Geometry, page 22

1. **B. Point B** Convert the improper fraction to a mixed fraction: $-\frac{16}{6} = -2\frac{4}{6} = -2\frac{2}{3}$, which is the value of Point B.

2. **C. 4** Substitute and simplify:
$$= 2x - (4y - 3) + 5xz$$
$$= 2(-3) - (4[2] - 3) + 5(-3)(-1)$$
$$= -6 - (8 - 3) + 15$$
$$= -6 - 5 + 15$$
$$= -11 + 15$$
$$= 4$$

3. **A. 54** To find the magnitude of the change in temperature, subtract the lowest temperature from the highest temperature: $46 - (-8) = 46 + 8 = 54$.

4. **B. 60** The tower, its shadow, and the distance between them form a right triangle. Use the Pythagorean relationship to find the missing distance:

$$61^2 = 11^2 + h^2$$
$$3721 = 121 + h^2$$
$$3600 = h^2$$
$$60 = h$$

5. **A. 18** To find the volume of a rectangular prism, multiply *base × width × height*. Here, however, the question asks for the volume in feet, while the measurements are given in inches. Therefore, start by converting the inches of model 413S to feet: 24 in × 72 in × 18 in = 2 ft × 6 ft × 1.5 ft = 18 ft^3.

6. **C. $2,600** The question stem gives us two equations. First, we know that $M + L = 4,680$. Also, since Levy earns $520 more than Matthew earns, that can be expressed as $L = M + 520$, or, put another way, $M = L - 520$. Since the question asks for a solution for Levy, substitute the value of M from the second equation in the first equation:

$$(L - 520) + L = 4,680$$
$$2L - 520 = 4,680$$
$$2L = 5,200$$
$$L = 2,600$$

7. **C. 16π** The formula for the surface area of a cone is: $SA = \pi rs + \pi r^2$. In that formula, *SA* means *surface area*, *r* represents the *radius*, and *s* is the *slant height*, or the distance from the bottom of one side of the cone to the point. The diagram indicates that the diameter of the base is 4, so its radius is 2. The slant height is 6. Substitute and simplify:

$$SA = \pi(2)(6) + \pi(2)^2$$
$$SA = 12\pi + 4\pi = 16\pi$$

8. **D. $5x^3 - 4x^2 - x + 12y$** Start by removing the parentheses:
$3x^3 + x + 2x^2 - 4x^2 + 14y - 2(y + x) =$
$3x^3 + x + 2x^3 - 4x^2 + 14y - 2y - 2x$.
Then, identify like terms that can be combined:
$3x^3$ and $2x^3$, which add to $5x^3$.
$-4x^2$ cannot be combined with any other term.
x and $-2x$ add to $-x$.
$14y$ and $-2y$ add to $12y$.
Combine into a new expression:
$5x^3 - 4x^2 - x + 12y$.

9. **(2, 4)** On scratch paper, draw the three points given in the question stem:

The fourth corner of the rectangle will be at (2, 4). Mark that point on the answer sheet.

10. **A. 18 − 2x** Simplify: $4x - 2(3x - 9)$
$= 4x - 6x + 18 = -2x + 18$. That can also be expressed as $18 - 2x$.

11. **D. 4** The simplest way to solve this problem is to try the values of x given in the answer choices in the equation. Starting with choice (A), where x equals −4: $3(-4)^2 - 10(-4) = 3(16) + 40 = 88$. That's a great deal more than 8. That result suggests that choice (B), where x equals −3, would also be likely to yield a result that's far too large. Try choices (C) or (D) to see what result a positive number yields. In choice (C), x equals 3: $3(3)^2 - 10(3) = 3(9) - 30 = -3$. That's a little too small, so the answer must be choice (D), x equals 4. Try it to confirm: $3(4)^2 - 10(4) = 3(16) - 40 = 8$. Choice (D) is correct.

12. **D. x < 4** Simplify the expression:
$$12(x - 2) < 24$$
$$12x - 24 < 24$$
$$12x < 48$$
$$x < 4$$

13. **B. 4.54 × 10⁹** Writing a number in scientific notation involves expressing it as the product of two terms: one term is a number and the other is 10 raised to some power. To find how large the power of ten should be, imagine counting spaces to the left of the decimal point. Choice (B) reflects the correct number and the correct power of 10, or places to the left of the decimal point.

14. **D. 204** The shape of Joe's new property is a trapezoid, and the formula for the area of a trapezoid is $A = \frac{1}{2}h(b_1 + b_2)$. In that formula, A is area, and h means the height, which is 12 yards here. The variables b_1 and b_2 are the two bases, which here are 10 yards and 24 yards. Plug those values into the formula: $A = \frac{1}{2}(12)(10 + 24) = (6)(34) = 204$. (You can tell that Joe's property is a trapezoid because the two bases are parallel; the right angles indicated at the two ends of the *height* line indicate this.)

15. **A. p = $5.00 − (n − 1) $0.50** If a customer requests only one monogram, the fee is $5.00. However, if a customer requests 2, the price per monogram drops by $0.50 (which you can think of as 1 × $0.50). If a customer requests 3 monograms, the price per monogram drops another $0.50, or 2 × $0.50 in total. Thus, the price per monogram is $5.00 minus a multiple of $0.50. The multiple is one less than the number of hats ordered.

16. **B. 70°** In any four-sided figure, all four interior angles add up to 360°. In a parallelogram, the two obtuse angles are equal to one another, and the two acute angles are equal to one another. Here, you know that the two obtuse angles add up to 220°. 360° − 220° = 140°. Since there are two acute angles, divide that number by two.

17. C. $y = \frac{2}{3}x + 2$ The answer choices are in slope-intercept form, so begin by finding the y-intercept, which is 2. Then find the slope, which represents $\frac{rise}{run}$. Find two points on line H, and count the difference between the y-coordinates for those two points in order to find the *rise*. Then count the difference between the x-coordinates for those two points to find the *run*. For each vertical increase of two (*rise*), the line moves three numbers on the horizontal axis (*run*). Thus, the slope is $\frac{2}{3}$, and the equation is $y = \frac{2}{3}x + 2$.

18. A. 20π The question asks for the circumference of the pool. The question stem gives the distance from the middle of the pool to the edge—that's the radius of the circle, which is half the diameter. Thus, the diameter of the circle is 20 feet. Plug that into the formula for the circumference of a circle: $C = d\pi$. $C = 20\pi$.

19. D. 2 The slope of a line can be expressed as $\frac{rise}{run}$. To find the slope using two points, subtract one y-coordinate from another to find the *rise*, and subtract one x-coordinate from another to find the *run*. It does not matter which point you subtract from the other, as long as you are consistent about which point you are subtracting when finding both rise and run. $\frac{-1-(-9)}{4-0} = \frac{8}{4} = 2$.

20. C. 192π The formula for the volume of a cylinder is $V = \pi r^2 h$. In that formula, V is volume, r is the radius of the base, and h is height. In this case, you know that the diameter of the base of the can is 8, so the radius is 4. Plug in the values: $V = \pi \times (4 \text{ cm})^2 \times (12 \text{ cm}) = \pi \times 16 \text{ cm}^2 \times 12 \text{ cm} = 192\pi \text{ cm}^3$

21. D. 4,100 To find the area of a compound figure like this one, split it up into simpler shapes. Here, the space can be split into two rectangles:

Find the area of the two rectangles and add those two areas together: $(70 \times 50) + (30 \times 20) = 3,500 + 600 = 4,100$.

22. D. (2, 5) There are two ways to solve this problem. First, you could graph both lines. After doing so, your scratchwork should have looked like this:

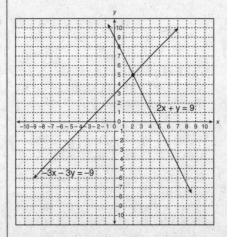

Based on that sketch, the two lines intersect at (2, 5), which means that those coordinates are the solution to the system of equations.

Alternatively, you could also have plugged each answer choice into both equations in order to find the answer choice that works in both equations. For example, to test choice (A) in this way:

Plug (2, −5) into the first equation: $3x − 3y = −9$

$3(2) − 3(−5) \overset{?}{=} −9$

$6 + 15 \neq −9$

Answer choice (A) does *not* work in the first equation. Therefore, it is incorrect, and there is no need to try choice (A) in the second equation. Try the other answer choices in a similar way. Only choice (D) will work in both equations.

SOCIAL STUDIES

Part I: Social Studies Practices, page 28

1. **C. The Voting Rights Act of 1965 gave the Federal Government oversight of state elections to end barriers against African American voting.** The passage described the historical events that led to the Voting Rights Act, and how this legislation ended the voting discrimination that certain states enacted after the passage of the Fifteenth Amendment.

2. **C. interpretation** According to the passage, the terms "strict construction" and "loose construction" refer to different ways in which people interpret the range of powers that the Constitution grants to the federal government.

3. **A. The FDA's new regulations would place a financial hardship on small food retailers.** According to the passage, smaller food retailers would feel more of the burden than larger establishments, and the Common Sense Nutritional Disclosure Act seeks to relieve this burden.

4. **C. "devastating"** This word highlights the author's point of view that the FDA's new regulations would be especially harmful to smaller food retailers.

5. **D. The argument is invalid, because it attempts to refute one reason against doing something while ignoring all the others.** The paragraph states that possible danger to the porcupine caribou is "one commonly cited" reason against drilling in the Arctic National Wildlife Refuge. This implies that there are other reasons as well. Thus, the author's conclusion that "we have no reason not to drill in the ANWR" is unsupported, since the author has attempted to refute only one of the possibly many reasons against drilling in the refuge.

6. **A. Some people depend on the porcupine caribou for food.** The primary evidence in this argument is that almost all of the species that have ever lived on Earth have gone extinct, and the vast majority of these extinctions happened naturally. The author uses this evidence to argue that the human threat to the porcupine caribou isn't a big deal. However, the author fails to consider the possibility that human-caused extinctions are worse than naturally-occurring ones. Choice (A) shows that the loss of the caribou by human hands would cause a severe problem: the loss of a major food source for some people.

7. **B. The map shows that most of the Warsaw Pact countries lay between the Soviet Union and Western countries, including France, West Germany, and Great Britain.** The passage states that the World War II Allies, which included France and Great Britain, formed NATO. It also states that West Germany was allowed to join NATO. And the map makes clear that the smaller Warsaw Pact countries lay geographically between those nations and the Soviet Union.

8. **A. In forming the Warsaw Pact, the Soviet Union greatly increased its access to oceanic coastlines.** Although most of the Warsaw Pact countries touched a body of water, most of their borders were land borders, and two of the Warsaw Pact countries were completely landlocked.

9. **A. $40\frac{2}{3}$** The three northernmost states are Maine (ME), New Hampshire (NH) and Vermont (VT). To find the average, sum the rainfall of each state and divide by 3: $\frac{41+42+39}{3} = 40\frac{2}{3}$.

10. **B. steadily increased, surpassing that of white voters in the 2012 elections** The solid gray line corresponds to the rate at which black voters participated in presidential elections. It increases consistently from year to year, and shows the highest rate of all groups in the 2012 election.

Part II: Social Studies Content, page 32

1. **B. the West Indies to the British colonies; the British colonies to Africa; Africa to the West Indies** According to the map, the West Indies exported sugar and molasses to the British colonies in North America. The British colonies exported rum to Africa. Finally, Africa exported slaves and gold to the West Indies. The trade routes formed a triangle.

2. **A. Cargo ships never had to sail empty on any leg of a profitable triangular journey.** This is a general conclusion that is supported by the details of the map, which show goods traveling along each leg of the triangular trade route. Therefore, a very profitable journey must have meant a ship carried cargo on each leg of the route. The remaining options state details that may or may not be confirmed by the map.

3. **B. Commercial bank** According to the descriptions, commercial banks provide services to businesses and other corporations. None of the other descriptions describe financial institutions making loans to companies. They focus either on national financial systems or on individual borrowers.

4. **B. tainted system** "Tainted" is a loaded word that indicates the author's belief that a "strong-mayor" system is inherently corrupt.

5. **D. No, because no indication is given that the current mayor will behave as past mayors did.** A strong-mayor system may enable, but does not guarantee, corruption. Past corruption is not by itself enough reason to have a strong suspicion toward the current government.

6. **D. serving on a jury** Serving on a jury, like voting, is a civic duty of each citizen. It is a way to participate in the judicial branch of government. Note that although choice (B), displaying the American flag, is a patriotic act, it does not involve participating in government

in any way and so is not a way of participating in the political system.

7. **D. law and order** The hallmark of military rule is strict control over the citizenry; in other words, law and order.

8. **C. The French president has the power to dissolve the legislature, while the U.S. president does not.** The checkmark in the last row under "France" indicates that the French president can dissolve the legislature. The U.S. president does not have this power.

9. **B. Of all the presidents shown, the French president has the greatest variety of powers.** This statement is a conclusion, a generalization based on the details in the chart. Choices (A), (C), and (D) are specific details from the chart.

10. **D. The U.S. Supreme Court ruling in *Plessy v. Ferguson* was wrong because it infringed on freedoms guaranteed in the Constitution.** This statement is a rephrasing of the dissenting justice's opinion, or belief, about the case. The other statements are all facts from the paragraph.

11. **A. The nation's debt increased at a faster rate than did the U.S. population during the period shown on the graph.** You can tell this is true because the per capita debt figure increased steadily from 1990 to 2010. This would happen only if the debt increased faster than the population of the United States.

12. **D. raise taxes and cut spending** You can conclude from the text that to cut the national debt, the U.S. government would have to increase income (raise taxes) and lower costs (cut spending).

13. **C. A drought was significantly worsened due to lack of native vegetation.** According to the passage, the deforestation caused a significant portion of the drought that led to the Mayan collapse. Choices (A) and (D) are both causes, not effects, of the deforestation.

14. **C. Many cities had large populations because nearby coal and iron ore deposits meant jobs.** Coal and iron ore were among the most important raw materials of the Industrial Revolution. By examining the relationship of the location of the cities to that of the coalfields and iron ore deposits, you can conclude that Great Britain's most populous cities (with the exception of London) were large partly because of their proximity to the important raw materials of the Industrial Revolution. The remaining statements are details from the map.

15. **B. Great Britain's acceptance of Germany's takeover of Austria and Czechoslovakia in the late 1930s** Of all the options, this is the only one that has the element of concession without opposition that is the hallmark of appeasement.

16. **D. People value the lives of their children more than they value money.** This is the underlying assumption of the poster: that Americans have been willing to send their sons into battle where they risk their lives, but haven't been donating money to the war cause with equal willingness. The poster thus plays upon their sense of guilt.

17. **B. World War I** The poster is dated 1917, so the war is World War I.

18. **D. television ads on prime time** Today, the government could probably reach the most people with television ads rather than print ads, because so many people watch television.

19. **D. The population of the colony of New York was smaller than that of Connecticut.** Since the chart shows the five colonies with the largest populations in 1750, it follows that any colony not listed has a population smaller than that of Connecticut, which ranked fifth. The other options are not supported by the data in the table.

20. **C. Applying for Civil Service Jobs** This title best describes what the flowchart shows—the steps in applying for a civil service job.

21. **A. salary** The GS rating of a job, based on the job description and the candidate's skills and experience, is directly related to the salary level of the position. The other options would not be affected by the GS rating.

22. **B. equal opportunity** Since Civil Service jobs are open to all who apply and are awarded on merit, they are designed to provide equal opportunity for employment, regardless of gender, race, ethnicity, party affiliation, or other factors.

23. **C. 6 percent and $12,000 billion** Locate 2005 on each graph. (Note that each tic mark on the horizontal axis indicates a year, even if it is not labeled.) The first graph shows the mortgage interest rate was about 6 percent in 2005. The second graph shows the total outstanding mortgage debt was about $12,000 billion in 2005.

24. **D. As interest rates rise and then fall, the total mortgage debt will move similarly but not at the same rate.** Look at the general trend shown by each graph. Note that as interest rates rise and fall, the mortgage debts rise similarly but fall at a different rate.

25. **D. Hollywood, California, which produces movies and television shows, enjoyed around the world** The movies and television shows that originate in Hollywood are distributed worldwide, helping to spread American popular culture to other nations.

Part III: Extended Response, page 40

Your responses to question 1 may vary but should be similar to the following:

1. **A.** Explain how the Supreme Court case applied the idea of free speech to students.

   B. Discuss what it means that school officials can prohibit some student conduct.

Your responses to questions 2 and 3 may vary. Sample responses are below.

2. The Supreme Court said that students have free speech, but only if that freedom doesn't lead to disorder in the classroom.

3. (1) The Supreme Court said that school officials can control speech that leads to disorder in the classroom. (2) It's very important that students be able to study without disruption. (3) But the ruling also means that it's up to the discretion of school officials to decide how much free speech constitutes a disruption.

4. **Drafting Checklist** Check off each task that you performed. Give yourself a score of 0–5 based on how many checks you made.

   _____ I wrote an introduction to my response based on my central idea (thesis statement).

   _____ I developed several paragraphs responding to the prompt.

   _____ In my response, I cited specific evidence from the text to support my central idea.

   _____ In my response, I provided additional relevant information based on my own knowledge and perspectives.

   _____ I wrote a conclusion that summarized my position or restated my central idea in a different way.

5. **Revising and Editing Checklist** Check off each task that you performed. Give yourself a score of 0–6 based on how many checks you made.

   _____ My piece was well organized, or I improved its organization so that one idea relates to another.

   _____ I made sure that my sentences were complete, clear, and correct.

   _____ Each of my paragraphs has a central idea and supporting evidence from the text.

   _____ My piece has a clear beginning, middle, and ending.

   _____ I corrected subject-verb agreement, pronoun agreement, and verb tense errors.

   _____ I have corrected punctuation, capitalization, and spelling.

Science

Part I: Science Practices, page 42

1. **C. "Hydrothermal Vents Suggest That Not All Life Is Solar-Powered"** The author's main point is that some of the life forms around hydrothermal vents derive energy from a source other than the sun. Choice (C) captures that idea. Choices (A) and (B) mischaracterize the subject matter of the passage, and choice (D) is far too broad.

2. **D. No sunlight penetrates to the world of hydrothermal ocean vents.** Only choice (D) supports the idea that some life forms derive energy from a source other than the sun. Choice (A) distorts the meaning of the first line of the passage. Choice (B) is true but does not serve to support this idea. Choice (C) is not stated in the passage.

3. **D. Pitchblende contains an element that is more radioactive than uranium.** A hypothesis is a guess made by a scientist before the scientist conducts an experiment. Before Marie Curie and her husband conducted their experiment with pitchblende, she guessed that pitchblende was more radioactive than pure uranium because pitchblende contained a radioactive element other than uranium. Curie already knew choice (A) to be true, so it was not a hypothesis she intended to test. Choice (B) is not stated in the passage. Choice (C) describes the outcome of the Curies' experiment, not their initial hypothesis.

4. **A. Pitchblende is more radioactive than pure uranium because it contains polonium.** As a result of their experiment, the Curies discovered that pitchblende contained polonium, a highly radioactive element. This suggests that Marie Curie's initial hypothesis was correct. The remaining choices are not supported by the passage.

5. **B. The hole in the ozone reached its largest size after CFCs were banned from production and use.** According to the passage, the hole in the ozone layer reached its largest size after CFCs were discontinued. The presence of CFCs that stayed in the atmosphere for years after use is a likely explanation for this phenomenon.

6. **B. While the ozone layer continues to thin, it is thinning at a rate much lower than it has in the past.** If the rate of ozone depletion has slowed significantly, it is likely that the CFC ban was at least partially effective.

7. **B. Adenosine triphosphate is broken down into adenosine monophosphate and a pyrophosphate, releasing energy.** The text describes this relation between ATP (adenosine triphosphate), AMP (adenosine monophosphate), and PP_i (pyrophosphate).

8. **D. Glycogen, which stores sugars that can be broken off in differing amounts when the body needs energy** Both glycogen and ATP store energy, and both can release different amounts of energy depending on the needs of the cell or organism.

9. **A. $\frac{1}{8}$** Because white is a recessive trait, a plant must have two white genes (ww) in order to be white. Of the eight possible outcomes illustrated in the Punnett squares, only one has this pair of genes.

10. **B. $3\frac{1}{2}$** The difference between the drop height and the first bounce height for the first drop was 1 foot. For the second, it was also 1 foot, and for the third, 2 feet. Find these differences for all the drops. The average of a set of items is the sum of the items divided by the number of items in the set. Thus, to find the average here, add all the differences and divide by the number of drops:

$$\frac{1+1+2+3+6+8}{6} = \frac{21}{6} = 3\frac{1}{2}$$

Part II: Science Content, page 46

1. **C. Neurons transmit instructions regarding movement to muscles.** Since neurons transmit information and the function of muscles is to move, it follows that neurons transmit instructions regarding movement to muscles. The paragraph and the diagrams show that all the other options contain incorrect information.

2. **D. Comets formed when the solar system was born.** Opinions are usually signaled by words like "believe," "think," or "feel." In this case, the last sentence of the paragraph states that scientists believe that comets formed when the solar system was born, showing that this is an opinion.

3. **D. photosynthesis, in which green plants use the energy from sunlight to make carbohydrates from water and carbon dioxide** The key element in a photochemical reaction is light. Of the options listed, only photosynthesis involves light.

4. **D. it helps control metabolism and growth** First, locate thyroxine in the "Hormone" column, then move along the row to the "Function" column to find the answer.

5. **D. uncontrolled blood sugar levels** The chart shows that insulin regulates blood sugar levels, so problems with insulin production will cause problems with blood sugar levels.

6. **A. Growth hormone is only one of several factors that determine a person's adult height.** Growth hormone alone does not determine height. A person's genetic make-up—the height of his parents and other family members—contributes, as do nutrition and the action of other hormones. Paul's expectations were therefore unrealistic.

7. **C. oil and vinegar salad dressing** This is an example

of an emulsion—two liquids mixed together but not dissolving. If you let oil and vinegar dressing stand, the oil will rise to the top. The other options are all solutions, which do not separate over time.

8. **C. a meteorologist who studies weather patterns and predicts weather** Knowledge gained from a study of the atmosphere and hydrosphere is closely related to the study of weather, which is influenced by both.

9. **D. They are decomposers.** Since earthworms are feeding on dead organic matter, which comes from dead organisms, they must be decomposers.

10. **B. switch from whole milk to 1 percent milk** The switch from whole milk to low-fat milk reduces fat intake by 3.5 grams/serving. While the difference in saturated fat per serving is greater in cheddar cheese than in milk, since the child drinks 4 servings of milk daily, this would be a reduction of 14 grams per day. The reduction from switching cheeses comes to 9.6 grams, since the child eats two servings of cheese per day.

11. **A. moving your hand closer to the center of the revolving door** Moving your hand closer to the center of the door decreases distance to the pivot point. Since the force remains the same in this case, when you multiply distance times force you will come up with a lower number, which indicates decreased torque.

12. **A. coal/peat and natural gas** Look on the circle graph for energy sources occupying wedges of approximately the same size. The only two that are about the same size are coal/peat and natural gas, indicating they provide about the same proportion of energy consumed in the United States.

13. **B. As European Americans moved from the East Coast westward between 1620 and 1850, they cut down forests to build farms.** The map shows, and the paragraph implies, that the virgin forests of the eastern United States were almost all cut down between 1620 and 1850. The paragraph further implies that the forests were cut down for farmland, which has since been abandoned. Based on this information, choice (B) is the only conclusion that is supported by the map and the paragraph. The map and the paragraph either lack support for or contradict the other options.

14. **B. the Northern Hemisphere** First, locate June 21 on the diagram, then examine the tilt of Earth. Note that at that time of year, the Northern Hemisphere tilts toward the sun, and it is summer there.

15. **D. On the first day of spring and fall, neither the Northern Hemisphere nor the Southern Hemisphere is tilted toward the sun.** According to the diagram, on March 21 and September 23, Earth's axis is tilted neither toward nor away from the sun, so neither hemisphere is tilted toward the sun. The remaining choices are not supported by the diagram.

16. **D. A quadrat makes plant distribution estimates more reliable.** This option is a conclusion, or a general statement, that is supported by all the details in the paragraph. The other options are specific details paraphrased from the paragraph.

17. **A.**

Charles's Law involves the relationship of a gas's volume and temperature. Since volume increases with increases in temperature, the first graph must be correct. Note that you can eliminate choice (D) immediately because it involves changes in pressure, and Charles's Law assumes that pressure remains constant.

18. **B. Atoms are composed of subatomic particles.** This is an assumption made by the writer of the paragraph. He or she does not explain this but assumes it is common knowledge. All the other options are statements made or strongly implied in the passage.

19. **D. The student should have divided the mass by the volume.** The paragraph states that density is calculated by dividing mass by volume. The student did the reverse, which is incorrect. All of the other steps the student followed were correct.

20. **C. a mixture of metals.** According to the passage, the Anthony dollar was made of a copper-nickel alloy, and the final Sacagawea dollar, of a manganese, zinc, copper, and nickel alloy. From these examples, you can infer that an alloy is a mixture of metals.

21. **B. Like nickels, dimes, and quarters, the Anthony dollar was silver-colored and therefore not distinctive.** The Mint wanted to replace the Anthony dollar with a distinctive coin—a coin that looked different from the coins already in circulation. Making the new coin out of the same metals as the silver-colored Anthony dollar would not accomplish this.

22. **D. hardy perennials** Hardy plants withstand frost, so they are more likely to survive than tender plants. Perennials come up and flower for many years. Therefore hardy perennials are likely to provide the most flowers with the least effort on the gardener's part.

23. C. **A viewer could not see any-thing through the telescope.** The function of the flat mirror is to redirect the light rays toward the eyepiece so the viewer can see the object in the telescope's sights. If the flat mirror were removed, the reflection of the object would no longer be visible through the eyepiece.

24. B. **They help scientists analyze large amounts of data in a systematic way.** The ability of a computer to process lots of data, far more systematically and quickly than a human being can, has helped speed up and refine the drug discovery process, although the older methods of running laboratory experiments and clinical trials are still also important.

25. B. **The typhoid fever vaccine is only 50 to 80 percent effective.** Because getting vaccinated against typhoid fever does not completely eliminate the traveler's chance of getting the disease, it makes sense that he or she should take extra precautions against contracting this food- and water-borne disease.

Part III: Short Answer, page 54

1. **Drafting Checklist** Check off each task that you performed. Give yourself a score of 0–3 based on how many checks you made.

   _____ I wrote a response based on my central idea (thesis statement).

   _____ I developed one to two well-developed paragraphs responding to the prompt.

   _____ In my response, I cited specific evidence from the text to support my central idea.

2. **Revising and Editing Checklist** Check off each task that you performed. Give yourself a score of 0–4 based on how many checks you made.

   _____ My piece was well organized.

   _____ My sentences were complete, clear, and correct.

   _____ I corrected subject-verb agreement, pronoun agreement, and verb tense errors.

   _____ I have corrected punctuation, capitalization, and spelling.

GED® UNIT ANSWERS AND EXPLANATIONS
REASONING THROUGH LANGUAGE ARTS

Interpreting Nonfiction and Informational Text

Lesson 1: Main Ideas and Details

Practice 1, page 63

1. **A. searching for a place to call home** The author states this feeling directly in the first two lines and in the last paragraph.
2. **D. the gods** The second sentence in the second paragraph says, "It was ordained by the deities."
3. **D. It was simply part of their beliefs to follow the pole.** The meaning of the pole is explained beginning with the fourth sentence of the second paragraph. The last sentence explains that the Chickasaws lacked sorrow because they trusted the pole's command.
4. **C. understands that her tendency to search is part of her Chickasaw heritage** The details about the author's search for a home, combined with the information that "the search for a homeland is part of the Chickasaw migration legend," helps you understand this main idea.
5. **D. accepts that she is Chickasaw** You can see that the writer is saying that her Chickasaw heritage is an inescapable part of who she is.

Lesson 2: Restatement and Summary

Practice 2, page 65

1. **C. lack of proper paperwork** As the writer discusses the problems, he states that he wants an "itemized list" and "a proper bill of sale." He does mention the premium price, choice (D), but that price is the reason he expects proper paperwork and is not a complaint in and of itself.
2. **B. the car to be repaired free of charge if the cause of the problem is discovered** This expectation is stated in the fifth paragraph of the letter.
3. **C. The service and warranty on the customer's car** have been unacceptable. The letter is a detailed list of the customer's complaints. They can be summed up by saying that both the service and the warranty have not been as promised.

Lesson 3: Application of Ideas

Practice 3, page 67

1. **A. overcoming a bad habit** The writer advises those trying to break free of credit card debt: "Stick with it until you're free again."
2. **B. never use the credit cards** The last paragraph implies that the author approves of using credit cards only once you have already gotten out of debt, and then only for convenience. Thus, if you are in debt, you should stop using your credit cards.
3. **C. losing weight by avoiding all-you-can-eat buffets** Basically, the advice is that you gradually lose your debt by not adding anything to it. This is similar to helping yourself lose weight by not adding to it with portions of food you don't need.
4. **C. "Live within your means."** This statement can be inferred from the advice "don't borrow any more," and "what I'm against is buying more on your credit cards than you can pay for at the end of the month."

Lesson 4: Cause and Effect

Practice 4, page 69

1. **C. It affected nearly everyone.** This answer summarizes the meaning of the first two sentences of the passage.
2. **A. Many people lost the mortgages on their homes.** This answer is stated in the first paragraph: "men and women who saw their mortgages foreclosed." Choices (B) and (D) are both mentioned as causes, not effects, of the depression.
3. **B. low worker incomes** The second paragraph states, "but the actual cause of the collapse was an unhealthy economy. . . . Most laborers . . . could not afford to buy the automobiles . . . because their incomes were too low."
4. **B. They had little effect.** The writer tells what Herbert Hoover did as president to curb the depression ("loans to businesses and banks") but then states that "his efforts proved to be too little and too late."
5. **D. The depression left people emotionally scarred.** The first paragraph states, "No one who lived through those years . . . could ever completely forget." The statement about eating mustard that is provided in the question addresses this emotional effect rather than issues related to farmers, workers, the economy, or the number of individuals affected.

Lesson 5: Compare and Contrast

Practice 5, page 71

1. **D. leave some of his possessions behind** This answer is found in the seventh and eighth lines of paragraph 1.
2. **C. They provided milk and pulled wagons.** The selection states that "cows . . . gave milk all the way to the sink of the Humboldt where they died, having acted as draught animals for several weeks after the oxen had perished."
3. **A. the provisions of each group of travelers** Each paragraph talks about a different group and what it had to offer the wagon train. For example, "Much in contrast to these men were four batchelors . . . who had a wagon drawn by four oxen . . . cows following behind."
4. **A. be happy to have people who could cook and sew** The writer was interested in assessing how self-sufficient the group could be and what each group could offer the entire wagon train. For example, she writes, "but as he was a wagon maker and his companion a blacksmith by trade and both were accommodating

there were always ready hands to 'pry the wheel out of mire.'"

5. **A. They must cooperate and work together.** Throughout the excerpt is evidence that all the travelers depended on each other for animals, food, and physical help, such as pulling wagons out of the mud.

Lesson 6: Conclusions and Generalizations

Practice 6.1, page 73

1. **A. It is rewarding and one of life's joys.** The passage states that "my teacher's genius . . . made the first years of my education so beautiful." She also delights in observing and learning from the tadpole.

2. **D. insightful and grateful** The writer has insight about the connection between herself and the tadpole: "Thus I learned from life itself. At the beginning I was only a little mass of possibilities." The writer is also grateful to her teacher: "nor has she ceased trying . . . to make my life sweet and useful."

3. **C. show Helen how addition is used in everyday life** You can apply what you learn in the diary entry: "Thus I learned from life itself. . . . She has never since let pass an opportunity to point out the beauty that is in everything. . . ." The teacher would therefore probably use everyday life situations to teach.

4. **D. as an anecdote followed by a generalization based on the anecdote** The writer tells the story of the tadpoles (an anecdote) and relates it to her attitude toward life and learning.

5. **D. Their development is not entirely smooth.** The writer describes the tadpole having difficulty after leaping out of the bowl. This is similar to the quotation about "the stony course" of a child's education.

Practice 6.2, page 75

1. **C. On the whole, temperatures are not rising.** The writer states that rising temperatures are "quite simply not what is happening," based

on the cold temperatures of the day before.

2. **A. Shady Hollow was hit with a record cold temperature yesterday.** This one piece of information is the example the author uses to support the generalization that temperatures, generally speaking, are not rising.

3. **D. nationwide data tables of temperatures from the 1980s through today** The author's generalization suffers from being based on one temperature reading. His generalization would be more likely to be valid if informed by many temperature readings over time.

Lesson 7: Word Choice

Practice 7, page 77

1. **D. the CoolForter blanket** The first sentence of paragraph 2 tells you two things about the CoolForter blanket: that "it works like an electric blanket," and that "it feels like a dream."

2. **B. to show that the blanket is a pleasant indulgence** To "coddle" is to treat gently or take care of a person. Choice (B) describes this idea.

3. **A. fluid** Many people associate the word *chemical* with toxicity or harm. A more neutral word to describe the cooling substance without inaccurate specificity is *fluid*.

4. **C. bland** The word *bland* indicates a lack of interesting features. Unlike the word *neutral*, which also indicates a lack of characteristic features, the word *bland* can carry a negative connotation.

5. **D. It allows the consumer to compare the CoolForter's energy usage to that of a familiar item.** The author's choice of a light bulb, an item with which most readers are probably familiar, emphasizes that the CoolForter blanket will not use excessive amounts of energy.

Lesson 8: Writer's Tone and Point of View

Practice 8, page 79

1. **C. the Internet writers** The writer mentions "Internet sass"

and then goes on to say that "you gotta love it" because it keeps writers "off the street and out of trouble."

2. **A. The Internet reviews were much more interesting than the TV show.** The review states, "They [Internet writers] were taking hours and hours of primetime dross and turning it into decadent, amoral, sharp, electronic gold."

3. **A. The show was boring.** The reviewer's main opinion of the show is that it was bad and boring ("non-goings-on of the non-people in the non-house"). Someone yawning supports the idea of boredom.

4. **C. informal and hip** Phrases such as "the dude" and "you gotta love it" contribute to an informal and modern, or hip, tone.

5. **C. someone knowledgeable about the media** The reviewer talks knowledgeably about both television and the Internet.

Lesson 9: Text Structure

Practice 9, page 81

1. **B. exposure to the cowpox disease** As seen in the text, James's recovery from cowpox followed his exposure to it. Note that choice (D) refers to Jenner exposing James to smallpox, not cowpox.

2. **C. "After being exposed to the disease"** The transition word *After* tells the reader that James's exposure came before his catching cowpox and recovery from it. Thus, it gives the reader explicit information about the order of the steps in the process.

3. **B. A number of factors can damage a garden.** As discussed in the passage, factors such as weather, pests, and diseases can affect plants and cause damage, undoing the time and work that have been invested.

Interpreting Nonfiction and Informational Text Practice Questions, pages 82–85

1. **D. hit a boy in the arm to get his attention** The writer talks about breaking a ruler over the head of a boy she likes; you can therefore conclude that she

would hit a boy in the arm to get his attention. She responds physically and without much thought to consequences.

2. **B. She was just pretending she didn't want to go to the principal's office.** The circumstances of Brer Rabbit pretending he was afraid to go into the briar patch where he was born and raised are similar to the speaker pretending to be afraid to go to the principal's office.

3. **C. unusual** From the different examples of how Frank Doleman behaved (allowing a young girl to play chess in his office and not punishing boys sent to his office), you conclude that he was an unusual principal.

4. **A. confident** The additional information you get from the new quotation and the examples of her behavior, plus the overall tone of the excerpt, suggest a confident young girl.

5. **C. concerned but hopeful** The author is worried about the health impact of soda consumption on teenagers. But she is also hopeful; in the last sentence, she states that more can be done to reduce the consumption of sugary beverages.

6. **D. Young people will choose healthier beverages if they are better educated about the dangers of regular soda consumption.** The last paragraph supports this choice. Choice (A) is unsupported by the passage: even though the author does not condemn the legal measures mentioned in paragraph 2, you do not know whether she would support an overall ban. Choice (B) is unsupported also; the author never mentions diet soda.

7. **C. Young people who drink these beverages regularly will eventually suffer from the same ailments as those who drink soda regularly.** The author points out that, even though juice and energy drinks have somewhat less sugar than soda, regular consumption of those products "is likely to be just as damaging in the long term."

8. **B. effective to some extent** After describing the measures, the author begins paragraph 3 by stating, "These efforts appear to be paying off" but goes on to explain why they may not fully solve the problem of sugar consumption among teenagers.

9. **C. Reducing excessive consumption of soda.** The author is referring to the efforts described in paragraph 2, all of which attempted to reduce soda consumption.

10. **C. The cost of mandated coverage will lessen the ability of NATS to hire and supply temporary workers.** This question is basically answered in paragraph 2: "the cost of mandates could weaken the ability of the temporary help industry to act as a 'jobs bridge.'"

11. **A. Many workers are losing their jobs and need temporary jobs until they find permanent work again.** The third paragraph explains this reason.

12. **D. to raise awareness of one side of an issue** The whole passage—plus knowledge of who Edward A. Lenz is—helps you see that its purpose is to explain the position of the NATS.

13. **B. Women will not resort to wearing pants or other restrictive men's clothing.** This statement and the lines that follow it help you see that Stanton is saying men can wear their restrictive clothing; women want no part of it.

14. **D. a cloth worn around the neck** By looking at the context clues—or words around the word *stock*—you can see that it is something worn around the neck.

15. **B. speak up about current events** This very direct speech of Stanton's indicates her straight-to-the-point personality. She is not interested in criticism for its own sake but rather speaks up about issues she strongly believes in.

16. **A. Women are fighting for the right to vote.** The phrase "over the horns of bigotry" helps you see that women are fighting for something. The last paragraph of the excerpt helps you see that they are fighting for the right to vote.

Analyzing Nonfiction and Informational Text

Lesson 1: Purpose of Text

Practice 1, page 87

1. **B. tell how creative engineers saved astronauts** This passage is a narrative about the process of saving the lives of the Apollo 13 astronauts, including in particular the role of engineers. Choices (A), (C), and (D) are all far too broad.

2. **B. supports the writer's main recommendation** The writer recommends that the state cut sales taxes on new vehicles. Preventing deaths with the modern safety features on new cars is one of the reasons for this recommendation.

3. **D. inform about the historical importance of silk** The passage begins by discussing the "historical importance" of silk, and continues throughout to introduce new points about this topic.

4. **C. It provides examples of silk's historical importance in trade and culture.** Nomads traveling to China for silk and the creation of the "Silk Road" are examples of silk's importance.

Lesson 2: Effectiveness of Argument

Practice 2, page 89

1. **B. The federal government should automatically raise the minimum wage to match price increases.** The author states that "[s]everal states have taken the sensible step of automatically raising their minimum wage to adjust for inflation and consumer price increases." Later, she also states that "the federal government should follow the lead of the states." Thus, the author is recommending that the federal government should adjust the minimum wage for price increases. The rest of the passage serves to support this recommendation.

2. **D. Those states have systems superior to the federal system of manual increases.** The author's main point is that the federal government should adopt automatic minimum wage increases, as some states currently have done. Thus, she believes that the states' systems are better than the current federal system.
3. **C. Over the past 40 years, the federal minimum wage has not kept pace with inflation.** Choice (C) is a historical fact provided in the second paragraph as evidence to support the writer's argument.
4. **B. Ensuring sustainable incomes for hardworking citizens is a responsibility of lawmakers.** The author states that lawmakers must ensure stability for workers but does not justify why they must do so. She assumes that this is part of the job lawmakers should do.

Lesson 3: Validity of Arguments

Practice 3, page 91

1. **C. DRE systems offer more security and accuracy than other voting systems.** The writer introduces DRE voting, describes several voting systems, and concludes by suggesting that DRE prevents the problems associated with these systems and is therefore better.
2. **B. DRE voting avoids problems associated with other voting systems.** The writer supports the assertion that DRE voting is the most accurate and secure voting system by listing problems that might be encountered with other voting systems and then stating that DRE voting avoids such problems.
3. **A. Each voter's choices are recorded in the DRE voting system.** This is one of the facts that the writer cites in support of the assertion that DRE is secure and accurate. The other three answer choices cite facts that are included in the passage, but those facts are all background information and do not give direct support to the writer's main point.

4. **C. The writer fails to consider that even if DRE voting addresses all the flaws of previous systems, it may introduce unique flaws of its own.** The writer's conclusion is based solely on the fact that DRE voting avoids problems that have been associated with the other systems mentioned in the passage. Because no information is given about possible flaws of DRE voting, the reader has no way to verify the writer's claim that DRE voting is the most accurate and secure system.

Lesson 4: Text Related by Theme or Topic

Practice 4, page 93

1. **C. online piracy of music files** Both passages are focused on reasons why online piracy is harmful and the need to take further action.
2. **B. additional action to combat online piracy is warranted because piracy causes financial loses to the music industry.** The first passage concludes that more must be done to prevent online piracy. The main factual information the writer uses to support this thesis is information about the financial damage that piracy causes.
3. **A. Fear of piracy makes it difficult for new, experimental acts to get signed.** Both passages reach the same conclusion: more must be done to prevent piracy of music files. Choice (A) is the only answer choice that provides direct support for the conclusion of Passage 2, and, therefore, also for that of Passage 1.
4. **A. Online piracy of digital files has a harmful effect on the music industry.** Both authors provide different reasons as to why piracy is potentially harmful, but both agree that it has a negative effect on the industry.

Lesson 5: Text with Opposing Arguments

Practice 5, page 95

1. **C. the MPAA movie rating system** Each writer is making an

argument about the relevance and trustworthiness of the MPAA rating system.
2. **B. The MPAA rating system is a useful tool for parents.** The writer of the Argument in Passage 1 uses information about the MPAA rating system to support her argument that the system helps parents to make sound decisions.
3. **D. The MPAA rating system should not be trusted.** In the second sentence, the writer indicates that the MPAA rating system is not a useful guide, and concludes by recommending that parents use a different source of advice.
4. **A. She largely approves of the MPAA rating system as a guideline for parents.** The passage provides no information about the writer's own child-rearing decisions, choice (B), or about her opinion of the effect of the Hays Code on the movie industry, choice (D). Also, her statements about the rating system are uniformly positive, making choice (C) incorrect.

Lesson 6: Texts with Related Graphic Information

Practice 6, page 97

1. **D. Governing parties can use their power to shape electoral districts to their advantage.** The passage and the figures focus on demonstrating how gerrymandering works. Choices (A) and (B) are not supported at all by the passage, and choice (C) is far too extreme.
2. **B. Through gerrymandering, a governing party can be elected to a greater number of seats than its voter support might otherwise allow.** The second paragraph describes how the second grid figure shows one party winning 75 percent of the seats from 60 percent of the vote, rather than the 50 percent of seats shown in the first grid figure.
3. **A. They illustrate the advantages a party can obtain through gerrymandering.** As discussed in the passage's second paragraph, the figures show how a party can benefit from the process.

While choices (C) and (D) may or may not be true statements, they do not describe how the figures support the passage.

Analyzing Nonfiction and Informational Text Practice Questions, pages 98–101

1. **D. to discuss whether communication technology helps or hurts relationships** This answer choice reflects the scope of the article introduced at the end of the first paragraph.

2. **B. how technology affects interpersonal connections** The question at the end of paragraph 1 introduces this topic. Paragraph 2 discusses positive effects of communication technology while paragraph 3 discusses a negative effect.

3. **D. The caption reveals that the woman's friends will use their phones during their visit.** The caption is similar to a scenario described in the first paragraph of the passage. In both cases, people are choosing to use technology rather than to enjoy the company of those with whom they have an established relationship.

4. **B. New communication technologies may adversely impact important human relationships.** The author's concluding paragraph discusses how communication technology can connect us with so many people that we have less time and energy to spend on relationships with friends and family, and the caption of the image reveals that the visiting friends plan to spend time on their phones rather than in conversing with one another.

5. **B. the giant squid is the world's longest cephalopod** The author's introduction and conclusion both raise this point, and the evidence in the paragraph supports this thesis.

6. **D. The giant squid is longer than the colossal squid.** The author provides scientific evidence about the colossal squid to support the passage's main idea about the giant squid.

7. **C. The length of the longest known colossal squid specimen is ten meters.** This factual evidence supports the author's main idea.

8. **A. The longest known colossal squid is ten meters long, so there is no colossal squid longer than the longest giant squid.** According to paragraph 2, there are very few samples of colossal squid, and all of them have been juveniles. It is improper to draw a conclusion about the entire colossal squid species on the basis of such limited evidence.

9. **B. mercury dental amalgam** Though the authors have somewhat different opinions on the subject, both passages are centrally about mercury dental amalgam.

10. **C. Mercury amalgam fillings should be banned because they are unhealthy and bad for the environment.** The first sentence of Passage 1 states that mercury amalgam should be banned for use in dental fillings. The first paragraph cites health reasons for this opinion. The second paragraph cites environmental reasons. Choice (D) is mentioned in Passage 1, but it serves as support for the author's main point.

11. **D. It is a convincing statistic from a reliable source.** The statement that 40–50 percent of mercury in wastewater is from an easily preventable source is a convincing statistic. The EPA is a large non-political government agency and so is likely to provide reliable information.

12. **A. Consumers have no other reason, such as cost or durability, to prefer mercury amalgam to composite fillings.** The author of Passage 1 states that "banning mercury amalgam would draw no consumer backlash" because resin composite fillings are better for cosmetic reasons. The author assumes that there is no other reason to prefer mercury amalgam.

13. **B. Resin composite fillings look better than mercury amalgam fillings when each is used on visible tooth surfaces.** The author of Passage 2 states that amalgam is preferable to resin composite whenever there is no cosmetic need for a tooth-colored filling. Thus, you can infer that he believes that resin composite fillings look more like natural teeth than mercury amalgam.

14. **A. Passage 1, because it cites no sources for the study or the statistic it cites** The author of passage 1 says that "it has been estimated" that 4 percent of the mercury in Lake Superior comes from dental amalgam, but the author cites no source. The author also gives no source for the 2001 study that is cited in the first paragraph.

15. **D. Mercury that accumulates in body tissues causes a variety of health problems.** The study cited in the first paragraph of Passage 1 found a correlation between mercury amalgam fillings and a number of health conditions. A correlation does not prove causation, but the author of Passage 1 states that "this accumulated mercury causes a variety of health problems."

Interpreting Fiction

Lesson 1: Plot Elements

Practice 1, page 103

1. **B. swearing that he was telling the truth** The following statement in the excerpt gives the context and meaning: "It is nevertheless God's own truth, the sacred truth. I repeat it on my soul and my salvation."

2. **D. confronted him and then asked to be searched** According to the excerpt, when the harness-maker comes in and repeats his story, the two "abused each other for an hour. At his own request, Maître Hauchecorne was searched."

3. **C. A peasant is accused of taking a pocketbook.** As you read the excerpt, you understand that a harness-maker has accused a peasant of taking a pocketbook, and the mayor of the town believes the harness-maker.

4. The elements go in this order:

3	The peasant and the harness-maker argue.
2	The peasant explains that he picked up a piece of string, not a pocketbook.
4	The mayor issues a warning to the peasant.
1	The mayor states that the harness-maker witnessed the peasant stealing the pocketbook.

Lesson 2: Inferences

Practice 2, page 105

1. **A. had always loved her** In the first paragraph, Josephine recalls her husband's face: "the face that had never looked save with love upon her." The term *save* means "except."
2. **C. spread her arms out in welcome** The first paragraph explains that although Josephine knew she would cry at the sight of her dead husband, "that bitter moment" would soon give way to years of freedom, which she welcomed.
3. **A. she was overcome and thrilled to see her husband** The doctors assumed that Josephine was so glad to learn her husband had not died in an accident that she was shocked and overjoyed to see him walk in the door.
4. **B. She was shocked that she would not be free.** Much of the excerpt is about Josephine looking forward to the freedom of being without her husband. When she learns that her husband is alive, she also learns that she will not be free.

Lesson 3: Character

Practice 3, page 107

1. **B. He is frightened about seeing the ghost of his wife.** The witch, supposedly speaking as Yaji's wife, says that she lies in her grave longing for Yaji to die and join her. She then asks, "Shall I come to meet you?" Throughout the passage, Yaji seems uncomfortable. At this moment you can infer that he is scared.

2. **C. untrustworthy** The witch is tricking Yaji. The witch has her own interests at heart when she pretends it is the wife requesting, "Give this witch plenty of money."
3. **D. neglectful** The information we are given about Yaji suggests that he treated his wife poorly when she was alive and now does not tend her grave.

Lesson 4: Theme

Practice 4, page 109

1. **B. finds a new explanation** After his father tells the boy he is dreaming, the boy states, "I decided that it was a magic horse and man that I'd seen."
2. **B. imaginative** The detailed description of the dream and the boy's insistence on believing in it are signs of his imaginative powers.
3. **A. He wants to reconcile what he saw with what his father told him.** Initially the boy seems to think that he saw a real, ordinary horse, but his father explains why this is unlikely. However, the boy does not accept the explanation that he was merely dreaming. Thus, he thinks of a new explanation.
4. **B. having enough money to pay some bills** The father is a practical man, a realist—"where were poor people like us going to find big gray stallions?" Because of the family's poverty, the father would probably enjoy having money to pay bills.
5. **D. Morning and youth are full of possibility.** The end of the excerpt states, "I believed that magic hides in the early morning . . . you might find something so beautiful . . . nothing else in life could ever be better."

Lesson 5: Style and Point of View

Practice 5, page 111

1. **B. He takes things in stride.** When Coach chides Bobby for having three malts, Bobby jokes with him and then pretends to hide them. Bobby is not angry or defensive in a way that could justify choice (D).

2. **C. the actions and speech of the characters** The narrator reports only what can be seen or heard by any observer. As a reader, you don't learn anyone's thoughts or feelings. You must infer them from their actions and speech.
3. **A. informal** Throughout the excerpt, people speak and act quite informally: Daphne washes up in a drinking fountain, Coach speaks with a spoon in his mouth, Bobby jokes with Coach, and so on.
4. **D. not entirely honest about his feelings** In his discussion with Daphne, Coach tries to explain his wife's need for an apartment of her own. Yet he sounds hostile and cuts his wife off when she speaks of her apartment. You can conclude he was hiding his real feelings from Daphne.

Lesson 6: Figurative Language

Practice 6, page 113

1. **B. rain clouds approaching** Lines 8–9 state, "patch of cloud spreads, darkening/Like a water-stain on silk." The following line mentions the coming rain: ". . . *quickly, before the rain!*"
2. **C. The rain caused their makeup to run.** The previous two lines mention "soaked by the shower" and "drenched." Immediately preceding the mention of "ruined faces" is a description of "streaked mascara." The girls' makeup is streaked because of the rain.
3. **B. the wind is so strong that it is blowing spray from the river into the boat** The figurative language helps you "see" the effects of the strong wind by painting a picture of curtains embroidered with white foamy water blown from the river.
4. **A. quick and easy** A knife cuts through a melon quickly and easily, and that is how cold, wet autumn weather has cut through the warm summer day.
5. **C. wry and observant** Throughout the poem, the speaker observes and comments on what is going on around him with a dryly humorous, or wry, attitude.

1. **C. self-concerned** Leroy's condition inspires Norma Jean to care for herself. She discusses herself and her body, and the passage gives no indication that any of the other answers fit her character.
2. **C. won't be driving his truck for a while** The passage tells us Leroy is injured and probably won't drive, so describing the truck as roosting, or sleeping, implies it will not be used.
3. **D. doesn't want to face what to do next** The passage says that Leroy is "not sure what to do next" and is making his crafts "in the meantime."
4. **A. It took some courage.** The fourth paragraph says the boy's "heart was in his mouth" and the sixth paragraph explains the boy was "scared as he looked down."
5. **B. alone** The boy has come to believe that you cannot rely on anyone but yourself. He is alone on the deck and sees the bird alone atop the mast. Even though it needs help, he is not going to help it at first.
6. **D. loneliness and sense of belonging** The sailor-boy begins the excerpt believing that everyone must look after himself. The final sentence of the excerpt states that his adventure leaves him with the belief that "the sky, the ship, the bird and himself were all one."
7. **D. triumphant** The mood of the piece rises as the boy climbs the mast to save the bird. At the top, he feels proud of what he has chosen to do and succeeded at doing and feels at one with everything.
8. **C. start singing again** A clue is given in the phrase "but his parched tongue clove to the roof of his mouth, he could not utter a stave." His mouth, dry from fear, could not utter a note of the song.
9. **A. panic** Reading those words both alone and in context gives you a sense of Ichabod's panic-stricken haste to get away.
10. **C. suspenseful** There is mystery and tension over whether the headless horseman will catch up with Ichabod and, if so, what

he will do. The events that are happening and the way they are told create suspense.
11. **B. too scared to think rationally** When you realize that Ichabod mistakenly thought he saw a head when it was in reality a pumpkin, you can see that he was letting his fear get the better of his judgment.
12. **B. reading** Reading had always been a "gentle thing" to Henry. He is not pleased with the students he has taught and not interested in the politics and history they bring to interpretations of literature.
13. **C. a dime a dozen** Henry thinks of the younger students as "mass produced" undergraduates. In other words, they are all the same.
14. **A. dissect literature too much and ruin the meaning** Henry views reading as delicate, the meaning comes "whole, unbroken." This is in contrast to the older students, who overanalyze everything they read ("carve and quarter") and apply their own modern interpretations to it ("stuffed with their political-sexual agendas").
15. **C. disapproving** Henry is critical and dissatisfied with college students.
16. **D. disapproving** Henry is displeased with college students and with college offerings such as the humanities courses taught by his brother. You can conclude that in general he disapproves of the state of college education.

Writing Effective Sentences

Lesson 1: Simple Sentences

Practice 1, page 119

A. The revisions are samples. Your rewrites may differ.
1. F It drives his girlfriend crazy.
2. F As soon as he comes home from work, he starts talking on the telephone.
3. C
4. F Dave's sister and his best friend like to talk on the telephone, too.
B. 5. **C. call from** Choice (C) correctly forms a complete sentence and avoids creating a sentence

fragment, as choices (A) and (B) do. "A conference calling" in Choice (D) is badly worded.
6. **C. if you're closing a deal, you can bring your lawyer into the conversation** Choice (C) includes a subject, thus creating a complete sentence. Choice (D) includes an incorrect verb form in *might could*.
7. **C. service can** Choice (C) uses the correct verb and avoids making a sentence fragment (as choice (D) does).

Lesson 2: Compound and Complex Sentences

Practice 2.1, page 121

A. 1. It was late, <u>and</u> I was walking home from work.
2. My co-worker, Judy, had offered to drive me, <u>but</u> I had refused.
3. It was a warm night, <u>so</u> I decided to get some fresh air.
4. It was really my choice. I could have taken a cab, <u>or</u> I could have walked.
5. I heard a loud noise, <u>so</u> I ran the last block to my house. Later, I learned that it was only a car backfiring.
B. 6. **B. An air courier carries shipping documents on an international flight and** A comma is required when two independent clauses are joined but not when two verbs are joined (*carries . . . gets*). All the incorrect choices have unnecessary commas.
7. **A. airlines, but** *But* is the most logical coordinating conjunction here. Most travelers on major airlines can check baggage. Because there are two clauses (*couriers . . . fly . . . they can't check*), a comma is needed.
8. **B. in advance, but they get their tickets on the day of the flight** A comma precedes a coordinating conjunction joining two independent clauses.

Practice 2.2, page 123

A. 1. Most fatal fires occur when a family is asleep.
2. Because a smoke alarm wakes you up, it can allow you to escape.

3. Try to replace the smoke detector's battery before it goes dead.
4. Although smoke detectors cost money, the expense is worth it.

B. 5. **B. are making a business call,** The subordinate clause should be followed by a comma. Choice (C) is incorrect because the present tense is needed for a statement that is generally true.
6. **A. After you identify yourself, ask** The introductory phrase should be followed by a comma. Choice (B) is incorrect because the word *Whenever* is not appropriate here.
7. **D. up, thank** Choice (D) correctly combines an introductory phrase and an independent clause to form a complex sentence.

Lesson 3: Run-Ons and Comma Splices
Practice 3, page 125

A. There are several possible correct answers. There may be other correct answers in addition to those listed.
1. Jeff just got his driver's license, and he's very excited. OR Jeff just got his driver's license. He's very excited.
2. He bought a car that has a lot of miles on it, so it wasn't very expensive. OR Because he bought a car that has a lot of miles on it, it wasn't very expensive.
3. He doesn't have a lot of free time, but he'd like to take a car trip. OR Although he doesn't have a lot of free time, he'd like to take a car trip.
4. He needs to find out about car insurance, get a good map, and join an auto club.

B. 5. **A. pictures if you just** Choice (A) correctly forms a complex sentence by adding a subordinating conjunction.
6. **B. Be patient and wait** Choice (B) correctly uses a coordinating conjunction. Don't be misled by the apparent lack of a subject; both clauses are commands, meaning the subject, *you*, is implied but unstated.
7. **C. the autofocus option, because most cameras** Choice (C) correctly forms a

compound sentence with a subordinating conjunction and a comma.

Lesson 4: Subordinate Ideas
Practice 4, page 127

A. There are several possible answers for each question. Sample answers:
1. Tornadoes and earthquakes can cause a lot of damage.
2. Earthquakes are somewhat common in California, but many Californians do not seem to mind.
3. On May 20, 2013, a tornado in Oklahoma killed twenty-three people and injured almost 400.
4. Tornadoes can occur anywhere in the United States and at any time of year.

B. 5. **D. repaired up** Choice (D) avoids forming two short, choppy clauses and instead forms one smooth sentence. The other choices are run-ons, excessively wordy, or both.
6. **A. may be brought or mailed to the service center** Choice (A) forms a compound predicate and avoids expressing ideas in short, choppy sentences.
7. **D. due to accidents, mishandling, or** Choice (D) makes one smooth, detailed sentence by forming a compound predicate.

Lesson 5: Modify Ideas
Practice 5, page 129

A. There are several possible answers for each question. Sample answers:
1. Trent's sister, who is a health professional, encouraged him to become a nurse.
2. When he wakes up the patients to take their blood pressure, they get rather annoyed.
3. He carefully writes their temperature and blood pressure on their charts.
4. It is hard to make visitors who are talking with the patients leave at 9:00 pm.

B. 5. **B. a person who is not the birth child of the adopter the rights of a son or daughter** Only choice (C) displays correct modifier placement.
6. **C. An agency requires a "home study" to determine**

All the wrong answer choices include misplaced modifiers.
7. **D. frequently handle these adoptions when parents ask them to** Choice (D) is the only answer choice that correctly places the modifier "frequently."

Lesson 6: Parallel Structure
Practice 6, page 131

A. There are several possible answers for each question. Sample answers:
1. Jenna has worked in a factory, in a store, and as a waitress.
2. She would like to put her kids in a better school and to get a better job.
3. She thinks the kids' father is irresponsible, lazy, and uncaring.
4. He doesn't have the time, the energy, or the money to give them what they deserve.

B. 5. **C. safer, more comfortable, and more pleasant** Choice (C) correctly makes all the adjectives into comparatives (*safer, more comfortable,* and *more pleasant*).
6. **D. computers, and** Choice (D) correctly forms a list in which all items display parallel construction.
7. **C. the secret code, press ON, and leave immediately** Only choice (C) makes all the verbs in the sentence (*punch, press,* and *leave*) parallel.

Writing Effective Sentences Practice Questions, pages 132–135

1. **B. Seal your windows so that cold air can't get through** When an independent clause comes before a subordinate clause in a complex sentence, there is no need to use a comma.
2. **B. day and 62° at night** Choice (B) is the only answer choice that avoids short, choppy sentences.
3. **D. sun, keep** Choice (D) is the only choice that correctly links the subordinate clause at the beginning of the sentence with the independent clause that starts with "keep."
4. **D. home. Do change** Choice (D) avoids making a comma splice or a run-on. It also is consistent with the theme of the paragraph as being a list of recommendations.

5. **A. will not cool down any faster when your air conditioner is on full blast** Only choice (A) correctly places the modifying phrase *any faster*.
6. **B. When I got the television home, I discovered** In this sentence, *When* begins a subordinate clause. A comma should be placed after a subordinate clause that begins a complex sentence.
7. **A. I returned to the store to see if the problem could** Only choice (A) correctly adds the subject "I" and uses the proper verb tenses.
8. **A. He claimed that because the TV had been used,** Only choice (A) correctly adds a subject, *He*, to make it clear who was claiming that the TV had been used.
9. **A. angry and frustrated about the treatment I received** Choice (A) makes a smooth complex predicate instead of a choppy run-on sentence, a run-on, or a comma splice.
10. **C. refund or get** Choice (C) puts both verbs in the same form. Choice (A) is grammatically correct but illogically suggests that Jeffrey will return *and* repair the TV.
11. **A. work productively if you feel alone** This choice correctly places *productively* close to the word it modifies (*work*) and avoids lengthy or wordy constructions.
12. **C. can make your day more pleasant and give you energy** A comma is not required before a coordinating conjunction that joins two verbs.
13. **B. Things get messy when the friendship unravels** A comma is not required in a complex sentence when the subordinate clause follows the independent clause. The verb form *get* is more appropriate than *are getting*, because the sentence does not refer to something that is necessarily happening right now.
14. **A. work or talk** Both verbs in the sentence should be in the same form. There is no need for a comma when a coordinating conjunction joins two verbs.
15. **B. may be hard, but it's worth the effort** A comma is required before the coordinating conjunction that

joins the two independent clauses in a compound sentence.
16. **D. hoaxes designed** Choice (D) efficiently turns the second part of the sentence into a descriptive phrase while avoiding wordiness.
17. **B. check a claim like this by contacting the agency** Choice (B) efficiently turns the second part of the sentence into a modifying phrase while avoiding wordiness.
18. **C. know. This** Choice (C) expresses the ideas as two independent clauses. Choice (A) is missing the comma required when joining two independent clauses with a conjunction.
19. **D. keep your computer equipment safe and avoid spreading hysteria** Choice (D) joins the two ideas in a compound predicate. A comma is not needed in a compound predicate.

Connecting Ideas

Lesson 1: Organize Ideas into Paragraphs

Practice 1.1, page 137

A. 1. The pharmacist at the local drugstore is very helpful.
2. No MI
3. Every vote counts, so let your voice be heard and vote!
4. When you are traveling, it's a good idea to mark your luggage clearly.
5. Listening to music can benefit you in many ways.
B. 6. **C. sentence 4** Sentences 1–3 explain who gets colds and how frequently. Sentences 4–6 are about the causes and prevention of colds.
7. **D. join paragraphs B and C** Sentence 10 in paragraph C is related to the main idea of paragraph B, the prevention of colds.

Practice 1.2, page 139

A. Your topic sentences should be similar to these:
1. Satellites have many different functions in today's world.
2. All signs show that the economy is headed for a slump.
3. The library has adopted a new dress code for employees.
B. 4. **D. Repetitive strain injury is a painful condition resulting from repeated use of the hands.**

The original topic sentence is too general. The other options don't tell the central point: what repetitive strain injury is.
5. **B. A number of factors contribute to repetitive strain injury.** This sentence covers the three causes of repetitive strain injury mentioned in the paragraph.

Lesson 2: Use Logical Order and Relevant Ideas

Practice 2, page 141

A. 1. Irrelevant detail: Getting very ill is one bad thing that could happen.
2. Irrelevant detail: Adult students can also use school supplies.
3. Irrelevant detail: This job will be extremely expensive!
B. 4. **D. remove sentence 3** This sentence adds no new information to what was given in the previous sentences.
5. **D. remove sentence 6** The information about the secretarial job is not relevant to getting a job in carpentry.
6. **D. move sentence 10 to follow sentence 8** It would be more logical to place sentence 9 at the end of the letter.

Lesson 3: Relate Sentences and Paragraphs

Practice 3, page 143

A. Your transitions should be similar to these:
1. Our marketing efforts need to be enhanced. Therefore, we will soon begin another marketing initiative.
2. Sales representatives say that their jobs are extremely demanding. However, the salary is attractive.
3. The marketing director has instructed sales representatives to try some new ideas. For example, sales representatives can give away free samples.
4. A new ad campaign will be launched in just a few weeks. As a result, we expect sales to increase.
B. 5. **B. Times are changing, however, and these days patrons can even buy coffee** This

position is the most logical for the transition. Also, because it is in the middle of a sentence, it should be set off by commas.

6. **B. restaurant. For example,** The second sentence offers an example of the broad menu described in the first sentence.

7. **A. In addition, having a cafe** This option inserts a helpful transition to move the reader smoothly from paragraph B to paragraph C.

Connecting Ideas Practice Questions, page 144–147

1. **C. sentence 5** Sentences 1–4 are about the general problem of sleep disruption, whereas sentences 5–8 are about reasons why people don't get enough sleep.

2. **B. High-achieving students get more sleep.** Both studies relate to the impact of lack of sleep on learning.

3. **A. grades. Similarly,** The ideas on either side of the "Select" button are similar, so they can be connected this way.

4. **D. remove sentence 13** The paragraph is about sleep, not losing weight.

5. **D. join paragraphs (C) and (D)** Both paragraphs contain tips for getting more sleep.

6. **B. sentence 4** Sentences 1–3 introduce the purpose of the passage. Sentences 4–7 contain general rules for stain removal.

7. **B. Choose the right water temperature for cleaning each stain.** This sentence is appropriate since the paragraph discusses hot, cold, and room-temperature water.

8. **D. juice, for example, removes** When a transition is placed in the middle of a sentence, commas should both precede and follow it.

9. **D. remove sentence 15** Sentence 15 explains a minor detail and moves away from the main idea of the paragraph.

10. **C. move sentence 19 to the beginning of paragraph D** Putting sentence 19 at the beginning of the paragraph lets readers know in advance what point the paragraph will make.

11. **C. remove sentence 5** Sentence 5 is a general statement about HMOs. It is not relevant to the explanation of which insurance carriers are being made available.

12. **A. However, you must pay the health providers when** A comma should follow when a transition begins a sentence.

13. **C. sentence 9** Until sentence 9, paragraph B is about the differences between the two insurance plans. Sentence 9 introduces the idea of the informational sessions.

14. **A. move sentence 14 to the end of paragraph C** Sentence 14 refers to the card that was mentioned in paragraph C and so continues that idea.

15. **A. move sentence 2 to follow sentence 3** The description of removing the wheel should start with the initial step.

16. **C. move sentence 11 to follow sentence 12** Sentence 11 tells what to do with the spot where there is a leak, so it should follow the information on finding that spot.

17. **C. The next step is to put the tire and tube back onto the rim.** Paragraph C describes the process of putting the tire and tube back on the rim.

18. **A. The final step is to reinstall the wheel.** Paragraph D describes the final step in the process; putting the wheel back on the bike.

19. **A. Then readjust the tire pressure, and you're** Of the choices given, *then* is the most appropriate transition for describing steps in a process.

Writing About Text

Lesson 1: Unpack the Writing Prompt

Practice 1, page 149

1. The topic of the writing prompt is **a pair of passages that discuss the safety of cell phones.**

2. The writing prompt asks me: **Do I agree with the writer of Passage A or the writer of Passage B, and what information led me to that decision?**

3. I am asked to include **specific information from *both* passages to support my response.**

4. Yes, I am being asked for **my position on the topic.**

Lesson 2: Identify a Writer's Argument and Assumptions

Practice 2, page 151

Your answers should be similar to this, but your wording may vary.

1. Mandatory military service
2. We should promote participation in volunteer programs rather than require mandatory military service.
3. There are a couple of assumptions you might have identified. One is: the potential drawback of mandatory military service (that is, the resentment it might generate) outweighs its potential benefit (preparing the U.S. military to face foreign threats). Another is: it would be better to heavily promote volunteer programs than to leave things the way they are now.
4. violence in video games
5. People should protest violent video games to protect children from portrayals of excessive violence.
6. There are a couple of assumptions you might have identified. First: the studies mentioned in the first paragraph, which indicated a correlation between violent video games and violent behavior, actually indicate a causal relationship. Second: the strategies effective in 1976 will still be effective today.

Lesson 3: Develop a Thesis Statement

Practice 3, page 153

These answers are samples; your answers may vary.

1. Prescription drug advertising on TV is harmful because it can lead patients to request or refuse medication for reasons that are not medically sound.

2. The author's argument against direct-to-consumer advertisement of prescription medication is unconvincing because it does not provide any statistical data about how drug advertisements have actually affected consumer behavior.

   Alternatively, you might have written something like this: The author's argument against direct-to-consumer advertisement of prescription medication is convincing because the author provides several potential dangers of the practice.

3. Because 18% of the U.S. population speaks a native language other than English, and because industries such as technology and business require contact with people who speak other languages, Americans should put a higher priority on learning foreign languages.

4. The author's argument in favor of foreign language education is compelling because she points out the large proportion of people living in the United States who speak foreign languages, as well as the many contexts where a native English speaker would come in contact with that 18%.

Alternatively, you might have written something like this: The author's argument in favor of foreign language education is not compelling because she does not explain the drawbacks of alternatives to foreign language education, such as enhanced English language education for those whose primary language is not English.

Lesson 4: Collect Supporting Evidence

Practice 4, page 155

These answers are samples; your answers may vary.

1. The passage states that alcohol is particularly harmful to parts of the brain that grow later in life. Another fact from the passage is that alcohol causes long-term damage to the heart and liver. In support of this position, the text further says that the United Kingdom allows younger individuals to drink and also has high rates of alcohol-related death.

2. Choose either agree or disagree.

3. You might have written something like this:

(Agree) One personal piece of evidence I would use to support my position is that teenagers are

already at higher risk of accidents when driving, and alcohol would only exacerbate this fact. (Disagree) One personal piece of evidence I would use to support my position is that 18-year-olds can enter combat in the military and can vote for the president. Claiming they are not responsible enough for alcohol is inconsistent with the responsibilities and privileges we otherwise give 18-year-olds.

Lesson 5: Plan Your Response

Practice 5, page 159

The following is a sample response. There is no objectively correct answer to the writing prompt. You may write your essay either for or against the author's position. Thus, answers to the following questions may vary.

1. **Sample thesis statement:** I think that the writer's position on owning a family pet is correct because the inconvenience and expenses cited outweigh the benefits, and because as someone allergic to cats, I agree with the writer's point that having pets can make it difficult for friends who visit.

2. **Sample outline:**
   I. The writer is correct that pets have more downsides than benefits and that families should not have pets.
   II. Monetary expenses; food, pet sitters, veterinary care, cleaning.
   III. Chores and time involved; kids may promise to help, but likely would not.
   IV. Friend can't visit; allergies, difficult with overnight guests.
   V. Pets are good friends and can be calming influence when people are stressed.
   A. Some people think this justifies any expense and difficulty in keeping animals.
      i. But, pets can keep away real friends and introduce stress as well, countering benefits.
      ii. Instead of petting a cat to relieve stress over money, it would be better to save the money you would spend on the cat's food and vet bills.

3. **Sample idea map:**
   The idea map below demonstrates how you might organize your thoughts to argue for pet ownership. Your idea map may vary.

Lesson 6: Draft Your Response

Practice 6.1, page 161

Your answers may vary.

A. Sample topic sentences:
Pet ownership is a major burden, and the time and money people invest in pets could be better spent elsewhere. The author of the passage says that keeping a pet is not worth the trouble, but he fails to consider all of the many benefits of pet ownership.

Your supporting statements may vary quite a bit, so no samples are given here. Check to make sure that your supporting statements are relevant to your topic statement.

B. Sample concluding statements:
And so, when all is taken into consideration, the conclusion is clear: the cost of a pet far outweighs the benefit. Don't let the long list of difficulties listed by the author scare you away, because a pet can be a friend to you and your children, one whose value can't be measured against time and money.

Practice 6.2, pages 162–163

Refer to the *Reasoning through Language Arts Extended Response Evaluation Guide* on page 722 to evaluate your response.

Practice 6.3, pages 164–165

Refer to the *Reasoning through Language Arts Extended Response Evaluation Guide* on page 722 to evaluate your response.

Lesson 7: Revise and Edit Your Response

Practice 7.1, page 167

A, page 167

Most of us are aware *that speeding has consequences*, which range from receiving a speeding ticket to getting into an accident. *Nonetheless*, a quick survey of any highway will show that many drivers exceed the speed limit. *This raises the question:* why do people speed?

¶One common reason is that people do not think they will suffer any consequences. If they have never been stopped by the police or ~~crashed their car,~~ been involved in a car crash, they don't see any reason to worry.

Another reason is that people simply need to get somewhere in a hurry. They realize that they are speeding but ~~they have such a need to arrive on time that they don't care~~ *their impatience gets the better of them.* ~~They've got ants in their pants~~.

¶A final reason is lack of respect for other drivers~~, one~~. One driver who is speeding makes road conditions less safe for everyone. Drivers who act as though they are in the Indy 500 ~~they~~ have no regard for the safety of others.

We know that people speed because ~~of impatience and they don't fear the consequences~~. they're impatient and don't fear the consequences. ~~Another reason is no respect~~. They also don't respect other drivers. Let's figure out what will make them stop speeding.

B, page 167

Refer to the *Reasoning through Language Arts Extended Response Evaluation Guide* on page 722 to evaluate your response.

Practice 7.2, page 169

Your revised paragraphs should be similar to the following.

One common reason for speeding is that people don't think they will suffer consequences. If they have never been stopped by the police or been involved in a car crash, they've never experienced the dangers of speeding first-hand.

Another reason is that people simply need to get somewhere in a hurry. They realize that they are speeding, but their impatience gets the better of them.

A final reason is lack of respect for other drivers. One driver who is speeding makes road conditions less safe for everyone. Drivers who act as though they are in a race have no regard for the safety of other drivers.

Writing About Text Practice, pages 170-173

A. Refer to the *Reasoning through Language Arts Extended Response Evaluation Guide* on page 722 to evaluate your response.

B. Refer to the *Reasoning through Language Arts Extended Response*

Evaluation Guide on page 722 to evaluate your response.

Polishing Your Writing

Lesson 1: Strengthen Sentences

Practice 1, page 175

A. Your revised sentences should be similar to the following. The underlined parts show where your revision marks should be:

1. First, write down what you know about your family. Then interview relatives. (Run-on sentence)
2. Videotaping or recording the interviews is a good idea. (Structure not parallel)
3. Ask relatives to provide exact names, dates, and other details. (Structure not parallel)
4. Make copies of documents such as birth certificates and marriage licenses. (Sentence fragment)
5. When older family members are interviewed, they'll often tell you stories you never heard. (Dangling modifier)
6. Carefully record all the information you get and put it in a three-ring binder. (Misplaced modifier)
7. Some people use their computers to do genealogy searches, and they get very good results. (Comma splice; coordinating conjunction needed)
8. However, one must have the time, the patience, and the know-how to use the Internet. (Structure not parallel)
9. If you do decide to learn more about your roots, don't be surprised to find yourself at a huge family reunion. (Comma needed after subordinate clause)
10. The whole process of putting together a family tree and contacting long-lost family members is rewarding. (Sentence fragment)

B. Sample revisions:
It was a beautiful day, and the blue ocean sparkled in the sunlight. It was a perfect day for going to the beach. As Renelle looked across the sand, she saw two little girls building a sandcastle and making a moat next to it. Renelle spread

out her <u>towel</u>, anchored it with her shoes and beach <u>bag</u>, and began to read a magazine. <u>Suddenly</u>, she heard a voice say, "Are you going to get in the water, or are you just going to lie there?" Renelle looked <u>up and</u> saw her friend Terry. She laughed softly <u>and got up to greet</u> Terry. Putting on her sandals, <u>she</u> walked <u>with Terry</u> across the burning sand to the water's edge.

Renelle loved going to the beach. <u>It relaxed her</u> and helped her forget about her problems. It didn't cost money like most other forms of entertainment. Most of Renelle's friends also spent a lot of time at the <u>beach, so</u> that was another incentive.

Lesson 2: Improve Organization

Practice 2, page 177

A. Your revised paragraphs should be similar to the following (starting after the first revision made for you):

Why do people continue to litter? One reason people litter is that they just don't care about others. It doesn't bother them to leave their trash in front of someone else's apartment building, forcing another person to deal with the problem. This inconsiderate attitude is also reflected in the refusal to recycle plastic, glass, and newspapers. People figure that they won't be around in the future when the landfills are used up, so who cares?

¶Another possible reason for littering is low self-esteem. If people don't feel good about themselves, they won't be motivated to keep their environment looking attractive. ~~Low self-esteem can cause many other problems, including depression and lack of self-confidence.~~ People who have high self-esteem believe that it's important to keep their home, the planet Earth, clean and beautiful.

B. Ask a friend or family member to evaluate your work.

Lesson 3: Word Choice

Practice 3, page 179

Sample answers:
A. 1. nonprofit organization
   2. thousands of

3. substandard
4. dollars
5. as soon as possible

B. If you ever order merchandise from a catalog, you should be aware of your rights. All companies, regardless of <u>the state in which they are located</u>, are required to ship your order within 30 days unless they have <u>advertised</u> a different shipping time. If a company is unable to meet the shipping deadline, it must send you an "Option Notice." You can choose to wait longer or get a refund.

Some consumers <u>have complained</u> about receiving merchandise that they did not order. <u>Companies</u> that <u>engage</u> in this practice <u>are breaking</u> the law. <u>If you receive</u> a product you haven't <u>ordered</u>, it is yours to keep.

If you receive a package that has been damaged, don't open it. Write "REFUSED" on the package, and return it to the seller. There's no need to add new postage as long as the package <u>came</u> by regular mail.

C. Have a friend or family member evaluate your work.

Polishing Your Writing Practice Questions, pages 180–183

1. **C. gardener, it's important that** Sentence 2 is a subordinate clause, not a complete sentence. Use a comma to combine it with the independent clause in sentence 3, creating a complex sentence.

2. **A. option if you live in a climate that is too extreme** The phrase *not good* is vague, since it provides no information about how a climate might be unsuitable. *Too extreme* allows the reader to anticipate the temperature and moisture requirements discussed in paragraph D.

3. **B. move sentence 8 to follow sentence 9** Sentence 9 is the topic sentence—it gives the main idea—for paragraph C. As such, it should be the first sentence of the paragraph.

4. **D. move sentence 11 to the beginning of paragraph D** The topic of paragraph C is choosing a garden spot, whereas the topic of paragraph D is choosing

plants. Therefore, sentence 11, which is about choosing plants, should appear in paragraph D.

5. **C. plants to** Choice (C) best expresses the relationship between the idea of investigating plants and the reason for doing so. These clauses should instead be joined with a word or phrase that expresses the relationship between them.

6. **A. Wales and had come to** The phrase *which had come* in the incorrect answer choices implies that Wales had come to the United States, not the boy. Replace *which* with *and* to clarify.

7. **D. ocean; it** A semicolon is required to separate two independent clauses, correcting the run-on sentence.

8. **C. Could he have crossed the vast** Describing the ocean as *vast* conveys the sense of size more precisely than does the phrase *really big*.

9. **B. kidding me** All of the wrong choices employ slang, which should be avoided.

10. **B. Sentence 12** Sentence 12 does not relate directly to the story of the narrator's great-grandfather's journey from Wales to the United States. Therefore it is unnecessary and should be removed.

11. **D. and morality. She also frequently** Only choice (D) avoids a run-on sentence.

12. **B. Many consider this** All of the incorrect answer choices are unnecessarily wordy. Additionally, choice (A) uses the informal phrase *figure*, which should not be used to express the idea of thinking.

13. **C. Combine the two sentences by replacing the period with a comma.** As written, the second sentence is not a sentence at all. It should serve as an appositive describing *lupus* in the previous sentence.

14. **A. Flannery maintained many fulfilling correspondences that gave her the insight into human behavior that is evident in her writing** This construction best avoids wordiness.

15. **A. will ensure you continue** The adverb *always* is

unnecessary when paired with the verb *continue*.

16. **B. Then we will replace** The adverbs *then* and *next* are redundant when used together.

17. **C. times. You** Insert a period and remove *and* between the two independent clauses.

18. **D. However, we will adjust your bill accordingly if your service is interrupted.** Unless *However* is followed by a comma, it seems that it is being used to modify the adjustment. Insert a comma to clarify that *However* introduces the sentence.

19. **B. about the scheduled repairs, please contact our office** Choices (A) and (D) create sentence fragments, and choice (C) is missing the comma that must follow an introductory phrase.

Using Grammar Correctly

Lesson 1: Noun and Pronoun Agreement

Practice 1.1, page 185

A. 1. They
   2. him
   3. it
   4. Her
   5. she
B. 6. **D. Bonetta and I** *Bonetta and I* is a compound subject, so a subject pronoun is required.
   7. **D. She always gets** The simple present tense and the subject form of the pronoun are appropriate here.
   8. **B. Walter or me** The phrase *Walter or me* is an object, so an object pronoun is required.

Practice 1.2, page 187

A. 1. Sally is moving to a small town. Her mother is concerned about the health care options it offers.
   2. Sally tried to reassure her mother, but it was hard for her mother to believe her.
   3. Sally asked a friend who lives in the town for information about its health care facilities. OR the town's health care facilities.
   4. The town has a freestanding clinic where a person can go when he or she is sick. OR

where people can go when they are sick.
5. There is also a nearby hospital, and it has a very good reputation.
6. If one is concerned about health care, one should sign up for a good insurance plan. OR If you are concerned about health care, you should sign up for a good insurance plan.
B. 7. **D. will learn only that they shouldn't make their** The word *children* earlier in the sentence is the antecedent to the pronoun; *their* agrees correctly with that antecedent, while the singular *one's* does not.
   8. **D. parents** Only choice (D) correctly identifies who should be clear about their expectations.
   9. **C. the child to play with the group** The term *play group* is a collective noun, so the plural *them* should not be used to refer to it. In this case, repeating the word *group* is the best way to make the meaning clear.

Lesson 2: Verb Forms and Tenses

Practice 2.1, page 189

A. 1. had ceased
   2. closed
   3. functions
   4. have visited
   5. will open
   6. looks
   7. are thinking
B. 8. **B. is offering** The action is taking place right now, so the present progressive is the correct tense.
   9. **D. If you sign up for Express Lane before April 9** The present-tense verb *sign* in the subordinate clause is appropriate, given the the future-tense verb *will receive* in the main clause.
   10. **D. will amaze you** The verb *will amaze* is in the simple future tense. The future progressive tense in *will be amazing you* is incorrect and overcomplicated.

Practice 2.2, page 191

A. 1. came
   2. showed
   3. had spoken

   4. took
   5. seen
B. 6. **D. began to appear on** The action takes place in the past tense, so the verb should be in its past form, *began*.
   7. **C. was broken** *Broken* is the correct past participle.
   8. **B. now give viewers** The clue word *now* tells you that the action is still true, so the present-tense form of *give* is correct.

Lesson 3: Subject-Verb Agreement

Practice 3.1, page 193

A. 1. is
   2. become
   3. is
   4. have
   5. seems
   6. is
B. 7. **B. have heard** In this sentence, the indefinite pronoun *most* is plural ("most of us"). The verb *have heard* agrees with the plural subject.
   8. **C. That noise occurs when a plane starts to** The verb *starts* agrees with the singular subject *plane*.
   9. **B. some other materials conduct sound** The verb *conduct* agrees with the plural subject *materials*.

Practice 3.2, page 195

A. 1. ~~on the market~~ carry
   2. ~~carrying the seal~~ are
   3. ~~an important ingredient in many toothpastes~~ strengthens, attacks
   4. are
   5. offer
   6. ~~with fluoride and good flavor~~ is
B. 7. **C. administers its own program and has** The verb *has* agrees with the singular subject *state*.
   8. **A. Wage level and length of employment** The verb *determine* agrees with the compound subject *Wage level and the length of employment*. The present tense is consistent with the rest of the passage.
   9. **C. draw benefits report regularly to their** The verb *report* agrees with the plural subject *workers*.

1. **C. highly paid coaches, but it didn't happen** The past tense is required because the second clause in the sentence is discussing what happened in the past.

2. **A. they** The antecedent of the underlined pronoun is *girls*, so it should be plural. *They* is clear; repeating *the girls* (as in Choice (B)) is unecessary. Choice (D), *them*, is incorrect because the pronoun is the subject of the dependent clause *while they practiced*.

3. **B. earned** The past tense is correct here because the action happened in the past over the course of a few years.

4. **D. who live in Palm Beach Gardens, Florida, are best friends** The verb *are* agrees with the plural subject *sisters*.

5. **D. there is no trace of sibling rivalry** The main clause needs the present tense verb *is* because the introductory subordinate clause has a present-tense verb, *face*.

6. **B. people where they have received** The present perfect is correct here because the point is to find out about other people's past experiences with auto shops, not their predictions about them.

7. **D. pick a shop just because it's close** Because this sentence is a command, the simple present tense is necessary.

8. **D. these often come with restrictions attached** The verb *come* agrees with the plural subject *specials*. Choice (C) is incorrect because the past tense is not consistent with the rest of the passage.

9. **D. what's wrong, the repair job will** The pronoun *it* in the incorrect choices has no clear antecedent.

10. **C. there are** The verb *are* agrees with the plural subject *limits*. The present tense is correct.

11. **B. changes and their effect** The antecedent *changes* is plural, so the plural possessive *their* should be used.

12. **C. send photocopies of your records** *Your* is used in the rest of the paragraph, so it is appropriate here.

13. **D. our calculations, which are appended to this letter** The word *which* is the subject of a subordinate clause. It refers to the plural noun *calculations*. Therefore, the verb *are*, not *is*, is required.

14. **A. has increased** The interrupting phrase *of taxes* does not change the fact that the subject of the new independent clause is *amount*, which is singular. The verb *has increased* therefore agrees with it.

15. **B. will credit** The future tense indicates an action that will take place at a later time, which is appropriate in this sentence.

16. **B. don't** The plural indefinite pronoun *many* is the subject of the sentence; the verb *don't* (don't = do + not) agrees with it. Changing to the past tense, choice (C), would be incorrect.

17. **C. is that people with disabilities have feelings** The verb *have* agrees with the plural subject *people*.

18. **B. him or her** The pronouns are objects of the preposition *with*, so the objective forms *him* and *her* are needed. The antecedent is *a person*, so the plural *them* in choice (D) cannot be used.

19. **B. such as a wheelchair, cane, or communication board, is the person's property** The verb *is* agrees with the singular subject *equipment*, and the interrupting phrase listing examples of assistive equipment is properly punctuated.

20. **B. it** *It* is the proper pronoun to use to refer to a dog.

Using Writing Mechanics

Lesson 1: Comma Use

Practice 1.1, page 201

A. 1. Train travel is more pleasant than riding a bus, but it can be more expensive.
2. When you're on a train, you can stand up and stretch if you need to.
3. NC
4. Unlike buses, trains sometimes have seats that face each other.
5. Traveling through a scenic area, you may find that your train has a double-decker car that offers a better view.
6. NC
B. 7. **A. For starters, use cooking methods that require little or no oil or butter,** A comma is required after an introductory phrase.

8. **A. dressing, and** A comma should come before a coordinating conjunction in a compound sentence.

9. **D. low-fat version, and though not all of them may be pleasing** The words *though not all of them may be pleasing to the palate* form a subordinate clause, and no commas are necessary in that clause.

Practice 1.2, page 203

A. 1. Kwanzaa is a week-long African American holiday that celebrates culture, community, and family.
2. Kwanzaa, a wintertime holiday, is based on an ancient African harvest celebration.
3. NC
4. Kwanzaa celebrations include rituals such as singing, dancing, drumming, and poetry reading.
5. The family lights one candle every day for each of seven principles: unity, self-determination, responsibility, cooperative economics, purpose; creativity, and faith.
6. NC
B. 7. **A. home accidents are responsible for more children's injuries than all childhood diseases combined** The subject and verb of a sentence should not be separated by a comma.

8. **B. medicines, poisons, or fragile objects are stored** Commas should be placed between items in a series.

9. **C. children, those ten and up,** You can mentally omit the phrase *those ten and up* and still understand the meaning of *older children*. Therefore, the appositive *those ten and up* should be set off by commas.

Lesson 2: Capitalization

Practice 2, page 205

A. 1. Last spring, I broke my arm in a car accident.
2. My internist, Doctor Claudia McNally, referred me to Waterside.
3. The center's director, Ilana Harris, assigned me a physical therapist named Ellie Royce.
4. Ellie studied physical therapy in her native London and used British methods of treat-

ment that relieved my pain quite effectively.

5. She also did therapy with me in the pool at Rainbow Health Club.

6. I finished my treatments just before Labor Day, and I feel 100 percent better, thanks to Ellie.

B. 7. **B. only emperors and nobles were** A title should be capitalized only when it comes directly before a person's name or is used in direct address.

8. **C. they were trained to hunt game and waterfowl in the mountains of Japan** A geographic feature is capitalized only when it is part of the name of a specific place, like *Rocky Mountains*.

9. **B. America by author Helen Keller** Proper nouns should be capitalized.

Lesson 3: Possessives and Contractions

Practice, page 207

A. 1. There's
2. can't, who's, it's
3. we're
4. theirs
5. ours

B. 6. **D. questions, we need your** In this phrase, the pronoun is showing ownership, so *your* is correct.

7. **B. In addition to our chain of stores, we're proud** *Were* is a verb and is incorrect in this sentence. Rather, an apostrophe should be inserted to create the contraction *we're*, the combined form of *we are*.

8. **B. parties should send their resumes** In this sentence, the pronoun is possessive, so *their* is correct.

Lesson 4: Homonyms

Practice 4, page 209

A. 1. fourth
2. know
3. whole
4. week
5. affect
6. past

B. 7. **C. have logged great achievements in the workforce, so why don't they receive fair pay** A *fare* is what you pay to get on the subway; *fair* means *just*.

Choice (A) is incorrect because the correct word is *great*, meaning large, rather than *grate*, meaning a metal frame. Choice (B) uses the wrong verb number: the word *women* needs a plural verb, *have*.

8. **A. In principle, the age gap could account for the wage gap because older women still work in jobs in which attitudes and conditions of the past** A *principal* is the head of a school; *principle* means *a guiding rule*. *Passed* in choice (C) and *four* in choice (D) are also incorrect homonyms.

9. **A. The effect is that, as women get older, the gap between men's and women's salaries becomes greater.** *Affect* is a verb meaning *to influence*; *effect*, which means *result*, is required here.

Using Writing Mechanics Practice Questions, pages 210–213

1. **B. Instead, children may have tantrums, erase phone messages,** The phrase *have tantrums* is the first item in series, so it should be followed by a comma.

2. **C. understand and show** A comma should not be used between two verbs, and avoiding the comma is simpler and cleaner than adding a new subject as in incorrect choice (D).

3. **D. your kids know that you feel you're** All the possessives, contractions, and homonyms in the sentence are spelled correctly. The comma following the introductory transition *However* cannot be removed, but the comma after *know* is incorrect.

4. **C. your children aren't at home** The apostrophe in a contraction must be placed in the spot where a letter has been removed.

5. **B. down, consider** An introductory subordinate clause should be followed by a comma.

6. **B. time is to save energy** The subject (*One*) and its verb (*is*) should not be separated by a comma.

7. **B. its standard time by an hour** The sentence is about ownership: each time zone has its own standard time. The possessive form *its* is correct.

8. **B. Congress passed a law making** The name *Congress* refers to a specific body of lawmakers and should therefore be capitalized.

9. **A. For example, radio and TV stations had** An introductory phrase must be followed by a comma.

10. **C. ending dates for daylight saving time in the spring and fall** There is no need to separate the final phrase from the rest of the sentence with a comma.

11. **C. for joining Spring Valley Community Center** When a proper name consists of more than one word, all the words should be capitalized.

12. **D. Please have your membership card with you at all times when you're in the building.** The sentence is saying, "when you are in the building," so the contraction *you're* is needed.

13. **A. If you are a weak swimmer, life jackets** A *week* is seven days. *Weak*, meaning *not strong*, is appropriate for this sentence.

14. **D. children's pool unless they're supervised** The clause beginning with *unless* does not need to be set off with commas.

15. **B. register and pay** Two items joined by *and* do not require a comma unless both are independent clauses.

16. **C. than their white counterparts, often for** The word needed in the sentence is *than*, meaning *compared with*. *Then* means *after that* or *at that time*.

17. **C. from 23 states show that this policy, called racial profiling,** The phrase *called racial profiling* is an appositive but is not essential to understanding the sentence. It needs a comma before and after it.

18. **B. distinctions, for nonwhites** The conjunction *for* is connecting two independent clauses in a compound sentence, so it must be preceded by a comma.

19. **B. Illinois, yet 30 percent** Names of states should be capitalized.

20. **B. However, police superintendents, chiefs of police, and other law enforcement officials** Three items are listed in the series: *police superintendents, chiefs of police, and other law enforcement officials*. There should be commas separating them.

MATHEMATICAL REASONING

Number Sense and Problem Solving

Lesson 1: Compare and Order Numbers

Practice 1, page 221

1. 4
2. 8
3. 9
4. 1
5. 6
6. 7
7. 3
8. 500
9. 80
10. 1100
11. 12,000
12. 2000
13. 100
14. 100
15. 341
16. 1145
17. 125,391
18. 18, 23, 39, 45
19. 89, 91, 109, 111
20. 909, 932, 1087, 1139
21. 1420, 1425, 1429, 1432
22. 11,098, 12,071, 12,131
23. 15,298, 15,309, 15,356
24. **C. 50, 48, 45, 40** Arrange the weights from heaviest to lightest.
25. **C. 1,500,000** The digit in the ten thousands column is less than 5, so round down.

Lesson 2: Whole Number Operations

Practice 2.1, page 223

1. 77
2. 100
3. 52
4. 36
5. 190
6. 4078
7. 43
8. 2117
9. 65
10. 114
11. 180
12. 293
13. 483
14. 456
15. 2419
16. 900
17. 11,308
18. 15,185
19. 131,197
20. 30,899
21. **B. 88** Calculate: 24 + 8 + 56 = 88
22. **C. $13** Calculate: $20 − $7 = $13

Practice 2.2, page 225

1. 484
2. 1000
3. 2736
4. 13
5. 105
6. 21
7. 1350
8. 2625
9. 3376
10. 28
11. 15
12. 6
13. 250
14. 44 r3
15. 300
16. 200 r4
17. 150
18. 67,068
19. 538
20. 384
21. 12,011 r8
22. **D. 96** Calculate: 16 × 6 = 96
23. **C. $75** Calculate: 15 × 5 = 75
24. **6** Calculate: 12 ÷ 2 = 6

Lesson 3: GED® Test Calculator Skills

Practice 3.1, page 227

1. 153
2. 1187
3. 784
4. 24
5. 27,084
6. 14,442
7. 11,704
8. 54
9. 1580
10. **B. 26,179** Press (clear) 42920 ⊖ 16741 (enter).
11. **D. $19,900** Press (clear) 995 ⊗ 20 (enter).

Practice 3.2, page 229

1. 25
2. 18
3. 35
4. 136
5. 125
6. 5%
7. 2
8. 135
9. 5%
10. **C. $336** Press (clear) 1680 ⊗ 20 (2nd) (((enter).
11. **A. 5%** Press (clear) 48 ÷ 960 (2nd))) (enter). The right side of the screen will display 5%.

Lesson 4: Word Problems

Practice 4.1, page 231

1. **C. 10** No paint is needed for the floor, so ignore the 700 square feet. 3500 square feet of wall space ÷ 350 square feet per gallon = 10 gallons.
2. **D. 22** 11 children × 2 party favors per child = 22.
3. **A. 5** Calculate: 30 − 25 = 5. The information that Sarah and Kate live 18 miles apart is not needed.
4. **90** Calculate: 450 gallons ÷ 5 gallons of *filtered* water use per day = 90 days.
5. **D. 90** The table states that it takes Joyce 30 minutes to give a pedicure. 3 × 30 = 90
6. **C. $25** Subtract the cost of the manicure & pedicure combination ($35) from the cost of a makeover ($60). $60 − $35 = $25
7. **42** Calculate: 7 × 6 = 42
8. **$162** Calculate: $189 − $27 = $162

Practice 4.2, page 233

1. **C. $103** Restaurant D ordered 2 cases of Boston lettuce and 3 cases of romaine lettuce in July. (2 × $17) + (3 × $23) = $103.
2. **B. $18** Calculate: 4 + 4 + 2 + 2 + 1 = 13 total cases, and delivery for the first 5 cases costs $2 each. 13 − 5 = 8 cases remained after the first 5, so delivery for those 8 cases costs $1 each. (5 × $2) + (8 × $1) = $18.
3. **B. Restaurant B** Calculate the totals for each restaurant:

Rest.	Asparagus	Tomatoes	Asparagus + Tomatoes
A	2 × $22	3 × $15	$44 + $45 = $89
B	4 × $22	1 × $15	$88 + $15 = $103
C	0 × $22	3 × $15	$0 + $45 = $45
D	1 × $22	4 × $15	$22 + $60 = $82

4. **C. 350** Calculate: 3 × 150 = 450 sheets will be used. Since the paper sells in packages of 400 sheets, 2 packages are needed, and 2 × 400 = 800. 800 − 450 = 350 sheets left over.
5. **A. 9** Calculate: 19 ÷ 2 = 9 r1, so the friends can make 9 whole batches using 2 cups of flour for each batch (and 1 cup will be left over).
6. **A. $1500** Calculate: (6 × $750) − $3000 = $1500.

Lesson 5: Distance and Cost

Practice 5, page 235

1. rate; $\frac{d}{t} = r$
2. distance; $d = rt$
3. time; $\frac{d}{r} = t$
4. price per unit; $\frac{c}{n} = r$
5. cost; $c = nr$
6. number of units; $\frac{c}{r} = n$
7. **$48** $c = nr$
   4 × $12 = $48
8. **$36** $c = nr$
   12 × $3 = $36
9. **$80** $\frac{c}{n} = r$
   $\frac{$320}{4} = 80
10. **5** $\frac{c}{r} = n$
    $\frac{$25}{$5} = 5$
11. **$2** $\frac{c}{n} = r$
    $\frac{$20}{$10} = 2

12. **180 miles** $d = rt$
$60 \times 3 = 180$

13. **200 miles** $d = rt$
$50 \times 4 = 200$

14. **1 hour** $\frac{d}{r} = t$

$\frac{\$25}{\$25} = 1$

15. **90 miles per hour** $\frac{d}{t} = r$

$\frac{270}{3} = 90$

16. **3 hours** $\frac{d}{r} = t$

$\frac{75}{25} = 3$

17. **A. 32** $\frac{c}{r} = n$

$\frac{\$640}{\$20} = 32$

18. **D. 55** $\frac{d}{t} = r$

$\frac{275}{5} = 55$

Number Sense and Problem Solving Practice Questions, pages 236–239

1. **D. 96** Multiply: 12 servings × 8 ounces = 96

2. **B. $2092** Add to find the total: $839 + $527 + 726 = $2092

3. **A. 4** Divide the length of the sample board by the length of the brace you want: 12 foot board ÷ 2 feet per brace = 6 braces per board. Since you can get 6 braces from each board, divide the total number of braces you want by 6: 24 ÷ 6 = 4 boards.

4. **B. 21** Use the square root function on your calculator or multiply each answer option by itself to find 441.

5. **A. 30,589** Subtract to find the difference in mileage: 70,040 − 39,451 = 30,589

6. **C. $656** You can use your calculator. Multiply: $3280 × 20% = $656

7. **A. $5625** Multiply: $125 × 45 = $5625

8. **B. 420** Divide distance by time to find Lydia's speed per hour: 180 ÷ 3 = 60. Then multiply by the number of hours she drove on Tuesday: 60 × 7 = 420

9. **B. 8** Divide the distance by the speed to find the time: 480 ÷ 60 = 8 hours.

10. **B. 96** Divide the total cost by price per item to find the number of items: $1440 ÷ 15 = $96

11. **A. $200** Multiply the late fee by the number of times Richard has paid his bill late: $25 × 8 = $200

12. **D. $53** Calculate: 7 × $5 = $35 and 18 × $1 = $18. Add the two amounts: $35 + $18 = $53

13. **A. 5** Divide. 17,500 total miles ÷ 3,500 miles between oil changes = 5 oil changes.

14. **A. 134** Divide: 536 total children ÷ 4 months = 134 children per month

15. **198** Subtract to find the difference: 636 − 438 = 198

16. **$1072** Multiply: $268 per payment × 4 payments left = $1072

17. **C. 51, 48, 44, 40**

18. **C. 2,350,000** Since the digit to the right of the ten thousands place is less than 5, the digit in the ten thousands place remains the same.

19. **A. 83** Calculate: 18 + 23 + 42 = 83

20. **A. $6** Calculate: $20 − $14 = $6

21. **B. 60** Since the question says "about," you can use approximate, or rounded, figures. Round the amounts and add: 8 + 33 + 18 ≈ 10 + 30 + 20 = 60

22. **62** Divide distance by time to find the rate of speed: 248 ÷ 4 = 62

23. **C. 18** Calculate: 144 ÷ 8 = 18

24. **B. 30** Since the question says "about," you can use approximate figures. Round 299 to 300 and 9 to 10 and then divide: 300 ÷ 10 = 30

25. **C. 1200** Use rounded figures: 33 rounds to 30, and 41 pounds rounds to 40: 30 × 40 = 1200.

26. **C. $9** Find the total and divide by 4: $21 + $15 = $36, then $36 ÷ 4 = $9

27. **A. $12** Subtract the amount David paid from the total: $128 − $20 = $108. Then divide the remaining amount by the remaining number of people in the group: $108 ÷ 9 = $12.

28. **D. 260** 65 miles per hour × 4 hours = 260 miles.

29. **B. $18** Add the cost of a 1-topping pizza and $2 for each of the 2 additional toppings: $14 + $2 + $2 = $18

30. **C. 14** Multiply by 2 for each dollar: 2 × 7 = 14

31. **24** Calculate: $1800 ÷ $75 per month = 24 months

32. **14** Divide the maximum capacity by the number of pages per document: 630 ÷ 45 = 14

Decimals and Fractions

Lesson 1: Decimal Basics

Practice 1, page 241

1. 3.8
2. 6
3. 0.43
4. 0.667
5. 8.1
6. 2.714
7. 0.45
8. 0.08
9. 4.68
10. 1.85
11. 1.029
12. 0.14
13. 5.08, 5.6, 5.8, 5.802
14. 0.1136, 0.115, 0.12, 0.2
15. 4.52, 4.667, 4.8, 14.005
16. 0.8, 0.8023, 0.803, 0.823
17. **C. 0.6 g, 0.572 g, 0.0785 g** The correct answer lists the weights from greatest to least. Since none of the weights has a whole number part, compare the tenths places.
18. **D. 1.38** This is the only choice that is rounded to the hundredths place. Since the number in the thousandths place of 1.3815 is less than 5, round down.

Lesson 2: Decimal Operations

Practice 2.1, page 243

1. 7.996
2. 10.508
3. 12.26
4. 5.85
5. 7.426
6. 2.11
7. 18.094
8. 5.117
9. 21.32
10. 0.895
11. 3.84
12. 2.35
13. 5.506
14. 21.16
15. 0.645
16. 2.426
17. 0.15
18. 4.88
19. 11.8
20. 14.016
21. 4.522
22. 2.36
23. 17.88
24. 17.225

25. **A. 22.25** Add the times: 7.2 + 6.8 + 8.25 = 22.25 minutes. You do not need to use the 3-mile distance to solve the problem.

26. **C. 4.25** Add to find Claudia's total hours for the week: 8.5 + 9.25 + 8.75 + 10 + 7.75 = 44.25. Then subtract 40 to find the number of overtime hours: 44.25 − 40 = 4.25 hours.

27. **A. 1.8** Add the lengths cut from the pipe: 2.8 + 1.4 = 4.2. Then subtract from 6: 6 − 4.2 = 1.8 meters.

28. **C. $55.26** Add the amounts: $16.98 + $31.78 + $6.50 = $55.26

Practice 2.2, page 245

1. 2.65
2. 12.8
12. 15,800
13. 34.1

3. 0.496
4. 0.52
5. 3.6
6. 4.09
7. 8.75
8. 3.375
9. 9.6681
10. 24
11. 14.2

14. 2.36
15. 0.656
16. 2.64
17. 1.65
18. 4.275
19. 3.696
20. 1.002
21. 0.0072

22. **D. 15.16** Multiply 3.79 liters by 4: 3.79 × 4 = 15.16 liters.
23. **B. $9.23** Multiply $0.45 × 20.5: $0.45 × 20.5 = $9.225, which rounds to $9.23.
24. **C. 92.9** Divide to find the average daily miles: 278.7 ÷ 3 = 92.9 miles.
25. **C. $0.26** There are 19 servings in a box of Toasted Oats. Divide: $4.94 ÷ 19 = $0.26.
26. **B. 50.0** Find the weight in the table and multiply: 12.5 × 4 = 50 ounces.

Lesson 3: Fraction Basics

Practice 3, page 247

1. $\frac{3}{5}$
2. $\frac{2}{4}$; $\frac{1}{2}$
3. $\frac{2}{3}$
4. $\frac{7}{3}$; $2\frac{1}{3}$
5. $\frac{7}{2}$; $3\frac{1}{2}$
6. $\frac{15}{4}$; $3\frac{3}{4}$
7. $5\frac{2}{3}$
8. $\frac{18}{5}$
9. 4
10. $\frac{47}{9}$
11. $4\frac{3}{4}$
12. $\frac{29}{12}$
13. $4\frac{7}{9}$

14. $\frac{7}{4}$
15. $8\frac{1}{4}$
16. $\frac{57}{10}$
17. $\frac{12}{16}$
18. $\frac{7}{21}$
19. $\frac{48}{60}$
20. $\frac{15}{40}$
21. $\frac{24}{100}$
22. $\frac{3}{4}$
23. $\frac{1}{6}$
24. $\frac{3}{5}$
25. $\frac{13}{15}$
26. $\frac{2}{3}$

27. **A. $\frac{3}{4}$** Of those surveyed, $\frac{18}{24}$ went to at least one movie. Reduce the fraction to lowest terms: $\frac{18 \div 6}{24 \div 6} = \frac{3}{4}$.
28. **C. $\frac{40}{100}$** Raise $\frac{2}{5}$ to an equivalent fraction with a denominator of 100 by multiplying both numbers by 20: $\frac{2 \times 20}{5 \times 20} = \frac{40}{100}$.

Lesson 4: Fraction Operations

Practice 4.1, page 249

1. $\frac{1}{2}$
2. 1
3. $\frac{1}{3}$
4. $\frac{1}{6}$
5. $\frac{11}{12}$
6. $1\frac{1}{8}$
7. $\frac{3}{10}$
8. $\frac{5}{18}$
9. $3\frac{13}{15}$
10. $1\frac{3}{4}$
11. $8\frac{1}{2}$
12. $11\frac{5}{8}$
13. $21\frac{7}{10}$

14. $7\frac{13}{18}$
15. $12\frac{5}{6}$
16. $2\frac{5}{8}$
17. $42\frac{5}{12}$
18. $22\frac{11}{20}$
19. $5\frac{1}{18}$
20. $11\frac{1}{8}$
21. $3\frac{23}{28}$
22. $1\frac{7}{24}$
23. $2\frac{3}{7}$
24. $8\frac{8}{9}$
25. $\frac{32}{35}$

26. **B. $1\frac{3}{16}$** Add to find the total: $\frac{5}{16} + \frac{7}{8} = \frac{5}{16} + \frac{14}{16} = \frac{19}{16} = 1\frac{3}{16}$ inches.
27. **C. $1\frac{5}{8}$** Subtract to find the difference in the lengths: $2\frac{7}{8} - 1\frac{1}{4} = 2\frac{7}{8} - 1\frac{2}{8} = 1\frac{5}{8}$ inches.
28. **A. $14\frac{3}{8}$** Subtract the amount sold from the amount on the bolt: $23\frac{1}{4} - 8\frac{7}{8} = 23\frac{2}{8} - 8\frac{7}{8} = 22\frac{10}{8} - 8\frac{7}{8} = 14\frac{3}{8}$ yards.
29. **C. $2\frac{11}{12}$** Add the amounts: $1\frac{2}{3} + \frac{1}{2} + \frac{3}{4} = 1\frac{8}{12} + \frac{6}{12} + \frac{9}{12} = 1\frac{23}{12} = 2\frac{11}{12}$ cups.

Practice 4.2, page 251

1. $\frac{1}{6}$
2. $\frac{11}{12}$
3. 14
4. $18\frac{3}{4}$
5. $\frac{7}{8}$
6. $\frac{21}{32}$
7. $7\frac{14}{15}$
8. $41\frac{1}{4}$
9. $2\frac{1}{32}$

10. 14
11. $1\frac{4}{5}$
12. 48
13. $2\frac{2}{5}$
14. $2\frac{1}{4}$
15. 27
16. 8
17. $9\frac{1}{2}$
18. $\frac{3}{4}$

19. **B. 75** Find $\frac{3}{16}$ of 400 by multiplying: $400 \times \frac{3}{16} = \frac{400}{1} \times \frac{3}{16} = \frac{75}{1} = 75$.
20. **B. 7** Divide: $20 \div 2\frac{3}{4} = \frac{20}{1} \div \frac{11}{4} = \frac{20}{1} \times \frac{4}{11} = \frac{80}{11} = 7\frac{3}{11}$. Ignore the remainder since the problem asks how many shirts can be completed.
21. **B. 33** You need to find how many $\frac{2}{3}$ hours there are in 22 hours. Divide: $22 \div \frac{2}{3} = \frac{22}{1} \div \frac{2}{3} = \frac{11}{1} \times \frac{3}{1} = \frac{33}{1}$.
22. **C. $37\frac{7}{8}$** Multiply $12\frac{5}{8}$ inches by 3, the number of panels: $12\frac{5}{8} \times 3 = \frac{101}{8} \times \frac{3}{1} = \frac{303}{8} = 37\frac{7}{8}$.

Lesson 5: Fraction and Decimal Equivalencies

Practice 5, page 253

1. **B. $20.00** Instead of multiplying $80 by 0.25, you can also find $\frac{1}{4}$ of $80.
2. **C. 480×0.3** Find $\frac{3}{10}$ of 480. "Of" in "of the workers" indicates multiplication, and the decimal equivalent of $\frac{3}{10}$ is 0.3.
3. **B. $4\frac{2}{3}$** The decimal part of the calculator display equals the fraction $\frac{2}{3}$.
4. **C. $18.00** Multiply 12 by 1.5. The decimal $1.5 = 1\frac{1}{2}$. Convert that fraction to an improper fraction: $\frac{3}{2}$ Now multiply: $12 \times \frac{3}{2} = \frac{36}{2} = 18$.
5. **B. $\frac{3}{4}$** Subtract: $1.875 - 1.125 = 0.75$, which equals $\frac{3}{4}$ inch.
6. **C. 0.375** Instead of dividing 3 by 8, think: $3 \div 8$ means $\frac{3}{8}$, which equals 0.375.

Lesson 6: Decimals and Fractions on the Number Line

Practice 6, page 255

1. **C. $\frac{2}{3}$** The number line is in increments of $\frac{1}{3}$, and the value you are asked to identify comes halfway between $\frac{1}{3}$ and 1.
2. **D. 2.8** The number line is in increments of 0.2, and the value you are asked to identify comes halfway between 2.6 and 3.
3. **C. 2** A minus B is $3\frac{1}{2} - 1\frac{1}{2} = 2$.
4. **$\frac{2}{3}$** Angela gave 16 of 24 cookies to her neighbor: $\frac{16}{24} = \frac{2}{3}$.

5. **4.625** Each increment on this number line is 0.125 greater than the previous increment.

6. **9.3$\overline{3}$** Each increment on the number line is 0.3$\overline{3}$ greater than the previous increment.

7. **3$\frac{1}{3}$** Each increment on the number line is $\frac{1}{3}$ greater than the previous increment.

8. **11$\frac{5}{6}$** Each increment on the number line is $\frac{1}{6}$ greater than the previous increment.

Lesson 7: Decimal and Fraction Calculator Skills

Practice 7, page 257

1. **7.379**
2. **2$\frac{1}{4}$** To work with mixed fractions on the TI-30XS MultiView™, use the (2nd) function above the $\boxed{\frac{n}{d}}$ key: (2nd) $\boxed{\frac{n}{d}}$ 3 ▶ 2 ▼ 3 ▶ ⊟ (2nd) $\boxed{\frac{n}{d}}$ 1 ▶ 5 ▼ 12 (enter). The number $\frac{9}{4}$ will appear on the right-hand side of the display.
3. **$380.25**
4. **42**
5. **$84.44** Multiply: $95 \times \frac{8}{9} = 84.44\overline{4}$. Round to get $84.44.
6. **$79.74** Divide: $956.88 ÷ 12 = $79.74.
7. **$1,475** Multiply: $118,000 × 0.0125 = $1,475
8. **4$\frac{1}{4}$ cups** Add: $1\frac{1}{2} + 2\frac{3}{4} = 4\frac{1}{4}$.
9. **B. $6.67** Multiply the weight of the quilt by $1.20: 5.56 × $1.20 = $6.672, which rounds to $6.67.
10. **C. 24** You need to find $\frac{3}{8}$ of 64. Multiply. $64 \times \frac{3}{8} = 24$ acres.

Decimals and Fractions Practice Questions, pages 258–261

1. **C. 15$\frac{3}{4}$** Subtract: $20\frac{1}{2} - 4\frac{3}{4} = 20\frac{2}{4} - 4\frac{3}{4} = 19\frac{6}{4} - 4\frac{3}{4} = 15\frac{3}{4}$
2. **B. $0.25** Divide the cost by the number of servings: $4.69 ÷ 19 ≈ 0.247, which rounds to $0.25.
3. **C. $1386.20** To find the amount the 12-month plan will cost a customer, multiply $98.85 by 12 and add $200: ($98.85 × 12) + $200 = $1386.20.
4. **C. $30.12** Multiply using your calculator. Use 10.5 for $10\frac{1}{2}$: $2.869 × 10.5 = $30.1245, which rounds to $30.12.
5. **B. 2.85** Since the answer choices are decimals, use your calculator.

Use decimals instead of fractions: $1\frac{1}{2} = 1.5$, $4\frac{3}{4} = 4.75$, and $2\frac{3}{10} = 2.3$. To find the average, add the three weights and divide the total by 3: $\frac{.5 + 4.75 + 2.3}{3} = \frac{8.55}{3} = 2.85$

6. **C. 32$\frac{1}{4}$** Divide: $258 ÷ $8 = 32.25, which equals $32\frac{1}{4}$.
7. **B. 57** Subtract $6\frac{1}{4}$ from $20\frac{1}{2}$ and divide the difference by $\frac{1}{4}$. To do the work quickly, use the fraction keys on your calculator or change the fractions to decimals: $20\frac{1}{2} - 6\frac{1}{4} = 14\frac{1}{4}$; $14\frac{1}{4} ÷ \frac{1}{4} = 57$.
8. **D. $90.00** Brand B costs $0.09 more than Brand A, so the school will save $0.09 on each marker. Multiply the savings by 1000: $0.09 × 1000 = $90.00.
9. **B. 3$\frac{1}{2}$** Add the times for the appointments: $\frac{3}{4} + \frac{3}{4} + 1\frac{1}{4} + \frac{3}{4} = 1\frac{10}{4} = 3\frac{2}{4} = 3\frac{1}{2}$
10. **C. 10** Divide $3\frac{1}{2}$ hours by the amount of time needed for a routine physical: $\frac{1}{2} ÷ \frac{1}{3} = \frac{7}{2} ÷ \frac{1}{3} = \frac{7}{2} × \frac{3}{1} = \frac{21}{2} = 10\frac{1}{2}$ Therefore, Jennifer can complete 10 physicals. Ignore the fraction remainder.
11. **D. $\frac{11}{12}$** Write the fraction and reduce it to lowest terms. You can save time by using the fraction key on your calculator, which automatically reduces a fraction to lowest terms. Press 5500 $\boxed{\frac{n}{d}}$ ▼ 6000 (enter). The right-hand side of the display will read $\frac{11}{12}$.
12. **C. $7.25** The first hour costs $3.50, and there are $1\frac{1}{2}$ hours left. There are 3 half hours, or $1\frac{1}{2}$ hours, so you will pay $3.50 + (3 × $1.25) = $7.25.
13. **$\frac{2}{3}$** Write a fraction and reduce: $\frac{56}{84} = \frac{56 ÷ 28}{84 ÷ 28} = \frac{2}{3}$
14. **0.84** Subtract to compare: $3.97 - 3.13 = 0.84$
15. **B. $\frac{3}{10}$** Subtract: $250 - 175 = 75$. Thus, 75 out of 250, or $\frac{75}{250}$, have not been loaded. Reduce: $\frac{75 ÷ 25}{250 ÷ 25} = \frac{3}{10}$
16. **B. $\frac{5}{8}$** $A - B = \frac{7}{8} - \frac{1}{4}$. Find a common denominator and subtract: $\frac{7}{8} - \frac{2}{8} = \frac{5}{8}$.
17. **A. 285** To find $\frac{3}{4}$ of 380, multiply. Change $\frac{3}{4}$ to 0.75. Then $380 × 0.75 = 285$.

18. **C. $\frac{5}{6}$** To find half of $1\frac{2}{3}$, either multiply by $\frac{1}{2}$ or divide by 2. Both results are the same: $1\frac{2}{3} × \frac{1}{2} = \frac{5}{3} × \frac{1}{2} = \frac{5}{6}$.
19. **D. core box, classic, bevel, cutter** You could change the fractions to decimals to solve the problem, but the quickest method is to rewrite the fractions with a common denominator of 32:
   cutter: $\frac{9}{16} = \frac{18}{32}$;
   core box: $\frac{5}{32}$;
   classic: $\frac{3}{8} = \frac{12}{32}$;
   bevel: $\frac{1}{2} = \frac{16}{32}$.
   Then arrange the like fractions from least to greatest by their numerators.
20. Points should be placed at $\frac{1}{8}$ and $\frac{1}{2}$. The most Joe will eat will be $\frac{7}{8}$ of his pizza, so the minimum he'll have left over will be $\frac{1}{8}$ of it. The least Joe will eat will be $\frac{1}{2}$, so the maximum he'll have left over will be $\frac{1}{2}$ of the pizza.
21. **C. 8** Divide: $60 ÷ 7.5 = 8$ days.
22. **C. 150** You need to find $\frac{5}{8}$ of 240. Multiply: $240 × \frac{5}{8} = \frac{\overset{30}{\cancel{240}}}{1} × \frac{5}{\cancel{8}} = \frac{150}{1} = 150$.
23. **A. $\frac{1}{2}$** Multiply: $\frac{2}{3} × \frac{3}{4} = \frac{\overset{1}{\cancel{2}}}{\cancel{3}} × \frac{\cancel{3}}{\cancel{4}} = \frac{1}{2}$.
24. **B. 56** Multiply: $140 × \frac{2}{5} = \frac{\overset{28}{\cancel{140}}}{1} × \frac{2}{\cancel{5}} = \frac{56}{1} = 56$.
25. **C. 17.9** Maya travels five segments of the route. Add to find the total distance: $2.4 + 4.3 + 3.6 + 3.6 + 4.0 = 17.9$.
26. **D. 5** Add to find the total amount to be cut off: $3\frac{3}{4} + 3\frac{3}{4} = 6\frac{6}{4} = 7\frac{1}{2}$. Subtract from $12\frac{1}{2}$: $12\frac{1}{2} - 7\frac{1}{2} = 5$.
27. **B. $535.60** Multiply $26.38 by 20 and add $8 to the result: $26.38 × 20 = $527.60. Then: $527.60 + $8.00 = $535.60.
28. **80.** Divide: $60 ÷ 0.75 = 80$.
29. **$\frac{7}{12}$** Add the fractions and subtract the total from 1: $\frac{1}{6} + \frac{1}{4} = \frac{2}{12} + \frac{3}{12} = \frac{5}{12}$. Then: $1 - \frac{5}{12} = \frac{12}{12} - \frac{5}{12} = \frac{7}{12}$.

Ratio, Proportion, and Percent

Lesson 1: Ratio and Proportion

Practice 1.1, page 263

1. $\frac{24}{6} = \frac{4}{1}$
2. $\frac{$250}{$1500} = \frac{1}{6}$

3. $\frac{180}{15} = \frac{12}{1}$

4. $\frac{12}{30} = \frac{2}{5}$ Add 12 + 18 = 30 to find the total workers.

5. $\frac{336}{14} = \frac{24}{1}$

6. $\frac{\$1500}{\$2400} = \frac{5}{8}$

7. $\frac{20}{12} = \frac{5}{3}$ Subtract 32 − 20 = 12 to find the free throws missed.

8. $\frac{14}{24} = \frac{7}{12}$ Add 10 + 14 = 24 to find the total students.

9. $\frac{1440}{6} = \frac{240}{1}$

10. **A. 9:11** Write the ratio in fraction form and reduce: $\frac{180}{220} = \frac{9}{11}$.

11. **B. 3 to 10** Calculate: $\frac{180}{600} = \frac{3}{10}$.

12. **B. $\frac{1}{3}$** Subtract to find the voters who have made a decision: 600 − 150 = 450. Write the ratio and reduce: $\frac{150}{450} = \frac{1}{3}$.

13. **C. 1 to 2** Subtract to find the amount owed: $1200 − $400 = $800. Write the ratio and reduce: 400 to 800 = 1 to 2.

14. **D. 8:3** Subtract to find the number of losses: 77 − 56 = 21. Write the ratio and reduce: $\frac{56}{21} = \frac{8}{3}$.

Practice 1.2, page 265

1. 12
2. 45
3. 2.5 or $2\frac{1}{2}$
4. 60
5. $371
6. 96
7. 2.1 or $2\frac{1}{10}$
8. 72
9. 12.5 or $12\frac{1}{2}$
10. $8.94
11. 1.25 or $1\frac{1}{4}$
12. 37.5 or $37\frac{1}{2}$
13. 18
14. 32
15. $45.50
16. 28
17. **B. $1.23** Calculate: $\frac{4}{\$0.98} = \frac{5}{x}$ $0.98 × 5 ÷ 4 = $1.225, which rounds to $1.23.
18. **C. 96** Calculate: $\frac{5}{8} = \frac{60}{x}$; 8 × 60 ÷ 5 = 96.
19. **B. 23** Calculate: $\frac{414}{18} = \frac{x}{1}$; 414 × 1 ÷ 18 = 23.
20. **B. 345** Calculate: $\frac{2 \text{ cm}}{150 \text{ km}} = \frac{4.6 \text{ cm}}{x \text{ km}}$; 150 × 4.6 ÷ 2 = 345.
21. **A. $6\frac{2}{3}$** Write the proportions using fractions. The process is the same: $\frac{2\frac{1}{2}}{1\frac{1}{2}} = \frac{x}{4}$; $2\frac{1}{2} × 4 ÷ 1\frac{1}{2} = 6\frac{2}{3}$.

22. **A. 155 × 7 ÷ 2.5** Set up the proportion and think about the order of operations you would need to solve for x: $\frac{155}{2.5} = \frac{x}{7}$; 155 × 7 ÷ 2.5 = x.

Lesson 2: Percents

Practice 2, page 267

1. base = $1000
   part = $200
   rate = 20%
2. base = 80
   part = 72
   rate = 90%
3. base = $13,700
   part = $2,740
   rate = 20%
4. base = $2000
   part = $500
   rate = 25%
5. base = 40
   part = 60
   rate = 150%
   60 is 150% *of* 40.
   The word *of* indicates that 40 is the base.
6. base = $38
   part = $3.23
   rate = 8.5%
7. base = $900
   part = $135
   rate = 15%
8. base = $10.70
   part = $1.07
   rate = 10%
9. base = 800
   part = 200
   rate = 25%
10. base = 12,500
    part = 5,000
    rate = 40%

11. **A. $\frac{9 \times 100}{12}$** Add the wins and losses to find the total games played: 9 + 3 = 12; then write the proportion: $\frac{9}{12} = \frac{x}{100}$. To solve the proportion, you need to find the expression that multiplies 9 and 100 and divides by 12. Only choice (A) does this.

12. **D. 50%** Bravo played 12 games (6 + 6 = 12). Then $\frac{6}{12} = \frac{x}{100}$ and 6 × 100 ÷ 12 = 50.

13. **C. $32** To find 25% of $128, solve the proportion: $\frac{x}{\$128} = \frac{25}{100}$; $128 × 25 ÷ 100 = $32. Since 25% = $\frac{1}{4}$, you can also find the answer by dividing $128 by 4.

Lesson 3: Using the Percent Formula

Practice 3.1, page 269

1. $5
2. 180
3. 140
4. 95%
5. 25%
6. 3%
7. 17
8. $60
9. 200%
10. 5%
11. 8%
12. $3.91
13. $6\frac{1}{2}$% or 6.5%
14. $364
15. 62.5% or $62\frac{1}{2}$%
16. 72
17. **C. 60%** Calculate: 72 ÷ 120 = 0.6 = 60%.

18. **B. $2,385** Calculate: $2,250 × 0.06 = $135, and $2,250 + $135 = $2,385.

19. **D. $6.90** Calculate: $46 × 0.15 = $6.90.

20. **D. 70%** Find what percent $45.50 is of $65 by dividing: $45.50 ÷ $65 = 0.7, which equals 70%.

21. **A. $\frac{\$3 \times 100}{\$50}$** You need to divide the part ($3) by the whole ($50) to find the rate; however, choice (D) states $3 ÷ $50, which equals 0.06. You still need to change 0.06 to a percent, which you can do by multiplying by 100. If you write a proportion to solve the problem, you will see that choice (A) is correct.

Practice 3.2, page 271

1. $175
2. 280
3. 6.4
4. $200
5. 30
6. $84
7. 200
8. 9
9. $13.50
10. 25%
11. $75
12. $9.30
13. 900
14. 90%
15. $780
16. $3120
17. 4000
18. 10%

19. **C. $1,230.00** Solve for the base: $\frac{\$369}{0.3} = \$1,230$.

20. **C. $1,200,000** Solve for the base. $\frac{\$72,000}{0.06} = \$1,200,000$.

21. **B. $\frac{160 \times 100}{5}$** Set up the problem as a proportion: $\frac{160}{x} = \frac{5}{100}$. To solve the proportion, you would multiply 160 × 100 and divide by 5. Only choice (B) carries out those operations.

22. **C. 720.** The base is 3600, the total number who received the application. The part is the unknown number who returned the application. Since 20% = 0.2, you can solve for the part by multiplying the base by the rate: 3600 × 0.2.

Lesson 4: Percent Calculator Skills

Practice 4, page 273

1. $59.80
2. $96
3. $15.12
4. 40
5. 3%
10. 79
11. 2.5% or $2\frac{1}{2}$%
12. 48
13. 78%
14. $16

6. 2080

7. 25%

8. 70

9. 25.2

15. 250

16. 14

17. 7%

18. 276

19. **C. $8.20** Chanel's order falls between $50.01 and $100. Find 5% of $84: press: 0.05 ⊗ 84 (enter). The right side of the display reads 4.2, or $4.20. Add $4: $4.20 + $4 = $8.20.

20. **A. $0.30** Find the shipping and handling for Jason's order: 8% of $110 = $8.80. Find the shipping and handling for Zola's order: 5% of $90 = $4.50, and $4.50 + $4.00 = $8.50. Then find the difference: $8.80 − $8.50 = $0.30.

21. **C. 88%** Press: 3190 ÷ 3625 (2nd)) (enter). The right side of the display reads 0.88. You could also simply divide: 3190 ÷ 3625 = .88. Then mentally translate .88 into 88%.

22. **D. 15%** Divide strikeouts (63) by at bats (410): press: 63 ÷ 410 (enter). The right side of the display reads 0.153658537, which rounds to 15%.

Lesson 5: Simple Interest

Practice 5, page 275

1. $360

2. $56

3. $420

4. $480

5. $1137.50

6. $1998. Note that 8 months = $\frac{2}{3}$ year.

7. $1700

8. **D. $1300 + ($1300 × 0.09 × 1.5)** Find the interest by multiplying the amount borrowed ($1300) by the interest expressed as a decimal (0.09) by the time period in years (1.5). To find the amount paid back, the amount borrowed must be added to the interest. Only choice (D) shows this series of operations.

9. **A. $2400** Multiply: $8000 × 0.06 × 5 = $2400.

10. **B. $1545** Find the amount of interest: for the time period, use $\frac{9}{12}$ months, which equals $\frac{3}{4}$, or 0.75; multiply: $1500 × 0.04 × 0.75 = $45. Add to find the amount paid back: $1500 + $45 = $1545.

11. **B. $144** Find the interest for each loan option: Option A: $2400 × 0.12 × 2.5 = $720; Option C: $2400 × 0.09 × 4 = $864. Subtract to find the difference: $864 − $720 = $144.

12. **D. $3640** Find the interest she will owe: $2800 × 0.1 × 3 = $840. Add to find the amount she will pay back: $2800 + $840 = $3640.

Lesson 6: Percent of Change

Practice 6, page 277

1. 50%

2. 38%

3. 200%

4. 45%

5. 20%

6. 32%

7. 21%

8. 86%

9. 420%

10. 34%

11. **B. 60%** Subtract $448 − $280 = $168. Divide by the original weekly pay: $168 ÷ $280 = 0.6, which equals 60%.

12. **B. 25%** Subtract $48 − $36 = $12. Divide by the original price: $12 ÷ $48 = 0.25, which equals 25%.

13. **C. 6%** Subtract $636 − $600 = $36. Divide by the original rent: $36 ÷ $600 = 0.06, which equals 6%.

14. **C. 125%** The wholesale price of the model is $63, and the retail price is $141.75. Subtract: $141.75 − $63 = $78.75. Divide by the wholesale price: $78.75 ÷ $63 = 1.25, which equals 125%.

15. **B. 30%** The retail price of the model is $150.50, and the member's price is $105.35. Subtract: $150.50 − $105.35 = $45.15. Divide by the retail price: $45.15 ÷ 150.50 = 0.3, which equals 30%.

Ratio, Proportion, and Percent Practice Questions, pages 278–281

1. **C. 1:11** Subtract to find the dollars spent on other costs: $360,000 − $30,000 = $330,000. Write a ratio and reduce: $\frac{\$30,000}{\$330,000} = \frac{1}{11}$.

2. **A. 2 × $\frac{50}{5}$** Write a proportion: $\frac{5}{2} = \frac{50}{x}$. To solve it, multiply 2 × 50 and divide by 5. Only choice (A) performs these operations.

3. **B. $7.56** Find 35% of $5.60: $5.60 × 0.35 = $1.96; add: $1.96 + $5.60 = $7.56. Another way to get the answer is to find 135% of $5.60. $5.60 × 1.35 = $7.56.

4. **D. $20,000** The current worth of the car ($12,000) is part of the base. Solve for the base: $12,000 ÷ 0.6 = $20,000.

5. **C. 42** Solve the proportion: $\frac{7}{3} = \frac{x}{18}$; 7 × 18 ÷ 3 = 42.

6. **A. 6%** The commission is part of the base. Solve for the part: $954 ÷ $15,900 = 0.06 = 6%.

7. **B. 1:6** Add to find the total time spent on the project: $2 + 1\frac{1}{2} + 2 + 3\frac{1}{2} = 9$ hours. $1\frac{1}{2}$ hours = 1.5 hours. Write a ratio using decimals and reduce: $\frac{1.5}{9} = \frac{1}{6}$.

8. **B. 36%** Add to find the acres used for grains, vegetables, or fruits: 5,200 + 9,200 = 14,400. Solve for percent: 14,400 ÷ 40,400 = 0.36 = 36%.

9. **A. 35,600** Calculate the decrease in acres of dairy farmland: 22,000 × 20% = 4,400. Subtract that amount from the total acreage of farmland to determine how many acres of farmland will remain: 40,000 − 4,400 = 35,600.

10. **A. $\frac{3}{16}$** The total fat is 3 + 13 = 16 grams. Write the ratio of saturated fat (3 grams) to the total (16 grams). The ratio cannot be simplified.

11. **B. 10** Write a proportion and solve: $\frac{4}{5} = \frac{x}{12.5}$. Then 4 × 12.5 ÷ 5 = 10 inches.

12. **138** Write a proportion and solve: $\frac{4}{3} = \frac{184}{x}$. Then 3 × 184 ÷ 4 = 138 female patients.

13. **$900** If 20% is the amount of the discount, then the sale price must be 80% of the original price. The sale price is the part, and the original price is the base. Solve for the base: $720 ÷ 0.8 = $900.

14. **B. 40** If the ratio of wins to losses is 5:4, then the ratio of wins to games played is 5:9. Write a proportion and solve: $\frac{5}{9} = \frac{x}{72}$; 5 × 72 ÷ 9 = 40 games won.

15. **C. 192** Add to find the number that did not answer "no": 16% + 32% = 48%. Find 48% of 400: 400 × 0.48 = 192.

16. **C. 20%** To find the percent decrease, subtract the lower price from the higher price and divide the difference by the original price. In this case, the original price is $25, the higher price. To change the answer to a percent, you must move the decimal point two places to the right or multiply by 100.

17. **A. 121** When the rate is greater than 100%, the part will be greater than the base. Solve for the part: 55 × 2.2 = 121.

18. **D. 18%** There are 6 grams of fat in the roast beef sandwich, so there are 6 × 9 = 54 calories in the sandwich from fat.

The total number of calories in the sandwich is 300. Find what percent 54 is of 300: $54 \div 300 = 0.18 = 18\%$.

19. **D. $264** Write a proportion and solve: $\frac{\$8}{\$3} = \frac{\$704}{x}$; $\$3 \times \$704 \div \$8 = \$264$.

20. **C. 175** The 140 employees who have more than 12 days of sick leave are part of the whole workforce. You need to solve for the base: $140 \div 0.8 = 175$.

21. **D. 825** If the ratio of sold to unsold tickets is 11 to 1, then the ratio of sold to total tickets is 11 to 12. Write a proportion and solve: $\frac{11}{12} = \frac{x}{900}$; $11 \times 900 \div 12 = 825$.

22. **C. $2464** Use the formula for finding simple interest: $i = prt$: $\$2200 \times 0.08 \times 1.5 = \$264$. To find the amount in the account at the end of the time, add the interest to the original investment: $\$2200 + \$264 = \$2464$.

23. **B. $328** Once you find the discount by multiplying 0.2 by $410, you will need to subtract the discount from $410 to find the sale price.

24. **D. 330** After changing $2\frac{3}{4}$ to the decimal 2.75, write a proportion and solve: $\frac{0.5}{60} = \frac{2.75}{x}$; $60 \times 2.75 \div 0.5 = 330$.

25. **C. $\frac{(140 - 91)}{140} \times 100$** There were 140 customers on Sunday, and 91 made a purchase. Therefore, $140 - 91$ did not make a purchase. To find the percent rate, divide the difference by 140, the total number of customers on Sunday (the base). Then move the decimal point two places to the right or multiply by 100 to change the answer to a percent. Only choice (C) shows this sequence of operations.

26. **270** Write a proportion and solve: $\frac{9}{14} = \frac{x}{420}$.

27. **$\frac{3}{5}$** If Marcie spends 15 hours answering telephones, she spends $40 - 15$, or 25 hours doing other tasks. Write a ratio and reduce: $\frac{15}{25} = \frac{3}{5}$.

Data, Statistics, and Probability

Lesson 1: Tables and Pictographs

Practice 1, page 283

1. **9** Calculate: $22{,}707 \div 2523 = 9$

2. **6%** Calculate: $(139{,}510 - 130{,}748) \div 139{,}510 \approx 0.06$, or 6%.

3. **300** There are $6\frac{1}{2}$ symbols in the "North" row and $4\frac{1}{2}$ in the "South" row. Two more symbols translates to 300 more books.

4. **3000** Count the number of symbols, 20, and multiply by 150.

5. **D. Reads or pretends to read** If 100 children were surveyed in each year, then the number of children who recognized all letters increased from 11 to 17. To find the percent change, use the percent change formula:
$$\frac{\text{amount of change}}{\text{original value}} = \frac{17 - 11}{11} = \frac{6}{11},$$
or a roughly 55% increase. Performing similar calculators for all categories will reveal that "reads or pretends to read" showed the least percent increase:
$$\frac{67 - 66}{6} = \frac{1}{66} \approx 2\%.$$
Note that simply subtracting 66 from 67 does not give you the percent of change.

6. **C. 119** In 2010, 34% of 3-year-old children could write their own names. Find 34% of 350: $350 \times 0.34 = 119$.

7. **C. 375** There are $7\frac{1}{2}$ car symbols. Each symbol represents 50 cars. Multiply: $7\frac{1}{2} \times 50 = 375$

8. **A. 75** Compare the symbols for the two rows. There are $1\frac{1}{2}$ more symbols for 8 A.M. to noon than there are after 4:30 P.M. Multiply: $1\frac{1}{2} \times 50 = 75$

Lesson 2: Bar and Line Graphs

Practice 2.1, page 285

1. **50**

2. **about 15** Estimate 38 complaints in 2011 and 22 complaints in 2006. Subtract and round.

3. **20%** The number of complaints decreased by 5, from 25 to 20. This represents a $\frac{5}{25} = 20\%$ decrease.

4. **about $20 million** Estimate values from the graph and subtract.

Be sure to use the black bars that represent cost.

5. **Film A** Film A has the biggest difference in size between the bar representing box-office receipts and the bar representing cost.

6. **150%** Calculate: $\frac{60}{40} = \frac{3}{2} = 150\%$

7. **A. 40** There are approximately 110 T-shirts, more than 40 books, and a little fewer than 30 toys sold. Combined, about 70 books and toys were sold. Subtract 70 from 110, and you have about 40.

8. **D. $1000** There were about 50 games sold, so 25 sold for $16 and 25 sold for $24. Calculate: $(25 \times 16) + (25 \times 24) = 1000$.

9. **C. 14:3** Write a ratio and simplify: $\frac{70}{15} = \frac{14}{3}$

10. **D. September** Add the 2-day and 5-day permits for each month. Only September's permits equal 80.

Practice 2.2, page 287

1. **October** The point representing October is lower than the point representing the previous month, and the line leading to it slopes downward. This indicates a decrease.

2. **270** Estimate totals for the three months and add.

3. **from June to July** The number of visits increased more from August to September, but because the number in June was so low, the percentage increase from June to July is nearly 100%.

4. **$10** Estimate values and subtract.

5. **20%** The price increased from about $25 to about $30, an increase of $5. $\frac{5}{25} = 20\%$.

6. **$30** The price increased from about $18 to about $45. This increase is almost $30.

7. **A. 1930 to 1940** The price of goods decreased over two decades, 1920 to 1940. Note the downward movement of the line. Only the time period 1930 to 1940 is included among the answer options.

8. **D. $\frac{1}{5}$** The price of the same goods was about $20 in 1970 and $100 in 2000. Write a ratio and simplify: $\frac{\$20}{\$100} = \frac{1}{5}$

9. **B. 50** There were about 390 sales in Store 2 and 340 sales in Store 1 in the sixth week: 390 − 340 = 50.

10. **D. Week 5** The steepest line segment leads from week 4 to week 5, indicating the largest increase in sales from the previous week.

Lesson 3: Circle Graphs

Practice 3, page 289

1. **29%** Find those two categories on the circle graph and add.
2. $\frac{2}{25}$ $8\% = \frac{8}{100} = \frac{2}{25}$
3. **$630** Use the total budget. $2250 × 28\% = $630.
4. **$30.60** 17 cents of every dollar are spent on water heating: $180 × 0.17 = $30.60.
5. **Heating and Air-Conditioning** The section labeled "Heating and Air-Conditioning" takes up more than half the circle.
6. **Cooking and Refrigeration** This section is 11 cents of every dollar, which is about 10%.
7. **A. 10** According to the graph, a records clerk spends 25%, or $\frac{1}{4}$, of his or her time preparing documents. Then 25% of 40 hours is 10 hours.
8. **D. 56%** If 44% of the time is spent on data entry, then 100% − 44%, which equals 56%, is spent on other tasks.
9. **B. 10%** Add: 3 cents plus 7 cents is 10 cents. Then 10 cents out of 100 cents is $\frac{10}{100}$, or 10%.
10. **C. $48** 40 cents out of every dollar, or 40%, is spent on public bonds. Then 40% of $120 is found by multiplying: $120 × 0.4 = $48.

Lesson 4: Measures of Central Tendency

Practice 4.1, page 291

1. **57** Count the number of tally marks and add.
2. **6** Count the number of tally marks and subtract.
3. **1:2** Calculate: $\frac{15}{30} = \frac{1}{2}$
4. **3:4** Calculate: $\frac{6}{8} = \frac{3}{4}$
5. **46** Count the tally marks and add.

6. **14%** Count the total number of tally marks, then divide: $\frac{10}{70} ≈ 0.14 = 14\%$.
7. **B. $\frac{4}{11}$** There are 16 tally marks next to the reason "wrong size." Add all the tally marks: 16 + 20 + 3 + 5 = 44. Write a ratio and reduce. $\frac{16}{44} = \frac{4}{11}$.
8. **C. 45%** Adding all the tally marks, you find that there were 44 clothing returns in all. Since there are 20 tally marks by "unwanted gift," $\frac{20}{44}$ or ≈ 45% of the total reasons given were "unwanted gift."
9. **D. 39%** Calculate: 35 applicants had a speed under 30 wpm, out of a total of 90 applicants, so $\frac{35}{90} ≈$ 39%.
10. **B. 1:2** To find those who could type above 45 wpm, add: 18 + 12 = 30. The number typing below 45 wpm is found by adding 35 + 25 = 60. Write a ratio and reduce: $\frac{30}{60} = \frac{1}{2}$.

Practice 4.2, page 293

1. mean: 80.14
   median: 80
   mode: 82
2. mean: $8487.17
   median: $8208.50
   mode: none
3. mean: $4.76
   median: $4.50
   mode: $4.50
4. mean: 309 miles
   median: 300 miles
   mode: none
5. mean: $101.83
   median: $101.81
   mode: none
6. mean: 86
   median: 88
   mode: 88
7. mean: 99.1°
   median: 99°
   mode: 98° and 100°
8. mean: 1.9 inches
   median: 1.8 inches
   mode: none
9. mean: 305
   median: 305
   mode: 305
10. mean: 38.8 hours
    median: 40 hours
    mode: 40 hours

11. **A. $117,100** Add the amounts in the column labeled "Asking Price" and divide by 6, the number of prices listed.
12. **C. $116,500** Arrange the selling prices in order: $124,800; $118,400; $116,500; $116,500; $109,000; $103,600. Since the number of items is even, there are two in the middle: $116,500 and $116,500. Since these are the same amount, the average of the two is also $116,500.
13. **A.** $\frac{790 + 1150 + 662 + 805}{4}$ To find the mean, add the numbers and divide by the number of items in the set. In this case, there are 4 numbers.
14. **C. $900** The median is the middle amount. Arrange the amounts in order and find the middle amount.
15. **B. 14** The mode is the number that occurs most often. Only 14 occurs more than once in the data.

Lesson 5: Line Plots

Practice 5, page 295

1. **C.** Look for a line plot that reflects that two zebras have 26 stripes, two have 28, two have 30, etc.
2. **B.** Look for a line plot that reflects three classes with 29 students, two classes with 32, etc.
3. Draw a dot for each person not already represented in the line plot. Your completed line plot should look like this:

4. **B. 3** Three people grew three vegetables—that's more people than grew any other specific number of vegetables.

Lesson 6: Histograms

Practice 6, page 297

1. **C.** Look for the histogram that begins with 30 and that has a second bar at 56, a third bar at 80, etc.
2. **D.** Look for the histogram that begins with 15 and that has a second bar at 22, a third bar at 35, etc.

3. **C. 36%** Estimate the percentages represented by the four bars that cover the time period of December 9 through January 5: 8%, 9%, 9%, and 10%. Add those estimates to find the approximate percentage of cases reported during that entire time period, resulting in 36%.

Lesson 7: Probability

Practice 7.1, page 299

1. $\frac{2}{5}$, **0.4, 40%** Calculate: $\frac{20}{50} = \frac{2}{5}$

2. $\frac{3}{10}$, **0.3, 30%** There were 12 non-blue spins out of 40 total spins: $\frac{12}{40} = \frac{3}{10} = 30\%$.

3. $\frac{1}{5}$, **0.2, 20%** Calculate: $\frac{2}{2+4+4} = \frac{2}{10} = \frac{1}{5} = 20\%$

4. $\frac{1}{4}$, **0.25, 25%** Calculate: $\frac{60}{180+60} = \frac{60}{240} = \frac{1}{4} = 25\%$

5. $\frac{1}{3}$, **0.33, $33\frac{1}{3}$%** Calculate: $\frac{2}{6} = \frac{1}{3}$

6. **C. 50%** There are 12 cards in the deck, and 6 are diamonds: $\frac{6}{12} = \frac{1}{2} = 50\%$

7. **A.** $\frac{3}{4}$ There are 3 clubs, so 9 are not clubs: $\frac{9}{12} = \frac{3}{4}$.

8. **D. 2 out of 5** Sixteen out of 40 trials resulted in tails: $\frac{16}{40} = \frac{2}{5}$.

9. **A. 3 out of 5** Twenty-four out of 40 trials resulted in heads: $\frac{24}{40} = \frac{3}{5}$.

Practice 7.2, page 301

1. $\frac{1}{36}$ The events are independent, so multiply: $\frac{1}{6} \times \frac{1}{6} = \frac{1}{36}$

2. $\frac{1}{4}$ Because the first card is replaced, the two choices are independent. The cards greater than 5 are 6, 7, 8, 9, 10. Multiply: $\frac{5}{10} \times \frac{5}{10} = \frac{1}{2} \times \frac{1}{2} = \frac{1}{4}$

3. $\frac{1}{8}$ Half of the sections are red, so there is a $\frac{1}{2}$ chance that the result will be red. Each spin is independent. Multiply: $\frac{1}{2} \times \frac{1}{2} \times \frac{1}{2} = \frac{1}{8}$

4. $\frac{9}{38}$ The marble is *not* replaced, so the probabilities are not the same. There is a $\frac{1}{2}$ chance the first marble is red. But once one red marble is removed, the odds of a second red become $\frac{9}{19}$. Multiply: $\frac{1}{2} \times \frac{9}{19} = \frac{9}{38}$.

5. $\frac{1}{16}$ Each flip is independent and has a $\frac{1}{2}$ chance of coming up heads: $\frac{1}{2} \times \frac{1}{2} \times \frac{1}{2} \times \frac{1}{2} = \frac{1}{16}$.

6. $\frac{1}{4}$ Half of the numbers on a standard die are odd: $\frac{1}{2} \times \frac{1}{2} = \frac{1}{4}$.

7. **A.** $\frac{1}{9}$ The probability of rolling a 5 is $\frac{1}{6}$. Of the six equal sections on the spinner, four are even numbers, so there is a $\frac{4}{6}$, or $\frac{2}{3}$, chance of spinning an even number. Multiply the probability of each outcome: $\frac{1}{6} \times \frac{2}{3} \times \frac{2}{18} = \frac{1}{9}$.

8. **D.** $\frac{1}{6}$ The only numbers that are on the spinner are 2, 3, and 4. There is only one 2 on the die, one 3 on the die, and one 4 on the die. So, no matter what number comes up on the spinner, there is a $\frac{1}{6}$ chance the die rolls that number.

9. **C. 1 out of 3** Of the 10 cards, 6 are marked with a square; therefore, there is a 6 in 10, or $\frac{3}{5}$, chance of getting a square on the first pick. Now there are only 9 cards left, and 5 are squares, so there is a $\frac{5}{9}$ chance of getting a square on the second pick. Multiply: $\frac{3}{5} \times \frac{5}{9} = \frac{15}{45} = \frac{1}{3}$.

10. **B. 80%** After the five white chips are removed from the bag, the bag contains 10 chips, with 8 green and 2 white. The probability of getting green is $\frac{8}{10}$, which equals 80%.

Lesson 8: Combinations

Practice 8.1, page 303

1. **5** Since Rob is choosing 4 team members, each possible team leaves out exactly 1 employee. There are 5 possible employees Rob could leave out, so there are 5 possible teams.

2. **10** Either an organized list or a table will work. To solve this problem using a list organized in columns, assign the books letters: A, B, C, D, and E. Count possible combinations:

A and B combinations	A and C combinations	A and D combinations	B and C combinations	B and D combinations	C and D combinations
ABC	ACD	ADE	BCD	BDE	CDE
ABD	ACE		BCE		
ABE					

3. **4** Use either a table or an organized list, as above.

4. **10** The problem does not give the names of the friends, so assign them letters: A, B, C, D, E. Then use a table or organized list, as above, to find possible combinations of two.

5. **A. 5** Use a table or an organized list.

6. **B. 6** Even though three people are going to the conference, you already know that one of them will be Regan. So the question is really asking how many combinations of two out of Regan's four employees could also go. Name the employees A, B, C, and D, and use a table or organized list.

7. **C. 10** The gender of the people sent to the signing is not relevant to answering this question, so you are being asked for possible combinations of 3 out of 5. Use a table or an organized list.

8. **A. 20** Assign letters to the six people (A, B, C, D, E, and F), and then use a table or organized list.

9. **B. 20** This question asks you to add the number of possible groups of 2 out of 5 to the number of possible groups of 3 out of 5. Perform each of those tasks separately, or realize that they will have the same solution because choosing 3 to be in the group is the same as choosing 2 to be out of the group. Then, add the possible combinations together.

Practice 8.2, page 305

1. **48** Use the fundamental counting principle: 4 (types of bread) × 3 (types of meat) × 4 (condiments) = 48.

2. **24** Use the fundamental counting principle: 3 (restaurant certificates) × 2 (T-shirts) × 4 (hats) = 24.

3. **27** Use the fundamental counting principle: 3 × 3 × 3 = 27.

4. **24** On Friday, Julio has 2 choices. On Saturday, he has 3. On Sunday, he has 4 choices. Use the fundamental counting principle: 2 × 3 × 4 = 24

5. **D. 5,184** There are three words in the passphrase: 24 choices for the first, 9 for the second, 24 for

the third. Use the fundamental counting principle: $24 \times 9 \times 24 = 5184$.

6. **A. 10.** You are asked for combinations from one set of items. Use either a table or an organized list. You can assign the superpowers letters A–E to make it easier to see how to combine them.

7. **C. 1,024** Use the fundamental counting principle:
4 (meats) × 4 (vegetables) × 4 (noodles) × 4 (broth) × 4 (spices) = 1024.

8. **A. 125** Use the fundamental counting principle:
5 (medications) × 5 (dietary changes) × 5 (vitamins) = 125.

Lesson 9: Permutations

Practice 9, page 307

1. **120** This is a permutations problem, because order matters. The question asks how many sequences of five items are possible. $5 \times 4 \times 3 \times 2 \times 1 = 120$.

2. **24** This question asks you how many sequences of four items are possible. $4 \times 3 \times 2 \times 1 = 24$.

3. **10** This is a combinations problem: you are being asked how many groups of three are possible, given five students. Order does not matter. Use a table or an organized list; you may name the students A–E if that is easier.

4. **720** This is a permutations problem, because order matters. $6 \times 5 \times 4 \times 3 \times 2 \times 1 = 720$.

5. **C. 360** This is a permutations problem, in which you are counting possible sequences of four out of six tasks. $6 \times 5 \times 4 \times 3 = 360$.

6. **B. 6** This is a permutations problem: the question asks you how many possible sequences of three types of flowers are possible. $3 \times 2 \times 1 = 6$.

7. **D. 5,040** This is a permutations problem, because you are told that the role of Bystander #1 is different from the role of Bystander #4. (Notice the phrase "specific roles" in the question.) Thus, order matters. The question is asking how many sequences of four are possible given ten people. $10 \times 9 \times 8 \times 7 = 5040$.

8. **B. 20** This is a combinations problem asking how many groups of

three out of six are possible. Use a table or an organized list.

9. **C. 120** This is a permutations problem asking how many sequences of three out of six are possible. $6 \times 5 \times 4 = 120$.

Data, Statistics, and Probability Practice Questions, pages 308–313

1. **B. 2007** Only the bar for 2007 falls between 500 and 600 on the scale.

2. **B. 40%** Estimate the values for 1998 and 1999. Then find the percent of decrease. Estimate roughly 650 and 390 for 1998 and 1999. Subtract. $650 - 390 = 260$. Divide by the original number. $260 \div 650 = 0.4 = 40\%$

3. **A. $\frac{3}{100}$** Jim and his friends bought a total of 12 tickets (4 people × 3 tickets). Then 12 out of $400 = \frac{12}{400} = \frac{3}{100}$.

4. **D. 50°** Arrange the low temperatures in order: 55°, 53°, 50°, 50°, 49°, and 48°. Find the middle of the list. Since there are two temperatures in the middle and both are 50°, the mean of the two must be 50°.

5. **C. 1.56** Add the six amounts, and divide by 6: $0.45 + 0.63 + 1.34 + 3.53 + 2.57 + 0.84 = 9.36$, and $9.36 \div 6 = 1.56$ inches. It makes sense to use your calculator on this question.

6. **C. Woodland Hills** Mentally subtract the low temperature from the high temperature for each area. The greatest difference is in Woodland Hills. $68° - 50° = 18°$.

7. **B. 2005** Ticket sales increased each year from 2001 through 2004. The first year in which they declined was 2005.

8. **C. 2008** The line graph shows the steepest increase (line rising from left to right) from 2007 to 2008.

9. **C. 32%** Eight customers chose a mouse pad. $8 \div 25 = 0.32 = 32\%$

10. **A. 1 in 2** Of the 52 cards, 26 are either hearts or diamonds: $\frac{26}{52} = \frac{1}{2}$

11. **3.5 or $\frac{7}{2}$** Add the hours, and divide by 6, the number of weeks: $5 + 3.5 + 4 + 0 + 1.5 + 7 = 21$ hours, and 21 hours $\div 6 = 3.5$ hours.

12. **$\frac{2}{5}$** Only the numbers 4 and 5 are greater than 3. The probability is

2 out of 5, $\frac{2}{5}$, or 0.4.

13. **B. 41%** The three candidates who received the smallest percentages of the vote also received the smallest number of votes. Add: $9\% + 14\% + 18\% = 41\%$

14. **C. Bowen and Utley** Since $\frac{3}{5} = 60\%$, look for two candidates whose combined percent is close to 60%. Since $24\% + 35\% = 59\%$, the correct answer is choice (C).

15. **D. 5100 × 0.09** Grace Reiner received 9%, which equals 0.09. You know the percent and the base. Multiply to find the part.

16. **B. March** The lines for both companies cross in March.

17. **B. 5900** Company A's orders continue to climb at about the same rate. Imagine extending the solid line to the next month. The line would reach to almost 6000. Choice (A) is too high an increase.

18. **C. 540** The graph indicates that about 3000 orders were placed in April. Multiply: $3000 \times 18\% = 540$.

19. **B. 24.5** Use only the Shots Attempted column. Put the numbers in order, and find the middle: 29, 27, 26, 25, 24, 24, 23, 18. The two in the middle are 25 and 24. Find the mean of those numbers: $25 + 24 = 49$, and $49 \div 2 = 24.5$.

20. **D. 10** Use the Shots Made column. The mode is the number that occurs most often. In this case the mode is 10, which occurs three times.

21. **B. $\frac{5}{36}$** The probability that a marble is red is $\frac{8}{24}$, or $\frac{1}{3}$. The chance that a marble is white is $\frac{10}{24}$, or $\frac{5}{12}$. Because the first marble is replaced, the two events are independent. Multiply: $\frac{1}{3} \times \frac{5}{12} = \frac{5}{36}$.

22. **B. $\frac{34 + 31 + 42}{3}$** To find the mean, add the three numbers and divide by 3, the number of months in the list. There are 36 employees, but you don't need this number to solve the problem.

23. **$\frac{1}{36}$** The probability of rolling one "one" is $\frac{1}{6}$. Multiply to find the chance of rolling two ones: $\frac{1}{6} \times \frac{1}{6} = \frac{1}{36}$.

24. 210 Arrange the numbers in order, and find the middle number: 305, 276, 210, 158, 54.

25. 625 Use the fundamental counting principle: $5 \times 5 \times 5 \times 5 = 625$.

26. 4 This is a combinations problem; use a table or an organized list.

27. 720 This is a permutations question, because the board is not simply picking three members. Rather, those members will also be ordered in a specific way. Multiply:
10 options for president × 9 options for secretary × 8 options for treasurer = 720.

28. 20% First find the total number of patients: 16 (colds and flu) + 13 (cuts and scrapes) + 12 (sprained muscles) + 7 (tetanus shots) + 12 (severe headaches) = 60. Now find what percent of 60 is represented by 12: $\frac{12}{60} \times 100 = 20\%$

29. B. 4:3 The ratio of patients with colds or flu to the number of patients with severe headaches is 16:12, which simplifies to 4:3.

30. B. 180–199 lbs The bar corresponding to this weight range is the tallest bar on the graph.

31. B. Participants weighing less than 200 lbs Choices (C) and (D) are both subsets of choice (B), and so cannot be correct. Add the totals of the columns in the graph to reveal that the total for choice (B) is greater than that of choice (A).

32. B. 20 miles per gallon Seven cars got 20 miles per gallon on average, more than in any other line of the table.

33. A. $\frac{1}{2}$ One car got 35 miles per gallon, and two got 15 miles per gallon.

34. Draw dots on the line plot so that it looks like the following:

35. D.

Only choice (D) reflects that 48% of visitors arrived during the fourth time period listed.

Algebra Basics, Expressions, and Polynomials

Lesson 1: The Number Line and Signed Numbers

Practice 1.1, page 315

1. 5	13. −50
2. 45	14. −11
3. 13	15. 25
4. 1	16. −35
5. 1	17. −11
6. 10	18. 11
7. −3	19. 10
8. 13	20. 75
9. −4	21. 12
10. 2	22. 2
11. −22	23. −1
12. 32	24. −13

25. B. 2 + (−5) The operation starts on + 2 and moves 5 units to the left (a negative direction).

26. C. 115° Begin with 92°. Then perform the following operations: $92° + 12° − 5° + 6° − 3° + 13° = 115°$

Practice 1.2, page 317

1. 20	15. 6
2. −21	16. −20
3. −48	17. −300
4. 18	18. 2
5. −10	19. −5
6. 3	20. 660
7. −3	21. 12
8. −5	22. −120
9. 2	23. −125
10. −5	24. −12
11. −28	25. 20
12. −3	26. −1
13. −1	27. 0
14. −75	

28. B. −7 Substitute the numbers from the spreadsheet for the cells in the expression and solve. Note that A1 is column A, row 1; A3 is column A, row 3; and so on: $\frac{(−3)(7)(−1)}{(3)(−1)} = \frac{21}{−3} = −7$

29. C. $\frac{2(8)}{(−8)}$ To find the product of two numbers, multiply: 2(8). Then divide by −8, as directed in the problem.

30. C. The result is a negative number. Do not do any calculations. Instead, examine the factors. Since there is an odd number of negative factors, the answer will be negative. This is the only possible option.

Lesson 2: Powers and Roots

Practice 2, page 319

1. 9	13. 6561
2. 4	14. 1296
3. 3	15. 12.2
4. 1	16. 8000
5. 9	17. 1
6. 7	18. $\frac{1}{16}$
7. 125	19. 15.6
8. $\frac{1}{16}$	20. 10.9
9. 16	21. 7.5
10. 8	22. 23.2
11. $\frac{1}{1000}$	23. 1
12. 11	24. 256

25. C. 6^3 To find the volume, you would need to solve $6 \times 6 \times 6$, which can be written as 6^3.

26. A. $3^{−3}$ Examine the choices. Choices (A) and (D) will result in a fraction, a value less than 1. Choices (B) and (C) will each have a value of 1 or greater

Choice (A): $3^{−3} = \frac{1}{3^3} = \frac{1}{27}$

Choice (D): $2^{−4} = \frac{1}{2^4} = \frac{1}{16}$

Since $\frac{1}{27} < \frac{1}{16}$, choice (A) is correct.

Lesson 3: Scientific Notation

Practice 3, page 321

1. 2.3×10^3	12. 480,000,000
2. $4.2 \times 10^{−4}$	13. 0.000017
3. 1.24×10^7	14. 0.0072
4. 1.432×10^{10}	15. 916,000
5. 3.6×10^7	16. 85,910,000
6. $9.5 \times 10^{−3}$	17. 0.00000956
7. $5.8 \times 10^{−7}$	18. 2.35×10^4
8. 1.5×10^{11}	19. 0.000000001
9. $9 \times 10^{−9}$	20. 2,670,000,000
10. 0.0005173	21. 3×10^8
11. 3,700,000	

22. **B. 4.356 × 10⁴** In scientific notation, the whole-number portion must be a digit from 1 to 9. Choice (B) is correct because the decimal place must be moved 4 places.

23. **D. 5 × 9.07 × 10⁻¹** In scientific notation, a ton = 9.07×10^{-1} metric tons. Multiply this by 5 to find the equivalent weight of five tons.

Lesson 4: Order of Operations

Practice 4, page 323

1. 24
2. 1
3. 29
4. 2
5. 7
6. 20
7. 14
8. 55
9. 10
10. 23
11. 161
12. 30
13. 360
14. 4
15. 6

16. **C. (1 − 0.75)(28)(30).** The total cost of the class can be found by multiplying 28 members by $30. Since the foundation pays 75%, or 0.75, the hospital will pay 100% − 75%, or (1 − 0.75). You must multiply the amount the class will cost by the percent that the hospital will pay. Only choice (C) performs these operations.

17. **B. Add 5** The operations in the brackets must be performed first. Once these are completed, multiply by 2 and then add 5. Notice that it is not necessary to find the value of the expression to answer the question.

18. **C. 76**
$22 + 6[(14 - 5) \div 3(17 - 14)]$
$= 22 + 6[9 \div 3(3)]$
$= 22 + 6[3 \times 3]$
$= 22 + 6[9]$
$= 22 + 54 = 76$

Lesson 5: Absolute Value

Practice 5, page 325

1. 18
2. 107
3. 423
4. 95
5. 7,026
6. 18
7. 5,708,432
8. 85.6
9. 42
10. 10.5
11. 163.24
12. 3.14
13. 11
14. −156
15. 156
16. 3
17. −91
18. 0
19. 620
20. −7
21. −20
22. −1
23. 2.125
24. −11

25. **D. 10 degrees** The change in temperature is the absolute value of the result of the new temperature minus the old temperature: $|(-5) - (-15)| = |10|$, or 10 degrees.

26. **D. 16** In order to find out how many blocks Bob walked in total, you also need to know how long the last leg of his journey (from the post office back to his apartment) was. To do this, you can think of movement east as having a positive value and movement west as having a negative value. So, on the first three legs of his journey Bob walked 5 + −6 + (−2), leaving him −3 blocks from his house. The last leg of his journey is 3 blocks, and you can simply add the absolute values of each part of the trip:
$|5| + |-6| + |-2| + |3| = 16$.

27. **C. 120** Add the absolute value of Milania's score to the absolute value of Chris's score:
$|-65| + |55| = 65 + 55 = 120$

28. **A. 1.5** The question defines absolute error as the absolute value of the difference between the actual and approximate values:
$23.5 - 25 = -1.5$, and $|-1.5| = 1.5$.

Lesson 6: Algebraic Expressions

Practice 6.1, page 327

1. $x - 7$
2. $3x^2 + x$
3. $8x - 10$
4. $-3x - 2y$
5. $\frac{10}{x} - 5$
6. $-8 + 7x$
7. $16x + x - 3y$
8. $x^2 + x^4$
9. $x^2 + \frac{4}{7}$
10. $15 + \sqrt{x}\, 6$
11. $x - (y + 13)$
12. $(x + 6)^2$
13. $17 - (2x + y)$
14. $x + \frac{24}{x}$
15. $2x - 15$
16. $4(x - y)$
17. $5(x^2 - 3)$
18. $x(11 - \sqrt{100})$

19. **C. $1500 + $0.50(x − 2000)** Let x represent the number of tickets sold. The expression $x - 2000$ is the number of tickets over 2000 sold. Multiply this expression by $0.50 to find the amount donated based on ticket sales. Then add $1500. Only choice (C) shows this sequence of operations.

20. **A. (3x + 4y) ÷ (2 + z)** The sum of 3 times a number and 4 times another number is represented by the expression $3x + 4y$. The sum of 2 and a third number is represented by $2 + z$. The first expression is divided by the second. Parentheses are necessary to clarify the order of operations.

21. **B. 6h + 0.03s** The correct sequence of operations shows the sum of 6 multiplied by the number of hours ($6h$) and 3% of the sales, or $0.03s$. Only choice (B) adds these two expressions.

Practice 6.2, page 329

1. $x^2 + 3x + 2$
2. $19y + 13$
3. $-3x + 54$
4. $6x^3 + 31x^2 + 4$
5. $7y + 14$
6. $3x + 8$
7. $22x - 12$
8. $2y^2 + y + 9$
9. $-5x - 17$
10. $4x - 7$
11. 31
12. 48
13. 8
14. 21
15. 72
16. 80
17. 85
18. −19
19. 9
20. 61

21. **D. $3x^2 + 4x + 1$** Simplify the expression:
$3x^2 + 3(x - 3) + x + 10$
$= 3x^2 + 3x - 9 + x + 10$
$= 3x^2 + 4x + 1$

22. **A. x = 2, y = 3** Substitute the values in the choices into the expression. Choice (A) equals −11.
$4x^2 - 3(y + 6)$
$= 4(2^2) - 3(3 + 6)$
$= 4(4) - 3(9)$
$= 16 - 27$
$= -11$.

23. **A. 20°** You need to convert a Fahrenheit temperature to Celsius.
$C = \frac{5}{9}(F - 32)$
$C = \frac{5}{9}(68 - 32) = 20$

Lesson 7: Expressions and Calculator Skills

Practice 7, page 331

1. 19
2. 15.9
3. 51
4. $16\frac{1}{2}$
5. 10
6. −98
7. 74
8. 146
9. 12
10. −76
11. 57
12. 36
13. −54
14. 24.8
15. 54
16. −45
17. 78
18. 108
19. 459
20. 1430

21. **B. 36.2** Use the formula stated in the problem.
$P = 2l + 2w$
$= 2(12.5) + 2(5.6)$
$= 25 + 11.2$
$= 36.2$

22. **D. −2xy** Try each expression, $x + y = -3$; $-x + y = 7$; $x - y = 3$; $xy = -10$; and $-2xy = 20$. The value of choice (D) is greatest.

23. **A. 32** If $x = 2$, then $2 \div x^{-4} = 2 \div \frac{1}{2^4} = 2 \div \frac{1}{16} = 32$.

Lesson 8: Understand Polynomials

Practice 8, page 333

1. Monomial
2. Monomial
3. Binomial
4. Trinomial
5. Binomial
6. Trinomial
7. Monomial
8. Monomial
9. Monomial
10. Binomial
11. Trinomial
12. Trinomial
13. Binomial
14. Monomial
15. Binomial

16. First term: $3x^4$, second term: $-2x^2$, third term: 3
17. First term: $12a^2bc$
18. First term: $3g$, second term: $-4h$
19. First term: x^2 second term: y
20. First term: $-4a$, second term: $-3b^2$, third term: c
21. First term: 25
22. First term: x^2, second term: $3x$, third term: -7
23. First term: $\frac{3x}{8}$
24. First term: $\sqrt{25}$
25. First term: $\frac{x^2}{9}$
26. First term: $49x^2y^2z^2$
27. First term: $18y^2$, second term: $-4y^2$, third term: 8
28. First term: $3h$, second term: -4
29. First term: x^2, second term: $-x$ third term: y^2, fourth term: -2
30. First term: ab, second term: ab^2, third term: b^2, fourth term: -4
31. **B. 5** Two variables in the expression have exponents: x^3 and x^2. Add the values of the exponents: $3 + 2 = 5$
32. **B. −1** The coefficients in this expression are 1, −3, −1, and 2. Add those values:
$1 + (-3) + (-1) + 2 = -1$

Lesson 9: Simplify Polynomials

Practice 9, page 335

1. Like
2. Like
3. Unlike
4. Unlike
5. Like
6. Unlike
7. Unlike
8. Like
9. Unlike
10. Unlike
11. Like
12. Unlike
13. Like
14. Like
15. Unlike
16. Like
17. Unlike
18. Like
19. Unlike
20. Unlike

21. $7x^2y$
22. $4b$
23. $-6a + 3$
24. $ab^2 + 16ab + 3$
25. $-2x^2 + 7$
26. $4ab$
27. $14g + 14gh$
28. $-4g^2h^2 + 2g^2 + 2h^2 - 4$
29. $-y^2 + 9y$
30. $-7x^2 + y - 3$
31. $22y - 7$
32. $6x^2y + 5y^2 - 23$
33. $4x^3 + 7x^2 + 3x + 5$
34. $-5x^2 - 4x + 5$
35. $-3x^3 + 7x^2 + x$
36. **B. $6a^2b + 9ab$** Identify and group like terms. Then combine:
$3a^2b + 4ab + 3a^2b + 5ab$
$= 3a^2b + 3a^2b + 4ab + 5ab$
$= 6a^2b + 9ab$
37. **B. 3** Identify and group like terms. Then combine:
$j^2 + k^3 - 2j^3 + 5k^3 - 2j^2$
$= j^2 - 2j^2 + k^3 + 5k^3 - 2j^3$
$= -j^2 + 6k^3 - 2j^3$
The expression has three terms.

Lesson 10: Add and Subtract Polynomials

Practice 10.1, page 337

1. $5x + 6$
2. $23y + 6$
3. $8x^2 - 5x + 2$
4. $15a^2 + 8a$
5. $11x^2 + 2x + 3$
6. $a + 1$
7. 1
8. $4x^2 + 16x - 9$
9. $24y - 3$
10. $-4a^2 - 2a - 9$
11. $y - 2$
12. $-3x + 13$
13. $3a + 2$
14. $3x^2 + x + 2$
15. $10y + 7$

16. $2x^2 + 3x + 13$
17. $2g + 1$
18. $a^2 - 10a + 2$
19. -16
20. $20x^2 - 5x + 1$
21. **A. $x^2y + 4xy$** Identify, group, and combine like terms:
$(2xy + 3xy^2 - 4x^2y) + (5x^2y - 3xy^2 + 2xy)$
$= 2xy + 2xy - 4x^2y + 5x^2y + 3xy^2 - 3xy^2$
$= 4xy + x^2y$
22. **C. $2x^2 + x + 3$** Distribute the negative sign to everything in the second polynomial. Then group and combine like terms:
$(5x^2 - 2x + 1) - (3x^2 - 3x - 2)$
$= 5x^2 - 2x + 1 - 3x^2 + 3x + 2$
$= 5x^2 - 3x^2 - 2x + 3x + 1 + 2$
$= 2x^2 + x + 3$

Practice 10.2, page 339

1. $a^2 + 5a + 4b^2$
2. $-4x - xy + y + 16$
3. $yz^2 - 4z^2 + 7yz + 5$
4. $7ab - b + c - 17$
5. $-4a^4 - c^2 + 3ac + 5$
6. $22xyz + x + 6$
7. $7ef + ef^2 + f - 10$
8. $4pq - 2q + 4$
9. $4ab$
10. 0
11. $3p^6 + 4pq - p^2 - q^2$
12. $x + y + 15$
13. $2bc - b$
14. $10xyz - 8y + 16$
15. $6a + 4b + d$
16. $7pq - q$
17. $-7ab + 2b + 12$
18. 0
19. $-2p^2 + 5q^2 + 7$
20. $x^4 + z^4 - z^5$
21. $bc^2 - bc + 2c$
22. $-3xy + xz - 2xyz$
23. $c^3d^7 - c^2 + 2d$
24. $ef^2g - ef^2 - 2fg + 8$
25. **D. $3x - y$** Distribute the negative sign. Then identify, group, and combine like terms:
$(x + y + z) - (-2x + 2y + z)$
$= x + y + z + 2x - 2y - z$
$= x + 2x + y - 2y + z - z$
$= 3x - y$
26. **B. $3g^2 + 5h - 2k$** Identify, group, and combine like terms:
$(2g^2 + 3h - 5k) + (g^2 + 2h + 3k)$
$= 2g^2 + g^2 + 3h + 2h - 5k + 3k$
$= 3g^2 + 5h - 2k$

Lesson 11: Multiply Polynomials

Practice 11, page 341

1. $30x^2$
2. $6xy^2$
3. $28ab^2c^2$
4. $12yz$
5. $9abc$
6. $10x^2y^3z^5$
7. $4ab^2c^2$
8. $34f^3gh^7$
9. $18xyz^2 + 12z^3$
10. $42x^2 - 36xz$
11. $-15ab^2 - 55abc$
12. $-18f^3h + 24f^4gh^2$
13. $70x^7z - 50z^2$
14. $z^2 + 6xyz$
15. $72ab^2 + 64ab$
16. $18x^4 - 27xy^2$
17. $x^2 - x - 30$
18. $x^2 + 2xy + y^2$
19. $z^2 - 81$
20. $y^2z^4 - 2xyz^2 - 3x^2$
21. $9x^2 + 24x + 15$
22. $x^2 - y^2$
23. $y^6 - 6y^4 + 10y^2 - 60$
24. $a^2b^2 - ab - 12$
25. **A. $12a^5b^2c$** The coefficients of each term are 4 and 3, so the coefficient of their product is 12. The product of a^3 and a^2 is a^5. Only choice (A) contains both of these elements.
26. **D. $12p^3c^3$** You need the product of $2pc^2$ and $6p^2c$, which can be calculated as $(2pc^2)(6p^2c)$. The product of the coefficients 2 and 6 is 12, the product of p and p^2 is p^3, and the product of c and c^2 is c^3. Only choice (D) has all three of these elements.

27. **B. $12a^2b^2 - 22ab - 14$** Use FOIL:
$(4ab \times 3ab) + (4ab \times [-7]) + (2 \times 3ab) + (2 \times [-7])$
$= 12a^2b^2 - 28ab + 6ab - 14$
$= 12a^2b^2 - 22ab - 14$

Lesson 12: Divide Polynomials

Practice 12, page 343

1. $y + 15$
2. $x + 3$
3. $x + 5$
4. $a + b$
5. $x^2 + 2x$
6. $2x^2 + 3x + 1$
7. $x + 2y$
8. $3a + 2b$
9. $\frac{3x}{2} + y$
10. $\frac{3a}{4} + \frac{5b}{4}$
11. $\frac{b + 4c}{3}$

12. $\frac{5a + b + 3c}{2}$
13. $6x + 2$
14. $5x + 3$
15. $8y + 2$
16. $6y + 7$
17. $2y + 2$
18. 3
19. $x - 6$
20. $y + 7$
21. $z - 5$
22. $2x + 6$
23. $x - 6$
24. $a + 3$
25. **C. $3a + 2b$** Break the fraction up into two separate fractions:
$\frac{(21a + 14b)}{7} = \frac{21a}{7} + \frac{14b}{7}$
Then divide each numerator by 7 to get $3a + 2b$.
26. **D. $9x + 17y + 20z$** The average of a set of terms is equal to the sum of terms divided by the number of terms in the set. In this case, that can be represented by the expression
$\frac{(27x + 51y + 60z)}{3}$
Break this up into three separate fractions:
$\frac{27x}{3} + \frac{51y}{3} + \frac{60z}{3}$
Then divide each numerator by 3 to get $9x + 17y + 20z$.
27. **A. $z - 5$** Distribute the 2 across the terms in the parentheses. Simplify the numerator. Then break the given expression into separate fractions:
$\frac{2z^2 - 12z + 2(z + 4) - 8}{2z}$
$= \frac{2z^2 - 12z + 2z + 8 - 8}{2z}$
$= \frac{2z^2 - 10z}{2z}$
$= \frac{2z^2}{2z} - \frac{10z}{2z}$
$= z - 5$.

Algebra Basics, Expressions, and Polynomials Practice Questions, pages 344–347

1. **D. $-4x - 6$**
2. **C. $3d - 75$** Since Heidi makes 75 less than 3 times Kris's wage, multiply Kris's wage, d, by 3 and subtract 75 to get $3d - 75$.
3. **B. 1.26×10^8** Calculate: $700 \times 180,000 = 126,000,000$. Scientific notation reduces to a single digit in front of the decimal, and to do this requires moving up 8 digits, so it would be 1.26×10^8.

4. **D. $84x^2y$** Total desks = schools × rooms per school × desks per room. $4x \times 3y \times 7x = (4)(3)(7)(x)(x)(y) = 84x^2y$.
5. **C. $(x + 5)(x - 5)$** Multiply the monomials and polynomials in the answer choices until you find an answer choice that results in the expression in the question stem. For answer choice (C), use FOIL: $(x + 5)(x - 5) = x^2 - 5x + 5x - 25 = x^2 - 25$.
6. **D. $18x + 2y + 13$** Tom has $9x$, Adam $9x + 13$, and Dave $2y$: $9x + (9x + 13) + 2y = 18x + 2y + 13$.
7. **B. $60y$** The diagram shows multiplication problems done using a table, so the horizontal number times the vertical number will yield the value in the table. The table tells you that $a = yc$ and $b = 5 \times 3 = 15$. So $ab = 15yc$. Now look for a value for c. Since $20 = 5c$, c must equal 4, and you have $ab = (15)(4)y = 60y$. There is not enough information to deduce the value of y, but since y appears in all the answer choices, you do not need to try to find its value.
8. **D. y** The diagram shows multiplication problems done using a table, so the horizontal number times the vertical number will yield the value in the table.
$d = 3y$ and $a = 4y$
so $a - d = 4y - 3y = y$.
9. **A. $7a^2c^2 + 35bc^2 + 49c^4$** Multiply each term by $7c^2$:
$7c^2(a^2) + 7c^2(5b) + 7c^2(7c^2)$
$= 7a^2c^2 + 35bc^2 + 49c^4$
10. **D. $\$\frac{150}{x}$** To figure out the individual pie cost, divide $900 by the number of pies, $6x$: $\frac{900}{6x} = \frac{150}{x}$.
11. **A. $\frac{a - 4}{a + 4}$** Cancel out $6b$ in the numerator and $2(3b)$ (which equals $6b$) in the denominator. Then, one $(a - 4)$ will cancel, leaving $\frac{a - 4}{a + 4}$.
12. **C. $\frac{xyz}{2}$** To find the total cost, multiply ounces per guest by the number of guests by the cost per ounce. Since $\$z$ is the cost per pound, the result needs to be divided by 16. $\frac{(x)(8y)(z)}{16} = xyz\left(\frac{8}{16}\right) = \frac{xyz}{2}$.
13. **B. -26** Substituting -2 for x and 5 for y leads to $6(-2 - 5) - 8(-2) = 6(-7) - (-16) = -42 + 16 = -26$.

14. **A. –88** Substituting 2 for x, 4 for y, and 3 for z leads to a product of $[2^2 + 6(3)] \times [2(4) - 4(3)] = (4 + 18) \times (8 - 12) = 22 \times -4 = -88$.

15. $1\frac{5}{11}$ Calculate: $\frac{4^3 - [3(12 + 2^2)]}{6 + 5(4) - 15} =$
    $\frac{64 - [3(12 + 4)]}{6 + 5(4) - 15} = \frac{64 - [3(16)]}{6 + 20 - 15} =$
    $\frac{64 - 48}{6 + 20 - 15} = \frac{16}{11} = 1\frac{5}{11}$

16. **D. $30kp + 20p^2 + 45hp$** Because $5p$ is paid to every member, each number of team members would be multiplied by $5p$, and the team totals would be added: $5p(6k) + 5p(4p) + 5p(9h) = 30kp + 20p^2 + 45hp$

17. **C. $-x + 9y - 10xy$** Solve: $7x - [(5y)2x - 9y + 8x] = 7x - [10xy - 9y + 8x] = 7x - 10xy + 9y - 8x = -x - 10xy + 9y$.

18. **A. $20cd - 75c$** Alyshia has $4d - 15$ DVDs. Multiply $5c$ by Alyshia's DVD total: $(4d - 15)$: $5c (4d - 15) = 5c(4d) - (5c)(15) = 20cd - 75c$

19. **A. $8x^2 + 7xy^3 - 12x - 1$** Factor out $7x^2$: $\frac{56x^4 + 49x^3y^3 - 84x^3 - 7x^2}{7x^2}$
    $= \frac{(7x^2)(8x^2 + 7xy^3 - 12x - 1)}{7x^2}$
    $= 8x^2 + 7xy^3 - 12x - 1$

20. **B. $16d - 4a$** The amount $80d$ is needed. Anything earned at the ball will be subtracted, and $64d$ and $4a$ were both earned: $80d - 64d - 4a = 16d - 4a$ left to raise.

21. **A. $\frac{x^4}{2y^2} + 2x^2y^2 - \frac{4x}{y^2} - \frac{1}{2}$** Split the fraction: $\frac{x^4 + 4x^2y^4 - 8x - y^2}{2y^2}$
    $= \frac{x^4}{2y^2} + \frac{4x^2y^4}{2y^2} - \frac{8x}{2y^2} - \frac{y^2}{2y^2}$
    $= \frac{x^4}{2y^2} + 2x^2y^2 - \frac{4x}{y^2} - \frac{1}{2}$

22. **B. $\frac{6k + 4f}{r} + 3$** The total of the three groups $(12k + 8f + 6r)$ should be divided by the number of squads, $2r$:
    $\frac{2k + 8f + 6r}{2r} = \frac{12k}{2r} + \frac{8f}{2r} + \frac{6r}{2r}$
    $= \frac{6k}{r} + \frac{4f}{r} + 3$
    $= \frac{6k + 4f}{r} + 3$

23. **A. $4x + 2$** Substitute 2 for q and 4 for r in the expression:
    $\frac{4^2x^2 + 2^3x}{2^2x} = \frac{16x^2 + 8x}{4x} = 4x + 2$.

24. **C. $-2x^4 + 5xy^4 - \frac{y^2}{x^2}$** Split the fractions and then simplify by factoring out $11x^2$:
    $\frac{11x^2(4x^4 + 5xy^4 + 8)}{11x^2} - \frac{11y^2}{11x^2} - 6x^4 - 8$

$= 4x^4 + 5xy^4 + 8 - \frac{y^2}{x^2} - 6x^4 - 8$
$= -2x^4 + 5xy^4 - \frac{y^2}{x^2}$

25. **A. $5xy^3 - 16x^2y^2 + 42x^2y$**
Distribute:
$(6x^2 + 5xy^2)(y) - (4xy - 9x)(4xy)$
$= 6x^2(y) + 5xy^2(y) - (4xy(4xy) - 9x(4xy))$
$= 6x^2y + 5xy^3 - (16x^2y^2 - 36x^2y)$
$= 42x^2y + 5xy^3 - 16x^2y^2$

26. **D. $20x^2 - 39x + 18$** The question states that the average salary of the non-managerial employees is $(5x - 6)$. That means that
$5x - 6 = \frac{Total\ of\ non-managers'\ salaries}{Number\ of\ non-managers}$
The question also states that the number of non-managers in the office is $4x - 3$. So,
$5x - 6 = \frac{Total\ of\ non-managers'\ salaries}{4x - 3}$
Then $(5x - 6)(4x - 3) = total\ of\ non-managers'\ salaries = 20x^2 - 39x + 18$

27. **B. 51** Factor before substituting. $\frac{5xy + 63y^2}{9y} = \frac{(9y)(5x + 7y)}{9y} = (5x + 7y)$
Substitute 6 for x and 3 for y:
$5(6) + 7(3) = 30 + 21 = 51$.

28. **D. $x - 1$** Split the fraction:
$\frac{x(x^2 + 3) - 2x(x^2 + 3) - (x^2 + 3)}{x^2 + 3}$
$= \frac{3x(x^2 + 3)}{x^2 + 3} - \frac{2x(x^2 + 3)}{x^2 + 3} - \frac{x^2 + 3}{x^2 + 3}$
$= 3x - 2x - 1 = x - 1$.

29. **D. $3h^2 + 4hk - 51h - 68k$** Add the populations of both countries $(3h + 4k)$ and multiply by the rice consumption: $(h - 17)$:
$(3h + 4k)(h - 17)$
$= (3h)(h) + (3h)(-17) + (4k)(h) + (4k)(-17)$
$= 3h^2 - 51h + 4hk - 68k$.

30. **A. $2x^2 + 2y^2 - xy$** Split the fraction:
$\frac{4x^2(x+y)}{(x+y)} - \frac{2(x+y)^2(x-y)}{(x+y)} - \frac{xy(x+y)}{(x+y)}$
$= 4x^2 - 2(x + y)(x - y) - xy$
$= 4x^2 - 2(x^2 - y^2) - xy$
$= 2x^2 + 2y^2 - xy$

31. **A. 2** The diagram shows multiplication problems done using a table, so the horizontal number times the vertical number will yield the value in the table. To figure out a, first look at the top right term. Since $5 \times a = ab$, $b = 5$. Another term with only a and b is the bottom middle, $4 \times ab = 40$. Substituting 5 for b shows that $20a = 40$, so $a = 2$.

32. **B. 40** The table tells you that $a^2 \times c = 8b$. Use the table to find a value for b. Since the top right cell of the table shows that $5 \times a = ab$, b must equal 5, and $8b = 40$.

Equations, Inequalities, and Functions

Lesson 1: Equations

Practice 1.1, page 349

1. $x = 9$
2. $m = 28$
3. $y = -1$
4. $x = -64$
5. $a = 125$
6. $y = -13$
7. $x = 27$
8. $c = 7$
9. $x = -4$
10. $b = -7$
11. $x = 31$
12. $s = -8$
13. $x = 108$
14. $t = 39$
15. $x = 48$
16. $y = -3$
17. $r = 110$
18. $x = 5$
19. $y = -9$
20. $d = -25$
21. $x = 4$
22. $x = -6$
23. $h = 26$
24. $x = 66$
25. $m = -10$
26. $y = 9$
27. $w = -28$
28. $y = 72$

29. **C. $x + 36 = 77$** Erin's hours (x) plus Kayla's hours (36) = 77 hours.

30. **C. $2y = 38$** Erin worked twice as many hours as Kayla ($2y$), and Erin worked 38 hours, so $2y = 38$.

31. **C. 128** A number (x) divided by 4 is 32. Solve for x: $\frac{x}{4} = 32$, $x = 128$.

32. **D. $12x = -60$** Try -5 for x in each equation. Only choice (D) is true when -5 is substituted for x.
    $12x = -60$
    $12(-5) = -60$
    $-60 = -60$

33. **B. $\$572.18 - c = \$434.68$** When you subtract the check from the amount in the checking account, the result will be the current balance.

Practice 1.2, page 351

1. $x = 50$
2. $y = -2$
3. $m = 2$
4. $x = -4$
5. $y = 6$
6. $z = 2$
7. $m = 3$
8. $x = 4$
9. $p = 7$
10. $s = -2$
11. $x = 6$
12. $r = -5$
13. $y = 11$
14. $b = 4$
15. $x = -1$
16. $h = 20$
17. $x = 9$
18. $z = 4$
19. $b = 3$
20. $n = 7$

21. **D. $3x + 9 = 6x - 15$** "Three times a number" is $3x$ and "increased by 9" means to add 9. "Six times the number" is $6x$, and "15 less" means to subtract 15. The word

"is" shows that the two expressions should be connected by the = symbol.

22. **D. 375** Solve:
$$3x + x = 500$$
$$4x = 500$$
$$x = 125$$
The variable x is the number of cards that Travis has. Eric has $3x$, or 3×125, which equals 375.

23. **A.** $4x - 7 = \frac{x}{3} + 15$ Remember that differences and quotients must be written in the order stated in the problem. The difference of four times a number and 7 is $4x - 7$. The quotient of the number and 3 plus 15 is $\frac{x}{3} + 15$.

24. **A. $54** Solve:
$$x + (2x + 12) = \$174$$
$$3x + 12 = \$174$$
$$3x = \$162$$
$$x = \$54$$

Lesson 2: Equation Word Problems

Practice 2, page 353

1. **1800 sq. ft.** Let the square footage of the first house be h, and the second house's square footage will then be $(2h - 1000)$. Then write an equation that combines both houses. The equation is $h + (2h - 1000) = 4400$. Solve for h.

2. **10 dimes** Let x equal the number of dimes in Julia's pocket. The equation is $0.10x + 0.25(24 - x) = 4.50$.

3. **24 games** Let w represent the number of wins, and then the number of losses will be half of w. Write an equation:
$$w + \tfrac{1}{2}w = 36$$
$$1\tfrac{1}{2}w = 36$$
$$\tfrac{3}{2}w = 36$$
$$3w = 72$$
$$w = 24$$
Alternatively, you could solve the equation by calculating the number of losses. Let l = losses. Wins will be twice that much. Then the equation would read $l + 2l = 36$. Once you find l, remember to multiply it by two to find the number of wins.

4. **54** The equation is $x + (x + 2) + (x + 4) + (x + 6) = 4x + 12 = 212$. Solve for $x + 4$, the third number.

5. **8 shirts** Let s represent the number of shirts Brenda bought, and then the number of pants she

bought will be equal to $13 - s$. Then, write an equation using the dollar amount she spent: $\$6(13 - s) + \$4s = \$62$. Solve for s.

6. **59** Let x equal the smallest of the three consecutive numbers. Then: $x + (x + 1) + (x + 2) = 180$. Solve for x.

7. **$1100** Andrew spends twice as much on rent, which means he spends half as much as his rent on food. The equation is $r + \tfrac{1}{2}r = \$1650$. Solve for r.

8. **28 hours** Let h represent the time he spends helping customers, and then stocking shelves will be one-fourth of h. Write an equation:
$$h + \tfrac{1}{4}h = 35$$
$$1\tfrac{1}{4}h = 35$$
$$\tfrac{5}{4}h = 35$$
$$5h = 140$$
$$h = 28$$

9. **C. 84** Let w = Wiley's points, $w + 10$ = Sylvia's points, and $w - 6$ = Greg's points. Write and solve an equation:
$$w + w + 10 + w - 6 = 226$$
$$3w + 4 = 226$$
$$3w = 222$$
$$w = 74$$
Wiley scored 74 points, so Sylvia scored $74 + 10 = 84$ points.

10. **B. $12** Let a = the price of an adult's ticket and $a - \$6$ = the price of a child's ticket. The question states that the cost of 2 adults' tickets and 4 children's tickets is $48. Write and solve an equation:
$$2a + 4(a - 6) = 48$$
$$2a + 4a - 24 = 48$$
$$6a - 24 = 48$$
$$6a = 72$$
$$a = 12$$

11. **B. 6** You know that in 12 years, Jenny will be twice as old as Tina. Therefore, if you multiply Tina's age in 12 years by 2, it will equal Jenny's age in 12 years. Write and solve an equation:
$$4x + 12 = 2(x + 12)$$
$$4x + 12 = 2x + 24$$
$$2x = 12$$
$$x = 6$$

Lesson 3: Inequalities

Practice 3, page 355

1. $x > 4$
2. $x > 7$
3. $x \leq -3$
4. $x \leq 36$
5. $x < -1$
6. $x \geq 5$
7. $x > -8$
8. $x > 4$
9. $x < -7$
10. $x < 2$
11. $x \geq 3$
12. $x < 6$
13. $x \geq 2$
14. $x > -10$
15. $x \leq 3$
16. $x < 21$
17. $x \geq -1$
18. $x < 3$
19. $x < 7$
20. $x \leq 3$
21. $-2 \leq x \leq 2$
22. $-20 < x < 6$
23. $6 < x < 16$
24. $4 \leq x \leq 9$

25. **A. $s \leq 16$** The perimeter must be less than or equal to 64, so solve the inequality: $4s \leq 64$, which leads to $s \leq 16$.

26. **D.**

Solve the inequality:
$$-4x + 3 < -3x + 5$$
$$-x < 2$$
$$x > -2$$
To graph the solution $x > -2$, place an open circle at -2, because -2 is not included in the solution. Then, extend the line to the right to include all values greater than -2.

Lesson 4: Quadratic Equations

Practice 4, page 357

1. $x^2 + 6x + 8$
2. $x^2 + 2x - 15$
3. $x^2 + 3x - 4$
4. $x^2 - 9x + 18$
5. $x^2 + 6x - 16$
6. $2x^2 - 3x - 2$
7. $x^2 - 14x + 45$
8. $3x^2 + x - 2$
9. $x^2 + 5x - 14$
10. $3x^2 + 14x + 16$
11. $x^2 - x - 30$
12. $x^2 - 13x + 30$
13. $4x^2 + 6x + 2$
14. $x^2 + 5x - 36$
15. $x^2 - 10x + 25$

For questions 16–30, the order of the factors does not matter: $(2x - 1)(x + 3) = (x + 3)(2x - 1)$

16. $(x + 1)(x + 3)$
17. $(x - 1)(x + 5)$
18. $(x + 2)(x + 6)$
19. $(x - 3)(x + 2)$
20. $(x - 2)(x + 7)$
21. $(x - 4)(x + 3)$
22. $(x - 5)(x + 7)$
23. $(x - 6)(x - 6)$
24. $(x - 7)(x + 1)$
25. $(x - 4)(x + 8)$
26. $(2x - 1)(x + 3)$
27. $(2x - 10)(x + 1)$ or $(2x + 2)(x - 5)$ or $(2)(x - 5)(x + 1)$
28. $(x - 5)(x + 10)$
29. $(2x - 1)(2x + 3)$
30. $(x - 7)(x + 8)$

31. A. –4 and 5 Get 0 on one side of the equation: $x^2 - x - 20 = 0$. Then, factor: $(x + 4)(x - 5) = 0$. Determine which values of x will make each factor equal to 0. The solutions 5 and –4 will make the equation true.

32. D. $2x^2 + 2x - 24 = 0$ Substitute –4 for x in the answer choices. Only choice (D) works.
$2(-4)^2 + 2(-4) - 24$
$= 2(16) + (-8) - 24$
$= 32 - 32 = 0$

33. B. 6 Substitute the answer choices for x in the equation. Only choice (B) makes the equation true: $2(6)^2 - 7(6) - 30 = 2(36) - 42 - 30 = 72 - 72 = 0$. You can also factor the original equation: $(x - 6)(2x + 5)$, so $x = 6$ or $x = -\frac{5}{2}$.

34. B. $x - 10$ You know that length × width = area. You need to factor the expression $2x^2 - 27x + 70$, and you know that one of the factors is the length, $(2x - 7)$. So $2x^2 - 27x + 70 = (2x - 7)(x - 10)$. The width is $(x - 10)$.

Lesson 5: Algebra Problem Solving

Practice 5, page 359

1. C. 24 Take each answer choice and divide it by 2. Then, check to see if the resulting number is 12 less than the answer choice. For example, choice (A): 12: 12 ÷ 2 = 6. And 6 is not 12 less than 12. Thus, choice (A) is incorrect. Only choice (C) works: 24 ÷ 2 = 24 – 12.

2. C. $200 Try each number. Choice (A) says Brenda raised $150. If she did, Sandra would have raised $450, and Matt would have raised $100. Also, the three of them together would have raised $150 + $450 + $100 ≠ $950. Since those numbers don't total to $950, choice (A) must be incorrect. Only choice (C) works: $200 + $600 + $150 = $950.

3. C. 5 The answer choices represent possible weights for the first package. Try choice (A): if the first package weighs 2, the second package would weigh 1, and the third package would weigh 3. Add them together to see if they total 15: 2 + 1 + 3 ≠ 15. So choice (A) is incorrect. Only choice (C) works:
5 + 2.5 + 7.5 = 15.

4. B. 82 The answer choices represent possible scores for the first test. If choice (A) 76 is Hannah's score on the first test, then her score on the second test would be 82, and 76 + 82 ≠ 170. Only choice (B) works: 82 + 88 = 170.

5. B. 10 The answer choices represent how old Nelson might have been six years ago. If choice (A) were correct, then Nelson would have been 5 six years ago, and he would be 11 now. Also, six years ago Maria would have been 1 year old, and today she would be 7. Now, the question is, is Nelson's current age twice Maria's age? 11 ≠ 2 × 7. So choice (A) is incorrect. Choice (B) does work: if Nelson was 10 six years ago, then Maria would have been 2. Today Nelson would be 16 and Maria would be 8, and 16 is two times 8.

6. A. –3 To solve by guessing, plug each answer choice into the equation. Try choice (A):
$2(-3)^2 + (-3) - 15 = 0.$
$2(9) - 18 = 0.$
$18 - 18 = 0.$

7. B. 6 If the group purchased 5 children's passes, as choice (A) suggests, then they would have purchased 15 adults' passes. Multiply each amount by the cost of that type of ticket, to see if the total equals $440: (5 × $15) + (15 × $25) = $450. Thus, choice (A) is incorrect. Choice (B) works: (6 × $15) + (14 × $25) = $440.

8. B. 20 The answer choices represent possible values for the width. If choice (A) were correct, then the width would be 15 and the length would be 30. Add to find out whether choice (A) would give the value of 120 for the perimeter: 15 + 15 + 30 + 30 = 90. Thus, choice (A) is incorrect. Choice (B) works: 20 + 20 + 40 + 40 = 120.

Lesson 6: The Coordinate Plane

Practice 6, page 361

1. (–4, 5)
2. (3, 6)
3. (0, –3)
4. (6, –7)
5. (–5, 0)
6. (–6, –4)
7. (2, 0)
8. (7, –2)

9.

10.

11. D. (–1, 0) Plot each point in the answer choices. Only choice (D) lies on the line that passes through points A and B.

12. A. (–3, –2) Find the two points discussed in the problem. Then locate the third corner of the triangle, and find the coordinates of the corner. The missing corner is 3 spaces to the left of the origin and 2 spaces down: (–3, –2).

Lesson 7: Graphing a Line

Practice 7, page 363

1.

If $x =$	Then $y =$
–2	2
0	3
2	4

2.

If $x =$	then $y =$
-1	2
0	-1
1	-4

3.

If $x =$	then $y =$
1	1
2	0
3	-1

4.

If $x =$	then $y =$
0	3
1	1
2	-1

5. C. point T and (0, 0) Try the coordinates for points S and T in the equation. Both lie on the graph of the equation. Check the remaining points in the answer choices. Only (0,0) will make the equation $y = \frac{1}{4}x$ true.

6. D. $y = -4x - 2$ Choose two points on line P. The easiest points to work with are the ones

represented by dots: (-1,2) and (0,-2). Try one of those points in the equations. If the point works in the equation, try the other point as well. (You must try both because any number of lines may pass through a single point. To establish that the equation represents line P, it must fit both points.) Both points work only in choice (D): $y = -4x - 2$.

7. B. $2x + 3y = 9$ Try the coordinates (-3, 5) in each equation. Only choice (B) is true.
$$2x + 3y = 9$$
$$2(-3) + 3(5) = 9$$
$$-6 + 15 = 9$$
$$9 = 9$$

Lesson 8: Slope of a Line

Practice 8, page 365

1. 1   **6.** 0
2. -2   **7.** $-\frac{1}{3}$
3. 0   **8.** 2
4. $\frac{3}{4}$ **9.** -3
5. $-\frac{1}{2}$

10. A. line A Of the answer choices, only line A has a negative slope, so it must be the correct answer. Line A moves down 1 space each time it goes 3 spaces to the right, a ratio of -1 to 3 or $-\frac{1}{3}$.

11. B. -2 You have more information than you need. Choose any two points and use the slope formula to solve for the slope. For example, if you choose points (0, 4) and (1, 2), your calculations would be: $\frac{2-4}{1-0} = -\frac{2}{1} = -2$.

12. C. (2, 3) The best way to solve the problem is probably to make a quick sketch. Because the line has a slope of 3, start at point (1, 0) and count 3 spaces up and 1 space to the right. You are now at point (2, 3),w which is choice (C). You can check your work using the slope formula.

Lesson 9: Slope and Equations

Practice 9, page 367

1. $y = -4x + 2$
$x = 1; y = -2; m = -4$
$-2 = -4(1) + b$
$b = 2$

2. $y = 2x - 2$
$x = -1; y = -4; m = 2$
$-4 = 2(-1) + b$
$b = -2$

3. $y = -\frac{1}{3}x + \frac{2}{3}$
$x = -4; y = 2; m = -\frac{1}{3}$
$2 = -\frac{1}{3}(-4) + b$
$b = \frac{2}{3}$

4. $y - 1 = 3(x - 2)$
$x_1 = 2; y_1 = 1; m = 3$

5. $y = -\frac{1}{3}(x - 2)$
$x_1 = 2; y_1 = 0; m = -\frac{1}{3}$

6. $y + 2 = x - 1$
$x_1 = 1; y_1 = -2; m = 1$

7. $y = -\frac{1}{3}x + \frac{4}{3}$
First, find the slope:
$m = \frac{3-1}{-5-1} = -\frac{1}{3}$
Choose either ordered pair to substitute for x and y:
$m = -\frac{1}{3}; x = 1; y = 1$
Follow the steps to find the equation of a line in the slope-intercept form.
$1 = -\frac{1}{3}(1) + b$
$b = \frac{4}{3}$

8. $y = 4x + 12$
$n = \frac{4-0}{-2-(-3)} = 4$
$0 = 4(-3) + b$
$b = 12$

9. $y = \frac{1}{2}x - \frac{5}{2}$
$m = \frac{1-(-4)}{7-(-3)} = \frac{1}{2}$
$1 = \frac{1}{2}(7) + b$
$b = -\frac{5}{2}$

10. C. $y = -x - 1$ Plug both points into the slope formula.
$m = \frac{-3-0}{2-(-1)} = -1$.
Then, use m and one of the points to solve for b.
$0 = -1(-1) + b$
$b = -1$

11. B. $y = 4$ Plug both points into the slope formula. $m = \frac{4-4}{1-(-3)} = 0$. Then, use m and one of the points to solve for b.
$4 = -3(0) + b$
$b = 4$
Because this line has a slope of zero, there is no x term in the equation. Rather, y is always equal to 4, no matter what the value of x is.

12. D. $y = \frac{1}{2}x - 1$ To answer this question, simplify the equation in the question to find an answer that matches:

$$y - 2 = \frac{1}{2}(x - 6)$$
$$y - 2 = \frac{1}{2}x - 3$$
$$y = \frac{1}{2}x - 1$$

13. **B.** $y = -x - 4$ Because the line on the graph slopes down from left to right, its slope is negative, so you can eliminate choices (A) and (C) immediately. Then note that the line crosses the y-axis at $(0, -4)$, so the y-intercept is -4. Therefore, the correct choice is (B).

Lesson 10: Systems of Linear Equations

Practice 10, page 369

1. **(7, 6)**

$$y = 3x - 15 \qquad x + y = 13$$

x	y
0	-15
5	0

x	y
0	13
13	0

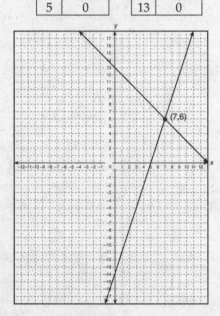

2. **(-3, 11)**

$$4x + 2y = 10 \qquad y = -5x - 4$$

x	y
0	5
$\frac{5}{2}$	0

x	y
0	-4
$-\frac{4}{5}$	0

3. **(3, -1)**

Isolate y:
$$-y = -7x + 22$$
$$y = 7x - 22$$
Substitute:
$$4x + 2(7x - 22) = 10$$
$$4x + 14x - 44 = 10$$
$$18x = 54$$
$$x = 3$$
Substitute back:
$$y = 7(3) - 22$$
$$y = -1$$

4. **(7, 2)**

Isolate y:
$$y = 9 - x$$
Substitute:
$$2x - 3(9 - x) = 8$$
$$2x - 27 + 3x = 8$$
$$5x = 35$$
$$x = 7$$
Substitute back:
$$y = 9 - 7$$
$$y = 2$$

5. **(-4, 3)**

y is already isolated.
$$y = 3x + 15$$
Substitute:
$$5x - 2(3x + 15) = -26$$
$$5x - 6x - 30 = -26$$
$$-x = 4$$
$$x = -4$$
Substitute back:
$$y = 3(-4) + 15$$
$$y = 3$$

6. **$(\frac{1}{2}, 6)$**

y is already isolated.
$$y = 12x$$
Substitute:
$$10x - (12x) = -1$$

$$-2x = -1$$
$$x = \frac{1}{2}$$
Substitute back:
$$y = 12\left(\frac{1}{2}\right)$$
$$y = 6$$

7. **A. (2, -1)** Isolate x in the first equation. $x = 2y + 4$. Then, substitute into the second equation to find a value for y.
$$6y + 5(2y + 4) = 4$$
$$16y + 20 = 4$$
$$y = -1$$
Finally, use that value of y in the first equation to find a value for x.
$$x = 2(-1) + 4 = 2$$

8. **C. (0,0)** The equation $y = x$ represents a line whose x-coordinate is always equal to the y-coordinate. The equation $y = -x$ represents a line whose y-coordinate is always equal to the negative of the x-coordinate. Neither line has a b term in its equation, so both lines have a y-intercept of zero, meaning that they both cross the y-axis at $(0,0)$.

9. **C. $\left(-\frac{9}{2}, -2\right)$** Since the only possible y-value for the line $y = -2$ is -2, simply substitute that value for y in the equation $3y = 2x + 3$ to find the intersection:
$$3(-2) = 2x + 3$$
$$-9 = 2x$$
$$x = -\frac{9}{2}$$

10. **C. $y = -4x + 2$** Two different lines cannot intersect if they are parallel. Lines are parallel if they have the same slope. Only choice (C) does not have a slope of 4, so this is the correct choice.

Lesson 11: Patterns and Functions

Practice 11, page 371

1. 0
2. 41
3. 2
4. 40
5. 23

6. -4
7. 31.25
8. -13
9. 32
10. -5

11. **B. 49** To highlight the pattern, it might be useful to make a table or list:

1st	2nd	3rd	4th
1 block	3 blocks	5 blocks	7 blocks

The number of blocks in each construction equals $2n - 1$, where n is the number in the sequence. The 25th construction would require $2(25) - 1 = 49$ blocks.

12. **C. 16** Each term is 6 greater than the term before it. The next (that is, the fifth) term in the sequence is 10, and the sixth term is 16.

13. **B. $c = \$5.00 - \$0.25 (n - 1)$** The original price per scarf ($5) is reduced by 25 cents starting with the second scarf.

14. **B. 1, 5, 9, 13, 17 . . .** Try the numbers 1, 2, and 3 for x in the function. This will result in the first three terms of the pattern: 1, 5, and 9. Only choice (B) contains these three terms.

Lesson 12: Function Applications

Practice 12, page 373

1. a. $99
   b. $265
2. a. 5.5 hours
   b. 4.25 hours
3. a. Plan A
   b. Plan B
4. **B. $29.50** Use the functions for the two jobs, substituting 30 hours for h:
   Job 1: $P = \$9.75h = \$9.75(30) = \$292.50$
   Job 2: $P = \$70 + \$8.40h = \$70 + \$8.40(30) = \$70 + \$252 = \$322$
   Subtract: $\$322 - \$292.50 = \$29.50$
5. **D. Alicia will earn the most at Job 2.** Use the functions to find Alicia's wages at all three jobs based on 40 hours:
   Job 1: $P = \$9.75h = \$9.75(40) = \$390$
   Job 2: $P = \$70 + \$8.40h = \$70 + \$8.40(40) = \$70 + \$336 = \$406$
   Job 3: $\$380 \times \frac{h}{38} = \$380 \times \frac{40}{38} = \$10 \times 40 = \$400$
   Compare the three results. Alicia will earn the most at Job 2.
6. **B. $19,400** Use the function to calculate the profit:
   $P = \$95,000 - \$5,400d$
   $P = \$95,000 - \$5,400(14)$
   $P = \$95,000 - \$75,600$
   $P = \$19,400$

Equations, Inequalities, and Functions Practice Questions, pages 374–377

1. **D. $-4x - 6$** Use the order of operations: $6 - 4 (x + 3) = 6 - 4x - 12 = -4x - 6$

2. **A. -3**
   $3 + 4x = x - 6$
   $3x = -9$
   $x = -3$
3. **B. $y = -4x + 6$** Choices (A) and (B) are the only two choices with the correct slope. Plug in $x = 1$ and $y = 2$ into both equations; only choice (B) works.
4. **C. $4x - y = -7$** Try $x = -2$ and $y = -1$ in each equation. Only choice (C) is true: $4(-2) - (-1) = -8 + 1 = -7$
5. **C. 510** Let t = Tom's earnings and $2t - \$150$ = Jan's earnings.
   $2t - \$150 + t = \$1380$
   $3t - \$150 = \$1380$
   $3t = \$1530$
   $t = \$510$
6. **D. D** The coordinates of D are $(-3, -2)$, which make the equation $y = -x - 5$ true.
   $y = -x - 5$
   $-2 = -(-3) - 5$
   $-2 = 3 - 5$
   $-2 = -2$
7. **C. $\frac{1}{3}$** Count the rise and run from C to B. The line moves up 3 spaces as it moves 9 to the right: $\frac{3}{9} = \frac{1}{3}$.
8. **A. $s \geq \$17,500$** Samuel's earnings can be represented by the expression $\$350 + 0.1s$, where s represents total sales. Since Samuel needs to earn at least $2,100, this expression must be greater than or equal to $2,100. Solve:
   $\$350 + 0.1s \geq \$2,100$
   $0.1s \geq \$1,750$
   $s \geq \$17,500$
9. **B. 5.35** Substitute 24 for n and solve:
   $F = \$3.95 + \$0.10(24 - 10)$
   $F = \$3.95 + \$0.10(14)$
   $F = \$3.95 + \$1.40$
   $F = \$5.35$
10. **D. 29** Let x = the first number. The remaining numbers are $x + 2$, $x + 4$, and $x + 6$. Solve:
    $x + (x + 2) + (x + 4) + (x + 6) = 104$
    $4x + 12 = 104$
    $4x = 92$
    $x = 23$
    The numbers are 23, 25, 27, and 29. The problem asks for the largest of these numbers.
11. **C. 3^6** Calculate: $3 \times 3 \times 3 \times 3 \times 3 \times 3 = 729$. The other expressions are less than 400. You could also use estimation to help with this problem. For

example, to evaluate choice (A), remember that $7 \times 7 = 49$. Then, since 49 is almost 50, round up to make the calculation easier: $7 \times 50 = 350$. So $7^3 < 350$, and it is definitely less than 400.

12. **B. $5x - 4 = 8 + 2 + 3x$** Translate each part of the problem to numbers and symbols and then connect the parts with the = symbol.
13. **B. 1** To find the slope of a line that crosses two points, find the difference between the y-coordinates and then divide by the difference in the x-coordinates: $\frac{6-4}{4-2} = \frac{2}{2} = 1$.
14. **B. 31** From 1 to 7, there is a difference of 6. From 7 to 14, there is a difference of 7. From 14 to 22, there is a difference of 8. To find the next term, add 9 to 22: $22 + 9 = 31$.
15. **C. 0** To find the y-intercept of a line when given the slope and a point, plug the x- and y-coordinates and the slope into the point-slope form, $y = mx + b$. This results in $2 = 2(1) + b$. Solve for b.
16. $(-2, 1)$

Create tables for each linear equation to find values of y when substituting values for x:

$y = x + 3$

x	y
0	3
-3	0

$y = -2x - 3$

x	y
0	-3
$-\frac{3}{2}$	0

Graph the two lines. They intersect at point $(-2,1)$.

17. **A. $-7x - (8 + y)$** The word *product* indicates multiplication, and the word *sum* indicates addition. Choice (B) means that y is added, rather than subtracted, from the product (due to order of operations), so it is incorrect.

18. **C. 8 and –3** Either solve by factoring or by trying each option in the equation. The correct factorization is as follows:

$x^2 - 5x - 24 = 0$
$(x - 8)(x + 3) = 0$
$x = 8$ or $x = -3$

19. **B. 4** Cynthia's age right now is six times Rebecca's, or $6r$. Thus, in six years, Cynthia will be $6r + 6$ years old, and Rebecca will be $r + 6$ years old. Write an equation and solve for r:
$6r + 6 = 3(r + 6)$.

20. **B.** $y = 2x - 3$ Try the given points in the equations in the answer options. Only choice (B) works with both points.

21. **B.**
$-2(x - 6) > 8$
$-2x + 12 > 8$
$-2x > -4$
$x < 2$

Remember to reverse the inequality symbol when you divide both sides by a negative number.

22. **B. (–5, 1)** Point L is 5 spaces to the left of the origin along the x-axis and 1 space above the origin along the y-axis.

23. **D.** $\frac{3}{2}$ The coordinates of point L are (–5, 1), and the coordinates of point M are (–3, 4). Find the slope by finding the difference of the y-coordinates, and divide by the difference of the x-coordinates: $\frac{1-4}{-5-(-3)} = \frac{-3}{-2} = \frac{3}{2}$.

24. **C. $18** Let s = Sam's gift. Then:
Daniel's gift = s.
Celia's gift = $s + 12$ (since Sam and Daniel gave the same amount).
Bob's gift = $0.5(s + 12)$ (that is, one-half of Celia's gift).
Add those four quantities together and set the sum total to $81:
$s + s + (s + 12) + .5(s + 12) = 81$
$3.5s + 18 = 81$
$3.5s = 63$
$s = 18$

25. **A.** $x \le 3$ Remember to reverse the inequality sign when dividing by a negative number:
$-7x - 4 \ge x - 28$
$-8x \ge -24$
$x \le 3$

26. **C.** $y = x + 2$ Start by finding the slope: $\frac{3-2}{1-0} = 1$. Now you know

that the equation will be $y = x + b$, and you can eliminate choices (A) and (B). And in this case, no calculations are required to find the y-intercept, because one of the points given in the question is (0, 2)—the point where the line crosses the y-axis.

27. **B. 8,652** Let x = votes for the leading candidate and p = votes for Perez. Write an equation:
$p = \frac{1}{3}x + 5,512$.
Additionally, you can say that $p + x = 18,072$, or $p = 18,072 - x$
Substitute for p:
$18,072 - x = \frac{1}{3}x + 5,512$
$12,560 = \frac{4}{3}x$
$x = 9420$
That number represents the number of votes the opposing candidate received. Now, substitute that value back into the simpler of the two original equations:
$p + 9,420 = 18,072$
$p = 8,652$

28. **B.** $x = -2$ Simplify:
$-4(x + 2) - 10 = 5x$
$-4x - 8 - 10 = 5x$
$-4x - 18 = 5x$
$-18 = 9x$
$-2 = x$

29. **D.** $\$5x + \$10(35 - x) = \$240$ The total value of the $5 bills is $5x$. Since there are 35 bills, the number of $10 bills must be $35 - x$. The value of the $10 bills is $\$10(35 - x)$. The sum of the value of the $5 bills plus the value of the $10 bills is $240.

30. **C. 75** Let x = the first number in the sequence. Then write an equation:
$x + (x + 1) + (x + 2) + (x + 3) + (x + 4) = 370$
$5x + 10 = 370$
$x = 72$
The first number in the sequence is 72. That means the fourth number (which equals $x + 3$) is 75.

31. **4** Substitute and solve: $E = \frac{9(8)}{18} = 4$.

32. **(–1, 1)** The given points lie in a vertical line. Since the distance between the points is 8 spaces, the midpoint is (–1, 1), which is 4 spaces from either point.

Geometry

Lesson 1: Plane Figures

Practice 1, page 379

1. rectangle, square
2. parallelogram, rectangle, square, rhombus
3. trapezoid
4. rectangle, square
5. none
6. rectangle, square, parallelogram, rhombus
7. square, rhombus
8. rectangle, square, parallelogram, rhombus, trapezoid
9. trapezoid
10. square
11. **C. 140°** Let h = the measure of $\angle H$. Then $3h + 20° = m\angle F$. The sum of the angles of a quadrilateral is 360°, so $3h + 20° + h + 90° + 90° = 360°$
Solve the equation:
$4h + 200° = 360°$, so $4h = 160°$, $h = 40°$, and $3h + 20° = 140°$.
12. **B.** $EF \parallel GH$ In other words, line EF is parallel to line GH. A trapezoid is a quadrilateral with exactly one pair of parallel sides.
13. **C. 90°** If the opposite sides of a figure are parallel and all four sides are equal, then the figure is either a square or rhombus. Since $\angle T$ is a right angle, the figure is square. Therefore, all the angles measure 90°.
14. **C. parallelogram** This quadrilateral has opposite sides that are equal and opposite angles that are equal. It has no right angles, and the two sets of sides are different lengths. The quadrilateral must be a parallelogram.

Lesson 2: Triangles

Practice 2, page 381

1. equilateral, acute
2. scalene, obtuse
3. isosceles, acute
4. 64°
5. 45°
6. 97°
7. **C. 14** Solve for $\angle BAC$: $m\angle BAC + 55° = 115°$, so $m\angle BAC = 60°$. Solve for $\angle BCA$: $\angle BCA + 35° = 95°$, so $\angle BCA = 60°$. If two of the angles of $\triangle ABC$ each measure 60°, the third angle also measures 60°. The triangle is equilateral,

and all the sides of *ABC* are equal to side *AB*.

8. **C. right** $55° + 35° + m\angle D = 180°$. Solve for the missing angle: $m\angle D = 90°$. Therefore, the triangle is a right triangle.

9. **C. 86°** The angles of a triangle add up to 180°. $38° + 56° = 94°$, so the third angle can be found by subtracting 94° from 180°: $180° − 94° = 86°$.

Lesson 3: Pythagorean Relationship

Practice 3, page 383

1. $c = 11.3$ in
2. $c = 15$ yd
3. $c = 2.5$ cm
4. $a = 5.2$ m
5. $b = 8$ mm
6. $a = 17.3$ ft
7. $c = 12.2$ cm
8. $b = 26.0$ in
9. $c = 6.4$ km

10. **B. 6.7** The distance from *A* to *C* is 3 units, and the distance from *B* to *C* is 6 units.
$$c^2 = a^2 + b^2$$
$$c^2 = 3^2 + 6^2$$
$$c^2 = 9 + 36$$
$$c^2 = 45$$
$$c = \sqrt{45} \approx 6.7$$

11. **C. 30** The shorter sides are the legs. Solve for the hypotenuse:
$$c^2 = a^2 + b^2$$
$$c^2 = 18^2 + 24^2$$
$$c^2 = 324 + 576$$
$$c^2 = 900$$
$$c = \sqrt{900} = 30$$

12. **D. 12.1** The brace divides the rectangle into two right triangles with the brace as the hypotenuse of each. Solve for the hypotenuse of one of the triangles:
$$c^2 = a^2 + b^2$$
$$c^2 = 5^2 + 11^2$$
$$c^2 = 25 + 121$$
$$c^2 = 146$$
$$c = \sqrt{146} \approx 12.08,$$ which rounds to 12.1.

13. **A. 36** Calculate:
$$c^2 = a^2 + b^2$$
$$39^2 = 15^2 + b^2$$
$$1{,}521 = 225 + b^2$$
$$1{,}296 = b^2$$
$$b = \sqrt{1{,}296} = 36$$

Lesson 4: Perimeter and Area

Practice 4, page 385

1. area: 39 sq units
   perimeter: 30.8 units
2. area: 16 sq units
   perimeter: 16 units

3. area: 640 sq units
   perimeter: 104 units
4. area: 29.6 sq units
   perimeter: 24.6 units
5. area: 616 sq units
   perimeter: 109 units
6. area: 38 sq units
   perimeter: 32 units
7. **C. 56** The shaded portion is a trapezoid: $\frac{1}{2} \times (5 + 9) \times 8 = 56$.
8. **C. 54** The area of a rectangle is its base times its height. $9 \times 6 = 54$.
9. **C. 324** Subtract the area of the patio from the area of the entire yard. Both are rectangles, so multiply length and width to find the area:
$(24 \times 18) − (12 \times 9) = 324$.
10. **B. 24** Add all four sides: $6 + 6 + 6 + 6 = 24$ centimeters.

Lesson 5: Circles

Practice 5, page 387

1. $C = 62.8$ in; $A = 314.2$ in^2
2. $C = 12.6$ cm; $A = 12.6$ cm^2
3. $C = 25.1$ m; $A = 50.2$ m^2
4. **C. 38** Use the formula $C = \pi d$, where $d = 12$. $12 \times 3.14 = 37.7$
5. **B. 3.14×6^2** The formula for the area of a circle is $A = \pi r^2$. The radius of a circle is half of the diameter. Half of 12 is 6. Substitute 6 for *r* and 3.14 for *π*. $A = 3.14 \times 6^2$.
6. **B. 13.0** The diameter of a circle is twice the radius. $6.5 \times 2 = 13$.
7. **C. 19** Find the circumference of the 10-point band. First find the diameter, which passes through the 10-point band, the inner circle, and the 10-point band a second time on its way from one edge of the circle to the other. Add the width of the 10-point band twice and the diameter of the inner circle: $2 + 2 + 2 = 6$ inches. Now you can use the formula for circumference: $6 \times 3.14 = 18.84$, which rounds to 19 inches.

Lesson 6: Volume

Practice 6.1, page 389

1. 160 cubic units
2. 27 cubic units
3. 141 cubic units
4. 420 cubic units
5. 3 cubic units

6. 236 cubic units
7. **A. 5.** $V = lwh$ You know that the length and width of the box both equal 4 and that the volume equals 80. Solve the equation:
$$80 = 4 \times 4 \times h$$
$$80 = 16h$$
$$5 = h$$
8. **C. 125** If each edge measures 5 feet, then the figure is a cube. $5^3 = 125$.
9. **C. 17** First, you must find the volume of the pool. The radius of the pool is 6 and the height is 3.
$$V = \pi r^2 h$$
$$\approx 3.14 \times 6^2 \times 3$$
$$\approx 3.14 \times 36 \times 3$$
$$\approx 339.12$$
Therefore, the volume is about 339. Solve the proportion $\frac{1}{20} = \frac{x}{339}$, where *x* equals the number of scoops Linda must add: $20x = 339$; $x = 16.95$, about 17.

Practice 6.2, page 391

1. 9 in^3
2. 127 in^3
3. 314 cm^3
4. 480 m^3
5. 11 in^3
6. 1060 cm^3
7. **A. 480** First, find the volume of the original package. Substitute the numbers given into the volume equation: $V = \frac{1}{3} \times 10^2 \times 15 = 500$. Then find the volume of the new package. Add 4 to the length and width of the base to get 14. Substitute into the volume equation again and solve: $V = \frac{1}{3} \times 14^2 \times 15 = 980$. Find the difference of the two volumes: $980 − 500 = 480$.
8. **C. 67** You know that the height of the cone is half of the diameter of the base. Since the radius of the base is also half of the diameter, the radius must equal the height. Therefore, the radius is 4. Now solve the equation: $V = \frac{1}{3} \times \pi \times 4^2 \times 4 \approx 67$
9. **D. The volume of *B* is less than the volume of *A*.** First, find the volumes of the two figures. Figure *A* is a rectangular solid. Use the formula $V = lwh = 4 \times 3 \times 2 = 24$. Figure *B* is a pyramid. Use the formula $V = \frac{1}{3}Bh = \frac{1}{3} \times 3^2 \times 6 = 18$. Now compare the

two volumes. Since 24 > 18, choice (D) must be the answer.

10. **D. 1,000** Use the formula $V = \frac{1}{3} \pi r^2 h = \frac{1}{3} \times \pi \times 8^2 \times 15 \approx 1,005$, which is about 1,000.

Lesson 7: Surface Area

Practice 7.1, page 393

1. 108
2. 39
3. 24
4. 336
5. 256
6. 384
7. **A. 5** If all the edges are the same length, then the box must be a cube, and each square face has the same area. There are 6 faces. Divide 150 by 6 to get an area of 25 for each face. Then $25 \div 5 = 5$, so each side has a length of 5 in.
8. **C. The surface area of Figure A is greater than the surface area of Figure B.** Calculate both surface areas. Figure A: $25 \times 6 = 150$. Figure B: $(30 \times 4) + (9 \times 2) = 138$. Therefore, Figure A's surface area is greater than Figure B's.
9. **C. 162** The original box has a side length of 3 centimeters, so the surface area is 54 square centimeters. When the dimensions are doubled, the new box has a side length of 6 centimeters, so the surface area is 216 square centimeters. The difference in surface areas is 216 cm – 54 cm, which is 162 square centimeters.

Practice 7.2, page 395

1. 168π 4. 378π
2. 40π 5. 400π
3. 36π 6. 96π

7. **B. 64π** The formula for the surface area of a sphere uses the radius, and the radius is half the diameter, so $8 \div 2 = 4 = r$. Now use the formula for the surface area of a sphere: $SA = 4\pi r^2 = 4 \times \pi \times 4^2 = 64\pi$.
8. **D. The new cone will have a surface area less than the surface area of the original cone.** The original cone has a radius of 4, so its surface area is $\pi(4)(8) + \pi(4^2) = 32\pi + 16\pi = 48\pi$. The new cone will have a slant height of 16, a diameter of 4 and a radius of 2, so its surface area is: $\pi(2)$

$(16) + \pi(2^2) = 32\pi + 4\pi = 36\pi$, which is less than 48π.

9. **C. 170** The surface area of the cylinder is $\pi(6)(6) + 2\pi(3^2) = 36\pi + 18\pi = 54\pi = 54(3.14) \approx 170$ square inches.

Lesson 8: Combined Figures

Practice 8, page 397

1. $P = 150$ units
   $A = 1050$ sq units
2. $P = 49.7$ units
   $A = 159.3$ sq units
3. $P = 72$ units
   $A = 168$ sq units
4. $V = 185$ cubic units
5. $V = 278$ cubic units
6. $V = 399$ cubic units
7. **D. 360** Find the volume of the main rectangular slab: $V = lwh$, so $V = 3 \times 8 \times 12 = 288$ cubic feet. Find the volume of one of the blocks: $V = lwh$, so $V = 3 \times 3 \times 2 = 18$ cu ft. Multiply by 4, the number of blocks: $18 \times 4 = 72$ cu ft. Finally, add the main slab to the blocks: $288 + 72 = 360$ cu ft.
8. **C. 134** The radius of both the cones and the cylinder is 2. The height of one cone is 4 inches. Find the volume of one cone: $V = \frac{1}{3}\pi r^2 h = \frac{1}{3} \times 3.14 \times 2^2 \times 4 \approx 16.7$ cu in. Multiply by 2 to find the volume of both cones: $16.7 \times 2 = 33.4$ cu in. Find the volume of the cylinder: $V = \pi r^2 h \approx 3.14 \times 2^2 \times 8 \approx 100.48$ cu in. Add to find the total volume: $33.4 + 100.48 = 133.88$ cu in, which rounds to 134 cu in.

Lesson 9: Geometry Calculator Skills

Practice 9, page 399

1. 42 in   4. 15.8 cm
2. 195 cm^2 5. 37.7 in
3. 43 ft^3 6. 3016 cm^3

7. **C. 520** Use the formulas for finding the area of a rectangle and the area of a triangle, and subtract the area of the cut-out triangle from the area of the rectangle. On the TI-30XS MultiView™ calculator, enter the following: 32 ⊗ 20 ⊖ 20 ⊗ 12 ⊗ .5 (enter). The right side of the display will read **520**. You can enter the entire calcula-

tion in this fashion because the TI-30XS™ understands the algebraic order of operations. If you press enter after each of those operations, your answer will be incorrect.

8. **B. 35** Use the formula for finding the volume of a cylinder. Press: (π) ⊗ 1.5 (x^2) ⊗ 5 (enter). The right side of the display will read **35.34291735**, which rounds to 35 meters.
9. **D. 5,056** Use the formula for finding the volume of a rectangular solid. Subtract the volume of Box B from the volume of Box A. Press: 26 ⊗ 12 ⊗ 32 ⊖ 22 ⊗ 8 ⊗ 28 (enter). The right side of the display will read **5056**.
10. **C. 608** Use the formula for finding the area of a rectangle. Combine the areas of the two faces. Press: 32 ⊗ 12 ⊕ 28 ⊗ 8 (enter). The right side of the display will read **608**.

Geometry Practice Questions, pages 400–402

1. **D. 150** If the edge length is 5 cm, then each square surface has an area of 25 cm^2. There are 6 faces, so multiply by 6 to get 150 cm^2.
2. **C. 192π** Substitute the values given in the question into the formula for the surface area of a cylinder:
   $SA = 2\pi rh + 2\pi r^2$
   $SA = 2\pi(6)(10) + 2\pi(6^2)$
   $SA = 120\pi + 72\pi = 192\pi$
3. **C. 66π** The surface area of a cylinder is calculated with the formula $SA = 2\pi rh + 2\pi r^2 = (2 \times \pi \times 3 \times 8) + (2 \times \pi \times 9) = 48\pi + 18\pi = 66\pi$.
4. **C. 16$\sqrt{3}$ + 16** The surface area of a pyramid with a four-sided base is $SA = \frac{1}{2}ps + B$, where p is the perimeter of the base, s is the slant height of a face of the pyramid, and B is the area of the base. The pyramid described in this problem has a square base with sides of length 4, so both the perimeter (p) and the area of its base (B) are 16. Each face of the pyramid is an equilateral triangle, the height of which represents the slant height (s) of the pyramid. Divide one of the equilateral triangles into two 30:60:90 triangles and use

the side length ratio $x : x\sqrt{3} : 2x$ to determine the slant height of the pyramid. Since the base of one of these 30:60:90 triangles is 2 (half the length of a side of the pyramid's base) and the hypotenuse is 4 (the length of a side of the equilateral triangles making up the faces of the pyramid), the height of each 30:60:90 triangle (and, therefore, of each equilateral triangle face of the pyramid) is $2\sqrt{3}$. That is the slant height (s) of the pyramid as well. Now, plug in all of the relevant measures and solve: $\frac{1}{2}ps + B = \frac{1}{2} \times (16 \times 2\sqrt{3}) + 16 = 16\sqrt{3} + 16$.

5. **D. 512π** The circumference is 16π so the diameter is 16, and the radius is 8. The surface area is $4\pi r^2 = 256\pi$. The paint covers the ball twice, so multiply by 2 to get 512π.

6. **D. 224** A closet is in the shape of a rectangular solid. To find the volume, multiply: $V = lwh = 7 \times 4 \times 8 = 224$ cubic feet.

7. **C. 48π** The cone has a surface area of $\pi rs = \pi \times 3 \times 10 = 30\pi$ (don't include the base of the cone). A sphere with radius 3 has a surface area of $4\pi r^2 = 4 \times \pi \times 3^2 = 36\pi$. The surface area of the ice cream is half of that, or 18π. Add to get $30\pi + 18\pi = 48\pi$.

8. **C. 8:1** The formula for the volume of a sphere is $V = \frac{4}{3}\pi r^3$. Find the volumes of both spheres and simplify the ratio between those volumes. Or think about it this way: the ratio of the volume of Sphere A to that of Sphere B would be as follows.
$(\frac{4}{3}\pi \times 2^3)$ to $(\frac{4}{3}\pi \times 1^3)$
Find the value of the exponents:
$(\frac{4}{3}\pi \times 8)$ to $(\frac{4}{3}\pi \times 1)$
You know that you can simplify a ratio by dividing both sides of the ratio by a number. Here, divide both sides by $\frac{4}{3}\pi$ to get: 8 to 1.

9. **24** The parallelogram has an area of 60 square cm. The area of the triangle is $\frac{1}{2}bh = \frac{1}{2}b \times 5 = 2.5b$, so $60 = 2.5b$ and $b = 24$.

10. **A. 1458.** The height of all three boxes is 9 in, the length is 18 in, and the width is 9 in. The total volume is $18 \times 9 \times 9 = 1458$.

11. **B. 500** Since Max hikes directly east after hiking directly due north, he has made a 90° turn. The distances hiked therefore form a right triangle. The legs are 300 and 400 yards. To solve for the hypotenuse, use the Pythagorean relationship:
$$a^2 + b^2 = c^2$$
$$300^2 + 400^2 = c^2$$
$$90,000 + 160,000 = c^2$$
$$250,000 = c^2$$
$$500 = c$$
A quicker solution would be to notice that the distances form a large triangle with sides in the 3:4:5 ratio. Then it is easy to see that the hypotenuse of a triangle with legs of 300 and 400 yards is 500 yards.

12. **C. 168** The volume of the container as drawn in the diagram is $V = lwh = 9$ in $\times$ 7 in $\times$ 12 in $= 756$ in^3. If you increase the length by 2 inches, the volume is 11 in $\times$ 7 in $\times$ 12 in $= 924$ in^3. Find the difference: 924 in^3 – 756 in^3 = 168 in^3. You can solve the problem more easily by multiplying the added length by the width and height: $2(7)(12) = 168$.

13. **D. $x^2 = 15^2 - 6^2$** Use the Pythagorean relationship. If $a^2 + b^2 = c^2$ and c is the hypotenuse, then $b^2 = c^2 - a^2$ and $x^2 = 15^2 - 6^2$.

14. **C. 36** Use the formula for finding the perimeter of a rectangle. Let $3w$ = length.
$P = 2l + 2w$
$96 = 2(3w) + 2w$
$96 = 8w$
$w = 12$
So the width is 12 inches, and the length is $3 \times 12 = 36$ inches.

15. **D. 1120π** The circumference is 16π, so $r = 8$ cm. A cone-shaped party hat does not have a base, so $SA = \pi rs = 56\pi$. Multiply by 20 to get 1120π.

16. **A. 3.43** To find the area of the shaded region, subtract the area of the circle from the area of the square. One side of the square is equivalent to the diameter of the circle. The radius is 2, so the diameter—and each side of the square—is 4. So $A = 4^2 - \pi \times 2^2 \approx 3.43$.

17. **B. 1,560** You may find it helpful to draw a sketch of the room. Two walls measure 40 by 12 feet. Two measure 25 by 12 feet. Find the total area: $2 \times 40 \times 12 + 2 \times 25 \times 12 = 960 + 600 = 1,560$.

18. **C. 12,000** Use the formula $V = lwh$. Multiply: $40 \times 25 \times 12 = 12,000$.

19. **A. 4** Begin by finding the total surface area of all three pyramids. The formula for the surface area of a pyramid is $SA = \frac{1}{2}ps + B$. For each pyramid, plug in the values and calculate:
Top left pyramid:
$SA = \frac{1}{2}(2 + 2 + 2 + 2)(3) + (2 \times 2)$
$= 16$
Top right pyramid:
$SA = \frac{1}{2}(3 + 3 + 3 + 3)(6) + (3 \times 3)$
$= 45$
Bottom pyramid:
$SA = \frac{1}{2}(4 + 4 + 4 + 4)(4) + (4 \times 4)$
$= 48$
Thus, the total surface area for all three pyramids is:

$16 + 45 + 48 = 109$

The problem states that Laura needs one tube of paint for each 30 square inches. Thus, she needs $109 \div 30 \approx 3.6$. In order to finish her project, she should buy four tubes of paint.

SOCIAL STUDIES

Social Studies Practices

Lesson 1: Determine Central Idea and Draw Conclusions

Practice 1, page 411

1. **C. the characteristics of Greek tragedy** The passage describes tragedy as "central to Greek culture" and supports this point with details about the plots, staging, characters, and themes of Greek tragedy.
2. **D. The main character in Greek drama has a tragic flaw that causes his downfall.** Choice (D) cites one of the details the author uses to try to establish the central role of tragedy in Greek culture. The other choices are all too broad (choice (A)) or misrepresent what the passage actually said (choices (B) and (C)).
3. **A. Ancient Greeks did not expect to see an original story each time they attended the theater.** Choice (A) is the only answer choice supported by information in the passage. The writer tells you that tragedies "told stories familiar from myths and epics," so it must have been the case that theatergoers knew the general story that would be acted out.
4. **D. Where do the incomes of senior citizens come from?** Choice (D) is correct because the graph tells you the sources of income for American senior citizens. The graph doesn't give any actual dollar amounts, nor does it state how many senior citizens there are in the United States You would need those numbers to answer the questions in choices (A), (B), and (C).
5. **B. Social Security benefits are the most widespread means of support for most senior citizens.** Each bar in the graph represents the percentage of all seniors who receive some of their income from that source. Since the Social Security bar is the tallest (representing more than 86% of all seniors), choice (B) must be true based on the graph.

Lesson 2: Interpret Words and Ideas

Practice 2, page 413

1. **C. political and social instability in some Northern European countries** In the first paragraph of the passage, the author mentions "riots, civil unrest, and open rebellion" as some of the factors that pushed German citizens to migrate. Those events are examples of "political and social instability," so choice (C) is correct.
2. **D. a painting of pioneers settling and farming productive prairie land** In the passage, the author discusses "abundance" in the second paragraph, giving examples of the kinds of optimistic messages that attracted people to the United States. The image of pioneers opening up productive farmland is symbolic of the economic opportunity promised to 19th century immigrants to the United States, so choice (D) is correct.
3. **C. a growth in the population of the United States** In the first paragraph, the author tells you that the number of immigrants arriving in the United States. between 1820 and 1870 was greater than the entire U.S. population just 10 years before that time period. You can conclude from the passage that the U.S. population grew.
4. **B. Internal migration led to overgrazing.** According to the timeline, aggressive agriculture occurred prior to 1930 and the "black blizzards," caused in part by overgrazing, began in 1931. Internal migration did not begin until around 1933. Inferring that internal migration (which began later) caused overgrazing (which had already occurred) would be illogical, so choice (B) is correct.
5. **C. depleted topsoil** The "aggressive, mechanized farming techniques" that depleted the topsoil in the American Midwest and Southern plains occurred prior to and contributed to the dust storms and "black blizzards" that characterize the Great Dust Bowl. Internal migration (choice (B)) and failed farms (choice (C)) were results, not causes, of the Dust Bowl.

Lesson 3: Analyze Author's Purpose and Point of View

Practice 3, page 415

1. **C. propagandistic** Page 414 explains that propaganda uses emotional language to influence readers' behavior. Here, asking the readers to "have a part in Victory" is just such language.
2. **C. Citizens who plant war gardens help supply the war effort with essential resources.** As the passage explains, war gardens were encouraged so that, with citizens supplying more of their own food, the government could use its limited resources to feed and equip soldiers, sailors, and airmen. Choice (C) paraphrases this nicely.
3. **A. describe war gardens and explain their popularity in the United States** The author's tone is neutral and explanatory; she simply wants to explain what war gardens were and why they were popular during the two world wars. The author is not advocating a point of view (choice (B)), trying to compare or contrast the United States with any other country (choice (C)), or arguing against anyone else's position (choice (D)).
4. **C. a cancer** By using a frightening and often fatal disease such as "cancer" to describe the impact of the proposed regulations, the citizen is making an emotional comparison. The analogy is especially aggressive given that the issue addresses health and safety.

Lesson 4: Evaluate Author's Reasoning and Evidence

Practice 4, page 417

1. **A. Damming the Mekong could solve Cambodia's energy problems.** The author argues for cooperation among Cambodia and its neighboring

countries, all of which share the Mekong river. The reason this is important, the author asserts, is because hydroelectric power from the Mekong would help solve Cambodia's energy problems. Nowhere in the argument, however, does the author support this contention.

2. **B. Strikes have a detrimental impact on workers.** The cartoon shows a laborer using a strike as a means of "cutting off" production, depicted as a tree branch. The joke is that the worker sits on the wrong side of the branch he's cutting. Once the worker is successful in cutting off production, the cartoonist implies, he will fall to the ground along with production. Choice (B) neatly sums up the cartoonist's point.

3. **D. Ancient Greece pioneered democracy.** The one reason the author gives for believing that Ancient Greece was the greatest of the early civilization is that it was the birthplace of democracy. Thus, choice (D) is correct. Choice (A) is the author's opinion, not a fact supporting that opinion. Choices (B) and (C) are both reasons that ancient Babylon and Egypt (and not the author's favorite, Greece) might be considered great.

4. **B. The Constitution grants more power to the federal government than did the Articles of Confederation.** In each category compared in the chart, the federal government has more power under the Constitution than it had under the Articles of Confederation, so choice (B) is a valid inference, though it is not explicitly stated anywhere on the chart. All three wrong answers cite specific facts stated in the chart.

Lesson 5: Analyze Relationships Between Materials

Practice 5.1, page 419

1. **A. housing and food** Study the circle graph (pie chart) to see that the two largest portions are labeled with white

(33%) and vertical lines (20%). Checking the legend to the right shows that these "slices" correspond to housing and food, respectively.

2. **D. Brazil has a higher divorce rate than Mexico.** This bar chart directly supports choice (D): Brazil's divorce rate is 0.6 per thousand, while Mexico's is 0.4 per thousand. Choice (B) is incorrect because this chart shows five countries in the Western Hemisphere, not all of them. One of the countries not shown on the chart may have a divorce rate even lower than Mexico's. Choice (C) is incorrect because this chart conveys nothing about how divorce rates have changed over time.

3. **fluctuated** As you read the line graph left to right, showing the change over time, you see that percentage of votes for third-party presidential candidates went up and down multiple times, so "fluctuated" is accurate.

4. **C. Third party candidates have never captured more than 10 percent of the popular vote in any presidential election.** The statement in choice (C) is disproved by 1968 (14 percent) and 1992 (more than 19 percent).

5. **C. how agriculture spread in the Americas** The map shows two places at which agriculture originated independently (indicated by black stars) and where agriculture spread out from those two points (indicated by the white arrows). The map shows no political boundaries (choice (A)) or physical features (choice (B)) of the Americas, nor does it claim to name all of the ancient civilizations on the two continents (choice (D)).

6. **B. Both the Andes civilization and Mesoamerica domesticated beans.** Check right below the names of the two civilizations named on the map and you'll find the crops they learned to grow. "Beans" is the only crop listed for both the Andes and Mesoamerican groups.

Practice 5.2, page 421

1. **D. Sea otters have been able to live in habitats from which they were once eliminated.** Choice (D) is directly supported by the third paragraph of the passage, which refers to successful "programs to reintroduce the sea otter into previously populated areas." Choice (C) is incorrect because, although the passage says that the sea otters in California have regained about two-thirds of their former habitat range, it does not indicate that they have reached two-thirds of their former population numbers. Choices (A) and (B) are not mentioned at all in the passage.

2. **D. The current range of the sea otter in California is larger than what it was in 1911.** According to the passage, the sea otter's range in 1911 "was limited . . . to a small area around Monterrey Bay." The map makes it clear that the sea otter's range now extends significantly to both the north and south of Monterrey Bay. Putting the information from the passage together with that from the map shows that choice (D) must be true.

3. **C. Without conservation efforts and reintroduction programs, the range of sea otters in California would be smaller than what is shown on the map.** In the third paragraph of the passage, the author states that conservation and reintroduction programs "have contributed to" the expansion of the sea otter's habitat range in California. This directly supports the statement in choice (C).

Lesson 6: Interpret Data and Statistics

Practice 6, page 423

1. **D. 36** Median refers to the middle term in a set of numbers arranged from smallest to largest. Since more than half of New Mexico's 2010 population was age 35 or older, the median age could have been 36. For that same reason, ages 30 (choice (A)), 32 (choice (B)), and 34 (choice (C)) are all too small to represent the state's median age in 2010.

2. **B. the average margin of victory was higher in years when a Democrat won than in years when a Republican won** In both years in which a Republican won the presidential election (2000 and 2004) the final electoral vote count was very close. In each of the four years in which a Democrat won (1992, 1996, 2008, and 2012) the Democratic candidate captured a much larger portion of the electoral vote. Thus, choice (B) is supported by the graph.

3. **C. 1920** Of the years shown on the graph, 1920 is the point when the rural and urban populations are closest in number. Prior to 1920, the rural population was much larger than the urban population. After 1920, the urban population begins to be much larger than the rural population.

4. **C. 34 million** To determine the correct answer to this question, you need to subtract the range of the rural population from the range of the urban population. The rural population was around 54 million in 1930, up from approximately 25 million in 1860. That's a range of approximately 29 million. The urban population was around 68 million in 1930, up from just 5 million in 1860. That gives a range of approximately 63 million. Subtracting 29 million from 63 million produces a difference of 34 million, choice (C).

Lesson 7: Write an Extended Response

Practice 7, page 425

Refer to the *Social Studies Extended Response Evaluation Guide* on page 723 to evaluate your response.

Social Studies Practices Practice Questions, pages 426–429

1. **B. The unemployment rate declined consistently until shortly before the war's end.** Checking the timeline, you can see that World War II began in 1939 and ended in 1945. Unemployment went down every year between 1939 and 1944, and rose just slightly in 1945. Thus, choice (B)'s description of the war's impact on unemployment is correct.

2. **A. the stock market crash** Immediately after the stock market crash in 1929, unemployment increases dramatically and directly until 1933. That makes choice (A) correct. After 1933, unemployment declines gradually until the end of the war, and the decline is interrupted by a small increase during 1937–1938.

3. **D. The Seneca Falls Convention was a shocking event that undermined the nature of women.** There is no objective way to prove that something is "shocking and unnatural." Those words reveal that the statement in choice (D) was the opinion of one newspaper's editors.

4. **D. The Seneca Falls Convention was important in the fight for women's rights.** The passage's primary purpose is to explain how the women's movement "gained strength" at the Seneca Falls Convention.

5. **A. More than half of the reported cases of human plague in the United States between 1970 and 2010 were reported in four states.** Even if you don't recognize the four states in question as Arizona, California, Colorado, and New Mexico, the map clearly shows the overwhelming concentration of reported plague cases as occurring there. Choice (A) is justified by the information in the map.

6. **C. Several cases of plague were reported on the East Coast of the United States between 1970 and 2010.** The statement in choice (C) is clearly false given the information in the map. No cases of plague were recorded east of Illinois during the time period depicted by the map.

7. **D. The effects of the cotton gin on the cotton industry actually led to an increased demand for slaves in the South.** The fact stated in choice (D) is directly supported by the end of the passage where the writer explains the effects of the cotton gin: "with the boom in the cotton industry, more slaves were used to pick cotton at a faster rate."

8. **C. 2,000,000** The increase in the number of cotton bales produced between 1840 and 1860 was approximately 3,500,000. The increase in the number of slaves living in the United States during the same twenty year period was approximately 1,500,000. The difference between the two figures is 2,000,000.

9. **C. In most years, the percent population increase in South Dakota was greater than that in North Dakota.** Choice (C) is correct. In seven of the eleven years shown (every year from 01–02 to 07–08) South Dakota's annual population increase was greater than that of North Dakota. The increases were approximately equal in 08–09, and North Dakota's increase was greater in the remaining three years. Choice (B) makes a statement about the populations of these states, but the graph only contains information about *percent increase*, or proportional increase, of the population.

10. **less than** Though North Dakota had far greater growth than South Dakota toward the end of the period, North Dakota averaged an increase of approximately 0.77 percent per year over the 11 years, while South Dakota averaged approximately 0.93 percent per year.

11. **70 percent** The mean voter turnout for the years shown is 39.67 percent in midterm elections, and 55.98 percent in presidential elections. 36.67 percent divided by 55.98 percent equals 70.9 percent.

12. **C. 13.8 percent** "Median" refers to the middle term in a set of numbers arranged from smallest to largest. Arrange the terms from the chart in order: 11.1 percent, 11.6 percent, 13.8 percent, 13.9 percent, 14.0 percent. The middle term is 13.8 percent, corresponding with the correct answer, choice (C).

13. Refer to the *Social Studies Extended Response Evaluation Guide* on page 723 to evaluate your response.

U.S. History

Lesson 1: Exploration, Colonialism, and the American Revolution

Practice 1, page 431

1. **the Spanish** According to the map and the key, Spain had the southernmost colony along the east coast of what would eventually become the United States.
2. **B. The English established several colonies in the New World.** The map shows several English colonies along the New England coast and in what is now Virginia and Maryland.
3. **D. Haitian refugees who fled to the United States to escape a dictatorship** Like the early colonists, the Haitian refugees of the mid- and late 1900s came to the United States seeking freedom from political persecution.
4. **B. increased British taxes and restrictions on the colonies** The fourth and fifth sentences of paragraph 4 link increased taxes and restrictions to the outbreak of the American Revolution.
5. **B. They were concerned about the government becoming tyrannical.** The first amendment guarantees citizens' rights to pressure their government. The passage explains that the framers of the U.S. Constitution did not want the government to become overly powerful. While choices (A) and (C) were both rights listed amongst the guarantees of the First Amendment, they do not explain *why* the Framers listed them. Choice (B) discusses their motivations and is correct.

Lesson 2: Westward Expansion, the Civil War, and Reconstruction

Practice 2, page 433

1. **D. whether slavery should be permitted in territories in the West** This is implied in the third and fourth paragraphs of the passage. Choice (B) is incorrect because the fourth paragraph says that Abraham Lincoln promised to halt the spread of slavery, not to end it where it already existed.

2. **C. To balance the admission of Missouri, they agreed to a compromise in which Maine was admitted as a free state.** The third paragraph of the passage describes how the U.S. government tried to maintain a balance of power between the North and the South by adding states in pairs: one slave state and one free state. Since Missouri was a slave state, the most likely response of Northerners would be to propose the addition of a free state. (Indeed, Maine and Missouri were the 23rd and 24th states to join the United States.)
3. **concluded with the reunification of the nation** The information in the question indicates that North and South Vietnam were reunited under the Communists at the end of the Vietnam War. The passage implies that at the end of the U.S. Civil War, the North and the South again were united under the United States federal government.
4. **C. In 1868, many African Americans served in the government of South Carolina.** There are more than 20 African Americans included in this composite photograph of the South Carolina legislature. The other choices are opinions that cannot be confirmed by the photograph.
5. **A. Over the course of Reconstruction, African Americans in the South gained and then lost political power.** The number of African Americans in the composite photograph of the South Carolina state legislature of 1868 indicates that near the beginning of the Reconstruction period, African Americans had considerable political power. The last paragraph of the passage on page 432 states that by the 1870s, whites were preventing African Americans from exercising their newly won right to vote. This indicates that African Americans were losing political power as Reconstruction ended.

Lesson 3: Industrialization, Immigration, and the Progressive Era

Practice 3, page 435

1. **B. an increase in manufacturing** By definition, industrialization is related to increased manufacturing. This meaning is implied in the passage in paragraphs one and two.
2. **C. the development of the Bessemer process, which made it easier to produce steel** The first paragraph of the passage relates rapid industrialization to the invention of new industrial processes. The Bessemer process was one such process. It made steel more readily available for tools, railroads, construction, and other uses.
3. **C. cooperation with others to improve worker safety** The fourth paragraph indicates that union workers pledged to work together (cooperate) for better working conditions. The passage states that better working conditions include improved worker safety.
4. **D. fairness** The fifth paragraph discusses the Progressive Era. The fact that reformers were working to improve conditions for poor people and to give people a greater voice in government indicates that fairness was a strong ideal for them.
5. **Asia and the Americas** The second circle graph indicates that, in the years 2000–2009, 77 percent of persons obtaining legal resident status came from Asia and the Americas.
6. **C. In the 1890s, that number was roughly three times what it was in the period of 2000–2009.** The question asks you to compare the number of persons from Europe in the first circle graph to the number of persons from Europe in the second circle graph. Keep in mind that the total numbers represented by the two graphs are different. Calculate that number for the period 1889–1890: 97 percent of 3,689,609 is about 3,578,920. (You could use your calculator or estimate to find an approximate number.) Then calculate that number for the

period 2000–2009: 13 percent of 10,299,430 is about 1,338,925. (Use your calculator or estimate.) Now, compare those two numbers: 3,578,920 is a little less than three times 1,338,925.

Lesson 4: The United States as an Emerging World Power

Practice 4, page 437

1. **Military** The building of a naval base indicates that the correct category is "military."
2. **B. In World War II, the Allies included England, France, and Russia.** The author assumes that you realize that the Allies of World War II included the same major powers as the Allies in World War I. If you do not recognize this unstated assumption, you will not understand who fought whom in World War II.
3. **C. Unemployment fell after the start of the New Deal and continued to fall as the United States entered World War II.** The graph shows a decline in the unemployment rate after the New Deal went into effect in 1934. It shows that unemployment went up in 1938 but then dropped after that and dropped considerably after the United States' entry into World War II in 1941.
4. **D. America took a strong leadership role during and after World War II.** The paragraph focuses on the role the United States played during and after World War II. The other choices are details from the paragraph or they bring up information not included in the paragraph.

Lesson 5: The Cold War and the Civil Rights Era

Practice 5, page 439

1. **Blank (1) no direct combat; Blank (2) dissolution of the Soviet Union** The first paragraph of the passage implies that the name "Cold War" was used because there was no direct fighting. The first sentence of paragraph two explains that the Cold War ended when the Soviet Union broke up.
2. **C. The buildup of nuclear arms increases fear and instability, not peace.** The statement about peace and stability made by the man on the right in the bottom frame of the cartoon is supposed to be ironic. The cartoonist's reference to the man's trembling arms suggests that the situation is not stable, and that perhaps we should be afraid.
3. **C. Americans were in complete agreement about pulling out of Vietnam.** Paragraph one states that even when defeat for South Vietnam seemed fairly certain, a few Americans still wanted to continue contributing to the fighting. Therefore, it is an overstatement to say that Americans were in complete agreement that pulling out of Vietnam was the right thing to do.
4. **B. petitioning for a city ordinance requiring those selling real estate to select a buyer without regard to race** Paragraph three states that the aim of the civil rights movement was to end segregation and discrimination in the United States. Preventing the selective selling of real estate was one important way civil rights activists worked to end discrimination, making decreased segregation possible.
5. **A. Reliance on technology has increased pollution.** This is a conclusion—a general statement about a topic. The other choices are details—facts or examples— that support this conclusion.

U.S. History Practice Questions, pages 440–443

1. **B. Although the Cherokee adopted many aspects of white culture, they were driven off their ancestral lands.** This statement is the only one with a large enough scope to be considered a conclusion. The other choices are details that are either included in, related to, or not based on the time line.
2. **A. If the government can't protect us from white settlers here, now, how could it protect us from whites moving west in the future?** This question shows the lack of logic in the government's claim that location was what made it difficult to protect Cherokee rights. Location had nothing to do with the government's lack of protection of Cherokee land in the South. The government did not have the political will to enforce laws protecting the Cherokee.
3. **D. equal rights and opportunities for women** Adams's statements that women are not inferior and her invention of the term *Lordess* both indicate that she advocated equality for women.
4. **Select any four of: Maryland, Delaware, West Virginia, Kentucky, and Missouri** The map shows that these were all slave states loyal to the Union.
5. **A. The nation's capital was located nearby.** If the nation's capital, located adjacent to the state of Maryland, had been surrounded by Confederate states, it would have been extremely difficult for the U.S. army to defend it. This would have given a great edge to the Confederacy during the Civil War. The other choices are untrue, irrelevant, or not verifiable by the map.
6. **D. to weaken the South by enlisting former slaves in the Union army** This was implied by the text of the Proclamation that is quoted. None of the other choices are supported by the text.
7. **the Voting Rights Act of 1965** The chart explains that this act prohibited literacy (reading) tests for voting.
8. **C. African Americans were granted the vote soon after the Civil War, but laws enforcing these rights had to be passed a century later.** This is implied by the passage of the 15th Amendment in 1870 and by the passage of the Voting Rights Act of 1965. Congress would not have passed the later law if the 15th Amendment were being upheld and enforced. Choice (A) is true, based on the chart, but is not a summary of the information in the chart.

9. **B. They both prohibited the legal separation of people by race in public places.** The chart shows that both the 1875 and the 1964 Civil Rights Acts banned racial segregation in public places.

10. **D. The telephone was the greatest electrical invention ever.** This statement is said to have been made by leading scientists of the time; this is not in the author's voice. It is the only opinion. Choices (A), (B), and (C) are all facts stated in the passage.

11. **B. the framers of the U.S. Constitution** The clothes of the men in the picture indicate that this cartoon is set in the late 1700s. Impeachment is discussed in the caption. Impeachment was a provision that the framers of the Constitution included in order to prevent the kind of abuse of presidential power carried out by Nixon. Impeachment of elected officials was not discussed in the Declaration of Independence, which laid out the reasons for the United States' independence from Great Britain, so choice (A) is incorrect.

12. **A. the pursuit of justice** By investigating the circumstances of Watergate, Congress was trying to make sure that the nation's laws were carried out.

13. **C. the escalation and failure of the Vietnam War** Of the choices listed, only choice (C) describes an event just prior to the Watergate scandal. The bloodshed and failure of the Vietnam War caused many people to question authority, including the government, and to question decisions made by the government.

14. **C. 1,000,000** The scale on the vertical axis of the bar graph shows that population is measured in millions. The bar for Cuba stands one unit high. This means that about 1,000,000 people of Cuban descent lived in the United States in 1990.

15. **B. Mexico** The bar graph shows that most people in the United States who are Hispanic originally came from Mexico. Therefore, Mexico is the most likely nation of origin of the unknown family.

Civics and Government

Lesson 1: Historic Basis for U.S. System

Practice 1, page 445

1.

Direct democracy	In Country D, laws are made by the vote of all citizens.
Monarchy	In Country B, laws are made by a sovereign king and are subject to no review.
Representative democracy	In Country C, laws are made by Congress, an elected group of representatives.
Aristocracy	In Country A, laws are made and administered by lords who inherit their land and titles.

2. **B. They were concerned about protecting the rights of individuals.** According to the passage on page 444, the Founding Fathers were influenced by the Enlightenment philosophers, who did place importance on the rights of the individual.

3. **C. Parliament of England** Similar to the United States Congress, the parliamentary system in England allows for citizens to elect representatives to a lawmaking body.

4. **D. England during the Age of Enlightenment** According to the passage on page 444, England adopted a bill of rights for the individual during the Enlightenment. This action limited the monarchy's power over the individual.

5. **D. The president would be appointed by the majority party in parliament.** In most parliamentary democracies, the majority party in the Parliament appoints the president. Nothing in the text indicates whether this would make the office of the president more or less powerful than it currently is, so choices (A) and (B) are unsupported.

Lesson 2: Constitutional Government

Practice 2, page 447

1. **B. elected representatives exercising government power on behalf of citizens** According to the first paragraph of the passage, the key characteristic of a republic is elected officials governing for the voters.

2. **C. The details of government would be worked out in the future, as the need arose, within the framework of the Constitution.** The leaders who drafted the Constitution were wise enough to realize that they could not anticipate every eventuality, so instead of trying to cover everything in the Constitution, they made it a general framework within which specific future decisions and laws could be made.

3. **C. the power of an office, not an individual** Roosevelt's long tenure worried many people as they saw his power growing with time. They pursued term limits to prevent any individual from amassing too much power as president.

4. **The U.S. Supreme Court declaring an Illinois state law unconstitutional** The supremacy clause asserts the supremacy of federal law when it conflicts with state law. Therefore, the declaration that a state law is unconstitutional is an exercise of the supremacy clause.

5. **A. State governments do not usually act together.** The third and fourth methods of passing a constitutional amendment both require concerted action by state governments. Therefore, choice (A) would explain why those methods have never been used. Choices (B) and (D) are contradicted by information in the chart. Choice (C) repeats information in the chart, but does not provide a useful explanation.

Lesson 3: Levels and Branches of Government

Practice 3, page 449

1. **A. division of power between national and state governments**

According to the second paragraph of the passage on page 448, a federalist form of government divides power between the national and state levels of government.

2. **D. the State Department** The State Department is part of the executive branch; its head is a member of the president's cabinet. The Democratic National Committee, choice (A), is not part of the government at all. Choice (B) is part of Congress, and therefore part of the legislative branch. Courts, choice (C), are in the judicial branch.

3. **A. Federal judges need not worry about pleasing their constituents in order to be reelected.** Because they do not need to please any constituents in order to be reelected, federal judges can preside without worrying about making unpopular decisions. This leaves them freer to be impartial judges of the law.

4.

Checks and balances	Limits that one branch of government can place on the other branches
Veto	The president's power to strike down a law
Senators	Legislators who serve six-year terms
Constituents	The people whom political leaders represent
Representatives	Legislators who serve two-year terms

5. **B. a member of Congress** Although this person subscribes to the idea that the government is divided into three branches, he can only think of one of them—the one to which he belongs. Since he is probably in the legislative branch, he is likely to be a member of Congress. The way the desks are arranged and the way the man is standing to make his point are visual cues that the setting of the cartoon is Congress.

6. **A. mutual respect and convenience** Although in theory each state could insist on its own laws being followed even by residents of other states, in practice that would be too cumbersome. So on many matters, such as driver's licenses, states respect one another's laws because it is convenient to do so.

Lesson 4: The Electoral System

Practice 4, page 451

1. **C. receiving a majority in the Electoral College** According to the second paragraph of the passage on page 450 a president must have a majority in the Electoral College to be elected.

2. **A. Exit polls may be inaccurate if the people polled are not representative of the political unit as a whole or if the election is very close.** It is more likely that a poll will be wrong if an unrepresentative sample is used or if the election is very close. Under those circumstances it is hazardous to call an election based on exit poll results, as was shown in the 2000 presidential election, in which the media gave Florida's vote first to Gore, then to Bush, and only hours later declared the state too close to call.

3. **D. Two city council members are on a ballot to determine which one will run for mayor as a Democrat.** A primary is an election to choose among candidates of the same party. The winner of the primary then faces an opponent of another political party in the general election.

4. **B. In total, individuals contributed a greater dollar amount to House candidates than they did to Senate candidates.** Although Senatorial candidates received a higher percentage (greater by 4 percent) of their contributions from individual donors, the total dollar amount received by the House candidates was much higher (greater by approximately $350,000,000). Therefore, the total dollar amount of individual contributions received by the

House candidates was ultimately greater than that received by the Senate candidates.

5. **A. In 2010, self-funding was a larger source of funds for Senate candidates than it was for House candidates.** The Senate candidates' own contributions accounted for 13 percent of the total Senate Candidates' Funds while the House Candidates' own contributions accounted for only 6 percent of the total House Candidates' Fund. In addition, calculations based on the total amount of funds reveal that Senate candidates spent more total dollars on self-funding than did House candidates.

Lesson 5: The Role of the Citizen

Practice 5, page 453

1. **The U.S. Constitution** According to the third paragraph of the passage, the Constitution sets forth the rights of citizens.

2. **A. resident alien** Because she moved here permanently as the wife of an American citizen, Louvina is a resident alien and will remain so until she qualifies for citizenship through naturalization.

3. **C. They would become enemy aliens.** If the country of aliens residing in the United States declares war on the United States, that nation becomes an enemy state, and the aliens become enemy aliens.

4. **B. privacy** The protection against unreasonable search and seizure is essentially a protection of citizens' privacy rights. The government must demonstrate a good reason before it is allowed to search or seize property.

5. **C. If the 2012 presidential election is representative of elections generally in the United States, voter turnout increases with age.** This is the only statement general enough to be a conclusion. All the other options are details from the graph that support this conclusion.

1. **B. In 2013, a different major party controlled the House than controlled the Senate.** According to the numbers of the 113th Congress, the Republicans had majority control in the House and the Democrats had majority control in the Senate. Choice (A) is too broad to be a summary of this chart which focuses on political divisions. The conclusions in choices (C) and (D) require more information than the chart provides.

2. **Bill of Rights of the U.S. Constitution, which guarantees citizens certain rights** Like the Magna Carta, the Bill of Rights of the U.S. Constitution accords citizens certain rights and protections. Note that the scope of the Bill of Rights is broader in that it protects the rights of all citizens, not just a special group, as the Magna Carta did.

3. **C. a $3,000 contribution to a party fund for TV ads on political issues** Of all the choices, this is the only donation that is going to a political party fund rather than to a specific candidate, so it is a "soft money" contribution.

4. **A. People were less aware of soft money because disclosure was not required.** During the 1980s, political parties did not have to reveal the amount and sources of their soft money contributions, so the extent of this type of campaign financing was not generally known. Only when a law was passed requiring disclosure did people become aware of the scale of soft money donations and so began to raise their concerns about the issue.

5. **C. Jill Stein won a greater percentage of the popular vote than of the electoral vote in 2012.** Jill Stein won 0.36% of the popular vote, but she did not win any electoral votes in the 2012 election.

6. **D. 2012 Presidential Election: Popular and Electoral Votes** This is the only option that covers the topic of the paragraph as well as that of the graphs.

7. **A. The board of election is the county, city, or town office responsible for local voting.** Nowhere in this excerpt from the voter's guide is the board of election defined or explained; the writer assumes that the reader knows what it is.

8.

The Democratic Party, which nominates candidates and tries to win elections	
The National Association of Manufacturers, which lobbies for businesses	★
The Federal Communications Commission, which regulates broadcasters	
The Cabinet, an advisory body for the president	
Public Citizen, a nonprofit consumer rights advocacy group	★

Of all the choices, these two are the only groups that consist of people with common interests and goals—in this case, manufacturers and consumers—working by lobbying to influence government policies. The other choices are either political parties or part of the executive branch.

9. **B. Most registered voters don't vote.** Despite the fact that voting is one of the obligations of citizens, in most elections, less than half of the nation's registered voters actually vote.

10. **C. civic duty** The cartoonist is appealing to voters to take their civic duty to vote more seriously.

11. **A. China, where the top leaders of the Communist party control the government** Of the national governments described, only China is an oligarchy, a government with rule by a small group of people. The other options are not oligarchies; they are either democracies or autocracies.

12. **A. retribution** These laws all embody the urge to take revenge on wrongdoers, or to exact retribution. The other principles underlie the modern criminal justice system and other modern legal systems.

13. **C. 32** Look for the map key to determine the symbol for death penalty states. According to the map, 18 states do not have the death penalty, so 32 out of 50 states have the death penalty.

14. **D. Two of the five states with the lowest per capita homicide rates have abolished the death penalty.** If that argument were correct, then the states with the lowest homicide rates should all be death penalty states, but that is not the case. Two states—Vermont and Hawaii—that have homicide rates among the lowest in the nation do not have the death penalty.

15. **C. The 1978 Panama treaties sold out U.S. interests to Panama.** Choice (C) states an opinion about the Panama treaties, not a fact that can be tested or proved. The word in the passage that signals an opinion is "believed."

16. **D. The mayor has ceremonial duties.** In both the mayor-council and the council-manager forms of city government, at least part of the time, the mayor plays a ceremonial role.

Economics

Lesson 1: Basic Economics Concepts

Practice 1, page 459

1. **B. to convert capital and raw materials into products and services** According to the first paragraph of the passage, labor transforms capital and raw materials into goods and services that may be sold.

2. **D. a plastic material** A producer good is something used in the production of a finished good. Of all the choices, only plastic is a producer good. The remaining choices are consumer goods, in other words, finished products.

3. **A. When the supply of houses is low, demand is high and sellers can raise their prices.** Because of the law of supply and demand, when the supply of houses is lower than the demand, sellers have more

control over the terms of sale. In that situation, they can raise the asking price. Because there are many potential buyers, chances are high that a seller will get a good price.

4. **B. Toys are not critical to a nation's economic and political well-being.** The U.S. government prefers the free-market system and generally provides price supports only for industries that are extremely important to the nation's welfare, such as agriculture and transportation.

5. **D. 16** On the vertical axis, locate $.30, and then see where a horizontal line drawn through $.30 would meet the sloping demand line. The answer is 16 apples.

6. **C. As the price of apples rises, Keisha buys fewer apples.** The demand line on the graph shows that Keisha's apple purchases are related to the price of apples. As the price rises, her demand for apples falls, and she buys fewer apples. None of the other choices is supported by the data on the graph.

7.

a tool manufacturer	a bicycle repair shop ★
a paper mill	a microchip factory
a car wash ★	a beauty salon ★

According to the passage, a service business does not produce or sell tangible goods but instead offers services. Of all the choices, a car wash, a repair shop, and a beauty salon all sell services; the remaining choices are businesses that produce goods for sale.

Lesson 2: The U.S. Economic System

Practice 2, page 461

1. **D. Monopolies shut out competition.** When a company has a monopoly on a market, it has great power to squelch competing firms that try to enter the market. This is implied in the last two sentences of the second paragraph of the passage.

2. **rising unemployment** Of all the economic factors listed, only high unemployment is associ-

ated with recessions, according to the third paragraph of the passage.

3. **A. Property owners have a stake in the future value of the property.** Since property can increase or decrease in value, its owner is motivated to do things that will maintain or increase its value.

4. **C. buying stock in a new company, such as an Internet startup** In general, investing in stocks is riskier than choice (A), saving money in a bank, or choice (B) buying a certificate of deposit (or CD, as they're commonly called). Choice (C), investing in a startup that has no track record of turning a profit, is also riskier than choice (D), investing in a big, well-established company like Microsoft.

5. **D. Despite ups and downs, the gross domestic product generally increases over time.** Even though the gross domestic product rises and falls with business cycles, the general trend shown by the graph is for the gross domestic product to rise over the long term.

6. **A. They provide capital for businesses to grow.** One of the similarities between saving and investing in stocks is the ultimate use of the money. In both cases, the money allows businesses to start or expand operations as banks loan money they hold in savings accounts and the purchase of stock directly funds the company issuing the stock.

Lesson 3: The Economy and the U.S. Government

Practice 3, page 463

1. **registers revenues that exceed its expenditures** As implied in the first paragraph of the passage on page 462, a budget surplus occurs when the government takes in more tax and other revenue than it spends.

2. **C. cutting the federal income tax** If Congress cut the federal income tax, consumers would have more money to spend. This strategy has been used to stimulate the economy. The other choices would decrease consumer

spending or have no direct effect on consumer spending.

3. **D. the air traffic control system** Like the federal highway system, the air traffic control system facilitates transportation, which is critical for economic activity.

4. **D. Both affect the amount of money circulating in the economy.** Fiscal and monetary policies are two tools the government uses to control the money supply. Increasing the money supply by lowering taxes or lowering interest rates stimulates the economy, and decreasing the money supply slows the economy.

5.

Money out of Circulation	Money into Circulation
Sell government securities (bonds and Treasury bills) to investors	Buy back government securities ●
Raise the discount rate member banks are charged to borrow from the Fed	Lower the discount rate member banks are charged to borrow from the Fed ●
Raise the reserve requirement, the amount banks must keep on hand to cover deposits	Lower the reserve requirement ●

According to the passage, policies that increase the amount of money in circulation are used to stimulate the economy. Therefore, all three of the choices listed on the chart under *Money into Circulation* could be used by the government to stimulate the economy.

6. **C. Our complex economy takes time to respond.** Since the economy is made up of the actions of millions of people, any Fed action takes time to have an overall effect that is measurable.

Lesson 4: Labor and Consumer Issues

Practice 4, page 465

1. **C. wages and benefits** According to the first paragraph

of the passage on page 464, the money a worker earns plus the value of his or her benefits equals total compensation.

2. **A. Workers must learn skills throughout their lives to be prepared for changes in their industries.** This is the conclusion that the writer comes to after describing the steelworkers who lost their jobs and had to retrain when much of their industry moved overseas.

3. **woman buying a computer** Of all the choices, this is the only one in which a person is buying a product, so that person is a consumer.

4. **A. All for one and one for all.** When workers unite in labor unions, all of them together have the power to benefit each of the individual members. Similarly, each member supports the goals of the union as a whole.

5. **A. in 2000** The lower line on the graph shows the number of unemployed civilians. That line is at its lowest point at the year 2000.

6. **B. As the number of employed civilians rose steadily from 2003 to 2006, the number of unemployed slowly declined.** The graph shows that the number of employed civilians rose from about 137 million to about 144 million from 2003 to 2006. At the same time, the number of unemployed civilians dropped slightly—by about 2 million.

Economics Practice Questions, pages 466–469

1. **B. the various types of resources needed for an economy to produce goods and services** According to the passage, the factors of production include all the resources—natural, human, and man-made—needed to produce products and services.

2. **D. entrepreneurs** In a communist nation with centralized economic decision making, there is no place for individual entrepreneurs. The government decides what will be produced and how it will be produced.

3. **A. an office building** An office building is a capital resource. Choice (B) is a natural resource, choice (C) is labor, and choice (D) is an entrepreneur.

4. **A. In a balanced budget, revenues equal expenditures.** This explanation of a balanced budget is a fact. The remaining choices express opinions held by many fiscal conservatives.

5. **A. More than half of all personal income was earned through work in February 2013.** According to the chart, the primary source of personal income in 2013 (approximately 60 percent) was from wages, salary, and other forms of employee compensation.

6. **D. an investor** The man in the plaid shorts represents an investor who buys and sells stock on the stock market.

7. **C. He is accustomed to stock market ups and downs.** Like the roller coaster in the background, stocks gain and lose value, often precipitously. The investor is calm because he has experienced the ups and downs of the stock market, so a roller coaster ride feels familiar to him.

8. **person who runs a home day-care center** This is a person who is running a business out of his home and so is self-employed. Therefore, no federal income tax is withheld from her earnings, and he must pay estimated tax.

9. **B. individualism** Individualism is one of the core values of a society with a free enterprise economic system, because each person is free to make his or her own economic decisions.

10. **2009.** A budget deficit occurs when the government is spending more money than it is collecting in revenue. The larger the gap between the revenues and the expenditures, the larger the country's deficit. In the five-year span depicted on the chart, the largest gap between the revenues and expenditures exists in the year 2009.

11. **B. income tax returns and expense records** The federal budget is similar to a family budget; it differs primarily in scale. For a family, income tax returns provide documentation of revenues (income), and expense records such as grocery receipts and credit card bills provide a record of expenditures. None of the other choices includes records of both income and expenditures.

12. **D. The national network of interstate highways is paid for mostly by federal excise taxes.** Of all the choices, (D) contains the main details of the paragraph. Choices (A), (B), and (C) each focus on only one supporting detail.

13. **A. When cheaper imported goods force out U.S.-made goods, U.S. factory workers often lose their jobs.** Free trade may benefit the economy as a whole in the long term, but as the economy adapts, some individuals (in this case, factory workers) lose in the short term.

14.

Agency	Function
Food and Drug Administration	Protects public from poorly processed and improperly labeled foods and drugs
Federal Trade Commission	Protects consumers from misleading and/or fraudulent advertising
Consumer Product Safety Commission	Protects consumers from risk of injury or death from hazardous products
Security and Exchange Commission	Protects investors from being misled about stocks and bonds
National Highway Traffic Safety Administration	Protects consumers by testing vehicle safely and monitoring nationwide speed limits

According to the chart, the Federal Trade Commission exists to protect consumers from misleading and/or fraudulent advertising.

15. **A shortage of the product** When a product's price falls below the equilibrium point, demand for

the product increases, and thus the supply decreases, causing a shortage of the product.

16. **B. what causes high rates of unemployment** The unemployment rate is a factor in the economy as a whole, so it is a subject of study to a macroeconomist. All of the other choices relate to the economic actions of individuals or companies, which are not the main interest of a macroeconomist.

17. **C. As the price per eraser increases, manufacturers supply more erasers.** According to the graph, as prices rise, manufacturers are willing to supply more erasers as they see an opportunity for more profit.

Geography and the World

Lesson 1: Early Civilizations

Practice 1, page 471

1. **B. the Maya** According to the passage, the Maya recorded their discoveries about mathematics and astronomy in a pictographic writing system.

2. **Ancient Greece; Ancient Rome** As stated in the passage, the Greek idea of democracy, in which citizens voted, and the representative government and laws of ancient Rome were great influences on the founders of the United States.

3. **A. Both developed flood control and irrigation technologies to boost food production.** Both ancient Egypt and the civilizations of the Fertile Crescent grew up along rivers. The passage points out that in both areas, people learned to control floods and irrigate fields in order to improve food production.

4. **B. towns** The food surpluses that result from agriculture mean that not everyone must grow or gather her own food. Therefore, some people are free to live in towns where they can pursue a craft or business in exchange for food from farmers. The other options occur without the gathering together of people in settlements.

5. **D. ancient Egypt** Ancient China developed along a great river, the Yellow River. Of the civilizations

listed, only ancient Egypt also grew up along a river, the Nile. In both ancient China and ancient Egypt, the river kept the soil rich and damp.

6. **C. The Yellow River was probably the main trade route between Loyang and Chengchow.** Not only were rivers the source of water for irrigation, they were major thoroughfares for the transport of goods. Since both cities are on the Yellow River, trade between them most likely took place by river at that time.

Lesson 2: Feudalism to Nation States

Practice 2, page 473

1. **C. to protect their noble's land from attack** According to the passage, the role of the knights in feudal society was to protect their noble's estate, or land.

2. **Spain** Of the lands mentioned in the passage that were conquered by the Muslims, only Spain is in Europe. Thus, of the European nations marked for selection in the map, Spain is the one in which you would most expect to find evidence of Muslim culture.

3. **B. the migration of people from farms to industrial cities in the 1800s** Like the migration to the cities in the 1800s, the migration from manors to towns in the late Middle Ages resulted from economic causes. In both migrations, people were seeking better economic opportunities than farming offered.

4. **A. Roman Catholics accepted the authority of the pope and Protestants did not.** According to the passage, this was one of the main differences between the two branches of Christianity.

5. **A. accepted legal principles** Since the manor court did not rely on a written body of legal rulings, its actions were unpredictable. Most people felt they would get a fairer ruling in the royal courts, which were bound by written common law that applied to everyone in the kingdom.

6. **C. The population of Western Europe showed almost constant**

growth with only brief periods of decline. This is the best summary because it contains the main idea (Europe's population rose from 500 to 1500) and important details (two brief periods of decline).

Lesson 3: The Age of Revolutions

Practice 3, page 475

1. **C. the U.S. Declaration of Independence** According to the passage, the American Revolution and its goals of democracy (as expressed in the Declaration of Independence and the Constitution) were big influences on the French.

2. **D. Members of the Third Estate owned the least amount of land per person.** With 98 percent of the population but only 70 percent of the land, the Third Estate owned the least land in proportion to its numbers. Members of the First and Second Estates owned more land in proportion to their percentage of the population.

3. **had a Parliament; did not have a parliament** This contrast is stated in the third paragraph of the passage. It is one of the reasons French citizens were dissatisfied with their lack of representation in the monarchy of Louis XVI.

4. **C. possessing large landholdings** The last paragraph of the passage on page 474 states that farmland had been the economic mainstay of the aristocracy up until the time of the Industrial Revolution, which began late in the eighteenth century.

5. **B. A sovereign nation is independent, having the power to govern itself.** In the passage, the word *sovereign* is used but not explained; the author takes for granted you know what it means. The remaining options are all stated in the passage.

6. **D. the Industrial Revolution** Like the Industrial Revolution, the Information Revolution is an economic revolution that has brought about social change. The other revolutions are all political in nature.

Lesson 4: Exploration, Colonialism, and Wars

Practice 4, page 477

1. **A. pay the Allies money to repair war damages** According to the passage, paying reparations was one of the provisions of the Treaty of Versailles.

2. **C. the invasion of Poland** The third paragraph of the passage indicates that to avoid going to war, the Allies permitted Germany to take over, or annex, Austria and Czechoslovakia. However, Germany's invasion of Poland spurred England and France to declare war.

3. **B. national pride** The Japanese had a great deal of national pride, which they found difficult to put aside. Thus it took the destruction of two cities and thousands of deaths to overcome their reluctance to surrender.

4. **D. Both were won by the Allies.** Of the options listed, the fact that the Allies won both wars is the only similarity. Choices (B) and (C) are true only of World War II, and choice A is not true: both wars involved other parts of the world.

5. **B. The United States sustained only a few civilian casualties.** The chart indicates "very few" civilian dead in the United States; every other cell in the chart has a number in the thousands or millions.

6. **A. the 1812 French invasion of Russia, which failed due to harsh weather and lack of supplies** Both the French and German invasions failed due to weather and lack of supplies, making them similar. The campaigns and actions mentioned in the other answer choices failed for different or unspecified reasons.

Lesson 5: Humans and the Environment

Practice 5, page 479

1. **C. the move of an individual or population from one geographic area to settle in another** The first paragraph of the passage on page 478 implies that the key characteristics of migration are the movement of people and their settling in a new place.

2. **B. the westward movement of the American population from the 1700s to the present** Because this migration took place within the U.S. borders, it is an internal migration. The other choices all involve people moving from one country to another.

3. **are more densely populated than** The passage describes suburban areas appearing as a consequence of urban areas becoming too crowded. Thus, the text implies that urban areas (cities) are more densely populated than suburbs (neighboring towns).

4. **D. the automobile** Automobiles make it possible for many people to live in the suburbs, where the distances between a home and retail stores and workplaces can be considerable and public transportation may be lacking.

5. **D..the projected total world population in 2050** To answer this question, first locate 9,039,000,000 on the graph. (Note that the figures are given in millions, so the number to locate is written as 9,039.) It represents a total world population figure. Then look at the bottom axis to see what year that bar represents.

6. **C. Most of the population growth in the 50 years from 2000 to 2050 will occur in the less developed nations.** The bar graph shows that the proportion of the world population living in the more developed nations (shown in gray) is relatively small, and shows that it is predicted to remain relatively small over the next 50 years. In contrast, the graph predicts that the population in the less developed nations (shown in white) will grow much more. The remaining choices are not supported by the data on the graph.

Lesson 6: Using Resources Wisely

Practice 6, page 481

1. **A. materials that will never run out or can be replaced if used**

According to the first paragraph of the passage on page 480, a renewable resource can be replaced (for example, replanting a field that's been harvested) or is in endless supply (for example, wind and solar power).

2. **D. rotating crops** In crop rotation, a farmer plants different crops in succeeding growing seasons in order to conserve nutrients in the soil. The other choices are all examples of a nonsustainable use of a resource; eventually, each will cause the resource to be used up.

3. **A. negotiating in an international forum** An international forum provides a framework for nations to work to resolve conflicts over resource use before the problems escalate.

4. **C. short-term benefit versus long-term benefit** Finding and using new oil deposits is a short-term solution to U.S. energy problems because it doesn't solve the underlying problem in the long run. Developing alternative sources of energy requires more investment of time and capital with an uncertain outcome, but it has the potential to help meet long-term U.S. energy needs.

5. **B. carpool to work and school** Carpooling saves gas, a nonrenewable resource.

6. **former U.S.S.R.** The second column lists current production figures; the highest figure in the column is 25.7, that of the former U.S.S.R.

7.

(1)	North America
(2)	Europe
(3)	former U.S.S.R.
(4)	Africa

To answer this question, look at the column labeled "Reserves to Production Ratio." This column indicates the relationship between the amount produced annually and the total amount the region has. Regions with lower ratios will run out of gas before regions with higher ratios.

Geography and the World Practice Questions, pages 482–485

1. **A. How Germanic Tribes Governed** The focus of the passage is the minimal governmental structure of the Germanic tribes.

2. **C. The Industrial Revolution started in Great Britain and spread to Europe, but by 1900 the United States was the leading industrialized nation.** This summary statement has all the major details from the paragraph—the start of the Industrial Revolution in Great Britain, its spread to Europe, and the lead taken by the United States. The other choices either focus too narrowly on a couple of details or are too broad to be an effective summary.

3. **Egypt (along the Nile River)** The map key gives the dates of each civilization shown on the map. Egypt, Kush, and Axum were the earliest civilizations. They are all located along the Nile River in the northeast part of Africa.

4. **A. Over 800 years, several civilizations succeeded one another in western Africa.** The civilizations of Ghana, Mali, and Songhai developed one after the other in the same region of Africa. None of the other choices is supported by information on the map.

5. **1498: Da Gama sails to India for Portugal by sailing around Africa.** Da Gama's voyage opened up new trading opportunities for the Portuguese. Note from the time line that the Portuguese dominated trade in the East Indies from about 1510 to 1600.

6. **A. Spanish and Portuguese domination of exploration gave way to that of the Dutch, French, and English.** According to the time line, most Spanish and Portuguese exploration and conquest took place during the 1500s. From the 1600s on, other nations such as England, France, and the Netherlands increased their activity considerably.

The other choices are incorrect or cannot be determined from the information in the time line.

7. **Pizarro** Like Cortés, Pizarro explored on behalf of the Spanish rulers. He conquered the Inca Empire in South America.

8. **B. The Age of Exploration** This title describes the era and events shown. The other choices are too narrow, too broad, or simply incorrect.

9. **D. After the Cold War ended, defense spending began to fall.** The graph shows defense spending decreasing in the period 1990–1995, after the Cold War ended in 1990. None of the other choices is supported by data on the graph.

10. **B. Colonies should be economically independent.** Of all the choices, only this one is an opinion. The other choices are facts that are stated in the paragraph.

11. **B. the migration of thousands of farm families to other regions** The Dust Bowl temporarily disrupted farming in the Great Plains, forcing farmers to migrate to find work. While the Dust Bowl contributed to the Great Depression, (choice (A)), it was not the Great Depression's only or primary cause.

12. **D. the spread of the Sahara into the grazing land on its southern border** The Sahara, the desert that covers much of northern Africa, has been spreading steadily southward into the Sahel, a dry grasslands region that has been overused as grazing land.

13. **D. The problem of feeding the world's population is a matter of political will rather than one of resources.** This is an opinion attributed to agriculture experts in the passage. The remaining choices are all facts stated in the passage.

14. **B. Nevada gained seats in the House.** The passage tells you that the population shifts were large enough that seats in the House were reallocated. Since Nevada had a large population

gain, it is likely that it also gained seats in the House. Choices (A) and (D) are stated outright rather than implied by the passage. Choice (C) does not have to be true based on the information in the passage. Because immigration also played a role in population changes, it does not have to be the case that people moved away from the Northeast and Midwest.

15. **B. a visitor to Philadelphia** This is a special-purpose map designed to help visitors find their way around the airport and locate transportation routes to and from the airport.

16. **D. Labels for terminals and parking areas are coordinated to provide convenient parking.** The map shows Terminal E by Lot E, Terminal D by Garage D, and so on.

SCIENCE

Science Practices

Lesson 1: Comprehend Scientific Presentations

Practice 1, page 493

1. **C. The causes of type 2 diabetes** The passage as a whole discusses the causes of type 2 diabetes. Choices (A) and (D) are not discussed in the passage. Choice (B) is mentioned in the second paragraph but is only a supporting detail.

2. **D. The causes of type 2 diabetes are not fully understood.** This question asks for the main point of just the first paragraph, which explains that scientists do not fully understand the role played by various factors in causing diabetes. Choices (A) and (B) both commit the same error: that is, they mention a specific detail from the first paragraph while missing the big picture. Choice (C) contradicts the paragraph.

3. **B. A study of 18- to 25-year-olds showed that a majority did not produce enough insulin to offset the high amounts of sugar they were consuming.** The question asks for a detail that serves to support the idea that high sugar consumption may contribute to the development of type 2 diabetes. Only choice (B) does so. Choice (A) is a detail that is indeed mentioned in the paragraph, but only as background information. It does not serve to support the author's point that sugar consumption may contribute to diabetes. Choice (C) brings in "genetic factors," which are not mentioned in paragraph two. Although choice (D) may be implied by the author's use of hesitant language, such as "one contributing factor *may* be high sugar consumption," this does not support the paragraph's main idea.

4. **A. As moist, flowing air encounters rising elevations, it cools, which causes condensation, a stage that precedes precipitation and cloud development.** In interpreting this diagram, follow the arrows. The diagram depicts air flowing toward hills or mountains. As it does so, the air cools and condensation happens. Based on the arrows, that stage happens before the stages of precipitation and cloud formation. Choice (B) suggests that the air becomes static at the highest elevations, which is not supported by the diagram. Choice (C) also contradicts the diagram. Choice (D) is unsupported because the diagram does not have an east-west orientation: just because the air is depicted flowing from the left-hand side of the picture does not mean that it's flowing from the west.

Lesson 2: Use the Scientific Method

Practice 2, page 495

1.

Independent variable	Dependent variable
combinations of bacteria	acne symptoms

The researchers were studying the question of how different combinations of bacteria affect acne symptoms. Because the researchers thought acne symptoms might depend on differences in bacteria, acne was the researchers' dependent variable. Combinations of bacteria are not affected by acne symptoms, but the researchers thought bacteria might affect those acne symptoms. Therefore, combinations of bacteria were the researchers' independent variable.

2. **B. Different kinds of bacteria may impact acne differently.** The last sentence of the first paragraph provides this answer as well. The researchers "began to wonder whether different strains of bacteria might impact acne in different ways": that statement represents the idea they sought to test—that is, their hypothesis. Choice (A) describes an assumption that was widely held before the researchers began their study. Choice (C) is a suggestion the researchers made after concluding their study, and choice (D) is their conclusion—not their starting hypothesis.

3. **D. Some combinations of bacteria may actually help ward off acne.** This question asks for the researchers' conclusion—that is, the idea they embraced after concluding their study. That idea is described by choice (D). Choice (A) is an assumption many people held before the research began. Choice (B) is not supported by the passage. Choice (C) is not supported by the passage: after drawing their conclusions, the researchers suggested a way to treat acne in the future, but they did not suggest that current treatments are misguided.

4.

a) Form a hypothesis.	iii. Based on your experience, you make a guess about which of the movements involved in playing softball puts the greatest stress on the knees. You suspect that it may be stopping suddenly after running a short distance.
b) Design a test for your hypothesis.	i. You make a list of each of the movements involved in softball. In the off season (when you are not playing entire games), you plan to perform each movement several times without performing the others.
c) Collect data to test your hypothesis.	iv. After performing each movement in isolation, record how your knee feels. Let your knee recover between tests of each type of movement.
d) Form a conclusion based on the data from your test.	ii. Based on the data you collected in your experiment, you think it is likely that stopping suddenly after running a short distance is indeed the cause of your knee pain.

Lesson 3: Reason with Scientific Information

Practice 3, page 497

1. **C. If both objects were currently sitting still, it would require more effort to push the brick across the floor than it would to push the block of wood across the floor.** According to the passage, a heavier object has more inertia, and the brick is heavier than the block. Therefore, you can conclude that it would be harder to move the brick across the floor. Choice (A), breakage, and choice (D), absorbing water, are not mentioned and are irrelevant to this question. Choice (B) is the opposite of the correct answer.

2. **A. The birds that the brown tree snake eats are the primary predators of spiders on Guam.** The scientist's conclusion is that the brown tree snake is the reason there are so many spiders on Guam. The question asks for a piece of information that makes that conclusion more likely—that is, a choice that makes the scientist's conclusion more reasonable or believable. Choice (A) explains why more brown tree snakes would lead to more spiders. Choices (B) and (D) don't link the spiders and snakes at all. Choice (C) describes a relationship between them, but it suggests that more brown tree snakes would lead to *fewer* spiders.

3. **B. If large areas of ice sheets sit on water, the rising of sea levels may proceed more quickly than had previously been predicted.** The main idea of the passage is that some ice sheets may be sitting on water and that those ice sheets may melt more quickly than ice sheets sitting on rock. The passage also states that melting ice sheets contribute to rising sea levels. Putting those two ideas together, a scientist could predict that ice sheets sitting on water might send more melted water into the oceans than would

ice sheets on rock. Choice (A) expresses the opposite of that idea. Choice (C) introduces a comparison that is not supported by the passage. Choice (D) goes too far by insisting that *all* of the quickly melting ice sheets are sitting on water.

4. **A. Most of the ice sheets sitting on water are covering inland lakes with no access to the ocean.** Choice (A) would make the prediction less likely, because if most ice sheets sitting on water have no way to send water into the ocean, then the link between the ice sheets and rising sea levels would be undermined. Choices (B) and (C) actually make the scientist's prediction more likely. Choice (D) may seem to undermine the information in the passage—until you notice that choice (D) criticizes the use of "radar alone" to assess ice sheets. The passage indicates that researchers used both satellite and radar data, which makes choice (D) irrelevant to the prediction.

Lesson 4: Express and Apply Scientific Information

Practice 4, page 499

1. **C. pure acetone; a solution of sugar in acetone** The passage states that, during osmosis, a liquid moves from a place where there is a higher concentration of dissolved material to where there is a lower concentration of dissolved material. Thus, to test the rate of osmosis of a liquid, Gillian would want to put that same liquid on two sides of the vat, with more dissolved material on one side than on the other. Only choice (C) describes that arrangement.

2. **D. formic acid** The solvent with the highest rate of diffusion would be the solvent that took the least time to reach equilibrium. Here it took formic acid the least time to do so.

3. **19.5 minutes** To find the average time, add the times of the

solvents, then divide by the number of solvents.
$$\frac{20+25+18+15}{4} = \frac{78}{4} = 19.5$$

4. **greater than** The passage explains that drinking seawater will result in a higher-than-normal concentration of dissolved material in your bloodstream. Then, according to the passage, water will flow from your tissues into your blood. For that to be an example of osmosis, it must be the case that the water is flowing from a place (your tissues) where the concentration of dissolved material is lower to a place (your blood vessels) where it is higher. Thus, your tissues would start to dry out when the amount of dissolved material in your blood vessels is greater than that in your tissues.

Lesson 5: Use Statistics and Probability

Practice 5, page 501

1. **rabbit** The median is the middle number of a set of numbers, and in this graph, the rabbit has a lower body weight than the dog, human, and horse and a higher body weight than the shrew, cactus mouse, and flying squirrel. It isn't necessary to know the animals' actual body weights to determine this.

2. **rabbit** Similarly, the graph shows that the rabbit has the middle metabolic rate of the seven species in the graph.

3. **lower than the previous average** To find an average, you add up all the numbers in a list and divide by the number of items in the list, like this:

$$\frac{shrew + c.mouse + f.squirrel + rabbit + dog + human + horse}{7}$$

Now, the shrew is the highest of those numbers: it has the highest metabolic rate. Therefore, if you removed it and recalculated the average, the new average would be lower than the previous average.

4. **C. Their metabolic rate would be slightly lower than that of horses.** The question states that elephants weigh more than

horses. Thus, elephants would be to the right of horses on the line graph. Based on the curve of the line, you can guess that elephants would have a slightly lower metabolism than that of horses. Because the line continues to decrease slightly, choice (B) is unsupported.

5. **C. 120** The question asks how many different orderings, or sequences, of the five crops are possible. This is a permutations question, because order matters. Thus, multiply to find the number of permutations: $5 \times 4 \times 3 \times 2 \times 1 = 120$

Lesson 6: Construct Short Answer Responses

Practice 6, page 503

1. **Short Answer Practice: Explanation**

   Moon Formation Writing Prompt

   3 points maximum

   Read your response and rate it as 3, 2, 1, or 0 based on these criteria:

   3—clear and well-developed explanation; complete support from two or more specific details in passage and/or graphics

   2—partially articulated explanation; partial support from passage and/or graphic

   1—minimal or implied explanation; minimal support from passage and/or graphic

   0—no explanation or support from the passage and/or graphic

   My score: _____

2. **Short Answer Practice: Experiment**

   Caffeine and Blood Components Writing Prompt

   3 points maximum

   Read your response and rate it as 3, 2, 1, or 0 based on these criteria:

   3—well formulated, complete controlled experiment design, hypothesis, data collection method, and criteria for evaluating the hypothesis

   2—logical controlled experimental design, hypothesis, data col-

lection method, and criteria for evaluating the hypothesis

   1—a minimal experimental design, hypothesis, data collection method, and criteria for evaluating the hypothesis

   0—an illogical or no experimental design, hypothesis, data collection method, or criteria for evaluating the hypothesis

   My score: _____

Science Practices Practice Questions, pages 504–507

1. **B. While Copernicus's theory was an important development, it included elements that are outdated today.** The first sentence of the second paragraph provides the main idea. The words "[f]or example" help to make clear that the second and third sentences are details supporting that main idea.

2. **C. The Significance and Limitations of the Copernican Theory** The title of a passage should reflect its topic or main idea. The topic of this passage is the importance, or significance, of Copernicus's theory, as well as the fact that Copernicus's theory was not completely correct. Choices (A) and (D) are both too broad, while choice (B) is incorrect because the passage is not about Copernicus's life.

3. **A. Astronomers now believe that the planets are not embedded in crystalline spheres.** The question asks for something that can be inferred, or deduced, from the passage. Choice (A) is supported by the passage. Copernicus's idea that the planets are embedded in crystalline spheres is mentioned in the second paragraph as an example of an idea that is today considered "primitive." This implies that astronomers today no longer believe this to be true. Choices (B) and (C) are contradicted by the passage. Choice (D) is not supported by the passage: primitive astronomers who came before Copernicus are not discussed.

4. **C. B and D** The passage describes what happens when you add heat to a substance: the

temperature of the substance increases, up to the point when the substance starts to change from a solid to a liquid or from a liquid to a gas. Then the temperature of the substance holds steady while the substance is undergoing that change. When more heat is added but the temperature of a substance remains constant, it must be undergoing a phase change. The places in the diagram where the temperature is flat—B and D—thus represent the two places where the substance is changing from solid to liquid or from liquid to gas.

5. For this question, read the passage carefully to find each type of cancer and identify the cause associated with it.

Type of Cancer	Cause
mesothelioma	long-term asbestos exposure
cervical cancer	human papillomavirus
liver cancer	hepatitis B
lung cancer	long-term regular inhalation of tobacco smoke

6. **B. Penrith** The black bars on the graph represent each city's previous record, and the gray bars represent its current record. Find the city for which the gray bar is furthest above the black bar: Penrith.

7. **C. Penrith** The median number is the middle of a list of numbers. Here, because there are seven cities, the city with the "previous record equal to the median of all the cities' previous records" simply means the city with the middle value (among the previous record values). Fortunately, the cities are represented in the graph in such a way that their previous records are in ascending order, and the median previous record belongs to Penrith.

8. **B. Temperatures increased 5 degrees or less** The largest increase was in the city of Penrith and was approximately 5 degrees.

9. **C. Why, when I touch the metal filing cabinet, do I experience**

more electrostatic shocks than my assistant does when she touches it? The first paragraph of the passage explains that the office manager "wondered why" she experienced more static shocks than her assistant. That's the question that prompted her experiment. While it is true that the office manager decided to switch to cotton clothing, she didn't begin by wondering whether it was better, so choice (A) is incorrect. Choice (B) distorts the office manager's thoughts. Choice (D) places too much emphasis on shoes, which were not the subject of the office manager's experiment.

10. **D. The office manager wore one type of clothing, while her assistant wore another type of clothing, and they recorded the number of shocks they experienced.** The office manager wanted to test her hypothesis that her nylon clothing was causing her to experience shocks when touching a metal filing cabinet. To do so, she conducted an experiment in which she wore cotton clothing for a week, while her assistant wore nylon clothing; both wore identical shoes. Then the manager and assistant recorded the number of shocks they each experienced during the course of a week. Choice (D) correctly describes this experiment. Choice (A) describes the office manager's hypothesis. Choice (B) describes the office manager's course of action after she had completed her experiment, while choice (C) is the opposite of what actually occurred during the experiment (both the manager and the assistant wore identical shoes).

11. **A. They wanted to test the effects of their clothing on the number of shocks they were experiencing, and wearing different types of shoes might have confused their results.** In an experiment, it is important to control factors other than the one thing the experimenter wants to study. In this case, the office manager wanted to study the effect of clothing on

the number of static shocks she was receiving. Choices (B) and (C) wrongly suggest that shoes were the subject of the office manager's experiment. Choice (D) distorts the passage: during her experiment, the office manager was trying to study static shocks—not avoid them.

12. **C. a new hypothesis** Remember, a hypothesis is a guess that a researcher starts with and then tests through an experiment. If the office manager formed a new guess about what was causing the static shocks, and she intended to study that new guess through an experiment, that would be a new hypothesis. It would not, at that point, be choice (A), a new conclusion based on findings. While she might, as choice (D) suggests, design an experiment to test this idea, the idea itself is not an experiment design. And the idea is certainly not choice (B), a general principle from the study of physics; rather, the office manager is making a guess based on observation.

13. **C. 15** This is a combinations question: you are asked for all possible groupings of two out of the six snails, and the order of snails within each group does not matter. Use a table or an organized list to find the number of possible groupings. Name the snails A–F if that makes it easier.

AB				
AC	BC			
AD	BD	CD		
AE	BE	CE	DE	
AF	BF	CF	DF	EF

Count the possible pairs: there are 15.

14. **6.3%** The question asks for the probability that any given star is a class G star, and we have to combine two probabilities to find it. We know that there is a 90 percent chance, or a .9 probability, that a star will be a main sequence star. We also know that, if it is a main sequence star, there is a 7 percent chance, or a .07

probability, that it will be a class G star. Multiply those two probabilities to find the probability of *both* of them happening: $.9 \times .07 = .063$. Express your answer as a percentage: 6.3%.

15. **Science Short Answer Practice: Explanation**
Swedish Men and Smoking
Writing Prompt
3 points maximum

Read your response and rate it as 3, 2, 1, or 0 based on these criteria:

3—**clear and well-developed explanation; complete support** from two or more specific details in passage and/or graphics

2—**partially articulated explanation; partial support** from passage and/or graphic

1—**minimal or implied explanation; minimal support** from passage and/or graphic

0—**no explanation or support** from the passage and/or graphic

My score: _____

Life Science
Lesson 1: Cell Structures and Functions

Practice 1, page 509

1. **mitochondrion** According to the diagram's labels, energy is produced in the cell's mitochondria (plural of *mitochondrion*).

2. **D. Cell walls cannot maintain a plant's shape and rigidity when the plant lacks water.** Even though cell walls contribute to keeping a plant firm and rigid, they cannot do the job without water-filled vacuoles. This conclusion follows from the fact that a plant that lacks water will wilt.

3. **A. the presence of a nucleus** According to the passage, the presence of a cell nucleus defines a cell as eukaryotic.

4. **A. Each time the microscope is improved, scientists can see cell structures more clearly.** Since cell structures are tiny, the more a cell is magnified, the more detail can be seen.

5. **B. Oxygen would diffuse from the unicellular organism into the pond water.** Since diffusion is the movement of molecules toward areas of lower concentration, if the organism had more oxygen than the surrounding water did, oxygen would pass out of the organism into the water until the concentrations were equalized.

Lesson 2: Cell Processes and Energy

Practice 2, page 511

1. **D. carbon dioxide, water, and energy** According to the equation that summarizes cellular respiration, the products of this process are carbon dioxide, water, and energy.
2. **A. increasing the amount of light the plants receive each day** Because light is required for photosynthesis, increasing light is the best choice for increasing the rate of photosynthesis. The other options either would have no effect or would decrease the rate of photosynthesis.
3. **B. increasing the number of green plants** Because green plants use up carbon dioxide during photosynthesis, increasing the amount of greenery on Earth would help reduce the amount of carbon dioxide in the atmosphere.
4. **stoma** According to the diagram, carbon dioxide enters the leaf through openings in the bottom, called stomata (plural form of *stoma*).
5. **B. Most of a leaf's chloroplasts are found in its palisade cells.** The diagram shows that most of the leaf's chloroplasts are in the palisade cells. Evidence to support the other choices cannot be found in the diagram.

Lesson 3: Human Body Systems

Practice 3, page 513

1. **A. the circulatory system** According to the passage on page 512, the circulatory system transports blood to all the cells of the body.
2. **C. Both are structures in which substances pass through capillary walls**

into the blood. Both alveoli and villi are tiny structures containing capillaries in which substances pass to and/or from the blood. In the alveoli of the respiratory system, oxygen and carbon dioxide pass into and out of blood; in the villi of the digestive system, nutrients pass into the blood.
3. **D. Veins have valves that allow blood to flow in one direction only.** Of the four facts given, this is the only one that involves the direction of flow of the blood. Therefore, it helps to support Harvey's conclusion that blood in the veins flows toward the heart.
4. **Ureters** According to the diagram, the ureters are the only structure connecting the kidney to the bladder, so urine must flow through them to reach the bladder.
5. **B. a patient with a painful kidney stone** Because a kidney stone forms in the urinary system, the patient is most likely to be treated by an urologist.

Lesson 4: Health Issues

Practice 4, page 515

1. **D. the skin** As implied by the passage, the skin is one of the first defenses against germs, along with mucous membranes, tears, and stomach acid.
2. **C. habituation** Although Sara feels an urge to drink wine, she feels no ill effects if she does not; this indicates that she is habituated to alcohol. She has a psychological dependence rather than a physical dependence on alcohol. If her dependence were physical, she would feel the effects of skipping her daily drink.
3. **A. Fats are a more concentrated source of energy than carbohydrates.** According to the table, carbohydrates provide 4 calories per gram while fats provide 9 calories per gram. None of the other statements is supported by the information in the table.
4. **B. Carbohydrates come from fruits as well as from bread and rice.** According to the table, bread and rice are not the only foods that provide carbohydrates; fruits and at least one type of vegetable

(potatoes) also do. Choices (A) and (D) are recommendations, not facts. Choice (C) is contradicted by the table.

Lesson 5: Reproduction and Heredity

Practice 5, page 517

1. **tall** According to the Punnett square, each parent has the same genotype: Tt. The capital letter *T* represents the tallness allele, and the lowercase *t*, the shortness allele. Because tallness is dominant, each parent plant is tall. The paragraph also states that the parent plants are tall.
2. **B. 1 out of 4** According to the Punnett square, only one out of four possible combinations yields a short plant (one with two recessive alleles for height: tt).
3. **D. TT** If you want to grow only tall plants, then it is better to use purebred tall plants (TT). If you use hybrid tall plants—(Tt) or (tT)—then in the next generation, you will likely get some short plants in your garden.
4. **2** According to the passage on page 516, in order to show a recessive trait, an organism must inherit two recessive alleles for that trait. If it inherits only one recessive allele, the dominant form of the trait will show.
5. **D. Organisms that reproduce sexually produce offspring that have inherited a mix of traits from their parents.** Because they are inheriting a mix of genes from two parents, the offspring of organisms that reproduce sexually are different from the parents and from each other, creating a more diverse population. When an organism reproduces asexually, the offspring are identical to the parent and to each other, which means less diversity in the population.
6. **B. The black male was actually a hybrid.** The only way a white rabbit and a black rabbit could produce a white offspring is if the black rabbit is carrying the recessive allele for white fur. That means the black rabbit was actually a hybrid, not purebred as the student had assumed.

Lesson 6: Modern Genetics

Practice 6, page 519

1. **C. the sequence of base pairs in a gene** According to the third paragraph of the passage on page 518, particular sequences of base pairs code for particular amino acids, which are the building blocks of proteins. Therefore, as the paragraph concludes, the order of bases on a gene forms a code for making a particular protein.

2. **D. a change in protein synthesis** Since DNA provides the blueprint for protein synthesis, any change in DNA may affect protein synthesis.

3. **D. Genetically engineered foods are safe for consumers and the environment.** This is an opinion; it is not a fact that can be proved true from the information in the text. All the other statements are facts, based on information given in the paragraph.

4. **B. so that each daughter cell receives a complete set of DNA** Cell division produces two daughter cells with genetic material, or DNA, that is identical to that of the parent cell. The DNA must be replicated in the parent cell first so that each daughter cell can receive an exact copy of it.

5. **B. The base guanine pairs only with the base cytosine.** According to both the diagram and the passage, in DNA sequences, the base guanine always pairs with the base cytosine. (Note that in the diagram, each base is represented by its initial.) The remaining statements are not supported by the passage or the diagram.

6. **amino acids** Amino acids are described as protein building blocks in the third paragraph of the passage on page 518.

Lesson 7: Evolution and Natural Selection

Practice 7, page 521

1. **B. Frogs' forelimbs contain carpal bones.** All four homologous structures in the diagram include the same layout of bones: humerus, radius, ulna, and carpal bones. Since frogs' limbs are homologous to those of the other three animals, they will likely have the same bones. Choices (A), (C), and (D) may be true, but they are not supported by the diagram.

2. **C. In penguins, flying birds, humans, and alligators, the forelimbs have similar structures despite performing different functions.** Even though the forelimbs of these organisms look alike, they all perform different functions. The arm helps to lift and hold things, the penguin's flipper helps it to swim, the bird's wing helps it to fly, and the alligator's foreleg helps it to walk.

3. **A. traits that make an organism better able to survive in its environment** According to the passage on page 520, adaptations are traits that some individuals possess that enable them to compete successfully in their environment.

4. **C. DNA analysis provides more objective data than observation does.** DNA analysis is more objective than observation, because the person doing the observing must interpret what he or she sees.

Lesson 8: Organization of Ecosystems

Practice 8, page 523

1. **D. the sun** The ultimate source of energy for the food web on the previous page is the sun. This is implied by the first paragraph, which explains that the green plants at the bottom of the food web produce their own energy from the sun. The other species in the food web ultimately depend on those consumers for food.

2. **B. The populations of hares and seed-eating birds would increase.** With fewer foxes to hunt them, more hares and seed-eating birds would survive long enough to reproduce, increasing the populations of these organisms.

3. **B. an aquarium with aquatic plants and herbivorous tropical fish** An aquarium is a human-made ecosystem with living organisms in balance with one another and with their physical environment. It includes both producers (the aquatic plants) and consumers (the herbivorous, which means plant-eating, fish).

4. **D. The natural replacement of lichens by mosses and ferns, and then shrubs, is an example of succession.** According to the information, succession is a naturally occurring replacement of one ecosystem by another.

5. **C. to turn atmospheric nitrogen into compounds plants and animals can use** According to the information, nitrogen-fixing bacteria on the roots of plants like peas and beans take nitrogen and use it to form compounds that plants and animals can use.

Life Science Practice Questions pages 524–527

1. **B. Active transport requires the cell to use energy, and passive transport does not.** According to the information given, the key difference between active and passive transport is the use of the cell's energy.

2. **C. The water level in the jar might have gone down because of evaporation.** Because the experiment did not control for evaporation, it does not prove that the water was absorbed by the ivy.

3.

The paragraph indicates that

squares stand for males and half-shading represents genetic carriers. Of all the choices, only the square that represents Megan's father is half-shaded, indicating that Megan's father is a carrier of cystic fibrosis.

4. **D. No one in either Megan's or Will's immediate family has cystic fibrosis except Cailin.** Since everyone in the pedigree except for Cailin has only the recessive gene for cystic fibrosis, no one else suffers from the disease. Thus, Cailin's family members were probably unaware that some of them were carriers for cystic fibrosis.

5. **B. metaphase** According to the diagram, the chromosomes line up across the middle of the cell during metaphase.

6. **B. After mitosis, the two daughter cells have their own nuclei.** The two daughter cells in the interphase section of the diagram each have their own nuclei.

7. **Science Short Answer Practice: Explanation**

    Spindle Fibers Writing Prompt

    3 points maximum

    Read and rate your response as 3, 2, 1, or 0 based on these criteria:

    3—clear and well-developed explanation; complete support from two or more specific details in passage and/or graphics

    2—partially articulated explanation; partial support from passage and/or graphic

    1—minimal or implied explanation; minimal support from passage and/or graphic

    0—no explanation or support from the passage and/or graphic

    My score: _____

8. **C. The fossil record for any given species may be incomplete.** Because fossils are found at random, scientists cannot be sure they have a complete fossil record for many species. An incomplete fossil record would also explain why evolution sometimes seems to take place in bursts rather than gradually.

9. **D. nutrient transport and immune defense** According to the information, plasma transports nutrients. White blood cells defend against infection.

10. **A. enamel** The diagram shows that the top surface of the tooth is made of enamel.

11. **few or no nerve endings** The diagram shows that decay must pass through dentin to reach the pulp. It suggests that decay is only painful once it reaches the pulp due to the many nerve endings located there. Thus, it is likely that the dentin has few or no nerve endings.

12. **B. grazing too many cattle on grassland** Overgrazing of domestic animals like cattle can destroy much plant life in grassland ecosystems. When that happens, the number of cattle the grassland can support decreases, as described in the paragraph.

13. **A. DNA analysis provides more fundamental, accurate data than does a visual analysis of structures and fossils.** Because DNA analysis involves genetic data at the molecular level, it is a better indicator of the relationships among organisms than visible similarities such as teeth. Thus DNA analysis has changed the way scientists previously classified some organisms.

14. **A. panting** A dog's panting and a human being's sweating are both processes that cause loss of body heat through the evaporation of water. In other words, they are body processes that function to cool off an overheated animal.

15. **3** Unintentional injuries, chronic lung diseases, and cancers all caused more deaths in 2011 than in 2005.

16. **biggest decrease** The gray bar representing 2011 is shorter than the black bar representing 2005, meaning the number of deaths decreased. The decrease is greater than that of cerebrovascular disease, and the other three causes of death all increased.

17. **B. 8% decrease** To find the percent change, first subtract to find the amount of the change. The number of deaths from heart diseases in 2005 was roughly 650,000, and the number in 2011 was roughly 600,000. So the amount of change was 50,000. Now, divide that by the original value: $\frac{50,000}{650,000} \approx .08$. To convert that number to a percent, multiply by 100: 8%. Since the number of deaths from heart diseases in 2011 was lower than in 2005, there was an 8 percent decrease.

Earth and Space Science

Lesson 1: Structure of Earth

Practice 1, page 529

1. **A. changes in Earth's crust** According to the passage on page 528, the theory of plate tectonics explains how major landforms are created, the continents move, and the seafloor spreads, all of which are changes in Earth's crust.

2. **(1) consist primarily of iron, (2) is mostly solid, (3) is mostly liquid** As the passage states, both the inner and outer core are made mostly of iron; the main difference is that the outer core is liquid and the inner core is solid.

3. **D. a destructive margin** According to the passage, destructive margins are places where one plate is being forced beneath another, and deep ocean trenches are characteristic of destructive margins between oceanic and continental plates.

4. **D. The west coast of Africa seems to fit into the east coast of the Americas.** Of the four choices, only this one provides evidence to support the idea that there used to be one continent made up of the pieces that are the continents we know today. The fact that two continents seem to fit together like the pieces of a jigsaw puzzle suggests that they were once part of one continent.

5. **C. The continents of North America and Europe are mov-**

ing apart. Since the Atlantic Ocean is getting wider, it follows that the continents on either side of the Atlantic are moving further apart.

6. **B. A single large landmass called Pangaea existed about 250 million years ago.** The existence of Pangaea is a theory based on evidence, not a fact. All the other choices are facts that can be proved true.

Lesson 2: Earth's Resources
Practice 2, page 531

1. **D. 177** To find the consumption of petroleum in 2011, locate 2011 on the horizontal axis. Then imagine a straight vertical line from 2011 to the graph line. Now imagine a straight horizontal line from that spot on the trend line to the vertical axis to find the approximate number of Btus. Note that Btus are British thermal units, a unit for measuring energy.

2. **14** The range of a data set is the difference between its highest value and its lowest value. In 2011, the world petroleum consumption was approximately 177 quadrillion Btus, and in 2003 it was approximately 163 quadrillion Btus. The difference between them is roughly 14 quadrillion Btus.

3. **A. World petroleum consumption increased by about 14 quadrillion Btus between 2003 and 2011.** This is the best summary of the graph because it includes the topic of the graph (world petroleum consumption) and the amount by which consumption changed during the period shown.

4. **D. Waste not, want not.** One of the basic approaches of conservationists is to reduce consumption of resources by decreasing waste ("waste not"). If that is done, in the future the resources will still be available ("want not").

5. **B. Developed nations have started using water more efficiently than they did in the past.** Since population and economic activity are increasing faster than water use in the developed nations, the most likely reason is that people have learned to conserve water, meaning they use water more efficiently now.

6. **D. Soil erosion is caused by both natural forces and the actions of people.** The first sentence mentions several causes of soil erosion. These include natural actions, such as wind, water, and ice, along with human actions, such as deforestation and poor farming practices.

Lesson 3: Weather and Climate
Practice 3, page 533

1. **D. southwest to northeast** The label describes the winds as "westerlies," and the arrows indicate that the winds generally move from the southwest to the northeast. It follows that weather patterns move along with the winds, from southwest to northeast.

2. **B. The winds in the Northern Hemisphere are a mirror image of those in the Southern Hemisphere**. If you compare the two sets of winds, you will see that those in the Northern Hemisphere are a reflection of those in the Southern Hemisphere, just as an image is reflected in a mirror.

3. **D. satellites, which transmit cloud photos and weather data** Satellite photos of cloud patterns help meteorologists identify hurricanes and follow their paths; weather data help them follow changes in the intensity of the storm. Thus, the photos and data from satellites help meteorologists make predictions about the development and movement of hurricanes.

4. **D. global wind and ocean current patterns** According to the passage, both global wind patterns and ocean currents redistribute heat from the solar heating of Earth.

5. **D. The highest temperatures in the atmosphere are in the thermosphere.** According to the chart, the thermosphere has temperatures of up to several thousand degrees Fahrenheit—much higher than temperatures in the other layers.

6. **Place your stick figure in the troposphere.** As the lowest layer of the atmosphere, the troposphere is where human beings live and work. Even many airplane flights stay within the troposphere.

Lesson 4: Earth in the Solar System
Practice 4, page 535

1. **D. Mercury** A planet's revolution is its orbit around the sun. Locate the column that shows the planets' revolution periods. Then review the data in the column until you find the shortest revolution period. That would be 88 Earth days, which is the time it takes Mercury to travel once around the sun.

2. **B. Venus** Of all the planets, Venus is closest in size to Earth. Venus's year is also closest in length to Earth's year. These features make Earth and Venus the most similar of the choices given.

3. **C. Uranus was not clearly visible with the telescopes generally in use at the time.** According to the information given, Herschel made excellent, powerful telescopes, so he probably saw a much sharper image of Uranus than did previous astronomers and was therefore able to recognize its unique color and shape.

4. **B. Saturn** Saturn has 53 moons according to the chart. That is many more than Uranus and Neptune, and three more than Jupiter.

5. **D. faith in human judgment and decision-making skills** This is the only value that relates to the possible benefits of sending a crewed mission rather than a robotic mission.

6. **B. an atom, with a dense nucleus and electrons orbiting the nucleus** Of all these choices, the structure of the atom is most similar to the structure of the solar system, even though the atom is much tinier.

Lesson 5: The Expanding Universe

Practice 5, page 537

1. **(1) Sirius; (2) Canopus** The brightest star as seen from Earth is the one with the lowest apparent magnitude. According to the chart, that is Sirius. Absolute magnitude is the measure of brightness of a star as if it were 32.6 light-years away from Earth. Therefore, the star with the lowest absolute magnitude would be the brightest, if all were seen at 32.6 light-years' distance. Canopus has the lowest absolute magnitude, so it is the brightest of the stars.

2. **C. The star's apparent magnitude would be equal to its absolute magnitude.** Since the absolute magnitude of a star is defined as the brightness an object would have at 32.6 light-years from Earth and the apparent magnitude is its brightness as seen from Earth, then an object that was actually 32.6 light-years from Earth would have the same apparent and absolute magnitude.

3. **D. Not all stars are located about 32.6 light-years from Earth.** The apparent magnitude is a measure of how bright the star looks from Earth. (A small, close star might look very bright compared to a large, distant star.) However, the absolute magnitude is a measure of how bright a star would be if it were a set distance from Earth. These numbers are not necessarily similar, since the apparent magnitude does not take the star's distance into account while the absolute magnitude does.

4. **B. It is a main-sequence star.** According to the passage on page 536, stars like the sun have about a 10-billion-year life cycle. Since the main-sequence stage is the longest, a star that is about 4.7 billion years old would be a main-sequence star, in the middle of its life cycle.

5. **D. Pluto should be classified as a dwarf planet.** Choices (A), (B), and (C) are factual details about Pluto. Choice (D) is not a fact but rather a recommendation (that is, an opinion) of the scientists.

Earth and Space Science Practice Questions, page 538–541

1. **A. The moon and the sun exert the greatest pull on Earth's oceans when these bodies are all in a line.** According to the paragraph, when the sun, moon, and Earth are in a line, the highest tides, called spring tides, occur. The paragraph also states that tides are caused by the gravitational pull of the moon and the sun on the oceans. Putting this information together, the paragraph supports the idea that the moon and the sun exert their greatest pull on the oceans when these bodies are all in a line, during spring tides. None of the other statements is supported by the paragraph.

2. **C. Iceland, an island nation in the Atlantic with active volcanoes** An area with active volcanoes has lots of magma near the surface, so it is ideal for geothermal energy, which is a renewable resource.

3. **D. 26 percent** According to the passage, dark matter is matter that does not interact with light, and according to the graph, dark matter may make up 26 percent of the universe.

4. **D. Ordinary matter is made of the chemical elements.** Of all the statements, only choice (D) is a fact that can be proved at this time. The other three choices are hypotheses, proposed explanations for things that have been observed but not proved.

5. **D. tropical-subtropical** First locate the equator on the map. Then consult the map key to identify the climate represented by the most common color that occurs near the equator.

6. **A. The continent with the least area of desert-steppe climate is Europe.** To find the answer to this question, you must check each statement against the map. If the map proves the statement is false, you can eliminate that statement. If the map doesn't show what the statement indicates, you can also eliminate that statement. Choice (A) is the only statement confirmed by the map.

7. **farm output** With a large food output, an area can easily support its human population. This not only contributes to the area's wealth, but it also frees a good portion of the population to do other work, producing wealth.

8. **4** Count the number of climate zones represented on each continent:
North America: 5
South America: 5
Europe: 2 (note the islands near Europe that have a polar climate)
Asia: 5
Australia: 3
Africa: 4
Find the average of those numbers: $\frac{5+5+2+5+3+4}{6} = 4$.

9. **(1) Earth; (2) the moon** According to the diagrams, a lunar eclipse occurs when the shadow (the umbra) of Earth falls on the moon, which happens when Earth is between the sun and moon.

10. **C. A lunar eclipse can be seen only at night, and a solar eclipse can be seen only during the day.** The lunar eclipse diagram indicates that a person on the daylight side of Earth would not be able to see the lunar eclipse; only a person on the nighttime side would see it. The solar eclipse diagram indicates that a person on the nighttime side of Earth would not be able to see the eclipse; only a person on the daytime side would see it.

11. **D. a catalytic converter, a device in the exhaust system of a vehicle that reduces harmful emissions from the engine** Of all the choices, only this one reduces the harmful pollutants of burning fossil fuel and so would reduce acid rain.

12. **Science Short Answer Practice: Explanation**

Acid Rain Writing Prompt

3 points maximum

Read your response and rate it as 3, 2, 1, or 0 based on these criteria:

3—**clear and well-developed explanation**; complete support from two or more specific details in passage and/or graphics

2—**partially articulated explanation; partial support** from passage and/or graphic

1—**minimal or implied explanation; minimal support** from passage and/or graphic

0—**no explanation or support** from the passage and/or graphic

My score: _____

13. **A. The rock cycle is a continuous process of rock formation, destruction, and reformation.** The diagram is a cycle diagram, which shows a process that occurs again and again; in this case, the process of the formation and destruction of rocks.

14. **sedimentary rock** An imprint can only occur in soft material like sand, mud, or silt. The diagram shows that when this material is compacted, sedimentary rock forms. This rock will contain the imprint as a fossil. Note that fossils sometimes also occur in metamorphic rock, but this is not presented as an option.

15. **A. melted rock** According to the diagram, igneous, sedimentary, and metamorphic rocks all form magma by melting.

16. **C. Open-pit mining destroys valuable land.** An open-pit mine destroys a huge area, so it is restricted in many countries to prevent large-scale destruction of land. There is no reason to suspect, based on the information given, that choice (B), open-pit mining, is more dangerous than shaft mining or choice (D)—it yields lower-grade minerals.

Physical Science

Lesson 1: Atoms and Molecules

Practice 1, page 543

1. **A. The sodium atom loses an electron, becoming positively charged, and the chlorine atom gains an electron, becoming negatively charged.** According to the diagram, the sodium atom gives up an electron to the chlorine atom. With one fewer electron than protons, the sodium becomes a positively charged ion. When the chlorine atom gains an electron, it has one more electron than protons, making it a negatively charged ion. The sodium and chloride ions are attracted to each other, forming an ionic bond.

2. **D. $C_6H_{12}O_6$** According to the passage on page 542 and the question text, a chemical formula represents the number of atoms of each element in a compound. Chemical symbols, which are letters, represent the elements, followed by subscripts, which represent the number of atoms.

3. **(1) not necessarily either positively or negatively charged, (2) either positively or negatively charged** The key difference between a non-ionized atom and an ion is the gain or loss of an electron, which gives the ion either a negative or a positive charge.

4. **B. Most of the alpha particles passed right through the gold foil.** Because most of the alpha particles passed right through the foil without being stopped or deflected, Rutherford concluded that atoms must consist mostly of empty space.

5. **B. 11** The atomic number of sodium refers to how many protons the atom has. An atom that is not an ion has the same number of protons as electrons. Therefore, a sodium atom has 11 electrons.

Lesson 2: Properties and States of Matter

Practice 2, page 545

1. **A. melting and boiling** According to the passage on page 544, adding heat to a solid melts the solid, and adding heat to a liquid causes it to boil, or change to a gas.

2. **B. Solids are usually denser than liquids and gases.** If you compare the densities of the solids, liquids, and gases in the chart, you will see that the solids are denser than the liquids and the gases.

3. **190** According to the paragraph, glycerin's boiling point is 190° greater than water's boiling point. To find the percentage by which glycerin's boiling point is greater than that of water, divide the difference between the two substances' boiling points by the boiling point of water and multiply the quotient by 100%. Thus, $\frac{190}{100} \times 100\% = 190\%$. Always read questions carefully. Glycerin's boiling point is 290 percent of water's boiling point, but this question asks for the percent by which glycerin's boiling point is *greater than* water's.

4. **A. Water is a unique substance on Earth.** This statement is a conclusion (a general statement) that is supported by the statements that give details about the properties of water.

5. **B. Antifreeze added to water in a car's radiator lowers the freezing point below 0°C.** Adding antifreeze (a solute) to water (a solvent) lowers the freezing point of the solution, the liquid in the radiator.

6. **D. Dusty air** Dusty air is the only choice with large suspended particles. Gold and oxygen are elements, not mixtures. Salt water is a solution; it has small particles that do not settle out of the mixture.

Lesson 3: Chemical Reactions

Practice 3, page 547

1. **C. $2Cu + O_2 \rightarrow 2CuO$** You can eliminate choice (A) because the product (CuO) is on the left side of the equation rather than on the right side. To determine which of the remaining answer choices is correct, you must look for the equation that has two copper atoms and two oxygen atoms on the left side to balance the two copper atoms and two oxygen atoms on the right side.

2. **B. Weigh the reactants, conduct the reaction in a sealed container,**

and weigh the products. This procedure should result in the weights of the reactants and products being equal, because none of the products would escape from the sealed container. The weight measurements would provide evidence for the law of the conservation of mass.

3. **Juanita ignites the gas = activation energy** Activation energy is the amount of energy required to start the reaction. **The gas burns = exothermic energy** Burning gas creates exothermic energy, given off in the form of heat and light. **The egg solidifies = endothermic energy** The energy the reactants absorb from their surroundings is endothermic energy.

4. **C. The time during which the reaction occurs** The horizontal axis is labeled "Time," so you can eliminate choice (D). The graph shows the progress of the reaction, which takes place over time, not just one instant of the reaction, so you can eliminate choices (A) and (B).

5. **A. Compounds are substances consisting of two or more elements chemically combined in a definite proportion.** The writer of the paragraph takes for granted that you know what a compound is and does not define the term *compound* in the paragraph. The other answer choices are stated explicitly in the paragraph.

6. **B. "Acids and Bases"** The passage gives an overview of acids and bases and describes what happens when they react with one another.

Lesson 4: The Nature of Energy

Practice 4, page 549

1. **C. Energy cannot be created or destroyed, but can only change in form.** According to the third paragraph on page 548, this is the law of conservation of energy.

2. **chemical, electrical, light** The batteries use chemical energy and convert it to electrical energy, which is converted to light energy in the filament of the lightbulb.

3. **B. power** Power is the rate at which work is done or, in this case, the rate at which energy is consumed. The wood stove has greater power than the oak tree because it consumes the tree's energy in much less time than it takes the tree to consume the sun's energy.

4. **B. the relationship between energy and mass** According to the passage, Einstein's equation explains how energy can be converted to mass, and vice versa.

5. **B. At the high point of its swing, a pendulum has potential energy.** The diagram shows that at the high point of its swing, the pendulum has potential energy, the energy of position. The information in the diagram does not support any of the other statements.

6. **A. The molecules in air are far apart.** Because the molecules of a gas like air are far apart, they are in contact with one another less frequently than are the molecules of a liquid or solid, since liquids and solids are much denser. That is why gases have lower conductivity than liquids and solids do.

Lesson 5: Motion and Forces

Practice 5, page 551

1. **D. anything that changes the rest or motion of an object** According to the passage on page 550, this is the definition of a force.

2. **D. the tendency of an object to remain at rest or in motion** According to the third paragraph on page 550, inertia is described in Newton's first law of motion as the tendency of objects to remain at rest or keep moving until acted upon by a force.

3. **B. the International Space Station orbiting Earth** The key concept regarding centripetal force is circular motion, and the orbit of the space station is the only example of circular motion among the options given.

4. **the momentum of a car decreases when its velocity decreases** The fifth paragraph on page 550 indicates that momentum is calculated by multiplying mass and velocity. Slowing a car before a collision decreases the car's momentum. Because momentum is a measure of energy of movement, slowing the cars will result in less energy on collision and so less damage to both cars.

5. **B. an object that has a constant speed** The graph shows a straight line that slopes upward. According to the paragraph, this type of graph shows an object that is moving at a constant speed.

6. **C. Some machines simply change the direction of a force.** According to the information given, a machine is a device that changes the direction *or* the size of a force, which means that some machines change only the direction of the force. An example is a simple pulley, which allows you to push down, rather than pull up, to lift a load.

Lesson 6: Electricity and Magnetism

Practice 6, page 553

1. **B. two poles repelling one another** According to the diagram, like poles repel, so a drawing of two north poles facing each other would look the same as the diagram of two south poles facing each other.

2. **A. Copper and aluminum are conductors.** Electrical wires need to be made of something that carries electricity easily, which is what conductors do.

3. **D. a flashlight** According to the passage, direct current is used in battery-powered devices. Choice (D) is correct because flashlights typically run on batteries.

4. **D. a transformer** According to the passage, transformers change the voltage of an incoming electric current.

5. **lightbulb** According to the paragraph, a device that gets power from a current is called a resistor. Since the battery in the circuit powers the lightbulb, the lightbulb is a resistor.

6. **C. Disconnecting the light bulb will also stop the current.**

To have current, you need to have a loop. Getting rid of any piece of the circuit—the battery, the switch, the lightbulb, or the wire—would break the loop and thus stop the current.

Physical Science Practice Questions pages 554–557

1. **B. 5,730 years** This information is in the table, in the row for carbon-14 and the column for half-life.

2. **D. Uranium produces radio-active waste that may harm living things for millions of years.** Since the question asks what an *opponent* of nuclear power would say, the correct answer should be a negative fact about uranium. According to the table, uranium is unstable for millions or even billions of years, so choice (D) is both negative and true. Choice (C) is a negative claim about uranium, but it's a false one—uranium is unstable for much longer than three days.

3. **D. Both involve the transfer of energy through matter or space.** According to the paragraph, a wave is something that transfers energy through matter or space, so both types of waves would have that in common. Longitudinal waves have forward-and-back displacement, while transverse waves have up-and-down displacement, so choices (A) and (B) are incorrect. Choice (C) is incorrect because only longitudinal waves involve compressions.

4. **A. A cork in water bobs up and down as waves pass.** The question asks for an example in which something stays in roughly the same place after a wave passes through it. If a cork merely bobs up and down as waves pass, then the cork will be in its original position after the waves stop. Thus, choice (A) is the right example.

5. **A. dust motes dancing in a shaft of sunlight** Brownian motion is the random movement of particles in a liquid or a gas. Choice (A) is correct because dust motes move about ran-domly in the air, which is a gas. Choice (C) is wrong because it doesn't involve movement, choice (D) is wrong because the raft is *on* a lake (not *in* it), and choice (B) is wrong because the ground is a solid.

6. **Increase rate of reaction: Use powdered marble. Decrease rate of reaction: Use larger chunks of marble.** The passage says that the greater the surface area of the reactants, the faster the reaction will go. *Surface area* in this case refers to the amount of marble in contact with the acid. Thus, using larger chunks of marble will slow down the reaction, since larger chunks will have more "inner" marble, which won't be exposed to the acid. This will reduce the surface area. On the other hand, using powdered marble will mean that practically all of the marble is exposed to the acid, making the surface area large and causing the reaction to go faster.

7. **decreases** The paragraph says that the bigger the pressure, the smaller the volume (and vice versa). So, when pressure increases, volume will decrease.

8. **C. xenon (Xe)** According to the chart, the noble gases are in column 18. Choice (C), xenon, is the only choice in this column.

9. **B. Chlorine (Cl) and iodine (I) have similar properties.** According to the information given, elements in the same column have similar properties. Since chlorine and iodine are in the same column, choice (B) is correct.

10. **A. microwaves** According to the diagram, wavelengths increase as you go left to right. Since microwaves are to the right of the visible spectrum, choice (A) is correct.

11. **C. People can see only a small portion of the electromagnetic spectrum.** In the diagram, the visible spectrum—the section that people can see—is only a small piece of the entire electro-magnetic spectrum.

12. **B. Its mass remains the same, and its weight decreases.** The mass of an object doesn't depend on anything; rather, mass is a property of the object. By contrast, the weight of an object gets smaller as the object gets farther from Earth. So, as a rocket travels away from Earth, its mass won't change, but its weight will get smaller.

13. **B. Coldness cannot be trans-ferred.** The paragraph directly states that heat can be trans-ferred, choice (A), a cold object can be warmed by your body (choice (C)), and that your body heat can be lost (choice (D)). What the passage assumes but doesn't say is that *only* heat can be transferred; coldness can't be. This is choice (B).

14. **D. the range** All of the engineer's recorded speeds are off by 3.7 km/hour, which skews the mean, mode, and median upward. However, the range is unchanged, because the difference between the largest value and the smallest value is the same in both columns (195.6 km/hour).

15. **C. $\frac{3}{5}$** This question asks about the planes' actual speeds, so be sure to use the "actual speed" column. Four of the five planes have a speed less than 360 km/hour, and once one of those planes is chosen, three of the four remaining planes will have a speed less than 360 km/hour. Thus, the probability that both chosen planes have a speed less than 360 km/hour is $\frac{4}{5} \times \frac{3}{4} = \frac{3}{5}$.

16. **Science Short Answer Practice: Experiment Design**

    Decongestant Writing Prompt

    3 points maximum

    Read your response and rate it as 3, 2, 1, or 0 based on these criteria:

    3—**well-formulated,** complete controlled experiment design, hypothesis, data collection method, and criteria for evaluating the hypothesis

    2—**logical** controlled experimental design, hypothesis, data collection method, and criteria for evaluating the hypothesis

    1—**a minimal experimental design,** hypothesis, data collection method, and criteria for evaluating the hypothesis

    0—**an illogical or no experimental design,** hypothesis, data collection method, or criteria for evaluating the hypothesis

    My score: _____

GED® PRACTICE TEST ANSWERS AND EXPLANATIONS
REASONING THROUGH LANGUAGE ARTS

Pages 560–581

1. **B. describe types of interviewers and how to approach them** The author is chiefly concerned with explaining that different interviewers have different personalities and that you should approach those interviewers differently.

2. **C. Our ability to "read" others makes us form instant, lifelong relationships with some people.** The author makes this general claim in the first paragraph but does not support it with evidence. Choices (A) and (D) are stated or implied in the first paragraph and then supported with evidence in paragraphs 2–4. Choice (B) is a generalization made in paragraph 3, not paragraph 1.

3. **D. interviewers with homey, comfortable offices and interviewers whose offices seem less welcoming** The author contrasts these two types of interviewers in the third and fourth paragraphs of the passage.

4. **A. Interviewers have some influence or control over their office arrangements.** In paragraphs 3 and 4, the author explains that you can learn a great deal about an interviewer's personality from the type and arrangements of furniture in the interviewer's office. However, in order for this to make sense, the author must be assuming that interviewers have some say about their office arrangements. If an interviewer had no influence over her office, then the office would not provide reliable information about the interviewer's personality. The passage does not discuss the virtues of email (choice (B)) or the relative importance of different aspects of preparing for an interview (choice (D)). Choice (C) is out of scope. This passage is about prospective hires, not employees.

5. Arrange the elements of the author's argument in the order in which they appear:

1st   c. The author makes a generalization about how your ability to "read" an interviewer can be useful.

2nd   a. The author claims that an interviewer's email style tells you something about that interviewer.

3rd   d. The author cites specific evidence about why an interviewer's email style may be helpful to you.

4th   b. The author claims that the arrangement of an interviewer's office tells you something about that interviewer.

6. **D. You should try to understand your interviewer's personality and tailor your responses to him or her accordingly.** Only choice (D) summarizes the author's overall argument. The other choices are either details (choice (A)) or not mentioned in the passage (choice (C)).

7. **A. jumping from a roof before an audience** Cleo loves attention. Her bet that she can swing upside down from an oak tree would have resulted in her either winning her sisters' money or gaining attention because she got hurt. Jumping from a rooftop would provide Cleo with attention whether it went well or poorly.

8. **D. Pa's** In this paragraph, the author describes Pa's love for Cleo and why she has so much influence over him.

9. Arrange the plot elements in chronological order:

1st   c. One day Cleo said that she did not want a kiss but wanted a copper instead.

2nd   d. Cleo asks her sisters to bet on whether she can swing from her feet in an oak tree.

3rd   a. Cleo envisions her own funeral.

4th   b. Cleo's sisters offer her their coppers.

10. **C. Serena felt that she had no choice but to give Cleo her copper to stop Cleo from doing something unsafe.** Serena does not want to give Cleo her copper; rather, Cleo is "compelling unnecessary sacrifice." Cleo does so by threatening to do something dangerous.

11. **D. Pa could not really afford to give Cleo and her sisters money.** The quote explains that Pa did not really have enough money to give some to Cleo and her sisters for doing chores. The phrase "dig deep" suggests that it was a sacrifice for him to do without that money, although he wanted to be generous. The language in the quote is figurative rather than literal, so choice (B) is incorrect.

12. **B. Cleo's boldness and her family's love for her sometimes make them feel powerless to resist her.** This passage is chiefly concerned with Cleo's character, which is bold and daring, and with the fact that her family members clearly love her. Both in the case of Pa giving the girls coppers and in the case of the sisters giving theirs to Cleo, Cleo's family members sometimes feel that they cannot refuse her.

13. **D. is a fast and inexpensive way to give that room a whole** A hole is a place that is dug out of the ground; whole means "entire."

14. **D. stripping paint and wallpaper, filling cracks, and adding** The verb "add" should end with -ing to match "stripping" and "filling." All the verbs in a series should be in the same form.

15. **C. is** The sentence should be in the present tense because the rest of the paragraph is in the present tense.

16. **A. missed, and go** Choice (A) uses the correct conjunction and correct verb form.

17. **B. are an ideal way for both children and adults** The verb "are" agrees with the plural subject "gardens."

18. **B. would like to start a community garden, first determine whether** In a complex sentence, a comma should follow the dependent clause at the beginning of the sentence.

19. **A. Next, choose a site for the garden.** Choice (A) is specific enough to be clear and general enough to cover all the details in the paragraph. It also includes a transition from the preceding paragraph.

20. **B. Start a new paragraph before sentence 3.** The first two sentences are about the benefits of community gardens. Sentence 3 begins a discussion of the steps involved in forming a community garden. Thus, a new paragraph is warranted.

Extended Response Evaluation Guide: Use the *Reasoning through Language Arts Extended Response Evaluation Guide* on page 722 to give your response a score between 0 and 6. Enter your score on the *Evaluation Chart* on page 707.

21. **D. Short-term profitability** The last sentence of paragraph 2 states that "these companies were too focused on their short-term profitability."

22. **A. Getting your product right the first time is more profitable than fixing mistakes later.** The correct answer comes from the first sentence of paragraph 4: "In the long run, the Detroit automakers learned the hard way that getting your product right the first time is less costly and more profitable than retrenching to play catch-up."

23. **C. wanted to build quality cars with few repair problems** The U.S. automakers produced cars with "far more problems than their foreign equivalents." This suggests that quality was a priority for the foreign automakers but not for domestic automakers looking to "keep their costs low and profits high."

24. **C. emphasize U.S. automakers' preoccupation with keeping costs low and profits high in the short term, at the expense of their long-term outlook** "Bean counter" is a derogatory term for an accountant or manager who is excessively concerned with keeping expenses low. The author uses this term to underscore the idea that the U.S. automakers failed to consider the "bigger picture"—that is, failed to consider their long-term outlook.

25.

Causes	Effects
a. U.S. automakers manufactured cars of low quality	d. U.S. automakers lost business to foreign automakers in the 1970s and 1980s
c. A customer has a bad experience when doing business with a company	b. A customer chooses not to do business with a company

26. **A. critical** The authors speak negatively of the cars produced by U.S. automakers in the 1970s and 1980s and include comments such as "to add insult to injury" and "weren't considering the bigger picture."

27. **A. U.S. automakers** The last paragraph states that U.S. automakers eventually "got their act together in the 1990s and have stopped the erosion of market share."

28. **D. is hoping her mother won't hear her asking for money** The narrator misinterprets Marjie's actions. She thinks Marjie is asking for money for herself, not her mother. She therefore interprets Marjie's actions as trying to hide her request from her mother.

29. **C. Jennie is perplexed when the narrator blames Marjie.** When the narrator explains that she thought Marjie wanted the money for herself, "Jennie looked doubtful."

30. **B. discuss it defensively** Jennie meets with the narrator directly to try to explain what happened and express concern. However, she misunderstands the narrator's explanation, apologizes for trying to borrow money, and reacts defensively when it is suggested that her daughter would ask for money on her own. Jennie would likely have this same defensive reaction if criticized by a boss.

31. **A. the narrator's thoughts** The passage is written with a first person point of view from the narrator's perspective. This allows the reader access to the thoughts of the narrator as well as a description of the action that the narrator sees.

32. **C. They know each other but are not close.** The narrator is visiting Jennie and her family and obviously knows them, yet there is a formal tone to Jennie's explanation about borrowing money, and the narrator is unable to explain how she misunderstood Marjie and is left "floundering." Those aspects of their relationship help you infer they are not on close, intimate terms.

33. **C. uncomfortable** Jennie feels she has to explain why she was going to borrow money from the narrator, and the narrator not only misinterprets Marjie's actions but has a difficult time explaining to Jennie "the whole of Marjie's act." Jennie appears to doubt her and states her children would never ask for money, leaving the narrator "floundering a bit." The entire situation ends with the narrator (and perhaps even the reader) feeling uncomfortable over the situation.

34.

Marjie	Obedient
Jennie	Proud
Narrator	Diplomatic

Marjie follows the instructions of the older characters. Jennie is defensive and quick to explain that she normally wouldn't ask for money or allow Marjie to. The narrator attempts to smooth over the misunderstanding.

35. **C. There may be more people in poverty than the Census Bureau official estimate suggests.** Overall, the passage conveys this main point. Choices (A) and (B) are details rather than main ideas, and choice (D) is not supported by the passage.

36. **A. The rate of poverty rose during each year from 2007 to 2011.** The main idea of paragraph 1 is that the rate of poverty is increasing. This detail supports that main idea. Choice (B) is the main idea of paragraph 1. Choices (C) and (D) are suggested in later paragraphs.

37. **C. The bar graph supports the claim that a different way to measure poverty would produce a different estimate of the rate of poverty.** The bar graph shows that the SPM would produce different estimates of how many people are poor, a claim that the author makes in paragraph 4.

38. **C. Higher rents can cause people to have less money for food.** Paragraph 3 explains that "higher rents may leave individuals with less money for food": higher rents are the cause, and less money for food is the effect. Choices (B) and (D) are too extreme. Choice (A) distorts the passage: the poverty thresholds measure who is poor—they don't cause people to be poor.

39.

Estimates that would be higher if the SPM were adopted	Estimates that would be lower if the SPM were adopted
The overall rate of poverty	The rate of poverty among people under 18
The rate of poverty among people 18–64	
The rate of poverty among people 65 and older	

Only the estimated rate of poverty among people under 18 would be lower if the SPM were adopted. (In your answer, the items in the left-hand column do not have to be in the order presented here.)

40. **B. The student has overlooked the fact that other factors might impact how much money local governments receive from the federal government.** The student has read in the passage that government spending on poverty is affected by the estimated rate of poverty. But even if the estimated rate of poverty were higher, that does not necessarily mean that government (at any level) would automatically spend more on poverty. After all, many factors go into governmental decision-making.

41. **C. wants governmental actions to be based on an accurate estimate of the rate of poverty** The author's chief concern is with the estimated rate of poverty and whether or not it is accurate. Moreover, the author states in paragraph 5 that this matters because government spending is involved. None of the other choices here are supported by the passage.

42. **D. how best to spend public money** Both writers discuss their thoughts about the best way to use funds to improve Glenwood.

43. **C. Improving them is a good use of funds right now.** While both writers agree that the parks are not in good repair, they disagree over whether improving them is the best way to use resources at the present time.

44. **A. They are good when done in the best locations.** The local business owner doesn't feel that improving the public parks is the best use of funds right now, but he does feel that using those resources to improve the appearance of the business district would contribute to economic growth.

45. **B. Investing in our community is important for the future of Glenwood.** Both writers are arguing that public resources should be invested in improving the community to help ensure its prosperity in the long term.

46. **C. often feel sick when at your workplace?** Because the workplace belongs to you, the possessive pronoun *your* is correct.

47. **A. symptoms seem to disappear magically once you leave work?** What happens magically is that the symptoms disappear, not that you leave work. Magically should be placed close to the part of the sentence that it modifies—symptoms disappearing.

48. **A. an older building isn't necessarily immune to** A sentence needs both a subject and a verb. Choices (B) and (C) are missing a noun to serve as the subject. Choice (D) is incorrect because it adds an unnecessary comma.

49. **D. the windows** Using a pronoun instead of the word *windows* would make it unclear what it was that originally opened.

50. **A. Tourism increases both air pollution and litter, which will further reduce the animals' chances for survival.** Choice (A) avoids wordiness while making it that tourists cause both pollution and litter.

51. **C. remove sentence 7** The flyer focuses on the land on Compton Point. This sentence about other areas in the county is irrelevant and should be deleted.

52. **B. and influx of tourism resulting from their development would boost the region's sagging economy** Choice B smoothly combines the two ideas into a single sentence with a compound subject.

53. **D. Saturday, May 7, in front of the mayor's office, 34 Wilton Road.** All parts of a proper noun must be capitalized.

Reasoning Through Language Arts Practice Test Evaluation Charts

Questions 1–53

Circle the numbers of the questions that you got correct and then total them in the last column of each row.

Content Area	Question Numbers	Number Correct/Total
Interpreting Nonfiction and Informational Text Pages 62–85	2, 3, 5, 21, 22, 23, 24, 25, 26, 27, 36, 38, 39, 41, 44	____/15
Analyzing Nonfiction and Informational Text Pages 86–101	1, 4, 6, 35, 37, 40, 42, 43, 45	____/9
Interpreting Fiction Pages 102–117	7, 8, 9, 10, 11, 12, 28, 29, 30, 31, 32, 33, 34	____/13
Writing Effective Sentences Pages 118–135	14, 16, 47, 48, 50, 52	____/6
Connecting Ideas Pages 136–147	19, 20, 51	____/3
Using Grammar Correctly Pages 184–199	15, 17, 49	____/3
Using Writing Mechanics Pages 200–213	13, 18, 46, 53	____/4
SUBTOTAL		____/53

Extended Response

Use the evaluation guide on page 722 and assign each category a number 0–2. Add to find the subtotal. On the GED® Test, your Extended Response score subtotal will be doubled. Multiply by 2 as shown in the table below.

Writing About Text Pages 148–173	**Creation of Arguments and Use of Evidence**	____/2
Connecting Ideas/Polishing Your Writing Pages 136–147, 174–183	**Development of Ideas and Organizational Structure**	____/2
Using Grammar Correctly / Using Writing Mechanics Pages 184–199, 200–213	**Clarity and Command of Standard English Conventions**	____/2
SUBTOTAL		____/6. Then multiply your subtotal by 2: ____/12.

Composite Score

Add both Subtotals to get the total number of points you earned on *Reasoning through Language Arts*.

Questions 1–53	____/53
Extended Response	____/12
TOTAL	____/65

If you do not have time to review the entire *Reasoning through Language Arts* unit, you may want to review the sections that need the most work. You can use your total above (____/65) to figure out your percentage correct for the entire *RLA* test. Divide the numerator by the denominator and multiply by 100.

To understand your performance on the practice tests, please see pages 719–720.

MATHEMATICAL REASONING

Pages 583–595

1. **C. $410** Use the formula Simple interest = principal × rate × time. Note that time is expressed in terms of a year, so 6 months = $\frac{1}{2}$ year: $I = \$400 \times 0.05 \times \frac{1}{2}$ which equals $10. This is the interest, so Mike will pay back the interest plus the $400 principal for a total of $410.

2. **B. 58** Plug in the values given for x and y and then follow the order of operations:
$3[2(4) - 5] + (3 + 4)^2 = 3(8 - 5) + 7^2 = 3(3) + 49 = 9 + 49 = 58$

3. **D. $15x^2 - 8xy - 12y^2$** Use FOIL to distribute the terms in the expression:
$(3x)(5x) + (3x)(-6y) + (2y)(5x) + (2y)(-6y) = 15x^2 - 18xy + 10xy - 12y^2 = 15x^2 - 8xy - 12y^2$

4. **C. 48** First, convert the length of the section of fence into inches: 22×12 in = 264. That number represents how many inches John must cover with new boards. Divide that number by the width of each board to find out how many boards will be required: $\frac{264}{5.5} = 48$.

5. **−76** Following the order of operations, first simplify anything in parentheses:
$(4 - 18)$ becomes −14
Next, simplify any terms with exponents:
$5^2 = 25$ and $3^3 = 27$
Now you have:
$-3 \times 25 + 2(-14) + 27$.
Next, do multiplication and division in the order in which they appear:
$-3 \times 25 = -75$ and $2(-14) = -28$
Last, add and subtract in the order in which they appear:
$-75 + (-28) + 27 = -76$

6. **Box A and Box D** All boxes share the same first digit in their weight. By comparing the second digit, you can eliminate Box B. Comparing the third digit of the remaining choices, you find Box A and Box D are the heaviest and should be placed on the bottom shelf.

7. **77** Brad's average golf score would be found like this:
$\frac{sum\ of\ scores}{number\ of\ scores} = average\ score$

Plug the information you are given in the question into the formula and solve for the unknown:
$\frac{78 + 86 + 82 + 81 + 82 + x}{6} = 81$
$78 + 86 + 82 + 81 + 82 + x = 486$
$409 + x = 486$
$x = 77$

8. **C. 4 mph** The kayaker traveled for a total of 12 miles: 6 miles upstream and 6 miles downstream. This took her 3 hours (2 hours upstream + 1 hour downstream). Divide the distance by the time to find her average rate of speed per hour: $\frac{12\ miles}{3\ hours} = 4$ miles per hour.

9. **10** Because sides AB and CD are parallel, the figure is a trapezoid. Use the formula for the area of a trapezoid: $A = \frac{1}{2}h(b_1 + b_2)$ and plug in the values given:
$A = \frac{1}{2}(2.5)(2 + 6)$
$A = \frac{1}{2}(2.5)(8)$
$A = 10$

10. **D. $2x(x + y)$** To begin adding the polynomials together, factor out any like terms: $2x(x - y + 2y)$. Then combine any like terms together: $2x(x + y)$

11.

```
    x
+--+--+--+--+--+--+--+--+--+--+--+
-5 -4 -3 -2 -1  0  1  2  3  4  5
```

Find the average of the three temperatures:
$\frac{-1 + 2 + (-4)}{3} = \frac{-3}{3} = -1$.

12. **16,384** Calculate: $4^7 = 4 \times 4 \times 4 \times 4 \times 4 \times 4 \times 4 = 16,384$. On the TI-30SX MultiView™, press 4 ⊗ 7 (enter). The right side of the display reads 16,384.

13. **C. 12** Substitute appropriate values from the spreadsheet, then multiply, add, and subtract carefully, using order of operations:
$-[-2 - (3 - 5) + 3 \times (-4)] =$
$-[-2 - (-2) + (-12)] =$
$-[-2 + 2 - 12] =$
$-[-12] = 12$

14. **B. $2x^4 + 7x^3 + 4x$** Combine like terms from the exponent with the largest degree, which is 4: $6x^4 - 4x^4 = 2x^4$. Combine like terms from the exponent with the next largest degree, which is 3: $5x^3 + 2x^3 = 7x^3$. Finally, combine the terms from the exponent with the smallest degree: $7x - 3x$

$= 4x$. The simplified polynomial is $2x^4 + 7x^3 + 4x$.

15. **D. 150** The perimeter of the trapezoid is given as 50. Since the three sides shown add up to 38, the remaining side must be 12. The missing side is the height, so use the height and the two bases in the formula for the area of a trapezoid, as found on the formula sheet:
$\frac{1}{2} \times 12(10 + 15) = 150$

16. **A. $214.40** Substitute 4 for b and 3 for n into the function. Then solve the equation:
$C = \$25.60(4) + \$14(4)(3 - 1)$
$= \$102.40 + \$112.00$
$= \$214.40$

17. **B. (8, −5)** Substitute the x and y values from each ordered pair into the equation. Only choice (B) makes the equation true:
$y = -\frac{3}{4}x + 1$
$-5 = -\frac{3}{4}(8) + 1$
$-5 = -6 + 1$
$-5 = -5$

18. **D. $y = \frac{1}{2}x + 3$** You can use the point-slope form to figure out the slope of the line first. Use $(-6, 0)$ and $(0, 3)$ as two points:
$0 - 3 = m(-6 - 0)$
$-3 = m(-6)$
$-3 = -6m$
$m = \frac{-3}{-6} = \frac{1}{2}$
Now you have the slope of the line, use either of the points to plug into the equation for a line, $y = mx + b$. Using $(0, 3)$,
$3 = \frac{1}{2}(0) + b$
$3 = 0 + b$
$b = 3$
The equation of the line is $y = \frac{1}{2}x + 3$.

19. **B. 63** The pattern is that the next number is 1 more than double the previous number. To find the 6th term, use the 5th term, in this case 31. $31 \times 2 + 1 = 63$.

20.

6	(	$24.50	−	$19	)

To determine how much Janice will save, she needs to determine the price difference between one evening and one afternoon ticket ($24.50 − $19) and then multiply that number by 6, the total number of tickets she intends to purchase. Thus, the equation that will supply her total savings is 6($24.50 – $19).

21. **2** Absolute change refers to the difference, either positive or negative, between two numbers. Over the three elections listed, party x gained 2 seats, lost 6 seats, and then regained 2 seats. That's a net loss of 2.

22. **B. 28π** Use the radius of 2 and the height of 5 in the formula for the surface area of a cylinder, which can be found on the formula sheet. $2\pi(2 \times 5) + 2\pi(2^2) = 20\pi + 8\pi = 28\pi$

23. **C. $x + 3$** Every term in the expression is divisible by two, so begin by simplifying: $\frac{2x^2 - 6x - 36}{2x - 12}$ $= \frac{x^2 - 3x - 18}{x - 6}$. Next, factor the numerator of the fraction and cancel: $\frac{x^2 - 3x - 18}{x - 6} = \frac{(x-6)(x+3)}{x-6} = x + 3$

24. **B. $65,000** About $130,000 was made from catalog sales. About $65,000 was made from online sales. Subtract $65,000 from $130,000.

25. **D.** The $\leq$ symbol indicates "greater than or equal to," which is indicated with a filled-in dot. The symbol $<$ indicates "less than" (but not equal to), which is indicated with an open dot.

26. **A. (–4, –5)** Solve by graphing or by substitution. The point of intersection will be where the lines cross each other. The lines intersect at the point (–4, –5). To solve by substitution, use the first equation to substitute the value of y in the second equation: $2x + 3 = -\frac{1}{2}x - 7$

$$2\frac{1}{2}x = -10$$
$$x = \frac{-10}{2\frac{1}{2}} = -4$$

Now use that value of x to find the value of y using the first equation: $y = 2(-4) + 3 = -5$ The solution of the equation set is (–4, –5).

27. **C. $\sqrt{9^2 + 12^2}$** The cable forms the hypotenuse of a triangle with side lengths of 9 feet and 12 feet. Use the Pythagorean theorem

($9^2 + [12]^2 = c^2$) to determine the length of the hypotenuse c: $c = \sqrt{9^2 + 12^2}$.

28. **6** This question is simply asking for the number of possible combinations of two differently colored chairs, so the order of the chairs does not matter. To determine the number of different pairs of chairs that could be selected for the design, draw a table to illustrate the possibilities. There are six possible ways that two different chairs could be chosen for Meg's design.

Yellow	Red	Green	Blue
X	X		
X		X	
X			X
	X	X	
	X		X
		X	X

29. **A. $600** Find 24% of $2500. $2500 × 0.24 = $600 You could estimate this answer by thinking 24% is roughly $\frac{1}{4}$, and choice (A) is closest to one-fourth of the Whitman's budget.

30. **$7.50** Six boxes of pasta will be purchased: 3 of ziti and 3 of spaghetti. Set up the proportion $\frac{4}{5} = \frac{6}{x}$ where x is the price of 6 boxes of pasta. Cross-multiply and divide to solve for x: 5 × 6 = 30 and 30 ÷ 4 = 7.5

31. Place four additional dots on the line plot to represent the data. Count this question as correct only if you placed all of the dots properly.

32. **C. 12** The formula for the area of a circle is $A = \pi r^2$ where r refers to the radius of the circle. The diameter of a circle (a straight line segment that goes from one edge of the circle to the other and passes through the center of the circle) is $2r$, or two times the length of the radius. The circle shown in this problem has an area of 36π. Plug that into the

area formula and find the length of the circle's radius:
$$36\pi = \pi r^2$$
$$\frac{36\pi}{\pi} = \frac{\pi r^2}{\pi}$$
$$36 = r^2$$
$$\sqrt{36} = \sqrt{r^2}$$
$$6 = r$$
Now that you know the radius has a length of 6, multiply that length by 2 to get the diameter: $6 \times 2 = 12$ The diameter of the circle has a length of 12.

33. **2.8%** To calculate the percent increase or decrease from Karen's 2011 earnings to her 2012 earnings, first find exactly how much she earned in each year. In 2011, she earned $52,500 + $6,250, which equals $58,750. In 2012, she earned $56,300 + $4,100, which equals $60,400.
To calculate the percent change from 2011 to 2012, use the percent change formula: $\frac{\text{amount of change}}{\text{original value}}$
In this case, that gives you $\frac{60,400 - 58,750}{58,750} = \frac{1,650}{58,750}$ which equals .028, or 2.8%.

34.

$157	$- y$	$=$	$101	$+ y$

Imtaez had $101 + y$ remaining after paying y to the runner. The equation would be $157 - y = 101 + y$.

35. Place a dot on the graph as shown:

You can solve either by graphing the lines or by substitution. To solve by substitution, use the first equation to substitute the value of y in the second equation:

$2(x + 4) + 4x = 44$

$2x + 8 + 4x = 44$

$6x + 8 = 44$

$6x = 36$

$x = 6$

Now use that value of x to find the value of y using the first equation:

$y = 6 + 4$

$y = 10$

36. **D. 28%** Probability is the ratio of the number of favorable outcomes to the number of possible outcomes. Add up the numbers of marbles to find out how many marbles are in the bag. $12 + 3 + 6 + 4 = 25$. Therefore, 25 is the number of possible outcomes. 7 marbles are either blue or yellow. 7 is the number of favorable outcomes. $\frac{7}{25} \times \frac{4}{4} = \frac{28}{100}$, or 28%.

37. **D. 514** To find the volume of a cone, use the formula from the formula sheet: $V = \frac{1}{3}\pi r^2 h$. Plug in values from the question stem and the approximate value of pi:

$V = \frac{1}{3}\pi(6.4)^2(12)$

$V = \frac{1}{3}(3.14)(40.96)(12) \approx 514$.

38. **720** This question asks how many orderings, or permutations, of three out of ten are possible. Multiply: $10 \times 9 \times 8 = 720$.

39. Place a dot on the number line as shown below:

Archie is giving away half his chili: $\frac{1}{4} + \frac{1}{8} + \frac{1}{8} = \frac{1}{2}$. So he will have one half left over.

40. **C. 240** Use the percent formula, $\% = \frac{part}{whole} \times 100\%$. We are given the part and the percent, and are solving for the whole.

$5\% = \frac{12}{x} \times 100\%$

$x = \frac{12 \times 100}{5\%}$

$x = 12 \times 20 = 240$

41. **C. $113.75** It takes Fabio 45 minutes, or $\frac{3}{4}$ of an hour to install a hard drive. It takes him exactly one hour to install an operating system. It will take him $1\frac{3}{4}$ hours to complete the job. Since he charges $65 per hour, multiply $1\frac{3}{4}$ by $65 to find the total charge:

$1\frac{3}{4} \times \$65 = \$113.75$

42. **D. 1.335×10^9** You move the decimal point 9 places to the left to get 1.335. Multiply this by 10^9 to get the scientific notation 1.335×10^9.

43. **−2** To find slope, calculate $\frac{rise}{run}$. In this case, the line moves up two units for each unit it moves to the left. Thus, the slope is negative: $\frac{2}{-1} = -2$

44. **D. −8 and −12** To solve this system of linear equations, first write two equations with the information given. Call the numbers x and y. The first sentence tells you that $x = 12 + 3y$, and the second sentence tells you that $x + y = -20$. Rewrite the second equation so that x is isolated on one side of the equals sign: $x = -20 - y$. Now that each equation is written in terms of x, set the two expressions for x equal to each other: $12 + 3y = -20 - y$.

Simplify this equation: $4y = -32$, so $y = -8$. Substitute this value for y back into the second equation: $x + -8 = -20$, so x must equal −12.

45. **D. −9 and 2** To find the solutions to this quadratic equation, start by setting it equal to 0. The equation then becomes $3x^2 + 21x - 54 = 0$. Then, divide each term by 3 to make the equation $x^2 + 7x - 18 = 0$. Now that the x^2 term has a coefficient of 1, factor the equation into two terms: $(x + 9)(x - 2)$. So $x + 9 = 0$, and $x - 2 = 0$. $x = -9$ and $x = 2$. The correct answer is D.

46. Match the solutions to the equations:

Equation	Value of the variable	Explanation
$x - 2 = 9$	11	$x - 2 + 2 = 9 + 2$ $x = 11$
$\frac{a}{10} = 5$	50	$\frac{a}{10} \times 10 = 5 \times 10$ $a = 50$
$3y = -21$	−7	$3y = -21$ $y = -\frac{21}{3} = -7$
$14 + m$ $= 6$	−8	$14 + m - 14 = 6 - 14$ $m = -8$

Mathematical Reasoning Practice Test Evaluation Charts

Circle the numbers of the questions that you answered correctly and then total them in the last column of each row.

Content Area	Question Numbers	Number Correct/Total
Number Sense and Problem Solving Pages 220–239	6, 8	____/2
Decimals and Fractions Pages 240–261	4, 39, 41	____/3
Ratio, Proportion, and Percent Pages 262–281	1, 30, 33, 40	____/4
Data, Statistics, and Probability Pages 282–313	7, 24, 28, 29, 31, 36, 38	____/7
Algebra Basics, Expressions, and Polynomials Pages 314-347	2, 3, 5, 10, 11, 12, 13, 14, 20, 21, 23, 42	____/12
Equations, Inequalities, and Functions Pages 348–377	16, 17, 18, 19, 25, 26, 34, 35, 43, 44, 45, 46	____/12
Geometry Pages 378–402	9, 15, 22, 27, 32, 37	____/6
TOTAL		____/46

If you do not have time to review the entire *Mathematical Reasoning* unit, you may want to review the sections that need the most work. You can use your total above (____/46) to figure out your percentage correct for the entire *Mathematical Reasoning* test. Divide the numerator by the denominator and multiply by 100.

To understand your performance on the practice tests, please see pages 719-720.

SOCIAL STUDIES

Pages 596–609

1. **D. The United States had an unfavorable balance of trade in merchandise during the 2000s.** According to the passage, the balance of trade is the difference between exports and imports. When imports are greater than exports, the balance of trade is unfavorable. Since the graph shows that imports consistently exceeded exports during the 2000s, you can conclude that the balance of trade in merchandise was unfavorable during the decade.

2. **39** To calculate the average percent of people surveyed who considered themselves independents, add up the January – June numbers, 38 + 38 + 36 + 40 + 39 + 41 = 232. Divide 232 by the total number of terms, 6, and round to the nearest percentage to get 39 percent.

3. Look for the continent with the highest percentage of countries colored in the lightest gray. Place a dot on **Africa**.

4.

Highest	United States
Second highest	Mexico
Third highest	India
Lowest	Democratic Republic of Congo

5. **2.1** The median is the middle number in a set of numbers. Here, the question asks for the median in the percent change figures, or the third column. Arrange those numbers in order, and 2.1 will be the middle number.

6. **1870, 1965** The 15th Amendment (1870) and the Voting Rights Act of 1965 expanded the right to vote.

7. **B. Both valued a stable political framework for society.** The paragraph indicates that this was one thing the ancient Chinese and the ancient Greeks had in common.

8. **C. The war created a huge demand for military equipment and supplies.** The chart shows that there was a substantial increase in manufacturing output between 1939 (when World War II began in Europe) and 1941. Even though the United States did not enter the war until late 1941, industry had already geared up to sell equipment and supplies to the Allies in Europe. Choices (A) and (B) may be true, but do not explain the war's impact.

9. **A. patriotism** The tendency of the American public to support a president's emergency foreign policy actions is sometimes called the "rally 'round the flag" effect.

10. **B. problems enforcing the Sherman Antitrust Act consistently led to further legislation to prevent monopolies** In the passage, the author explains the intention behind the Sherman Antitrust Act: to make monopolies illegal. He goes on to outline the limitations of the act, arguing that its broad language rendered it insufficient to solve the problems created by monopolies. He concludes the paragraph by telling how Congress responded to the problems in the Sherman Antitrust Act by passing additional laws to control monopolistic practices.

11.

The author would agree with this statement:	The author would disagree with this statement:	The author does not address this information:
b. The dangers of climate change are more significant than the possible benefits.	a. The United States has failed to take any action against carbon emissions.	c. Wind energy is preferable to solar energy.
	d. Climate change will not impact the world food supply.	

12. **B. Whites wanted to take over Indian lands in the eastern states.** The graphic shows the Indians being moved away from eastern states to Kansas and Oklahoma. The question asks about "forcible" relocation, so the correct answer can't be about what Indians wanted.

13. **D. the Seminole** The Seminole tribe's home territory was in Florida, which was farthest from the new, government-declared Indian Territory in the Midwest.

14. **C. Special interest groups are treated better than voters by members of Congress.** The cartoonist is using irony in the caption to indicate that he thinks members of Congress treat voters badly, but treat people who represent special interest groups well.

15. **C. Industrialization and urbanization caused many changes in family life in the late 1800s.** This covers the main points of the passage, which discusses the impact of industrialization and urbanization on the American family. The other choices are all supporting details.

16. **C. It did not impose direct economic costs on the colonists.** All of the other acts of Parliament shown in the chart cost the colonists money, whether by having to pay import taxes, buy revenue stamps, or use their own resources to shelter British soldiers.

17. **A. The Declaration of Independence, which explained why the colonies broke away from Great Britain** The acts of Parliament listed in the chart were grievances used to justify declaring independence.

18. **A. 0% to 4%** First find the United States on the map and see what shade it is colored. Then consult the map key to see the percentage of undernourished people that shade represents. The map indicates that the percentage range is 0% to 4%.

19. **D. Hunger is a major problem in many countries in Africa.** More than 20 nations in Africa have a very high percentage of undernourished people. The remaining options are not supported by the data on the map.

20. **C. Both established methods of self-government in the English colonies.** Both documents set forth rules and laws for the self-government of specific English colonies.

21. **D. the English Bill of Rights** The English Bill of Rights tied the king's right to rule to the consent of the people's representatives, and the colonists' major grievance was taxation without representation. The colonists felt they should be granted the same representation and rights as other British citizens, which were listed in the English Bill of Rights.

22. **A. the Magna Carta** The Magna Carta, signed in 1215, was the first document to set limits on the British king's powers.

23. **D. Slavery destroyed the culture of the slaves, diminishing their self-respect.** According to the paragraph, this is an opinion, or belief, held by some historians. The other choices are all facts stated in the paragraph.

24. **B. 30 cents** According to the passage, market price is reached under equilibrium conditions—when supply equals demand. According to the graph, supply and demand cross each other—and so are equal—at 30 cents.

25. **D. The market price would go up.** When the supply decreases and demand stays the same, the market price increases. The same number of people want to buy fewer apples, so the people will generally be willing to pay more for the apples.

26.

Belonged to the Confederacy before the battle of Fort Sumter	Belonged to the Confederacy after the battle of Fort Sumter
Alabama	Alabama
	North Carolina

Iowa and Delaware never seceded, so they never belonged to the Confederacy. Alabama seceded before the Battle of Fort Sumter, so it belonged to the Confederacy both before and after the Battle of Fort Sumter. North Carolina also belonged to the Confederacy, but it didn't secede until after the Battle of Fort Sumter.

27. **C. the Court of International Trade** International trade" is commerce with foreign companies, so the case would most likely be filed in the Court of International Trade.

28. **B. The volume and variety of federal cases were too great for a single court to handle.** It would be impractical to have just one court handling all cases; the workload would be too great.

29. **A. the Supreme Court of the United States** According to the passage, cases are appealed to higher level courts; according to the diagram, the Supreme Court is the highest court of appeal.

30. **B. The war effort needs the help of everyone, including men, women and children.** The focus of the poster is to enlist the help of everyone in the country for the war effort. The sleeping woman represents an American population that needs to take action.

31. **D. at 0° latitude** On both of these projections the distortions are greatest near the north and south poles. Along the equator (0° latitude), the maps look most alike and most similar to a globe; the distortions increase as you go north or south toward the poles.

32. **B. The interrupted projection distorts distances across the oceans.** The interrupted projection was a poor choice because ocean areas are cut apart on the map, making it very difficult to measure distances on an around-the-world voyage.

33. The one segment (the bottom right box) of the Roman frontier that the map legend identifies as land frontiers would see "Heavy" fortification, the one river frontier (the top right box) would see "Light" fortification, and the two sea coasts (the two left-hand boxes) would see "None." Rivers served as natural barriers, making fortifications less necessary, and the emperors saw no need to defend ocean frontiers.

34. **C. The Fifth Amendment applies to the federal government, and the Fourteenth Amendment, to state governments.** According to the passage, this is one of the main differences between the two amendments.

Extended Response Evaluation Guide Use the *Social Studies Extended Response Evaluation Guide* on page 723 to give your response a score between 0 and 6. Enter your score on the *Evaluation Chart* on page 714.

Social Studies Practice Test Evaluation Charts

Questions 1–34

Circle the numbers of the questions that you got correct and then total them in the last column of each row.

	United States History Pages 430–443	Civics and Government Pages 444–457	Economics Pages 458–469	Geography and the World Pages 470–485	Points
Social Studies Practices					
Determine Central Idea and Draw Conclusions Pages 410–411	10, 15	7, 17	(no questions)	(no questions)	___/4
Interpret Words and Ideas Pages 412–413	12	9, 16, 20, 27	8, 25	33	___/8
Analyze Author's Purpose and Point of View Pages 414–415	11, 30	14	(no questions)	(no questions)	___/3
Evaluate Author's Reasoning and Evidence Pages 416–417	23	21, 28, 34	1	32	___/6
Analyze Relationships Between Materials Pages 418–421	13, 26	6, 22, 29	3, 4, 24	18, 19, 31	___/11
Interpret Data and Statistics Pages 422–423	(no questions)	2	5	(no questions)	___/2
SUBTOTAL	___/8	___/14	___/7	___/5	

Extended Response

Use the evaluation guide on page 723 and assign each trait a value. Add to find the subtotal. On the GED® Test, your Extended Response score subtotal will be doubled. Multiply by 2 as shown in the table below.

Creation of Arguments and Use of Evidence	___/2
Development of Ideas and Organizational Structure	___/2
Clarity and Command of Standard English Conventions	___/2
SUBTOTAL	___/4. Then multiply your subtotal by 2: ___/8.

Composite Score

Add both Subtotals to get the total number of points you earned on the *Social Studies Test*.

Questions 1–34	___/34
Extended Response	___/8
TOTAL	___/44

If you do not have time to review the entire *Social Studies* unit, you may want to review the sections that need the most work. You can use your total above (___/44) to figure out your percentage correct for the entire *Social Studies* test. Divide the numerator by the denominator and multiply by 100.

To understand your performance on the practice tests, please see pages 719–720.

SCIENCE

Pages 610–621

1. **A. lift** As the diagram shows and the paragraph implies, the wing's weight and the opposing force of the air under it result in an upward force called *lift*.

2. **C. "Why We Sleep"** The topic of the paragraph is why sleep evolved in humans, and the paragraph cites several reasons for sleeping. The other options are too specific.

3. **17** If the mean is 23 degrees, then the sum of all six angle measurements must be $23 \times 6 = 138$ degrees. Since the five given angles add up to 121 degrees, the sixth angle must make up the difference, or $138 - 121 = 17$ degrees.

4. **B. the air and rainwater in the soil** According to the diagram, nitrogen-fixing bacteria take nitrogen from both the air and rain found in soil.

5. **C. The recycling of nitrogen through the biosphere involves many complex processes.** This is a general statement, or conclusion, that is supported by the various details in the diagram. The other statements are details from the diagram.

6. **B. compost with plant and animal wastes** According to the diagram, plant and animal waste contains nitrogen compounds that decomposers, including nitrite bacteria and nitrate bacteria, break down. In this way, composting with plant and animal wastes results in the addition of usable forms of nitrogen to the soil. So composting with organic waste (plant and animal materials) would be an alternative to synthetic fertilizers.

7. **D. For the three compounds shown, solubility increases as temperature increases.** The graph shows all three substances having increased solubility as the temperature rises from 0°C to 50°C. None of the other statements is supported by information in the graph.

8.

Step of the scientific method	The scientist's action
Step 1. Formulate a question about a phenomenon	b. The scientist wondered whether water at different temperatures might affect houseplants differently.
Step 2. Collect data	c. The scientist researched the growth rate of plants at various greenhouses, some of which use cool water and some of which use warm water to water their plants.
Step 3. Form a hypothesis	e. The scientist guessed that warm water might be better for plants than cool water.
Step 4. Test the hypothesis through an experiment	a. For 6 weeks, the scientist used water at 75 degrees to water plants in Group A and used water at 55 degrees to water plants in Group B. He recorded their growth during this period.
Step 5. Draw a conclusion	d. At the end of 6 weeks, the plants in Group A were, on average, 2″ taller than plants in Group B. The scientist interpreted this to mean that warm water is better for plants than cool water.

9. **A. Its charge would become positive.** If an atom loses an electron, it has more protons than electrons, and thus it has a net positive charge. (Such an atom is called a positive ion.)

10. **A. the cracking of granite from the expansion of freezing water** This is an example of physical weathering because it involves changes of temperature causing physical effects on rock. Choice (C) is not an example of weathering because transport is involved.

11. **C. how special fluids keep insects alive during subfreezing weather** Understanding how insects can survive freezing may be a key to finding a way to freeze organs without destroying them.

12. **B. sea star** Of the four animals shown, only the sea star has a center section from which similar parts radiate. All the other animals are bilaterally symmetrical.

13. **C. Hydrogen peroxide is decomposing into water and oxygen.** The chemical reaction begins on the left hand side of the equation, which represents two hydrogen peroxide molecules. Thus, it is incorrect to say that hydrogen peroxide is being made (choices (A) or (D)). Rather, hydrogen peroxide is decomposing, or breaking up, into two substances. What remains after the chemical reaction is written on the right hand side of the equation. The question stem explains that water is composed of two hydrogen atoms and an oxygen atom, so the results of the reaction are water and O_2, which you can infer represents oxygen. Choice (B) is incomplete and (C) is correct.

14. **A. Mercury and bromine are liquids at room temperature.** Room temperature is about 70°F. The chart indicates that both mercury and bromine are liquids at that temperature: each has a melting point—the temperature at which it becomes a liquid—well below room temperature.

15. **D. Bacteria quickly evolved resistance to antibiotic drugs.** In 1969, the Surgeon General did not anticipate that bacteria would evolve to be resistant to the antibiotics that had been so effective until that time.

16. **B. The student should have used books of the same height for all of the ramps.** The height of the ramp affects how far the ball rolls. So the height of the ramp should be a controlled variable in this experiment. By using one ramp that is not as high as the others, the student is introducing a second variable into the experiment, which makes her data invalid for the ramp that is lower than the others.

Short Answer Response: Explain
Based on the following criteria, give yourself a score from 3 to 0 on your short written answer.

Score	Quality of Your Explanation	Support from Passage
3	Well Developed	Complete
2	Adequate	Partial
1	Minimal	Minimal
0	None	None

My Score: _____

17. **D. The dog has canines and the sheep does not.** If you compare the two diagrams, you will see that the sheep does not have any canines; instead the sheep has a large gap where the canines would be.

18. **C. The five largest asteroids are all farther from the sun than Earth is.** According to the chart, Earth's distance from the sun is set at 1, so any value greater than 1 indicates that the asteroid is farther from the sun than Earth is. All the asteroids have distance values of 2 or greater, so they are all farther from the sun than Earth is.

19. **less than** If all the lobsters weighed the maximum of 9 lbs, the 220 million pounds of lobster would still account for more than 20 million individual animals. Two blue lobsters out of 20 million lobsters is substantially less likely than the estimated 1 in 2 million occurrence of the blue mutation.

20. **A. Pressure builds up inside the magma chamber and vent.** If you examine the diagram, you will see that hot magma wells up into the volcano's cone. You need to infer that when the pressure builds up sufficiently, the volcano explodes, or erupts. None of the other events described would cause a violent explosion from the inside of the volcano.

21. **B. when food is digested, as when an enzyme in saliva called ptyalin breaks down starch into sugars without itself changing** The catalyst is the enzyme ptyalin; you can identify ptyalin as the catalyst, because it aids the chemical reaction of digestion but itself remains unchanged after the reaction. None of the other reactions include a substance that remains unchanged.

22. **B. People can reduce their chances of developing age-related hearing loss by not smoking.** Of all the options, this is the only one that is a hypothesis that the researchers could have been testing with their experiment. Choice (A) is too general to be a hypothesis for this experiment and is stated more like a conclusion than a hypothesis. The other options are facts relating to the study.

23. **D. Humans contain a higher percentage of carbon than bacteria do.** To find the correct answer, you must check each statement against the graphs to see whether the information in the graphs supports the statement. The graphs show that humans have a higher percentage of carbon than bacteria have.

24. **B. Both involve effort applied with circular motion.** The diagrams show that the effort applied to each of these machines is circular.

25. **A. During an ice age, temperatures drop and ice covers vast areas of Earth.** According to the passage, scientists aren't sure what causes ice ages. Choices (B), (C), and (D) each offer a different hypothesis for what causes an ice age. By contrast, choice (A) is an objective fact.

26. **D. The arrangement of the carbon, hydrogen, and oxygen atoms in the two hydrocarbons is different.** Although ether and ethanol both have the same number of carbon, hydrogen, and oxygen atoms, the different arrangements of atoms in each compound results in two substances with different properties.

27. **D. Observation is useful as long as the results are used to support or disprove a hypothesis.** According to Darwin's remarks, it is a waste of time to observe phenomena if you do not use what you observe to evaluate your theories.

28.

Type of process	Example of process
Magmatic	b. A gradual increase in temperature in the mantle, followed by a sudden drop in temperature
Hydrothermal	c. Movement of seawater through fractured rock underground
Metamorphic	d. Fault lines fracturing rock into particles underground, and then those particles undergoing great heat and pressure
Surficial	a. Wind eroding away the softer components in sandstone

29. **Crescent City** Begin by finding each increase in rainfall:

Crescent City	13.42
Eureka	14.76
Ukiah	17.84
Redding	6.74
Sacramento	4.41

The median is the middle value in a group of numbers. Arrange the numbers above in order; the middle value belongs to Crescent City.

30.

Experiment outline	Brock's steps
Step 1. Formulate a question about a phenomenon	d. Brock asked, "Does size affect the buoyancy of an object in water?"
Step 2. Collect data	b. Brock noted that ice floats in water, whether it is a small ice-cube or a huge iceberg.
Step 3. Form a hypothesis	e. Brock thought: "For an object made of a given material, increasing the size of the object won't affect its buoyancy in water."
Step 4. Test the hypothesis through an experiment	a. Brock placed wooden cubes that were 1 cc, 10 cc and 100 cc in water. He observed their buoyancy. Then he placed iron cubes of 1 cc, 10 cc and 100 cc in water and observed their buoyancy.
Step 5. Draw a conclusion	c. Brock said: "Since all wooden cubes float and all iron cubes sink, size does not affect the buoyancy of an object in water."

31.

Since the dam was built to stop fluctuation, or change, in reservoir levels, 1993 must be the final year that reservoir levels changed.

32. A. A teacher's perfume can be detected at the back of the classroom. This is an example of diffusion, the spreading of gas molecules (perfume vapor) throughout a container (the classroom).

Short Answer: Experiment Design
Based on the following criteria, give yourself a score from 3 to 0 on your short written answer.

Score	Experiment Design	Data Collection Method	Criteria for Hypothesis Explanation
3	Complete	Well Formulated	Complete
2	Logical	Logical	Logical
1	Minimal	Minimal	Minimal
0	None	None	None

My Score: _____

Science Practice Test Evaluation Charts

Questions 1–32

Circle the numbers of the questions that you got correct and then total them in the last column of each row.

	Life Science Pages 508–527	Earth and Space Science Pages 528–541	Physical Science Pages 542–557	Number Correct
Science Practices				
Comprehend Scientific Presentations Pages 492-493	2, 4, 17, 23	20	1, 24	____/7
Use the Scientific Method Pages 494–495	8, 11, 22	27, 28	16, 30	____/7
Reason with Scientific Information Pages 496–497	5, 15	18, 25	7, 9, 14	____/7
Express and Apply Scientific Information Pages 498–499	6, 12	10, 29	13, 21, 26, 32	____/8
Use Statistics and Probability Pages 500–501	19	31	3	____/3
SUBTOTAL	____/12	____/8	____/12	

Science Composite Score

Add your Subtotals as shown below to get the total number of points you earned on the *Science Test*.

Questions 1-32	_____/32
Explanation Short Answer	_____/ 3
Experiment Design Short Answer	_____/ 3
TOTAL	_____/40

If you do not have time to review the entire *Science* unit, you may want to review the sections that need the most work. You can use your total above (____/40) to figure out your percentage correct for the entire *Science* test. Divide the numerator by the denominator and multiply by 100.

To understand your performance on the practice tests, please see pages 719-720.

Evaluating Your Practice Tests

Scoring of the new GED® test works very differently from that of the 2002 series GED® test. The following are some major differences:

- Scoring is based on the number of points a test-taker earns in each section rather than on the number of questions the test-taker gets correct. Different questions have different point values. For example, questions in which a test-taker is asked to fill in two blanks or choose options from two drop-down menus are worth two points.

- The number of questions a test-taker will see on test day may vary from one form of the test to another. What remains the same across different test forms is the number of points on each test. The total number of points available on each test is as follows:

  - Reasoning Through Language Arts: 65 raw points
  - Mathematical Reasoning: 49 raw points
  - Social Studies: 44 raw points
  - Science: 40 raw points

- The number of points a test-taker earns is translated into a scaled score, on a scale of 100 to 200 for each subject test:

  - 100-149: below passing
  - 150-169: passing
  - 170-200: passing at the "GED with Honors" level, intended to indicate career and college readiness

- Test-takers must earn a minimum of 150 on *each* subject test in order to pass overall. It is no longer the case that a high score on one test can compensate for a below-passing score on another test. If a test-taker scores below 150 on any of the subject tests, the test-taker must retake those subject tests regardless of her performance on other subject tests.

While the number of raw points needed to earn a 150 or 170 on each subject test is confidential test-maker information, we can make inferences regarding the performance levels that will be required for test-takers to pass. Please see the next page for this information.

We also encourage test-takers to take the GED Ready™ Official Practice Tests as a final step before scheduling their actual GED® test. The GED Ready™ Official Practice Tests are available from the MyGED™ portal. Register at https://ged.com.

For each subject test from Kaplan's book or website:

If you got this percentage of questions correct . . .	then you are . . .	Kaplan recommends . . .
0% to 50%	unlikely to pass that subject test on Test Day.	an in-depth review of the subject matter. Be sure to look for commonalities among the questions you got wrong, and study those topics in greater depth. Review the questions you got wrong on the practice tests until you understand how to avoid similar mistakes in the future.
50% to 65%	somewhat unlikely to pass that subject on Test Day, but this is still uncertain.	setting a goal by which you would like to complete a final review of the material. As you do that review, focus on the material you have struggled with the most. Review the questions you got wrong on the practice tests until you understand how to avoid similar mistakes in the future.
65% to 75%	moderately likely to pass that subject on Test Day.	considering scheduling a date to take that subject test. You may want to give yourself a few more days or weeks to do a final comprehensive review of this subject before testing. If you must take all the GED® subject tests at the same time, be sure to review this material once per week as you prepare for the other subject tests.
75% or higher	highly likely to pass on Test Day.	considering scheduling this subject test for the near future. If you do, be sure to do a comprehensive, high-level review of the material and a final brush-up of any concepts you've struggled with before test day. Also, get yourself ready to test by getting on a regular sleep schedule, keeping yourself healthy, and managing stress. If you must wait before taking the official GED® test for this subject, review the material once per week until Test Day so that your skills do not rust.

GED® Test Resources

Reasoning through Language Arts Extended Response Evaluation Guide

You can use this guide to evaluate your own writing. You can also provide the guide to another person whom you ask to read your paper. Read a paper three times—once for each trait. Circle a score for each trait in the chart at the bottom of this page. Add to find your total score and then analyze your results.

Trait 1 – Creation of Arguments and Use of Evidence

Rate the response as 2, 1, or 0 based on these criteria:

2 – makes **text-based argument** with **clear thesis;** uses **relevant and specific evidence** from the text; **analyzes the validity** of the **claims** and **reasoning** in the source text(s)

1 – makes **argument** with **some connection to text;** cites **some relevant evidence;** makes **limited analysis** of the **claims** and **reasoning** in the source text(s)

0 – makes **little or no argument** with **minimal or irrelevant evidence** from the text; makes **little or no analysis** of the **claims** and **reasoning** in the source text(s)

Trait 2 – Development of Ideas and Organizational Structure

Rate the response as 2, 1, or 0 based on these criteria:

2 – demonstrates **logical organization;** uses a **clear progression of ideas** with well-chosen **transitions;** uses **adequate supporting details** and connects them to the main idea; utilizes **appropriate style, tone**, and **word choice**

1 – demonstrates **inconsistent organization** with **vague reasoning;** uses **disjointed ideas** with few **transitions;** contains **some supporting details** but may not explain their connection to the main idea; utilizes **inappropriate style or tone** and **vague and misused word choice**

0 – demonstrates **insufficient or illogical development** with **unclear progression of** ideas; uses **few, no, or irrelevant supporting details;** utilizes **incorrect** or **inappropriate style, tone, and word choice**

Trait 3 – Clarity and Command of Standard English Conventions

Rate the response as 2, 1, or 0 based on these criteria:

2 – exhibits **mainly correct and varied sentence structure; avoids awkward or overly wordy constructions;** uses **transitional words and phrases** to connect ideas; **competent application of grammar, capitalization, punctuation,** and **spelling -** with some mistakes allowed

1 – exhibits **inconsistent control** of **sentence structure;** may display **some awkward or wordy constructions;** inconsistent use of **transitional words and phrases; frequent errors** in **grammar, capitalization, punctuation,** and **spelling**

0 – exhibits **flawed or highly repetitive sentence structure;** may use **overly wordy, awkward, or confusing constructions; lacks transitional words and phrases;** little or no control of **grammar, capitalization, punctuation,** and **spelling**

Trait	Circle Score
1	0 1 2
2	0 1 2
3	0 1 2
Added Total	

Analysis of Score Total

0 to 3	Weak – needs improvement with all three traits
4 to 5	Fair – needs work with traits with a score of 0 or 1
6	Strong – mastery of all three traits

NOTE: This guide is Kaplan's simplified interpretation of the official GED® *Reasoning through Language Arts Extended Response* rubric. It has been developed for ease of use in evaluating extended written responses to one passage or paired passages.

Social Studies Extended Response Evaluation Guide

You can use this guide to evaluate your own writing. You can also provide the guide to another person whom you ask to read your paper. Read a paper three times—once for each trait. Circle a score for each trait in the chart at the bottom of this page. Add to find your total score and then analyze your results.

Trait 1 – Creation of Arguments and Use of Evidence

Rate the response as 2, 1, or 0 based on these criteria:

2 – makes **logical, explicitly stated claim(s)** based on a close reading of text(s); utilizes **mainly accurate analysis of ideas, events, or figures**; provides **largely accurate and relevant understanding** of **historic context** of sources

1 – makes **one strongly stated claim or an implied claim** which may be unclear or inconsistent; **limited analysis of ideas, events, or figures**; provides **limited understanding** of **historic context** of sources

0 – makes **vague, illogical, or no claims**, with **minimal or no analysis of ideas, events, or figures**; makes **little or no analysis** of the **claims**; presents **no understanding of historical context** of source texts

Trait 2 – Development of Ideas and Organizational Structure

Rate the response as 1 or 0 based on these criteria:

1 – demonstrates **logical organization;** uses a **clear progression of ideas** with well-chosen **transitions;** connects **supporting details to the main idea;** utilizes **appropriate style, tone**, and **word choice**

0 – demonstrates **insufficient or illogical development** with **unclear progression of** ideas; contains **few supporting details** and/or **does not connect them to the main idea**; utilizes **incorrect** or **inappropriate style, tone, and word choice**

Trait 3 – Clarity and Command of Standard English Conventions

Rate the response as 1 or 0 based on these criteria:

1 – exhibits **mainly correct and varied sentence structure;** uses **transitional words** to connect ideas; **avoids awkward or overly wordy constructions; competent application of grammar, capitalization, punctuation,** and **spelling -** with some mistakes allowed

0 – exhibits **flawed or highly repetitive sentence structure** may use **overly wordy, awkward, or confusing constructions; lacks transitional words and phrases;** exhibits **frequent errors** of **grammar, capitalization, punctuation, and spelling**

Trait	Circle Score
1	0 1 2
2	0 1
3	0 1
Added Total	

Analysis of Score Total

0 to 1	Weak – needs improvement with all three traits
2 to 3	Fair – needs work with some traits
4	Strong – mastery of all three traits

NOTE: This guide is Kaplan's simplified interpretation of the official GED® *Social Studies Extended Response* rubric. It has been developed for ease of use in evaluating extended written responses to one passage or paired passages.

2015 GED® Test Mathematics Formula Sheet

Area of a:

square	$A = s^2$
rectangle	$A = lw$
parallelogram	$A = bh$
triangle	$A = \frac{1}{2}bh$
trapezoid	$A = \frac{1}{2}h(b_1 + b_2)$
circle	$A = \pi r^2$

Perimeter of a:

square	$P = 4s$
rectangle	$P = 2l + 2w$
triangle	$P = s_1 + s_2 + s_3$
Circumference of a circle	$C = 2\pi r$ OR $C = \pi d$; $\pi \approx 3.14$

Surface area and volume of a:

rectangular/right prism	$SA = ph + 2B$	$V = Bh$
cylinder	$SA = 2\pi rh + 2\pi r^2$	$V = \pi r^2 h$
pyramid	$SA = \frac{1}{2}ps + B$	$V = \frac{1}{3}Bh$
cone	$SA = \pi rs + \pi r^2$	$V = \frac{1}{3}\pi r^2 h$
sphere	$SA = 4\pi r^2$	$V = \frac{4}{3}\pi r^3$

(p = perimeter of base with area B; $\pi \approx 3.14$)

Data

mean	mean is equal to the total of the values of a data set, divided by the number of elements in the data set
median	median is the middle value in an odd number of ordered values of a data set, or the mean of the two middle values in an even number of ordered values in a data set

Algebra

slope of a line	$m = \dfrac{y_2 - y_1}{x_2 - x_1}$
slope-intercept form of the equation of a line	$y = mx + b$
point-slope form of the equation of a line	$y - y_1 = m(x - x_1)$
standard form of a quadratic equation	$y = ax^2 + bx + c$
quadratic formula	$x = \dfrac{-b \pm \sqrt{b^2 - 4ac}}{2a}$
Pythagorean Theorem	$a^2 + b^2 = c^2$
simple interest	$I = Prt$ (I = interest, P = principal, r = rate, t = time)
distance formula	$d = rt$
total cost	total cost = (number of units) × (price per unit)

Provided by GED® Testing Service.

3. **4** Question 3 requires you to predict an outcome because it uses the words "In the next convention, it is most likely...." Since the presidential candidate has won on the first ballot for over twenty years in both parties' political conventions, and since a simple majority is all that is required to win, it is safe to predict that this will be true of future conventions. Therefore, Choice 4 is correct.

4. **2** Question 4 is somewhat tricky. All of the choices contain correct associations but one. Thus, the Organization Committee chooses the convention chairperson; the nominees make acceptance speeches; the states make nominations; a simple majority results in a nomination. Only Choice 2 is in error; the *temporary* chairperson makes the keynote address.

5. **3** Question 5 pinpoints the one difference between the Republican and the Democratic conventions. Skimming to a point halfway through the selection, looking for the words *Republican* and *Democratic*, you find that the actual nominations are made differently—by alphabet in one and by lottery in the other. The correct choice, therefore, is 3.

6. **3** Question 6 calls your attention to the organization of the article. To find the answer, you note how the various paragraphs in the passage follow one another. In this instance, the second paragraph indicates the length of the convention—four days—and tells how it opens. The third paragraph deals with the second day; the fourth paragraph, with the third day. The next to the last paragraph indicates what has happened by the fourth day. Since the passage follows the time sequence of the convention, it is organized chronologically. Choice 3 is the correct answer.

HISTORY, WITH ANSWERS AND ANSWER ANALYSIS

The United States is often considered a young nation, but in fact it is next to the oldest continuous government in the world. The reason is that its people have always been willing to accommodate themselves to change. We have been dedicated to equality, but have been willing to realize it by flexible means. In the European sense of the term, America's political parties are not parties at all, because they do not divide over basic beliefs. Neither wishes to overturn or replace the existing political and economic order; they merely desire to alter it at slower or faster rates of speed.

One of our proudest achievements has been the creation of a system of controlled capitalism that yields the highest living standards on earth, and has made possible a society as nearly classless as man has ever known. The profit system as it has developed in America shares its benefits with all parts of society: capital, labor, and the consuming masses. Yet even this was the result of trial and error. Unprincipled businessmen had first to be restrained by government, and by the growing power of organized labor, before they came to learn that they must serve the general good in pursuing their own economic interests. Now labor is feeling the restraint.

Even our creed of democracy is not fixed and unchangeable. Thus the statesmen of the early republic, though they strongly believed in private enterprise, chose to make the post office a government monopoly and to give the schools to public ownership. Since then, government has broadened its activities in many ways. Americans hold with Lincoln that "the legitimate object of government is to do for a community of people whatever they need to have done but cannot do at all, or cannot do so well for themselves, in their separate and individual capacities."

NOTE:

The terms in the passage and in the questions that are defined in the "Glossary of Social Studies Terms" are *capitalism, democracy, party, profit, monopoly, republic,* and *standard of living.*

1. The main quality of the United States stressed in this passage is its

   (1) youth
   (2) equality
   (3) high living standards
   (4) profit system
   (5) flexibility

2. The widely held belief about the United States with which the passage mentions disagreement concerns American

   (1) political parties
   (2) capitalism
   (3) private enterprise
   (4) labor
   (5) public ownership

3. All of the following are characteristic of the United States, according to the passage, EXCEPT a

   (1) dedication to equality
   (2) classless society
   (3) belief in democracy
   (4) profit system
   (5) controlled capitalism

4. An agency that performs a function of which Lincoln, according to his quoted words, would most approve is the

   (1) U.S. Office of Education
   (2) U.S. Chamber of Commerce
   (3) National Guard
   (4) Public Service Commission
   (5) Federal Aviation Administration

5. The creation of the U.S. government post office monopoly is cited as an example of a

   (1) replacement of the existing economic order
   (2) restraint of unprincipled businesspersons
   (3) control of organized labor
   (4) flexible view of private enterprise
   (5) system of shared profits

6. According to the passage, which of the following statements is true?

   (1) Our political parties agree on goals but not on methods.
   (2) Business has a larger share of profits than labor.

   (3) Government has tended to restrict its role in American life.
   (4) Americans are conservative where change is required.
   (5) Americans have kept their democratic beliefs intact.

7. The author's view of change in America is

   (1) critical
   (2) cautious
   (3) favorable
   (4) qualified
   (5) unclear

ANSWER KEY

1. **5**   2. **1**   3. **2**   4. **5**   5. **4**   6. **1**
7. **3**

ANSWER ANALYSIS

1. **5** This question requires you to determine the author's main purpose in writing this passage. Each of Choices 1 through 4 refers to a quality of the United States, but none of them is central to the selection. Flexibility is mentioned in many ways: "willing to accommodate themselves to change"; "flexible means"; "trial and error"; "not fixed and unchangeable."

2. **1** The question calls for selecting a common belief about the United States that is called into question in the passage. While two exceptions to private enterprise are cited, the belief in private enterprise is not challenged. Three other beliefs are mentioned, but none of them except political parties is called into question. The passage states that Europeans would not consider America's political parties parties at all. So Choice 1 is the correct answer.

3. **2** Here location of a detail in the passage is required. Of the five characteristics mentioned, four are true characteristics of the United States. The fifth, a classless society, is not, although a society "as nearly classless as man has ever known" is a quality of American life.

4. **5** This difficult question involves applying the principle stated by Lincoln to

TI-30XS Calculator Reference Sheet

An on-screen calculator reference sheet, similar to what appears on these two pages, will be available to you on Test Day. However, you should understand how to use the calculator before you take the GED® Test. Refer to the *Mathematical Reasoning Unit* on pages 215–403 for information about how to use the Texas Instruments TI-30XS MultiView™ calculator.

To perform basic arithmetic, enter numbers and operation symbols using the standard order of operations.

Example: [8] [×] [(–)] [4] [+] [7] [enter]   –25

To calculate with percentages, enter the number, then [2nd] [( ]

Example: [4] [0] [2nd] [( ] [×] [5] [6] [0] [enter]   224

To perform calculations with scientific notation, use the [×10ⁿ] key.

Example: [7] [.] [8] [×10ⁿ] [8] [◉] [–] [1] [.] [5] [×10ⁿ] [8] [enter]   630000000

To perform calculations with fractions, use the $\frac{n}{d}$ key. The answer will automatically be formatted in reduced form.

Example: [n/d] [2] [◉] [9] [◉] [×] [n/d] [3] [◉] [7] [enter] $\frac{2}{21}$

To perform calculations with mixed numbers, use [2nd] [n/d]

As with fractions, the answer will automatically be formatted in reduced form.

Example: [1] [2] [2nd] [n/d] [5] [◉] [6] [◉] [–] [1] [2nd] [n/d] [1] [◉] [2] [enter] $\frac{34}{3}$

To perform calculations with powers and roots, you will use the following keys:

$\sqrt{}$ / x^2 $x\sqrt{}$ / $\wedge$ 2nd $\sqrt{}$ / x^2 2nd $x\sqrt{}$ / $\wedge$

Example: 1   .   2 $\sqrt{}/x^2$ enter   1.44

Example: 7 $x\sqrt{}/\wedge$ 4   enter   2401

Example: 2nd $\sqrt{}/x^2$ 5   2   9   enter   23

Example: 3   2nd $x\sqrt{}/\wedge$ 1   7   2   8   enter   12

_____

The answer toggle key ◂▸ can be used to toggle the display result between fraction and decimal answers, exact square root and decimal, and exact pi and decimal.

Example: $\frac{u\frac{n}{d}}{}$ 9   ◂✛▸   1   0 reset   enter   ◂▸   0.9

Æ Symbol Tool Explanation

Starting in 2014, test-takers will take the GED® Test on the computer. On the computer-based test, some fill-in-the-blank questions require you to insert mathematical symbols.

You can access the "Symbol Selector" by clicking on this icon when it appears on the computer screen:

Æ Symbol

Choose the symbol you want, and click on Insert at the bottom of the screen. When you are done, close the screen.

Æ Symbol

| ∏ | ƒ | ≥ | ≤ | ≠ | ² | ³ | | | × | ÷ | ± | ∞ | √ |
| + | − | (|) | > | < | = |

Below are the meanings of the symbols. Learn the meanings before you take the test because only the symbols will be available to you.

∏ "pi" symbol π

ƒ "function" symbol

≥ greater than or equal to

≤ less than or equal to

≠ not equal to

² 2 exponent ("squared")

³ 3 exponent ("cubed")

| "absolute" value

× multiplication sign

÷ division sign

± "positive-or-negative" sign

∞ "infinity" symbol

√ "square root" symbol

+ plus sign or "positive" symbol

− minus sign or "negative" symbol

(open (or left) parenthesis

) close (or right) parenthesis

> "greater than" symbol

< "less than" symbol

= "equals" sign

INDEX

Direct current, 552
Direct democracy, 444
Distance problems
    absolute value, 324
    formula, 234
    scales on maps, 418
Distribution of data, 294
Distribution of goods/services, 458
Distribution of population, 479
Distribution of wealth, 462
Distributive property, 328
Dividend, 224, 244
Division
    decimal numbers, 244
    fractions, 250
    on calculator, 227, 256, 727
    order of operations, 316, 322
    polynomials, 342
    reducing fractions, 247, 250
    signed numbers, 316
    symbols for, 234, 316, 729
    whole numbers, 224–225
    word problems, 230
Divisor, 224, 244, 250
Dominant alleles, 516
Double-bar graph, 284
Drafting response
    in text box, 60, 407, 489, 491, 502
    read aloud, 166
    time management, 156, 160
    wide margins, 176
Drag-and-drop questions, 59, 217, 407, 489
Drop-down questions, 58, 216, 406, 488
Drugs, 514

E

Earthquake origins, 528
Earth science
    resources, 531. *See also* Natural resources
    solar system, 534
    structure of Earth, 528
    weather and climate, 532
Economics
    basic concepts, 458
    capitalism vs. communism, 438
    depression, 436, 460, 476
    industrialization, 434, 436, 474
    labor issues, 465. *See also* Labor
    Middle Ages, 472
    natural resources, 480
    political campaigns, 450
    United States, 432, 460, 462

Ecosystems, 480, 522
Editing and revising responses
    computer tools, 166, 176, 408, 491
    organization of text, 176
    questions to ask, 167, 168, 174, 176
    read draft aloud, 166
    revision marks, 174, 177
    time management, 156, 165
    word choice, 178
Effect. *See Cause* and effect
Egypt (ancient), 470
Einstein, Albert, 548
Elaboration text structure, 80
Elections. *See also* Voting
    Electoral College, 450
    general elections, 450
    primary elections, 450
    swinging, 450
Electricity, 474, 548, 552
Electromagnet, 552
Electrons
    atoms, 542
    electricity, 552
    molecular bonding, 542
Elements, 542
Emigration. *See* Immigrants
Emotional appeals, 90
Empires
    Greek, 470
    imperialism, 436, 476
    Inca, 470
    Islamic, 472
    Roman, 470
Endangered species, 480
Endocrine system, 512
Endothermic reactions, 546
Energy
    activation energy, 546
    as natural resource, 530
    cell processes, 510
    conservation of, 548
    definition, 548
    ecosystems, 522
    endo- vs. exothermic reactions, 546
    forms of, 548
    heat, 536, 544, 546, 548
    mass relationship, 548
    momentum, 550
    nuclear reactions of stars, 536
    potential vs. kinetic, 548
    quasars, 536

England
  Church of England, 472
  colonialism, 430, 474
  Magna Carta, 444
  monarchy, 472
Entrepreneurs, 460
Environment
  ecosystems, 522
  natural resources, 480, 530
  population stress, 478, 531
Enzymes, 512
Equations
  equals sign on toolbar, 729
  linear, 362
  multi-step, 350
  one-step, 348
  slope and, 366–367
  word problems, 352–353
Equator, 528, 532
Equilateral triangles, 380
Erasable board. *See* Wipe-off board
Esophagus, 512
Essay main idea statement, 138
Eukaryotic cells, 508
Europe
  explorers, 430
  imperialism, 429, 436
  Industrial Revolution, 474
  Magna Carta, 444
  Middle Ages, 472
  Renaissance, 472
  world wars, 436, 476
Evaluating expressions, 322, 328
Evaluation of writing, 722–723
Evaporation, 522, 544
Evidence. *See also* Evidence-based writing
  arguments, 88, 90, 94, 150
  citing, 153, 160, 722–723
  collecting, 154, 156
  conclusions from, 72
  evidence statements, 154
  generalizations from, 74
  paragraph logical order, 140
  Science, 492, 496, 502
  Social Studies, 416, 424
  thesis statement vs. opinion, 152
  wipe-off board, 154
Evidence-based writing
  Extended Response, 57, 59, 60–61, 409, 722, 723
  prewriting strategies, 157
  purpose of, 148
  Short-Answer questions, 502
  successful answers, 722, 723

Evolution, 520
Examples
  Social Studies details, 410
  text structure, 80
  transition words for, 142
Exclamation point, 118
Executive branch, 448, 462
Exothermic reactions, 546
Experimental probability, 298
Experiments, 494, 502
Explorers, 430
Exponents
  as multiplication, 318, 332
  order of operations, 322, 330
  scientific notation, 320–321
  Symbol Selector toolbar, 729
Expressions
  algebraic, 326, 327
  distributive property, 328
  evaluating, 328
  guess-and-check, 358
  order of operations, 322–323
  polynomials, 332–342
Extended Responses
  arguments and assumptions, 150
  evaluation of, 722–723
  highlighter tool for, 60, 154, 156, 409, 424
  practice for, 174
  pretests, 1
  Reasoning through Language Arts, 57, 148–173, 722
  Social Studies, 407, 409, 424, 723
  strategy for, 156, 424
  successful answer qualities, 61, 722–723
  thesis statements, 153, 424
  wipe-off board, 60, 154, 156
  writing prompt then passages, 148, 154, 156
  writing prompt unpacked, 148–149, 156

F

Factories. *See* Industrialization
Factoring expressions, 356
Facts, 416, 492
Farming. *See* Agriculture
Fascism, 436
Fats as nutrients, 515
Faults in crust, 528
Faulty generalizations, 74
Favorable outcomes, 298
Federal Deposit Insurance Corporation (FDIC), 462
Federalism, 447, 448
Federal judges, 448

S

Saliva, 512
Satellites, 532, 534
Saturation of market, 460
Saturn, 534
Savings and loan associations, 460
Scalene triangles, 380
Scales on maps, 418
Science
  calculator for, 490, 500
  computer-based format, 488–491
  designing experiments, 502
  earth science, 528–541
  Flag for Review, 488, 516, 546
  highlighter tool, 491, 502
  life science, 508–527
  math problems on, 490
  physical science, 542–557
  science practices, 487, 492–507
  scientific method, 494, 502
  score needed to pass, 487
  Short-Answer questions, 1, 489, 491, 502
  space science, 528–541
  test overview, 487
  wipe-off board, 490, 502
Scientific notation, 320–321, 727
Scores needed to pass
  Mathematical Reasoning, 215
  Reasoning through Language Arts, 57
  Science, 487
  Social Studies, 405
Sea floor spread, 528
Season capitalization, 204
Secession of states, 432
Semicolon, 124, 142
Semiconductors, 552
Senate, 446, 448
Sentences
  assessed, 57
  comma splices, 124
  complex, 122, 124, 126
  compound, 120, 124, 126
  effective paragraphs, 136, 137
  effective sentences, 118–135, 173
  flow of, 126, 142
  fragments, 119, 122
  independent clauses, 120
  inverted structure, 194
  logical order, 140
  parallel structure, 130
  run-ons, 124
  simple, 118, 120, 124, 126
  topic sentences, 138

Serial comma, 130, 202
Services (economics), 458, 460
Setup problems, 326
Sexual reproduction
  asexual versus, 516
  cloning, 518
  genetics, 518
  natural selection, 520
Sharecropping, 432
Short-Answer questions
  five-step process, 502
  pretest, 1
  Science, 489, 491, 502
Short sentences, 126
Signed numbers
  absolute value, 324
  addition, 314
  coordinate planes, 360
  division, 316
  exponents as, 318, 320
  inequalities, 354
  multiplication, 316
  on calculator, 314, 330
  polynomials, 334, 336
  subtraction, 314–315
  Symbol Selector toolbar, 729
Silica in Earth structure, 528
Silicon in semiconductors, 552
Similes, 76, 112
Simple interest, 274, 403, 725
Simple probability, 298
Simplifying
  expressions, 328
  polynomials, 334, 338, 342
Skeletal system, 513
Slang
  as writing style, 78, 110
  avoiding, 178
Slavery
  abolishment, 432, 446
  African Americans, 431, 432
  Civil War, 432, 446
  Egyptian, 470
  Native Americans, 430
Slope
  equations and, 366–367
  formula, 364–365, 403, 725
Small intestine, 512
Smith, Adam, 460
Social changes
  Age of Enlightenment, 444
  civil rights movement, 438
  industrialization, 434, 436, 474
  Middle Ages, 472

Tone of writing, 78
Topic, 92, 138, 410
Trachea, 512
Traits, 516, 520
Transformers (electricity), 552
Transform margins, 528
Transition words, 61, 80, 142
Transpiration, 523
Trapezoids, 378, 384, 403, 725
Treaty of Versailles (1918), 476
Tree diagrams, 302, 304
Trends, 422, 458, 496
Triangles, 380–383, 383, 398
Trinomials, 332

U

Unanswered test questions, 104, 112
Unconstitutional laws, 449
Unemployment, 464, 476
Unicellular organisms, 509
Union (Civil War), 432
Unions (labor), 434, 464
United States (U.S.)
  branches of government, 446, 448
  citizenship, 453. *See also* Voting
  Cold War, 436, 476
  Constitution, 430, 446, 448
  economics of, 432, 460, 463. *See also* Economics
  electoral system, 450
  free market economy, 458, 462
  government, 444–457
  history, 430–438, 473
  immigrants, 432, 434, 452
  imperialism, 436
  political parties, 450
  population, 434
  slavery, 430, 432, 446
  voting, 432, 434, 438, 444, 446
  wars, 436, 438, 448
Universe, 536
Unlike terms, 334
Uranus, 534
Urban centers. *See* Cities
Urinary system, 513
U.S. House of Representatives, 446, 448
U.S. Senate, 446, 448
U.S. Supreme Court, 447

V

Validity, 74, 90
Variables
  algebraic expressions, 326
  coefficients, 332
  dependent vs. independent, 494
  equations, 348
  formulas, 234, 274
  inequalities, 354–355
  polynomials, 332
  simplifying expressions, 328
  word problems, 352–353
Variations in traits, 520
Veins, 512
Velocity, 550
Venus, 534
Verbs
  compound predicates, 200
  helping verbs, 188
  irregular verbs, 190
  parallel structure, 130
  regular verbs, 188
  simple sentences, 118, 120
  subject-verb agreement, 57, 61, 192, 194
  subordinate ideas, 126
  tenses of verbs, 188, 189
Veto, 448
Vietnam War, 438
Villi, 512
Viruses, 514
Visualization
  combinations, 302
  fractions, 246
  percents, 268
  sketching for, 354
Vitamins as nutrients, 515
Volcano sources, 528
Voltage, 552
Volume
  capacity formulas, 388–390, 397, 403, 725
  states of matter, 544
Voting
  African Americans, 432, 438, 446
  Athenian democracy, 444, 470
  direct democracy, 444
  independent voters, 450
  primary elections, 450
  representative democracy, 444, 448
  republic, 446, 447
  voting age, 446
  women, 434, 446, 470

W

Wages, 464, 474
Warm fronts, 532
Washington, George, 430

Water (H$_2$O)
cellular respiration, 510
Earth's surface, 534
ecosystems, 522
formation equation, 545
natural resource, 530
nutrient, 514
photosynthesis, 510
rust, 546
states of matter, 544
universal solvent, 544
Watts, 548
Weather, 532
Weight, 544
White dwarfs, 536
Wind, 480, 530, 532
Wipe-off board
evidence gathering, 154
Extended Responses, 60, 156
frequency tables, 290
Mathematical Reasoning, 215, 219, 342
Science, 490, 502
Social Studies, 408, 424
sketching for visualization, 354
Wire (electricity), 552
Witnesses in court, 452
Word choice
figurative language, 76, 112
polishing writing, 178
Reasoning through Language Arts, 57, 61, 76
restating ideas, 64
Word problems
equations, 350, 352–353
five-step process, 230, 232
of as base of percent, 266
per meaning, 234, 264
translating to math, 326, 350
Work and energy, 548
Workers. *See* Labor
World wars, 436, 476

Write-on board. *See* Wipe-off board
Writing invented, 470
Writing prompt
read before passages, 148, 154, 156
unpacking, 148–149, 156
Writing skills. *See also* Clarity in writing; Word choice
effective paragraphs, 136, 137
effective sentences, 118–135, 173
evaluation of, 722–723
flow of writing, 126, 142
mechanics of writing, 200–213
polishing your writing, 174–183
prewriting strategies, 157
Reasoning through Language Arts, 57, 59–61
tone of writing, 78
writing about text, 148–173

X

x-axis, 360

Y

y-axis, 360
y-intercept, 366

Z

Zero (0)
as placeholder, 224, 242, 244
as signed number, 314
decimal numbers, 240
exponents, 318
horizontal line slope, 365
probability, 298
quadratic equations, 356, 358
scientific notation, 320